D0217847

Encyclopedia of

GARDENS

History and Design

CHICAGO BOTANIC GARDEN

Encyclopedia of

GARDENS

History and Design

Volume 2

G–O

EDITOR

CANDICE A. SHOEMAKER

FITZROY DEARBORN PUBLISHERS
CHICAGO LONDON

For information write to:

FITZROY DEARBORN PUBLISHERS
919 N. Michigan Avenue, Suite 760
Chicago, Illinois 60611
USA

or

FITZROY DEARBORN PUBLISHERS
310 Regent Street
London W1B 3AX
UK

Library of Congress and British Library Cataloging in Publication Data are available.

ISBN 1-57958-173-0

First published in the USA and UK 2001

Index prepared by Hughes Analytics, Chicago, Illinois
Typeset by Argosy Publishing, Waltham, Massachusetts
Printed by Edwards Brothers, Ann Arbor, Michigan
Cover design by Chicago Advertising and Design, Chicago, Illinois

Cover illustration: Patio de la Acequia, Generalife, Granada, Spain. Copyright Juan Luis de las Rivas Sanz.

CONTENTS

LIST OF ENTRIES

VOLUME 3

G

Garden City

A garden city is an ideal self-contained community of predetermined area and population surrounded by a greenbelt. Early examples of Garden Cities are Adelaide in Australia and Christchurch (1850) in New Zealand, which were planned with parks or greenbelts. Before the great fire of 1870, Chicago could be justified as a garden city, due to the designing of the city's ambitious park system in 1869. Possible origins for the term *garden city* include Alexander T. Stewart, who first used the term in 1869 to describe his layout for a model city on Long Island, New York, known as Garden City. Other examples were Robert Owen's workers' village at New Lamar, Scotland, built in the early 19th century, Sir Titus Salt's Saltaire (West Yorkshire, England) in 1853, the Cadbury Brothers' Bournville (West Midlands, England) in 1879, and the Lever Brothers' Port Sunlight (Merseyside, England) in 1887. In 1880 the term was applied to the industrial village at Bornemout by the lord mayor, who proclaimed the village to be the "Garden City of the South." In 1905 it became the title of a book, *Garden Cities in Theory and Practice,* by A.R. Sennett. In terms of theoretical application, however, the model devised and drawn by Sir Ebenezer Howard stands out as the first book to outline the basic elements and tenets of garden-city planning.

Howard's book *Tomorrow: A Peaceful Path to Real Reform* (1898), later revised as *Garden Cities of Tomorrow* (1902), encapsulates many of the then-prevailing ideas about town and city planning. As formulated by Howard the garden city was intended to bring together the economic and cultural advantages of both city and country living, with landownership vested in the community, while at the same time discouraging metropolitan sprawl and industrial centralization.

Howard illustrated his ideas in a diagram of three magnets: the city, the country, both which presented advantages and disadvantages, and the town-country, his conception of the garden city, combining the best elements of city and country. Industry and commerce would be integrated with homes, gardens, and farms in the garden city. Each garden city, surrounded by a greenbelt, was to be one of a constellation of garden cities,

Advertisement in *Punch Almanack* for Welwyn Garden City, ca. 1921
Courtesy of Mary Evans Picture Library

each with population limited to 30,000, separated from each other by countryside.

In 1899 Howard organized the Garden City Association to promote the ideas presented in his writings. In 1902 the Garden City Pioneer Company Limited was created to build the first genuine garden city, Letchworth in Hertfordshire, where work began in 1903. The company acquired a 3,822-acre (1,547-ha) site 35 miles (56 km) north of London and held a design competition that was won by architect-planners Barry Parker and Raymond Unwin. Parker and Unwin's plan was based on an area of 1,250 acres (506 ha) for 30,000 inhabitants (24 persons per acre [0.4 ha]), with 2,500 acres (1,012 ha) reserved as a rural belt. Welwyn Garden City, begun in 1919 and designed by Louis de Soissons, was Howard's second garden city. Although neither were successful in demonstrating Howard's ideal of the entirely self-contained garden city, his theories continued to have enormous influence. A New Towns Act, enacted by Parliament in 1946, led to the development of over a dozen new communities based on his ideas.

Howard's influence extended far beyond England but commonly resulted in residential suburbs of individually owned homes. After World War II countries throughout the world experimented with government-planned new towns. Among the most noteworthy were the new-town programs of Sweden, Finland, France, and Israel. In the United States Howard's ideas were realized under the auspices of the Regional Planning Association of America. Examples in the United States include Radburn, New Jersey, designed by Clarence Stein and Henry Wright, and Forest Hills, Queens, New York, designed by Frederick Law Olmsted. The concepts behind the ideal garden city have had a great influence on the development of modern city planning.

Further Reading

Ashworth, William, *The Genesis of Modern British Town Planning: A Study in Economic and Social History of the Nineteenth and Twentieth Centuries,* London: Routledge and Paul, 1954

Barnett, Henrietta Octavia, *A Garden Suburb at Hampstead,* London: Headley, 1905

Creese, Walter L., *The Search for Environment: The Garden City, Before and After,* New Haven, Connecticut: Yale University Press, 1966; expanded edition, Baltimore, Maryland: Johns Hopkins University Press, 1992

Girouard, Mark, *Cities and People: A Social and Architectural History,* New Haven, Connecticut: Yale University Press, 1985

Howard, Ebenezer, *Tomorrow: A Peaceful Path to Real Reform,* London, 1898; reprint, London: Routledge/Thoemmes, 1998

Mumford, Lewis, *The Culture of Cities,* New York: Harcourt Brace, and London: Secker and Warburg, 1938; reprint, London: Routledge/Thoemmes, 1997

Osborn, Frederic James, *Green-Belt Cities: The British Contribution,* London: Faber and Faber, 1946; new edition, London: Evelyn Adams and Mackay, and New York: Schocken Books, 1969

EVIE T. JOSELOW

Garden Club

In the late 19th century, as the industrial age was in full swing and Americans were enjoying their prosperity, an ironic result of the newfound wealth was the leisure time it afforded the wives of the wealthy. Often faced with boredom and a feeling of uselessness, the women began forming clubs of all kinds. One sort that has lasted is the garden club.

The clubs started as small groups of acquaintances meeting at each others' homes to talk about their gardens, exchange plants with one another, and perhaps read poetry lauding their flowers. If weather permitted they would take a tour of the hostess's garden and then sit down to tea. These informal clubs were by invitation only, keeping them small and exclusive. Two major clubs eventually evolved from these beginnings, similar in mission but following different paths.

The Ladies Garden Club of Athens organized in January 1891, with 12 women convening at the house of Mrs. E.F. Lumpkin in Athens, Georgia, to begin the first garden club in the United States. Their mission was "the exchange of plants and ideas for the betterment of the community." This is the earliest recorded garden-club meeting. This club would later become part of the National Council of State Garden Clubs (NCSGC).

The idea of garden clubs soon began to flourish. Each club adopted a mission similar to the Garden Club of Athens, each wanting to be of service to the community. While the community appreciated the beautification efforts, the women's impact was not really felt outside their own circle. As cities and factory towns multiplied, natural beauty disappeared.

In 1913 a member of the Garden Club of Philadelphia suggested uniting the local clubs into a larger group that would allow them to make a greater contribution. Other clubs quickly embraced the idea. In April of the same year 22 representatives of various clubs met in Philadelphia to draw up plans for a national organization. Among the items agreed upon was that the local clubs should retain a large measure of independence. They would be allowed to set their own dues, develop their own programs, and establish their own membership criteria. The national organization would be known as the Garden Club of America (GCA).

The GCA's first efforts to educate the public were met with indifference. The approach of World War I made matters even worse. The media ridiculed the members for being foolishly interested in ornamental gardening when people were going hungry. The membership responded to the challenge by replacing their perennial borders with rows of vegetables and organizing the Women's Land Army, a volunteer effort that endeavored to replace farmhands who had gone to war with shop girls and factory workers. This time their efforts did not go unnoticed. It was also at this time that the GCA first established a relationship with the U.S. government, with some of its members serving on civilian advisory boards.

The GCA was still the exclusive, invitation-only domain of wealthy women. Less-well-to-do women had at the same time been forming clubs of their own, and the GCA offered them assistance but not inclusion. In 1924, the non-GCA clubs in New York decided to become federated to pursue a common goal. By 1929, 19 states had federated. Later that year, representatives of eight state federations met in New York City to lay the groundwork for a national federation. The NCSGC actually formed in Washington, D.C., on 1 May 1929. Georgia was not among the original members because they felt the five-cent dues too high. They eventually joined three years later.

In the aftermath of World War II, garden clubs needed to find fresh avenues to continue their community involvement. Promoting tasteful gardening no longer seemed a satisfying credo. The GCA formed a committee to study and chart the group's future direction. They settled on conservation and began a crusade to educate and to affect legislation. They held an advantage because so many of the members were married to influential businessmen.

The idea of conservation took hold, and committees formed to take on roadside littering, billboard advertising, protecting national parks, and even enforcing ethical standards among seed houses and nurserymen. The GCA extended its reach to preserving historic houses and town planning. While the group does not lobby, members will put pressure on legislators when it concerns one of their issues; members often observe Washington hearings on, for example, solar energy, pesticides, endangered species, and water conservation.

The NCSGC has also flourished. Today it is the largest volunteer gardening organization in the world, with over 8,000 clubs and more than 250,000 members in all states and the District of Columbia. While still active in promoting gardening, their mission has broadened also including the objective, "To aid in the protection and conservation of natural resources, to promote civic beauty and encourage the improvement of roadsides and parks." They also maintain a scholarship fund.

The current GCA is no longer an exclusive enclave of the wealthy, with almost 200 clubs and a total membership exceeding 17,000. A portion of annual dues supplemented with fund-raising projects goes toward national conservation projects each year.

Although in essence begun out of boredom, the clubs are still seeking ways to be useful to their communities. While men have never been excluded from the clubs, no special efforts have been made to attract them, and very few have ever joined. An unexpected bonus of both organizations was that friendly competition among the members inevitably developed, a competition credited with broadening the plant material used in American gardens.

While organized garden clubs first took hold in the United States, the idea continues to spread internationally, particularly in areas that have been under Great Britain's influence. Oddly, the concept of community garden clubs is far more popular in England's former colonies that in England itself. The British favor gardening societies that provide a shared interest and education but that do not necessarily meet on a regular basis or afford a social aspect.

One finds a good cross section of local garden clubs in Canada. Many were started in recent years and remain small and social, such as the Mission Garden Club in British Columbia. These clubs are strictly social and have no dues or business agenda. Other groups are highly organized, such as the Nova Scotia Association of Garden Clubs, which has over eight districts and more than 50 clubs. The South Surrey Garden Club began in 1989 with the goal to "advance horticulture in all its branches, beautify our homes and surroundings, and sponsor tours of particular interest to club members." They have been so successful that they have had to limit their membership to 375 members.

Membership in the Garden Clubs of Australia is much broader, welcoming any gardening oriented organization, whether or not they are an actual garden club. Founded in 1950, there are currently over 500 affiliate organizations encompassing over 34,000 members. Some are quite traditional, such as the Fairfield Garden Club, founded in 1972, which meets monthly and holds a competition among its members at each meeting. Others are less conventional, such as the Weed Society of New South Wales, the first Australian group devoted to weeds, but so many have followed that there is now an umbrella organization, the Council of Australian Weed Science Societies.

While all of these clubs share common goals, ideals, and interests, what distinguishes them from broader societies is their focus on the local community. The idea of the garden club grew out of a desire to bestow some benefit on the community while enjoying the company of like-minded friends and neighbors.

Further Reading

Battles, Marjorie, *Fifty Blooming Years, 1913–1963: The Garden Club of America,* New York: The Garden Club of America, 1963

Cochran, Mary L., "From Athens to Atlanta," *The National Gardener* 70, no. 2 (1999)

Goodman, Ernestine Abercrombie, *The Garden Club of America: History, 1913–1938,* Philadelphia, Pennsylvania: Stern, 1938

Martin, Mrs. James Bland, *Follow the Green Arrow: The History of the Garden Club of Virginia,* 2 vols., Richmond, Virginia: Dietz Press, 1970–97

Speller, Florence C., *Garden Clubs: Their Activities and Organization,* New York: Mohawk Press, 1931

MARIE IANNOTTI

Gardener in Society

The short verse "When Adam delved and Eve span/ Who was then the gentleman?" which was in use during the English Peasants' Revolt of 1381, points to the importance of examining the position of the gardener in society. Ownership of land and the division of labor have constantly affected gardening, even in mythological representations. According to the Bible, life began in a garden, and gardening is the oldest profession. The work in the Garden of Eden was originally pleasant, but, after their banishment by God, Adam and Eve were confronted with the hard labor of dealing with thorns and thistles. The Aborigines of Australia interpreted this as a tale about injustice. They saw God as white and Adam and Eve as black. The expulsion from Eden explained why the Aborigines had so little and why the white settlers had all the power and the food they needed.

The power of ownership and control has had a continual effect on gardeners, seen, for example, in the massive labor involved in the construction of royal gardens. The Hanging Gardens of Babylon, constructed in the sixth century B.C., were made up of a series of huge terraces and galleries built on a hillside, supported by arches up to 57 yards (52 m) high, with walls almost eight yards (7 m) thick. Elaborate machines were used to draw water from the river Euphrates to the top of the gardens, which was then channeled through conduits.

Similarly, a century before the Spanish arrived, an aqueduct of baked clay was erected in the Aztec hanging gardens of Texcotzingo to supply the terraces with water from a distance of 11 miles (approximately 18 kilometers). Mountains and valleys were leveled to let the water flow under its own power to the gardens, which had been built on top of a hill. There the water was fed through a system of wells, fountains, and canals to irrigate all the plants. A flight of 520 steps led to the top.

At the end of the 13th century, Marco Polo saw Kubla Khan's gardens in what is now Beijing. A mound had been created about 99 yards (91 m) in height and more than a mile (more than 1.6 kilometers) in circumference. The mound was covered with a dense growth of evergreen trees. Many of the trees had been dug up and transported to the mound by elephants.

Medieval monks also employed laborers to cultivate their monastery gardens, including digging, planting, weeding, and repairing walls and ditches. As Teresa McLean has documented in *Medieval English Gardens,* monasteries hired casual labor to do "all the unskilled jobs that should not take up too much of the monks' time."

In 1680 at Boughton in Northamptonshire, the first duke of Montagu, who had been ambassador at Versailles, had avenues laid out that stretched for miles in all directions. Later his son even contemplated having an avenue planted which would extend in straight line for 70 miles (approximately 114 kilometers), all the way to London.

Evictions were particularly common in 18th-century England, when whole villages were often removed to provide a pleasing prospect for the aristocratic landowner. The work involved in constructing the famous landscape gardens was immense. At Rousham in 1738 more than 70 men were employed in digging and damming the river. In the duchess of Marlborough's personal garden at Blenheim in 1708, gardeners planted thousands of bulbs, including 4,600 tulips and 18,500 Dutch yellow crocuses.

In 1786 Thomas Jefferson visited England and toured some of the famous landscape gardens to find out how much they cost to make and maintain. At Stowe he found 15 men and 18 boys employed in keeping the pleasure grounds. At Blenheim, with its 2,500 acres (1,000 ha), 200 people were employed to keep it in order and to make alterations and additions, 50 of whom worked in the pleasure grounds.

The same scale of work continued in the 19th century. The village of Edensor near Chatsworth House in Derbyshire had already been destroyed once in the 18th century because the fourth duke of Devonshire thought it spoiled his view. It was rebuilt after designs by Lancelot "Capability" Brown. In the 19th, century the village was again pulled down and redesigned by Joseph Paxton. In 1831, 22 men were employed just to work in the Chatsworth kitchen garden.

All the famous gardens in the world have been created by hard physical labor, and often that labor was forced, carried out by servants, convicts, or slaves. The Calcutta Botanic Garden, for example, used to be cultivated by convicts in chains. Their labor was replaced by peasants hired by the day or week, when it was realized that the labor of freemen was cheaper than that of slaves.

Usually these gardeners have been hidden from history. Even language conspires to conceal them. We hear, for example, of Gertrude Jekyll "making" her 15-acre (6 ha) garden at Munstead Wood, but not of the 11 gardeners she employed; of Ellen Willmott "making" her garden at Warley Place, near Brentwood in Essex, with no mention of the 86 gardeners she employed. In his poem "The Task" (1785), the English poet William Cowper satirized the way in which "Capability" Brown is seen in the same light, as an omnipotent magician who has only to wave his wand and the landscape is transformed:

> He speaks. The lake in front becomes a lawn,
> Woods vanish, hills subside, and vallies rise,
> And streams as if created for his use,
> Pursue the track of his directing wand
> Sinuous or strait, now rapid and now slow,
> Now murm'ring soft, now roaring in cascades,
> Ev'n as he bids.

Traditionally, in many societies there has been a split between the royal and aristocratic owners of the land and gardens, the middle-class professional designers of gardens, and the working-class laborers who construct the gardens. This division of labor is reflected in the ancient Egyptian saying, "The scribe is released from manual tasks: it is he who commands." Similarly, in China the literati despised physical work, although they enjoyed helping to design their own gardens. The manual work would have been seen as labor fit for the artisan class, in a land "where men who worked with their heads were thought to rule naturally over those who worked with their hands" (McDermott). The actual makers of the gardens are usually unidentified in the records.

As well as being unidentified in history, gardeners were often kept out of sight so that gardens could be enjoyed without reference to how they were constructed and maintained. In 1644 John Evelyn visited the Luxembourg Palace in Paris, describing in his *Diary* (1 April) the "beautiful and magnificent" gardens: "What is most admirable, you see no gardeners, or men at work, and yet all is kept in such exquisite order, as if they did nothing else but work; it is so early in the morning, that all is despatched and done without the least confusion."

The invisibility of gardeners is mirrored in 17th-century poetry, which generally leaves out any reference to the violent labors of the countryside, as James Turner points out: "There is virtually no mention of land-clearance, tree-felling, pruning, chopping, digging, hoeing, weeding. . . . Almost everything which anybody *does* in the countryside is taboo."

There has also been a division of labor *within* gardening work. In his *Encyclopaedia of Gardening* (1822) John Claudius Loudon distinguishes four groups engaged in the practice and pursuit of gardening, including tradesmen, designers, and patrons. The remaining group he calls "operators or serving gardeners," of which there are ten categories, ranging from royal gardener to garden laborer:

> The garden labourer is the lowest grade in the scale of serving gardeners. He is occasionally employed to perform the common labours of gardening, as trenching, digging, hoeing, weeding, &c.: men for the more heavy, and women for the lighter employments. Garden labourers are not supposed to have received any professional instruction, farther than what they may have obtained by voluntary or casual observation.

As Loudon indicates, another division of labor is between men and women, although again the women have often been hidden from history. Nevertheless, women were almost certainly the first gardeners. Edward Hyams concludes that "the earliest agricultural communities were matriarchal and feminine in their social values" and that "women long remained in charge of their discovery of agriculture." In Asia and Africa almost all women who are employed work in agriculture. In Mozambique, for example, 90 percent of working women are engaged in the production of food.

In 16th-century England, Thomas Tusser's gardening books express the concept of separate spheres of gardening for men and women. Tusser indicates that the orchard and fruit lie within the man's province and that flowers, plants for the kitchen, herbs, and salads come within the housewife's. Similarly, in Tommaso Campanella's utopian work *La città del sole* (1602, *The City of the Sun*), the men gather fruit and the women work in the gardens near the city, gathering vegetables and herbs and performing other light duties.

In 19th-century England vegetable gardening came to be seen as a male occupation. Flora Thompson has described the division of labor in Oxfordshire during the 1880s as a code whereby only the men worked in the vegetable gardens, although the women could cultivate flower gardens and an "herb corner, stocked with thyme and parsley for cooking, rosemary to flavour the home-made lard, lavender to scent the best clothes, and peppermint, pennyroyal, horehound, camomile, tansy, balm, and rue for physic."

In England plant lore was traditionally a female area of knowledge and was handed down from mother to daughter, in the same way that Mary Seacole, the famous West Indian nurse in the Crimean War, had learned traditional African remedies from her mother. Women looked after the herb garden and were expert in the medicinal use of plants. Midwives relied on their knowledge of plants and flowers, and herb women were often more skilled than the formally educated male doctors. In the Middle Ages, women healers organized themselves in groups as pharmacists, cultivating herbs and exchanging their knowledge. In the 18th century, herb women taught Joseph Banks his early botanical knowledge.

Hired gardeners on the whole were men. Women would, however, be employed for weeding, hoeing, collecting insects, sweeping up dead leaves, cutting off decayed flowers, and tying up straggling shoots. Men cutting the grass with scythes would be followed by lawn women who gathered up the cuttings. The gendered division of labor may be changing, but it still existed in an English survey conducted in 1988 by the Garden Centre Association. It found that more men dig the vegetable patch and mow the lawn, while more women look after the plants and weed.

Another sphere in which women found a place has been illustrating gardening books. In the 16th century, for example, Christophe Plantin of Antwerp employed women illustrators to color by hand the botanical books he produced. In England the prints in early 19th-century gardening books were colored by women and children in assembly-line factory conditions.

Throughout the 19th century, male gardeners gradually managed to gain some horticultural qualifications, but these were not available to women until the end of the century. The first female students were admitted to the Horticultural College at Swanley in 1891. By 1896 there were 39, and in 1903 the college was given over completely to women students, numbering 63.

Female gardeners were at last allowed at the Royal Botanic Gardens, Kew, in 1896, but they were ridiculed in the press and laughed at by male passengers passing on buses. The women had been instructed to wear clothing similar to that of the ordinary gardener, which consisted of thick brown bloomers, woolen stockings and boots, tailored jackets, waistcoats and ties, and peaked caps. The director ordered them to wear long mackintoshes on their way to work to hide the bloomers.

The working conditions of gardeners have normally been harsh: long hours and low pay, often with the added insecurity of casual work. In the 18th century, the head gardener was often the only permanent member of the garden staff. Living conditions could be atrocious. On large estates they usually had to live next to the gardens in a bothy that was often less important than the area in the same building set aside for tools and seeds. Sometimes they had to be on duty more or less 24 hours a day, seven days a week, in case of emergency. They were treated as servants and sometimes were not paid at all. At the beginning of the 19th century, the job of gardening was so poorly paid and precarious that gardeners often had to beg or advertise for charity in the gardening press. In 1839 the Benevolent Institution for the Relief of Aged and Indigent Gardeners and Their Widows was formed to deal with such cases.

In his *Gardener's Magazine* (1826–44) John Loudon constantly called for better wages, hours, and lodgings for the hired gardener. He compared an illiterate bricklayer, with wages of between five and seven shillings a day, to a journeyman gardener who, despite having studied geometry, land surveying, and botany, received only two shillings and sixpence a day. In 1841 even head gardeners were paid only about a tenth of a cook's salary and half that of a footman.

When Victoria Park, in the East End of London, was constructed in the 1840s, the workers who built it were paid three shillings and threepence a day if they were unskilled laborers and five shillings and fivepence if skilled, such as bricklayers, carpenters, and painters. About 70 to 80 men were employed daily and more than 32,000 trees were planted. In 1868 the Board of Works decided to extend the bathing lake, and eventually 100 men, many of them skilled workers, were employed, but all at the unskilled rate. The board complained that progress was too slow, to which the park superintendent, Mr. Merrett, who was in charge of the work, replied that the main reason for the delay was the physical weakness of the laborers, many of whom had been close to starvation.

At the beginning of the 20th century, the National Union of Horticultural Workers was set up in England to negotiate wages for its members, but by the end of the century gardeners were still the lowest-paid workers. The New Earnings Survey of April 1987, for example, gave the average gross weekly earnings of male manual workers in Britain. At the bottom of the list were general farm workers, with 124 pounds, and second to last were gardeners and groundsmen, with 132 pounds. The average wage for all male manual workers was 185 pounds.

Gardening work has not always been an alienating part of the division of labor. There have always been gardeners who have gardened for themselves and their families, without constraint or orders, uniting design and planning, labor and consumption, although not always ownership. According to Ralph Austen, the 17th-century gardening writer, such gardeners included the Roman emperor Diocletian and Cyrus, king of Persia. John Evelyn, in *A Discourse of Sallets* (1699), also mentions Cicero as one who used to prune and water his garden with his own hands.

But more generally the history of cottage gardens and allotments shows how laborers can spend a whole day doing harsh physical labor and still have the energy and enthusiasm to garden in their own time. Similarly, at the end of the 18th century, florists' clubs were organized throughout Britain by factory workers and artisans to cultivate flowers. Derbyshire miners raised pansies; Lancashire cotton workers auriculas; Sheffield workers polyanthus; colliers of Northumberland and Durham pinks. Norwich was noted for its carnations, Manchester for its gooseberries, and Spitalfields in London was famous especially for its auriculas and tulips. Paisley and Glasgow were famed for pinks. The most famous pinks were produced by Paisley weavers, who obtained seeds from London between 1785 and 1790. Some of the seedlings showed a pattern of lacing. Through careful selection, these laced forms were propagated, and, by the early 19th, century Paisley pinks were being exported to the rest of the country. During this time more than 300 new varieties of pinks were raised.

An anonymous writer of this period writes of the difference between hired labor and free labor in the garden:

> The auricula is to be found in the highest perfection in the gardens of the manufacturing class, who bestow much time and attention on this and a few other flowers, as the tulip and the pink. A fine stage of these plants is scarcely ever to be seen in the gardens of the nobility and gentry, who depend upon the exertions of hired servants, and cannot therefore compete in these nicer operations of gardening with those who tend their flowers themselves, and watch over their progress with paternal solicitude.

At the beginning of the 21st century amateur gardening in Britain is a six billion pound-a-year industry. But throughout the world there are still gardeners working in atrocious conditions to provide the West with flowers. The 40,000 women working in the Colombian flower industry, for example, are suffering deadly diseases caused by pesticides, and they have a saying: "Behind every beautiful flower is a death. Flowers grow beautiful while women wither away."

The position of the gardener in society has usually been lowly and despised. As the creator of things of beauty and use, however, the gardener should be honored, as Wordsworth expresses in "To the Spade of a Friend": "Thou art a tool of honour in my hands; / I press thee, through the yielding soil, with pride." Even in prison, the gardener has the secret of life, as Nelson Mandela demonstrated: "A garden was one of the few things in prison that one could control. To plant a seed, watch it grow, to tend it and then harvest it offered a simple but enduring satisfaction. The sense of being custodian of this small patch of earth offered a small taste of freedom."

Further Reading

Austen, Ralph, *A Dialogue (or Familiar Discourse) and Conference betweene the Husbandman and Fruit-Trees in His Nurseries, Orchards, and Gardens,* Oxford, 1676

Campanella, Tommaso, *The City of the Sun* (1602), translated by A.M. Elliott and R. Millner, London and West Nyack, New York: Journeyman Press, 1981

Critchley, Laurie, editor, *A Glimpse of Green: Women Writing on Gardens,* London: Women's Press, 1996

Evelyn, John, *Acetaria: A Discourse of Sallets,* London, 1699; 2nd edition, 1706; reprint, edited by Christopher Driver, Devon: Prospect Books, 1996

Evelyn, John, *The Diary of John Evelyn,* 6 vols., edited by E.S. de Beer, Oxford: Clarendon Press, 1955

Hadfield, Miles, *Gardening in Britain,* London: Hutchinson, and Newton, Massachusetts: Branford, 1960; 3rd edition, as *A History of British Gardening,* London: John Murray, 1979

Hoyles, Martin, *The Story of Gardening,* London and Concord, Massachusetts: Journeyman Press, 1991

Hoyles, Martin, *Bread and Roses: Gardening Books from 1560–1960,* London: Pluto Press, 1995

Hyams, Edward, *Soil and Civilization,* London and New York: Thames and Hudson, 1952; new edition, London: John Murray, and New York: Harper and Row, 1976

Jefferson, Thomas, *Thomas Jefferson's Garden Book, 1766–1824,* Philadelphia, Pennsylvania: American Philosophical Society, 1944

Loudon, John Claudius, *An Encyclopaedia of Gardening,* 2 vols., London, 1822; new edition, 1835; reprint, New York: Garland, 1982

Mandela, Nelson, *Long Walk to Freedom,* London and Boston: Little Brown, 1994

McDermott, Joe, "Review of Ji Cheng's *The Craft of Gardens*," *Garden History* 18, no. 1 (1990)
McLean, Teresa, *Medieval English Gardens*, New York: Viking Press, 1980; London: Collins, 1981
Thompson, Flora, *Lark Rise to Candleford*, London and New York: Oxford University Press, 1945
Turner, James, *The Politics of Landscape: Rural Scenery and Society in English Poetry, 1630–1660*, Oxford: Blackwell, and Cambridge, Massachusetts: Harvard University Press, 1979
Tusser, Thomas, *A Hundreth Good Pointes of Husbandrie*, London, 1557; reprint, Amsterdam: Theatrum Orbis Terrarum, and New York: Da Capo Press, 1973
Tusser, Thomas, *Five Hundreth Points of Good Husbandry*, London, 1573; new edition, as *Five Hundred Points of Good Husbandry*, London, 1812; reprint, Oxford and New York: Oxford University Press, 1984

MARTIN HOYLES

Gardenesque Style

The term *gardenesque* was employed throughout the 19th century to describe a style of landscape gardening. More recently it has occasionally been used as a term of abuse to describe the confused taste of the Victorian garden. As the structure of the word indicates, it was derivative of and, in a sense, complementary to the picturesque. It was first used by John Claudius Loudon (1783–1843) in the *Gardeners' Magazine* of 8 December 1832 in a review of William Sawrey Gilpin's *Practical Hints upon Landscape Gardening* (London, 1832) where Loudon castigated the author, an avowed disciple of the picturesque, for his ignorance of American trees. He commented:

> Mere picturesque improvement is not enough in these enlightened times: it is necessary to understand that there is such a character of art as the gardenesque, as well as the picturesque. The very term gardenesque, perhaps, will startle some readers; but we are convinced, nevertheless, that it is a term which will soon find a place in the language of rural art.

Loudon betrayed the source of his new concept when he complained that Gilpin's work simply imitated nature and, therefore, could not be regarded as an art form. To be a true modern gardener he needed to appreciate the value of the new species of trees which, when carefully introduced into a garden and allowed to flourish, would be a valid expression of artistic creativity—the gardenesque. Loudon borrowed this idea from A.C. Quatremère de Quincy, whose *Essai sur...l'Imitation* (1823) had dismissed the picturesque style as a form of art in terms similar to those used by Loudon. It is also likely that he translated the term *gardenesque* from the French *jardinique*, which distinguished artistic gardening from mechanical gardening and was in vogue when Loudon visited Paris in 1828.

Modern writers have been quick to point out that the espousal of the artificial as a true measure of garden art had a long pedigree, which predated the English landscape movement led by Lancelot (Capability) Brown and Humphry Repton. In a sense the gardenesque reconnected landscaping with the flower gardens of William Mason, William Chambers, and Richard Bateman, as well as with the tradition of the *ferme ornée* of Philip Southcote and William Shenstone. In fact, Loudon had no intention of detaching the gardenesque from the picturesque, as he made clear in his introduction to *The Landscape Gardening and Landscape Architecture of the Late Humphry Repton Esq.* (1840). Whereas the picturesque had been built upon a taste for landscape painting and poetry, to be relevant in the 19th century it had to account for the prevailing interest in botany, horticulture, and exotic planting. The new plants needed to be displayed where they could develop their natural potential, while picturesque principles would still govern the overall effect of the planting. "In short, the aim of the gardenesque is to add, to the acknowledged charms of the Repton School, all those which the sciences of gardening and botany, in their present advanced state, are capable of producing."

Loudon realised that by the early 19th century the picturesque had won the hearts and souls of those who delighted in landscape gardening and would provide the philosophical base for gardening activities for many years to come. However, its promoters—Uvedale Price, Richard Payne Knight, Repton, and Gilpin—had several blind spots. They had failed to take account of the vast number of exotic plants that had suddenly become available in the Regency period. The interest in the flower garden revived. The new plants needed to be displayed with artifice and, perhaps, in a formal setting. Furthermore, the new middle classes with small villa gardens needed a modified form of the picturesque as a framework for their new botanical acquisitions. If necessary, they might require an arboretum or an American garden. All this necessitated a degree of artifice that could be accommodated within the gardenesque.

Well before the term had been proposed, Loudon's experiments at Tew Lodge (1808–11) showed the gardenesque in practice. Trees and shrubs were planted on the lawns of the house grouped according to species, forming a "botanical shrubbery" which was both useful and ornamental. Beyond the lawns was a productive, populous, and picturesque farm modeled on Foxley, Price's estate in Herefordshire, England, a true revival of the *ferme ornée*.

The gardenesque was eminently suitable for the botanical gardens and public parks that sprang up in the early 19th century. These projects frequently had an educational purpose, making Loudon's methods of discrete planting within a picturesque framework the perfect vehicle. In 1831 he designed the Birmingham Botanical Garden, where the centerpiece was an ornamental shrubbery laid out on the Linnaean system with an attached American garden. The garden had a flowing design, exploiting its elevated position, and demonstrated the key Pricean tenet of connection. By 1834 the garden had 9,000 species of plants on display. The Derby Arboretum followed in 1839, where Loudon recommended that trees should be planted on mounds of earth to display their roots, so that they took on the symmetry of a classical column. Similar gardenesque principles were applied by Joseph Paxton (1803–65) to the arboretum at Chatsworth and the style reached its apogee at Crystal Palace Park, Sydenham Hill, in 1854 and at Biddulph Grange in Staffordshire (ca. 1850). Loudon had also proposed a farsighted scheme of metropolitan improvement in 1839 that would have divided London into town and country zones. The latter would have been improved by employing gardenesque and picturesque canons.

The gardenesque was adopted enthusiastically by the suburban dwellers who read Loudon's periodicals. Their evergreen shrubberies surrounded garden plots where, often within a formal framework, they propagated rarities. Such artistic creations were far removed from those of Price and Repton, but their makers had learned from Loudon that their efforts counted as a creative art form. Some commentators have noticed that the gardenesque advocacy of the artificial underpinned the revival of formality, which reached its zenith in the mid-19th century with the great parterres of W.A. Nesfield (1793–1881). Both Price and Knight admired ancient formality, and the latter had predicted in *The Analytical Inquiry* (1805) that the Italian garden would soon be revived.

After Loudon's death the gardenesque was reinstated by Edward Kemp (1817–91) as a mixed or irregular style, a blending of art and nature. It was no longer specifically associated with the display of plants, but in this form it continued to hold sway in the post-Nesfield era of the 1870s and 1880s. Eventually, the gardenesque became linked with the "old English" landscape style of the 18th century where, from the perspective of the late 19th century, its roots lay. William Robinson's *English Garden* (1883) has been seen as a reassessment of gardenesque principles. These concepts also figured prominently in the plans of Edward Milner (1819–84) published in *The Art and Practice of the Landscape Gardener* (1890) by his son Henry. It is not impossible to view the Arts and Crafts movement as the final refuge of the gardenesque, since the term was still being used periodically in the Edwardian era.

See also Loudon, John Claudius and Jane Webb Loudon

Further Reading

Ballard, Phillada, *An Oasis of Delight: The History of the Birmingham Botanical Gardens,* London: Duckworth, 1983

Bisgrove, Richard, *The National Trust Book of the English Garden,* London and New York: Viking, 1990

Elliott, Brent, *Victorian Gardens,* London: Batsford, 1986

Jacques, David, *Georgian Gardens: The Reign of Nature,* London: Batsford, 1983

Loudon, John Claudius, editor, *The Landscape Gardening and Landscape Architecture of the Late Humphry Repton, Esq.,* London, 1840

MacDougall, Elisabeth B., editor, *John Claudius Loudon and the Early Nineteenth Century in Great Britain,* Washington, D.C.: Dumbarton Oaks, 1980

Simo, Melanie L., "John Claudius Loudon: On Planning and Design for the Garden Metropolis," *Garden History* 9 (1981)

Simo, Melanie L., *Loudon and the Landscape: From Country Seat to Metropolis, 1783–1843,* New Haven, Connecticut: Yale University Press, 1988

DAVID WHITEHEAD

Garden Show and Flower Show

Starting in winter, flower and garden shows throughout the horticultural world mark the beginning of the gardening year. The shows are commonly sponsored by a horticultural society and started as a way to champion a society's mission, which generally includes the furthering of the science and practice of horticulture, as well as public understanding and appreciation of gardening and the environment. A theme is usually designated for each year's show, and the displays are designed accordingly. Although entertaining, such shows are basically commercial. They feature the latest in plant material and showcase the latest trends. They are also a venue for manufacturers to introduce new gardening supplies, tools, and gadgets. The main draw for the public, however, is not the market but the exhibitions. The landscape displays can be so grand in scale, incorporating stonework, water elements, and full-size trees, that one can forget that they are assembled on site in a matter of days.

Garden shows took place before the 20th century, but they were essentially demonstrations of horticultural skills. With the idea of displaying flowers in a more natural looking setting, public interest in flower and garden shows developed, as even the most novice gardener could glean some inspiration from the scenic displays featured at modern shows.

Those partial to a particular flower joined together to form specialty plant societies. These societies often host public shows of their own. Most every variety of flower has a devoted society showcasing its attributes. The proliferation of garden clubs in the United States gave rise to annual flower shows in many cities across the country. The enthusiasm for competitive shows has resulted in a shortage of qualified judges, and courses are held regularly to train new recruits.

The grand-scale shows attract the most attention in horticultural societies. Unrivaled to this day is the oldest recurring garden show, the annual Chelsea Flower Show, produced by the Royal Horticultural Society (RHS) on the grounds of the Royal Hospital in Chelsea, England. The first Chelsea show in 1827 was actually advertised as a public breakfast and was held in part to raise funds for the society. The idea was an immediate success, and the event continued to grow in both size and glamour. The British royal family has supported the event since its inception, further bolstering the show's prestige. The Royal Preview, a private showing the night before the show opens to the public, began in 1912 with King George V.

Awarding prizes began in the late 1850s at Chelsea. While exhibiting at the show was always good advertising, winning a medal would establish a company's or designer's reputation. Competition to present the new, the rare, and the unusual increased once the award system was in place. Fortunately, such competition supports the universal theme of educating the public, and even plant breeders participate in the competitions for the honor of creating the most exciting new plant of the season.

Amateurs and professionals compete separately at most shows, but the categories often overlap. Plant material plays an important role for judges. As in garden design color, texture, and scent are all primary considerations. Judges are also interested in the use of unusual plant material, perhaps new cultivars or varieties that may not be readily available to the public. The landscape-design exhibits are judged on many levels, including creativity, design, use of plant material, quality of plant material, outstanding horticultural interest, use of features such as walls, water, walkways, and structures, and excellence in demonstrating a theme or issue to the public. More and more frequently, show themes underscore the link between horticulture and environmentalism. With the vast number of categories it is not uncommon for an exhibit to win multiple awards, the most coveted being the best of show, which generally goes to the favorite exhibit of the majority of judges.

Flower arranging was not an initial feature at garden shows. It was only introduced as a category in 1937 at the Chelsea Flower Show. Constance Spry, an Englishwoman renowned for flower arranging, made a presentation that year, but the event did not become a regular feature of the show for another 20 years.

The run of the Chelsea Flower Show has been interrupted only twice, once during World War I when the RHS used the show to educate the public on vegetable gardening and food preservation and to raise money for War Horticultural Relief, and again during World War II when the War Office took over the hospital grounds as an anti-aircraft site. For three days in May the Chelsea Flower Show becomes the focal point for avid gardeners and marks the start of the British gardening season.

Chelsea, the beginning of the modern garden show, is still a leader in the gardening world. However, it is far from alone. Garden shows have proliferated, from the coral island of Anguilla to Van Dusen, Canada, and in virtually every state in the United States. The Melbourne International Flower and Garden Show in Australia is one of the country's largest tourist events, although for Australians the show season is their autumn. The Philadelphia Flower Show is the largest show in the United States and the largest indoor garden show in the world. Held on the 33 acres (13.4 ha) inside the Pennsylvania Convention Center, the show generally encompasses about 60 landscape exhibits, 3,000 floral displays, and a thriving marketplace. This one-week show, held in March, attracts in excess of 250,000 visitors. The Pennsylvania Horticultural Society held its first annual exhibition in the summer of 1829, when 25 society members gathered to display their finest plant treasures. Some years later the official show was originally produced by a group of nurserymen and growers established as the Philadelphia Flower Show. At that time the society was only responsible for the show's amateur competitive sections.

In July the British turn their attention to the Hampton Court Palace Flower Show, sponsored by the RHS and the largest outdoor annual flower show in the world. Held over six days and visited by some 200,000 people each year, the show spreads out over 25 acres (10.1 ha) on the banks of the Thames.

Billed as the longest continually running garden show, the New England Flower Show is held in Boston in March. Although small by show standards (covering only five-and-a-half acres [2.2 ha]), according to the Massachusetts Horticultural Society, the show includes over 2 million blossoms, 1,500 varieties of flowers, trees, and shrubs, and enough bark mulch to cover 15 football fields. The concord grape and the Bartlett pear were both introduced at the New England Flower Show.

While the shows last only a brief time, revenue from garden shows can be considerable, and the proceeds are used to further the societies' educational and research projects. For example, the Philadelphia show benefits several of the society's outreach projects, including their neighborhood greening program, Philadelphia Green. The RHS is able to fund their advisory and research undertakings. The communities involved enjoy the boom in tourism, and the visiting public takes their newly gained knowledge back into their own communities.

Further Reading

Geddes-Brown, Leslie, *Chelsea: The Greatest Flower Show on Earth,* London: Dorling Kindersley, 2000

Marsden-Smedley, Hester, *The Chelsea Flower Show,* London: Constable, 1976

Moreland, John, *Chelsea Gold: Award-Winning Gardens from the Chelsea Flower Show,* London: Cassell, 2000

Wearn, E.D., *The Flower Show: A Guide to Exhibiting Flowers, Plants, Fruit, Vegetables, and Handicrafts at Local and National Level,* London and Dover, New Hampshire: Croom Helm, 1985

Whiten, Faith, and Geoff Whiten, *The Chelsea Flower Show,* London: Elm Tree Books, 1982

MARIE IANNOTTI

Garzoni, Villa

Collodi, Pistoia province, Tuscany, Italy

Location: approximately 10 miles (16 km) east-northeast of Lucca, and 30 (48 km) miles west-northwest of Florence

The Villa Garzoni, Collodi, now the seat of the family of the Gardi dell'Ardenghesca, is one of the most spectacular villas of Tuscany, most famous for its great gardens and terraces that run down the slope of the hill upon which the villa stands. Situated near Lucca, in the small town of Collodi (the birthplace of Carlo Lorenzoni, the author of *Pinocchio,* who took the name of the town as his pseudonym), the villa itself is set on the site of a medieval fortress built by the Garzoni family in the 14th century. Being Ghibellines, with the rise of the Guelfs, the Garzonis had to flee Florence to seek protection in neighboring Lucca. We know little about the history of the later villa, and few famous names are associated with it. But it is clear from a surviving drawing that, whenever it was begun, the building was completed by 1633 as it is now. To judge from lines in a poem by Francesco Sbarra, *Le pompe di Collodi,* the main work of terracing and leveling of the ground below was completed by 1652. By 1692, according to another contemporary description, the garden was essentially finished.

Much of the style of the decoration at the Villa Garzoni can be seen in the more general history of taste in Lucca. In earlier villas in the area, as in all Tuscany as a whole, gardens were defined by notions of privacy. By the 17th century, however, the plans and designs for the parts of these villas designed for a newly enriched merchant class now reflected the form of magnificence—both inside and out—of the great palaces built in that time in Rome. The house, perched high on the hill, with the village behind it, is plain on its facade, three floors with a basement level, with few exterior details except for an entrance arch and decorations around the windows. Inside all is different; the entrance leads to a courtyard and to a richly decorated summer house, with a receding front, marked by a projecting bow at the center that becomes a small tower. All the details are marked out by pebbles and small rocks. This design has been attributed to a local Lucchese artist Ottaviano Diodati (1716–86), who worked in the garden in the later 18th century, but it has also been associated with the famous Torinese architect Filippo Juvarra (1678–1736), who had been in Lucca a half century earlier and produced villa designs for several patrons there.

Below and to the side of the main axis of the house is the garden. This skewed placing was necessitated by the lie of the land, but it also allows parts of the garden, in particular the grand parterres and the fountains, to be clearly visible from the windows of the villa. The design of the garden was such that one could walk from the house to the highest terraces and gaze on the view below, cooled by breezes sent up by the torrents in the long water staircase. This staircase was based on a similar feature found at the Villa Aldobrandini, Frascati, but in a detail typical of the visual virtuosity here, the one at the Villa Garzoni widens as it ascends, thus making it seem more abrupt when seen from below and longer when seen from above.

At the highest point of the staircase is a semicircular pool, presided over by the statue of Fame and two other figures, symbolizing Florence and Lucca. Behind it to the right, amid the trees, Diodati added a little bathhouse, the inside of which is divided by screens into compartments, each with a sunken bath, with a musicians' gallery above, screened off to give the bathers privacy. Below the water staircase, terraces lead down, in three levels, with a niche at each point similar to those at the Villa d'Este, Tivoli, with statues of Neptune and Triton. The floor had sunken water jets that were turned on by a hidden tap. All these were invisible from above, giving the effect of an almost headlong incline to anyone looking down the staircase. In a similarly amusing manner are humorous figures all around: in niches peasants and beggars and ruffians, along the water cascade monstrous birds that seem to drink, and on the balustrades terracotta monkeys, dressed in long jackets and armed with spiked gloves, ready to play the game of *pallone.*

The lower parterre on the flat ground, as the base, is decorated more soberly with two circular pools, which are outlined with the forms of countercurves with double scalloped hedges. The higher level is marked out with two main plots, again subdivided. The center of each plot is set in the arms of the Garzoni family, with a box hedge and the fillings added with all the appropriate heraldic colors. Around this are set what are called knots, laid out also in box and framed with four simple straight lines, the inner sides being more decorative than the outside. All the beds, as was apparently the case when first planted, are filled with low growing flowers.

Gardens change, and it is clear from visual records that the statues, made of terra-cotta, were at one time painted white to simulate marble. Otherwise, remarkably little has changed, beyond a simplification of some of the plantings. Few gardens from the 17th and 18th centuries have survived in such perfect preservation, down to the details of the pebble mosaics. The garden is now owned and kept by the Commune of Collodi.

Synopsis

1633	Villa Garzoni completed in present form
1652	Terracing and leveling of ground completed
1692	Gardens completed
present day	Villa and gardens owned and maintained by the Commune of Collodi

Further Reading

Binney, M. "Villa Garzoni, Collodi, Tuscany," *Country Life* (April 1976)

Elgood, George S., *Italian Gardens,* London and New York: Longmans, 1907

Masson, Georgina, *Italian Villas and Palaces,* London: Thames and Hudson, and New York: Abrams, 1959l new edition, London: Thames and Hudson, 1966

DAVID CAST

Gatchina

Palace Khotchina, Russia

Location: approximately 28 miles (45 km) southwest of St. Petersburg

The park at Gatchina Palace, which incorporates one of the earliest examples of an English landscape garden in Russia, is on the site of the old lakeside village of Khotchina, first mentioned in a chronicle in 1499. The land that fell to the Swedes in the Swedish Livonian war was reclaimed by Russia under Peter I (1672–1725). In 1765 the estate was bought by Catherine the Great,

Park at Gatchina Palace
Copyright Paul Miles Picture Collection

widow of Peter III, who presented it to her favorite of the moment, Count Grigory Orlov.

The accepted style for the gardens of St. Petersburg had been governed by Peter the Great's taste for formality. He had founded the new city in 1703, and his palace gardens emulated those at Versailles. It was only following Peter III's edict of 1762, giving greater freedom of movement to the aristocracy, and the end of the Seven Years' War in Europe in 1763, making travel possible, that Russia became open to wider influences. However, it was Catherine the Great, who did not herself travel abroad but who possessed an impressive collection of engravings, contemporary texts, and Wedgwood's Green Frog dinner service depicting English stately homes in their gardens, who embraced the new style of the English landscape garden. In 1772 she wrote to Voltaire

> I adore English Gardens with their curved lines, pente-douces, ponds, . . . and I despise deeply straight lines and identical allées. . . . In a word Anglomania is more important to me than plantomania.

This knowledgeable patron sent her architects, Vasily and Peter Neyelov, to England for six months specifically to visit English stately homes in their parkland settings and to engage a British gardener. They hired John Bush, who was born Johannes Busch in Hannover. He had lived in England since the 1740s and owned a nursery garden in Hackney that he sold when he left for Russia in about 1774 to take up the appointment.

Catherine's gift of a simple hunting lodge to Orlov was transformed by Antonio Rinaldi (1709–94), the empress's Italian architect, into a substantial limestone palace more in the spirit of an English castle of the period than a Russian one. Work on the castle took 15 years, and the park and gardens inevitably took considerably longer. Unfortunately, no archival evidence is available in St. Petersburg to make definitive attributions with regard to gardeners. It appears that the work was largely the responsibility of Charles Sparrow, a Scot who is believed to have arrived in 1769. A German, F. Helmholtz, was also involved, and James Hackett continued Sparrow's work in the 1790s. Bush may have been involved at Gatchina for a few months between his work at the Oranienbaum and Tsarskoye Selo and possibly again when the estate was given to Grand Duke Paul in 1783, following Orlov's death. (At Catherine's instigation the estate, with the contents of the palace, had been bought from the Orlov family for one million rubles.) At Oranienbaum, where Rinaldi had designed the Little Dutch House for Catherine, a new garden with a lake, streams, bridges, winding paths, and garden pavilions was laid out. All these ingredients are to be found at Gatchina, where it is clear that Catherine herself took a great interest in the garden. She was pleased that Orlov acknowledged her "merite jardinier."

While continental influence is also evident in the park, the landscaping of the lakes and islands and surrounding area is the work of Sparrow and Hacket, perhaps aided by Bush.

The natural fall of the land was enhanced by man. Water was manipulated and hills created. Islands, planted with fir, birch, or pine trees, were added to lakes for their Picturesque effect. Even the clay lining of the Silver Lake may have been added to give an emerald color to the water in contrast to the White Lake. The hunting area lies to the north of the park, separated by the Menagerie Gates with limestone piers from the 1770s. Limestone was used for the many garden buildings, gates, and bridges in the 18th century, while in the 19th century the use of iron for bridges and, more surprising, for balustrades is apparent.

We know that work in the garden was well under way in 1774 when a foreign visitor noted that

> The garden is being arranged in the English taste by an English master invited for the purpose. The character of the locality and the closeness to the house of an enchanting lake afford him every opportunity to display his genius. (Tretyakov)

Later, an English visitor admired Sparrow's planting: "The noble plantations are the most conspicious, and draw the most attention" (Cross).

The garden temples, designed by various architects, had elaborately decorated interiors for their illustrious guests; the wooden Temple of Venus of the 1780s, situated on the Island of Love in the White Lake, with its pedimented portico and French windows opening onto the lake, was inspired by one at Chantilly. It acted as the most glamorous pier from which one could step onto a boat, while the interior was decorated with gilded mirrors and fountains. The Birch House disguises the splendid decoration of its interior with what appears, from one side, to be piles of wooden logs, while from the other, shielding the exit, an Ionic screen by Vincenzo Brenna stands dramatically in front of the logs.

The fact that Grand Duke Paul was presented in 1783 with an estate that had belonged to his mother's old lover, a man involved in the death of Paul's father, Peter III, inevitably led to a number of changes on the estate. Much work was carried out while he waited to succeed as emperor at Catherine's death in 1796. Rinaldi was replaced by Brenna, who enlarged the palace while formal gardens were added around it. These included the Upper and Lower Dutch Gardens, a garden with Italian sculptures, botanical gardens and geometrically shaped ponds, and additional buildings, including the Sylvia, Admiralty, and Birch Gates as well as the Birch House and Venus Pavilion already mentioned. The pasture land in front of the palace was replaced by a parade ground for the military exercises of Grand Duke Paul's own army, which he modeled on Prussian lines.

An impressive farm was built in 1796 by Andreyan Zakharov, the central entrance based on a triumphal arch but with the addition of a dome and extending wings. Two years later Nikolai Lvov was responsible for the Prioratsky (Priory) at one end of the lake. It was named after the headquarters of the Great Priory of the Russian Order of Malta of which the czar was grand master. Built in a Gothic style, it is in marked contrast to all the classical limestone buildings, with only its tower, an "eye catcher," and plinth made of stone.

It is ironic that many of Paul's additions to Gatchina, following the dismissal of the empress's architect, merely contributed features that were in accord with the concept of the English landscape garden so admired by Catherine.

Synopsis

1499	Khotchina mentioned in chronicle
1708–10	Farm occupied by Peter the Great's sister, Natalia
1719–32	Owned by I. Blumentrost
1734–65	Owned by Prince Kurakin
1765	Bought by Catherine the Great, who presented it to Count Grigory Orlov
1765–83	Owned by Orlov; new palace built by Antonio Rinaldi, and park laid out
1770s	Orangery, Earthwork Amphitheatre, Menagerie Gate, wildflower hill, Echo Grotto, and Chesme Column created
1780s	Private Garden, Upper Dutch Gardens, Birch House, Admiralty Gate, Eagle Column, Hump-Backed Bridge

1783–1801	Grand Duke Paul (from 1796 Emperor Paul I)
1790s	Eagle Pavilion created; Venus Pavilion created; Brenna's screen to Birch House created
1796	Andreyan Zakharov's farm created
1798	Nikolai Lvov's Priorstsky (Priory)
1851	Ivan Vitali's sculpture of Paul I
1918	Nationalized

Further Reading

Cross, Anthony, "British Gardeners and the Vogue of the English Garden in Late Eighteenth Century Russia," in *British Art Treasures from Russian Imperial Collections in the Hermitage,* edited by Brian Allen and Larissa Dukelskaya, New Haven, Connecticut: Yale University Press, 1996

Les palais des émpereurs de Russie, St. Petersburg: Société Lenart, 1989

Shvidkovskii, Dmitrii Olegovich, *The Empress and the Architect: British Architecture and Gardens at the Court of Catherine the Great,* New Haven, Connecticut: Yale University Press, 1996

Shvidkovskii, Dmitrii Olegovich, *St. Petersburg: Architecture of the Tsars,* New York: Abbeville Press, 1996

Tretyakov, Nikolai S., *Gatchina Palace and Park,* St. Petersburg: P-2, 1997

ANNE PURCHAS

Generalife

Granada, Andalusia, Spain

Location: east side of the Alhambra, or approximately .75 mile (1 km) east of Granada city center

Generalife (*jinan al-'arif* in Arabic) is a magical composition of hanging gardens and intimate patios. It was once the summer palace of the sultans, built for the Nazarite dynasty. From its breezy miradors, the Moorish governors of Granada viewed the misty distances of the fertile Genil river valley, their last foothold on the Iberian Peninsula. The Arab, observes author Laurie Lee, here "achieved for a while a short sweet heaven before the austere swords of the Catholic Kings drove him back to Africa and to oblivion." The oldest parts of the Generalife are from the prosperous mid-13th century, a golden age of court patronage for the arts and sciences that ended abruptly with the siege of Granada in 1492. The Generalife survived because its owner, an aristocratic Moor, converted to Christianity.

The garden, which is now open to the public, maintains many original characteristics. The two patios, despite incorrect modern plantings, give a good idea of Moorish sensitivity to the design of personal space. The southwest orientation means the spaces are warmed by June sunshine, ready for the first visit of the governor's entourage. The larger patio is the Court of the Pool (Patio de la Acequia). A long, arcaded, space bisected by a long pool, it is animated by parabolic fountains and fed from lotus-form bowls set in the richly decorated north and south arcades. To the west is a long arcade of sturdy pillars offering views of the Alhambra. The fourth, or east side, is cut into the hillside and serves as part retaining wall, part range of service rooms.

The composition resembles the Persian *chahar-bagh,* or four-quartered garden, with the pool as the major axis and the minor axis formed by a path. Their intersection was once marked by a columned pavilion, an aesthetic device that would have corrected the almost excessive linearity of the space. Ancient irrigation pipes once watered what may have been a flower-studded mead, a recurrent feature in Islamic miniatures. The canal form is Persian and was found in gardens as early as the third millennium B.C., as well as being influential in Roman gardens.

The Patio de la Sultana was the domain of the harem, whose exalted status was recognized by the patio's elevated position above the principal patio. It contains a U-shaped pool enclosing an island with a smaller pool, with the whole enveloped by air-cooling fountains. Its ancient columnar cypresses, pink oleanders, and myrtles are authentic plantings. Also of Moorish date is the Camino de las Cascades, a remarkable water stairway descending to this patio from a higher mirador, an invention that predates a characteristic feature of the baroque garden.

The remaining terraces are modern and executed in a neo-Spanish Renaissance style. A plan in Count

Patio de la Acequia (Court of the Pool) of the Generalife, Granada, Spain
Copyright Juan Luis de las Rivas Sanz

Alexandre Laborde's *Voyage pittoresque et historique de l'Espagne* (1812) shows a park covering the slopes above the patio. Colmenar, in his *Délices de l'Espagne,* confirms this and says that the park was stocked with wild animals, suggesting that this area resembled a Persian or Mesopotamian *pairidaeza* or hunting park.

Synopsis

mid-13th century	Gardens built under Moorish rule
1492	End of the siege of Granada; gardens survived because their owner, a Moor, converts to Christianity
1921	Gardens became property of the state

Further Reading

Brookes, John, *Gardens of Paradise: The History and Design of the Great Islamic Gardens,* London: Weidenfeld and Nicolson, 1987
Byne, Mildred Stapley and Arthur Byne, *Spanish Gardens and Patios,* London and Philadelphia, Pennsylvania: Lippincott, and New York: The Architectural Record, 1928
Casa Valdés, Teresa Ozores y Saavedra de, *Spanish Gardens,* Woodbridge, Suffolk: Antique Collector's Club, 1987
Dickie, James, "The Islamic Garden in Spain," in *The Islamic Garden,* edited by Elisabeth MacDougall and Richard Ettinghausen, Washington, D.C.: Dumbarton Oaks, 1976
George, Michael, and Consuelo M. Correcher, *The Gardens of Spain,* New York: Abrams, 1993
Nichols, Rose Standish, *Spanish and Portuguese Gardens,* Boston: Houghton Mifflin, and London: Constable, 1924
Villiers-Stuart, Constance Mary, *Spanish Gardens: Their History, Types, and Features,* London: Batsford, 1929

JOHN H. MARTIN

Gen Yue

Kaifeng, Henan Province, China

Location: northeast part of Kaifeng City, approximately 450 miles (724 km) northwest of Shanghai

Gen Yue was a famous Chinese palatial garden of the Song Dynasty (960–1279) that holds a special artistic status in the history of Chinese gardens. It represented the highest level of the palatial garden, combining the natural environment with artificial scenes. The construction of Gen Yue indicates that the palatial garden with picturesque composition in China was already at a mature stage in the 12th century and also that the palatial garden was affected by private gardens. Architecture in the garden played an important role, taking advantage of advanced construction technology. In this period Chinese culture and art had reached a high level, which was reflected also in the construction of gardens. In Bianjing, the east capital of the Chinese Empire, there were already more than 150 private and palatial gardens, not including the temple gardens. The whole urban area became a garden city.

Gen Yue was constructed in 1117–22, but it had a very short history; the whole garden was destroyed in 1127 by the Jin Minority of North China when it occupied the capital Bianjing of the Song Dynasty. Therefore, the garden today exists only in the literature. Before construction began there was an innovative layout and painting supervised by the Emperor Song Huizhong (Zhao Ji) who was also a famous painter and calligrapher. The construction work was under the supervision of a talented eunuch, Liang Shicheng.

The name *Gen Yue* has a special meaning for the garden. *Gen* means the northeast direction, according to ancient Chinese literature; *Yue* is the name of a landmark divine mountain. The garden was originally named Wanshou Mountain before being named Gen Yue. The total area of this palatial garden was about 124 acres (50 ha). This garden represented the first time that poetic meaning and picturesque composition had been introduced into the Chinese garden. The stone cliff and water became the main motif of the garden, which contained various well-known flowers. The stonework and its layout were a highlight of garden development in China, which greatly changed the country's artistic and intellectual taste in gardens. The transportation of the precious and strange stones from south China became a historic event as well.

According to the literature the garden consisted of three parts. The first was Shou Shan (Longevity Mountain), an earth and rock-filled hill that was the focal point and summit of the garden, located at its very center. The mountain was an ideal copy of the Phoenix Mountain of Hangzhou. The second part, Wan Song Ling (Thousands Pines Ridge), was located in the west part of the garden. Yan Chi (Wild Goose Lake), the third section, contained a water system located in the south part of the garden. The water originated from the Jinglong River located in the northwest part of the garden. There were more than 70 species of plants distributed in different scenic areas of the garden, which was also a natural zoo containing thousands of rare animals and birds.

Architecture played an important role in the garden with more than 40 complexes of buildings for resting, entertaining, and viewing. After Gen Yue, architecture became one of the four important elements in the Chinese garden: water, stone, plants, and architecture. The pavilions, temples, villages, studios, housing, and market had both scenic and living functions and were positioned throughout the whole garden. The artistic setting of the garden communicated the essence of the natural landscape in China but was not just an imitation of nature. The stonework is another main characteristic of the garden and construction of stonework became the model for future development.

The composition of Gen Yue, referred to as the model of one lake and three mountains, served to change the prototype of the palatial gardens from ancient times. Gen Yue also introduced to the gardens of China the skill of landscape painting with the goal of representing an ideal surrounding.

Synopsis

before 1117	Garden design perhaps painted by Emperor Song Huizhong (Zhao Ji)
1117	Construction begun
1122	Garden completed
1127	Garden destroyed

Further Reading

Yang, Chia-lo, *Hsin chiao pen Sung shih ping fu pien san chung* (History of Song Dynasty), 18 vols., Taipei Ting-wen shu chü, 1978; 8th edition, 1994

ZHENG SHILING

Georgian Period

Cultural change rarely coincides with the reigns of kings, but the use of the term *Georgian* in referring to the rule of the Georgian monarchs from 1714 to 1830 has become a useful way to classify various forms of art and literature, not least among which is gardening. The early 20th-century histories of gardening in England, with their Arts and Crafts interest in the formal, usually dealt with the Georgian garden in a single chapter. Such is the case in Alicia Amherst's *A History of Gardening in England* (1895) and the popular history by Eleanour Sinclair Rohde, *The Story of the Garden* (1932). In these books the Georgian period is regarded as a postscript to the great formal centuries that preceded it, and any account of the "landscape school" is reduced to a few pages.

With the revival of interest in Georgian architecture in the 1920s and 1930s came a slow appreciation of the landscape garden. World War II created a sense of yearning for the English countryside and particularly the pastoral landscapes surrounding the country house, largely unaffected by the wartime necessity to grow more corn. Frank Clark's *The English Landscape Garden* was conceived during the war, although not published until 1948. It was followed in 1950 by Dorothy Stroud's *Capability Brown* and a decade later by Miles Hadfield's *Gardening in Britain* (1960), in which the Georgian garden finally received its due attention. More definitive was Christopher Hussey's *English Gardens and Landscapes 1700–1750* (1967) and two recent monographs by David Stuart (1979) and David Jacques (1983), both of which employ as their titles *Georgian Gardens*. In the last two decades the conservation movement in Britain has sharpened perceptions of the sacred qualities of the finest landscape gardens in Britain, if not the world. Restoration has been inaugurated, if not completed, at some notable examples such as Stowe, Stourhead, Painshill, Studley Royal, and the Leasowes, while several Picturesque landscapes, hitherto forgotten, at Downton, Hackfall, Hafod, and Piecefield have also received academic attention. Moreover, English Heritage has begun to compile a register of historic landscapes, and a majority of these date from the Georgian century.

There is a certain symmetry about the Georgian era. When George I (r. 1714–27) ascended the throne, all the great houses of Britain were surrounded by formal gardens with great parterres enclosed within yew and box, replete with statuary and rectangular canals. The basic source of ideas was the Continent—Italy, France, and the Netherlands—modified to a degree by the British climate, its topography, and the tastes of its elite. When George IV (r. 1820–30) died in 1830, terraces were back in fashion. Richard Payne Knight, in search of the visual delights of the antique, had saved the terraces at Powis Castle; Humphry Repton had laid out the geometric flower gardens at Beaudesert, Staffordshire (1814); and the Italianate layouts of W.A. Nesfield were just around the corner. In between was the great era of the landscape garden or the "Natural Style" (Jacques), or what was "Modern Gardening" to Horace Walpole and William Mason writing in the 18th century. On the Continent the style was called the *jardin anglais* to distinguish it from the *jardin régulier* derived from the great formalists such as André Le Nôtre.

In the reign of George I all gardens remained regular, and notwithstanding the recommendations of literary figures such as Addison and Pope, there was little indication that whole estates were being "thrown into a kind of garden" (Addison, *Spectator,* 25 June 1712). As was frequently the case in this era, landscape theory was well ahead of practice. Charles Bridgeman's plan of Eastbury in Dorset (ca. 1716) shows the mansion held tightly in a gridiron plan that stretches as far as the boundaries of the park. Only later did his designs relax and at Stowe ca. 1730 display serpentine walks connecting wooded glades, set within forest scenery. It was Horace Walpole who complimented Bridgeman on the first use of the ha-ha, which realized Addison's counsel, opening up the countryside and creating a succession of pictures from within the garden. Many formal schemes were depicted by Johannes Kip (1653–1722) and by later topographers who demonstrated how long the formal style survived into the late 18th century. Some geometric schemes, such as that at Melbourne Hall in Derbyshire, survived against the odds and the compulsive fashion for extensive gardening. In Herefordshire the great avenues of Croft Castle escaped the landscaper's axe to become objects of veneration in the eyes of Picturesque writers such as Sir Uvedale Price. Nearby, at Hampton Court (Herefordshire), the gardens of George London and Henry Wise, laid out for Lord Coningsby, appear to have survived until the 1780s. Even in the age of Lancelot "Capability" Brown, Thomas Wright could produce in 1766 a remarkably geometric design for St. James's Park. Throughout the 18th century regularity was always recommended close to the house and especially for the small garden, such as that illustrated in Miller's *Gardener's Dictionary* (1732), where flowers were to be displayed. These had been all but banished from the landscape garden. Thus, the typical Georgian garden frequently contained elements of the formal past—as at Stowe—unless it had been established *de nouveau*.

Stephen Switzer, who recommended the *ferme ornée* or ornamental farm in his many publications between 1715 and 1742, mixed pleasure grounds with the profitable parts of the estate (the farm) and brought paddocks, cornfields, and hedgerows into the garden. Two influential gardens exemplified this style: Robert Southcote's Woburn Farm and William Shenstone's the Leasowes. It continued to be recommended by Price and John Claudius Loudon at the end of the period and represents an important subtext of the Georgian style, and one that was also carried to the United States.

However, it was the pursuit of the natural style that epitomized the Georgian garden. Not only was there a strong literary input into these landscapes, based on a rereading of the familiar texts by Virgil and Horace, but beginning with Pope there was an increasing sense that garden making was allied with painting. Many of its practitioners, such as William Kent and Repton, were talented painters able to manipulate nature in a painterly manner. Empirical observation of real landscapes in

Italy, as well as England, also sharpened perceptions of the beauty of nature, which, as the paintings of Claude and Poussin showed, could be enhanced by humankind's sensitive intervention.

The craze for follies and garden ornaments also had its roots in the current admiration for decaying classicism but additionally in a patriotic appreciation for the venerable relics of Britain's Gothic past. William Gilpin celebrated such scenes on the Wye and in the lakes, although, ironically, his discriminating eye, which poured scorn on the "paltry" imitations of real antiquities, killed off the fashion for follies. But Gothic as a serious style, which seemed correct for the English landscape, went from strength to strength. Price and Knight in the last decade of the 18th century reaffirmed the importance of Italian and Dutch landscapes of the 17th century as a stimulus for landscaping in the Picturesque style, and this was reiterated by Thomas Hope early in the 19th century.

No other period saw so much theorizing on the garden. Burke, Gilpin, Price, and Loudon produced the framework, but there were legions of minor figures. Even Repton was eventually forced into print to defend his landscaping style. It was also the era of the practical gardening book, for example, Miller's *Dictionary,* which went through many editions. More significant for the polite classes were literary works such as Thomas Whately's *Observations* (1770) and William Mason's *The English Garden* (1772), which described existing examples of the landscape style and stimulated new ones.

The landscape garden was ever varied, and Clermont, Painshill, Stowe, Rousham, and many more were all distinct not simply because of topography but also as a result of the ever-changing kaleidoscope of fashionable influences and individual taste. Most gardens until mid-century were improved with little input from professional designers, except in the case of follies and other buildings. However, Capability Brown in the 1750s came close to creating a standard landscape park with undulating pasture, a serpentine lake, scattered clumps, and individual trees, all enclosed within a wooded belt. Hogarth's line of beauty had become a cliché, which was applied to almost every planned feature. Brown spawned many imitators or "mechanic improvers," as his critics called them, and among them was his self-appointed successor, Repton, whose early work was criticized by writers such as Price and Knight. As a result of this and pressure from patrons, Repton was forced to embrace a more eclectic style, which included the Picturesque but also acknowledged the growing interest in the flower garden.

The great weakness of the Georgian landscape garden was that it ignored the innumerable exotic plants that were daily being imported into Britain. Knight poured scorn on the lovers of floristry, regarding the cultivation of flowers as the preserve of the lower classes. In mid-century, William Mason and William Chambers were lonely voices, promoting the artificial environment necessary for the successful propagation of herbaceous plants. At the Royal Botanic Gardens, Kew, which was laid out by Chambers, there were 3,400 species of plants growing in 1765. Nurserymen issued regular catalogs promoting exotic plants. For example, a provincial seedsman such as James Clarke of County Durham could issue a 52-page catalog in 1779. It has been estimated that, whereas in 1700 there were only 1,400 plants available to the gardener in Britain, by 1830 there were 25,000.

Repton's great achievement in the context of the Regency garden was to combine Picturesque sensibilities with the desire to exploit this massive flora. He improved over 400 places and, following in the main the wishes of his patrons, provided them with the mixed gardens they required. The Picturesque theorists had given their approval to the "moss-grown" terrace, and with the aid of an amazing diversity of glasshouses and other props such as treillage, baskets, pots, etc., the flower garden was the final achievement of the Georgian era.

When he died in 1830, George IV had all but turned his back on the landscape garden and was yearning for a geometric garden at Windsor.

Further Reading

Bisgrove, Richard, *The National Trust Book of the English Garden,* London: Viking, and New York: Viking Penguin, 1990

Carter, George, Patrick Goode, and Kedrun Laurie, editors, *Humphry Repton: Landscape Gardener, 1752–1818,* Norwich, East Anglia: Sainsbury Centre for Visual Arts, 1982

Cecil, Evelyn, *A History of Gardening in England,* London, 1895; 3rd edition, London, John Murray, and New York: Dutton, 1910

Clark, H.F., *The English Landscape Garden,* London: Pleiades Books, 1948; 2nd edition, Gloucester, Gloucestershire: Sutton, 1980

Hadfield, Miles, *Gardening in Britain,* London: Hutchison, and Newton, Massachusetts: Branford, 1960; 3rd edition, as *A History of British Gardening,* London: John Murray, 1979

Harvey, John Hooper, *Early Gardening Catalogues: With Complete Reprints of Lists and Accounts of the 16th–19th Centuries,* London: Phillimore, 1972

Hussey, Christopher, *English Gardens and Landscapes: 1700–1750,* London: Country Life, and New York: Funk and Wagnalls, 1967

Jacques, David, *Georgian Gardens: The Reign of Nature,* London: Batsford, and Portland, Oregon: Timber Press, 1983

Rohde, Eleanour Sinclair, *The Story of the Garden,* London: The Medici Society, 1932; Boston: Hale, Cushman, and Flint, 1933

Stuart, David C., *Georgian Gardens,* London: Hale, 1979

David Whitehead

Germany

From a global perspective garden culture north of the European Alps had a late start. In Germany it was introduced from Italy. Little evidence exists of horticultural and gardening activities—except of those by the Romans—in the territories of present-day Germany before the Middle Ages. Categories such as Renaissance, baroque, and rococo, which have been used in the field of traditional art history for many years, offer only a limited approach to garden history. They tend to neglect the social dimensions of garden culture, which relate to the bourgeoisie and other social groups.

Gardens in the Middle Ages

Garden culture evolved gradually during the medieval period. Unfortunately, knowledge of gardens from medieval times is limited; in particular, little is known about the gardens of lower social groups up until the 19th century.

Monasteries, which gradually moved north across the Alps, were important centers of garden culture in central Europe. During the reign of Charlemagne (742–814), who ruled an empire that encompassed much of Italy, all of France, and large parts of what later became Germany, monasteries stood out as spiritual and intellectual centers of the country. The document *Capitulare de villis vel curtis imperii,* dating from the last decade of the ninth century and issued by Charlemagne, lists about 70 plant species with practical hints for cultivation in the garden. It also contains plant knowledge from antiquity and the Byzantine Empire. No evidence exists of pleasure gardens in Germany during this period.

The plan for the St. Gall monastery in Switzerland (ca. 820), one of the most important documents surviving from this period, shows formal garden beds and clearly reflects the utilitarian predominance of garden culture, as does the poem of the abbot Walahfrid Strabo (809–49), *Liber de cultura hortorum* (Book on the Cultivation of Gardens) on horticulture, gardening, and garden plants. It is unclear whether the St. Gall plan was realized or whether it remained a model plan for an ideal monastery. Hildegard von Bingen's (1098–1179) *Liber simplicis medicinae* (Book of Medicinal Herbs) gives evidence of the evolution of botanical knowledge; it comprises more than 200 plants and, probably for the first time in Germany, lists such plants as lilies and roses separately as ornamental plants.

The 12th and 13th centuries produced numerous poetic garden descriptions and garden paintings. However, it is difficult to deduce from these works of art the actual appearance of the gardens. In the course of the 13th century the first signs of pleasure gardens emerge. The seven books of *De Vegetabilibus* (ca. 1260), written by the monk Albertus Magnus, contain a special treatise on "De plantatione viridariorumque" (About Planting and Fruit Gardens), probably the first description in Germany of how to design a pleasure garden. During the 13th and 14th centuries cities became more powerful, and their bourgeoisie developed an urban garden culture.

Garden Culture in the 16th Century and Early 17th Century

In many of the German states, garden culture experienced an enormous impetus during the Renaissance. Strongly influenced by examples from Italy, as well as France and the Netherlands, designers created increasingly refined gardens during the 16th century. The ruling nobility, the clergy, and members of merchant families who profited from the widening and intensification of commercial contacts invested some of their wealth in pleasure gardens. The emerging bourgeoisie made cities such as Nuremberg, Augsburg, and Frankfurt into centers of garden art. Particularly in the second half of the 16th century, garden art came fully to bear. Mazes, grottoes, artificial mounds, elaborate water fountains, fishponds, *berceaux* (tunnel arbors), and other garden features found their way into German gardens. The garden became an artistic representation of the world. The impact of antiquity on Renaissance gardens is reflected in the placement of sculptures, which often followed sophisticated programs.

Other developments of the time, including humanism, travels to Italy and France, the evolution of science and engineering, the discovery of new countries, and the resulting introduction of hitherto unknown plant species, affected garden design in the 16th century. Early botanical gardens in Germany were established in

Königsberg (1551), Leipzig (1580), and Heidelberg (1593). Numerous publications from the period, such as Hieronymus Bock's *Kreüter Buch* (1539), reflect a growing interest in botany and plants. Numerous garden owners with botanical interests began to collect plants systematically and publish inventories of their collections. The bishop of Eichstätt's *Hortus Eystettensis* (1613) is an outstanding example.

Over time a distinction developed between gardens for practical use and gardens mainly for pleasure. Many of the early pleasure gardens consisted of garden rooms separated by such garden features as *berceaux*. Designs by Hans Vredemann de Vries, as published in his treatise *Hortorum viridariorumque elegantes et multiplices formae* (1583; Elegant and Manifold Forms of Gardens and Fruit Gardens), characterize this stage in the evolution of German garden culture.

The garden of the Stuttgart residence developed after 1550 by Duke Christoph of Württemberg in south Germany, which dates to the 15th century, became one of the most important gardens of late 16th-century Germany. It included a maze and one of the first orangeries in Germany. Emperor Rudolf II influenced further development of garden art in Prague, as well as in Vienna. During this period most gardens were enclosed by walls, palisades, and *berceaux*. The garden of the Rantzau Water-Palace in Schleswig-Holstein is an example.

One of the most impressive gardens in Germany was the Hortus Palatinus in Heidelberg, Rhineland-Palatinate, designed for Friedrich V, the elector palatine, and his wife, Elizabeth, by the French architect and engineer Salomon de Caus (1576–1626), whose treatise *Hortus Palatinus* (1620) explains the design. The Thirty Years' War proved detrimental to pleasure gardens. However, the architect and architectural writer Joseph Furttenbach (1591–1667), who had lived in Italy for ten years, enlarged the theoretical basis for garden design with his treatises *Architectura Civilis* (1628; Civil Architecture), *Architectura Recreationis* (1640; Architecture for Recreation), and *Architectura Privata* (1641; Private Architecture). He addressed the garden interests of various social groups and especially promoted bourgeois garden culture.

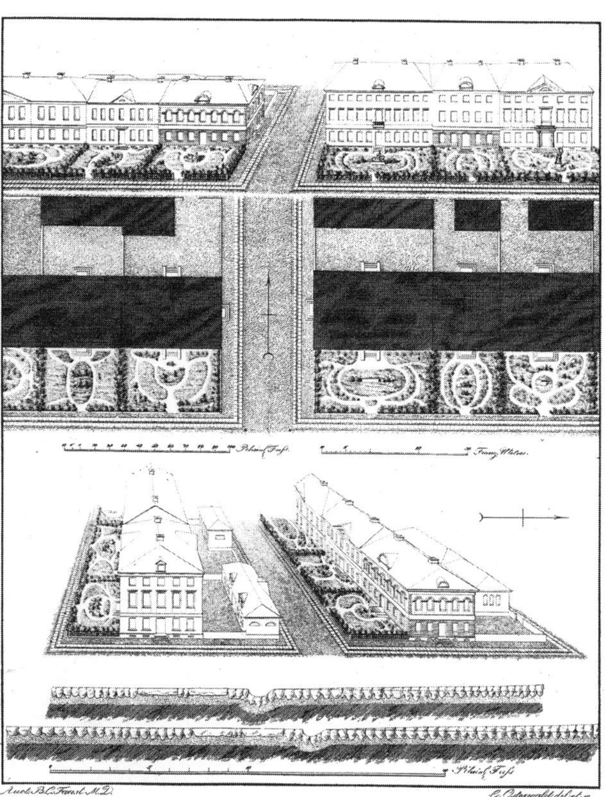

Stereotyped landscape gardens for row houses in Germany in the 1820s; from Bernhard Christoph Faust, *Zur Sonne nach Mittag sollten alle Häuser der Menschen gerichtet seyn*, 1824
Courtesy of Joachim Wolschke-Bulmahn

Late 17th and Early 18th Century

After the end of the Thirty Years' War, in the second half of the 17th century, the design of pleasure gardens received fresh impetus. The economic situation improved, and the old empire had split up into numerous individual states. The respective courts needed palaces and gardens. For many of the new palatial gardens, the gardens of Louis XIV of France at Versailles served as an example. André Le Nôtre's conception of the ideal baroque garden, with its emphasis on the central axis, the symmetrical integration of the other garden parts and axes, and the central position of the palace, can be seen in many contemporary gardens in Germany, such as Nymphenburg near Munich, as well as Veitshöchheim, Sanssouci, near Potsdam, and Augustusburg, near Brühl, with various deviations. Johann Conrad Schlaun designed for Elector Clemens August in the early 18th century the palace and the gardens in Augustusburg, which were considerably changed beginning in 1728 by François Cuvilliés the Elder (1695–1768) and Dominique Girard. The main part of the garden strongly reflects French baroque traditions.

Rulers often viewed their palatial gardens as a way to affirm their claim to power, as straight alleys would stretch far out into a palace's rural surroundings. In some instances kings and princes tried to embellish their entire territory and created systems of parks and palaces, which related to each other both economically and visually. The gardens and parks of Johann Moritz of Nassau-Siegen near Kleve, designed in the second half of the 17th century, provide an early example of such land embellishment in Germany.

Baroque garden art reached its climax toward the end of the 17th century. Such publications as Matthias

Diesel's *Erlustierende Augenweide* (1717–22; Pleasure to the Eyes) give evidence of the richness of baroque gardens of this period. The Große Garten in Herrenhausen near Hanover was begun in 1666 under Duke Johann Friedrich. Due to Electress Sophie, who had close ties to Holland, the garden also reflects Dutch traditions. Since Elector Georg Ludwig became King George I of England in 1714 and the court consequently moved from Hanover to London, the Herrenhausen garden escaped the change to a landscape garden that other gardens frequently underwent.

Also in the state of Brandenburg, French and Dutch design ideas influenced the newly created gardens. During the reign of August the Strong, Dresden in Saxony became a focus of the latest garden design ideas from France and Italy. Here a system of parks and palaces along the river Elbe was created at the beginning of the 18th century, serving such different needs as representation of social status, pleasure, plant collection, and hunting. The palace with its orangery (also named the Zwinger), the Große Garten, Großsedlitz, Pillnitz, and Moritzburg are part of this feudal park system. In particular, Großsedlitz has been underrated in its significance for garden culture.

Developments in Bavaria under Elector Max Emanuel of Bavaria also demonstrate French influence. Enrico Zuccalli and Charles Carbonet, a pupil of Le Nôtre, worked on the gardens of Schleißheim in the late 17th and early 18th centuries. Nymphenburg is an outstanding example of baroque garden art in Germany. Electress Maria Henriette Adelaide initiated work on the palace and gardens. Under Elector Max Emanuel the design of the palace and the gardens developed further into a summer residence comparable to Versailles. Major parts of the final design are based on ideas from Joseph Effner. The architect Antonio Petrini supervised construction of the palace and gardens of Seehof near Bamberg beginning in 1686. The garden reached its peak in the second half of the 18th century under Prince-Bishop Adam Friedrich von Seinsheim.

The design of the Karlsberg or Wilhelmshöhe near Kassel was initiated by Landgrave Karl of Hesse-Kassel (1670–1730). The gardens display Italian influence in general and show some similarities to the Villa Aldobrandini in particular.

Some garden historians label gardens of the late baroque as rococo gardens. Characteristics typical for gardens ascribed to the rococo include the use of "exotic" architecture (e.g., Chinese architecture in the gardens of Sans Souci, Pillnitz, and Veitshöchheim).

A major distinction between baroque and rococo also seems to be the impression that gardens are no longer subordinated to one powerful idea, as the gardens during the time of Absolutism are said to have been. Rather, they would follow a variety of themes. The gardens of the Prussian king Friedrich II in Rheinsberg near Neuruppin, at the palace in Berlin-Charlottenburg, the Tiergarten in Berlin, and most important, the gardens at Sanssouci, near Potsdam, fall into this category. In 1744–45 Friedrich gave orders to design a terraced vineyard, a new garden, and "Marly" garden in what had been the kitchen garden of his father. (Friedrich deliberately called this modest garden his Marly garden in order to demonstate how much more economically he ran this part of his estate that Louis XIV did at Marly.)

After the Seven Years' War (1756–63) the prince-bishop of Würzburg developed the Hofgarten in Würzburg and the garden of Veitshöchheim into masterpieces of late baroque garden art. Duke Karl Eugen's garden around his Solitude Palace near Stuttgart—begun in 1763—is another important example of this period of garden culture in Germany. Some of these gardens clearly mark the transition to the following English landscape garden, such as the early 18th-century garden near Kukus in the Riesengebirge, called "Bethlehem," and the rock garden Sanspareil, built 1745 to 1746 for Margravine Wilhelmine von Bayreuth, with its naturalistic design.

Late 18th Century and 19th Century

While many feudal gardens were still designed in an architectonic style in the second half of the 18th century, a new design idea began to fascinate the ruling classes in the German states. The Picturesque style that came from England transformed into a *Landschaftsgarten* (landscape garden) in Germany. Instead of clipped shrubs and trees and a rectilinear design for garden beds and water basins, what was then seen as nature became the ideal; curved lines, seemingly natural forms for garden beds and water basins, and unclipped shrubs and trees replaced formal garden design. This was also a period of intellectual reflection about garden art, which resulted in a rich body of literature about garden theory, including Christian Cay Lorenz Hirschfeld's five-volume *Theorie der Gartenkunst* (1779–85; Theory of Garden Art), Wilhelm Gottlieb Becker's treatises *Das Seifersdorfer Thal* (1792; The Seifersdorfer Valley) and *Der Plauische Grund bei Dresden* (1799; The Plauen Ground near Dresden), Johann Gottfried Grohmann's *Schöne Gartenkunst* (1798; Beautiful Garden Art), Christian August Semler's *Ideen zu einer Gartenlogik* (1803; Ideas for a Garden Logic), and Friedrich Ludwig von Sckell's *Beiträge zur bildenden Gartenkunst für angehende Gartenkünstler und Liebhaber* (1819; Contributions to Formative Garden Art for Garden Artists-to-be and Amateurs). Becker, Grohmann, and Hirschfeld were professors of philosophy.

Early examples of the landscape garden in Germany include Schwöbber near Pyrmont and Harbke near Helmstedt. The Hinübersche Garden in Marienwerder near Hanover, described at length in Hirschfeld's *Theorie der Gartenkunst,* was created by Jobst Anton von Hinüber, who was inspired by a journey to England in 1766, where he visited Windsor Park, Royal Botanic Gardens, Kew, and Chiswick. Prince Leopold Friedrich Franz von Anhalt-Dessau (1740–1817) created the so-called Dessau-Wörlitz garden empire with its park in Wörlitz, probably the best-known early landscape garden in Germany. The architect, Friedrich Wilhelm Erdmannsdorff, accompanied Franz on his Grand Tour to a new destination, England. Dessau-Wörlitz is also a notable example of land embellishment. In the 1770s Johann Wolfgang von Goethe contributed to the landscape design of Ilm Park in Weimar.

Many formal gardens either partially or completely transformed into landscape gardens, among them the parks in Biebrich, Lütetsburg near Norden, Wilhelmshöhe near Kassel, and Schwetzingen. After his return from a journey to England, Friedrich Ludwig von Sckell (1750–1823) added landscape forms into the formal garden of Schwetzingen, beginning in 1777. Peter Joseph Lenné (1789–1866) and Hermann Prince Pückler-Muskau (1785–1871) also promoted the landscape style in Germany. An eccentric aristocrat, Pückler started work on his Muskau Park at the Neisse River in 1815 after his first journey to England and continued over three decades. In his *Andeutungen über Landschaftsgärtnerei* (1833; *Hints on Landscape Gardening*) he described in detail his design ideas. After Pückler had to sell Muskau Park for financial reasons, Eduard Petzold (1815–91) worked in Muskau as director of gardens from 1852 to 1881. Earlier, Petzold had been in Ettersburg near Weimar and was made court gardener in Weimar in 1848, where he was involved in the redesign of Ilm Park.

Pückler's parks in Muskau and Branitz created particular interest with park enthusiasts in the United States.

Commemorative stone, "Der Natur" (For Nature), from Karl Lang, *Ideen aus dem Gebiete der schönen Künste,* 1804
Courtesy of Joachim Wolschke-Bulmahn

Samuel Parsons, Charles Eliot, and others visited Muskau Park and emphasized its significance for U.S. landscape architecture. In 1917 Parson edited a translation of Pückler's *Andeutungen über Landschaftsgärtnerei.* Eliot remarked in 1891 on Muskau's significance for landscape architecture in the United States: "When shall a rich man or a club of citizens, an enlightened town or a pleasure resort, do for some quiet lake-shore of New England, some long valley of the Alleghanies, some forest-bordered prairie of Louisiana, what Pückler did for his valley of the Neisse?" Pückler himself had plans to visit the United States and view the beautiful landscape along the Hudson River, but he was not able to realize them.

In 1824 Lenné became the Royal Prussian Director of Gardens, a position he held until his death in 1866. He made significant contributions to the professionalization of landscape architecture in Germany. In his early years as garden designer (1815–30), he developed plans for the Neue Garten in Sanssouci, the Tiergarten in Berlin, the park for the Charlottenburg palace, and Klein-Glienicke. His later, and more mature, works include designs for the Marlygarten and Charlottenhof in Sanssouci. Lenné's plan "Projected Ornamental and Park Ways for Berlin and Its Surroundings" (1840) was an important contribution to the evolving discipline of city planning. In the 1820s he developed a land-embellishment concept for a plantation in Reichenbach in Pommerania that resembles earlier ideas from England known as ornamented farm (*ferme ornée*). In 1822 he was one of the founders of the Verein zur Beförderung des Gartenbaues in den Königlich-Preussischen Staaten (Association for the Promotion of Horticulture in the Royal Prussian States), and in 1823 he played a leading role with the establishment of the Königlich Gärtnerische Lehranstalt Wildpark near Potsdam, the first college for horticulture and garden design in Germany.

Lenné also contributed to the evolution of the park movement with his design for the first German communal public park for the city of Magdeburg (1824). With the help of Count Rumford, who had fought for the British cause in the United States and had returned to England after it was lost, Elector Karl Theodor had already in 1789 turned his idea of a garden for the military into a large public park for the city of Munich, which was executed by Sckell. As communal self-administration and industrialization developed in Germany in the mid-19th century, numerous cities began constructing public parks. Outstanding examples include the Bürgerpark in Bremen, designed by Wilhelm Benque (1814–95), and the Humboldthain in Berlin, designed by Gustav Meyer (1816–77).

In the course of the 19th century, bourgeois garden culture developed further. An increasing number of well-to-do people could afford to hire professional landscape gardeners to design their gardens. The landscape style became commonplace, applied not only to the parks of the nobility but also to those of the bourgeoisie, and continued to the turn of the 20th century. Carl Hampel's (1849–1930) book *Die Deutsche Gartenkunst* (1902; The German Garden Art) contains typical design examples. Particular impulses to bourgeois garden culture date from the early 1870s, after Germany had won the war against France (1870–71) and consequently experienced an economic boom due to the reparations France had to pay.

Late 19th and Early 20th Century

The land-embellishment movement, with Gustav Vorherr (1778–1847) as its leading figure, and the nature preservation movement, led by Ernst Rudorff (1840–1916) and others, in the 19th century aided in the establishment of a landscape architecture profession in Germany during the course of the early 20th century.

Landscape architecture as a profession came to Germany in the late 19th century with the establishment of the Verein Deutscher Gartenkünstler (VDG, Association of German Garden Artists) in 1887. The association strove to maintain a standard of garden design that its approximately 70 members felt had been set by Lenné and Gustav Meyer (1816–77). Meyer, a former student of Lenné who collaborated with Lenné until his death, appeared to be the natural successor to Lenné. However, his openly displayed democratic leanings left him unacceptable to the Prussian court. From 1870 until his death in 1877, Meyer was the first municipal garden director of the city of Berlin, the capital of Prussia, which gradually emancipated itself from royal Prussian rule during those years. In the course of the second half of the 19th century, many cities established parks departments as part of the emerging communal self-administration. In 1860 Meyer pubished the *Lehrbuch der schönen Gartenkunst* (Manual of Beautiful Garden Art), which contains many examples for the design of gardens and landscapes. A second edition appeared in 1873, and a third one in 1895. Although a number of design books in landscape architecture appeared in the late 19th and during the 20th centuries, Meyer's book is still considered important; the 1860 edition was reprinted in 1999. Already in the late 19th century a Lenné-Meyer school of landscape design had developed. It became so widespread that a landscape-style design was applied to almost every kind of open space.

After 1900 the number of freelance garden architects gradually increased. When in 1906 many members of the Verein deutscher Gartenkünstler seriously questioned the design conventions that had been distilled from Lenné's and Meyer's designs, the association renamed itself the Deutsche Gesellschaft für Gartenkunst (German Association for Garden Art). This new

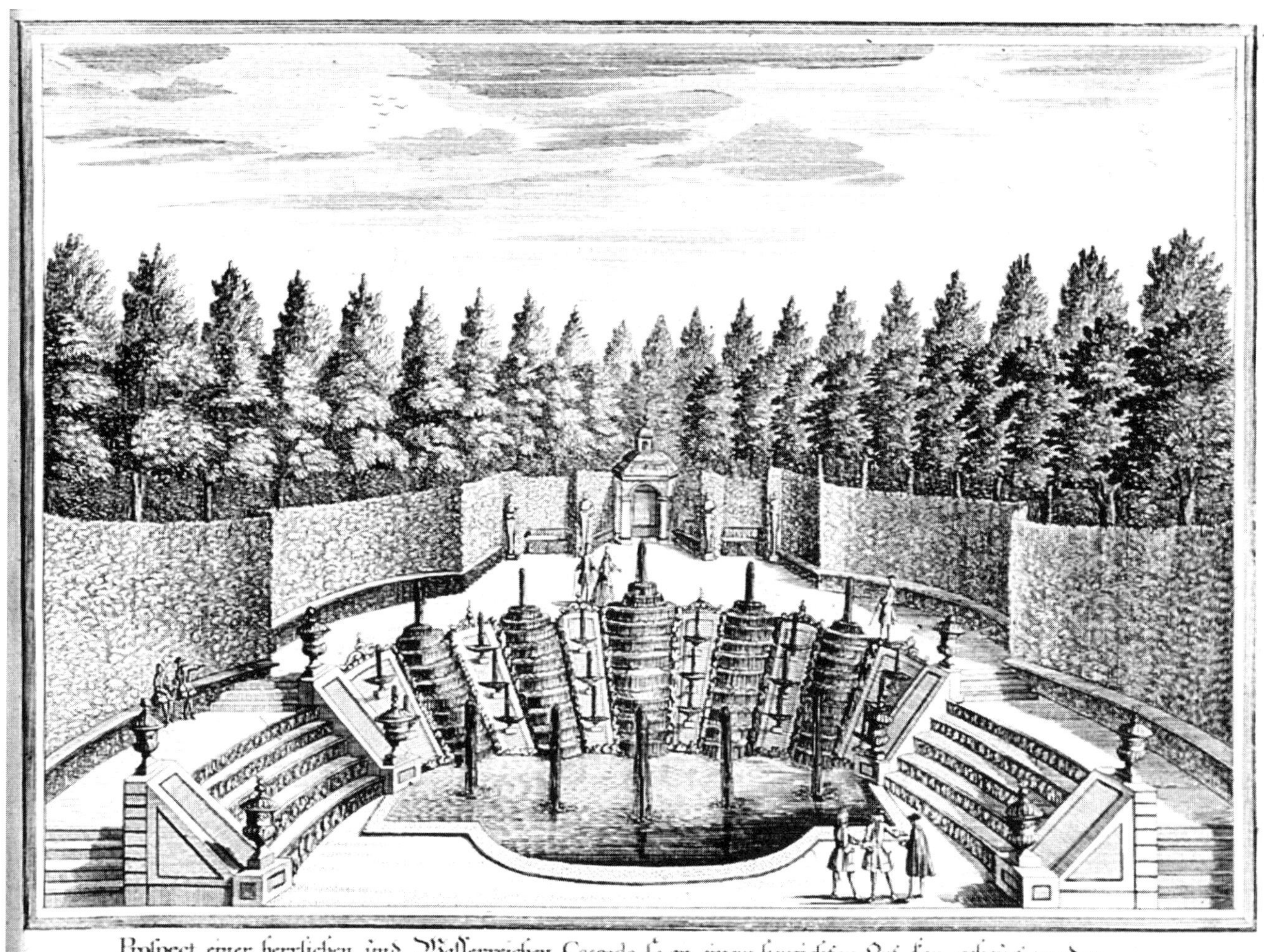

Example of a "cascade as to design at a mountaineous place," from Matthias Diesel, *Erlustierende Augenweide,* 1717–22
Courtesy of Joachim Wolschke-Bulmahn

direction signaled an opening of the association to lay people who shared an interest in garden art. Julius Trip (1857–1907), then municipal garden director of the city of Hanover and opposed to the preservation of the Lenné-Meyer style, realized the need for a separate organization for professional garden designers within the association. He suggested in 1905 it be called Bund Deutscher Gartenkünstler (League of German Garden Artists). His proposal, however, went unheeded.

In the last years of imperial Germany before World War I, many perceived the situation in landscape design as stagnant. In response, artists, architects, and garden and landscape architects looked for new solutions. The art historian Alfred Lichtwark, (1852–1914), the architects Hermann Muthesius (1861–1927), Joseph Maria Olbrich (1867–1908), and Paul Schultze-Naumburg (1869–1949), the artist and self-taught garden designer Max Laeuger (1864–1952), and others argued for an architectonic future as opposed to the "landscape" future of garden architecture, as did such landscape architects as Fritz Encke (1861–1931), Carl Heicke (1862–1938), Jacob Ochs (1870–1927), Leberecht Migge (1881–1935), and Camillo Schneider (1876–1951). Of special significance to the early reform movement in garden art were the contributions of Muthesius. His idea to correspond the garden design to the spatial arrangement of the house resonated widely. Muthesius himself had been strongly influenced from his study of country houses and gardens in England, as were many of the garden architects in Germany in the years before World War I.

With respect to park planning and park design in the early 20th century, the public park movement in U.S. cities such as Boston, Chicago, New York, and Philadelphia was considered exemplary in Germany. Mutual comparisons of park-related statistics between the situation in German and U.S. cities were common. The city of Boston even decided to shape the Charles River Basin according to the Alster Basin in Hamburg. In Bremen, Wilhelm Benque, who emigrated to the United States in the mid-19th century for political reasons, designed the Bürgerpark (Citizens' Park) in Bremen in 1866 with U.S. park designs in mind.

New Phase of Professionalism in Landscape Architecture

In 1913 two separate associations for garden architects formed in Kassel and in Frankfurt on Main, a new stage in the process of professionalization in German landscape architecture. In Kassel the Verband deutscher Gartenarchitekten (VDG) (Union of German Garden Architects) and in Frankfurt the Bund Deutscher Gartenarchitekten (BDGA) (League of German Garden Architects) established themselves. World War I interrupted the activities of both groups, and after the war the socioeconomic situation in Germany had changed considerably. For the first time in Germany governments were formed based on a democratic constitution, the so-called Weimar Constitution. Whereas the BDGA clearly oriented toward the economic interests of landscape architects and landscape gardeners, the VDG claimed in a somewhat elitist way to orient toward the artistic achievements of its members. Members of the BDGA not only designed gardens; most of them also operated tree nurseries and acted as landscape contractors. Members of the VDG preferred its image as an association of outstanding garden artists. Along this line the VDG complained in 1923 about the "Kulturlosigkeit in Gartendingen," the lack of culture in garden matters, which many people were said to display in Germany.

Socially Oriented Landscape Architecture and the Design of People's Parks

Despite the social and economic difficulties during the Weimar Republic (1918–33), a number of design issues in landscape architecture developed and propelled the profession. Based on examples of urban park planning in New York, Boston, Chicago, and other cities in the United States, which had been popularized in Germany around 1910 by the city planner Werner Hegemann, democratically elected city councils supported the implementation of people's parks during the Weimar Republic. These parks would not only allow for walking and scenic views but would also provide facilities for track-and-field activities, swimming, canoeing, specially designed areas for children, wading pools, restaurants, etc. People's parks such as Jungfernheide (1923) and Rehberge (1929), both in Berlin, designed by the landscape architect Erwin Barth (1880–1933), Rüstringen near Wilhelmshaven, designed by Leberecht Migge (1881–1935), and Raderthal (1923–24) in Cologne, designed by Fritz Encke (1861–1931), are outstanding examples. *Volksparke heute und morgen* (1927; People's Parks Today and Tomorrow), written by the landscape architect Ludwig Lesser, encapsulates in a characteristic way the hopes associated with the design of people's parks. Lesser later was forced by the National Socialists to leave Germany because they considered him to be "of fully Jewish origin." He ultimately emigrated to Sweden in 1939, where he died in 1957.

Aspects of Private Garden Design in the Early 20th Century

As a concomitant to a widespread feeling for a new beginning after centuries of feudalistic government, many freelance landscape architects engaged after World War I in a design debate about the *Kommende Garten* (garden of the future), a term probably introduced by Gustav Allinger. This was a private garden to be designed according to the needs and interest of the private owner rather than what were considered representative design standards. Landscape architects such as Hans Friedrich Pohlenz introduced avant-garde ideas into garden design. Pohlenz's Sonderbarer Garten (peculiar garden) for the Juryfreie Kunstschau Berlin (jury-free art show) 1925 is an outstanding example. Such design may have been inspired by the work of members of the Dutch group De Stijl, such as Gerrit Thomas Rietveld, Cornelis van Eesteren, and Theo van Doesburg.

Whereas many landscape architects primarily focused on design issues for the *Kommende Garten,* the landscape architect Leberecht Migge approached it as a standardized and industrialized version of the provision of gardens for everybody. In Dessau, Saxony-Anhalt, the Bauhaus city, Migge designed his most advanced scheme for the Siedlung am Knarrberg (Knarrberg residential quarter) in 1928.

Barth, Heicke, Migge, Lesser, Georg Béla Pniower (1896–1960), and other landscape architects also supported activities for allotment gardening and school gardening, views they could for the first time voice publicly as part of a democratic decision process. Whereas many cities had previously had *Kleingärten* and allotment gardens, the allotment-garden movement spread as a social movement in the late 19th and early 20th centuries. Similarly, the garden-city movement, the *Lebensreformbewegung* (movement for a reform of life), and the *Jugendbewegung* (youth movement) actively demanded open space to be part of the cities in a rapidly industrializing society.

An influential means of garden design associated with the term *Naturgarten* (nature garden) was introduced again in the early 20th century by the landscape architect Willy Lange (1864–1941). Contrary to the architectonic design of gardens and landscapes, Lange argued for what he called a biologistic aesthetic in garden design. He referred to Darwin and the development of science and created an idea for gardening that was strangely dissociated from people. In the United States the landscape architect Frank A. Waugh, who had studied with Lange in Berlin, was strongly influenced by Lange's ideas. The landscape architect Jens Jensen (1860–1951) advocated related concepts in the United States. Lange's thoughts on natural garden design turned more and more racist, nationalistic, and chauvinistic over the years. His interest in Germanizing garden art became especially clear in his idea for heroes groves that he promoted in 1915 during World War I.

The landscape style in cemetery design developed by the German-American landscape architect Adolph Strauch for Spring Grove in Cincinnati, Ohio, in the 1860s had been adopted in Germany in the decades to come. In 1904 landscape architect Hans Pietzner concluded his comprehensive book about landscape-style cemeteries, *Landschaftliche Friedhöfe, ihre Anlage, Verwaltung, und Unterhaltung* (1904; Landscape Cemeteries, Their Design, Administration, and Maintenance), with the prediction that the landscape style would be the style of the future. During the first decade of the 20th century, however, the cemetery reform movement in Germany changed the shape of cemeteries from landscape style to architectonic design.

During the Weimar Republic, a new stage of professionalization was reached with the university training for landscape architects. The debate concerning whether landscape architects should have academic training had begun in the first half of the 19th century. It was finally decided in 1929 when the first chair for landscape architecture was established at the Landwirtschaftliche Hochschule (Agricultural University) in Berlin. The chair was given to Erwin Barth. Barth's career ended in 1933 after the National Socialist takeover when he committed suicide after being pressured by National Socialist students and feeling the lack of support from his colleagues, many of whom gradually also turned National Socialist.

Era of National Socialism

Many of the professional design prospects that progressive landscape architects had opened during the Weimar Republic closed during the period of National Socialism. Professional organizations such as the BDGA and the VDG were dissolved or dissolved voluntarily. Garden architects were forced to join the Reich Chamber of Fine Arts, which declared some ineligible for racial or political reasons. Such restriction of professional prospects was actively pursued by landscape architects who became National Socialists, such as Gustav Allinger (1891–1974), Alwin Seifert (1890–1972), and Heinrich Friedrich Wiepking-Jürgensmann (1891–1973). The National Socialist blood and soil ideology seemed to allow for a natural

The "peculiar garden," designed by Hans Friedrich Pohlenz for an art exhibition in Berlin, 1925
Courtesy of Joachim Wolschke-Bulmahn

design in gardens and landscapes only because it assumed a close connection of the Germans to the landscape. Since both late landscape-style and architectonic-style designs were suggested for gardens, parks, cemeteries, and landscapes during the era of National Socialism, authorities had to apply criteria other than design when deciding about truly Germanic designs for gardens and landscapes. The landscape-style design Kleine Landschaft (little landscape) by Pniower may serve as an example. Designed for a 1935 exhibition in Berlin, it was first celebrated in newspapers as exemplary for the new German *volkish* design. When authorities learned that its designer was in their terms "half-Jewish," the design was leveled and Pniower was forbidden to practice.

Wiepking-Jürgensmann succeeded Barth in 1934 at the Landwirtschaftliche Hochschule in Berlin as the only chair for landscape architecture in Germany during the era of National Socialism. With the Nazi attack on Poland in 1939, and in compliance with National Socialist expansionist politics, Wiepking-Jürgensmann felt that gigantic tasks awaited future generations of landscape architects in the East, that is, Poland and the Soviet Union. For Wiepking-Jürgensmann the urban issues in park and garden design diminished in light of the vast areas in the East where the landscape needed, from the Nazi point of view, to become Germanized once the earlier population of Slavs, Jews, and others considered *Untermenschen* (subhuman beings) had been deported or exterminated. Wiepkingian landscape architects would then proceed, under the leadership of Heinrich

Himmler, as Reich Commissioner for the Strengthening of Germandom, to change the vast areas in the East into truly Germanic landscapes. There, the true German would feel at home in *Wehrlandschaften* (military defense landscapes), a term corresponding to the *Wehrwirtschaft* (the National Socialist economy). These landscapes, as described in Wiepking-Jürgensmann's *Landschaftsfibel* (1942; Landscape Primer), would be structured by long triple rows of strong trees in deep ditches that would cut through the land from north to south and were meant to be unsurpassable for tanks that were expected to attack from east to west. Here, Wiepking-Jürgensmann collaborated closely, under the leadership of Himmler, with Professor Konrad Meyer from the Institute for Agriculture and Agricultural Politics (Institut für Agrarwesen und Agrarpolitik) at Berlin University. Meyer was mainly responsible for implementing the 1942 *Generalplan Ost* (General Plan East). This plan provided for the expulsion and extermination of Slavs, Jews, and other people from the so-called annexed areas East, that is, the land taken from Poland during World War II, which would then have to be designed in a way that made German settlers feel at home.

National Socialism almost completely succeeded in extinguishing the memory of the prospects for landscape architecture that had appeared during the Weimar Republic. In landscape design this precipitated in an almost ubiquitous prevalence of a late landscape style in parks and gardens after the liberation from National Socialism in 1945. Designers no longer put forth progressive ideas about public parks as reflected in the people's parks movement, and any attempts for avant-garde and other modernist or progressively oriented garden design were rejected. For example, Pniower's 1947 design for the Berlin Tiergarten, the central park of Berlin, which had been completely destroyed in the final weeks of the battle for Berlin, was rejected as too modern. Instead, the Tiergarten was reconstructed along the lines Lenné had drawn some 100 years earlier. Again, landscape architecture design in Germany seemed stagnant.

Post–World War II

The design of gardens, parks, and other open spaces during the second half of the 20th century recovered slowly from the blows of National Socialism. A kind of late landscape style prevailed until the last decade of the 20th century, when new and vigorous designs in an architectonic style appeared again.

The emergence of two German states after World War II, the Federal Republic of Germany and the German Democratic Republic, led to the establishment of new university curricula for landscape architects in Hanover, Munich, Berlin, and Dresden. Landscape architecture courses had been taught at a polytechnic level in Berlin and Potsdam (since 1824), Proskau, Silesia (1868–1945), Geisenheim, Hessen (since 1872), Köstritz, Thuringia (since 1887), Weihenstephan, Bavaria (since 1920), and Pillnitz, Saxony (since 1922). The second half of the 20th century saw the additional establishment of landscape architecture courses at polytechnic schools (*Fachhochschulen*), such as Osnabrück, Northrhine Westphalia (1950), Nürtingen near Stuttgart, Baden-Württemberg (1969), Oranienburg, Brandenburg (1948), Bernburg near Erfurt, Saxony-Anhalt (1948), Neubrandenburg, Mecklenburg-Vorpommern (1996), and at university level in Essen (1966) and in Höxter-Paderborn (1978), both in Northrhine Westphalia. Many curricula for architecture at technical universities and art schools in Germany established positions for landscape architecture during the course of the century, such as the Kunstgewerbeschule at Düsseldorf, Northrhine Westphalia (1910), and the Hochschule der Künste, Berlin (1948).

In Berlin, which was made a separate political unit after World War II, landscape architect Georg Bela Pniower in 1946 received the academic chair Wiepking-Jürgensmann had vacated in 1945. From 1951 until his death in 1960, Pniower, who had been forbidden to work during the era of National Socialism, promoted for the first time in academic landscape architecture historical-, technical-, and science-based research related to the provision of open space in urban and rural areas. After Pniower's death his chair was split, and landscape architect Reinhold Lingner (1902–68) was professor of garden design until his death. After 1968 academic training in landscape architecture remained nearly absent in the German Democratic Republic for the next 20 years. The university curriculum for landscape architecture at Humboldt University in Berlin closed, and a science-oriented curriculum for landscape planning was opened at the Technical University, Dresden.

After Pniower went to Humboldt University in East Berlin in 1951, a new chair for landscape architecture was established at the Technical University in West Berlin and given to landscape architect and former National Socialist Gustav Allinger (1891–1974), who held it from 1952 to 1961. Allinger was succeeded by landscape architect Hermann Mattern (1902–71), who designed most of his many projects in a late landscape style that he had already developed in the late 1920s. The last decade of his professional career he devoted to *Landschaftsaufbauplanungen*, plans for the reconstruction of landscapes, such as Landschaftsaufbauplanung Marl (1962–63) and Landschaftsaufbauplanung Insel Fehmarn (1966–68).

In Hanover, Lower Saxony, which belonged to the Federal Republic of Germany, landscape architect Wiepking-Jürgensmann, who had left his chair at Berlin University when the Russian army approached Berlin, established in 1946 a new curriculum for landscape architects as part of the College for Horticulture and Land Culture. The college was incorporated into Hanover University in

1952. In 1955 Wiepking-Jürgensmann arranged for the former head of Himmler's planning board, Konrad Meyer (1901–73), to be given a chair for agriculture and land planning at the department of land maintenance of Hanover University, where he himself held a chair for landscape maintenance, landscape, and design.

In 1958 landscape architect Werner Lendholt (1912–80) succeeded Wiepking-Jürgensmann and represented the field of green planning and garden architecture, the landscape and garden design part of Wiepking-Jürgensmann's chair, until 1974. Lendholt focused on design and planning issues for parks, gardens, and other kinds of open spaces, such as cemeteries, playgrounds, parks, and allotment gardens. As Pniower had done earlier, Lendholt supported scholarly historical-, technical-, and social science-based research and thus increased the theoretical and methodological body of knowledge in landscape architecture.

In 1974 landscape architect Günther Grzimek (1915–96) succeeded Carl-Ludwig Schreiber (1903–76) for the chair, established in 1956, in garden and landscape design in Weihenstephan near Munich, Bavaria, against strong opposition from conservative forces such as landscape architect Alwin Seifert. Grzimek had developed an unusually progressive concept for the open-space plan of the city of Ulm, Baden-Württemberg, in the early 1950s and had worked as professor at the Hochschule für bildende Künste at Kassel from 1965 to 1972.

Professional Development of Landscape Architecture in Second Half of 20th Century

Whereas the Bund Deutscher Gartenarchitekten (BDGA; Association of German Garden Architects), the professional organization of freelance landscape architects, began to recover in 1948 in the Federal Republic of Germany, no comparable organization formed in the German Democratic Republic, reflecting the virtual absence of freelance landscape architects there. The *Essener Beschlüsse* (1953; Essen Resolutions) of the BDGA marked a new stage of professional development in the Federal Republic of Germany. Now only landscape architects who were not active as landscape contractors or entrepreneurs could apply for membership. In 1972 the organization changed its name to Bund Deutscher Lanschafts-Architekten (BDLA; League of German Lanscape Architects).

Bild 252. Doppelte und hohe Wallhecken ohne Straße mit tiefen Grabenaushüben und engen Hartholzbestand von über 50 cm Stammdurchmesser bilden ein unüberwindliches Hindernis auch für Panzer gegen überraschende Angriffe. Die „Wurzelfüße" der Bäume bilden ein dichtes, äußerst festes Wurzelgeflecht, das auf viele hundert Jahre erhalten bleibt und bei sachgemäßer Pflege des Bestandes Ewigkeitswert besitzt. Die Bewirtschaftung des Bestandes ist aber nur von geringster Nutzung. Dagegen hoher agrarwirtschaftlicher Wert durch naturwirtschaftliche Nutzungseffekte. Pflanzung möglichst in Nord-Süd-Richtung.

Sketch by Heinrich Friedrich Wiepking-Jürgensmann of his concept of the "Wehrlandschaft" (defense landscape)
Courtesy of Joachim Wolschke-Bulmahn

The professional organization of landscape architects working as leading officials for cities in the Federal Republic of Germany established itself as the Ständige Konferenz der Gartenamtsleiter beim Deutschen Städtetag in 1958. Johannes Joachim Sallmann (1912–1996), who headed the parks department of the city of Frankfurt on Main from 1957 to 1977, strongly promoted this project. He also was the first chairman of the Permanent Conference, from 1958 to 1964.

In addition to design competitions, garden shows on federal, state, and local levels publicly promoted landscape architecture both in the Federal Republic of Germany and German Democratic Republic during this period. Such exhibitions, which indicated an increasing interest in landscape architecture, had emerged in Germany during the second half of the 19th century. In the Federal Republic of Germany federal garden shows began in Hanover, Lower Saxony, in 1951 and after that took place every other year.

During the 1970s and 1980s the concept of a bio-, eco-, or nature garden became a major issue in landscape architecture in Germany due to a variety of factors, including a widespread "no-future" perspective, emerging environmentalism, ecologism, and nativism, as well as anticivilizationism, preindustrialism, and a lack of understanding for the history of garden culture throughout civilization. Although the concept of the nature garden had been popular during the early 20th century, advocates of the nature garden in the late 20th century in a characteristic ahistorical way believed to have invented a new way of design for parks and gardens.

From 1975 onward the garden conservation movement in Germany established itself as another field of professional activities for landscape architects. Although comparable activities had taken place since the late 1920s, the establishment of the Institute for Monument Maintenance with a department for historical parks and gardens in the German Democratic Republic in 1975 and the perseverance of Dieter Hennebo to establish similar positions in some of the states in the Federal Republic of Germany helped propel the movement. Hermann Schüttauf, Harri Günther, and Hugo Namslauer were important representatives of this movement in the German Democratic Republic, as were Christian Bauer, Gerda Gollwitzer, Dieter Hennebo, and Martin Sperlich in the Federal Republic of Germany.

The last decade of the 20th century was marked by the process of the political unification of Germany, which began in 1989–90. Similar processes have been occurring as well within lay and professional organizations, within universities and polytechnics, within journals, and on all levels of private and public engagement in landscape architecture. There have been some cautious attempts to mutually understand what political debates about landscape architecture can mean under both capitalist and communist premises. A fuller understanding of the differences between the Federal Republic of Germany and the German Democratic Republic concerning the approaches to the various tasks for landscape architects during the second half of the 20th century may perhaps be possible after continued research in the 21st century.

See also Berlin, Tiergarten; Berlin-Dahlem, Botanischer Garten; Branitz; Charlottenburg; Eremitage; Grosser Garten; Großsedlitz; Hortus Palatinus; Klein-Glienicke; Kleve; Nymphenburg, Palace of; Sanspareil; Sanssouci; Schleissheim; Schwetzingen; Veitshöchheim; Wilhelmshöhe; Wörlitz Park; Zwinger

Further Reading

Buttlar, Adrian von, *Der Landschaftsgarten,* Munich: Heyne, 1980; expanded edition, Cologne, Germany: DuMont, 1989

Eliot, Charles, "Muskau—A German Country Park," in *Charles Eliot: Landscape Architect,* by Charles William Eliot, Boston and New York: Houghton Mifflin, 1902; reprint, Freeport, New York: Books for Libraries Press, 1971

Franz, Günther, editor, *Geschichte des deutschen Gartenbaues,* Stuttgart, Germany: Ulmer, 1984

Gothein, Marie Luise, *Geschichte der Gartenkunst,* Jena, Germany: Diederichs, 1914; 2nd edition, 1926; as *A History of Garden Art,* 2 vols., edited by Walter P. Wright, translated by Mrs. Archer-Hind, London: Dent, and New York: Dutton, 1928; reprint, New York: Hacker Art Books, 1979

Gröning, Gert, "The Idea of Land Embellishment: As Exemplified in the *Monatsblatt für Verbesserung des Landbauwesens und für zweckmäßige Verschönerung des baierischen Landes,*" *Journal of Garden History* 12, no. 3 (1992)

Gröning, Gert, "Ideological Aspects of Nature Garden Concepts in Late Twentieth-Century Germany," in *Nature and Ideology: Natural Garden Design in the Twentieth Century,* edited by Joachim Wolschke-Bulmahn, Washington, D.C.: Dumbarton Oaks Research Library and Collection, 1997

Gröning, Gert, "Aspects of the Political and Social Context of the Garden Conservation Movement in Twentieth-Century Germany," *Garden History* 28, no. 1 (2000)

Gröning, Gert, and Joachim Wolschke-Bulmahn, *DGGL, Deutsche Gesellschaft für Gartenkunst und Landschaftspflege e. V., 1887–1987: Ein Rückblick auf 100 Jahre DGGL,* Berlin: Boskett, 1987

Gröning, Gert, and Joachim Wolschke-Bulmahn, "Politics, Planning, and the Protection of Nature: About Political Abuse of Early Ecological Ideas in Germany between 1933 and 1945," *Planning Perspectives* 2, no. 2 (1987)

Gröning, Gert, and Joachim Wolschke-Bulmahn, *Von Ackermann bis Ziegelhütte: Ein Jahrhundert Kleingartenkultur in Frankfurt am Main,* Frankfurt: Kramer, 1995

Gröning, Gert, and Joachim Wolschke-Bulmahn, *Grüne Biographien: Biographisches Handbuch zur Landschaftsarchitektur des 20. Jahrhunderts in Deutschland,* Berlin: Patzer, 1997

Gröning, Gert, and Joachim Wolschke-Bulmahn, "Landschafts- und Naturschutz," in *Handbuch der deutschen Reformbewegungen, 1880–1933,* edited by Diethart Kerbs and Jügen Reulecke, Wuppertal, Germany: Hammer, 1998

Hartmann, Kristiana, "Gartenstadtbewegung," in *Handbuch der deutschen Reformbewegungen, 1880–1933,* edited by Diethart Kerbs and Jürgen Reulecke, Wuppertal, Germany: Hammer, 1998

Hennebo, Dieter, *Gärten des Mittelalters,* Munich: Artemis Verlag, 1987

Hennebo, Dieter, editor, *Gartendenkmalpflege: Grundlagen der Erhaltung historischer Gärten und Grünanlagen,* Stuttgart, Germany: Ulmer Verlag, 1985

Hennebo, Dieter, and Alfred Hoffmann, *Geschichte der deutschen Gartenkunst,* 3 vols., Hamburg, Germany: Broschek, 1962–65

Lesser, Ludwig, *Volksparke heute und Morgen,* Berlin: Rembrandt Verlag, 1927

Migge, Leberecht, *Gartenkultur des 20. Jahrhunderts,* Jena, Germany: Diederichs, 1913

Migge, Leberecht, *'Der soziale Garten': Das grüne Manifest* (1926), Berlin: Gebrüder Mann, 1999

Pückler-Muskau, Hermann Fürst von, *Andeutungen über Landschaftsgärtnerei verbunden mit der Beschreibung ihrer praktischen Anwendung in Muskau,* Leipzig, 1833; reprint, Stuttgart, Germany: Deutsche Verlags-Anstalt, 1996

Reinsch, Günter, "Wilhelm Benque: Der Gestalter des Bürgerparks," in *Der Bremer Bürgerpark, 125 Jahre: Jahrbuch der Wittheit zu Bremen,* edited by Werner Barkemeyer and Walter Hubert, Bremen: Döll, 1991

Rippl, Helmut, editor, *Der Parkschöpfer Pückler-Muskau,* Weimar, Germany: Böhlau, 1995

Wimmer, Clemens Alexander, *Geschichte der Gartentheorie,* Darmstadt, Germany: Wissenschaftliche Buchgesellschaft, 1989

Wolschke-Bulmahn, Joachim, *Auf der Suche nach Arkadien: Zu Landschaftsidealen und Formen der Naturaneignung in der Jugendbewegung und ihrer Bedeutung für die Landespflege,* Munich: Minerva, 1990
Wolschke-Bulmahn, Joachim, "The 'Wild Garden' and the 'Nature Garden'—Aspects of the Garden Ideology of William Robinson and Willy Lange," *Journal of Garden History* 12, no. 3 (1992)
Wolschke-Bulmahn, Joachim, "Avantgarde und Gartenarchitektur in Deutschland," *Zolltexte* 7, no. 26 (1997)
Wolschke-Bulmahn, Joachim, and Gert Gröning, *1913–1988: 75 Jahre Bund Deutscher Landschafts Architekten BDLA,* Bonn: BDLA, 1988
Wolschke-Bulmahn, Joachim, and Gert Gröning, "The Ideology of the Nature Garden: Nationalistic Trends in Garden Design in Germany during the Early Twentieth Century," *Journal of Garden History* 12, no. 1 (1992)
Zander, Robert, *Geschichte des Gärtnertums,* Stuttgart, Germany: Ulmer, 1952

GERT GRÖNING AND JOACHIM WOLSCHKE-BULMAHN

Ge Yuan

Yangzhou, Jiangsu province, China

Location: at the city center of Yangzhou, which is approximately 150 miles northwest of Shanghai

Gardens are an important characteristic scenery in Yangzhou. As a scholar of the Qing dynasty has noted in his book "Notes of Painted Boats of Yangzhou": "Hangzhou is famous for its lake and mountains, Suzhou is famous for its city and shops, and Yangzhou is famous for its gardens." Ge Yuan was constructed in 1818 on a ruined vegetable garden named "Shou Zhi Yuan" by a rich salt merchant, Huang Yingtai (Zhijun; his other assumed name was Geyuan), who was also a painter. There is lots of bamboo planted in the garden, and the form of bamboo's leaf is very similar to the Chinese character form; therefore, the owner of the garden took a half of the character and named the garden Ge Yuan, which became his assumed name as well. Originally, the area of the garden was about 0.6 hectares (1.5 acres); today it is about 4,500 square meters (5,382 sq. yd.) and it is located behind the residence.

The piled rockeries are the essence of the gardens in Yangzhou. The rockeries of Ge Yuan, which remain from the former Shou Zhi Yuan, are one of the highlights of classical Chinese gardens. It is said that the rockeries of Shou Zhi Yuan were designed by the great painter and calligrapher Shi Tao (1642–ca. 1718). Because Shi Tao had traveled many famous mountains and rivers, the artist was able to design a landscape consisting of innumerable mountains, valleys, deep streams, and pools within a limited piece of land and to absorb the essence of all mountains. The unique art of the rockeries was created to represent the four seasons; the designer used considerably varied colors and sizes of stones, which came from different parts of the country. The stone bamboo shoots symbolized spring, the lake stone summer, the yellow stone autumn, and the white snow stone winter. The four seasons rockeries are arranged in a clockwise sequence from west to east in the garden.

The Spring Mountain is located at the entrance of the garden. Upon entering the garden, one sees the rockeries, the bamboo, and stone bamboo shoots of varying heights standing upright in the front of a moon gate. A main hall, Osmanthus Hall, is located in front of the garden.

The Summer Mountain, with 12 caves, is built of piled lake stone and covered with shady trees and canopy-shaped cypresses and is located in the northwest side of the main hall. A stream flows under the foot of the rockeries to present a cool and refreshing atmosphere in summer. The Summer Mountain is divided into two peaks, both of which are connected to the picturesque Autumn Mountain.

The Autumn Mountain consists of three peaks built with yellow stone and is located in the eastern part of the garden, facing the sunset. There is a plateau on the top of the Autumn Mountain to which one can ascend in order to enjoy a distant view of the city. With the setting sun reflecting on the yellow rockeries and the red leaves of maple trees, it contributes to the poetic atmosphere of the season. The Autumn Mountain is the highlight of the garden.

For the Winter Mountain the designer used white round-shaped snow stone and piled up the rockeries at the foot of the northern part of the garden wall to create a scene of nonmelted snow covering the peak. The acoustics have been manipulated to create a sound to remind one of the winter north wind.

The only weakness of the garden is the excessive size of the main building, with seven bays, which is in the northern part of the garden. It overwhelms the small space of the garden.

Synopsis

ca. 1710 Artificial hill representing four seasons built in original garden (Shou Zhi Yuan), perhaps designed by Shi Tao

1818 New garden constructed on the ruins of Shou Zhi Yuan by the rich salt merchant Huang Yingtai

Further Reading

Wu, Zhaozhao, *To t'ien Kung; For the Art Excelling Nature: Collected Works on Chinese Gardens* (bilingual Chinese-English edition), Peking: Zhongguo Jian Zhu Gong Ye Chu Ban She, 1992

Yang, Hung-hsün, *Chian nan yüan lin lun; A Treatise on the Garden of Jiangnan*, Shanghai: Shang-hai Jen Min Ch'u Pan She, 1994 (with English summary)

ZHENG SHILING

Gilpin, William Sawrey 1762–1843

English Landscape Gardener

William Sawrey Gilpin came to landscape gardening late in life, but his early training as a painter and his family connections played a major part in the development of his career in the field. He came from a landed family in the northwest of England, whose home was Scaleby Castle in Cumberland. His grandfather, John Bernard Gilpin, an army captain, was described as "probably one of the best gentlemen painters of his time" (Williams). He had a number of children, of whom his sons William and Sawrey are of interest to those concerned with garden design. William, the elder of the two, was the celebrated cleric and author-illustrator of several important volumes of "observations relative chiefly to picturesque beauty," as they were called. The appreciation of picturesque scenery was a topic of great interest in the latter part of the 18th century, and Gilpin's ideas influenced the thinking of his own and subsequent generations. His younger brother Sawrey, John Bernard's seventh child and the father of William Sawrey, developed his career as a painter specializing in the depiction of animals.

William Sawrey Gilpin did not emerge as a real talent in the field of painting, though he became a competent painter of landscapes. Significantly his early training does seem to have helped him to develop an eye for siting objects in the landscape, for their relationships, and for three-dimensional composition. Through his uncle, Gilpin became familiar with Sir Uvedale Price and Richard Payne Knight, the other two main protagonists in the "Picturesque discussion," an ongoing dialogue over the characteristics and merits of the picturesque style—a principal aesthetic preoccupation in the latter part of the 18th century in Britain. Gilpin's ideas had evidently developed along the same lines as those of Price, and when he finally decided to take up a career in landscape gardening, Price reported his pleasure, commenting that he had "been long wishing that a person such as Mr Gilpin might be induced to take up the profession." Gilpin's own view of the profession, as Price's before him, and as had been expressed by John Claudius Loudon at the beginning of the century, was that landscape gardening was concerned only with visual composition, the practical details of planting and construction being suitably left to a head gardener. Landscape gardening, as described by the *Quarterly Review* in 1821, was "the disposition of the external scenery of a country residence."

A site for which Gilpin's advice has long been considered particularly significant in terms of successful composition is Scotney Castle in Kent, home of the Hussey family from 1778 and now in the ownership of the National Trust. Here he was asked advice on the location of a new house to take the best advantage of the picturesque qualities of the site, centered on the moated medieval castle. This was in 1836; two years later, at the age of 77, he was back, this time to mark out the positions of terraces, a water feature, and new plantations to complete the composition. Much of his work was of this informal and intermittent character, so it is no surprise that of the "hundreds of sites" in which he claims to have been involved, there is indisputable evidence for his work in only 62, with strong indications in a further 23. Written reports were infrequent, other records brief and scrappy, and drawings few and far between. A typical situation obtained at Trentham, Nottinghamshire, where the duchess of Sutherland had employed the

Scotney Castle, Kent, England
Copyright M.F. Downing

English architect Charles Barry. The latter had produced several alternative designs, and Gilpin's "practised eye" was sought to determine which should be put into effect.

On some sites Gilpin produced more complete reports and drawings. Bowhill in Selkirkshire is particularly well documented. Here Gilpin laid out the terrace in front of the house and provided detailed advice on the creation of new plantations, the arrangement of paths, and the treatment of the lake. Adherents of the picturesque might be said to occupy a place somewhere between the complete informality of the earlier landscape school and the more rigorously architectural style that was beginning to take hold at the time of Queen Victoria's accession to the throne in the late 1830s. Gilpin recognized the artificiality of buildings and believed that their immediate surroundings should reflect this quality. Hence, his enthusiasm for terraces, which he said were not only aesthetically correct but also contributed to the comfort and convenience of the house. Like a painter, he divided landscapes into the distance, middle distance, and foreground. The distance would be natural scenery. This part of the landscape was not usually susceptible to design changes, although Gilpin was very particular in his advice about planting tree groups in irregular clumps, for continued variation in form as seen from different directions. As one approached the foreground through the middle distance, the level of obvious art could increase. His term for this intermediate area was "dress ground," and the art of improvement lay, he said, in uniting into one harmonious whole the dress ground and the scenery beyond.

Other sites worth visiting include Clumber Park in Nottingham, where Gilpin created the "dress ground"—ornamental pleasure grounds—around the duke of Newcastle's now demolished mansion and laid out the formal Lincoln lakeside terrace. Here he is also credited with laying out the great avenues of this extensive park. At Audley End, Essex, in the late 20th century, a new flower garden was created to Gilpin's design.

Of the well-documented sites, Sudbury Hall in Derbyshire is an example for which one of Gilpin's plans survives, for the re-creation of a formal element. This was a range of terraces in a comparatively closed landscape—there were virtually no distant views—replacing in the contemporary idiom a lost formal garden of the time of the original house around 1682. Others were Wolterton in Norfolk, Gorhambury in Hertfordshire, and Sedbury Park, Yorkshire, the home of a relative, where Gilpin died at the age of 81.

Biography
Born probably in Windsor, England, 1762. Trained as a watercolor painter; helped his celebrated uncle, the Rev. William Gilpin, with illustrations for his volume *Observations on the River Wye* (1783); exhibited landscapes at the Royal Academy, London, 1797, 1799, 1800, and 1801; most of his early life spent in the London area; elected president of the newly founded Society of Painters in Water Colours, 1804; appointed third drawing master at the Royal Military College then at Great Marlow, in 1806, but was at Sandhurst from 1814; after the end of the Napoleonic Wars, lost his position as a drawing master, 1820, and at age 58 took up landscape gardening; records exist of his work at 62 sites in the British Isles, with a further 23 probable; his volume *Practical Hints* was published in 1832. Died at Sedbury Park, Yorkshire, England, 1843.

Selected Designs

1820	Kinfauns Castle, Perthshire, Scotland
1830	Clumber Park, Nottingham, England
1830	Nuneham Courtney, Oxfordshire, England
1832	Bowhill, Selkirkshire, Scotland
1836–38	Scotney Castle, Kent, England
1837	Sudbury, Derbyshire, England

Selected Publications
Practical Hints upon Landscape Gardening: With Some Remarks on Domestic Architecture, as Connected with Scenery, 1832

See also Nuneham Courtenay

Further Reading

Hussey, Christopher, *The Picturesque: Studies in a Point of View,* London and New York: Putnam, 1927
Hussey, Christopher, "Scotney Castle, Kent," *Country Life* 146 (16 October 1969)
Piebenga, Sophieke, "William Sawrey Gilpin (1762–1843), Picturesque Improver," *Garden History* 22, no. 2 (Winter 1994)
Tait, Alan Andrew, *The Landscape Garden in Scotland, 1735–1835,* Edinburgh: Edinburgh University Press, 1980
Williams Iolo A., "The Artists of the Gilpin Family, with Particular Reference to William S. Gilpin," *Old Water Colour Society's Club Annual Volume* 29 (1951)

M.F. DOWNING

Girard, Dominique d. 1738

French Garden Architect

Dominique Girard was one of the most outstanding French garden architects, although little is known about his personal life. He was presumably born in Paris, the son of Jean Girard, who himself worked as an architect at the court of Louis XIV of France. However, there is no evidence of Dominique's birth or where he might have studied. He is listed in the royal accounts of Versailles, where he worked from 1708 to 1714 as a *garçon fontainier* (waterworks and hydraulic apprentice). Here he learned the art of planning and designing gardens in the style of André Le Nôtre. At that time Versailles, with its fabulous gardens, was an example for all other garden architects, and Le Nôtre's forms and ideas were realized in many other European gardens of the 17th and 18th centuries.

Girard's career is closely related to Max Emanuel's personal history. During his exile years in Paris, Max Emanuel, elector of Bavaria, visited Versailles and other French baroque gardens. Delighted by the gardens he saw adjoining French castles, Max Emanuel looked for a French artist. On Louis XIV's recommendation he brought back with him the young Dominique Girard, from whom a distinctively French gardening style was to develop in Bavaria.

In the contracts of 1715 drawn up in Munich, "D. Girard" was appointed as *Prunnmeister* (head of water and fountains) with a regular yearly income of 1,200 florins. This can be compared to Enrico Zuccalli's 1,600 florins and to Joseph Effner's 1,500 florins as architects directing the works in Schleissheim and Nymphenburg in Munich.

Girard's first recorded design was for the garden of Schloß Nymphenburg. Most famous are the gardens of Schloß Schleissheim, where Girard could make use of all he learned during his years in Paris. In Schleissheim the choice of ground for the garden was limited by existing situations. He placed the baroque garden between the two buildings, the Neues Schloß Schleissheim and Lustheim.

Symmetry and axiality determined the layout. Recurrent geometry and garden parts relate to each other as well as to the house, creating a high degree of unity. The middle axis is flanked by two long, slightly sunken areas, and each end is accentuated by a round basin with a fountain. In these low gardens clipped boxwood, flowers, and colored gravel trace ornate patterns that derive from the art of embroidery. The style of Girard's parterres, which he also used later in Vienna and Brühl, derived from instructions given by Dézallier d'Argenville or by Le Nôtre, trailing plantlike forms of box with interlacing bands of turf or colored earth; but Girard's parterres are on the whole more open, with a pronounced use of the volute, particularly in the border. He also created more varied and complex contours. In Schleissheim Girard used the *parterres de pièces coupées* (cutwork parterre), in which flower beds make up the individual pieces of the design.

Canals play a dominant part in Schleissheim: not only is the garden bounded by canals, but the middle axis is formed by a canal, which terminates the cascade at the end of the parterre nearest the Neues Schloß. Bosquets containing garden rooms were placed on either side of the canal. All the paths in the bosquets are hedged. Girard's distinctive ability as a landscape architect becomes apparent at Schleissheim: the creation of great level spaces around the house, with trees pushed well back to display the architecture; the siting of the main elongated vista on the axis of the house with a great canal at right angles; the hierarchical arrangement of parterres and *pièces d'eau* (water parterre). Water was a crucial feature of the French formal garden, and as a *garçon fontainier.* Girard was well able to create admirable water features. As the garden was never turned into a English landscape park, it now ranks next to Belvedere, Schloßhof, and Herrenhausen as the best-preserved baroque gardens in Germany.

Besides designing, Girard was also in charge of the care for all of Max Emanuel's gardens. As a *Generalinspektor* (superintendent) beginning in 1727, Girard oversaw the workings of the fountains and maintenance of the aqueducts. He was also responsible for a great number of craftsmen. His duties included the upkeep of the parterres and the allées surrounding them. He was also required to stock the flower beds and to keep the garden between the parterre and the terrace full of flowers.

The gardens in Munich are among Girard's greatest achievements. But Girard also became famous in Austria. In the service of Prince Eugen of Savoy during the years 1717, 1719, and 1722, Girard designed the grounds of Schloß Belvedere in Vienna and in 1729–30 the Schloßhof nearby. The main garden of the Belvedere are rectangular, joining the two palaces so ingeniously as to form a whole that is unique among gardens of any period. Girard dominated the terrain by imposing a strong main axis, siting it across a shallow valley. This enabled him to play with differences of levels, for which he skillfully devised architectural features and surprises. The garden still exists in its original form thanks to the effort of today's garden director. For the great unity between palace and garden in the different sites a close cooperation with the architects must be assumed. Joseph Effner, François Cuvilliés, Lucas von Hildebrandt, and Johann Conrad Schlaun are some of the important architects with whom Girard must have worked closely.

In 1728 Girard obtained permission to visit the gardens in the middle part of Germany and to work in the services of Clemens August, archbishop and elector of Cologne, and a son of Max Emanuel. Girard's close collaboration with Schlaun and Cuvilliés played an important part in the development of the gardens of Augustusburg in Brühl. These gardens exhibit the quintessential traits of the French formal garden: symmetry, grandeur, and great expanse. The essence of Girard's artistry was a sense of scale, balance, and proportion, but always with an eye to the ground and attention to the visual effect.

Girard spent the last years of his life in Munich. His son Phillip followed in his footsteps; a plan for the garden in Nymphenburg is signed "Girard le fils."

See also Belvedere Palaces; Schleissheim

Biography

Born in Paris?, France, date unknown. Worked at Versailles, 1708–14; hired by Max Emanuel, Elector of Bavaria, 1715, a gardener and landscape architect in Bavaria; applied his Paris training to the design of the garden of Schloss Schleissheim in Munich; became inspector general for all of Max Emanuel's gardens, 1727; visited central Germany, 1728. His son Phillip followed in his footsteps and became a notable landscape architect in his own right. Died in Munich, 1738.

Selected Designs

1715	Garden of Schloß Nymphenburg, Munich, Germany
1715–17	Garden of Schloß Schleissheim, Munich, Germany
1717–22	Garden of Schloß Belvedere, Vienna, Austria
1728	Garden of Augustusburg, Brühl, Germany
1729–30	Garden of Schloßhof im Marchfeld, Austria

Further Reading

Aurenhammer, Hans, "Der Garten des Prinzen Eugen," in *Prinz Eugen und sein Belvedere,* Vienna: Österreichischen Galerie, 1963

Bader, Walter, and Walter Kordt, *Die Gärten von Bruehl,* Cologne, Germany: Du Mont Schauberg, 1965

Brauneis, Walther, *Die Schlösser im Marchfeld,* Vienna: Niederösterreichisches Pressehaus, 1981

Fox, Helen M., *André Le Nôtre, Garden Architect to Kings,* New York: Crown, 1962; London: Batsford, 1963
Hager, Luisa, "Der Schloßgarten zu Schleissheim," *Deutsche Kunst und Denkmalpflege* 2 (1965)
Hansmann, Wilfried, "Gartendenkmalpflege im Rheinland am Beispiel des Parterres von Schloß Augustusburg in Brühl," *Deutsche Kunst und Denkmalpflege* 43 (1985)
Hansmann, Wilfried, "Parterres: Entwicklung, Typen, Elemente," in *Gartendenkmalpflege,* edited by Dieter Hennebo, Stuttgart, Germany: Ulmer, 1985
Hansmann, Wilfried, "Dominique Girard und Antoine Joseph Dézallier d'Argenville," in *Garten, Kunst, Geschichte: Festschrift: für Dieter Hennebo zum 70. Geburtstag,* Worms, Germany: Werner, 1994
Hauttmann, Max, *Der kurbayerische Hofbaumeister Joseph Effner,* Strassburg, Germany: Heitz, 1913
Hazlehurst, F. Hamilton, *Gardens of Illusion: The Genius of André Le Nostre,* Nashville, Tennesse: Vanderbilt University Press, 1980
Imhof, Gabriele, *Der Schleissheimer Schloßgarten des Kurfürsten Max Emanuel von Bayern,* Munich: Wölfle, 1979
Ludwig, Wilhelm, "Belvederegarten in Wien wird restauriert—Eine Zwischenbilanz," *Historische Gärten* 2 (1996)
Ross, Stephanie, *What Gardens Mean,* Chicago: University of Chicago Press, 1998
Strandberg, Runar, "The French Formal Garden after Le Nostre," in *The French Formal Garden,* edited by Elisabeth MacDougall, Washington, D.C.: Dumbarton Oaks, 1974
Wimmer, Clemens-Alexander, "Broderie," *Das Gartenamt* 35 (1986)

UTE-HARRIET GLADIGAU

Giulia, Villa

Museo Nazionale di Villa Giulia, Rome, Italy

Location: approximately 0.5 miles (0.8 km) north of the Piazza del Popolo, at Pizzale Villa Giulia 9

The Villa Giulia was called the "eighth wonder of the world" in the 16th century and is still one of the most famous complexes in Europe. The villa, described as such by contemporaries because it was then the center of a notably large estate, was built for Pope Julius III between 1551 and 1555. Julius III, while he was still Cardinal Giovanni Maria Ciocchi del Monte, had inherited some land outside the walls of Rome near the Porta del Popolo. With his brother Baldovino he started to develop the property, buying extra parcels of land. Cardinal Poggio then gave him his own nearby villa, designed by Pellegrino Tibaldi. As a result the *vigna,* or estate, ran from the Tiber across the valley with the palazzo to the slopes of the hills beyond.

There were a number of other buildings on the land including the church of S. Andrea in Via Flaminia erected by Vignola. Although there were several enclosed gardens, the land was planted with 36,000 trees, many of them trained on extensive trelliswork. According to the *Lex Hortorum,* the pope wanted the public to enjoy his property as well.

The models for the design of this grand estate varied from the architectural complex of the Temple of Fortuna Primigenia at Praeneste and the gardens of Lucullus on the Pincian Hill in Rome to Donato Bramante's Belvedere Court at the Vatican in Rome. A long pergola shaded the walk from the river to the remodeled public fountain on the Via Flaminia. The palazzo was then reached either by the main avenue or by one of the side paths, which were lined with fruit trees. All the avenues met in a semicircular piazza, like a *patte d'oie,* in front of the palazzo. Perpendicular to the long axis of the palazzo, wide paths led to a bosky wood. Throughout the *vigna* were grottoes, pavilions, statues, fishponds, loggias, and aviaries, and there was a wonderful view of the city from the highest point of the estate. Sculptor and architect Bartolommeo Ammannati stated in a 1555 letter to his former patron Marco Benavides that "in constructing this palace we wanted to respect this beautiful and pleasant valley." He also remarked that the major building work was complete when the pope died but the decoration was not. The painters Taddeo Zuccaro and Prosper Fontana both worked at the villa.

Giacomo Barozzi da Vignola designed the entrance and courtyard facades of the casino and the original

Nymphaeum at the Villa Papa Giulia, Rome, Italy
Copyright Gian Berto Vanni/Art Resource, New York

layout. The entrance facade derives from the Palazzo Farnese in Rome and supports the belief that Michelangelo consulted on the design of the villa. Giorgio Vasari claimed credit for the overall layout and was involved with the project until he returned to Florence in December 1553, but extant documents make clear that Ammannati was responsible for most of the design. The casino of the villa is a small two-story house with three rooms on each floor; the principal rooms lie on either side of the large entrance vestibule. The salon on the upper floor is painted with a landscape frieze that includes views of the seven hills of Rome. The semicircular loggia with arched vaulting, painted with now vanished *topia* decorations (little landscape paintings), leads out of the vestibule to the first courtyard, which was originally richly decorated with sculptures and plants in pots, centered on the magnificent antique porphyry basin from the Baths of Titus, now in the Vatican. The design of the casino derives from various sources, including the Villa Madama, Pliny the Younger's writings about his own villa, and the buildings of Sebastiano Serlio. The subtle design of a semicircle interlocked with a rectangle is echoed in the second courtyard.

From the first courtyard the second loggia leads to the *nymphaeum* via the superb semicircular stairway, which is clearly influenced by Bramante. From the second courtyard the third loggia leads to the gardens beyond, with a row of rusticated arches at the end of the vista. The vertical axis leads visually down to the inaccessible real *nymphaeum,* where four caryatids support the upper level; the walls are also decorated with *topia*. The water of the Fontana Giulia of the *nymphaeum* is called Aqua Virgo after the Roman aqueduct that supplied the villa. The design of the *nymphaeum* courtyard, with four plane trees around a low fountain, echoed Pliny's description of his villa in Tuscany.

The Villa Giulia has been extremely influential in the history of garden design. For example, when the villa was only recently completed it was echoed in the Villa Barbaro at Maser, at the casino of Pius IV at the

Vatican, and later in the design of the Boboli Gardens at the Palazzo Pitti.

After Pope Julius III died 160 boatloads of sculpture were removed from the villa and taken to the Vatican. After its completion the villa was used as a guesthouse for distinguished visitors to Rome, including Cosimo I, duke of Tuscany, and Queen Christina of Sweden. The villa belonged to the papacy until the Risorgimento. After being used for a variety of purposes, in 1889 the building was restored and extended and became the National Museum of pre-Roman antiquities from Latium, Umbria, and S. Etruria.

Synopsis

ca. 1550 Cardinal Giovanni Maria Ciocchi del Monte, later Pope Julius III, inherits estate outside Rome, near Porta del Popolo, and begins acquiring neighboring land

1551 Work started on main casino, designed by Giacomo Barozzi da Vignola

1552 Bartolommeo Ammannati presents Pope Julius III on Easter day with model for the *nymphaeum;* work begins in May

1553 Pope Julius III deeds villa to brother Baldovino

1555 Work on villa completed

1555 Pope Julius III dies; villa taken over by Apostolic Chamber

1569 Villa stripped and sculpture removed

1889 Villa extended for museum

Further Reading

Bafile, Mario, "I disegni de Villa Giulia nella collezione Burlington-Devonshire," *Palladio* 2 (January–June 1952)

Carunchio, Tancrede, *La Villa di Papa Giulio III,* Roma: Il Ventaglio, 1987

Cocchia, Stanislao, Alessandra Palminteri, and Laura Petroni, "Villa Giulia: Un caso esemplare della cultura e della prassi costruttiva nella metà del Cinquecento," *Bollettino d'Arte* 72, no. 42 (March–April 1987)

Coffin, David R., editor, *The Italian Garden,* Washington, D.C.: Dumbarton Oaks, 1972

Coffin, David R., *The Villa in the Life of Renaissance Rome,* Princeton, New Jersey: Princeton University Press, 1979

Coffin, David R., *Gardens and Gardening in Papal Rome,* Princeton, New Jersey: Princeton University Press, 1991

Coffin, David R., "The Self-Image of the Roman Villa during the Renaissance," *Architectura: Zeitschrift für Geschichte der Baukunst* 28, no. 2 (1998)

Coolidge, John, "The Villa Giulia: A Study of Central Italian Architecture in the Mid-Sixteenth Century," *Art Bulletin* 25, no. 3 (September 1943)

Davis, Charles, "Villa Giulia e la 'Fontana della Vergine,'" *Psicon* 3, nos. 8–9 (July–December 1976)

Davis, Charles, "Four Documents for the Villa Giulia," *Römisches Jahrbuch für Kunstgeschichte* 17 (1978)

Fagiolo, Marcello, *Roman Gardens: Villas of the Countryside,* New York: Monacelli Press, 1997

Falk, T., "Studien zur Topographie und Geschichte der Villa Giulia in Rom," *Römisches Jahrbuch für Kunstgeschichte* 13 (1971)

Gere, J.A., "The Decoration of the Villa Giulia," *The Burlington Magazine* 107 (April 1965)

Hunt, John Dixon, editor, *The Italian Garden: Art, Design, and Culture,* Cambridge and New York: Cambridge University Press, 1996

Lazzaro, Claudia, *The Italian Renaissance Garden: From the Conventions of Planting, Design, and Ornament to the Grand Gardens of Sixteenth-Century Central Italy,* New Haven, Connecticut: Yale University Press, 1990

Letarouilly, Paul Marie, *Édifices de Rome Moderne,* 4 vols., Paris, 1840–57; as *Letarouilly on Renaissance Rome,* New York: Architectural Book, 1984

Masson, Georgina, *Italian Villas and Palaces,* London: Thames and Hudson, and New York: Abrams, 1959

Masson, Georgina, *Italian Gardens,* London: Thames and Hudson, and New York: Abrams, 1961

Nova, Alessandro, *The Artistic Patronage of Pope Julius III (1550–55): Profane Imagery and Buildings for the De Monte Family in Rome,* New York: Garland, 1988

Stern, Giovanni, *Piante, elevazioni, profili e spaccati degli edifici della villa suburbana di Giulio III,* Rome, 1784

Stevens, G.P., "Notes on the Villa di Papa Giulio, Rome," *Journal of the American Institute of Architects* 2 (1914)

Tagliolini, Alessandro, *Storia del Giardino Italiano,* Florence: La Casa Usher, 1988

Tuttle, Richard J., "Vignola e Villa Giulia: Il disegno White, Vignola, Villa Giulia," *Casabella* 61, no. 646 (June 1997)

JULIA KING

Giverny

Giverny, Eure, France

Location: village of Giverny, near Vernon, 34 miles (55 km) northwest of Paris

Giverny is probably the most famous artist's garden in the world. It is the name generally given to the house and garden of the great Impressionist painter Claude Monet (1840–1926) in the village of the same name in the lower Seine valley. The long, pink-painted, green-shuttered house is actually called the Maison du Pressoir (House of the [Cider] Press) (see Plate 13). The village is near the right bank of the Seine on its tributary, the river Epte, which is the boundary between Normandy and Île-de-France.

Giverny is a unique garden, created almost entirely by Monet himself, who stamped on it a style peculiarly his own. Here Monet's extraordinary ability to see and depict the interaction of light, color, sky, and water came together with his boundless enthusiasm for flowers and horticulture, the one talent feeding off the other. The garden was designed to give delight and inspiration to his eye. In developing it he used color boldly; flowers were grouped in masses of the same color, often with whole beds given over to a single flower variety.

Monet and his large household rented Giverny in 1883. The existing garden was a typical bourgeois one of the day—prim, gloomy, with box-edged beds and nothing of botanical interest. Monet rejected most of it, liking only the yews and lime trees. The central walk, the *Grande Allée,* was flanked by stiff borders and alternating spruce and cypress trees. The latter were removed, but the trunks of the former remained for a long time, used as supports for climbing roses. Initially Monet did much of the gardening himself, planting flowers and organizing the kitchen garden. By the 1880s Monet's paintings were selling well, and in 1890 he was able to buy the Maison du Pressoir. A head gardener, Félix Brueil (who stayed until after World War I and was succeeded by Léon Lebret, who remained in the post for 30 years), and six under gardeners were hired, and two greenhouses built. In 1893 Monet bought the small pond across the road from the main garden and soon afterward built the Japanese bridge over it. The water garden was begun, and it became the principal subject of his paintings from the end of the 1890s. Soon Monet found the pond too small and in 1901 bought a further 30 acres (12 ha) in order to enlarge it. This he was eventually allowed to do, although not without local opposition, and the garden was laid out in its present form.

Monet had a number of friends in the neighborhood, particularly the writer Octave Mirbeau and fellow Impressionist Gustave Caillebotte, who were equally enthusiastic gardeners. Caillebotte's garden, on the opposite bank of the river Seine, had many similarities to Monet's flower garden. Together the friends would scour gardening magazines and plant catalogs and attend horticultural shows. Plants were always being given and exchanged between friends, invariably sent by rail. Monet's preference for simple flowers led to plants from the kitchen garden and cottage garden—and even wildflowers—being brought into the main garden. He also had an enthusiasm for the new and exotic, however; his hothouse plants, including orchids, were carefully tended, and when new flower varieties caught his eye,he snapped them up. Monet's friend, the distinguished horticulturalist Georges Truffaut, took a great interest in the garden, and both Truffaut and Monet were given many Japanese plants, including rare irises and tree peonies, by their Japanese friend, the art dealer Mr. Kuroki.

The garden is divided into two areas. To the south of the house is the flower garden, which started life as a traditional *clos Normand* (apple orchard) and kitchen garden. To the south of this, beyond a road, the *chemin du Roy,* and railway line, lies the water garden. The two parts, now joined by a tunnel, could not be more different, but the characters of both were molded by Monet. There are no records of how he planned the garden, only notes, letters, and the descriptions by his friends. His instructions to his head gardeners, however, show a great attention to detail; much time was spent deadheading the flowers.

The flower garden is formally laid out, dominated by a central axis, the *Grande Allée.* This is a wide gravel path aligned with the central bay of the house and is the main survivor of the earlier garden that Monet took over. At its head are two large yews, also from the earlier garden, and at its lower end is the main gate onto the road. The path is flanked by colorful borders and crossed at intervals by rose arches. In high summer, nasturtiums (*Tropaeolum*) trail across the path. Parallel borders are filled with massed flowers, particularly irises. Roses, including Monet's favorite, "Mermaid" clematis, and Virginia creeper (*Parthenocissus quinquefolia*) grow on the house walls. Next to the house are some large island beds, planted in Monet's day with climbing nasturtiums on bamboo *tuteurs,* pelargoniums, cannas, and sages, with borders of pinks (*Dianthus*). To their west are two rows of pleached lime trees, which Monet retained from the earlier garden. The west side of the garden has a lawn planted with roses, fruit trees, and square flower beds, beyond which are 15 closely spaced long, narrow, parallel beds filled to capacity with annuals, biennials, perennials, and climbers, which throughout the garden are grown upon green-painted iron *tuteurs.* Beyond, on the edge of the garden, are two greenhouses and cold frames. To the east of the *Grande Allée* are 38 small, narrow, parallel beds, called the paint-box beds (or *les tombes* by the gardeners), where Monet experimented with color and grew flowers for cutting. Alternate beds have frames over them on which *Clematis montana* varieties are trained. Beyond are three further lawns bounded by borders and paths.

The water garden is Monet's most celebrated horticultural creation and was the subject of many of his paintings, including the famous *Grandes Décorations,* a series of murals in the Orangerie, Paris. The pond lies on the river Ru, a minor tributary of the river Epte. When the pond was enlarged, the Ru was diverted around its south side. Monet spanned the narrow west end of the pond with an arched wooden bridge, which he described as *genre Japonais* (in the Japanese style), on the axis of the *Grande Allée.* A path on this axis led to the bridge from a gate onto the road. A framework was made over the bridge, on which white and mauve wisterias were trained. Simple paths wind along the banks of the pond and along the Ru, which is crossed by a number of small bridges. This part of the garden is planted very differently from the flower garden, with weeping willows, bamboos, and other water-loving plants, such as Japanese iris, meadowsweet (*Filipendula ulmaria*), marsh marigold (*Caltha*), and sweet coltsfoot (*Petasites*) on the banks of the pond. A Japanese influence is clear here, but the mix is eclectic. Flowering shrubs, including roses, tree peonies, azaleas, and rhododendrons, grow around the boundaries, and rambling roses (originally 'Belle Vichyssoise', which is still grown, and 'Crimson Rambler') are trained over frames and up trees. The existing poplars on the marshy ground that Monet bought were left in place.

The still water of the pond, so necessary for water lilies, was achieved by a system of sluices. The water lilies, painted repeatedly by Monet for almost 30 years, are perhaps the most famous plant in the garden. They are hardy hybrids, bred by Joseph Bory Latour-Marliac from 1877 onward at his nursery in Temple-sur-Lot, near Bordeaux. Latour-Marliac brought specimens to the *Exposition Universelle de Paris* in 1889, and Monet was an instant enthusiast. When he began his pond there were 15 varieties to choose from, and the red *Nymphaea* 'Marliacea Ignea' (1893) was the model for the water lilies of some of his early pond paintings.

After Monet's death in 1926, his stepdaughter Blanche lived at Giverny until her death in 1947. Thereafter, the garden declined, and by the time Monet's son Michel left it to the nation on his death in 1960, it was in a sorry state. Its restoration was masterminded by Gérald van der Kemp and his American wife, Florence. Kemp was an extraordinarily effective fund-raiser who had previously done the same for Versailles. The garden had to be almost completely rebuilt and replanted, as only the major trees, including one weeping willow by the pond, and a few shrubs and tenacious perennials had survived. Since 1976 Gilbert Vahé has been in charge. Great efforts have been made to retain the spirit of Monet's gardens, but some concessions have had to be made in the interests of the throngs of visitors. The main difference in the planting is that whereas Monet planted flowers of a single variety in blocks, they are now intermingled. Giverny is the ultimate expression of human creativity, not only in the physical reality of the garden but also in the paintings of its creator, which capture the garden's every mood and fleeting moment.

Synopsis

1883	Monet rents the Maison du Pressoir, Giverny, and moves in with Alice Hoschedé and children
1890	Monet buys the Maison du Pressoir
1892	Two greenhouses built; head gardener Félix Breuil and six gardeners hired
1893	Monet buys the pond; soon afterward the Japanese bridge is built; Monet purchases and plants the water lilies that were to become famous in his paintings
1895	Monet first paints water garden
1899	Japanese bridge series of paintings
1901	Monet buys an additional 30 acres (12 ha) and enlarges pond to present size
1910	River Seine bursts banks and floods water garden for two months
1916	Third studio finished in garden to enable Monet to paint large *Nymphéas* canvases
ca. 1920	Rose arches erected over the *Grande Allée*
1926	Death of Monet
1966	Monet's son Michel leaves Maison du Pressoir and its garden to the state through the Académie des Beaux-Arts; a program of restoration begun
1976	Gilbert Vahé put in charge of gardens by Gérald van der Kemp

Further Reading

Breuil, Félix, "Les iris aux bords des eaux," *Jardinage* 21 (October 1913)

Elder, Marc, *A Giverny, chez Claude Monet,* Paris: Bernheim-Jeune, 1924

Joyes, Claire, *Monet at Giverny,* London: Mathews Miller Dunbar, 1975

Russell, Vivian, *Monet's Garden: Through the Seasons at Giverny,* New York: Stewart, Tabori, and Chang, 1995; London: Frances Lincoln, 1998
Russell, Vivian, *Monet's Water Lilies,* London: Lincoln, and Boston: Little Brown, 1998
Truffaut, Georges, "Le jardin de Claude Monet," *Jardinage* 87 (November 1924)

ELISABETH WHITTLE

Glasnevin, National Botanic Gardens

Dublin, Ireland

Location: 2 miles (3.2 km) northwest of central Dublin

The National Botanic Gardens, Glasnevin is Ireland's principle botanical institute possessing a research library and herbarium as well as a delightful garden with excellent specimen trees, colorful borders, and glasshouses of outstanding architectural merit. For over two centuries it has served as a focal point for Irish gardeners, professional horticulturists, and botanists.

In 1790 the Dublin Society was empowered by the Irish parliament to establish a botanic garden and was granted funds to maintain it; by the time the society had formed a plan and acquired land, £2,200 were available. On 25 March 1795 a lease was purchased for the site covering 16 Irish acres (approx. 27 statute acres) on which the botanic gardens still flourish. When established it was the largest publicly supported botanic garden in the world. Until 1877 the Glasnevin Botanic Gardens was managed by the Royal Dublin Society (prior to 1836, named the Dublin Society) although largely funded by the government. In 1878, when the administration was handed over fully to the state, the title changed to Royal Botanic Gardens, Glasnevin. In 1922, on the formation of the Irish Free State, the title was altered again to National Botanic Gardens. Today the National Botanic Gardens is part of Dúchas, the Heritage Service of the Department of Arts, Heritage, Gaeltacht, and the Islands.

Dr. Walter Wade, the prime mover of the scheme to establish a public botanic garden in Dublin, was in charge from the beginning. In 1796 the Dublin Society elected him as its first Professor of Botany. With Head-Gardener John Underwood, a Scottish horticulturist, Wade laid out and planted the gardens. The original plan included glasshouses for subtropical and tropical plants, a pond, arboretum, and shrubberies, as well as sections to display labeled collections of useful and harmful plants, vegetables, and medicinal herbs. The original outline of the Glasnevin Botanic Gardens is still discernible, although the total area has increased to about 48 statute acres. The present arrangement of paths can be traced on maps dating from the 1830s. A chain-tent (a circular pergola), draped with wisteria, is one of the few structures that survives from this early period.

The climate of eastern Ireland is not as moist, mild, or equable as that of southwestern Ireland. Mean annual rainfall at Glasnevin is 725 millimeters (28.5 inches); mean summer (July) maximum temperature is 19.3 degrees C (66.7 degrees F) and mean winter (January) minimum temperature is 1.7 degrees C (35 degrees F) (absolute minimum recorded was minus 20 degrees C [minus 4 degrees F]). Thus heated glasshouses have always been an important feature of the gardens. The most remarkable is the Curvilinear Range, built from cast and wrought iron with a curving roof. This structure was commenced in 1843 and has a complicated history in which the Dublin ironmaster Richard Turner played a crucial role. Turner submitted designs for an iron conservatory that were adopted, but he lost the tender to William Clancy, who built the first section. Clancy went bankrupt, so Turner was given the contract to complete the range, finishing it in 1848. When the wings were doubled in size 20 years later, Turner and his son William produced the designs and built the extensions. The Curvilinear Range, perhaps Richard Turner's most beautiful glasshouse, was restored in the 1990s and re-commissioned in 1995 to mark the Glasnevin Botanic Gardens' bicentenary.

The Victoria Regia House was built in 1854 to house the Amazon waterlily (*Victoria amazonica*). A palm house was erected in 1866, but had to be replaced by the present building in 1884. With its excellent glasshouse facilities, Glasnevin has always boasted good collections of tropical species. Especially under Sir Frederick Moore, who had a passion for small-flowered orchids and for cycads, the indoor collections were outstanding, even excelling those at the Royal Botanic Gardens, Kew.

Consequently, numerous new orchid species were named from plants that first flowered in Glasnevin.

Glasnevin Botanic Gardens played a significant role in the introduction into cultivation of exotic hardy plants. For example, pampas grass (*Cortaderia selloana*) from Argentina was raised at Glasnevin from seed sent by the Scottish collector John Tweedie in the 1840s. Also around this time, Major Edward Madden sent seeds of *Abelia triflora* and *Cardiocrinum giganteum* (among others) from the Himalaya. Among cultivars that originated in the National Botanic Gardens are *Escallonia* 'C.F. Ball', *Garrya* × *issaquahensis* 'Glasnevin Wine', and *Erica cinerea* 'Glasnevin Red'.

Although the National Botanic Gardens has not made any unique contribution to garden design, several significant horticultural developments occurred there. In the mid-1840s, under the supervision of David Moore, orchid seeds were germinated, and seedlings of four different tropical orchids were grown on to flower, something no one had succeeded in doing before. In the late 1860s, again under Dr. Moore's direction, several species of North American pitcher plants (*Sarracenia*) were artificially cross-pollinated and the hybrids *Sarracenia* × *moorei* and *Sarracenia* × *popei* were raised.

A more melancholy achievement must also be noted. Alerted by reports of the spread of a devastating potato "murrain," David Moore observed the first signs of this disease on potato plants in Glasnevin on 20 August 1845. He tried to find a method of preventing or curing the disease. Now called late blight, it wiped out the Irish potato crop in 1845 and 1846, resulting in the Great Famine. Subsequent observations caused Moore to accept the theory that the disease was caused by a fungus; few of his contemporaries agreed with him.

Throughout its existence, the National Botanic Gardens, Glasnevin has been a center for horticultural education. Gardeners have been trained there since 1800, including women since 1898. It has also been a center for research on Ireland's native flora. Walter Wade and David Moore both published works about the indigenous flora. During the late 1800s and the first half of the 20th century, there was greater emphasis on horticulture, but in 1970, when the herbarium of the National Museum of Ireland was moved to the National Botanic Gardens, scientific research resumed and continues to the present day. The herbarium, including perhaps half a million specimens, is supported by an outstanding botanical library and archive including a unique collection of botanical watercolors.

Synopsis

1795 Dublin Society takes lease on 16 Irish acres at Glasnevin and establishes its Botanic Gardens

1795–1800 Gardens planted; Dr. Walter Wade elected professor of botany to the Dublin Society, and John Underwood appointed head gardener

1800–1805 Open to visitors; first catalogs published by Wade and Underwood

1834–38 Ninian Niven elected curator, revitalizes the gardens

1836 Dublin Society becomes Royal Dublin Society

1838 David Moore elected curator

1843 William Clancy commences east wing of Curvilinear Range of glasshouses

1844–49 Richard Turner continues building Curvilinear Range

1845 David Moore detects fungus that causes late blight in potatoes at Glasnevin on 20 August 1845; the consequence was destruction of the potato crop and the Great Irish Famine

1845–48 Orchid seedlings raised and grown to flowering stage

1854 Victoria Regia House built to house the Amazon waterlily *(Victoria amazonica)*, which flowers in 1855

1868–69 Curvilinear Range expanded by Richard and William Turner

late 1860s Hybrid pitcher plants (*Sarracenia* (*moorei*) and *S.* (*popei*) artificially created

1878 Royal Botanic Gardens administered by state

1879–1922 Frederick Moore, son of David Moore, appointed curator; title changed to Keeper in 1890; gardens reach peak of excellence and renown; Moore knighted in 1911

1884 Great Palm House erected to replace one severely damaged in storm

1922 Irish Free State established; name of gardens altered to National Botanic Gardens

1970 Herbarium moved to National Botanic Gardens from the National Museum of Ireland

1995 Bicentenary of gardens celebrated by restoration and recommissioning of Curvilinear Range; 150th anniversary of arrival of potato blight also marked

1997 New herbarium and library building completed

Further Reading

Nelson, E. Charles, "A Select Annotated Bibliography of the National Botanic Gardens, Glasnevin, Dublin," *Glasra* 5 (1981)

Nelson, E. Charles, *The Cause of the Calamity: Potato Blight in Ireland, 1845–1847, and the Role of the National Botanic Gardens, Glasnevin,* Dublin: The Stationery Office, 1995
Nelson, E. Charles, and Eileen M. McCracken, *The Brightest Jewel: A History of the National Botanic Gardens, Glasnevin, Dublin,* Kilkenny, Ireland: Boethius Press, 1987

E. CHARLES NELSON

Göteborgs Botaniska Trädgård

Göteborg, Sweden

Location: 2 miles (3.2 km) southwest of Göteborg town center, approximately 250 miles (402 km) southwest of Stockholm

The Göteborgs Botaniska Trädgård (Göteborg Botanic Garden) differs in many respects from most traditional botanical gardens on the European continent. It was conceived and planned by the municipality of Göteborg in the 1910s as a botanical garden with an emphasis on horticulture and as a contribution to Swedish community life. The town, located on the Swedish west coast and Sweden's second largest city, has a long history of private donations benefiting the cultural life of its inhabitants. The garden was initially financed by such a donation.

The garden is situated on vast and richly varied premises. The area totals 175 hectares (432 acres), most of which constitutes a nature reserve created for the combined purposes of research, interpretation, and leisure. The garden proper is 20 hectares (49 acres). It is the largest and perhaps the finest botanical garden in northern Europe. The difference in altitude from the main entry to the highest point (outside the main garden) exceeds 90 meters (98 yd.). A glasshouse complex with an area of about 1,200 square meters (1,435 square yd.) is open to the public and covers climate zones from tropical to cold temperate. In addition, the garden runs the Palm House (1878) in central Göteborg with its area of some 900 square meters (1,076 square yd.).

Great emphasis is laid on using material collected in the wild or of well-documented wild origin. Around 13,000 taxa from the wild are cultivated, as well as some 3,000 hybrids and cultivars. Taxonomic research is carried out in the garden and at the University Department of Botany using plant material under cultivation. Several doctoral theses and various publications on a number of topics have been produced over the years, such as on the horticulturally valuable and taxonomically intriguing genera *Calceolaria, Colchicum, Corydalis, Dionysia, Fritillaria,* and *Tulipa.* Within this framework, the shifting interests of the garden staff have shaped the garden's development. From its inception and up to about 1950, the garden was developed into a general botanical garden with representative living plant collections and a herbarium. Perhaps the most spectacular early single achievement is the rock garden, about one hectare (2.47 acres) of semi-natural rock landscape that is extremely favorable for its purpose, not the least due to its variation in exposure to sun. A continuous interest in alpine plants among the staff has made the rock garden one of Göteborg's areas of excellence. It houses some 6,000 species from the temperate parts of the world in an attractive setting with steep rock faces, huge boulders, an artificial waterfall, mountain streams, and a pond. It is laid out geographically.

The 1950s saw the development of the arboretum, mainly within the nature reserve. Its 15 hectares (37 acres) contain over 500 stands, with over 300 woody plant species and some 6,000 specimens. The Asiatic section contains particularly valuable material, including a *Cercidiphyllum japonicum* and a *Sorbus commixta* 'Ullung'; both are of highly decorative quality and good hardiness for northern Europe. The Japanese glade, the rhododendron valley, the Smith valley, and the bamboo grove date from more or less the same time. Along with the arboretum, they were laid out during the period when an interest in dendrology was prevalent at the garden.

From the mid 1960s onward there has been a focus on southwest and central Asiatic bulbous and tuberous plants. The bulb garden was created in the mid 1980s. There and in the alpine glasshouses are found collections, probably the most comprehensive in one single place, of *Dionysia, Corydalis, Iris, Fritillaria, Tulipa, Crocus, Colchicum,* and others. A tropical house, an epiphyte house, three orchid houses (tropical, subtropical, and warm temperate), a begonia house, an Australian–South African house, a dry alpine house, a moist alpine

Rock Garden, Göteborgs Botaniska Trädgård, Sweden
Copyright Gunnar Weimarck

house, a succulent house, and an exhibition house were completed in the early 1980s. The plant material is selected with a view to university and school teaching, to geographical and taxonomical representation, and to general interest.

The historic Palm House in central Göteborg was restored in the first half of the 1980s and presents some of the late-19th-century fashions of plant arrangement. The central Palm House contains high-altitude tropical plants; in addition, the range consists of a bird house with a parrot cage, a water house, a Mediterranean house, and a camellia house, all run by the botanical garden since 1986 as a complement to its glasshouses. Emphasis is slighty less on interpretation in the Palm House than in the garden. Among its remarkable specimens is the cactus *Cereus hexagonus*, a direct clonal offspring of the specimen introduced to Uppsala by Linnaeus some 250 years ago.

During the late 1980s and the 1990s, extensive remodeling and redesign was done in some of the earliest gardens. For example, when a restaurant with an adjoining outdoor service area claimed the place of the vegetable garden and order beds, these elements were moved to new positions and given a new design. The order beds created in 1997 present the angiosperm families in close accordance with the views of the late 1990s, based on molecular information, and are intended to be both informative and decorative.

Yet another innovation is the creation of decorative annual flower beds that welcome visitors at the garden entrance. They confirm the message to the public that the Göteborg Botanic Garden aims to provide something of value to everyone.

Synopsis

1910	Financial donation by private will to Göteborg "to the adornment and embellishment of the city and the development of botanical or zoological gardens"
1914	Proposal to create botanical garden on grounds of former estate Stora Änggården
1915	Carl Skottsberg project leader
1919–48	Carl Skottsberg director
1923	Garden officially inaugurated
1923–38	First-generation public glasshouses constructed
1924–66	Scientific periodical, *Acta horti got(h)oburgensis*, published
1929	First version of rock garden completed
1936	Herbarium wing added to office building
1949	Henning Weimarck director
1950–63	Bertil Lindquist director
1950s	Start of development of rhododendron valley, Japanese glade, and arboretum
1961	Agreement with Swedish government to serve as university garden; herbarium and parts of library handed over to state university
1965–81	Per Wendelbo director
1969	University Department of Botany built on part of garden's grounds
1973–83	New generation of public glasshouses constructed
1978–93	Extensive remodeling of rock garden
1983–2000	Gunnar Weimarck director
1986	Historic palm house in city center reopened to public; run by Botanical Garden

1987	Society of Friends established
1989–94	Extensive remodeling of rhododendron valley
1995	Environment Research Information Centre opened in former cafeteria; joint project with university
1998	Botanical Garden and Natural History Museum in Göteborg joined under same board and directorship
1999	Responsibility for Botanical Garden and Natural History Museum taken over from Municipality of Göteborg by Region of Västra Götaland
2001	Arne Strid director

Further Reading

Celander, Rigmor, and Mona Holmberg, *Nordiskt ljus och italiensk hetta: Sommarblommor à la Göteborgs Botaniska Trädgård,* Göteborg: Göteborgs botaniska trädgård, 1996

Eriksson, Folke, *Göteborgs Botaniska Trädgård. Liv och utveckling 1914–1991,* Göteborg: Tre Böcker Förlag AB, 1991

Fredriksson, Allan, *Det blommar i Botaniska,* Göteborg: Göteborgs botaniska trädgård/TreBöcker Förlag AB, 1992

Neuendorf, Magnus, and Gunnar Weimarck, *Palmhuset,* Göteborg: Göteborgs botaniska trädgård, 1986

GUNNAR WEIMARCK

Grass

Grasses dominate 30 percent of the world's terrestrial vegetation and are found in nearly all habitats. Typically hardy and adaptable to various climates, temperatures, soils, and water supplies, they are the first plant group to establish in disturbed landscapes. With 650 genera and over 15,000 herbaceous species, true grasses (*Gramineae* family) comprise the most abundant plant group on earth and include lawn grasses, bamboos, cereals, fescues, fountain grasses, and switchgrasses. Their importance for humankind, as food, animal forage, construction material, and material for household goods, is inestimable; they are considered instrumental in the shift from nomadic- to agrarian-based societies. Although not true grasses, rushes (*Juncaceae* family) and sedges (*Cyperaceae* family) are often included with ornamental and native grasses by landscape and garden designers.

While the vast majority of grasses have hollow culms (stems) and are unbranched, growing anywhere from 15 centimeters (5.8 in.) to 24 meters (26 yd.) in height, their varying structures, seasonal growth patterns, and root systems are key in classifying and choosing them for design purposes. Grass plant forms are often classified as tufted, mounded, upright, upright divergent, upright arching (or fountainlike), and arching. Most grasses have long and flexible leaves and, because they are wind pollinated and have no need of showy flowers, are lightweight. They may be warm season or cool season, clumping or running. Designers use grasses' variations in seasonal changes, color and color variegation, seed head shape, and height, as well as the movement and sound that grasses may bring to a garden. Linearity is the predominant grass feature considered in design.

The Chinese have used bamboo, which flourishes throughout the Far East, for shelter, food, household utensils, and other uses for thousands of centuries. Researchers have discovered bamboo writing tablets containing Chinese history dating from the 23rd century B.C. and evidence of bamboo plantings in Chinese gardens over 2,000 years old. In the seventh century A.D. the Chinese introduced bamboo to Japan, where it became an essential part of Japanese gardens and a common building material.

Grasses have been used in the West as ground cover throughout history, providing a backdrop for other plantings. Pliny the Younger's writings note such application in first-century Roman villas, as do plans and written works compiled in monasteries from the fifth through the tenth centuries.

In the later Middle Ages Job's tears (*Coix lacryma-jobi*) and reed canary or ribbon grass (*Phalaris arundinacea* 'Picta') were cultivated, in part, for ornamentation, while other grasses were used to cover lawn areas in pleasure gardens and raised turf seats in some herb gardens. These grasses were likely a mix of natural grasses, chosen for their ease of establishment and durability, and were kept short using a rolling technique. Through the 17th century grasses were primarily used for manicured lawns, although garden view sheds contained more natural grass plantings, as meadows, woodland edges, and pastures.

European designers in the 18th century began to capitalize on grasses' natural forms. The picturesque aesthetic of that era embraced views of, and walkways through, naturalized areas, such as meadow plantings and grassy woodland transitions. Grasses mixed with flowers at garden edges also provided transition zones from formal gardens to the countryside. In these cases grasses were not cut or rolled but left to grow to their natural height and form. During the latter 19th century William Robinson recommended ornamental grasses in his writings on English gardens, and his fellow Victorians celebrated the "wild," "natural," and "flamboyant" aspects of grasses in their gardens.

Gardening and designing with ornamental grasses increased considerably at the turn of the 20th century. Gertrude Jekyll, an English landscape architect known for designing herbaceous borders, often used grasses as accents and backdrops to emphasize color, and her writings about design helped popularize such plantings. The propagation of grasses also increased, bringing further attention to their use in design. The work of German nurseryman Karl Foerster in plant propagation and ornamental garden design, as well as published accounts of his work, resulted in international acclaim. His success centered on six key plants, *Miscanthus, Pennisetum, Calamagrostis, Molinia, Festuca,* and *Panicum,* which have maintained their popularity.

In the United States Wolfgang Oehme, one of Foerster's protégés, helped popularize design with ornamental grasses in the mid-20th century. At the same time Brazilian Roberto Burle Marx used grasses boldly in his tropical garden designs, both to frame the ground plane and as sculptural elements. His exploration of the textures, forms, and impact of grasses planted en masse often led him to place them as centerpieces in his design and ensured their importance in the design world.

While grasses enjoyed a surge as ornamental plantings in the 20th century, the ecological movement supported their use in more natural settings. Landscape architect Jens Jensen pioneered (with Frank Lloyd Wright) the Prairie style, in which native prairie grasses were used in the Midwestern United States. In the Netherlands biologist Jaques Thijsse and his gardener C. Sipkes created "ecological gardens" using indigenous grasses in marshes, cereal fields, and dune landscapes. Although an increased understanding of ecology was apparent, interest in naturalistic planting was not yet widespread.

The latter decades of the 20th century brought Ernst Pagels (another Foerster pupil) and Piet Oudolf of the Netherlands into the forefront. Pagels is known internationally as a plant breeder, particularly for his work in the 1970s with the narrow-leaved maiden grass *Miscanthus sinensis* 'Gracillimus' (also known as Japanese silver grass, a native grass of Japan and China), now popularized in many countries. One of the world's leading landscape designers today, Oudolf has made extensive use of grasses in his naturalistic planting designs.

Although ornamental plantings of grasses remain popular worldwide, current trends include increasing use of grasses in native stands (e.g., meadow plantings and prairies) and in combination with more prolific flowering plants in beds and borders. The importance of grasses in creating humus, preventing erosion, and retaining water has long been recognized. Now, however, the ecological benefits of grasses are also increasingly exploited in wastewater treatment systems and as a natural means of mitigating air and water pollutants. At the same time, the greatest use of grasses in the United States—lawns—is being reevaluated. Criticisms of the time, money, and environmental impact implicit in traditional lawn care began appearing late in the 20th century. As watering, chemical-based fertilizers, and mowers powered by fossil fuels have all come under close scrutiny, low-maintenance substitutions for close-cropped lawns have appeared in the form of different kinds of plantings, including lawn grasses that do not require mowing. Despite such shifts in the kinds and uses of grasses in design, they remain a mainstay of both beauty and utility throughout the world.

Further Reading

Chapman, Geoffrey Peter, and W.E. Peat, *An Introduction to the Grasses (Including Bamboos and Cereals),* Tucson, Arizona, and Wallingford, Oxfordshire: CAB International, 1992

Chase, Agnes, *First Book of Grasses,* New York: Macmillan, 1922; 4th edition, as *Agnes Chase's First Book of Grasses,* edited by Lynn G. Clark and Richard W. Pohl, Washington, D.C.: Smithsonian Institution Press, 1996

Colston, Burrell C., "Ornamental Grasses," *Landscape Architecture* 90, no. 3 (2000)

Darke, Rick, *The Color Encyclopedia of Ornamental Grasses: Sedges, Rushes, Restios, Cat-Tails, and Selected Bamboos,* Portland, Oregon: Timber Press, and London: Weidenfeld and Nicolson, 1999

Foerster, Karl, *Einzug der Gräser und Farne in die Gärten,* Radebeul, Germany: Neumann, 1957; 7th edition, Stuttgart, Germany: Ulmer, 1988

Greenlee, John, *The Encyclopedia of Ornamental Grasses: How to Grow and Use Over 250 Beautiful and Versatile Plants,* Emmaus, Pennsylvania: Rodale Press, 1992

Grounds, Roger, *The Plantfinder's Guide to Ornamental Grasses,* Portland, Oregon: Timber Press, and Newton Abbot, Devon: David and Charles, 1998

Hubbard, Charles Edward, *Grasses: A Guide to Their Structure, Identification, Uses, and Distribution in the British Isles,* London and Baltimore, Maryland: Penguin, 1954; 3rd edition, revised by J.C.E. Hubbard, London: Penguin, 1984

King, Michael, and Piet Oudolf, *Prachtig gras,* Warnsweld, The Netherlands: Tierra, 1996; as *Gardening with Grasses,* Portland, Oregon: Timber Press, 1998; London: Lincoln, 1989
Oakes, Albert J., *Ornamental Grasses and Grasslike Plants,* New York: Van Nostrand Reinhold, 1990
Ottesen, Carole, *Ornamental Grasses: The Amber Wave,* New York: McGraw Hill, 1989
Reinhardt, Thomas A., Martina Reinhardt, and Mark Moskowitz, *Ornamental Grass Gardening,* Los Angeles: HP Books, 1989
Taylor, Nigel, *Ornamental Grasses, Bamboos, Rushes, and Sedges,* London and New York: Ward Lock, 1992

MARTHA A. HUNT

Great Mosque of Córdoba. *See* Córdoba, Great Mosque of

Greece

The earliest archaeological evidence of a vegetable component in the diet of inhabitants of what is now Greece comes from the Frankhthi Cave in the southern Argolid, where two species of wild pulses (species of lentil and vetch) were being gathered about 10,000 B.C. Some scholars have suggested that three millenia later these plants were being cultivated. Although the gradual dietary addition of plants introduced from Asia Minor also suggests cultivation, nothing is known about the distribution or nature of utilitarian gardens and orchards in Greece even as late as the Greek Mycenaeans or the non-Greek Minoans in Crete during the Bronze Age. The latter, however, under Egyptian influence, may well have had pleasure gardens. Floral landscapes are to be found in their murals, painted pottery, metal work, and glyptic art. At Amnisos, a villa northeast of Knossos, the formal setting of lilies in a restored fresco probably represents a garden, while at Phaistos in central Crete a rocky outcrop adjoining the palace was both cut back and furnished with round holes that were presumably once filled with soil and planted with flowers to create a tiny garden. Cultivation of flowers in the Aegean area in the second millenium B.C. is proven by finds of flowerpots (clay or faience pots with apertures in the base). Moreover, a few of the flowers depicted in Minoan and Mycenaean frescos have been identified as cultivated varieties, and late Mycenaean Linear B tablets (used for palatial inventories) mention roses for the production of perfume.

Although evidence is even more scant for the dark age from the 11th to early eighth century, gardens are described in Homer's *Odyssey,* which is generally considered to reflect the culture of this period more than that of the Mycenaean. Most notable are the descriptions of the gardens of Alcinous and Laertes, both of which are primarily enclosed orchards, the former with two fountains and what are probably vegetable beds. Homer's delight in both cultivated and wild vegetation contrasts sharply with the harsh realities of agriculture depicted in Hesiod's *Works and Days* (ca. 700 B.C.), but is echoed in lyric poetry of the archaic age from the early eighth to early fifth century.

Archaeology and literature furnish more, but still frustratingly insufficient, information for the ensuing classical period. Partly owing to the choice of man as almost the exclusive conceptual artistic form, no vase-painting has an incontrovertible garden setting.

The defining features of a garden, as opposed to agricultural land, were a wall or fence and usually a permanent form of irrigation. Private gardens were always chiefly, if not entirely, utilitarian rather than aesthetic; any flowers grown were probably for the production of perfume or garlands. The vast majority of urban houses possessed no garden at all because they were densely crowded together and their interior courtyards were paved (although pots, presumably for herbs rather than flowers, could be found there). Evidence from Athens and Tegea suggests that for the upper classes gardens were usually attached or close to their houses and probably more common on the periphery than in the center of the city. On the tiny island of Delos (probably an atypical example) gardens were concentrated in a single area and in Athens there was also a district just outside the walls known as "Gardens." Nothing is known about the layout of these productive gardens except that the proverb "not even in the celery" is explained in the *Suda* (a tenth-century A.D. lexicon) by the statement that celery and rue were planted at the edges.

There is a single reference by Demosthenes to a garden devoted solely to flowers (roses). Although no Greek horticultural manual is known to have existed, the later fourth-century writer Theophrastus details in his botanical works methods calculated to enhance longevity, sweetness, and tenderness. Thus the garden came to symbolize not only civic responsibility in enhancing productivity but also unnecessary luxury.

Other productive gardens belonged to temples (nearby or at some considerable distance) and were leased out. They are thus quite distinct from the generally unwalled sacred groves, meadows, and *orgades* (rich tracts of land dedicated to a divinity), which were untended, inviolate spaces and are known from remote antiquity in Greece, Cyprus, and elsewhere in the Greek world. Urban temples to gods and shrines to heroes could, however, have attached gardens of more aesthetic than practical utility. The latter were sometimes associated with gymnasia, which included shady groves of trees. Plato took over one such complex, that of the hero Academus, for his philosophical school. The sole temple garden to have been excavated surrounds the Hephaesteion in the Athenian agora and dates from about 300 B.C. Here two straight rows of square pits in the bedrock indicate the planting of shrubs or small trees on three sides of the building, while small flowerbeds lay directly adjoining the precinct wall. Deliberately broken pots in pits attest layering by circumposition for propagation. The so-called Gardens of Adonis had a religious purpose but were not real gardens, being merely lettuce, fennel, wheat, and barley sowed at midsummer in broken amphorae placed on rooftops so that they should wither before maturation and thus symbolize the early death of the god.

Although information is again sparse, the Hellenistic period (323–31 B.C.) saw genuine pleasure gardens come into existence. The causes were growing affluence, the influence of the Persian *paradeisos*, the building of new cities (which made possible a more generous disposition of buildings with space for public parks) and the changed political conditions that spawned autocrats focused on private luxury and public ostentation. Athens, where the philosopher Epicurus (d. 270 B.C.) bequeathed his garden to the city as a public park, became a greener place. Still, it could not compare with Alexandria, the capital of the Ptolemies, where Pharaonic influence was also evident. Gardens became furnished with artificial grottos, fountains, scuptures, and an increasing range of plants. Funerary plots had also grown into gardens planted with cypress, poplar, and willow. The height of luxury was attained by Hieron II of Syracuse, who had a gymnasium with bowers of vines and flower beds on a cruise ship.

Greek gardens during the period of Roman rule were largely Roman in inspiration. With the fall of Constantinople to the Ottoman Turks in 1453, political conditions allowed only small, productive gardens. Towns and cities built since the War of Independence (1821–29) usually contain small, formal squares with shady avenues and occasional geometric parterres. Among palatial gardens, that at Tatoï outside Athens is mainly notable for successful afforestation in unpromising soil. Most landscape designers, apart from Queen Amalia, who designed what is now the National Garden in Athens, have been foreigners, usually English. Unfortunately most of the plans of Thomas Mawson dating from after World War I were not carried out, although he was responsible for the initial landscaping on the Acropolis, Lykavittos, and Philoppapos Hill in Athens. From the mid 1960s to early 1980s, Robert and Marina Adams encouraged the integration of both public and private gardens into the landscape by the use of native materials. More recently some good work has been done by Greek designers, but no true indigenous style has yet developed.

See also Byzantium

Further Reading

Carroll-Spillecke, Maureen, *Κῆπος: Der antike griechische Garten,* Munich: Deutscher Kunstverlag, 1989

Carroll-Spillecke, Maureen, "The Gardens of Greece from Homeric to Roman Times," *Journal of Garden History* 12, 2 (1992)

Carroll-Spillecke, Maureen, "Griechische Gärten," in *Der Garten von der Antike bis zum Mittelalter,* edited by Carroll-Spillecke, Mainz, Germany: Von Zabern, 1992

Karageorghis, V., and Carroll-Spillecke, Maureen, "Die heiligen Haine und Gärten Zyperns," in *Der Garten von der Antike bis zum Mittelalter,* edited by Carroll-Spillecke, Mainz, Germany: Von Zabern, 1992

Osborne, R., "Classical Greek Gardens: Between Farm and Paradise," in *Garden History: Issues, Approaches, Methods,* edited by John Dixon Hunt, Washington, D.C.: Dumbarton Oaks Research Library and Collection, 1992

Schäfer, J., "Gärten in der bronzezeitlichen ägäischen Kultur?" in *Der Garten von der Antike bis zum Mittelalter,* edited by Maureen Carroll-Spillecke, Mainz, Germany: Von Zabern, 1992

Shaw, M.C., "The Aegean Garden," *American Journal of Archaeology* 97 (1993)

A.R. LITTLEWOOD

Greenhouse

The purpose of a greenhouse is to protect plants from the climate outside. The earliest known experiments in plant protection were by the Romans at Pompeii, where there was a brick structure heated by a furnace and covered with thin sheets of mica, transparent enough to let light pass through it. By the Renaissance in Italy, citrus trees, pomegranates, and myrtles were highly prized for the garden, but those in northern Italy or the Apennines required protection in winter. Two methods were common: trees in pots were overwintered in a frost-proof building called an *aranciera* or *limonaia;* and larger trees planted in the ground had a wooden shed with a tiled roof built up around them in winter, for example, at the Villa Pratolino near Florence (from 1569). This was copied in England at Beddington, Surrey (ca. 1570).

The temporary wooden structure was described in 1600 in *Le theatre d'agriculture* by Oliver de Serres, whose name was eventually used as the French term for greenhouse: *serre*. Salomon de Caus published a design for an elegant stone-built orangery in *Les raisons des forces mouvantes* in 1624, and it was this version that was generally adopted in northern Europe, from St. Germain-en-Laye (ca. 1610) to Heidelberg (1618) to Wimbledon Manor (1642) and, the grandest one of all, Versailles (1685). With a solid roof, south-facing windows, and heat from charcoal during frosty weather, this form of building for protecting tender evergreens was called a *greenhouse* or *conservatory* by John Evelyn in the late 17th century. The term *orangery* meant the garden where orange trees were displayed.

Edward Anderson's conservatory, Stockholm Botanic Garden, Sweden
Copyright Garden Matters

In the kitchen garden subtropical and tropical flowers and fruit from southern Africa, the Caribbean, India, and the Far East were grown in stove houses or stoves, so called because they were often heated with Dutch or Continental stoves. The alternative method of heating was a furnace with underfloor flues, but when mortar between flagstones cracked and shrank through heat, noxious fumes regularly escaped to kill plants.

Plants that liked dry conditions were grown in the dry stove; those that preferred heat and humidity were kept in the hot stove. Hotbeds made from rotting manure or tanner's bark provided extra heat for tropical fruit such as pineapples, which a Dutch grower, Agnes Block, was the first to fruit successfully in 1687. Daturas, aloes, hibiscus, bananas, and papaya were all grown by the early 1700s, and the duchess of Beaufort's guavas produced perfect fruit on a Christmas day in the 1720s.

In the 1752 edition of his *Gardener's Dictionary,* Philip Miller of the Chelsea Physic Garden advises putting flues up the rear wall. With these improvements Miller was growing avocados, coconuts, cashew nuts, and mahogany trees. The Dutch and the English were acknowledged masters in the field of greenhouse design.

Early in the 19th century, several changes in design took place. First, because overhead light was beneficial for all plants, many new greenhouses were built with glass roofs. Experiments were made by Sir George Mackenzie and W. and D. Bailey, who devised versions of the glazed semidome, and John Claudius Loudon who introduced the ridge and furrow roof. Second, because the profusion of flowers in the stove house was tantalizingly distant in the kitchen garden, a new glasshouse with planting beds, called a conservatory, was built adjoining the house. Third, techniques in the manufacture of cast iron meant that it could be easily molded while retaining its strength and was, therefore, ideal for slender, curving glazing bars. This development liberated design and led eventually, with an increase in the size of a pane of glass, to the soaring curves in the Palm House at the Royal Botanic Garden, Kew. Fourth, in the 1830s heated walls were replaced by hot-water pipes by which temperature could be controlled efficiently and reliably. Finally, terminology in English underwent a change that still causes confusion. The greenhouse of the 18th century was given the more chic French name of *orangery;* the term *greenhouse* was used instead for an all-glass house with staging for flowers, usually in the walled garden; and the term *stove* was dropped in favor of *hothouse.*

By the middle of the 19th century, the well-equipped country estate in the United States or northern Europe would have a variety of decorative and functional glasshouses, while many middle-class houses had a greenhouse for sowing seeds and growing flowering plants. Grand public glasshouses were springing up in cities and botanic gardens to satisfy public curiosity about exotic plants, including the Summerhouse at Stuttgart (1846), the Palm House at Kew by Burton and Turner (1848), the Jardin d'Hiver in Paris by Hector Horeau (1848), the Kibble Palace by Boucher and Cousland in the Glasgow Botanic Garden (1865), the Palm House in Golden Gate Park, San Francisco (1879), and the conservatory at the New York Botanical Garden (1902) by Hitchings and Company.

From these sparkling peaks of popularity and achievement, there followed much decay and destruction during world wars and the depression, but in the last 20 years of the 20th century the private conservatory and greenhouse became fashionable for living space and growing plants. For climatic reasons, the market is especially buoyant in the United Kingdom.

In the public domain architects have yet again been working with new materials and technology to produce Climatron, Murphy, and Mackay's huge geodesic dome in the Missouri Botanical Garden (started 1959), Emilio Ambasz's progressive design at the San Antonio Botanic Garden (late 1980s), and Gordon Wilson's multiclimated Princess of Wales Conservatory at Kew (1987). For the National Botanic Garden of Wales, Norman Foster designed a gracious oval greenhouse made of concrete, steel, and glass (2000).

Nicholas Grimshaw's design for the Eden Project in Cornwall (2001) uses steel and featherlight fluoropolymer in place of glass for clusters of domed conservatories that sit around the lip and down the sides of a deep pit. These are grouped into two climates, each of which display representations of wild flora in a natural environment and explore man's use of plants and trees.

Public greenhouses are used now for conservation, education, and economic botany as well as for display, and, as always, forms and materials are constantly evolving.

Further Reading

Abercrombie, John, *The Hot-House Gardener,* London, 1789

Coppa and Avery Consultants, *Botanical Gardens, Arboretums, and Greenhouses: A Bibliography,* Monticello, Illinois: Vance Bibliographies, 1984

Cowell, John, *The Curious and Profitable Gardener,* London, 1730; 3rd edition, London, 1733

Evelyn, John, *Kalendarium Hortense; or, The Gard'ners Almanac,* London, 1664; 10th edition, London, 1706; reprint, Falls Village, Connecticut: Herb Grower Press, 1963

Hibberd, Shirley, *The Amateur's Greenhouse and Conservatory,* London, 1875

Hix, John, *The Glass House,* Cambridge, Massachusetts: MIT Press, and London: Phaidon, 1974

Kohlmaier, Georg, and Barna von Sartory, *Das Glashaus,* Munich: Prestel, 1981; as *Houses of Glass: A Nineteenth-Century Building Type,* translated by John C. Harvey, Cambridge, Massachusetts: MIT Press, 1986

Koppelkamm, Stefan, *Gewächshäuser und Wintergärten im neunzehnten Jahrhundert,* Stuttgart, Germany: Hatje, 1981; as *Glasshouses and Wintergardens of the Nineteenth Century,* translated by Kathrine Talbot, London and New York: Granada, and New York: Rizzoli, 1981

Lockwood, Alice G.B., *Gardens of Colony and State: Gardens and Gardeners of the American Colonies and of the Republic before 1840,* 2 vols, New York: Scribner, 1931

Loudon, John Claudius, *Sketches of Curvilinear Hothouses . . . ,* s.l., 1818

Loudon, John Claudius, *The Green-house Companion,* London, 1824; 3rd edition, London, 1832

Marston, Peter, *Garden Room Style,* London: Weidenfeld and Nicholson, and New York: Rizzoli, 1998

McIntosh, Charles, *The Greenhouse, Hothouse, and Stove: Including Selected Lists of the Most Beautiful Species of Exotic Flowering Plants, and Directions for their Cultivation,* London, 1838

McKenzie, Sir George, "Paper to the Horticultural Society," *Transactions of the Horticultural Society* 2 (1817)

Miller, Philip, *The Gardener's Dictionary,* London, 1731, 1752; as *The Gardener's and Botanist's Dictionary,* London, 1807

Serres, Olivier de, *Le theatre d'agriculture et mesnage des champs,* Paris, 1600; reprint, Arles, France: Actes Sud, 1997

Taft, Levi Rawson, *Greenhouse Construction: A Complete Manual,* New York, 1894

Tallack, J.C., *The Book of the Greenhouse: With a Special Chapter on the Little Town Greenhouse,* London and New York: Lane, 1901; 2nd edition, 1908

Tod, George, *Plans, Elevations, and Sections of Hothouses, Greenhouses,* London, 1807

Vance, Mary A., *Garden Rooms and Greenhouses: A Bibliography,* Monticello, Illinois: Vance Bibliographies, 1983

Woods, May, and Arete Warren, *Glass Houses: A History of Greenhouses, Orangeries, and Conservatories,* London: Aurum Press, and New York: Rizzoli, 1988

MAY WOODS

Greenough, Horatio 1805–1852

American Sculptor and Aesthetic Theorist

Horatio Greenough, the first American to select sculpture as a profession, is most widely known for his sculpture of a toga-clad George Washington originally intended for the rotunda of the United States Capitol. Greenough was also an important aesthetic theorist, who, through his writing and theoretical studies on the nature of American art, was able to directly influence the fledgling profession of landscape architecture. He developed his aesthetic theories in concert with the renowned transcendentalist philosopher Ralph Waldo Emerson (1803–82). After attending a boys school in Lancaster, Massachusetts, managed by the parents of the pioneer landscape architect Horace Cleveland, Greenough earned a liberal arts degree from Harvard. After his graduation he moved to Italy, where he studied classical sculpture. He met Emerson for the first time in Florence in 1833. The Italian experience helped Greenough develop as a sculptor, but it also caused him to consider how an American aesthetic in any art might differ from the timeworn artistic conventions of Europe.

During the early 1840s, Greenough developed his theories on a new American aesthetic. He first published that perspective, termed a "theory of structure," in the *United States Magazine and Literary Review* (1843). In that article, titled "American Architecture," Greenough argued that American art and architecture should be adapted to the American climate, landscape, and people. He believed that the archaic and corrupt art of Europe was not appropriate for the new nation. In assessing the nature of a new American aesthetic, he suggested the importance of truth in design. American art, Greenough proposed, should be stripped of meaningless ornament (artificial embellishment). Moreover, he contended, all works of art should be carefully fitted to the subject and place.

In his writings he provided multiple examples of this view of integrity in design. He presented the design of a ship as one example: "Mark the majestic form" as it "rushes through the water, observe the graceful bend" of the "body, the gentle transition from round to flat, the grasp . . . [of the] keel, the leap of . . . [the] bows, the symmetry and rich tracery of [the] . . . spars and rigging, [and] those grand wind muscles, . . . [the] sails." The design of the ship, according to Greenough, perfectly and elegantly fit its purpose free of superfluous decoration.

Emerson developed a similar theory often referred to as the organic principle and engaged in a correspondence with Greenough on the general subject of American aesthetics. When Greenough published a number of his essays in *The Travels, Observations, and Experience of a Yankee Stonecutter,* Emerson was impressed enough to write that the book "contains more useful truth than anything in America I remember." After Greenough died in 1852, Emerson continued to develop the organic principle in essays titled "The Poet" and "Art."

While both Greenough and Emerson thought deeply about the need for a new American aesthetic, neither was able to adequately suggest what those ideas might mean to the actual making of art. Emerson was a poet and philosopher not an artist, and Greenough was not able to effectively test his aesthetic theories in practice during his short life. However, Greenough's aesthetic theories were developed in the practice of landscape architecture by Horace William Shaler Cleveland (1814–1900). Cleveland was acquainted with both Greenough and Emerson and was directly inspired by Greenough's call for integrity in art and elegant simplicity in design. Cleveland, along with his partner Robert Morris Copeland, designed Sleepy Hollow Cemetery in Concord, Massachusetts (the final resting-place of Emerson, Henry David Thoreau, and Nathaniel Hawthorne). At Sleepy Hollow Cemetery, Cleveland worked in a way that was true to Greenough's aesthetic principles. The design was carefully fitted into a natural amphitheater, and native plantings were used. In an "Address to the Inhabitants of Concord at the Consecration of Sleepy Hollow" Emerson wrote that art was employed "only . . . to bring out [the] natural advantages" of the landscape and that the "lay and the look of the land" suggested the design. A biographer of Hawthorne commented about the use of native plants in the cemetery: "Around the edge of the basin winds an avenue bordered by beautiful wild [native] plants—woodbine, raspberry, goldenrod, flower, vine and shrub." Cleveland interpreted the integrity principle espoused by Greenough and Emerson as a charge to incorporate the very plants that naturally occur in the place.

While Copeland died a relatively young man (he was only 44), Cleveland carried forward with this organic perspective throughout a career that spanned the second half of the 19th century. As he shaped new parks in the burgeoning cities of Chicago, Minneapolis, and Omaha, and laid out numerous suburban communities, Cleveland stayed true to the aesthetic principles developed by Greenough. Cleveland also echoed Greenough's perspective on truth in design, a general disdain for artificial embellishment, and a desire to appropriately fit each designed landscape to its place in numerous publications. These included "Landscape Gardening" (1855), *Landscape Architecture as Applied to the Wants of the West; with an Essay on Forest Planting on the Great Plains* (1873), and *The Aesthetic Development of the United Cities of St. Paul and Minneapolis* (1888).

Biography

Born in Boston, Massachusetts, 1805. Graduated from Harvard, 1825; studied sculpture in Rome and Florence, Italy, during the late 1820s and early 1830s; returned to the United States after apprenticeship and became first professional sculptor in United States; was also important 19th-century aesthetic theorist; his aesthetic theories developed in concert with transcendentalist leader Ralph Waldo Emerson also influenced practice of early landscape architects such as Horace Cleveland; published essays on aesthetics in *The Travels, Observations, and Experience of a Yankee Stonecutter,* 1852. Died in Somerville, Massachusetts, 1852.

Selected Publications

"American Architecture," *United States Magazine and Democratic Review,* 1843

The Travels, Observations, and Experience of a Yankee Stonecutter, 1852

Letters of Horatio Greenough, American Sculptor, edited by Nathalia Wright, 1972

Form and Function: Remarks on Art, Design, and Architecture, edited by Harold A. Small, 1947

Further Reading

Hopkins, Vivian C., *Spires of Form: A Study of Emerson's Aesthetic Theory,* Cambridge, Massachusetts: Harvard University Press, 1951

Matthiessen, Francis Otto, *American Renaissance: Art and Expression in the Age of Emerson and Whitman,* London and New York: Oxford University Press, 1941

Metzger, Charles Reid, *Emerson and Greenough: Transcendental Pioneers of an American Aesthetic,* Berkeley: University of California Press, 1954

Nadenicek, Daniel Joseph, "Sleepy Hollow Cemetery: Transcendental Garden and Community Park," *Journal of the New England Garden History Society* 3 (1993)

Nadenicek, Daniel Joseph, "Civilization by Design: Emerson and Landscape Architecture," *Nineteenth-Century Studies* 10 (1996)

Nadenicek, Daniel Joseph, "Emerson's Aesthetic and Natural Design: A Theoretical Foundation for the Work of Horace William Shaler Cleveland," in *Nature and Ideology: Natural Garden Design in the Twentieth Century,* edited by Joachim Wolschke-Bulmahn, Washington, D.C.: Dumbarton Oaks Research Library and Collection, 1997

Neckar, Lance, "Fast-Tracking Culture and Landscape: Horace William Shaler Cleveland and the Garden in the Midwest," in *Regional Garden Design in the United States,* edited by Therese O'Malley and Marc Treib, Washington, D.C.: Dumbarton Oaks Research Library and Collection, 1995

Wright, Nathalia, *Horatio Greenough, The First American Sculptor,* Philadelphia: University of Pennsylvania Press, 1963

DANIEL JOSEPH NADENICEK

Grishko National Botanic Gardens

Ukraine

Location: Kiev, Ukraine

The M.M. Grishko National Botanical Garden of the National Academy of Sciences of Ukraine (NBG) was founded in September 1935 in the city of Kiev. It lies on the high hills over the deep river Dnieper. Numerous splendid gardens, parks, avenues, and squares supplement the beauty of the locale and the monumental architecture of Kiev. An area of 132 hectares (326 acres) in the center of Kiev was chosen for the construction of the garden, which includes gently sloping hills and valleys, providing ideal conditions for growing introduced plants with due account for their biological characteristics. The soil and climatic conditions also favor the NBG's work on plant introduction and construction. The climate in Kiev is temperate continental. The soil in the garden is light and fertile.

The garden's area, its rich collections of plants, and the qualification and size of its scientific staff have made the garden one of the largest in Europe. In 1967 it achieved the status of a scientific research institute. At present, eight departments and one laboratory in the garden employ a staff of more than one hundred researchers. The garden contains unique collections consisting of approximately 11,970 taxa (1,437 genera) belonging to 220 families.

The NBG is a leading biological institution in Ukraine. Its scientists carry out research work on plant introduction; conservation of endemic, relict, and endangered plants; selection and genetics of ornamental, fruit, vegetable, and forage plants; biotechnology of tropical and subtropical plants; medical botany; chemical interaction of plants; dendrology; and park building. From the beginning the basic direction of the garden's activity has been the conservation of nature, including the study of rare and endangered plants.

A series of floristic complexes have developed in the garden, including the Forests of Ukranian Plains, Ukranian Steppes, Carpathians, Crimea, Caucasus, Central Asia, Altai, and the Far East, which provide excellent ecological niches for endemic, relict, and endangered plants. The section Rare Plants of Ukranian Flora was built in 1970 with over 100 rare, endangered, relict, and endemic species represented.

The arboretum's collection of trees, shrubs, and lianas (1,416 species, 23 forms, 158 varieties, and 46 hybrids) includes 165 genera and 59 families (1,858 taxa) covering 30 hectares (74 acres). The arboretum includes a rich collection of *Pinopsida* (*Coniferae*) of more than 100 species. Well represented in the collections are such genera as *Pinus* (20 species), *Juniperus* (15), *Picea* (13), *Abies* (11), and *Larix* (18). The arboretum includes a lilac garden with over 1,500 shrubs (21 species and over 70 varieties). Varieties 'Taras Bulba', 'Bogdan Khmelnitsky', 'Poltava', and 'Lights of Donbass' developed in the garden are characterized by attractive large blossom clusters. It also includes an interesting collection of *Magnolia* (11 species and 16 forms).

A unique and valuable resource of local plants not native to Ukraine has also been collected and selected (*Armeniaca, Cydonia, Persica, Cornus, Actinidia, Schisandra*), and a gene bank of *Chaenomeles, Lonicera, Actinidia chinensis, Elaeagnus multiflora,* and *Rubus* has been created. Distinctive features of the new varieties bred at the NBG include high yields, good quality, cold resistance, and high resistance to diseases and pests.

A topiary fruit garden laid out in 1957 has been continuously expanded. It contains over 800 fruit and berry cultures of 50 varieties aesthetically arranged, together with flowering and ornamental plants near artificial pools on a one-hectare (2.47-acre) plot.

At present over 3,800 species and varieties of flowering and ornamental plants have been studied and bred at the NBG. New varieties of *Chrysanthemum, Dahlia, Aster, Phlox, Iris, Gladiolus, Paeonia, Clematis,* and ornamental grasses have been created, many of which have received awards at international exhibitions.

Plots of forage, vegetables, and spicy and aromatic plants started in 1969 now contain over 300 species in cultivation. As a result of breeding, scientists at the garden have developed alternative varieties of forage crops, including *Raphanus sativus, Brassica, Amaranthus, Galega orientalis, Silphium perfoliatum, Bunia orientalis,* and vegetable plants. The use and composition of native spice plants are being researched.

The garden includes collections of tropical and subtropical plants (over 3,000 taxa) under glass (total area of 5,000 square meters [5,980 sq. yd.]). Methods of microclonal propagation of tropical plants and nutrient media have been developed in the garden. The largest collection is of tropical orchids, which contains over 600 species and varieties belonging to 150 genera. The primary aims of this collection are to study the biology of orchid development and to develop methods for commercial cultivation. This research will help conserve rare and threatened species.

Commercial propagation of orchids is confined to *Cymbidium* varieties, *Calanthe vastita,* and commercial varieties of *Phalaenopsis amabilis. Cymbidium* propagated in vitro flowering with three mature tuberidea can produce three to five inflorescence and 30 to 75 flowers. *Calanthe vestita* is propagated by tuberidia, and *Phalaenopsis amabilis* is propagated by seeds and micropropagation of dominant buds of the inflorescence.

The studies and biotechnologies gave rise to in vitro reproduction and optimum cultivation methods for *Calanthe vestita* hothouse growing that ensure a mass blooming in December, the most bloomless month, of the *Dendrobium phalenopsis* and its species blooming all the year round, the *Cymbidium hubridum* of the winter blooming, the *Phalaenopsis amabilis* and its species that also bloom practically year-round.

The conservation collection of orchids includes a number of endemics such as *Angraecum ebumeum Bory* and *A. sesquipedale Thouars* from Madagascar, species of *Aeranthes* from the Mascarene Islands, and South American species of *Cattleya* and *Laelia,* which have local distributions in Brazil and Venezuela. Vietnamese orchids have also begun to be collected.

In 1965 A.M. Grodzinsky, academician of the Ukranian Academy of Sciences, initiated at the NBG the study of chemical plant interaction (allelopathy). He developed a number of important and fundamental directions at the garden, including formulating a new approach to determine chemical plant interactions as physiological active substances circulation in biocenoses.

Medicinal botany is a new research direction at the NBG. Scientists here have researched plant immunomodulators and developed phytocompositions correcting immunocompetence. Native medicinal plants are studied in the wild, together with their efficient use, propagation, and protection. Conservation of nature, plant gene banks, and biological research, combined with educational activities in ecology and plant use, remain the principal responsibilities of the NBG.

The M.M. Grishko National Botanical Garden publishes the scientific magazine *Plant Introduction.* The NBG has also become a favorite place for recreation. Approximately 500,000 people visit every year.

Synopsis

1935 Botanical garden founded
1957 Topiary fruit garden added
1965 Study of allelopathy begins on premises
1967 Botanical garden becomes scientific research center
1970 Plot containing rare Ukrainian flora planted

Further Reading

Cherevchenko, T.M., and N.B. Gaponenko, "M.M. Grisko Central Botanical Garden of the National Ukrainian Academy of Sciences," *Botanical Garden Conservation News* 2, no. 5 (1995)

Lapin, P.I., *Botanicheskie sady SSSR; Botanical Gardens of the USSR* (bilingual Russian-English edition), Moscow: Kolos, 1984

NIKOLAY B. GAPONENKO

Grosser Garten

Dresden, Germany

Location: southeast of Altstadt, between Lennéstrasse, Karcherallee, and Stuebelallee

Outside the municipal center of Dresden is found its largest and oldest public park, the Grosser Garten, which comprises not only an elegant pleasure palace but also a garden that has experienced much change over the centuries. As the largest connected park system in the city with an estimated 470 acres (190 ha) of developed grounds, the Grosser Garten holds a history that reaches back to 1676 during Germany's dynastic wars of expansion when one of the Saxon princes, Elector

Johann George II, secured fields outside of Dresden ostensibly for a hunting park and pheasantry. Purchased during the Dutch War, the land was soon augmented with more parcels of property and turned over to master gardener Martin Goettler, who steadily enlarged the scope of the preserve over the next two years. At that same time construction for the palace began under the direction of Johann George Starcke and lasted for seven years. Many deem this pleasure palace, or *Lustschloss,* historically significant because it was the first large-scale project in the German territories to be built by a native architect. The palace has since been declared the first Saxon baroque monument of its kind.

Once the palace, which stands at the center of the park, was complete, attention turned toward transforming the parklands into a level, geometric garden with rigid avenues, including three longitudinal avenues and a transverse avenue. Landscape architect Johann Friedrich Karcher introduced this French-inspired baroque style. Over the next ten years eight pavilions (*Kavalierhauser*) were established around the palace near the orangery and yew groupings, and by 1693 the rectangular shape that the garden bears today had taken hold. Between 1699 and 1719 an ornamental parterre was sculpted near a newly built pheasant enclosure, and a palace pond, nature theater, hedge labyrinth, and shooting hut quickly followed. By the early 18th century, over 1,500 marble and sandstone statues had been installed throughout the grounds. Sadly, few of the originals exist today.

King Augustus II of Poland, also known as Augustus the Strong, experienced great success in perpetuating the baroque flavor that had established Dresden as the "Florence on the Elbe." Under his hand Dresden grew into a leading cultural center, and Augustus worked with architect Matthäus Daniel Pöppelmann (primary architect of the Zwinger Palace and Pillnitz palace gardens) to stress the French emphasis on lines and open spaces so emblematic of the Saxon baroque style. The Seven Years' War (1756–63) levied much damage on both Dresden and its parks: many sculptures were stolen and garden structures wholly destroyed. Reconstruction efforts began shortly after the war and included the framework of a new enclosure system for the pheasants that were becoming the garden's most famous residents. Other sculptures were recruited from neighboring gardens to replace the stolen art, among them several classical works by Balestra and marble vases crafted by Antonio Corradini. Unfortunately, Napoléon's retreat from Moscow and the resulting War of Liberation in 1812 inflicted still further damage, but by 1829 the palace had been refurbished, and several decades later, in 1861, Peter Joseph Lenné partitioned 32 acres (13 ha) of the property to allow for a zoological garden. Today this garden is the Dresden Zoo, a popular attraction that houses approximately 2,700 animals.

The Grosser Garten had its first international horticulture exhibition in 1887, and two years later seven-and-a-half acres (3 ha) were set aside for the dedication of a botanical garden that currently houses rare tropical plants, orchids, and succulents within both a greenhouse and open-air arrangements. By the time the botanical garden opened, the general public had access to these collections, and the Grosser Garten was no longer a private pleasure retreat. (In 1814 Johann Gotthelf Huebler had demolished a wall that had previously formed the perimeter of the garden, and Repnin Wolkonski, the governor general at the time, subsequently opened the garden for public use.)

Perhaps due to a combination of past damage and regional trends, restoration efforts in the 19th century began to take a different turn, and the intensely baroque park evolved into a more romantically inspired landscape garden. This metamorphosis also occurred elsewhere in Germany as classically baroque gardens slowly absorbed the influence of rococo and English-style designs. The six bosquets and adjacent pheasant enclosures were modified during the tenure of garden director Johann Carl Friedrich Bouché, who eased through a redevelopment program that cautiously preserved a certain level of the original baroque character, particularly around the palace. Other areas were remodeled into more exotic landscape terrain, with the transformation of a gravel pit into the Carolasee (1881–86) and plans for a new pond begun in 1890. Before the turn of the 20th century, the garden director had developed a restaurant and a stately exhibition palace on the Stuebelplatz (inaugurated with great fanfare in 1896). Work continued at a modest tempo during the reign of William II and throughout the years of the Weimar Republic (1919–33). One of the last additions before World War II included a beautiful mosaic water well fashioned after the design of Hans Poelzig (restored in 1993).

The fire bombing of Dresden in 1945 effectively destroyed the large garden, the pavilions, and the palace. Efforts to restore the devastated park and burnt palace structure began immediately after the war. By 1950 a narrow-gauge railway had been introduced—a feature that increased the park's popularity as a public entertainment and recreation venue over the years. Several outdoor theaters were also built or enhanced, and in the mid-1950s reconstruction work on five of the pavilions had been largely completed. Refurbishments continue, and the Grosser Garten enjoys its status as a historical German monument, perhaps the most important member of a system of public gardens fondly referred to as the "green lung" of Dresden.

Synopsis

1676 Fields purchased by Johann George II for hunting garden and pheasantry

1677 Garden grounds gradually expanded
1683 Karcher begins to impose baroque style on garden design
1684 Garden pavilions begun
1699 Parterre and pheasant enclosure constructed
1715 King Augustus II initiates further park development; palace pond built
1719 Nature theater, hedge labyrinth, orangery, and shooting hut begun
1720 Introduction of sandstone and marble sculptures
1756–63 Seven Years' War
1812–13 War of Liberation; Napoléon's retreat damages portions of park
1814 Grosser Garten opened to public
1829 Palace is refurbished
1861 Zoo established on 32 acres (13 ha) of park
1873 Johann Carl Friedrich Bouché redesigns portions of garden
1887 First international botanical exhibition
1888 Botanical garden begun
1890–94 New pond system developed
1896 Introduction of exhibition palace on Stuebelplatz
1945 Destruction of garden during World War II
1946 Restoration work begun
1950 Railway finished
1954–55 Refurbishment of five of original eight pavilions

Further Reading

Clayton, Anthony, and Alan Russell, editors, *Dresden: A City Reborn,* Oxford and New York: Berg, 1999
Hansmann, Wilfried, *Gartenkunst der Renaissance und des Barock,* Cologne, Germany: DuMont, 1983
Heckmann, Hermann, *Matthäus Daniel Pöppelmann und die Barockbaukunst in Dresden,* Stuttgart, Germany: Deutsche Verlags-Anstalt, 1986
Helas, Volker, *Architektur in Dresden, 1800–1900,* Braunschweig, Germany: Vieweg, 1985
Hunt, John Dixon, *Gardens and the Picturesque: Studies in the History of Landscape Architecture,* Cambridge, Massachusetts: MIT Press, 1992
Nafziger, George, *Napoleon's Dresden Campaign: The Battles of August 1813,* Chicago: Emperor's Press, 1994
Schreiber, Hermann, *August der Starke: Leben und Lieben im deutschen Barock,* Munich: List, 1981
Staszewski, Jacek, *August II,* Warsaw: Zamek Królewski w Warszawie, 1986

KRISTIN WYE-RODNEY

Großsedlitz

Saxony, Germany

Location: approximately 7.8 miles (12.6 km) southeast of Dresden

Though never completed, Großsedlitz is one of the most magnificent baroque gardens in Germany. It is situated on a plateau on the Elbe Valley near the Saxon capital of Dresden. King Friedrich August I took the estate over from his minister Count Wackerbarth in 1723. The garden had been designed for Wackerbarth in 1719 but only partially executed. The king implemented changes in some parts of the design up to 1732. His architects Matthäus Daniel Pöppelmann, Zacharias Longelune, and Johann Christoph Knöffel were responsible for the garden layout.

The little three-winged castle occupies the highest point of the area and was intended to form the middle part of the garden, but only the eastern half of the garden plan was executed. Beneath the castle is the upper orangery with its modern grass-and-flower parterre (1958) on the south side, which replaces the former *parterre de broderie* executed with colored gravel and box. The two basins on the south side of this parterre are original. A grand axis stretches from this parterre over a sunken bowling green and a little bosquet eastwards into the valley. Here, the boundary of the garden is formed by a ha-ha. The borders of the bowling green were originally ornamented with *broderie* elements. The whole bowling green area was surrounded by trelliswork. On the eastern end a trelliswork pavillion was erected. These elements no longer exist. South of the bosquet mentioned previously, another little bosquet followed, containing a bowling alley between sweet chestnut trees (*Castanea sativa*).

The lower orangery is located in front of the bowling green. Before this building lies the most famous part of the garden, the lower orangy parterre. It ends in a great

Aerial view of Großsedlitz
Copyright Herbert Boswank, courtesy of Sächsische Schlösserverwaltung

curved set of double stairs, called the "Silent Music," in the south. The axis between the orangery and the stairs is bordered by two small channels accentuated by little fountains, termed in French *chandeliers*. Just before the doubled stairs a water jet rises up 46 feet (14 m). The lawn of this parterre was ornamented by orange trees in tubs and many box trees clipped into balls, pyramids, and fowl shapes. Now it is bordered by columnar hornbeams on the top of the grass slopes, first described around 1830.

At the level of the upper orangy parterre there is a great basin, never filled with water, surmounted by a great cascade, never completed, on the south side. Both the "Silent Music" stairway and the cascade led into the vast adjacent baroque park on the slope of a hill. This wooded area is crossed by allées in the main axes and by some paths in the parts beneath the garden. The compartments of the bosquets were bordered with hornbeam (*Carpinus*) hedges.

Many sculptures are erected, mostly accompanying the hedges. They were partly attributed to the famous Saxon sculptor Balthasar Permoser. A couple of sphinxes stand watch on the east side of the upper orangy parterre.

Both the buildings and the gardens were damaged in the wars of 1756–63 and 1813. Due to its bad condition the castle was demolished in 1871, and only the eastern wing was rebuilt (1872–74). The lower orangery was demolished also in 1861–64 and rebuilt afterward. Considerable reconstruction work took place during the time of the German Democratic Republic (1949–90), and the garden was again famous and well-kept at this time. The actual main entrance for visitors is from the parking area and dates from 1960, when a baroque gate from Dresden was relocated here.

Synopsis

1719–23 Construction of garden begun for Count Wackerbarth
1723–32 Alterations made for King Frederick Augustus I
1871 Castle demolished
1872–74 Eastern wing of castle rebuilt
1932 Preservation work begun

Further Reading

Buby, Simone, "Raumbildung und pflanzliche Ausstattung im Barockgarten Großsedlitz," in *Jahrbuch der Staatlichen Schlösser, Burgen und Gärten in Sachsen* (1997)

Kempe, Lothar, *Schlösser und Gärten um Dresden,* Leipzig: Seemann, 1979

Koch, Hugo, *Sächsische Gartenkunst*, Berlin, Germany: Deutsche Bauzeitung, 1910

Koitzsch, Herbert, *Der Barockgarten Großsedlitz, Stadt Heidenau,* Heidenau, Germany: Stadt Heidenau, 1984

Mertens, Klaus, "Der Park zu Großsedlitz," Ph.D. diss., Dresden, Technische Universität, 1962

CLEMENS ALEXANDER WIMMER

Ground Cover

The ancient Greeks were fortunate to have a natural landscape that resembled a lush garden paradise. The countryside was replete with native ground covers of periwinkle (*Vinca minor*), English ivy (*Hedera helix*), and honeysuckle (*Lonicera*), and very little effort was needed to transplant these plants into their courtyard gardens. Early gardens in the more remote areas of Europe, Britain, and later North America contained ground covers that were native plants. These early ground covers were grown for food purposes; little space was available in a garden for plants that did not provide something toward basic human survival.

The Renaissance period signaled the change from the medieval way of life as people gained a wider cultural horizon. A revival of the arts and learning ensued. Florence grew to achieve a high degree of peace and prosperity, which eventually elevated the garden to an art form. Many Renaissance philosophies originated in gardens, as gardens were places of dialogue and enjoyment of the senses. Gardens for the first time were now being planned on a generous scale, and garden design was being done by architects and painters (not practical gardeners). Much of the inspiration for these gardens came from studies of ancient Roman life, and other countries soon strove to duplicate the gardens of Florence. Renaissance gardens used massed ground-cover plantings of asarabaca (*Asarum europaeum*), carpet bugleweed (*Ajuga reptans*), chamomile (*Chamaemelum nobile*), houseleek (*Sempervivum*), lily-of-the-valley (*Convallaria majalis*), marigold (*Tagetes patula*), mint (*Mentha*), orache (*Atriplex hortensis*), pansy (*Viola cornuta*), periwinkle, stocks (*Matthiola*), wallflower (*Erysimum cheiri*), tarragon (*Artemisia dracunculus*), and violets (*Viola odorata*). Ground covers were fast spreading and grown for their flowers (in contrast to the present-day trend to grow ground covers for their foliage effects). Many of these ground-cover-type plants could be found inside knot gardens or parterres.

The Momoyama period of Japanese garden history (1583–1603) led to the creation of the *roji,* which is the dewy path through a tea garden. This natural garden was designed to take the visitor on a journey in preparation for arriving at the teahouse. The main features of a tea garden are the stepping stones that slow the pace of visitors. Along the way is a simple sea of green moss. The moss ground cover is kept meticulously weeded and watered. Fastidious sweeping of the moss ensures that the subtle green colors are always seen.

The artificiality of the early 18th-century garden in Europe paved the way for a pendulum swing in gardening styles. Designers in England began implementing a more natural style of design. With this new style, in the first half of the 18th century, ground covers started to become more prominent. The sweeping park-like landscaped garden emerged with Lancelot "Capability" Brown as the designer to instigate this change. For the next century, trade with North America opened up a tidal wave of new plants heading to England. In the late 19th and early 20th centuries, William Robinson moved garden design away from the formal Italian parterres still favored in Victorian England toward a more natural style.

From the late 19th century to the early 20th century, the emerging middle class, striving to emulate the upper classes, wanted to surround their town homes in a landscape that gave the impression of the countryside. They used ground covers, predominantly English ivy, in the shady locations where more desirable plants refused to grow. Space was limited, and a diversity of plants in the garden meant a higher status. As a result many wildflowers occupied the unmown lawn areas near trees.

Plants arriving from Asia and North America in the beginning of the 20th century had a dramatic effect on the garden landscapes in England. Plant collectors now had easier access to the plant treasures in many Asiatic regions. An influx of native American plants also made their way into English nurseries. Pioneer gardeners in the United States at the end of the 19th century had created an entirely new gardening style of their own, using indigenous plants as the main components of their homestead gardens. This opened up a new pallet of plants that could be used as shady ground covers in England and Europe. Mayapples (*Podophyllum peltatum*), Virginia bluebells (*Mertensia virginica*), wood poppy (*Stylophorum diphyllum*), twinleaf (*Jeffersonia diphylla*), and woodland phloxes (*Phlox divaricata*) were now being propagated and sold at premium prices in England. Although the influx of Asian plants did not have a significant impact on gardening styles (unlike the American plants), they added more choices to achieve the naturalistic style. An English garden of the time could have mayapples, European wild ginger (*Asarum europaeum*), and Asian primulas all in the same bed. New arrivals from the Far East were placed in the English-style, large herbaceous flower borders or the naturalistic, informal Robinson-style landscapes. Astilbes, hosta, and daylilies (*Hemerocallis*) that had been grown for centuries in Chinese and Japanese gardens were instant hits.

As time progressed nurseries in New England started to import plants from England. Gardens in the major settlements now could include ground covers of carpet bugleweed from Europe and Iran, star-of-Bethlehem (*Ornithogalum umbellatum*) from Europe and North Africa, periwinkle from Spain and France, and moneywort (*Lysimachia nummularia*), goutweed (*Aegopodium podagraria*), and deadnettles (*Lamium galeobdolon, L. maculatum*) from Europe. One plant called marvel of Peru (*Mirabilis jalapa*) was imported to Britain from Peru and then sent to North America. Unfortunately, many of these new exotic plants excelled as vigorous ground covers and have since become naturalized in North America. They are now considered invasive pests.

In South America during the mid-1900s, Roberto Burle Marx endeavored to translate his interest in abstract art into the landscape. The culmination of his biology, painting, fabric, and stage-designing skills gave him an unusual background from which to draw for his landscape-design projects. By gathering inspiration from Brazilian forests and the Amazon River, Burle Marx used repetitive plantings to emphasize the plants' texture. His design at Kronforth Garden features flowing masses of plants that resemble a paisley river of ground covers.

Burle Marx's work in Rio de Janeiro inspired many future designers around the world, including landscape architect and urban designer James van Sweden, who formed a partnership with Wolfgang Oehme in 1975. The partnership brought a dramatic change to North American landscapes during the next decades. They have been credited with developing the new American garden style that brought the illusion of a natural meadow to the landscape. They selected plants so that they could grow, bloom, and set seed without training, pruning, or artificial shaping. Plants and designs were chosen to be naturally self-sufficient without the need for extensive maintenance. Low-growing perennials and ornamental grasses were used as ground covers. These plants were the mainstays of the designs, with taller grasses, perennials, and shrubs becoming the "walls" of the design. The use of plants as ground covers for the purpose of lower maintenance was launched. The garden at Nelson A. Rockefeller Park in New York is one example that has changed the public's views of ground covers. Roses, ornamental grasses, succulents, and perennials in masses were now considered ground covers. No longer are ground covers considered lower-class plants used just to hold the soil, stop weeds, and conserve moisture. Through the efforts of Oehme and van Sweden, ground covers now have an integral place in the landscape as fully contributing components in the design.

Ground covers are an important part of the landscape today. While they certainly do conserve moisture and soil, control weeds, and cool soil temperatures, they can also be used to create lower-maintenance gardens for busy homeowners. They are essential in creating a subtle garden that gives the visitor a pleasurable, restful, and peaceful location for meditation and reflection. Ground covers soften the landscape, presenting an alternative to hard surfaces. In addition, evergreen ground covers offer year-round interest in the garden. Ground covers are usually easy to propagate and divide, making them ideal for sharing with others.

Further Reading

Elliott, Brent, *Victorian Gardens,* Portland, Oregon: Timber Press, and London: Batsford, 1986

Hobhouse, Penelope, *Plants in Garden History,* London: Pavilion Books, 1992; as *Penelope Hobhouse's Gardening through the Ages,* New York: Simon and Schuster, 1992

Huxley, Anthony, *An Illustrated History of Gardening,* New York: Paddington Press, 1978; London: Macmillan, 1983

Jellicoe, Geoffrey, and Susan Jellicoe, *The Landscape of Man: Shaping The Environment From Prehistory to the Present Day,* London: Thames and Hudson, and New York: Viking Press, 1975; 3rd edition, New York: Thames and Hudson, 1995

Leopold, Allison Kyle, *The Victorian Garden,* New York: Potter, 1995

Masson, Georgina, *Italian Gardens,* New York: Abrams, and London: Thames and Hudson, 1961; revised edition, Woodbridge, Suffolk: Antique Collector's Club, 1987

Phillips, Roger, and Nicky Foy, *A Photographic Garden History,* London: Macmillan, and New York: Random House, 1995

Plumptre, George, *The Garden Makers: The Great Traditions of Garden Design from 1600 to the Present Day,* London: Pavilion Books, and New York: Random House, 1993

Plumptre, George, *Great Gardens, Great Designers,* London and New York: Ward Lock, 1994

Smit, Daan, *Baroque Gardens,* New York: Smithmark, 1996

Stroud, Dorothy, *Capability Brown,* London: Country Life, 1950; new edition, London: Faber, 1984

Symes, Michael, *A Glossary of Garden History,* Princes Risborough, Buckinghamshire: Shire, 1993; 2nd edition, 2000

Thacker, Christopher, *The History of Gardens,* Berkeley: University of California Press, and London: Croom Helm, 1979

Thomas, Graham Stuart, *Plants for Ground-Cover,* London: Dent, 1970; revised edition, London: Dent, and Portland, Oregon: Sagapress/Timber Press, 1990

Van Sweden, James, *Gardening with Nature,* New York: Random House, 1997

ANNE MARIE VAN NEST

Grove

Groves have a long history in mythology, with some of the earliest sacred groves being connected with temples in ancient Egypt. In ancient Greece groves sometimes achieved a higher status in religious worship than the associated temples. During Homer's time these groves were surrounded with a wall and planted with large forest trees. Later they gradually turned into the more gardenlike surroundings of temples, the grove becoming as important as the temple. Influenced by Oriental traditions, the Greeks also planted groves around the graves of their dignitaries to prevent them from being desecrated. Such graves were normally located in gymnasiums, parks, or game places.

In ancient Rome groves had a completely different appearance; they were basically untouched tracts of land, which were considered sacred. However, by the first century A.D. (about the time of Pliny the Elder), only the names of these groves survived, and occasionally a single tree, which was still considered sacred. At that time new groves were created that appeared natural but adhered to a certain aesthetic ideal. Gradually, however, the more gardenlike influence from the Greeks was introduced, and groves were embellished, probably with rockeries and marble basins. Later they also included burials and associated monuments.

Groves—small woodlands or groups of trees—have generally been imbued with mythical meanings, serving as places of worship for heathen deities. Such meanings continued throughout the ages of more rational thinking and are visible, for example, in the work of John Evelyn and Thomas Traherne in the 17th century. By this time, however, the grove had become a woody component of the formal garden of the 17th and 18th centuries. Equivalent to the French word *bosquet,* this type of grove was referred to by a series of names, most commonly *wilderness,* but also *thicket, boscage, coppice* or *copse, wood, forest, plantation,* and sometimes even *maze.* In England Alexander Pope, in his *Epistle to Burlington* (1731), wrote, "No artful Wilderness to perplex the Scene. Grove nods at Grove, each Ally has a Brother and half the Platform just reflects the other." This essay announced a change in fashion and ultimately served as a death knell to formal gardens and to wildernesses by their association, although they continued up to about 1750, when they were finally replaced by shrubberies. To 18th-century improvers the word *grove* became synonymous with *woodland,* while to poets it was equated with a stand of trees along Elysian fields.

In England the first literary references to wildernesses as an element of the formal garden occurred in the description of Nonsuch by Anthony Watson (*Magnificae et plane regiae domus quae vulgo vocatur Nonesuch brevis et vera descriptio,* ca. 1582). Watson, writing in Latin, refers to the grove as a *desertum* but notes that it was "neither wild nor deserted." Apparently it did not consist of wild, rugged, uncontrolled vegetation, nor did it remind him of a wilderness in the biblical sense, the barren desert, the wilderness of Jews. John Parkinson in *Paradisi in Sole paradisus terrestris: or, The Garden of All Sorts of Pleasant Flowers* (1629) was the first author to use the word *wilderness* as part of the garden. He does not, however, explain its meaning and continues to define the three parts of the garden as being the kitchen garden, flower garden, and orchard. The wilderness did not feature in this, but the various ornamental shrubs and trees included in the section of Parkinson's book under the discussion of the orchard could be found in wildernesses from about 1650, when they became normal adjuncts to any important country house. By then conceived as densely planted areas, wildernesses formed a contrast to the flatter parts of the garden. These areas were used for "studious retirement" or, alternatively, for "recreation with friends." It is no coincidence that the first London pleasure gardens, such as Vauxhall, were laid out on the model of the wilderness or grove. They were also appreciated as havens for songbirds, while the Italians appreciated such thickets as places to net birds, the so-called *ragnaia.*

The design of a grove or wilderness generally consisted of a series of walks cutting through a plot of ground creating variously (often geometrically) shaped areas, referred to as squares or quarters. These quarters were generally filled with woody plants and surrounded by hedges, although there were a number of variations to this. The usual form was to lay out the walks in the form of a star (at least three walks crossing each other in a central point), a direct cross, St. Andrew's cross, or goosefoot (*patte d'oie*). Several features were normally included in these arrangements, such as cabinets, halls, natural and artificial arbors, and cloisters. Contemporary texts, such as the standard work of the period *La theorie et la practique du jardinage* (1709; *The Theory and Practice of Gardening*), written by the Frenchman Dézallier d'Argenville and translated into German and English, elaborated on these and other features. The first English translation of this work, by the architect John James, was published in 1712 and discussed the planting practice distinguishing various types of groves.

Forests or great woods of tall trees were promoted in England by the writings of John Evelyn, Moses Cooke, and Stephen Switzer, who wrote of "forest, or in a more easie style rural gardening." These were promoted to counter the great lack of trees in 17th-century England and were planted with forest trees for "pleasure and profit." In France, however, such woods did not form part of the pleasure garden and had neither hedges nor rolled walks. They were usually planted in the form of a star with a large circle in the middle where all ridings meet, with famous examples including Fontainebleau and Bois de Vincennes. A well-known English example was Moseley near Cookeridge (between Leeds and Otley).

Coppice woods in France were also meant for commercial purposes; they consisted of trees that were cut back to the base at regular intervals, depending on tradition and species, once per nine years or so. In England Richard Bradley referred to coppices as "close wildernesses" and Switzer as "set wildernesses," which clearly showed that they were intended for pleasure as well. They were generally planted without hedges.

Woods of a middle height with tall hedges formed the most common type of wilderness. Here the quarters were filled with a very dense planting of a mixture of trees and shrubs, left to grow in a dense thicket or "sort of green knot." Switzer vilified these as "promiscuous plantations" because they were not profitable. They were maintained to a maximum height of 30 or 40 feet (9.1 or 12.2 m) and could be found in most gardens of the period.

Groves open and in compartments had no trees planted in the center of the squares, which were left open, and the avenues planted with trees such as lime and horse chestnut. The hedges were kept low, at three feet (0.9 m) or breast height, to enable views across the different compartments. In the squares there would be mown walks and some ornamental flowering shrubs or shaped yew trees. A well-known example of such a grove was at Ham House, Richmond, London, England (replanted in the 1970s; changed ca. 1996 to a wood of middle height).

Open groves only consisted of trees with high stems and tufted crowns, which meant trees wherein the bottom branches had been removed to such an extent that the tree lost its apical dominance and grew various leaders, which each formed tufts. Open groves were sometimes referred to as quincunxes, even if they were not planted in a quincunx fashion, that is, in staggered rows. Other customs were planting in squares (in opposite rows) and in an irregular manner. During the 17th and 18th centuries, there were distinct fashions for specific trees, with the sycamore favored early in the 17th century, being surpassed first by elm and then by lime. One example of an open grove was that at Hartwell House, Aylesbury, Buchs, England, depicted by Balthasar Nebot in the 1730s.

Woods of evergreens were favored because of their continuing beauty, but they were not much applied since they took a long time to establish. There were continuing debates among gardeners as to whether evergreens should be planted in separate areas or whether they should be intermixed with deciduous plants. A variation on this type is the golden or gilded grove, which was an assembly of various variegated evergreens. Examples of evergreen groves were at Castle Howard, North Yorkshire, England, and Nimmerdor, Netherlands.

A separate manner of planting first developed at Kensington Palace in London, in the early 18th century, whereby shrubs and trees were planted in a theatrical manner, arranged according to height, with the highest trees in the center. From this time onward there was a great emphasis on the use of ornamental shrubs, which when copied on the Continent became referred to as *bosquet a l'Angloise.*

Further Reading

Biddle, Martin, "The Gardens of Nonesuch: Sources and Dating," *Garden History* 27, no. 1 (1999)
Bradley, Richard, *A General Treatise of Husbandry and Gardening,* London, 1726
Coffin, David, *The English Garden: Meditation and Memorial,* Princeton, New Jersey: Princeton University Press, 1994
Cook, Moses, *The Manner of Raising, Ordering, and Improving Forest Trees,* London, 1676
Dent, John, *The Quest for Nonsuch,* London: Hutchinson, 1962
Dézallier d'Argenville, Antoine-Joseph, *La théorie et pratique du jardinage,* Paris, 1709; as *The Theory and Practice of Gardening,* translated by John James, London, 1712; reprint, Farnborough, Hampshire: Gregg, 1969
Evelyn, John, *Sylva; or, A Discourse of Forest Trees,* London, 1664; reprint, Menston: Scolar Press, 1972
Gothein, Marie Luise Schroeter, *Geschichte der Gartenkunst,* Jena, Germany: Diederichs, 1914; as *A History of Garden Art,* 2 vols., London: Dent, and New York: Dutton, 1928; reprint, New York: Hacker Art Books, 1979
Grimal, Pierre, *Les jardins romains à la fin de la république et aux deux premiers siècles de l'empire,* Paris: Boccard, 1943; 3rd edition, as *Les jardins romains,* Paris: Fayard, 1984
Hunt, John Dixon, and Peter Willis, *The Genius of the Place: The English Landscape Garden, 1620–1820,* London: Elek, 1975
Jacques, David, and Arend Jan van der Horst, *The Gardens of William and Mary,* London: Helm, 1988
Langley, Batty, *New Principles of Gardening,* London, 1728; reprint, New York: Garland, 1982
Miller, Philip, *The Gardeners Dictionary,* London, 1731
Mollet, André, *The Garden of Pleasure,* London, 1670
Parkinson, John, *Paradisi in Sole Paradisus Terrestris,* London, 1629
Prest, John M., *The Garden of Eden: The Botanic Garden and the Re-creation of Paradise,* New Haven, Connecticut: Yale University Press, 1981
Switzer, Stephen, *The Nobleman, Gentleman and Gardener's Recreation,* London, 1715; new edition, as *Ichnographia Rustica; or, The Nobleman, Gentleman and Gardener's Recreation,* 3 vols., London, 1718; reprint, New York: Garland, 1982
Traherne, Thomas, *Groves,* edited by D.D.C. Chambers, Toronto: Stone Press, 1987

JAN WOUDSTRA

Guévrékian, Gabriel 1900–1970

French Landscape Architect

The professional life of landscape architect Gabriel Guévrékian spanned nearly half a century, yet he is best known for three French gardens he designed within the span of three years, 1925–27. These gardens comprise some of the 20th century's most important explorations in early modernist garden design. The Garden of Water and Light (Jardin d'eau et de lumière), designed for the 1925 Paris Exposition des Arts Décoratifs et Industriels Modernes, the garden at the Villa Noailles in Hyères, in collaboration with the architect Robert Mallett-Stevens (1927), and the terrace garden at the Villa Heim in Neuilly (1927) captured forever the spirit of the emerging modern movement and its ultimate influence on the design of the Western garden. Described in contemporary accounts as "modern" or "Cubist," they also were perceived to be reinterpretations of Persian gardens. They represent the high point of Guévrékian's inquiry and invention concerning the garden as an expressive medium of the age.

These three gardens broke radically from earlier garden designs. Guévrékian's innovative use of traditional garden materials and his explorations of new materials; new expressions of time, movements, and change; color;

abstractions of nature; and the interrelationships between the garden and the interior architectural spaces place these gardens at the forefront of the developing modern garden. They suggest what the American landscape architect Fletcher Steele saw as the potential of the modern garden to "bring a new meaning into the whole contemporaneous movement of thought and art, for the field of gardening is particularly adapted to interpreting these ideas, and to making all of us conscious of new aspects in materials, colors, and dimensions." Guévrékian explored in some depth nontraditional uses of plants. Often using a limited palette of plants in color or textural masses, he incorporated plants into the garden's architectural palette. At the Villa Noailles he used plants within the garden as a counterpoint to the natural vegetation of the site.

The Garden of Water and Light was commissioned by J.C.N. Forestier, who specified that the garden be "in the modern spirit with elements from Persian decor." Guévrékian responded to this challenge by creating a highly geometric garden of concrete, glass, and low plantings clearly influenced by Cubist paintings and the color theories of the Simultaneists. Guévrékian played on the temporary nature of the exposition as he created a garden in which time itself appeared frozen. It was a garden composed as a strictly visual experience. Steele (1930) praised the Garden of Water and Light as "startling in geometrical forms, resulting in an utterly new quality and design in gardening," further noting that, for Guévrékian, "Materials whether water, concrete, earth, or plants are frankly used for their aid in carrying out the artist's ideas. . . . Horticulture, as such is important, not for the love of plants, but for what one can do with them." The garden earned Guévrékian numerous other accolades and was awarded one of the exposition's Grand Prizes.

One influential patron who saw the Garden of Water and Light was the Vicomte de Noailles, who commissioned Guévrékian to design a garden for his villa at Hyères that was being designed by Mallett-Stevens. Completed in 1927, this walled garden was a highly geometric composition, with an expressive use of color that made the most of its restricted palette of concrete, glass, water, and a few plants. Again influenced by Cubist paintings, the garden presented three different visual compositions depending on the viewers' vantage point as they moved through the house and into the garden. The changing vantage points further revealed the tensions between the garden within the walls, the architecture of the villa, and the surrounding landscape. It was clear to Steele that "M. Guevrekian feels and visualizes, and hence, designs in three dimensions." In 1928 the villa served as the setting for Man Ray's film *The Mystery of the Château of the Dice* (*Les Mystères du Château du Dès*). By 1993 the garden had been partially restored to its original design by the city of Hyères, a restoration that Dorothée Imbert has called "probably the first true re-creation of a modernist garden."

Guévrékian's third French garden of note was the Villa Heim in Neuilly. Here, the landscape architect was in total control and created his most integrated composition and the most thorough exploration of the potential relationships and interactions between interior space and garden space. As at the Villa Noailles, part of the garden was a visual composition to be seen from above, but here the clear distinctions between architectural elements and garden elements were blurred. So seamless was the integration of compositional elements that the villa has been described as having the "archetypal modernist roof terrace." For Steele the Villa Heim was "the most livable of the modernistic houses which I happened to see. . . . It is particularly interesting, because, so far as I know, the first in which the roofs and terraces all over the house are designed as integral elements of the garden" (1930).

The pictorial quality of these gardens was a critical aspect of their popularity and influence. They photographed beautifully. The images clearly revealed the aesthetic sensibilities expressed in the garden of modern art in general and Cubism in particular. Images of Guévrékian's French gardens were widely distributed and, along with the work of other designers such as Pierre-Emile Legrain and André and Paul Vera, highly influential. Guévrékian's work together with the other garden designers in the 1925 Paris Exposition stimulated debate not only in Europe but in the United States as well. His work was greatly admired by Steele and featured prominently in Steele's essay "New Pioneering in Garden Design" in the April 1930 issue of *Landscape Architecture*, the monthly publication of the American Society of Landscape Architects. Imitations of Guévrékian's work quickly appeared but lacked both the certainty of his inquiry and the contextual moment of these highly original garden explorations.

Biography

Born in Constantinople, Ottoman Empire, 21 November 1900. Raised in Tehran, Iran, until age ten; educated as architect at Academy of Applied Art, Vienna; worked in office of Josef Hoffman, and in Paris office of Henri Sauvage; collaborated with architect Robert Mallett-Stevens on several projects; attended Congress International d'Architecture Moderne, 1932, and served as its secretary; office in Tehran from 1933 to 1937, where he had numerous private and public commissions, including from Ministry of War, Ministry of Foreign Affairs, and Palace of Justice; on eve of World War II, relocated to London; returned to France upon outbreak of war; following the war, taught briefly at the Sarrebruck Beaux-Arts Academy; taught at Auburn University, Auburn, Alabama, United States,

1948; spent 20 years at University of Illinois, Champaign-Urbana. Died in Antibes, France, 1970.

Selected Designs

1925 Garden of Water and Light (Jardin d'eau et de lumière), Paris Exposition des Arts Décoratifs et Industriels Modernes, Paris, France
1927 Villa Noailles Garden (with architect Robert Mallett-Stevens), Hyères, France; Terrace garden, Villa Heim, Neuilly, France
1934 Villa Panahy, Iran
1935 Villa Siassy, Iran; Villa Aslani, Iran
1936 Villa Khosrovani, Iran; Villa Taleghani, Iran
1937 Villa Firouze, Iran; Villa Mafi, Iran

Selected Publications

"Villa a Neuilly," *Cahiers d'art* 4 (1929)
"Maisons en pays de soliel," *Art et decoration* (1946)

Further Reading

Briolle, Cecile, "An Uncommon Work: Cubist Style Garden by Gabriel Guévrékian," *Monuments historiques,* no. 143 (1986)
Briolle, Cecile, Agnes Fuzibet, and Gerard Monnier, "La villa de Noailles a Hyères, 1923–1933," *Casabella* 48 (July/August 1984)
"Gabriel Guevrekian's Cubist Gardens," *Diadalos* 46 (1992)
Imbert, Dorothée, [book review of *Gabriel Guévrékian, 1900–1970,* by Vilou, Deshoulières, and Jeanneau], *Journal of the Society of Architectural Historians* 49, no. 4 (1990)
Imbert, Dorothée, *The Modernist Garden in France,* New Haven, Connecticut: Yale University Press, 1993
Imbert, Dorothée, "Unnatural Acts: Propositions for a New French Garden, 1929–1930," in *Architecture and Cubism,* edited by Eve Blau and Nancy J. Troy, Montreal, Quebec: Canadian Centre for Architecture, and Cambridge, Massachusetts: MIT Press, 1997
Mosser, Monique, and Georges Teyssot, editors, *L'architettura dei giardini d'Occidente,* Milan: Electa, 1990; as *The Architecture of Western Gardens,* Cambridge, Massachusetts: MIT Press, 1991; as *The History of Garden Design,* London: Thames and Hudson, 1991
Pasquali, Michela, "Il giardino cubista," *Ville giardini* 280 (1993)
Shand, Morton, "An Essay in the Adroit: At the Villa of the Vicomte de Noailles," *Architectural Review* 65 (1929)
Steele, Fletcher, "New Styles in Gardening," *House Beautiful* (1929)
Steele, Fletcher, "New Pioneering in Garden Design," *Landscape Architecture* 20, no. 3 (April 1930)
Vitou, Elisabeth, Dominique Deshoulières, and Hubert Jeanneau, *Gabriel Guévrékian, 1900–1970: Une autre architecture moderne,* Paris: Connivences, 1987

BRIAN KATEN

Gu Yi Yuan

Location: town of Nanxiang, Jiading County

Gu Yi Yuan is located in Nanxiang, Jiading County, Shanghai, covering an area of 97,236 square meters (116,300 sq. yd.). The size of the garden is presently ten times larger than the original garden. As a private garden Gu Yi Yuan has become a popular scenic area.

Bamboo-carving specialist Zhu San-song, designed the garden, planting it throughout with bamboo. Because of the abundance of green bamboo, the garden was called Yi Yuan (Splendid and Beautiful Garden). Ye Weitang rebuilt the garden in 1746 and changed its name into Gu Yi Yuan. Zhu San-song had created the Xie Pond at the center of the garden, the main hall, Yiye Tang, to the west, and Chunzao Tang and Liudai Xuan to the north. The southeast side of the pond includes a painted land boat called Buxi Zhou. Across the lake facing the south of Buxi Zhou is a bamboo-made villa called Fuyun Ge. On the south side of Fuyun Ge is a rectangular pavilion, called Buque Ting, on a hill. The northeast section of the roof is missing, to remind the Chinese of the Japanese invasion of Manchuria in northeastern Chinese province. Recently, some ancient relics have been moved to the garden, such as the Buddhist Sutra Pillar (A.D. 867) from the Tang dynasty and Putong Stone Pagoda (A.D. 1222) from the Song dynasty. These changes make the garden even more elegant. The scenic combination of nature with splendid halls, fine pavilions, painted boats, buildings, and bamboo and flowers forms a fine example of the traditional garden in southern China.

There are two types of hills in Gu Yi Yuan. One is made out of yellow stones; Fucui Ge, for example, is built on a yellow stone hill. The other type is made out of lake rocks, exemplified by the rockery in Yuanyang Lake. The winding paths and corridors on the hills have become important main structures. Unfortunately, these artificial structures destroy the natural beauty of Gu Yi Yuan.

The arrangement of water in Gu Yi Yuan has been quite successful. Yuanyang Lake and Guishan Lake have recently been built on the south and east banks, respectively, of Xie Pond. The water surrounding the hills creates a harmonious balance in the landscape. The irregular shape of the lakes, with heavily shaded plants at waterside, creates the illusion of flowing water.

The pathways in Gu Yi Yuan are carved with patterns of animals, plants, and flowers. These artistic hand carvings represents the highest form of traditional garden design in southern China.

Plants form another important part of the Gu Yi Yuan scheme. Year-round color comes from the flowers and trees. Evergreen bamboo and flowering *Prunus* are planted throughout, with twisting paths in between. The banks of the lakes are decorated with flower beds. The overall plant layout, however, is simplistic and lacks subtlety and variation.

Although many pavilions, small villas, and pagodas have been well conserved and maintain their traditional shapes, the layout and spatial arrangement do not make this a site of cultural sophistication. However, Gu Yi Yuan is a favorite destination for travelers in Shanghai.

Synopsis

1522–66 Min Shiji, high-ranking official, builds garden and names it Yi Yuan

1746 Ye Weitang renovates Yi Yuan and changes name to Gu Yi Yuan

1789 Civic leaders purchase garden and transform it into local god temple's incense burning field

1806 More temple halls and nunnery added; estate becomes public worship and gathering place

1946 Some patriots raise funds and reconstruct garden into public park

1958 Shanghai Garden Bureau rebuilds and expands property into tourist spot in Shanghai metropolis

Further Reading

Chi, Ch'eng, *The Craft of Gardens* (1634), translated by Alison Hardie, New Haven, Connecticut: Yale University Press, 1988

Johnston, R. Stewart, *Scholar Gardens of China: A Study and Analysis of the Spatial Design of the Chinese Private Garden,* Cambridge and New York: Cambridge University Press, 1991

Keswick, Maggie, and Charles Jencks, *The Chinese Garden: History, Art and Architecture,* New York: Rizzoli, and London: Academy Editions, 1978

Liu, Tun-chen, *Su-chou ku tien yüan lin,* Beijing: Chung-kuo chien chu kung yeh ch'u pan she, 1979; as *Chinese Classical Gardens of Suzhou,* translated by Chen Lixian, edited by Joseph C. Wang, New York: McGraw Hill, 1993

Tsu, Frances Ya-Sing, *Landscape Design in Chinese Gardens,* New York: McGraw Hill, 1988

Wang, Joseph C., *The Chinese Garden,* Oxford and New York: Oxford University Press, 1998

XU DEJIA AND JOSEPH C. WANG

TRANSLATED BY SYLVIA CHOI

H

Hammerbacher, Herta 1900–1985

German Landscape Architect

Herta Hammerbacher was the most important female landscape architect in 20th-century Germany. Her practice spanned more than four decades, during which time she also gained influence as a teacher of garden design. Her work focused on the private house garden. In all, Hammerbacher designed about 3,000 gardens, parks, cemeteries, and open spaces for schools and hospitals. After her apprenticeship in the palace gardens at Sanssouci in Potsdam and her studies at the Lehr- und Forschungsanstalt für Gartenbau (Teaching and Research Institute for Horticulture) in Berlin-Dahlem in the 1920s, she worked as a gardener in the Bodensee region. Later she was employed as a landscape architect at the famous Ludwig Späth nursery in Berlin, where she was inspired by the landscape architect Otto Valentien. In 1928 she started a long collaboration with another member of the profession, Hermann Mattern (1902–71), to whom she was married until 1935, and with Karl Foerster (1874–1970), a breeder of herbaceous perennials. From 1934–35 on she ran her own landscape architecture practice. She collaborated with many architects of the Neue Sachlichkeit (New Functionalism), among them Egon Eiermann, Richard Neutra, Peter Poelzig, and Hans Scharoun. Hammerbacher was strongly influenced by the garden writer and landscape architect Willy Lange (1864–1941).

Starting in 1900 Lange had developed concepts of natural garden design that gained particular ideological influence in Germany under National Socialism because they corresponded to the National Socialist "blood-and-soil" ideology, which saw the Germans rooted like plants in the soil and in their home landscapes. Important components of Lange's gardens were an informal design and a preference for the use of native plants. Lange also sought foreign plants similar in appearance (physiognomically) to the native flora. Hammerbacher interpreted the garden as part of the natural landscape and, like Lange, promoted informal design and the use of both native plants and foreign plants that were in harmony with them. In 1977 she described her own design motifs: "I see the garden as part of the landscape to which it should lead from the house. The plantings ought to correspond to the particular laws of their growth (Eigengesetzlichkeit ihres Wuchses) and their plant associations (Vergesellschaftungen)." Hammerbacher's ideas about garden design and the use of hardy perennials were also influenced by Foerster, who was in turn influenced by the English landscape designers William Robinson and Gertrude Jekyll. Her ideas on natural garden design were further reinforced through her membership in a group of landscape architects that included Foerster, Mattern, Valentien, and Alwin Seifert.

Hammerbacher's habit of modeling the ground by creating hollows earned her the nickname Mulden-Herta (Hollow Herta). Her own garden in Nikolassee, Berlin, planned together with the gardens of Poelzig and the painter Vincent Piper, serves as a characteristic example of her design style: the native oaks and pines were preserved, and the intervening spaces were sown with wild grasses and planted with wild roses, yews, hornbeams, and other indigenous species.

Hammerbacher entered many design competitions. She won numerous awards, among them a prize for the Reichsgartenschau (Reich garden exposition) in Stuttgart in 1939 and a first-place prize in the Bundesgartenschau Kassel (Kassel Federal Garden Exposition) competition in 1955. She contributed to many garden expositions, for example, the Reichsgartenschauen in Dresden (1936), Essen (1938), and Stuttgart (1939).

Garden design by Herta Hammerbacher
Courtesy of Joachim Wolschke-Bulmahn

Hammerbacher was critical of the National Socialist dictatorship. Considering her reputation as a respected landscape architect and compared with such colleagues as Gustav Allinger, Alwin Seifert, and Heinrich Friedrich Wiepking-Jürgensmann, she apparently got few commissions from the Nazi state agencies and prominent National Socialist officials. In her own words, during National Socialism she was in a state of "inner emigration." Nevertheless, after the liberation from National Socialism, she did not promote a critical discussion of the role of landscape architecture under that regime. To the contrary, she even wrote a letter of reference for Seifert, a fanatical anti-Semite and supporter of National Socialism. Her support helped him to continue his career as a landscape architect and teacher of garden design under the Federal Republic.

After World War II Hammerbacher started a career as a teacher of garden design. In 1946, in addition to her work as a freelance landscape architect, she began teaching garden and landscape design in the department of architecture at the Technische Universität (Technical University) in Berlin. She was a professor—the first female professor in Germany in the field—from 1950 on and in 1969 became an emeritus professor. She was a member of the Karl-Foerster-Stiftung für angewandte Vegetationskunde (Karl Foerster Foundation for Applied Vegetation Science) and of the Gesellschaft für experimentelle und angewandte Ökologie (Society for Experimental and Applied Ecology). During her career, Hammerbacher published numerous articles about her own designs and principles of landscape architecture. She died in 1985.

Biography

Born in Nuremberg, Germany, 1900. After an apprenticeship in palace gardens at Potsdam-Sanssouci, worked as gardener at Bodensee Lake; studied at Higher Teaching and Research Institute for Horticulture, 1924–26; worked in Department of Garden Art, Späth nursery, Berlin, 1926–28; worked in collaboration with plant breeder Karl Foerster and landscape architect Hermann Mattern, beginning 1928; ran own landscape architecture practice, 1934–35; after World War II, received teaching assignment at architecture department of Technical University Berlin, 1946–48; appointed associate professor in newly established program of landscape and garden design, 1950, and worked as full professor, 1962–69. Died in Niederpöcking, Bavaria, 1985.

Selected Designs

1929–30 Garden of Hermann Engel, Berlin-Charlottenburg, Germany (architect Otto Firle)

ca. 1930 Grounds of IG Farben administration buildings, Frankfurt on Main, Hesse, Germany, together with Hermann Mattern (architect Hans Poelzig)

1930–35 Garden of Dr. Felix Baensch, Berlin-Weinmeisterhöhe, Germany (architect Hans Scharoun)

1931 Together with Karl Foerster and Hermann Mattern, garden of Prof. Hans Poelzig, Berlin-Charlottenburg, Germany (architect Marlene Poelzig)

1933–34 Together with Hermann Mattern, garden of Mattern/Hammerbacher, Bornim, near Berlin (architect Hans Scharoun)

1934 Gardens for Siedlungsausstellung (Settlement Exposition), Munich-Ramersdorf, Germany

1935 Garden of Dr. Alfred Fuchs, Berlin-Steglitz, Germany (architect Ludwig Hilbersheimer)

1936 Garden of Kurt Dienstbach, Berlin-Nikolassee, Germany (architect Egon Eiermann)

1936 "Garten des blauen Fortschritts" (Garden of Blue Progress) for the Reich garden exposition Dresden, Germany

1937 Garden of Dr. Joseph Steingroever, Berlin-Charlottenburg (architect Egon Eiermann)

ca. 1938 Garden of Hakeburg, Klein-Machnow (residence of the Reich post minister)
1939 Contributions to Reich garden exposition, Stuttgart, Germany
1940 Garden Günther Werner-Ehrenfeucht, Berlin-Dahlem, Germany (architect Wilhelm von Gumbertz)
ca. 1940 Gardens and grounds of Albrecht Dürer School, Bydgoszcz, Poland
ca. 1942 Dam of river Inn near Ering
1946–47 Waldfriedhof (wood cemetery), Berlin-Zehlendorf, Germany
1950s Gardens and grounds of elementary school, Leverkusen-Manfort, Germany
1953–54 Dam of river Inn near Braunau
1955 Garden Hans Schilling, Cologne, Germany (architect Hans Schilling)
1956 Garden Paul Schwebes, Berlin-Dahlem, Germany
1958 Gardens of Paracelsus hospital, Marl, Westphalia, Germany
1958 Garden Harald Schweitzer, Berlin-Grunewald, Germany (architect Ernst Pfitzner)
1959–60 Grounds of B.A.T. cigarettes factory, Berlin-Siemensstadt, Germany
1963 Garden Herta Hammerbacher, Vincent Piper and Peter Poelzig, Berlin-Nikolassee, Germany
1967 Botanical Garden, Athens, Greece (architect Bernhard Hermkes)
1968 Garden André and Günther Vollberg, Berlin-Charlottenburg, Germany
1969 Plaza at Hilton Hotel, Berlin, Germany
1971 Open-air theater and Brunnengarten (well garden) for Bundesgartenschau (Federal Garden Exposition), Cologne, Germany
1973 Parts of grounds of Technical University Berlin, Germany (architect Bernhard Hermkes)

Selected Publications

"Aus Hausgärten: Arbeiten der Arbeitsgemeinschaft Karl Förster, Hermann Mattern und Herta Hammerbacher, Bornim," *Monatshefte für Baukunst und Städtebau* (1933)
"Wie sollen wir gestalten?" *Die Gartenkunst* (1934)
"Ein Luzerner Landhausgarten," *Die Gartenschönheit* (1938)
"Ein Hausgarten," *Die Gartenkunst* (1938)
"Die Gartenanlagen an der Albrecht-Dürer-Schule in Bromberg," *Die Gartenkunst* (1941)
"Haus und Garten an einem märkischen See," *Monatshefte für Baukunst und Städtebau* (1941)
"Der Gartenarchitekt und seine Pflanzung," *Garten und Landschaft* (1950)
"Beziehungen zwischen dem Haus und seiner Umgebung," *Garten und Landschaft* (1952)
"Gedanken über den Friedhof-Waldfriedhof Berlin-Zehlendorf," *Garten und Landschaft* (1955)
"Landschaftsverbundener Städtebau," *Garten und Landschaft* (1957)
"Ein Hausgarten am Rande von Köln," *Pflanze und Garten* (1957)
"Rund um die Paracelsus-Klinik," *Marl Mosaik in grün: Festschrift aus Anlaß des 25 jährigen Bestehens der Stadtgartengesellschaft Marl, 1938–1963* (1963)
"Wettbewerb 'Ratingen-West' IV: Sonderankauf," *Der Architekt* (1967)
"Über das Studium 'Landschafts- und Gartenplanung' an der Technischen Universität Berlin, Fakultät für Architektur, Lehrstuhl für Landschafts- und Gartenplanung," *Garten und Landschaft* (1968)
"Häuser und Gärten an der Rehwiese in Berlin-Nikolassee," *Garten und Landschaft* (1970)
"Die Hausgärten," in *Berlin und seine Bauten,* part 4, *Wohnungsbau,* vol. C, *Die Wohngebäude–Einfamilienhäuser* (1975)
"Gruß an Wilhelm Hübotter," *Garten und Landschaft* (1976)
"Eine Entgegnung," *Bauwelt* (1977)

Further Reading

Amberg, Kristin, "Die Gartenarchitektin Herta Hammberbacher: Werdegang und Werk," Master's thesis, Technical University Munich-Weihenstephan, 1990
Gröning, Gert, and Joachim Wolschke-Bulmahn, "Changes in the Philosophy of Garden Architecture in the Twentieth Century and Their Impact upon the Social and Spatial Environment," *Journal of Garden History* 9, no. 2 (1989)
Gröning, Gert, and Joachim Wolschke-Bulmahn, *Grüne Biographien: Biographisches Handbuch zur Landschaftsarchitektur des 20. Jahrhunderts in Deutschland,* Berlin: Patzer-Verlag, 1997
Hottenträger, Grit, "New Flowers–New Gardens: Residential Gardens Designed by Karl Foerster, Hermann Mattern, and Herta Hammerbacher (1928–c. 1943)," *Journal of Garden History* 12, no. 3 (1992)
Jacobshagen, Axel, and Karin Sommer-Kempf, editors, *Beiträge zur Problematik der Beziehungen zwischen Freiraum und Bauwelt: Festschrift Herta Hammerbacher, der Garten- und Landschaftsarchitektin und Hochschullehrerin zum 75. Geburtstag,* Berlin: Library of the Technical University Berlin, 1975
Mattern, Hermann, "Drei kleine Gärten: Arbeitsgemeinschaft Karl Förster, Hermann Mattern, und Herta Mattern-Hammerbacher, Bornim,"

Monatshefte für Baukunst und Städtebau, no. 5 (1934)

Wolschke-Bulmahn, Joachim, "The 'Wild Garden' and the 'Nature Garden'—Aspects of the Garden Ideology of William Robinson and Willy Lange," *Journal of Garden History* 12, no. 3 (1992)

Wolschke-Bulmahn, Joachim, and Gert Gröning, "From Open-Mindedness to Naturalism: Garden Design and Ideology in Germany during the Early Twentieth Century," in *People–Plant Relationships: Setting Research Priorities*, edited by Joel Flagler and Raymond P. Poincelot, New York: Food Products Press, 1994

JOACHIM WOLSCHKE-BULMAHN

Hampton Court Palace and Bushy Park

Middlesex, England

Location: East Molesey, on A 308 at junction with A 309; Park Road, Richmond, London, England

Hampton Court Palace Gardens is a good example for the changing tastes of garden design over the centuries. Since their creation early in the 16th century, the gardens have been considerably designed and extended or changed by consecutive owners far into the 18th century.

When Cardinal Thomas Wolsey had a palace built for himself on the banks of the river Thames about 1515, he had the surrounding land converted into two parks, one fenced in with palings or brick walls, the other surrounded by a moat. The integrated concept of house, garden, and park was translated into reality with the first gardens planted shortly after the construction of the palace.

In 1525 Wolsey presented Hampton Court to Henry VIII (r. 1509–47) in order to mollify the king, although this did not prevent the cardinal's final downfall in 1529—with all his possessions falling into the hands of the crown. As the new owner of Hampton Court, Henry VIII began the tradition of extending and redesigning the gardens—as well as the palace, which was his favorite residence—that his successors to the English throne in subsequent centuries would follow. Intent on competing with his rival in France, François I, Henry VIII altered Hampton Court on a scale hitherto unknown in England. Design and layout were of major significance for the whole development of garden design in the country up to the beginning of the following century. Moreover, with acquisitions turned into royal parks spread all over England—Painshill in Surrey being one of them—Henry proved himself "the parkmaker par excellence" (Lasdun).

Similar to Renaissance gardens on the Continent, Hampton Court was laid out in a series of square enclosed knots with colored sands and earths in elaborate patterns and geometrically arranged beds of plants. The king added a new garden (later Privy Garden), bowling greens, tennis court, labyrinth, and mount. He also planted a rose garden and had the flower beds filled with primroses, violets, carnations, and mint surrounded by rails that were painted green (for eternity) and white (for purity), the Tudor colors. Although the gardens were full of flowers, the most colorful time was limited to spring and early summer, the time of bloom of most of the European plants. At that time bushes of juniper, yew, cypress, bay, and holly dominated; the rose garden offered as great a variety as 400 different roses. The apricot, introduced at that time, may well have had its place at Hampton Court. In addition, effigies of heraldic animals, such as dragons, bulls, rams, and greyhounds, made of either stone or wood and mounted on posts, embellished the parterre and other parts. A great number of sundials—20 had been supplied for Hampton Court in June 1534 alone—were scattered throughout the gardens.

With the mount, built in 1533, Henry set a particularly effective example in garden design; a form of this mount became part of large English gardens until late in the 17th century. A pile of over a quarter million bricks was covered with soil and planted with hawthorns spiraling upward to a building of three stories with windows on all sides, called the Great Round Arbor, the Lantern Arbor, or South Arbor. On top of the lead cupola was a vane in the form of a heraldic lion.

In 1537 Henry walled in a large area called the Course, where the sport of coursing, a form of hunting, would take place. In the same year he extended the estate to include another 183 acres (74 ha) to the northwest, which was to form Bushy Park. As the gardens were subject to numerous alterations in subsequent centuries, most of the elements of the Tudor garden were removed later. Elements that still remain today are the small pond garden and the kitchen gardens to the north of the palace.

The years of the Commonwealth in the middle of the 17th century saw the sale or even destruction of many royal pleasure grounds, 93 in all, including Nonsuch and Wimbledon. Hampton Court and Bushy Park nearly followed suit; they were sold but quickly bought back again, when Oliver Cromwell, lord protector, was granted the palace and gardens as a residence in 1653. He devoted some attention to the gardens, for example, having the fountains and ponds repaired.

It was Charles II (r. 1660–85), with the impression of Versailles still vivid on his mind, who devised an ambitious scheme to alter the gardens at Hampton Court. He had a canal dug, the Long Canal, inspired by Versailles and one mile (1.6 km) long, with limes planted in a semicircle in avenues that radiated from the palace.

Many of the schemes were only carried to completion after the Glorious Revolution of 1688 by William III (r. 1689–1702) and his wife, Queen Mary (r. 1689–94). During their reign the gardens took the form they are in today. With the aid of Sir Christopher Wren, the palace was transformed and the gardens altered. However, only part of Wren's ambitious plan for the gardens could be put into effect. In Bushy Park a wide and majestic avenue lined with triple rows of trees was built, more than 1,000 lime trees originally, to which were added horse chestnut trees in 1690 that have given the avenue its name. The Chestnut Avenue enclosed a large pool also designed by Wren, with a statue of Diana by Francesco Fanelli—both still exist. George London was appointed to the post of royal gardener, who, together with his partner Henry Wise, acted in concert with Wren. They supplied the flowers, bushes, and trees and planted the chestnut avenue. They also laid out the Long and Broad Walks in Hampton Court Gardens and shifted the avenue of lime trees farther eastward. It has been estimated that by 1700 there were more than 4,000 trees lining the grand avenues. In addition, Daniel Marot, following in the footsteps of André Le Nôtre, designed and created the great parterre in front of the palace with box hedges as a characteristic feature.

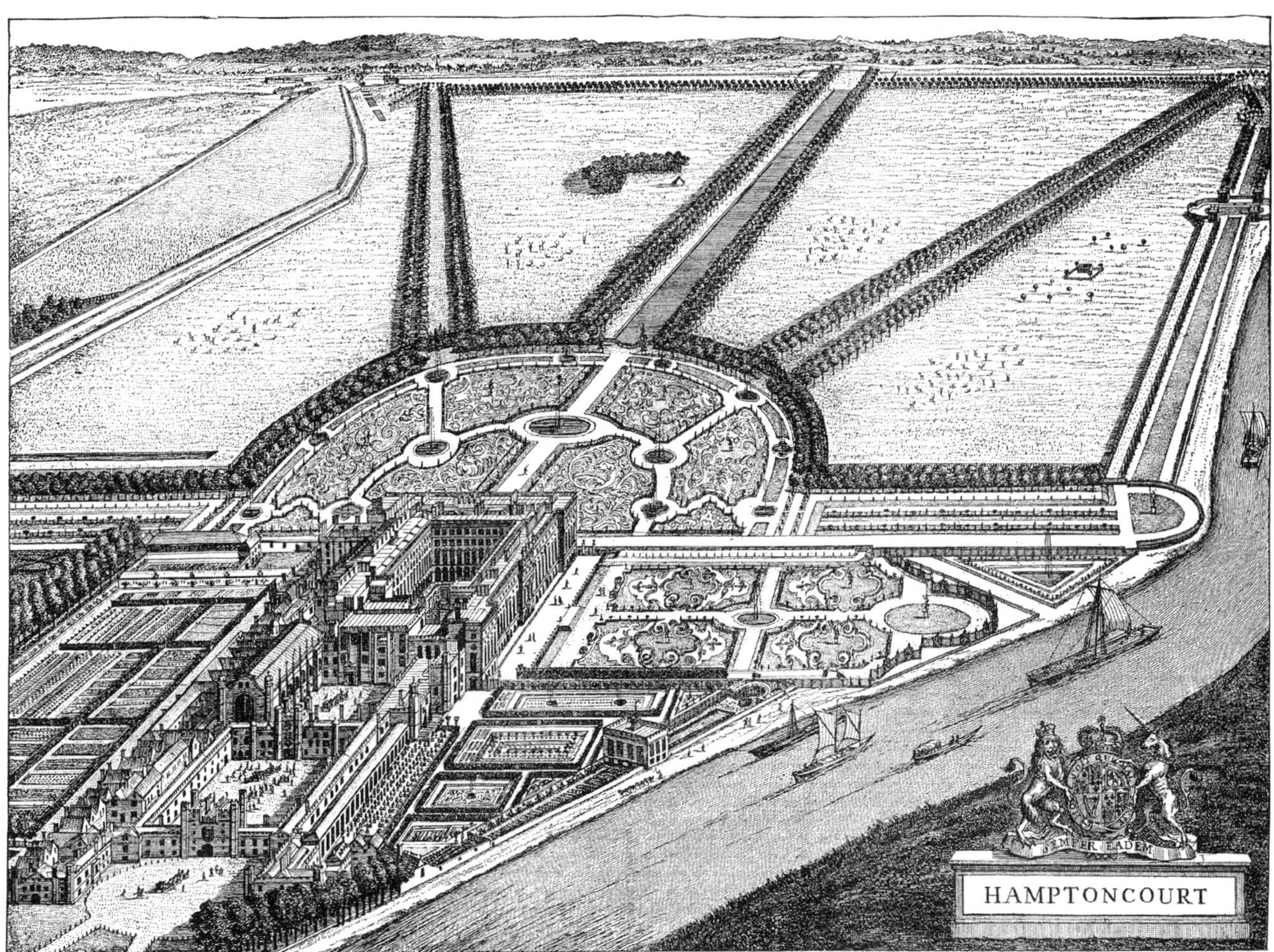

General plan of Hampton Court under William and Mary, from an engraving by John Bowles

With the mount—the earth used to form the banks that enclose the beds of shrubs and trees in the Privy Garden—and Henry VIII's tilt yard, some of the few vestiges of the Tudor garden that had survived were swept away. To add the Great Fountain Garden below the east facade of the palace, it was necessary to fill in some of the canal Charles II had built. The Fountain Garden probably reflects most the influences that had a decisive effect on the design of Hampton Court Gardens in the late 16th and early 17th centuries: there was the influence of William's native Holland—some elements can be traced back to Het Loo gardens—and an indebtedness to the French style, such as the semicircle for the *patte d'oie* of radiating avenues and the *broderie* of box trees in flower beds of hyacinths, tulips, or powdered brick (*brique pilée*) for a colorful effect. The fountains were constructed to display the initials of William and Mary, as well as motifs of classical gods symbolizing the monarchs' role as harbingers of peace and prosperity.

Since the Glorious Revolution, the facility for obtaining rare plants, especially from the East Indies and Japan, increased. While William had promoted the introduction of new plants to the royal gardens generally, Mary concentrated on the collection of rare and delicate plants. Thus, Hampton Court was supplemented by a new greenhouse, subdivided into several rooms, and furnished with a stove to house the specimens of exotic plants.

When Queen Anne (r. 1702–14) came into possession, the gardens were again altered. She had not only the box of the parterre uprooted (it made her sneeze) and replaced by lawn but also a maze planted in the wilderness, a garden with symmetrical paths where, in Tudor times, orchards had been. The triangular maze, designed by Wise and planted in 1714, was formed of hornbeam hedges that lined paths nearly half-mile (0.8 km) in length. In the words of Daniel Defoe, the wilderness and the maze in it were placed "on the North Side of the House, where the Gardens seem'd to want skreening from the Weather, or the view of the Chapel, and some Part of the old Building requir'd to be cover'd from the Eye" (*A Tour thro' the Whole Island of Great Britain* [1724–26, 1742]).

George II (r. 1727–60) engaged William Kent and Charles Bridgeman to do some work on Hampton Court. In deference to the fashion of the day for "natural gardening," some of the elements of the formal gardens were swept away. The Fountain Garden was changed to the state it is at present. When Lancelot "Capability" Brown was appointed royal gardener or surveyor to His Majesty's Gardens and Waters at Hampton Court in 1764, the final victory of the landscape-gardening movement seemed imminent. Surprisingly enough, Brown, who retained his post under George III (r. 1760–1820), refrained from making new alterations to the gardens "out of respect to himself and his profession," as he put it.

Up till then, Hampton Court and Bushy Park had been the pleasure grounds of English monarchs. In 1838 Queen Victoria (r. 1837–1901) took the unusual step to open the Royal Gardens at Hampton Court and Bushy Park to the public shortly after her coronation, and people thronged to see the gardens. As many as 120,000 came in the first year.

Several additions have been made to the gardens in more recent decades. In 1924 a new knot garden was created to recapture the Tudor flavor of the original design. Tulips have been planted to endow the gardens with a blaze of color in spring, and a great variety of flowers have been arranged to provide two spectacular herbaceous borders. Some parts of the gardens have been altered once again, transformed back to the state of one of the earlier centuries of the garden's existence. Between 1992 and 1995 one of the two parterres created during the reign of William III, the Privy Garden on the site of Henry VIII heraldic garden and mount, has been restored.

On the whole, the gardens have never suffered a period of neglect. Hampton Court, more than Bushy Park, has been the place changed by its consecutive owners over centuries to epitomize the fashion of the day. Despite the changes, the extent and the basic concept of the gardens have prevailed to the present.

Synopsis

ca. 1515	Hampton Court Palace built by Cardinal Thomas Wolsey on banks of Thames; surrounding land turned into two gardens
1525	Wolsey presents Hampton Court to Henry VIII
1529	After Wolsey's downfall, his possessions become King Henry VIII's, who starts to extend Hampton Court Palace and gardens
1532–33	Work begins on Mount Garden, Pond Garden, and king's New Garden (or Privy Garden)
1533	Construction of mount with Great Round Arbor on summit
1537	Bushy Park created by Henry VIII
1653	Oliver Cromwell takes possession of palace and gardens
1660–	Conversion to baroque style begun under Charles II
1689	William III orders Christopher Wren to extend palace, and gardens redesigned according to French ideal
1689–	George London and Henry Wise, royal gardeners to William and Mary (as well

as to Queen Anne), plant avenues of lime trees *(Tilia)*

1702 On death of William III, Queen Anne alters some changes brought about by her predecessor

1714 Wilderness garden with triangular maze of hornbeam hedges *(Carpinus)* created from design by Wise

1760 After death of George II, Hampton Court Palace no longer residence of British monarchs

1764 Lancelot "Capability" Brown appointed royal gardener at Hampton Court

1838 Queen Victoria opens gardens of Hampton Court to public

1924 Knot garden laid out

1992–95 Privy Garden restored to state it was in during reign of William III

Further Reading

Batey, Mavis, and Jan Woudstra, *The Story of the Privy Garden at Hampton Court,* London: Barn Elms, 1995

Clifford, Derek, *A History of Garden Design,* London: Faber and Faber, 1962; New York: Praeger, 1963; new edition, London: Faber and Faber, 1966; New York: Praeger, 1967

Lasdun, Susan, *The English Park: Royal, Private, and Public,* London: Deutsch, 1991; New York: Vendome Press, 1992

Law, Ernest, *The History of Hampton Court Palace,* 3 vols., London, Bell, 1885–91

Law, Ernest, *The Chestnut Avenue in Bushey Park, Hampton Court: Illustrated with Wren's Original Designs and Plans,* London: Bell, 1919

Law, Ernest, *Hampton Court Gardens, Old and New: A Survey,* London: Bell, 1926

Sands, Mollie, *The Gardens of Hampton Court: Four Centuries of English History and Gardening,* London, 1950

Strong, Roy C., *The Renaissance Garden in England,* London: Thames and Hudson, 1979

Triggs, Henry Inigo, *Formal Gardens in England and Scotland: Their Planning and Arrangement, Architectural and Ornamental Features,* London: Batsford, and New York: Scribner, 1902; 2nd edition, Woodbridge, Suffolk: Antique Collectors' Club, 1988

ANGELA SCHWARZ

Hårleman, Johan 1662–1707

Swedish Garden Designer

Johan Hårleman was one of the most talented gardeners of Sweden's baroque period, able to combine his roles as gardener and garden architect with his royal official responsibilities. For a quarter of a century, Hårleman had his hand in both the royal garden projects and most of the larger private landscape designs in the country. Hårleman was literally born into the profession of garden art in Stockholm, during the most expansive decades of imperial Sweden. His father, garden master Christian Horleman, was born in Delmenhorst just west of Bremen. Horleman was called permanently to Sweden's Queen Dowager Hedvig Eleonora of Holstein-Gottorp (1636–1715), King Karl XI's mother. Horleman was known as an apprentice at the queen's childhood home near the court of Gottorp. He passed his interest for plants on to his son Johan.

Hårleman worked during his short life both in parallel and together with the famous architect Nicodemus Tessin the younger. Tessin arranged Hårleman's practice as well as his travels abroad. The first trip consisted of a five-year grand tour to Europe (1680–85), during which time Hårleman traveled to England, Holland, Germany, France, Italy, and Spain. In Versailles and Chantilly Hårleman practiced under the guidance of Jean Baptiste de la Quientinie and met the landscape architect Claude Desgots, André Le Nôtre's nephew. The next trip was to Holland and France in 1699. There, Hårleman met Le Nôtre himself, shortly before the older man's death. The close collaboration with Tessin generally makes it difficult to explain what clearly distinguishes Hårleman's own architectural landscape vision.

Hårleman's work is found in about 20 castles and larger properties throughout Sweden. In his younger years he worked as a gardener in Stockholm with his father. Here, his work is evident at Drottningholm, Ulriksdal, Strömsholm, and Kungsträdgården. During his travels as the inspector of all of Sweden's royal gardens and pleasure gardens from 1688, he was busy with gardens in Våstergotland, such as Läckö and Höjentorp, and the Uppland garden of Ekolsund. Among his later

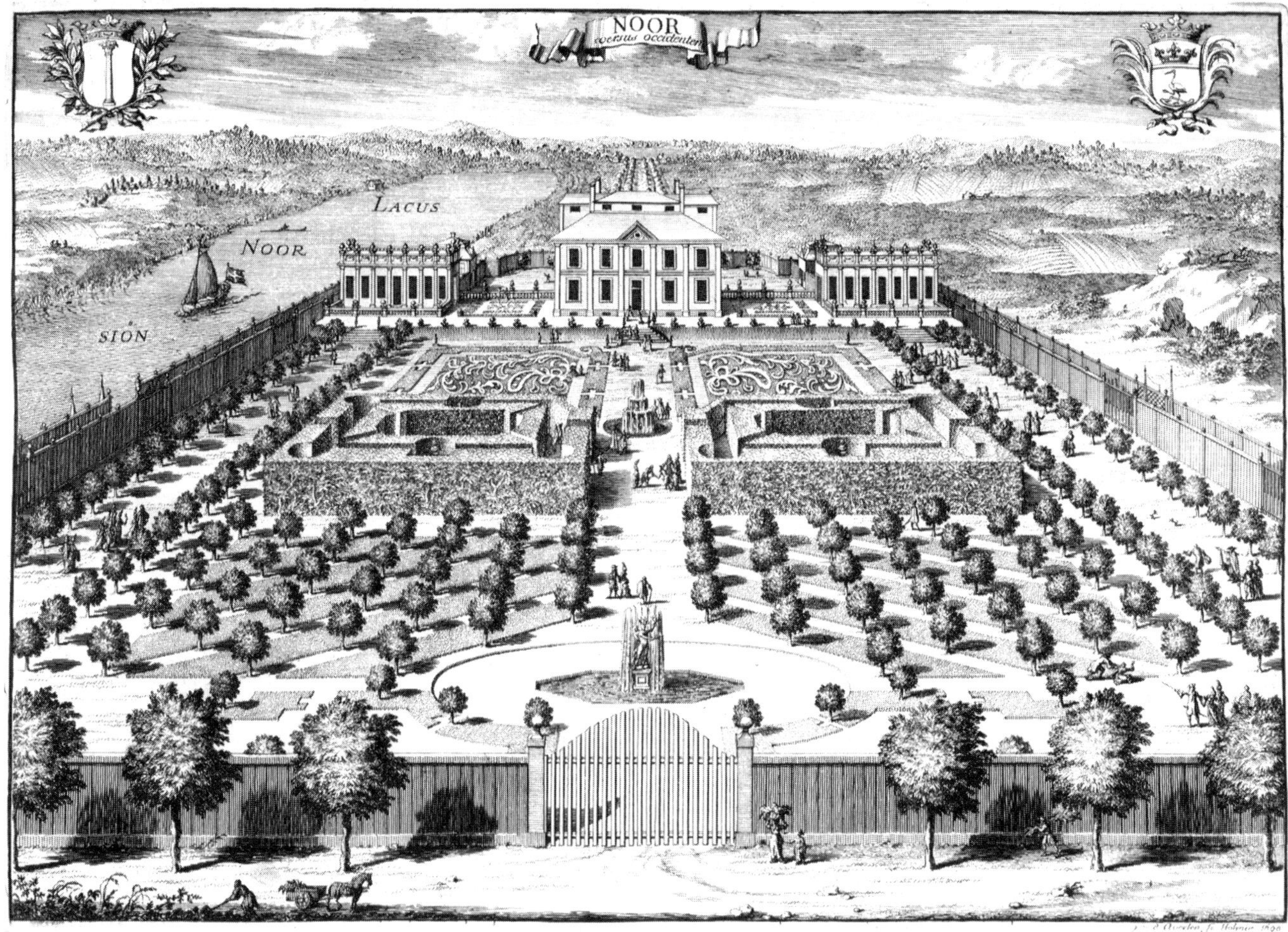

An engraving by Johannes van den Aveelen of the garden at Noor, designed by Johan Hårleman, from *Suecia Antiqua et Hodierna,* 1698

architectural commissions were Stora Wäsby, Leufsta, Östanå, and Noor in Uppland, from about 1690 until his death.

All aspects of the garden design of Noor's manor house, 12 miles (19 km) south of Uppsala, were created and designed by Hårleman. It is representative of the late 17th-century Le Nôtre style in which Hårleman worked. Landscape and garden design began at the end of the 1690s under the mandate of the Swedish king Karl XII's teacher, Count Nils Gyldenstolpe.

A copper-plate engraving of Noor by the Dutch engraver Johannes van den Aveelen (1698) provides a good picture of Hårleman's work at Noor. A symmetrical and precisely defined garden is enclosed by double wood fencing. The scenery is both seemingly peaceful and embellished along the powerful axis that cuts through the entire design and around which both the manor house and the elements of the garden are grouped and subordinated. The single avenues from this axis merge into the distant scenery both to the east and the west, and they are transformed into double walls that hold together and protect the garden compartments. Inside the garden at Noor are equally important building blocks, including the parterres, arbors, fountains, and woodlands. Even in this respect the landscape design at Noor abides by the rules and norms of the time concerning balance and proportion. In this context there are ample grounds to recall the whole arsenal of garden components that André Mollet had introduced a few decades earlier for the baroque garden in Sweden.

On both sides of the manor house are two smaller parterres in palmette design (*parterre de pièces coupées*), similar to those Hårleman also designed for Läckö and for Östanå. Two longer oblong embroidered parterres extend out on the lower terrace behind the building. This continues a succession of well-known parterres by Hårleman with various variations. The parterres are characteristic in the rectangular ground form, with an outer flower bed edged by boxwood but broken by notches (*plates-bandes*). These are decorated with figures in boxwood, spruce, and a group of newly introduced expensive and select bulbs and perennials. Each parterre's interior has elegant and large embroideries of cut boxwood in wreaths.

Earlier designs for embroidered parterres by Hårleman are often characterized by order and structure, with freer improvisations of the acanthus vine or similar plant ornamentation terminating in heads of animals and fish. Later designs are freer in form but still adhere to symmetrical and balanced designs. The embroidered parterres for Count Fabian Wredes Östanå (1692) are elegant patterns of vines and pearls, which discreetly pass in *enrollements.* Around the parterres, the notches or the *plate-bandes,* furnished with Hårleman's typical hooks, form a vault against the stairs.

In the cross section between the subsidiary cross axis between the boat dock and the barn lay both of Noor's fountains. It is the fountains at Noor that balance the garden. Beyond this axis lies the baroque garden with traditionally cut arbors. The large interior space, narrow pathways and many smaller polished *cabinets* that have a strong resemblance to the arbors that Hårleman had created in Kungsträdgården, and the rhythmic placement are reminiscent in their strong and balanced form of the garden design at Drottningholm. In the eastern part of Noor is a simple *plantage* or pleasure garden, with fruit trees, which was common in both Dutch and Swedish baroque designs.

The feeling for plants and their tender handling is a decided characteristic of Hårleman's work. One example of this is found in his embroidered parterres at Drottningholm (1695–96). His years here were formative ones for Hårleman. The notched *plate-bandes* around the embroidered parterre's two straight edgings inside contain, according to a description in 1723, 100 cut trees (topiaries of *Picea abies*), 62 junipers (*Juniperus communis*) formed into pyramids, 194 blue and white lilacs (*Syringa vulgaris*), spirea, elders, and privet bushes, together with a large number of flowering bulbs.

Hårleman traveled in 1699–1700 to France and, from February to April, Holland. This trip was mainly for purchasing plants and trees. It seems that primarily orange trees were bought, among other plants, for the already-completed orangery in Kungsträdgården as well as for Östanå. Orangery production started during Erik XIV's time in 1565; however, it was only in the middle of the 17th century that the production of orangeries and the propagation of orange trees began in earnest in Sweden. This was due to Olof Rudbeck's engineering art, European trips and contacts, and the nobility's new garden ambitions and resources. Rudbeck's better known (Seville) orangeries are in the Uppsala Botanical Garden and the botanical garden at Jakobsdal (Ulriksdal), among others.

Hårleman's involvement in the orangery tradition entailed many parts; buildings in themselves, the orange parterres, the plant collection, and the actual cultivation of the plants. Many building blueprints in his hand are well known. He designed the orangeries at Karlberg, which were apparently the basis for the newer orangery in 1705 at Ulriksdal. Kungsträdgården's orangery was designed by Nicodemus Tessin and was Hårleman's special love. In 1703 Hårleman asserted that the plant collection there was "next to Versailles as the best to find in Europe."

Hårleman's work with the orangeries at Drottningholm, Östanå, and Noor is also well recognized. The orangery at Noor deserves special recognition. In September 1708, the year after Hårleman's death, it was at the center of attention in Sweden. For the first time Sweden's Century plant, or American aloe (*Agave americana,* earlier *Aloe americana*) from Mexico bloomed. It exploded with 4,863 flowers from seven different stems, bringing attention and recognition from all around. In Denmark a Century plant was not noted until 1736, more than 100 years after the one at Noor arrived. A blooming aloe at the beginning of the 18th century was a major cultural event. The plant at Noor originally came from Holland by way of Haag. To the newly constructed Noor the aloe was given in 1698 as a gift to Nils Gyldenstolpe from King Karl XII. In Noor we can also trace a local apple type, Noor's glass apple. This apple is one of Europe's oldest apple varieties from the 16th century. It most likely arrived in Sweden via Holland.

In 1688 Hårleman married Anna Grill, daughter of a goldsmith, who died in childbirth. Later, in 1695, he married Eva Johanna Bartz, of Dutch ancestry and with whom he had eight children. One of their children, Carl Hårleman, carried forth the Hårleman garden legacy further, becoming a respected architect and landscape design worker. Carl Hårleman also became during the period of 1718–72 the most important garden architect in Sweden, and his fame spread throughout Europe.

Biography

Born in Stockholm, Sweden, 28 August 1662. His parents were the gardeners Christian Horleman and Elisabeth Boegels (von Beugeln), who had been called in from Holland to Sweden, in 1666; traveled (grand tour) to England, Holland, Germany, France, Italy, and Spain, 1680–85; royal gardener in Stockholm (at the Kungsträdgården) together with his father, from 16 January 1685; sole proprietor of service from 26 February 1687; inspector of all royal gardens and pleasure grounds of Sweden, 1688; gardener at Drottningholm, Sweden, 1692, and at Karlberg, 1697; comptroller of all royal gardens and pleasure grounds of Sweden, 1697; ennobled, 16 November 1698; traveled to France and Holland, 1699–1700. His son Carl Hårleman (1700–1753) carried on, developed, and crowned his work as garden architect in Sweden and Europe. Died in Stockholm, Sweden, 26 May 1707.

Selected Designs

1685 Kungsträdgården, Stockholm, Sweden
1690–92 Lindholmen, Västergötland, Sweden; Läckö, Höjentorp, Västergötland, Sweden; Ekolsund (*parterre en broderie*), Uppland, Sweden
1692– Drottningholm (partly), Stockholm, Sweden; Östanå, Uppland, Sweden; Leufsta, Uppland, Sweden; Stora Wäsby, Uppland, Sweden; Ulriksdal (*orangerie*, 1705), Uppland, Sweden; Karlberg (*orangerie, parterres*), Uppland, Sweden; Rosersberg, Uppland, Sweden (in collaboration with Nicodemus Tessin the Younger; *parterre en broderie*, 1701)
1694– Steninge, Uppland, Sweden (in collaboration with Tessin the Younger); Noor, Uppland, Sweden; Sandemar, Uppland, Sweden

Further Reading

Dahlbergh, Erik, *Suecia Antiqua et Hodierna*, Stockholm, 1715

Karling, Sten, "Östanå," in *Svenska trädgårdskonsten . . . Arkitekturminnesföreningen*, edited by Hakon Ahlberg, vol. 1, Stockholm: Nordisk Rotogravyr, 1930

Karling, Sten, "Stora Wäsby," in *Svenska trädgdskonsten . . . Arkitekturminnesföreningen*, edited by Hakon Ahlberg, vol. 1, Stockholm: Nordisk Rotogravyr, 1930

Karling, Sten, *Trädgårdskonstens historia i Sverige intill Le Nôtrestilens genombrott*, Stockholm: Bonnier, 1931

Lundberg, Erik, "Sandemar," in *Svenska Trädgårdskonsten*, vol. 1, Arkitekturminnesföreningen, edited by Hakon Ahlberg, Stockholm: Nordisk Rotogravyr, 1930

Lundquist, Kjell, "Om Salomon, Maria och 'Trägårdzmestaren på Dråningaholm' 1693," *Lustgården* 72 (1992)

Lundquist, Kjell, "Johan Hårleman (1662–1707)," in *Svensk trädgårdskonst under fyrahundra år*, edited by Thorbjörn Andersson, Tove Jonstoij, and Kjell Lundquist, Stockholm: Byggförlaget, 2000

Stavenow, Åke, "Johan Hårleman: En trädgårdsarkitekt under stormaktstiden," *Tidskrift för konstvetenskap*, (1923–24)

Wollin, Nils G., "Noor i Uppland," *Saisonen* (1923)

Wollin, Nils G., "Kungsträdgården," *Samfundet S: t Eriks årsbok* (1923–24)

Wollin, Nils G., "Drottningholms lustträdgård och park," *Lustgården* 7 (1926)

Wollin, Nils G., "Drottningholms lustträdgård och park II," *Lustgården* 8 (1927)

KJELL LUNDQUIST

Hellbrunn

Salzburg, Austria

Location: approximately 1.7 miles (2.7 km) south of the city center

Hellbrunn, with its famous grottoes, water jokes, and the so-called Stone Theater, is Austria's most important mannerist garden. It was built in 1613–19 under a strong influence of late Renaissance Italian architecture and garden design. It is the earliest *villa suburbana* to be built north of the Alps. Although some minor alterations have been made to it over the years, its original character has been well preserved. Hellbrunn is well maintained and has been a tourist attraction since the 18th century. It is the only garden where mannerist hydraulic automatons have survived and are still functioning.

The patron of Hellbrunn, Markus Sittikus of Hohenems (1574–1619), was archbishop of Salzburg from 1612 to 1619. He was a humanist who had lived in Italy and was well acquainted with Italian gardens. His ancestors had settled in Hohenems in Vorarlberg (Austria) but were related to distinguished Italian families, such as the Medici and the Borromei. Educated in Milan under the care of his uncle, Archbishop Carlo Borromeo, Markus Sittikus lived in Rome for several years, where another uncle, Cardinal Marco Sittico d'Altemps, owned the famous Villa Mondragone in Frascati. Markus Sittikus commissioned the Italian architect Santino Solari (1576–1646), who was born near Lake Como, to continue the construction of Salzburg's cathedral, and Solari was certainly also the designer of Hellbrunn's villa and gardens.

The estate of Hellbrunn extends over an area of 60 hectares (148 acres). It is connected with the city of Salzburg by a straight southbound allée that runs into the southeast-oriented central axis of the villa in front of the two gatehouses. The axis continues with a driveway, flanked by walls and outbuildings, the horseshoe-shaped *cour d'honneur,* the villa itself, and finally the Altems Fountain at the rear of the building.

The gardens consist of three sections: (1) the Lustgarten (Pleasure Garden) behind the villa, with its well-known ponds, fountains, and water jokes; (2) the Ziergarten (Ornamental Garden, or *giardino segreto*), with a large water parterre east of the villa; and (3) the Hellbrunner Berg (Hellbrunn Hill), with a zoo occupying the area of the old game preserve, the *casino* Waldems (also named Monatsschlössl because it is said to have been built in one month), and the Stone Theater.

Villa and Lustgarten

The ground floor of the villa contains five grottoes, decorated with stucco, tuff, shells, and mirrors. The Neptune Grotto in the center, with a statue of Neptune in a niche, opens toward the garden through a rusticated portal. Neptune stands on top of the "Germaul," a mask whose tongue and eyes move by hydraulic power. By means of hidden water jets, an artificial rain shower can drench unsuspecting visitors. North of the Neptune Grotto are two grotto rooms: the first is decorated with frescoes, colored stucco, and shells; the second, the Ruin-Grotto, with its broken lintels and cracks all over the walls and the ceiling, creates the terrifying impression that the house might collapse at any moment. South of the Neptune Grotto are the Grotto of Mirrors and the Birdsong Grotto, where the songs of birds are imitated by water automatons.

The Altems Fountain opposite the Neptune Grotto is the final point of the main axis and constitutes at the same time the center of the Lustgarten, which extends from both sides of it with various ponds, fountains, and grottoes that are fed by several sources in the adjoining slope. It consists of three ponds on different levels that are backed by an exedra ranged against the slope. The shape of the third pond is a semicircle of seven star points that corresponds with the exedra. The small cascades between the ponds are decorated with stone mosaics and flanked by sculptures of ibex and lions, the heraldic animals of Markus Sittikus. The grotto in the center of the exedra contains the statue of a young man in Roman armor, while above stands a statue of Perseus flanked by the Four Seasons.

The Altems Fountain was certainly inspired by the Italian *teatro delle acque* of the late 16th century. At the Villa Barbaro in Maser (constructed in 1557–62) and at the Villa Aldobrandini in Frascati (constructed in 1598–1604), the *teatro* is situated in the end of the main axis opposite the villa as in Hellbrunn. In the Villa Barbaro, there is even also a semicircular pond in front of the *teatro*.

To the northwest of the Altems Fountain a sequence of three connected ponds forms an axis that begins at the side of the villa and ends at the Roman Theater, an exedra flanked by two small pavilions. The walls are decorated with pebble mosaic and tuff. The central niche contains the sculpture of a Roman emperor, while in the side niches there are two conquered barbarian rulers. The building is crowned with a statue of *Roma victrix* and four obelisks. In front of it stands a stone table with a central water channel (as at the Villa Lante in Bagnaia) and with water jets concealed in the surrounding stone seats. Parallel to the axis of the three ponds, one can still see the surrounding walls of the pheasantry, which existed until the first half of the 18th century.

Water gardens with surprise water table at Hellbrunn
Courtesy of Wildlife Matters

The Orpheus Grotto, a cube-shaped pavilion, is situated beside the pond near the Roman Theater. The inside is covered with tuff and shells. It contains a small fountain, a statue of Orpheus playing the violin (as in the grotto in Saint-Germain-en-Laye), and at his feet a sleeping nymph, a lion, an ibex, and other wild beasts.

Through the bosquet southeast of the Altems Fountain runs a path, the Fürstenweg, accompanied on both sides by an irregular sequence of statues, fountains, and grottoes with waterworks. Their subjects are taken from ancient mythology, although there are secular images as well. The "Crown Grotto" is decorated with statues of Apollo and Marsyas and a metal crown that can be lifted up by a water jet. A water-powered marionette theater, showing the life of an 18th-century town, was added in 1748–52 by Lorenz Rosenegger.

Ziergarten

The Fürstenweg leads to the Ziergarten with an extended water parterre. Its main axis directs to Goldenstein castle (one kilometer [0.67 mi.] farther east) and differs approximately 30 degrees from the central axis of the villa. Originally, the garden was surrounded by walls on three sides and separated from the villa by a bosquet. Two symmetrical mazes and two obelisks flanked the central access from the villa. The Ziergarten was clearly organized along two crossing axes. The center of the parterre was a rectangular island with eight compartments and in the middle a pavilion located on top of a "strawberry hill."

From about 1720 until 1735, the Ziergarten was transformed by the head gardener, F.A. Danreiter (ca. 1695–1760), who had traveled to France as a young man. His German translation of Dézallier d'Argenville's garden treatise was published in 1731. Danreiter removed the hill and the two mazes and designed larger parterres and new bosquets in the style of André Le Nôtre and Dézallier d'Argenville. In the main axis, an allée was planted against Goldenstein castle. Danreiter published his new design in several etchings.

Around 1790, most of the walls around the Ziergarten were removed and the parterres simplified. In the triangle between the Ziergarten and the driveway to the villa, an English garden was planted.

Hellbrunner Berg

On the small ridge south of the Ziergarten, a large area was occupied by a game preserve, which is now a zoo. In 1615, Solari erected the *casino* "Waldems" on the top of the hill overlooking the Ziergarten and the surrounding landscape.

The Stone Theater, a little farther south, was originally a quarry used for the construction of the villa. In approximately 1617 it was transformed into an open-air theater with an artificial stone stage that was probably used for pastoral plays.

There exists no earlier example of this type in architecture, but it may have been inspired by contemporary Italian grottoes and stage sets (e.g., the *scena satirica* in Serlio's *Tutte le opere d'architettura,* 1619, vol. 2). Later, stone theaters were constructed near Bayreuth, at Eremitage, and at Sanspareil in the 1740s. Still farther south, at the far end of the estate at the foot of Hellbrunn Hill, a contemplative area with several chapels, hermitages, and a calvary was laid out about 1616. It has delapidated since the 18th century and has now completely disappeared. This "meditation park" was inspired by contemporary *sacri monti* in Northern Italy (Varallo, 1486 and 1560s; Varese, 1604; Arona, 1614) and represented a Christian counterpart to the pagan grottoes around the villa.

Synopsis

1421 Archbishop of Salzburg installs game preserve on Hellbrunn Hill

1613–19 Archbishop Markus Sittikus of Hohenems (r. 1612–19) commissions construction of villa (completed 1615) and surrounding gardens (completed 1619)

1720–35 Transformation of Ziergarten from mannerist to late baroque design by F.A. Danreiter

ca. 1790 English garden laid out between parterre of Ziergarten and central driveway to villa

1816 Archdiocese of Salzburg becomes part of Habsburg Empire and Habsburgs become owners of Hellbrunn

1922 Hellbrunn passes into ownership of city of Salzburg

Further Reading

Bigler, Robert R., *Schloss Hellbrunn: Wunderkammer der Gartenarchitektur,* Vienna: Böhlau, 1996

Saiko, Wolfgang, "Hellbrunn," in *Historische Gärten in Österreich,* edited by Géza Hajós et al., Vienna: Böhlau, 1993

Woods, May, "Italian Water Jokes and Automata at Schloss Hellbrunn in Austria," *Follies* 10, no. 4 (1999)

BEATRIX HAJÓS

Herbal

Although the term *herbal* dates from only the 16th century, books describing plants survive from antiquity. They were normally more concerned with the often medicinal and quasi-magical properties of plants and the practicalities of their cultivation than with botanical description and so are generally more closely related to handbooks for physicians, pharmacopoeias, and works of horticulture than to plant science. Collectively, their amalgamation of herbal remedies and folklore with magic, religion, and superstition offers an absorbing insight into social history. They were normally conservative documents, codifying for their own generation what was considered to have been the reliable medicinal practice of the past for the guidance of the future.

The earliest written examples of books about plants record practices in Egypt, Sumeria, and China that antedate the invention of writing. The *Papyrus Ebers* (ca. 1550 B.C.) contains material from at least 5 and perhaps 20 centuries earlier, while a Sumerian tablet records a dozen items from some physician's repertoire dating about 2700 B.C. Frank J. Anderson has noted that its few ingredients, including cassia, thyme, figs, milk, salt, and saltpeter, could be used to create laxatives, detergents, antiseptics, salves, filtrates, and astringents.

Records exist of plant books in Western antiquity from the third century B.C., as well as fragments of a book from the first century B.C., but the first full herbal that survives, the most influential of all, is Dioscorides's *De materia medica* (ca. A.D. 65; On Medical Materials), which was still considered authoritative in parts of Europe in the 19th century. Modern pharmacy has its roots in this essentially practical book about the medicinal properties of plants, while the difficulty in identifying Dioscorides's plants a millennium and a half later powerfully influenced the rise of botany. Like the works of major philosophers of Greek antiquity, Dioscorides's text was translated first into Syriac, then into Arabic and Persian, before entering into Islamic culture and being transmitted through North Africa to southern Spain. The text was divided into five "books," although the surviving early sixth-century manuscript, which seems to reproduce faithfully the original illustrations, orders the material alphabetically.

Dioscorides was followed by Pliny the Elder's nearly contemporaneous *Naturalis historia* (A.D. 77–79; Natural History) a huge compilation drawing on some 400 authors and approximately 2,000 manuscripts and containing an herbal. Of its 37 books, 16 deal with plants and sometimes their medicinal properties, and 18 address medicines and diseases. Unlike Dioscorides, Pliny was not a physician, but a lawyer, administrator, and military commander. The major medieval herbals quote him frequently.

Few other plant books from antiquity are known. *The Herbal of Apuleius,* which is not by the Apuleius who wrote *The Golden Ass,* probably dates from about A.D. 400. Its origins are mysterious, and its 130 (or in some versions, 131 or 132) chapters contain much that is superstitious. One northern European manuscript simply replaced the unavailable Mediterranean plants with northern varieties. The work's later popularity astonishes. Its interest today has little to do with gardens or medicine but testifies to the medical practices prevailing in the transitional period when paganism had not yet been banished from the relics of the imperial Roman world, the ascendancy of Christianity was still only in the process of becoming clear, and the cure of sickness was, like so much else, being left to the monks. Verbena, for example, apparently had 24 names, 12 remedial uses, and if worn, protected from snakebite.

The ascendancy of Apuleius and his antecedents was not challenged in Latin-speaking Europe for half a millennium. The rhymed *De viribus herbarum* of "Macer," still heavily dependent on the folklore collected by Pliny, was probably composed in the late ninth or early tenth century. In an 11th-century manuscript the poem describes the medicinal properties of 77 plants, increased to 88 in the first printed edition of 1477. According to the poem merely to look at marigolds strengthens the sight; an English verse translation of 1373 includes lengthy instructions for picking them, which must be when the moon is in the sign of the Virgin, but not when Jupiter is in the ascendant; they are not to be picked by anyone in mortal sin, and the picker must recite three Paters and three Aves.

The displacement of the authority of Apuleius was also due to three Latin texts normally ascribed to a supposedly Arabic author of the late tenth century, known as Mesue. The first book, known by three different names, concerns laxatives, graduated by potency up to and including the sometimes lethal juice of the root of Syrian bindweed or scammony. The work is sometimes called *De simplicibus,* the "simples" being the basic substances in medicinal use. The second book is a widely used apothecary's manual, the *Grabadin,* and the third is an unfinished treatment of curative agents. Mesue, who pressed the rose into medicinal service, is mentioned frequently in later herbals and was translated into Italian. His was among the earlier books to be printed, with 19 editions between 1471 and 1501. The herbal at this date is not yet what one would call a botanical work but is still mostly pharmaceutical in inspiration.

A second author thought to be Arabic and now known as Serapion quotes from works of the very early 12th century but was unknown until he was himself translated into Latin, possibly from a Spanish translation from Arabic or Hebrew, by the physician of Pope Nicholas V at the end of the 13th century. Serapion was massively used. He is quoted nearly twice as often as Avicenna in three of the important early herbals and is also important because he draws on Persian and Indian sources, as well as those in Arabic and Greek. The text's Greek origins explain its comparative diminution of superstition.

The *De simplici medicina* of Matthaeus Platearius, known as the *Circa instans* after its opening words, also was highly influential. It attempted to classify and describe the unmixed simples, whether produced by nature (such as aloes) or art (ammonia) as elaborated by

Page from a 12th-century Arab manuscript depicting cinnamon, balsam, nard, and valerian
Courtesy of Mary Evans Picture Library

the incipient school of medicine established at Salerno in the mid-12th century, and discusses over 200 drugs derived from plants. It was regarded as authoritative until the invention of printing in the late 15th century made the rapid dissemination of other herbals possible. Its contemporary, the *Physica* of Hildegard von Bingen, is the first major work of natural science written on German territory. As an abbess from 1136 to 1179, Hildegard held titular responsibility for the welfare of the monastic community and all its dependents, which no doubt accounts for the *Physica*'s emphasis on the practical aspects of medicine. Hildegard's work hands down much impractical procedure from the folklore of earlier generations but can also be shrewdly practical, relying on her own experience.

During the high Middle Ages the universities in Oxford, Cambridge, and Paris slowly replaced the peripatetic teachers, as well as the medical school of Salerno and the legal teaching of Bologna. In place of monastic and cathedral schools as centers of learning, concentrations of the best teachers, the best pupils, and the best sources of ecclesiastical patronage began to form. This was the period of the great theological *Summae* and the adoption of Aristotle by the schools. Oxford, Cologne, and Paris became known for their interest in the natural sciences, and herbals began to become more systematic treatises.

Bartholomaeus Anglicus wrote his much-translated encyclopedia on the properties of things (*De proprietatibus rerum*) some time before 1283, on the formal pattern established by Isidore of Seville in the seventh century, but with an herbal section mentioning about 12 dozen species. This was the only original treatise on herbs written by an Englishman during the Middle Ages that has survived; a well-known English translation appeared in 1398.

The *De proprietatibus rerum* easily outdid in popularity its rivals, which included the *Speculum* of Vincent of Beauvais and the *Natura rerum* of Thomas de Cantimpré, later adapted and enlarged as Conrad von Megenberg's *Buch der Natur* (Book of Nature), written in a Middle High German dialect at Regensberg in the mid-14th century with women particularly in mind. Like Bartholomaeus, Conrad produced an encyclopedia in which plants come in the traditional order of being between animals and precious stones, with trees preceding vegetables and herbs. The printed edition of 1475 contains the first woodcut ever made to present plants as they appear, and not simply for ornament or as part of a landscape.

Due to their medicinal lore, herbals were in great demand, and the speed of dissemination allowed by the invention of the printing press ensured that they were frequently and speedily printed. However, the herbals so far discussed, all originally circulated in manuscript, do not tell the whole story of the study of the medicinal properties of plants before the invention of printing.

An eighth-century letter sent from England to Boniface, the English missionary to the Franks, asks him to send to England foreign herbs known only from books. The Anglo-Saxons knew more about the medicinal properties of herbs than did their Norman conquerors in 1066 and even the doctors of Salerno. The oldest complete Anglo-Saxon manuscript of a book on plants is known as the *Leech Book of Bald*, a doctor's manual that shows traces of pre-Christian practice and which dates from the early tenth century. It must, however, have been written earlier than that since its author had access to material sent to Alfred the Great (A.D. 849–99) from Syria. A "leech" was a doctor, and Bald was probably the owner rather than the author of the surviving vellum carrying the text.

The Anglo-Saxons had named and used 500 plants, far more than Dioscorides and Apuleius together and more than the earliest printed German herbals half a millennium later. Their "herb yards" were typically filled with marigolds, sunflowers, peonies, and violets, but if the Anglo-Saxons knew more about herbs than the doctors from Salerno, their herb lore was much more intricately intermingled with superstition and depictions of monsters, elves, and the malevolent supernatural enemies of the human race who lurked in forests and marshes.

After the Norman conquest the Latin books of the victors replaced as the source of medical authority the Saxon folklore preserved in the leech books. Most Anglo-Saxon herbal manuscripts derive directly from Macer, and even Bartholomaeus devoted only part of an encyclopedia to plants. Strictly speaking, the first printed English herbal was the small quarto volume printed by Richard Banckes and known simply as *Banckes's Herbal* (1525), an anonymous compilation from earlier manuscripts, known in several versions, under different titles and in various editions. One edition, dated 1550 and known as *Askham's Herbal,* advertises a supplementary almanac advising on the times and days of the moon that are "best and most lucky" for administering the herbs, although it does not print the almanac.

Eleanour Sinclair Rohde's *The Old English Herbals* reproduces the five rose-leaf recipes from Askham, which are variants of rose petals and sugar boiled in water or oil, and notes the faith of the medieval herbals in the power of perfume. This trust came to its apex under Charles II when rosemary was thought to protect against the plague and fetched an accordingly exorbitant price. Binding violet leaves to the temples and bathing the feet up to the ankles in water in which violets had been soaked were said to induce sleep. Askham also gives notes by which some herbs can be recognized, appending directions for their medicinal application.

Most appealing about the early printed English herbals is their charm. The authors must have deliberately repeated old wives' tales in which at best they only half believed, handing down traditional lore about improbable monsters and whimsical remedies mixed in with what may well have been more practical information such as that concerning plant recognition. The Renaissance belief in the hermetic properties of stones and small animals extended to plants and is amply reflected in the herbals. The application of celandine to a sick person's forehead, for example, was thought to provoke song or tears according to whether death or recovery was to take place. In addition, the herbals provide recipes for all manner of charms as well as for the confection of aphrodisiacs. There was even a recipe for the reviving of drowning flies and bees; by placing them in the warm ashes of pennyroyal, they were said to recover within the hour.

More direct is the *Grete Herball* (1526; Great Herbal), for which only the printer's name is known. It claims to draw on an impressive list of forerunners, including Avicenna, Platearius, Mesue, Albertus (Magnus), and Bartholomaeus, but is in fact somewhat sporadically a translation of the French *Le grant herbier,* itself once improbably thought to be a translation of an early version of the *Circa instans,* from which it borrows its preface and whose contents it reproduces. The relationship of the Latin, German, French, and English herbals of the 16th century is complex and confused and has given rise to a host of bibliographical problems and anomalies, many of which have been the subject of academic debate for well over a century, and not all of which have yet been resolved by consensus. The *Grete Herball* itself is chiefly important because of its popularity in England and perhaps because of the importance it attaches to smoked herbs and their use as amulets. It claims to be a full compendium of "the perfect knowledge and understanding of all manner of herbs and trees" and of their medicinal applications.

The advent of printing had much earlier led to the composition of the *Herbarius* (1484), printed by Peter Schoeffer at Mainz and known in Latin, Dutch, German, and Italian versions. The *Herbarius zu Teutsch* (Herbal in German) is not the same book but is another name for a different herbal known as *Der Gart.* The *Herbarius (Latinus)* is profusely illustrated to aid people finding their own plants and making their own medicines. The first section identifies 150 plants, together with their use and description; all are indigenous to Germany, and the book gives their German names. The second section, wholly derivative from a variety of sources but especially Vincent of Beauvais, deals alphabetically with spices and the medically necessary substances available for purchase at apothecaries, divided into categories such as laxatives, aromatics, fruits, gums and resins, and salts. It also treats animal products and stones, including some expensive items such as crushed lapis lazuli.

A year after the *Herbarius* Schoeffer published *Der Gart der Gesundheit* (1485; The Garden of Health), written in Bavarian dialect and including among its 379 large woodcuts approximately 65 based on the plants themselves. The rest came from the Salerno depictions still generally used. Schoeffer also provided an index of ailments and the location in his text of the remedies, as well as of the medical simples. Lofty in tone as befitted a printer who was revealing to the populace the remedies granted to humankind by the creator of the universe, it was the best compendium of medicine available, instantly and frequently plagiarized. *Le grant herbier,* originally called the *Arbolayre,* borrows not only its preface but also just over half its chapters from *Circa instans,* almost all of which it incorporates. It uses woodcuts made for *Der Gart,* and it includes a whole list of passages from other works, some of which were probably Arabic. Its length varied considerably in different printings, but it was popular and influential in France.

The last major herbal to make no reference to the New World was the 1491 *Hortus sanitatis,* compiled by or for its publisher Jacob Meydenbach of Mainz the year before Columbus discovered America. With 1,066 chapters, of which 530 concern plants, it was the largest herbal to date. It was also the most heavily illustrated, with 1,073 woodcuts, most of those of plants based on smaller designs made for *Der Gart.* Its indexes were even more detailed and its sources amply identified. Frequently printed, it was translated from the original Latin into French, English, German, and Dutch, usually with treatises on animals and minerals and often with modified illustrations appropriate to the country whose language was being used. Some of its text is as picturesque as the illustrations. A magnetic stone under the head, for example, is said to cause a faithful wife to open her arms to her husband and an unfaithful one to suffer evil dreams and trembling severe enough to cause her to fall out of bed.

The herbal had already become an integral part of more extensive works of natural science, and for a period few new works appeared that solely concerned plants. The role of the humble surgeon began to rise to challenge those of the apothecary and the physician, and works on herbs gave way to treatises on how to distill essences from plants. Not surprisingly, herbals also gave way to works of botany, not essentially medical in conception and bereft of the mixture of superstition, folklore, and traditional curative practices that had characterized the old herbals. Some of the earlier manuscripts had been individually embellished with fine botanical paintings, but the *Herbarum vivae eicones* (1530) of Otto Brunfels inaugurated a new high standard for woodcuts, regarded by the author as more important than the text itself. When the woodcuts were copied, the printer successfully sued the plagiarist. Some of the watercolors on which the woodcuts were based have survived.

Brunfels, a monk who left the Carthusians, preached, married, taught, and settled as town physician in Bern, was neither original nor scientific as a botanist. The *Kreüter Buch* (1539) of his disciple Hieronymus Bock is the first truly scientific herbal, discussing the characteristics, effects, and names of German plants and introducing a rudimentary scheme of plant families based on outward similarities of appearance. Bock studied medicine, became a teacher, and was appointed garden superintendent of the palatine count, finally becoming a Lutheran pastor.

It is still possible to refer to *De historia stirpium* (1542) of Leonhart Fuchs, physician and university professor, as an herbal, but although it mentions a hundred hitherto unrecorded plants, it is interesting principally for the splendid hand-colored illustrations. In England William Turner's *New Herball* was published in three parts (1551, 1562, and 1568), after two slighter works, a *Libellus* (1538) and a 1548 guide to the names of plants in Greek, Latin, English, Dutch, and French. Banished twice for religious nonconformity, Turner described 200 new English native plants and eliminated much medieval fantasy from his work.

From the mid-16th century onward, herbals gave way definitively to works either of compilation and vulgarization, such as Adam Lonitzer's *Kreüterbuch* (1557) or the *Cruÿdeboeck* (1554) of Rembert Dodoens, or to works more interesting for their woodcuts than their text, such as Pier Andrea Mattioli's *Commentarii* (1544), or to works of incipiently scientific botany, such as John Parkinson's large folio, the *Theatrum Botanicum* (1640). Some of the old superstition still lingered in these works, such as belief in the unicorn, but the discovery of the New World resulted in the increasing need for scientific description, and botany, the forerunner of plant science, was born, leaving the story of the herbals to reveal an absorbing section through the evolving plant lore of Europe as revealed by the need to seek medicinal remedies in the natural world.

Further Reading

Anderson, Frank J., *An Illustrated History of the Herbals,* New York: Columbia University Press, 1977

Arber, Agnes, *Herbals: Their Origin and Evolution: A Chapter in the History of Botany, 1470–1670,* Cambridge and New York: Cambridge University Press, 1912; 3rd edition, 1986

Blunt, Wilfrid, *The Art of Botanical Illustration,* London: Collins, 1950

Rohde, Eleanour Sinclair, *The Old English Herbals,* London and New York: Longmans, Green, 1922; reprint, New York: Dover, 1971

ANTHONY H.T. LEVI

Herbarium

A herbarium is a collection of labeled specimens of plants. These specimens are collected in the wild or from cultivated plants, and they can represent all groups of nonmicroscopic plants from fungi and lichens to ferns and flowering plants. They are usually pressed, dried, and fixed permanently to stiff sheets of paper, but specimens preserved in other ways (for example, in alcohol) are also held in herbaria. Today a herbarium is usually connected with a museum, botanic garden, university, or with a department of state directly concerned with forestry, horticulture, agriculture, or the conservation of natural environments.

The origin of the modern herbarium is generally traced back to the *hortus siccus,* literally a "dry garden," invented in Renaissance Europe during the early 16th century, perhaps by the Italian botanist Luca Ghini. There is some dispute about whether Ghini himself devised this method of preserving plant specimens, but he was the first to develop the idea and use it.

From his surviving correspondence, it is known that Ghini not only assembled his own *hortus siccus* but sent pressed and mounted specimens to fellow botanists. He recognized that this method of preservation not only allowed botanists to study plants at any season but also enabled them to create reference collections for future study. A further benefit of this simple technique was that botanists could acquire plants from distant regions for comparison with the flora of their home territory. By the 17th century, the compilation of a *hortus siccus* or *herbarium* was often a part of the training received by medical students for whom accurate knowledge of medicinal herbs was essential. Gradually the *hortus siccus* (containing examples of real plants) replaced printed herbals, which often had poor and sometimes fictitious illustrations of plants, as an essential tool for students of botany—indeed the word *herbarius* was originally applied to books about plants but gradually changed in meaning and replaced *hortus siccus* as the term for a collection of dried plants.

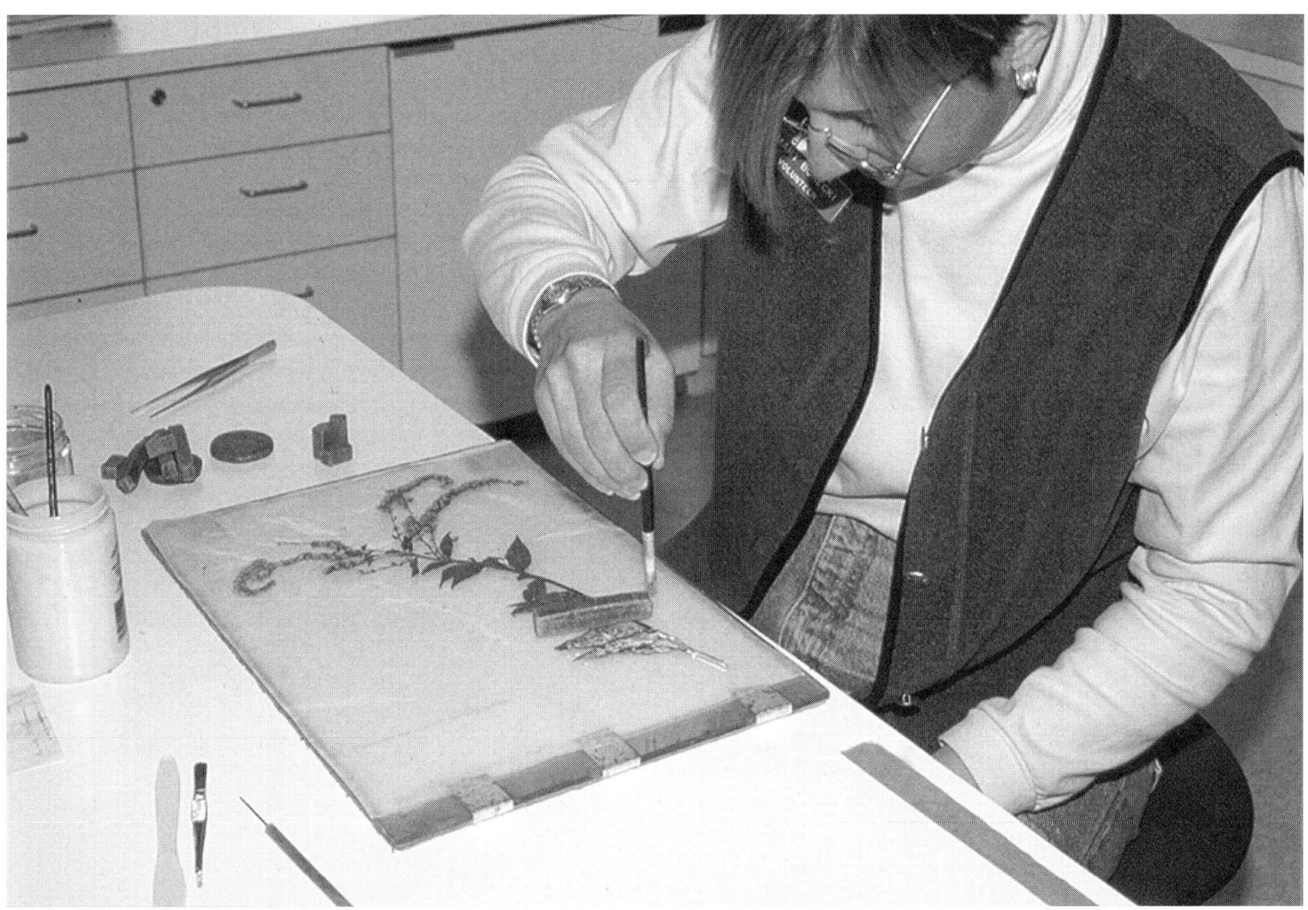

Researcher working with a plant specimen
Photo by William Biderbost, copyright Chicago Botanic Garden

To compile a *hortus siccus*, a person gathered fresh pieces of plants, usually including the flowers as well as the leaves, and pressed these flat, using moderate pressure, while allowing them to dry. Pressing and drying a specimen not only arrested decay but also permanently preserved, albeit in two dimensions, most of a plant's critical characteristics, including sometimes (but not always) flower color. When the pressed pieces were dry, they were glued or in some other manner (perhaps sewed) attached separately or in groups to sheets of paper, which might have been loose or bound as a book (see Plate 14). Such specimens can survive for, and be identifiable after, many centuries as long as they have been protected from attack by insects and molds. Countless old specimens have been lost because of irreparable damage, especially by insects. Pressed and dried plant specimens must be kept in dry, insect-free places and in the dark.

As exploration of remote regions progressed, naturalists made use of this labeling technique to collect new plants and bring specimens back to their base for study. The vast majority of plant species have been described and named using such preserved specimens and not freshly picked samples.

To be of scientific value each individual specimen has to be labeled at least with the plant's name—today the data recorded will also include the exact locality and date of collection, the habitat in which the plant grew and its associated species, and the name of the collector. Often, however, the earliest examples lack such complete data.

Almost every nation had its own herbarium. The most important, scientifically and historically, remain those in the principal cities of Europe, although very important herbaria are active on the other continents. Increased awareness of the need to conserve species has meant that botanists collect fewer specimens of well-known plants, but the rules governing the naming of new species require a permanent specimen, called a type specimen, to be preserved in a herbarium.

Herbarium specimens gathered from gardens have, in the past, formed a significant proportion of collections and were frequently used as type specimens when new species were named. Today, botanists tend to prefer specimens collected in the wild, if these can be procured. However, specimens from cultivated plants are of considerable value to garden historians because they can indicate, often more precisely than written records, the species and cultivars grown at particular periods and in certain gardens. In this regard herbarium specimens are at least as valuable as illustrations.

Further Reading

Arber, Agnes Robertson, *Herbals, Their Origin and Evolution: A Chapter in the History of Botany, 1470–1670,* Cambridge: Cambridge University Press, 1912

Morton, Alan G., *History of Botanical Science,* London and New York: Academic Press, 1981

E. CHARLES NELSON

Herb Garden

The popular idea of a herb garden of old-fashioned plants grown together for aesthetic effect is of remarkably recent origin. This idealization of presumed early practice dates to no earlier than the late 19th century, a product of the Arts and Crafts movement of which William Morris, that amazing polymath, was an archpriest. The excesses and successes of the industrial revolution were seen to have demoted men and their labor into mere mechanistic activity. Work and its product should be a finer thing inseparable from art. William Robinson and Gertrude Jekyll were horticultural protagonists of that movement, first in the rejection of the vastly extravagant displays of tropical and subtropical plants for summer display and the adoption, inter alia, of traditional flowers grown in "traditional" ways. In Britain the 20th-century ornamental herb garden, as exemplified by the still-extant garden created by Vita Sackville-West at Sissinghurst Castle, grew from that. In continental Europe such rebirth was less necessary; the formal French *potager* (kitchen garden) had maintained a herbal dimension, and a robust culinary tradition insisted on the availability of a wide range of herbs. In the United States, too, a continuum can be traced from early colonial gardens of the 17th century—formal, fenced enclosures of food plants—to the 20th-century restorations and re-creations throughout the eastern states. The important Shaker tradition and its huge herb-growing industry of the 19th century provides a cultivational link.

The growing of herbs is as old as gardening itself. Indeed, the Western ethic, developing as it did from the ancient civilizations of Asia Minor, produces both the plant and the place. Any list of species accepted as herbs is mainly Mediterranean in origin, with a concentration in a few botanical families whose adaptations to succeed in the cold moist winter and hot dry summer often included the production of aromatic and essential oils. Humankind has seen these as desirable attributes, the very essence of "herbness," but they presumably evolved as protective mechanisms against destructive browsing (although the condition of a Cretan hillside after the passage of a herd of goats shows that it is only partially effective).

The origin and habitat of these wild plants are particularly significant in that these are the lands of the classical and preclassical worlds, where so much of science and medicine began. No doubt their use as food additives and flavorings (herbs by their very nature are never staple foods) and as medicines encouraged their early cultivation, but they were also, as they still are today, gathered from the surrounding countryside.

The most significant groups are the Labiates—which include sage, thyme, savory, lavender, rosemary, lemon balm, mint, marjoram, and many more—and the Umbellifers—which include fennel, coriander, dill, lovage, caraway, angelica, and parsley. Many members of both groups are used in modern cooking; however, the line between culinary and medicinal herbs is very thin, and some medicinal herbs are virulent poisons that are close relations of culinary herbs. Hemlock is a classic example, as are mandrake and true deadly nightshade, members of the potato family (*Solanaceae*).

While herb production today both for culinary and medicinal use is of considerable commercial importance, herb gardens as such are seen more as ornamental to evoke an earlier age or to provide a suitable period setting for a historic building. This is a mere vestige of their original role when herbs were central to mainstream medicine rather than being considered as alternatives. Early collections of herbs were brought together for convenience, for use, and for study. A well-documented plan at the Abbey of St. Gall, near Lake Constance in Switzerland, dates from A.D. 820–30 and shows the whole monastic estate. Next to the physician's house is a square infirmary garden with 16 labeled beds, one plant for each. A kitchen garden some distance off also lists its plants, some of which—for example, coriander and poppy—one would consider today to be herbs rather than vegetables. Clearly the divide was not then so clearly made. Such places, for the religious community itself and for the local population, were centers of healing and of plant knowledge for hundreds of years.

The second millennium A.D. saw the beginnings of university foundations that gradually built upon the Church's monopoly of learning. Faculties of medicine and then of botany were set up, and these demanded demonstration gardens where teaching could be based on living materials. Physic or botanic gardens were founded first in the Italian city-states of Pisa and Padua (1540s) and then throughout Europe in Montpellier, Lieden, and Oxford (1621). The Chelsea Physic Garden was founded by the Society of Apothecaries of London in 1673. The invention of printing and the vastly greater availability of texts facilitated this explosion of learning. Among the new texts were the early herbals such as Fuchs's *De historia stirpium* (1542; A History of Plants) and William Turner's *New Herball* (1562), which predates the better-known work by John Gerard by 25 years.

These early texts list, describe, and illustrate medicinal herbs that had been known and used since classical times, almost all natives of Europe and adjacent Asia Minor. A few species had traveled along the spice and silk routes from further east. This was also the beginning of the age of discovery, and from the early 16th century plants began to be imported from the New World and the East Indies. As there was still the presumption that a beneficent deity had provided all such plants to benefit humankind, all were considered of value if only that use could be discovered. Culpeper's *Herball* (1649) continued to uphold the doctrine of signatures ("like cures like"). If, therefore, all were worth cultivating, the repositories of these new plants provide in their layout and in their libraries information of the first professional herb gardens. Those gardens already mentioned still exist on their original sites.

Throughout the 18th century the Chelsea Physic Garden was perhaps the most significant institution for teaching about and research concerning herbs. Philip Miller, its curator for 50 years, was a renowned horticulturist ("Hortulanorum princeps," said Linnaeus), and his great *Gardeners Dictionary* (1731) went into eight editions and remained the standard text in Europe and the New World well into the 19th century. It remains, as does the Chelsea Physic Garden, a vital link in the unbroken chain of humankind's employment of herbs, for use and for delight, from the earliest times.

Further Reading

Harvey, John Hooper, *Mediaeval Gardens,* Beaverton, Oregon: Timber Press, and London: Batsford, 1981

McLean, Teresa, *Medieval English Gardens,* London: Collins, and New York: Viking, 1981

Paterson, Allen, *Herbs in the Garden,* London: Dent, 1985

Rohde, Eleanour Sinclair, *A Garden of Herbs,* London: Warner, 1920; revised and enlarged edition, London: Dover, 1969

ALLEN PATERSON

Herbs: Culinary

Herbs are commonly defined as aromatic plants used especially for medicinal purposes, cooking, or as seasoning. The word *culinary* comes from the Latin word *culina,* which means "kitchen" and refers to cooking. Therefore, any part of a fruit, plant, or vegetable, such as the roots, stems, seeds, or leaves, can be used as a culinary herb to season or flavor foods. Unlike spices, culinary herbs are usually leafy and locally grown; their use extends further back into history than spices. Most culinary herbs come from the four plant families *Umbelliferae, Cruciferae, Labiatae,* and *Compositae.*

The use of roots, stems, and seeds of plants for flavoring food has been a practice of humans for more than 5,000 years. The Assyrians, Sumerians, and Egyptians used herbs for this purpose, and the Bible contains many references to the use of herbs in food. Some culinary herbs originated in the East and were gradually imported to the Middle East. Many others are natives of Mediterranean coastal regions and were introduced to Europe as the Romans expanded their empire westward. About 400 new plants were introduced into Britain after the Roman invasion of A.D. 43, including rosemary, fennel, sweet bay, dill, and chervil. Many disappeared after the Romans' departure to be reintroduced during the medieval period

The Greeks and Romans gained their herbal knowledge from Assyrians, Sumerians, and Egyptians. The Greek physician Hippocrates, who lived between 460 and 377 B.C., was also well known as an herbalist. He is credited with having coined the phrase, "Let your foods be your medicines, and your medicines your food." The Romans used herbs so extensively that even Roman armies carried herbs in their baggage on all journeys. As a result previously unknown herbs were introduced in every part of the Roman Empire.

After the fall of the Roman Empire, herbs continued to be used for their flavor, as medicine, and as perfume. Gradually, herbs became rather obscure as the literature tended to ignore them, only occasionally appearing in the Middle Ages. During the Dark Ages, from about 641 to 1096, and after the Crusades, monks throughout Europe and Britain began to plant large herb gardens to grow herbs to heal the sick.

A list of culinary herbs produced in A.D. 812 by the Emperor Charlemagne includes mint, rosemary, rue, sage, savory, tansy, sweet bay, parsley, dill, fennel, and chervil. There were herbs for the pot or pottage (a kind of vegetable stew), and herbs for sallets (salads). A looser definition of culinary herbs than we have today included leaf vegetables such as colewort or kale, kohlrabbi, orach, leaf beet, sorrel, and chicory. Herbs for sauces included costmary, sage, hyssop, rosemary, clary, and rue.

The establishment of Christianity in Europe and the foundation of cathedrals, abbeys, and monasteries ensured the continuity of a horticultural tradition in which herbs and especially medicinal herbs played an important part. Similarly, within the precincts of castle walls and manorial estates, enclosed gardens bounded by walls, hedges, or ditches were devoted to the cultivation of vegetables and herbs. The monks made copies of old herbals and manuscripts such as Dioscorides's *Materia medica,* sources of knowledge about plants until the Renaissance and the beginning of the scientific study of botany in the 16th century. They cultivated herbs in enclosed gardens, planting them in beds arranged geometrically on a grid system, one type of plant to each bed. They also distributed plants and seeds, which were sold at the monasteries or at markets in nearby towns. Gardeners on manorial estates also sent plants and seeds of herbs and vegetables to markets.

A list of herbs written at the end of the 12th century by Alexander of Neckham suggests the plants that a garden should contain, classifying herbs according to their culinary uses. Another list, produced by Master John the Gardener in his *The Feate of Gardening,* includes flowers such as dandelions, daisies, and violets for salads. Some culinary herbs were picked from the hedgerows; others, such as rosemary, borage, chives, and basil, were gradually introduced into England from the continent by foreign queens such as Eleanor of Aquitaine and Philippa of Hainault.

Gradually, herb gardens began to spread throughout Europe and were found in the gardens of both the rich and the poor. The herbs were used to prepare food, wine, beer, perfumes, and candles. By the mid-16th century, herbal use was so common that herbs were grown everywhere. They were also given a superstitious and magical quality, as herbs were planted and harvested based on astrology.

Beginning in the 1550s, books called herbals were produced that outlined the medicinal properties of herbs, such as herbal remedies, treatments, and herb culture. This period became known as the Great Age of Herbals and lasted until the end of the 17th century and the onset of the scientific era. One of the best-known herbalists was John Parkinson, who wrote the famous *Theatricum Botanicum* (1640; *Theater of Plants*), considered the last great herbal. In it he advocates the use of herbs to season foods in order to prevent illnesses. Other well-known herbals of the time include John Gerard's *Herbal* (1597) and Nicholas Culpeper's *The Complete Herbal* (1651).

In England, the social upheavals brought about by the Civil War generally consolidated the tradition of gardening among the country gentry who turned to the development of their country estates during the Cromwellian period. During this period the Puritans, seeking a new life away from religious persecution, sailed to

America and established the colony of Virginia, taking with them many English traditions of plant cultivation.

European settlers brought herbs and spices to the New World, and the Shakers (a Quaker sect) were among the first to grow, dry, package, and sell herbs commercially. As in times past, the colonists counted on their herbs to combat illness and to mask the smell and flavor of bad or bland food. After herbs came to the Americas, their use quickly spread, and between 1600 and 1800 American kitchen gardens were planted with herbs based on astrological calendars. Herbs remained popular throughout the 18th and 19th centuries. Their use waned with the increase in scientific knowledge that enabled humans to develop synthetic substitutes for plants. A few favorites survived this decline, such as mint and parsley, but most herbs became obsolete.

French ideas of cooking and growing herbs influenced English Royalists who had escaped to France during the Civil War and who returned during the Restoration in 1660. John Evelyn comments on the cultivation and use of herbs for sauces, sallets, and pottage in his *Kalendarium Hortense* (1669; The Gardener's Almanac).

After 1850, the importance of culinary herbs declined. They remained of interest during the late Victorian period in England to those members of an intellectual elite, followers of John Ruskin and the Pre-Raphaelites, who, with their intense interest in and reverence for nature and the values of the medieval world, preserved the plants and flowers of the period. Books on herbal folklore, such as Canon Ellacombe's *The Plant Lore and Garden Craft of Shakespeare,* followed by Eleanour Sinclair Rohde's *Shakespeare's Wild Flowers,* were an expression of this sentiment.

In the 20th century culinary herbs went through a revival as scientists demonstrated the nutritional value of plants. In the 1930s Maud Grieve published the two-volume *A Modern Herbal*, and in 1933 the Herb Society of America was founded, for "furthering the knowledge and use of herbs." Herbs became increasingly popular beginning in the 1970s due to an increased awareness of the environment and ecology, which led to a greater reliance on natural products. Their use has continued to the present day. In response to demand, nurseries specializing in herbs have proliferated, and sales of plants, seeeds, and cut herbs have soared. Supermarkets now stock fresh cut herbs and plants. The public is enlightened about culinary herbs as never before.

Some of today's most popular culinary herbs are also some of the world's oldest. These include coriander, in use for over 3,000 years, which was brought to Europe by the Romans, who used it to preserve meat and as a spice; dill, whose use dates back to ancient Egyptian times as a medicine; oregano, used by the ancient Greeks as a symbol of happiness and by the Egyptians to preserve food, to heal, and to disinfect; parsley, which was used by the Greeks as a medicine and by the Romans to make garlands and to get rid of strong odors; mint, used as symbol of hospitality by the Romans; and thyme, which was used by the Greeks to denote graceful elegance.

Further Reading

Anderson, Frank J., *An Illustrated History of the Herbals,* New York and Guildford, Surrey: Columbia University Press, 1977

Bown, Deni, *Encyclopedia of Herbs and Their Uses,* London and New York: Dorling Kindersley, 1995

Clarkson, Rosetta E., *Green Enchantment: The Magic Spell of Gardens,* New York: Macmillan, 1940; reprint 1991; also published as *The Golden Age of Herbs and Herbalists,* New York: Dover, 1972

Clarkson, Rosetta E., *Herbs, Their Culture and Uses,* New York: Macmillan, 1942

Dowden, Anne Ophelia Todd, *This Noble Harvest: A Chronicle of Herbs,* New York: Collins, 1979

Grieve, Maud, *A Modern Herbal,* 2 vols., London and Toronto, Ontario: Cape, 1931

Keville, Kathi, *The Illustrated Herb Encyclopedia,* London: Grange and New York: Mallard Press, 1991; as *Herbs: An Illustrated Encyclopedia,* New York: Friedman/Fairfax, 1994

Stuart, Malcolm, editor, *The Encyclopedia of Herbs and Herbalism,* London: Orbis Books, and New York: Grosset and Dunlap, 1979

Van Brunt, Elizabeth R., editor, *Handbook on Culinary Herbs,* Brooklyn, New York: Brooklyn Botanic Garden, 1982

DIANA BASKERVYLE-GLEGG AND JUDITH GERBER

Herbs: Medicinal

Medicinal herbs are plants used to treat both physical and psychological illnesses. Renewed interest in medicinal herbs has resulted in part from the feared destruction of the Amazon rain forest and the possible extinction of potentially medically useful plants. The lack of confidence that many people have in modern medicine also explains why medicinal herbs are becoming more widely recognized as acceptable remedies.

The application of medicinal herbs is the oldest form of medicine practiced by humankind. Chinese historians identify Emperor Shen Nong (3494 B.C.) as the father of Chinese herbal medicine. This emperor not only acquainted his people with agriculture but also tested plants in order to determine their medicinal value. Chinese herbal medicine developed significantly during the Han period in Chinese history (206 B.C.– A.D. 230) with the appearance of systematic records of herbal prescriptions along with recommended dosages. In addition, the territorial expansion that characterized the dynasty brought new plant remedies into the Chinese pharmacopoeia. Finally, the trade undertaken during this era introduced medicinal herbs from India and the Persian Gulf into China. *Ben cao,* or herbal medicine, has remained an important part of Chinese medicine for thousands of years. For instance, a tea made from *Huperzia serrata,* a type of club moss traditionally consumed by elderly Chinese, has been shown to benefit memory. It now is being clinically evaluated in China, and plans are under way in other nations to study its effects.

Medicinal herbs also formed part of classical medicine, a tradition upon which Western medical practice depended for centuries. The first herbal, or text that describes medically useful plants and lists their effects on the parts of the body, owed its existence to Diocles of Carystius, who wrote *Rhizotomika* in the fourth century B.C. Crateuas (ca. 100 B.C.) created the first illustrated herbal. Although his original text is lost, his descriptions survive through the works of Pliny the Elder, especially in Pliny's *Natural History.* The most famous of the ancient herbals is that of Dioscorides, a Roman who may have worked as an army surgeon during the first century A.D., who wrote *De materia medica,* a text that remained influential into the 19th century. Roman physician Galen (A.D. 131–200) classified medicinal herbs by evaluating them according to how they reacted to one of the body's four humors (blood, yellow bile, phlegm, and black bile). The term *simple* came from this theoretical scheme. Galen employed the word in order to describe an herb that possessed a particular attribute, such as heat or dryness. Eventually, *simple* referred to one of the herbs in a compound prescription.

The Islamic world served as the repository of classical herbal knowledge from the seventh century until the 11th century, when Greek and Roman works were once again made available to the Western world through the efforts of scholars studying at the famous medical school at Salerno in southern Italy. The Islamic herbal tradition not only incorporated the wisdom of the ancient Greeks and Romans but also depended on the investigations undertaken by Islamic doctors to understand the effects of particular plants on the human body. The records that these physicians kept indicate that Islamic practitioners were well aware of the importance of proper dosage, potency, and possible side effects. The herbal medicine practiced by Muslims also relied on Indian therapeutics and pre-Muslim Arabic folk medicine. Practitioners from India emphasized the influences that both the natural and supernatural had on human existence and human health. The use of herbs and a proper diet were key parts of the Indian system, which stressed the maintenance of health over the treatment of illness. *Ayurvedic* or Indian medicine provided the world with an important tranquilizer, reserpine, made from the Indian snakeroot plant *Rauwolfia serpentina.* For centuries Indian practitioners have employed this medicinal herb as a remedy for mental disorders and insomnia. Manufacturers continue to derive reserpine from this plant.

The discovery of the Americas in the late 15th century was an important event in the history of medicinal herbs. Many practitioners questioned their dependence on herbs when plants were unable to cure the dreaded disease syphilis, which many believed had been transmitted from the New World to the Old. They instead relied on a chemical cure, mercury, whose side effects were often worse than the disease they aimed to treat. Their faith in herbal remedies was restored when they heard of a plant called *guaiac* used by native Caribbean women to heal this disease. Its import became big business, and colonizers realized they might make huge

1. 2. *Suber latifolium & anguſtifolium.*
The Corke tree with broad and narrow leaues.

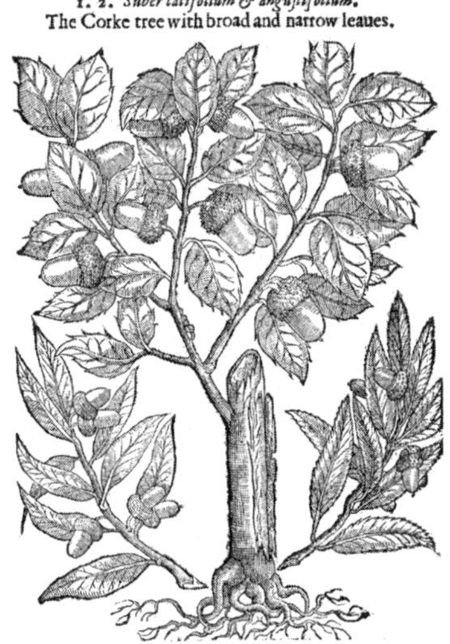

¶ *The Temperature and Vertues.*
Thisbarke doth moſt manifeſtly dry,with a binding faculty. A
Being beaten to pouder and taken in water it ſtancheth bleeding in any part of the body. The B
Corke which is taken out of wine veſſels,ſaith *Paulus* being burnt,maketh aſhes which doe mighti-
ly dry,and are mixed in compoſitions diuiſed againſt the bloudy flix.
Corke is alſo profitable for many things : it is vſed (ſaith *Pliny*) about the anchors of ſhips, Fi- C
ſhers nets, and to ſtop veſſels with ; and in Winter for womens ſhoos, which vſe remaines with vs
euen to this day : fiſhermen hang this barke vpon the wings of their nets for feare of ſinking : and
ſhoo-makers put it in ſhooes and pantofles for warmneſſe ſake.
CHAP.

The Corke tree and its therapeutic benefits, from John Gerarde, *The Herball; or, Generalle Historie of Plantes,* 1636 profits by exporting medically useful plants from the Americas. Ipecacuanha and quinine are only two of the many American plant remedies that became essential to Western therapeutics.

Many of the herbal remedies that European colonizers brought back from the Americas were gained from Native Americans. Other groups outside of mainstream Western medicine contributed herbal information that eventually became part of the modern pharmacopoeia. One of the most famous examples of this transfer of knowledge from traditional herbalists to formally trained medical practitioners concerns foxglove, or *Digitalis purpurea.* William Withering, an 18th-century English practitioner, learned of the beneficial effects of foxglove in the treatment of dropsy, or the excessive accumulation of fluid that often characterizes heart disease, from local Shropshire female herbalists. After conducting tests on patients at a free clinic, he published his findings as *Account of Foxglove* in 1785.

Like Withering, modern ethnopharmacologists explore, identify, describe, and experiment with the ingredients and effects of indigenous drugs, especially medicinal herbs. This emphasis on traditional herbal knowledge has become standard practice for several drug companies in the United States and Britain. These manufacturers devote portions of their research and drug discovery budgets to uncover remedies used by local herbalists across the globe.

Further Reading

Bellamy, David, and Andrea Pfister, *World Medicine: Plants, Patients, and People,* Oxford and Cambridge, Massachusetts: Blackwell, 1992

Blunt, Wilfrid, and Sandra Raphael, *The Illustrated Herbal,* New York: Thames and Hudson, 1979

Farnsworth, Norman R., "A Treasure-house of Herbs," *World Health* (June 1983)

Griggs, Barbara, *Green Pharmacy: A History of Herbal Medicine,* London: Jill Norman and Hobhouse, and New York: Viking Press, 1982

Reid, Daniel P., *Chinese Herbal Medicine,* Boston: Shambhala, 1987

KAROL K. WEAVER

Hestercombe

Taunton, Somerset, England

Location: approximately 2 miles (3.2 km) north of Taunton and 35 miles (56.3 km) southwest of Bristol

Hestercombe is famous today for the survival of two historic gardens: a picturesque landscape garden of the mid-18th century created by Coplestone Warre-Bampfylde and a formal Arts and Crafts garden of the Edwardian era designed by Sir Edwin Lutyens and Gertrude Jekyll. The landscape garden was rediscovered in 1992, after two centuries of neglect, by Philip White, director of the Hestercombe Gardens Trust. The trust is restoring both gardens to their original condition.

Coplestone Warre-Bampfylde inherited Hestercombe from his father in 1750 and began to develop his valley Elysium in the well-watered combe behind his early Georgian house. A talented landscape painter, Bampfylde was at the heart of the movement that produced the English landscape garden and numbered among his friends many important practitioners and admirers of this new art form. Through Richard Graves he was known to William Shenstone and visited the latter's famous garden at the Leasowes. Shenstone promised to visit Hestercombe but never did. He nevertheless wrote about it in flattering terms. Bampfylde is mentioned in several of Graves's poems, and it seems likely that Graves's story *Columella; or, the Distressed Anchoret* (1779) was an affectionate parody of Bampfylde's gardening activities rather than Shenstone's. Bampfylde married Mary, the daughter of Edward Knight of Wolverley in Worcestershire, who was also familiar with a large circle of West Midland garden improvers, including George Lyttleton of Hageley, Shenstone, and Richard Payne Knight of Downton Castle, Edward Knight's nephew.

Bampfylde's paintings were regularly compared with Gaspard Dughet and Claude and Salvator Rosa, and as with Bampfylde's friend Henry Hoare of Stourhead, the work of these artists clearly influenced the formation of the Hestercombe landscape. Just as Shenstone engaged in "poetical gardening," so Bampfylde's creation displayed his visual sensibility. The centerpiece of the landscape was the Pear Pond, which also served as a mill

General view of Hestercombe
Copyright Robert M. Craig

pool. Its serpentine curves reflected Hogarth's "line of beauty" and was repeated elsewhere, especially in the footpaths. Bampfylde's own painting of the pond in the 1770s shows its smooth outline, flanked by open glades grazed by sheep. There are woodlands, a cascade where the stream enters the pond, and diagonally on the rising ground above the pond, a white Doric temple.

A well-made path leads off from Bampfylde's painting toward the high ground and woods to the west. The path enjoys views across the Pear Pond toward the mausoleum, the most architectural structure in the garden, which was probably designed by Bampfylde, who was a competent architect, providing the design for a market hall at Taunton. The mausoleum is constructed with rusticated stonework, painted pink, and has a chimneylike obelisk on its roof. Close to the path there is a memorial urn on a pedestal, dedicated to two fellow landscapers. The inscription alludes to Virgil and emphasizes the pastoral rather than the picturesque theme of the garden. The path continues upward, passing the site of a Chinese Seat, still planted around with *Robinia pseudoacacia* to provide oriental associations, and then drops down to the stream where in the thickening woods the "most romantick object" in the garden is revealed—the cascade. The setting was inspired by Virgil's Grove at the Leasowes, but here a natural rock face, 45 feet high, provides the only near-sublime experience in the garden. Around the base of the falls there was originally a "rock lawn" created using quartz blocks quarried on the estate. Henry Hoare was so impressed by the cascade that he asked Bampfylde to design one for Stourhead. The path runs back up the hillside to view the serpentine rill—similar to the one at Rousham—that carries the water from an upper lake. The penstock or sluice that controlled the flow was so effective that Bampfylde was asked to provide a design for a similar mechanism for George III to control the water feeding a falls at Virginia water in Windsor Great Park.

After passing the dam, the path rises zigzag through pollarded laurels toward a bastioned mount projecting into the surrounding fields where an alcove, shaded with bay and perfumed with virburnum (which is still growing) embraces a panorama of the Vale of Taunton with the Blackdown Hills beyond. Once back in the woods the path passes the Doric Temple; a newly restored Witch House, enhanced with suitable emblems; and the site of a Root House. More views are provided through the trees of the falls, the Pear Pond and its mill, and the Vale. Past the pond a gate in the garden wall invites visitors into the formal gardens. Edwin Lutyens designed the gate, which signals his appreciation of the juxtaposition of the contrasting garden styles that makes Hestercombe such a complete landscape experience today.

Viscount Portman gave Lutyens and Jekyll their greatest challenge at Hestercombe in 1903. The essential feature of most Arts and Crafts gardens was the relationship between the house and the garden. But at Hestercombe the ugly Victorian house had to be ignored, and in a rather 18th-century way the new garden turns its back on the house and looks through the long pergola into the pastoral countryside of Taunton Vale. Also like the Stuart gardens reflected in the prospects of Kip and Knyff, the intricacy of its design has to be appreciated from the windows of the house or the elevated Victorian terrace. And yet, unlike the two-dimensional gardens it imitates, the Great Plat—as its designers called it with Stuart models in mind—is a garden of enticement, drawing the visitor down into its compartments and providing a sense of enclosure. The garden has a strong architectural framework, but compared with many of Lutyens's later "classical" designs, the hard landscaping does not dominate, and Jekyll was able to exploit the many varied opportunities to demonstrate her painterly skills in planting.

Much of the grayish sandstone used in the walls and for paving was rough cut and laid with little pointing to allow for the immediate colonization of wall plants, especially *Santolina,* catmint (*Nepeta*), and *Stachys,* which occur throughout the garden, together with *Erigeron karvinskianus*, which has colonized everywhere. Where a degree of formality is required in the gate piers, balustrade, and edging to the rills, yellow Ham Hill stone is employed as ashlar.

The garden was planned in two contrasting elements—the Great Plat laid out beneath the Victorian terrace and the orangery terrace set awkwardly at 102 degrees to the northeast. Lutyens provided an easy marriage between the gardens by building a rotunda that provides access to both. Taking the steps down to the south leads eventually to the eastern water garden, raised on a terrace, which has a long paved rill, derived from the Deanery Garden at Sonning, where Lutyens and Jekyll collaborated in 1899. The rill runs the full length of the garden and is repeated on the west. The flags, which separate the rill from the grass, enclose occasional circular "tankets," which Jekyll compared with "gathered ribbon" from ancient needlework. Arum lilies are planted in the "tankets" while irises, forget-me-nots (*Myosotis*), water plantain (*Alisma*), and arrowheads (*Sagittaria*) flourish informally in the rills

Rondel at Hestercombe
Copyright Robert M. Craig

themselves. Eventually, the water falls into ornamental tanks at either end of the great pergola. This has alternately square and round pillars carrying climbing roses, *Clematis,* other vines, and *Forsythia,* which provides a sense of enclosure for the garden but also a raised terrace from which to view the countryside. Throughout the garden great advantage is made of changing levels, which provides endless opportunities for steps and retaining walls.

From the water gardens, quadrant steps at each corner lead on to the Great Plat—regarded as one of the great triumphs of Edwardian garden design. Lutyens insisted on a diagonal design with broad panels of grass leading toward a central sundial, which left Jekyll with triangular patches for planting. She eventually abandoned her original "hot" scheme of *Canna, Gladiolus,* and *Phlox* for a softer scheme of *Paeonia*, China roses, *Delphinium,* and *Bergenia*—the last were allowed to flop over the stone edging. The general effect is of a strong architectural framework, especially when seen from the terrace, but a sense of richness and repose from within the garden.

The orangery terrace has a much more intimate feel. The backdrop in Lutyens's time was a group of great elms (*Ulmus*) that Tipping described as "cast[ing] a desirable air of humility over the work of man." These are now gone, however, making the terrace much more open. The various levels require steps and balustrades down to the orangery and then up again into the Dutch Garden, which was laid out as a raised parterre on a pile of builder's rubbish. The orangery is the one major building in the scheme, a low classical building in the "Wrenaissance" style composed of a well-blended mixture of sandstone and Ham Hill stone. In the Dutch Garden Lutyens engaged in some complex geometry, cutting beds of intricate design in the stonework. This challenge was taken up by Jekyll, and today the formal framework is lost in mid-summer beneath a sea of blue-gray foliage of lavender and its flowers with an under planting of *Stachys* and catmint. The effect is heightened by the pink of an occasional China rose. Jekyll also instructed the gardeners to have available for instant planting some *Clarkia*, white, pale yellow and pink snapdragons (*Antirrhinum*), and blue ageratum to fill the gaps. From the elevation of the Dutch Garden there is a south prospect of an orchard and a rolling lawn with fine sweet chestnuts (*Castanea*), survivors, no doubt, of the 18th-century landscape. Tipping commented that at Hestercombe Lutyens and Jekyll showed that "a formal garden can be part of a landscape."

Synopsis

1750 Coplestone Warre-Bampfylde begins creating landscape garden at Hestercombe

1761 Description provided by his father-in-law Edward Knight

1762 Bampfylde visits William Shenstone at The Leasowes and then builds his cascade at Hestercombe

1770s Bampfylde paints a picture of Pear Pond, centerpiece of the landscape

1791 Bampfylde dies

Pergola at Hestercombe
Copyright Robert M. Craig

1872 House and garden passed out of Warre-Bampfylde family and purchased by Lord Portman
1903 Viscount Portman commissions Sir Edwin Lutyens and Gertrude Jekyll to create gardens at Hestercombe
1944 Hestercombe sold to Crown Estates
1973 Gardens begin to be restored by Somerset County Council
1997 Hestercombe Gardens Trust becomes responsible for restoration of both gardens

Further Reading

Bisgrove, Richard, *The Gardens of Gertrude Jekyll,* Boston: Little Brown, and London: Lincoln, 1992
Bond, James, *Somerset Parks and Gardens: A Landscape History,* Tiverton, Devon: Somerset Books, 1998
Brown, Jane, *Gardens of a Golden Afternoon: The Story of a Partnership, Edwin Lutyens and Gertrude Jekyll,* London: Allen Lane, and New York: Van Nostrand Reinhold, 1982; updated edition, London and New York: Penguin Books, 1994
Elliott, Brent, *Victorian Gardens,* London: Batsford, and Portland, Oregon: Timber Press, 1986
Fricker, L.J., "Gardens at Hestercombe House," *Journal of the Institute of Landscape Architects* (1963)
Ottewill, David, *The Edwardian Garden,* New Haven, Connecticut: Yale University Press, 1989
Plumptre, George, *Great Gardens, Great Designers,* London: Ward Lock, 1994
Richardson, Tim, "Deep in the Woods a Garden Was Sleeping," *Country Life* (8 January 1998)
Weaver, Lawrence, *Houses and Gardens by E.L. Lutyens,* London: Country Life, 1913; reprint, Woodbridge, Suffolk: Antique Collectors' Club, 1985
White, Philip, *A Gentleman of Fine Taste: The Watercolours of Coplestone Warre Bampfylde, 1720–1791,* London: Lloyds Bank, 1995

DAVID WHITEHEAD

Het Loo Palace

Apeldoorn, Gelderland, Netherlands

Location: approximately 1 mile (1.6 km) northwest of Apeldoorn, and 45 miles (72.5 km) east of Amsterdam

The new palace of Het Loo in Gelderland near the small town of Apeldoorn was the creation of Prince William of Orange (1650–1702), stadtholder of Gelderland and subsequently king of England, where he ruled jointly with his wife and cousin, Mary. The overall plan of the palace and its gardens owes much to French models fashionable in the 17th century, with the palace approached through a forecourt flanked by buildings. The central axis leading through a tree-lined avenue to the front of the palace continues on the other side of the house to the end of the garden, where it is now virtually stopped by colonnades and the planting that backs them. As originally conceived the central vista extended much further into the distance. The garden itself, however, was only to be seen or entered after passing into and through the house, as at Vaux-le-Vicomte or Versailles. The main or Great Garden comprises two parts, the lower and the upper gardens. The lower garden is a parterre garden of eight large and complex compartments of parterre work viewed from a higher level terrace in front of the house. This terrace extends the full width of the garden and continues to enclose the parterres along the lateral boundaries. Immediately in front of the house are copies of four of the King's Vases, the marble originals of which are now inside the house.

The garden is known particularly for its ornamental elements, especially statuary and water features, fountains, and canals; at the central point of the lower garden stands a statue of Venus. Her supporters are gilded tritons with fountains, and in the pool that surrounds are figures of swans, similarly gilded. Spaced on either side of this statue between the four parterres on either side are the Fountain of the Terrestrial Globe to the west and the Fountain of the Celestial Sphere to the east. The upper garden lies beyond the lower and is separated from it by the Middenwarslaan, as it is called. This comprises a wall and beyond it a canal and a double row of small oak trees. The central feature of the upper garden is the King's Fountain, set in an octagonal basin; beyond this is a circular space defined on its far side by the colonnades and with the Fountain of the Peacock as its central feature.

Formal parterre and fountain, Het Loo, Apeldoorn, Netherlands
Copyright Marijke Heuff/Garden Picture Library

On either side of the main block of the house are two separate gardens, both at the lower level and separated from the main garden area by the line of the terrace. On the east is the Queen's Garden, originally that of Queen Mary, and below her apartments on that side of the building. This originally consisted of formal patterns of box and flowers and more particularly of *berceaux,* a pattern of arbors constructed in timber with climbing plants. On the west side is the King's Garden, a wider open space devoted to more active pursuits, with a bowling green as its major feature. What is notable about this garden is that it is a complete reconstruction. In the late 18th century it had been allowed to deteriorate. By the time of Napoléon it was taken over as a residence by Louis Napoléon, the emperor's brother. He had the entire formal garden obliterated to be replaced by a garden in the English landscape manner. In 1970 it was decided that the palace should become a museum, and four years later a decision was made to restore the formal garden as completely as possible to its original form. The original works had always been attributed to Daniel Marot and Jacob Roman, and illustrations, a bird's-eye view by the latter, and other plans were used as a basis for the reconstruction. In addition, a good deal of valuable archaeological evidence was discovered in the course of work on the grounds. It was not always possible to reproduce the original sculptures, and a number are copies of work by those working contemporaneously for the king in England or for others.

From the time of their coronation William and Mary were making improvements not just at Het Loo but also in England at Kensington Palace and Hampton Court near London, where extensive formal gardens were laid out. Although the fashion for great gardens such as this was short-lived, it is unusual to find a royal family working like this on both sides of the channel. Royal families intermarried, and William's mother was the eldest sister of Charles II. He married his cousin Mary, the daughter of James II. His father William was the second of that name in the succession of princes of Orange. He was thus William III both as king of England and prince of Orange, in England ruling jointly with Mary until her death.

In 1672 William had been named stadtholder of Gelderland, with which title came the hunting rights over the

Velue area of Holland. A keen huntsman, he decided to develop a palace in the country and in 1684 bought the old castle of Loo, a fortified house surrounded by a wide moat set in an extensive estate. Here he proposed to build a new and magnificent palace. Work began in the same year, and although he and his wife succeeded to the English throne in 1689 they continued to take a close interest in the palace and its gardens throughout their lives.

Synopsis

1684	Purchase of Het Loo by Stadtholder Prince William III
1684	Designs for new palace sought in Paris by Dutch Ambassador for person of high rank
1685	Work begins on palace based on French designs
1686–1702	Gardens laid out and continuously developed and improved by Daniel Marot and Jacob Roman
1807	Louis Napoléon, King of Holland (1806–10) takes Het Loo for summer residence, covering formal garden with layer of soil and creating English-style garden
1970	Decision to convert Het Loo into national museum
1974	Decision to remove all 19th- and 20th-century additions and return exterior to original state, including garden, which is integral to design
1977–84	Comprehensive restoration completed under direction of J.B. Baron von Asback

Further Reading

Harris, Walter, *A Description of the King's Royal Palace and Gardens at Loo,* London, 1699; reprint, 1983

Hunt, John Dixon, and Erik de Jong, editors, *The Anglo-Dutch Garden in the Age of William and Mary; De Gouden eeuw van de Hollandse tuinkunst* (exhib. cat.; bilingual English-Dutch edition), London: Taylor and Francis, 1988

Journal of Garden History 8

Strong, Roy C., *Royal Gardens,* London: BBC Books, Markham, Ontario: Octopus, and New York: Pocket Books, 1992

Vliegenthart, A.W., et al., *Het Loo: Palace and Gardens,* S.l: Stichting 'T Konings Loo, 1988

M. F. DOWNING

Hidcote Manor Garden

Hidcote Bartrim, Gloucestershire, England

Location: 4 miles (6.5 km) northeast of Chipping Campden, approximately 30 miles (48 km) southeast of Birmingham

Gardens divided into a sequence of rooms were not uncommon by the time Lawrence Johnston (1871–1958) started laying out his garden at Hidcote in 1907. Among other Edwardian designers, Harold Peto, Edwin Lutyens, and Gertrude Jekyll had created several such gardens. Theirs were quite architectural, however, subdivided by walls and terraces, using considerable amounts of brick and stone to achieve the desired effect. Johnston opted for the much cheaper approach, using hedges instead of walls to divide the spaces. Others were to follow his example, most notably Vita Sackville-West and Harold Nicholson at Sissinghurst. As in contemporary Arts and Crafts gardens, there was the mixed, cottage garden–style planting crammed into beds, with no bare earth showing, preventing weeds from emerging. Instead of using common traditional plant varieties, Johnston would satisfy his plantsman's desires by pursuing the uncommon, filling his garden with many unusual trees, shrubs, and perennials.

The estate's location, perched on a windy hillside overlooking the beautiful Vale of Evesham, forced Johnston to create an essentially introversive garden, sheltering it from the strong winds, and developing a series of microclimates for his special plants. Only the two main axes, the long walk and the view through the red borders, offer a glimpse of the surrounding countryside. To create shelter, he planted deciduous and evergreen trees and shrubs and miles of hedges. Where serenity was required Johnston planted single-species hedges such as hornbeam or box. In other garden areas he planted his famous tapestry hedges, consisting of a mixture of two or more species such as holly, hornbeam, and copper and green beech, which during the summer months would create a plain, dull backdrop for the flowers, while in the spring and autumn they would come alive with the different shades of each plant.

The development of the garden can be divided into three phases, with distinctive design styles. The initial development around the house (1907–14), consisted of small, intimate spaces regimented by formally shaped beds and parterres, which in turn were softened by opulent planting and the rounded shapes of topiary birds. The design of these spaces is more akin to the contemporary Arts and Crafts gardens with interesting details in paths and steps combined with the use of topiary to give added interest. The old garden, white garden, maple garden, red borders, and original bathing pool garden all date back to this period, and the lily pool in the pine garden probably does as well. The second phase (1914–20) saw the introduction of the grander, more classical features, such as the theater lawn, and the completion of the main view axis from the old garden. The view was extended through the circle and the red borders (see Plate 15), with the addition of the twin gazebos and the stilted hedges, in turn framed by ornate iron gates flanked by large brick gateposts and two splendid holm oaks. They frame the view beyond a ha-ha, across the Vale of Evesham. During the last phase (1920–30) Johnston completed the long walk, an elongated space with tall hornbeam hedges on either side, terminating in the distance with a pair of magnificent gates. This is the second of the two main axes in the garden, running at right angles to the first one. Parallel to the long walk he planted Westonbirt, an informal area named after the famous Gloucestershire arboretum he was so taken by, where, unlike everywhere else, the lie of the land was left untouched. In between the undulations of the old ridge-and-furrow agricultural system, Johnston expanded his collection of unusual trees and shrubs. This last phase was the most generous in scale, providing a breathing space, an opportunity to take a rest from all the other areas where the eye is constantly overwhelmed by vivid impressions created by the interesting color and plant combinations.

A keen amateur gardener, Johnston felt confident enough to supervise the development of his garden with its five gardeners, and it was not until 1922 that he employed Frank Adams as professional head gardener. Although he did not employ anybody to design his garden, he had many gardening friends and was a close friend of Norah Lindsey, who advised on the design and planting of several major English gardens, among them Blickling Hall and Cliveden. Her love for formal layouts, packed with perennials and shrub roses, can be seen in Johnston's planting style. The garden is a testimony not only to Johnston's skills as a plantsman but also as a designer. The visitor is effortlessly drawn from one room to the next, walking up gentle slopes, descending flights of steps, or strolling along terraces, all devised to accommodate the awkwardly sloping site and to create intriguing views and appealing archways.

Nowadays, Hidcote is best known for its structural layout, its cottage-style opulent planting, and its color schemes. Johnston's contributions as a plantsman have recently become appreciated as more information has surfaced about his plant-hunting expeditions to Kilimanjaro in Tanzania and to North Burma with George Forrest. He was an avid collector and created many sheltered pockets within the garden to grow some of the more unusual plants. Those too tender to withstand the outdoor climate, such as *Arbutus canariensis, Dendromecon rigida,* and *Haemanthus katherinae,* which he collected on Mount Kilimanjaro, were protected by makeshift constructions in the garden or were kept in the large lean-to winter shelter opposite the pool in the pine garden. This acted as a three-quarter-span greenhouse in winter; in spring the glass side panels were removed, creating a covered walk. For acid-loving plants he dug out special planting areas, replacing the soil with sawdust and peat, enabling rhododendrons and other ericaceous plants to thrive.

Johnston used to spend his summers at Hidcote but would migrate to the French Riviera to spend the winter months at his garden in Serre de la Madonne. In 1948 he moved there for good, leaving Hidcote to the National Trust, making it their first property taken on solely for its garden. Although it had before been opened occasionally to the public for charity fund-raising events, it was permanently opened in 1948.

Synopsis

1897 American Lawrence Johnston obtains history degree from Cambridge

1900 Lawrence Johnston becomes naturalized British subject, and joins army, where he later gains rank of major

1907 Gertrude Winthrop, Johnston's mother, purchases 280 acres (113 ha) of farm land, including 17th-century farmhouse, farm buildings, and several cottages

1907–14 Lawrence Johnston begins to lay out garden and creates area within existing brick walls, including original pool garden, red border, and areas now known as white garden and maple garden

1914–20 Creation of stilt garden, gazebos, Mrs. Winthrop's garden, theater lawn, and main axis views

1920–30 Creation of southern-most part, including long walk, Westonbirt, and pillar garden;

	bathing pool garden also redesigned during this period to its present form
1922	First professional head gardener employed, Frank Adams
1926	Death of Gertrude Winthrop (b. 1845)
1948	Hidcote handed over to National Trust by Johnston, who moves permanently to his property on French Riviera, La Serre de la Madonne
1958	Lawrence Johnston dies in France

Further Reading

Bisgrove, Richard, *The National Trust Book of the English Garden,* London and New York: Viking Penguin, 1990

Brown, Jane, *Eminent Gardeners: Some People of Influence and Their Gardens, 1880–1980,* London: Viking Press, 1990

Clarke, Ethne, *Hidcote: The Making of a Garden,* London: Joseph, 1989

Jekyll, Gertrude, and Lawrence Weaver, *Gardens for Small Country Houses,* London: Country Life, 1912

Lees-Milne, Alvilde, "Lawrence Johnston, Creator of Hidcote Garden," *National Trust Year Book* (1977–78)

Lord, Tony, *Best Borders,* London: Lincoln, 1994; New York: Viking, 1995

Ottewill, David, *The Edwardian Garden,* New Haven, Connecticut: Yale University Press, 1989

Pavord, Anna, *Hidcote Manor Garden, Gloucestershire,* London: The National Trust, 1993

Sackville-West, Vita, "Hidcote Manor," *The Journal of the Royal Horticultural Society* 74, no. 11 (1949)

Thomas, Graham Stuart, "How Past Became Present at Hidcote," *The Field* 5 (1966)

Tipping, H. Avray, "Hidcote Manor Garden," *Country Life* 67 and 68 (1930)

ISABELLE VAN GROENINGEN

Hill, Thomas 1529–1576

English Garden Writer

By the middle of the 16th century in England, many books had been written on herbs and agriculture, but none in English on gardening. Gardens had become status symbols, an indication of wealth and taste, and garden owners as well as gardeners were keen to improve their knowledge of the practical art of gardening. In 1558, the year of Elizabeth I's ascension to the throne, Thomas Hill (or Hyll, as he often spelled his name) published a small, insignificant-looking book that was to herald a vast body of gardening literature. The book was entitled *A Most Briefe and Pleasaunt Treatyse, teachyng how to dresse, sowe, and set a garden* and was the first gardening book written in the English language.

Little is known about Thomas Hill. He was born in 1529 in London and became a writer of popular books on topics as wide ranging as dreams, physiognomy, and astrology, as well as gardening matters. *A Most Briefe and Pleasaunt Treatyse* was one of his earliest books and was an immediate success, a second edition being printed in 1563. The popularity of the book was undoubtedly due to Hill's informal and enthusiastic style as well as to the practical gardening information it contained. These early editions were mainly comprised of text giving detailed instructions for choosing a garden site, setting out the garden in "knots" and "mazes," preparing raised beds, planting with herbs such as hyssop, cotton lavender, and thyme, and dealing with pests including "the Garden wormes, the great Moths and Snayles with shelles and without shelles." The title page has a beautiful woodcut of Hill's layout for a formal, enclosed Tudor garden, such as contemporary maps indicate were common in 16th-century London.

Hill's popularity as a garden writer was later assured by the publication of an enlarged version of his book, entitled *The Newe and Profitable Arte of Gardening* (1568), which included new sections on beekeeping and fruit trees. This book was reprinted at least six times, and in 1577, the year after Hill's death, a more comprehensive version, *The Gardener's Labyrinth,* was published under the name Didymus Mountaine (a pseudonym) with additional woodcuts to illustrate the text. Information on vegetables, herbs, and flowers was featured in these later versions, including the medicinal properties of plants, an important part of 16th-century culture. For example, Hill wrote, "Onions maintaine health, cure ulcers, remove spottes in the bodie . . . recover the haires shed away, the biting of a mad dog!" Contemporary belief in astrological intervention also influenced Hill's gardening hints and tips, and he often referred to the best times for planting according to the phases of the moon.

Thomas Hill provided entertaining and accessible gardening literature at a time when no other such works existed. However, as he admitted in his frontispiece, he did not provide original information, but based his writings on "the principallest Authors which have writte of gardening," and he named classical writers such as Palladius and Cato as his sources. Notwithstanding, Hill is a joy to read, and his comments on contemporary gardening practice, including the introduction of new tools such as thumb pots and "the great squirt" (a watering device illustrated in *The Gardener's Labyrinth*), are of particular importance for garden historians because they provide information about a period for which no British gardens remain intact.

Biography

Born in London, 1529. Published the first gardening book written in the English language, *A Most Briefe and Pleasaunt Treatyse, Teachyng How to Dresse, Sowe, and Set a Garden,* 1558. Died 1576.

Selected Publications

A Most Briefe and Pleasaunt Treatyse, Teachyng How to Dresse, Sowe, and Set a Garden, 1558; enlarged edition as *The Profitable Arte of Gardening,* 1568

The Gardener's Labyrinth, 1577 (under the name of Didymus Mountaine); reprint, edited by Richard Mabey, Oxford and New York: Oxford University Press, 1987

Further Reading

Hoyles, Martin, *Gardeners Delight: Gardening Books from 1560–1960,* London and Boulder, Colorado: Pluto Press, 1994

Thacker, Christopher, *The Genius of Gardening: The History of Gardens in Britain and Ireland,* London: Weidenfeld and Nicolson, 1994

BARBARA SIMMS

Hirschfeld, Christian Cay Lorenz 1742–1792

German Garden Writer

A theologian by profession, Hirschfeld asserted himself as one of the leading guides to gardens and garden aesthetics in Europe in the Age of Enlightenment. Characteristically enough, all of his writings have an unambiguous ethic undertone. In his later years Hirschfeld turned to fruit growing in theory as well as in practice. He looked upon his life and professional activities as part of a large-scale endeavor to enlighten, improve, and embellish.

Hirschfeld's sphere of activity was intimately connected with the north German duchies of Schleswig and Holstein, which at that time were governed by the Danish king. Hirschfeld's language was German, yet as a professor in aesthetics at the University of Kiel, he was a Danish public servant. As tradition called for, he dedicated his works to the Danish heir presumptive.

Hirschfeld's name is first and foremost associated with his fervent propagation of the aesthetics of landscape gardens. Starting with a sound knowledge about empirical and aesthetic theories, as well as about art and archaeology, he emphasized the role of color, light, composition, and architectural styles in his discussions about the sentimental or romantic aspects of the landscape genre. With the years Hirschfeld also obtained an insight in botanical matters, and several of his writings served as guides to the construction of planting schemes. From 1784 he involved himself in the building up of a nursery that ideally was to feature utility plants, fruit trees, and a wide selection of the then new North American trees and shrubs. In practice, however, the Düsternbrook nursery specialized in fruit growing and set up distribution of trees to local farmers. One of the side effects of Hirschfeld's fame is represented by the garden monuments raised in his honor (e.g., the Seifersdorfer Garden near Dresden).

As far as practical garden art is concerned, Hirschfeld seems only to have involved himself with the layout of the garden at Bad Meinberg in Lower Saxony. Yet sources show that dozens of garden patrons and garden artists were familiar with and made practical use of his written guidelines. His theories concerning the layout of public gardens were to have significant influence until well into the 19th century. Hirschfeld was also one of the first theorists to ascribe garden art to the fine arts. Many of his aesthetic viewpoints are indebted to mid-18th-century European garden theory, and Hirschfeld may be said to have taken the role of an intermediary rather than that of an innovator. Yet his insight was appreciably renowned among leading intellectuals, artists, and patrons of the period; for example, Goethe pointed to Hirschfeld in the latter's capacity as catalyst and consultant.

It was the five-volume *Theorie der Gartenkunst* (1779–85; Theory of Landscape Gardening), published simultaneously in German and French, that cemented Hirschfeld's reputation. The *Theorie* reached an extensive readership not only in Germany and Scandinavia but also in most central European countries. Lengthy passages were translated and published in Italy and in Russia. In England and France, on the other hand, the need for literature on horticulture and garden aesthetics was largely met through native authors.

Hirschfeld only gradually approached the field that was to give him fame throughout Europe. His early writings, several of which testify to his distinct literary gifts, primarily touch upon social, educational, and moral issues. Following a stay in Switzerland (1765–67), Hirschfeld moved to Leipzig and subsequently to Halle, and influence from the erudite milieus of these university towns was to mark *Das Landleben* (1767; Country Life) and other of his didactic essays.

In 1770 Hirschfeld began teaching at the University of Kiel; simultaneous to building up survey courses in art and archaeology, he also specialized in gardens and country-house architecture. His first publication devoted to this subject came out in 1773 (*Anmerkungen über die Landhäuser und die Gartenkunst*; Remarks about Country Houses and Landscape Gardening). Hirschfeld ideally wanted to make contemporary landscape gardening match or even surpass the best works of the past. In this his scope comes close to trends typical of neoclassical art theories of the time (e.g., J.J. Winckelmann). Hirschfeld carefully looked for suitable sources of inspiration. His garden discourse owes much to Thomas Whately's *Observations on Modern Gardening* (1700), and the importance of the Scotch philosopher Henry Home's *Elements of Criticism* (1762) should be emphasized as influencing the general aesthetic apparatus in Hirschfeld's writings. In addition, the English writer J. Addison and his thesis about nature's immediate effect on humankind's emotional habits should also be singled out for its exemplary significance to Hirschfeld's reflections. Hirschfeld's continuous occupation with the parallels between landscape painting and landscape gardening was primarily inspired by French thinking of the time, in particular Laugier's *Essai sur l'Architecture* (1753; Essay on Architecture). Interestingly enough, this aspect later was to find resonance with several other German garden writers (e.g., F.L.von Sckell).

In 1775 Hirschfeld's first edition of *Theorie der Gartenkunst* came out. As for its size and its review of the new gardens of the age, it lacks much of what a few years later would evolve into the immense five-volume addition. Yet the essay of 1775, which should be seen as a continuation of Hirschfeld's previous discussions of humankind's connectedness with nature, holds all the basic principles. New in the large-scale edition is the inclusion of lengthy garden descriptions. The latter are based first on the contemporary garden literature, second on reports and surveys furnished by colleagues or diplomats, and third on impressions Hirschfeld gathered during a few travel campaigns to German, Swiss, and Danish gardens. The landscape and portrait painter J.H. Brandt made the larger part of the illustrations in the *Theorie*. Lengthy recordings on waters, pavilions, and planting schemes, as well as on the seasons, light, poetic inscriptions, etc., made parts of the *Theorie* highly applicable as a collection of recipes.

Hirschfeld did not define his goal as that of bringing about a revolution in landscape gardening. He primarily wanted to call forth a consciousness about garden art as a universal phenomenon. To that end he encompassed data and reflections on the evolution of gardens from all over the world and continuously emphasized peace, virtuous manners, and a historic landscape as prerequisites to the prospering of garden art. And conversely, what may be termed the unprofitable, ideal occupation with nature, in his view, ultimately acquires a practical value because it induces man to apply the right ethic norms in his general conduct of life. Whether in the botanical or architectural appointments of the garden program, Hirschfeld deemed a national historic message highly desirable. Another aspect to be stressed is a twofold religious and moral dimension in his writings. The closing sentence of *Theorie der Gartenkunst*, "God created the world, and man embellishes it," thus has a truly existential meaning in Hirschfeld's interpretation.

Biography

Born in Kirchnüchel, near Eutink, Holstein, Germany, 1742. Trained as a theologian; worked for the prince-bishop of Lübeck as private tutor and secretary, 1764–67; journeyed to Switzerland, 1765–67; studied and engaged in literary activities in Leipzig and Halle, Germany, 1767–69; lecturer at the University of Kiel, Germany, 1770; appointed professor in aesthetics, 1773; wrote on garden aesthetics and horticulture, from 1772; journeyed to Denmark, 1780; founded the Düsternbrook nursery near Kiel, 1784. Died in 1792.

Selected Designs

1782 Bad Meinberg, Lower Saxony, Germany

Selected Publications

Das Landleben, 1767
Anmerkungen über die Landhäuser und die Gartenkunst, 1773
Theorie der Gartenkunst, 1775

Theorie der Gartenkunst, 5 vols., 1779; as *Théorie de l'art des jardins,* 1779
Gartenkalender, 1782 (also published as *Taschenbuch der Gartenfreunde* and *Kleine Gartenbibliothek*)
Handbuch der Fruchtbaumzucht, 2 vols., 1788

Further Reading

Buttlar, Adrian von, Margita Marion Meyer, and Birgit Alberts, editors, *Historische Gärten in Schleswig-Holstein,* Heide, Germany: Boyens, 1996
Kehn, Wolfgang, *Christian Cay Lorenz Hirschfeld, 1742–1792: Eine Biographie,* Worms, Germany: Wernersche Verlagsgesellschaft, 1992
Kehn, Wolfgang, "Hirschfeld in Kiel: Dokumentation einer Ausstellung," *Die Gartenkunst* 2 (1993)
Schepers, Wolfgang, *Hirschfelds Theorie der Gartenkunst, 1779–85,* Worms, Germany: Wernersche Verlagsgesellschaft, 1980

MARGRETHE FLORYAN

History

Garden history includes the evolution of garden structures and garden layout, landscape gardening and associated architecture, the house and its cultivated surroundings, the introduction of plants, plant collecting, and exploration, and the raising of hybrids and their propagation. The works of previous generations have benefited the present, designing the great gardens we admire, planting the saplings that are now tall spreading trees, and bringing plants into cultivation often at great cost or risk.

The earliest attempts to document such work were in 301 B.C., with Theophrastus's *Enquiry into Plants* (usually known by its Latin title, *Historia Plantarum*) and in A.D. 90 with Frontinus's *De aquae ductibus,* which addresses waterworks in the garden and farm. In the ninth century the monk Walahfrid Strabo, as abbot of the Benedictine abbey of Reichenau on Lake Constance, had a small garden within the abbey grounds, about which he wrote a Latin poem, *Hortulus: Liber de cultura hortorum* (Book concerning the Cultivation of Gardens), which existed for many centuries in manuscript and was first published in 1510. The poem includes a section for each of 28 garden plants that interested Walahfrid. In 1085 the great Arab libraries in Toledo, Spain, provided European access to sophisticated Islamic and Greek writings in science and agriculture. Almost a century later, in 1180, Al-Awwam wrote on Andalusian agriculture and garden design; in 1259 Chen Jingyi's *Quanfang Beizu* (Complete Chronicle of Fragrances), one of the first encyclopedic works about ornamental plants, was written in China; and in 1305 the first European book on agriculture in a thousand years was produced in Italy by Pietro de' Crescenzi.

In medieval times monasteries were the main repositories of gardening knowledge and important herbal lore. The earliest account of gardening in English, *The Feate of Gardening* (ca. 1400), mentions the use of more than a hundred plants, with instructions on sowing, planting, and grafting trees and advice on the cultivation of herbs. Later works included Thomas Hill's *Profitable Arte of Gardening* (1569), Francis Bacon's essay "On Gardens" (1625), in which he advocates a modern conception of gardens, and Wang Xiangjin's ten-volume encyclopedia of ornamental plants, *Qunfang Pu* (1644; Assembly of Perfumes).

A number of treatises and books on gardening from the mid-17th century to the mid-19th century were known to be read in the New World. Examples include *The Compleat Gard'ner* (1663) by John Evelyn, English writer, government official, diarist, and landscape garden expert; *La theorie et la pratique du jardinage* (1712; Theory and Practice of Gardening) by Dézallier d'Argenville; and *Philosophia Botanica* (1751) and *Species Plantarum* (1753), compiled by Carl Linnaeus, from which began scientific nomenclature for plants. The first notable British garden historian was Horace Walpole (1717–97), who published articles on the subject, but the first major gardening history book focusing on England was George William Johnson's (1802–86) *History of English Gardening, Chronological, Biographical, Literary and Critical* (1829), primarily a catalog of horticultural writers and their books that can still be consulted with interest. Johnson later wrote *A Dictionary of Modern Gardening* (1846), which was much revised. He then felt the need for a journal concerned with small gardens and in 1842 founded the *Cottage Gardener* (later *Journal of Horticulture and Cottage Gardener*). After a reviewer remarked that the *Cottage Gardener* was "for the occupiers of a cottage to which a double coach-house was attached," it became the *Journal of Horticulture.* Percy Edward Newberry (1869–1949) made his chief contribution to garden history when he began to publish in the *Gardener's Chronicle* of 1888–89 a series of scholarly articles, mostly initialed "P.E.N.," on English vineyards and the history of English gardening down to the 16th century. These were largely based on manuscript sources and constituted an original piece of horticultural scholarship.

During the 19th century gardening books became quite popular and were written to keep up with the demand from readers who began to develop gardening as a hobby and wanted to find out as much as they could about various flora and fauna. Most had fairly direct titles, such as *American Gardener* (William Cobbett, 1821) and *Ladies' Companion to the Flower Garden* (Jane Loudon, 1841), which were directed to specific audiences, and more scholarly volumes, such as *Treatise on the Theory and Practice of Gardening Adapted to North America* (Andrew J. Downing, 1845), *Heirloom Vegetable Gardening: A Master Gardener's Guide to Planting, Seed Saving, and Cultural History* (William W. Weaver, 1865), and the four-volume *Cyclopedia of American Horticulture* (Liberty H. Bailey, 1900).

Next came Alicia Amherst (1865–1941) and her *History of Gardening in England* (1895), whose research led to the discovery of a medieval gardening manuscript by Ion (or John) Gardener in Trinity College Library, Cambridge, which was printed in *Archaeologia,* vol. 5 (1894). As Alicia Cecil, her married name, she published *Children's Gardens* (1902) and *London Parks and Gardens* (1907). In 1938 she published *Historic Gardens of England.* In November and December 1899 she and her husband visited Rhodesia and Mozambique, where she collected botanical specimens; in subsequent years she visited the dominions of the British Commonwealth. From her travels she wrote *Wild Flowers of the Great Dominions of the British Empire* (1935); one section was enlarged and issued separately as *Some Canadian Wild Flowers* (1937).

Another important work was *History of Garden Art* by Marie Luise Gothein, published in Heidelberg (1913), complete with engravings of monkeys in ancient Egypt being used to harvest figs.

Gregor Konrad Michael Kraus (1841–1915) made important contributions to the study of fossil plants and to plant physiology, but his scholarly and original excursion into garden history arose from his directorship of the Halle Botanic Garden, which had been under the care of the celebrated botanist and historian Kurt Sprengel (1766–1833). In studying the historical background of the Halle Botanic Garden and comparing the lists of plants grown at different times in European botanic gardens, Kraus noticed that there appeared to be five main periods of plant introduction into botanic gardens, each with plants from a particular region that were most striking. He elaborated this theme, with ample detail, in his *Geschichte der Pflanzeneinfuhrung in die Europaischen Botanischen Garten* (1894).

A different type of contribution was made by Kurt Wein (1883–1968), who began to publish in 1905 with a note on the occurrence of *Geranium phaeum* in the Lower Harz and on historical botanical matters with papers on Johann Thal (1542–83), a pioneer investigator of the plants of the Harz Mountains who lived most of his life in Nordhausen. These studies led Wein into a detailed examination of pre-Linnaean literature, notably old botanic and other garden catalogs, and local floras in search of facts about the introduction and spread of garden plants and weeds. Wein bought much of this literature, building up a remarkable private library; his publications deal with the history of individual species, garden flowers of Germany in the mid-16th century, North American trees in Europe, garden weeds in Nordhausen, and the history of garden plants. He evaluated the introduction and spread of such plants against a background of general history and culture and related them to trends and fashions in art and landscape gardening and to historical factors such as European acquisition of overseas territories. Wein's detailed studies on the history of the introduction and spread of individual plants, particularly those later naturalized or economically exploited, are invaluable to those concerned with the restoration of historic gardens or the care of archaeological sites.

In the United States, where European methods and craftsmen greatly influenced gardening methods and techniques, efforts were made by writers such as Alice Morse Earle (1853–1911), who wrote on gardening, and landscape architects such as Frederick Law Olmsted (1822–1903), who designed public parks in several major cities (e.g., Central Park, New York, and the Fenway, Boston), to make gardens available, if only through the written word, to the working classes, who usually only glimpsed them, if at all, through the great country estates of the rich. Other important sources in the United States, especially for garden historians, were Thomas Jefferson, who left detailed diaries of his gardening and farming activities at his Virginia estate, Monticello, that were later published, and George Washington at Mount Vernon. From them one learns much about the gardening activities of early Americans. Also noteworthy was the 1968 publication of *America's Garden Heritage: Explorers, Plantsmen, and Gardens of Yesterday,* edited by Dorothy S. Manks.

Resources in the United States became more accessible as organizations were created that allowed members to share concerns and publish their research, but trends were often 30 years or so behind Europe. The American Society for Horticultural Science began in 1903 as a respected scientific society. In 1945 the American Horticultural Society, the counterpart of the Royal Horticultural Society, which itself started in Great Britain (1804) as the first society devoted to horticulture, was founded to allow its members to share gardening concerns; in 1922 it started publication of *Horticulture Magazine* (1922). Another important association is the National Gardening Association, with its publication *Gardens for All* and its on-line site, which offers articles, tips, online courses, gardening links, industry research, a children's classroom, advertising, and a library, as well as a seed-swapping service.

Popular interest in the 1960s coincided with the movement to preserve historic buildings. Popular histories of garden history were written by Miles Hadfield (*A History of British Gardening* [1960]), Alice Coats and her groundbreaking *History of Garden Shrubs* (1963), and Peter Hunt (*Shell Gardens Book* [1964]), but the major organization for garden history must be the Garden History Society, founded in November 1965 by Hadfield and Hunt, the first body in Great Britain to advocate the preservation and restoration of historic gardens. In 1983 its register of important gardens was taken over by English Heritage, a government-funded body. During its early years members were kept in touch by a newsletter, along with two volumes of *Occasional Papers* (1969, 1970), but in September 1972 the society started publishing its journal, *Garden History.* In the United States the Garden Conservancy, a group with similar aims, was established in 1989.

The Garden History Society brings together those interested in the history of gardens, gardeners, and gardening to study all aspects of garden history and the gardens, both old and new, in which this history is contained; it publicizes this study and encourages its wider diffusion by means of conferences, visits both at home and abroad, and the publication of appropriate bulletins, articles, and documents, especially important non-English literature on the subject that otherwise might go unread. For example, anyone writing on the general history of orangeries and glasshouses should read A. Tschira's *Orangerien und Gewachshauser, ihre Geschichtliche Entwicklung in Deutschland* (1939) and Marie Louise Gothein's *Geschichte der Gartenkunst* (1914; *A History of Garden Art*).

More gardening history books appeared in the 1970s by authors ranging from populist Edward Hyams to the scholarly Christopher Thacker to support the restoration of historic gardens to something reaching their original form.

In 1977 a Museum of Garden History was established in a restored church in London to explore all aspects of gardening, including plants and shrubs, their history, who introduced them and how they can be examined today, major gardens in the world, garden history societies, horticultural and landscape architects, and bibliographies of garden-related materials.

The Museum of Garden History is only one of hundreds of libraries and archives that have been created to support garden history research. The oldest and most comprehensive horticultural research center in the Western Hemisphere, the Massachusetts Horticultural Society Library, opened in Boston (1829) and today holds more than 100,000 books, periodicals, botanical prints, seed catalogs, and videotapes; it is linked by computer to 16,000 libraries worldwide. Two major research collections, both part of the Smithsonian Institution's Horticultural Services Division, are in the same building only a few feet from each other: the Archives of American Gardens and the Horticulture Branch Library. The archives maintain a collection of approximately 60,000 photographic images and records documenting historic and contemporary American gardens. The library holds more than 5,000 books, 2,700 volumes of periodicals, 10,000 trade catalogs, and vertical files and videotapes. In Beltsville, Maryland, the National Agricultural Library, part of the U.S. Department of Agriculture, holds the largest collection of documents related to agriculture in the United States; gardening is only a division of the collection.

There are also garden symposiums that address garden history, such as the annual event held every April in Colonial Williamsburg, its longest running symposium series, which also designates a Historic Garden Week, also in April; they attract the best garden lecturers and writers of the day. Similar events take place throughout the United States and Europe. One unusual meeting, held in early August 1994, was the "Out of the Garden" symposium, jointly sponsored by the American Horticultural Society and the Montessori Foundation; it drew some 450 educators, horticulturists, and others from around the United States. The New England Wild Flower Society, which has developed its own botanic garden, the Garden in the Woods, focuses on education and is dedicated to stimulating young people's curiosity about plants, birds, insects, and ecology. The Smithsonian Associates gives annual garden tours and lectures as part of its programming; these are some of the most popular programs offered.

The media has also played an important role in promoting gardening. In 1923 Marian Cran started a popular garden show on British Broadcasting Corporation (BBC) radio that began a trend; other radio networks both in Europe and in the United States developed their own shows, mostly addressed to local audiences. There are now garden shows on television and videotape that both teach and entertain in the comfort of home. A major production was the 1993 television series, later produced as a six-part videotape collection, hosted by Audrey Hepburn on gardens of the world. The series presented different garden themes, covering formal gardens, Japanese gardens, tropical gardens, roses and rose gardens, flower gardens, and country gardens; the programs visited many of the world's most beautiful gardens, exploring each from a historical, cultural, and aesthetic perspective. With more home gardeners creating their own plots on everything from apartment rooftops to backyard showplaces, the demand for such educational materials has become its own industry as witnessed by the publication and sale of gardening books and videotapes in local bookstores and libraries.

Closely tied to symposiums, lectures, and media programs are garden fairs and exhibitions, which draw visitors of all ages. The World's Columbian Exposition, Chicago (1893), included many old-style American gardens, a project that was continued at most of the world fairs that followed during the 20th century. By the end of the century, garden festivals were separate events whose primary objective was the appreciation of the value of gardens and greenery to human life. Major ones included the Glasgow (Scotland) Garden Festival (1988), the Osaka (Japan) International Garden and Greenery Exposition (1990), and the Columbus (Ohio) Floriade (1992), in observance of the Columbus quincentenary.

Further Reading

Bell, Susan G., "Women Create Gardens in Male Landscapes: A Revisionist Approach to Eighteenth-Century English Garden History," *Feminist Studies* 16 (Fall 1990)

Best, Clare, and Caroline Boissett, editors, *Leaves from the Garden: Two Centuries of Garden Writing,* London: John Murray, 1986; New York: Norton, 1987

"The Curious History of Herbaceous Borders," *Economist* 343, no. 8023 (June 1997)

Dietsch, Deborah K., "A Garden of Hope and Recovery," *Architectural Record* 177, no. 13 (November 1989)

Griswold, Mac, and Eleanor Weller, "Green Grandeur: American Estate Gardening in the French Style, 1890–1910," *The Magazine Antiques* 140, no. 3 (September 1991)

Hill, May B., "'Grandmother's Garden,'" *The Magazine Antiques* 142, no. 5 (November 1992)

Huxley, Anthony Julian, *An Illustrated History of Gardening,* New York and London: Paddington Press, 1978

Martin, Carol, *Cultivating Canadian Gardens: A History of Gardening in Canada,* Ottawa, Ontario: National Library of Canada, 1998

O'Malley, Therese, "Appropriation and Adaptation: Early Gardening Literature in America," *Huntington Library Quarterly* 55, no. 3 (Summer 1992)

Pollan, Michael, "Digging into the Past," *House Beautiful* 133, no. 10 (October 1991)

Stearn, William T., "The Garden History Society's Tenth Anniversary and Some Historians of Garden History," *Garden History* 4, no. 3 (Spring 1977)

Stocker, Carol, "1,000 Years of Progress in Horticulture," *Boston Globe* (30 December 1999)

Strong, Roy C., compiler, *A Celebration of Gardens,* London: HarperCollins, and Portland, Oregon: Sagapress/Timber Press, 1991

Wheeler, David, editor, *The Penguin Book of Garden Writing,* London and New York: Viking, 1996

MARTIN J. MANNING

Hluboká

České Budějovice district, South Bohemian region, Czech Republic

Location: six miles north of České Budějovice, and 70 miles south of Prague

The Hluboká nad Vltavou château, standing on a rocky point over the Vltava River, is a dominant feature of a large part of the south Bohemian countryside. Together with the landscaped gardens, a parklike landscape in the *ferme ornée* style, a pond network, and extensive enclosures, it forms an area of exceptional importance in Europe. The landscaped gardens next to the castle are extraordinary due to their simple composition and many specimens of introduced tree species as well as their location on a plateau, which provides a view of the distant countryside.

The original château was a Gothic castle built in the second half of the 13th century. The present look of the château in the Tudor neo-Gothic style (1839–71) was designed by a Viennese architect, Franz Beer.

The reign of the Schwarzenberg family (1661–1945) influenced the development of the surroundings in a significant way, especially due to the popularity of hunting and game keeping. In 1664 the prince ordered the planting of oak and beech trees so that the game stayed on the manor premises. During this period a great number of oak avenues were planted along roads and on the dikes of lakes, which has been a typical feature of the local countryside up to the present time. Many of the oaks planted at that time still exist.

To meet the demand for a state venue for organizing magnificent hunts, a hunting château, Ohrada, was constructed not far from the Hluboká château on the bank of the Munický Lake. Paul Ignatz Bayer built the hunting château Ohrada (1708–21), one of the most accomplished baroque compositions in south Bohemia. Extensive enclosures were established close to the château—the Old Enclosure (1766–71) and the New Enclosure (1853). The Old Enclosure boasts remarkably tall trees, mainly oaks and beeches, that have been preserved until the present day.

Until the second half of the 19th century, the Hluboká castle had no significant garden area—only relatively small vegetable gardens. In the area of today's gardens, avenues divided the fields. Not until the reconstruction of the château in the neo-Gothic style was a landscaped park, with an area of 90 hectares (222.3 acres), established in the environs of the château and on the adjacent plateau.

A regular neobaroque parterre forms the immediate surroundings of the park with box tree ornaments supplemented with roses and in summer also with annuals. The parterre was renewed at the beginning of the 1970s, from plans dating from the beginning of the 20th century. Visitors can enjoy the fascinating view of the romantic parklike countryside with meadows, solitary and groups of trees, ponds, and the outline of the Vltava River. A neo-Gothic fountain with a two-winged stairway and a group of stately beeches closes the parterre area in front of the château entrance and the riding hall.

A large number of exotic tree species originating from the second half of the 19th century can be found in Hluboká, many of which were first introduced into the Czech lands at this park. In the parterre, for example, are examples of *Ginkgo biloba*—both the male and female plants—*Cladrastis lutea, Carya ovata, Platanus × acerifolia, Gymnocladus dioica, Quercus petraea* 'Mespilifolia', *Thuja gigantea, Tsuga canadensis, Picea bicolor,* and *Liriodendron tulipifera.*

Princess Eleonora Schwarzenberg, inspired by journeys to England with her husband, initiated the establishment of a natural landscape park situated next to the symmetrically arranged surroundings of the château. The park construction was at first supervised by the court gardener, G. Immeline, who was replaced in 1851 by Theodor Heinrich Rehder—a son of Jacob Heinrich Rehder, the head manager of the Prince Pückler park and seed plots in Bad Muskau in Germany. It is documented that Theodor H. Rehder worked at the Schwarzenberg manor between 1851 and 1854. His style of work, inspired by the work and ideas of English landscape designers Lancelot "Capability" Brown and Humphry Repton, corresponds with the generous compositions of the park on the Podskalská meadow below the Hluboká castle, close to the Červený Dvůr château garden (about 30 kilometers [18.5 mi.]). The next projects until the park's completion in 1864 were managed by the head gardener, Rudolph Wacha. At that time 106 genuses of deciduous trees and 25 species of coniferous trees were planted there.

The simple but magnificent park composition takes great advantage of the rugged topography, in particular the situation on the plateau, which gives a wonderful view of the open countryside with the calm surface of the Munický Lake and with oak avenues surrounded by a range of the Šumava Mountains and the Blanský Forest Mountains.

The regular parterre arrangement is situated beside a sloping meadow, which offers the most beautiful view of the château especially if one is standing at the water tower. Three large meadows with solitary trees and tree groups bordering the picturesque view of the enclosure form the heart of the park composition. A small lake with two rocky islands brightens the first meadow. A significant dark point—a circle of spruce firs—is a dominant feature on the largest meadow in the center of the park. The lookout meadow at the edge of plateau, which is an extensive stage with a scene of solitary trees, provides an amazing view of the valley, with the lake, the Ohrada hunting château, the forest growth of a baroque pheasantry, and a distant range of mountains on the horizon.

Despite the importance of the introduced tree species, domestic types—oaks (*Quercus robur*), lime trees (*Tilia cordata, T. platyphylla*), beeches (*Fagus sylvatica*), maples (*Acer platanoides, A. pseudoplatanus*) and ash trees (*Fraxinus excelsior*)—form the core of the composition; spruce fir (*Picea abies*) is a significant representative of coniferous trees. The border growth of the meadows is mostly formed by only one tree species: a contrast between the dark green spruce firs and the silver trunks of beeches in the foreground, the meadows are bordered by oaks with gorgeous tree tops. Curving pathways lead the visitor.

The introduced tree species include *Sophora japonica, Gleditsia triacanthos, Coryllus colurna, Cercidiphyllum japonicum, Pseudotsuga menziesii, Acer cissifolium, A. monspessulanum, Quercus palustris, Q. cerris, Q. frainetto,* and *Carya tomentosa.*

Since 1945 the château, gardens, and park have been owned by the state and open to the public.

Synopsis

1285	First references to Hluboká in official records
1490	First reference to the largest lake, Bezdrev, in official records
1630–60	The first fallow-deer enclosure established under the reign of the Marradas family
1661–1945	The Schwarzenberg family owns the manor

1664	Prince Schwarzenberg has oaks planted on the landscape
1680	Beginning of pheasant rearing
1708–21	Ohrada hunting chateau built by P.I. Bayer
1766–71	Old Enclosure built
1839–71	Reconstruction of the chateau in neo-Gothic style
1851–54	Theodor Heinrich Rehder lays out park in English landscape style
1853	New Enclosure built
1864	Completion of landscape park by Schwarzenberg's head gardener, Rudolf Wacha
1945	Czechoslovak state takes over the chateau
1970s	Renovation of the parterre
1990s	Gradual regeneration of the natural landscape park

Further Reading

Dokoupil, Zdeněk, *Historické zahrady v Čechách a na Moravě* (Historic Gardens in Bohemia and Moravia), Prague: Nakladatelství československých výtvarných umělců, 1957

Hieke, Karel, *České zámecké parky a jejich dřeviny* (Czech Castle Parks and Their Tree Species), Prague: Stání zemědělské nakladatelství, 1985

Pacáková-Hošt'álková, Božena, et al., *Zahrady a parky v Čechách, na Moravě a ve Slezsku* (Gardens and Parks in Bohemia, Moravia, and Silesia), Prague: Libri, 1999

MARIE PAVLÁTOVÁ AND MAREK EHRLICH

Hooker, William Jackson 1785–1865 and Joseph Dalton Hooker 1817–1911

English Botanists

The father-and-son team of William Jackson Hooker and Joseph Dalton Hooker were instrumental in the development of the Royal Botanic Gardens, Kew, into a national botanic garden and center of botanical science for Great Britain. The 18th and 19th centuries were times of extensive exploration for England. It was not uncommon for botanists to accompany sea expeditions around the world. These plant explorers brought back their observations, writings, drawings, and plant discoveries and in doing so contributed greatly to the growing interest in plant sciences.

William Jackson Hooker

William Jackson Hooker was born in Norwich, England. He showed an early interest in and aptitude for natural history. During the early part of the 19th century, this interest had brought him in contact with many of the leading figures of the day, including Sir Joseph Banks, Kew's first unofficial director; the British botanist Robert Brown; and Augustin de Candolle, the renowned Swiss botanist who developed a system of plant classification that would be expanded on by William's son Joseph and become the foundation for the method used today. While all of these men had some influence on William, it was the Norwich doctor and founder of the Linnaean Society, James Smith, who helped him focus his interest on botany.

As a young man in need of an income, Hooker elected to study estate management and purchased a quarter share in Halesworth Brewery, moving into the house to superintend operations. Hooker's main attraction to the house was that it came with a large garden and a heated greenhouse, providing him with a place to grow orchids. His reputation as a botanist also began to grow.

While retaining his partnership in the brewery, Hooker accepted a professorship in botany at the University of Glasgow. During his tenure at the university, he expanded his reach beyond a personal interest in botany and plant collecting and established the Botanic Garden at Glasgow. He spent the remainder of his tenure developing this garden and pursuing his newfound interest in ferns. The Kibble Palace, erected shortly after Hooker's tenure, still contains an extraordinary collection of ferns from Australia and New Zealand.

After the deaths of King George III and Sir Joseph Banks, Kew Garden declined into an incidental garden for the royals. Parliament accepted a recommendation to make Kew a national institution, and Hooker was offered and accepted the directorship. He held this position until his death.

At Kew, Hooker set about expanding the diversity and breadth of the displays. The present herbarium and library were developed from his own private collections. Constantly confronted with a lack of space, he was also responsible for the creation of the Palm House and began the construction of the Temperate House.

With the opening of the gardens to the public, it was felt that there was a need for a house to showcase palms and other tropical fauna. As this was "the age of iron," the glasshouse was constructed of iron and curved glass. Wrought-iron "deck beams" generally used in shipbuilding were used to create large spans of otherwise unsupported space and give the house its colloquial description of an upturned hull. Situated near what was then George II's lake, you could see the reflection of this wonderful structure in the water. Inside, curator John Smith needed the help of engineers to install the first palms, *Sabal mauritiiformis* and two species of *Phoenix*.

The Temperate House was designed to complement the Palm House. The construction took almost 30 years, resulting in the largest glasshouse at Kew, about twice the size of the Palm House. Inside this imposing structure is housed a variety of tender woody plants from the temperate regions of the world.

Perhaps Hooker's greatest legacy to Kew was the founding of the first museum of economic botany. He wanted the Economic Botany Collections

> to render great service, not only to the scientific botanist, but to the merchant, the manufacturer, the physician, the chemist, the druggist, the dyer, the carpenter and the cabinet maker and artisans of every description, who might here find the raw materials employed in their several professions correctly named.

A tall order, but one he took seriously. The museum now houses over 76,000 items, reflecting the history of Kew and its role in showcasing British life. Included are one of the world's finest wood collections (32,000 samples from 12,000 species), thousands of bottles of oils, and plant-related treasures from explorers and collectors such as Hooker himself.

Hooker wrote extensively on his botanical work and was instrumental in establishing the natural system of plant classification in Great Britain. The herbarium he established now has specimens representing 98 percent of the known plant species.

Joseph Dalton Hooker

Joseph Dalton Hooker was the second son of William Jackson Hooker and arguably the leading British plant geographer and taxonomist of the late 19th century. He was also one of the chief proponents of the principle of evolution and became a close friend and trusted colleague of Charles Darwin. His vast knowledge and curiosity of the distribution of plants made him of invaluable assistance to Darwin in his research. While in the United States, Hooker met the English naturalist Alfred Russel Wallace, who was about to make public his findings on evolution, which were very similar to Darwin's. Helping to arrange for a joint presentation of both men's papers to the Linnaean Society of London, Hooker earned several enemies because of his support of Darwin and evolution theories.

A medical doctor by training, Hooker had an interest in botany that no doubt was fostered by the time spent in his father's herbarium. Combining his interests and his fondness for travel, Joseph Hooker served as assistant surgeon-naturalist on the *H.M.S. Erebus* while it explored Antarctica, New Zealand, Tasmania, and the Falkland Islands. On his return, he published his first botanical findings. He also left behind a namesake daisy species, *Pleurophyllum hookerii.*

Hooker's second expedition took him to India. He spent three years exploring the Himalayas, Sikkim, and Nepal, sending England its first rhododendrons. The plants and data he gathered gained him an international reputation as a plant geographer. Plants new to science were brought home to England for cultivation. Many still grow in Kew. He also introduced the Himalayan birch and reported the largest of all magnolias, *Magnolia campbellii.*

During the period he was engaged with the Royal Geological Survey, he was also appointed assistant director at Kew, working under his father. He eventually succeeded William and remained at Kew until his retirement. As director, he oversaw the founding of the Jodrell Laboratory. The Jodrell was established for physiological research, and Hooker used the laboratory as his office.

Hooker's last major botanical expedition would be to the Rocky Mountains and the Sierra Nevada Mountains in the United States. There he studied the relationship of American and Asian floras. Throughout his career, he was intrigued by how plants were disbursed from one place to another. His work studying and charting this phenomenon cemented his reputation as a plant geographer. Among his most significant contributions to the science of botany was his explanation of the observed geographic distribution of plants and why there seemed to be such peculiar variations, such as the Asian natives he found growing in the western United States.

In 1883, in collaboration with George Bentham, he published the final volume of "Genera Plantarum," describing in detail 200 families, 7,569 genera, and approximately 97,000 species of seed-bearing plants, most of which he had personally examined and many of which are still in the Kew collection today. To classify the plant material, Hooker and Bentham adopted a system similar to that of de Condolle. The work of writing the three volumes consumed over 20 years.

Hooker, William Jackson 1785–1865

Biography

Born in Norwich, Norfolk, England, 6 July 1785. Studied estate management and purchased quarter share in Halesworth Brewery, where he pursued his botanical interest in the greenhouse; accepted professorship in botany at University of Glasgow, 1820, and established Botanic Garden at Glasgow; accepted directorship of Royal Botanic Gardens, Kew, 1841; oversaw creation of Palm House at Kew, 1844–48; began construction of Temperate House at Kew, 1860–61; founded Museum of Economic Botany at Kew, 1847. Knighted, 1836. Died in Kew, Surrey, 12 August 1865.

Selected Publications

British Jungermanniae, 1816
Flora Scotica, 1821
British Flora, 1830; 8th edition, revised and corrected (with George A. Walker-Arnott), 1860
Genera Filicum, 1838
Species Filicum, 5 vols., 1846–64
Handbook of the New Zealand Flora—Part I, 1864
Synopsis Filicum, 1868
Handbook of the New Zealand Flora—Part II, 1868

Hooker, Joseph Dalton 1817–1911

Biography

Born in Halesworth, Suffolk, England, 30 June 1817. Graduated from University of Glasgow with medical degree, 1839; served as assistant surgeon-naturalist aboard *H.M.S. Erebus* on its famous Antarctic expedition, 1839–43; met and befriended Charles Darwin, 1843; invited to teach botany at Edinburgh University for spring term, 1845; became paleobotanist with Royal Geological Survey, 1846–55; went on a natural history expedition to India, 1848; became assistant director at Royal Botanic Gardens, Kew, 1855; explored Syria and Lebanon, 1860; made director of Kew, 1865; explored Atlas Mountains in Morocco, 1871; became president of Royal Society, 1873–78; conducted exploration of Rocky Mountains and California, 1877; retired from Kew, 1885. Knighted, 1877. Died in Sunningdale, Berkshire, 10 December 1911.

Selected Publications

Antarctic Flora, 1844–47
Botany of the Antarctic Voyage of H.M. Discovery Ships Erebus and Terror in the Years 1839–1843, 6 vols., 1844–60
Rhododendrons of Sikkim-Himalaya, 1849–51
Flora Tasmaniae, 1860
Genera Plantarum (with George Bentham), 3 vols., 1862–83
Handbook of the British Flora (with George Bentham), 1866
Vegetation of the Rocky Mountain Region and a Comparison with That of Other Parts of the World, 1880
Student's Flora of the British Islands, 1870; 3rd edition, 1884
Flora of British India, 7 vols., 1875–97

Further Reading

Allan, Mea, *The Hookers of Kew, 1785–1911,* London: Joseph, 1967
Curtis, Winifred M., "Hooker, Sir Joseph Dalton (1817–1911), Botanist and Explorer," in *Australian Dictionary of Biography,* edited by Douglas Pike et al., vol. 4, Melbourne: Melbourne University Press, and London and New York: Cambridge University Press, 1972
Desmond, Ray, *Sir Joseph Dalton Hooker,* Woodbridge, Suffolk: Antique Collectors' Club, 1999
Huxley, Leonard, *Life and Letters of Sir Joseph Dalton Hooker: Based on Materials Collected and Arranged by Lady Hooker,* 2 vols., New York: Appleton, and London: Murray, 1918; reprint, New York: Arno Press, 1978
Kantvilas, Gintarus, "A Brief History of Lichenology in Tasmania, Australia," *Proceedings of the Royal Society of Tasmania* 117 (1983)
Stevens, P.F., "J.D. Hooker, George Bentham, Asa Gray, and Ferdinand Mueller on Species Limits in Theory and Practice: A Mid-Nineteenth-Century Debate and Its Repercussions," *Historical Records of Australian Science* 11, no. 3 (1997)
Turrill, William Bertram, *Pioneer Plant Geography: The Phytogeographical Researches of Sir Joseph Dalton Hooker,* The Hague: Nijhoff, 1953

MARIE IANNOTTI

Hortus Botanicus Leiden. *See* Leiden, Universiteit Hortus Botanicus

---

Hortus Conclusus

The *hortus conclusus* (enclosed garden) was the medieval garden of the Virgin Mary, inspired by the Old Testament book Song of Songs (also called Song of Solomon or Canticles). An enduring symbol, the Canticlean garden is referred to in early Christian texts, widely represented in 15th-century European painting, and a flourishing literary theme from the Middle Ages until the 17th century. In practice the *hortus conclusus* became the model for medieval romance gardens, thus becoming associated with the more secular manifestations of courtly love; yet it was also regarded as a representation of Paradise, frequently as an enclosed garden within a garden, an earthly but exquisite refuge. Although an essentially medieval phenomenon, later vestiges of the *hortus conclusus* may be found in 16th- and 17th-century palace gardens in the guise of the *giardino segreto*.

The Song of Songs is a celebration of love and nature based on a central theme of the garden, which, following Middle Eastern tradition, is described as an enclosed orchard or vineyard with fountains and springs, perfumed breezes, flowers, sweet fruits, milk and honey, and exotic spices. In what is both a sensuous love poem and an allegory of divine love, the garden symbolizes the beloved: "She is a garden enclosed, my sister, my promised bride." As early as the fourth century St. Jerome and St. Ambrose linked the garden imagery with the Virgin Mary; but it was in the 12th century that such exegesis blossomed in Western Christendom, with the Virgin's intact womb seen as "a garden enclosed, a sealed fountain." Regarded as the mystical bride of Christ, Mary was symbolized by the Canticlean garden; and, at the same time, "a fountain of gardens, a well of living waters" was taken to be a metaphoric description of her extraordinary progeny.

In this Marian vision of a garden, which is protected and pure yet also fecund, key elements of the medieval *hortus conclusus* became its sealed enclosure, most commonly a wall, wattle fence, or hedge, and its water source—a fountain, pool, trough, or spring. Commonly it would have stood within, but well separated from, a larger garden, sometimes at the end of a path to signify it as a special destination, and occasionally it was viewed from an upper story. Usually a square or rectangular herbarium, the *hortus conclusus* often contained paths intersecting a lawn or floral meadow, planted borders, and climbing shrubs, perhaps a few trees, turf seats, and arbors.

The 15th century delighted in depicting Madonnas or scenes of the Annunciation in the *hortus conclusus,* a practice perhaps fueled by innovations in the courtly garden, and invaluable to us now in lieu of the gardens themselves. *Paradise Garden,* by an unknown painter of the Cologne school, is a detailed vignette of a garden surrounded by a crenellated stone wall with border flowers and trees. The Virgin is depicted as a charming medieval mother quietly reading while her son and a handmaid play music on the flowery lawn, here without paths or individual beds. The picture is outstanding for its detailed depiction of many individual plants: borage, rose campion, cowslip, daisy, purple flag iris, hollyhock, Madonna lily, lily-of the-valley, peony, vinca, sweet rocket, rose, sage, strawberry, violet, cherry, and yellow wallflower have all been identified. Such scenes of pastoral domesticity were possibly intended to captivate personal and lay sentiments, and the gardens portrayed are aristocratic rather than monastic. In fact the prestige and romance of palace gardens may have contributed to the popular appeal of these images.

The detailed, jewel-like quality of such garden representations may indicate the influence of Islamic gardens, if not directly then through the introduction of Persian miniatures into Europe at least by the 14th century. In a similar vein the rich meadow of the *hortus conclusus,* as in Stefano da Zevio's *Madonna in a Rose Garden* in Verona, recalls Muslim floral carpets. Nonetheless, the iconography of the *hortus conclusus* is Christian. Each detail carries symbolic meaning, biblical or contemporary, attractive to medieval notions of virtue. White lilies and lilies-of-the-valley represent the purity of Mary, the reclusive violet her humility, and the purple iris her royal lineage from King David. The trifoliate leaves of the strawberry symbolize the Trinity while apples recall the fall of humanity and later redemption by Christ. Goldfinches were associated with Christ for their red stigmata-like markings and diet of thorn seeds; peacocks were symbols of resurrection; fountains and pools were the "living waters" of Christ.

Most of all, roses were essential features of the *hortus conclusus.* Trellises carried climbing varieties—white blooms symbolized Marian virtue, and red the Passion of Christ. The rose of Sharon, which appears in the Song of Songs, was probably a crocus or narcissus, but in Europe it was understood as the more exotic *Rosa* where, through Persian import via the Crusades and Muslim conquest of Spain and Sicily, it gained great popularity in the 12th century. Highly valued for its associations with the cult of the Virgin Mary and the Mystical Rose that had materialized in the early Middle Ages, the rose offered a metaphor for Mary's love and pure beauty and especially for her intact womb, which in carrying Christ was understood to enclose all of the world. In this combination of human capacity and cosmic meaning, it became a perfect motif for the *hortus conclusus* as medieval love garden, for medieval courtly love aspired to divine charity in the belief that God sanctioned human love that was pure in thought and deed. Mary was the perfect object of such devotion, and likewise the *hortus conclusus* that symbolized her was the ideal place to

The Little Paradise Garden, ca. 1410, by an Upper Rhine Master
Courtesy of Städelsches Kunstinstitut Frankfurt am Main, Loan of the Historisches Museum, Frankfurt

express sanctified human love in its many forms, as described in the great romances of the 13th and 14th centuries such as *The Pearl* and *The Romance of the Rose*. In effect the *hortus conclusus* became a garden of pleasure; sacred and profane were happily intermingled, separated only by the temporality of the earthly garden and the eternity of the one symbolized in heaven.

In the early Renaissance the *hortus conclusus* became the secluded or secret walled enclosures in palace gardens known as *giardini segreti*. Although no longer imbued with the ideals of medieval courtly love, these planted rooms, with sweet-smelling flowers and herbs and perhaps some topiary around a small lawn, ensured privacy within large Italian gardens. By the 16th century they were a major feature at the Villa Lante, Palazzo Farnese at Caprarola, and the Villa Medici at Fiesole. Although still distinct and walled, these gardens were quite transformed, sometimes of considerable size with elaborate sculpture and fountains, and occasionally commanded expansive views, as a *giardino pensile* or hanging garden.

In literature the tradition of the *hortus conclusus* endured, eventually becoming more emblematic. The locked Marian garden of Henry Hawkins's *Partheneia Sacra; or, The Mysterious and Delicious Garden of the Sacred Parthenes* (1633) is a good example of its culmination in the 17th century, after which time it quickly fades.

Further Reading

Crisp, Frank Bart, *Medieval Gardens, Flowery Medes, and Other Arrangements of Herbs, Flowers, and Shrubs Grown in the Middle Ages,* 2 vols., edited by Catherine Childs Paterson, London: Lane, 1924; reprint, New York: Hacker Art Books, 1966

Daley, Brian E., "The 'Closed Garden' and the 'Sealed Fountain': Song of Songs 4:12 in the Late Medieval Iconography of Mary," in *Medieval Gardens,* edited by Elisabeth B. MacDougall, Washington, D.C.: Dumbarton Oaks, 1983

Harvey, John Hooper, *Mediaeval Gardens,* London: Batsford, 1981

Hawkins, Henry, *Partheneia Sacra, 1633,* edited by John Horden, Menston, Yorkshire: Scolar Press, 1971

Masson, Georgina, *Italian Gardens,* Woodbridge, Suffolk: Antique Collectors Club, and London: Thames and Hudson, 1961; revised edition, 1987

McLean, Teresa, *Medieval English Gardens,* London: Collins, 1981

Pearsall, Derek Albert, and Elizabeth Salter, "The Enclosed Garden," in *Landscapes and Seasons of the Medieval World,* by Pearsall and Salter, London: Elek, 1973

Stewart, Stanley, *The Enclosed Garden: The Tradition and the Image in Seventeenth-Century Poetry,* Madison: University of Wisconsin Press, 1966

WENDY PULLAN

Hortus Palatinus

Heidelberg, Baden-Württemberg, Germany

Location: on large terraces east of castle above city of Heidelberg, approximately 0.5 mile (0.8 km) east of city center

The Hortus Palatinus, the mannerist garden of the Heidelberg castle, owes its name to its creator, French architect and engineer Salomon de Caus (1576–1626), who under this title published an extensive description of the garden containing 30 plates. Hortus Palatinus was created between July 1614 and October 1619, replacing an existing garden near the castle. Friedrich V, elector Palatine, commissioned de Caus to create the new garden.

De Caus's engineering skills were certainly an advantage for the mastery of the difficult topographic situation in Heidelberg. Important engineering work was necessary for the construction of high retaining walls built up from the Neckar valley to support the large superimposed terraces beneath the castle. The terraces are organized into a large L; that is, two arms arranged in several tiers and at right angles to each other. This technical conquest over nature, commented on extensively by de Caus in his book, emphasized the determination of the elector to accomplish the plan despite the difficulties. A similar technical achievement was the transporting and transplanting of thirty 60-year-old bitter orange trees from the Herrengarten in downtown Heidelberg. They were protected from cold temperatures by an ephemeral wooden construction against the eastern garden wall. De Caus's project for a stone greenhouse was not realized.

As shown in the plates of de Caus's publication, the structure and elements of the Hortus Palatinus display typical features of a mannerist garden. As there were no axes dominating the visitor's view, the structure of the garden invites one to admire the different attractions of the garden and the plant beds, which are one of several types and follow French models. The circular flower garden, next to the greenhouse, is divided into flower beds dedicated to the four seasons.

The numerous grottoes, fountains, and statues spitting water and producing musical effects prove their designer's skill in hydraulics and reflect Italian models (Pratolino, Villa di Castello). A general political and panegyrical meaning of the Hortus Palatinus is demonstrated in several features: a statue of Friedrich V dominates the highest point of the garden and stands directly above that of Neptune, the ruler over the element of water in nature, suggesting Friedrich's sovereign control. Statues of the river gods such as the Rhine, Neckar, and Main under Neptune's government define the garden as equivalent to the elector's territory. The dedication to Vertumnus, god of the four seasons, and the statues of the goddesses of fruit and farming, Ceres and Pomona, make clear that the iconography of the garden emphasizes the contrast between the artifical garden and the surrounding uncultivated nature. In one of the garden quarters containing statues of the Muses, an inscription refers to the young Elector, thus characterizing Friedrich as patron of the arts, as leader of the Muses, and as equivalent to Appollo.

As shown in the plates of de Caus's publication, the structure and elements of the Hortus Palatinus carry typical Renaissance elements such as a maze, gazebos, *bassins* (ornamental ponds or lakes), statuary, and tubs of plants. There were innumerable waterworks and grottoes designed by de Caus, many of which were musical. The structure of the garden guided the visitor to visit one element after the other, to admire the different attractions of the garden, as there were no axes dominating the visitor's way or view. Friedrich V became King of Bohemia in 1619 and soon after was forced to leave Bohemia for exile in the Netherlands, and as a result the garden was never finished. There still remain today the terraces, a number of grottoes, and the ruins of the bathing grottoes and heating chambers.

An illustration of Hortus palatinus, *Grottoe,* taken from Salomon de Caus, *Hortus Palatinus,* 1619
Copyright Zentralinstitut für Kunstgeschichte, München

Synopsis

1614	Friedrich V commissions Salomon de Caus to create new garden at Heidelberg castle
1618	Peter Leonhardt appointed gardener
1619	Friedrich V accepts Bohemian crown and transfers court to Prague
1620	De Caus's book *Hortus Palatinus* published
19th C.	Partly transformed into irregular garden
late 20th C.	Reconstruction of several basins and individual architectural and sculptural elements

Further Reading

Caus, Salomon de, *Hortus Palatinus a Friderico, Rege Boemiae, Electore Palatino Heidelbergae Exstructus,* Frankfurt, 1620 (both a German and a French edition identical in substance); reprint of the German edition, Worms, Germany: Werner'sche Verlagsgesellschaft, 1980; reprint of the French edition, with a postface by Michel Conan, Paris 1981

Zimmermann, Reinhard, *Kommentar* (on de Caus's German *Hortus Palatinus*), Worms, Germany: Werner'sche Verlagsgesellschaft, 1986
Zimmermann, Reinhard, "Iconography in German and Austrian Renaissance Gardens," in *Garden History: Issues, Approaches, Methods,* edited by John Dixon Hunt, Washington, D.C.: Dumbarton Oaks Research Library and Collection, 1992

IRIS LAUTERBACH

Hospital Garden

The role of gardens at hospitals has varied throughout history depending on time, culture, and medical technologies. Many people throughout history have believed that gardens are strongly connected to life cycles and as such are linked to renewal and healing. Today, gardens are often considered to be an important element of complementary and integrative medicine; as a result, gardens are appearing in more health care settings. Gardens as places of healing can often be found at health care facilities where the focus is on the care of terminal patients; gardens can serve a crucial role by providing a comfortable, homelike setting. Traditional hospitals have also begun to include gardens in and around their buildings, both to take advantage of the garden's healing powers for patients, visitors, and staff and to appeal to the potential hospital "customer."

A hospital garden meant as a restorative garden is intended as a place for relaxation, stress relief, connection to nature, and escape from the otherwise institutional setting. In offering these things the garden helps to enhance the recuperative powers of the individual. If recovery is not possible, the garden can provide a calming setting through its connection to life cycles and other natural processes. The effects of a successful garden can be experienced throughout the entire hospital facility, by patients as well as by hospital staff and visitors.

Some studies have shown that the inclusion of a well-planned garden in a health care setting can have demonstrable healing effects. It is thought that when people are most stressed they crave familiarity, comfort, and support, and that a garden has the potential to provide this type of environment. The positive effects of the garden include reducing or eliminating withdrawal, isolation, depression, disinterest, and other symptoms commonly experienced by hospital patients. Restorative gardens support the healing process by providing opportunities for sensory stimulation that in turn stimulates body movement and cognitive functioning. Gardens that include a hands-on component provide outlets for creative and constructive activities that contribute to patients' feelings of well-being and competence. Gardens also provide nonthreatening and comfortable locations for social interaction and can provide privacy and spaciousness, which is often lacking in patients' rooms.

Gardens as a restorative or healing component of a hospital first appeared during the Middle Ages, emerging as a part of the monastery and other healing places. The design of most monasteries included an enclosed courtyard space surrounded by an open but covered walkway, a setting that allowed for meditation as well as various degrees of sun, shade, warmth, and shelter. St. Bernard (1090–1153) described the benefits of a healing garden at Clairvaux, France, referring to the therapeutic effects of green plants, fragrance, privacy, and the songs of birds. Toward the end of the Middle Ages, the ability of monasteries to provide these healing environments declined as they were overwhelmed by a number of factors, including increasing numbers of people and plagues. As monasticism declined so did the inclusion of the healing courtyard in health care facilities.

A few hospitals throughout Europe, in cities such as Paris, Florence, Marsailles, and Vienna, did adopt the monastic courtyard setting. Les Invalides (1671) in Paris included in the design of the facility courtyards planted with trees in rows. All of these hospitals' gardens included many opportunities for exposure to nature, including views through windows and doors and walks through the gardens.

The development of scientific medicine during the 17th and 18th centuries at first encouraged the reemergence of outdoor hospital garden spaces for use by those in the hospital. Published recommendations for hospital garden design written in the late 18th century refer to the benefits of window views of the garden to invigorate patients. Nearby gardens were thought to encourage patients to take walks outdoors and to promote health. Suggested garden features included fragrant plants, winding pathways, benches, and wildlife, all of which could help encourage a patient's positive outlook.

Due in large part to the work of Florence Nightingale and the development of the germ theory of disease during the 19th century, the idea of the hospital as a place where patients returned to health emerged. Nightingale wrote about the importance of fresh air, hygiene, cross-ventilation, and the physical design of hospital spaces to promote these things. These discoveries in medicine led to the pavilion style in hospital design that dominated the 19th century, and a style that can be seen in both the Royal Naval Hospital in Plymouth, England, and the rebuilt Hôtel Dieu in Paris. Both consist of buildings with large windows, two and three stories tall, linked to each other by colonnades. Outdoor garden spaces are located between the buildings, with windows allowing for green views, fresh air, and sunlight. These outdoor spaces were regarded as an important component in the therapeutic recovery of patients. Nightingale also promoted individual nursing care for patients, and by the end of the 19th century, good nursing practices included taking patients outside to roof terraces and gardens.

Reforms in the treatment of patients with mental illness and in the design of psychiatric hospitals also took place in the 19th century. Physical punishment began to be replaced by psychological counseling in treatment methods. New psychiatric facilities included extensive grounds that were landscaped to shield patients from the public. The protective landscapes also served as settings for therapeutic programming in farming and gardening. Outdoor spaces were now being perceived as an integral component of the healing environment.

After World War I, some hospitals began to recognize that gardening activities could be used as a therapeutic treatment for individuals with physical disabilities. The horticultural therapy profession was established in the United States following World War II, and gardens were increasingly included in facilities for veterans, individuals with mental illness, and older adults. These gardens were included to serve specific therapeutic purposes. In 1918 architect Edward Stevens published a book on modern hospital design that also addresses the landscape architectural design of hospitals. Stevens's writings reveal the philosophy of hospital design during the first part of the 20th century as one in which the recovery and comfort of the patient was of primary importance in the planning, siting, and landscaping of the hospital. His book came out at a time when it was thought that tuberculosis patients benefited from recuperation in an outdoor environment.

Other types of patients were thought to benefit from recovery in the outdoors as well, including those suffering from physical and mental illnesses. Stevens's book describes and illustrates the outdoor areas of many modern hospital facilities, referring to extensive parklike grounds with trees and curving walks that would benefit not only the patients but also the staff. Stevens also considered it important for patients to be in contact with sunlight, which could be achieved through the inclusion of large windows, sleeping porches, and areas where the patient's bed could be rolled out into the sunlight. His book cites the Newton Hospital outside of Boston as an example of a nearly ideal healing environment. Stevens's architectural firm collaborated with a landscape architect over a number of years to create here a sort of hospital "estate," which combined small buildings, landscaped grounds, and various patient gardens. Due to its growth, the hospital has since changed the original design and no longer contains the series of gardens.

A shift took place in hospital design during the 1920s as land costs in many cities grew. The low-rise pavilion-style building turned into multistory cubes whose various levels were accessed by elevator, changes made possible by advances in high-rise construction. The new style reduced land costs, lowered heating costs, and saved time in walking from ward to ward. Developments in increasingly sophisticated approaches to medical treatment also contributed to the steady separation of healing and nature. As more and more medical specialties emerged and patients were being treated by different specialists for each body part, the attention to body and spirit in the healing process was lost. Accordingly, landscaping became peripheral and decorative, and the use of gardens as therapeutic environments steadily declined. Although there continued to be a variety of outdoor gardens options available to incorporate into hospital design, by the 1970s many hospitals looked more like high-rise office buildings than the earlier rambling pavilion-and-garden-style facilities.

By the 1990s landscaping again became an important component of hospital design. The increasingly competitive health care industry found itself needing to attract potential "customers," and as a result hospitals began to look more like hotels and resorts. These new hospitals often include lush landscaping both indoors and out, art in hallways and patient rooms, and private rooms with decorative schemes. They also include large atriums with plants, seating, pools, and fountains, as one might find in hotel lobbies or indoor shopping malls. One goal of these areas is to appear as familiar and accommodating places, easing the often terrifying experience of coming to the hospital. While outdoor courtyard spaces or roof terraces are sometimes included in this new style of hospital, they are usually treated as areas to view from a window rather than as a destination.

Many argue that the role of the modern hospital has changed, which also explains the lack of planned outdoor healing gardens. Tremendous economic pressures on the health care system have led to greatly shortened patient stays following illness, surgery, or other treatments. As a result, the treatment takes place in the hospital, while recovery often happens elsewhere.

During the last two decades, much research has been done on the relationship between people and plants. Some of these studies have looked at the role of gardens and other outdoor settings in the healing of people. Roger Ulrich, in *Healing Gardens* (1999), found that gallbladder surgery patients in an urban hospital who had windows that looked out over a natural setting recovered faster, required less pain medication, and made fewer demands on nursing staff than those whose windows looked out on a brick wall. Ulrich theorizes that viewing natural landscapes reduced stress and promoted a sense of well being that contributed to health and recovery.

It has also been shown that particular scents stimulate bodily organs to release neurochemicals that help eliminate pain, induce sleep, or create a sense of well-being. Research has also shown a link between the scent-sensitive hypothalamus and the immune system, drawing a connection between scent and the body's ability to fend off disease. Another study comparing rates of delirium in intensive care units found that patients in the unit without windows had a higher rate of delirium on the whole than those in the unit with windows. Certainly, more research is needed in this area, but studies conducted so far show a clear and strong relationship between access to nature and healing.

As particular categories of health care settings grow in numbers, including facilities for people with Alzheimer's disease, Ronald McDonald Houses, and cancer and AIDS hospices, many have once again recognized the importance of the healing garden. These types of facilities emphasize care not cure, and in doing so they stress homelike comfort, familiarity, and spiritual well-being. Gardens have become an important component in providing this atmosphere. Recently, the Joint Commission on Accreditation of Healthcare Organizations in the United States now requires that long-term care and pediatrics patients be given access to the outdoor landscape through the use of the hospital grounds and nearby green areas.

Many people have recently become more interested in alternative medicines and healing techniques. Clare Cooper Marcus and Marni Barnes in their book *Gardens in Healthcare Facilities* (1995) suggest that this rising interest is due to widespread dissatisfaction with conventional medicinal practices. They point out that the 1990s saw an increase in people's interest in taking care of their own health, and many have recognized the calming effect that nature can have on feelings of stress. Alternative medicines and therapies have adopted the garden and nature as an intricate part in the healing experience.

Hospitals are beginning to once again look at the value of the landscapes within and surrounding their facilities as restorative gardens. A restorative hospital garden is a healing environment beyond, but still part of, a hospital facility. By its very nature it serves many purposes, all emphasizing relaxation, recuperation, stress relief, invigoration, and recovery. A well-planned hospital garden allows for interaction in several ways, both passive and active. The garden should be the subject of the view out of many windows, allowing patients who cannot get to the garden to still benefit from its adjacency. The garden should also take the needs of visitors and staff into consideration, allowing for quiet contemplation and privacy as well as active participation and social interaction. Access to gardens and their views throughout all phases of hospitalization and recovery has been proven to enhance healing, recovery, and recuperation. Hospitals administrators are beginning to understand that which has been known since the Middle Ages, and the healing effects of nature are being reintroduced into health care settings, garden by garden.

Further Reading

Bennett, Paul, "Golden Opportunities," *Landscape Architecture* 88, no. 3 (1998)

Burrell, C. Colston, "Plants with Power," *Landscape Architecture* 90, no.1 (2000)

Gerlach-Spriggs, Nancy, Richard Enoch Kaufman, and Sam Bass Warner, *Restorative Gardens: The Healing Landscape,* New Haven, Connecticut: Yale University Press, 1998

Marcus, Clare Cooper, and Carolyn Francis, editors, *People Places: Design Guidelines for Urban Open Space,* New York: Van Nostrand Reinhold, 1990; 2nd edition, 1998

Marcus, Clare Cooper, and Marni Barnes, *Gardens in Healthcare Facilities: Uses, Therapeutic Benefits, and Design Recommendations,* Martinez, California: Center for Health Design, 1995

Marcus, Clare Cooper, and Marni Barnes, editors, *Healing Gardens: Therapeutic Benefits and Design Recommendations,* New York: Wiley, 1999

Stevens, Edward Fletcher, *The American Hospital of the Twentieth Century: A Treatise on the Development of Medical Institutions, both in Europe and in America since the Beginning of the Present Century,* New York: Architectural Record, 1918; 2nd revised edition, 1928

Thompson, J. William, "A Question of Healing," *Landscape Architecture* 88, no. 4 (1998)

Thompson, J. William, "Healing Words," *Landscape Architecure* 90, no. 1 (2000)

ELIZABETH R. MESSER DIEHL

Hothouse Plant

Hothouse plants are tender plants that require the artificial warmth of a hothouse or stove to survive the winter season in temperate climates. Most are exotic plants that are native to tropical and subtropical regions of the globe and are not frost hardy.

Today horticulturists interchange the terms *hothouse* and *greenhouse* as well as the types of plants that are grown in each, but this nomenclature was more precise during the 18th and 19th centuries. A hothouse, also called a stove, was a plant house in which heat was supplemented, whereas a greenhouse was warmed by the sun, which entered through large, south-facing windows. Greenhouses were built to overwinter temperate climate plants such as oranges and myrtles, which go dormant during the winter season but cannot withstand freezing temperatures. Inside the greenhouse they were not expected to grow but simply to remain alive or "green." Potted plants were staged on a tiered frame where they gradually rose above each other in regular rows, like a pyramid. When the weather turned warm, they were taken outside into the garden or orangerie.

Tender succulent plants, such as aloes and sedums, *Cereus, Cotyledon, Euphorbia, Mesembryanthemum,* and *Pedilanthus tithymaloides,* are hothouse plants from the Cape of Good Hope, Jamaica, and Barbados, that were grown in a hothouse called the dry stove because they required a dry winter season. Philip Miller gave detailed directions for dry stove construction in the 1752 edition of his *Gardener's Dictionary.*

Two dry stove designs were most common: an upright front glass that was combined with a sloping ceiling glass, or a front glass that sloped from floor to ceiling at an angle of 45 degrees. Both were heated by air warmed from coal or wood-burning furnaces at one end of the house, which was then transported through flues under the pavement of the floor or along the back of the house. In the center of the dry stove, about 2.5 feet (0.76 m) from its front and back, a scaffold was erected to display the plants. Movable shelves were raised or lowered according to the plant heights so that a pyramid of plants was formed, similar to that in the greenhouse.

To bring pineapples into fruit, a second kind of hothouse, the bark stove, came into use in Holland about 1720. In it a large hotbed, nearly the length of the house and about 6 to 7 feet (1.8 to 2.7 m) wide and 3 to 5 feet (0.9 to 1.5 m) deep, replaced the staging scaffold of the dry stove. The hotbed consisted of a layer of horse manure that was covered with tanner's bark (i.e., oak bark that was chopped or ground into a powder for tanning). During its fermentation a gradual heat was produced. Pots of pineapples were then plunged into the bark, where the bottom heat initiated root growth. By 1730 bark stoves for the cultivation of pineapples were found in almost every garden.

Other exotic plants that require high heat were also grown in bark stoves. Miller recommended that "most sorts of trees, shrubs, and herbaceous plants which are natives of the hottest parts of the East and West Indies should be plunged into the bark bed." Among them he included the cashew nut, coconut, custard apple, mamea apple, Barbados cherry, papaya, ginger, Barbados flower fence (*Caesalpinia pulcherrima*), *Plumeria, Thevetia,* and *Guaiacum officinale.*

In the 19th century, partly as the result of the Wardian Case, a rush of new tender species entered England. Collections of one kind of plant, such as palms, orchids, or exotic ferns, often filled an entire hothouse. John Claudius Loudon classified over 300 flowering hothouse or bark stove plants according to their habit (woody, climbing, or bulbous), their life cycle (annual or perennial), and their habitat (aquatic or reedy). Each group was subdivided by its month of bloom.

Nineteenth century technologies, such as cast iron manufacture, hot water heat, and the design of the hemispherical roof by Sir G. Mackenzie in 1815 to increase sunlight penetration, enabled hothouses to evolve into elegant crystal palaces. Strong and slender cast iron frames could support large glass panes that became available in Great Britain after the repeal of the glass tax in 1845. Hot water from boilers produced a more uniform heat that circulated faster through pipes than did the smoky hot air from stoves or furnaces, which traveled through flues.

Hothouse environments may have begun to mimic the tropics, but the rare and beautiful plants within them were unfortunately tightly packed together "like merchandise in a warehouse." N.N. Humphrey, in the 1862 *Journal of Horticulture,* pleaded for a picturesque arrangement of hothouse plants in order to create the illusion of a tropical scene rather than a walk under glass. When hothouse plants were given adequate space to display their wildest habits amid flowing streams and fragments of rock and boulders, Humphrey claimed, an imitation of an Indian or Brazilian forest occurred. In his hothouse, climbing passionflowers were interspersed with the heads of large foliated bananas and palms; the undergrowth beneath them was intermingled with gigantic ferns.

By the fourth quarter of the 19th century, gardeners knew that all plants indigenous to hot countries did not grow in the same habitat and at the same temperature and moisture level. Hothouse plants, therefore, required different environments for their successful cultivation. It was recommended to have two hothouses kept at different temperatures, but if only one was possible, the grower should locate the temperature differentials within the hothouse at various distances from the boiler. Then plants such as poinsettia and Amazon lily (*Eucharis amazonica*), which preferred night temperatures near 70 degrees Fahrenheit (21.1 degrees C), could be grown with South American gesneriad hybrids, such as *Gloxinias* and *Achimenes,* which preferred night temperatures around 65 degrees Fahrenheit (18.3 degrees C), as well as with the various begonias that ranged in their temperature requirements from 55 to 60 degrees Fahrenheit (12.7–15.5 degrees C). Bulbous flowering and foliage plants, such as amaryllis and caladium, that required dormancy could be moved to different temperatures at different seasons.

The precise distinction between *stove, hothouse, greenhouse,* and *conservatory* had become vague by the end of the 19th century. A plant house heated to 80 or 90 degrees Fahrenheit (26.6–32.2 degrees C) for orchids may have been called a stove or hothouse, but when the orchids were replaced with pelargoniums and the temperature lowered to 40 or 50 degrees Fahrenheit (4.4–10 degrees C), it became a greenhouse. If camellias were planted into the ground, it was called a conservatory. In the United States Liberty Hyde Bailey favored the word *greenhouse* for any glass building in which plants are grown, and all the plants within it are generally called greenhouse plants.

Further Reading

Bailey, Liberty H., editor, *Cyclopedia of American Horticulture,* 4 vols., Toronto, Ontario: Virtue, and New York: Macmillan, 1900–1902; revised edition, as *The Standard Cyclopedia of Horticulture,* 6 vols., New York: Macmillan, 1914–17

Hibberd, Shirley, *The Amateur's Greenhouse and Conservatory,* London, 1873

Loudon, John Claudius, *An Encyclopaedia of Gardening,* 2 vols., London, 1822; new edition, 1835; reprint, New York: Garland, 1982

Miller, Philip, *The Gardeners and Florists Dictionary,* 2 vols., London, 1724; 8th edition, as *The Gardener's Dictionary,* London, 1768

Thompson, Robert, *The Gardener's Assistant: Practical and Scientific,* London and Glasgow, 1859; new edition, revised by William Watson, London, 1902

Woods, May, and Arete Swartz Warren, *Glass Houses: A History of Greenhouses, Orangeries, and Conservatories,* London: Aurum, 1988

RICHARD R. IVERSEN

Howard, Ebenezer 1850–1928

English City Planner

Ebenezer Howard devoted the greater part of his creative energies to city reform. His book *Tomorrow: A Peaceful Path to Real Reform* was published in 1898, with a slightly revised second edition appearing in 1902 as *Garden Cities of Tomorrow.* In his writing he outlined the principles that led to the building of his two Garden Cities, Letchworth (1903) and Welwyn Garden City (1919). He was knighted in 1927 in recognition of his services in furthering the cause of rational city planning in England and throughout the world.

Howard was born in the city of London, the son of a store owner. His formal education completed at age 15, Howard spent some years working in London before immigrating to the United States at the age of 21. Failing as a Nebraska homesteader, he moved to Chicago in 1872, the year following that city's devastating fire, to work as a news and court stenographer. These were impressionable years; there was the debate to rebuild the city and its economy, and there were the financial scandals associated with the planning of Riverside (1868), an innovative planned suburb by Frederick Law Olmsted and Calvert Vaux, the designers of New York City's Central Park (1858). Howard returned to England in 1876, working the rest of his life as a court stenographer. This provided him with income and also left him time for his principal concern, urban social reform and the promulgation of his invention, the Garden City.

Speculation about the need for new towns has been a recurrent aspect of British town planning, a debate that intensified with the industrial revolution. The industrial city of the 19th century was a response to the new economy of mass production, involving a rapid shift from dispersed cottage industries to centralized, large-scale factory production in urban centers. The results were as rapid as they were devastating on the quality of life. Crowded and unsanitary living conditions caused epidemic disease, while thousands of others succumbed to industrial injuries. Loss of manpower to the cities caused severe economic problems in rural areas. The physical impact was equally severe, the insatiable demand for raw materials creating extraction industries that scarred the landscape that enfolded William Blake's "dark Satanic Mills": the squalid, unplanned manufacturing and mining towns. Two strategies to reform were evident. The first sought to modernize and sanitize the existing city. The second advocated starting anew, believing, with Charles Mulford Robinson, that a "mended article is never as good as one well made at first." Howard's life work was to pursue the second option in his new towns or Garden Cities. He followed a thin trail of utopians and pragmatic city builders.

Decisively influential among the utopians was Edward Bellamy's novel *Looking Backward* (1889) and William Morris's socialist dream in *News from Nowhere* (1890). Earlier was James Silk Buckingham's proposal for a new town, *Victoria,* published in *National Evils and Practical Remedies* (1849), the same year as Minter Morgan's *Christian Commonwealth,* which advocated self-supporting housing trusts and other ideas. Added to these was a mix of artistic and economic theories from John Ruskin to Henry George's single-tax concept.

Among industrial city builders were Samuel Greg and Samuel Oldknow, who established textile towns at Styal (1784) and Mellor (1787). Best known is New Lanark, Scotland, founded by David Dale (1784) and taken over by Robert Owen (1799). They established a tradition of industrial paternalism. All were nonconformists who believed the condition of their workforce was their Christian and paternal concern, holding the unorthodox belief that fostering a happy workforce could make profits. Titus Salt, who built Saltaire, near Bradford (1849–53), was inspired as much by this tradition as by *Sibyl,* a novel by Benjamin Disraeli that describes a model factory town. Salt was a Congregationalist, as was W.H. Lever, the soap manufacturer, who built Port Sunlight (1887). The Cadburys built Bournville (from 1879) and were Quakers, like the Rowntrees, who laid out New Earswick (1902). Few as they were, these new cities sought to integrate profit with social happiness, within a harmonious physical environment set in open country. All were attempts to reverse the concentration of manufacturing within or adjacent to the dysfunctional city.

Howard had a profound grasp of the problems as well as a pragmatic, even impetuous, approach in seeking remedies. Starting afresh with the Garden City was the direction advocated by Howard in *Garden Cities of Tomorrow.* A Garden City, according to Sir F.J. Osborn, can be defined as a town "designed for healthy living and industry; of a size that makes possible a full measure of social life, but not larger; surrounded by a rural belt; the whole of the land being in public ownership or held in trust for the community." Self-sufficiency, employment opportunity, and good living conditions, Howard argued, would create a reverse migration from city to Garden City.

According to Howard a garden city should have a regional context and possess a number of characteristics. First, size would be limited to a total land area of 6,000 acres (2,429 ha), with an ultimate population of 30,000. There would be a central urban core of 1,000 acres (405 ha) and an outlying 5,000-acre (2,024-ha) agricultural zone, the latter free of building to maximize agricultural production and to act as a protective armature from the outside world. Second, the site would have the benefit of railway or canal connections. Third, land would be in public trust, leased to occupiers, to prevent speculation and to retain betterment for the community. Fourth, all development would be subject to municipal-planning approval. Aesthetics would be limited to overall form; architectural individuality was to be encouraged. Fifth, planning would be based on neighborhoods, each with a population of 5,000, and planned around a school. Sixth, homes would occupy ample sites without regard for the means of the occupants. Each neighborhood would focus on a spacious green. Next, there would be a central green core containing public gardens, with adjacent shopping and civic and cultural buildings. Eighth, there would be provision for employment in manufacturing. Industry would be zoned away from residential areas and be smoke free, taking advantage of electric power. Ninth, town and country would be married to mutual advantage. Finally, given the finite population, there would be overspill into adjacent Garden Cities, forming satellites about a larger "Central City" of 58,000, producing a total population of 250,000.

Howard was a policy maker of genius but no designer, so at Letchworth the practical planning and architectural design was awarded in 1904, after a competition, to the brilliant architectural-planning partnership of Barry Parker and Raymond Unwin; both were utopians. Unwin was a socialist, influenced by Ruskin and a friend of William Morris. Both had put Howard's ideas to work earlier at New Earswick. The architecture at Letchworth was in the Arts and Crafts tradition. Later, at Welwyn, Howard was less well served by the town architect Louis de Soissons and others, much of it in a dull neo-Georgian style.

The British social revolution following World War II brought a socialist government with a sweeping program of reforms. One important component was the New Towns Act of 1946. Fourteen new towns were begun between 1946 and 1950, eight to relieve population pressure on London. Many more followed. The early new towns observed many of Howard's planning principals, although postwar planners had scant imagination in adapting them to the automobile age. Elsewhere, Howard's principles can be found in Israel, Sweden, and Canada. In the United States the pioneering but incomplete Radburn, New Jersey (1929), and the depression-era Greenbelt Towns (1933–38: Greenhills, Ohio; Greenbelt, Maryland; Greenbrook, New Jersey; Greendale, Wisconsin) were brilliant adaptations of Howard's ideas not only to a different society but to a world shortly to become dominated by the automobile. His influence endures still in Reston, Virginia (1962), and Columbia, Maryland (1963), and more recently in Seaside and Celebration, Florida (1981). None, however, attained the total integration of social form and landscape achieved at Letchworth.

Howard's vigorous pragmatism was allied with a gift for persuading practical businessmen that his ideas were not only socially desirable but also financially sound. His classic polemic, *Garden Cities of Tomorrow,* and his Garden Cities forever changed town planning, and today his inspiration enjoys something of a revival in the town-planning aesthetic known as the New Urbanism.

Biography

Born in London, 1850. Worked as clerk in City of London; emigrated to United States, 1871; failed as Nebraska homesteader and moved to Chicago, 1872; returned to London and took up lifetime employment as court stenographer, 1876; began writing on Garden City movement; published *To-morrow: A Peaceful Path to Real Reform,* 1898; was responsible for developing two of first garden cities in England: Letchworth, 1903, and Welwyn Garden City, 1919, both in Hertfordshire; knighted, 1927. Died in Welwyn Garden City, Hertfordshire, England, 1928.

Selected Designs

1903 Garden city of Letchworth, Hertfordshire, England
1919 Welwyn Garden City, Hertfordshire, England

Selected Publications

To-morrow: A Peaceful Path to Real Reform, 1898; 2nd edition, as *Garden Cities of To-morrow,* 1902

Further Reading

Creese, Walter L., *The Search for Environment: The Garden City, Before and After,* New Haven, Connecticut: Yale University Press, 1966; expanded edition, Baltimore, Maryland: Johns Hopkins University Press, 1992

Katz, Peter, *The New Urbanism: Toward an Architecture of Community,* New York: McGraw Hill, 1994

Kostof, Spiro, *The City Shaped: Urban Patterns and Meanings through History,* Boston: Little Brown, and London: Thames and Hudson, 1991

Osborn, Frederic James, and Arnold Whittick, *The New Towns: The Answer to Megalopolis,* London: Hill and New York: McGraw Hill, 1963; 3rd edition, as *New Towns: Their Origins, Achievements, and Progress,* London: Hill, 1977

Stein, Clarence Samuel, *Toward New Towns for America,* Liverpool: University Press of Liverpool, 1951; 3rd edition, Cambridge, Massachusetts: MIT Press, 1966

Taylor, Ray, Margaret Cox, and Ian Dickins, editors, *Britain's Planning Heritage,* London: Croom Helm, 1975

JOHN MARTIN

Huaxtepec Park

Oaxtepec, Morelos, Mexico

Location: approximately 15 miles (25 km) east of Cuernavaca and 60 miles (96.5 km) south of Mexico City

On 15 May 1522 Hernán Cortés wrote to Charles V describing his exploits in Mexico. In the course of conquering the empire of the Aztecs of Tenochtitlán (later Mexico City) in the Basin of Mexico, Cortés had traveled through the more tropical environment of the Valley of Morelos, where, at a small regional capital called Huaxtepec, "We were all quartered in a chief's country house amid the most beautiful and refreshing gardens ever seen." Cortés's lieutenant, Bernal Díaz del Castillo, recalled Huaxtepec as "an orchard within the town, which was so beautiful and contained such fine buildings that it was the best worth beholding of anything we had seen in New Spain. . . . The garden . . . is the best that I have ever seen in all my life, and so said . . . our Cortés."

Considering that the Spanish conquistadores included widely traveled men who had no doubt seen the Moorish gardens in Spain, their praise for Huaxtepec carries weight. The Spaniards found gardens everywhere in Mexico because gardening was one of the most popular pastimes of the nobility there. Lords vied for status in informal (but serious) contests of aesthetic and horticultural skill, as they designed gardens representing paradise, incorporating sculptured monuments to their own dynastic power as well as unusual plants whose cultivation was forbidden to commoners by sumptuary laws. In the 1460s Huaxtepec (a Nahuatl term that combines the words for a plant name and a hill and is pronounced "washTAYpeck") was developed by the Aztec emperor Motecuzoma Ilhuicamina, or Motecuzoma I (r. 1540–69), lord of Tenochtitlán, to counter Texcotzingo, the garden of his royal cousin and rival, King Nezahualcoyotl of Texcoco. Texcotzingo, in turn, had been established as a counterpoint to Tenochtitlán's dynastic gardens at Chapultepec.

Cortés described the Huaxtepec gardens as being "two leagues round about and through the middle of them runs a pleasant stream. There are summer houses spaced out at distances of two crossbowshots, and very bright flower beds, a great many trees with various fruits, and many herbs and sweet-smelling flowers." Díaz added that the gardens also had medicinal plants, fruits, and vegetables. The stream had been dammed to form a lake, part of which was for raising fish, and there were also baths, the *temascal* sweat baths so necessary to health and hygiene among the Aztecs. Thus the Huaxtepec gardens formed a pleasure park as well as horticultural gardens.

The Aztecs also had a strong interest in botanical gardens, the systematic gathering together of a wide variety of plants representative of many regions, regardless of their perceived value as decoration, food, or medicine. While contemporaneous European gardens included the pleasure park and horticultural/medicinal types, botanical gardens were not established until the 1540s and 1550s in Italy, apparently inspired by the accounts of Mexican gardens such as Huaxtepec. In a sense Mexican botanical gardens expressed dynastic power because they offered plants found in all the areas forced into tributary status; these represented native habitats ranging from coastal tropical jungles to alpine glaciers.

The 16th-century chronicler Fray Diego Durán described how Huaxtepec and other gardens were stocked and how this process was part of the complex tribute empire of the Aztecs. Motecuzoma I's decision to establish his garden at Huaxtepec, a tributary province 60 miles (approximately 96.5 kilometers) south of his capital, Tenochtitlán, took advantage of the tropical climate there. After ordering various alterations to the site, Motecuzoma sent tribute demands for rare plants to another province, Cuetlaxtla, on the Gulf coast. The plants included cacao (*Theobroma cacao*), "ear flower" (*Cymbopetalum penduliforum*), "heart flower" (*Talauma mexicana*), "flower of the cacao" (*Quararibea funebris*), "carrying crate flower" (*Philodendron pseudoradiatum*), and "raven flower" (*Plumeria rubra*). The plants were sent to Tenochtitlán and after Motecuzoma's approval taken to Huaxtepec and planted around the springs.

Durán recounted the ceremony following the planting:

> After the Cuetlaxtla gardeners had taken the plants to Huaxtepec and had sown them there, these men fasted for eight days and slashed the upper parts of their ears as sacrifice, and smeared the blood upon the leaves. . . . They performed a sacrifice in honor of the god of flowers, offering him quail and scattering the birds' blood upon the plants and upon the earth where they had been sown. They did this because they believed that with that rite no plant would be lost and that soon all would burst forth with flower and fruit. And thus it was that the devil . . . let not one plant be lost. On the contrary, in the third year they gave abundant flowers and the gardeners from Cuetlaxtla were amazed. They said that in their country no flowers bloomed as quickly as here and that Huaxtepec was a more fertile and better land for the plants than their own.

After the conquest of Mexico in 1521, Cortés appropriated many of the personal gardens of the Aztec lords, and in 1526 he sought control of Huaxtepec. The gardens were visited in the 1570s by Francisco Hernandez, the Spanish authority on medicinal plants sent by Philip II to study the resources of Mexico. The Spaniards recognized Huaxtepec's importance as a source of medicines to supply their hospitals. Today, the gardens still provide a retreat and are administered by the Mexican government as a national park and vacation spot for Mexico's social security administration.

See also Chapultepec Park

Synopsis

1460s Landscape alterations to Huaxtepec, during the reign of Motecuzoma I (1440–69)
1521 Conquest of Mexico by Spain
1526 Court case by Hernán Cortés to gain control over Huaxtepec
1570s Visited by Francisco Hernandez

Further Reading

Cortés, Hernán, *Cartas de relación* (1519–26), Mexico City: Editorial Porrúa, 1960; as *Letters from Mexico,* edited and translated by Anthony R. Pagden, New Haven, Connecticut: Yale University Press, 1986

Díaz del Castillo, Bernal, *Historia verdadera de la conquista de la Nueva-España* (1560s), Madrid, 1632; as *The Discovery and Conquest of Mexico: 1517–1521,* edited by Genaro García, translated by A.P. Maudslay, New York: Farrar Straus, 1956

Durán, Fray Diego, *Historia de las Indias de Nueva-España y Islas de Tierra Firme* (1581), 2 vols., Mexico City, 1867–80; as *The History of the Indies of New Spain,* edited and translated by Doris Heyden, Norman: University of Oklahoma Press, 1994

Evans, Susan Toby, "Aztec Royal Pleasure Parks: Conspicuous Consumption and Elite Status Rivalry," *Studies in the History of Gardens and Designed Landscapes* 20 (2000)

Maldonado Jiménez, Druzo, *Cuauhnáhuac y Huaxtepec: Tlalhuicas y Xochimilcas en el Morelos Prehispánico,* Cuernavaca, Mexico: Universidad Nacional Autónoma de México Centro Regional de Investigaciones Multidisciplinarias, 1990

Rocha Herrera, Octavio, and Susan Toby Evans, "Huaxtepec," in *Archeology of Ancient Mexico and Central America: An Encyclopedia,* edited by Susan Toby Evans and David L. Webster, New York: Garland, 2001

SUSAN TOBY EVANS

Hungary

The Hungary of today lies in the heart of the Carpathian Basin in central Europe. The climate of the whole area is continental; in the center summers are hot and dry and winters are cold with rain. The climate of the range of the Carpathians is colder with more rainfall. Cold weather in the mountains and summer drought in the plains mean a challenge to plant cultivation, but in general the area is favorable to horticulture. Originally, the whole basin was covered with woods.

The area was populated already in prehistoric times, but no trace of activities exists concerning the changing of the landscape. The Romans, on the other hand, changed the landscape in the ruled territories significantly. The borders of the Roman Empire ran along the Danube River, the region of Transdanubia belonged to the Roman province of Pannonia. The Romans built villas in the hills above Lake Balaton, known to them as Pelso, which was already a popular resort area at that time. It is likely that these villas contained not only kitchen gardens and orchards but also ornamental gardens. Romans also naturalized the cultivation of grapes in the region in the Carpathian Basin and cleared large areas for agriculture.

In the first half of the fifth century A.D., Romans lost this province, and until the Hungarian conquest the Carpathian Basin was ruled by different nations. The Magyars (known as Hungarians today) arrived in 895 from central Asia after centuries of migration and in a short time occupied the whole area of the Carpathian Basin. Cultivation of plants spread slowly among the nomad Magyars, who were animal keepers, and involved more and more clearing of land over the centuries. Western monks who led missions to the Magyars already during the first millennium brought their methodical horticultural knowledge here. Almost nothing is known about the layout and plants of the gardens of medieval monasteries in the country, but they probably corresponded to the ones elsewhere in Europe.

Construction of cities and fortified places began in the 12th century and continued in the 13th century. The sovereign and the members of the aristocracy created gardens next to their residences and town houses, mostly outside the city walls. These gardens had a utilitarian function at first, but by the reign of Sigismund of Luxemburg (1387–1437), they were transformed to ornamental gardens. The king himself had several gardens in Buda, Visegrád, and Pest.

Renaissance garden art found its way to Hungary relatively early, in the second half of the 15th century, although its influence did not extend beyond the royal court and the humanist circle connected with it. King Matthias Corvinus (r. 1458–90) had contacts with the Italian Renaissance through his wife, Princess Beatrix of Naples, and created a hanging garden in his palace of Buda similar to the *giardino pensile* of the princely palace of Urbino. The designer of this garden was probably Chimenti Camicia (ca. 1431–after 1505), who probably also played a role in the creation of the king's other gardens. These included a larger ornamental garden outside the walls of the Buda castle, a deer park surrounded by a wall in the neighboring hills, and flower gardens and a large ornamental orchard next to the summer residence in Visegrád.

The Hungarian army suffered defeat by the Turks in 1526 in a battle that fundamentally affected the

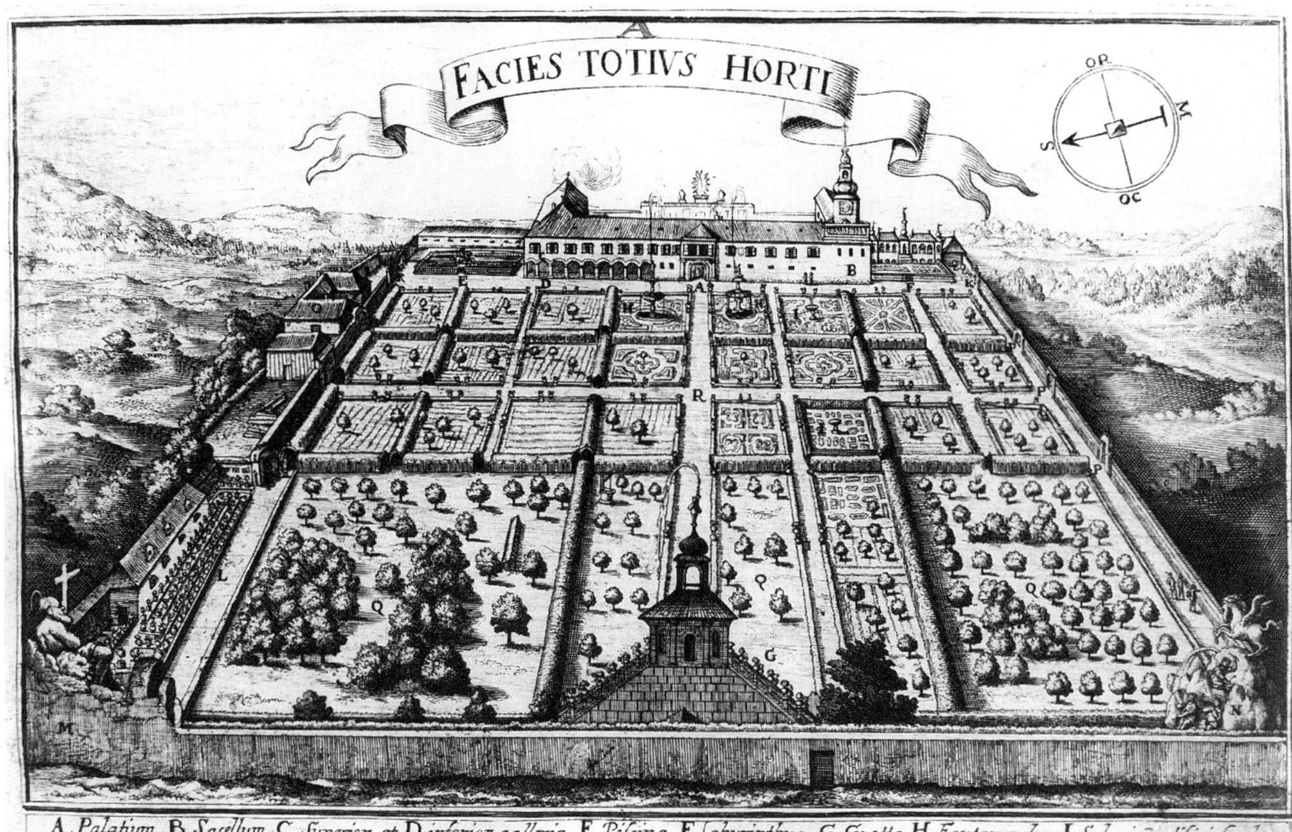

The Primate's Garden, which was the summer residence of György Lippay, Archbishop of Esztergom, Pozsony (now Bratislava, Slovakia)
Courtesy of Department of Manuscripts and Rare Books, Library of the Hungarian Academy of Sciences

subsequent history of Hungary. The Ottoman Empire occupied the central region of the country and ruled it for the next century and a half. The country was broken up into three parts. The Turks controlled the southern and central territories, the northwestern part of the country remained the kingdom of Hungary, while in the east the region of Transylvania and the adjacent eastern counties formed an independent, although vassalic to the Turks, state.

Horticulture was different in the three territories. Sources do not show any trace of ornamental gardening in the part of the country ruled by the Turks, but utilitarian gardening mostly remained. In Royal Hungary and in Transylvania the Turkish threat and the pauperization of the country did not allow the creation of luxury gardens; the financial resources of the nobility were spent on the defense of the remaining territories. The gardens of the 16th and 17th centuries were usually decorated utilitarian gardens, generally surrounded by board fence. Quite often the flower garden was not separated from the kitchen garden and the orchard but formed a part of it. Besides the few flowers planted purely for aesthetic reasons, mainly herbs were cultivated. In such modest ensembles garden structures such as bowers and garden pavilions had special significance. Appreciated for shade, bowers were also used to cultivate grapes or were made from different fruit trees. These gardens were often called bower gardens, the bowers designating the main axes of the garden. The carpentered garden pavilions, on the other hand, were specifically designed for joy and entertainment and were used in flower gardens as well as in kitchen gardens or in orchards. They were often connected to the bowers, standing either at their end or at the point of intersection. The pavilions were frequently built onto a lime tree or between a few lime trees and in many cases had several stories.

In the second half of the 16th century, the most significant gardens of the country belonged to the leading families of the western Hungarian humanist circle, the Batthyánys and the Nádasdys. Besides the prominently developed utilitarian horticulture they practiced, these families also turned their attention to ornamental gardening and brought many notable botanists into their courts. Carolus Clusius (1526–1609) visited the Batthyány estates several times and studied and described plants from Hungary. He also designed the ornamental garden of Szalónak (today Stadtschlaining, Austria), which probably was a kind of plant collection that served scientific purposes as well.

Among the ornamental gardens of the 17th century, the garden of the Hungarian lord chief justice, Count Ferenc Nádasdy (1625–71), must have had a grandiose layout, since he was famous for his generosity and desire for splendor; he also had plants and gardeners brought in from the Netherlands in 1660. Since Buda was occupied by the Turks, the capital of the country was Pozsony (today Bratislava, Slovakia), where several noteworthy gardens were constructed between 1630 and 1670. Little is known about the gardens of the Count Pálffys and of Palatine Wesselényi (1605–67); the garden of the summer residence of Primate György Lippay, Archbishop of Esztergom (1600–1666), the so-called Primate's Garden, is the only well-documented garden in Pozsony from that era.

The Primate's Garden was the most significant and famous garden work of the 17th century in Hungary. Travelers noted in particular in their descriptions the water display. The garden was subdivided into regular squares by walks and bowers. The units closer to the main entrance of the palace contained parterres, each of a different pattern, the more distant ones filled with kitchen garden beds and orchards. A large orangery, called the Hortus Italicus, in the garden held the more delicate plants. A grotto crowned with a look-out terrace closed the main axis of the garden. In the back corners of the garden stood two artificial hills; one was the Parnassus with Pegasus on top, the other a hermitage with the figure of St. Hyeronimus on it. Both hills concealed grottoes inside. These hills were inspired by the ones in Pratolino, Italy. Apart from some baroque elements, the Primate's Garden was a typical late Renaissance ensemble.

The Primate's Garden was also connected with the creation of horticultural literature in Hungarian. János Lippay (1606–66), the primate's brother, published a book titled *Posoni Kert* (The Garden of Pozsony). The first part concerned flower gardening in Nagyszombat (published in 1664 in Nagyszombat, today Trnava, Slovakia), while the other two parts discussed kitchen gardening and orchards (published in 1664 and 1667 in Vienna). A horticultural treatise, the work draws upon the Primate's Garden for its drawings and plant list.

Graphic representations of gardens from the last decades of the 17th century also show *parterres de broderie*, but the regular square units still recall the Renaissance tradition. After the Turks were chased from the country, French gardening came into fashion. The earliest works showing this influence were created in and around Pozsony in the first decades of the 18th century. Little is known about the ensembles of this period; only the new layout of the Primate's Garden and the garden in Királyfa (today Král'ová pri Senci, Slovakia) were described in detail by contemporaries. In the second quarter of the century, the most significant designer in the country was Anton Zinner, a pupil of Dominique Girard, who laid out the gardens in Féltorony (today Halbturn, Austria) and Pozsony for the sovereign, and in Süttör (today Fertõd) and Kismarton (today Eisenstadt, Austria) for the widow of Prince Esterházy.

In general, Hungarian baroque gardens can be characterized by a rather modest layout. Even the exactingly arranged gardens of the aristocracy often lacked size and costly water displays. Although the proportion of nobility in the population was one of the highest in Europe, most of them had no land. Many landowners also lived in poverty. Therefore, as in previous centuries, regularly arranged and somewhat decorated utilitarian gardens replaced the ornamental ones. The only luxury most nobility could afford was the cultivation of delicate plants, especially oranges. The citizens' gardens were similarly modest.

By the mid-18th century the country's economic growth allowed the creation of more ornamental gardens. The most important gardens were still laid out in and around Pozsony as part of the aristocrats' urban residences. Naturally, the estates of the wealthy landowners also included manors and ornamental gardens; among the most significant were Kismarton (today Eisenstadt, Austria), Cseklész (today Bernolákovo, Slovakia), and Gödöllô, Nagycenk, Darufalva (today Drassburg, Austria).

Baroque garden art in Hungary reached its peak in Eszterháza (today Fertõd) (see Plate 16). When Prince Miklós Esterházy "the Sumptous" (1714–90) began to enlarge the old hunting lodge in the 1760s, the name of the settlement was Süttör, but the prince renamed it after his family name. Contemporaries regarded the uniquely equipped ensemble as the "Hungarian Versailles," although it was no match for Louis XIV's residence. Eszterháza was a perfect baroque ensemble. The parterres, bosquets, and park followed each other successively; next to the building were the intimate chamber gardens. The utilitarian gardens were arranged behind the lateral walls of the ornamental garden. Opera house, theater, grotto, coffeehouse, Chinese dance hall, and a number of pavilions and subsidiary buildings completed the ensemble. The composer Joseph Haydn lived here in the service of the prince.

From the 1760s onward descriptions mention the *parterre de gazon* in many gardens. In this period of the rococo, Chinese taste was fashionable and reigned in Hungarian gardens. Few gardens were without a Chinese pavilion or at least Chinese mural decoration or objects.

Concurrent with the taste for the exotic, elements of landscape gardening began to spread throughout the country. The period of the transitional landscape garden lasted from 1760 until 1790. Almost all of the formal gardens were reshaped into landscape gardens; the few exceptions were simplified or neglected. The fact that the climate of the central part of the country is not favorable for the English style—due to the summer drought the grass turns to a yellowish color by early summer—did not prevent the owners from following the new fashion.

English romantic gardens started to spread in the 1770s. The most important among them was the garden of Csákvár, which was continuously improved in the last decades of the century; a whole series of garden structures was set up there in neoclassical, Gothic, Chinese, Turkish, Egyptian, Native American, and other styles. Following the European fashion, artificial ruins, hermitages, and weeping willows were also popular elements in the Hungarian gardens. Other significant gardens of the sentimental movement include Tata, Körmend, Hotkóc (today Hodkovce, Slovakia) and the Sanssouci in Illésfalva (today Iliasovce, Slovakia).

The designer of the first classic English landscape gardens in Hungary was Bernhard Petri (1767–1853). Another important planner from the turn of the 19th century was Charles de Moreau (1758–1840), who created one of the most significant Hungarian landscape gardens in Kismarton; he also worked elsewhere in the country. In Kismarton he transformed the terraced formal garden and the adjacent vineyard into a vast landscape garden in the purest classic style. The third important designer of this style, active in the first decades of the 19th century, was Heinrich Nebbien (1779–1841). He created the gardens of Alsókorompa (today Dolná Krupa, Slovakia) and Martonvásár for the Brunszvik family, but his most significant work was the plan for the City Park in Pest.

The most influential person in the landscape gardening movement of the first half of the 19th century was not a designer but a statesman. Palatine Joseph (1776–1847), a Habsburg archduke, played a leading role in the development of agriculture, horticulture, and arboriculture. His famous garden in Alcsút was created on bare land, which inspired others to win over nature by laying out gardens on marshy land or on almost pure sand. His other gardens in the Margareth Island in Pest, around the royal palace in Buda, and his ornamented utilitarian garden in Lágymányos also enjoyed fame throughout the country.

During the second half of the 19th century, owners put more emphasis on collecting exotic plants, which resulted in the construction of large glasshouses, a denser system of walks, and less open areas in the gardens. This period lasted until World War II with minor changes. In the first half of the 20th century the formal layout found its way back to the gardens, although it was used simultaneously with the landscape style.

The first public gardens were created in the last decades of the 18th century, first in Pozsony in 1775 and then in the restored capital of Buda in 1785. These gardens were almost entirely formal in their layout, with some irregular details. The city of Pest conducted a competition for the City Park in 1813, which was won by Heinrich Nebbien in 1816, although the park's final design was more modest than Nebbien's original designs. In the second half of the century more and more public parks were established in the capital as well as in other cities.

After World War I Hungary was subdivided; nine countries now share its former territory. After World War II the almost complete elimination of private property included the nationalization of all the significant gardens, most of which were destroyed due to lack of maintenance and care in the second half of the 20th century. Important gardens were not created during Communist rule, and following the political change of 1990 there are still only few noteworthy works of garden art.

Further Reading

Feuerné, Tóth, Rózsa, "A budai vár függõkertjei és a Cisterna Regia" (The Hanging Gardens of Buda Castle and the Cisterna Regia), in *Magyarországi reneszánsz és barokk. Mûvészettörténeti tanulmányok,* edited by Géza Galavics, Budapest, Akadémiai Kiadó, 1975

Galavics, Géza, *Magyarországi angolkertek* (English Gardens in Hungary), Budapest: Balassi Kiadó, 1999

Galavics, Géza, editor, *Történeti kertek: Kertmûvészet és mûemlékvédelem* (Historic Gardens: Garden Art and Monument Conservation), Budapest: MTA Mûvészettörténeti Kutatóintézet, and Mágus Kiadó, 2000

Gombocz, Endre, *A magyar botanika története* (History of Hungarian Botany), Budapest: Magyar Tudományos Akadémia, 1936

Lippay, János, *Posoni Kert* (The Garden of Pozsony), Nagyszombat-Wien, 1664–67; facsimile, Budapest: Akadémiai Kiadó, 1966

Mõcsényi, Mihály, *Eszterháza fehéren-feketén* (Esterháza in Black and White), Budapest: Mõcsényi Mihály, 1999

Ormos, Imre, *A kerttervezés története és gyakorlata* (The History and Practice of Garden Design), Budapest: Mezõgazdasági Kiadó, 1955; 2nd edition, 1967; reprint of 2nd edition, Budapest: Ormos Imre Alapítvány, 2001

Rapaics, Raymund, *Magyar kertek* (Hungarian Gardens), Budapest: Királyi Magyar Egyetemi Nyomda, 1940

Sisa, József, "A csákvári Esterházy-kastély parkja" (The Park of Esterházy Mansion in Csákvár), *Mõvészettörténeti Értesítõ* 46 (1997)

Stirling, János, *Magyar reneszánsz kertművészet a XVI–XVII. században* (Hungarian Renaissance Garden Art in the 16th and 17th Centuries), Budapest: Enciklopédia, 1996
Zádor, Anna, "The English Garden in Hungary," in *The Picturesque Garden and Its Influence outside the British Isles,* edited by Nikolaus Pevsner, Washington, D.C.: Dumbarton Oaks Trustees, 1974
Zádor, Anna, "The History of the English Garden in Hungary," *Acta Historiae Artium* 33 (1987–88)

KRISTÓF FATSAR

Huntington Library and Botanic Gardens

San Marino, California, United States

Location: 2 miles (3.2 km) south of Pasadena, or approximately 15 miles (24 km) northeast of Los Angeles city center

The Botanic Garden at the Huntington Library in San Marino, California, is one of the foremost public gardens and botanical research institutions in southern California. From 1903 until 1925, it was one of the region's major estate gardens, exemplifying the trend for gardens to both reflect their owners' social status and serve as centers of horticultural experimentation. Since 1925 it has become a major center of scientific research and a public garden that has been embellished with new plant collections in the last three decades.

In 1903 Henry Edwards Huntington, a leading developer of real estate and transportation and a distinguished collector of books and art, purchased the 600-acre (approximately 243 ha) San Marino ranch close to the base of the San Gabriel mountains and began transforming it into an elaborate estate. Like many such enterprises, it combined competitive plant collecting as a form of status and experimentation with plants valuable for both ornamental and commercial use.

In 1904 Huntington hired William Hertrich, an expert German horticulturist, as garden superintendent. Hertrich satisfied Huntington's desire for a mature garden by taking advantage of the long growing season and pioneering the transplantation of large trees in boxes, including 650 California live oaks, many species of palm, and specimen trees such as *Araucaria bidwillii* and deodar cedars. In introducing these and other nonnative plants, Hertrich made the tacit assumption that adequate water would be available in this semi-arid landscape.

The garden developed without a master plan prior to the selection of the site for the new house, one garden project succeeding another. The earliest gardens typified the prevalent passion for specialized gardens and an atmosphere of lush tropicality. The four-acre (1.6-ha) palm garden was developed as an ornamental and experimental collection of palms from the semitropical regions of Australia, Asia, Africa, and the Americas for use in Huntington's numerous real estate enterprises. The palms include pinnate-leaved species such as *Archontophoenix, Arecastrum, Arenga, Butia, Chamaedorea, Cocos, Collinia, Howea, Jubaea,* and *Phoenix* and palmate-leaved species such as *Chamaerops, Erythea, Livistona, Pritchardia, Rhapidophyyllum,* and *Sabal.*

In 1905 Hertrich initiated a small cactus collection from local deserts. This was expanded to 5 acres (2 ha) in 1908 and 1912, and other desert plants from Arizona, New Mexico, Texas, and Mexico were added. By 1925 it had increased to 15 acres (6 ha) and was the largest collection of desert plants in the world outside a natural desert containing cacti such as *Opuntia, Echinocereus, Echinocactus, Cireus, Carnegiea, Selenicereus, Monvillea,* and *Harrisia.* Succulents included *Aloe, Euphorbia, Crassula, Mesembryanthemum, Kleinia,* and *Stapelia.* Fibrous desert plants included *Agave, Yucca, Puya, Furcraea, and Pitcairnia.*

Unlike the naturalistic layout of the early gardens, the North Vista and the rose garden were laid out as formal areas with an anticipated axial relationship to the formal Italianate mansion. However, Huntington's insistence on preserving two large oak trees resulted in an awkward visual relationship to both gardens. The North Vista, a long axial vista oriented toward the mountains, bisects a large grove of oak trees, beneath which are collections of azaleas and camellias. The vista to the mountains is flanked by *Cocos* palms alternating with 17th-century Italian marble statues and is terminated by a large Renaissance fountain. Outstanding classical garden temples were placed in other gardens near the house.

The Japanese garden was created in 1912 in a canyon west of the rose garden; all of the plants and structures came from a failing commercial tea garden. The camellias, azaleas, cherries, Chinese and Japanese wisterias, dwarf maples, pines, and cycads were supplemented by a moon bridge built by a Japanese craftsman and lanterns and miniature pagodas brought from Japan. In 1914 Hertrich developed a rock and cycad garden near the house. For this garden he acquired a major collection of cycads, successfully outbidding one of Huntington's rival plant collectors.

As an estate garden, the Huntington ranch was designed to be at its peak when the Huntingtons were in residence, normally in late winter and spring. It was therefore known only to a small group of horticultural experts. In 1915 a group of visiting park superintendents declared that the Japanese garden was "the finest that they had ever seen in that style." Two Japanese members of this group declared that the cycads "were better looking than any they had seen in . . . their native country." The park officials declared the San Marino Ranch the "cream of California."

In 1917 Hertrich first broached the idea of establishing a botanic garden. This was undoubtedly intended to complement the 1916 proposal to create a scholarly library and art collection. The Huntington Library and Art Gallery was legally established in August 1919 as a free public library, art gallery, museum, and park, and by 1925 the original ranch had been reduced in size to 207 acres (84 ha). The Library and Art Gallery, North Vista, palm garden, desert garden, rose garden, and Japanese garden were first opened to the public in 1928.

The transformation of the private garden into a botanic garden initiated Hertrich's career as a major horticultural scholar. In 1933 Dr. Eric Werdermann, curator of the botanic museum at Dahlem, Germany, came to assist him in classifying the desert collection. The garden remained unchanged, apart from some refurbishing, until the 1960s, when numerous developments occurred. The camellia collection was expanded; additions were made to the collections of roses, magnolias, rhododendrons, and azaleas; and new gardens were created, including the herb garden, Shakespeare garden, Zen garden and bonsai court, jungle garden, and Australian garden.

The Huntington ranch was one of the largest early 20th century examples of wealthy Californians competing in the collection and display of rare plants. It was also a pioneering and influential display of classical garden art, such as fountains, temples, and statues. Its subsequent role as a public and botanic garden has been equally important. It serves as a major visitor destination and is a center of botanical and horticultural research of equivalent value to the very distinguished library and art collection.

Synopsis

1903	Henry E. Huntington purchases Rancho San Marino
1904–5	Lily ponds installed
1905	Palm garden laid out
1906–8	Desert garden and North Vista laid out
1907–8	Rose garden laid out
1908–10	Mansion designed by Myron Hunt and Elmer Grey (occupied as winter residence in 1914)
1911–12	Japanese garden laid out
1914	Cycad garden laid out
1919–22	Huntington Library designed by Myron Hunt and H.C. Chambers
1922	Rose garden reduced in size
1925	Huntington Mausoleum designed by John Russell Pope
1927	Garden of director's house designed by Beatrix Jones Farrand
1928	Huntington Botanic Gardens first opened to the public
1938	Rose garden altered
1948	Rose garden replanted
1959	Shakespeare garden laid out
1964	Australian garden developed
1965	New plantings in the Japanese garden
1966	New Japanese rock and sand garden
1980	New northern entrance developed

Further Reading

Brown, Jane, *Beatrix: The Gardening Life of Beatrix Jones Farrand, 1872–1959,* New York: Viking, 1995

Hertrich, William, *A Guide to the Desert Plant Collection in the Huntington Botanical Gardens,* San Marino, California: Henry E. Huntington Library and Art Gallery, 1940

Hertrich, William, *The Huntington Botanical Gardens, 1905–1949: Personal Recollections of William Hertrich, Curator Emeritus,* San Marino, California: Huntington Library, 1949

Hertrich, William, *Palms and Cycads: Their Cultivation in Southern California as Observed Chiefly in the Huntington Botanical Gardens,* San Marino, California: Henry E. Huntington Library and Art Gallery, 1951

Hertrich, William, *Camellias in the Huntington Gardens: Observations on their Culture and Behavior and Descriptions of Cultivars,* San Marino, California: Huntington Library Botanical Gardens, 1955

Lyons, Gary W., "The Development of the Huntington Desert Garden: Past and Future," *Cactus and Succulent Journal* 41, no. 1 (1969)

Lyons, Gary W., "The Huntington Desert Garden Today," *Cactus and Succulent Journal* 41, no. 1 (1969)

Padilla, Victoria, *Southern California Gardens,* Berkeley: University of California Press, 1961

Pomfret, John E., *The Henry E. Huntington Library and Art Gallery: From Its Beginnings to 1969,* San Marino, California: Huntington Library, 1969
Thorpe, James Everest, "The Creation of the Gardens," in *The Founding of the Henry E. Huntington Library and Art Gallery: Four Essays,* San Marino, California: Huntington Library, 1969

DAVID C. STREATFIELD

Hu Qiu

Gansu Province, China

Location: approximately 3 miles (5 km) outside of Suzhou, situated on the northwest side of Suzhou

Hu Qiu (Tiger Hill), surrounded by a river and covering approximately 188,700 square meters (225,700 sq. yd.), derives its reputation from its beautiful scenery and mythical events.

Tiger Hill is particularly well known for its Buddhist pagoda. Yun Yan Temple, 47.7 meters (52.2 yd.) high, is a tower serving as depository of holy relics of Buddhism. This pagoda, over a thousand years old, has been recently restored. Hufu temple, originally built in A.D. 327, has been destroyed and rebuilt many times. The main hall was burned down during the reign of Xianfeng in the Qing dynasty. The southeast side of Tiger Hill contains Guan Yin Hall, which has 53 stone stairs. One can see a statue of the Buddha while walking up the stairs. To the west side of the stone stairs is a flat rock that can accommodate about a thousand people; it was once a preaching place for a monk, Zhu Dao-sheng. According to ancient legend Zhu Dao-sheng's preaching could make rocks move and lotuses blossom. Diantou Shi (Nodding Head Stone) remains at the center of the Bailian Chi. On the west side of the Bailian Chi is a pavilion called Erhxianting, built against the cliff. According to legend the immortals had played chess in the pavilion. The combination of Buddha and immortals creates the main theme of Tiger Hill.

Another feature is the Sword Pond, which lies between two cliffs at the foot of Tiger Hill. The sides of the stone cliffs are inscribed with ancient scholars' calligraphy. A bridge over the Sword Pond connects the cliffs. There are two holes, named Shuangdiao Tong (Double-Hanged Barrels), on the surface of the bridge. It was said that the monks used barrels to scoop water through the holes. According to Lu Yu, the king of tea in the Tang dynasty, the water in the Sword Pond was the third-best water in the world for making tea. The Sword Pond is also called Lu, Yu Jing (Lu, Yu Well). A pavilion on the hill is called Sanquan Ting (Three-Spring Pavilion). Several stories exist about the Sword Pond. According to one version, the Sword Pond was formed naturally, while another legend indicates the emperor of Wu Kingdom during the Spring and Autumn period was buried under the pond. The charming scenery and the historical background combine to make the Tiger Hill more attractive and impart a feeling of eternity.

On the trail up to the hill is a unique and rare stone, called Shijian Shi (Sword-Testing Stone), split into two parts. According to legend the sword-making couple Ganjiang and Moxie were making swords at Tiger Hill and cracked the stone when testing their swords on it. Kankan Quan (Kankan Spring) was dug by the monk Kankan during the Jin dynasty. On the way to "53 Stairs" is a natural cave that was the immortals' passage to the East Sea, the immortals' gathering place.

The Ershan Men and Duanliang Dian halls were built in 1338 (Yuan dynasty). Both are made entirely of stones and match the surrounding environment. In 1961 both sites came under government protection. Mei-flowers and winter sweet are planted around the halls and pavilions. In 1884 a residential garden, called Yongcui Shanzhuang, was built on the spot of Yuejia Xuan hall, located on the west side of the trail. It is a rectangular-shaped garden with the area of approximately 1,000 square meters (1,196 sq. yd.). The main construction includes the Wenquan Ting pavilion, the Baoweng Xuan lounge, and rockeries.

Camphor trees and elm trees are planted in the Pehjing Yuan garden. In addition, Tiger Hill contains Siberian elms and plum trees that are over 500 years old. These old trees enrich the historical nature of Tiger Hill.

Synopsis

496–76 B.C. Wu emperor Fu-chai buries father (Helu) at Haiyong Shan mountain in northwestern par of Suzhou; three days after burial a white tiger appears on top of Haiyoun Shan mountain;

	emperor thus changed name to Hu Qiu (Tiger Hill)
210 B.C.	Qin Shihuang Di travels to south, stops by Suzhou, makes search at Tiger Hill but fails to locate legendary sword that once belonged to Helu
A.D. 222–28	Sun Quan of Wu kingdom goes to look for sword of Helu at Tiger Hill; digs pond in search (jien chi, or Sword Pond), and creates hill with excavated earth
327	Brothers Wang Xun and Wang Min donate households to build Hufu Chansi (later Wuqiu Baoen Si Temple)
434	Monk Zhu Dao-sheng preaches lessons to stones and rocks at Tiger Hill to make them move; One Thousand People stone and Nodding Head Stone created
505–10	Nobleman Han Han digs spring Han Han Quan
959–61	Yunyan Si Ta (also called Hu Qiu Pagoda) built
1338	Construction of Ershan Men Duanliang Dien completed
1884	Yongcui Shanzhuang built on old site of Yuejia Xuan
1952–95	Additional scenes, such as Haiyong Qiao, Taying Qiao, Wanjing Shanzhuang, Pehjing Yuan, etc., built

Further Reading

Ji Ch'eng, *The Craft of Gardens* (1634), translated by Alison Hardie, New Haven, Connecticut: Yale University Press, 1988

Johnston, R. Stewart, *Scholar Gardens of China: A Study and Analysis of the Spatial Design of the Chinese Private Garden,* Cambridge and New York: Cambridge University Press, 1991

Keswick, Maggie, *The Chinese Garden: History, Art and Architecture,* New York: Rizzoli, and London: Academy Editions, 1978

Tsu, Frances Ya-Sing, *Landscape Design in Chinese Gardens,* New York: McGraw Hill, 1988

Wang, Joseph Cho, *The Chinese Garden,* Oxford and New York: Oxford University Press, 1998

XU DEJIA AND JOSEPH C. WANG
TRANSLATED BY SYLVIA CHOI

Hydraulics

Hydraulics has played an extremely important role in the history of garden design and development. This science, which essentially examines the motion of liquids (such as water) and deals with the application of these liquids in machinery, was employed for the upkeep and maintenance of gardens. On one level, therefore, it facilitated the transportation of water across large distances and occasionally over difficult terrain, irrigating landscaped areas devoted to trees and plantation. Beyond this functional role, mechanical devices based on the principles of hydraulic science also served as elements of visual delight within the garden environment, taking the diverse form of devices such as sprays, fountains, and ingenious automata.

The Hanging Gardens of Babylon, completed under Nebuchadnezzar II (604–562 B.C.), were the first complex application of hydraulics in the ancient world. Located on the eastern bank of the river Euphrates, 31 miles (50 km) south of Baghdad (present-day Iraq), these gardens were built by Nebuchadnezzar supposedly to please his wife or concubine who had been "brought up in Media and had a passion for mountain surroundings." Accordingly, these legendary gardens sloped like a hillside, and several parts of the structure rose on terraced tiers, supported on massive brick vaults. Earth was piled on these platforms and thickly planted with trees of every kind to, with their great size and other charms, give pleasure to the beholder. Most significant, innovative machines raised water in great abundance from the nearby river, transporting it to the highest of the terraces. In the detailed descriptions of Strabo and Philo of Byzantium, streams of water emerged from elevated sources and flowed down sloping channels, thereby irrigating the garden and keeping the area moist.

The impressive application of hydraulics at the Hanging Gardens with its massive water machines was only part of the complete picture from the ancient world. Hero's experiments with enchanting automata in the gardens at Alexandria in the first century B.C. added yet another dimension. This may be characterized as a new emphasis on aesthetics and visual delight achieved through the use of hydraulic devices in the garden environment, a preoccupation that was to serve as an important antecedent for future developments. In yet

Ovata Fountain, Villa d'Este, Tivoli, Lazio, Italy
Copyright John Bethell/Garden Picture Library

another geographical context, and still at a monumental scale, an aqueduct during the time of Augustus Caesar provided water to the entire city of Pompeii. It fed into the courtyards of dwellings, filling pools, basins, and fountains. Lead pipes, preserved in the volcanic eruptions of A.D. 79, caused jets of water to emerge from elaborate fountain-statues, while water basins combined with niches formed nymphaeums, essential elements of the Roman garden. Further evidence that the ancient Romans were aware of the principles of hydraulic science comes from excavated gardens at Fishbourne in Britain. Here, elevated distribution tanks provided a sufficient head of water, thereby generating efficient circulation through ceramic pipes laid along the paths to all parts of the garden.

The next evidence for extensive use of hydraulics comes from Iran and is first seen within the Persian *pairidaiza* (paradise gardens). Among Xenophon's accounts of the legendary Achaemenid gardens with a typical water axis, excavations at Pasargadae have revealed a large palace complex overlooking a vast garden with two pavilions, watered by stone-lined channels. These are clear indicators that the movement of water within the garden environment was the subject of substantial concern in this early period. In any case, the incorporation of intersecting water channels in orthogonally organized gardens (later quadripartite or *chahar-bagh* gardens) was a development that necessitated other technological and mechanical hydraulic innovations to ensure that water works (fountains, sprays) and running bodies of water (channels, aqueducts) functioned as desired. Gradually, aqueducts and sluice gates, traditionally meant for irrigating tracts of arable land, evolved into more complex hydraulic devices, thereby supplementing their original functional role. Several of these devices watered the *hayrs* (suburban parks or zoological gardens) of ancient Mesopotamia and Syria.

These developments served as models for gardens in the Islamic world, a substantial part of which was concentrated in the regions of Iran, central Asia, and the Indian subcontinent. The extensive Abbasid palaces at Samarra, those of the Spanish Umayyads at Madinat al-Zahra in Spain, and the Gahaznavid palaces at Lashkari Bazar in Afghanistan incorporated water as an integral part of garden layouts. Literary sources from the period boast of specialized hydraulic devices, such as the legendary Birkat al-Mutawakkil at Hayr al-Wuhush in Samarra, with animal-shaped fountains made of precious materials. In terms of surviving evidence, the so-called Pharaoh's Tray Fountain, originally located in the courtyard of the Great Mosque at Samarra in A.D. 850, would have sent a jet of water in the air to fall back into its large, circular basin. Its overflow would have fallen into a thin meandering channel around the base and escaped through a long spout into a lower pool.

Islamic gardens also provide evidence of technology that made such hydraulic innovations possible in the first place. This could involve layout and siting, such as locating the garden or pavilion near an elevated source of water and simply controlling the natural flow of water down the slope. Such technology could also incorporate certain water-raising mechanisms, of which at least two were popular throughout the Islamic world and were initially used for irrigation purposes before they became a part of garden hydraulics. The *naura* or *noria* was the first among these. It was a water wheel with hinged compartments that dipped into a moving stream and carried water to the top of the wheel where it was discharged into an aqueduct. Because *norias* relied on the flow of water for their motion, they could only be used in fairly rapid streams, which in the Islamic world restricted their usage to Syria, parts of North Africa, and Spain. More practical for the arid climate in several other parts of the Islamic world was the *saqiya*—a water-elevating machine that used animal power. Its central mechanism consisted of two gears meshed at right angles to each other. The vertical gear was mounted on an axle over the source of water, usually a well, while a drum suspended on its other side carried a chain-of-pots or "pot garland." A second gear moved the first vertical gear on the horizontal axis powered by a drawbar pulled by an animal tethered to it, thereby causing water to be raised to the surface and discharged into a head tank.

Beyond such functional devices, which appear to have been standard equipment for irrigation, certain other exotic and visionary mechanisms were used specifically in palatial Islamic gardens. These were the automatas, known primarily from the 11th-century treatise of Banu Musa and the 1206 treatise of Banu al-Jazari. Al-Jazari's work contains an entire chapter entitled "On the construction in pools of water which change their shape, and of machines for the perpetual flute." While the text illustrates and discusses several types of water-raising mechanisms, an initial idea about their aesthetics and effect may be derived from briefly examining one of them, called the water-elevating mechanism. In this device, explained by al-Jazari, water from a nearby lake filled a tank whose bottom contained a drain that discharged a steady stream of water over a mechanism concealed in a lower basin. The water in turn turned a wheel with scoops, setting it in motion. Through a system of meshed gears, this motion was transferred vertically to a pot garland that dipped into the top tank and in turn carried water to a channel, which emptied into the lake as a cascade. Since all of the lower mechanism was cleverly hidden from sight, all that the amazed viewers could see was a *saqiya,* which appeared to be propelled by a model of a wooden cow.

While the elaboration of automata, seen in Hero's gardens at Alexandria and in the palatial gardens of the Islamic world, served as an important element of hydraulic science in western Europe, there was also considerable experimentation on the mechanics of hydraulic devices themselves. No longer were automatas considered mere tricks and stage sets, using concealed devices to create visual effect. Instead, these devices increasingly relied on an understanding of complicated mechanics for their operation. Interest in hydraulics and waterworks was first apparent in Leonardo da Vinci and Niccolò Machiavelli's fantastic scheme to build a system of canals that would extend the Arno River to the sea, thereby making Florence a world power. Da Vinci's own sketches from this period reveal a particular concern for water-raising and water-pumping equipment, an important requirement for large civic and architectural commissions. Agostino Ramelli's *Le diverse et artificiose machine* (1588; Diverse and Ingenious Machines) illustrates the rotary pump, mechanical details of windmills, and a cofferdam of interlocking piles, effectively building on da Vinci's work. Equally important in this respect was Salomon de Caus's *Les raisons de forces mouvantes avec diverses machines tant utiles que plaisantes* (1615; The Relations of Motive Forces, with Various Machines as Useful as They Are Pleasing). With an array of workable, hydraulic devices now at his command, de Caus was preoccupied with the production of pleasure gardens incorporating hydraulic displays. His work describes elaborate grottoes and fountains, which served as prototypes for actual constructions.

Michel de Montaigne's account of 1581 in his "Journal" documents the best 16th-century examples of ingenious hydraulic and pneumatic machines in Italy. At the Villa d'Este at Tivoli, he noted the fine statuary adorning the villa and the gardens, reproduced from the finest sculptures of Rome. Montaigne was particularly impressed by the organs that played music to the accompaniment of the falling water and devices that imitated the sound of trumpets; he observed similar displays at the archducal Villa of Scarperio in Tuscany and at the casino of the archduke of Florence, with its mills motivated by water and air power to operate small church clocks, animals, soldiers, and countless other automata. Montaigne described similar curiosities in Germany at the famous residence of the Foulcres, the banking family of Augsburg.

Undoubtedly the automata and waterworks of the Renaissance reached their peak in the gardens of the royal château of Saint-Germain-en-Laye, which had often served as the residence of the kings of France. In the late 16th century, Henri IV considerably enlarged the château so that it became the principal royal residence. To effect these changes Henri requested from Archduke Ferdinand I de Medici the services of Tommaso Francini, a young Florentine architect and mechanician. Accompanied by his younger brother, Alessandro, Francini arrived in France in 1698. His first assignment was to design a series of terraces with grottoes and fountains at Saint-Germain-en-Laye. These terraces, lying between the garden and the Seine, were sustained with vaulted galleries of sufficient size to permit passage from one to another. Francini devised an elaborate waterworks system with a great fountain as the main feature. From the basin of this fountain, water descended by means of intricate channels and accumulated in the reservoirs placed within the vaults of the galleries beneath. Through a multitude of secondary tubes, these reservoirs supplied the grottoes and fountains of the galleries and provided the force to motivate the various mechanisms. Identical systems were repeated in the galleries below so that the water was finally collected and combined to give life to the fountains adorning the Italian-style garden. The Francini brothers also embellished the park at Fontainebleau with a series of fountains and grottoes and in 1661 designed a series of waterworks for the palace of Versailles for Louis XIV. Despite the unusual difficulties created by a limited water supply on the site, they produced numerous fountains as well as the Grotto of the Teti, considered superior even to Saint-Germain-en-Laye.

Between the Renaissance and modern times, while gardens became substantially larger and more elaborate, often occupying a relatively more urban location than their medieval predecessors, there was an increasing tendency to reduce the role of hydraulics to its earlier, more utilitarian function, that of irrigation itself. Therefore, while modest fountains and canals have existed in several cases, hydraulic displays no longer attracted as much attention as did the diversity of plant material imported from around the world, paving material and garden furniture, or evening light displays. Hydraulic devices now mainly operate "under the scenes" in the garden environment.

Further Reading

Glick, Thomas F., *Irrigation and Society in Medieval Valencia,* Cambridge, Massachusetts: Harvard University Press, 1970

Goblot, Henri, *Les Qanats: Une technique d'acquisition de l'eau,* Paris and New York: Mouton, 1979

Hasan, Ahmad Yusuf, and Donald Routledge Hill, *Islamic Technology: An Illustrated History,* Cambridge and New York: Cambridge University Press, and Paris: Unesco, 1986

Hill, Donald Routledge, *Arabic Water-Clocks,* Aleppo, Syria: University of Aleppo, Institute for the History of Arabic Science, 1981

Hill, Douglas Routledge, editor and translator, *On the Construction of Water-Clocks,* London: Turner and Devereaux, 1976 (translation of a treatise ascribed to Archimedes)

MacDougall, Elisabeth B., editor, *Fons Sapientiae: Renaissance Garden Fountains,* Washington, D.C.: Dumbarton Oaks Trustees, 1978

MacDougall, Elisabeth B., and Wilhelmina F. Jashemski, editors, *Ancient Roman Gardens,* Washington, D.C.: Dumbarton Oaks Trustees, 1981

Masters, Roger D., *Fortune Is a River: Leonardo da Vinci and Niccolò Machiavelli's Magnificent Dream to Change the Course of Florentine History,* New York: Free Press, 1998

Petruccioli, Attilio, editor, *Gardens in the Time of the Great Muslim Empires: Theory and Design,* Leiden and New York: Brill, 1987

Schiøler, Thorkild, *Roman and Islamic Water-Lifting Wheels,* translated by Pauline M. Katborg, Odense: Odense University Press, 1973

Stronach, D., "Excavations at Pasargadae: Third Preliminary Report," *Iran, Journal of the British Institute of Persian Studies* 3 (1965)

Tabbaa, Y., "The Medieval Islamic Garden: Typology and Hydraulics," in *Garden History: Issues, Approaches, Methods,* edited by John Dixon Hunt, Washington, D.C.: Dumbarton Oaks Research Library and Collection, 1992

Vercelloni, Virgilio, *Atlante storico dell'idea del giardino Europeo,* Milan: Jaca Book, 1990; as *European Gardens: An Historical Atlas,* New York: Rizzoli, 1990

MANU P. SOBTI

I

India

Archaeological evidence indicates that the Indus Valley civilization (3000–2000 B.C.) had a reverence for specific trees that were believed to be the abode of "tree spirits." The care of these trees and their arrangement in the performance of rituals forms the historical basis for garden and landscape design in India. An emperor of the Mauryan dynasty, Asoka (ca. 270–232 B.C.), directed a large landscape planning scheme: "On the roads, I have had banyan trees planted which will give shade to beasts and man. I have had mango groves planted and I have had wells dug and rest houses built every nine miles." (inscription on a monumental stone). Asoka also insisted that forests should be maintained to protect woodland plants used in Ayurvedic medicine, the traditional system of Indian healing. He also insisted on the establishment of gardens for the cultivation of medicinal herbs.

Many references to gardens occur in early Indian literature including this passage in the celebrated epic the *Mahabharata*.

> The walls of the pavilions shone like mirrors. There were numerous arbours covered by climbers, charming artificial hillocks, lakes filled to the brim with clear water, fish ponds carpetted with lotus and water lilies, and ponds, covered by many delicate aquatic plants, on which swam red geese, ducks and swans. . . . The gardens echoed to the cry of the peacock and the song of the kokila [the Indian cuckoo].

The *Kama Sutra* has lots of interesting general information, including discussions of gardening, in addition to the erotic material for which if is most famous in the West. Early records of actual rather than fictional gardens are found in the writings of Western observers. The historian Aelian, writing during the reign of the Roman emperor Hadrian (A.D. 117–38), provides a glimpse of an Indian royal garden.

> Among cultivated plants there are some to which the king's servants attend with great care, for there are shady groves and pasture lands planted with trees, and branches of trees which the art of the woodsman has deftly interwoven. And their very trees, from the unusual benignity of the climate, are ever in bloom, and, untouched by age, never shed their leaves; and while some are native to the soil, others are brought with circumspect care from other parts, and with their beauty enhance the charms of the landscape.

The garden of the Gupta kings at Patilaputra (present-day Patna) in the fourth century A.D. was described by Megasthenes, the Seleucid envoy at the royal court. He refers to fish-filled tanks of remarkable beauty, tame peacocks and pheasants, cultivated plants and shaded groves, and parterres planted with trees apparently trained or pleached.

After the Mauryan Empire disintegrated, the art of gardening in northern India lost its central force. However, two Chinese Buddhist pilgrims, Fa Hsien and Hsuan Tsang, writing in the fifth century A.D. and the seventh century A.D., respectively, have left us with an idea of gardening in India during these periods. Fa Hsien relates that vegetarianism was already well-established, and Hsuan Tsang notes that a wide variety of fruits and vegetables were grown together with sugar cane, herbs, peppers, and spices to flavor the bland staple diet of wheat in the northwest and rice in the northeast. Thus, kitchen gardens were likely well-organized and productive.

The Chinese writers also recorded the use of garlands and the scattering of flowers during religious rituals. It

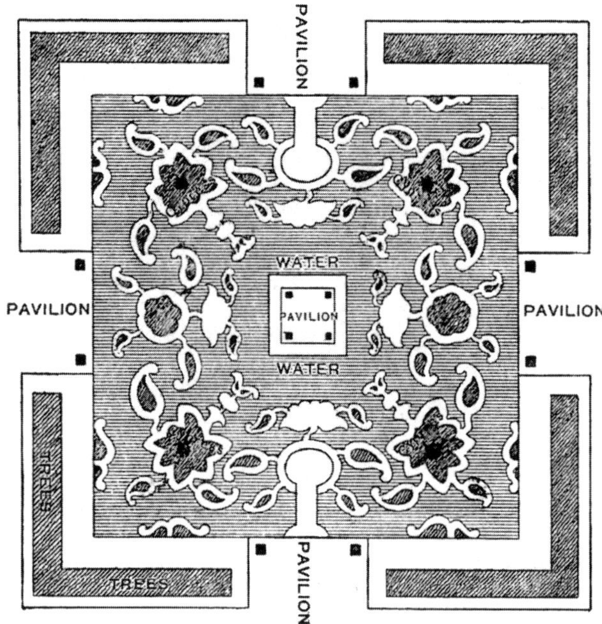

Plan of a garden located in one of the island palaces at Udaipur, from C.M. Villiers Stuart, *Gardens of the Great Mughals,* 1913

is still an important function of gardening in India today to provide the appropriate flowers for each ritual. Fa Hsien describes flowering trees surrounding a temple and shrine located by the Sarasvati river: "the water in the pools was clear, the trees luxuriant of foliage, with flowers of various hues, truly so beautiful to behold that it was named 'The Shrine of the Garden of Gold.'" Hsuan Tsang relates how the shrine at the spot where Buddha died had four trees of equal height, one opposite each corner of the shrine—an early example of formal tree planting.

Formal water tanks were an adjunct of Buddhist shrine gardens. Hsuan Tsang describes one at Bodhi Ghaya, the place where Buddha gained enlightenment: "The southern gate of its enclosure borders on a great flower tank." By a monastery at Nalanda, in eastern India, he saw "deep, translucent pools bearing on their surface the blue lotus intermingled with the Kie-ni of deep red colour and, at intervals, the Amra groves spread over all their shade." The pool constructed in the ninth century at Bengarh, in eastern India, was in the shape of a lotus.

The conventional Indian garden evolved to reflect not only western preoccupations with sensual and representational effect, but also the traditional Indian consideration of "auspiciousness." Formulae for planting in sacred gardens were gradually codified in treatises known as *shastras,* some of which are still followed today. An old Indian treatise on gardening designates the auspicious orientation of particular species of trees in a garden; which species, for example, should not be planted at the gate of the house or in such a place that its shadow may fall on the building.

Later documentation gives descriptions of sophisticated gardening in India during the centuries leading to the establishment of the Mogul empire in India in the early 16th century. During this era, the outlets of water-tanks were sometimes sculpted in the form of elaborate stone masks. The water spouts at the 13th-century Suryan temple at Konarak are in the form of open-mouthed beasts. At the 14th-century Jain temple at Abu, a stone water spout is in the form of a cow's head, as is another at Chittorgarh. Large reservoirs were sometimes ornamented with island gardens. The island known as Jag Mandir in Lake Pichola at Udaipur, laid out in 1551, is a notable example. The reservoir at the 14th-century temple at Pandoh boasted a floating island.

The 12th-century invasion of northern India by a Turko-Afghan dynasty began the long and complex interaction between the Muslim world and the established Hindu culture. This interplay produced the Mogul gardens of India. The Hindu contribution to their design is found in formal features such as lotus-shaped pools, lotus-bud fountains, and marble swings, as well as in the exquisite Indian sculptural tradition seen in the surface decoration of garden architecture and ornaments. Native Indian trees were integral to the planting of the Mogul garden: avenues of tamarinds, groves of mangos, and free-standing areca nut palms were part of their distinctive visual impact.

Suprisingly little attention has been paid to the gardens laid out by Hindu rulers during the Mogul period. Surviving examples include the garden at Deeg, created during the 18th century by a maharajah of Bharatpur, and the spectacular garden in Maota Lake at Amber, created by a maharajah of Jaipur. Not all of the Hindu gardens of this period exhibit the conventional Mogul plan. Some boast a conception that is not found in Mogal design and therefore can be considered distinctly Indian. A water parterre on Jag Niwas, an island on Lake Pichola in Udaipur, illustrates Rajput originality in garden design. The garden's stone-edged flower beds, conceived in a sinuous geometry of foliate and floral shapes, are designed to seem to float on the surface of a formal pool of water.

During the 19th century the long tradition of Indian gardening was influenced by British gardening practices. In 1823 Bishop Heber described the garden of the Hindu *thakur* (or baron) Babu Hurre Mohum as being laid out in formal parterres of roses, intersected by straight walks, with some fine trees and a chain of tanks, fountains, and summerhouses. There were also swing whirligigs and other amusements for the females of the family. The strangest element in the garden was a sort of *Montagne Russe*, a very steep hill of masonry that was covered with plaster, which the ladies reportedly used as a slide. Heber also described the house and gardens of a wealthy Hindu shawl manufacturer near Delhi. They comprised three small courts surrounded by stone cloisters; two were planted with flowering shrubs and orange trees, and the third was ornamented with a beautiful marble fountain. In 1829 Colonel James Tod described the princely gardens of the maharanis of Udaipur.

> Parterres of flowers, orange and lemon groves, intervene to dispel the monotony of the buildings, shaded by the wide-spreading tamarind and magnificent evergreen khirni; while the graceful palmyra and coco hang their plume-like branches over the dark cypress or cooling plantain.

Tod also noted lakeside pavilions.

> Detached colonnaded refectories are placed on the water's edge for the chiefs, and extensive baths for their use. Here they listened to the tale of the bard, and slept off their noonday opiate amidst the cool breezes of the lake, wafting delicious odours from myriads of lotus-flowers which covered the surface of the waters.

Later in the 19th century, some remarkable gardens were maintained by Indian princes. The German botanist Otto Warburg noted the "numerous extensive and costly gardens" belonging to the Indian princes and nobles, mentioning those at Baroda and Travancore specifically. In 1912 the English garden designer William Goldring was asked to lay out a series of new gardens and parks in Baroda in the neighboring state of Gujurat. On his return from India, Goldring wrote an account of his visit listing the notable princely gardens that he had seen.

> That of Jaipur, over 70 acres in extent, designed by Dr. de Fabeck; Durbangha which was, at one time, under the direction of Mr. Maries but who is now, I hear, doing a great deal of work at Gwalior. There are also fine gardens at Patiala and Chikalda while I hope the various palace gardens and parks that I am designing for the Gaekwar of Baroda will in time compare with any in India.

However, earlier in his article he states unequivocally that the garden of the maharanis of Udaipur, Sajjan Niwas Bagh, begun in 1874, was the most important princely garden of them all.

During the latter part of the 19th century, public interest in gardening became more widespread. A number of Indian rulers established horticultural schools such as those at Baroda and Cossipore. A series of important nurseries was established, the best known being those in the vicinity of the Mysore State Botanical Garden in Bangalore. British seed merchants like Sutton and Sons opened outlets in Calcutta; flower shows and horticultural exhibitions were held. Seeds and plants were exchanged not only through the network of Indian botanical gardens but also through the worldwide network of imperial botanic gardens headquartered at the Royal Botanic Gardens at Kew, near London. Public parks were opened, most notably in Jaipur, Udaipur, and Baroda. These sometimes boasted museums with botanical and horticultural exhibits as well as extensive herbariums.

The interest in gardening was not confined to Indian rulers. At the flower show held at Udaipur in 1889, many of the nobility and gentry won prizes, including the prime minister of the state. For centuries prosperous urban families maintained walled orchards, often developed in an ornamental way, on the outskirts of the cities. Villages continued to maintain their sacred groves of trees, safeguarding these reservoirs of herbal medicines.

Significant gardens laid out by Indian rulers during the 20th century include those at the Rambagh Palace, Jaipur (ca. 1920), and the Umaid Bhawan Palace, Jodhpur (1929–44). One of the most outstanding private gardens was created between 1907 and 1964 at the Retreat in Ahmedabad. L.N. Birla's *Planning a Landscape Garden* (1962) had an important influence on the planning of suburban villa gardens (known as "farms") on the outskirts of big cities. Important institutional gardens include those of the Theosophical Society (begun in 1907) in Madras, of the Sri Aurobindo ashram (1968) at Auroville, and of the cultural institution Sanskriti Kendra (1979) near Delhi, where the contemporary landscape design is planted with native Indian species mentioned in the great *Mahabharata* epic.

See also Agra Fort; Babur; Calcutta Botanic Garden; Chashma Shahi; Islamic Gardens; Mogul Gardens; Nishat Bagh; Red Fort; Taj Mahal

Further Reading

Birla, L.N., *Planning a Landscape Garden,* Calcutta: Royal Agri-horticultural Society of India, 1962

Firminger, Thomas Augustus Charles, *Firminger's Manual of Gardening in India,* 8th edition, Calcutta: Thacker Spink, 1947

Gopalaswamiengar, K.S., *Complete Gardening in India,* Madras, India: Huxley Press, 1935

Patnaik, Naveen, *The Garden of Life: An Introduction to the Healing Plants of India,* New York: Doubleday, 1993

Randhawa, G.S., K.L. Chadha, and Daljit Singh, *The Famous Gardens of India,* New Delhi: Malhotra, 1971

Swarup, Vishnu, "History of Flowers and Gardening in India," in *Garden Flowers,* by Swarup, New Delhi: National Book Trust, 1967

PATRICK BOWE

Indonesia

Indonesia is an archipelago nation strongly influenced by Dutch and British colonial botanical exploration and economic agriculture imperatives. Contemporary authors perceive a recent evolution in Indonesian gardening and landscape history. However, the legacy goes back much earlier to 2500–100 B.C., when an extensive and highly engineered irrigation system was devised to service terraced rice fields and paddies. This hydraulic knowledge and much of the ancient designed landscape, structured around village communities, exists on the islands of Java (Batavia), Sumatra, and Bali.

Indonesia's garden traditions lie in the myriad of villages that sought to cultivate staple tropical vegetation and species. Many of these staples are still in mass production, including rice on irrigated terraces. With European colonial settlement and trade, part of the emphasis shifted to spice and economic plant cultivation, especially rubber in the mid-1900s. This tradition underlies the cultural landscape of many of the Indonesian islands today. They developed as a series of fiefdoms and turned into royal kingdoms with *kratons* (royal palaces) accompanied by sacred groves of trees and open decorative *sitihinggil* (pavilion) courtyards.

With the advent of Javanese and Sumatran kingdoms in the fifth century A.D., numerous temples and palaces were erected to Buddhist and Hindu religions. Borobudor, erected ca. 780–833 near Yogyakarta, with its extensive galleries, terraces, and bell-enclosed statues, was the culmination of Buddhist structures on Java and is the world's largest stupa. It is a symmetrical temple without an interior, consisting of nine square terraces built upon a knoll, with about 4.8 km (3 mi.) of decorative galleries consisting of about 1,500 relief panels depicting the life and teachings of Buddha and 504 large Buddha statues enclosed within bell-like stone structures. In contrast, the Hindu complex of Prambanan, including the Siva temple (Loro Jonggrang), built during the 800s, displays a temple-like configuration scattered throughout a valley.

With the advent of European colonialism, the Portuguese first established trading posts in Indonesia in the 1600s in an attempt to exploit the profitable European spice market. Commercial profits led British and Dutch merchants to establish the British East India Company and the rival Dutch East India Company; their respective governments stood back as the merchant navies struggled to gain territory, which the Dutch eventually achieved in 1682 with the withdrawal of the British. Progressively, the Dutch took control of various ports, kingdoms, and principalities, as Javanese and Sumatran rulers attempted to deal with internal rebellions and economic difficulties. Under the Dutch intensive agriculture was promoted, and the commercial opportunities of spice and plant cultivation were expanded before the Dutch government assumed control of the company's assets and territories in 1799 as the Dutch East Indies. During the Napoléonic wars Stamford Raffles captured Batavia for the British in 1811, but the territories were returned to the Dutch in 1815.

During the Dutch occupation the Bogor Botanic Gardens (Kebun Raya) were established. Kebun Raya was founded with the decision of Dutch Governor-General Baron Gustaaf von Imhoff to erect a summerhouse at Buitzenzorg (meaning "without a care") in 1744. The gardens were officially opened in 1817 to the design and planting strategy of C.G.L. Reinwardt on a 111-hectare (274-acre) estate that includes the former presidential palace. Raffles's impetus was to establish and expand the botanical agenda at Bogor, and he set about establishing of satellite gardens such as the cool-climate Cibodas Gardens in 1886, to encourage greater economic agricultural research and experimentation, rediscover and survey Borobodur to bring it to international attention, and enable botanical information and specimen exchanges with Malaya, the Singapore Botanic Gardens, and the Royal Botanic Gardens, Kew.

The Dutch instigated a major period of development and construction works in the 1920s and 1930s, anticipating that the Dutch East Indies would remain a colony under their control. However, internal unrest, followed by World War II, promulgated Indonesian independence in December 1949.

Batavia, renamed Jakarta, formed the central pivot of the Dutch, British, and then Indonesian administration

Water garden of Tirta Gangga illustrative of Hindu cosmology of *ramé* (overcrowded abundance) with a contrasting *sepi* (empty stillness)
Copyright Mel Watson/Garden Picture Library

of the archipelago. The suburb of Mentang within Jakarta, established between 1920 and 1940, was conceived as a Dutch garden city under architect P.A.J. Mooyen's plan, *Bebouwingsplan Nieuw Gondangdia 1910*. The final plan for Mentang and Nieuw Gongangdia was drawn up by F.J. Cubbatz and developed by *Bouw Maatschppij De Bouwploeg* to create "een ideale tuinstad met moderne Hollandsche villas in de tropen" (ideal tropical garden city with modern Dutch villas).

Indonesia's third largest city is Bandung in central Java and is also called Kota Kembang (the flowering city). It possesses a rich accumulation of Art Deco architecture, including the Savoy Hotel, as it was established between 1920 and 1940 as a Dutch garrison town. Dutch colonial architect Ir. Frans Johan Luwrens Ghijsels had a major impact on this period by exploring tropical interpretations of Art Nouveau during his residency on Java (1910–29), particularly in the design and landscape of Bandung. Hospitals, colleges, hotels, swimming pools, private residences (including Ziekenhuis Onder de Bogen Djocjakarta [1928] in Yogyakarta), the design for the Training College (1917), the Capellen School (1926) in Bandung, the Hotel des Indes (1928) in Jakarta, the Tjikini Swimming Pool (1924) at Cikini, and the Dominique W. Beretty house "Villa Isola" (1932), are minor compared to Ghijsels's master planning for government precincts in Bandung. These precincts (1917) relied on axes to accentuate the role that Bandung was proposed to serve as the future capital of the archipelago.

Yogyakarta was established in 1755 with the formation of two central states: Surakarta (Solo) and Yogya. The Yogya Kraton is the highest-ranking court in Indonesia today, and the city remains an important center for learning and culture. The *kraton* is classical Javanese in its series of courtyard gardens and *pagelaran* (buildings), dating from 1755, with various *sitihinggil* enclosed within a four-meter-high (4.3 yd.), three-meter-thick (3.2 yd.) walled fortress. Including five gateways, it is laid out in a symmetrical northerly aligned design stretching north-south more than 1.3 square kilometers (0.5 sq. mi.), with the central courtyard representing the sacred mountain Mahameru and a western courtyard to enable prayer to Mecca. The central portion of the complex, Proboyekso, is still the private domain of the sultan of Yogyakarta and his family. Plant positions within the complex were determined according to symbolic and religious principals. This spatial layout is similar for many traditional Javanese palaces. Within the *alun-alun lor* (northern square) and *alun-alun kidul* (southern square) of this *kraton* grow the old sacred *waringen* (banyan) trees, which still receive offerings.

An extension of the rice terracing was developed by the sultans of Yogyakarta in the nearby Taman Sari (water castle). An extensive pleasure park, with an ingenious aquatic garden with numerous moats, canals, ponds, and intimate bathing pools, was commenced in 1758.

Senapati, the founder of the kingdom of Mataram, also founded nearby Kota Gede in 1579; his grave is now within a moss-covered graveyard in this settlement. One enters this series of courtyards through a broad pathway, flanked by two enormous banyan trees. His original *kraton* is now occupied by the beautiful garden cemetery established by Hamengkubuwono VIII, which includes a walled garden full of roses, jerberas, and frangipani trees.

The *kraton* of Surakarta Hadiningrat, at Solo (opened in 1745), has similar characteristics to that at Yogyakarta but is less known. The entry road runs a short distance to the *alun-alun lor,* down between two royal banyan trees, and stops in front of the pale blue Pagelaran pavilion. Much of this complex has been converted into the grounds of the university.

On the island on Lombok an extensive palace and garden at Cakranegara, including the huge Mayura (peacock) Garden with its vast pond and floating pavilion, now lies destroyed due to the 1894 Dutch invasion and 1980s earthquakes.

On the island of Bali contemporary cultural and ecological tourism goals have resulted in the development of numerous tropical gardens associated with hotel and resort developments on the island. Thematically, Bali, with its Hindu predominance, maintains a garden design philosophy of *ramé* (overcrowded abundance) with a contrasting *sepi* (empty stillness). The banyan is the symbolic tree, and the Pura Taman Ayun, part of the former capital of Mengwi, and the garden temples of Pura Baturkau, Pura Ulun Danu Bratan, and the water gardens of Tirta Gangga (Ganges water) and Tirta Empul (fountain of immortality) are illustrative of Hindu cosmology. Before the Dutch only the Balinese kings had gardens, often as garden temples with pavilions, fountains, and water spouts in the form of animals, mimicking an amalgam of Indian Mogul and Hindu design principles with Chinese architectural aesthetics. The palaces of Klungkung (Pura Smarapura [palace of the god of love]) and Denpasar, featuring *balé kambang* (floating pavilions), were partially destroyed with Dutch invasions in 1906 and 1908, while Gianyar and Karangasem (Amlapura) survived. Tourism developments have sought to draw inspiration from these complexes at Sanur, Kuta, Ubud, Nusa Dua, resulting in projects such as the Bali Hyatt, Grand Hyatt, the Batujimar Estate, Amandari, and have also encouraged the maintenance of the Eka Karya Botanic Gardens at Candi Kuning, and the creation of the Bali Barat National Park (19,366 ha [47,834 acre]) in 1947. Many of the recent landscape design projects on Bali have been influenced by designers Bill Bensley and Michael White.

Since the 1960s garden design and landscape architecture have been maturing in Indonesia. Garden and landscape architecture education at Bogor and Trisakti have foreshadowed the growth in this sphere, which has largely been driven by hotel and resort development and monument creation.

See also Kebun Raya Botanic Garden

Further Reading

Akihary, Huib, *Ir. F.J.L. Ghijsels, Architect in Indonesia, 1910–1929,* Utrecht, Netherlands: Seram Press, 1996

Beng, Tan Hock, *Tropical Architecture and Interiors: Tradition-Based Design of Indonesia, Malaysia, Singapore, Thailand,* Singapore: Page One, 1994

Helmi, Rio, and Barbara Walker, *Bali Style,* Singapore: Times Editions, 1996

Holttum, Richard Eric, and Ivan Enoch, *Gardening in the Tropics,* Singapore: Times Editions, 1991

McCracken, Donal P., *Gardens of Empire: Botanical Institutions of the Victorian British Empire,* London: Leicester University Press, 1997

Raffles, Thomas Stamford, *The History of Java,* London, 1817

Soekmono, R., J.G. de Casparis, and Jacques Dumarçay, *Borobudor: Prayer in Stone,* London: Thames and Hudson, 1990

Tettoni, Invernizzi, and William Warren, *Balinese Gardens,* Singapore: Periplus Editions, 1995

Warren, William, *The Tropical Garden,* New York and London: Thames and Hudson, 1991

DAVID JONES

Indoor Garden

Cheerful houseplants arranged into fanciful window gardens were an essential part of American and European interior decoration during the second half of the 19th century, especially in northern climates. Indoor environments conducive to plant growth, those with adequate sunlight and with temperatures that were neither too cold nor too hot, supported containerized flowering and foliage plants from around the world. Elaborate plant collections, with exotic vines that twined their way around windows, transformed the sitting room or parlor into a jungle-like oasis.

Before the 19th century, the use of houseplants was limited. It was common for parlor plants to freeze during cold winter nights. The advent of stoves in the sitting room in the early 1800s, followed by furnaces later in the 19th century, allowed for the indoor cultivation of tender plant species.

Household manuals advocated houseplants to purify the air and replace moisture lost from dehumidifying heat, although 19th-century horticulturists lamented the dry conditions that stoves and furnace heat provided plants. Boston seedsman Joseph Breck commented in 1866 that

> a choice collection of plants in the sitting room or parlor adds much to the charm of a home; but as we often see them—weak, struggling, drawn-up, crowded together, and infested with insects—they give pain rather than pleasure.

Too much heat and water, or too little light, air, and water were the most frequent causes of plant death.

By the 1870s, according to Rochester, New York seedsman and editor James Vick, most plants were injured by too much heat. It was known to horticulturists that the dry heat of the furnace harmed plants, causing an excessive loss of water through the foliage. Vick recommended that the thermostat should not go above 70 degrees Fahrenheit (21 degrees Celsius) and preferably closer to 65 degrees Fahrenheit (18 degrees Celsius). Night temperatures of 50 degrees Fahrenheit (10 degrees Celsius) were high enough, but Edward Sprague Rand, director of the Massachusetts Horticultural Society, warned that they should never fall below 40 to 45 degrees Fahrenheit (4.5 to 7.2 degrees Celsius); "To grow plants to perfection in a room is not an easy thing. Careful and constant attention to details is necessary to insure any degree of success" (Rand, 1864).

The recommended situation for growing plants indoors was a window that faced east and received the full rays of the morning sun. If such a window did not exist, a window that received afternoon sun was better than one with no sun at all. It was considered useless to attempt to grow plants in rooms where windows faced north. A bay window facing south, which provided the maximum amount of sunlight, was the best interior environment for an indoor garden.

Bay windows were integral to the rural architecture aesthetic espoused by Andrew Jackson Downing, and they were a component of many of the designs in his publications. A room in the Italianate style was recognized by the large opening of the bay window, which was "admirably adapted" to terra-cotta hanging baskets filled with flowers. Several of Downing's cottage designs in the rural Gothic style show parlors where "elegance is conferred on them by the bay window."

When glass doors separated the bay window from the parlor, a separate apartment was formed where the atmosphere could be artificially supplied with moisture by syringing water freely. In this indoor garden temperatures remained lower than what would be comfortable in the adjacent living room. Plants were also saved from dust. The "terrible infliction" of carpet sweeping, according to James Vick, caused clouds of dust dense enough to kill elderly people who were forced to breath it. Dusty plants were not healthy ones and needed to be washed and cleaned.

A window garden design favored by Henry T. Williams featured the well-known calla lily. He urged that it was "exceedingly ornamental in a bay window" when eight to ten flowering tubers were "planted in a hollow stand lined with zinc .. . three or four feet long, 18 inches wide, and eight inches deep." There was "no better plant for the center of a group of flowers" (Williams, 1876). Calla lilies were easily cared for with plenty of water, a weekly sponging of the leaves, and occasionally by turning the stand as the large leaves turned towards the light.

The parlor during the Victorian era was the domain of the ladies, and within it feminine taste prevailed. Flowers and plants were considered to be harmonious with costly parlor furniture, pictures, and statuary. Since gardening was a subject suited for women, garden related furnishings such as stands for "ladies work" and flower baskets evoked a feminine style. Mrs. Loudon's *Gardening for Ladies* addressed window gardening and the management of plants in pots.

Indoor gardeners found that plants grew best when they were potted in porous clay pots that did not retain moisture. Fancy painted pots of non-porous glazed earthenware, china, or glass were common products of the 19th century, but plants seldom thrived when planted directly in them. If decorative containers were to be used for plants, they needed to be large enough so that the clay pot could be set inside them. Window garden designs, at the height of their popularity in the last quarter of the 19th century, included a multitude of

Example of a window garden, from Henry T. Williams, editor, *Window Gardening,* 14th ed., 1878

ornamental plant receptacles: jardineres, window boxes, hanging baskets, bulb glasses, flower stands, rustic stands, cast-iron vases, and wardian cases.

Through improved greenhouse cultivation and hybridization, mid-19th century American florists sold a diverse number of plants with varying cultural requirements to indoor gardeners. Rand's 1863 *Flowers for the Parlor and Garden* lists camellia, citrus, *Daphne odorata, Azalea indica,* and cyclamen as plants that require cool temperatures. Oleanders, jasmine, and gardenias were also grown. Bedding plants like geranium, verbena, heliotrope, and roses were grown outdoors during the summer months and were to be brought into the window garden for winter bloom. When bulbs, especially hyacinths, arrived from Holland in early September, they were potted, plunged into a cold frame, brought indoors in December, and forced to flower during the winter months.

Palms became fashionable parlor decorations during the last quarter of the 19th century when the aesthetic movement popularized things exotic. Not only did palms evoke images of the tropics, they could also conjure visions of the Orient or Morocco and fit into those decorative schemes as well. Prior to the 1870s palms were considered too large for parlor decoration, and few species were cultivated. However, the South American explorations of Alexander von Humboldt acquired seeds of many species that proved easy to grow. It was discovered that seedling plants were useful and durable parlor plants and could be purchased at a low price. "No home of taste is now considered complete without its window garden," asserted Williams in 1876; "Where flowers reign, grace of mind and manner soon follow."

Further Reading

Breck, Joseph, *New Book of Flowers,* New York, 1866

Downing, Andrew, J., *The Architecture of Country Houses,* New York, 1850

Henderson, Peter, *Practical Floriculture: A Guide to the Successful Cultivation of Florists' Plants for the Amateur and Professional Florist,* New York, 1869

Hibberd, Shirley, *Rustic Adornments for Homes of Taste and Recreations for Townfolk in the Study and Imitation of Nature,* London, 1857; reprint, London: Century, 1987

James Vick Company, *Vick's Flower and Vegetable Garden*, Rochester, New York: James Vick, 1876

Loudon, Jane Webb, *Gardening for Ladies and Companion to The Flower Garden,* edited by A.J. Downing, New York, 1843

Martin, Tovah, *Once upon a Windowsill: A History of Indoor Plants,* Portland, Oregon: Timber Press, 1988

Rand, Edward Sprague, *Flowers for the Parlor and Garden,* Boston, 1863

Williams, Henry T., *Window Gardening, Devoted Specially to the Culture of Flowers and Ornamental Plants for In Door Use and Parlor Decoration,* 12th edition, New York, 1876

RICHARD R. IVERSEN

Informal Garden

At the dawn of the 20th century, a new design approach to gardens developed throughout the Western world. Called the informal or naturalistic garden, it grew from a British tradition of design innovation. English designers were among the first to embrace the organic freedom of the flora and fauna, and they simulated it in their gardens and landscapes. Characteristically natural and relaxed, the informal garden drew its aesthetic justification from the apparent freedom of plant life. In a naturalistic garden plants grew unhindered, maturing to their natural form in untamed compositions.

The early English proponents of the informal or natural style stoutly opposed the formal garden traditions of Italian, French, and Dutch models. These English gardeners of the 18th century abandoned the classic geometries, axes, and symmetries of their Renaissance predecessors. Rolling green hills, casually placed copses of trees, meandering rivers, and sudden views of lakes replaced the formal arrangements of the previous centuries. The British landscape and climate ideally suited this new design concept. Its pastoral countryside and rich collection of native plant material created the illusion of endless landscape. Foregrounding the natural elements, the informal garden emphasizes those characteristics most harmonious with nature's intentions.

Landscape designer Lancelot "Capability" Brown is closely associated with garden design from this period. Brown softened the stiff, formal elements in his landscapes, eliminating straight lines and de-emphasizing geometry to expose the natural forms of the landscape. His talent for envisioning the "capabilities" of a site, combined with a widely accepted passion for the simple charms of nature, brought about a revolution in design. Brown and other similarly minded designers no longer thought of nature as merely something to be tamed and organized, embracing the natural environment for its unique qualities.

Sir Uvedale Price, a leading figure in English culture and society, was among several exponents of the 18th-century Picturesque concept of landscape. Designers of the Picturesque believed they could improve upon the "sublime" composition of nature. They aimed to intensify nature's beauty, accentuating the rough, rugged, savagely dramatic, and anything that might induce strong feelings of fear or amazement. The aesthetic of the Picturesque endured into the 19th century, now reflecting a wilder, more chaotic view of nature.

This preoccupation with wildness may have developed partly from the spread of industrialism—mines, factories, and mills dominating once-rural landscapes. Western civilization has always struggled to harness and tame the wilderness, and by the end of the 19th century, the culture had spread imperialistically to other "untamed" landscapes. The naturalistic garden resembles in this light something of a museum, an organic memento of wilderness frontiers. Deriving primarily from British design innovations, the naturalistic garden may be seen as a remembrance of vanquished wildernesses, but it is also a reminder of imperial rule.

The landscape movement in the so-called English way or natural tradition inspired subsequent garden styles in both Europe and the United States. William Robinson, an Irishman, developed in his work and writing in the late 19th century the idea of the ecological return to nature. Condemning the artificiality of the formal style, Robinson expressed the need for a greater respect of nature and garden design. Revered as the "grandfather of the natural tradition," he promoted the virtues of naturalistic plantings in a variety of settings—in woodland gardens, along streambeds, as shrub borders, and in open areas as meadows. He developed several concepts of importance to the process of garden making: harmoniously combining various flower colors and forms, planting self-seeding perennials to foster the self-cultivating garden, and carefully selecting plants to reduce maintenance and plant loss. Robinson envisioned the garden as a reflection of personality or cultural influences. He argued that a love of nature should inspire the gardener to create a space that transcended

The garden of Castle Howard, designed in 18th-century English Landscape style
Copyright Paul C. Siciliano, Jr.

novelty or mere spectacle. The true gardener would design a garden space to live in, a space that would delight, whether arranged formally or informally. The naturalistic garden should be harmonious and alluring; it should complement rather than contradict nature.

This informal attitude provoked considerable opposition among landscape and garden designers. Most prominent among the opponents of the new, informal style was Reginald Blomfield, who stated his position in *The Formal Garden in England* (1892). Blomfield insisted on laying out gardens with regularity and symmetry, based on a strong axial design.

The general shift of taste favored naturalism. English landscape designer Gertrude Jekyll championed naturalistic planting in the rural cottage gardens that she designed during the late 19th and early 20th centuries. She has been recognized for establishing the fashion of the herbaceous garden borders, planting hardy perennials, biennials, and annuals in informal drifts, often within formal constraints of ordered geometries extending from the associated dwelling. The resulting display appeared to be without plan, a luxuriant accident of nature harmonizing with the strict geometries and orders of a classical arrangement.

Jekyll collaborated with architect Sir Edwin Lutyens on many projects. This partnership narrowed the gap between the opposing views of the formal versus the informal philosophies for design. Lutyens and Jekyll united in their gardens the architectural garden theories of Reginald Blomfield and the informal, naturalistic opinions of Robinson. Each garden theory has its value, but they are both contrived forms. As Edith Wharton pointed out in her book *Italian Villas and Their Gardens* (1904), "sympathies are divided between the artificial-natural and the frankly conventional (formal). The time has come, however, when it is recognized that both of these manners *are* manners, the one as artificial as the other, and each to be judged, not by any ethical standard of 'sincerity,' but on its own aesthetic merits." Landscape design in the United States has employed both the formal architectonic style as well as the informal naturalistic approach.

Designers in the United States who were influenced by earlier exponents of the informal, naturalistic style included landscape architect Frederick Law Olmsted, who adapted the Picturesque imitation of nature popularized by designers in England as a method for improving the civilization of the United States. Several 19th-century urban parks, including Central and Prospect Parks, both in New York, provide restorative antidote to the stresses of urban life through "natural scenery." The landscape parks that Olmsted designed provided city inhabitants a place in which to escape the hectic urban lifestyle and experience the redeeming power of nature in tranquil surroundings.

Example of a garden designed in an informal style
Copyright James van Sweden

Landscape architects Wolfgang Oehme and James van Sweden embrace nature in their work as garden designers. Their distinctively American work has engendered a new aesthetic of 20th-century design that has come to be known as the New American Garden Style. Internationally renowned, Oehme and van Sweden have worked on public and private projects and lectured on their design philosophies in U.S. and European universities. Their gardens are natural, free spirited, and informal, perhaps even wild. Inspired by Robinson, Jekyll, and other proponents of a freer style of gardening, Oehme and van Sweden's garden style reflects the beauties of the American countryside, especially its meadows and prairies. They juxtapose drifts of flowering perennials against great sweeps of native grasses, achieving a feeling of grandeur with massed plantings and dramatic scale by varying colors and textures. Most important, their gardens accommodate all the seasons. Plants flourish naturally in spring and summer with little or no maintenance. By autumn the garden glows with the splendid color of ripened foliage and persistent seed heads. The drama continues through winter, revealing fascinating textures against snow. Oehme and van Sweden's work does not attempt to copy the arrangement of plants in nature but rather attempts to translate nature's motives into designed landscapes. Their gardens arouse the senses and engage the imagination.

In the postindustrial age, such gardens may evoke once-wild landscape, but they also suggest the ordered chaos of the contemporary world. The informal style of gardening continues to thrive today, opposing strict formalities. In creating such gardens, designers accommodate nature, yielding to its unsolicited contribution.

Further Reading

Hobhouse, Penelope, *Garden Style,* Boston: Little Brown, and London: Windward, Lincoln, 1988

Hobhouse, Penelope, and Jerry Harpur, *Penelope Hobhouse's Natural Planting,* London: Pavilion, and New York: Holt, 1997

Oehme, Wolfgang, James Van Sweden, and Susan Rademacher Frey, *Bold Romantic Gardens: The New World Landscapes of Oehme and Van Sweden,* Reston, Virginia: Acropolis, 1990; revised edition, Washington, D.C.: Spacemaker Press, 1998

Pizzoni, Filippo, *Il giardino: Arte e storia,* Milan: Arte, 1997; as *The Garden: A History in Landscape and Art,* translated by Judith Landry, London: Aurum Press, and New York: Rizzoli, 1999

Robinson, William, *The English Flower Garden,* London, 1883; 15th edition, London: Murray, 1933; reprint, Sagaponack, New York: Sagapress, 1995

Tankard, Judith B., and Michael Van Valkenburgh, *Gertrude Jekyll: A Vision of Garden and Wood,* London: Murray, and New York: Abrams/Sagapress, 1989

Turner, Roger, *Capability Brown and the Eighteenth-Century English Landscape,* London: Weidenfeld and Nicholson, and New York: Rizzoli, 1985

Van Sweden, James, and Wolfgang Oehme, *Gardening with Nature,* New York: Random House, 1997

Wharton, Edith, *Italian Villas and Their Gardens,* London: John Lane, 1904; New York: Century, 1907

PAUL C. SICILIANO, JR.

Iran

The creation of orchards and gardens has a long history in Iran; the earliest evidence dates to the early sixth century B.C., during the time of the Achaemenid dynasty. Flowers, trees, and herbs have long held a special place in Iranian culture. This is evidenced primarily by the remains at Persepolis and the various Sassasian monuments.

Iran has several climactic and geophysical regions, but the dominant one is the central plain of Iran, an elevated plateau shaped like a basin and surrounded by several ranges of high mountains. These mountains are largely of alpine origin and rise sharply high above the plain. Only in the northeast does the land vary, where the Elburz Mountains lead to the Caspian Sea, and where a Mediterranean climate persists. Here, one finds more vegetation, more rainfall, and a more temperate climate, as opposed to the hot, dusty plain. But it is the Iranian plain that has a persistent culture of irrigation and of garden design, given the scarcity of water and vegetation.

The plain is flat and desertlike, with reddish-brown soil. Where water has collected into lagoons, the reddish-brown soil changes to a shade of a dull yellow, since the water is brackish and slow moving. To see a splash of green in such an area is certainly a welcome sight. Hence, there is a need for gardens, where vegetation and water serve as much-needed relief from the monotony of the plain.

Much of Iran has scant vegetation, but because of irrigation agriculture is the dominant way of life. Until recent times, before the oil industry, water lay at the heart of Iranian civilization (as with many other Middle Eastern cultures). It was this old economy that gave richness to Persian civilization and made it into a world power in the fifth century B.C. This economy also made Iran the center of learning in the Middle Ages and lent a deep-seated respect for water in the Persian psyche, which found its fullest expression in the paradise garden.

Rainfall in the plain is seldom more than five inches (12.7 cm) per year, and most of that falls within a space of a few days, and sometimes even one day. As a result few rivers are permanent; little water remains on the surface for long, given the high seepage through the porous ground and excessive evaporation, and little exists to contain the rain when it does fall, resulting in flooding of the land with devastating effects. Therefore, the precious commodity of water is managed by way of elaborate canals. The only river that is permanent is the

Zaindeh, which flows through Isfahan. This great river feeds many oases for approximately 40 miles (64 km) and keeps a swath of green vibrant some 10 to 15 miles (16 to 24 km) deep into the desert. Fed by the snows of the high Zagros Mountains to the west, the river runs for several hundred miles before finally being lost in the salt flats of Gavkaneh to the east. Along the upper reaches of the Zaindeh, where the river is strongest, the water is directed away by small aqueducts or jukes and channeled into villages and even cities. These jukes form a familiar Persian scene, with many trees and shrubs lining the coursing river.

Other types of irrigation methods include the Persian well and the *qanat* well. The Persian well uses large scoops fixed to a moving belt stretched between two wheels (often turned by oxen, mules, or asses) to haul water and dump it into a trough, where it then flows into a conduit, from where it is diverted into a series of smaller irrigation ditches.

The need for water engendered many types of garden designs, which used the various traditional methods of Persian irrigation. For example, well gardens made use of the area around a well as a place for flowers and other vegetation and shade-giving trees. Canal gardens lined the banks of canals; typically, poplar and willows trees would be planted for shade, along with shrubs and other plants. All along the length of canals were fields of wheat. Tank gardens surrounded a tank of water, where shady trees were planted. In addition, gardens were created where a pool of water naturally occurred, at which people could come to rest and to take their water supply for the day.

The second method of irrigation is the uniquely Persian *qanat,* a complex underground aqueduct that terminates in a large cistern where the water accumulates. The entire process begins when water is located. Then a straight shaft is bored to the level of the water, which can be found at about 50 yards (46 m). Thereafter, the placement and distance of the cistern is determined. In between the water source and the cistern, a series of vertical shafts are drilled (usually at about 22 or 33 yards [20 or 30 m]), at the same depth as the master shaft. Then the entire series of shafts is linked at the bottom by a tunnel, with a breakthrough on the master shaft. This tunnel is some 1.5 yards (1.4 m) in diameter. The water rushes forward, flowing from one shaft to the next until it empties into the cistern at the far end of the *qanat.* However, a *qanat* does not have to end in a cistern; the water can be channeled from one enclosure to another until it reaches the desired final depository.

The cistern directly led to the Persian garden tank, the crossing piece of the paradise garden. In some cases the cistern is below ground level and a flight of steps leads down into the subterranean well, where the temperature is always pleasantly cool. This is the origin of the *birchet* or *ambar,* the resting house, which became a typical feature of the classic paradise garden.

The roots of Iranian or Persian culture span many millennia. A fundamental component of this continuing tradition is the paradise garden, which has a long history and is linked with the Iranian love for flowers, trees, and water. Records from the Achaemenid period show that gardening was a viable and flourishing trade. During this time horticultural knowledge and many plants and trees were introduced to various Western nations. It is said that King Cyrus the Great in the sixth century B.C. planted the garden at Sardis with his own hands, arranging the trees carefully into ordered rows. King Darius (r. 522–486 B.C.) had large gardens constructed at Persepolis. In one of these gardens King Xerxes (r. 486–465 B.C.) had a favorite chenar tree whose branches he adorned with golden amulets and bangles. King Khusru II constructed a vast paradise garden, contained within 300 acres (122 ha). Many large gardens have been found in the archaeological record dating from the Umayyad dynasty (ca. A.D. 750).

According to the fifth-century B.C. Greek historian Herodotus, the Iranian people used spray perfumes derived from various flowers in their religious festivals and victory parades. Much later, in the 11th century A.D., the poet Ferdowsi referred to this tradition, recounting that during the Pishdadian dynasty it was customary to sprinkle perfume and saffron (along with gold and silver coins) during festivals. Ferdowsi's writings also relate that the Pishdadian kings invented the art of perfume distillation and herbal essences.

Persia was one of the first countries to come under Muslim rule, after the defeat of the Sassanian dynasty, around A.D. 642. By this time Persia had a well-established and highly developed culture, with many traditions that the conquering Arabs did not possess. These various traditions were overlaid with Islamic ideology and freely adopted by the conquerors. Thus what is normally considered Islamic in the Islamic garden (the paradise garden) is in fact ultimately Persian in origin. This is also true of many elements of the Islamic garden. For example, the garden at Pasargadae (early sixth century B.C.), a palace complex built by Cyrus the Great, certainly shows features that came to be typically Islamic. The present-day ruins of Pasargadae comprise a large expanse of meadows, where once stood two palaces, two pavilions, and a stone waterway interspersed with pools. As in the Islamic garden, the waterway served two functions: it was a formal element and it irrigated the garden. Pasargadae was probably meant to be seen and enjoyed from large pavilions as a beautiful vista, rather than a place for promenading, with walkways and footpaths. This aspect certainly continued in the later Persian gardens, where the view was an integral part of the design. The complex at Persepolis and the palace at Susa also show the inclusion of gardens in palace architecture. Persopolis, constructed by Darius, had many garden areas, where various trees, flowers, and shrubs were planted, along with the inclusion of water. The palace at Susa shows a garden courtyard, around which the buildings were arranged. Thus even at this early date gardens had become an important and indispensable part of official architecture.

By the time of the Sassanian period (A.D. 224–642), earlier elements of the garden combined with newer ones. Thus, for example, at the Imarat-e-Khusrow complex near Kirmanshah (ca. A.D. 620) built for Khusrow Parvez II, contemporary accounts relate that the building was enclosed by a paradise garden, which in turn was encompassed by a wall. A great pool stood in an inner garden. As before, this garden was probably meant to be seen rather than used. *Qanats* were incorporated as decorative elements and were not merely functional. Not far from the Imarat-e-Khusrow complex is the Howsh Kuri Palace (ca. A.D. 620), with an avenue running from the north to the entrance of the large central garden, where stood a number of pavilions from where the garden could be viewed.

The paradise garden is certainly an important concept in Persian garden design, although the marriage of trees, flowers, and water in a harmonious whole is a far older concept in the cultural history of the Middle East. Indeed, the Garden of Eden, the first paradise, was certainly construed as a garden. The basic design of the paradise garden, also known as *chahar-bagh* (quartered garden), is inherently simple, in which water is shown to be the source of life both symbolically and physically. Four channels converge in the center of the garden, dividing the rectangular area into four quarters. These waterways are raised above ground level and used for irrigation purposes. On each side of the channels, straight lines of trees are planted, while the quarters themselves are filled with flowers or shrubs and more trees; sometimes trees are also planted at each side of the garden to form a woodland. The entire garden is then surrounded by a wall to lend privacy and to keep out dust-laden winds, and a pavilion is set at the juncture where the four channels meet, where the coolness from the flowing water may be enjoyed. This is the basic design upon which many variations were created across Iran, Afghanistan, and northern India.

The design of the *chahar-bagh* was also imbued with symbolic significance. The cross formed by the intersection of the water channels came to represent the meeting of humanity and the divine. Later, the octagon, which is the squaring of a circle, was also included in the paradise garden and represented the meeting of the mundane (denoted by the square) with the circle of eternity. Present also were other Islamic symbols. For example, the division of the garden into eight parts designated the eight divisions of the Koran. The water tanks were always ten cubits by ten cubits, thus copying the water tanks where the faithful did their ablutions before the daily prayers (Muslims are enjoined to pray five times a day). In addition, the conventional planting of cypress trees alternatively with fruit trees came to symbolize immortality (the evergreen cypress) with the season renewal of life (the flowering fruit trees).

Typically, a paradise garden contains extensive geometric designs within which exuberant flowers and plants flourish. The colorful roses, irises, and tulips and the rising cypress poplar and chenar trees offset the formal interlacing of geometric patterns, thus ensuring that order is wedded to freedom and growth.

Originally, the paradise garden was flat, but soon waterfalls were introduced wherever gardens stood beside hills that rose from the plain, as in Shiraz. Common also were dovecotes, which were placed at the corners of the enclosing walls. These can still be seen in the countryside, especially around the city of Isfahan. The purpose of these dovecotes was to provide a source of food, but they were in fact the architectural ancestors of the later pavilions and gazebos that would be placed within gardens, especially in the later Mogul gardens.

Trees commonly found in a paradise garden included almond, apple, apricot, cherry, fig, date, lemon, lime, mulberry, orange, plum, pomegranate, quince, and walnut. Flowers too were abundant, such as carnation, stocks, wallflower, saffron, narcissus, lilac, delphinium, violet, sunflower, rose, marigold, poppy, peonies, crown imperial, lily, tulip, iris, and cyclamen.

Although most of the garden elements were certainly in existence before the Islamic conquest of Iran, the Muslim conquerors did provide the garden with many metaphors. One important metaphor is that of the garden as paradise. In the Koran paradise is often depicted as a beautiful garden, where running water flows from bubbling fountains, where there are two kinds of every fruit and delightful foods of a great variety, and where couches are laid out for the blessed, where they can recline and enjoy the beauties of the heavenly garden. The garden was also described as an oasis, an escape from the harsh realities of the world outside, where rest, relaxation, and quiet could be found. Consequently, Muslim gardens were always secluded and private, surrounded by a high wall or contained in the courtyards of buildings. The garden surrounded by a wall was certainly the garden of choice in Islamic Iran. A good example is the Hasht Behisht ("Eight Paradises") in Isfahan, which was built during the Safavid period by Shah Suleiman (1667–94).

Some of the early paradise gardens are found in Afghanistan, such as the Bagh-e-Babur Shah, Bagh-e-Wafa, and Bagh-e-Baba Wali. Bagh-e-Babur Shah ("Garden of Babur the King") is found in Kabul and is the tomb of Babur, the first Mogul emperor of India (r. 1508–30). The remains of the garden show a four-terraced construction on the Shah-e-Kabul hill. Originally, Babur wished his grave to be simple and open to the elements. Because of great deterioration a modern shelter has been placed above the grave proper for protection. One of Babur's sons, Hindal, is buried beside him. In 1640 Shah Jahan (the builder of the Taj Mahal) added a mosque to the garden, where it still stands. Throughout the garden various flowering shrubs were planted, as were wild cherry trees, one of the trees favored by Babur.

Babur described his favorite garden, the Bagh-e-Wafa ("Garden of Fidelity"), in his autobiography. It was perhaps located in Kabul, Afghanistan, and was a classic *chahar-bagh* with running water and a reservoir, according to Babur's description. Here, Babur planted such trees as citron, orange, plantain, pomegranate, and even sugarcane. It is believed that Babur himself directed the construction of this garden. He often came here to rest after his campaigns in India. As to its location, remains of a garden in the Mogul style have been found outside the city of Kabul proper, lower down near the Kabul River at Nimla, close to Jelalabad. However, there can be no precise identification.

The Bagh-e-Baba Wali ("Garden of Baba Wali") houses the tomb of the Sufi mystic Baba Wali Kandahari (popularly known as Baba Hasan Abdal), who lived during the latter part of the 14th century through the late 15th century. Approximately four miles (6.5 km) west of the city of Kandahar in Afghanistan are the ruins of the old city. Historians believe that the name "*Kandahar*" is derived from "*Alexandria*"—Alexander the Great indeed founded a city in this area and named it "Alexandria the Furthermost." Down the rocky slopes of a ridge, into the plains, are the ruins of old Kandahar. From the top of the ridge a small citadel overlooks the half-buried ruins. Within the walls of this ruined city is the Bagh-e-Baba Wali, a famous shrine that once attracted many pilgrims. Although the place is now only ruins, visible still on the northeast face of the hill are 40 steps cut into the living rock that lead up to a small domed niche, where inscriptions by Emperor Babur can still be read, in which he records details of his conquests and his Indian empire. There is also an inscription by his grandson Akbar. The garden itself once was a beautiful example of the paradise garden; many fruit trees and flowers grew in plots, irrigated by water channeled from a long-dried nearby spring and from the Argandab River.

Other gardens have continued the tradition of the Persian garden. Bagh-e-Dilgusha ("Garden of the Heart's Delight") in Shiraz dates from the mid-18th century and is located in the northeast part of the city, near the Mausoleum of Saadi (a 13th-century Persian poet). The garden is set at the foot of a barren mountainside to the north, and one can easily discern that a long canal once ran through it, with a pool and many fountains. The garden was renowned for its flower beds and flowering trees.

Bagh-e-Eram ("Garden of Eternal Rest"), also found in Shiraz, was constructed in the early 19th century, at the foot of a mountain range. The garden is extensive, covering some 57 acres (23 ha). A path leads from an entry on the north to a royal pavilion (from the Qajar period) situated in the very center of the garden. At the lower level of this pavilion, a water channel runs through a tiled room. In front is a large water tank from which a narrow canal extends, from which in turn many offshoots flow into the garden. These offshoots are lined with straight paths and high trees, as well as various shrubs, flowers, and roses.

Bagh-e-Fin ("Garden of Fin"), also called Bagh-e-Shah ("Garden of the King"), is located in the town of Kashan and is named after the oasis spring of Fin, some 3.7 miles (6 km) off, close to the great desert Dasht-e-Kavir. The early buildings in the garden, from the time of Shah Abbas I (r. 1588–1629), have long vanished. The current buildings date from the mid-19th century. Inside the walls of the garden, the spring provides a constant source of flowing water to all the channels and the large pool located in front of a pavilion. All around are many fountains, with plane and cypress trees bordering most of the pathways. Scattered across the 3.7-acre (1.5-ha) garden are plots where flowers of many colors grow in profuse abundance.

Bagh-e-Gulshan ("Rose Garden"), also known as Afifabad, was created in 1863. Located to the west of Shiraz, it is over 547 yards (500 m) long and extends well over 49.9 acres (20 ha). It was formerly owned by the late shah of Iran. The garden contains a small courtyard with pool and fountain. From here a long tank leads to a large pavilion, built of stone quarried locally, with a large reception hall and many smaller adjacent rooms. The grounds contain many beds of roses, several pools with fountains, long paths lined with trees, and large swaths of grassy areas.

Bagh-e-Takht ("Throne Garden") was once located on the northern edge of the city of Shiraz and extended over 3.5 acres (1.4 ha) of land, at the foot of a rocky hillside. It was established in the 11th century by Atabeg Qaracheh; the original name of the garden is unknown. The 17th-century French traveler Jean-Baptiste Travernier referred to this same garden as Bagh-e-Firdaus ("Paradise Garden") and described it as always full of fruit trees, rose trees, and abundant flowers. The water from a spring in the rock, which supplied this hillside garden, was enough to fill a small artificial lake, on which boats glided. The pressure of the water was enough to maintain jets of water that could be opened or closed. Presently, Bagh-e-Takht is a neglected ruin, where housing complexes are now being built.

See also Islamic Gardens

Further Reading

Brookes, John, *Gardens of Paradise: The History and Design of the Great Islamic Gardens,* New York: New Amsterdam, and London: Weidenfeld and Nicolson, 1987

Khansari, Mehdi, M. Reza Moghtader, and Minouch Yavari, *The Persian Garden: Echoes of Paradise,* Washington, D.C.: Mage, 1998

Lehrman, Jonas, *Earthly Paradise: Gardens and Courtyards in Islam,* Berkeley: University of California Press, and London: Thames and Hudson, 1980

Moynihan, Elizabeth B., *Paradise As a Garden: In Persia and Mughal India,* New York: Braziller, 1979; London: Scolar Press, 1980

Wilber, Donald Wilber, *Persian Gardens and Garden Pavilions,* Rutland, Vermont: C.E. Tuttle, 1962; 2nd edition, Washington, D.C.: Dumbarton Oaks, 1979

NIRMAL DASS

Ireland

Ireland has long been renowned for its mild, equable climate, warmer than would be expected for its latitude. In recent times it has also become renowned for its gardens.

There are few explicit records of ornamental gardens in Ireland prior to the 16th century, and archaeological investigations have not yet contributed significantly to our knowledge of gardens before that period. Gardens certainly were ubiquitous but were little more than small-scale agricultural plots containing vegetables and herbs. Accounts indicate that orchards and gardens were associated with the monasteries established by continental religious orders that came to Ireland in the late 12th century and also with the castles and fortified houses built after the Norman invasion of Ireland in 1170. Those gardens would have contained edible plants, vegetables, and medicinal herbs and may also have had a few primarily ornamental plants such as roses and lilies, both of which, along with almost all medicinal and culinary herbs, had to be imported as they are not native to Ireland.

Among indirect evidence for gardening in Ireland in the Middle Ages are carvings and manuscripts. The capitals of columns in the chancel of the ruined abbey of Sancta Maria de Petra Fertilis, Corcomroe, County Clare, are carved with flowers and seed pods, apparently representing exotic plants (lily-of-the-valley, henbane, poppies) such as would have been grown in a cloister garden; the abbey dates from 1205–10, meaning that the carvings predate, by about a century, better known botanical carvings in English and French cathedrals. The manuscripts are copies of the earliest gardening manual in English by one Master Jon Gardener and were made in the 14th century, probably by a scribe working in County Kildare. They include references to "the herbs of Ireland," this phrase being absent from later copies.

Early maps and plans of towns and castles, compiled in the late 16th and early 17th centuries, show gardens within the walls and castle bawns (fortified enclosure). These gardens had regular patterns of beds similar to the knot gardens typical of Elizabethan England. Thus, garden design at this period copied the style prevalent in other countries, especially England, which was the principal home of most of the landowners. However, none of these gardens survives, and to date none has been revealed by excavations. Exotic ornamentals were certainly being imported into Ireland by gardeners in the late 16th century, and at least one Irish native species, the strawberry tree (*Arbutus unedo*) found around Killarney, County Kerry, was exported to England to adorn gardens there. It is said that Sir Walter Raleigh introduced wallflowers (*Erysimum* spp.) and cherries in the late 16th century and that he brought the first potatoes to Ireland, but this latter claim is contradicted by other evidence.

Unexcavated, relic gardens dating from the early 17th century include those at Dunluce Castle, County Antrim, and at Lemaneh, County Clare, where traces of fishponds, terraces, walls, and a summerhouse survive. However, the series of wars and rebellions that unsettled Ireland during the mid- to late 1600s, until the end of the campaign of William III in the 1690s, meant that during much of the 17th century gardens were not a priority for the landed class and certainly not for the peasantry. There were exceptions: especially notable was Sir Arthur Rawdon of Moira, County Down, who employed a collector to travel to Jamaica to collect tropical plants for his conservatory. The project was uniquely successful; James Harlow brought about 1,000 plants from the Caribbean to Moira in 1692. A few late 18th-century gardens survive. The best example, in the French style with canals and formal hedges, is at Kilruddery, Bray, County Wicklow; another is Antrim Castle, County Antrim. Others remain as unexcavated sites, as at Castle Coole, County Fermanagh.

In the 18th century stability and prosperity prevailed. Many fine large houses were built and demesnes laid out, again according to the prevailing fashion in England. Most demesnes were designed as spacious landscaped parks, with clumps of trees (in the style promoted in England by Lancelot "Capability" Brown), ha-has, vistas, follies, and artificial lakes. There were few Irish-born landscape architects active during this period, so men were usually brought from England to supervise the work, some of which may have been carried out as famine relief. Native designers whose names and works are known include W. King (fl. 1780), who worked at Florence Court and Castle Coole, County Fermanagh, and James Sutherland (ca. 1745–1826), whose earliest known work was at Derrymore, County Armagh. Examples of early 18th-century gardens include Castle Hyde, County Cork; Castletown House, Celbridge, County Kildare, which includes the Connolly Folly; and Howth Castle, Howth, County Dublin. Later examples include Florence Court, Crom Castle, and Castle Coole, all in County Fermanagh; Carton House, County Kildare; Curraghmore, County Waterford, which contains a famous shell house; and Powerscourt, County Wicklow. At the same time there was considerable interest in florist's flowers—auriculas and carnations, for example—and a Florists Club flourished briefly in Dublin during the 1740s.

The first botanic garden was established on the campus of Trinity College, Dublin, in 1687, and by the 1720s it contained novel exotic plants as well as traditional medicinal herbs; its prime purpose was medical education. A publicly funded botanic garden, to benefit and educate the general public, was formed under the auspices of the Dublin Society at Glasnevin, one of Dublin's northern suburbs, in 1795. This continues to flourish as the National Botanic Gardens.

Ireland in the 19th century was a place of stark contrasts, even more so than in previous centuries. The landed classes enjoyed their gardens and embellished them with the latest novelties and restyled them according to the prevailing fashions. Powerscourt, County Wicklow, is a good example of a garden spectacularly remodeled in the mid-19th century by, among others, Daniel Robertson. Such gardens required a large labor force to keep them in prime condition, and unskilled laborers were plentiful. There was comparatively little horticultural training available in Ireland, however, so owners were often obliged to engage head gardeners from Scotland, where the system of education and garden apprenticeships encouraged young men to become expert plantsmen as well as good practical gardeners.

Horticultural societies were established and flourished in the towns, attracting membership from the landed gentry and middle classes. The membership was almost without exception drawn from the minority Protestant community. The Royal Horticultural Society of Ireland, which continues to function, was formed in 1816. Horticultural shows also flourished, and those in Dublin attracted fashionable crowds. The three main botanic gardens—the Royal Dublin Society's at Glasnevin, that belonging to Trinity College Dublin at Ballsbridge, and the one run by Belfast Horticultural Society—distributed new species and cultivars to favored gardeners, thereby ensuring these plants were tried and tested outdoors and indoors.

For the vast majority of the population, the peasant tenant farmers, who were predominantly Roman Catholics, ornamental plants were luxuries. As the population increased rapidly, reaching more than 8 million in early 1840s, these people struggled to grow enough food on the land that they rented—potatoes were the universal staple. In 1845 the potato crop was wiped out by late blight, and again in 1846. Famine ensued, causing immigration and death.

At the same time, elaborate parterres, bedded out for the seasons with gaudy annuals, ornamented the gardens of the "big houses." Splendid greenhouses were erected, many built by Richard Turner of Ballsbridge, Dublin. Arboretums were formed by gardeners passionate about the many new plants flooding in from newly explored lands on other continents. James Hugh Smith Barry started the arboretum at Fota House, County Cork, about 1830. Thomas Acton commenced an outstanding plant collection at Kilmacurragh, County Wicklow, about 1850. They were followed by, among others, the Knight of Kerry at Glanleam and Samuel Heard at Rossdohan (both in County Kerry), Viscount Powerscourt, and most notably Earl Annesley at Castlewellan, County Down, and the marquis of Headfort at Headfort, Kells, County Meath.

At least some of the new plants, especially those from the Himalaya and New Zealand, flourished in the equable climate. In the prevailing circumstances of postfamine Ireland, there was a decline in standards of management, and so a more informal style of gardening emerged. William Robinson, a native of Ireland who started his horticultural career as a garden boy at Curraghmore, County Waterford, recognized this—he saw bamboos growing at Fota, County Cork, in a way that seemed to him to resemble the natural vegetation of the Far East. He promoted this less formal style of gardening in his book *The Wild Garden* (1870) and later continued the campaign in his periodicals and his most famous book, *The English Flower Garden* (1883). Released from the necessity of raising thousands of annuals for bedding plants, gardeners began to develop gardens that were less regimented. Today, there are many so-called Robinsonian gardens of note in Ireland, rich in plants allowed to grow as naturally as possible—Mount Usher, Ashford, County Wicklow, which Robinson sometimes visited; Annes Grove, Castletownroche, County Cork, with its river and rhododendron collection; and Rowallane, Saintfield, County Down, are just three examples.

The 20th century may be characterized by a return to formality, especially gardens composed of disparate compartments, at the same time retaining informality in the plant collections. But there was further disruption: the formation of the Irish Free State in 1922 resulted in the departure of some Protestant, Anglo-Irish families and, consequently the division of estates.

Prior to 1922 a remarkable Japanese garden was designed for Lord Wavertree by Tassa Eida, at Tully, County Kildare. Edwin Lutyens and Gertrude Jekyll designed a number of gardens in Ireland; Heywood, Ballinakill, County Laois, is regarded as one of the finest of Lutyens's small gardens, while Lambay Island, off the coast of County Fingal, is outstanding because both house and garden are by Lutyens. Other architects also added jewels. Harold Peto's formal garden on Ilnacullin (Garinish Island), Glengarriff, County Cork, is an outstanding garden enriched by an exceptional, informal collection of tender plants. In Northern Ireland, the superb, eccentric garden at Mount Stewart, Newtownabbey, County Down, deserves World Heritage Site status. Several large formal gardens were created after the partition of Ireland; Lutyens's National War Memorial at Islandbridge on the outskirts of Dublin is majestic, while the grounds of the Northern Ireland Parliament Building at Stormont, near Belfast, County Down, include a great axial drive bordered by double avenues of trees.

A final trend may be noted. The last quarter of the 20th century saw the formation by An Taisce in the Republic of Ireland of the Heritage Gardens Committee, which published a carefully considered inventory of gardens and parks of international significance according to the criteria established by International Council on Monuments and Sites (ICOMOS); this was first issued in 1980 and revised in 1988. In 1985 a unique inventory of trees and shrubs cultivated in gardens throughout Ireland was also published by the An Taisce Heritage Gardens Committee. A similar committee was established in Northern Ireland in 1980; it published a companion list for the province in 1982. Ten years later in 1992, the Northern Ireland Heritage Gardens Committee with the Institute of Irish Studies, the Queen's University of Belfast, published a more complete *Heritage Gardens Inventory,* including gardens of regional importance as well as ones of international significance. Stimulated by trends in Great Britain, the Irish Garden Plant Society was established in 1981 to work for the conservation of Ireland's garden plants. These and other projects were made possible by the considerable research into the history of gardening in Ireland, and while much remains to be discovered, a substantial corpus of publications now exists about the progress of gardening on the island.

In the 1990s interest in historic parks and gardens was further stimulated by the Great Gardens Restoration Programme initiated by the Irish government. It provided substantial grants to restore derelict gardens in the Republic and open them to the public. Gardens that have benefited from this program include Kylemore Abbey, County Galway, and Ballinlough, County Westmeath. Other refurbishment programs have restored glasshouses in the National Botanic Gardens, Glasnevin, Dublin, and in Northern Ireland at Belfast Botanic Gardens Park.

Gardeners continue to create gardens, and the best gardens are ones that are actively maintained and continually renewed. Notable gardens of the present day include Helen and Val Dillon's garden at Ranelagh, Dublin, and Jim Reynold's at Butterstream, Trim, County Meath. Darina Allen has created a new series of gardens around a reclaimed 1830s garden at Kinoith, Shanagarry, County Cork, including a spectacular modern shell house. In addition, Kate and Nicholas Mosse have recovered the 18th-century romantic garden at Kilfane, County Kilkenny, and added modern sculpture.

See also Glasnevin, National Botanic Gardens; Mount Stewart

Further Reading

Bowe, Patrick, "The Renaissance Garden in Ireland," *GPA Irish Arts Review Yearbook* 11 (1995)

Bowe, Patrick, and E. Charles Nelson, editors, "A List of Gardens and Parks of International and National Significance in the Republic of Ireland," *Moorea* 7 (1988)

Fitz-Gerald, Desmond, and Patrick Bowe, editors, *Gardens of Outstanding Historic Interest in the Republic of Ireland,* Dublin: An Taisce, 1980

Jupp, Belinda, *Heritage Gardens Inventory 1992,* Belfast: The Queen's University, 1992 Lamb, Keith, and Patrick Bowe, *A History of Gardening in Ireland,* Dublin: National Botanic Gardens, 1995

Malins, Edward Greenway, *Lost Demesnes,* London: Barrie and Jenkins, 1976

Malins, Edward Greenway, *Irish Gardens and Demesnes from 1830,* London: Barrie and Jenkins, 1980

Nelson, E. Charles, "The Dublin Florists' Club in the Mid-Eighteenth Century," *Garden History* 10 (1982)

Nelson, E. Charles, "Some Records (1690–1830) of Greenhouses in Irish Gardens," *Moorea* 2 (1983)

Nelson, E. Charles, *An Irish Flower Garden: The Histories of Some of Our Garden Plants,* Kilkenny, Ireland: Boethius Press, 1984

Nelson, E. Charles, "Towards an Historical Inventory of Irish Cultivars," *Acta Horticulturae* 182 (1986)

Nelson, E. Charles, "Scottish Connections in Irish Botany and Horticulture," *Scottish Naturalist* (1987)

Nelson, E. Charles, "'This Garden To Adorne with All Varietie'-The Garden Plants of Ireland in the Centuries before 1700," *Moorea* 9 (1990)

Nelson, E. Charles, editor, *Trees and Shrubs Cultivated in Ireland,* compiled by Mary Forrest, Kilkenny, Ireland: Boethius Press and An Taisce, 1985

Nelson, E. Charles, and Aidan Brady, editors, *Irish Gardening and Horticulture,* Dublin: Royal Horticultural Society of Ireland, 1979

Reeves-Smyth, Terence, "The Natural History of Demesnes," in *Nature in Ireland: A Scientific and Cultural History,* edited by John Wilson Foster and Helena C.G. Chesney, Dublin: Lilliput, 1997

Reeves-Smyth, Terence, *Irish Gardens and Gardening before Cromwell,* Carrigtwohill, Ireland: The Barryscourt Trust, 1999

Robins, J., "Social Influences on Irish Gardening," *Glasra* 5 (1981)

Ulster Architectural Heritage Society, *Northern Gardens: Gardens and Parks of Outstanding Historic Interest in Northern Ireland,* Belfast: Ulster Architectural Heritage Society, 1982

Walsh, Wendy F., Ruth Isabel Ross, and E. Charles Nelson, *An Irish Florilegium: The Wild and Garden Plants of Ireland,* London and New York: Thames and Hudson, 1983

E. CHARLES NELSON

Islamic Gardens

Despite Islam's vast territory from Spain to India and beyond and the many centuries since its inception in A.D. 622, gardens of Islam exhibit enough significant common aspects to be able to categorize them "Islamic gardens." This is visually apparent in the persistence of a surrounding enclosure and the widespread use of water within, creating a moist and protected microclimate in the hot and dusty lands typical of many Islamic regions. Much garden terminology is Persian, such as the apt and widely used *bustan,* which refers to an orchard or grove in a walled enclosure. Spatial interiority, a critical aspect of Islamic architecture in general, prevails in the garden as well. Public open space in the Western sense of a civic square or public park is not found. Instead, the palace, pavilion, or funerary garden, the courtyard of the mosque or madrassa, and the market passages and enclosures that constitute the Islamic landscape in its widest sense are contained within individual or groups of built structures, whether in the small, dense spaces of Fez and Cairo or the larger expanses of Isfahan and Lahore. Although these outdoor places are not normally visible from the outside, they are critical for orienting the world around them; the courtyard in all of its manifestations may be considered a primary ordering device of the Islamic physical environment, and even modest houses and residential complexes will focus on a courtyard with a water source and a small tree or vine. Outside of cities royal gardens, game parks, and funerary gardens are also enclosed, and even in these large areas there is a sense of introversion.

Other broad themes contribute to the identity of Islamic gardens, most fundamentally the Muslim concept of *tawhid,* or unity. This idea is ultimately identified with the perfection of the divine, but it is manifested through the ordered harmony and equilibrium of all material elements. Gardens are almost always rectangular with straight paths and water channels, and geometric symmetry is usually observed; patterns and colors are repetitive and contribute to a well-balanced whole. Pictorial representation in the Western manner of garden statues is absent, and no one decorative element prevails over any other. Cosmic symbolism is also a synthesizing force, most often embodied in the *chahar bagh,* Persian for fourfold garden, a quartered square or rectangular plan deriving most directly from Muslim Iran but rooted in extensive pre-Islamic precedents where the number four acts as a fundamental division of the earth. In Islam this quadripartite sectioning of the garden, often by tile-, stone-, or lead-lined water channels with a fountain or pavilion at the center, was generally understood to represent the water source and four rivers of Eden as described in the Koran. Symbolically the central structure may allude to a cosmic mountain; this is perhaps reflected in tiered construction, but it is generally apparent less in its visible form than in the orientation it provides. Even a modest pool will be geometric, usually rectangular or polygonal, made of marble or tiles, sometimes with lobed edges.

Most significant, the Islamic garden on earth is understood to be a representation of Paradise, that heavenly garden that is described in the Koran and promised to the righteous after Judgment. From the Old Persian *pairidaeza,* for walled garden, comes the word *paradise* (via *paradeisos* in Greek), but in the Koran the word *djanna,* meaning simply "garden" in Arabic, is favored. *Djanna* is mentioned many times in the Koran and later Muslim literature, often in highly specific and hospitable terms; it is the Koranic description of a garden of delights—four rivers of water, wine, milk, and honey, lotus trees without thorns, laden banana trees, shade trees, pomegranates, palms, fountains and pavilions, golden brocade settees, beautiful youths and virgins—that served as inspiration for Islamic pleasure gardens often built as part of palace enclosures. At the same time the notion of an eschatological paradise characterizes funerary complexes, particularly in today's India and Pakistan, of which the Taj Mahal is the best known. Despite the Islamic injunction to refrain from elaborate tomb structures, large mausoleums were surrounded by extensive gardens in what is thought by some to anticipate the final paradise for which the deceased lies in wait.

The paradise garden may be seen in contrast to the desert, which also acted as a powerful force in the Islamic landscape, both in its own dormant possibilities for life and in the verdant oases in its midst. The courtyard of the Prophet Mohammed's house at Medina (ca. 622), available to us only in limited reconstruction but arguably the first Islamic garden, is certainly indicative of early attitudes to nature. It is described as combining the complementary opposites of an open sunlit courtyard and the shady palm trees that sheltered the Prophet as he preached to his followers. Built a little later, the courtyard of the Umayyad Great Mosque in Damascus (705) articulates the dialectic further: a large and mostly empty courtyard constructed of reflective white stone is enclosed by a portico encrusted with elaborate mosaics that show gardens with many types of trees and shrubs interspersed with pavilions and bridges over streams. Although the austere courtyard remained common in mosques, there are examples of planting such as at Cordoba's Great Mosque (tenth century) where the courtyard is filled with a citrus grove in the Spanish tradition. In all mosque courtyards water is incorporated in pools, fountains, or even a simple urn for ritual ablutions.

Beyond the prevalence of the courtyard in Islamic countries, extant Islamic gardens are concentrated in Andalusia in southern Spain, where they date from the medieval period, in Persia from the 14th century, and in Mogul India from the 15th century. However, from the earliest centuries of Islam, gardens are known from archaeological and textual sources. In the Levant from at least the eighth century, Iraq from the ninth, Spain and North Africa from the eighth and ninth centuries, and Turkey by the tenth. Garden traditions developed somewhat later in the 14th and 15th centuries in central Asia and the Indian subcontinent. Where Islam spread gardens were established and flourished, often to the astonishment and admiration of foreigners. A tenth-century account by Byzantine ambassadors refers to the extraordinary palace gardens in Baghdad, and a 15th-century Flemish traveler to Tunis reports 4,000 gardens and the lingering smell of flowers and fruit in the air.

A long pre-Islamic history of horticulture exists in Iran; written sources and miniatures reveal the use of the *chahar bagh,* sophisticated irrigation systems that bring water from mountain sources in underground channels called *qanats,* and royal hunting parks and gardens (going back to at least that of Cyrus the Great in the fifth century B.C.). From the gardens of the great palace-cities of Mesopotamia, we can see continuity with the later Islamic palace gardens. Eighth-century desert palaces in Syria, Palestine, and Jordan were centers for caliphal hunting parties and themselves often contained huge irrigated courtyards (*hayr*) seemingly used for crops and keeping animals. The Abbasid palace, Jawsaq al-Khaqani in Samarra (833–42), contains courtyards that were surrounded by royal apartments, but much of its 172 acres (70 ha) of garden was part of terraced esplanades, perhaps reminiscent of the hanging gardens of Babylon, with the whole area dotted by pools and fountains and enclosed by a canal and rampart.

These two types of garden—courtyard and esplanade—became typical of Islam for many centuries to follow. Courtyard gardens within palaces were often divided fourfold with a central fountain or pool and incorporated flowers and trees; by nature they were introverted in their aspect, offering an intensity of experience with songbirds, running water, perfumed blossoms, and a variety of fruits in a relatively small enclosure. The esplanade gardens could be of enormous scale, with many subdivisions of the *chahar bagh*, vistas over planted beds and hydraulic works, and in Kashmir and parts of Persia, sometimes a backdrop of distant mountains. Spanish examples such as the Alhambra, Generalife, and Madinat al-Zahra' are clearly adaptations of the courtyard and esplanade, generally smaller than in Persia and India and without large areas of water, although with elaborate irrigation systems and extensive views. In a wide variety of Islamic gardens, the full *chahar bagh* is easily comprehensible from its parts or even fully visible, but this is not as a distant aerial view in the Western manner, for the vantage points in the Islamic gardens—a pavilion in the center, a gate or palace at one end, or a series of reception rooms around a courtyard—were integral to the space. The nonperspectival nature of Persian and Mogul miniatures, themselves an excellent source for Islamic gardens, make this clear. Much of the pleasure of the garden was seen to be in viewing and contemplating it from a place of comfort, although ceremonial functions were also important.

The Persian garden may be regarded as the source and model of the classical Islamic garden, and many of the greatest examples still exist in modern-day Iran, particularly in Isfahan and Shiraz. Terraces and stepped pathways were made to take advantage of natural slopes to enable water to run gently between channels and ponds. Large trees, such as poplar, ash, plane, elm, pine, and sycamore, were planted next to garden walls and for shade along walkways; the beds contained orchard trees (including apricot, quince, mulberry, almond, pistachio, fig, peach, and pomegranate), citrus and palms in warm regions, and grapevines. Certain trees were important for their proximity to each other: the dark cypress, a symbol of death and eternity because it never rejuvenates after being chopped down, was often juxtaposed with the willow, which easily sprouts from a stump, or with flowering plum or cherry, which represent regeneration and new life.

In establishing the Mogul Empire in the early 16th century, Babur brought the Persian garden eastward to Afghanistan and India. Conditions in India, with its great open plains, precluded the productive *bustan* or flower garden, and the Mogul garden tends to be more expansive and open, with larger areas of water. Nonetheless, Babur retained the *chahar bagh* and irrigation systems of Persia, these being well depicted in a 16th-century miniature. The water channels flowing through the earth, which are basic to many Islamic gardens, very simply articulate a complement of light and dark, dynamic and static materials.

Many of the flowers well known in Western gardens are found in Islamic gardens: bulbs, such as narcissi, tulips, grape hyacinth, and lilies; small flowers, such as carnations, violets, anemones, poppies, and cyclamen; and flowering shrubs and vines, such as jasmine, honeysuckle, and passiflora. But roses have a long history of being most admired, and rose gardens (*gulistan* is the widely used Persian term) remain common. The rose (*gul*) pervades much of Islamic culture in perfumes and rose water used for scent and as a gastronomic ingredient. Persian and Arabic poetry is filled with metaphors based on the beauty of this flower, and painted tiles often depict it along with other favorite blossoms.

The representation of nature was not confined only to ceramic tiles; textual sources inform us that plants, trees, and flowers were modeled with paper, paste, and wax, and even gold, silver, and precious stones. The more expensive fabrications were generally commissioned by royalty: Timur (Tamerlane) had a particularly sumptuous oak tree with jeweled fruit and enameled birds on the branches. Such esteem for artifice reflects the Muslim belief that, as part of the divinely made natural world, human beings are the means through which God continues to create. To some extent floral carpets, which bring gardens year-round inside the building, may be seen as part of this tradition: one genre of paradise carpets commonly displays the *chahar bagh* with a central fountain, four rivers of paradise, and a tree of life in the weaving or knotting.

See also Agra Fort; Alhambra; Babur; Chashma Shahi; Córdoba, Great Mosque of; Generalife; Iran; Madinat al-Zahra'; Mogul Gardens; Nishat Bagh; Red Fort; Seville, Real Alcázar; Spain; Taj Mahal; Turkey

Further Reading

Ansari, A.S. Bazmee, "Bustan," in *The Encyclopedia of Islam,* vol. 1, Leiden: Brill, 1958

Begley, Wayne E. "The Myth of the Taj Mahal and a New Theory of Its Symbolic Meaning," *Art Bulletin* 61 (1979)

Blair, Sheila S., and Jonathan M. Bloom, editors, *Images of Paradise in Islamic Art,* Hanover, New Hampshire: Hood Museum of Art, Dartmouth College, 1991

Dickie, James, "The Mughal Garden: Gateway to Paradise," *Muqarnas* 3 (1985)

Gardet, L., "Djanna," in *The Encyclopedia of Islam,* vol. 2, Leiden: Brill, 1958

Lehrman, Jonas, *Earthly Paradise: Garden and Courtyard in Islam,* London: Thames and Hudson, 1980

Macdougall, Elizabeth B., and Richardson Ettinghausen, editors, *The Islamic Garden,* Washington, D.C.: Dumbarton Oaks, 1976

Marcais, G., "Les jardins de l'Islam," *Mélanges d'histoire et d'archéologie de l'Occident Musulman,* Algiers: Impr. Officielle, 1957

Moynihan, Elizabeth B., *Paradise as a Garden: In Persia and Mughal India,* London and New York: Braziller, 1979

Petruccioli, Attilio, editor, *Il giardino islamico: architettura, natura, paesaggio,* Milan: Electa, 1994

Tabbaa, Yasser, "The Medieval Islamic Garden: Typology and Hydraulics," in *Garden History: Issues, Approaches, Methods,* edited by John Dixon Hunt, Washington, D.C.: Dumbarton Oaks, 1992

Wescoat, James L., Jr., and Joachim Wolschke-Bulmahn, *Mughal Gardens: Sources, Places, Representations, and Prospects,* Washington, D.C.: Dumbarton Oaks, 1996

Wilber, Donald Newton, *Persian Gardens and Garden Pavilions,* Washington, D.C.: Dumbarton Oaks, 1979

WENDY PULLAN

Israel

The key to understanding garden and landscape design in Israel is its location as a geographical and cultural crossroads. Israel is situated at the periphery of three continents and is simultaneously a center of civilization and home to historic and sacred sites of Judaism, Christianity, and Islam. Environmental, historical, and cultural conditions set the framework for design in the modern era, beginning with the inception of Zionism a century ago and the establishment of the State of Israel in 1948. The physical area is small, but it encompasses great diversity, ranging from 35 inches (889 mm) of rain at the northern border to 4 inches (102 mm) in the desert, from almost 3,500 feet (1,067 m) elevation to 1,295 feet (395 m) below sea level at the Dead Sea, from Mediterranean vegetation to desert. Garden designs of the Mediterranean, desert oasis gardens, and Middle Eastern *bustan* all have exerted their influence. These forms are coupled with garden types and ideals brought by immigrants from over 80 nations, especially those of central and eastern Europe.

A distinct Israeli landscape design language is evolving that speaks eloquently in stone, is frugal with water, uses indigenous and naturalized vegetation, is intimate in scale, and creates places that are intensively used. Inspired by the native landscape, there is the Mediterranean iconography of olive groves, vineyards, wheat fields, terraced agriculture, arbors, and irrigation. Planting design is a complex mix of native and non-native species, a cultural mix of biblical and historic association, internationalism and localism. In the desert, design is focused on ameliorating the extremes of climate. At the same time, garden design has oscillated between an appreciation and preservation of the indigenous landscape and the desire for transformation and a "greening of the desert."

Ben Gurion National Park, designed by Yahalom Zur, Negev Desert, Israel
Copyright Kenneth Helphand

The modern history of the Israeli landscape reflects dramatic social change: absorbing millions of immigrants with great rapidity, housing them, and creating communities. Most landscape design has been sponsored by the public sector and there is little private garden tradition. The unique Israeli communal models of the kibbutz and moshav evolved distinct garden forms as did new development towns. Landscape architects also were instrumental in the development of national parks, campuses, roads, landscape preservation, afforestation, and regional planning.

Late 19th century communities of the German Templars, agricultural colonies, and the Mikve-Israel agricultural school experimented with appropriate plants and forms. They took little heed of indigenous garden traditions. A professional tradition began in the 1920s and 1930s with a wave of immigrant designers, largely from Germany, who settled in Palestine. These pioneers included Shlomo Oren-Weinberg, Itzhak Kutner, Meir Victor, Avraham Karavan, Yechiel Segal, and Haim Latte. Some had received professional design training, and all had experience as gardeners and possessed fine horticultural knowledge. Their work included the designs of scores of kibbutz settlements and parks in major cities. Their designs were distinguished by their idealism and social commitment, and they engaged in intense ideological debates over design principles, the nature of community, and the creation of a symbolic landscape. Their work set a tone and standard for subsequent Israeli design. Landmark projects included Haifa's Gan Benjamin (*gan* is Hebrew for garden or public park) by Segal, Gan Hatzmaut in Tel Aviv by Karavan, and Ramat Hanadiv by Oren-Weinberg, the garden and tomb of the Baron Rothschild. A gardener's association was formed in the 1930s, followed by the Israel Association of Landscape Architects in 1951, and professional education for landscape architects in 1975.

The next era was dominated by several partnerships, those of Lippa Yahalom and Dan Zur, Zvi Miller and Moshe Blum, Joseph Segal (son of Yehiel) and Zvi Dekal. Extraordinarily active for almost 50 years, their collective work paralleled the establishment of the state and its accompanying mass immigration and construction. Work during this period included the planning and design of the open space framework and infrastructure of communities and the establishment and design of national parks. The designs for the communities of Kfar Saba, Carmiel, Ashkelon, Arad, and Modiin are particularly notable.

Yahalom and Zur, the 1998 winners of the prestigious Israel Prize for their body of work, have designed projects which are now national icons. They include the grave of David Ben-Gurion in the Negev desert—distinguished by its abstracted wadi (dry river) entry passage—and the Valley of the Destroyed Communities at Yad Vashem (Holocaust Memorial) in Jerusalem. After the 1967 Six-Day War attention turned to Jerusalem, resulting in the design of the Jerusalem National Park, a greenbelt of open spaces encircling the Old City. In the 1970s a younger generation of designers, educated largely in the United States, established their practices including Gideon Sarig and Shlomo Aronson. The latter's work, especially in Jerusalem, has combined traditional materials and motifs with a modernist sensibility. At Jerusalem's Haas (designed with American landscape architect Lawrence Halprin) and Sherover Promenades (*tayelet* in Hebrew) he made masterful use of stone and native landscape forms and plants. Other promenades are the Louis Promenade in Haifa by Miller and Blum, Tel Aviv's promenade by the architect Yaakov Rechter, and the Albert Promenade in Mitzpe Ramon by Tichnun Nof (the successor firm to Segal-Dekal) overlooking an immense geological crater. The deep sense of time, the archeological aspect of many sites and the design of memorial landscapes are distinguishing characteristics of many places. Artist Danny Karavan (son of Avraham) has created two dramatic sculptural environments of great impact, the Negev Memorial outside of Beersheva and the White City in Tel Aviv.

In a half century Israel transformed from a developing to a prosperous nation. Designers now confront problems of density and affluence, and seek to preserve the traditional agricultural and rural landscape that is rapidly disappearing.

Further Reading

Aronson, Shlomo, *Making Peace with the Land: Designing Israel's Landscape,* Washington, D.C.: Spacemaker Press, 1998

Ben-Arav, Joseph, *Ganim ve-nof be-Yisra'el* (Gardens and Landscapes in Israel), Tel Aviv: ha-Kibbuts ha-Me'uhad, 1981

Enis, Ruth, and Ben-Arav, Joseph, *Ganim ve-nof Ba-kibuts: 60 Shenot Hitpathat 1910–1970* (Sixty Years of Kibbutz Gardens and Landscape 1910–1970), Tel Aviv: Israel Ministry of Defense, 1994

Gaon, Galit, and Paz, Iris, editors, *Point of View: Four Approaches to Landscape Architecture in Israel*, Tel Aviv: The Genia Schrieber University Art Gallery, Tel Aviv University, 1996

KENNETH HELPHAND

Italy

Garden design in Italy can be traced to ancient times, when the Romans borrowed a whole philosophy of gardens from the Greeks. Italian Renaissance garden design was dominated by the reworking of Greek and Roman antiquity, particularly in its exploitation of water and shade and in the mythological themes of its neoclassical statuary.

Italy is a Mediterranean country with flat to mountainous topography and extremely hot and dry to cool and temperate climates. Modern garden design as an art form started principally in locations where shade was a critical component of the garden. Colorful flowers, a considerable luxury, were both less cultivated and thrived less easily than tall hedges and trees that provided shade, with evergreens for decorative effect and potted orange trees to mark the corners of box-edged parterres.

The quest for summer coolness drove the moneyed classes to the hills and is ultimately responsible for the creation of gardens whose designs were subsequently considered paradigms of excellence. They often incorporated uneven terrain, rocks, cliffs, and boulders and were laid out in a characteristically layered format around a central axis, with steps culminating in a colonnade. Terraces were frequently joined by stone steps, sometimes at the sides, and visually connected by waterfalls, with such indigenous green flora as cypress, box, holly, ivy, and rosemary.

As all traces of the gardens of ancient Rome gradually disappeared after the fall of the Roman Empire, the great horticultural and gardening tradition of antiquity was lost. Fortunately, the classical treatises survived in monastic libraries, and the catastrophic eruption of Vesuvius in A.D. 79 preserved the gardens of Pompeii. Varro wrote of pleasure gardens in 36 B.C., complaining that in Rome they were crowding out the market gardens, leaving the city short of vegetables. From Pompeii we know that villa gardens, planned in axial relation to the house, generally had a central watercourse, often lined with marble adorned with fountains and statues, on each side of which were symmetrical plantations, often in quincunx formation. Together with fruit trees, such as the peaches and cherries introduced from Asia Minor by Lucullus, favorite plants included cypress, bay, oleander, almond, pomegranate, pear, quince, and apple, with ivy, myrtle, box, and laurel used for bordering and even topiary. Vineyards often extended up against the villa walls. Color came largely from mosaic decorations and probably painted statues and stone ornaments. Shade-giving plane trees were introduced from Greece.

The flowers were those of Greece—roses, lilies, and violets—to which were added field flowers such as the daisy, as well as, among other cultivated species, the iris, daffodil, narcissus, crocus, anemone, cyclamen, foxglove, gladiolus, jasmine, lavender, and marigold. Pliny the Elder's *Naturalis historia* (A.D. 77; *Natural History*) also mentions dwarf planes and acanthus. Georgina Masson in *Italian Gardens* (1961) remarks on the erotic themes of the ornamentation of the Pompeian villa gardens and the evident design for "convivial supper parties . . . when host and guests reclined upon couches built under a vine-covered pergola beside a rippling water-staircase or wall fountain lit by gilded statues carrying clusters of small oil-lamps."

Grander Roman villas would have one or more porticoes, sheltered walks still known by their Greek names as *gymansia* or *palaestrae*. The large Roman villas had a vegetable garden (the *hortus*) and an animal enclave for stock reared for the table and including deer, goat, duck, boar, and small birds. Villas also included fishponds, aviaries, and thickets planted to attract songbirds for netting. Large gardens also included painted representations of historical events and wild landscapes and seascapes, creating a symbiotic relationship with scenic stage settings explained by Vitruvius late in the first century B.C.

Some large gardens contained swimming pools, and Pliny the Younger, like the historian Sallust, had a hippodrome in the form of an elongated horseshoe surrounded by plane trees garlanded with ivy, backed by box and cypress for deeper shade. Cypresses were planted at the round end, backed by concentric circles of rose-lined paths. The paths behind the cypresses in Pliny's hippodrome led to small enclosures, one of which contained the names of Pliny and his gardener in clipped box; others contained lawn or fruit trees with obelisks. Beyond was a small landscape garden planted with dwarf plane and acanthus clumps where a fountain cooled from below a marble seat covered by a vine pergola. The fountain's water was collected in a basin on which food could be floated for bucolic suppers, although there was also a pavilion with a dining room, a feature to be found later in early English gardens. The amphitheater at the Boboli gardens in Florence and the Piazza di Siena of the Villa Borghese in Rome are the lineal descendants of these hippodromes.

Medieval Italian literary accounts present gardens in heavily idealized forms deriving from the French romances. Water springs out of tree stumps, Tristan and Iseut (Isolde) meet in the garden of King Mark's palace, and a garden features as the setting for the idealized relationship of Guenièvre and Lancelot. Gardens also retained in the corporate subconscious overtones of their medieval roles as sites for lovers' meetings, as in the 12th-century treatise on love by Andreas Capellanus, or as settings for music and outdoor sports symbolizing a purity and tranquillity removed from the sycophancy and corruption of court life, an oasis separated from the world as at Pisa's Campo Santo. Italian gardens sometimes also retain an association with their original function as a place of conversation, discussion, companionship, and social intercourse, where ancient divinities presided over love and fertility and into which the Middle Ages incorporated the conditions and metaphors of spiritual progress.

Of medieval Italian gardens we know relatively little except that the inherited antique paradigms never entirely faded from memory and that the sensitivity to natural advantages afforded by slopes, wind directions, sun angles, watercourses, springs, orientations, and setting never disappeared completely. The 13th-century emperor Frederick II, enlightened and tolerant ruler of the southern half of the Italian peninsula and patron of the arts, created around his palaces gardens and hunting enclosures that were also part zoo, consciously modeling his garden architecture on antique models. His gardens contained the usual vine trellises, myrtle groves, and fishponds, with violets and roses the predominant flowers.

Frederick's practice is probably reflected in Pietro de' Crescenzi's famous treatise on farming, *Liber ruralium commodorum* (1305). De' Crescenzi's sources included Arabic writings, classical treatises, and other 13th-century works. The eighth of the 12 books deals specifically with the art of gardens, describing three types of gardens, their size varying according to the owners' means. The small gardens envisaged had a lawn with a fountain surrounded by borders of sage, basil, marjoram, mint, lilies, and roses, to which the medium gardens of two to four acres added an orchard and an arbor, shrub fencing, and a perimeter of pomegranates or hazel and quinces. The large 20-acre (8-ha) garden had extensive fauna and fountains throughout, with aviaries, meadow, and wood, as well as evergreens and fruit trees. De' Crescenzi came from Bologna but mentions palms, which suggests familiarity with practices in the south of the peninsula. He is enthusiastic about topiary, clipping, and what can be achieved by grafting.

It is usual to place the 14th-century poet Petrarch at the beginning of the Italian cult of the antique, and he has left a record of his gardening failures with spinach, beet, parsley, and fennel in Milan. Despite ignoring the instructions of Virgil's *Georgica* (36–29 B.C.) Petrarch had more success with vines at Parma in 1348. The 15th-century Careggi garden of Cosimo de' Medici was a deliberate re-creation of the antique, innovative only in its carnations, which had come to western Europe with returning crusaders. Cosimo inaugurated the fashion for a return to antique models of garden design and to gardens suitable for the neoclassical building style advocated by Leon Battista Alberti in his ten-volume treatise on architecture, *De re aedificatoria* (completed in 1452; printed in 1485). Alberti drew heavily from such classical texts as those of Pliny the Younger and Vitruvius, who taught that beauty came from a harmony of all the parts. Alberti's work was to be a fundamental point of reference for artistic developments in the Renaissance.

The garden design of 15th-century Italy was influenced, as in the rest of Europe, by the technology of armaments. Structures originally designed and used as forts gradually became useless for that purpose and were slowly being converted throughout western Europe into residential palaces, the largest of them for princes and their courts. Heavy stone fortifications became steadily less able to provide defense against contemporary artillery, and as the forts were reconstructed to become palaces, their interior courtyards were adapted for the social purposes of courts.

Among the gardens reconstructed for Cosimo by Michelozzo Michelozzi is that of his hunting lodge Il Trebbio (ca. 1451), situated on a hilltop and commanding a fine panoramic view of the Tuscan landscape. Michelozzi lightened the enclosed character of a fortress by adding a loggia and covered the passages on the bastions and tower. He laid out a modest walled garden at some little distance from the house. A vine pergola once ran along one wall of the garden, and another, with original columns still standing, shades a terrace overlooking square beds of flowers and vegetables. In contrast is Cosimo's garden with a similarly spectacular view wedged into a hillside at the Villa Medici in Fiesole (1458–61). Fiesole took a decisive step in the direction the Renaissance villa was to increasingly go. The incline is steep, and the outline of the garden terraces can still be traced. The view is again spectacular, and a series of garden rooms makes the most of the villa's outstanding situation, but it is an early garden, created about 1460, and the lower terraces can be reached only from the cellars or through a side road from the avenue leading to the house. The exploitation of ramps and steps on hillside locations chosen partly to show them off was a later development.

The fashion that swept through continental Europe in the early 19th century to restore the wildness and irregularity of the "English" garden is a principal reason why comparatively few of the 15th-century garden layouts have survived. Not all followed the prescriptions of Alberti, even when their owners consciously strove for the archaism of the antique, creating symmetrically arranged parterres filled with small evergreens in decorative geometric straight-edged patterns. Descriptions of them survive in paintings and prints, as well as occasional literary accounts such as that of Montaigne, who visited Castello in Tuscany in 1580 and was delighted by the alleys perfumed with cedar, cypress, orange, lemon, and olive trees. Montaigne was enthusiastic, too, about the famous grotto with seashell mosaics, the hidden fountains, and the evergreens clipped in animal shapes. Characteristically, he showed more interest in the technicalities of the waterworks and the ingenuity of the mechanics of the garden's surprises than in the aesthetic delights of the garden itself and its position or in the integration of the terrain into the monumentality of the aesthetic effect achieved. The way in which the terrain is not allowed to determine the desired aesthetic effects is one of the more remarkable features of the Boboli gardens behind the Pitti Palace in Florence.

Illustrating the intensity of Tuscan conservatism in garden design at this period, by 1550 the major gardens designed in or near Rome, the Cortile del Belvedere by Donato Bramante, the Caprarola of Giacomo da Vignola, and the Villa d'Este at Tivoli by Pirro Ligorio, all started out from the nature of the site, developing from it their aesthetic effects. During this time the Medici and Este families and Pirro Ligorio and Vignola stand out as having made significant contributions to garden design. Ligorio had studied the Temple of Fortune at Praeneste (modern Palestrina), not quite 19 miles (30 km) south of Tivoli, and had completed Bramante's Belvedere.

The Villa d'Este shows the effect of both projects on Ligorio's imagination. It exists today very nearly as it appears in a print of 1575, which shows one or two features that were planned but never built. Cardinal Ippolito d'Este II intended the garden of the Villa d'Este to be the world's finest, and a section of the town was torn down to make room for it. It takes almost to extremes the principles of Roman garden architecture of the mid-16th century and marks a determined return to the antique foundations of the Roman *nymphaeum* or pleasure palace, including within its boundaries a depiction of the mythological foundation of Rome. The Villa d'Este, however, is more than a reconstruction of a Roman villa, being one of the finest Renaissance gardens in its own right. Ligorio took his inspiration from the nearby ruins of Hadrian's Villa, adapting its use of water from what had been achieved on an undulating site to its exploitation on a steep slope, going far beyond what Bramante had achieved with wall fountains at the Cortile del Belvedere. The Villa d'Este is a series of hillside terraces originally to be approached from below, where they offer an impressive series of vistas as the visitor ascends from the fishponds through the stepped waterfalls and the grottoes. Its most memorable feature is its water system and profusion of lavish water displays.

Vignola, the most accomplished philosopher/landscape architect of the Renaissance, is most noted for his designs of one of the most exquisite of the Italian Renaissance villas, the Villa Lante in Bagnaia (1560). The garden is the main subject of the design; the two symmetrically arranged casinos are discreetly relegated to the second plane, as if mere garden ornamentation.

The reanimated cult of classical antiquity marked garden design as much as other cultural forms on the Italian peninsula during the later 15th and 16th centuries. This period of the Italian Renaissance is a milestone in the development of garden art, both by ideas that it has generated and by its compositional techniques. The Italian garden dominated the European scene during this time. The architectural complexes linking the villa and garden into a seamless whole was the fullest expression of the Renaissance ideals. By the later 16th and 17th centuries, the style changed to what is conventionally known as baroque. Simplicity, symmetry, and small-scale intricacy gave way to more flamboyant and complicated classical references, with more elaborate decorative features. Movement took over from stillness, and ornamentation became larger and more prominent, aesthetic norms more restless, and mythological references more violent. Older gardens were transformed, their formal patterns loosened until eventually, another century later, they would be more fully merged into the landscape in the English style.

In Italy, however, and more intensely from Tuscany southward, the need remained for the provision of tranquility and shade. The baroque had begun to intrude before the Villa d'Este gardens were finished, and gardens were conceived elsewhere in the new style. Designers created more play with light and shade and less with the boundaries between the cultivated and the natural. Grass did not grow well, and the natural was allowed to merge into the manmade, a development symbolized by the use, as at the Villa Mondragone in Frascati, of hidden fountains that could be used to drench unsuspecting visitors unaware that nature had been so mischievously tampered with.

By the late 16th century Frascati, one of the 13 "Castelli Romani" in the Alban hills just beyond the city's southern boundary, had become to Rome the fashionable summer retreat of preference and played a role analogous to that which Fiesole played for Florence. By 1620 Frascati was covered with villas, the outstanding examples being the Villa Mondragone (1565), the Villa Muti (1579), and the Villa Aldobrandini (1598–1603), the last anticipating the large-scale dramatic effects of the Roman baroque manner.

The garden of the Villa Aldobrandini clearly foreshadows the baroque ground plan, with an emphasized axis starting out from the entrance, at the bottom, and moving toward the castle as a trimmed allée. The axis continues on the other side of the palace with a *nymphaeum* and ends by a cascade. The niches of the *nymphaeum*, which offers magnificent views over Rome, the *campagna*, and the sea, contain a figure of Atlas, a centaur, and two figures of Pan. The gardens consist of terraces connected by slopes or steps, with paths shaded by clipped trees. The formally arranged *nymphaeum* also contains semi-underground rooms, but it no longer included a series of terraces with clipped hedges and geometrically decorated parterres as there would have been a century earlier. Instead, a single small terrace is above the water staircase, with informally placed trees around a stone fountain and a central perspective leading into a wood, and the formal allées gradually give way to woodland paths.

Not all the developments in 17th-century Italian garden design moved in the direction of blurring the distinction between the formal and the natural, and in some respects they differed from what was happening elsewhere in Europe. In particular Italy resisted French innovations much longer than did England. Georgina Masson has cogently argued from the intertwining of initials in the design that the date of what she regards as "the most magnificent box parterre in Italy" laid out by Ottavia Orsini at Vignanello must have been about 1612, and certainly between 1600 and 1618. The house had been a castle and had to be converted into a villa, which entailed linking it to its large garden by a bridge and laying out the parterre. Interestingly, the design is still purely geometrical, without the curls and arabesques popular in France from the 16th century, but in Italy only later in the 17th century.

The French in the 16th century had been using colored earths for their parterres, whose rounded decorative forms became so elaborate that the parterres did not need flowers. In Italy flowers appeared extensively in parterres late in the 16th century; by the end of the first quarter of the 17th century, box was everywhere replacing clipped herbs. Italy shared the general European rage for exotica, generally expensive bulbous flowers imported from the Middle East, India, and the Americas, which were cataloged, cultivated, painted, studied, classified, and traded. An interest in rare plants developed, leading to the establishment of Vignola's Orti Franesiani on the Palatine as a botanical center. A list of the rare plants there was published in 1625.

During the 17th century, shortly after the completion of the Villa Aldobrandini, Cardinal Scipione Borghese, the nephew of Paul V, inaugurated another massive innovation, purchasing huge quantities of land just outside the walls of Rome near the Porta Pinciana in order to create the massive park that is now the Villa Borghese. The buildings were incidental to the main purpose, which was to create the park, and the main house was not designed as a residence but as a picture gallery and library, with facilities for lavish entertaining. The circumference was already approximately 2.5 miles (4 km) in 1650 and has subsequently grown.

An account from 1700 gives a detailed description of the park, which was divided into four sections, making clear between them the transition from contrived baroque garden to natural parkland. There was no symmetrical plan, but dense plantations of trees crossed by straight allées lined with clipped hedges. A circular clearing at the intersections allowed for a fountain, statue, or ornament around which were stone benches. It was this type of garden that André Le Nôtre brought to the peak of its perfection in 17th-century France.

A set of prints made in the 1650s shows that the late 17th-century Roman garden of Camillo Pamphilii, with a circumference of some five miles (8 km), was not very different in style from the Villa Borghese. The design may have been more free, and there is more open land, but straight avenues in the park still divide the clumps of trees. Again, the residential building was separate from the garden pleasure casino and was surrounded by the more elaborate gardens, which consisted of groups of geometrical parterres with two pools, still lacking the French influence that first appears in late 18th-century prints. The Pamphilii line died out in 1760, when the villa passed to the Genoese female Doria line, and in the late 18th century the stream feeding the fishponds was diverted through a series of waterfalls into an ornamental pond.

Rome was the center of conservative garden design in Italy, and Italy as a whole was resistant to the French style that conquered the rest of Europe until its position was usurped by the English landscape style. Two outstanding 18th-century Italian gardens outside Rome, however, should be mentioned. One is the garden of the Villa Corsi Salviati at Sesto in Tuscany, whose development is documented from the early 16th century and continued through five different periods of history. Unusually, the terrain is flat. The early 16th-century garden at Sesto was simple, consisting of some squares of grass with paths and a circular fountain with a statue. In 1593 an enclosed tennis court was built. In the 17th century another tower was added to the house, and an aviary and gallery were built. The garden consisted of four enclosed spaces, of which the first was a rectangular parterre garden next to the house, with the usual circular space with fountain at the intersection of the principal paths. It had a plantation at one end and a fishpond at the other. Behind it was a lemon garden, and it also included walled vegetable gardens, a winter orangery, and a bowling green. The house and garden were modernized in 1738: the boundaries between the four rooms were removed, the pond was enlarged, French-style fountains at surface level were introduced, and the fishpond was converted into an urn-bordered canal with statues of the four seasons at the corners. Frescos of classical ruins were painted on the old aviary, now converted to a loggia, and the square parterres were altered to the diamond layout that can still be seen. A maze was added. Except for the maze, this was the garden's 18th-century form to which it was largely restored in 1907. In the 19th century it had been further landscaped, and added to it was a mound, a mock castle, and a Romantic lake. The villa became famous for its collection of rare plants, some of them tropical. As with numerous other gardens, the garden at Sesto has shown itself amenable to change and has constantly reflected cultural change, even in its 20th-century removal of 19th-century accretions.

La Reggia, almost on the periphery of garden design, is also noteworthy. The palace is one of many inspired by and intended to rival Versailles. (Others include Potsdam and the St. Petersburg summer palaces.) La Reggia is at Caserta, approximately 18.5 miles (30 km) from Naples, and the palace, begun in 1752 for the Bourbon king Charles III with Luigi Vanvitelli as architect, is built to a rectangular plan approximately 275 meters (300 yd.) long and 220 meters (240 yd.) wide. The building is said to contain 1,200 rooms. The work of the Parisian Martin Biancour, the park consists chiefly of a long vista enclosed by thickets and stretches for about two miles (3 km). It is scattered with fishponds and fountains and ends in a huge cascade whose water falls more than 80 meters (87 yd.). An overflow basin contains a sculpture group of Diana bathing among the nymphs and surprised by the hunter Acteon, whom she turns into a stag to be devoured by his own hounds. An English garden was created in 1782, complete with rare plants and inevitably, fake Roman ruins.

After Caserta, no major gardens were created in Italy in either the Italian or French style. The 19th century saw the decay of most of the major gardens, as these were converted into a parody of the English landscape or swallowed up in urban expansion. At the end of the 19th century, renewed interest in the classic Italian gardens resulted in an assortment of garden designers, such as Charles Platt and Thomas Church, incorporating various features of the Italian tradition into their own practices.

See also Adriana, Villa; Aldobrandini, Villa; Boboli Gardens; Caserta, La Reggia di; Este, Villa d'; Garzoni, Villa; Giulia, Villa; Lante, Villa; Madama, Villa; Orsini, Villa; Padova, Orto Botanico dell'Università di; Palermo, Orto Botanico dell'Università de; Pisa, Orto Botanico dell'Università di; Roman Gardens

Further Reading

Hunt, John Dixon, editor, *The Italian Garden: Art, Design, and Culture,* Cambridge and New York: Cambridge University Press, 1996

Masson, Georgina, *Italian Gardens,* New York: Abrams, and London: Thames and Hudson, 1961; revised edition, Woodbridge, Suffolk: Antique Collectors' Club, 1987

Platt, Charles Adams, *Italian Gardens,* New York, 1894; reprint, London: Thames and Hudson, and Portland, Oregon: Sagapress/Timber Press, 1993

ANTHONY H.T. LEVI AND CANDICE A. SHOEMAKER

J

Jäger, Hermann 1815–1890

German Garden Writer

Hermann Jäger was unparalleled by other German gardeners of the 19th century, having written over 40 specialty books and innumerable articles on all areas of garden architecture and horticulture. His position from 1845 up to his death as court gardener and later as court garden inspector in Eisenach in the grand duchy of Sachsen-Weimar-Eisenach, where he redesigned the Kartausgarten and regenerated Park Wilhelmsthal, enabled him to be so extensively active as a writer.

Jäger collaborated on several German specialist journals, such as the *Illustrierten Monatshefte für Obst und Weinbau* (Illustrated Monthly Periodical for Fruit and Wine-Growing), the *Wochenzeitschrift für Gärtnerei* (Weekly Periodical for Gardening), and *Möllers Deutsche Gärtner-Zeitung* (Möller's German Gardening Newspaper). From 1857 he coedited *Gartenflora,* where among other things he reviewed significant expert literature by Gustav Meyer, Rudolph Siebeck, Eduard Petzold, Eduard Lucas, Lothar Abel, Gustav Eichler, and Camillo Schneider.

Since Jäger's written works were only partially based on his own experiences, his opinions were supported by observations, discussions, and particularly the study of already-existing literature. Jäger wanted to address the large circle of interested laity as well as experts. He therefore commented on horticultural issues that related to gardening, for example, the growing of fruit and vegetables, tree nurseries, and floral and ornamental gardening, and produced corresponding lists and dictionaries of plants. The discussion from the middle of the 1870s onward concerning whether a college for garden architecture should be established presented him with the opportunity of making rather conservative statements about the professional training of gardeners.

In reference to the basic knowledge of the gardener, principles of design, the handling of park elements, and rules on maintaining gardens and parks, Jäger's views on garden architecture are situated between those of Meyer and of Petzold. Jäger, however, also refers to the opinions of other garden architects, to whom he refers as teachers and models, and either adopts them as his own or reevaluates them. This particularly includes the opinions of Prince Pückler-Muskau, Friedrich Ludwig von Sckell, John Claudius Loudon, Georg Adolph von Hake, Humphry Repton, and Andrew Jackson Downing, as well as those of Thomas Whately and Christian Cay Lorenz Hirschfeld. Jäger discusses tendencies in foreign garden architecture, for example, the park systems of Paris, or the U.S. parks movement, in relation to which he not only praises the villa gardens and squares but also, and especially, the city parks and park-like cemeteries.

On the one hand Jäger's function was that of a chronicler of the tendencies and trends in garden architecture during the second half of the 19th century; on the other hand as a critic he discussed their terms and design tendencies. Time and again he provided important stimulation, which was recognized and discussed by his contemporaries.

Jäger's *Lehrbuch der Gartenkunst* (1877; Textbook on Garden Architecture) takes up many topics. He belonged to the most eager supporters of landscape beautification but soon recognized any hope of its implementation to be an illusion. By bringing up the problematic issue of water and water systems as park elements, he also elaborated on questions of style in contemporary garden architecture. He attributed equal value to the "naturally" and "artificially" implemented arrangement of regular forms of water elements. Therefore he also accepted regular plantings and tree-lined avenues in conjunction with the architecture and the "modern regular gardens."

Jäger defined and categorized the gardens according to function and form, for example, by explaining the term *gardens of a mixed style* and by making a distinction between gardens, parks, and garden-like enhancement. The latter, according to Jäger, included private grounds, public squares, and park-like cemeteries but also certain garden types, such as flora, society, and restoration gardens, as well as roof and hospital gardens and those found at horticultural exhibitions.

Jäger concerned himself with the question of preserving plantings in garden systems, suggesting that for each park a kind of legacy of its creator be drawn up. This was meant to serve as a guide, with detailed information for the ensuing treatment of the park, a kind of last will with a written decree concerning the most important plantings and how these were to be preserved and regenerated in the future.

In 1888 Jäger published his important work, *Gartenkunst und Gärten sonst und jetzt* (Garden Architecture and Gardens Then and Now), a scientifically sound history of garden architecture from classical antiquity to the present.

Biography

Born in Münchenbernsdorf, near Gera, Thuringia, Germany, 1815. Trained at commercial garden nursery of C. Wagner, Gera, 1831–34; continued at court nursery and gardens of Belvedere, near Weimar, Germany, under garden inspector Johann Conrad Sckell; journeyman years brought him to Hamburg for two years, where he worked under garden inspector Ohlendorff in the Botanical Garden; inspection assistant, Schönbrunn, near Vienna, 1837; undertook several short trips to Hungary and Austria; worked in plant garden of Nymphenburg, Germany, 1837–40; took advantage of large range of cultural and educational possibilities in Munich, studying in its libraries and mixing in artistic circles; Maria Paulowna, Grand Duchess of Sachsen-Weimar-Eisenach, made it possible for Jäger to make educational trips to Italy, where he visited Venice, Bologna, Florence, Pisa, Milan, and Genoa, 1840; spent autumn in Paris, working at cemetery of Mont Parnasse and in Botanical Garden; accepted position of head gardener and botanist at Schloss (the castle of) Verneuil, France, 1841; managed to visit England and Belgium before finally returning to Thuringia, Germany, 1841, where he worked as assistant in the Belvedere; briefly worked as assistant in Berlin-Schönefeld, 1844; position of court gardener in Eisenach, Germany, April 1845; started career as prolific writer, 1850. Died 5 January 1890.

Selected Publications

Katechismus der Ziergärtnerei, 1853
Die Baumschule, 1855
Die Verwendung der Pflanzen in der Gartenkunst, 1858
Der Apothekergarten, 1859
Allgemeines illustriertes Gartenbuch, 1864
Die Ziergehölze der Gärten und Parkanlagen, 1865
Der Hausgarten, 1867
Frauengarten, Illustriertes Gartenbuch, 1871
Die schönsten Pflanzen des Blumen- und Landschaftsgartens, der Gewächshäuser und der Wohnungen, 1873
Lehrbuch der Gartenkunst, 1877
Katechismus der Rosenzucht, 1882
Pflege des Zimmer- und Hausgartens, 1882
Die Zimmer- und Hausgärtnerei, 1883
Gartenkunst und Gärten sonst und jetzt, 1888

Further Reading

Beissner, Ludwig, "Zum 71. Geburtstage Jäger's," *Garten-Zeitung* 13 (1885)
Falkenried, Ariane von, "*Der Gartenschriftsteller Friedrich Hermann Jäger, 1815–1890*: Ein Memorandum zum 100. Todestag," diploma diss., Technische Universität Berlin, 1991
Lucas, Eduard, "Hermann Jäger, großherzoglicher Hofgärtner in Eisenach," *Illustrierte Monatshefte für Obst- und Weinbau* (1870)
Rohde, Michael, "Eduard Petzold—Weg und Werk eines deutschen Gartenkünstlers im 19. Jahrhundert," diss., University of Hannover, 1998
Rohde, Michael, *Von Muskau bis Konstantinopel: Eduard Petzold, ein Europäischer Gartenkünstler, 1815–1891,* Dresden: Verlag der Kunst, 1998
Rümpler, Theodor, editor, "Hermann Jäger," in *Illustriertes Gartenbau-Lexikon,* Berlin: Paul, 1882
Springer, Leonard A., "Die Holländischen Gärten in Jägers 'Gartenkunst und Gärten Sonst und Jetzt'," *Gartenflora* 37 (1888)

MICHAEL ROHDE

Japan

Geophysical and Prehistoric Roots

Japan comprises an archipelago of four large islands and more than 1,000 lesser adjacent ones that extend in an elongated northeast-southwest crescent. The four main islands extend approximately between latitude 46 in the north and 31 in the south (the Ryūkyū or Okinawan Islands extend as far south as the 24th parallel), a distance and latitude that roughly corresponds to the span from Montreal, Canada, to the northern border of the state of Florida. Although the country is not large in land mass (slightly smaller than California), this extreme north-south orientation gives rise to a number of ecological zones and is partly to explain for the wide range of flora there. The archipelago lies along the fault line that separates the Pacific, Eurasian, and Philippine tectonic plates, and the islands themselves are mostly the result of the corresponding volcanic activity. Furthermore, the archipelago rests amid the warm ocean and atmospheric currents that flow north from the South China Sea, which tempers the climate and yields annual precipitation rates that typically range from one to two meters (one to 2.2 yd.). This geophysical situation affected the development of gardens in Japan in several ways. First, as an island nation composed of myriad narrow valleys, social characteristics were fostered that were fundamental to its cultural development. For instance, the habit of not applying overlying, geometric design solutions to the land but instead working with the peculiarities of a site to create a garden is indicative of that mentality. Second, the dramatic landscape of steep volcanic mountains rising from the sea became one of the primary images incorporated into gardens, as were the swift rivers, waterfalls, meadows, and rough ocean shores inherent to the islands, which were developed into stylized gardening techniques. A third influence resulted from the development in Japan's fertile, well-watered volcanic soils of a complex flora, which became the focal point of animistic religious practices and in later years provided a rich palette for garden design. Over the past several centuries that flora has also been the objective of European plant hunters and has thus affected the worldwide horticultural trade as well.

Historically, the central part of the main island, Honshu, was the site of most garden development, and the physical climate of that region, with its four clearly defined seasons and broad mix of deciduous and coniferous flora, set the tone of garden design in Japan. It can be postulated that all gardens throughout the world fall into two groups: those built in severe (usually arid) climates, where the intent of the garden is specifically to modulate the existing harsh physical environment, and those built in temperate climates, which reflect the hand of gardeners who revel in their natural surroundings. Due to its geophysical conditions, Japanese gardens developed into classic examples of the latter type.

Long before gardening culture was imported from the ancient kingdoms of Korea and China, the Japanese people had developed an animistic perception of the natural world, a vision that influenced all later cultural development, including garden design. According to that animism, certain natural elements, such as waterfalls, boulders, ponds, and large trees, were believed to be abodes of the gods (*kami*) or, more properly, to be points of connection through which contact with the god world could be made. The area around these sites was considered sacred, cleared to some extent, and demarcated by an encircling rope. The act of tying and binding developed into highly elaborate forms for religious practices and was expressed in gardens of later eras in the form of ornamental rope work. The purified sacred spaces (*yuniwa, saniwa*) themselves can also be perceived in gardens, for instance in the empty spaces of medieval dry gardens (*karesansui*). Of the many sacred natural objects, the boulders (*iwakura*) and ponds (*kami ike*) are of particular interest because when the concept of garden making was introduced from the continent, stones and ponds were considered fundamental elements of the design, and the newly imported Buddhist and geomantic meanings attributed to stones and ponds overlaid the preexisting Japanese animistic perception but did not entirely replace it.

Sacred trees are still common and can be found in nearly all Shinto shrines. Sacred ponds, sacred stones, and/or cleared scared spaces can be found at the following ancient religious sites: Achi jinja, Okayama; Ise jingu, Mie; Ishizukadera, Hyōgo; Kibitsu jinja, Okayama; Kuramadera, Kyoto; Ōmiwa shrine, Nara; and Ryūsenji, Ōsaka.

Early Gardens

During the Asuka period (A.D. 552–710) a hierarchical system of clans began to develop, eventually culminating in the imperial and aristocratic families of later eras. This development was fostered by a studied attempt on the part of Japanese rulers to introduce Korean and Chinese culture and technology. Many foreign craftsmen and scholars immigrated to Japan during this period to contribute their skills, and as a result Japanese culture was refashioned after continental models, including architecture, textile and fashion design, writing, speech, religion, poetry, and painting. The first gardens were little more than agricultural enclosures; ponds and orchards of plums feature frequently in ancient texts. The Chronicles of Ancient Times (*Nihon*

Shoki) mention ponds for fish and birds in entries as early as the third century. Winding streams (*kyokusui*), which could refer to a Chinese form of garden, are mentioned as early as 486, but the first certain record of an ornamental garden being made is found in an entry for 612, in which an immigrant named Shikomaro (Shikimaro), from the Korean kingdom of Paekche, is entreated to do some garden work in the southern courtyard of Empress Suiko. The work included building a Chinese-style bridge (*kurehashi*) and a symbolic image of Mount Shumisen (Sanskrit *Sumeru*), the central mountain of Hindu and Buddhist cosmology. Archeological work has uncovered a three-part stone sculpture of Shumisen from that period that was hollowed out in order to be used as a water fountain; this may be the sort Shikomaro installed. Other sculptural garden pieces from this period have been found that depict distinctly Central Asian faces, implying that the Japanese court was also entertaining other craftsmen from farther along the Silk Road. Other literary references from the Asuka period also hint at the beginnings of ornamental gardens, for instance, the building up of mountain forms (*tsukiyama*) and ponds with rocky shores (*iso, araiso*). The detached palace of one minister, Soga Umako (d. 626), often mentioned in poetry had a curved pond and a rocky shoreline with inlets planted with azaleas. Both the palace and minister became so associated with the garden as to receive the appellations Island Villa and Minister of the Island, in which the island refers to the garden as a whole.

During the Nara period (710–94) a new imperial city was built, the structure of aristocratic society became more stable, and culture was more fully developed. Consequently, gardens became more common at aristocratic residences, and we even find a "department of pond gardens" (*enchi shi*) mentioned as part of the imperial household agency, although their responsibilities had more to do with overseeing imperial agricultural plots than with ornamental gardens. Two gardens from this period have recently been excavated and restored. Tōin, the eastern garden of the imperial palace, was entirely surrounded by a high wooden wall and featured several wooden pavilions placed around a central pond. The northern end of the pond has some prominent rock work in the rocky-shore style (*araiso*). At the other garden, named only by its ancient address (Heijōkyō Sakyō Sanjō Nibō Miya), a wooden pavilion overlooks a winding stream (*kyokusui*) punctuated by boulders along the edge. Wooden boxes buried into the streambed most likely held aquatic plants such as irises. In both of these gardens the bed of the pond or stream was made with clay that had a layer of uniform, fist-sized rounded pebbles embedded into the surface for aesthetic reasons as well as to prevent erosion. The gardens were designed with a formal, stylized method of composition and reflect the level to which the society had internalized continental culture.

During the Asuka period the names associated with gardens were initially those of foreign craftsmen and the Japanese aristocrats to whom they were lending their expertise; while in the Nara period, Japanese aristocrats appear as owner/designers. Asuka and Nara period garden personae include the following: Ōtomo no Tabito (665–731), a poet often cited in the *Manyōshū* anthology (in one well-known poem he speaks of the tall trees in a garden he built with his wife); Shikomaro (Michiko no Takumi), a seventh-century Korean immigrant gardener; and Soga Umako (?–626), government minister and owner of the detached palace, *Shima no miya*, famous for its island, who was referred to as Minister of the Island, *Shima no ōomi*.

A section of an Asuka period garden was recently excavated. It reveals square-shaped, walled sides to its pond similar to those found in ancient Korean gardens yet dissimilar to Japanese gardens of later eras. Nara period gardens include Heijōkyō Sakyō Sanjō Nibō Miya (Nara) and Tōin (Nara) (both archaeological restorations).

Heian Period (794–1185)

The Heian period marks the peak of Japanese aristocratic society, during which time the aristocrats terminated official relations with China and embarked on a period of cultural introspection. The gardens reflect this new internal focus, as well as the concerns of aristocratic society in general, which included geomancy, Buddhist allegory, nature imagery, and taboos. The incorporation of these aspects of aristocratic concerns in garden design is clearly recorded in the Heian-period gardening treatise called *Sakuteiki* (mid-11th century; Records of Garden Making).

As were all of the imperial capitals in Japan before it, Heian was fashioned after Changan (present-day Xian), capital of Tang-dynasty China. Heian was a large rectangle, subdivided into a grid of smaller blocks, the basic unit of which was a *chō*, approximately 120 square meters (143 sq. yd.). Within those rectangular, walled properties, the layout followed certain basic forms: there was a central hall (*shinden*); annex halls (*tainoya*), usually to the east and west and, at times, north; corridors (*chūmonrō*) that ran southward from the annex halls; and garden pavilions (*tsuridono, izumidono*) at the terminus of the corridors. All this formed a south-facing, U-shaped architectural complex, within which was a sand-covered court that served as an entry to the main hall and as a stage for various events, including formal meetings, dances, poetry competitions, and sports events such as archery or cockfights.

To the south of the court was a garden that usually was dominated by a central pond containing one or more islands connected to shore by bridges. The entire arrangement of sand-covered entry court and ornamental garden were collectively referred to as the southern court (*nantei, dantei*). Although there were large pond gardens built on the outskirts of the city and very small courtyard gardens (*tsubo*) built in the spaces left between the various outbuildings of the *shinden* complex, the Heian period is most commonly represented by the gardens of the southern court. These gardens contained many more plants than was typical for Japanese gardens built since the medieval period, including many herbaceous plants such as grasses, flowers, and vines that are rarely used these days. Gathering the multitude of beauty from the natural world—referred to as "plantings" (*senzai*)—into the garden is indicative of Heian-period garden design. The gardens were not like the holistic sculptural or painterly arrangements found from the late medieval period onward but rather were collections of several styles or scenes, arranged together on one property and available at once to the eye but discerned separately by the mind.

Another kind of garden indicative of the Heian period was built at temples more often than private residences and is now referred to as a Pure Land garden. These gardens symbolically re-created in the landscape the Western Pure Land of the Buddha of Infinite Light (Japanese, Amida Nyorai; Sanskrit *Amitābha*) by placing a prayer hall in which sculptures of Amida were enshrined on the western side of a large pond, symbolic of the vast ocean one needed to traverse in order to arrive at the Pure Land—in other words, the difficult process required for spiritual purification and enlightenment.

The names associated with gardens during the Heian period fall into two categories: aristocratic owners/designers and semiprofessional designers, artists, or priests whose main profession was not gardening but who advised on garden matters for others. Chief among the latter were the *ishitatesō*, or rock-setting priests, whose names are mostly associated with Ninnaji in Kyoto, a head temple of the Buddhist Shingon sect. There was no clearly defined profession called *ishitatesō* or any such rank in the social hierarchy. Rather, those priests who had expertise in, and gave advice on, matters related to garden design and construction were casually referred to by that appellation.

Known personae from this period include Enen Ajari, an 11th-century *ishitatesō,* mentioned as gardening master in *Sakuteiki* and associated with Kayanoin (the residence and garden of Fujiwara no Tadamichi); Eshin, son of imperial regent Fujiwara no Tadamichi and a priest at Kōfukuji, Nara, associated with Jōruruji; Fujiwara no Yorimichi (992–1074), imperial regent and owner/designer of Kayanoin and Byōdōin; Kose no Hirotaka (10th–11th century), descendent of Kose no Kanaoka and mentioned in *Sakuteiki;* Kose no Kanaoka (ninth century), court painter associated with the following works—Shinsenen (imperial garden), Kaninke residence, and Daikakuji pond; Renchū, 11th-century *ishitatesō*, mentioned in *Sakuteiki* as having possibly committed a taboo; Rinken, a 12th-century *ishitatesō* (perhaps identical with priest Rinjitsu mentioned in *Senzui narabini yagyōzu*) and associated with the original construction of the waterfall at Hōkongōin and waterfall at Ninnaji; Tachibana no Toshitsuna (1028–94), aristocrat, minister, purported author of *Sakuteiki,* and owner of Fushimitei; Tokudaiji Hōgen Seii, a 12th-century *ishitatesō* and priest of Ninnaji, who oversaw the reconstruction of Toba Rikyū, rebuilt the waterfall at Hōkongōin, and is mentioned in *Senzui narabini yagyōzu* (Kamakura-period gardening treatise); and Zōen, an *ishitatesō,* whose history is unclear, mentioned as original source of *Senzui narabini yagyozu.*

Heian-period gardens (all extant) include Byōdōin, Kyoto; Enjōji, Nara; Hōkongōin, Kyoto; Jōruriji, Kyoto; Mōtsuji, Iwate; and Ōsawa pond, Kyoto.

Kamakura Period (1185–1333)

The Kamakura period marks a shift away from aristocratic society to one controlled by feudal military lords. The seat of government was moved from Heian to Kamakura to escape the intrigues of society in the older capital, yet the gardens of that period are still for the most part derivative of the aristocratic *shinden* gardens that predate them. Although the teachings of Zen Buddhism were brought to Japan from China in the early Kamakura period and some new Buddhist allegory was introduced to garden design, the distinctive dry gardens (*karesansui*) now found in Zen temples do not yet appear in this period. The shift from aristocratic to military society, however, did initiate a change in the form and usage of architecture at the estates of military lords that set the stage for the development of the *karesansui.* With smaller courtyards (*tei*) associated with their residences and a new entry to the main hall from side corridors, formal meetings occurred more often in the southern half of the main hall rather than the southern court, allowing the use to change from entry court to viewing garden.

The main change in persons associated with gardens during the Kamakura period is that the Kamakura-period *ishitatesō* were more likely to be associated with the new Zen temples than the older esoteric Buddhist sects. The following are persons active during this period: Kamōhoin Teisei, an *ishitatesō,* associated with the northern garden of Kamakura shogunate; Musō Soseki (Musō Kokushi [1275–1351]), a prominent Zen priest and *ishitatesō,* associated with Saihōji and Tenryūji (Kyoto), Zuisenji (Kamakura), and Erinji (Yamanashi); Seigen, an *ishitatesō,* associated with Eifukuji, Kamakura; and Shinjakubō, an *ishitatesō* who consulted with Fujiwara no Sadaie (Fujiwara no Teika [1162–1241]) on the design of the Kyōgoku palace garden.

Kamakura-period gardens include Eihoji, Gifu; Erinji, Yamanashi; Rokuonji (Kinkakuji, Golden pavilion), Kyoto; Saihoji (Moss Temple); Shomyoji, Kanagawa; Tenryuji, Kyoto; and Tokoji, Yamanashi.

Muromachi Period (1333–1568)

The Muromachi period commenced with the return of the political seat to the Muromachi district of Kyoto (formerly Heian) and is culturally defined by a broad mixing of classes—military lords and their retinue, aristocrats, newly affluent merchants, and Zen priests—that spawned the development of many medieval arts: flower arranging (*ikebana*), *No* theater, and dry garden design, to name but a few. The dry gardens developed first around the main hall (*hōjō*) of temples especially in spaces adjoining the northern private half of the hall and later in the southern court, which adjoined the more formal, public half.

The mix of classes during the Muromachi period is clearly revealed in the relationship between "riverbank people" (*kawaramono*) and gardens. Riverbanks, subject to flooding and pestilence, were the least desirable place to live and thus the abode of an unofficial untouchable class. Excluded from other work, they performed those tasks that others refused: execution, butchering, tanning, hauling of feces, and earthwork. Their experience with earthwork meant they were useful in garden building and eventually became a de facto gardening class. In the Muromachi period some members of that class became so well associated with their gardening skills as to earn the appellation *senzui kawaramono* (*senzui* meaning garden) and are recorded as building gardens for the emperor and highest-ranking military lords. Many names of *senzui kawaramono* are left in estate records or diaries from the 15th and 16th centuries, although few details are known of their lives. One record mentions that *kawaramono* scouted for garden materials in existing gardens, a practice still common among modern gardeners.

Persons known from this period include the following: Ashikaga Yoshimasa (1436–90; r. 1449–74), eighth shogun (head of military government), patron of the arts, and owner of Marinokōjiden and Higashiyamadono (now known as Ginkakuji, the Silver Pavilion); Daishō kokushi (Kogaku Sōkō), a Zen priest and the founder of Daisenin, who is also associated with the design of that temple's garden; Hikosaburō, a *senzui kawaramono* whose name is associated with Marinokōjiden; Ichi, *senzui kawaramono,* associated with work on imperial gardens; Matashirō, a *senzui kawaramono,* grandson of Zenami, and who reputedly had great knowledge with regard not only to gardening techniques but also to the history, geomancy, and taboos associated with garden design; Kotarō and Seijirō, whose names are carved on a rock in the garden at Ryōanji; Sesshū (1420–1506), Zen priest and painter associated with Manpukuji (Shimane), Ikōji (Shimane), and Jōeiji (Yamaguchi); Shiken (Zean), priest of Sōkokuji, painter in Sesshū's style, associated with the restoration of Saihōji, Ryōunin (Reiunin, Myōshinji); Tora, a *senzui kawaramono* associated with the Sentō Gosho; Toragiku, a *senzui kawaramono* associated with the residence of the sixth shogun Ashikaga Yoshinori (1394–1441; r. 1429–41); and Zenami, a *senzui kawaramono* and member of Shogun Ashikaga Yoshimasa's artistic salon, who worked on Onryōken (Sōkokuji) and Higashiyamadono (Ginkakuji).

Muromachi-period gardens include Daisenin, Kyoto; Hōkokuji, Ehime; Ikōji, Shimane; Jishōji (Ginkakuji, Silver pavilion), Kyoto; Joeiji, Yamaguchi; Manpukuji, Shimane; Ryōanji, Kyoto; Ryōgenin, Kyoto; Shijūan, Kyoto; and Taizōin, Kyoto.

Momoyama Period (1568–1600)

The Momoyama period spans only 32 years and yet is known for various cultural developments, foremost being the tea ceremony (*chanoyu*). As part of the development of the culture of tea gatherings, a particular form of garden was created to act as an entryway to the teahouse as well as a place for guests to prepare themselves, both physically and inwardly, before partaking of tea.

The names associated with tea culture, *sadō* or *chanoyu,* are from mixed classes: wealthy merchants, Zen priests, and those of the military class. While today tea masters are referred to as *chajin,* the terms *chanoyusha* and *sukisha* were originally used. Names associated with gardens of this period include Kentei, a gardener who reworked Sanpōin after the death of Toyotomi Hideyoshi (1537–98) and who worked on the garden at the temple Konchiin; and Kansaiji Sōshin, a Zen priest and tea master, who related gardens with seven principles of flower arrangement and who is associated with Shōjuraigōji, Shiga.

Momoyama-period gardens include Entokuin, Kyoto; Honpōji, Kyoto; Mushanokōji Senke (Kankyūan), Kyoto; Nijōjō ninomaru, Kyoto; Nishihonganji taimensho (Tiger Glen garden), Kyoto; Omote Senke (Fushin'an), Kyoto; Sanpōin (Sanbōin), Kyoto; Senshūkaku, Tokushima; Shōjuraigōji, Shiga; Ura Senke (Konnichian), Kyoto; and Yabunouchi, Kyoto.

Edo Period (1600–1868)

The Edo period is marked by a coincident development of two social classes—provincial lords (*daimyō*) and townsfolk (*chōnin*)—and correspondingly two forms of gardens: large stroll gardens of the *daimyō* estates and tiny courtyard gardens in the urban residences of the *chōnin.* The former was encouraged by the stabilization of the nation during the Edo period, which took place under the central rule of a top single military leader (shogun) whose seat was in Edo (present-day Tokyo). Provincial lords oversaw provinces (*han*) of various sizes, where they each maintained an estate that served both as private residence and administrative headquarters. They were also required to maintain three estates in Edo—*kami yashiki, naka yashiki,* and *shimo yashiki* (upper, middle, and lower estates). The stability of the era allowed for the successive growth of the estates, especially those in the provinces, with each new generation of lords adding to the property or elaborating on the garden's design. Edo-period gardens thus developed into the largest in Japan's history. Travel was severely limited, yet at the same time advances in wood-block print technology meant that written descriptions and graphic images of famous places (*meisho*) were commonly available, with the limitation on travel adding to the interest. As a result owners of large gardens created in abstract form various landscape scenes along a winding path that were alternately hidden and revealed, allowing a person passing along the trail to take an imaginary excursion within the space of the garden. The scenes included Kyoto, Edo, famous provincial landscapes, China, and imaginary scenes from literature. The act of walking being primary to the experience, these gardens are now referred to as stroll gardens (*kaiyūshiki teien*). Edo-period stroll gardens are not limited to *daimyō* estates; some of the most elegantly designed were the property of the imperial family or members of the aristocratic class. Katsura Rikyū, Shugakuin Rikyū, and Sentō Gosho in Kyoto, as well as Shiba Rikyū and Hama Rikyū in Tokyo, are examples.

Along with the development of the *daimyō*, the urban merchants and craftsmen, also known as *chōnin,* began to assert an influence on the culture of the era, especially the latter half of the Edo period. Well-known aspects of Japanese culture, such as *kabuki* theater and wood-block prints, stem more from support by the *chōnin* as a class than from singular patrons among the aristocratic or *daimyō* class. In the mid-Edo period, the *chōnin,* especially the merchants, began to develop a unique form of architecture that suited their particular needs. The street frontage was narrow (to avoid a "frontage tax"), and the site was correspondingly deep. Along the street was a building called *omoteya,* or front house, that served as a shop downstairs and as residence for the servants upstairs. Further into the site was a second structure called *omoya* that served as residence for the owner. In the rear were thick-walled, fireproof storehouses called *kura.* The spaces left in between these separate structures had gardens built in them over the years that incorporated elements of tea gardens: stone lanterns, water lavers (hand-washing basins), stepping stones, and so on. The smaller of these gardens are called *tsubo niwa* or *naka niwa*, while the larger ones (usually in the rear) are called *senzai.*

Daimyō families are associated with the construction of gardens at their own provincial estates as well as those in Edo. The following names are the most noted: Ii of Ōmi (presently Shiga), Genkyūen; Ikeda of Bizen (presently Okayama), Kōrakuen; Maeda of Kaga (presently Ishikawa), Kenrokuen; Matsudaira of Takamatsu, Ritsurin Park, Kanagawa; Tokugawa of Mito (presently Ibaraki), Koishikawa kōrakuen, Tokyo, Kairakuen, Mito; Yanagizawa (shogunal grand chamberlain), Rikugien, Tokyo; Gomizunoo Tennō (1596–1680), emperor from 1568 to 1611, associated with construction of Sentō Gosho and Shūgakuin Rikyū; Hachijōmiya Toshihito (1579–1629), imperial prince and original builder of Katsura Rikyū; Hachijōmiya Toshitada (1619–62), imperial prince, son of Toshihito, enlarged Katsura Rikyū; Hon'ami Kōetsu (1558–1637), artist and tea master who studied tea under Furuta Oribe, retired to Takagamine (northern Kyoto) in 1615, and formed artist's community, and whose works include Honbōji Mitsutomoe no niwa and a Kōetsu-style bamboo fence; Ishikawa Jōzan (1583–1672), Confucian scholar, tea master, and poet, associated with the construction of Shisendō (his own villa), Shōseien, and Rengeji, all in Kyoto; Kobori Enshū (1579–1647), a *daimyō,* tea master, architect, and garden designer, born Kobori Masakazu in Ōmi province (presently Shiga prefecture), the son of commissioner of public works (*fushin bugyō*), became *daimyō* in 1608, served as commissioner of public works under first three Tokugawa Shoguns, studied tea under tea master Oribe, and subsequently became tea master for shogun Tokugawa Iemitsu, founder of the style of tea practice known as Enshūryū, and known for skills in a variety of arts, associated with many architectural projects (Nijō, Edo, and Fushimi castles) and gardens, including Sentō Gosho, Nijōjō ninomaru, Konchiin, and Kohōan; and Ryōshō Hōshinnō, priest of imperial descent and nephew to Hachijōmiya Toshitada, who worked on Manjuin (Manshuin) while resident head priest.

Early Edo period gardens include Daichiji, Shiga; Daitokuji Honbo, Kyoto; Fushinan, Kyoto; Genkyūen, Shiga; Hama Rikyū, Tōkyō; Kanjiin, Kyoto; Katsura Rikyū, Kyoto; Konchiin, Kyoto; Matsuo Shrine, Shiga; Rikugien, Tōkyō; Sentō Gosho, Kyoto; Shinnyoin, Kyoto; and Shūgakuin Rikyū, Kyoto.

Mid- to late Edo period gardens include Chishakuin, Kyoto; Emmanin, Shiga; Entsūji, Kyoto; Jikōin, Nara; Jōjuen, Suizenji, Kumamoto; Jōjuin, Kyoto; Kenrokuen, Ishikawa; Koishikawa korakuen, Tōkyō; Kōrakuen, Okayama; Manjūin, Kyoto; Nanzenji, Kyoto; Risturin, Kagawa; Sanzenin, Kyoto; Shisendō, Kyoto; and Shōdenji, Kyoto.

Meiji (1868–1912), Taisho (1912–26), and Early Showa (1926–89)

The Meiji era marks the beginning of Western technological, social, and cultural influence in Japan. The emperor was reinstated as the head of society, replacing the shogun, and Western influence appeared in the residences of some aristocrats, usually expressed in a Western-style annex hall and an associated geometrically designed garden. As capitalism took hold in the nation, certain merchant families rose to great prominence; many of the large gardens left from the Meiji period were (or still are) residences of those families. One of the changes in gardens most indicative of the era is the use of grass. Grass (*shiba*) had been used in gardens before then, in fact it is mentioned in the Heian-period *Sakuteiki* as a plant to be used in certain areas, but its use in Meiji-period gardens extended to not only include covering of hill forms but also to create large flat areas for outdoor gatherings; thus the idea of a lawn came into Japanese gardens. Another change was a shift toward naturalism as garden design became more evocative of actual natural scenes rather than stylized artistic forms. The trends that were begun in the Meiji period continued through the following Taisho and Showa periods, until World War II.

Names from this period include Yamagata Aritomo (1838–1922), a political and military leader who oversaw the construction of gardens at his various villas. The best known is Murinan, Kyoto (with Ogawa Jihei). Ogawa Jihei (1860–1933) was the Meiji period's most prominent gardener. Seventh in line of his family in the trade, he was well known for designing villas for the patricians of his day, including Murinan, Tairyūsansō, Hekiunsō, Shinshin'an, Keitakuen, I'en, and Shokuhōen, all in Kyoto. Public works by Ogawa Jihei include Heian Shrine and Maruyama Park.

Early modern gardens include Furukawa residence, Tokyo; Heian jingū, Kyoto; Isuien, Nara; Keitakuen, Osaka; Kiyosumi residence, Tokyo; Murin'an, Kyoto; and Sankeien, Kanagawa.

Postwar Gardens

Postwar Japanese society was marked by the national effort to rebuild and modernize and the accompanying dramatic and widespread shift in cultural values. During the 1960s and 1970s, a period of rapid economic expansion, a trend began in which elements of traditional society, from kimono to town houses, were discarded in favor of Western models, which were seen as being of the new age. The 1980s witnessed a massively inflated bubble economy in Japan, and land prices skyrocketed. The result of the shift in cultural taste, high cost of land, and correspondingly high inheritance tax was that many traditional residences and their gardens were destroyed to be replaced by high-rise structures with no gardens at all. For the past few years, English cottage gardens have been in fashion, and many gardening magazines feature Western-style motifs in favor of traditional Japanese gardens. Another development recently is the advent in Japan of American-style garden centers catering to home owners who wish to work on their own gardens. These garden centers also focus almost exclusively on Western garden motifs.

Despite the overall trend toward Westernism, there is also a movement among modern artists and garden designers to create gardens that are based on the aesthetics of traditional Japan and at the same time match the environment of modern Japan. To this end, for instance, many garden designers now use chunks of split granite in their designs rather than the natural boulders used in the past, the new material thought to fit better with the glass, concrete, and steel that surround the gardens and which is more widely available and less expensive than naturally weathered boulders.

See also Jōruri-ji; Katsura Imperial Villa; Konchi-in; Kyoto Botanic Garden; Ryoan-Ji; Saiho-ji; Shisen-dō; Shoden-ji; Shugaku-in; Tenryu-ji

Further Reading

Keane, Marc Peter, *Japanese Garden Design,* Rutland, Vermont: C.E. Tuttle Company, 1996

Kuck, Lorraine, *The World of the Japanese Garden: From Chinese Origins to Modern Landscape Art,* New York: Walker/Weatherhill, 1968

Kuitert, Wybe, *Themes, Scenes, and Taste in the History of Japanese Garden Art,* Amsterdam: Gieben, 1988

Nitschke, Günter, *Gartenarchitektur in Japan: Rechter Winkel und natürliche Form,* Cologne, Germany: Taschen, 1991; as *Japanese Gardens: Right Angle and Natural Form,* translated by Karen Williams, Cologne: Taschen, 1993

Takei, Jirō, and Marc Keane, *The Sakuteiki, Vision of the Japanese Garden,* Boston: C.E. Tuttle, 2001

MARC PETER KEANE

Jardim Botanico do Rio de Janeiro. *See* Rio de Janeiro, Jardim Botanico do

Jardin Anglais

The *jardin anglais* is the English landscape garden style adapted on the European continent, especially in France in the 18th and 19th centuries, that succeeded the formal, architectural style of André Le Nôtre. The *jardin anglais* was known for asymmetry, informality, variation, expanses of lawn, association of structures with characters, and the blending of gardens and parks. It overlapped with the Romantic, Picturesque, and Naturalesque styles. English influence was paramount in its evolution, although much of the impetus came from within France. Joseph Addison's "The Pleasures of the Imagination" (*The Spectator,* 1712) which introduced irregular plantations, winding streams, and a blending of the garden into nature, was translated into French in 1720. William Chambers's *Designs of Chinese Buildings* (1757) and *A Dissertation on Oriental Gardening* (1772) popularized the romantic garden with its strong contrasts as well as the idea that English gardens were derived from the Chinese.

During the 1760s the *jardin anglais* emerged as a concept, as a romantic or melancholic place with a wild air, bodies of water, and artificial ruins, where visitors could retreat and meditate. Such a notion was also linked to the idealization of nature and the virtue of simplicity expressed in *Julie; ou, La nouvelle Héloïse* (1761; Julie; or, The New Heloise) by Rousseau, who was critical of the ostentatious formal garden. Another text in the spirit of Rousseau was *Essai sur les jardins* (1774; An Essay on Gardens) by C.H. Watelet, which recommended modifying the formal garden by allowing more natural elements. The picturesque gardening theory was another important influence. Views were framed so as to create "pictures" inspired by paintings of Dutch, Italian, or Alpine landscapes. In *Observations on Modern Gardening* (1770), Thomas Whately discusses the associational properties of elements such as hills, fruit trees, lawns, fountains, rocks, and buildings that can evoke different emotions, as well as four types of farm: ornamental, simple, ancient, and pastoral.

From the 1770s French architects and garden designers visited English gardens, especially Stowe, an ornamental garden-park, and The Leasowes, a pastoral farm. The *jardin anglais* was initially often small and was added to a formal garden as a labyrinth or a sinuous grove. Rustic hamlets began to be introduced, as at Chantilly (1775) or at the Petit Trianon of Versailles (1775). One of the first large-scale landscaped estates was Louis-René Girardin's pastoral Ermenonville (1766–76). It was inspired by Rousseau and featured Rousseau's tomb on an island, as well as Julie's garden from *La nouvelle Héloïse*. Plantation was limited to beeches, oaks, and poplars. Famous for picturesque views, Ermenonville marked the transition from the poetic and philosophical toward the practical and methodic, for purely visual effects.

The more elaborate and theatrical type of the *jardin anglais* is the *jardin anglo-chinois*, which multiplied from the 1770s through the 1790s. This type of garden included numerous *fabriques,* or follies, such as obelisks, huts, pavilions, Chinese bridges, and statues without any transition so that the visitor would feel different sensations associated with distant times and places. The Désert de Retz was famous for its numerous *fabriques,* including Chinese pavilions, a Turkish tent, and a monumental ruined column that served as the owner's residence. At Bagatelle Thomas Blaikie designed a garden of undulating surfaces, paths with mazes, expanses of grass, exotic trees, cottages, grottoes, and an artificial river with islets. A "Chinese" corner featured willows, bridges, brooks, and Chinese pavilions. At Folie Saint-James (1778–85) Blaikie and its proprietor François-Joseph Bélanger, who studied in England, created an artificial lake and a vast grotto framing a Doric portico from which a river flowed. There were numerous statues, Chinese structures, and bridges of different styles. Inside an innovative underground promenade were a Gothic dairy and corridors with moss vaults and grass seats.

The vogue of the ornamental *jardin anglo-chinois* ended with the French Revolution. As part of a reaction against oversophistication, *fabriques* tended to be replaced with botanical elements. At Méréville (1784–94) Bélanger planted 225 species of trees and shrub. Another highlight was a "scene" composed of a waterfall with a rustic hut on a rock and a bridge. Blaikie redesigned Parc Monceau from 1781 to 1793 in the landscape style. A winter garden inside an immense hothouse was filled with lilacs, vines, walnut trees, banana trees, palm trees, cherry trees, coffee trees, and sugar canes. Structures were limited to a Chinese facade, pavilions of different colors, and a deep grotto with a fountain above. Music played by musicians hidden in the grotto echoed as an element of surprise.

After 1800 the French began to see the English garden as a practical landscape style emphasizing nature rather than the imitation of nature through artifice. Returning émigrés restored their estates in the landscape style. Fontainebleau (1809–12) is one of the best preserved. Louis-Martin Berthault designed the new, vast park of La Malmaison with little ornamentation. There was a celebrated collection of 250 species of painted roses, hydrangeas, dahlias, camellias, peonies, and hibiscus, plus a variety of trees such as beech, cedar of Lebanon, magnolia, white lime, larch, and Mediterranean hackberry. In 1806 Berthault converted the estate of the Palace of Compiegne into an English-style park garden with 70,000 trees and shrubs.

From the mid-19th century *jardin anglais* took a major turn into a more functional style for public recreation.

Baron Haussmann and Adolphe Alphand created several public parks, such as Buttes-Chaumont and Parc Montsouris, and rearranged Bois de Boulogne. These parks incorporated a scheme of walks connected to a circular allée that enclosed lawns of diverse surfaces. Here the ideas of John Claudius Loudon and Joseph Paxton were influential. They suggested balancing the urban with the natural through a systematic inclusion of public parks in urban planning, in order to meet the needs of the urban population for air, hygiene, and pleasure. Public parks would fuse the landscape style, which permitted promenade and meditation, with botanical gardens and pleasure gardens. A unique public garden is the Père-Lachaise Cemetery, which is an evolved *jardin anglo-chinois,* with numerous unexpected vistas that helped dramatize the great variety of tombs. The *jardin anglais* spread to other countries. Best-known examples are the Englischer Garten in Munich, Villa Borghese in Rome, Drottningholm Park in Stockholm, and Tiergarten in Berlin.

Further Reading

Laborde, Alexandre, *Description des nouveaux jardins de la France et de ses anciens chateaux,* Paris, 1808; reprint, Farnborough, Hampshire: Gregg, 1971

Le Rouge, Georges-Louis, *Détails des nouveaux jardins à la mode,* 21 parts, Paris, 1776–87; see especially part 11, *Jardins anglo-chinois*

Mosser, Monique, and Georges Teyssot, editors, *L'architettura dei giardini d'Occidente,* Milan: Electa, 1990; as *The Architecture of Western Gardens,* Cambridge, Massachusetts: MIT Press, 1991; as *The History of Garden Design,* London: Thames and Hudson, 1991

Nourry, Louis-Michel, *Les jardins publics en province: Espaces et politique au XIXe siècle,* Rennes, France: Presses Universitaires de Rennes, 1997

Pevsner, Nikolaus, editor, *The Picturesque Garden and Its Influence outside the British Isles,* Washington, D.C.: Dumbarton Oaks, 1974

Quest-Ritson, Charles, *The English Garden Abroad,* London: Viking, 1992

Sirén, Osvald, *China and Gardens of Europe of the Eighteenth Century,* New York: Ronald Press, 1950; reprint, with an introduction by Hugh Honour, Washington, D.C.: Dumbarton Oaks, 1990

Wiebenson, Dora, *The Picturesque Garden in France,* Princeton, New Jersey: Princeton University Press, 1978

HAZEL HAHN

Jardin Botanique National de Belgique. *See* Belgique, Jardin Botanique National de

---

Jardin des Plantes

Paris, France

Location: approximately .6 miles (1 km) southeast of Notre Dame cathedral, in the fifth arrondissement, by the Seine

The Jardin des Plantes is one of the oldest gardens of Paris, dating from the 17th century. It is divided into two parts: the Botanical Garden and the Zoological Park. The Jardin des Plantes is one of the most prestigious research centers in France. Many of the trees and flowers now common in Europe were introduced and naturalized here. It represents a utopian vision of mastering and collecting all forms of nature.

The first botanical garden in France appeared in Montpellier in the 16th century. In 1630 the court physician Guy de la Brosse persuaded Louis XIII to lay out the Royal Garden of Medicinal Herbs on a 24-acre (9.8 ha) site in Paris. At the time Richelieu opened the palace and garden of the Palais Royal to the public, and the king opened his new garden to the public as well. The garden was a tremendous success; a lemonade seller sold refreshments, and each day at noon a crowd gathered to listen to a Chinese gong strike 12 times on a globe. The garden was set on a varied landscape of mounds, valleys, meadows, and woods. The plan of 1640 included an artificial mound, a hillock planted with mountain trees, rectangular parterres for medicinal plants, a botanical garden, an orchard, hotbeds for delicate plants, a grove planted with wild trees, a garden of Indian plants, kitchen gardens, a terrace commanding the marshy grounds, an amphitheater, an orangery and a fountain basin. Guy de la Brosse, who also collaborated in the creation of the Luxembourg Gardens, created the School of Natural Sciences and the Pharmacy. Later a School of Botany was also founded, and the garden became a leading botanical research institute. In 1653 the Belvedere, the oldest structure in the garden, was built on a site that provided a splendid view of the surrounding areas. The garden had a celebrated collection of *vélins,* exquisite 17th-century flower paintings on parchment, notably those by Nicholas Robert. A succession of renowned scientists administrated the garden. In the early 18th century the era of physicians ended, to be replaced by naturalists and botanists: Joseph PittonTournefort, Bernard de Lacépède, Antoine de Jussieu, Jean-Baptiste Lamarck, and Etienne Geoffroy de Saint-Hilaire. In 1718 the name changed to Jardin Royal des Plantes. In 1732 Charles-François de Cisternay Du Fay created the first large hothouses.

In 1739 a new era began as 26-year-old Georges Buffon was appointed director, with Jean Thouin as head gardener. Buffon, who would be the garden's director for 49 years, until his death in 1788, founded collections in every department of natural history and worked on his vast *Histoire naturelle* (36 vols., 1749–1804; *Natural History*). He dispatched naturalists all over the world to collect for the garden. The Grand Labyrinth on the artificial mound is one of Buffon's most noted creations. From 1773 he extended and rearranged the garden, replacing the taxonomy of Tournefort with that of Carl Linnaeus. Buffon also doubled the size of the garden by extending it to the Seine.

During the French Revolution the garden was again transformed. Saved from destruction, in 1793 its name was officially changed to the Museum of Natural History, to include the Jardin des Plantes, and strictly "scientific" aims were laid out. Along with other royal parks such as the Tuileries, the Palais Royal, and the Jardin du Luxembourg, the museum became much more accessible to the public. André Thouin reformed the garden according to his ideas about the public's need for green space for moral and physical health and leisure. At the same time Louis Daubenton, the director, set out to create a menagerie, starting with the animals from the menagerie of Versailles. Several intellectual and political trends gave momentum to the museum's research in botany and horticulture. The 18th-century sensualist theory emphasized direct observation as the unique source of knowledge. The pre-Romantic aesthetic validated the moving power of nature, God's creation. In addition the revolutionary political project sought to identify the transparent order of nature as part of the formation of the new citizen.

Between 1789 and 1823 the garden grew from 43 to 79 acres (17.5 to 32 ha). In 1798 the large collection of Captain Nicolas Baudin arrived from the West Indies, for which a new hothouse was built. During the consulate and the empire the collection expanded with specimens from newly conquered regions. Thouin distributed material to the botanical gardens of all the departments of France and also abroad. By that time there was a botanical garden in each department. The menagerie, completed in 1822, was created as a landscape garden. About 1823 the garden featured large avenues of linden trees, cultivated squares, groves of forest trees, and the garden of economical plants.

The garden became very popular in the mid-19th century. The arrival of a giraffe in 1827 in Paris was greeted with extraordinary enthusiasm. Another source of popularity were glasshouses. Orangeries had multiplied in the last years of the ancien régime. In the 19th century a remarkable range of iron-and-glass structures were produced in Europe, many of them greenhouses in gardens and later at universal expositions. The public was fascinated with exotic plants, and they also admired the designs of the glasshouses. The greenhouses designed by Rohault de Fleury (1833) at the museum are masterpieces. These marked the first load-bearing cast-iron facades made of prefabricated parts in a two-story structure. The success of the glasshouses at the garden was later undermined by competition from the sumptuous and vast winter gardens on the Champs Elysées (1846–48; demolished ca. 1860), new sites of entertainment. In 1889 the garden was equipped with its own winter garden.

Today the Jardin des Plantes occupies about 70 acres (28.3 ha) and is the fourth most visited spot in Paris. The most famous plants include the first acacia introduced into Europe, planted in 1636; a legendary Cedar of Lebanon (*Cedrus libani*) with a three-meter circumference, planted by Bernard de Jussieu in 1735; and a Japanese pagoda tree (*Sophora japonica*), planted in 1747 and which flowered for the first time 30 years later. The tropical and Mexican hothouses shelter 50,000 tropical plants. An alpine garden created in 1931 contains species of origins as diverse as Morocco, Caucasus, and Himalaya. Several other establishments are attached to the garden, notably the arboretum of Chèvreloup near Versailles.

Synopsis

1626	Louis XIII buys 24 acres of uncultivated land in the quarter of the Saint-Victor abbey
1630–35	Development of the Royal Garden of Medicinal Herbs, by the court physician Guy de la Brosse
1635	Garden founded by an edict of Louis XIII, and registered by parliament
1636	First acacia introduced into Europe planted here

ca. 1640	Creation of the artificial mound, later incorporated into the Grand Labyrinth
1653	Construction of the Belvedere, the oldest structure in the garden
1718	Name changed to the Royal Garden of Plants
1732	Creation of the first big hothouses, by Cisternay Du Fay
1739	Comte de Buffon appointed director at 26 years of age, with Jean Thouin as head gardener
1773–88	Extensions completed under Buffon, garden doubled in size since foundation
1788	The first large hothouse built by Edme Verniquet, named after Buffon
1788	Building of the kiosk (Buffon's Summer House), the oldest metal structure in Paris
1793	The Convention gives a definitive organization to the garden, renamed officially as the Museum of Natural History
1794–95	Amphitheater finished and opened
1795–1800	Building of the greenhouse, designed by Molinos
1798	Construction of Nicolas Baudin's hothouse for housing his collection from the West Indies
1802	Publication of the first volume of *Annals du Muséum*
1822	Completion of the new menagerie set in the English landscape garden
1833	Construction of greenhouses, designed by Rohault de Fleury
1889	Winter garden inaugurated
1931	Creation of the alpine garden
1937	The *grande serre* or new winter garden built

Further Reading

Blanckaert, Claude, et al., editors, *Le muséum au premier siècle de son histoire*, Paris: Éditions du Muséum National d'Histoire Naturelle, 1997

Deleuze, J.P.F., *Histoire et description du Museum d'histoire naturelle, ouvrage redigé d'après les ordres de l'administration du museum*, Paris: Royer, 1823; as *History and Description of the Royal Museum of Natural History, Published by Order of the Administration of That Establishment*, Paris: Royer, 1823

Kohlmaier, Georg, and Barna von Sartory, *Das Glashaus: Ein Bautypus des 19. Jahrhunderts*, Munich: Prestel-Verlag, 1981; as *Houses of Glass: A Nineteenth-Century Building Type*, Cambridge: MIT Press, 1986

Letouzey, Yvonne, *Le Jardin des plantes à la croisée des chemins avec André Thouin, 1747–1824*, Paris: Muséum National d'Histoire Naturelle, 1989

Marrey, Bernard and Jean-Pierre Monnet, *La grande histoire des serres et des jardins d'hiver, France, 1780–1900*, Paris: Graphite, 1977

Mazas, Alain, "Le Belvédère du Jardin des Plantes de Paris," in *Journal of Garden History* 10, no. 1 (1990) and 10, no. 2 (1990)

HAZEL HAHN

Jardins d'Annevoie. *See* Annevoie, Jardins d'

Jefferson, Thomas 1743–1826

American President

Thomas Jefferson, statesman and third president of the United States, made noteworthy contributions to architecture, landscape gardening, and city and land planning during the United States's early period of nation building. Formally educated to be a lawyer, he was a self-taught expert on many subjects, a true member of the Enlightenment. Jefferson was a gifted amateur designer and helped bring architecture, landscape gardening, and land planning into a discourse about the aesthetics, symbolism, and practicalities of these disciplines as they expressed the new republic's ideals. Jefferson drew his design ideas from an array of sources. Extremely well read, he was conversant about the literature on architecture, preferring Palladian forms, and landscape gardening. He had a special interest in English landscape gardening and recommended William Hogarth and Edmund Burke, whose writings on nature, aesthetics, and the naturalistic style appealed to his own sensibilities about the native Virginia landscape. Jefferson also drew inspiration from American and European landscapes that he observed and wrote about, and in *Notes on the State of Virginia* (1788), he published his well-informed commentary about nature. In addition, he acted on the creative impulses that arose from curiosity and the need to solve particular problems.

In 1784 Jefferson accepted an appointment as minister to the French court and subsequently lived in Paris for five years. During this extended stay abroad he participated in and studied Parisian urban life. He also took advantage of his situation to travel to other parts of Europe and documented the quality and practicalities of life in the agrarian countryside as well as the city. On one notable trip to England, he and another future president of the United States, John Adams, recorded their impressions of the parks and gardens they saw. Using *Observations on Modern Gardening* by Thomas Whately (1770) as a guidebook, Jefferson noted his reactions to estates such as Blenheim and Stowe. Inspired by the English travel experience, he later wrote, "The gardening in that country is the article in which it surpasses all the earth."

Statesman and patriot first, Jefferson nonetheless found occasion to develop his talent in the design arts. He used as his laboratory for his ideas Monticello, his primary residence, in Charlottesville, Virginia. Here, he experimented with architecture, landscape design, horticulture, and scientific farming throughout his adult life. Acquiring Monticello—the plantation on the "little mountain"—in his early twenties, Jefferson idealized the property as a *ferme ornée,* or gentleman's farm, that combined agricultural operations with pleasure parks and gardens. He adapted ideas of English picturesque landscapes rather than borrowing the tradition of formal gardens then current in Virginia. With the main house and connected dependencies, which were configured like a head with attached arms, sited at the mountain's summit, Monticello's plan took advantage of the remarkable vistas. In order to maximize these views, Jefferson designed the buildings with low profiles, even constructing the dependencies partially underground. One of the masterful strokes of planning was the circulation system that included a series of roughly concentric drives, referred to as "roundabouts," which followed the mountain's contours and centered on the mountaintop residence. The drives served to separate various planting and crop areas as well as to afford visitors the experience of "unfolding" and changing views. Monticello featured both park environments intended for deer and wildlife and more highly cultivated spaces near the main residence.

Jefferson also envisioned Monticello as a botanical garden. To this end he avidly collected and experimented with plants, exchanging samples with other horticulturists throughout the country and overseas. The extensive list of plant species known to have been grown at Monticello shows that he was interested in the scientific, practical, and aesthetic potential of horticulture. Inspired by and devoted to gardening throughout his life, in his later years he wrote, "though an old man, I am but a young gardener."

Another of Jefferson's significant works was within view of Monticello, in nearby Charlottesville. In 1817 he began work on the University of Virginia. He proposed a unique concept of campus design, an ordered "academical village." A group of connected buildings enclosing three sides of a terraced lawn, Jefferson's plan integrated architecture with the site. In addition to the signature lawn, often referred to as the "most beautiful outdoor room in America," the plan provided for garden spaces at a more intimate level yet also linked to the distant mountain landscape through an axial view.

Jefferson's ideas are most visible on the larger American landscape. He believed that, unlike Europe, the United States offered a blank canvas for experimentation with government, aesthetics, freedom, and equality, among other concepts. One aspect of this experiment was the physical disposition of the land itself. He took a rational approach to land planning and advocated the grid as the basis for organization at two levels. One was the idealized town plan, which used a checkerboard pattern. Similar to plans of Philadelphia and Savannah, Georgia, Jefferson's towns were intended to foster a healthy environment by alternating blocks of concentrated building with blocks of green space. At another level he influenced the Ordinance of 1785, which called for the geometric subdivision of newly acquired territories. The large-scale grid was based on individually owned farmsteads as units of planning and the democratic ideal. Jefferson resisted using cities and industrialization as national symbols of growth and progress but instead celebrated the agrarian lifestyle and the citizen-farmer as appropriate strongholds of republican virtue. Still clearly evident in the United States, the grid imposed on the larger landscape demonstrates Jefferson's agrarian ideal as translated into physical form.

Biography

Born in Shadwell, Virginia, 1743. Educated at College of William and Mary, Williamsburg, Virginia; best known for activities as statesman, notably as third president of United States, 1801–9; also surveyor, lawyer, farmer, plantsman, and gifted amateur architect and landscape designer; accepted overseas political appointment and lived in Paris, France, and traveled in Europe, 1784–89, including tour of English gardens; ideas about design and horticulture evolved from reading, experiments, and observations; major laboratory for his concepts about architecture, horticulture, husbandry, and landscape design was Monticello, his primary residence, 1768–1826; designed original campus of University of Virginia, 1817; institutionalized land planning at national level. Died at Monticello, Albemarle County, Virginia, 4 July 1826.

Selected Designs

1768–1826	Monticello, Albemarle County, Virginia, United States
ca. 1785	Hotel de Langeac garden, Paris, France
1793	Edgemont, Albemarle County, Virginia, United States
ca. 1798	Edgehill, Albemarle County, Virginia, United States
1806–26	Poplar Forest, Bedford County, Virginia, United States
1817	Barboursville, Orange County, Virginia, United States; University of Virginia, Charlottesville, Virginia, United States

Selected Publications

Notes on the State of Virginia, 1788
Garden and Farm Books of Thomas Jefferson, 1987

Further Reading

Adams, William Howard, editor, *The Eye of Thomas Jefferson* (exhib. cat.), Washington, D.C.: National Gallery of Art, 1976
Betts, Edwin Morris, and Hazelhurst Bolton Perkins, *Thomas Jefferson's Flower Garden at Monticello,* Richmond, Virginia: Dietz Press, 1941; 3rd edition, Charlottesville, Virginia: Thomas Jefferson Memorial Foundation, 1986
Brawne, Michael, *University of Virginia: The Lawn,* London: Phaidon Press, 1994
Chambers, S. Allen, *Poplar Forest and Thomas Jefferson,* Forest, Virginia: The Corporation for Jefferson's Poplar Forest, 1993
Dumbauld, Edward, "Jefferson and Adams' English Garden Tour, " in *Jefferson and the Arts: An Extended View,* edited by William Howard Adams, Washington, D.C.: National Gallery of Art, 1976
Hatch, Peter J., *The Gardens of Thomas Jefferson's Monticello,* Charlottesville, Virginia: Thomas Jefferson Memorial Foundation, 1992
Hatch, Peter J., *The Fruits and Fruit Trees of Monticello,* Charlottesville: University Press of Virginia, 1998
Lambeth, William Alexander, and Warren H. Manning, *Thomas Jefferson As an Architect and a Designer of Landscapes,* Boston and New York: Houghton Mifflin, 1913; reprint, 1989
Leighton, Ann, *American Gardens in the Eighteenth Century: "For Use or for Delight,"* Boston: Houghton Mifflin, 1976
McLaughlin, Jack, *Jefferson and Monticello: The Biography of a Builder,* New York: Holt, 1988
Mullen, William, "Roses for the Rotunda," *Modulus* 16 (1983)
Nichols, Frederick Doveton, and Ralph Griswold, *Thomas Jefferson, Landscape Architect,* Charlottesville: University Press of Virginia, 1978
Reps, John, "Thomas Jefferson's Checkerboard Towns," *Journal of the American Society of Architectural Historians* 20, no. 3 (1961)

CECILIA RUSNAK

Jekyll, Gertrude 1843–1932

English Horticulturist and Garden Designer

There are few gardens made in the 20th century that do not in some way reflect the influence of Gertrude Jekyll, the great English gardener whose lifetime spanned the Victorian and modern eras. The author of a dozen books and hundreds of articles and the designer of several hundred gardens, Jekyll was above all a keen horticulturist and a consummate planting artist. Her theories of planting in naturalistic drifts, using harmonious colors and contrasting textures of foliage, were revolutionary in her day and still resonate among garden designers today.

Jekyll's ideas about garden design owe a debt to her early training as an artist. As a young woman she studied anatomical drawing, painting, and color theory, and she copied paintings in art galleries in London, Rome, and Paris. Her study of the atmospheric paintings of J.M.W. Turner, Hercules Brabazon, and other English

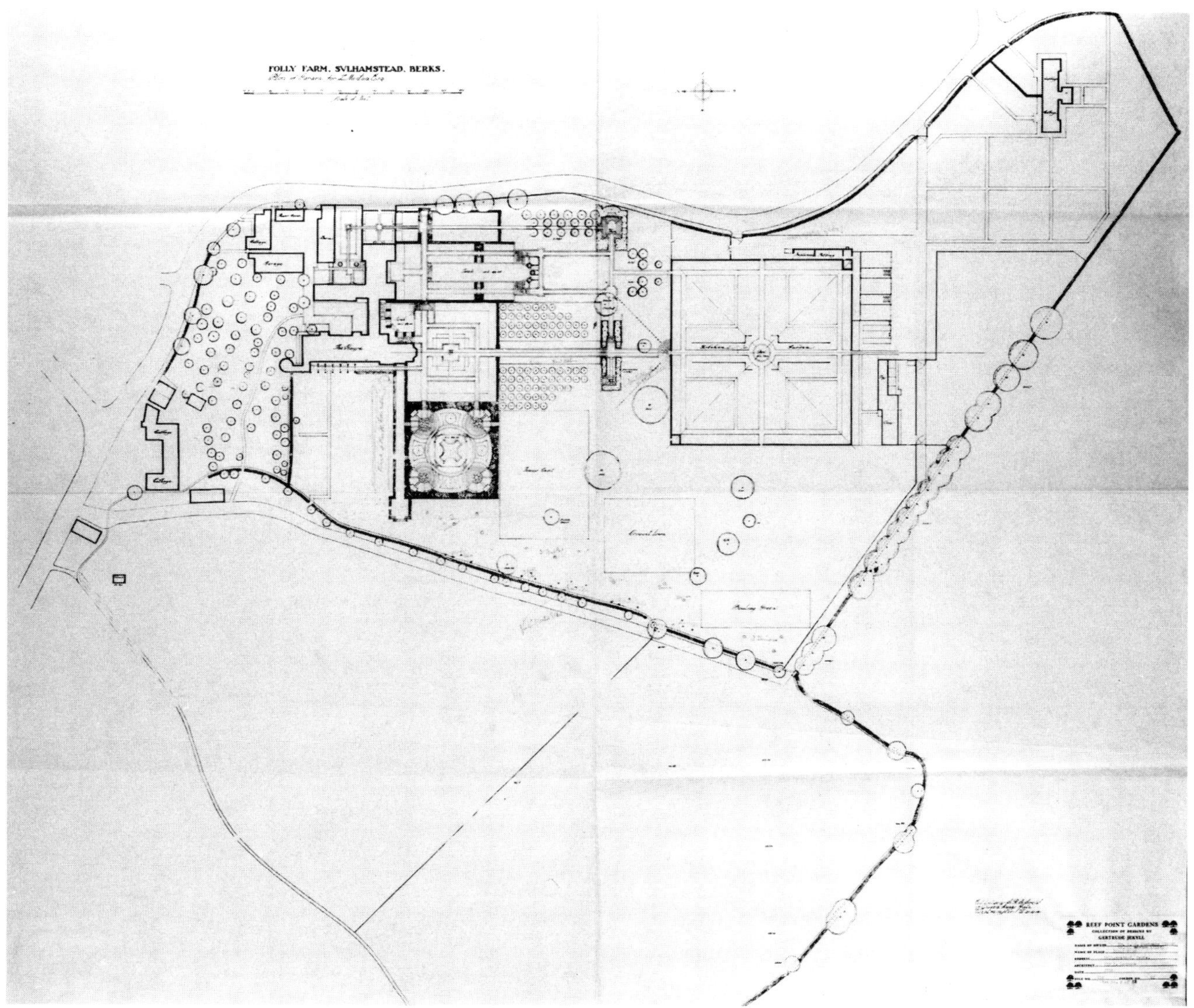

Plan of Folly Farm, Berkshire, England
Courtesy of Gertrude Jekyll Collection, Environmental Design Archives, University of California, Berkeley

Impressionist artists played a major role in the development of her special approach to garden design, which involved the use of plants to translate the artist's theories of composition and color into a living, three-dimensional work. Jekyll's practical studies of silversmithing, wood inlaying, embroidery, and other crafts helped develop the keen eye for detail that characterized her affinity for plants. Travels to Algeria and the Mediterranean during these formative years introduced her to exotic flora, in particular silver-foliaged and scented plants, both of which would become hallmarks of her planting style. Closer to home, she was inspired by indigenous country cottage gardens filled with a jumble of old-fashioned plants.

Jekyll laid out her first garden at Munstead House, her family's home in Surrey, in 1878. Many of the features of this garden—the long herbaceous border, spring garden, azalea garden, and naturalistic plantings of rhododendrons—found their way into her own, more famous garden, Munstead Wood, begun five years later. By the early 1880s, Jekyll's impressive working knowledge of plants earned her recognition in the horticultural world. Foremost among her colleagues at this time was William Robinson, the author of *The Wild Garden* (1870) and *The English Flower Garden* (1883) and an influential editor. Jekyll wrote many articles for Robinson's magazine *The Garden,* using as illustrations her own photographs, which she began taking in 1885.

Jekyll's first book, *Wood and Garden* (1899), with its engaging prose style and enchanting photographs, introduced her ideas to a wider world. Many books followed on subjects including roses, lilies, annuals, water gardens, and flower decoration, but *Colour in the Flower*

Garden (1908) best expresses her theories of gardening. Instead of relying on the seasonal rotation of colorful annuals bedded out in regimented patterns (the style that had dominated the Victorian era), she advanced the idea of naturalistic groupings of hardy plants, using her gardens at Munstead Wood as an example. She clearly showed her prowess in implementing and maintaining seasonal gardens and borders emphasizing color and texture, arranged with an artistic hand. Her October aster borders, composed in pale hues of blues and purples, and her celebrated hardy border, its composition arranged in the same manner as a Turner painting, served as inspiration to gardeners around the world.

At Munstead Wood, the whole garden was planned as a series of "pictures." She began by laying out naturalistic woodland gardens inspired by Robinson's theories, followed by extensive kitchen and nursery gardens, as well as numerous color and seasonal borders. The legendary house at Munstead Wood, which was not built until long after the gardens were laid out, was designed to be in perfect harmony with nature. The architect, Edwin Lutyens, later became Jekyll's professional design partner. Jekyll had begun designing small gardens in the 1880s, mainly at the request of friends who acquired plants from her surplus nursery stock, but it was not until 1899, when she and Lutyens laid out the gardens at Orchards, that she embarked on a serious garden design career. There followed nearly 50 commissions, including Deanery Garden, Hestercombe, Millmead, and Folly Farm, to name a few of the better-known examples. Most of their projects received widespread coverage in *Country Life* magazine and in books of the period, accounting for familiarity with their work among Americans.

One of the most innovative commissions by Lutyens and Jekyll is Folly Farm, Berkshire. When enlarging a medieval cottage on a small dairy farm by adding a William-and-Mary-style house in 1906, Lutyens included in his architectural framework several courtyards connecting the buildings, each designed and planted with a different character. In addition to overseeing the courtyard plantings, Jekyll also planted a rhododendron walk and numerous herbaceous borders, but much of this early scheme was obliterated six years later when Lutyens added another wing. On this occasion, Lutyens and Jekyll laid out new gardens as a series of geometric "rooms," each delineated with high, clipped hedges, predating those at Hidcote, Sissinghurst, and other pivotal gardens of the modern era. The layout, which exists to the present day, includes a rectangular canal garden (perpendicular to the 1906 addition), an unusual sunken rose garden (hidden behind dense yew hedges) with interlocking descending circular steps at each corner, a lily tank cloister garden nestled into the junction of the two additions, a walled kitchen garden, and other areas that were dramatically conceived and artfully planted. Notations on surviving planting plans clearly show that Lutyens and Jekyll worked together on this garden layout, querying each other as to where critical features were to be located. Even though the plantings were simplified somewhat in the 1960s by the American landscape architect Lanning Roper, Folly Farm still retains its magical character.

During the course of Jekyll's career, which spanned nearly 50 years, she designed at least 400 gardens, most of which were located in southeast England, with some in the English West Country, Scotland, and Ireland. She also designed at least three gardens in the United States, where her clients were garden club women. These commissions included the cottage gardens at the Glebe House in Woodbury, Connecticut (replanted in the 1990s); a woodland garden in Greenwich, Connecticut; and the design for stone terrace gardens in Cincinnati, Ohio, that were never built. In addition to Lutyens, Jekyll worked with M.H. Baillie Scott, Herbert Baker, Oliver Hill, Sidney Barnsley, Robert Lorimer, Walter Brierley, and other architects associated with the Arts and Crafts movement. Examples of these commissions are described in *Gardens for Small Country Houses* (1912), which she wrote with Lawrence Weaver, a well-known architecture critic.

One of the most surprising aspects of Jekyll's activities as a garden designer is that she seldom traveled to any of the sites involved (after World War I, she was almost entirely reclusive). Instead, she worked with a site plan, photographs, and soil samples supplied by her clients or their architects. In later years when her eyesight was failing, she drew upon her unusual facility for laying out borders using a varied palette of plants recalled entirely from memory. On larger projects, her work was made somewhat easier when an architect was involved, as was the case at Barrington Court, Somerset. In the early 1920s, when she was in her late seventies, Jekyll was approached to prepare a planting scheme for gardens laid out by the architectural firm Forbes and Tate. Working directly on the architects' plan, she created more than a dozen individual enclosed garden rooms, each with a distinct character, all tied together by an enclosing wall and the remains of an ancient moat. Although the garden has been simplified, Jekyll's basic layout survives today under the care of the National Trust.

Only a handful of Jekyll's gardens survive, and with the exception of Barrington Court and Hestercombe, most are privately owned. Jekyll's principles of garden design are best appreciated in her numerous books. Her professional planting plans and photograph albums are held at the College of Environmental Design Documents Collection of the University of California, Berkeley, to which they were donated in 1956 by the U.S. landscape architect Beatrix Farrand. Additional collections of her albums and notebooks are held at the Godalming Museum (Surrey), the Surrey History Centre (Woking), and the Lindley Library, London.

See also Color; Hestercombe; Lutyens, Edwin; Mount Stewart; Munstead Wood

Biography

Born in London, 29 November 1843. Studied at Kensington School of Art, South Kensington, 1861; traveled to Turkey, Rhodes, and Greece, 1863; informally studied painting with Hercules Brabazon; studied gilding, woodcarving, silversmithing, embroidery, 1870s; moved to Munstead, Surrey, England, 1878, where she laid out her first garden; began writing articles for *The Garden,* 1882; acquired land for Munstead Wood, 1883; took up photography, 1885; met Edwin Lutyens (with whom she collaborated on 50 gardens), 1889; carried out approximately 400 garden design commissions between the early 1880s and 1932; awarded Victoria Medal of Honour by Royal Horticultural Society, 1897; wrote first book, *Wood and Garden,* 1899; coeditor of *The Garden,* 1900; received George Robert White Medal of Honor from the Massachusetts Horticultural Society, 1929. Died at Munstead Wood, 9 December 1932.

Selected Designs

1883 Munstead Wood, Godalming, Surrey, England
1899 Orchards, Godalming, Surrey, England
1901 Deanery Garden, Sonning, Berkshire, England
1904 Hestercombe, Cheddon Fitzpaine, Somerset, England
1905 Marsh Court, Stockbridge, Hampshire, England
1906 Folly Farm, Sulhamstead, Berkshire, England
1907 Lambay Castle, Lambay Island, County Dublin, Ireland
1908 King Edward VII Sanatorium, Midhurst, West Sussex, England
1909 Millmead, Bramley, Surrey, England
1911 Lindisfarne Castle, Holy Island, Northumberland, England
1917 Barrington Court, Ilminster, Somerset, England
1919 Heywood, Abbeyliex, County Laois, Ireland
1920 Mount Stewart, Newtonards, County Down, Northern Ireland
1925 Gledstone Hall, North Yorkshire, England
1926 Glebe House, Woodbury, Connecticut, United States

Selected Publications

Wood and Garden, 1899
Home and Garden, 1900
Wall and Water Gardens, 1901
Some English Gardens, 1904 (with George Elgood)
Old West Surrey, 1904
Colour in the Flower Garden, 1908 (later editions entitled *Colour Schemes for the Flower Garden*)
Gardens for Small Country Houses, 1912 (with Lawrence Weaver)
Garden Ornament, 1918 (1927 revised edition with Christopher Hussey)
Gertrude Jekyll on Gardening, 1984

Further Reading

Bisgrove, Richard, *The Gardens of Gertrude Jekyll,* London: Lincoln, and Boston: Little Brown, 1992; reprint, Berkeley: University of California Press, 2000
Brown, Jane, *Gardens of a Golden Afternoon: The Story of a Partnership: Edwin Lutyens and Gertrude Jekyll,* London and New York: Penguin Books, 1985
Festing, Sally, *Gertrude Jekyll,* New York: Penguin Books, and London: Viking, 1991
Gunn, Fenja, *Lost Gardens of Gertrude Jekyll,* London and New York: Macmillan, 1991
Hobhouse, Penelope, editor, *Gertrude Jekyll on Gardening,* London: Collins, and Boston: Godine, 1984
Jekyll, Francis, *Gertrude Jekyll, a Memoir,* London: Jonathan Cape, 1934
Jekyll, Francis, and G.C. Taylor, editors, *A Gardener's Testament: A Selection of Articles and Notes by Gertrude Jekyll,* London: Country Life, and New York: Scribner, 1937
Massingham, Betty, *Miss Jekyll: A Portrait of a Great Gardener,* London: Country Life, 1966
Tankard, Judith B., and Martin A. Wood, *Gertrude Jekyll at Munstead Wood,* Stroud, Gloucestershire: Sutton, and New York: Sagapress, 1996
Tankard, Judith B., and Michael R. Van Valkenburgh, *Gertrude Jekyll: A Vision of Garden and Wood,* New York: Sagapress, and London: Murray, 1989
Tooley, Michael, editor, *Gertrude Jekyll: Artist, Gardener, Craftswoman: A Collection of Essays to Mark the 50th Anniversary of Her Death,* Witton-le-Wear, Durham: Michaelmas Books, 1984
Tooley, Michael, and Primrose Arnander, editors, *Gertrude Jekyll: Essays on the Life of a Working Amateur,* Witton-le-Wear, Durham: Michaelmas Books, 1995

JUDITH B. TANKARD

Jellicoe, Geoffrey Alan 1900–1996

English Architect and Landscape Designer

Sir Geoffrey Jellicoe was one of the most influential landscape architects of the 20th century, resulting from professional work that spanned more than half a century. He explored new ideas and discovered original, functional, and meaningful landscape solutions. He also helped lead the movement to establish landscape architecture as a profession. At the age of 23, following qualification as an architect, Jellicoe and fellow student J.C. Shepherd made a tour of Italian Renaissance gardens. While the practical result of their survey and recordings was the publication *Italian Gardens of the Renaissance* (1925), exposure to the philosophy of classical gardens also had a profound influence on Jellicoe's career. His experiences deepened his appreciation of a fundamental historic continuum, and he was to return to the Italian Renaissance garden throughout his life, lecturing and publishing on the meaning of the gardens "not only the visible and conscious . . . but also the invisible and subconscious" (Jellicoe, 1993) and their importance in his own developing theories of garden design.

After his return from Italy, Jellicoe spent several years in private architectural practice before establishing his own practice in 1931 at Bloomsbury Square, London. Here he was able to indulge his preference for landscape rather than architectural commissions, working on both private traditional gardens such as Mottisfont Abbey and numerous corporate commissions for restructuring after World War II. Notwithstanding his admiration for Italian Renaissance garden design, Jellicoe felt that the philosophy from which it had sprung was inadequate. His own design ideas were additionally influenced by contemporary trends—by the modern movement, by modern art, and by theories of the unconscious, particularly those of Carl Jung. Jellicoe often drew inspiration from natural forms, as well as from shapes derived from the unconscious or "the invisible idea," to suggest a theme or hidden message which would bind the design elements into a coherent whole. Examples from the late 1950s are the curving, snake-shaped watercourse at Hemel Hempstead and his design for a roof garden on a Guildford store that was symbolic of the earth as seen from space and built as the first Sputnik circled the earth. Jellicoe sometimes used specific works of art as the basis for exploration in design. Examples are his landscape proposals for a nuclear power station in Gloustershire (1960), clearly influenced by a Ben Nicholson abstract painting, and his adoption of a flowing, organic design for a rose garden at Cliveden (1961), inspired by Paul Klee's painting *The Fruit.*

During his epic work on the Kennedy Memorial at Runnymede (1964–65), Jellicoe was able to apply to landscape design the modern artist's conception of the viewer as participant, and to further explore his interest in the link between the conscious and subconscious mind. The hillside landscape chosen for the memorial for John F. Kennedy was designed as an allegory of Bunyan's *Pilgrim's Progress,* in which the visitor makes a journey representative of "life, death and spirit." Jellicoe attributes his use of allegory to a visit to Japan, where he made the first sketches for the design stating that "it was probably the local historic influence that suddenly brought forward the idea the memorial was in fact a design in continuous progress" (Jellicoe, 1970). Symbolism at Runnymede includes a granite pathway with individual pavers representing pilgrims traveling to the top of the hill and through a wood, where a slab of Portland Stone bears a quotation from Kennedy's inaugural speech. By the stone are hawthorn trees (*Crataegus*) representing Catholicism and an American scarlet oak (*Quercus coccinea*) with its red autumn leaves to symbolize death. A pathway called Jacob's Ladder leads down to the Seats of Contemplation, which expands the setting of the memorial to the surrounding countryside with its views over the Thames and London.

It is interesting that much of Jellicoe's later work, including Sutton Place (1980–86), Shute House (1970–93), and his proposal for the Moody Gardens, Galveston (1984), was designed as similar journeys of discovery. It was, indeed, during this later period of retirement, when he accepted more than 33 commissions, that Jellicoe's most creative work took place. The commission for Sutton Place, a 16th-century house and existing garden in Surrey, is undoubtedly one of his most important projects. Although it came nearly 20 years after the construction of the Kennedy Memorial, Jellicoe's design for Sutton Place is generally considered a development of his investigation into the conscious and subconscious mind: "The landscape at Sutton Place is of the mind as well as the eye; a study in humanism emanating from the interior of an historic mansion enriched with modern art" (Jellicoe, 1983). The original design, described by Jellicoe as "a grand allegory of Creation," incorporates paradise, secret gardens, a grotto, and a cascade and is a dramatic fusion of historical associations, surrealist concepts and modern art. Surrealist ideas, for example, are seen in the distorted prospective created by the giant urns in the Magritte

Pond and sculpture at Sutton Place, Surrey, England
Copyright Clive Boursnell/Garden Picture Library

Walk, and modern art is represented by the celebrated Nicholson Wall, an imposing white marble sculpture by the artist Ben Nicholson contained in a 19th-century hedged enclosure.

Due to financial limitations, Jellicoe's design for Sutton Place was never completed, but his intricate designs clearly trace the journey of the subconscious through "creation, the good life and aspiration." Surprisingly, Jellicoe had always considered himself poor at drawing and was content to leave the detailed design work to others, once he had sketched the conceptual framework. It was only in retirement, when he was able to give free rein to his originality, that his drawings became confident, unique works of art. He generally drew freehand; plans were sometimes overlaid with color and were invariably accompanied with annotations and smaller sketches of individual features or sections of the landscape. Jellicoe also claimed to possess limited horticultural knowledge and regarded trees and shrubs as design elements that could be used to enhance the atmosphere of his landscapes. He relied on his wife Susan, or other members of the design team, to produce detailed planting plans for his landscapes.

Jellicoe was a prolific writer and lecturer. His epic work *The Landscape of Man* (1975), co-authored with his wife, is a definitive study of the designed landscape past and present, encapsulating his belief that "All design . . . derives from impressions of the past, conscious and subconscious." The publication, begun in 1958, emphasizes the importance of landscape architecture as a fine art and a profession. Subsequent revisions provided Jellicoe the opportunity to comment on his developing theories and designs, work which continued until his death at the age of 95.

Biography

Born in Chelsea, London, 8 October 1900. Studied at Architectural Association, London, 1919–23; study tour of Renaissance gardens in Italy, 1923; in practice with Tubbs, Son, and Duncan, Architects, and private practice as Shepherd and Jellicoe, 1925–31; established practice at 40 Bloomsbury Square, London, 1931; principal, Architectural Association School of Architecture, 1939–42; president, Institute of Landscape Architects, 1939–49; editor of *Journal of the Institute of Landscape Architects,* 1941–45; first president of International Federation of Landscape Architects, 1948; awarded Commander of the British Empire, 1961; Knight Bachelor, 1979; elected to Royal Academy, 1991; received Victoria Medal of Honour from Royal Horticultural Society, 1995. Died 17 July 1996.

Selected Designs

1934–36	With Russell Page, garden for restaurant, Cheddar Gorge, Somerset, England
1936–39	Mottisfont Abbey Gardens, Hampshire, England
1947	New Town, Hemel Hempstead, Hertfordshire, England
1956–57	Roof garden, Harvey's Department Store, Guildford, Surrey, England
1957–59	Water gardens, Hemel Hempstead, Hertfordshire, England
1960	Oldbury-on-Severn power station, Gloucestershire, England
1961	Rose garden at Cliveden, Buckinghamshire, England
1964–65	Kennedy Memorial, Runnymede, Surrey, England
1970–93	Shute House, Donhead St. Mary, Wiltshire, England
1971–72	Royal Horticultural Society Gardens, Wisley, Surrey, England
1980–86	Sutton Place, Guildford, Surrey, England
1984	Moody Gardens, Galveston, Texas, United States
1992–93	Atlanta Historical Gardens, Atlanta, Georgia, United States

Selected Publications

Italian Gardens of the Renaissance (with J.C. Shepherd), 1925
Studies in Landscape Design, 3 vols., 1960
The Landscape of Man: Shaping the Environment from Prehistory to the Present Day (with Susan Jellicoe), 1975
Geoffrey Jellicoe: The Studies of a Landscape Designer over 80 Years, 3 vols., 1993

Further Reading

Brown, Jane, *The English Garden in Our Time from Gertrude Jekyll to Geoffrey Jellicoe,* Woodbridge, Suffolk: Antique Collectors Club, 1986
Harvey, Sheila, editor, *Geoffrey Jellicoe,* Reigate, Surrey: Landscape Design Trust Monographs, 1998
Museum of Modern Art, *Denatured Visions: Landscape and Culture in the Twentieth Century,* New York: Museum of Modern Art, 1991
Spens, Michael, *Gardens of the Mind: The Genius of Geoffrey Jellicoe,* Woodbridge, Suffolk: Thames and Hudson, 1994

BARBARA SIMMS

Jensen, Jens 1860–1951

United States Landscape Architect

Jens Jensen was a leading figure in U.S. landscape architecture. He was born near Dybbøl, on the Jutland peninsula of Denmark, the eldest son of Christian Jensen and Magdalen Sophia Petersen, who were prosperous farmers. When Jensen was four, a major battle in the Danish-Prussian War raged in the Slesvig area around his family's farm. The Danes lost the war, and the region fell under German rule, but the nationalistic Danes promoted their heritage in the folk schools Jensen attended by advocating a close relationship to the land and to traditional Danish culture. After conscription into the German army, Jensen served for a time in Berlin. There he developed an interest in the city's array of grand parks, boulevards, and gardens, which he studied and sketched.

At the age of 24, Jensen came to the United States with his wife, Anne Marie Hansen. He worked for a short time in Florida and Iowa and then moved to Chicago's Scandinavian enclave near Humboldt Park, where he took a job as a laborer with the West Park System. Jensen honed his horticultural skills through part-time work with a local nursery, and he quickly developed a fascination for the Chicago area's indigenous plants. In 1888 he created his popular "American Garden," a display of native trees, shrubs, and wildflowers, in Union Park. It contrasted sharply with the more formal and rigid landscape designs in many of Chicago's parks at that time. This became the first of Jensen's many park designs and landscape innovations that marked his more than 60-year career. Assuming greater responsibilities, he rose to become superintendent of Humboldt Park, a position he held from 1894 to 1900. In 1900 a series of sharp disagreements between Jensen, who maintained high standards of integrity, and corrupt park administrators led to his abrupt dismissal. However, in 1906, with reform measures underway in Chicago politics, Jensen was rehired as landscape architect and superintendent of the West Park System. He was active in this capacity until 1909, and he remained a consultant to the parks until his resignation in 1920.

Early in the 20th century, Jensen started what would become a prolific and highly successful private practice, completing masterful designs for what he termed "natural parks and gardens." Soon his work became fashionable among some of the Midwest's most elite citizens, including the Florsheims, Kuppenheimers, McCormicks, and Fords. Jensen's landscape designs were both democratic and spiritual, expressing the fervent belief that the United States would develop a new culture rooted in its own regional landscapes. His symbols became the hawthorn, with its horizontal branches mimicking the prairie; flowing outdoor spaces with gentle contours reflecting the Midwestern plains; and spectacular rock work suggesting ravines and bluffs found along Lake Michigan and the Mississippi River.

One of his most visible symbols was a low stone circular gathering place called a council ring. His concept for this feature was steeped in ancient Nordic traditions and Native American lore. He believed it symbolized the democratic ideals of his new homeland by creating a place where all would have equal seating around a central campfire to commune with nature and with each other. The details of Jensen's brilliant designs were often carried out by a series of talented foremen, some of whom, including Alfred Caldwell, went on to establish their own distinguished careers.

Toward the end of World War I, Jensen began working on Columbus Park, which he regarded as the most successful of his park designs. His inspiration for its creation grew from the park's geology and natural topography. The plan included the re-creation of a nearby prairie and a dramatic prairie river built on an ancient glacial beach running through the site, as well as council rings, a "players hill" for outdoor pageants, and an innovative playground. Jensen became one of the leading figures in the Prairie School of design centered in Chicago. A friend and admirer of Louis Sullivan, at times he collaborated with such Prairie style architects and Hugh Garden, John van Bergen, Dwight Perkins, and Frank Lloyd Wright. His relationship to the latter was sometimes stormy, since both men were strong-willed individuals, and Jensen disliked some aspects of Wright's controversial lifestyle. Ultimately Jensen's work would spread from Nebraska to Maine and from Kentucky to Michigan's Upper Peninsula.

Jens Jensen was also significant for his conservation activities—a steadfast passion that continued throughout his career. He helped establish three influential conservation organizations: the Friends of Our Native Landscape, the Chicago Playground Association, and the Prairie Club. Each involved active participation in outdoor activities and extensive efforts to save and restore large natural preserves and interconnected systems of open spaces. In Illinois and Wisconsin, such organizations were an important early influence for setting aside state and local parks. These organizations were also active in promulgating better roadside management practices, establishing the Cook County Forest Preserve, saving part of the Indiana Dunes at the south end of Lake Michigan, initiating pioneering rural land use planning activities, and other important conservation projects.

During the 1920s, Jensen and his family began vacationing at their Wisconsin retreat in a remote corner of Door County near Ellison Bay. The area reminded him of his Danish homeland and was a catalyst for his dream of some day establishing a "school of the soil" patterned after the Danish folk schools he attended as a young man. In 1934 his wife died, and several months later his grandson Kenneth Jensen Wheeler, whom Jensen favored to carry on his practice, died shortly after completing his studies in landscape architecture at the University of Wisconsin. Devastated, Jensen, who was growing increasingly restless with city life and politics, closed his Ravinia office and moved to the Door County peninsula to establish his school on what would become a 129-acre (52.2 ha) tract of land overlooking the waters of Green Bay. He patterned this unique learning environment after his Danish folk school experiences and envisioned it as a place where people could find a deeper understanding of nature and themselves. Today, The Clearing flourishes as a unique school of the arts and humanities. It remains the most visible and intact legacy of Jensen's masterful contributions to U.S. landscape architecture.

Biography

Born on farm in Dybbøl, Denmark, 1860. Studied city parks and gardens as conscripted German soldier in Berlin, 1881–83; emigrated to America in 1884 and eventually settled in Chicago; worked for Chicago West Parks Commission, 1886–1900, and for varying periods of time thereafter; superintendent of Humboldt Park, Chicago, 1894–1900; in early 1900s, established what eventually became flourishing private practice that continued for more than three decades; this involved design of projects that varied in scale and included private estates, parks, recreational developments, subdivisions, and numerous institutional projects; early in his career active in several conservation causes; founded Friends of Our Native Landscape, 1913; became leading figure in Prairie style of garden design, 1920s; also became vigorous spokesman for setting aside natural areas, a passion he championed for the rest of his life; closed his office, 1935, and moved to Wisconsin's then remote Door County Peninsula: established "The Clearing," in Door County, a "school of the soil" based on his childhood experiences in Danish folk schools. Died in Door County, Wisconsin, 1951.

Selected Designs

1888	American Garden, Union Park, Chicago, United States
1907	Garfield Park, Chicago, Illinois, United States
1910	Luther College, Decorah, Iowa, United States
1909–11	Racine, Wisconsin, Park System
1911–29	Julius Rosenwald Estate (now Rosewood Park), Highland Park, Illinois, United States
1912	E.L. Ryerson commission, Lake Forest, Illinois, United States
1914	Henry Ford estate, Dearborn, Michigan, United States
1917–20	Columbus Park, Chicago, Illinois, United States
1934–36	Lincoln Memorial Garden, Springfield, Illinois, United States
1935–51	The Clearing, Door County, Wisconsin, United States
1945	Glenwood Children's Park, Madison, Wisconsin, United States

Selected Publications

Parks and Politics, in *American Parks and Outdoor Art Association*, vol. 6, 1902

Greater West Park System, 1920

"The Park Policy," *A Park and Forest Policy for Illinois*, by Friends of Our Native Landscape, 1926

"Swimming Pool and Playground at Columbus Park," *Parks and Recreation* (1928)

"Natural Parks and Gardens," *Saturday Evening Post*, 8 March 1930 (with Ragna B. Eskil)

Siftings, 1939

The Clearing, 1949

"Siftings," The Major Portion of "The Clearing," and Collected Writings, 1956

Further Reading

Caldwell, Alfred, "Jens Jensen, the Prairie Spirit," *Landscape Architecture Quarterly* 60 (January 1961)

Christy, Stephen, "The Metamorphosis of an Artist," *Landscape Architecture* 66, no. 1 (January 1976)

Christy, Stephen, "Jens Jensen," in *American Landscape Architecture: Designers and Places*, edited by William H. Tishler, Washington, D.C.: The Preservation Press, 1989

Domer, Dennis, *Alfred Caldwell: The Life and Work of a Prairie School Landscape Architect*, Baltimore, Maryland: Johns Hopkins University Press, 1997

Eaton, Leonard K., *Landscape Artist in America: The Life and Work of Jens Jensen*, Chicago: The University of Chicago Press, 1964

Egan, Dave, and William H. Tishler, "Jens Jensen, Native Plants, and the Concept of Nordic Superiority," *Landscape Journal* 16 (1999)

Fulkerson, Mertha, and Ada Corson, *The Story of the Clearing: A Door County Legend*, Chicago: Coach House Press: 1972

Grese, Robert E., *Jens Jensen: Maker of Natural Parks and Gardens*, Baltimore, Maryland: Johns Hopkins University Press, 1992

Grese, Robert E., "The Prairie Gardens of O.C. Simonds and Jens Jensen," in *Regional Garden Design in the United States*, edited by Therese O'Malley and Marc Treib, Washington, D.C.: Dumbarton Oaks Research Library and Collection, 1995

Miller, Wilhelm, *The Prairie Spirit in Landscape Gardening*, Urbana: University of Illinois Agricultural Experiment Station: 1915

Sniderman, Julia, "Bringing the Prairie Vision into Focus," in *Prairie in the City: Naturalism in Chicago's Parks, 1870–1940*, Chicago: Chicago Historical Society, 1991

WILLIAM H. TISHLER

Ji Chang Yuan

Wuxi, Jiangsu Province, China

Location: approximately 70 miles (116.6 km) west of Shanghai

The garden Ji Chang Yuan is listed as a Chinese national heritage site. The garden was originally part of a Buddhist monastery called Nan Yin. In 1506–21, a classical garden was created at the monastery by Qin Jin. The original name of the garden was Feng Gu Xing Wo (Wind Valley Villa); it was then renamed Ji Chang Yuan, which means "delighted garden." As the emperors Kang Xi and Qian Long traveled to southern China, they both visited the garden. Emperor Qian Long was so impressed with the design of this very small garden (about 2.5 acres [1 ha]) that he had the inner garden Xiequ Yuan of the Summer Palace in Beijing built to imitate it.

Ji Chang Yuan is divided into two areas. The main feature of the eastern area is a spacious water surface and rockeries around the pool called Jing Hui Qi (Splendid Wave Pond), created by Zhang Yue, son of a famous garden designer of the Ming dynasty, Zhang Nanyuan. A long corridor was built alongside the pool. The Bridge of Seven Stars in the northeastern part of the garden divides the water surface into two sections and gives an impression of profound space. A pavilion called Zhiyu Jian (Knowing Fish Pavilion) provides the central scene of the pool. The western part of the garden is mainly for rockeries and trees.

The pool, corridor, bridge, pavilion, rocks, and trees are skillfully used to create illusions of depth and distance. In the northwest part of the garden is an artificial mountain of earth and yellow rock that is so cleverly made that it seems part of Hui Hill, visible in the distance beyond it. This technique of borrowing scenery is called *jie jing* and is used very effectively here to open the small space of the garden into a vast environment.

The garden was totally destroyed during the Taiping Revolution in the 1860s. In the garden were old trees, including a one thousand-year-old camphor tree, all of which were also destroyed during this period. Only the rockeries and central pond are original; the other part of the garden was rebuilt in the 1920s.

Synopsis

1506–21 Classical garden constructed on the site of a monastery by Qin Jin; owned since then by Qin family
1864 Garden destroyed
1920s Garden rebuilt

Further Reading

Luo, Zhewen, *Zhong guo gudai yuan-lin* (Ancient Chinese Gardens), Beijing: China Architecture and Building Press, 1999

Tong, Jun, *Jiang-Nan yuan-lin zhi* (Notes on Jiangnan Gardens), Beijing: China Architecture and Building Press, 1984

ZHENG SHILING

Jones, Inigo 1573–1652

English Set Designer, Architect, and Landscape Designer

Inigo Jones was the first British architect to earn the title of *Vitruvius Brittanicus* (The British Vitruvius) and was instrumental in introducing mature Classical architectural forms to England. To chronicle his contribution to landscape design, his work in other genres has to be dissected. His promotion from scenery designer for court masques to architect and landscape designer was the result of study during continental travels, particularly his visits to Heidleberg, Germany, and Italy accompanying the Earl of Arundel. Jones was influenced by the Frenchman Salomon de Caus. It is recorded that the garden at Heidelberg Castle by de Caus was furnished with grottoes, foundations, statues, and water features similar to some of the details designed by Jones for the court masques. An engraving of the Heidelberg garden indicates a romantic panorama with elements providing surprise and contrast. This was clearly in the same aesthetic mold as Jones's approach to masque scenery, including some of the mechanically operated devices.

Jones visited Italy on two occasions. The second established his reputation as a master of classical design. A major point in his design philosophy was the adoption of severe classical forms for his buildings. He recognized that visual impact on the spectator was all important. Regarding landscape, Jones argued in his Roman sketchbook that mannerist design was not appropriate to "Sollid Architecture" but should be reserved for composed ornaments in garden architecture. The contrast of austere, disciplined architectural forms with a free, almost mannerist landscaping foretold the Romantic movement more than a century later. Jones argued that design should start with a disciplined plan leading to a geometric ensemble of architectural elements. To enable the spectator to appreciate the design, especially its symmetry and relationship with the parterre, pavilions, and artistic elements, a responding external space must be created. This is shown in the design for Whitehall (ca.1638), in which formal internal courts allowed controlled views of the internal classical facades.

It is unfortunate that Jones rarely had the type of site to develop this principle freely, for almost all his work was in urban locations. The block plan of his development at Covent Garden displays the application of his classical form in such a setting. The 1631 plan shows Jones forming a piazza by designing a range of houses around a square in which the major element, St. Paul's Church and its relatively small church yard, is situated on the axis of the entrance gate.

Control of external spaces by the layout of paths and approaches is a common feature of Jones's designs. One of his later works, the south facade of Wilton House, shows this principle at work. The creation of a level area and a water feature some distance from the house allows the composition to be seen and appreciated. The response of landscape to buildings can also be seen in his uncompleted work at Stoke Bruerne (1629–35). Paths and low balustrades run from curved colonnades and show how each secondary element had its own parterre. A stone staircase leads down into the formal landscape at the center of the composition, creating a hierarchy of landscaped areas reflecting the architectural composition.

Jones's greatest influence on English landscape is the way in which he linked solid, proportional structures with subordinated exterior responses, thus foreshadowing later cultural forms in the relationship of buildings to their surroundings.

Biography

Born in Smithfield, London, 1573. Traveled to Italy, 1590s to 1603; may have served with Christian IV of Denmark, 1603; scenery designer for court masques in England, 1605; traveled second time to Italy, via Heidelberg, Germany, with Earl of Arundel, 1613–14; surveyor of King's Works to James I and Charles II, 1615–42; designed Covent Garden, London, including piazza and surrounding houses, 1631; resigned as surveyor of King's Works, estates confiscated with outbreak of Civil War, 1642; pardoned by House of Lords, estates restored, 1646. Died in Somerset House, Strand, London, 1652.

Selected Designs

1615–25 Grounds, Arundel House, Arundel, West Sussex, England
1631–38 Covent Garden piazza, Covent Garden, London, England
1638 Gardens, Lincoln's Inn Fields, London, England

Further Reading

Summerson, John Newenham, *Inigo Jones,* London: Penguin, 1966

KENNETH HALL MURTA

Jōruri-ji

Kamo-chō, Sōgaku-gun, Kyoto Prefecture, Japan

Location: on the border with Nara Prefecture, near route 24

Jōruri-ji is a temple of an esoteric Buddhist sect called Shingon Risshū, located among low hills on the border between Kyoto and Nara prefectures in central Japan. The garden at the temple is of significance for two reasons: it is one of the few extant gardens reflective of Heian-period (794–1185) design, and the form of the garden contains allegorical Buddhist meaning, making it a classic example of what is now known as a Pure Land garden.

By tradition the history of the temple stems from the eighth century, but the first date of certainty is the construction of a main hall in 1047 under the direction of the priest Gimyō. At that time a sculpture of Yakushi Nyorai (the Healing Buddha [Sanskrit Bhaisajya-guru]) was enshrined as the temple deity. According to the Yakushi sutra the Yakushi Buddha presides over a paradisiacal land known as Jōruri Sekai, Land of Pure Lapis Lazuli, thus the name Jōruri-ji, in which the suffix *ji* means temple. *Ruri,* lapis lazuli (Sanskrit vaidūrya, sometimes translated as emerald), is one of the seven precious jewels of Buddhism. In 1107 a new main hall was built under the direction of Awakōkōshin, the presiding head priest. Within that hall a set of nine sculptures of Amida Nyorai (Buddha of Infinite Light [Sanskrit Amitābha]), which is attributed to the Heian-period sculptor Jōchō, was enshrined as the temple deity along with the original sculpture of Yakushi Buddha, which was moved to a western hall.

The next major influence on the temple's development came with a priest named Eshin, son of imperial regent Fujiwara no Tadamichi and an administrator of Kōfukuji, a large temple of the Hossōshū sect in Nara. In 1150, having placed Jōruri-ji under the auspices of the larger temple, Eshin directed the reconstruction of the central pond and rock work in the garden. In 1157 the large hall housing the Amida sculptures was due to be reroofed, so Eshin took the opportunity to completely rebuild it, relocating it to the west side of the pond. At the same time the hall holding the image of the Yakushi Buddha was moved to the east side of the pond into a refurbished hall. The central pond that lays between these two structures was developed at this time to create the proper setting for the Amida Hall, which ideally sits before a body of water. Eshin's father, Tadamichi, and grandfather, Tadazane, are reputed to have been involved in garden design, so it is understandable that Eshin had a background in those matters. Eshin left Jōruri-ji for Izu Province in 1163 and died on a trip back to Kyoto in 1170 at the age of 58.

In 1178, by the decree of Emperor Takakura (r. 1161–81), a three-story wooden pagoda was moved from Ichijō Ōmiya in Kyoto, rebuilt on the east side of the pond, and the Yakushi statue was enshrined within it. Additionally, in 1205 a well-known gardening priest, Shōnagon Hōgen, came to repair the rock work. The stones remaining in the garden may stem from this time, although there is also a record that in 1410, 450 workmen came to Jōruri-ji to clean out the pond, and that project may have affected the garden design to some degree. Nevertheless, the overall garden design, as well as the rock work extant in the garden, is indicative of the Heian period. The stone lantern in front of the Amida hall and the statue of Dainichi nyorai (the Universal Buddha [Sanskrit Mahāvairocana]), enshrined in a hall to the north of the central pond, are believed to date from the Kamakura period (1185–1333). In 1343 fire broke out in the southern gate, burning several buildings, but the Amida Hall and pagoda were spared. Jōruri-ji is presently entered from a northern gate, but the record of this fire reveals that a traditional southern entry once existed.

The result of this progressive development was the establishment of a temple garden that expresses Buddhist ideals in an allegorical manner. In the center of the complex is a large pond that contains a small island and some rock work in the rocky-shore (*araiso*) style. A single prominent rock, which stands at the very tip of the island, lies directly on axis with the center of the Amida hall and the pagoda. This is in accord with the *Sakuteiki,* a garden manual from the mid-11th century, which notes that the tip (side) of the central island should be aligned with the center of the main hall. This rock arrangement is also meant to be representative of Shumisen (Sanskrit Sumeru), the central mountain of Buddhist and Hindu cosmology, and the entire garden correspondingly revolves around it. To the east of the pond, atop a small rise, Yakushi Buddha is enshrined in the pagoda, while the nine Amida Buddha are enshrined in a hall that sits to the west of the pond. This placement corresponds to the fact that Yakushi Buddha's Land of Pure Lapis Lazuli is traditionally believed to exist in a place far to the east, while the Pure Land of Amida Buddha is ascribed to a location far to the west on the other side of a great ocean, which is symbolized in the garden by the pond. The well-known literary images of the deities' respective paradises has been given physical form in the garden. Disciples who come to Jōruri-ji first approach the pagoda to offer prayers to Yakushi Buddha and then turn to face the Amida hall across the pond to the west. During the annual equinoxes they will be able to see the sun set directly behind the center of the Amida hall.

The positioning of the deities also describes a timeline of past, present, and future in the garden. The Butsumyōkyō, a sutra that names over 3,000 Buddhas, describes Yakushi as a Buddha of the past who offers salvation from past suffering; Shakamuni (Sanskrit Śākyamuni) as a Buddha of the present age, teaching the proper way of living; and Amida as a Buddha of the future, offering salvation in the afterlife. Relating east, center, and west with past, present, and future is typical of Chinese geomantic thought and can be seen expressed, for instance, in the main hall (Kondō, Golden Hall) of Hōryūji temple, which positions sculptures of Yakushi in the east, Śākyamuni in the center, and Amida in the west. Although Śākyamuni is not clearly expressed at Jōruri-ji, Yakushi and Amida have been positioned accordingly, and Dainichi Buddha, the Universal Buddha, from whom all other deities are born, oversees the entire arrangement from its seat in the north.

Synopsis

mid-8th century Traditional date of temple's original founding

1047	Temple revived by the priest Gimyō Jōnin from Taima-dera temple; hall built to house Yakushi Buddha
1107	Awakōkōshin moves the Yakushi sculpture to a western hall; new hall built to hold nine sculptures of Amida Buddha
1150	Eshin works on constructing pond and guiding rock work in garden
1157	Amida Hall reconstructed in its present location on west side of pond; Yakushi Buddha hall moved to east side
1178	Three-story wooden pagoda moved from Ichijō-miya in Kyoto
1205	Shōnagon Hōgen comes from Kyoto to perform repairs on garden rockwork
1343	Fire breaks out in southern gate; Amida Hall and pagoda are spared damage
1410	During fifth month, over period of four days, 450 workmen clean out pond

Further Reading

Keane, Marc Peter, *Japanese Garden Design,* Rutland, Vermont: C.E. Tuttle Company, 1996

Kuck, Lorraine, *The World of the Japanese Garden: From Chinese Origins to Modern Landscape Art,* New York: Walker/Weatherhill, 1968

Kuitert, Wybe, *Themes, Scenes, and Taste in the History of Japanese Garden Art,* Amsterdam: Gieben, 1988

Nitschke, Günter, *Gartenarchitektur in Japan: Rechter Winkel und natürliche Form,* Cologne, Germany: Taschen, 1991; as *Japanese Gardens: Right Angle and Natural Form,* translated by Karen Williams, Cologne, Germany: Taschen, 1993

Takei, Jiro, and Marc Keane, *The Sakuteiki, Vision of the Japanese Garden,* Boston: C.E. Tuttle, 2001

MARC PETER KEANE

Journalism

Just as gardens and gardening date back to ancient times, so does the desire to capture the essence of gardens in written or printed form. The history of garden books, newspapers, magazines, and journals can be traced back to the ancient Greeks and even as far back as the ancient Egyptians. However, most of the earliest garden writing is found within other types of literature, such as novels and poetry, and focuses mainly on descriptions of gardens as a setting to a story or as imagery to accompany the story.

Prior to the eighth and ninth centuries, for example, gardens were often described in Greek novels and in the romantic novels of the Byzantine culture. There were, however, a small number of books written on both techniques and plant history. For example, in 301 B.C. Theophrastus (whom many consider to be the father of botany) wrote his *History of Plants and Theoretical Botany,* in which he describes plant diseases such as rusts and mildews and explains how to hand pollinate fig trees to maximize productivity.

Other early examples of gardening books include *The Book Concerning the Cultivation of Gardens* by Walafridus Strabo (A.D. 850); *The Book of Agriculture* by Ibn Bassal, an Arab botanist, horticulturist, and plant collector (1080); and *A Japanese Treatise on Garden Design* by Sakuteiki (1094).

By the beginning of the 12th century, books on gardening techniques began to be written in Europe, spurred by the fact that gardening was embraced by noblemen who were impressed by the gardens found in European churches and monasteries. This was particularly true in Italy, where traveling clergy members brought the upper classes garden ideas they had seen in their travels through Norman Sicily. Soon, the Sicily style made its way through Italy, France, and Germany.

By the 14th century gardens and interest in gardens began to spread from the nobility to the lower classes, particularly in Paris and throughout Germany and Italy. This led to a proliferation of books and almanacs on gardening. It was during this time that one of the first known gardening technique books ever known was published, *Opus ruralium commodorum* (1305), by Pietro de' Crescenzi, which was about creating and caring for gardens. It not only dealt with layout and design but also explained how to make turf seats, shady arbors, waterways, and walks and discussed the arts of grafting, budding, and topiary.

The earliest known technical and objective work on gardens in England was published around 1400. The nine-part book, called *Feate of Gardening,* is credited to a "Mayster Ion Gardener." It includes sections on planting trees, grafting, and grapevines and explains how to sow seeds and grow green vegetables, herbs, parsley, and saffron. The book names over 97 plants, including daffodil, foxglove, hollyhock, honeysuckle, lavender, lily, and rose, most of which were grown as medicinal herbs rather than as ornamentals. It was during the 15th century that one of the first textbooks on gardening was written, Leon Battista Alberti's *De re aedificatoria* (1485).

Garden journalism continued to grow throughout the Renaissance, and a number of writings had a profound influence on the style of the French Renaissance garden. These include works by Jacques Boyceau, such as *Traite du jardinage* (1638), in which he describes the new parterre design, and Claude Mollet, Henri VI's head gardener, who after retiring in 1613 wrote about gardening in *Le theatre des plants et jardinages,* which was published in 1652, after his death. Another well-known French book on gardening from this period was Olivier de Serre's *Theatre de'agriculture,* which describes gardens mainly for cultivating vegetables, fruits, and herbs. It also gives one of the first descriptions of French flower gardens, helping to elevate the status of flowers in French gardening.

During the English Renaissance Francis Bacon's essay "Of Gardens" (1625) was famous for originating a specifically English type of garden. In it he describes the ideal 30-acre (12.1 ha) farm, which includes the use of lawns, a wilderness area in the garden, and the rejection of topiary. However, Bacon's ideal would not become popular until much later.

One of the first English catalogs for gardens, *Catalogus arborum fruticum,* a list of over a thousand plants, was published by John Gerard in 1596. He later wrote *Herbal* (1597), which remained popular for centuries and which can still be found in bookstores today.

In 1629 John Parkinson published what is considered by many to be the first great gardening book of England: *Paradisi in Sol Paradisus Terrestris.* As a result of its publication, Parkinson earned the title Botanicus Regius to Charles I. Parkinson followed this success with *Theatre of Plants,* which describes over 3,750 kinds of plants.

Also during the 17th century John Evelyn became the best-known gardening writer of his time. His works include *The Compleat Gard'ner* (1693), a translation from the French by Jean de la Quintinie, which became the standard English authority on the subject, and *Kalendarium Hortense,* one of the first gardening almanacs. In 1664 he published *Sylva, or a Discourse of Forest Trees,* which remained the standard work on trees until the end of the 18th century.

The 18th century saw the establishment of several books, magazines, and almanacs that are still influential today. *The Gardener's Dictionary* (1731) was published by Philip Miller, the head of Apothecaries Garden in Chelsea. In 1753 one of the most important gardening books ever written was published, *Species Plantarum,* by the Swedish naturalist Carl Linnaeus. In it, he presents his taxonomic arrangement of classifying and organizing plants and animals using binomial nomenclature (two-word naming: one for genus, one for species). This is the same system still used today.

Other notable publications of the 18th century include works by renowned English gardener Humphry Repton, such as his *Sketches and Hints on Landscape Gardening* (1794). The Royal Botanic Gardens, Kew, also published in 1768 the first *Hortus Kewis, a Catalogue of Plants Cultivated in the Gardens of H.R.H. the Dowager Princess of Wales at Kew,* by Sir John Hill. William Aiton published the second *Hortus Kewensis,* listing 5,500 species grown at Kew, in 1789. In 1837 the third *Hortus Kewensis* was published, listing 11,000 species. Another important development of the time was the creation of the first gardening magazine, the annual *Botanical Magazine,* established by William Curtis in 1787.

It was also during the 18th century that we find the earliest description of U.S. gardens, in a book by English botanist Mark Catesby (*Natural History of Carolina, Florida, and the Bahama Islands* [1731–43]). By the end of the century *The Farmer's Almanack* (1793) was first published in the United States by Robert B. Thomas. This was a major breakthrough; prior to its inception the New England gardener had to rely on English herbals published in the 17th century as a guide to choosing traditional flowers and herbs for cooking and other chores.

In the 19th century the first mass-produced garden magazines were established in England. These include the *Gardener's Magazine,* founded in 1826 by John Claudius Loudon, which ran for almost 20 years. He also edited several other periodicals along with his wife Jane; at one point they were producing five monthly publications at a time. Joseph Paxton also created a well-known periodical in 1841 called *The Gardener's Chronicle.* Another well-regarded and long-standing publication, the *Journal of the Royal Horticultural Society,* was founded in 1866.

Perhaps the most famous of the British magazines and journals were those published by William Robinson. *The Garden,* founded in 1871, was also noteworthy for featuring the writing of famed gardening expert Gertrude Jekyll, who started writing for the magazine in 1875. Robinson also founded *Gardening Illustrated,* beginning in 1879.

In 1806 the first important book on gardening in the United States, *The American Gardener's Calendar; Adapted to the Climate and Seasons of the United*

States, was published by Bernard McMahon. The book was a large work that detailed a month-to-month approach to cultivating. McMahon names over 1,500 species of trees, shrubs, and plants. The book was reprinted 11 times in the 50 years after its publication, serving as the standard authority for every gardening procedure from how to plant and maintain flower and kitchen gardens to building greenhouses. In 1845 Andrew Jackson Downing founded the U.S. magazine *The Horticulturist,* which became the United States's leading gardening magazine. Other U.S. magazines created during this time include *The American Gardener,* by William Cobbett (1821), and *Sunset Magazine* (1898).

The same experts also published a number of encyclopedias and reference books that became the standard authorities for years to follow: *The Encyclopedia of Gardening* by Loudon (1822), *Landscape Gardening: A Treatise on the Theory and Practice of Landscape Gardening* by Downing (1841), *A Treatise on the Theory and Practice of Gardening Adapted to North America* by Downing (1841), and *The English Flower Garden* by Robinson (1883).

The period from 1900 to 1940 in the United States saw a dramatic increase in both the popularity of amateur gardening and gardening journalism, particularly in the growth of garden magazines. Many of the best-known magazines of the present day began during this time, including *Better Homes and Gardens, House and Garden,* and *House Beautiful,* which featured writing from such noted garden experts as Louise Beebe Wilder, Grace Tabor, Fletcher Steele, Wilhelm Miller, and Francis King.

One of the most important modern gardening encyclopedias was published during the period 1900–1902: the four-volume *Cyclopedia of American Horticulture* by Liberty Hyde Bailey. In 1914 other technical works followed, including *The Encyclopedia of Practical Horticulture* by Granville Lowther and William Worthington, *Fundamentals of Plant Breeding* by John M. Coulter, and Liberty Hyde Bailey's follow-up to his own book, *The Standard Cyclopedia of Horticulture,* now at six volumes. In 1935 *Sunset Magazine* published the first edition of *The Sunset Western Garden Book.*

Also during this time books on the modern English garden flourished by such authors as noted English writer and gardener Gertrude Jekyll, who wrote standards such as *Wood and Garden* and *Home and Garden.* The new medium of radio also became a popular venue for garden journalism in the 1920s. For example, Marion Cran started her popular British Broadcasting Corporation (BBC) radio gardening broadcasts in 1923.

During World War II gardening became more than just a hobby when those on the home front took to the garden, creating "victory gardens" to aid in the war effort. It is estimated that in 1942, 40 percent of all U.S. vegetables were produced in victory gardens. During that same year organic gardening became more popular, when the magazine *Organic Gardening and Farming* was first published by Jerome I. Rodale.

The postwar years represented a lull in the amount of garden writing that lasted well into the 1960s. Nonetheless, during this period some prominent garden columns in both newspapers and magazines were established. For example, noted garden writer Vita Sackville-West began a weekly gardening column in the British newspaper *The Observer* in 1946. Her column was popular until her retirement in 1961.

In the early 1970s amateur gardening again became popular due to the increase in concern for the environment and the start of a back-to-the-land movement. In addition to reaching amateur gardeners through traditional print media, gardening experts began to reach their audiences through television. The first nationally syndicated program aimed at the home gardener in the United States was *The Victory Garden,* which first aired on the Public Broadcasting System (PBS) in 1974. Today it remains the oldest running gardening show on television and is broadcast to 30 million viewers each week.

Following the success of *Victory Garden,* PBS started a similar show called *This Old House* in 1979. Although not focused on gardening, *This Old House* helped to make the idea of the home-and-garden how-to show more popular. Over the years such shows became increasingly popular, such as the 1991 PBS series *Gardens of the World,* hosted by Audrey Hepburn, which included a companion book with over 200 photographs of gardens that had been featured on the program. By the middle of the 1990s, as gardening became even more popular, more new shows were introduced, such as *Martha Stewart's Living.*

In 1995 an entire television network devoted exclusively to home and garden programs was launched. This was HGTV (Home and Garden Television), which today features 24-hour-a-day home and gardening programming. Currently it presents 18 decorating and interior-design programs, 11 building and remodeling shows, 13 gardening and landscaping segments, 4 on crafts and hobbies, and 17 other special-interest shows. Some of the more popular programs on HGTV include *Victory Garden, Rebecca's Garden, Martha Stewart's Living,* and *Gardens by Design,* hosted by noted British garden writer Penelope Hobhouse. The success of HGTV has spawned versions around the world.

New gardening radio programs also became popular during the 1990s, including HGTV's radio network. It features programming from HGTV, which brings some of the more popular television hosts to the radio format. Other popular radio shows include the weekly nationally syndicated radio program *The Cultivated Gardener.*

The end of the 20th century also saw the introduction of some of the most popular gardening books of all time, such as *The Readers Digest Complete Library of the Garden* (1980), *The Scented Garden* by Rosemary Isabel Verey (1981), and the *Encyclopedia of Garden Plants* (1989) and *Encyclopedia of Gardening* (1993), both by the American Horticultural Society.

Further Reading

Griswold, M, *The Golden Age of American Gardens: Proud Owners, Private Estates, 1890–1940,* New York: Abrams, 1991

Hobhouse, Penelope, *Penelope Hobhouse's Gardening through the Ages: An Illustrated History of Plants and Their Influence on Garden Styles—From Ancient Egypt to the Present Day,* New York: Simon and Schuster, 1992

Hoyles, Martin, *The Story of Gardening,* London and Concord, Massachusetts: Journeyman Press, 1991

Isaacson, Richard, *Gardening: A Guide to the Literature,* New York: Garland, 1985

Lyon, Thomas, *This Incomparable Land: A Book of American Nature Writing,* Boston: Houghton Mifflin, 1989

Marranca, Bonnie, *American Garden Writing: Gleanings from Garden Lives Then and Now,* New York: PAJ, 1988

Smith, Roger, *Guide to the Literature of the Zoological Sciences,* Minneapolis, Minnesota: Burgess, 1942; 8th edition, as *Guide to the Literature of the Life Sciences,* 1972

Strong, Roy, *A Celebration of Gardens,* London: Harper Collins, and Portland, Oregon: Sagapress/ Timber Press, 1991

Thacker, Christopher, *The History of Gardens,* Berkeley: University of California Press, and London: Croom Helm, 1979

Wheeler, David, editor, *Penguin Book of Garden Writing,* London and New York: Viking Press, 1996

JUDITH GERBER

K

Katsura Imperial Villa

Kyoto, Japan

Location: approximately 3 miles (4.8 km) west of Kyoto station

The Imperial Villa at Katsura was created between 1615 and 1645, the early decades of the Edo period (1603–1867). The heart of the garden is the pond. Paths trace their way around its edge, taking guests to simple yet refined teahouses, or pavilions, and across bridges until, in gentle culmination, the villa itself comes into sight. A rural retreat rather than a permanent residence, Katsura served as a venue for exquisite aesthetic entertainments—poetry writing and moon viewing, boating on the nearby Katsura River and the pond, tea drinking, and admiring of the cherry blossoms.

Prince Toshihito acquired the site in 1615. By 1617 the section of the villa now called the Old Shoin was in place and before it a small pond with islands. The famous collection of cycads (*Cycas revoluta*) on Cycad Hill had its beginnings then too. The Lord of Satsuma in the subtropical province of Kyushu presented Toshihito with a gift of five cycad cuttings. Botanical testing has confirmed that some of today's 20 or so cycads date back to that time. In the colder climate of Kyoto, they are nursed through the winters in wrappings of rice straw.

Under the care of Toshihito's son, Prince Toshitada, the Middle Shoin was added in the early 1640s and the pond extended. By the time priests from the Konchi-in temple attended a tea ceremony at Katsura in 1649, the garden had five teahouses. Some years later, the New Palace and the Music Suite were planned in preparation for a visit by the retired Emperor Gomizuno-o. Completed in 1663, these extensions did not disturb the view of the garden from the Old Shoin, for they were stepped back in the "flying geese" pattern. This configuration gave the whole villa a diagonal alignment within its garden space and effectively maximized visual enjoyment of the garden from the interiors.

The next member of the family to actively engage himself with the villa was Prince Yakahito (1703–67). He supervised renovations to the buildings and the garden and may have initiated the unsubstantiated claim that the renowned Kobori Enshu (1579–1647) had been Katsura's original designer.

There is no single vantage point from which the whole garden can be taken in. Instead, through the strategy known as "hide-and-reveal" (*miegakure*), the visitor's experience of the garden is built up progressively. The tea masters of the 16th century had employed this technique on a much smaller scale in the *roji*, the quiet, secluded passageway through which guests for the tea ceremony would approach the teahouse. At Katsura "hide-and-reveal" comes into full expression. The line of the paths gently dictates the movement of the guests and their corresponding line of vision. At times, the nature of the ground underfoot plays a crucial role in this process. Rough, well-spaced stepping stones sometimes demand that the walkers watch their step. When this need passes, and they lift their gaze, yet another view in the continuous sequence rewards them. Planting is also used to control the viewing, permitting glimpses but not vistas. The *Sumiyoshi* pine, for instance, standing at the tip of its promontory, screens the Shokintei pavilion on the other side of the pond from clear view.

Literary associations layer Katsura with meanings not readily apparent today. These are best appreciated by considering the making of the garden against a backdrop of the political realities of the time. Kyoto had been the home of the imperial family since the city's founding in A.D. 794. In the first three years of the 17th century, the Tokugawa shogunate came to power and relocated the country's capital to Edo, present-day Tokyo. The imperial family was physically isolated in Kyoto. Furthermore, shogunal decree prohibited the

Katsura Imperial Villa, Kyoto, Japan

court from political involvement, confining it instead to seemingly innocuous artistic pursuits.

Forced into such a nominal role in the affairs of state, the court looked back to the cultural achievements of its golden age, the Heian period (794–1185). Of these, *The Tale of Genji* by Lady Murasaki informed the Katsura Villa perhaps more than any other. The book's main character, Prince Genji, admired the moon's reflection upon the Katsura River. When Toshihito planned the Old Shoin, he sited it at precisely the right angle to best see the reflection of the mid-autumn moon on the pond. The Moon-Viewing platform, which extends out into the garden at the front of the Shoin, was specifically designed for the enjoyment of this event. So too was the nearby Gepparō, the Moon Wave pavilion. Another of the structures, the Shōkintei, the Wind in the Pines pavilion, is named after one of the chapters in *The Tale of Genji*.

There are also geographical references, Ama-no-hashidate for instance. This pine-clad sandbar in Wakasa, the birthplace of Toshihito's wife, is suggested at Katsura by a small chain of islands and bridges. A pine, trained as if bent by the sea breezes, completes the allusion.

Such are the fine details that compose Katsura. Even the construction of the stone pathways reveals infinite care, for they are of three types: the formal, made of cut slabs; the semiformal, which juxtapose cut and naturally shaped stone; and the informal, which employ only natural shapes. The fence of living bamboo along the eastern border similarly exhibits the subtle artifice that has formed Katsura's naturalness. Black bamboo is planted about six feet (1.8 m) behind the fence line; its leafy tops are bent over and woven through a rigid frame to give a hedgelike effect.

Today Katsura Imperial Villa enjoys the status of the oldest extant example of a Japanese garden in the "stroll style." As the Edo period progressed, some provincial lords (*daimyo*) had sufficient wealth to create stroll gardens far larger than Katsura's relatively small 11 acres (4.5 ha). Some of these, Ritsurin-koen in Takamatsu and Kenroku-en in Kanazawa, for example, are now among Japan's most beautiful gardens. Katsura cannot be held up as the single inspiration for such places, as a number of other factors were to seed the full flowering of the stroll garden over the next two centuries. Nevertheless, it undoubtedly set a precedent of extraordinary quality.

Synopsis

1615	Prince Toshihito acquires site and begins planning villa
1617	Illustrated records show Old Shoin and *soan*-style teahouse in place
1619	Construction of *sukiya*-style teahouse
1629	Prince Toshihito dies, and Katsura falls into disrepair
1641	Prince Toshitada takes interest in Katsura, and Middle Shoin added
1649	Tea ceremony held for priests of Konchi-in (five teahouses built by this time)
1651	Toshitada writes *waka* (31-syllable poem) on Katsura while staying there
1662	Death of Prince Toshitada; New Palace and Music Suite completed for visit by retired Emperor Gomizuno-o
1708	Floods covered some of islands and caused damage to Shōkintei
1876	Visit by Meiji Empress
1877	Visit by Meiji Emperor
1878	Repairs and decoration of Shoin and teahouses in preparation for Kyoto exhibition when site was open to public for 100 days
1883	Officially designated Imperial Villa
1893–98	Renovations to Shoin and re-thatching of roofs
1933	German architect Bruno Taut escorted through villa

Further Reading

Baba, Shozo, editor, *Katsura,* Tokyo: Shinkenchiku-sha, 1983

Fujioka, Michio, *Kyoto Country Retreats: The Shugakuin and Katsura Palaces,* translated by Bruce A. Coats, Tokyo and New York: Kodansha, 1983

Gropius, Walter, *Katsura Tradition and Creation in Japanese Architecture,* New Haven, Connecticut: Yale University Press, 1960

Hayakawa, Masao, *Niwa,* Tokyo: Heibonsha, 1967; 2nd edition, 1979; as *The Garden Art of Japan,* translated by Richard L. Gage, New York: Weatherhill, 1973

Inaji, Toshiro, *Teien to jukyo no "ariyo" to "misekata, miekata": Nihon, Chugoku, Kankoku,* Tokyo: Kodansha, 1998; as *The Garden as Architecture: Form and Spirit in the Gardens of Japan, China, and Korea,* translated and adapted by Pamela Virgilio, New York and London: Kodansha, 1998

Isozaki, Arata, *Katsura Rikyu: Kukan to Katachi,* Tokyo: Iwanami Shoten, 1983; as *Katsura Villa: Space and Form,* translated by John D. Lamb, New York: Rizzoli, 1987

Itoh, Teiji, *The Gardens of Japan,* Tokyo and New York: Kodansha, 1998

Iwamiya, Takeji, and Teiji Itoh, *Kyutei no niwa,* Kyoto: Tankosha, 1977; as *Imperial Gardens of Japan: Sento Gosho, Katsura, Shugaku-in,* New York: Weatherhill, 1970

Koh, Jusuck, "Katsura: Why Is It So Beautiful?" *Landscape Architecture* 74, no. 5 (1984)

Moore, Charles Willard, William J. Mitchell, and William Turnbull, Jr., *The Poetics of Gardens,* Cambridge, Massachusetts: MIT Press, 1988

Nitschke, Günter, *Gartenarchitektur in Japan: Rechter Winkel und natürliche Form,* Cologne, Germany: Taschen, 1991; as *Japanese Gardens: Right Angle and Natural Form,* translated by Karen Williams, Cologne, Germany: Taschen, 1993

Treib, Marc, and Ron Herman, *A Guide to the Gardens of Kyoto,* Tokyo: Shufunotomo, 1980

FRAN NOLAN

Kebun Raya Botanic Garden

Bogor, Indonesia

Location: 48 kilometers (30 m) south of Jakarta

The Kebun Raya Garden, on Java, remains one of the great botanic gardens of the world. The Buitenzorg Gardens, as it was first called, was founded by Caspar Georg Carl Reinwardt on 18 May 1817, while the Dutch East Indies was under British occupation. Buitenzorg translates as "without a care." The garden was renamed the Kebun Raya Botanic Garden, or "Hortus

Bogoriensis," following Indonesian independence in 1949.

The gardens comprise 87 hectares (215 acres) within the grounds of the former palace of the Hindu kingdom of Padjadjaram. They are situated at an altitude of 235–60 meters (257–85 yd.) in the shadow of Mount Salak, with an annual rainfall of 4,000 millimeters (157 in.). The gardens were primarily developed under the guidance of Reinwardt (director, 1817–22), C.L. Blume (director, 1822–26), Johannes Elias Teysmann (curator, 1830–69), R.H.C.C. Scheffer (director, 1870–79), and Melchior Treub (director, 1880–1909). The site was selected by the Dutch Governor-General van Imhoff in 1756 for a recreation ground and two-story palace that was rebuilt as a single-story structure in 1856 following the 1832 earthquake.

Although Java was a Dutch colony, British botanist Joseph Banks and botanist and colonial gardener Stamford Raffles encouraged Reinwardt in his endeavors, with avid support from the British horticulturist William Kent and Royal Botanic Gardens, Kew gardener James Hooper. Reinwardt, formerly a professor of botany at Amsterdam University, later became a professor of botany at the University of Leiden. From 1826 to 1868 Buitenzorg experienced a period of decline, although Blume did compile the first catalog of plants in the gardens. To Teysmann's credit, he changed the appearance of the garden, introducing many ornamental and economic plants, rearranging the gardens by taxonomic families (with assistance from assistant curator Justus Karl Hasskar), introducing the flame tree (*Delonix regia*), and establishing the majority of the species in the garden during his curatorship (he is honored in the genus *Teijsmaniodendron*).

The most significant botanist to manage Buitenzorg was Treub, who noted in 1893 that he was "greatly indebted to Kew" for establishing the foundations of the gardens. During Treub's tenure no British colonial botanic garden equaled the scientific direction and staffing profile at Buitenzorg. Treub, a graduate of Leiden, succeeded Scheffer as director at the age of 29 years. One of his obituaries states: "Through his energy and perseverance he raised the position of the Buitenzorg Gardens to the highest rank of any gardens in the world. Aided by a sympathetic government and his own powers of administration he developed the economic functions of the establishment to the utmost, increasing the area under cultivation, and the staff, and adding the finest Botanical Laboratories in the world." He continued the *Annales du Jardin Botanique de Buitenzorg*, founded by Scheffer, as a major conduit for the garden's research.

Buitenzorg especially assisted the British in the introduction of cinchona (*Cinchona officinallis* and *C. succiruba*) from South America via Kew Gardens. Ironically this function enabled the Dutch, with the assistance of Javanese planters, to gain a monopoly on cinchona production by undercutting Ceylonese production with mass cultivation of *C. ledgeriana*. Cinchona was the source of quinine, viewed in the Victorian era as the "miracle cure" for malaria.

Upon independence, Kusnoto Setyodiworjo served as the first indigenous curator of the newly named Kebun Raya Garden. In 1962, the garden became part of the Lembaga Biologi Nasional (National Biological Institute; NBI), and Otto Soemarwoto was appointed director in 1964, before the NBI was reorganized and split in the 1980s, enabling the appointment of Suhirman as the head of the garden. Under Soemarwoto, Repelita I and II commenced, focusing on increased quality and production of economic crops, and Kebun Botani Serpong (Serpong Botanic Garden; 350 hectares [864 acres]) was established in 1978, as well as an extensive orchid glasshouse complex.

The garden consists of several tree-lined avenues, notably the long avenue of majestic *Canarium* trees (1832), where each tree is festooned by a climbing member of the Arum family and many are linked by a giant *Entata* liana. The avenues are spread over the undulating former palace grounds with the river Tjiliwung sweeping through part of the gardens. The palace has served as the residence of the Dutch governors-general and presidents of Indonesia. A large lake accommodates water lilies and artificial pools for aquatic and marsh plants such as papyrus. Impressive palm and bamboo collections are positioned to strengthen their aesthetic qualities. An extensive collection of some 3,000 registered hybrid orchids (including the giant orchid *Grammatophyllum speciosum*) is cultivated in the orchid house, and cactuses are grown in open-air gardens. The gardens today contain a collection of some 15,000 species of tropical plants.

The gardens also instigated extensive economic crop trials that established or improved the agricultural production base of the Dutch East Indies (Indonesia) and the revenues of the Dutch East India Company. Trials included African oil palms (*Elaeis guineenis*) from West Africa (1848), *Cinchona* from Peru (1852), Assam tea from British India (1873), rubber from Brazil (1876), Chinese tea from Taiwan (1826), arabica coffee from Ethiopia (1699), cocoa from Ecuador (1826), vanilla, sugarcane, corn, beans, taro, and cassava (*Manihot esculenta*) from Sumatra. The gardens became and continue today to be a major center for the research, cultivation, and propagation of Malaysian and Indonesian flora and economically important plants. Many crops and ornamental plants associated with this region commenced their journey to the Northern Hemisphere from Bogor.

Part of this research was aided by the establishment of the library (Bibliotheca Bogoriensis; 1842), the herbarium (1884; new building, 1970), which under Cornelis Gijsbert Gerrit Jan van Steenis orchestrated the *Flora Malesiana* (1948–), the Treub Laboratory (1914), and the zoological museum (Museum Zoologicum Bogoriense; 1894). The gardens also were instrumental in the development of satellite or regional gardens in the colony, including the cooler climate Cibodas (Tjibodas) Mountain Garden near Bogor in 1866, the Parwodad (Purwodadi) Garden in East Java in 1941, the Sibolangit Garden in east Sumatra (1941), and the Eka Karya Botanical Garden in Bali (1954). Cibodas actually started as "acclimatization gardens" under Teysmann in 1830 and was annexed in 1860.

Synopsis

1817 Gardens established by Dr. Caspar Georg Carl Reinwardt, and Reinwardt appointed director
1830 Johannes Elias Teysmann appointed curator
1842 Library established
1866 Cibodas (Tjibodas) Mountain Garden established
1879 *Annales du Jardin Botanique de Buitenzorg* founded
1880 Melchior Treub appointed director
1884 Herbarium established
1894 Zoological museum established
1914 Treub Laboratory established
1940 Parwodad (Purwodadi) Garden established
1948 Publication of *Flora Malesiana* begun
1949 Indonesia granted independence; Buitenzorg Scientific Centre renamed Kebun Raya Botanic Garden
1954 Eka Karya Garden established
1970 New herbarium building opened
1978 Serpong Botanic Garden established

Further Reading

Buitenzorg Scientific Centre, *Buitenzorg Scientific Centre: A Description of the Scientific Institutions at Buitzenzorg,* Buitzenzorg, Indonesia: Archipel Drukkerij en 't Boekhuis, 1948
Huitema, W.K., *Guide to the Economic Gardens at Buitenzorg*, Buitenzorg, Indonesia: Archipel Drukkerij en 't Boekhuis, 1929
Luca, Invernizzi, and William Warren, *Balinese Gardens,* Singapore: Periplus, 1995, and New York: Thames and Hudson, 1996
McCracken, Donal P., *Gardens of Empire: Botanical Institutions of the Victorian British Empire,* London and Washington, D.C.: Leicester University Press, 1997
"Obituary: Dr. Melchior Treub," *Agricultural Bulletin of the Straits and Federated Malay States* 9, no. 12 (1910)
Zeijlstra, H.H., *Melchior Treub: Pioneer of a New Era in the History of the Malay Archipelago,* Amsterdam: Koninklijk Instituut voor de Tropen, 1959

David Jones

Kemp, Edward 1817–1891

English Garden Designer and Commentator

Edward Kemp was an assistant of Joseph Paxton at Chatsworth, Derbyshire, in the 1830s, where he was also a colleague of Edward Milner. In 1843 Paxton designed the first of the "people's parks" at Birkenhead, near Liverpool, and left Kemp to execute the design. The site, being low and marshy, was drained by the creation of two lakes, each with an irregular outline and an island. The spoil from their construction was used to create artificial mounds, around the lakes and at the junctions of the paths. These were planted with shrubs and trees, thus producing an intimate environment with a series of concealed views. The network of paths were serpentine in design, imitating the "line of beauty" much loved by 18th-century landscapers. The design principles were Picturesque, introducing an aristocratic landscape to the proletariat. The center of the park was kept open for games, such as cricket and archery, but essentially it was designed for quiet contemplation. There were classical lodges and a boathouse in the same style, with an observation platform overlooking the eastern lake. The lower classes were thus introduced to, in John Ruskin's words, "noble scenes and civilisation." emphasizing the park's didactic purpose as an arena of education. It was much imitated, and Frederick Law Olmsted, who visited the park in 1850, commented on its popularity with the people of Birkenhead and used it as a model for Central Park in New York City. Birkenhead Park was finally opened in 1847, and Kemp, who lived in one of the lodges, remained its superintendent for 40 years.

The success of Birkenhead Park, its high degree of maintenance, and Paxton's patronage brought Kemp a number of private commissions. One of the earliest in 1849 was for a flower garden designed for James Barratt of Lymm Hall, near Warrington in Cheshire. Kemp provided a forward-looking geometrical design as an accompaniment for an Elizabethan mansion surrounded by a moat. He displayed his sensitivity to historical styles by providing a yew enclosure containing a series of circular beds, planted with fuchsias and different varieties of verbenas. Summer flowers filled the long side borders. The design avoided the use of gravels and thus would have been applauded by the Arts and Crafts enthusiasts of the next generation—had they seen it.

In 1850 Kemp published *How to Lay Out a Garden.* A second edition, including illustrations of 35 private commissions, was published in 1860, with a third edition in 1864. It was one of the most influential gardening books of the mid-Victorian era and set out to follow in the footsteps of John Claudius Loudon, providing practical advice for the suburban middle classes who owned gardens ranging from a quarter of an acre to 25 acres (10 ha). Kemp mentioned Humphry Repton and William Gilpin in the preface but regarded Sir Uvedale Price's essay on the Picturesque (*Essay on the Picturesque*, 1794) as "probably the most valuable thing of its kind in our language." The *Essays* had recently been republished in 1842, and many of Kemp's preoccupations—variety, connection, intricacy, and his antipathy to clumps and belts and mansions painted white, etc.—indicate his debt to Price. Nature, aided by a sensitive hand, was to rule in the park and on the lawns, but close to the house the terrace reigned supreme as a highly polished example of formality. Price's predilection for ancient gardens had been reborn via Repton and Loudon. Kemp recommended bedding for his terraces and had doubts about the honesty of the gravel parterres being promoted by William Andrew Nesfield. Kemp was also an early supporter of the mixed summer border but consigned it to a position well away from the house and its lawns. He also banished the Picturesque in its most rugged guise to a sequestered dingle or a retired position where it could be sublimated as a quarry, rock, or root garden. He believed that the mixed style, "with a little help from both the formal and the picturesque, is altogether best suited for small gardens." The "mixed style" was Loudon's gardenesque style, but without the emphasis on the display of individual plants and trees; Kemp had a special aversion to landscapes "spotted" with specimen trees, which again shows shades of Price. Essentially, Kemp promoted a new sense of propriety in gardening, condemning brashness, eccentricity, and pretentiousness but praising simplicity, "snugness," quietness, and congruity. His goal was to provide the complete setting for a life of constraint and sobriety much admired by the Victorian middle classes. For a "little freshness" in the garden he recommended manipulating the "scenes of nature" that were ever changing, such as giving prominence to a "chosen tribe of plants" or even putting a bell-shaped tent on a lawn.

Like Price's *Essays, How to Lay Out a Garden* was full of excellent practical advice, provided by a practical gardener, and yet set within a sound philosophical and aesthetic framework. Its influence was long lasting. When Edward Milner's son, Henry Milner, provided an account of his father's work in *The Art and Practice of Landscape Gardening* (1890), he followed Kemp's model. Similarly, Thomas Mawson's *The Art and Craft of Garden Making* (1900), the most celebrated book of the Edwardian era, followed *How to Lay Out a Garden,* a work much admired by Mawson. Like Kemp, Mawson tried to reconcile a variety of styles, and his early parks, such as Hanley in Staffordshire (1891), owe a great deal in their sinuous design to Kemp.

In 1856 Kemp discovered his ideal garden at Biddulph Grange in Staffordshire, the creation of James Bateman and his artist friend Edward Cooke. Two series of articles by Kemp, in 1856 and 1862, for the *Gardeners' Chronicle,* as well as a separate pamphlet, *Description of the Gardens at Biddulph Grange* (1862), made this garden the most famous in mid-Victorian England. In it much had been put into practice that Kemp had recommended in *How to Lay Out a Garden:* dividing the landscape into a series of regions and themes, allowing for a diversity of planting and treatment, but retaining congruity through judicious screening. The compulsion to display a "wondrous multitude of curious or ornamental plants," as Kemp wrote, combined with picturesque canons produced a composition that was "a very high achievement of art."

During the 1850s Kemp's career flourished. Many of his private commissions were in the northwest of England, close to Birkenhead, where he laid out modest estates, often about 20 acres in extent, for successful businessmen, on the edge of the Liverpool conurbation, or in Cheshire or the Lakes. There were also a number of schemes close to London, in a similar social milieu, and a scattering of grand country houses across the shires. The largest included parkland, pools, shrubberies, picturesque valley gardens, and rockeries, but Kemp was equally at ease with the formal flower garden or the kitchen garden. Indeed, he seems to have provided a floristic alternative to the gravel parterres of Nesfield, which were very much in vogue at the time. At Daylesford in Gloucestershire Kemp proposed an uncomplicated plan for a terrace, which contained display beds for China and standard roses, accompanied by vases for annual flowers. At Knightshayes in Devon he worked up the preliminary design by William Burges into a series of geometrical beds full of color, covered the house with creeper, and planted tall yew hedges around the bowling green. Much of this can still be seen today. Probably his most extensive commission was for the Liverpool banker John Naylor, who bought a 1,000-acre (405 ha) estate at Leighton Hall, near Welshpool in Powys, about 1850. The Gothic house, designed by W.H. Gee of Liverpool, cost £275,000, albeit unfinished; the grounds, laid out by Kemp, were on a similar scale. A great enclosed flower garden, divided into four patterned compartments, was dedicated to summer bedding and herbaceous planting. He also designed a circular rose garden, set within a shrubbery with two glasshouses for tender roses. Brass figures enhanced a winter garden for evergreens, and numerous garden buildings were greatly embellished. One of the longest terraces in England led to the High Bridge or viaduct, which revealed the whole garden and passed over a series of cascades developed below. A new church by Gee was set within the grounds, and the views of the famous landscape surrounding Powys Castle were appropriated to enhance the new estate.

Kemp continued to design public parks, including Hesketh Park, Southport (1864), Stanley Park, Liverpool (1868), and Anfield Cemetery, Liverpool (1856). In 1851 he published *The Parks and Gardens of London and Its Suburbs,* which placed the capital's open spaces under the critical eye of the park keeper from Birkenhead. He condemned the Long Walk at Windsor for not being laid out on flat ground. He felt Nesfield's parterre at Kew destroyed the landscape of a famous royal park.

See also Birkenhead Park

Biography

Born in 1817. Worked at Chatsworth, Derbyshire, England, ca.1830–43; laid out Birkenhead Park, Merseyside, England, to design by Joseph Paxton, 1843–7; superintendent of Birkenhead Park until retirement, ca.1880; published *How to Lay Out a Garden,* 1851; occasional correspondent of *Gardeners' Chronicle,* ca. 1850–70; main period of private commissions, 1850s and 60s. Died in 1891.

Selected Designs

1843–47	Birkenhead Park, Merseyside, England (designed by Joseph Paxton)
1849	Flower garden, Lymm Hall, Warrington, England
1856	Anfield Cemetery, Liverpool, England
1850–51	Pleasure grounds, Holmefield, Aigburth, Liverpool, England
1851	Acton Burnell, Shropshire, England, flower garden.
1854–55	Park, Shendish, Hemel Hamstead, England
1854	Park, Roby, Liverpool, England
1855	Pleasure ground, Mollington, Chester, England
1858	Pleasure grounds and park, Leighton Hall, Powys, Wales
1864	Hesketh Park, Southport, England
1866	Parkfield, Hallow, near Worcester, England
1867	Grosvenor Park, Chester, England
1868	Stanley Park, Liverpool, England
1874	Terrace garden, etc., Knightshayes, Devon, England

Selected Publications

How to Lay Out a Small Garden, 1850; 2nd edition, as *How to Lay Out a Garden,* 1860
Parks and Gardens of London and Its Suburbs, 1851
Gardeners' Chronicle, 1856, 1862 (on Biddulph Grange)
Description of the Gardens of Biddulph Grange, 1862

Further Reading

Elliott, Brent, *Victorian Gardens,* London: Batsford, and Portland, Oregon: Timber Press, 1986
Hayden, Peter, *Biddulph Grange, Staffordshire: A Victorian Garden Rediscovered,* London: Philip, 1989
Jackson-Stops, Gervase, *An English Arcadia: Designs for Gardens and Garden Buildings in the Care of the National Trust, 1600–1990,* London: National Trust, and Washington, D.C.: American Institute of Architects Press, 1991
Lasdun, Susan, *The English Park: Royal, Private, and Public*, London: Deutsch, and New York: Vendome Press, 1991
Ottewill, David, *The Edwardian Garden,* New Haven, Connecticut: Yale University Press, 1989
Taylor, Hilary, "Urban Public Parks, 1840–1900: Design and Meaning," *Garden History* 23, no. 2 (1995)
Thacker, Christopher, *The Genius of Gardening: The History of Gardens in Britain and Ireland,* London: Weidenfeld and Nicholson, 1994

DAVID WHITEHEAD

Kensal Green Cemetery

Kensington and Chelsea, London, England

Location: west London, between Harrow Road and the Grand Union Canal, 2 miles (3.2 km) west-northwest of Paddington station, and approximately 6 miles (9.7 km) from the center of London

The fear of pollution and disease was the impetus for the garden cemetery movement in England, which led to the creation of London's Kensal Green Cemetery and was also the precursor of the movement to create public parks. By the early 19th century the country's graveyards and crypts were filled to bursting, and many corpses were dug up before they had decomposed. The population of London increased by 20 percent in the 1820s, and in 1832 there was a particularly severe cholera epidemic. In July 1832 the act of parliament for "establishing a General Cemetery for the Interment of the Dead in the Neighbourhood of the Metropolis" achieved its final reading, and Kensal Green Cemetery became the first of the six joint-stock cemeteries that encircle London (the others being Norwood, Highgate, Nunhead, Abney Park, and Brompton).

The idea for the Cemetery of All Souls at Kensal Green was put forward by George Frederick Carden (1798–1874), a barrister, who wanted to establish in London a cemetery comparable to Père Lachaise in Paris. With the advice and financial backing of Sir John Dean Paul, a governor of the Bank of England, about 55 acres (22 ha) of the Fillingham estate were bought in what was then the village of Kensal Green on the outskirts of London. Later a further 22 acres (9 ha) were purchased. The original capital of £45,000 (later increased to £60,000) was divided into £25 shares.

Richard Forrest, head gardener to the Duke of Northumberland at Syon Park, designed the landscape with a broad avenue bisecting a circular road. The style was similar to John Nash's recently completed Regents Park, with some geometric layout within a general landscape, in the form of a gentleman's small country park. Hugh Ronalds, the Brentford nurseryman, supplied the plants and acted as contractor. John Griffith of Finsbury (1796–1888) produced designs in the Greek revival style for the Main Gate, Dissenters' Chapel, Anglican Chapel, and North Terrace Catacomb.

The sum of £300 was allowed for the initial planting in November 1831. This included a line of shrubbery along the north wall to exclude noise from the Harrow Road, a central cedar avenue, and some flower beds, which were planted just before the public opening on 24 January 1833, when the cemetery was consecrated by the bishop of London. Sheep were allowed to graze the cemetery, and the ground not yet allocated for burial was planted with potatoes and other market crops. Because of the waterlogged clay soil, the cedars began to die as early as 1834, and those surviving were killed by the frost in 1838. The avenue was replanted with silver firs, but by 1842 it was decided to abandon conifers and plant horse chestnuts and other deciduous trees instead.

The choice of Kensal Green for the burial of George III's son, Prince Augustus Frederick, in 1843 assured the fortunes of the cemetery company. Stocks in cemetery companies generally provided investors with above-average profits, and already by 1839 the original shares had doubled in value. The prince's burial also made the cemetery fashionable: there are more eminent Victorians buried in Kensal Green than in any other cemetery in England. Some of the most famous are the railway engineer Isambard Kingdom Brunel, the mathematician Charles Babbage, who invented the first computer, Blondin, the tightrope walker, the architect Decimus Burton, Wilkie Collins, the pioneer of detective fiction, the Chartist leader Feargus O'Connor, whose funeral was attended by 50,000 people, and the novelists Thackeray and Trollope.

As regards garden history, the most celebrated people buried there are John and Jane Loudon. John Loudon thought that the cemetery could also serve as a botanic garden and saw Kensal Green Cemetery as a way of improving the architectural taste of the public and providing them with an education in horticulture. In a series of articles on cemeteries published in *The Gardener's Magazine* in 1843 (the year of his death), Loudon listed literally hundreds of trees and shrubs, climbers, bulbs, herbaceous plants, and ferns that he considered suitable for a cemetery.

In 1862 a conservatory was built to provide flowers for the graves, as pollution in London prevented many flowers from growing in the open air. In 1897 the *Gardeners' Chronicle* refers to the difficulty of cultivating plants in Kensal Green, owing mainly to the presence of several very large gasholders.

In 1938 Edward White was hired to design the Garden of Remembrance, a rectilinear garden in an Arts and Crafts style. Work began in 1939 with the firm of J. Burley and Sons as contractors. The garden was planted with shrubs from Walter Slocock of Knap Hill and perennial flowers from Samuel Ryder of St. Albans; the latter included Russell lupins, which had been launched commercially the year before. The main features now are rose beds and an avenue of clipped beeches.

During the second half of the 20th century, the pressure for new grave space began to erode the landscape and paths, and in the older areas the cemetery began to suffer from reduced maintenance and became overgrown with vegetation. During the 1980s parts of the cemetery began to be managed for the benefit of the wildlife, in consultation with the London Wildlife Trust. There are about 500 varieties of native plants in the cemetery.

The General Cemetery Company still runs Kensal Green Cemetery, with a staff of more than 30. In the late 1990s there were some 68,000 graves; 250 new graves are dug every year, and at that rate, the space will last only until 2015 to 2020. The cemetery is the longest surviving English cemetery remaining in private ownership.

Kensal Green is still used for recreation as well as burials, just as when Charles Dickens made his tour in 1863. Children play in it, picking conkers from the chestnut trees and gathering raspberries from the canal bank. Every Sunday, regardless of weather, there are guided tours starting at 2 P.M. at the Anglican Chapel, organized by the Friends of Kensal Green Cemetery, founded in 1989.

Synopsis

1830 General Cemetery Company founded
1831 Land at Kensal Green purchased by Sir John Dean Paul, planting begun to landscape design by Richard Forrest
1832 Royal assent given to a bill for establishing a cemetery
1833 Cemetery consecrated by Bishop of London
1834–37 Chapels and catacombs built, designed by John Griffith
1840 Cemetery's first gardener fired for receiving fees illicitly
1843 George III's son, Augustus Frederick, buried in the cemetery
1862 Conservatory built to provide grave flowers
1866 Conservatory augmented by additional building
1896 Conservatory complex rebuilt
1939 Work begun on construction of Garden of Remembrance, designed by Edward White
1980s Parts of cemetery start to be managed for wildlife
1997 Dissenters' Chapel restored

Further Reading

Clark, Benjamin, *Hand-Book for Visitors to the Kensal Green Cemetery,* London, 1843
Croft, H.J., *Guide to Kensal Green Cemetery,* 2nd edition London, 1871
Curl, James Stevens, "The Architecture and Planning of the Nineteenth-Century Cemetery," *Garden History* 3, no. 3 (1975)
Curl, James Stevens, *A Celebration of Death,* London: Constable, and New York: Scribner, 1980; revised edition, London: Batsford, 1993
Curl, James Stevens, "John Claudius Loudon and the Garden Cemetery Movement," *Garden History* 11, no. 2 (1983)
Dickens, Charles, "Kensal Green," *All the Year Round* 10 (1863)
Dunk, Julie, and Julie Rugg, *The Management of Old Cemetery Land,* London: Shaw, 1994
Etlin, Richard A., "Père Lachaise and the Garden Cemetery," *Journal of Garden History* 4, no. 3 (1984)
Friends of Kensal Green Cemetery, *Paths of Glory,* London: FKGC, 1997
Latham, J.B., "A Survey of the Flora of Kensal Green and St. Mary's Cemeteries, 1981–1983," *London Naturalist* 63 (1984)
Litten, Julian, *The English Way of Death: The Common Funeral since 1450,* London: Hale, 1991
Loudon, John Claudius, *On the Laying Out, Planting, and Managing of Cemeteries and on the Improvement of Churchyards,* London, 1843; reprint, Redhill, Surrey: Ivelet Books, 1981
Meller, Hugh, *London Cemeteries,* Amersham, Buckinghamshire: Avebury, 1981; 3rd edition, Aldershot, Hampshire: Scolar Press, and Brookfield, Vermont: Ashgate, 1994
Worpole, Ken, *The Cemetery in the City,* London: Comedia, 1997

MARTIN HOYLES

Kensington Gardens

Kensington, London, England

Location: west London, between Kensington Road and Bayswater, adjoining Hyde Park

When William III and Mary II came to the throne of England and Scotland in 1689 after the deposing of James II, William had not yet finished the garden at his beloved estate in Holland, Het Loo. Mary Stuart and William, who married in 1677, were both keen gardeners and plant collectors, and their shared pleasures were of a domestic nature rather than the ceremony of court life. The Dutch court had been small, relaxed, and orderly, in contrast to the pomp and intrigue typical of the huge courts of the Stuart kings. At the time Whitehall Palace was the sovereign's principal London residence, but the damp, polluted air aggravated William's asthma, and Mary complained that all she could see was "water or wall." They both preferred Hampton Court Palace, but it was more than 12 miles (19.3 km) from Westminster, and so they immediately began looking for a residence closer to the affairs of government. In the summer of 1689 William purchased a Jacobean-style house in Kensington, dating from about 1605. The small town of Kensington was then still separate from London, but several wealthy families had already built villas there.

It may have been the beauty of the existing gardens (then about 17 acres [6.9 ha]) that attracted William and Mary to Kensington. In 1664 Samuel Pepys had described the gardens as "a mighty fine cool place with a great laver of water in the middle and the bravest place for musique I ever heard." Daniel Defoe in *A Tour through the Whole Island of Great Britain* (1726) wrote that he had been present when Queen Mary gave orders for "enlarging the gardens" and "had the honour to attend her majesty, when she first viewed the ground, and directed the doing it." Shortly after ascending the throne, William appointed Hans Willem Bentinck, who had been the chief steward of the king's gardens at Het Loo, as superintendent of the Royal Gardens. Bentinck appointed George London as his deputy. It was London who laid out, and probably also designed, the garden of 12 acres (4.9 ha) to the south of Kensington House between 1689 and 1691.

London had founded the Brompton Park Nursery in 1681 and had a major influence on garden design and horticulture in Britain. The nursery was located within a mile (1.6 km) of Kensington House. David Jacques suggests that Daniel Marot may have been in part responsible for the design of the gardens at Kensington. Marot was a Huguenot who had fled from France, and he joined the team led by Willem Bentinck at Het Loo as a garden designer. Marot had been trained as a mathematician, and his designs relied heavily on mathematics, as was the contemporary taste. The gardens were in the Dutch style with parterres, evergreen hedges, and topiary work, but no visual record exists of the exact plans before Queen Anne made alterations.

The king also had constructed a private road, illuminated by a row of lamps, from Kensington House to Hyde Park Corner. It was called the Rue de Roi, soon corrupted by Londoners to "Rotten Row." The road later became a fashionable place to be seen on horseback. Only that part of Rotten Row in Hyde Park survives today. Mary had a privy garden under the east range of the house that was reached by a marble bridge from her apartments. The queen enjoyed much better health than did William, but she died of smallpox in December 1694, at the age of 32.

In 1701 William instructed Henry Wise to begin the layout of a 30-acre (12.1 ha) formal wilderness north of the house on the site of an old orchard. Wise had purchased a share in the Brompton Nursery in 1689 and was George London's partner until the latter retired. But the work on the wilderness was halted when later in 1701 William had a riding accident at Hampton Court and died at Kensington a few months later. During William and Mary's reign, botanical and horticultural development had been vigorously pursued with enthusiastic royal patronage. Gardening not only became fashionable but popular. Jacques has noted that both Stephen Switzer and Daniel Defoe wrote that William and Mary had revived a love of gardening in the kingdom. Unfortunately, almost all traces of their garden at Kensington have disappeared.

On William's death, Mary's sister Anne became queen. She had detested her brother-in-law but shared his love of gardening. She made no substantive alterations to the house but quickly put Wise back to work on the wilderness. This work included the reclamation of a disused gravel pit as a series of concentric terraces. Near the entrance to the wilderness, the orangery was built (1705) to Nicholas Hawksmoor's design, which was somewhat altered by Sir John Vanbrugh. In the same year Anne further extended the palace gardens by acquiring 100 acres (40.5 ha) of Hyde Park as a paddock for deer and antelope. It had become fashionable to have a menagerie of exotic animals. The queen apparently hated the smell of boxwood and had the offending plants removed from William and Mary's formal parterres south of the palace. But the basic structure of the Dutch style gardens, as shown in the Overton and Hoole engraving (ca. 1720) was probably little changed, with yew and other evergreens used to replace the boxwood. As John Dixon Hunt writes, "her gardens still invoke the heavy green hedges of Dutch garden 'rooms' and their topiary decorations"; he suggests that it was the relatively small scale of the garden at Kensington that gave it "a Dutch feeling." Anne also embellished the garden with fountains and placed an alcove (designed by Sir Christopher Wren) at the south end of Dial Walk. This building was moved to its present location near the Italian Gardens in the late 19th century.

After George I succeeded Anne in 1714, he spent most of his time at Hampton Court. Defoe, writing in 1726, suggested that the reason the monarch preferred not to live at Kensington was that so many of his predecessors, including King William, Prince George of Denmark (Queen Anne's husband), and Queen Anne, had died there. Even if George was superstitious about the palace,

Overton and Hoole engraving of Kensington Gardens, London, England, ca. 1720
Copyright Royal Borough of Kensington and Chelsea

in 1726 he directed that the paddock be enlarged; cages were built for a number of exotic animals, including three tigers and two civet cats. This work was under the direction of Charles Bridgeman in partnership with Wise, who had continued to manage the gardens after Anne's death. From 1722 William Kent was active at Kensington Palace but had little to do with the gardens. He was first commissioned to paint the Cupola Room, and although his paintings were widely criticized, the king evidently was pleased as Kent went on to decorate ceilings for nearly all the royal apartments in the palace.

When George II came to the throne in 1727, he and Queen Caroline evidently liked Kensington Palace, spending four to six months each year in residence. Queen Caroline saw the paddock as an opportunity for a grand scheme east of the palace. The animals were removed and changes carried out that gave the gardens their present basic structure. The Broad Walk was constructed running north-south alongside the old gardens and wilderness. In 1728 a large octagonal basin, the Round Pond, was completed, from which radiates a series of wide tree-lined avenues in a *patte d'oie.* The design is attributed to Bridgeman, although it may have been done before 1728, when Wise retired from royal service and a contract had been drawn up for Bridgeman alone. The quarters that were defined by the avenues were mostly lined with espaliered limes, and a *berceau* or "walk of shade" was made around the perimeter of the gardens. In 1731 the Serpentine was completed by removal of the balks that separated the Long Water and a series of ponds. A ha-ha with bastions was built along the boundary with Hyde Park (the only evidence of the ha-ha today is a shallow depression). The new gardens also included a mount with a revolving summerhouse at its summit that was designed by William Kent. Neither mount nor summerhouse have survived, but another summerhouse designed by Kent, known as the Queen's Temple (1734–35) still exists, and its siting epitomizes the Arcadian landscape style. In *The History of the Modern Taste in Gardening* (1771), Horace Walpole criticized Kent, who "followed nature, and imitated her so happily, that he began to think all her works were equally proper for imitation." As an example of this inappropriate imitation, Walpole noted that Kent had planted dead trees in Kensington Gardens "to give greater truth to the scene—but he was soon laughed out for his excess." Walpole offered no evidence for his statement, but there are instructions in Bridgeman's account to plant "1195 standard elms already dead."

Bridgeman also eliminated the wilderness to the north of the palace and William and Mary's Dutch garden south of the palace, sweeping away the ornate parterres and topiary and replacing them with simple grass panels. The north-south axis of the Dial Walk, the main east-west path, and the walk along the west side of the garden are the only features that have survived. Bridgeman's plan (ca. 1733) shows Kensington Gardens at the completion of his work. George II opened Kensington Gardens to the public, at first only on Sundays when the court was at Richmond. He outlived Queen Caroline, but after his death in 1760 Kensington Palace never again served as the seat of a reigning monarch.

George III preferred to live at Buckingham Palace, but his fourth son, Edward, duke of Kent, was allocated rooms in Kensington Palace. Edward's first child, Victoria, was born there in May 1819. Only 17 years later in her apartments at Kensington Palace, Victoria was informed of her uncle William IV's death and that she was queen of England. Her accession council, depicted in the painting by David Wilkie, was held at Kensington the next day. Victoria moved at once to Buckingham Palace, and although the private apartments at Kensington continued to be used by members of the royal family, the state apartments were sadly neglected. It was not until 1897 that Parliament agreed to pay for restoration on condition that the apartments were opened to the public, which occurred in 1899 on Victoria's 80th birthday.

During Victoria's reign the structure of the gardens as laid out by Bridgeman for Queen Caroline lost much of its definition. The espaliered limes enclosing the quarters were removed and the tree canopy became thin and far from continuous. New features included the Flower Walk, laid out in 1843; flowers had been absent from the gardens since the 18th century. The association of Kensington Gardens with children also became firmly established. This had much to do with the character Peter Pan, since Kensington Gardens was his home. In 1906 J.M. Barrie published *Peter Pan in Kensington Gardens,* illustrated by Arthur Rackham. Rackham's depiction of the landscape is remarkably accurate. The visual importance of the English elm as the predominant species in the gardens is clear in his drawings. This dominance came to an abrupt end when two outbreaks of the Dutch elm disease, the last in the 1970s, destroyed all the elms. Today there is more diversity of tree species with lime (*Tilia* spp.) being the best-represented genus. The iron rail fencing in Rackham's drawings is evidence of the contemporary management of the gardens, which were grazed by sheep. This practice ceased during World War II when the iron railings were taken down for war metal. The popularity of Barrie's story was such that the Symbolist sculptor Sir George Frampton was commissioned to do a bronze of Peter Pan that was erected in 1912.

Victoria's reign also saw the erection of monumental sculptures that add yet another dimension to the historic significance of the gardens. The most prominent is the Albert Memorial (1863–76) designed by Sir George Gilbert Scott, which appropriately overlooks the site in Hyde Park where the Crystal Palace was erected for the Great Exhibition (1850), an event that had been inspired by Albert, Queen Victoria's consort. The Albert Memorial features a large number of works by Victorian sculptors. The main figure of Prince Albert and a group depicting Asia, one of the four continents at each corner of the monument, are by John Henry Foley. Other monuments at focal points on Bridgeman's avenues include a granite obelisk for John Hanning Speke (1866), who discovered the source of the Nile, *Physical Energy,* a colossal bronze horse and rider (designed in 1883, but not erected until 1907) by George Frederick Watts, and a sculpture of Queen Victoria (1893) by her sixth child, Princess Louise, who lived at Kensington Palace.

Also during Victoria's reign, land on the western edge of the gardens were sold for Kensington Palace Gardens, a private residential development inspired by Regents Park and designed by James Pennethorne in 1843. Distinguished architects designed several of the houses, some of which are now embassies.

Diana, Princess of Wales, lived in the private apartments in Kensington Palace following her divorce from Prince Charles. After her death in 1997, a proposal was made to create a memorial garden south of the palace. However, as the well-being of children was one of her greatest concerns, it was decided instead to commission the design of a children's garden in her memory.

Synopsis

1689 William III and Mary II come to the throne and shortly thereafter purchase Nottingham House as a suburban retreat; George London instructed by the queen to lay out a garden south of the house

1690 Rue de Roi (Rotten Row) constructed through Hyde Park to Kensington Palace

1701 Henry Wise begins work on a formal wilderness north of the palace, but work stopped with the death of the king at Kensington in 1702

1702 Anne, Mary's sister, becomes queen (1702–14), and immediately instructs Wise to resume work on the wilderness; Anne removes the boxwood from the William and Mary garden but retains much of the original design

1705 Orangery built near the entrance to the wilderness, designed by Nicholas Hawksmoor

1705 One hundred acres of Hyde Park acquired to build a paddock for deer and antelope
1714 Anne dies at Kensington Palace and is succeeded by George I (1714–27), who rarely resides at the palace
1722 William Kent commissioned to paint the Cupola room and goes on to decorate ceilings for nearly all royal apartments at Kensington
1726 Paddock doubled in size under the direction of Charles Bridgeman; king introduces a number of exotic animals to the paddock, including three tigers and two civet cats
1727 George II and Queen Caroline (1727–60) make Kensington one of their principal residences
1728 Queen Caroline orders gardens to be "repaired"; gardens to south of palace and wilderness to north swept away and replaced by grass, under the direction of Bridgeman
1728–31 Broad Walk, running north-south alongside old gardens and wilderness, and Round Pond, from which radiates a series of wide tree-lined avenues, constructed; Serpentine completed by joining a series of existing ponds, culminating a series of changes by Bridgeman that effectively eliminate most traces of earlier layouts of the gardens
1733 Kensington Gardens opened to public on Sunday evenings
1734–5 Queen's Temple built, probably to William Kent's design; in both its siting and design it typifies the Arcadian landscape then fashionable
1760 George III (1760–1820) came to the throne; preferred Buckingham Palace, and Kensington never again served as the seat of a reigning monarch (though Edward, Duke of Kent, lived at Kensington Palace)
1819 Victoria, the Duke of Kent's first child, is born at Kensington Palace
1837 Victoria becomes queen but moves at once to Buckingham Palace
1842 Construction of residences in Palace Gardens begun "after the manner of Regent's Park"
1843 Flower Walk constructed
1851 Great Exhibition held in Hyde Park; Crystal Palace erected adjacent to Rotten Row
1861 Italian Water Gardens at Victoria Gate constructed, which included Calder Marshall's statue of Edward Jenner
1863–72 Albert Memorial constructed on a strip of land taken from Hyde Park; Kensington Gardens then covered about 275 acres (111.3 ha), its present size
1905 Inventory of trees shows 1,400 English elms
1906 J.M. Barrie's *Peter Pan in Kensington Gardens* published
1912 Statue of Peter Pan by Sir George Frampton erected in Kensington Gardens
1942 Removal of iron railings to be melted down for war metal (replaced 1968–70)
1950s Many elms lost in outbreak of Dutch elm disease, including the Broad Walk Avenue
1970s All remaining elms killed in second outbreak of elm disease
1980 Henry Moore's Arch erected on west bank of Long Water
1981 After loss of elms, species of lime *(Tilia)* made up the most important genus numerically in the gardens, with 58 percent, followed by horse chestnut *(Aesculus)* with 31.1 percent
1997 Diana, Princess of Wales, who had lived at Kensington Palace since her divorce from Prince Charles, dies in an automobile accident in Paris
1998 Proposal to commemorate Princess Diana by restoring the William and Mary garden rejected in favor of a children's garden north of the palace

Further Reading

Colvin, Howard Montagu, editor, *The History of King's Works,* 6 vols., London: HMSO, 1963; see especially volumes 5 and 6
De Jong, Erik, "Netherlandish Hesperides: Garden Art in the Period of William and Mary, 1650–1702," *Journal of Garden History* 8 (1988)
Green, David Brontë, *Gardener to Queen Anne: Henry Wise (1653–1738) and the Formal Garden,* London and New York: Oxford University Press, 1956
Hunt, John Dixon, "Reckoning with Dutch Gardens," *Journal of Garden History* 8 (1988)
Jacques, David, and Arend van der Horst, *The Gardens of William and Mary,* London: Helm, 1988
Jones, J.R., "The Building Works and Court Style of William and Mary," *Journal of Garden History* 8 (1988)
Lucas, Edward Verrall, *A Wanderer in London,* London: Methuen, 1906; 29th edition, 1936
Piper, David, *The Companion Guide to London,* London: Collins, 1964; 7th edition, London: Harper Collins, 1992

Walker, Annabel, and Peter Jackson, *Kensington and Chelsea: A Social and Architectural History*, London: Murray, 1987
Wijnands, D.O., "Hortus Auriaci: The Gardens of Orange and Their Place in Late 17th-Century Botany and Horticulture," *Journal of Garden History* 8 (1988)

RICHARD WESTMACOTT

Kent, William 1685–1748

English Architect, Painter, and Garden Designer

Architect, garden artist, designer, and painter, William Kent is generally recognized as the founder of landscape gardening. Before he achieved his position as revolutionary in the field of artistic gardening, Kent had already had considerable experience in the other disciplines of plastic arts. He was accepted first as apprentice to a coach painter but soon left that workshop to seek more opportunities in London.

Thanks to the support of a wealthy art lover, Kent traveled to Italy in 1709, where he intended to complete his artistic training. During his ten years of study in Rome, he met Englishmen making grand tours of the country, who turned out to have a decisive influence on his future. At the beginning of 1715 he became acquainted with Richard Boyle, the third earl of Burlington, who became Kent's patron. Burlington persuaded Kent to return to England as part of his entourage in 1719. Burlington imagined with this step to have won a historical painter worthy of his support.

With tireless eloquence Burlington recommended his protégé among the English nobility, with the result that Kent, against all odds, received the commission to decorate the newly built apartments for the king at Kensington Palace. This prestigious project increased Kent's visibility and led to further commissions.

Although Kent primarily pursued a career in painting in the first years after his return to England, Burlington devoted himself to the study of architecture. His preoccupation with the Palladian architectural style became the foundation of his own designs. The best-known outcome of Burlington's work was his suburban villa in Chiswick, where Kent first decorated the rooms and then later partially rearranged the garden.

Ongoing discussions with his patron led Kent to take a growing interest in problems of architecture. After several years of work Kent published two volumes entitled *Designs of Inigo Jones* (1727). Kent's concentration on Jones, a painter, stage designer, and architect, is not surprising especially since Jones was known as Palladio's most important successor in England and was the revered inspirational ancestor of the Burlington circle. In particular the central perspective of Jones's theater sets and the stage scenery produced by Ferdinando Galli-Bibiena on the principle of *scena per angolo* (a special kind of painted stage scene) influenced Kent. Both opened up perspectives in a way that Kent could capitalize on when he found spatial problems to solve in garden design.

Kent was able to prove his landscaping talents, his ability to form spaces with earth, plants, and water, at the city residence of the crown prince in London. Kent's contemporaries acknowledged that the artist had created a new pastoral style, surprising in its variety and its emphasis on the beauty of nature, without betraying any involvement with art. Horace Walpole, however, did recognize how decisively Alexander Pope had inspired Kent's landscape artistry. Through Burlington's connections Pope and Kent had known each other for many years, and Kent had had the opportunity to study Pope's garden at Twickenham, thereby seeing firsthand the earliest attempts toward a new ideal in garden design. Above all, however, he had Pope to thank for recognizing the Augustan ideals of nature, as laid out in his poetry.

Between Burlington and Pope, Kent developed the ability to synthesize landscape and pictorial art, to represent nature in painterly forms. No doubt his Italian experiences proved useful as well, for Kent had seen the landscape paintings of Claude Lorrain, whose motifs and configurations were ready at hand to imitate. When Alexander Pope in 1734 wrote, "All gardening is landscape-painting, . . . just like a landscape hung up," he formulated the artistic ideal of the epoch that Kent sought more and more to realize.

In contrast to his predecessor, the royal gardener Charles Bridgeman, who conceptualized the layout of a garden with ground plans, Kent switched to using full drawings. This change in the manner of presentation

Temple of the British Worthies in the Garden at Stowe, designed by William Kent, from Osvald Sirén, *China and Gardens of Europe of the Eighteenth Century,* [1950], 1990
Courtesy of Dumbarton Oaks

suggested a different understanding of space. Bridgeman determined the placement of objects in his gardens in a quasi-negative way, by cutting away from thickets of vegetation spaces in the realization of cabinets, rooms, and theaters. Kent, on the other hand, started with empty spaces, into which he placed positive elements. He composed so-called clumps, made up of several trees of the same sort, placing them into the acreage to be landscaped—an accomplishment that his successor Lancelot "Capability" Brown would take up as well. The basic element of clumps, once placed, allowed Kent to build up a whole landscape structure on that foundation, or even to break up the vegetation pattern into groves. The repertory he developed in the placement of vegetation, including rows of bushes, edge plantings, and freestanding individual elements, made it possible for him to form a continuity of spaces flowing into each other with easy transitions. Kent handled each portion of the total landscape as a distinct artistic view.

In order to give the visitor a sequential picture of such contrived spaces, Kent needed to arrange them in a perceptible order. By inventing the circuit walk, a path leading around the periphery of the garden, he could see to it that the visitor was led from one view of nature to the next, each seen as a distinct picture. Background plantings, similar to side scenery on the stage, served to separate each tableau from the next. This translation of theatrical principles to the artistic presentation of garden landscapes is Kent's most significant accomplishment.

Botanical knowledge was not Kent's forte. An observer of his convoluted landscape designs can see that the plants he drew are hard to classify. It is clear, however, that he was able to shape distinct spaces with attention to variety, contrast, and surprise. As far as gardening itself was concerned, Kent relied on the help of knowledgeable experts. The artist, however, looked at the land with the eye of a painter. Walpole said of him that "the great principles on which he worked were perspective, and light and shade."

Kent became an unopposed authority on garden design and received numerous contracts to reshape either in whole or in part the gardens conceptualized by his predecessor, Charles Bridgeman. In the early 1730s Kent drew up designs for the gardens of Charlton

Temple of Venus in the Garden at Stowe, designed by William Kent, from Osvald Sirén, *China and Gardens of Europe of the Eighteenth Century*, [1950], 1990
Courtesy of Dumbarton Oaks

House, Claremount, Esher, Chiswick, and Stowe. In addition he designed individual park buildings such as the Eremitage in Richmond Park for Queen Caroline. His artistic garden designs include drawings for the country seat of Holkham Hall. After 1738 he worked at Rousham; about the same time he devoted himself to the plans for Euston Hall. In the early 1740s the earl of Beaufort took him into his service to redesign his family holdings at Badminton.

See also Kew, Royal Botanic Gardens; London Parks; Rousham House

Biography

Born in Bridlington, Yorkshire, England, 1685. Apprenticed to coach painter, Hull, Humberside, England; left for London at age of 20; went to Italy, 1709; studied art in Rome until 1719; met Richard Boyle, third Earl of Burlington, at end of 1714 or beginning of 1715, who became his patron; with Burlington's help received commission to decorate king's new apartments and staircase in Kensington Palace, London, begun 1721, completed in 1727; appointed to London Board of Works, May 1726; received post of Master Mason and Deputy Surveyor, 1735, positions he retained until his death; became interested in landscape design, encouraged by friend Alexander Pope; dominant figure in landscape design in England from mid-1730s; often credited with inventing English landscape style of garden design. Died in London, 1748.

Selected Designs

ca. 1727	Garden building, Holkham Hall, Holkham, Norfolk, England
ca. 1730	Garden building, Alexander Pope's residence and gardens, Twickenham, Middlesex, England
after 1731	Garden buildings and gardens, Stowe, Buckinghamshire, England
1732	Garden building, Richmond Middlesex, England
after 1733	House and gardens, Esher Place, Surrey, England
ca. 1732–38	Gardens, Chiswick House, Chiswick, Middlesex, England
ca. 1733–36	Gardens, Carlton House, London, England
after 1734–38	Gardens, Claremont, Surrey, England
ca. 1738	Gardens, Euston Hall, Euston, Suffolk, England
1738–42	House and gardens, Rousham House, Rousham, Oxfordshire, England

after 1741 Lodgings and gardens, Badminton House, Badminton, Gloucestershire, England

Selected Publications

Designs of Inigo Jones, 2 vols., 1727

Further Reading

Hunt, John Dixon, *William Kent: Landscape Garden Designer: An Assessment and Catalogue of His Designs,* London: Zwemmer, 1987

Jourdain, Margaret, *The Work of William Kent: Artist, Painter, Designer, and Landscape Gardener,* London: Country Life, and New York: Scribner, 1948

Wilson, Michael I., *William Kent: Architect, Designer, Painter, Gardener, 1685–1748,* London: Routledge, and Boston: Kegan Paul, 1984

ULRICH MÜLLER

Keukenhof

Lisse, South Holland, Netherlands

Location: approximately 40 kilometers (25 miles) southwest of Amsterdam

The description of Keukenhof as the world's largest flower garden is based on its spring display of more than 6 million flowering bulbs (see Plate 17). It is one of the few garden parks that has successfully united what seems to be an infinite variety of flowers. Visitors from around the globe trek to the gardens to enjoy the blooming sights. A trip to Keukenhof will confirm why the Dutch have been leaders in the bulb trade for over 400 years.

The word *Keukenhof* literally means "kitchen garden." The gardens bear this name because they were formerly a kitchen garden during the early 15th century, where vegetables and herbs were grown to feed the castle inhabitants. The kitchen garden was part of the 15th-century castle and lands belonging to Countess Jacoba van Beieren of Bavaria. Keukenhof, which is now so famous for its bulb displays, did not contain tulips until the late 16th century, after Carolus Clusius introduced them to the Netherlands. Much of the present Keukenhof grounds were originally used as hunting grounds for the countess.

The castle and land had many owners through the centuries and resembled a country park in the early 20th century. In 1949 a group of prominent Dutch bulb growers wanted to create a flower exhibition to show visitors the splendor of the Dutch flower-bulb industry. They found a 70-acre (28.3-ha) country park in the heart of the bulb district between Haarlem and Leiden. It was here that they created the present-day Keukenhof.

Each year the gardens are open from about the third week in March until the end of May. The seven- or eight-week display of spring-flowering bulbs fluctuates slightly each year because of weather conditions. Each year over 500,000 people visit in the spring to witness the masterful painterly display of flowers. Over 6 million bulbs bloom in the gardens during eight short weeks. Huge bold banks of tulips, narcissi, daffodils, hyacinths, grape hyacinths (*Muscari botryoides*), checkered fritillary (*Fritillaria meleagris*), iris, and pansies appear throughout the garden. Included in this display are over 1,000 different varieties of tulips.

A newly opened area at Keukenhof is the Jacoba van Beieren Historical Garden. Wooden gates designate the division between old and new themes. The historical garden is representative of the period when Countess Jacoba van Beieren flew her falcons in the area. The garden has a variety of medicinal and cooking herbs, including lovage, sage, common bistort, and mint. It also has a large collection of 17th- and 18th-century bulbous plants.

A Japanese Garden nestled between the windmills and the Music Garden is a modern interpretation of a traditional Japanese garden. The garden was planted in collaboration with the Hanakairo Park in Tottori, Japan, as a tribute to the 400th anniversary of Dutch-Japanese relations.

An indoor spring garden show installed under a large 7,000-square-meter (8,372 sq. yd.) glass pavilion highlights displays of bulbs as cut flowers. Huge flower arrangements can be seen in ten indoor flower shows, each named for a member of the royal family. Over 500 different varieties are present, including the major groups of amaryllis, hyacinths, freesia, lilacs, orchids, anthuriums, gerbera, chrysanthemums, alstroemeria, roses, carnations and lilies.

During the eight weeks that the spring show is blooming, bulbs come into flower at different times. The first bulbs to bloom are the daffodils, crocuses, and narcissi, followed by tulips and hyacinths. The best time to visit is the last half of April, when everything is blooming.

The bulb displays are presented by 90 bulb-producing companies. Each year a new design template is given to the bulb companies, who design a spectacular show with their products. Different designs are used each year for two reasons: tulips don't grow well in the same spot year after year, and the new designs are meant to inspire fresh ideas for visitors' home gardens. Often the design resembles streams of water, using thousands of grape hyacinth bulbs. The gardens also have complementary permanent plantings of shrubs and trees that bloom at the same time as the bulbs. Azaleas and Japanese cherries are particularly attractive with the bulbs.

After the bed designs are completed, the 22 Keukenhof gardeners start the task of planting the 6 million bulbs. These gardeners are employed throughout the year to keep the garden immaculate. Bulbs shipped from the growers in the fall are immediately planted by Keukenhof staff. The beds are then maintained until the bulbs bloom the following spring. After the gardens close in late May, the bulbs are lifted and sent back to the growers.

The bulbs are planted in tiers, with three bulbs atop each other. This multibulb stacking is planned to ensure constant color in each flower bed. The deepest bulbs are the late-blooming tulips. The middle layers are early blooming tulips, and the top layers are small crocuses that bloom first. The deeper the bulbs, the later they will bloom.

Keukenhof provides innovative ways to see the bulbs. Visitors can climb the steps of a Groningen-type corn mill (windmill) to see the bulbs from a higher elevation. To add an auditory dimension to the garden, a clock-carillon plays tunes every 15 minutes.

In 1999 Keukenhof celebrated its 50th anniversary with the inauguration of a Zomerhof or Summer Garden. This show runs from the beginning of August until mid-September with an additional 1 million bulbs in bloom. A special sculpture walk was also set up in the park to mark the anniversary. At the center of the fan-shaped garden is a 3,000-square-meter (3,588-sq. yd.) Oranje Nassau Pavilion nestled between a labyrinth and a 150-meter (164-yd.) fountain. A three-part section of the garden with the creation of a dune landscape, a dike body, and a terp (man-made mound of soil) features the Netherlands' age-old battle with the sea. The Eikenlaan (oak lane) connects this new section with the rest of the garden and boasts 120 oaks each over 50 years old.

Synopsis

1401–36 Kitchen gardens laid out on site, near castle of Countess Jacoba van Beieren of Bavaria
1900s Gardens remain country park after many centuries
1949 Dutch bulb growers purchase site for flower exhibition
2000 Jacoba van Beieren Historical Gardens opened

Further Reading

Abbs, Barbara, *The Garden Lover's Guide to the Netherlands and Belgium,* New York: Princeton Architectural Press, 1999
Coats, Peter, *Great Gardens,* New York: Putnam, and London: Weidenfeld and Nicolson, 1963

ANNE MARIE VAN NEST

Kew, Royal Botanic Gardens

Location: 6 miles (9.6 km) southwest of central London via the A4 and the A205

During the 450 years that botanical exotica have been cultivated on the site of the present Royal Botanic Gardens, Kew, several functions have competed to shape the terrain. Between 1718 and 1904, as a convenient two-hour row or carriage ride up the Thames from the capital, once large though diminishing portions of the site provided royal residences or hunting grounds. Under the direction of Sir Joseph Banks from the 1770s until his death in 1820, glass conservatories for specimens from the growing empire's five continents dominated the garden's northeast sector. With three generations of the Hooker family in charge through Queen Victoria's reign, Decimus Burton's Palm and Temperate Houses rose to rival George III's Pagoda for vista orientation. Supervised by government bureaus beginning in 1841, most of Kew's 330 acres (133.5 ha) assumed the primary function of safe, healthy cultivation for botanical study of, by now, some 6 million specimens representing a quarter of the world's named plants. The principles of siting and grouping this largest botanical collection are naturally less picturesque than taxonomic. Yet since

George II's residence in the 1720s, visitors without professional interest in botany (a million each year during the 20th century) have sought recreation and beauty at Kew. Their challenge to Kew's national commitments as laboratory, museum of economic botany, seed repository, and clearinghouse for international specimens, has kept aesthetic and lay-educational concerns alive there.

The site is hardly conducive for a global garden. The Thames is tidal here, hence brackish and polluted by the capital; the terrain is "one continued dead flat," as the Pagoda's architect William Chambers described it (1763); and the soil—river sand and gravel some 23 yards (21 m) deep over London clay—requires constant amendment. Yet political power matched with curiosity about plants rooted botanical research here. William Turner, the respected "father of English botany," based his mid-16th-century herbal on work in his own garden at Kew or just across the Thames at Sion House, home of the duke of Somerset, lord protector, whom he served as physician. Some 125 years later John Evelyn's diary records visits to Sir Henry Capel's exotics in the garden surrounding his Kew house. Leased in 1731 by Frederick, prince of Wales, Capel's home became known as the White House or Kew House, the royal residence for which by 1757 Chambers unfolded the most comprehensive landscaping program in Kew's history.

An adjoining royal property within Kew's current bounds was landscaped before Chambers's work. At the next bend upriver Frederick's parents, crowned George II and Queen Caroline in 1727, resided at Richmond Lodge. About 1725 Charles Bridgeman designed for Caroline a landscape transitional in its labyrinthine woodland paths and its vistas over cultivated fields but traditional with its royal Dairy overlooking a canal, its aisles of trees, an amphitheater of elms, and a round Tuscan belvedere yielding panoramic views from its mount. To judge from published praise, satires, and prints, however, Richmond Park's major attractions were two follies designed by William Kent. His Hermitage (1731) of rough "Gothic" stone yet classical alignment, shouldering a hillside Bridgeman raised behind it, contained busts of Boyle, Newton, and others to embody the Enlightenment's reconciliation of theology and science. Merlin's Cave (1735) was actually a pavilion flanked by octagonal wings, capped by several thatched cones. Entered through a Gothic ogee arch, it too purported—responding perhaps to the whiggery of Lord Cobham's statues at Stowe—to interpret the national character through life-size wax figures of King Arthur's wizard, Queen Elizabeth, possibly Britannia, and three others. Yet the impact of Caroline's Richmond Park was surpassed 20 years after her death in 1737 by the adjoining park, facing Kew's White House and sponsored by her daughter-in-law Augusta, princess of Wales.

Augusta's husband, Prince Frederick, died in 1751 while implementing landscaping plans for the 110 acres (44.5 ha) their residence overlooked—plans yoking concerns botanical and patriotic. (Frederick had hoped, from earth dredged to make a lake before the White House, to raise a "Mount Parnassus" on which statues would pair British and classical scientists, poets, architects, etc.) Within five years Augusta had enlisted Frederick's friend John Stuart, earl of Bute, to direct both the botanical and landscaping vectors of her property's development. With the outbreak of global warfare with France, the "Great War for Empire" whose seven years synchronized with Augusta's alterations at Kew, the patriotic vision shifted from the past to the present and future. Near the White House Frederick was commemorated by the erection of a Temple of Solitude, and his House of Confucius was transferred to a suraquatic setting typifying English treatment of Chinese garden structures. Not far off, Chambers's orangery and Great Stove housed plants from warmer climates, while scattered temples dedicated to the Sun, Arethusa, Aeolus, and Pan saluted natural forces on which Bute's plants depended. Far beyond the northeast corner of the Physic Garden stretched two prominent sheep's meadows defined by ha-has within a circuit path. The flocks that cropped and animated these meadows represented both a national industry and particular concerns of Augusta's firstborn, crowned George III in 1760 but admired as "Farmer George." He set to improve here the English breed with his merino sheep smuggled out of Spain. Yet architectural signals in the extreme southern two-fifths of the White House vista beckoned beyond a pragmatic, personal, or even a dynastic scale toward an imperial destiny that the Seven Years' War was securing Britain.

The belvedere, whose circling panorama embraced that imperial vision and connected it back to Augusta's White House, capped an artificial hilltop: the Temple of Victory at Minden was named for a battle her brother won in 1759, the year that saw power shift decisively to Britain and its allies. Visible in the foreground to the south and southeast of it, two structures represented intercontinental powers of the past. The triumphal shape and statue fragments of the Roman arch Chambers designed as "ruined" may also have once commemorated conquest, although it served a practical contemporary function as an overpass from the London road into the sheep pasture and bent the circuit path it straddled to focus strollers' eyes on the recent Victory Temple. Across the sheep's meadow a pastiche replica of a Gothic cathedral, its two spires approximately 13 yards (12 m) apart, bespoke another supranational institution of ebbing power. Farthest from the White House, framed between these two icons of former power, in the view from Victory Temple (or visited between them along the peripheral footpath), rose three exotic buildings: a quasi-Moorish Alhambra on the left, the Pagoda, and a Turkish Mosque at right. Britain's trading future lay across the Mediterranean, but now also decisively into the Far East; not incidentally, by 1763 Chambers's Pagoda offered visitors a ten-story-high panorama over Kew and the Thames Valley. It is a mind-broadening layout once its spatial dimension and cross-cultural allusiveness are clear. The ways in which some of Chambers's many buildings, pocketed in greenery, would continually appear and vanish as one walked the circuit path, may have slightly vindicated the channeling of the visitor's spatial experience that Chambers criticized in print. Keen Whig satire and Banks's botanical initiatives soon obscured this imperial emblem Augusta had inscribed in Kew's landscape. But when Princess Diana in 1987 opened the Princess of Wales Conservatory, Kew's most capacious glasshouse with its ten climatic zones, she commemorated the vision of Augusta, who would see her son's coronation but not her own.

While residing summers at Richmond Lodge with his growing family, George III hired Lancelot "Capability" Brown to sculpt Caroline's Thameside terrace into sloping lawns, convert Kent's Hermitage to a ruin, and quite efface Merlin's Cave. This work resulted in readier vistas toward the river, a more "natural" curvature to the walks, and Brown's most enduring contribution, yielding a welcome vertical dimension, the "Hollow Walk" (1773), renamed Rhododendron Dell a century later when its laurels gave way to the Chinese and Indian imports cherished by Victorian visitors. Two buildings associated with George's consort Charlotte survive with significant floral adornment: the Queen's Cottage amid wildflowers and Kew Palace (the former "Dutch House" of 1631) backed by the Queen's Garden, a pastiche of 17th-century idioms dedicated by Elizabeth II in 1969.

Since Brown's work, many of Kew's developments toward its current state originated from considerations of utility. Perhaps the earliest of Joseph Banks's gifts to Kew were the spongy lava chunks, ballast for his return voyage from Iceland, which hosted Kew's first moss garden. Sir William Hooker floated his wooded and islanded lake in a pit 4.5 acres (1.8 ha) long, from which gravel had been dug for terraces of the Temperate House. In the mid-19th century Kew nourished hundreds of thousands of trees and shrubs for transplantation to public parks as the "lungs" of British cities. And in wartime years—1813, 1917, and 1940—Kew's lawns and parterres have yielded to grains, turnips, and potatoes. Yet Kew's sturdiest practical nudges to global economy and world history leave no traces on its landscape: Kew provided supervision and a clearinghouse for the transfer of quinine and rubber from South America to India and Indonesia; for retrotransfer of bananas, cocoa, and coffee to the West Indies (after the dubious "bounty" of Banks's scheme for Tahitian breadfruit); and for ongoing training in cultivation, control of pests and disease, and maintenance of a sustainable environment.

In 1965 the nearly 500 acres (202.5 ha) of Wakehurst Place, a respected woodland park in the Sussex Weald, brought, under Kew's management, vitally needed space, as well as variety in soil, climate, and terrain, thereby enriching Kew both botanically and aesthetically.

Synopsis

before 1549	William Turner starts herbal garden at Kew
1680s	Henry Capel plants exotic garden around his house at Kew
1718	Future King George II and Queen Caroline take up residence at Richmond Lodge, adjacent to Capel's Kew house
1725	Charles Bridgeman landscapes Richmond Gardens for Richmond Lodge
1731	Capel's Kew house leased by Frederick Louis, prince of Wales, and renamed White House (or Kew House); Hermitage built in Richmond Gardens, designed by William Kent
1735	Merlin's Cave built in Richmond Gardens, designed by William Kent
1751	Frederick Louis dies and his widow, Augusta, princess of Wales, continues work on Kew Park
1756	Augusta commissions John Stuart, earl of Bute, to direct landscaping and development of botanical garden for Kew Park
1757–63	Building program for Kew Park completed by William Chambers, including Temple of Solitude, Temple of Victory at Minden, Pagoda, Orangery, and Great Stove
1759–93	William Aiton the Elder superintends botanic garden established at Kew
1772–1820	Joseph Banks supervises global operations and construction of glass conservatories for botanical specimens at Kew
1773	Hollow Walk created, designed by Capability Brown
1789	William Aiton publishes *Hortus Kewensis,* a catalog of Kew, listing 5,600 species
1841	Supervision of Kew transferred to government department
1844–48	Palm House built to design by Richard Turner and Decimus Burton

mid-19th C.	Kew propagates trees and shrubs for public parks as "lungs" of British cities
1917and 1940	Grains, turnips, and potatoes raised during wartime
1965	Wakehurst Place, in the Sussex Weald, acquired as extension of Kew
1969	Queen's Garden dedicated by Queen Elizabeth II
1987	Princess of Wales Conservatory opened by Diana, princess of Wales

Further Reading

Blunt, Wilfrid, *In for a Penny: A Prospect of Kew Gardens: Their Flora, Fauna, and Falballas,* London: Hamish Hamilton, 1978

Carter, H.B., *His Majesty's Spanish Flock: Sir Joseph Banks and the Merinos of George III of England,* Sydney: Angus and Robertson, 1964

Chambers, William, *Plans, Elevations, Sections, and Perspective Views of the Gardens and Buildings at Kew in Surry,* London, 1763; reprint, Farnborough, Hampshire: Gregg Press, 1966

Colton, Judith, "Merlin's Cave and Queen Caroline: Garden Art As Political Propaganda," *Eighteenth Century Studies* 10, no. 1 (1976)

Desmond, Ray, *Kew: The History of the Royal Botanic Gardens,* London: Harvill Press, 1995

Hepper, F. Nigel, editor, *Kew: Gardens for Science and Pleasure,* London: HMSO, 1982

Quaintance, Richard, "Toward Distinguishing among Theme-Park Publics: William Chambers' Landscape-Theory vs. His Kew Practice," in *Theme Park Landscapes: Antecedents and Variations,* edited by Terence Young and Robert Riley, Washington, D.C.: Dumbarton Oaks Research Library, 2001

Rorschach, Kimerly, "Frederick, Prince of Wales: Taste, Politics, and Power," *Apollo* 34 (1991)

Thiselton-Dyer, William T., "Historical Account of Kew to 1841," *Kew Bulletin* 60 (December 1891)

RICHARD QUAINTANCE

Kienast, Dieter 1945–1998

Swiss Landscape Architect

Zürich-born Dieter Kienast was a renowned Swiss landscape architect and one of the most influential landscape architects in Europe at the end of the 20th century. He learned the gardening profession at his father's nursery in Zurich. Working with important Swiss garden architects such as Fred Eicher, he soon learned to reduce the elements in garden design to a few substantial items. Another important source of inspiration for Kienast throughout his professional career was the Swiss garden architect Ernst Cramer, who was well known for his abstract gardens dating from the 1960s. With large earth pyramids and concrete objects, Cramer inspired the student Kienast as much as the successful landscape architect more than 30 years later.

After his professional training Kienast studied landscape architecture at the University in Kassel in Germany, where he earned his degree in landscape architecture. Soon afterward he began research in plant sociology, specializing in the study of spontaneous vegetation in the urban environment. In this work he learned to balance his more intuitive way of design with a more scientifically structured approach. After earning his doctorate in Kassel, he decided not to continue in specialized scientific work but to concentrate again on landscape design; in 1979 he joined the landscape architectural firm Stöckli, Kienast, and Koeppel in Wettingen, Switzerland. Kienast felt that poetic sensibility would unfold in the dialogue between nature and architecture: "We contrast architectural order with natural chaos, knowing that the order will serve as an essential backbone in our landscape projects." Kienast considered the design process to be a constant oscillation between chaos and order, rationality and intuition, nature and culture, Arcadia and residual places. In his garden designs he cultivated both the paradise and the ordinary.

In 1995 Kienast left the office of Stöckli, Kienast, and Koeppel and founded his own successful office in Zürich and Bern together with landscape architect Guenther Vogt and his wife Erika Kienast-Lueder. Kienast, Vogt, and Partner realized numerous remarkable projects in Switzerland, Germany, Austria, England, and the United States. Among these were the Swiss embassy in Berlin with the architects Diener and Diener, the open-space planning for the EXPO 2000 in Hanover, and the landscaping for the new Tate Gallery of Modern Art in London with the architects Herzog and De Meuron. In addition to his strong cooperation with renowned European architects and urban planners Kienast was especially interested in American Minimalist art. He worked with various artists such as Jenny Holzer, Fischli and Weiss, Richard Long, and Ian Hamilton Finlay, whose work he particularly admired. Finlay's strategy to insert written texts in the form of inscriptions as a new layer of meaning into the context of the garden inspired Kienast to some of his most remarkable projects. Just as the artistic avant-garde of the 1960s fought against the flood of arbitrary images, Kienast introduced a certain minimalist approach to garden design, trying to create places of a certain authenticity. His pronounced interest in the theory and history of the garden architecture prevented him from producing purely formal gardens.

As a professor at the Technical School (Interkantonales Technikum) in Rapperswil, Switzerland, the University of Karlsruhe, Germany, and lastly, at the Swiss Federal Institute of Technology (ETH), where he founded the chair of landscape architecture, Kienast developed a strong interdisciplinary cooperation with city planners and architects. His teaching and research activity contributed to the improvement of cooperation between architects, landscape architects, and environmental planners in Europe. Kienast, who died at the age of 53, educated some of the most successful Swiss landscape architects of the next generation.

Biography

Born in Zürich, Switzerland, 1945. Apprenticeship as gardener in nursery of father, 1962–65; studied landscape architecture at University of Kassel, Germany, 1970–75, with dissertation in plant sociology, 1978; partner in office for landscape architecture Stöckli, Kienast & Koeppel, Wettingen, Switzerland; professor of garden architecture at Technical School (Interkantonales Technikum), Rapperswil, Switzerland, 1980–91; technical head of botanical garden in Brügglingen near Basel, Switzerland, 1981–85; lecturer for landscape architecture at Swiss Federal Institute of Technology, Zürich, 1985–97; professor at Institute of Landscape and Garden, University of Karlsruhe, Germany, 1992–97; cofounder, together with wife and landscape architect Günter Vogt, of landscape architecture office Kienast, Vogt, and Partner, Zürich and Bern, 1995–98; professor of landscape architecture at Swiss Federal Institute of Technology, Zürich, 1997–98. Died in Zürich, 1998.

Selected Designs

1982 Municipal park, Wettingen, Switzerland
1987–93 Municipal Park, Sankt Gallen, Switzerland
1988–94 Open space planning for Inselspital Bern (with U. Strasser, A. Roost, architects), Bern, Switzerland
1991 Ecole cantonale de langue francaise (with Haflinger, Grunder, von Allmen, architects), Bern, Switzerland
1992 Vogelbach residential development (Riehen with M. Alder, architect), Basel, Switzerland
1994 Waldhaus psychiatric clinic (with F. Chiaverio and F. Censi, architects), Chur, Switzerland
1995 Hotel Zürichberg (with M. Burkhalter and C. Sumi, architects), Zürich, Switzerland
1996 Furstenwald cemetery (with U. Zinsli, architect), Chur, Switzerland
1997 Center of Art and Media Technology, Karlsruhe, Germany
1998 Spa gardens, Bad Münder, Germany; municipal savings bank, art and landscape, Fürstenfeldbruck, Germany
1999 Federal Labor Court (with C. Weinmiller, architect), Erfurt, Germany; new building for Ministry of Foreign Affairs of the Federal Republic of Germany (with Müller Reimann Architekten), Berlin, Germany
2000 International horticultural show Steiermark 2000, Graz, Austria; Swiss Embassy (with Diener und Diener, architects), Berlin, Germany; Federal Institute of Technology, open space design (with Campi Pessina, architects), Zürich, Switzerland; EXPO 2000 (with architects T. Herzog, A. Speer, Arnaboldi/Cavadini), Hannover, Germany; New Tate Gallery of Modern Art (with Herzog and de Meuron, architects), London, England

Selected Articles

"Die Sehnsucht nach dem Paradies," *Hochparterre* 7 (1990)
"Die Form, der Inhalt und die Zeit" (with G. Vogt), *Topos* 2 (1993)
"Die Natur der Sache—Stadtlandschaften," in *Stadtparks,* edited by T. Koenigs, 1993
"Un decalogo: A Set of Rules," *Lotus* 87 (1995)
"Stadt und Natur Gartenkultur im Spiegel der Gesellschaft," *Archithese* 14 (1997)
"Funktion, Form und Aussage" (with R. Schafer), *Topos* 18 (1997)

Further Reading

Dieter Kienast: Zwischen Arkadien und Restfläche (exhib. cat.), Lucerne, Switzerland: Architekturgalerie Luzern, 1992

Kienast, Dieter, and Christian Vogt, *Kienast: Gärten; Gardens* (bilingual German-English edition), Basel, Switzerland, and Berlin: Birkhäuser, 1997

Kienast, Dieter, *Kienast Vogt: Aussenräume; Open Spaces* (bilingual German-English edition), Boston: Birkhäuser Verlag, 2000

Weilacher, Udo, *Zwischen Landschaftsarchitektur und Land Art*, Basel, Switzerland, and Boston: Birkhäuser, 1996; as *Between Landscape Architecture and Land Art*, translated by Felicity Glath, Basel, Switzerland, and Boston: Birkhäuser, 1996

UDO WEILACHER

Kiley, Daniel Urban 1912–

United States Landscape Architect

Acclaimed as the United States' "master landscape architect," Daniel Urban Kiley uniquely balances place, space, and nature. His projects foreground and enhance the social possibilities of the organic landscape. They poise between the beautiful and the functional, achieving a regal quality, a confidence, and a presence of detail through their skillful structuring of space.

Kiley established himself as an iconoclast, along with Harvard classmates Garret Eckbo and James Rose, rebelling against the prescribed and uninspired classicism of their Beaux-Arts professors. Ironically, as he subsequently traveled the world, Kiley reassimilated some of the classicism, tempering it with seemingly unhindered organic variations. Kiley's interpretation of modernism arose from those stylistic juxtapositions.

Unlike many modern thinkers, Kiley invokes historical design precedents in his work, although revitalizing them in a contemporary perspective. He uses natural elements to organize space for both function and visual enjoyment, inspired yet not controlled by historical examples. He has been a master of reinventing tradition in unique and interesting ways.

The essence of Kiley's theory of design is nature itself. He has compared his work to the experience of a walk in nature, where everything is always changing spatially toward the infinite. Design for Kiley is a process of discovery, a revelation of spatial continuity taking the designer from the immutable past to the limitless future. To design landscapes successfully, one must be connected physically and spatially to the natural environment.

Kiley's connection to nature and the environment began as a child. He spent many summers at his grandmother's farm near the White Mountains of New Hampshire exploring the fields and piney woods with his sisters. He was drawn to the richness of the rural landscape and was fascinated by the influence of nature. He connected physically and spiritually to this landscape, an experience of nature that formed the basis of his design principles. He argues that, if performed with sensitivity and knowledge, human intervention can reveal the power of nature and reconnect people with physical spaces. Central to Kiley's work is a passionate search for human intimacy with the natural environment.

Living modestly on a forest property of northern New England, Kiley maintains a small international practice from this mountain setting. He has had some of the most prestigious landscape commissions of his time, working with highly respected architects on projects ranging from residential gardens to major institutions. He has designed landscapes for the Lincoln Center in New York City, the Mall and the National Gallery in Washington DC, the Gateway Arch in St. Louis, Missouri, the Art Institute in Chicago, Independence Mall in Philadelphia, and the famous Miller Garden in Columbus, Indiana.

Kiley's work displays a modernist desire for spatial continuity and dynamic movement in the landscape. Hedges, orchards, allées, and simple rows of trees organize space for both function and visual pleasure. Precise geometries give way to relaxed, open spaces of lawn and orderly groves. Kiley's designs present a spatial diversity in the landscape that stimulates the surprises and originality that one might experience in wild nature. His design for the Miller Garden, a private residence, may be one of his finest accomplishments. Indeed, the design community holds it as a standard by which to judge other modern landscapes.

The function and organization of the interior spaces of the Miller house informed Kiley's overall planning of

The South Garden of the Art Institute of Chicago, designed by Dan Kiley
Copyright Office of Dan Kiley

the garden. He addressed several functional concerns as a practical basis for his design. For example, two weeping beeches *(Fagus sylatica* f. *pendula)* drape like green curtains before the glass walls of the west side of the house during the summer months, shading the living areas from the afternoon sun. Along the western edge of the terrace, 18 moraine honey locusts *(Gleditsia triacanthos* 'Moraine') create an allée, shielding the living areas from western exposure and wind. But function is not Kiley's only intent for this arrangement of trees. The allée is situated at the edge of a carefully graded plateau that falls to a vast floodplain. Normally intended to direct views down its path, the allée is deployed here in a untraditional way, drawing the viewers eye westward across the line of trees to the grassy meadow below.

Kiley arranged privacy hedges along the property boundaries in a unique way. Arborvitae grow in interrupted rows with sections stepped back to suggest, while actually denying, entry. This alternating rhythm recurs in the design of the architectural screen that extends from the house at the car park. Numerous clearly defined garden spaces create aesthetic diversity—apple orchard, adult garden, and swimming pool area—yet all are bound together in an order of spatial flow extending from the house. The Miller Garden is truly one of Kiley's masterpieces—a timeless work of modern spatial harmony and continuity.

Kiley developed another of his successes, the Chicago Art Institute's south garden, under the keen aesthetic sensibilities of a discriminating patron. A garden of strong geometric order that respects the grand stature of the institute, it nonetheless responds eloquently to the distinctive urban setting. The garden is situated 18 inches below street level, bound by Michigan Avenue and East Jackson Boulevard. A bosquet of hawthorns along the southern boundary (East Jackson Boulevard) screens the busy roadway. Kiley repeated this idea with three rows of honey locust in a raised planter along

Miller Garden, designed by Dan Kiley for a private residence
Copyright Paul C. Siciliano, Jr.

Michigan Avenue, providing a peaceful transition from the neighboring road. Kiley selected the honey locust for its graceful form and light, airy foliage as well as for its tolerance of the stresses of urban environments.

The garden is pristinely simple. A plane of crushed rock covers the ground on either side of a central pool. Marble-capped planters order the space, creating focal points where visitors may gather to socialize. Cockspur hawthorns (*Crataegus crus-galli*) gracefully unite the ordered rhythm of the planters, their latticed canopies forming a translucent ceiling over the garden. The hawthorn bosquet and central pool establish a new relationship between the fountain sculpture on the northern wing and the street. This garden scheme surprises passersby, intriguing them with a sudden grove of trees in the cityscape. A splendidly colored and textured seasonal display encourages the onlooker to enter this peaceful natural landscape. At the Art Institute one may enjoy art, culture, and flora, and within this extraordinary garden that experience begins.

Kiley's legacy to the profession of landscape architecture derives from his blend of classicism and modernism. His lasting innovations include the techniques of rhythmically modulating geometric grids, extending interior spaces outward, and extending ground planes. Concerned with the architectural balance of form and space, he discovers the poetry of space in recurrence and variation. Kiley's work counterpoints civil society with wilderness freedom. Always he foregrounds how place informs life and how life in turn gives meaning and value to place—all within the order of nature—timelessly expressing his talent, sensitivity, and spirit.

Biography

Born in Roxbury, Boston, Massachusetts, 1912. Spent summers on grandparents' farm in New Hampshire, experiencing nature unhindered; during high school, while a caddy at a local country club, became interested in designed landscapes; graduated high school, 1930; enrolled in postgraduate class in horticulture (without any undergraduate education), which led to his interest in landscape architecture; apprenticed to landscape architect Warren Manning of Cambridge, Massachusetts, beginning 1932; at Manning's office, gained unique understanding of plant characteristics, construction methods, and other activities of landscape architecture; entered Harvard Graduate School of Design as special student, 1936, where he and two other students, Garrett Eckbo and James Rose, began legendary rebellion against conservative historicist ideas of design in favor of functionalist freedom of modern thinking; left Harvard, 1938; worked for city planning commission, and later National Park Service, both in Concord, New Hampshire; moved to Washington, District of Columbia, where he was employed by Public Housing Authority, and later United States Housing Authority, before enlisting in army; married and settled in New Hampshire, 1942; traveled to Europe, 1945, touring French gardens, which gave him an appreciation for spatial order and structure in the landscape, leading to many classic French qualities and the influence of historical precedents in his work; established Office of Dan Kiley, 1951, a highly respected international Landscape Architecture practice located in Charlotte, Vermont. Currently lives and practices in Charlotte, Vermont.

Selected Designs

1955 Miller House, Columbus, Indiana, United States
1958 Rockefeller University, New York City, New York, United States
1960 Lincoln Center for the Performing Arts, New York City, New York, United States
1962 South garden, Chicago Art Institute, Chicago, Illinois, United States
1963 Third Block of Independence Mall, Philadelphia, Pennsylvania, United States
1963 Dulles Airport, Chantilly, Virginia, United States
1965 Rochester Institute of Technology, Rochester, New York, United States
1967 Tenth Street Overlook, Washington, District of Columbia, United States
1968 U.S. Air Force Academy, Colorado Springs, Colorado, United States
1977 Pedestrian connection between gallery and east wing, National Gallery of Art, Washington, District of Columbia, United States
1978 Dalle Centrale, La Defense, Paris, France
1983 Dallas Museum of Art, Dallas, Texas, United States
1985 Fountain Place, Dallas, Texas, United States
1988 Henry Moore Sculpture Garden, Nelson-Atkins Museum of Art, Kansas City, Missouri, United States
1989 Design created to revitalize 6-acre National Sculpture Garden, west side of gallery, National Gallery of Art, Washington, District of Columbia, United States
1992 Corning Riverfront Centennial Park, Corning, New York, United States

Selected Publications

Dan Kiley: The Complete Works of America's Master Landscape Architect (with Jane Amidon), 1999

Further Reading

Brown, A., "Kiley Kudos," *Landscape Architecture* 65 (October 1995)

Columbus Area Chamber of Commerce, *Columbus, Indiana: A Look at Architecture,* Columbus, Indiana: Visitors Center, 1974; 7th edition, 1998

Dean, A.O., "Modern Master," *Landscape Architecture* 66 (February 1996)

Dillon, D., "The People Commandeer a Plaza," *Landscape Architecture* 81, no. 1 (January 1991)

Eckbo, Garrett, Daniel Urban Kiley, and James C. Rose, "Landscape Design in the Rural Environment," *Architectural Record* 86 (August 1939)

Eckbo, Garrett, Daniel Urban Kiley, and James C. Rose, "Landscape Design in the Primeval Environment," *Architectural Record* 87 (February 1940)

Gill, B., "Landscapes of Joy," *Architectural Digest Magazine* 50 (March 1993)

Gillette, Jane Brown, "Kiley Re-visited," *Landscape Architecture* 88, no. 8 (August 1998)

Hilderbrand, Gary R., *The Miller Garden: Icon of Modernism,* Washington, D.C.: Spacemaker Press, 1999

Korab, Balthazar, *Columbus, Indiana,* Kalamazoo, Michigan: Documan Press, 1989

Saunders, William S., editor, *Daniel Urban Kiley: The Early Gardens,* New York: Princeton Architectural Press, 1999

Walker, Peter, and Simo, Melanie, *Invisible Gardens: The Search for Modernism in the American Landscape,* Cambridge, Massachusetts: MIT Press, 1994

Yamada, Michiko, editor, *Dan Kairi no rando sukepu dezain II: katari kakeru shizen; Dan Kiley, Landscape Design II: In Step with Nature* (bilingual Japanese-English edition), Tokyo: Process Architecture, 1993

Zapatka, Christian, *The American Landscape,* New York: Princeton Architectural Press, 1996

PAUL C. SICILIANO, JR.

Kingdon-Ward, Francis 1885–1958

English Plant Hunter

In a plant hunting career that spanned 47 years, Frank Kingdon-Ward made 23,000 collections of seeds during 22 trips to China, Burma, and Tibet. He published 137 papers on botany and geography and more than 20 books. Some of his best-known plant introductions include *Rhododendron wardi, Primula burmanica, Meconopsis betonicifolia, Primula florindae, Cotoneaster conspicuous, Rhododendron macabeanum,* and *Lilium macklinae.*

Kingdon-Ward may have inherited his interest in botany from his father, Henry Marshall Ward, who held the chair of botany at Cambridge University. As a boy he overheard a conversation that included the offhand comment, "Up the Brahmaputra where no white man has ever been," words that he said inspired his fascination with the unexplored regions of the world. Soon after completing his education, Kingdon-Ward took a job as a teacher in Singapore; although he had little interest in teaching, the job brought him closer to his dream of exploring tropical forests.

Kingdon-Ward's first opportunity to travel into the interior of China in 1909 involved collecting animal specimens on an expedition with Malcom Anderson, an American zoologist. He managed to assemble a small plant collection on the side, which he sent to the Botany School at Cambridge. His career as a plant collector began in earnest with his second trip. When Arthur Kilpin Bulley, founder of the Bees Seed Company, lost his previous collector, George Forrest, he asked Kingdon-Ward to make an expedition to Yunnan on behalf of the company. Kingdon-Ward leapt at the chance and left Shanghai early in 1911. After a harrowing journey that involved two boats, a train, a steamboat, and a mule, he arrived in Yunnan in February. At one point he became separated from his guides and could not find his way back to camp. Starving, he ate rhododendron flowers, which made him sick, and a finch, which he blasted at point-blank range with his only bullet. During this same trip he was thrown by a mule and forced to travel to safety 180 miles (290 km) out of his way because of a threat that the Chinese revolutionaries planned to kill any Englishman they found. As a plant collecting expedition the trip was not particularly successful. Although he sent back several new species to Bulley, including *Saxifraga wardii* and *Gentiana wardii,* the plants did not do well in cultivation. He returned to Yunnan twice more, in 1913 and 1921, making large collections of rhododendrons and primulas. His most significant contribution to botany, however, came during his later trips to Assam, Burma, and Tibet.

The eastern Himalayas, where the borders of Burma, China, and Tibet come together, had many unexplored areas that were rumored to have the most spectacular flora in the world. Kingdon-Ward made numerous expeditions to these regions and brought back many new plants, including *Primula burmanica* and the slipper orchid, *Paphiopedilum wardii.* His most famous journey was the 1924–25 trip to the region of the Tsangpo River, where 50 miles (80 km) of unexplored gorges were thought to have spectacular waterfalls. Here, he found some of his most celebrated plants, including the blue poppy.

The history of the blue poppy, *Meconopsis betonicifolia baileyi,* is an interesting one. The flower was first collected by the French missionary J.M. Delavay, who found a specimen in the Chinese province of Yunnan and sent back mounted samples to Paris in 1886. It was classified as a new species in 1889 and named *M. betonicifolia* because its leaves resembled betony. In 1913 Colonel Frederick Bailey—whose primary purpose was to map the Tsangpo River through the unexplored, near-vertical gorges that were rumored to contain waterfalls the size of Niagara—found fields covered with spectacular blue poppies near the Rong River in southeastern Tibet. Bailey was not a professional plant collector and was not particularly excited by what he had found, but he had the foresight to send specimens back to the Royal Botanic Gardens, Kew, in England, where they were classified as a new species and given the name *M. baileyi.* Neither Delavay nor Bailey collected seeds. This task was left to George Forrest, who, after many years of searching, found Delavay's original site. He collected seed, which he sent back to England. Unfortunately, every one of the cultivated plants failed, and the blue poppy was set aside as a horticultural curiosity.

Surprisingly, 75 percent of the blue poppy seeds collected by Kingdon-Ward during his 1924 expedition to the Tsangpo region germinated, and the resulting plants were displayed at the 1925 Royal Horticultural Society Chelsea Flower Show. They were an immediate and enduring success; today, more blue poppies grow under cultivation than are growing in the wild. Kingdon-Ward himself painted one of the best word pictures of the plant: "The flowers flutter out from amongst the sea-green leaves like blue-and-gold butterflies; each is borne singly on a pedicel, the plant carrying half a dozen nodding, incredibly blue four-petalled flowers, with a wad of golden anthers in the centre." Examination of the specimens collected by Kingdon-Ward led to the determination that *M. baileyi* was the same species as *M. betonicifolia.* The only remaining mystery was why the Chinese blue poppy did so poorly while the Tibetan variety proved to be so easy to cultivate. Specialists now feel that Bailey's plant was actually a variety within the species. On this same expedition Kingdon-Ward found *Lilium wardii* and *Cotoneaster conspicuous,* as well as at least ten new species of rhododendron. He also solved the mystery of the Tsangpo waterfall. Instead of the spectacular 165-foot (50-m) drop that had been rumored, he found several smaller cascades.

Kingdon-Ward made five more expeditions to the eastern Himalayas after World War II, accompanied by his second wife, Jean Macklin, after whom he named a species of the pink Manipur lily, *Lilium mackliniae.* On one of their trips the couple was camped 25 miles (40.2 km) from the epicenter of one of the most powerful earthquakes ever recorded in Burma, in which even the crests of mountains were broken off. Because Kingdon-Ward had noticed slight tremors earlier in the week and had pitched his tents on open ground, he and his wife were unscathed.

The Royal Geographical Society honored Kingdon-Ward in 1930 with its Founder's Gold Medal. In 1932 the Royal Horticultural Society awarded him its highest honor, the Victoria Medal of Honour in Horticulture, as well as the Veitch Memorial Medal in 1933. He also received the Royal Scottish Geographical Society's Livingstone Gold Medal in 1936 for his contributions to geography and travel literature. In 1952 he received the Order of the British Empire for his contributions to horticulture. Systematic botanists gave the names of the genera *Kingdon-wardia* and *Wardaster* and the epithets *kingdonii, wardii,* and *kingdonwardii* to the many plants Kingdon-Ward introduced. He was particularly successful in finding hardy plants, many of which are garden staples today.

Biography

Born in Lancaster, England, 6 November 1885. Read natural sciences at Christ's College, Cambridge, but was forced to cut studies short by sudden death of father, 1906; served as second lieutenant in Indian infantry during World War I; served in World War II teaching jungle survival to airmen in Poona, India; after World War II, employed by United States to find aircraft lost in mountains between India and China; scaled Mount Victoria, Burma, then traveled on to Sri Lanka, 1956. Died in London, 8 April 1958.

Selected Publications

Land of the Blue Poppy, 1913
Mystery Rivers of Tibet, 1923
Riddle of the Tsangpo Gorges, 1926
Plant Hunter's Paradise, 1937
Assam Adventure, 1941
Pilgrimage for Plants, 1960
Himalayan Enchantment: An Anthology, 1990

Further Reading

Elliott, Charles, *The Transplanted Gardener,* New York: Lyons and Burford, 1995; London: Viking, 1996
Healey, Ben J., *The Plant Hunters,* New York: Scribner, 1975
Lyte, Charles, *Frank Kingdon-Ward: The Last of the Great Plant Hunters,* London: John Murray, 1989
Musgrave, Toby, Chris Gardner, and Will Musgrave, *The Plant Hunters,* London: Ward Lock, 1998

KAREN MEYERS

Kirstenbosch National Botanical Garden

Cape Town, South Africa

Location: 8 miles (13 km) from Cape Town city center

Kirstenbosch, situated in the heart of the Cape Floral Kingdom, is a world-renowned botanic garden and center of scientific research. The world is divided into six floral kingdoms, each of which represents a community of plants. The Cape Floral Kingdom, although the smallest in area, supports a rich variety of plants known as *fynbos.* Many of the plants of the *fynbos* are found in the Cape Peninsula, where Kirstenbosch is situated. This great diversity of plants has made it possible for Kirstenbosch to cultivate and display only plants indigenous to southern Africa. The variety of plants and the natural beauty of the area have contributed to Kirstenbosch being of intense interest to both researchers and laypeople. Situated on the eastern slope of Table Mountain, Kirstenbosch is one of the most beautiful botanic gardens in the world.

The origin of the name Kirstenbosch is uncertain; a number of families with the name Kirsten lived in the vicinity, and with time the area became known as Kirstenbosch (Kirsten's Forest). Kirstenbosch was inhabited long before the arrival of the European settlers in the 17th century. Traces of large pear-shaped stone implements and round perforated stones that were used as weight-pointed digging sticks have been found. The boundary of the Cape colony was established by early settlers, who in 1670 planted a hedge of *Braebejum stellatifolium*, a member of the family *Proteaceae*. This hedge, which was 3,673 roods (.25 acres [.1 ha]) long, was established to prevent the Hottentot tribes from stealing the settler's cattle. Today it is the oldest living relic of the first European settlement in South Africa and can be seen along the southern boundary of the garden. The mountain slopes were covered with indigenous trees that for two centuries were a source of firewood and building materials. South African trees and forests are slow growing, and the early colonists were soon faced with shortages. To alleviate this problem the settlers planted rapid-growing trees from Australia and Europe. Kirstenbosch was directly affected by these activities and inherited its full share of aliens. The dominant species were *Quercus robur, Populus canescens, Pinus pinaster, Alnus glutinosa, Eucalyptus* spp., *Acacia longifolia,* and *A. melanoxyon.*

In 1811, while the area was under British occupation, a Colonel Bird and Henry Alexander were granted land there. Both built houses, one at the foot of Window Gorge and the other on the site where the original Tea House was situated. Colonel Bird discovered a fountain with a constant stream of clear water on his property, and he built a pool around it for protection from silt and mud. It was built in the shape of a bird and has become a focal point of the garden today. In 1823, the Eksteen family acquired both these properties, which were later passed on to the Cloete family. The area was farmed, and oaks, fruit trees, and vines planted. Cecil John Rhodes purchased the property in 1895 and appointed a caretaker. The area became run-down, with many pigs feeding on acorns and wallowing in the muddy pools. In 1898 an avenue of camphor trees was planted, which provided a wonderful shady walk up to the higher areas of the garden. Sadly, an airborne fungus has attacked some of these majestic trees. However, the disease has been arrested, and the Kirstenbosch staff are hopeful of a complete recovery to the trees' former glory. Rhodes died in 1902, bequeathing Kirstenbosch to the people of South Africa as part of his great Groote Schuur estate. For some time Kirstenbosch was abandoned and neglected; in fact it was almost 20 years before Kirstenbosch came under the control of its trustees. Hundreds of pigs continued to grub for acorns under the shady oak trees. The orchards and vineyards were overwhelmed with alien weeds, brambles, wattles, and pines, while Colonel Bird's bath was filled with sand and rubbish, and the old buildings of the Kirstenbosch homestead crumbled into ruins.

Harold Pearson came to South Africa in 1903 from the Royal Botanical Gardens, Kew, to fill the newly established Chair of Botany at the South African College. Pearson's drive and determination contributed a great deal to the eventual realization of Kirstenbosch. In February 1911 Pearson hired a Cape cart (a horse-drawn, two-wheeled vehicle with suspension and a canopy for the transportation of people), and upon a suggestion of his friend Neville Pillans, visited Kirstenbosch to assess its suitability as a site for a botanic garden. They were accompanied by G.H. Ridley, who was the curator of the Cape Municipal Gardens. On 18 July 1913 the wild and overgrown estate of Kirstenbosch was set aside by the government with a grant of £1,000 per annum. Pearson was the obvious choice for director, but there was no money for his salary. He accepted the task in an honorary capacity. In the winter of 1913, Pearson and his wife left their comfortable suburban home to occupy a dilapidated woodsman's cottage at Kirstenbosch. Margaret Levyns, a botany student from Cambridge invited to tea at their temporary home, described the house as "consisting of two, small, rat-infested rooms, damp in winter and dusty in summer. Cooking is carried out under a lean-to structure outside." Four days each week Pearson worked at the South African College. He devoted Wednesdays and weekends to Kirstenbosch.

Finance was a great problem, and in the early days the government grant of £1,000 was supplemented by the sale of firewood and acorns. When work started on the garden, Pearson was confronted by the ruins of the Cloete homestead, thousands of pigs grubbing in the orchards, and bush obscuring the bath. He had to clear the area of undergrowth and pigs and create the order of a botanic garden. He began with what is known as the Dell, planting cycads. The curator, Joseph William Mathews, also from Kew, assisted Pearson. Their expertise complemented each other, and when they set to work with vigor and determination they achieved great results. The first task was to lay out a nursery. Before the end of the first year, a nursery of 2,000 square meters (2,392 sq. yd.), complete with terracing and fencing, had been organized. Mathews and his staff cleared the ruins of Kirstenbosch's old homestead, built a shed in the nursery, constructed pathways (approximately 2.5 miles, or 4 km, in total), and began planting indigenous grass to establish the first lawns. They planted about an acre (.4 ha.) of oats on the slopes, where Mathews's rockery stands today, to provide forage for their horses, and they built 19 benches, which were placed at suitable sites. Within the garden itself, Pearson and Mathews started in the area in which Colonel Bird had built his bath and which they soon named the

Dell because of its extraordinary beauty. With the bath cleared, the bed of the stream flowing from the springs was paved with flat-topped stones so that water could flow in between. Even a waterfall, designed to look as natural as possible, was included. *Streptocarpus* and ferns were planted. Today it is difficult for people to realize that water from the bath once flowed down a gentle slope and that shade was provided by oak trees, affording welcome shelter until the indigenous trees, well known today, became large enough to replace them. In the natural amphitheater above, what was soon to be the impressive collection of one of South Africa's botanical curiosities, the cycad collection (*Encephalartos*) (see Plate 18), was planted. Pearson was interested in gymnosperms, and his enthusiasm and drive resulted in a large collection of cycads, being established in the amphitheater.

In 1915 Pearson moved to the newly built director's house, and his temporary dwelling became his office. Tragically, in 1916, at the age of 46, he died from pneumonia. This was a severe blow to the garden. He was buried on the slopes overlooking the Dell and the cycad amphitheater that he had lovingly created. Beside his grave grows one of the most beautiful gymnosperms, a blue Atlas cedar (*Cedrus atlantica* var. *glauca*), donated by the Royal Botanic Gardens, Kew. His epitaph reads, "If ye seek his monument, look around."

Finances continued to pose challenges, and a scheme was introduced whereby Mathews trained gardeners to work in the garden in return for free lodging. World War I and the Great Depression handicapped these early years, but from about 1919 Kirstenbosch began to make progress again.

In 1919 Professor Robert Harold Compton arrived from England to assume directorship. He and Mathews were responsible for an enormous amount of development. By 1926 the developed features in the garden were the *Protea* Garden, the Horseshoe Path, Cycad Amphitheater, the Dell below Colonel Bird's Bath, the Annuals and *Pelargonium* Garden, *Mesembryanthemum* Bank, *Aloe* Kopje (hill), the *Erica* Garden, and the Great Lawn. Abundant water and the natural suitability material of Table Mountain sandstone for building made possible the development of the garden's basic infrastructure. Due to the interesting and sometimes challenging topography, a great deal of construction work was necessary. Drystone walls to support terracing on the steep slopes, bridges over many streams, rockeries, roads, drinking fountains, pathways, steps, rock features, and entrance gates have all been built of the Table Mountain sandstone. This stonework has been created by local garden staff, which has become very skilled in stonemasonry. The layout of Kirstenbosch is informal, and the natural stone features provide a strong and harmonious thread throughout the garden. Not all features were a success. Rocks and soil were transported to create a kopje, which Pearson had hoped would be one of the most prominent features in the garden. It was planted with a number of *Aloe* species that, if they had been successful, would have provided a magnificent display of color in the winter months.

Unfortunately, the aloes succumbed to diseases, and the climate at Kirstenbosch was not very suitable. The kopje remains and has merged, with age, into its surroundings. Spring and summer annuals, pelargoniums, and the only surviving aloe, *Aloe plicatilis*, now grow in this area. Another feature that Pearson attempted was the establishment of an avenue of Cape chestnut (*Calodendron capense*) leading up to Colonel Bird's house. Initially, the trees did well, but one by one they died. Only one or two remain today; it is probable that the Cape summers are too dry for their survival. Sadly, the dream of establishing a magnificent flowering chestnut avenue was not to be. Although some of the original plants were not successful, many did flourish, and today the Dell, the Cycad Amphitheater, and the lawn are living testimonies to the flare, imagination, skill, and hard work of the Kirstenbosch staff.

The prime objective of Kirstenbosch was to conserve, study, promote, and display the flora of southern Africa. In the early days the garden was inundated with plants donated by the public in support of the garden's development. By 1925 Kirstenbosch had received 32,647 contributions of seed and plants. Garden staff had great difficulties coping with all the plant material because of their limited resources. As the infrastructure of the garden developed, greater emphasis was placed on the living plant collections, and plant-collecting expeditions were arranged to gather material for the garden. The focus was on cycads (*Encephalartos*) and *Proteaceae* (including *Protea, Leucospermum*, *Leucadendron*, *Serruria,* and *Aulax*).

Heath plants (*Erica*) form another important Kirstenbosch collection; today many of the 600 species that occur in the Cape are displayed (see Plate 19). Early on, another important group of plants that was concentrated on was the spring-flowering annuals from Namaqualand. These included numerous daisies of *Ursinia, Dimorphotheca, Arctotis, Nemesia Heliophila,* and many other species that provided breathtaking displays of color in the spring. As the infrastructure in the nursery improved, the succulent and bulb collections were able to develop. High winter rainfall called for shelter for succulents, and many of the bulbs required protection from moles and porcupine. Unfortunately, many of these bulbous plants could not be displayed in the garden. *Agapanthus* and *Dietes,* which flower in midsummer, and the spring-flowering *Watsonia* were exceptions and could be planted throughout the garden.

With the increase in horticultural staff during the 1960s, the living plant collections continued to grow. Important collections that developed were the restios (*Restionaceae*), an important component of the *fynbos* with great horticultural potential. During the 1990s a restio garden was developed in the upper reaches of Kirstenbosch. The herbaceous collection contributed many fascinating horticultural subjects, such as the *Wahlenbergia* species, *Scabiosa, Leonotis,* and *Hypoestes,* which contributed largely toward the improvement of summer displays.

The early garden development involved the construction of many pathways for easy access. With the installation of an extensive water reticulation system in the 1970s, many pathways were removed and instead flowing lawns established, which considerably reduced maintenance, enhanced the beauty of the garden, and provided a sponge to absorb much of the heavy winter rainfall.

No history of Kirstenbosch would be adequate without emphasizing the vital role of the Botanical Society of South Africa. The first general meeting of the society was held on 31 July 1913—one month after the official handing over of Kirstenbosch to the board of trustees. The objectives of the society were to encourage the public of South Africa to take an active part in the development of Kirstenbosch and to augment government grants. These intentions have been fully realized, and much of the success of Kirstenbosch can be attributed to the dedicated and ongoing support from the Council and members of the botanical society.

Buildings at Kirstenbosch have developed in a rather fitful fashion. When Pearson arrived at Kirstenbosch, the only building left standing was an old woodsman's cottage, and until the 1990s, it was often a case of making do. One of the first important buildings to materialize was the Bolus Herbarium (later renamed the Compton Herbarium). The Lecture Hall was built to provide a venue to hold nature study classes for local schools. The Kirstenbosch Tea House provided a popular place for tea and scones and in the last 30 years has also become famous for its Sunday lunches. The meager staff facilities remained unchanged until the 1990s, when a large capital development program was undertaken. This has resulted in the Kirstenbosch Research Center, Botanical Society Conservatory for the display of plants from arid regions, a Visitors' Center that includes shops, a conference center, and a first-class restaurant. With the completion of this extensive building program, Kirstenbosch is in a strong position to move into the 21st century.

Synopsis

1913 Kirstenbosch Estate under control of Trustees

1914 Work begun on Director's House on Wynberg Hill, Cape chestnut avenue, rockwork along Bath stream; tree ferns planted; cycad Amphitheater planted with over 200 plants of 13 species

1915 Government grant reduced; only one gardener left during WWI; orchids and pelargonium gardens laid out; cycad collection greatly increased; meteorological records started

1916 Two acres (.8 ha.) cleared for *Protea* garden above Cycad Amphitheater (400 protea planted); 1,111 square m (1,330 square yd.) dug in main lawn for aquatic plants

1917 Female gardeners trained; construction of Fern Dell completed

1918 Six cottages for workers built on protea village boundary; cave constructed below outlet to bath

1919 Transfer of Bolus herbarium from University of Cape Town

1920 Government grant increased; horseshoe path around cycad Amphitheater started; construction work at Bath completed; *Erica* garden laid out

1921 Stone bridge built over Nursery-Skeleton stream at foot of lawn, providing better entrance for visitors; water system constructed; transfer of 680 acres (272 ha) to trustees from the Forestry Department (Upper Kirstenbosch Nature Reserve)

1922 Building of Bolus Herbarium begun

1923 Tea House built using funds from Botanical Society and private subscriptions

1926 Curator's office, glasshouse, potting shed, and succulent house built; *Protea* and *Erica* gardens extended; water reservoir extended to supply entire garden

1927 Succulent garden planned and curator's house built

1929 Area around historical Van Riebeeck's Hedge cleared

1934 Government undertakes to maintain buildings; horseshoe path completed

1935 Van Riebeeck's Hedge declared national monument

1939 Large glasshouse for winter care of small succulents built; trustees establish a garden herbarium

1962 Mrs. I.G. Lübbert donates approximately 87.5 acres (35 ha) of Fernwood Estate (adjoins Kirstenbosch); becomes known as Lübbert's Gift

1970 Upgrading of *Protea* garden; plans for water reticulation system

1972 Re-landscaping and development of *Erica* garden

1976–77 Removal of paths and establishment of lawns

1980 Establishment of Braille Trail and Fragrance Garden

1992 Computerization of the irrigation system
1996 Botanical Society Conservatory opened
1997 Opening of the Water-Wise Garden

Further Reading

Compton, Robert Harold, *Kirstenbosch, Garden for a Nation: Being the Story of the First 50 Years of the National Botanic Gardens of South Africa, 1913–1963,* Cape Town: Tafelberg, 1965

McCracken, Donal P., and Eileen M. McCracken, *The Way to Kirstenbosch,* Cape Town: National Botanic Gardens, 1988

Paterson-Jones, Colin, *A Visitor's Guide to Kirstenbosch,* Claremont, South Africa: National Botanical Institute, 1993

Rycroft, Brian Hedley, and Ray Ryan, *Kirstenbosch,* Aylesbury: Timmins, 1980

JOHN WINTER

Kitchen Garden. *See* Potager (Kitchen Garden)

Klein-Glienicke

Berlin, Germany

Location: northeast of Potsdam on the banks of the river Havel, approximately 6 miles (9.7 km) southwest of Berlin city center

In 1816 the Prussian state's chancellor Prince Karl August von Hardenberg commissioned the young gardener Peter Joseph Lenné to create a pleasure ground in front of the prince's villa, Klein-Glienicke, near Potsdam. This estate, which now is a part of Berlin, is situated on the banks of the Havel River and touches the main road from Berlin to Potsdam, called Königstrasse. Magnificent views stretch over the river, widened here to lakelike dimensions, to the distant hills and the town of Potsdam in the west. The garden was Lenné's first work in Prussia.

After Hardenberg's death in 1822, the new owner, Prince Karl, who used it as his summer residence, ordered alterations on a large scale. Each of the sons of King Friedrich Wilhelm III became owner of an impressive estate and park: Karl at Klein-Glienicke in 1822, Friedrich Wilhelm IV at Charlottenhof in 1826, Wilhelm I at Babelsberg in 1833, and Albrecht at Albrechtsberg near Dresden in 1850. Karl Friedrich Schinkel and his successors designed the buildings and Lenné the park for Prince Karl. The idea was to create the impression of an Italian estate. Prince Karl had visited Italy with his elder brother, the future king Friedrich Wilhelm IV, in 1822. Several antique fragments brought back from this tour were integrated into the new ensemble. The villa, the casino on the river, two outlook buildings facing the road, and the cloister court were either built or transformed in an Italianate style. The courtyard of the villa is laid out as a flower garden, characterized by a pergola with climbing *Passiflora* and *Aristolochia,* little beds, orange tubs, and a fountain crowned by the *Ildefonso* group reminiscent of Goethe's mansion in Weimar. Ludwig Persius constructed the glasshouse with curvilinear roofs in 1839 after the then fashionable English model. The visitor is overwhelmed by magnificent views from the terrace and the pergola of the casino, with the Italianate towers of the belvedere and the silhouette of Villa Henckel (Potsdam) on the horizon and—at the right hour—the sun setting behind the distant hills. A semicircular bench (*stibadium*) in the eastern background of the pleasure ground offers another fascinating view toward the cupola of Potsdam's Saint Nicolai Church. The bench faces a granite bowl, an arrangement clearly inspired by the fountain in front of the Villa Medici in Rome. Each son of Friedrich Wilhelm III inherited a granite bowl from his father. Prince Karl transformed his into a fountain. The monumental gilded lion's fountain in front of the villa was inspired by the Villa Medici as well.

From 1840 onward Lenné transformed the large park on the northern and eastern sides of the villa into a vast landscape garden, thereby simulating a journey from Italy via the Alps and Germany into Britain. Included is an alpine Devil's Bridge, a beech wood, and a hunting court in the Tudor style. From the northern end the Heilandskirche (Savior's Church) near Sacrow appears on the opposite bank of the river, constructed mainly as a visual focus.

After Prince Karl's death in 1885 the estate was neglected and all of its interior sold. In 1979 the Berlin Garden Preservation Board began reconstruction of the pleasure ground. Filled-in paths, basins, and flower beds were excavated and statues were recast. Present preservation work is focused on the state of development around 1850. Alternating views from the garden to the Havel grounds and toward Potsdam have been reopened. The original garden structure, its flower beds, fountains, and benches have been restored. A special feature is the tile-work edging of the beds in the shape of palmettes, lilies, corals, and acanthus. The greater park, however, has not been reconstructed. For example, the romantic lake on the east side of the villa is still without water.

Extending along Königstrasse to the south is the Jagdschlosspark. Originally created around a hunting lodge of the great elector in the late 17th century, it was redesigned into a landscape garden in 1862 by Lenné or Gustav Meyer for Prince Friedrich Karl, the son of Prince Karl. Different views link this small park with the larger one on the northern side and with the Havel River and the Babelsberg estate in the south. In 1939 construction work to widen the Königstrasse caused large soil deposits on the banks of both parks.

From 1984 to 1987 the Jagdschlosspark was reconstructed. Approximately 20,000 cubic meters (26,160 cu. yd.) of soil were removed, and the network of paths and the pond were restored. This pond connects with the Havel and the pleasure ground on the northern side. An avenue lined with lime trees leads eastward from the castle. It has survived from the original 17th-century conception. In the 1860s Prince Karl had several Swiss-style cottages constructed along this alley by the royal architect Ferdinand von Arnim, who also redesigned his castle. The surrounding somewhat hilly land was also designed in alpine style with artificial rockwork borders and serpentine pathways up to "Boettcherberg," a wooded hill offering open views to Babelsberg, Potsdam, Sanssouci, and the Havel River. Its top is crowned with an open lodge, devoted to the Czaress Alexandra, a sister of Prince Karl (1869).

From 1961 until 1989 the wall between Potsdam and West Berlin divided the Glienicke ensemble into several parts. Because of their location immediately joining the border, some important buildings dating from Prince Karl's time were demolished.

Synopsis

1816 Peter Joseph Lenné creates pleasure ground for Prince Hardenberg

1822 Death of Hardenberg, estate passed to Prince Karl, who made large-scale alterations

1824–60 Integration of surrounding woods and hills by Lenné for Prince Karl

1839 Curvilinear glasshouse constructed by Ludwig Persius

1840– Lenné designs and builds landscape park

1860–62 Creation of Jagdschlosspark by Lenné for Prince Karl's son, Prince Friedrich Karl

1961 Berlin Wall between Potsdam and West Berlin divides Glienicke estate into several parts

1979–85 Preservation work in pleasure grounds by Berlin Garden Preservation Board

1984–87 Jagdschlosspark restored

Further Reading

Landesdenkmalamt Berlin, *Gartenkunst Berlin: 20 Jahre Gartendenkmalpflege in der Metropole,* Berlin: Schelzky and Jeep, 1999

Ostergard, Derek E., and Ilse Baer, *Along the Royal Road: Berlin and Potsdam in KPM Porcelain and Painting, 1815–1848,* New York: Bard Graduate Center for Studies in the Decorative Arts, 1993

Seiler, Michael, "Die Entwicklung des Landschaftsgartens Klein-Glienicke, 1796–1883," Ph.D. diss., Hochschule für Bildende Künste, Hamburg, 1986

CLEMENS ALEXANDER WIMMER

Kleve

North Rhine-Westphalia, Germany

Location: 66 miles (106 km) west-southwest of Münster

A castle on the cliff (Kleve) is mentioned in writings before the end of the first millenium A.D., and Kleve received its town charter from its duke, Dietrich VI, on 25 April 1242. The present town consists of three elements that have grown and combined: the castle enclave; the village lying beneath it; and the town created by Dietrich on the Heideberg, the opposite side of a valley created by a dried-up stream of the Rhine estuary.

In November 1647, the elector of Brandenburg appointed as governor the founder of the modern town and the creator of its garden layout, Prince Johann Moritz von Nassau-Siegen, former governor of Brazil (1636–44). Moritz was to oversee the integration of parks and gardens with the city, the first such development effort in Germany. Inspired by the woods, the multiple springs, and the falling away of the terrain from the height of the cliff, Moritz resolved first to create a garden of the arts with an amphitheater at its center that would blend with the forest and the garden site on Springenberg hill. The symmetrical rectilinear baroque garden, with a long straight-sided canal and geometrically patterned beds designed by the Dutch landscape architect Jacob von Campen, exploited garden architectural techniques that would soon be used at Versailles and Potsdam and that took their own inspiration from Italy and Holland.

By 1664 the castle had been converted into a baroque palace by the master-builder Pieter Post, and Moritz was building the governor's residence, the Prinzenhof. Helped by the team of artists and scholars he had assembled, he investigated, collected, and documented as appropriate whatever he could of the natural world, adopting as his working principle "Build, Dig, and Plant." He created a zoo and opened it to the public, thereby creating one of Germany's earliest public parks. His motto *Qua patet orbis* (as far as the earth's sphere reaches) reflects his preference for immensely long paths through the woods and unblocked vistas.

The high point and center of the landscape he created was the amphitheatre, the Italian terraced garden created around a spring on the north face of the Springenberg, in which Campen placed choice trees, fountains, and sculptures. Campen brought plants from Rome and planted Brazilian exotics, using souvenirs of the Thirty Years' War as decoration. At the center, from which radiated twelve vistas, was the marble statue of Minerva by Artus Quellinus given to Johann Moritz in 1660 by the town of Amsterdam. Hailed as a masterpiece of the harmonization of art and nature, the ensemble was finished by 1660. Its magnificent long canal stretching out toward the plain from the Schwanenburg remains to this day.

In 1741 a doctor, Johannes Blanckenhorn, discovered a curative spring at the bottom of the amphitheater. It became the foundation for the town's development into a spa, Bad Kleve. A Kurhaus was built next to the baroque gardens between 1846 and 1872 (now an important museum and gallery). In 1782 Ernst Julius von Büggenhagen started the construction of a forest garden on the opposite side of the road, near where the modern zoological gardens are to be found. He planted 156 different species of trees and shrubs. Within a score of years, however, Kleve had again been ravaged by the Napoleonic armies, and the Düsseldorf garden architect Maximilian Friedrich Weyhe changed the character of all the gardens in 1821 to make an English landscape park with serpentine paths, fountains with tall water jets, patches of lawn, and picturesque views. The straight canals of the original design, however, survive today, as do the 17th-century ponds surrounded by rhododendron, jasmine, and roses.

During the Prussian ascendancy of the 18th and 19th centuries, the gardens were not wholly neglected. Frederick I had the gallery restored for strollers in the old baroque garden, while Wilhelm IV himself took an interest in planning the temple (1858) and obelisk (1853–56), in order to terminate the earlier open vistas, as per the fashion of the day. More recently, since 1975 the garden designers Gustav and Rose Wörner have worked on restoring the town's gardens in order to respect the different periods of the past, and in 1993 the ensemble was designated a European Memorial Garden. The museum, completing the restoration, was opened in 1997.

Synopsis

1242	Kleve granted town charter
1453	Completion of Schwanenburg
1647	Johann Moritz von Nassau-Siegen becomes governor
1650–60	Creation of baroque gardens
1664	Conversion of Schwanenburg into baroque palace
1679	Death of Johann Moritz
1741	Discovery of spring water with curative properties
1782	Construction of forest garden
1846–	Construction of Kurhaus
1944–45	Destruction of Kleve by air raids
1950	Rebuilding of Schwanenburg and tower
1975	Restoration of gardens
1997	Opening of museum

Further Reading

Diedenhofen, Wilhelm A., *Klevische Gartenlust: Gartenkunst und Badebauten in Kleve,* Cleves, Germany: Freunde des Städtischen Museums Haus Koekkoek, 1994

Geisselbrecht-Capecki, Ursula, and Guido de Werd, *An den Wassern zu Cleve: Studien und Beiträge zur Garten- und Badegeschichte Kleves,* Cleves, Germany: Freunde des Städtischen Museums Haus Koekkoek, 1994

Anthony H.T. Levi

Knight, Richard Payne 1751–1824

English Scholar and Author

Richard Payne Knight was an English connoisseur, writer, and collector, famous for the estate he designed at Downton, Herefordshire, and for his writings about the picturesque. Educated privately and inheriting a fortune from his father in 1764, like many gentlemen of his class he traveled widely in Europe, first in 1772 in France and Italy and then in 1776 in Switzerland with the landscape painter John Robert Cozens. In 1777 he went to Sicily with the German artist Philipp Hackert and his pupil Charles Gore. Of this journey, which was undertaken perhaps in part to collect antiquities later to be sold, Knight kept a fully detailed and illustrated journal that is now preserved in the Goethe Archive in Weimar.

Before beginning all these travels, Knight had begun work on the designs for his house at Downton, assisted by a local architect, Thomas Pritchard. When Knight returned to England in 1778, the house was complete, asymmetrical in plan and built in a style that, for all the seemingly medieval battlements, he believed to be derived from Roman architecture. The interiors were filled out with clearly classical details. The principal room in the largest of the south towers, completed in 1782, was done like the Pantheon, with a coffered dome and an eye in the center. The exterior, which rises dramatically over the Teme, for all its irregularity and castellation, is in its effect similar to the fortified houses

House and grounds of Downton Castle, Herefordshire, England
Courtesy of British Library

House and grounds of Downton Castle, Herefordshire, England
Courtesy of British Library

often seen in the background of works by Claude Lorraine, as in the painting *The View of La Crescenza,* which Knight once owned.

It was such an idea of what can be called the picturesque style that Knight used in the gardens, completed over the next ten years, and wrote of also in *The Landscape, a Didactic Poem* (1794). The term *Picturesque* had been found in Italian as early as 1654. If it may sometimes refer to what in 1791 William Gilpin spoke of as objects "proper for painting," more generally by the end of the 18th century it had come to be reserved for a particular idea of landscape design, a style that led to more varied, even rougher plantings than those seen immediately before this in the gardens of Lancelot "Capability" Brown or Humphry Repton. In place of the undulating lawns that Brown would bring right up to the windows of the house, along the south front of Downton, Knight built a terrace, deliberately contrasting nature and the manmade, the wildness and ruggedness of the Teme valley with the structure placed within it. Throughout the park there were what a visitor of the time enthusiastically called wild and solitary paths.

Behind this was a theory, elaborated both by Knight and by his friend Sir Uvedale Price and also Gilpin, in which a category was established between the accounts of the beautiful and the sublime, which Edmund Burke had so famously laid out in his *Philosophical Inquiry into the Origin of Our Ideas of the Sublime and the Beautiful* (1756). Something of the delight in mountains that Knight expressed or in irregular and half-seen shapes, even the low viewing points that the Picturesque called for often, came from the idea of the experiences Burke set in the sublime. But to this, Knight added something of the idea of association of which Archibald Allison had written in his *Essays on the Nature and Principle of Taste* (1790), arguing for an account of our perception of the world that is colored as much by our experiences of it as from anything reason would suggest; hence Knight's delight in sites such as Loch Tay and the Falls of the Clyde, or the streams at Betws y Coad and a waterfall nearby that had what he called "a hard Welsh name." All this Knight laid out in his volume *An Analytical Inquiry into the Principles of Taste* (1805). In arguing that art was concerned with associations and memory, Knight went further than anything his former colleague Price had said. Yet in believing that painting was essentially about visual appearances, he was also contradicting the new notions of neoclassicism that held, as classicism had in the past, that the value of art came from the idea of a selection and discrimination in what of nature was represented.

In 1781 Knight had been elected to the Society of the Dilettanti, and it was under their auspices that Knight worked with the collector Charles Townley on the two-volume *Specimens of Ancient Sculpture* (1809–1835). And in 1805 he was one of the founder members of the British Institution, set up to encourage native artists; indeed he was an active patron of British painters, commissioning works by Thomas Lawrence, John Hamilton Mortimer, and especially Richard Westhall. Knight had also long been a collector of both antiquities and drawings and paintings, many of which he bequeathed to the British Museum. All this made him, for a moment, a supreme arbiter of taste in England; but he also had his critics. His volume *An Account of the Remains of the Worship of Priapus* (1786), based on both the work of the French scholar Baron d'Hancarville and on information from Sir William Hamilton, had been considered obscene and blasphemous. When later, in 1815, in giving evidence for the Parliamentary Select Committee on the purchase of the Elgin Marbles, Knight criticized their quality, he found himself isolated from what was by then the general artistic opinions. His influence now over, he busied himself with scholarship, as in his *Inquiry into the Symbolical Language of Ancient Art and Mythology* (1818); but this work was too learned to attract much attention.

Biography

Born 1751. Designed own home, Downton Castle, Herefordshire, England, ca. 1771, before leaving to tour Europe, 1772–78; returned to England, 1778, and became one of supreme arbiters of taste in England; elected to the Society of Dilettanti, 1781; founding member of British Institution, 1805. Died in London, 1824.

Selected Designs

ca. 1771 Downton Castle, Herefordshire, England

Selected Publications

An Account of the Remains of the Worship of Priapus, 1786; 2nd edition, as *A Discourse on the Worship of Priapus,* 1865

The Landscape, a Didactic Poem in Three Books, 1794

An Analytical Inquiry into the Principles of Taste, 1805

Specimens of Ancient Sculpture, 2 vols., 1809–35

An Inquiry into the Symbolical Language of Ancient Art and Mythology, 1818; 2nd edition, as *The Symbolical Language of Antient Art and Mythology: An Inquiry,* 1876

Further Reading

Ballantine, A., "Downton Castle: Function and Meaning," *Architectural History* 32 (1989)

Clarke, Michael, and Nicholas Penny, editors, *The Arrogant Connoisseur: Richard Payne Knight, 1751–1824,* Manchester: Manchester University Press, 1982

Hussey, Christopher, *The Picturesque: Studies in a Point of View,* London and New York: Putnam, 1927; reprint, London: Cass, 1983

Pevsner, Nikolaus, *Studies in Art, Architecture, and Design,* 2 vols., London: Thames and Hudson, and Princeton, New Jersey: Princeton University Press, 1968

DAVID CAST

Knot Garden

The knot garden was the most fashionable type of garden in Tudor England. The overall design was in the form of a square, subdivided into a variety of shapes that were then outlined on the ground with low hedges of herbs such as thyme, hyssop, lavender, and marjoram. The garden derives its name from the way these herbs were grown with the hedges appearing to weave over and under each other to imitate interlacing knots. The spaces between the hedges were filled with other herbs or colored materials such as brick dust, marble chips, and sand.

Although there are no accounts of knot gardens in the medieval period, the use of knots as a decorative and symbolic element has a long history. The use of knotted designs is one of the distinguishing features of Celtic

Examples of different knot garden styles, taken from Gervase Markham's *Country Fair,* 1615

decoration, for example. It is not until the late 15th century, however, that the earliest known illustrations of knot gardens appear in the *Hypnerotomachia Poliphili* (The Dream of Polyphilus) written by an Italian monk, Francis Colonna, and published in Venice in 1499. One of the first mentions of knot gardens in England comes early in the 16th century in the love poem by Stephen Hawes, *The Passetime of Pleasure* (1509), in which he refers to a garden with "dyveres knottes, of mervaylous gretenes." No other descriptive details of the knots are given in this poem, but it is assumed that the form of the garden was similar to those illustrated in the *Hypnerotomachia.* Documents show that by the middle of the 16th century the use of the knot motif in gardens was found widely in Europe. Particularly good examples in French gardens can be seen in the drawings of the French architect Jacques Androuet du Cerceau, which were published in *Les plus excellents bastiments de France* (1576), showing geometric patterns in the gardens of French Renaissance palaces. In France these designs were called *parterres,* broadly equivalent to the *knot garden,* which was the name specifically used for this kind of garden in England.

There are an increasing number of references to knot gardens as the Tudor period progresses, but it was the publication in London of Thomas Hill's *The Proffitable Arte of Gardening* (1568) and *The Gardeners Labyrinth* (1608) that provided the first printed illustrations of knot patterns to be used in gardens. Although little is known about the personal life of Hill, he published a number of books on popular science, and his titles on gardening are sometimes described as the first gardening books in England. Such was their success that *The Gardeners Labyrinth* was reprinted regularly over the next hundred years. Although knot designs are included in the book, virtually no practical information is given as to how the knot should be laid out. Hill does, however, list the plants that he recommends and declares that thyme, hyssop, and winter savory are the best for making the hedges.

The next most important contribution to the history of knot gardens came with the publication of Richard Surflet's *Countrie Farme* in 1600, which was a translation of the comprehensive French work *Maison rustique* (1586 was the date of the first French edition illustrated with knot designs). In this work much more practical

Herb knot garden at Tradescant Garden, London
Copyright Clive Boursnell/Garden Picture Library

information is given as to how the designs should be laid out on the ground. Other significant garden books followed in England containing knot patterns: Gervase Markham's *The English Husbandman* (1635), which relies heavily on *Maison rustique,* and William Lawson's *The Countrie Housewifes Garden* (1617), which introduces new knot designs, some of which were clearly borrowed from the pattern books of carpenters, glaziers, and plasterers. Although a few of the designs are similar to those of Thomas Hill, gradually there is a move to more simple geometric shapes, and the use of knotted hedges begins to disappear, leaving simply a regular pattern of compartments.

The herbs thyme and hyssop continued to be the favored plants for making the hedges, and it was not until the publication of John Parkinson's famous book *Paradisi in Sole* (1629) that the advice comes that the best plant to use is box, "Which lastly, I chiefly and above all other herbes commend unto you." In this recommendation Parkinson is taking up the practice of the French royal gardener Claude Mollet, who first used box for the parterres at Saint-Germain in 1595. Parkinson also uses the term *open knots* to describe a garden of simple geometric shapes, which he says should be used for "outlandish flowers," by which he means plants that were then being introduced into England for the first time.

Fashions were changing in England in the first half of the 17th century, and during the 1630s Isaac de Caus, the garden designer and hydraulic engineer, laid out magnificent gardens at Wilton House near Salisbury in the latest continental style of *parterres de broderie.* However, the use of knots continued well past the middle of the century with such influential books as Stephen Blake's *Compleat Gardeners Practice* (1664) containing the "True Lovers Knott," which is still reminiscent of 16th-century Tudor designs. It is not until the end of the 17th century that the knot garden drops completely out of fashion to be replaced by the French *parterre de broderie.*

To some extent there has been a revival of interest in knot gardens in the 20th century in Britain, and a number of interesting restorations and recreations have taken place. Edzell Castle in Scotland, with its original garden walls and the date 1604 carved over the entrance portal, has a knot garden dating from the 1930s that is an attempt to recreate the kind of garden that would have been there in the early 17th century. At Moseley Old Hall (Staffordshire) and Little Moreton Hall (Cheshire) striking late 20th-century knot gardens have been created, based on early drawings and printed designs. A small but authentic knot garden was designed for the Tudor House in Southampton (Hampshire) using features from early 16th-century examples, with the pattern outlined by traditional herbs. A most magnificent garden has been planted at Hatfield House (Hertfordshire), where box hedges have been used to make a large-scale knot garden based on a variety of designs from early sources. Other examples can be seen at Red Lodge in Bristol and the Museum of Garden History in London.

Further Reading

Androuet du Cerceau, Jacques, *Les plus excellents bastiments de France,* 2 vols., Paris, 1576–79; reprint, Paris: Sand and Conti, 1988

Blake, Stephen, *The Compleat Gardeners Practice,* London, 1664

Colonna, Francesco, *Hypnerotomachia poliphili,* Venice, 1499; as *Hypnerotomachia Poliphili: The Strife of Love in a Dream,* translated by Joscelyn Godwin, London: Thames and Hudson, 1999

Estienne, Charles, and J. Liebault, *L'agriculture et maison rustique,* Paris, 1570; as *The Countrie Farme,* translated by Richard Surflet, London, 1600

Hawes, Stephen, *The Pastime of Pleasure,* London, 1509; reprint, Oxford and New York: Oxford University Press, 1928

Hill, Thomas, *The Proffitable Arte of Gardening,* London, 1568; 2nd edition, 1574

Hill, Thomas, *The Gardeners Labyrinth,* London, 1577; reprint, Oxford and New York: Oxford University Press, 1987

Lawson, William, *The Countrie Housewifes Garden,* London, 1617; reprint, Herrin, Illinois: Trovillion Private Press, 1948

Markham, Gervase, *The English Husbandman,* London, 1613–15; reprint, New York: Garland, 1982

Parkinson, John, *Paradisi in sole paradisus terrestris; or, A Garden of All Sorts of Pleasant Flowers,* London, 1629; reprint, as *A Garden of Pleasant Flowers,* New York: Dover, and London: Constable, 1976

Rockley, Alicia Margaret Tyssen-Amherst Cecil, Baroness, *A History of Gardening in England,* London, 1895; reprint, Detroit, Michigan: Singing Tree Press, 1969

Strong, Roy, *The Renaissance Garden in England,* London: Thames and Hudson, 1979

Verey, Rosemary, "Knots and Parterres: A Bibliography," *Garden History* 2, no. 2 (1974)

Whalley, Robin, and Anne Jennings, *Knot Gardens and Parterres: A History of the Knot Garden and How to Make One Today,* London: Barn Elms, 1998

ROBIN WHALLEY

København Botanisk Have

Copenhagen, Denmark

Location: central Copenhagen

The present day botanical garden was landscaped during the years 1871–74 on the old ramparts surrounding Copenhagen's inner city. The ten hectares (24.7 acres) of garden feature about 13,000 species, with the plants arranged partly by type and partly by geographic origin. The garden is affiliated with the Botany Department of the University of Copenhagen.

Copenhagen's first botanical garden was given to Copenhagen University by King Christian IV in 1600. It was a moderately sized medicinal herb garden laid out in connection with one of the professors' residences. Its early history parallels that of other botanical gardens of the time. In the 1620s, during a reformation of the university's teaching in medicine and botany, the scientist Ole Worm expanded the native herbs selection. He also introduced rare plants from collections abroad. In 1696 a private grant allowed for a gardener to be hired. A contemporary source gives an alphabetical list of the plants being replanted in 1719.

In 1752 King Frederik V commissioned the German botanist G.C. Oeder to lay out a botanical garden in the new city quarter of Frederiksstad. Initial works were carried out, but Oeder's plans for the garden were not fully realized. The public was first admitted to this garden in 1763. Oeder is best known for creating the scholarly publication on Danish national flora, *Flora Danica*

Palm House at København Botanisk Have
Photo by Omar Ingerslev, courtesy of København Botanisk Have

(1761–1883). The original copper plates and hand-colored engravings form part of the botanical garden's rich library holdings.

In 1778 the King bought back the land by the university and began the construction of a third garden. It was placed on the harbor front, as a continuation of the former Charlottenborg gardens. A museum and library formed part of the new facilities, and initiatives to strengthen their scientific activities were gradually implemented. The first botanical gardener had been appointed in Oeder's garden in 1770. There followed the appointment of a reader in 1778 and a professor in 1797. The earliest descriptions of the plant collections are by F.L. Holbøll, who was the botanical gardener from 1793 to 1829. The practice of registering every new acquisition, whether a seed or a plant, was introduced in 1790. The death of plants has also been registered continuously since then.

By the middle of the 19th century, the garden had developed into a repository of botanical collections. A section devoted to Danish plants was an important innovation. The flora of Danish colonies was featured in another section. In the well-equipped hothouses some 3,550 of the garden's 9,000 species were eventually displayed. Until 1841 the garden made money by selling plants and seed. The administrative influence of the Royal Court was eliminated in 1817. The botanical garden has since been under the auspices of the University of Copenhagen.

Lack of space and continuous environmental problems convinced the garden administration and staff to look for a new site outside the old city walls. In 1871, thanks to an extraordinary appropriation, the university could move the botanical garden to the fourth and present location. It was now to form part of a vast new green belt, including the Tivoli Gardens, on the former city ramparts (which were destroyed in the 1860s). The landscape architect Henrik A. Flindt (1822–1901), then Denmark's leading figure in landscape gardening, was assigned to draw up the plans. The botanist Johan Lange, who was the director of the Botanical Gardens, and the head gardener Tyge Rothe collaborated closely with Flindt in defining the botanical schemes. The scientific approach, however, did not inhibit Flindt's virtuoso style, which threw the aesthetics of the plants and scenery into relief. The garden was inaugurated in 1874 and the first guidebook was published in 1875.

Flindt's purpose was to create intriguing yet harmonious spaces. The city moat was only partly filled in, and the surroundings of what now became a lake were picturesquely planted with Danish as well as foreign trees. By means of a few strategically placed lines of vision, Flindt succeeded in connecting key motifs within the garden and the surrounding cityscape. To the visitor this creates an inspiring interplay between movement and absorption. A large rockery with alpine and calcicole plants was laid out on a double hill left by the old bastions. This terrain rises further to the Observatory, while large flat areas, crisscrossed by winding pathways, spread out to the other sides. Partly geometric, partly irregular beds and shrubberies alternate with extensive lawns. Despite the largely systematic planting scheme, some sections appear as natural settings. The hothouses (1872–74, thoroughly restored 1980–82) occupy the northern part of the grounds. The beautiful glass structure, shaped like a waterlily, makes the large Palm House not only the emblem of the gardens but one of the landmarks of Copenhagen. The famous brewer Carl Jacobsen drew up the plan using London's Crystal Palace as his model. His large donation of antique-inspired sculptures, and portraits of leading botanists, still adorn the lush garden landscape.

Individual plants, as well as more complex setups from the former Charlottenborg gardens, were integrated with the new layout. The only tree known to have been moved is the monumental swamp cypress (*Taxodium distichum*) by the lake. All remaining trees have been sown or planted after 1871. Several specimens are now full-grown. As of 1999 the botanical garden comprises 22,000 plants representing approximately 13,000 species. Plants from almost all climatic areas are featured. The garden also has a number of special plant collections, the *Cycas* and *Begonia* holdings being the oldest.

The garden's rich representation of Danish flora comprises 1,200 native species. The old moat offers an ideal surrounding for the many water and marsh plants; the moor section is also particularly well executed. Part of the collection of Greenlandic and Arctic species has been planted in a rocky outdoor area, while other specimens thrive in a special Arctic house (1959–60). A large section of the garden is re-sown every year with approximately 1,000 different species of annuals, including plants which have their natural habitat in warmer countries. The section devoted to perennial plants is comprised of 1,500 species. A fine collection of Greek and other Mediterranean species forms part of the alpine section. The collection of Thai orchids is the largest in the world. Other highlights in the hothouses are a nearly complete *cryptocoryne* collection, mangroves, and succulents. The arboretum comprises some rare *Bambusoideae, Rhododendron,* and *Salix* species. Among the finest specimen trees are the *Platanus acerifolia*, *Gingko biloba,* and *Sophora japonica.*

A close collaboration with botanical gardens abroad continues to be crucial to the upkeep of the garden's high scientific standards. In addition to serving as a teaching garden, the Copenhagen Botanical Garden is a valuable source of knowledge and inspiration for professional and amateur gardeners. Furthermore, it has developed into one of Copenhagen's most popular public parks.

Synopsis

1600	First botanical garden given to the university by Christian IV
1752–63	New garden laid out near Frederik V's Amalienborg Palace
1778–83	Construction of new botanical garden next to Charlottenborg Palace
1817	Copenhagen University solely in charge of garden
1871–74	Layout of fourth botanical garden on old city ramparts; landscape design by H.A. Flindt
1980–82	Restoration of the historic Palm House (originally constructed 1872–74)
2000	Inauguration of two new hothouses

Further Reading

Dahl Møller, *Botanisk Have 400 år,* Copenhagen: Botanisk Have, 2000

Friis, Ib, and Leif Blohm Edlefsen, *Oversigt over Botanisk Haves plantesamling,* Copenhagen: Kobenhavns Universitets Fond til Tilvejebringelse af Laeremidler, 1970

Olsen, Olaf, "Botanischer Garten der Universität København," in *Botanische Gärten Mitteleuropas,* edited by Friedrich Ebel, Fritz Kümmel, and Christine Beierlein, 2nd edition, Halle, Germany: Martin-Luther-Universität, 1990

Ostenfeld, Carl Emile Hansen, *Botanisk Have gennem 50 Aar: 1874–1924,* Copenhagen: Schultz, 1924

MARGRETHE FLORYAN

Kokushi (Muso Soseki) 1275–1351

Japanese Priest and Garden Designer

Muso Soseki was one of the most reverend priests (*Kokushi* in Japanese) during his era. He played an important role in developing design theory as well as practical techniques of the Japanese garden and had an enormous influence on subsequent Japanese gardens.

Japanese gardens are characterized by their naturalistic composition, such as asymmetrical arrangements, with naturally curved lines and land forms, and natural stones and naturalistic tree forms. This character had already been presented in the principles and methods of garden design set forth in the *Sakuteiki,* which is thought to have been written in the late 11th century (Heian period). During this period the Japanese introduced picturesque sceneries into their residential gardens according to the natural conditions of the site. Through his work Muso deepened the significance of the natural landscape and landscaping in the Japanese garden.

Muso studied the Buddhist writings, including esoteric Buddhism, as a priest of the Tendai sect of Buddhism; and he became a Zen priest at age 19. There, he tried to attain spiritual enlightenment with a *mondo* or a catechism under the priest of high virtue and by sitting in religious meditation facing nature, not through the study of the Buddhist writings. He selected various places with caves and with splendid natural scenery to sit for religious mediation. The places ranged from the northern Kanto region to Shikoku in the southwestern region of Japan. He would stay in one place for only a few years before moving to experience different scenery; he also rejected an invitation from an emperor and the feudal government in order to concentrate on religious mediation.

Until he was 45 years old, the places in which Muso stayed were in natural environments, with few artificial elements, such as a ravine or a bluff with a splendid view. He then changed his selections to seminatural areas that included artificial elements, such as a rural area, until he was 50. He gradually became engaged in the instruction of the laity, including an emperor in Kyoto and the regent of feudal government in Kamakura.

After the age of 50 Muso began creating gardens in several temples, including Zuisenji in Kamakura, Erinji in Kohu, and Nanzenji, Rinsenji, Saihoji, and Tenryuji in Kyoto. He had pursued higher spiritual enlightenment with gardening as he affirmed in his text in verse and the literature of *Muchu mondo,* which documented his answers to the questions from Naoyoshi Ashikaga, a younger brother of Takauji Ashikaga of the first *Ashikaga* shogun. One could say, therefore, that he began his training by sitting in religious mediation and finally pursued spiritual enlightenment with landscape gardening.

The gardens of Nanzenji, Zuisenji, Tenryuji, and other temples have similarly steep slopes, each with a pond at its foot facing Muso's chamber. These gardens would have given him a severe impression in his daily life. His intention can be clearly seen in the composition of the Tenryuji temple, where he created a steep waterfall on the slope with many rugged stones. Another characteristic of his gardens is the splendid view from the height of the garden. For instance, at the top of the steep slope in Zuisenji temple is a magnificent view of Mount Fuji.

Muso designed his garden with two different landscapes, of closed and open sceneries, using them to attain higher spiritual enlightenment in his daily life. In the closed landscape one can easily become engaged in introspection, while in the open landscape one's view can broaden.

In the garden of the Saihoji temple, which is called Kokedera because of its beautiful moss, Muso created a complex landscape in comparison with his other gardens, but he still created places of closed and severe landscape in Koinzan, as well as open landscape in Shukuentei, at the top. Koinzan is composed of many large natural stones creating an effect similar to a rugged mountain trail. According to the chronological record of Muso written by one of his disciples, Myoha Shunoku, he made it with the motif of Yu-Shusai asking Ryo-zasu, a famous hermit of high virtue in northern Sung. Climbing this trail one reaches the Shukuentei or an arbor where one can look down on the Kyoto basin. Koinzan is considered one of the earliest examples of *karesansui,* or sand and stone garden, in which water is positively denied to imagine more splendid and various water sceneries with sand and stone. One can understand the gardens of Ryoanji and Daitokuji temples as an extension of the Koinzan.

The Kinkakuji temple and its garden in Kyoto, designed by Yoshimitsu Ashikaga of the third *Ashikaga* shogun in Muromachi period, uses a composition similar to the Saihoji temple. The Ginkakuji temple and its garden, also in Kyoto and designed by Yoshimasa Ashikaga of the eighth *Ashikaga* shogun, is similar in composition to the Kinkakuji temple. These two examples show the enormous influence that Muso's gardens had on succeeding gardens in Japan.

The types of plants and vegetation used in Muso's gardens have not yet been clarified. The original floral composition has of course changed with plant succession. Moreover, related writings regrettably do not refer to plants, and an archeological investigation to analyze plant relicts in accumulated soils in ponds and swampy areas has not yet been done in his gardens.

See also Tenryu-ji

Biography

Born in Ise, 1275. Moved to Koshu with family, 1278; received commandments of Buddhism, Nara, 1292; became Zen priest, 1293; until 1318, tried to attain spiritual enlightenment from priests and through religious meditation in various locations having splendid natural landscapes; from ca. 1325 engaged in instruction of laity including an emperor; started to make gardens in Buddhist temples. Died 1351.

Selected Designs

1325	Garden of Nanzenji, Kyoto
1327	Garden of Zuisenji, Kamakura
1330	Garden of Erinji, Kohu
1333	Garden of Rinsenji, Kyoto
1339	Garden and related buildings of Saihoji, Kyoto
1341–45	Garden of Tenryuji, Kyoto

Further Reading

Eijiro, Fujii, *Miru niwa to fureru niwa: Nihonjin no ryokuchikan* (Gardens to See and Gardens to Touch), Kyoto: Tankosha, 1995

Kawase, Kazuma, and Katsuo Meikyo, *Muso Kokushi Zen to teien* (Zen Buddhism and Gardens), Tokyo: Kodansha, 1968

Mori, Osamu, *Nihon no teien* (Gardens of Japan), Tokyo: Yoshikawa Kobunkan, 1964; 5th edition, 1976

Muso Soseki, *Muchu mondo,*1344; revised by Taishun Sato, Tokyo: Iwanami Shoten, 1934; reprint, 1976

Toyama, Eisaku, *Muromachi jidai teienshi* (Garden History of the Muromachi Period), Tokyo: Iwanami Shoten, 1934

Yoshikawa, Matsu, *Karesansui no niwa* (The Garden of Karesansui), Tokyo: Shibundo, 1971

Yoshinaga, Yoshinobu, *Jishoji teien no hensen o ronzu* (Consideration on the Changes of Jishoji Garden), Tokyo: Yoshinobu Yoshinaga, 1940

EIJIRO FUJII

Kolomenskoye Palace and Gardens

Moscow, Russia

Location: approximately 4.5 miles (7.3 km) southeast of the Kremlin, Moscow

The state museum-reserve Kolomenskoye was founded in 1923–24 by P.D. Baranovsky and is situated not far from the center of Moscow. It represents a unique natural landscape and a historical, architectural, and cultural complex. It occupies an area of 963 acres (390 ha), replacing the territory of the former villages Kolomenskoye, Diakovo, and Sadovniki on a high bank of the Moscow River and the adjoining meadow on the opposite bank. It is a unique place in which the ancient landscape and architectural monuments are in unusual harmony.

In the early 16th century, Kolomenskoye was the summer residence of the grand prince of Moscow, Vassily III, who began active construction on the site. The Church of the Ascension has been preserved in its original state. It was erected in 1532 in honor of the heir to the throne, the future Czar Ivan IV, known as Ivan the Terrible. This cathedral is one of the most beautiful in Russia, rising up on the high bank of the Moscow River. Wild spans of low-lying meadows are seen from its gallery. The czar's throne of carved white stone was placed at the east end of the gallery, a peculiarity usually absent in orthodox churches. In 1994 the Church of the Ascension was included on the United Nations Educational, Scientific, and Cultural Organization (UNESCO) World Heritage list.

Kolomenskoye was of the greatest importance in the 17th century during the reign of Czar Aleksey Mikhaylovich, the second Czar of the Romanov dynasty. Construction of the new Czar's palace on an unprecedented level began in 1667. Its architecture expressed the traditions of ancient Russian wooden construction. The palace struck contemporaries with its uniqueness and its beauty. It was decorated with wooden carvings, the roofs were made of colored wooden shingles, and forged decorations on the roofs were gilded. Three thousand windows made of mica sparkled, and the ceiling and walls inside the palace were painted by the best artists. There was a free combination of separate buildings, and

View of Tzar's Palace in Kolomenskoye Village from Midday Side to Garden
Courtesy of Kolomenskoye Museum

absence of symmetry, picturesque roofs, porches, and passages everywhere. The czar's children's tutor, the poet Simeon Polotsky, called it the eighth wonder of the world for its unusual architectural riches. Being constructed entirely of wood, however, the palace fell into decay quickly and was dismantled after 100 years during the reign of Catherine the Great.

It is supposed that the inhabitants of Kolomna, near Moscow, resettled here in 1237, in order to save themselves from the Tatarian and Mongolian conquerors, and it was they who started gardening here. In the 12th and 13th centuries there were kitchen gardens. Apple, pear, cherry, and plum trees imported primarily from the southern regions (Byzantia, Caucus, Kiev) were planted here at that time. Berry bushes such as raspberry, gooseberry, and black and red currant, as well as various types of rose, were being cultivated. Turnips, horseradishes, carrots, peas, and beets, as well as medicinal herbs, were planted in the kitchen gardens. Wild trees were planted near private dwellings and businesses as well. Oak trees, trees considered to be sacred in Russia, of up to 75 feet (22.8 m) high and near 6 feet (1.8 m) in diameter, still survive in the old oak tree grove of Kolomenskoye. Most of these trees are situated in a line, confirming the opinion that these giant trees are the oldest artificial plantings in the territory of modern Moscow.

Gardening and vegetable gardening developed intensively in the 16th and 17th centuries. Gardens and kitchen gardens started appearing widely in Russia, becoming a symbol of prosperity. Food, medicinal, and textile plants were being planted for peasants' needs, commerce, and exchange. Rest gardens appeared at that time, too. Contemporary thought dictated that a garden must please not only the senses of sight and taste but of sound and scent as well. A fruit was perceived as an object as beautiful as a flower, and therefore as an element of garden aesthetics. Gardens also included ponds, fountains, rare plants, and birds. A garden's importance was not only economic but also aesthetic. It was thought that gardens should influence all human feelings and that a visitor should feel at rest and peace. Flowers and medicinal herbs were therefore planted along with fruits and berries.

Kolomenskoye included fruit gardens, meadows, and a park as well as the palace and trade buildings. It was surrounded by a ring of oak, lime, elm, and ash tree woods. There were excellent squares for the czar's amusement, such as duck hunting with falcons. Czar Aleksey Mikhaylovich hunted bears, wolves, foxes, hares, and elk in the winter at Kolomenskoye. There were six large gardens around the czar's residence in which thousands of apple trees, hundreds of pear trees and plum trees, numerous cherry trees, and berry bushes (gooseberry, raspberry, and currant) were growing. In Kazansky garden, which still remains, at the square of six hectares (15.8 acres) there grew 912 apple trees, 93 pear trees, 13 white berry bushes, 110 red berry bushes, 50 gooseberry bushes, 50 plum trees, 14 raspberry beds, two walnut trees, seven cedars, and one silver fir. The old large garden occupied almost 20 hectares (49.5 acres). In spring the czar's residence was overwhelmed by white fragrant clouds of flowering gardens. Multiplan panoramas on the Moscow River and churches at the czar's court opened up from the allées.

From the middle of the 17th century, at the czar's order, trees were brought in from other climatic zones, such as walnuts, Siberian silver firs, Siberian pines, and sweet cherries. The gardeners covered the warm-loving plants in an effort to protect them from the cold in winter, but they could not grow in open soil and perished in a few years. Siberian plants grew well, and they gathered good cedar nut harvest even in the time of Aleksey Mikhaylovich's son Peter the Great. Several pines and silver firs were growing in Kolomenskoye in the early 20th century. Today there are three European larches that are over 100 years old on the grounds of the czar's court.

The gardens of Kolomenskoye were the place where the czar's children played in the summer. For a long time, there grew the oak in the shadow of which former Czar Peter I liked to do his homework. The candlestick made of wind-broken secular cedar under which Czar Alexander I studied in childhood is preserved as well.

The 17th and 18th centuries were the time of physic gardens and physic-kitchen gardens. Medical herbs such as tansy, mint, hyssop, butterfly orchid, and sagebrush were seeded between fruit trees and bushes in kitchen gardens.

Allées between lines of apple trees and pear trees were created. One such road (which still exists today) in Kazansky garden goes from west to east. It is lined with pear trees and leads to the high bank terrace of the Moscow River, where the palace of Catherine II was built in the second half of the 18th century. From here the delightful panoramic view of the residence's landscape can be observed. Flowers and decorative, food, and medicinal herbs are planted around the garden roads and paths. Flower beds, fountains, and arbors were constructed in the path crossings. The yellow acacia (a decorative bush from Siberia) became popular in the 18th century, and it was planted as a green hedge around the czar's palace. Fragments of these plantings are still preserved today. Harvests were large in the Kolomenskoye gardens. Various drinks were made out of the berries and fruits in Sitny Palace, which came into the czar's farmstead complex in the 17th century. White cherries and cedar nuts were sent to the czar's table in St. Petersburg until 1776. Part of the harvest was sold. Later, the gardens were leased, and by the 19th century, they began to be of economic significance.

At the beginning of the 19th century, construction of a palace in the classic style was begun for Alexander I on a high bank hill not far from the Church of the Ascension. Designed by architect E.D. Tiurin, its fragments still exist today. Tiurin constructed the lime allées from the front to the back gates of the czar's court. From reliable accounts, we know that the trees were planted in 1825. From that time, Tiurin's pavilion of 1825 is preserved, but Alexander's palace did not last long and was dismantled.

Three of six gardens created at Kolomenskoye still exist: Kazansky, Voznesensky, and Diakovsky. Currently they are filled with apple and pear trees, planted in the 1940s and 1950s. There is a park at the old location of the czar's court; its base is a lime tree allée and ancient oaks.

Since 1990 Kolomenskoye, known as an art, history, and architectural museum-reserve, has the title of nature landscape as well. There are several landscape lots picked out of the museum's territory that represent nature monuments for Moscow's conditions. One of the most interesting of them is landslide steps at the hill under the Church of the Beheading of St. John the Baptist.

Near the hill's foot is the Palace (Golosov) ravine's mouth, situated with a stream, springs, slopes covered with mixed wood, and restored ponds of the 19th century. Two hundred-year-old specimens of lime, oak, and ash grow there, and one can hear the nightingale's song in the dense thicket of bird-cherry trees.

Future plans for the museum's development include restoration of fragments of the historical landscape, reconstruction of the czar's road from the Kremlin to Kolomenskoye, development for ecological tourism, and the creation of landscape excursion routes. The first efforts to restore the historical landscape of the central part of the museum reserve have already been completed. The 18th century plan for the Kazansky garden has been restored with flowerbeds in path crossings. Beds of medicinal herbs typical of Moscow gardening in the 17th century are placed in the Voznesensky garden. The restoration of the gardens' plans and plant compositions in Kolomenskoye allows visitors to imagine for the first time since their original creation these gardens of Russia's past.

The famous French composer Hector Berlioz visited Russia in 1868 and wrote that nothing struck him in his life like the architecture in Kolomenskoye.

> The beauty of the whole appeared before me. Everything in myself shook. It was mysterious silence, finished forms beauty's harmony. I saw a kind of architecture. I saw aspiration upwards, and I stood long stupefied.

Although these words refer to the Church of the Ascension, the church is combined into the surrounding landscape so naturally that the impression it makes is conditioned by its natural unity with the environment. This harmony is characteristic of all of Kolomenskoye. Much of what was created in the 17th and 18th centuries is lost, but the preserved part represents the harmony of the whole, in which nature, garden art, and architecture are in perfect unity.

Synopsis

1237	Founding of Kolomenskoye village
1336	First mention of Kolomenskoye as prince's village in will and testament of Ivan Kalita, Grand Prince of Moscow
1532	Construction of Church of Ascension finished
1533	Kolomenskoye belongs to Vassily Vassilievich, grand prince of Moscow
1547	Church of Beheading of St. John the Baptist built
1641	Construction of Church of Kazan Icon of Mother of God begun
1645	Government of Czar Aleksey Mikhaylovich begins
1667–71	Wooden palace of Aleksey Mikhaylovich built
1750–	Kazansky garden planned
1825	Construction of Alexander I's palace by architect Egraf D. Tyurin; English park "Lipki"; planting of lime tree alley in Czar's Court
ca. 1900	Dismantling of Alexander I's palace
1923–1924	Organization of art, historical, and architectural museum-preserve by P.D. Baranovsky on 64 acre (26-ha) site
1924–50s	Monuments of wooden architecture brought to territory of Kolomenskoye, including house of Peter I from Archangelskoye (1702), the tower of St. Nicholas's monastery from Karelia (1692), and the tower from Bratsk (1652)
1990	Reorganization of Kolomenskoye into art, historical, architectural, and natural landscape museum-preserve, increased to 390 hectares (963 acres)
1994	Church of Ascension added to UNESCO World Heritage list
1995–99	Planning and organization of public services in central part of park; restoration of gardens and park plantings

Further Reading

Goldin, I.I., et al., *Kolomenskoye,* Moscow: Interbook-Business, 1998

The Kolomenskoye Museum-Preserve: A Guide, translated by C. Rosenberger, Moscow: Raduga, 1985

Likhachev, Dimitrii Sergeevich, *Poeziia sadov* (The Poetry of Gardens), Leningrad: "Nauka," Leningradskoe Otd-nie, 1982; 3rd edition, Moscow: OAO Tipografiia "Novosti," 1998

Vergunov, Arkadii Pavlovich, and V.A. Gorokhov, *Russkie sady i parki* (Russian Gardens and Parks), Moscow: Nauka, 1988

ALEXANDER N. LUFEROV, LOUBOV I. LYASHENKO, AND ARKADIY VERGUNOV

Komarov Botanical Institute Botanic Garden

St. Petersburg, Russia

Location: Aptekarsky island in the center of St. Petersburg, approximately 1 mile (1.6 km) north of the Fortress of St. Peter and St. Paul

The Botanic Garden of the Komarov Botanical Institute of the Russian Academy of Sciences (RAC) has its origins in the Aptekarsky Ogorod (Pharmaceutical Garden), which was established in 1714 by an act of Peter the Great. The edict was signed by Robert Erskine of Scotland, who was *Leib-Medic* (chief physician) to the czar. Erskine was "Archiater et Physicus primarius" and had overall responsibility for medicine throughout the Russian Empire; he was also the creator and first manager of the garden. The founding of this garden in effect signaled the beginning of scientific botany in Russia. The garden is situated at Aptekarsky Island and is nearly at the center of Saint Petersburg. The park *dendrarium* (trees arranged geographically) and nurseries occupy 16.5 hectares (41 acres). There are 23 greenhouses occupying a total of one hectare (2.5 acres). Modern collections exceed 12,000 taxa.

After Peter I died in 1725, the garden was renamed The Garden of Her Imperial Majesty Catherine I and was under supervision of the imperial court. The documented history of the garden began in 1735 when Ioann Siegesbeck was invited from Germany to be its director. The garden at that time was named Meditzinsky Sad (Medical Garden), and Siegesbeck published the garden's first catalog—*Primitiae Florae Petropolitanae* (1736; First Flora of St. Petersburg). The catalog enumerated 1,275 species, many of which had been brought from Siberia, Mongolia, China, and other remote countries. Plants that had been collected during the first Russian expeditions for natural history by D.G. Messerschmidt, T. Gerber, I.G. Gmelin, and other great explorers began to be cultivated here, from which they spread throughout the world. Swedish botanist Johan Falck, a student and follower of Carl Linnaeus, was the director of the garden from 1765 to 1768. After Falck's departure on a long expedition (from which he never returned), the garden was placed under the directorship of Russian botanist Martin Terekhowsky. In 1793 Terekhowsky compiled the second catalog of the species under cultivation in the garden (published in 1796). Terekhowsky was succeeded by G.F. Sobolewsky, and in 1798 the Medical Garden became the Medico-Botanic Garden of the Academy of Medicine and Surgery. After Sobolewsky the garden was directed for a time (1806–8) by F.H. Stephan and (1809–23) by Ja.V. Petrov. Despite their considerable and experienced efforts, however, it continued to deteriorate.

In 1823 the Medico-Botanic Garden was reorganized as the Saint Petersburg Imperial Botanic Garden, and it became an independent institution and took on a scientific character. The eminent botanist F. Fischer now became its director. The 19th century was a period of great expansion and growth at the garden, during which time it became the most important botanical institution of Russia as well as a major international botanical center. The *Index Seminum* was published beginning in 1835. The garden supported many expeditionary efforts, especially inside Russia but also throughout the world. Expeditions by G. Kangsdorff, N.S. Turchaninov, C.I. Maximowicz, N.M. Przewalsky, G.N. Potanin, V.L. Komarov, B.A. and O.A. Fedchenko, and A.E. Regel are some of the most notable. Great achievements in the garden were connected with E.L. Regel, who was its director from 1855 to 1892. A.A. Fischer von Waldheim was in charge of the garden from 1896 until the Russian Revolution in 1917. Under his directorship a record number of 27,793 taxa was reached in 1905.

After the revolution the garden was ruled by the People's Commissariat of Land Use and was first named the Main Botanic Garden of the Russian Federation and then the Main Botanic Garden of the USSR. In 1930 it was transferred to the USSR Academy of Sciences. Since 1931, when the garden was united with the Botanical Museum and the Botanical Institute of the USSR Academy of Sciences was formed, the garden has been a scientific department of the Botanical Institute. In 1940 the Botanical Institute was named in honor of V.L. Komarov, who was then its most distinguished botanist and who had also been president of the Academy of Sciences.

The living plant collections suffered from frequent floods and unfavorable weather conditions, but they were most severely damaged during the wars. Enormous losses occurred during World War II and the siege of Leningrad. Many greenhouses were destroyed and most plants perished in the winter of 1941–42. At present the garden's collections in both quality and quantity exceed the prewar level. The whole institute in modern times has broadened its scope to include virtually all branches of botanical research. The structure of the Komarov Botanical Institute RAC includes the division into departments of Higher Plants, Botanic Garden, Botanic Museum, and laboratories: Lichenology and Bryology, Algology, Vegetation of Extreme North, Geography and Cartography of Vegetation, Plant Resources, Paleobotany, Anatomy and Morphology, Embryology and Reproductive Biology, Ecological Physiology of Plants, Biosystematics and Cytology, Systematics and Geography of Fungi, Biochemistry of Fungi, Ecology of Fungi, Analytic Phytochemistry, Vegetation of the Steppe Zone, Vegetation of the Forest Zone, Ecology of Plant associations, and Palinology. The botanic garden is a department of living plants, and its main aim is to do research in the field of the introduction and acclimatization of plants, to collect and maintain the most botanically interesting species of plants, and to promote conservation in situ and ex situ of the biodiversity of the Russian flora.

Synopsis

1714 Aptekarsky Orgorod (physic garden) established by Czar Peter the Great, created and directed by Scottish chief physician to the Czar, Robert Erskine

1725 Garden renamed Garden of Her Imperial Majesty Catherine I

1735 Ioann Siegesbeck comes from Germany to act as director

Plate 13. Gravel path leading to Monet's house and studio, Giverny, France

Plate 14. Plant specimen
Photo by William Biderbost, copyright Chicago Botanic Garden

Plate 15. The red borders at Hidcote Manor Gardens
Copyright John Feltwell/Garden Matters

Plate 16. Plan of the Esterházy Palace and Gardens, ca. 1827
Courtesy of Országos Széchényi Könyvtár

Plate 17. Flowering bulbs at Keukenhof Gardens

Plate 18. Cycads at Kirstenbosch, National Botanical Garden of South Africa, Cape Town

Plate 19. An Erica garden and Fernwood Buttress at Kirstenbosch, National Botanical Garden of South Africa, Cape Town
Copyright Colin Paterson-Jones

Plate 20. Watercolor of Shalamar gardens at Lahore, Pakistan, by Charlotte Lady Canning
Courtesy of the Earl and Countess of Harewood and the Trustees of Harewood House Trust

Plate 21. Villa Lante, Bagnaia, Lazio, Italy
Copyright John Bethell/Garden Picture Library

Plate 22. Lavin Garden at the Chicago Botanic Garden
Photo by William Biderbost, copyright Chicago Botanic Garden

Plate 23. The maze in Anne Boleyn's garden at Hever Castle, Kent
Copyright Nick Meers/Garden Picture Library

Plate 24. Models of various garden types, from Leberecht Migge, "Der technishe Gartentypus unserer Zeit," in *Die Gartenschönheit* (1927)
Courtesy Joachim Wolschke-Bulmahn

Plate 25. *Sommerabend auf dem Barkenhoff* (Summer Evening at the Barkenhoff), Heinrich Vogeler, 1905

Plate 26. Rosendal Barony Garden, 1993
Copyright Ola Bettum

Plate 27. Spring tulip gardens at Royal Botanic Gardens, Ontario, Canada
Courtesy of Royal Botanic Gardens, Ontario

1736	Siegesbeck publishes *Primitiae Florae Petropolitanae,* first catalog of the garden
1798	Garden became Medico-Botanic garden of Academy of Medicine and Surgery
1823	Garden reorganized as independent botanical research center, becoming main botanical institution of Russia
1835	*Index Seminum* begins publication
1917	People's Commissariat of Land Use takes charge of garden and renames it Main Botanic Garden
1930	Garden transferred to USSR Academy of Sciences
1931	Garden becomes part of the Botanical Institute of USSR Academy of Sciences
1940	Botanical Institute renamed after V.L. Komarov, its most distinguished botanist
1941–43	Severe damage to gardens during the siege of Leningrad
1946–present	Under initial leadership of dendrologist Sergei Sokolov, gardens returned to and surpassed their pre–World War II levels

Further Reading

Firsov, Gennady A., "Robert Erskine: A Scotsman in Peter the Great's Russia," *The Newsletter of the Botanical Society of Scotland* 66 (March 1996)

Firsov, Gennady A., and Yuri S. Smirnov, "The Role of the Saint-Petersburg Botanical Garden in the Introduction and Distribution of Plants," *The Newsletter of the Botanical Society of Scotland* 68 (March 1997)

Shetler, Stanwyn G., *The Komarov Botanical Institute: 250 Years of Russian Research,* Washington, D.C.: Smithsonian Institution Press, 1967

GENNADY A. FIRSOV

Konchi-in

Kyoto, Japan

Location: 86-12 Fukuchi-cho, Nanzen-ji, Sakyo-ku, Kyoto

Konchi-in is a subtemple of the Nanzen-ji monastery, an important center of the Rinzai sect of Zen Buddhism, located within the monastic grounds in the eastern part of Kyoto. It is renowned for its Tsuru-Kame—the crane and tortoise garden created in 1631, a dry landscape garden (*kare-sansui*) with a Buddhist theme centering on the sacred Mount Horai. Its style is known as *Horai-kare-sansui.* It is a contemplative Zen garden, a lavish composition of silver sand, with a rich variety of rocks and large-scale topiary crowned with distant views of the Higashiyama Mountains. The large compositions of the tortoise and crane are its prominent features.

Konchi-in is an outstanding work of Enshu Kobori, the most renowned arbiter of taste of his time; it is also a vivid document of the political power of the Rinzai sect in the early decades of the Tokugawa shogunate. The establishment of Konchi-in as an aesthetically sophisticated center for religious practices, with its works of art, tea garden, and a tea pavilion (*Hasso-no-Seki*), was due to one man, Ishin Suden, abbot of Nanzen-ji and superior of Konchi-in. The Rinzai monks, with their diplomatic skills and intellectual refinement, had always been close to the ruling courts, especially to the Ashikaga shoguns in the 14th and 15th centuries. The continuing wars of the 16th century were disastrous for temples, but by aligning itself with the Tokugawa shogunate, the sect recovered spectacularly.

Ishin Suden achieved an outstanding position as an adviser to Ieyasu Tokugawa and to two of his successors, dealing with foreign policy, trade laws, with the legislation intended to control the warrior clans, and imperial court and religious houses; he was also involved in the suppression of Christianity. Suden was instrumental in moving the ruined Konchi-in from its original location in the Kitayama area onto its present site at the turn of the 17th century. After he was awarded the rank of *kokushi* (national teacher) by the imperial court and granted the right to wear purple robes (1626), Suden turned his attention to Konchi-in.

With its large grounds the temple was to embody Buddhist beliefs, mark the strength of the Rinzai sect, and express loyalty to the authority of the shogunate. In

1627 he engaged Enshu Kobori, who was already working in Nanzen-ji. Kobori was a Tokugawa official, a master of all the Zen arts, poet, pottery connoisseur, calligrapher, tea master, and garden designer. A year later (1628) Suden built the Toshogu Shrine devoted to the memory of Ieyasu Tokugawa in the upper part of the temple grounds. For the abbot's quarters, he installed a building brought from the Fushimi Castle, once the stronghold of Hideyoshi Toyotomi, which had been destroyed by Tokugawa. Suden asked Kobori to design the garden in front of this building. Although Suden was absent from Konchi-in during its creation and never saw it completed, his presence is now symbolized by the shrine *Kaizan-dou,* dedicated to his memory, facing the garden on the west side.

Suden's intention to build a garden soon resulted in copious donations of precious stones, the names of ingratiating hopefuls having been preserved in the temple diary called *Honko Kokushi nikki.* The diary also records Kobori's protests and frustrations at the gifts, which were not of his choice or to his liking. But one of the stones, donated by a government official Matsudaira, now occupies a central position as the worshiping stone. The monastic diary marked 12 July 1631 as the completion date of the garden. The name Kentei is also mentioned as the foreman responsible for the actual work in the garden. A skilled *kawaramono* (riverside worker), he worked on Sambo-in and other renowned gardens. With the help of a contemporary painting of the garden called *Torinsenmeikastuzukai,* it is possible to trace later additions to the garden, such as a flying stone (a stone cut on one side) from the west part of the garden.

The Tsuru-Kame garden is laid out on the rectangular area in front of the abbot's quarters, facing south. Its single-depth composition involves an empty plane of white gravel, which terminates abruptly in a vertical wall of shaped trees and clipped shrubs. At the base of this green background, several groups of rocks are positioned in a narrow line, and before them the two large-scale compositions, of the turtle and the crane, are placed asymmetrically to the right and to the left. A wide slab of worshiping stone (*reihaiseki*) between them binds the two together into a tight, dynamic composition. It is a monastic contemplative garden, which should be viewed from a single vantage point, ideally from the veranda of the *hojo* (abbot's quarters), in accordance with the meditative practices of Zen Buddhism. The garden presents itself to the viewer as a panoramic sweep of forms on a monumental scale, with a baroque richness of colors and a precious quality of detail.

The boldness of working with topiary on this scale is striking, as are the two compositions of the turtle and the crane, each approximately seven meters (7.6 yd.) long. They face each other, and both carry huge loads on their backs. The crane, to the right of the scene and sharply outlined, carries as a wing stone a Buddha Triad of rocks about 1.5 meters (1.6 yd.) high and their companions, shaded by a mature Japanese red pine. The turtle, with its head lowered, a vast heavy creature, carries an ancient Japanese cypress. The tree looks petrified, but green branches grace its extremities, and the combination of its gray, fantastically twisted split trunk and green clouds of young growth makes for an exquisite art form. The sophisticated exuberance more akin to the courtly aesthetics is tempered in this garden by the gravity of religious thought. The theme pursued here is the Buddhist ideal of immortality. The turtle and the crane participate in a symbolic discourse on longevity—the turtle an old creature, the crane a young one, full of vitality—while the rocks and plants, especially the cypress, are seen to bridge life and death.

The two creatures dip their heads in the ideal ocean of blue pebbles, on which floats an archipelago of rocks, signifying the Islands of the Immortals. A series of 11 large rocks half a meter to a meter high (.55 to 1.1 yd.) at the very back of the composition re-create the Horai ridge. Colors of rocks and shades of topiary create a sense of distance, giving a long perspective toward the misty dissolving shapes of the unreachable sacred mountains. The combined color effects of the stones—the whiteness of the sand, the black area around the worshiping stone, and the darkness of the recesses around the furthermost rocks—create an optical distance to the view of the mountains and brings out their full roundness, something that Enshu Kobori had already perfected in his topiary compositions.

The human longing for the land of the immortals is given a prime acknowledgment in the forming of the whole of the stretch of silver sand into a boat traveling in the direction of the Islands of the Blessed. On the border between the silver sand and the blue pebbles, between the realm of the accessible and the unreachable, lies the flat worshiping stone (1.95 by 4.2 m [2.1 by 4.6 yd.]). With its strong perpendicular line it provides a visual aid to the perspective of the Horai Mountains. It also becomes a mental and physical place to enter the garden and to participate in its world. The stone acts as a focal point for the worship of all the Buddhas of the Three Worlds, for the reverent acknowledgment of Ishin Suden, whose shrine is visible from the west, and for honoring Ieyasu Tokugawa, commemorated in the Toshogu shrine on the hill above the garden.

Synopsis

1394–1427 Foundation of Konchi-in in Kitagate by shogun Yoshimochi Ashikaga, with Daigo as first priest

ca. 1600 Ensho Honko Kokushi Ishin Suden, abbot of Nanzen-ji (1569–1633),

	moves Konchi-in into Nanzen-ji complex
1627	Suden commissions Enshu Kobori to design garden
1629	Garden finally mapped out on ground; foundations finished; first delivery of rocks
1631	Completion of garden

Further Reading

Ito, Teiji, *The Gardens of Japan,* Tokyo and New York: Kodansha, 1984

Nitschke, Günter, *Gartenarchitektur in Japan: Rechter Winkel und natürliche Form,* Cologne, Germany: Taschen, 1991; as *Japanese Gardens: Right Angle and Natural Form,* translated by Karen Williams, Cologne, Germany: Taschen, 1993

Slawson, David A., *Secret Teachings in the Art of Japanese Gardens,* Tokyo and New York: Kodansha International, 1987

AGNIESZKA WHELAN

Krieger, Johan Cornelius 1683–1755

Danish Gardener, Architect, and Garden Designer

Johan Cornelius Krieger (Krüger) is traditionally named as Denmark's first garden architect. He combined a sound knowledge of the European fashions with a pronounced virtuosity. His name is linked to the many grandiose building and garden projects initiated by King Frederik IV (1671–1730). Next to his design activities and his long-standing position as head gardener of the royal garden at Rosenborg, Krieger consecutively occupied the highest posts in the royal building administration. He was also involved in manufacturing various kinds of building materials.

According to family lore, J.C. Krieger was trained as a gardener. He also followed in his father's footsteps in working for the royal house. In 1705 he completed his apprenticeship at the royal gardens at Frederiksberg and soon thereafter left for a several years' journey abroad, probably to the Netherlands and England. His first assignment after returning home was at the royal garden of Vallø, where he remodeled the grounds and laid out a formal garden with herbaceous parterres. In 1711 Krieger became gardener of the orangery in the royal garden at Rosenborg. That same year he created what became one of the landmarks of Danish urban planning, the great ring of lime trees on Kongens Nytorv in Copenhagen (now ruined). Krieger's prominent position in Danish garden history rests on the projects he carried out for the royal house from 1719 to 1749. Following extensive travels in France and Italy, King Frederik IV gained considerable insight into garden matters, and he contributed actively to some of the projects to which Krieger was assigned. This patronage proved of major importance to the prospering of Danish garden art in the wake of the Great Nordic War (1700–1721).

Like most other garden architects of his time, Krieger was strongly indebted to the French formal tradition as defined and practiced by André Le Nôtre. Krieger probably knew A.J.D. d'Argenville's highly normative *La théorie et la pratique de jardinage etc.* (1709), yet this book was not in his comprehensive library. Most of Krieger's designs were based on a marked central axis embracing the main building as well as the grounds. Several of his preparatory drawings have been handed down, along with prints and other sources documenting the historic gardens. He had an exceptional eye for utilizing the characteristics of existing topography, and he typically relished creating a dynamic interplay between open and closed spaces. Compared to his Swedish contemporary and colleague Tessin the Younger, Krieger was more inclined to use rather bold approaches.

There was a clear Dutch influence on Krieger's views and working schemes. It can be assumed that he gained first-hand experience in the planting and care of French-inspired bosquets and parterres during his likely sojourn in the Netherlands—thus taking part in a traditionally intense Dutch-Danish exchange of ideas. Krieger's predilection for drawing up labyrinthine bosquets indicates Dutch schooling because this motif had largely gone out of fashion in France. In his parterres Krieger mainly applied the *broderie*-scheme, using box and pyramidal yew in the outer flower borders.

Amongst the architectural treatises and pattern books in his book collection, the majority were of German origin. Several of his designs were decidedly kindred to the pleasure gardens laid out by Maximilian von Welsch and Dominique Girard, and more than once he borrowed a plan or an elevation from L.C. Sturm's *Vollständige Anweisung Grosser Herrenpaläste* (1718).

At an unusually rapid pace Krieger designed or redesigned a series of Denmark's finest gardens, and he concurrently proved to be one of the most industrious architects of the period. He also played a leading role in the rebuilding of Copenhagen following the fire of 1728 and wrote the first architectural pattern book to be published in Denmark (1729).

In the Fredensborg garden (1719–23) Krieger's topographical sense manifested itself when he took the existing facilities for hunting as point of departure for a fan-shaped layout of the grounds. Parterres and bosquets were placed adjacent to the palace building. The vegetable garden was furnished with a menagerie and a voliere, the latter in the form of an octagonal timber house in an octagonal pond; Krieger subsequently created several variations on this motif in other gardens. It was Frederik IV who envisioned the plan for extending the central axis of the Fredensborg complex across the lake to the very spot where the sun sets on 8 August, the very date the light northern nights come to an end. Krieger's layout was modified in the 1750s, but many of its elements are still detectable. As of 1999, Fredensborg was one of Queen Margrethe II's summer residences.

While working at Fredensborg, Krieger also constructed a number of gardens with a more typical French stamp: Odense, Amalienborg, and Frydenlund. In the last garden he introduced the *parterre à l'anglaise*. A challenge of a different order awaited him at Frederiksberg (1720–26), where the existing garden layout had proven aesthetically and technically insufficient. Krieger demonstrated a unique boldness in turning the height difference between the palace and the garden into the key motif. The hill was hollowed out; seven terraces were created in an amphitheatrical setup; and a cascade was placed in the center. In his last garden design, Ledreborg (1742–48), Krieger elaborated even further on this basically Italian-inspired motif. The main axis here runs through the palace and two very steep slopes above a natural brook. Broad grass-covered terraces, bordered by a dense planting of trees, were constructed on the slopes, with stairs and zigzag ramps leading from one ledge to the other.

Distinctive elements of the French as well as the Italian garden traditions were brought together in Krieger's layout of Frederiksborg (1721–29) in Hillerød. This garden was his most comprehensive work. Three natural lakes and an impressive hillside called for the creation of cascades, with bosquets, lime alleys, a boulingrin, and large parterres allocated to the four landings. The Frederiksborg cascades worked until 1779, whereafter several changes were imposed upon the baroque layout. The ensemble has recently been restored (1993–96) to its former glory and thus constitutes, together with the National Portrait Gallery which is housed in the Frederiksborg castle, one of Denmark's most popular sights. As the baroque tradition prescribed, one of the big four parterres has been given a colorful planting scheme representing the monogram of the reigning monarch, Margrethe II.

See also Frederiksberg

Biography

Born 1683. Trained as a gardener at Frederiksberg, Denmark, 1705; traveled abroad (probably to the Netherlands and England), 1705–8; appointed royal gardener at Rosenborg, Denmark, 1711; numerous assignments for designing and redesigning royal pleasure gardens, from 1719; supervisor of the royal nursery, 1721; inspector of the royal building office, 1722; national building inspector, 1725; ended his career as a gardener and architect, 1749; appointed counsellor the same year. Died in Copenhagen, 1755.

Selected Designs

1719–23 Redesign of the Fredensborg Garden, North Zealand, Denmark
1720–26 Redesign of the Frederiksberg Garden, Copenhagen, Denmark
1721–25 Odense Palace Garden, Odense, Denmark
1722 Frydenlund, north of Copenhagen, Denmark
1721–29 Frederiksborg Garden, Hillerød, Denmark (recreated 1993–96)
1725 Redesign of Amalienborg, Copenhagen, Denmark
1731 Redesign of Hirschholm, North Zealand, Denmark
1735 Redesign of Rosenborg, Copenhagen, Denmark
1742–48 Ledreborg, Mid Zealand, Denmark

Further Reading

Hendeliowitz, Jens, and Mette Kromann, editors, *Barokhaven ved Frederiksborg slot: Genskabelsen af det Kriegerske anlæg, 1993 til 1996*, Copenhagen: Slots- og Ejendomsstyrelsen, 1996

Lund, Hakon, *De kongelige lysthaver,* Copenhagen: Gyldendal, 1977

Lund, Hakon, editor, *Danmarks arkitektur,* 6 vols., Copenhagen: Gyldendal, 1979–81

Margrethe Floryan

Kroměříž

Moravia, Czech Republic

Location: 35 miles (56 km) east of Brno, Moravia, Czech Republic

The city of Kroměříž is situated in the middle of Europe and the province of Moravia, in the fertile plain of Haná, on the Morava River. Destroyed in the 17th century during the Thirty Years' War, the medieval fortified city was reconstructed between 1664 and 1695 and converted to a princely residence by the bishop of Olomouc, Karl II of Liechtenstein-Castelcorn. He rebuilt the Renaissance castle and concurrently created two ambitiously laid-out gardens, Květná zahrada (the Flower Garden) and Podzámecká zahrada (the Castle Garden).

The bishop created Květná zahrada (the Flower Garden) outside of the ramparts, on the site of an orchard. Begun in 1665, the garden took ten years to complete. It formed a rectangle 485 by 300 meters (530 by 328 yd.) on an area of 10.9 hectares (27 acres). The imperial engineer-architect Filiberto Lucchese designed the garden and castle; he died soon after work on the garden was started, and his successor, Giovanni Pietro Tencala, continued the work. The result was a significant late Renaissance garden, which has been conserved and which is now again being restored.

The garden was composed of two different parts bound by a common axis and enclosed in a common framework of clipped espaliers. Half of the garden consisted of bosques on a square network interwoven with eight diagonal alleys that converged on an octagonal pavilion, the Rotunda. The bosques were filled with ornamental "embroidery." The other half of the garden, more intimate and planted with utility plants, consisted of an orchard enclosed in espaliers and divided by the main alley into two identical parts. Along the city side were situated enclosed special gardens and the farmyard.

The entrance to the garden was on its northern side. In front of the entrance a large water basin extended along the garden's whole width and fed several pools and water jets. Important guests came through the main entrance to the covered arcade corridor, the 224-meter-long (245 yd.) Colonnade, which borders the garden along its entire width. From the entrance a through vista opened into three high clipped espalier alleys, the central one of which was terminated by the pavilion of the Rotunda with a high cupola. The portals on the Rotunda's eight sides opened vistas into eight espalier alleys. Sculptured fountains were placed in the intersection of alleys, between the Colonnade and the Rotunda. In the interior of the bosques were decorative embroideries; in two of them were created clipped square labyrinths, one with rectangular paths and the other with circular paths and a target tree in the center.

The arcade corridor of the Colonnade offered a shadowed walk along a procession of 44 larger than life-size antique statues placed in the nooks of the gallery. On both ends the stairway led to the terrace, which offered a view of the whole garden.

The Rotunda was a garden pavilion for indoor entertainment, with a dance hall under a monumental cupola decorated with Italian polychrome ornamentation by Q. Castelli and C. Borsa. On its perimeter the hall is bordered by a circular corridor connecting four grottoes with statues of satyrs, fountains, and hidden triggers of water jests and lined with tufa and conch shells.

The garden's main axis passed from the entrance in the middle of the Colonnade through the Rotunda and between the espaliers of the orchard to a small piazza between them, with a paved skittle alley decorated on both sides with statues and hiding triggers of water jests, which visitors involuntarily touched off. In the bosques, on both sides of the main axis, were situated orchards, each with a square trout pond with a central sculpture and a water jet. Above the basins towered the Strawberry Hill, with a direct stairway and a spiral way to the top, on which was built a pavilion that offered a hiding place and a bird's-eye view of the garden.

Along the garden's eastern side, which was enclosed by clipped espaliers, special entertainment and pleasure gardens were aligned in a row and enclosed by a wall: a garden with an aviary in a special pavilion on the islet in the Swan Lake; a *vivarium* featuring an artificial Rabbit Hill with statue of Diana, the goddess of hunting, situated on top and with statues of hunters on the perimeter (the rabbits living in the warrens in the hill could be flooded out before the waiting hunters); a breeding pheasantry; behind the farmyard an orangery with trees in vessels placed around the water basin with a statue of Neptune; and a Dutch garden with flowering bulbous plants. A sophisticated water supply system fed the pools and many water jests, especially in the Rotunda.

The Flower Garden aroused great interest, evidenced by a luxurious publication edited for the bishop by Canon U.F.A. Heger in 1691 when the garden was already mature and fully equipped. Justes van den Nyport of Utrecht engraved the plans and drawings by G.M. Vischer. That the garden was much in favor and frequently visited is demonstrated by the fact that, during the baroque period, which in Moravia was characterized by intensive artistic and building activity, the

General view of Kroměříž, Moravia, Czech Republic, from an engraving by J. van den Nyport, 1691

Flower Garden remained respected in its concept; after 1770 three glasshouses were erected at the farmyard, as well as a building for pineapple growing.

The following period stigmatized the garden in a coarse way: before 1820 a quarter of the espaliers around the Rotunda were felled, chestnut tree bosques were planted in the southern part of this area, and an "English Park," which also included conifers, was established in the triangle between the Rotunda and the Colonnade. Some of the statues were relocated to the Castle Garden, and one labyrinth was converted into a rosary. The system of water jests was abolished some time before 1900. However, a new Empire-style entrance, developed in 1840–45 by Anton Arche, the archbishop's architect, on the site of the farmyard, was regarded a success. Although it was illogically situated on the garden's flank, it brought the garden nearer to the city. It included new glasshouses with the entrance courtyard between. The glasshouses were equipped with decorative cast-iron garden benches made in the archbishop's ironworks.

Restoration of the garden's historic character began in 1952–54, after the garden's nationalization. Architect Pavel Janák removed tree plantings from the anglicized area of the triangle between the Colonnade and the Rotunda and opened the view of both dominant buildings. The parterre thus created was articulated in the original outline and decorated with flower embroidery consisting of estival plants with a box border. In 1964 architect Dušan Riedl designed the garden's further restoration, which has been gradually implemented: instead of tree bosques, espalier bosques with box "embroidery" in sand have been restored, as well as espaliers and labyrinths; a 300-year-old work has also been uncovered.

Podzámecká zahrada (the Castle Garden), which links directly to the castle, has a much different character from the Flower Garden in both its development and its present form. Already in 1509 Bishop Stanislav Thurzo had invited the king of Bohemia to visit Kroměříž and offered the garden as a convenient place for the amusement and pleasure of the prince. In 1564–72 Bishop Vilém Prusinovsky of Vickov had extended the garden and created in it a rosary.

During the reconstruction by Bishop Karl II of Liechtenstein-Castelcorn of the Renaissance-style castle into a manneristic one (1686–98), after the design of Giovanni

Pietro Tencalla, the garden had obviously been rearranged. The original garden formed a long fenced rectangle extending along the castle's facade to the Morava River, which formed several branches here. The garden consisted of a field of *parterres de broderie* decorated in the corners with statues and intersected by a transversal axis leading from the castle's entrance to the bridge across the river branch, with a monumental fountain in the intersection of the axes. The castle, monumentally rising above the garden, had a broad *salla terrena* connecting the castle with the garden. It was richly decorated with stuccowork and colored mosaic by Baltasar Fontana and with frescoes by P.A. Pagani. Alongside the *salla terrena* two grottoes were erected: one with statues of fauns, incrusted shells, and tree reliefs, and the other with a remarkably realistic representation of a mine and of ore-mining methods used in the bishop's domains in northern Moravia. Only this part of the baroque garden has been preserved and bears evidence of its artistic ensemble.

An anonymous plan dating from about 1760 shows the greatest expansion of the baroque form of the parterre, extending in the castle's axis up to a transversal basin that obviously made use of a river branch to close the parterre. The parterre was divided into six regular fields, four of which were planted with decorative plantings and two with tree plantings, filling up two semicircular fields on both sides. The whole was enclosed by a clipped pergola and alleys.

Under the influence of Rousseau's return to nature, the hitherto formal garden began to change. In the years 1777–1811, under Archbishop A.T. Colloredo-Waldsee, the garden was extended, enriched with new water areas, and converted into a Romantic natural park. In 1795, still in a baroque spirit, a new entrance to the garden from the castle was built, with an arcade corridor, a double-flight stairway, and a terraced intimate small garden (*giardinetto*). Although the design of 1802 preserves the extant baroque parterre in front of the castle and a system of straight alleys of the original layout, the garden itself had already been filled with many Romantic nooks and playthings, as well as some statues relocated from the Flower Garden. On a lake formed by a river branch an islet was created that included a Temple of Friendship, a Chinese pavilion, once with figures of bowing Chinese, artificial ruins with a waterfall as a stage for antique plays, and an observation arbor on an artificial hill. The Long Pond was established, and the park extended up to the Morava River and, in the spirit of the time, passed into a natural landscape. The garden's appearance at this time is preserved in an album of engravings by J. Fisher (1802).

The Castle Garden's definitive transformation into a natural landscape park took place under the Archbishops Ferdinand Chotek and Maxmilian Sommerau-Beckh in the second quarter of the 19th century. The parterre was abolished, the statues removed, and the park further extended after the new concept of the archbishop's architect Anton Arche. The concept was characterized by extensive meadows, sceneries of trees, and plantings of solitary trees and groups of trees, usually of imported exotic species. Water courses were trained and decorated with cast-iron bridges made in the archbishop's ironworks, new fountains were erected, and in 1846 the so-called Pompeian Colonnade, a semicircular column pavilion, was erected.

The Castle Garden extended over an area of 47 hectares (117 acres), including three ponds. Beginning in 1841 trees were planted in new areas, reaching a peak in 1913–14 when thousands of trees, particularly exotic species stemming mostly from southern Europe, North America, and East Asia, were planted. The park contains 63 species of conifers, including *Abies homolepis, Larix leptolepis, Picea bicolor, Pinus jeffreyi,* and *P. ponderosa.* In 1966 a *Gingko biloba* 'Chotek', with a ball-shaped crown, was grown here. The 290 species of deciduous trees include *Aesculus octandra, Cercidi phylum japonicum, Liriodendron tulipifera, Magnolia obovata, Phellodendron amurense, Quercus conferta, Robinia vascosa, Sophora japonica,* and *Tilia tomentosa.*

In 1950 the Castle of Kroměříž and both parks were nationalized. In 1998 they were included in the United Nations Educational, Scientific, and Cultural Organization (UNESCO) World Heritage List. They belong to the most important historic parks of central Europe.

Synopsis

Květná zahrada (Flower Garden)

1665	Bishop Karl II of Liechtenstein-Castelcorn founds garden after plan made by Filiberto Lucchese
1666	Giovanni Pietro Tencalla continues construction of garden
1674	Carpoforo Tencalla paints decoration of garden pavilion
1675	Garden completed at cost of 75,000 guldens
1691	U.F.A. Heger publishes pictorial monograph on garden
1770	Three new glasshouses and building for pineapple growing built
1840–45	Anton Arche builds new entrance to garden, with new glasshouses
before 1820	Some of bosks abolished and "English" park planted instead
1950	Garden nationalized
1952–54	Reconstruction of anglicized part of garden by Pavel Janák
1964–	Restoration scheme of whole garden by Dušan Riedl begins
1998	Garden included in the United Nations Educational, Scientific, and Cultural

Organization (UNESCO) World Heritage List

Podzámecká zahrada (Castle Garden)

1509	First mention of garden and castle
1564	Bishop Vilém Prusinovský of Víckov extends garden and founds rosary
1686	Modification of garden after design of Giovanni Pietro Tencalla under Bishop Karl II of Lichtenstein-Castelcorn
1688–92	*Salla terrena* and grottos decorated by Baltasar Fontana
1795	Terraced *giardinetto* built, with new entrance to garden
1802	Romantic modifications of garden under archbishop Colloredo-Waldsee; album of engravings of garden by J. Fischer
1825–50	Conversion of garden into natural landscape park under Archbishops Chotek and Sommerau-Beckha
1841	Plantings on new areas
1846	Anton Arche builds Pompeian colonnade
1913–14	Extensive tree planting, in particular exotic species
1950	Garden and castle nationalized
1998	Castle and park included in United Nations Educational, Scientific, and Cultural Organization (UNESCO) World Heritage List

Further Reading

Birnbaumová, Alžběta, "Historické zahrady v Kroměříži (Historic Gardens in Kroměříž)," in *Kroměříž: Městská památková rezervace, státní zamek a památky v okolí* (Kroměříž: Historic Town Reserve, State Castle, and Monument in the Environs), by Jarmila Vacková, Prague: STN, 1963

Jůza, Vilém, "Kotázce ideového konceptu květné zahrady v Kroměříži (On the Idea of the Concept of the Flower Garden in *Kroměříž*)," in *Historická Olomouc a její současné problémy* (Historical Olomouc and Its Present Problems), Olomouc: Univ. Palackého, 1985

Jůza, Vilém, et al, *Kroměříž,* Prague: Státní naklaadatelství krásne literatury a umění, 1963

Kříž, Zdeněk, *Historické zahrady okresu Kroměříž* (Historic Gardens of the District of Kroměříž), Brno, Czech Republic: ONV, 1984

Kříž, Zdeněk, Dušan Riedl, and Jan Sedlák, *Významné parky Jihomoravského kraje* (Important Parks of the South Moravian Region), Brno: Blok, 1978

Kuča, Otakar, "Zámecké zahrady v Kroměříži (Castle Gardens in Kroměříž)," *Umeni* 6 (1958)

Peřinka, František Václav, *Dějiny města Kroměříže* (History of the City of Kroměříž), 3 vols., Kroměříž: Nakl. Obecní Rady Města Kroměříže, 1913–48

Petrů, Jaroslav, "Bischof Karl von Liechtenstein-Castelcorn als Bauherr," *Stadt und Grün* 46, no. 1 (1997)

DUŠAN RIEDL

Kuskovo

Moscow, Russia

Location: 7 miles (11.3 km) southeast of Moscow

Kuskovo is the estate of the counts Sheremetyev near Moscow, where the regular garden of the mid-18th century, the palace, and many garden pavilions have been preserved. These lands were given to the Field Marshal Boris Petrovitch Sheremetyev by the Emperor Peter the Great no later than 1715. In the 1720s the creation of the first estate was begun, probably in the traditional Russian medieval manner.

The son of B.P. Sheremetyev, Count Piotr Borisovitch Sheremetyev, decided to transform Kuskovo into a residence of a new type, according to the European manner, which had become popular in court circles. He wanted to create a country pleasure estate. In 1737 the new church was built near the old wooden palace, and in 1749, the Dutch house—the first stone pavilion—appeared in the small regular garden. Near it flower beds were made with plants brought from the Netherlands.

The main construction work for the estate took place from 1750 to the 1780s. By the year 1754 the architect and gardener Kologrivov was the main figure in the development of Kuskovo. From 1755 to 1764 the works were headed by the serf-architect F. Argunov, and in the period from 1765 to the 1780s by Karl Blanc, the famous architect from Moscow.

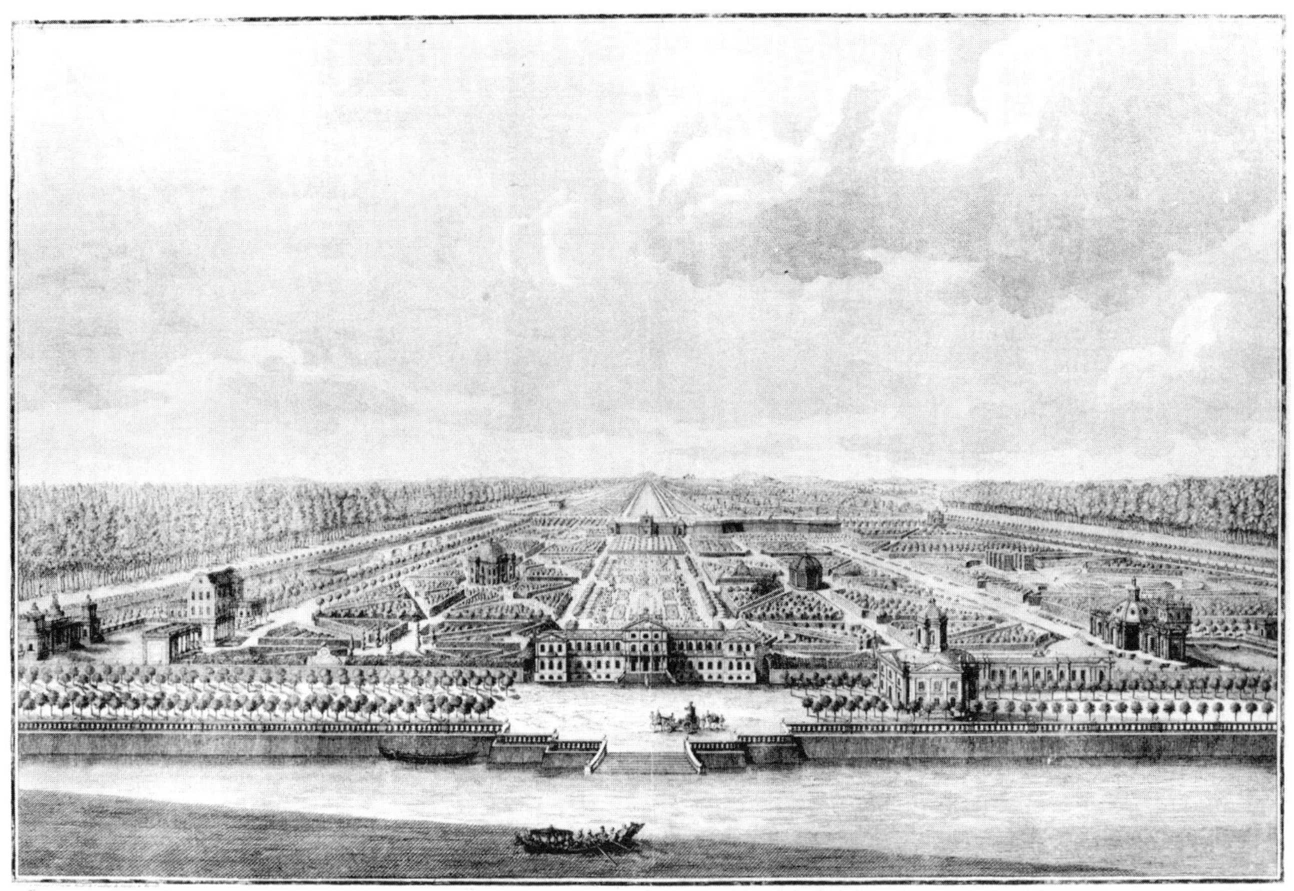

Kuskovo garden, ca. 1770s
Courtesy of Moscow Institute of Architecture

In 1755 the large lake was dug, with the palace and church standing on its bank. In the 1770s the palace was rebuilt in neoclassical style but was still made of wood. The main axis of the complex crossed the center of the palace and the lake, and then was continued by a long channel surrounded by groves. The beginning of the channel near the lake was marked by two columns—lighthouses—while its end was decorated by a cascade. Nearby was situated the large menagerie with some hundreds of animals.

At the other side of the palace the regular garden was developed; a long greenhouse building was placed on the same main axis, at the garden's end. The central part of the garden was covered by a low parterre of ornamental patterns. In summer the pots containing exotic southern plants and trees were taken from the greenhouse and put around the parterre. On both sides of the parterre there were bosquettes of pruned shrubs and trees, while in between stood the pavilions: the Dutch house, the Italian house (1754–55), the Grotto over the Italian pond (1756–62), the Hermitage (1765–67), and the Menagerie (1761–63).

The special American greenhouse was built in the 1770s for the plants brought from the New World. In the main greenhouse were grown different types of palms, laurels, bitters, orange trees, lemon trees, coffee trees, and tea trees. In the garden cut limes were used as well as box and yews. Attempts to prune the birches were undertaken.

In the 1780s the territory of the park in Kusko was greatly enlarged. The picturesque garden was made with the Philosophical House, the House of Solitude, the Temple of Silence, the "ideal" peasant's estate similar to that at Versailles, and the Chinese Pagoda in the manner of William Chambers at the Royal Botanic Gardens, Kew.

In the 18th century Kuskovo became popular for its festivals and fireworks. Here the famous Sheremetyev's theater was organized with serf actors. During the holidays the owners of Kuskovo received more than 1,000 privileged guests, while the gardens were opened for the common people. According to some accounts, during summer festivals nearly 50,000 visitors came to Kuskovo from Moscow.

During the 19th century Kuskovo was neglected, as the Sheremetyevs preferred to stay in other residences.

Nevertheless, the palace and gardens were restored in the 1850s and again in the 1870s. In the second half of the 20th century, several additional restorations were undertaken.

Synopsis

1715	Field Marshal B.P. Sheremetyev receives lands of Kuskovo
1720s	Layout of gardens begins
1737–54	Works of architect U. Kologrovov constructed
1737	Construction of church
1749	Construction of Dutch house garden pavilion
1755	Creation of large pond
1755–65	Works of architect and gardener F.S. Argunov constructed
1765–80	Works of architect K.I. Blank constructed
1770	Construction of existing estate palace
1782	Plan for whole complex by architect serf A. Mironov
1850s	First restoration of garden
1958–68	Restoration of garden by architect L. Soboleva
1985–97	Latest restoration of garden and buildings of Kuskovo

Further Reading

Chvidkovski, D., and J.M. Pérouse de Montclos, editors, *Moscou: Patrimoine architectural,* Paris: Flammarion, 1997

Glozman, Iosif Moiseevich, and Leonard Vladislavovich Tydman, *Kuskovo*, Moscow: Iskusstvo, 1966

DMITRY SHVIDKOVSKY

Kyoto Botanic Garden

Kyoto, Japan

Location: bank of Kamo River, northern part of Kyoto

Kyoto Botanical Garden, one of the oldest and foremost in Japan, was founded in 1917 as a place for botanical study and relaxation for the general public. It is positioned on the bank of the Kamo River in the northern part of Kyoto, a flat area of 24 hectares (59 acres) surrounded with the Kitayama and Higashiyama mountain ranges visible in the distance. Its wide alleys—shaded by mature camphor trees (*Cinnamomum camphora*), a large central lawn, secluded spots, and easy access to the plants—provide for a variety of activities for individual and group visitors. A heaven of quiet in the midst of the busy town, it is considered a scenic spot where the aesthetic qualities of planting are heightened by the careful framing of the views of the distant mountain ranges.

The Garden was created in response to a call for a socially beneficial and instructive project to mark Emperor Taisho's accession to the throne in 1912. The Taisho period was remarkable for the increased democratization and liberalization of Japan and for a social policy that encouraged openness to the developments in the West. The Garden aimed to create an environment in which plants could be appreciated in a wide cultural and social context, where they could be touched and studied, collected, grown, and exhibited as a service for the general public. These are still the aims today.

The original idea, however, involved staging a great exhibition called the Taisho State Ceremony Memorial Kyoto Exhibition, for which the area of 33 hectares (82 acres) was cleared in April 1913. The plans were changed because of economic circumstances. Shouichi Omori, governor of Kyoto Prefecture, decided on the establishment of the botanical garden, and with the financial help of the Mitsui family, the garden became one of the earliest botanical gardens to be created in Japan. It shares this distinction with the Tokyo University Botanical Garden (the Koishikawa Botanical Garden) and the Hokkaido University Botanical Garden.

In April 1917 building works were begun under the direction of Ryousaku Terasaki from the Meiji Jinguu shrine construction department. The site was a largely uninhabited area still within the borders of the city with easy access for visitors. The first director of the garden (1921–29) was Kan Kooriba (1882–1957), a professor in the Kyoto University Department of Science. The work was completed on 10 November 1923 on the anniversary of Emperor Taisho's accession to the throne, and the garden was opened to the public on 1 January 1924. It was then called the State Ceremony Memorial Kyoto Botanical Garden and housed the largest collection of plants in Japan (2,500 species). An entry fee was charged.

In the aftermath of World War II, the site was requisitioned by the Allied forces, who used it between 1946 and 1957. Houses and roads were constructed, and the site was ruined (70 to 80 percent of the collections were lost), but the 200-meter-long (219 yd.) promenade of camphor (Kusunoki) trees survive from the original planting, as do the *Zelkova* trees, bordering the approach road to the main entrance. These are now 70 years old. Some plants, veterans from the first phase of the garden's history, are now especially cherished as witnesses to these historical events and as examples of mature beauty; these include the *Keteleeria davidiana* var. *formosana* (1930), *Sophora japonica* var. *pendula* (1934), *Photinia serrulata* (1935), and *Juniperus chinensis* 'Pyramidalis' (1938).

When the Allied forces returned the Garden to the Kyoto Prefecture Council, the Japan Association of Botanical Gardens suggested the restoration of the garden. In December 1957, a Botanical Garden Round Table Conference Group was formed, a new management structure was created, the Kyoto Botanical Gardens Corporate Foundation was established, and finally, reflecting all these developments, the name of the garden was changed to the Kyoto Botanical Garden. The ceremony of groundbreaking in August 1960 began a year of extensive restoration works, and the Garden reopened to the public in April 1961.

The restoration has remained true to the original conception of the garden while at the same time allowing for the modernization and addition of new features. The present garden has essentially the same ground plan as before: wide, gently curving alleys circling the area in an unhurried, clear manner. The southeastern part was designed from the start in a European manner. The Sunken Garden, with a fountain and a waterfall, presented European seasonal flowers against the background of turf and clipped evergreens. Now it forms a part of the European Style Garden, which consists of three formal courts along one axis directed toward the distant Mount Hiei. Two of the courts, called the Approach Garden and the Rose Garden, feature 2,000 bushes of 300 cultivars of roses, while the Sunken Garden, the last one, retains its old form. The European feel continues across the large adjacent lawn provided for recreation and into the freely planted Perennials and Useful Plants Garden, while the undulating paths lead to the Japanese flora enclaves. The Japanese Iris Garden, with wooden walkways over a pond, contains 250 cultivars of iris, including the Edo, Ise, and Higo lines. The Japanese Native Plants Garden contains 1,000 species of wild and traditionally cultivated plants in a near natural habitat. The Bamboo Garden displays 100 taxa of bamboo chosen for their relevance to daily life: for food, furnishings, and building.

The new conservatory, completed in 1992, was designed to reflect in its architecture the continuity of the Japanese gardening tradition and its unity with the natural environment. Its ideological expression and architectural form have been specifically commissioned by the Kyoto Prefecture Council. The conservatory recalls the form of the Kinkaku-ji temple (known as the Golden Pavilion or by its official name, Kitayama Rokuon-ji Temple), surrounded with water, while the two undulating halls reflect the peaks of the nearby Kitayama Hills. It houses 25,000 plants representing some 4,500 tropical species, divided into nine environmental zones, creating humid, dry, and alpine habitats. This is the most comprehensive collection of tropical plants in Japan, while the bromeliad collection is the greatest in the world.

To mark the 100th anniversary of Kyoto Prefecture, a new Japanese Forest in the northern part of the garden was established in 1970. This area of 9 hectares (22.2 acres) now comprises several zones: the Nakaragi-no-Mori Wood, the adjacent Coniferous Plantation, the Ume Grove, and the Cherry Grove. The Coniferous Trees area gives preference to trees of economic importance, uniting Japanese varieties of pine and cedar with sequoias and other nonnative conifers. Unique to the Botanical Garden are specimens of trees once native to the Shimogamo area of the Yamashiro Basin that form the 0.5-hectare (1.2-acre) Nakaragi-no-Mori wood enclosed by five ponds.

The Camellia Garden, the block planting of cherries and plums, the maple trees, and large areas of peonies, *Iris laevigata,* and rhododendron cultivars provide sweeping seasonal displays, and the annual splendor of cherry blossom and autumn color is especially admired. Both these and the establishment of the permanent bonsai exhibition site relate to and promote the national cultural and aesthetic tradition, which is reinforced by the establishment of a Shinto shrine in the Nakaragi-no-Mori, a teahouse, and the traditional rock dressing of the ponds.

The Kyoto Botanical Garden is already home to 120,000 specimens of 12,000 varieties and aims to continue as the main center for plant collections in Japan. The garden's most representative plants are the tropical plant collection (Maranthaceae, Heliconia, Gesneliad, Acanthaceae, and Rhipsalis) and the Japanese wild collection (camellia, Japanese iris cultivars, and hydrangea). The most prized sites are the Nakaragi-no-Mori Wood, the Japanese Native Plants Garden, and the Bamboo Garden.

The Omori Bunko Library, a memorial to Shoichi Omori, houses 3,000 valuable books, an example of which is *Honzokomoku,* a 1590 Chinese edition, one of only three in existence.

Synopsis

1913 33.5 hectares (82.7 acres) cleared for Taisho State Ceremony Memorial Kyoto Exhibition

1917 Work begins on creation of botanical garden under direction of Meiji Jinguu Shrine construction engineer Ryousaku Terasaki
1921–27 Kan Kooriba takes up post of first director of Kyoto Botanical Garden
1923 Completion of construction works; garden named State Ceremony Memorial Kyoto Botanical Garden
1924 Garden opened to public
1929–49 Akio Kikuchi second director of garden
1945 Garden requisitioned by Allied Forces
1957 Ruined garden returned to Kyoto County Council
1959 Name changed to Kyoto Botanical Garden; new management structure put into place
1960 Start of restoration work
1961 Completion of conservatory, visitor center, and amenities; opening ceremony; garden reopens to public
1962–78 Jirou Fumoto third director of garden
1966 Work begins on 9-hectare (22.2-acre) Japanese Forest as part of celebrations to mark centenary of Kyoto Prefecture Council
1980 2.5-hectare (6.2-acre) European style garden remodeled and enlarged in southeastern part of garden
1992 Opening of new conservatory and visitors center to public; New Kitayama gate completed

Further Reading

The Kyoto Botanical Garden Guide Book/Kyoto Furitsu Shokubutsu-en Gaido Bukku, Kyoto: Kyoto Botanical Garden, 1997

Kyoto Furitsu Shokubutsu-en Shi (The History of the Kyoto Botanical Garden), Kyoto: Kyoto Prefecture, 1959; 2nd edition, Kyoto Botanical Garden, 1961

Nippon no Shokubutsu-en (The Botanical Garden in Japan), Kyoto: Japan Association of Botanical Gardens, 1987

Reischauer, Edwin O., *Japan: Past and Present,* New York: Knopf, 1946; London: Duckworth, 1947; new edition, as *Japan: The Story of a Nation,* New York: Knopf, and London: Duckworth, 1970

AGNIESZKA WHELAN

L

Labels, Plant

Considering the time, trouble, and expense plant labels have caused gardeners in the past, it is strange that these vital accessories of the garden have not received serious attention from garden historians. Plant labels are essentially the product of the 18th-century Enlightenment and the quest for scientific knowledge. Of course botanic gardens predate this time, and occasional references before this may be found to the labeling of plants. In 1720 nurseryman Adam Holt wrote of numbered lead labels that were to be nailed to a wall beside various plants: "It's thought four penny nails will be big enough."

The 18th-century kitchen and garden calendars are largely silent on the subject of labels and lettering. This is perhaps understandable. Prior to the industrial revolution, pleasure gardens were less numerous than they were later. Most of the gardens that did exist were privately owned with their own gardeners. Ever keen to retain for themselves knowledge of plants, the caretakers disclosed information only to the privileged few. This secretiveness was a phenomenon that sometimes existed even into the 19th century when gardeners or curators deliberately did not label plants. Pride in being able to announce the name of a plant to a visitor was all very well, but once the gardener died or left, too often no one knew what was what, and confusion reigned.

The Enlightenment witnessed great strides in scientific botany. The desire to list and catalog plants, the influx of exotic plants to America and Europe, and the dramatic increase in the variety of printed source material on plants (dictionaries, floras, and botanical magazines) all encouraged the serious gardener to label plants.

The sharp rise in the number of botanic gardens and public parks also encouraged the use of labels, although the latter were slower and less diligent about labeling. Two further developments also helped to popularize the use of labels: the increase in the transport of plants across the globe, especially after the invention of the Wardian case, and the blossoming of the commercial nursery trade in exotic plants.

By the 19th century labeling was regarded in botanical circles as desirable. The variety of types of labels in the 19th century was considerable. The old system of painting a number on wooden stakes or directly onto tree trunks continued throughout the century, even for a while at the Royal Botanic Gardens, Kew. A catalog giving the numbers and then the name and details of the plant was sometimes printed and sold to the general public. But more often a handwritten ledger listing the numbers and names was kept in the garden office, thus effectively retaining knowledge of the plants within a privileged inner circle. This was sometimes justified with the dubious argument that the system discouraged thieves who did not know what was what and thus what was valuable.

Wooden labels were the most common. Sometimes made of pine wood, those of teak, oak, or elm were more durable. Wooden labels could be varnished, painted, or soaked in solutions of lime or sulfate of iron.

Cast-iron labels were more expensive (about sixpence each). They were often T-shaped, the "T" placed directly into the ground in front of the plant. Usually these were painted black or soaked in a solution of copper, ammonium, hydrochloric acid, and water. The lettering was then painted on in white paint. Iron-framed labels with a glass front became quite common in the middle of the 19th century, with the name of the plant written on a piece of paper covered by the glass. These were not successful, as the damp warped the paper and the sun dried out the putty or resin that kept the glass in place. Steel labels and those of slate or terra-cotta were less common. The most attractive, and most expensive, were the white enamel labels with blue or black lettering that became popular in the late Victorian era.

All shapes and sizes were used for labels, but most were either the T-shaped labels or oval or rectangular disks that could be fixed to a stake or nailed to a tree, preferably using copper or zinc-coated nails. The labels in Melbourne Botanic Gardens were especially unusual and described in 1873 as similar to "miniature tombstones."

The problems associated with plant labels seemed endless to 19th-century gardeners. Slate or enamel labels tended to chip or break. The weather was perhaps the worst enemy: frost, rain, humidity, and especially sunlight attacked labels and their lettering. Rust, rot, expanding metal, warping, and fading all contributed to the problem. Wood-eating borer insects were a common culprit as destroyers of labels or their stakes. Damage caused by pesticide also created a challenge, with the lampblack, copper, ammonium, and water solution of the French chemist Brainnot sometimes being used to counter this.

A problem facing many gardens was procuring a good "letterer." In Australia sometimes a convict was found with a clear and steady hand. In Oodeypore, India, in 1880 it was said that Shiu Charan was "a good printer with the pen as the labels in the rose garden prove."

A constant complaint of a newly arrived gardener was that labeling was inadequate. Initial enthusiasm for labeling soon diminished as the task became more daunting. So many different species, uncertainty as to exact identity, the deterioration of existing labels, and the general changing nature of a garden through the death of plants, new introductions, climate, and fashion all countered a successful labeling initiative. And of course there were, and still are, many complaints about inaccuracies on labels, whether through ignorance or a later change of nomenclature.

The general public could also be a problem, rearranging labels as a practical joke; garden workmen also frequently put the labels back in the wrong place in error after weeding. Theft of plant labels was commonplace as was the vandalizing of labels. In 1864 a boy was fined 18 shillings for shooting at labels with a catapult in Belfast Botanic Garden.

Finally there was the problem of expense. In 1786 Kew Gardens was paying threepence per dozen for "flower sticks." Letterers also had to be paid. In Glasnevin, Ireland, this could cost as much as threepence per label. In the 26 years from 1839 to 1865, that botanic garden spent on average more than £21 a year on labels and lettering, David McArdle succeeding his father Pat as a letterer. In some years the cost of the lettering at Glasnevin was the equivalent of the annual wage of an undergardener.

In 1892 Kew Gardens introduced a new type of label, which was cut out from a sheet of smooth lead and then stamped with a name. The lettering was then painted white. These labels lasted many years. A generation later, well into the 20th century, machine-stamped aluminum labels with raised letters became popular in gardens. But the old wood and hand-painted labels continued to be used. More recently a revolution in labeling has occurred with the use of various forms and combinations of plastic. While some of these become brittle and discolor, plastic has nonetheless disposed of many of the problems of labels. Still, too many public gardens and botanic gardens are inadequately labeled. In 1880 Dr. Trimen of Ceylon commented that without labeling, "little more than a feeling of admiration can be experienced by even intelligent visitors. . . . It has been customary here to accompany visitors over the ground and attempt to supply by word what could be far better conveyed by the eye."

Further Reading

Bailey, Liberty H., editor, *The Standard Cyclopedia of Horticulture,* 6 vols., New York: Macmillan, 1914–17

Desmond, Ray, *Kew: The History of the Royal Botanic Gardens,* London: Harvill Press, 1995

Hadfield, Miles, *Gardening in Britain,* London: Hutchison, 1960; 3rd edition, as *A History of British Gardening,* London: Murray, 1979

McCracken, Donal P., *Gardens of Empire: Botanical Institutions of the Victorian British Empire,* London: Leicester University Press, 1997

McCracken, Eileen M., *The Palm House and Botanic Garden, Belfast,* Belfast: Ulster Architectural Heritage Society, 1971

Nelson, E. Charles, and Eileen M. McCracken, *The Brightest Jewel: A History of the National Botanic Gardens, Glasnevin, Dublin,* Kilkenny, Ireland: Boethius Press, 1987

Donal P. McCracken

La Granja

Segovia Province, Spain

Location: 7 miles (11.2 km) southeast of the city of Segovia, from Madrid via Navacerrada

One of the favorite pastimes of the Castillian monarchs was hunting in the Sierra de Guadarrama near the city of Segovia. This affinity led Henry III of Castile to build a hunting lodge in the nearby Valsaín forest. Henry IV would add a second lodge, as well as a hermitage dedicated to San Ildefonso. The Catholic monarchs transferred the lands to the Jerónimos from El Parral who, besides converting them into a spiritual retreat, also put them to use as farmland. It is from the Spanish word for "farm" that the name *La Granja* derives. The region was highly valued by the Spanish Habsburgs both for the beauty of the landscape and the quality of the hunting. Philip II (1527–98) in the 16th century ordered the construction of a palace at Valsaín, which was later destroyed by fire. But it was Philip V, the first Spanish Bourbon, who in 1720 decided to repurchase the lands from the monks. Enamored of the area, he ordered that a palace and an extensive network of gardens be built.

Philip V (1683–1746), the grandson of Louis XIV, was born in Versailles. He ascended to the Spanish throne after the War of Spanish Succession. Memories of the French palaces and gardens would come to play a role in the La Granja project. Philip's second wife, Isabella Farnese, was also very fond of La Granja. An Italian princess, she had a great deal of influence on the king. Consequently, elements not only of the French baroque garden but also of the Italian Renaissance garden can be detected at La Granja. According to Kubler, only the alcazar proper was Spanish; the gardens and fountains, in contrast, were French inspired, while the palace wings, the north and south courtyards, and the garden facade were Italian influenced. La Granja therefore had a Spanish nucleus, a French park, and Italian surfaces. The Marqués de Lozoya, however, claimed that the gardens were derived from the Italian model and were conceived of as a sort of theater where stone and metal actors would play out pagan scenes on a verdurous stage. Whatever the case may be, the French artists René Carlier and Esteban Boutelou worked on the first layout of the garden, and French artists such as Carlier, René Frémin, Jacques Bousseau, and H. Dumandré designed the fountains and its sculptures.

La Granja's most outstanding feature is the siting of the ensemble and the way in which it has been adapted to the surrounding environment. This was probably directed by the French engineer Etienne Marchand, the creator of the hydraulic system. Beginning at an elevation of 1,192 meters (1,304 yd.), La Granja is situated at the foot of the Sierra de Guadarrama; from the point at which the Eresma River meets the Cambrones, the ensemble follows a slope that runs toward the southeast into a natural cirque, where a cluster of hills known as the Silla del Rey provides a natural backdrop to the setting. The garden—today, the park—extends from the main facade of the palace to this cluster of hills. A green area with an abundance of water, the vegetation ranges from small stands of trees to larger woodlands. In the lower-lying areas along the river, stands of elm, ash, and black poplar are typical, while in the foothills of the mountains are forests dominated by oak and Valsaín pine. In the garden proper, lime, maple, and horse chestnut, as well as a variety of conifers, were introduced along with the plants and shrubs planted there.

Pond with fountain, La Granja, Segovia, Spain
Copyright Paul Miles Picture Collection

Taken together these areas form a large rectangle—over 162 hectares (400 acres)—surrounded by a six-kilometer-long wall with four gates located on the north face, which contains the town, the palace, and the gardens. Twenty-six fountains and 54 statues, along with other minor elements, ornament the parterres. The figures and vases are of varnishing lead; there are also statues, pedestals, and benches made of marble from Genoa, Granada, and El Paular, a region north of Madrid. The iconography was influenced by the works of Cesare Ripa and by the illustrations of Charles Le Brun; however, while the central motif at Versailles is Apollo—the symbol of the king—at La Granja the principal figure is Diana, the huntress.

Opposite the king's apartments, and practically at an axis with the main body of the facade, lies the Great Cascade. It is made up of 11 stepped pools that rise from a central parterre—encircled by statues and patterned designs of myrtle and yew—to the fountain of the Three Graces. The work of Frémin, the fountain stands out against a verdurous background with the mountains in view behind.

Near the main facade to the north lies a series of fountains. The *Carrera de los Caballos* (Horse Race) marks the beginning of a spectacular view, where three small reservoirs with sculpted figures form an axis with the fountain of *El Abanico* (the Fan). This is followed by a larger reservoir containing the fountain of *Neptune*; separated from Neptune by two stairways, the cascade fountain of *Apollo* rises from a half-moon-shaped reservoir. It is from here that the Ría descends to surround the ensemble. The final touch to this vista is provided by the fountain of *Andromeda* rising up from a small plateau. Descending from the north facade, the fountain of *Pomona* depicts the moment at which Vertumnus reveals his true identity to the Roman goddess of garden fruits.

Lying at the extremity of the garden, about 900 meters (984 yd.) in a straight line from the palace facade, is the artificial lake that provides water to the garden and fountains. At an elevation of 1,245 meters (1,362 yd.), El Mar (the Sea) collects water from three streams that descend from the nearby mountains. The small woodland of pine and oak trees surrounding the reservoir blends with the preexisting vegetation in the area.

The system of parterres at the southern end of the garden is organized around a central *glorieta* (plaza) known as the Plaza of the Eight Avenues. At each of the eight corners is a fountain and an allée leading to other fountains: the fountain of *Latona*, the *Fountain of the Frogs* (designed by Jean Thierry and executed by Jacques Bousseau, Pierre Pitué, and the Dumandré brothers), the fountain of the *Canastillo* (Basket), and others.

Palace with reflecting pond, La Granja, Segovia, Spain
Copyright Paul Miles Picture Collection

The most architecturally involved fountain is that of *Diana.* Among the last to be built, the fountain was executed in 1742 by H. Dumandré and Pitué using the designs of Bousseau and may have been modeled after the fountain of the *Triton* at Versailles. It is contained by a wall of Sepulveda stone bordered by cascade fountains; on the jets are groups of sculpted figures including children and nymphs among deer, dogs, and aquatic birds. Of the fountain, Philip V is said to have commented, "It has cost me three million and amused me three minutes."

Also outstanding is the Parterre de la Fama (renown), which extends longitudinally opposite the Patio de la Herradura (horseshoe courtyard). In the shape of a bowling green, the parterre includes meticulously patterned box hedges, statues, and vases. In the center is a circular reservoir from which rises the fountain of *La Fama,* with a jet 47 meters high.

Between the gardens and the walls were enclosed beds of fruit trees and flowering plants. Each of these beds is named for a specialized operation of the garden. To the northeast, for example, are El Plantel (the nursery), La Estufa (the hothouse), El Invernáculo (the greenhouse), La Huerta Grande (the fruit and vegetable garden), and El Laberinto (the maze). To the southeast are La Partida de la Reina (the Queen's orchard) and the garden of La Botica (the apothecary).

The king was less than fond of El Escorial, and his choice of site, combined with Isabella's contributions, made the creation of a garden designed for summer possible. St. Louis's Day in August offers an excellent opportunity to view the spectacular ensemble of water effects and to admire the singular union of elements in what is a collective work of art.

Synopsis

1450 Henry IV of Castille builds hunting lodge and hermitage dedicated to Saint Ildephonsus
1477 Catholic monarchs donate lodge, sanctuary, and surrounding grounds to monks *Jerónimos* (Hieronymite)
1686 Fire devastates Valsaín Palace
1713 Treaty of Utrecht; end of War of Spanish Succession; Philip V crowned king of Spain
1720 Philip repurchases lands from monks
1721 Philip V orders construction of palace (to be summer residence) on grounds of former monastery; Teodoro Ardemans chosen to construct palace; gardens entrusted to René Carlier—brother-in-law of Mansart—and Etienne Boutelou
1722 René Carlier dies; replaced by Renato Frémin, who takes charge of sculpture studios
1723 December 22, Cardinal Borja, Patriarch of the Indies, dedicates church (Colegiata)
1724 Philip V abdicates and retires to La Granja; upon death of son Louis, former king returns to throne
1725 Andrea Procaccini, assisted by Sempronio Subisati, in charge of palace works;
1728 Royal Glassworks founded at La Granja
1734 Alcazar of Madrid burns; Juvara summoned to Spain to design garden facade of palace
1736 Upon death of Juvara, J.B. Sacchetti takes charge of project
1742 H. Dumandré and P. Pitué finish Fountain of Diana
1746 Death of Philip V; buried in church (Colegiata) at palace
1796 Treaty of San Ildefonso between Spain and French Republic
1836 Sergeants Rebellion at La Granja
1844 Under Isabella II, Fountain of Diana restored
1853 Under Isabella II, cascade restored
1918 Fire at palace; Casa de los Canónigos and other pieces destroyed
1933 Restoration of the palace undertaken
1983 ICONA (formerly the Spanish Institute for the Nature Conservation) manages the gardens

Further Reading

Bottineau, Yves, *L'art de cour dans l'Espagne de Philippe V, 1700–1746,* Bordeaux: Féret, 1960
Breñosa, Rafael and Joaquín María de Castellarnau, *Guía y descripción del Real Sitio de San Ildefonso,* Madrid: Rivadeneyra, 1884; reprint, La Granja: Biblioteca Nueva-Icaro, 1991
Casa Valdés, Maria Teresa Ozores y Saavedra, Marquesa de, *Jardines de España,* Madrid: Aguilar, 1973; as *Spanish Gardens,* Woodbridge, Suffolk: Antique Collector's Club, 1987
Digard, Jeanne, *Les jardins de La Granja et leurs sculptures décoratives,* Paris: Ernest Leroux, 1933
Kubler, George, *Arquitectura de los siglos XVII y XVIII,* Madrid: Plus-Ultra, 1957
Lozoya, Juan Conteras y López de Ayala, Marqués de, *The Royal Palaces of La Granja de San Ildefonso and Riofrio,* Madrid: Patrimonio Nacional, 1962
Sancho, Jose Luis, *La arquitectura de los sitios reales: Catálogo histórico de los palacios, jardines y patronatos reales del patrimonio nacional,* Madrid: Patrimonio Nacional y Fundación Tabacalera, 1995

JUAN LUIS DE LAS RIVAS SANZ

Lahore, Shalamar Bagh

Lahore, Pakistan

Location: on the Grand Trunk Road, 6 miles (9.7 km) east of the Delhi Gate of the old walled city of Lahore

Shalamar Bagh in Lahore is the second and best known of the three Mogul gardens having this name (see Plate 20). It is the only Mogul garden on the United Nations Educational, Scientific, and Cultural Organization (UNESCO) World Heritage list. The third was completed in Delhi in 1650 but had been mostly destroyed by the end of the 18th century. The first, completed near Srinagar in Kashmir in 1620, gave all three gardens their name. This name is often said to mean abode of love, for *shala* means abode and *mar* means love or, more precisely, bliss. A likelier—though more prosaic—explanation is that *shali* in both Sanskrit and Kashmiri means rice cultivation, while *mar* means the black, loamy soil suitable for this crop. The Kashmir garden is situated in just such a rich rice-growing region.

Based on Persian prototypes, Mogul gardens were the earliest pleasure gardens to be laid out in India, where they also took on some indigenous characteristics, particularly in the patterns of their brickwork. Like the great Persian gardens, they were walled, rectilinear in form, and harmonized a profusion of plants through the orchestration of running water. Water for the first Shalamar in Kashmir was provided by diverting a stream to flow through the terraced garden built on the slope of a hill. This garden had been built at the order of the emperor Jehangir, and it was added to by his son and successor, the fifth Mogul emperor, Shah Jahan.

At Lahore, where Shah Jahan created the second Shalamar, he was first faced with the problem of obtaining a supply of water. This was accomplished by his talented engineer Ali Mardan Khan, in 1633, who brought the waters of the Ravi River more than a hundred miles through a canal that began at Madhupur, now in India. The site was so well chosen that the British later used it as the place to take off water for their great Bari Doab Canal. Adjacent to the garden, the Moguls built a three-level filtration plant to purify the water before it entered Shalamar. This structure survived until 1999, when it was demolished to make way for a widening of the road. At Shah Jahan's direction, the garden itself was begun under the supervision of Khaliullah Khan and, after 18 months, was completed in 1642 at a cost of six lakhs of rupees.

Enclosing about 40 acres (16.2 ha), its towering red brick walls exclude wind-blown dust and make the garden an orderly sanctuary from the chaotic clutter of everyday life outside. The British spoiled the aesthetic effect of the garden by opening a new entrance in the middle of the south end. The original entrances were on either side of the lowest of the three terraces, each of which ascends about 15 feet (4.6 m). Thus, as one was intended to mount from the Faiz Bakhsh (Bountiful) level toward the final Farah Bakhsh (Delight) level, new sensual pleasures of sight, sound, and aroma would be revealed. Spilling over the lip of the middle terrace was an unbroken sheet of water, *sawan-bhadon* (meaning monsoon time, the monsoon being a season of rejoicing in the subcontinent), which fell past niches containing twinkling oil lamps at night, golden vases of flowers by day. On either side of this cascade, steps led up to the middle level, where 150 red sandstone fountains jetted plumes of water 12 feet (3.7 m) high to cool the sultry air. Beyond the shallow tank from whose surface some of these jets still arise, the white marble throne of the emperor also remains, framed by more jets and a marble *abshar,* a carved chute, 20 feet (6 m) wide, down which water ripples from the uppermost terrace of the garden.

In the time of Shah Jahan, this loftiest terrace was the domain of the royal family when they were in residence in Lahore, with separate apartments for the emperor and empress and an audience hall for the reception of guests. A Turkish-style bath was located on the east side of the middle terrace, and a domed tower stood at each corner of the garden, while other small pavilions were scattered elsewhere. All these structures were elaborately decorated, with marble and tile work and perhaps *pietra dura* (inlaid semi-precious stones), most of which was removed by the Sikh successors (1767–1848) either to sell or to adorn their own buildings. The architectural structures seen today in Shalamar are brick-and-plaster reproductions.

Structurally, the Lahore garden consists of two *chahar-baghs* separated by a central reservoir. The *chahar-bagh* (literally, four gardens) is a Persian form, and in Lahore each *chahar-bagh* is itself further divided into four quadrants. The plants in the quadrants are watered from a narrow canal separating each *chahar-bagh* from its neighbors, while the great central reservoir has a narrow walkway crossing it to enable a visitor to reach the stone platform at its center. A somewhat wider longitudinal canal runs the entire length of the garden, linking all the pools and subsidiary canals into one hydraulic system.

Flower beds lie slightly lower than these canals, making it convenient for the gardeners to dip irrigation water from an ever-ready source. In addition to beds of massed flowers alternating with patches of grassy lawns, the original Mogul garden design emphasized trees, both for the sake of providing shade and especially for the agreeable sensations of taste and aroma.

Records show that there were fruit trees such as mango, cherry, apricot, peach, plum, apple, almond, quince, mulberry, and both sour and sweet orange. It is not known what flowering plants filled the beds or what aromatic plants and bushes may have been used. It is known, however, that the plantings of deciduous trees were punctuated by occasional evergreen cypresses, symbolizing eternity in the midst of fleeting fecundity. Although never wholly neglected, Shalamar changed over time with the changing tastes of its owners. In one period, it is said, it was wholly planted in mango trees.

As late as 1711, when the garden already had lost much of its splendor, it still took 128 gardeners to maintain it. Even though the Sikhs are blamed for stripping away most of the architectural embellishments, they too loved flowers. The first professional naturalist to leave a record, Victor Jacquemont, who was lodged in Shalamar in 1831 as a guest of the Sikh ruler Ranjit Singh, described his experience thus:

> We alighted at the entrance of a delicious oasis, consisting of a large parterre of carnations, irises, and roses, with walks of orange trees and jasmine, bordered with basins, in which a multitude of little fountains were playing. In the centre of this beautiful garden was a little palace, furnished with extreme luxury and elegance. This is my abode.

Synopsis

1630s	Gardens laid out by Ali Mardan Khan, by command of Shah Jahan, Mogul emperor of India
1633	Completion of Shah Nahar canal bringing water from Ravi River to the garden site
1641	Planting of fruit trees begun
1642	Completed garden opened by Emperor Shah Jahan
1654	First mention of name "Shalamar" (Abode of Love, or perhaps Rice Soil, depending on the translation), in *Bahar e Sakhun*, a book compiled by Shah Jahan's historian
1659	Aurangzeb, Shah Jahan's son and successor, visits Shalamar
1712	John Ketelaar, ambassador of Dutch East India Company, leaves account of his visit
1747–72	During time of Ahmed Shah Abdali, garden suffers from neglect
1767–98	During reign of Lahna Singh, agate and marble embellishments stripped away, and Shalamar became so overgrown it was said to be the haunt of tigers
1820	English visitor William Moorecraft, as guest of Ranjit Singh, reports that many architectural elements have been "suffered by the Sikh prince to fall into decay"
1831	French visitor Victor Jacquemont, as guest of Ranjit Singh, calls garden a delicious oasis and is impressed by abundance of flowers
1849	Renovation of Shalamar begun after Second Sikh War, when Punjab came under control of British
1876	Visit of Prince of Wales (later Edward VII), who inaugurates practice of using Shalamar Bagh as site for receptions for important visitors
1956	Reception given at Shalamar Bagh to Chou En-lai during his state visit to Pakistan
1981	Shalamar becomes only Mogul garden on UNESCO World Heritage list
1999	Garden's water filtration plant, only such Mogul works remaining, bulldozed to widen Grand Trunk Road

Further Reading

Aijazuddin, F.S., *Lahore: Illustrated Views of the 19th Century,* Middletown, New Jersey: Grantha, 1991

Crowe, Sheila, et al., *The Gardens of Mughul India,* London: Thames and Hudson, 1972

Hussain, Mahmood, Abdul Rehman, and James L. Wescoat, Jr., editors, *The Mughal Garden: Interpretation, Conservation, and Implications,* Rawalpindi, Pakistan: Ferozsons, 1996

Jacquemont, Victor, *Correspondance avec sa famille et plusieurs de ses amis: Pendant son voyage dans l'Inde (1828–1832),* Paris, 1833; new edition, 2 vols., Paris, 1869

Moorcroft, William, and George Trebeck, *Travels in the Himalayan Provinces of Hindustan and the Panjab,* 2 vols., London, 1841; reprint, edited by Horace Hayman Wilson, Pakistan and New York: Oxford University Press, 1979

Moynihan, Elizabeth B., *Paradise As a Garden: In Persia and Mughal India,* New York: Braziller, 1979

Osborne, William Godolphin, *The Court and Camp of Runjeet Sing,* London: Colburn, 1840; reprint, Karachi, Pakistan: Oxford University Press, 1973

Waliullah Khan, Mohammad, *Lahore and Its Important Monuments,* Lahore, Pakistan: Department of Archaeology, 1959–61; 3rd edition, Karachi: Department of Archaeology and Museums, Ministry of Education, Government of Pakistan, 1973

CHARLES BOEWE

Landscape Architecture

Landscape architecture is one of the seven fine arts. As such it is viewed as an environmental-design profession and as a discipline of broad scope concerned with the design, planning, and management of landscapes. At the heart of the profession is the belief that planning and design for a healthy society rests on the commitment to stewardship of the earth and the conservation and reservation of landscape as the foundation of human experience and culture. Landscape architects strive toward the creation of landscape that respects the land processes and integrity, aids in the fulfillment of human potentials, and aspires to art. Tracing the evolution of the profession is an interesting journey that can only be highlighted here. An overview of the main themes of the profession reveals the influences that shaped the practice of landscape architecture in the United States and the rest of the Western world.

Although the term *landscape architecture* and the profession itself are relatively modern, people have been practicing both the art and science of this field for thousands of years. The design and installation of ancient times were carried out by individuals who had the training and experience to complete the project. The selection of these designers was based on their leadership skills as well as their knowledge of handling natural materials and of construction. Historian Kenneth Helphand has stated that agriculture is perhaps the most significant process from which gardens have derived and that agriculture's symbiotic relationship between humans and plants is idealized and beautified in the garden: "The craft of agriculture—the development of an artful skill in the manipulation of materials and space—is the basis of garden craft and design." The evolution of the garden over time brought about change, and the original agricultural function was lost in the transformation. Water, planting patterns, enclosure, support, and protection of plants are good examples of this ritualization process that took place in landscape design. The linear pattern of irrigation is transformed by the garden design into patterns of pools, basins, channels, and fountains. Other examples of the ritualization process occur when original features become complicated beyond recognition and the garden design is removed from its agriculture roots. For example, the parterre, elaborate geometric patterns of planting beds that were originally laid out for producing vegetables, herbs, and flowers, became a central design element of the pleasure garden.

Historical Perspective

Following the fall of the Roman Empire and during the medieval period, only monastic monks carried on the art of gardening. These cloister gardens in monasteries were formal, with small water features planted with medicinal plants and fruit trees. The decline of the feudal system and the rise of the Renaissance, with a free-market economy, opened a new era in the arts. The semiskilled labor and the early development of the crafts during the medieval times gave way to the establishment of specialized professions. Together with the emergence of science, the profession of landscape architecture delighted the Europeans in creating idealized landscapes. In Italy the tradition and records of the old Roman villas served as inspiration for new work, as was the case in architecture and the other arts. This inspiration is reflected in the Renaissance garden just as in its architecture and paintings. The 16th-century villa gardens provide some of the finest examples of the conscious application of architectural design to the outdoor setting. The Villa Lante, Villa d'Este, and Villa Medici are but a few examples. The native vegetation of Italy was well adapted to the garden's formal design. H. Hubbard and T. Kimball note that the "cypress, the stone pine and the ilex—the vegetation and the architecture of the Italian Garden form a complete and aesthetically sufficient whole to a degree that can be matched in few other styles." The site qualities were respectfully molded into a strong architectural composition, creating a strong contrast between natural and manmade forms—a contrast that provides the essence of visual satisfaction in landscape design. Whereas the Italian gardens of this period were designed mainly by architects, in France they were designed by professional gardeners trained in design. Such was André Le Nôtre (1613–1700). His two masterpieces, Vaux-le-Vicomte and Versailles, represent the ultimate expression of the geometrically designed landscape with carefully set proportions and optical effects.

The emerging Romantic movement in the 18th century produced painting and poetry that praised the beauty of nature and landscape. The English garden (also called the landscape garden) was a product of that movement. The garden form was derived from observation of nature and the period's principles of painting. Undulating lines and articulation of light and shade in the design became the preoccupation of 18th-century England and Europe and in the 19th century, the United States. The French parterres and terraces of the formal gardens were replaced with rolling grass, lakes, meandering rivers, and groups of trees. The English school also eliminated the visual break between the garden and the landscape. The wall that separated the garden from the surrounding land was replaced by a sunken barrier—the ha-ha. William Kent (1685–1748) was the first professional to design gardens in the new manner. Lancelot "Capability" Brown (1716–86) worked under

Kent's direction and later became the head designer at Stowe. Brown continued to clear the formal layout and bring grass up to the house foundation. Sunken fences eliminated the visual boundaries of the site, and groups of trees blended into the landscape. To be successful, these picturesque landscapes required the understanding of ecological principles. Humphry Repton (1752–1818) published a theory of landscape gardening (*Observations on the Theory and Practice of Landscape Gardening,* 1803). He was successor to Capability Brown at Stowe, restoring the terrace and connecting it to the house. He was best known, however, for his Red Books (so-called because they were bound in red morocco), which illustrated his proposals with "before" and "after" drawings and with watercolors to sell his designs to clients.

The Romantic movement, well established by the 19th century, is a tradition that continues in England and many parts of Europe to the present time. Both the Renaissance and the Romantic styles also found fertile ground in the United States, beginning with George Washington (1732–99) at Mount Vernon, Virginia (1737), and Thomas Jefferson (1743–1826) at Monticello in Virginia (1809). Some of the completely new landscape gardens were designed by André Parmentier (1780–1830), who established a nursery in Brooklyn, New York, and who in 1828 was commissioned to develop plans for a number of estates from Canada to the southern United States. He was succeeded by Andrew Jackson Downing (1815–52) as the champion of the landscape garden in the United States.

Downing further advanced the application of the Picturesque in the United States and published his theories in 1846, based on the work of Repton. Downing's *Treatise on the Theory and Practice of Landscape Gardening Adapted to North America* (1841–49) influenced four decades of landscape architects. The theories of landscape design were developed in large part as a response to a concern for public health threatened by the ever-increasing and unhealthy condition in the eastern cities, and Downing had established himself as the tastemaker in gardening matters on the East Coast. The public park movement had its start during this period and used curvilinear drives, irregular-shaped lakes, informal landscape planning, and rustic furnishings. Park planning emerged as a distinct area of growth and practice for the designers offering their services as landscape architects.

By the end of the 19th century, two prototypes of modern gardens achieved their definition: the landscape or flower garden and the architectural garden. These two garden types led to sharp controversy; Gertrude Jekyll (1843–1932) brought sense and resolution to the debate. She approved of formal garden layout near the house and the wilderness of small woodlands with trees and shrubs selected because of their ecological compatibility away from the house. Many attribute the invention of the herbaceous border, a collection of hardy perennial flowering plants providing a succession of flowers throughout the spring, summer, and fall, to Jekyll.

Frederick Law Olmsted (1822–1903) greatly influenced the nature of the practice of landscape architecture in the United States. Like Downing, Olmsted saw landscapes as a cure for the social ills of the ever-increasing urban population density. He was interested in integrating green open spaces into the cities. Prior to 1857 public open spaces were of two types: the small city square and the public garden. Both were elaborate plantings with many ornamental features. While the public gardens were fairly large, they did not block the city traffic, noise, or the noxious odors and for the most part were horticulturally oriented amusement parks. Olmsted was able to apply his theory when, with the English architect Calvert Vaux (1824–95) (who had field experience under Downing), he designed Central Park in New York City (1858). This park drastically changed the nature of open public parks in the United States. While designing Central Park, Olmsted coined the term *landscape architecture* and used it on his letterheads and drawings. He believed that the term *landscape gardening* limited the focus of the profession to the garden. He established his firm and designed or was involved with hundreds of parks and park systems through his lifetime. Central Park was his pivotal work, one that vastly expanded the scale of landscape architecture. Philip Pregill and Nancy Volkman note that Central Park "demonstrated that function as well as appearance was important in the arrangement of outdoor spaces. It proved that properly designed landscapes were not merely civic amenities, but critical to both the physical and economic development of cities."

In addition to designing parks, cemeteries, and communities, Olmsted introduced environmental conservation ethics to the profession, and in 1865 he petitioned to preserve the Yosemite region (known today as Yosemite National Park) for future generations to enjoy, thus contributing to the development of the National Park Service which was later established in 1916.

In 1899 the American Society of Landscape Architects (ASLA) was established. In 1900 the first formal educational program in landscape architecture was offered at Harvard University. Other universities soon followed Harvard's lead. In 1902 the University of Massachusetts became the first land-grant institution to include landscape architecture as a technical program. In 1904 Cornell established a comprehensive professional program. By 1920 six other universities offered landscape architectural degrees.

In 1917 Harvard educators Hubbard and Kimball suggested that in the history of landscape design, design styles fall into two groups or classes: one formal and the other informal or natural. Michael Laurie reinforces the same view: "In time, essentially two systems of landscape design evolved. One based on geometry and the other on nature, although the rationale and meaning has varied with time and place." These two styles combined during the first part of the 20th century when formal style was practiced in estate design in the United States. One of the best examples of this neoclassical approach was Dumbarton Oaks, designed by Beatrix Jones Farrand (1872–1959) beginning in 1920 over a 30-year period. Along with Olmsted, Hubbard, and nine others, Farrand was a founding member of the ASLA. Between 1900 and 1930 the landscape architecture profession entered a somewhat less ambitious phase where at least 90 percent of all landscape architectural projects were residences of various scales.

The neoclassical style created eclectic "rooms" in the garden of different historic styles, all linked along sightline paths. While these were formal, the entry area was designed as a naturalistic site. The plantings were arranged in irregular groupings to frame a broad lawn. An end to the neoclassical design period began with the crash of the stock market in 1929. The early formal and naturalistic styles gave way to a new freedom. There was increasing interest in new forms laid out in nonsymmetrical compositions. This was the movement toward modernism and abstract landscape design. The designs of Thomas Church (1902–78) are associated with the early application of this movement. His work popularized the concept of creating strong connections between indoor and outdoor spaces and making the garden a primary living area.

The Great Depression and two government programs of the New Deal of 1933 had direct repercussions for landscape architecture: the formation of the Civilian Conservation Corps (CCC) and the Works Progress Administration (WPA). Landscape architects were involved in these programs and were again engaged in large-scale planning, playing significant roles in various public programs and involved in physical development and conservation of resources. They worked across the country on planning national and state parks, housing projects, and urban recreation. Community planning was part of the New Deal, and the most successful communities developed during this period were the so-called green cities: Greenbelt, Maryland; Greenhills near Cincinnati, Ohio; and Greendale outside Milwaukee, Wisconsin. These are the best examples of the effort by the designers to create a sense of community and offer social amenities. This period was one of social, economic, and political reorientation, where progressive ideas of conservation, creating pleasant functional urban environments, were implemented and designs that responded to site conditions rather than historical styles were the norm.

Following World War II, Garret Eckbo (b. 1910) was the leader who stressed that landscape architects had a social responsibility. Eckbo, Church, Geraldine Knight Scott, and others who worked for the WPA and the U.S. Forest Service earlier in their careers established a tradition of public and social service. Eckbo's peers, James Rose and Dan Kiley, advanced the importance of regionalism ecology and the multidisciplinary approach to design and design education. The work of Lawrence Halprin (b. 1916) and his writings were an influential force in the 1960s. He sought, through a creative design process based on ecological principles and forms found in nature, to accommodate people in public spaces. Ian McHarg's (b. 1920) *Design with Nature* (1969) is considered a modern classic in environmental planning literature. In it, he advances an approach to design that bases land-planning decision making on natural and social scientific factors. Perhaps more than any other person, McHarg promoted ecological planning and helped make "ecology" the household word that it is today. His design methods are taught in all schools of landscape architecture in the United States and many European countries. Roberto Burle Marx (1920–98), in Brazil, developed an approach to design based on modern planting and botany. In his designs he demonstrated that native or naturalized materials can be used to create bold design statements that reflect the nature and that are well adapted to its conditions.

In the modern era landscape architecture has returned to three concerns: aesthetics, environmentalism, and social needs. Present-day landscape architects have been inspired by modern art, have viewed nature as an inspiration for design forms and a resource to be conserved, and recognize the need for design to improve society's life.

The history of landscape architecture reveals cycles of change in the popularity and importance of landscape and environmental issues. Landscape architecture design and the design process have been strong parts of the tradition of landscape education for some time and have a strong historical context. Various opportunities, creation of governmental agencies, and educational influences left their mark on the profession in the United States. In addition, the U.S. academic model of landscape architectural education is becoming increasingly prevalent in the rest of the world.

The Practice of the Profession

Over time, the realm of landscape architecture has diversified in response to society's needs. Today there are four related types of practice. First is the practice of landscape evaluation and planning. It is concerned with the study of large land areas and the systematic analysis of the area. It has a strong ecological and natural science base (a method developed by McHarg), and it addresses concerns for the area's visual quality and history of the area land uses. The process involves a team of specialists including soil scientists, economists, planners, plant scientists, and geologists. The end result of such studies is a land-use policy or a land-use plan. At times, such studies are made to determine the environmental impact of a proposed development on the area or the study of suitability for development.

The second type of practice is site planning. The real issue of site planning is not whether sites should be planned but rather how systematic and extensive that planning should be. As more buildings are executed with standardized units on a large scale and at a rapid rate, a formal design process becomes imperative. The site is a crucial aspect of our environment. It has a biological, social, and psychological impact that goes beyond its accepted influence on cost and technical function. It limits what people can do and at the same time opens new opportunities for them.

Thus, site planning is the process in which the characteristics of the site and the proposed functions for it are brought together in a creative synthesis. Writer Harvey Rubinstein compares site planning to other types of problem solving, noting that "the critical thinking process of research, analysis and synthesis makes a major contribution to the formation of design decisions. . . . The site planner must constantly strive to ward off preconceived thoughts or influences which might close his mind to worthwhile ideas."

The third activity of the practice is detailed landscape design. Detailed design involves the selection of materials, components, their fabrication, and plant materials for a well-defined problem on a specific site. Solutions are for such areas as subdivision entrances, playgrounds, clubhouses, enabling gardens, etc. Detailed design deals with design solutions to the surfaces, edges, steps, ramps, paving, and drainage.

The fourth type of practice is urban design. This type of practice is not new to the profession of landscape architecture; it was the main portion of the pioneers of the profession. It entails the organization of public open spaces in the urban areas and the location of structures. In urban design the major design focus is on public use and pedestrian circulation. Urban design includes such projects as streetscapes, plazas, riverfront development, commercial centers, and urban renewal of neighborhoods. Due to the complex problems of the urban environment, such projects are rarely given to one designer. These are team projects. The planners are involved in the infrastructure: architects with the buildings and landscape architects with the public spaces. The design of these areas are crucial to the success of the urban environment.

Landscape Architecture Design Process

The landscape architecture design process creates a framework and lines of action by which the landscape is to be modified in accordance with ecological principles to meet the development needs. According to Ian McHarg, one should view manmade change to the landscape in terms of creativity. He argues that humankind, as part of nature, is required to be creative in the evolutionary process and that changes should be judged in terms of the law of nature and evolution. Nature, to McHarg, is exhibiting both opportunities and constraints for human use.

The design process starts with site investigation made concurrently with the formulation of a program. The program is developed from specific needs and wishes of the client. The formal process begins with an understanding of the persons for whom the site is being planned. Next comes an analysis of the situation: a study of the site itself and also the whole structure of power, values, and technology within which the work must be carried out.

Every site, natural or manmade, is to some degree unique, a web of things and activities. The web must be understood: it imposes limitations and constraints; it contains new possibilities; and the plan, however radical, must maintain some continuity with the preexisting locale. Understanding the locality demands time and effort. The landscape architect, through understanding the site, can become familiar with "the spirit of the place." This understanding comes from the assessment and analysis of facts and forces that have formed the landscape. It involves studying the landscape ecological factors, the human, socioeconomic, and cultural factors, and the visual appearance representing the interaction of these two. Since each site is complex and somewhat difficult to comprehend, dissecting it into single elements or layers that are overlaid on the topographical map simplifies the study and makes it more manageable. The site is analyzed with the program in mind. The natural factors that are interpreted and assessed include topography, geology, soils hydrology, micro climate, vegetation, macro climate, and wildlife. The social factors studied include the human impact on the site, its historical land use, landmarks, land ownership and political jurisdictions, utilities, traffic, and zoning. The visual quality analysis is part of the process as it is a potential resource that should be evaluated according to its uniqueness. The National Environmental Policy Act of 1969 requires an evaluation of unquantifiable environmental amenities and protection of aesthetic, natural, and historical environmental qualities.

Each layer of analysis is mapped and illustrated graphically and given a numerical value for its suitability for the development program. Then the layers are added to form a composite. The flexibility of details with which the factors are investigated and the order in which they are studied depends on the complexity of the project. The composite ensures sensitivity to the site analysis and forms the base for providing, locating, and connecting all the program elements to each other and to the region, with minimum destruction of the area. To arrive at a design solution the design process, upon completion of the analysis, moves into synthesis phase in which the designers study design options on paper in graphic forms. Options are developed in the form of concepts. The concepts put into action all the conclusions and proposals that have emerged from the site analysis and program development. The graphic form of the concepts are general and loose arrangements of the solution. The first phase in formulating the concept is the ideal functional diagram. It is not site related and its purpose is to identify the best possible relationship between the proposed functions and spaces as outlined in the design program. The intent of the ideal functional diagram is to develop a clear understanding of the different functions and to gain insight about the ones that should be associated with each other and the ones that should be separated. This diagram takes the form of bubbles or outlines. The bubbles should be arranged to establish an ideal relationship among the various spaces and functions and can be drawn to any scale. The diagram should include the major activities, the relative distance of one activity to another, type of space needed, the space dividers (buffers), views, and access to the area.

The next step is to adapt the ideal diagram to the site composite map. The site-related functional diagram should show the same information as the ideal functional diagram, with the added consideration of relating to the site conditions; in addition, it should be drawn to the activities' approximate size and scale. The site-related diagrams will vary from the ideal one as they respond correctly to the site opportunities and constraints. The landscape architect should develop and study the site-related diagrams as overlays placed directly on the composite drawing. The overlay technique helps the designer to see the location and size of the proposed functions and spaces in the proper relation to the site conditions. Many alternatives have to be generated and based on many themes. These alternatives must be evaluated to ensure the best solution. That solution, at times, will be a combination of several alternatives. Once this is done, more refinement is needed.

The preliminary master plan is drawn with more details of content and graphic representation. With the basic theme of forms in mind, the designer converts the abstract symbols into exact forms. This is again done with the overlay technique on top of the concept drawing to ensure that the basic concept arrangement is retained. The overlays will reflect the designer's composition of forms. The forms address the design's hard surfaces and open spaces, and the existing and proposed plant materials are drawn as masses and individual plants, although no plant species are identified. All the design elements are considered, and their locations, functions, and space are drawn within the framework established in the early phases.

The preliminary master plan will undergo many overlay refinements on many layers of tracing paper to ensure the best solution. Once it is completed, the designer must check it against the program to verify that all the program's intentions have been implemented. The review of the preliminary master plan is done by the client and the agencies involved in the project.

After making the needed revision, the designer proceeds to develop the master plan, which is the refinement of the preliminary master plan. This plan will include the changes and revisions to the preliminary plan. The master plan presents a different graphic style from the early plan, which is loose. Here, the drafting shows more control and higher level of details and refinement.

The final step of landscape architecture design process is the construction drawings. Here, the designer is concerned with the detail appearance and the fabrication and integration of the various materials. In addition to detailing, this phase includes the drawings needed to carry out the proposed design. These include such drawings as site demolition, layout plans, grading plans, planting plans, circulation layout, etc. The construction drawings are accompanied with written specifications. The project drawings, technical specifications, bidding documents, special instructions, and other bidding materials together are called the project manual.

Once the contract has been signed, the contractor proceeds to build and install the design. This is the construction contract administration phase. The degree of involvement by the landscape architect in this phase is determined by the client. The activities include evaluating the contractor-supplied materials and equipment, monitoring the actual construction performance, and documenting these evaluations. The landscape architect also has the responsibility of representing the client and the client's interests on the job site. Thus, his or her role is to ensure that the contractor's materials and workmanship throughout the installation of the project meet or exceed the quality specified. The design process does not end when the project is complete. The designer should observe the site years after its completion and engage in post occupancy evaluation (POE) to see how well the project works and how the site users interact and behave in it. A great deal can be learned from the built project so that well-functioning areas can be carried forward to future jobs while areas that do not serve the user well can be done differently on the next project.

The maintenance of a project is of utmost importance. Too often well-constructed projects look and function poorly due to low-quality maintenance. If the design did not take into account the maintenance aspect or if the maintenance people are not sensitive to the designer's intentions, the result will be project failure.

Norman Booth, in discussing the design process, suggests that "there are no esoteric formulas or secret states of mind that produce good designs effortlessly and the design process itself is no guaranteed recipe either." Instead, he argues, one must view the design process as merely a "framework or outline of various steps. Its success relies upon the designer's observations, experience, knowledge, ability to make proper judgments and creativity."

All the phases and steps listed suggest a structure of a design process. This process does not inhibit the designer's creativity. There can be an endless source of design forms and alternatives to any given problem, and keeping an open mind during the design process can produce unique design solutions.

Landscape architecture is a profession that suggests a continuum and a process of growth as well as change. It starts with one's completion of formal education. After the apprenticeship period is ended, the next step is passing a license examination. Like most design professionals, landscape architects are licensed under state statutes. In the United States 45 states have laws for individuals who practice or call themselves landscape architects. The purpose is to protect the health, safety, and welfare of the public.

Landscape architecture practice continues to grow at the present time. The breadth and complexity of projects in the profession have also greatly increased. At the same time, the increasingly complex work performed by landscape architects must draw upon the expertise of scientists in many fields. Areas of specialization such as wetland restoration, environmental assessment, botanical gardens, and zoos require the input of such diverse sciences as herpetology, silverculture, horticulture, and entomology. The information revolution has brought about an increasing awareness of the great diversity of human populations and cultures, and diverse communities have articulated special needs.

Landscape architecture in the United States is practiced by professionals who are trained and have experience working with complex design problems on challenging sites. The historical precedent that influenced the evolution of the profession in the United States and its adaptability to meet new challenges placed landscape architecture in the forefront and its practitioners in a strong strategic position among their peers throughout the world.

See also Education: Landscape Architecture

Further Reading

Booth, Norman K., *Basic Elements of Landscape Architectural Design,* Columbus: Department of Landscape Architecture, Ohio State University, 1979

Cetron, Marvin, and Owen Davies, *The Gardening of America: Prosperity for the Gardening Business and Landscape Professions into the 21st Century,* Radnor, Pennsylvania: Chilton, 1991

Church, Thomas Dolliver, *Gardens Are for People: How to Plan for Outdoor Living,* New York: Van Nostrand Reinhold, 1955; 3rd edition, Berkeley: University of California Press, 1995

Eckbo, Garrett, *Landscape for Living,* New York: Architectural Record 1950

Eckbo, Garrett, *The Art of Home Landscaping,* New York: McGraw Hill, 1956; revised and enlarged edition, 1978

Fein, Albert, *Frederick Law Olmsted and the American Environmental Tradition,* New York: Braziller, 1972

Giedion, Sigfried, *Space, Time, and Architecture: The Growth of a New Tradition,* Cambridge, Massachusetts: Harvard University Press, and London: Oxford University Press, 1941; 5th edition, Cambridge, Massachusetts: Harvard University Press, 1982

Graff, M.M., *Central Park, Prospect Park: A New Perspective,* New York: Greensward Foundation, 1985

Hubbard, Henry Vincent, and Theodora Kimball Hubbard, *An Introduction to the Study of Landscape Design,* New York: Macmillan, 1917; reprint, New York: Macmillan, 1967

Hunter, John Michael, *Land into Landscape,* London and New York: Godwin, 1985

Jellicoe, Geoffrey Alan, and Susan J. Jellicoe, *The Landscape of Man: Shaping the Environment from Prehistory to the Present Day,* London: Thames and Hudson, and New York: Viking Press, 1975; 3rd edition, New York: Thames and Hudson, 1995

Laurie, Michael, *An Introduction to Landscape Architecture,* New York: American Elsevier, 1975; 2nd edition, 1986

Leighton, Ann, *American Gardens of the Nineteenth Century: For Comfort and Affluence,* Amherst: University of Massachusetts Press, 1987

McHarg, Ian L., *Design with Nature,* Garden City, New York: Natural History Press, 1969, reprint, 1992

Newton, Norman T., *Design on the Land: The Development of Landscape Architecture,* Cambridge, Massachusetts: Harvard University, 1971

Pregill, Philip, and Nancy Volkman, *Landscapes in History: Design and Planning in the Western Tradition,* New York: Van Nostrand Reinhold, 1993

Rowling, Marjorie, *Life in Medieval Times,* New York: Perigee Press, 1968

Rubenstein, Harvey M., *A Guide to Site and Environmental Planning,* New York: Wiley, 1969; 4th edition, 1996

Scott, Mel, *American City Planning since 1890: A History Commemorating the Fiftieth Anniversary of the American Institute of Planners,* Berkeley: University of California Press, 1969

Sharky, Bruce G., *Ready, Set, Practice: Elements of Landscape Architecture Professional Practice,* New York: Wiley, 1994

Thacker, Christopher, *The History of Gardens,* Berkeley: University of California Press, and London: Croom Helm, 1979

Tishler, William H., editor, *American Landscape Architecture: Designers and Places,* Washington, D.C.: Preservation Press, 1989

Tobey, George B., *A History of Landscape Architecture: The Relationship of People to Environment,* New York: American Elsevier, 1973

ALON KVASHNY

Landscape Garden Style

Each great 18th-century English country house inevitably imposed its own constraints on its garden or parkland. While, therefore, no English garden synthesizes the totality of the features that make up the landscape garden style, sufficient constants make the style, as it originated in 18th-century England, instantly recognizable. In continental Europe at the time, such gardens were known as "English gardens" and called by that name in French, German, and Italian. Some of them, transformed into parks, continue to exist in cities such as Munich and Paris. Even in the United States, Manhattan suspended its traffic grid for Central Park, allowing its normally parallel streets to bend as they cross it, as landscape style dictated. A superb and partly artificial landscape park was created there at Fort Tryon.

Landscape style denotes informality and irregularity of layout, clumps of trees arranged for shade and views of the surrounding countryside, serpentine lakes instead of rectangular canals, winding avenues through parks rather than stiff allées through rectilinear garden beds, and vistas leading to statuary, monuments, gazebos, temples, and obelisks. Real topography was to be made

Bridge in landscape over New River, Castle Howard, Yorkshire, England
Copyright Robert M. Craig

to resemble more closely the idealized fantasy landscapes of 17th-century painters such as Nicolas Poussin and Claude Lorraine and later the 18th-century fantasies of Jean-Honoré Fragonard and François Boucher. It is not infrequently said that the landscape garden is England's only original indigenous art form, with Stourhead its greatest example.

Although generally landscape-style gardens have water to supply waterfalls, cascades, torrents, pools, and the ubiquitous fountains, the only essential original feature of the complete landscape style, without which it could never have been adopted, is the ha-ha, a deep ditch and a retaining wall that permitted a house both to keep a carefully cultivated formal garden and to create the illusion of perfect unity with the surrounding pastures. The ditch and wall, which prevented the livestock from straying into the formal gardens, were invisible to anyone in the house. There are great landscape gardens without water, but scarcely any great English 18th-century examples without a ha-ha, unless other natural features, such as rivers, sea, or mountains, make one redundant.

A simple fence would not do. The landscape style came into being as part of a much wider cultural phenomenon that was reflected partly in those attitudes to ambient natural surroundings found, for instance, in the writings of Jean-Jacques Rousseau. With the ha-ha's safety net in place, a new possibility could be explored that promoted the illusion that human beings were part of a seamless unity with the natural world, with its once threatening wildness, menacing mountains, treacherous watercourses, and cattle incompatible with formal flower beds. Later, after the industrial revolution, this pleasure pier enabled people to feel a similar union with the might of the ocean without actually having to incur the danger of sailing on it.

Strictly speaking, the landscape style refers to that portion of the parkland lying beyond the intensively cultivated formal flower, kitchen, and herb gardens. It would no doubt accommodate woods, rides, perhaps a pheasantry or a deer park, and, where the land was extensive enough, perhaps even sporting facilities, as medieval archery, bowls, and real tennis yielded to such shooting or fishing as might be naturally available or artificially contrived. Trees could be planted and watercourses moved. The precise configuration of parkland wood and water was often, even generally, determined by the need for windbreaks to protect sheep or cattle and by the type of sport to which it could be adapted or modified. The picturesque also assumed greater importance. At Blenheim it required Lancelot "Capability" Brown to put adequate water under the magnificent bridge that Sir John Vanbrugh had already constructed over what was not much more than a ditch.

Blenheim is an exception. Woodland and water were normally arranged for purely decorative purposes only on the smaller estates such as Rousham. Large estates surrounding vast country mansions needed to be managed with a particular eye to features such as slopes over which game might be driven, moors or marshes where grouse or snipe might be shot, or coverts where a fox might be drawn. Which way game would fly out of a wood or a field depended on the direction of the wind; a wood might be planted on a hillside for the primary purpose either of holding game to be driven or offering it an attractive refuge when disturbed. Wood could also provide cover for a pond where wild duck might flight. As a consequence, the decorative function of landscape gardening often became intricately interwoven with the pattern of country pursuits adopted by the owners of the great houses and, with them, the large areas of park or moorland to be landscaped.

The landscape gardens attached to country houses must therefore be distinguished both from the cultivated beds of their formal gardens and from their more widely laid out estates, managed with agricultural, sporting, and forestry considerations in mind. The major designers of England's most famous landscape gardens—such as Stourhead, Stowe, Castle Howard, Rousham, and Blenheim—including Charles Bridgeman, William Kent, Humphry Repton, John Vanbrugh, and Lancelot "Capability" Brown—did not create entirely typical landscape-style gardens. These gardens are outstanding if very different examples of it. The landscape style itself was often reduced to something much simpler.

A more typical lesser-known example of the style is Heythrop Park, only a few miles from Blenheim and Rousham, between 700 and 800 acres (280 and 320 ha), with enough woodland to provide some rough shooting and celebrated for the exotic trees planted in the 19th century. Similar to Ralph Allen's magnificent Prior Park, also an 18th-century creation, the house itself at Heythrop has undergone numerous internal and external transformations and is not itself of the greatest architectural distinction, although it does have Italianate reversed pediments to decorate the roofline.

Heythrop's country undulates. The house is set on a ridge, and from its portico front an avenue over a mile long sweeps round and down behind the house, from which, as at Prior Park, can be seen the formal gardens giving way over an invisible ha-ha to a falling and narrowing meadow. Here, the prospect focuses in the center on a characteristic "acre pond," nearly a mile away, in which can be seen from the house the reflection of the avenue on its sweep toward the gate. In the artificial lake, too shallow for fish, one can also see a highly effective and characteristically 18th-century mirror image of a plantation of silver birch behind it. In front of the Heythrop house, beyond the avenue going off to the left, the land is too stony for arable farming; it was intended to be pasture, although it is now a golf course. The back, as at

Prior Park, offers the view over the lake. On each side of the Heythrop house, beyond outhouses and gardens, are woods through which wide swathes have been cut to provide rides and straight vistas of a mile (1.6 km) or more.

Farnborough, near Banbury in Warwickshire, is another minor gem of the landscape style, showing yet other features of the style adopted by a modest but elegant country mansion. To the front an avenue leads to the gates and farther to the main road, through what is now lawn but must earlier have been parterres. To the sides are the functional gardens, outhouses, and the stable block. But to the rear, in quite restricted space, vistas have been contrived more spaciously than at Rousham, although similarly blocked by obelisks, vases, statues, and ornaments.

In its original forms the landscape style tried almost obsessively to highlight the invariably neoclassical temples, statuary, summerhouses, ruins, and other sculpted or architectural ornamentation, as if to give structure to the garden. The "praeneste" terrace at Rousham, with its dying gladiator and arcade by Kent, is modeled on the Roman temple at Palestrina and was an early manifestation of the English Palladian movement. Later, the ornamentation would be used to capture the eye at the end of the vistas with some generally neoclassical object, such as the obelisk at Blenheim. Later still, the vistas were left open to foster the illusion of continuity with the natural ambiance, and the landscape style moved beyond the artificial creation of a landscape to delight the senses and finally merged into the cult of nature in its unretouched condition.

The landscape style was not created as suddenly as used to be thought, based partly on the literary advocacy it enjoyed and of the impact of the letter on the subject published by Joseph Addison in *The Spectator* of 6 September 1712, buttressed by the satire by Alexander Pope published in *The Guardian* in 1713, and followed by the celebrated fourth epistle of Pope's *Moral Essays,* published in 1733: "Consult the genius of the place in all:/That tells the waters or to rise or fall."

In the 17th century, English poets John Dryden and Andrew Marvell had regarded mountains as frightening and ugly. Gardens by and large after the restoration of the Stuarts in 1660 favored the formal but fashionable French or more intricate Dutch styles, but there was also discussion of allying art and nature, linking personal introspection to scientific examination. The *Britannia illustrata* (1709) shows Hampton Court, Chatsworth, and Badminton with gardens laid out in the French style, with long axial avenues, intersecting allées bordered by pollarded trees, and straight-sided canals. Although that style was still gaining adherents, even in much smaller gardens, John Aubrey in the 18th century had begun to praise irregularities "both natural and artificial" in garden design.

As usual, taste in architecture and garden design moved more slowly than taste in literature and the visual arts. It started with a vogue for designing parts of gardens visible from the house to imitate the contours and irregularities of natural landscape, with the walls of summerhouses and open terraces decorated with pictures of idealized "landskips," such as at Wilton, with scenes of hunting, shooting, fishing, and their prey. In a 1657 letter to Thomas Browne, John Evelyn advocated "Caves, Grotts, Mounts, and irregular ornaments," as morally elevating and contributing "to contemplative and philosophicall Enthusiasms."

What the landscape style was to realize in garden design was first drawn to public attention by landscape paintings, such as Peter Paul Rubens's *The Castle of Steen* and much Dutch genre painting, to which must be added the work of artists such as Claude Lorraine, Nicolas Poussin, Gaspard Dughet, Salvator Rosa, and their imitators. It was for the early 17th-century idealized landscape painters that Richard Blome (*The Gentleman's Recreation* [1686]) used the definition in Peacham's 1612 *Graphice,* "landskip is the expression of the perfect vision of the Earth." For Addison such a landscape included fields and woods, cattle, and bees. The neoclassicism of the 18th century nourished itself, too, on the bucolic poems of antiquity, especially Virgil and Horace, and on the Italian cult of antiquity encountered on the grand tour.

Addison's important pieces for garden design appeared in *The Tatler* and *The Spectator* from 1710 to 1712, extolling the imitation of nature, more "Grand and August" than "the Curiosities of Art." The first professional gardener to adopt the new design philosophy was probably Stephen Switzer, foreman of the Brompton nursery of the celebrated consultants, designers, and nurserymen George London and Henry Wise, who published an *Ichnographia rustica* in 1718 advocating paths with "as many twinings and windings" as possible and with diversified views, vistas rather than panoramas. The first garden to adopt the new style was Castle Howard, whose owner, the earl of Carlisle, fell out with an architect who normally employed London and Wise. In the end the garden was designed chiefly by Switzer for Vanbrugh. The house was set in the first great ornamental landscape in British gardening history, populated by elaborate garden buildings, including Vanbrugh's Temple of the Four Winds, architecturally related to the house itself, and Nicholas Hawksmoor's mausoleum.

Castle Howard was soon followed by Stowe—where Bridgeman and Kent worked and "Capability" Brown began in the kitchen garden—and Rousham, where Kent realized ideas acquired on the grand tour by the third earl of Burlington. Originally a sign painter and inspired chiefly by paintings, Kent filled the garden with ornamental structures. Kent's primarily visual imagination is well illustrated by his suggestion that dead trees should be planted in Kensington Gardens for visual effect. Planting dead trees is only one step more incongruous than creating false ruins to catch the eye at a distance, as at Rousham and Prior Park.

Horace Walpole, who first credited Bridgeman with the invention of the ha-ha, described the device at length, regarding it as a liberating force that permitted the emergence of the landscape style. "Levelling, mowing, and rolling followed," and "the garden might assort with the wilder country outside," without drawing "too obvious a line of distinction between the neat and the rude." In the blurring of that line lies the essence of the landscape style.

Further Reading

Conan, Michel, *Dictionnaire historique de l'art des jardins*, Paris: Hazan, 1997
Fleming Laurence, and Alan Gore, *The English Garden*, London: Joseph, 1979
Hadfield, Miles, *Gardening in Britain*, London: Murray, 1960; 3rd edition, as *A History of British Gardening*, 1979
Hadfield, Miles, *The English Landscape Garden*, Aylesbury, Buckinghamshire: Shire, 1977; 2nd edition, 1998
Hunt, John Dixon, *The Figure in the Landscape: Poetry, Painting, and Gardening during the Eighteenth Century*, Baltimore, Maryland: Johns Hopkins University Press, 1976
Hunt, John Dixon, *William Kent, Landscape Garden Designer*, London: Zwemmer, 1987
Hunt, John Dixon, and Peter Willis, editors, *The Genius of the Place: The English Landscape Garden, 1620–1820*, London: Elek, and New York: Harper and Row, 1975
Jackson-Stops, Gervase, *The Country House Garden: A Grand Tour*, London: Pavilion, and Boston: Little Brown, 1987
Jackson-Stops, Gervase, editor, *An English Arcadia: Designs for Gardens and Garden Buildings in the Care of the National Trust, 1600–1990*, Washington, D.C.: American Institute of Architecture Press, 1991; London: The National Trust, 1992

ANTHONY H.T. LEVI

Lange, Willy 1864–1941

German Garden Writer, Garden Theorist, and Landscape Architect

Willy Lange was an early 20th-century German landscape architect and teacher of garden design who gained particular importance as a garden writer and theorist. He developed and promoted ideas about natural garden design that gained particular ideologicial significance during the period of National Socialism.

Lange's professional career began in the 1880s as a gardener's apprentice. From 1884 to 1886 he studied at the Königliche Gärtnerlehranstalt Wildpark-Potsdam (Royal Horticultural College). From 1886 to 1889 Lange worked for the firms of Weber and Company in Wiesbaden and Franz Degen, Jr., in Köstritz, Thuringia. From 1889 to 1896 he ran his own gardening firm in Leipzig. Lange withdrew from business and public life from 1896 to 1903, while he pursued his own studies in natural science, art history, and cultural history and worked, mainly as a garden writer.

In the following phase of his professional career, Lange influenced garden design in Germany and other countries with numerous treatises. Especially significant was his concept of the nature garden. He was also influential as a teacher at the Royal Horticultural College, which had been moved in 1903 from Wildpark-Potsdam to Berlin-Dahlem. From 1903 to 1915 he worked as a teacher and department head for plant production at the college. In 1906 he was appointed Royal Garden Inspector and in 1911 Royal Garden Director. About the same time he served, in collaboration with the architect Otto Stahn, as a consultant to the land agency Landgesellschaft Kleines Wannsee.

Lange traveled widely in countries south of Germany, including France, Italy, Spain, Morocco, and the Canary Islands, and north in Denmark, Sweden, and Norway. These travels apparently supported his biased ideas about garden design as an expression of race and about specific nordic, southern, or south-alpine approaches toward garden design. In a series of articles in the journal *Die Gartenwelt*, Lange systematically developed his concept of natural garden design. On the one hand, he attempted to find new and modern garden forms. On the other hand, he tried to fight architects and artists who increasingly competed with garden architects and

Nature garden motif in the garden of Willy Lange, Berlin-Wannsee: carpet of *Sedum spurium* with junipers
Courtesy of Joachim Wolschke-Bulmahn

promoted architectonic gardens. Lange claimed that his approach required aesthetic expertise as well as considerable knowledge about plants. Lange's own nature gardens were informal. His style was opposed to the architectonic, which he believed expressed the anthropocentric and unnatural attitude of other cultures and lower stages of cultural evolution.

Lange was impressed by the rate of scientific developments since Charles Darwin. In his concept of the nature garden he wanted to apply the most up-to-date scientific concepts of ecology and plant sociology. He described this in 1913:

> Today we have a natural science that is based on the history of development. It teaches us, as far as the interrelations between creatures with their homeland and their fellow creatures are concerned, to understand the laws of life. Biology penetrates all previous knowledge, which was only superficial. Biology, applied to arts, establishes a new, a biological aesthetic (Lange, 1913).

Lange's "biological aesthetic" provided a theoretical basis for his approach to garden design. From a social perspective it was reactionary. It was racist and assumed a dubious special relationship between the German people and nature. Lange's concept of natural garden design also meant to fight modern and international trends in garden design and to create a specific German garden style.

In a period of increasing nationalism and racism, a period in which the Nazi ideology of *Blut und Boden* (blood and soil) asserted a close connection between the German people and their soil and landscape, Lange's ideas about the nature garden fascinated many German landscape architects. They followed Lange's interpretation of the garden as something to be subordinated to the surrounding landscape. Lange's other tenet was that so-called laws of nature should guide garden design. The designer should be spiritually heightened in order to produce an artistic display of nature in the garden. Accordingly, Lange preferred so-called native plants. For Lange, garden art was a constituent of national culture, and culture could only be national. He vehemently rejected the idea that art could be international, declaring: "Let us find the national style for our gardens, then we will have art, German garden art. As long as there exist different nations, there must exist different national styles" (Lange, 1900). Nevertheless, Lange explicitly promoted the use of those non-native plants which he believed fit physiognomically with local plants and helped heighten their artistic appearance.

Lange saw the German nature garden as a high point of cultural evolution, thus furthering the idea of the superiority of the German people. During the imperial period many Germans believed in this superiority; some in the Weimar Republic continued to do so even after World War I and felt confirmed in their belief when it became a state doctrine under the Nazi program of National Socialism. Consequently, every German was thought to require and deserve an appropriately designed environment. The subordination of the garden to the landscape became an essential criterion of Lange's nature garden. He considered the German landscape or "physiognomy" to be the foundation, inspiration, and frame for garden design, from which all artistic impulses must be derived. Over time, Lange expressed his ideas in a more and more racist and nationalist way. His reactionary ideas received new impetus during National Socialism. Hans Hasler, Lange's student and later his assistant and a fanatic follower of National Socialism, published *Deutsche Gartenkunst* (German Garden Art) in 1939, in which he presents Lange's ideas about natural garden design.

Lange also influenced ideas about garden design in the United States. The U.S. landscape architect Frank Albert Waugh (1869–1943) supported Lange's ideas about natural garden design and believed that in landscape gardening "styles are national—perhaps, more strictly speaking, racial" (Waugh, 1917). Waugh studied under Lange for several months in 1910. He was fascinated by Lange's concepts and named him an outstanding writer in the field of garden design in a *Country Gentleman* article. Waugh compared Lange to the American Warren H. Manning and recommended at least a partial adherence to his methods. The U.S. landscape architect Jens Jensen promoted similar racist ideas about natural garden design in his 1939 book *Siftings*. In Scandinavia Lange's ideas about garden design also were highly influential. Lange's impact on garden design in other countries has only been partially researched.

Lange was less influential as a designer, and only a few of his designs for gardens are still known today. He created a number of gardens for wealthy clients in conjunction with houses designed by Stahn along Lake Kleiner Wannsee in Berlin. These gardens were located across from the site where Lange built his own *Gartenheim* (garden home) in 1906.

Lange was a member of the Kaiserlich und Königliche Gartenbaugesellschaft Wien (Imperial and Royal Horticultural Society Vienna, Austria) and the Verein deutscher Gartenkünstler (Association of German Garden Artists), which he served as president in 1906. He also was a member of the National Socialist German Workers Party. Although Lange retired in 1915, he accepted an offer from the headquarters of the German army near the end of the war to lecture to German soldiers along the Lothringian front in 1918. In 1934 Lange was made honorary professor at the agricultural college in Berlin, and on the occasion of his 75th birthday the National Socialist *Führer* confered on him the Adolf Hitler Medal. Lange died in March 1941.

Biography

Born in Berlin, Germany, 1864. Served apprenticeship in private enterprise, 1882–84; attended Königliche Gärtnerlehranstalt (Royal Horticultural College), Wildpark-Potsdam, Brandenburg, Germany, 1884–86; worked as journeyman with Weber and Company, Wiesbaden, Hesse, Germany, 1886–87; served as head and representative of horticultural firm of Franz Degen in Köstritz, Thuringia, Germany, 1887–89; operated horticultural business at Leipzig-Lindenau, Saxony, Germany, 1889–96; withdrew from business, and retreated to *Waldhaus* (forest house) at Dietharz, near Gotha, Thuringia, where he studied nature, art, art history, and cultural history, and published numerous articles in professional journals developing racist and nationalist ideas for garden design later embraced by National Socialists, 1896–1903; teacher and head of department for horticulture and plant production (Pflanzenbau) at Royal Horticultural College, Berlin, Germany, 1903; retired from teaching for health reasons, 1915; served as consultant to land agency in Berlin, from 1906, and designed number of gardens for houses of wealthy clients designed by architect Otto Stahn on lots along southern shore of Lake Kleiner Wannsee, Berlin. Died in 1941.

Selected Designs

1906	Willy Lange's Gartenheim (garden home), Berlin-Wannsee, Germany
1906(?)	Garden Johannes Bolle, Berlin-Wannsee, Germany
ca. 1906–7	Grounds, Royal Horticultural College, Berlin-Dahlem, Germany (the so-called Dorfanger)
1908	Garden Franz Fieseler, Berlin-Wannsee, Germany
1908(?)	Garden Benjamin, Berlin-Wannsee, Germany
1910	Setting for the Kleist memorial, Berlin-Wannsee, Germany
1911(?)	Garden Electricity Works, Berlin-Wannsee, Germany

Selected Publications

"Garten und Weltanschauung," *Die Gartenwelt* 4, no. 31 (1900)
Gartengestaltung der Neuzeit, unter Mitwirkung für den Architekturgarten von Otto Stahn, 1907
Land- und Gartensiedlungen, 1910
Der Garten und seine Bepflanzung, 1913
Deutsche Heldenhaine, 1915
Gartenbilder, 1922
Gartenpläne, 1927

Further Reading

Gröning, Gert, and Joachim Wolschke-Bulmahn, *Grüne Biographien: biographisches Handbuch zur Landschaftsarchitektur des 20 Jahrhunderts in Deutschland,* Hannover and Berlin: Patzer-Verlag, 1997

Gröning, Gert, and Uwe Schneider, *Die Heide in Park und Garten: zur Geschichte und Bedeutung Heidemotivs in der Gartenkultur,* Worms: Wernersche Verlagsgesellschaft, 1999

Schneider, Uwe, and Gert Gröning, "Nature Mystification and the Example of the Heroes Groves," *Environments by Design* 2, no. 2 (1998)

Waugh, Frank Albert, "German Landscape Gardening," *Country Gentleman* 25 (August 1910)

Waugh, Frank Albert, *The Natural Style in Landscape Gardening*, Boston: Badger, 1917

Wolschke-Bulmahn, Joachim, "The 'Wild Garden' and the 'Nature Garden': Aspects of the Garden Ideology of William Robinson and Willy Lange," *Journal of Garden History* 12, no. 3 (1992)

Wolschke-Bulmahn, Joachim, and Gert Gröning, "The Ideology of the Nature Garden: Nationalistic Trends in Garden Design in Germany during the Early Twentieth Century," *Journal of Garden History* 12, no. 1 (1992)

Wolschke-Bulmahn, Joachim, editor, *Nature and Ideology: Natural Garden Design in the Twentieth Century*, Washington D.C.: Dumbarton Oaks, 1997
Wolschke-Bulmahn, Joachim, "The Search for 'Ecological Goodness' among Garden Historians," in *Perspectives on Garden History*, edited by Michel Conan, Washington, D.C.: Dumbarton Oaks, 1999

JOACHIM WOLSCHKE-BULMAHN AND GERT GRÖNING

Langley, Batty 1696–1751

English Gardener and Garden Writer

The fluidity of ideas about landscape and architecture in the early 18th century enabled Batty Langley to play an important role in popularizing both the natural style in gardening and Gothic architecture. Langley, who spent most of his early life in Twickenham, on the outskirts of London, followed his father in the trade of gardener. Nothing is known about this phase of his career, and he soon took up writing books on building and gardening. The title of his first publication, *Practical Geometry Applied to the Useful Arts of Building, Surveying, Gardening, and Mensuration* (1726), suggests that he was experienced in laying out grounds. This is confirmed, after his move to London, by his advertisement in the *City and Country Builder's Treasury* (1740), which states that he was prepared to make designs for "Buildings, Gardens, Parks etc. in the most grand Taste." But apart from a garden pavilion for his neighbor in Westminster and a greenhouse for the duke of Kent at Wrest Park in Bedfordshire, nothing else is known of his architectural or garden work. His reputation rests entirely upon his publications.

In 1728 Langley published *New Principles of Gardening; or, The Laying Out and Planting Parterres, Groves, Wildernesses, Labyrinths, Avenues, Parks etc.* Langley appreciated that the avant-garde were turning away from formality in the garden and was determined to provide a book that defined the principles of the natural style and gave some practical advice. He commenced by excoriating those who "deviate from nature, instead of imitating it" and promoted the old style as "that abominable mathematical regularity and stiffness." The rest of the book, with its many illustrations and breathless text, was designed to provide "general directions for laying out gardens in a more grand and delightful manner than has been done before." What follows is by no means a revolutionary book but a distillation of the style promoted by Addison, Pope, Lord Burlington, and their circle. There are still avenues, mounts, basins, and parterres, but scrollwork has been banished, to be replaced by "beautiful carpets" of grass. The avenues are planted with sweet-smelling flowers—honeysuckle, stock, jasmine, and pinks—while serpentine paths wriggle their way through the "pleasing meanders of shady delightful plantation(s)" and make a detour through an agricultural landscape of cattle enclosures, cornfields, and a farmyard. Without naming it, Langley stumbled on the *ferme orneé* five years before its official appearance in Stephen Switzer's *Practical Husbandman* (1733).

Many of Langley's illustrations in *New Principles of Gardening* are pure confectionery, gleaned in some cases from French sources. Frequently the book degenerates into a catalog, for example, of statues suitable for all locations in the garden—"Philomela, a young woman ravished by Tereus"—for the wood or grove. Nevertheless, this was for some time the only readily available book of gardening that conveyed to property owners something of the new style. In the West Midlands its influence was long lasting, for William Shenstone (1714–63) borrowed a copy from a neighbor in 1749 and lent it to his confidante, Lady Luxborough, hoping it would be of service in "modelling the crooked walks in your shrubbery." Shenstone, who certainly had his finger on the pulse of the landscape movement, admitted that, although he found the work amusing, "I have never seen any book that treated modern design in gardening before." Serpentine walks running through shrubberies "in the Batty Langley manner" (Jacques) became exceedingly common in the 1730s and 1740s.

Langley knew his strengths, and when he sensed a new fashion developing in architecture, he produced in parts during 1741–42 his book on Gothic design, reissued as *Gothic Architecture Improved* in 1747. The garden buildings proposed here provided the perfect destination for the serpentine walks recommended in *New Principles of Gardening*. Again the aesthetes—Horace Walpole, Thomas Gray, Charles Lyttleton—were already discussing the style, but Langley popularized it and, in their view, vulgarized it. Initially, however, even members of the elite could see its value. Shenstone learned of the book from Sanderson Miller in 1749 and felt that it exhibited "tolerable good native taste" and was grateful for the assistance it provided to "sketch out some charming gothic temple and gothic benches for garden seats." He gave his mason, Pedley, a view of it, and soon "gothick turrets" were going up on his summerhouse. Lord Stamford's craftsmen at Enville in Staffordshire presumably also got sight of Miller's copy and reproduced the style in the museum and elsewhere on the estate. The cognoscenti such as Walpole soon detached themselves from such a tasteless source and sought authentic precedents for the style in England's many medieval buildings. But many garden owners, including Charles Hamilton of Painshill in Surrey, found it useful, albeit Walpole (in private) might have poured scorn on his Gothic temple "taken from Batty Langley's book (which does not contain a single design of true or good gothic). . . . [T]he Goths never built a summerhouse or temples in a garden." Even today the British Isles are full of mid-18th century Gothic buildings that are justifiably described as "Batty Langley gothick."

Biography

Born in Twickenham, England, 1696. Worked as a gardener; published *New Principles of Gardening,* 1728, in which he advocated the laying out of serpentine walks running through shrubberies, a feature for which he became well known; moved to London in ca. 1735; opened a school offering lessons in architectural drawing, ca. 1740; manufactured an artificial stone, which could be employed in making statues and garden ornaments; published *Gothic Architecture Improved,* 1747. Died in Soho, London, 1751.

Selected Publications

Practical Geometry Applied to the Useful Arts of Building, Surveying, Gardening, and Mensuration, 1726

New Principles of Gardening; or, The Laying Out and Planting Parterres, Groves, Wildernesses, Labyrinths, Avenues, Parks, etc., 1728

A Sure Method of Improving Estates, by Plantations of Oak, Elm, Ash, Beech, etc., 1728

Pomona; or, The Fruit Garden Illustrated, 1729

The Landed Gentleman's Useful Companion, 1741

Ancient Architecture: Restored and Improved, 1742

Gothic Architecture, Improved by Rules and Proportions, 1747

Further Reading

Colvin, Howard Montagu, *A Biographical Dictionary of British Architects, 1600–1840,* Cambridge, Massachusetts: Harvard University Press, 1954; 3rd edition, New Haven, Connecticut: Yale University Press, 1995

Dutton, Ralph, *The English Garden,* London: Batsford, 1937; New York: Scribner, 1938

Hunt, John Dixon, and Peter Willis, editors, *The Genius of the Place: The English Landscape Garden, 1620–1820,* London: Elek, and New York: Harper and Row, 1975

Jacques, David, *Georgian Gardens: The Reign of Nature,* Portland, Oregon: Timber Press, and London: Batsford, 1983

McCarthy, Michael J., *The Origins of the Gothic Revival,* New Haven, Connecticut: Yale University Press, 1987

Mowl, Tim, *Horace Walpole: The Great Outsider,* London: Murray, 1996

Rowen, A., "Batty Langley's Gothic," in *Studies in Memory of David Talbot Rice,* edited by Giles Robertson and George Henderson, Edinburgh: Edinburgh University Press, 1975

Williams, Marjorie, editor, *The Letters of William Shenstone,* Oxford: Blackwell, 1939; New York: AMS Press, 1979

DAVID WHITEHEAD

Lante, Villa

Bagnaia, Viterbo, Lazio, Italy

Location: 3 miles (5 km) northeast of Viterbo, toward Madonna della Quercia-Soriano nel Cimino, and approximately 40 miles (64.5 km) northwest of Rome

Cardinal Gianfrancesco Gambara, a member of the Farnese family, commissioned Giacomo Barozzi da Vignola to design the gardens of the Villa Lante on the edge of Bagnaia (see Plate 21), a hill village enlarged into a residence town in the 16th century. It was begun as a summer retreat after the cardinal's election as bishop of Viterbo in 1566 and must have been influenced by his relatives' great garden, also by Vignola, at the Palazzo Farnese at Caprarola, 20 miles (32 km) away. His successor, Cardinal Alessandro Montalto, altered most of the fountains in the park and added a fountain in the lowest square terrace but preserved the garden's basic structure. In 1656 the villa was granted for a peppercorn rent to the Lante family, from whom it takes its name. The architectural structure of the gardens has changed little over the centuries, although some modern plantings of rhododendrons, azaleas, camellias, and hydrangeas are out of keeping.

The garden is divided into two interrelated parts. A geometrically arranged formal garden of a series of terraces gently rising about 15 meters (16.5 yd.) up the hillside, incorporating fountains, cascades and waterfalls, groves, and statues, is situated adjacent to an irregular wooded hunting park with axial alleys and fountains scattered among groves of evergreens, oaks, and fruit and olive trees. At the entrance to the park is a huge fountain, the only one still in its original form, with Giambologna's statue of *Pegasus,* surrounded by water nymphs. A change of mood and concentration occurs from one end of the garden to the other, and its general theme is the dominance of reason over the forces of nature. Water emerges from the surrounding wilderness, flows down the rugged hillside, and ultimately supplies the town's fountains.

The gardens were designed to be experienced from the highest level, as the water descends in stages on a central axis from the top of the garden, beginning in a grotto sheltered by plane and *Ilex* groves where two pavilions flank the Fountain of the Deluge. The water passes through the Fountain of the Dolphins, previously the Fountain of Coral (1596), and then down an elaborately sculpted channel, the *catena d'acqua,* or water chain, inspired by the joints of the leg of a crayfish or *gambero,* Cardinal Gambara's family symbol. The water feeds through the claws of a large crayfish into the Fountain of the Giants, set centrally in the wall of the next terrace, the balustrade of which is lined with vases shooting out vertical jets of water. This is laid out as a room for open-air banquets, with the water diverted into a trough cut into the top of a large stone table, designed to cool the cardinal's wine, perhaps inspired by Pliny the Younger's Tuscan villa. Staircases descend on either side to the Fountain of the Lights, a circular fountain surrounded by small stone "lamp-lights" issuing jets of water, designed as an exedra, flanked by grottoes dedicated to Neptune and Venus.

On the lowest level are twin casinos, built on either side of the central axis, each about 22 square meters (26 sq. yd.) and functioning as decorative parts of the overall design. The Palazzina Gambara (on the right looking down the hill) was completed in 1578, and its loggia contains wall paintings illustrating the Villa d'Este at Tivoli, the Palazzo Farnese at Caprarola, and the Villa Lante itself, as well as the estates of the Gambara, Farnese, and Este cardinals. The ceilings are decorated with mythological stories and iconographical themes featuring the *gambero,* which are repeated in the garden. The Palazzina Montalto (on the left looking down the hill) was completed later by Carlo Moderno.

The features become more grand and spacious with each terrace, culminating in the spectacular lowest square with a central, theatrical fountain described by Montaigne as a "high pyramid which spouts water in a great many different ways. . . . Around this pyramid are four pretty little lakes, full of pure and limpid water. In the centre of each is a stone boat, with musketeers who shoot and hurl water against the pyramid, and a trumpeter in each, who also shoots water." The fountains and pools were originally surrounded by flower parterres containing fruit trees, later replaced with scroll *parterres de broderie,* executed in box and gravel probably in the 17th century. Cardinal Montalto added a central island with four moors holding aloft the Montalto coat of arms, surmounted by a "star" of water.

The garden has aroused endless admiration through the centuries, from Montaigne in 1581 to Sir George Sitwell, who described it as follows: "pool, cascade and water-temple are threaded like pearls upon a string, . . . a colour harmony of cool refreshing green and brighter flowers, of darkest bronze, blue pools and golden light."

The garden's formal symmetry predates Versailles by a hundred years. André Le Nôtre may have been involved in transforming the parterres at the Villa Lante while in Italy in 1678.

Cardinal Gambara wrote to Ottavio Farnese, duke of Parma, in 1576 of his plans to level his garden and plant a grove of plane trees in the *bosco;* these trees remain a feature of the garden. An inventory taken after Cardinal Gambara's death in 1587 lists the plants grown in the garden and park (reproduced in Lazzaro). Outside the gates elms were planted in rows of seven on a side. An upper terrace called the Piazza dell'Auro Regia was shaded by plane trees and probably planted with cherry laurel. Fir trees surrounded groves of myrtle, arbutus, and juniper; there was also a wood of quinces and pomegranates and, higher still, oak, olive, and peach trees. Quince, plum, pomegranate, and medlar, as well as vines and figs, covered the walls. The park also included sweet chestnuts and orchards of apricots and dwarf fruit trees grafted on quince.

Synopsis

1566 Property purchased by Cardinal Gianfrancesco Gambara as summer retreat

ca. 1568	Vignola commissioned to design gardens
1578	Palazzina Gambara completed
1581	Montaigne visits and describes garden in his *Journal*
1587	Death of Cardinal Gambara
1590	Villa owned by Cardinal Montalto
1596	Fountain of Dolphins, formerly Fountain of Coral, built
1656	Leased to Lante family
1953	Lease to Lante family ends

Further Reading

Coffin, David R., *The Villa in the Life of Renaissance Rome,* Princeton, New Jersey: Princeton University Press, 1979

"Italian Flower Collectors' Gardens in Seventeenth Century Italy," in *The Italian Garden,* edited by David R. Coffin, Washington, D.C.: Dumbarton Oaks, 1979

Lazzaro, Claudia, *The Italian Renaissance Garden: From the Conventions of Planting, Design, and Ornament to the Grand Gardens of Sixteenth-Century Central Italy,* New Haven, Connecticut: Yale University Press, 1990

Mader, Gunter, and Laila Neubert-Mader, *Jardins italiens,* Paris: Vilo, 1987

Masson, Georgina, *Italian Villas and Palaces,* New York: Abrams, and London: Thames and Hudson, 1959

Masson, Georgina, *Italian Gardens,* New York: Abrams, and London: Thames and Hudson, 1961

Montaigne, Michel de, *Journal du voyage de Michel de Montaigne en Italie, par la Suisse et l'Allemagne en 1580 et 1581,* Paris and Rome, 1774; new edition, edited by Maurice Rat, Paris: Garnier, 1955; as *Montaigne's Travel Journal,* translated by Donald M. Frame, San Francisco: North Point Press, 1983

Shepherd, J.C., and Geoffrey Alan Jellicoe, *Italian Gardens of the Renaissance,* London: Benn, and New York: Scribner, 1925; reprint, Princeton, New Jersey: Princeton Architectural Press, and London: Academy Editions, 1986

Sitwell, George Reresby, *An Essay on the Making of Gardens: Being a Study of Old Italian Gardens, of the Nature of Beauty, and the Principles Involved in Garden Design,* London: John Murray, 1909

Triggs, H. Inigo, *The Art of Garden Design in Italy,* London and New York: Longmans Green, 1906

Wharton, Edith, *Italian Villas and Their Gardens,* New York: Century, and London: Lane, 1904; reprint, New York: Da Capo Press, 1988

CHARLOTTE ANN JOHNSON

Lawn

In a nation containing thousands of carefully manicured gardens and parks, the standard home in the United States is often surrounded by what many call a "private park" and what others term an "unnatural disaster." The ubiquity of the American lawn stands as a symbol of an aesthetic that took shape in the United States after World War II. Turf grass is not indigenous to North America, yet if all lawns in the United States were joined, the "American savanna" would currently spread over about 25 million acres (10 million ha), or 40,000 square miles (103,600 sq. km)—a bit larger than the state of Pennsylvania. The lawn can often seem more closely related to a two-by-four than to a garden; placed within its historical context, however, this landscape form can be viewed for its "natural" significance in the lives of many Americans.

A green sward generally surrounds nearly 60 percent of U.S. homes, offering a border between public and private space. While there are certainly utilitarian purposes for the lawn, particularly for children's play, it remains largely an aesthetic creation. Imported from France and England, the lawn was normally a transitional zone into manicured gardens (see Plate 22). While lawns were not uncommon in the United States at the turn of the 18th century, the more purposeful design was not devised until the mid-19th century. Starting with the rural cemetery movement of the 1830s, Andrew Jackson Downing and other landscape architects created a general aesthetic that relied on the green space as a multipurpose setting to help civilize the wild vista beyond one's property. This was particularly important in the country estates that Downing normally designed.

After Downing's death in 1842, Frederick Law Olmsted and Calvert Vaux moved this aesthetic program forward. With the creation of Central Park in New York City in 1863, the designers brought a model to the public of a lawn used for the public welfare. Olmsted designed parks for many communities while also devising the model for the first suburban homes—complete with private green spaces. Nearly a century later, when Arthur Levit and others streamlined the suburban model to its bare bones, the lawn survived the cut. It became one of few aesthetic features in the nondescript housing developments that swept the nation after World War II.

Particularly in the suburban model of the late 20th century, the lawn can be divided into different zones governed mostly by use. The front lawn is the most heavily manicured and managed zone. Often constructed to most effectively frame the home's presentation, the front lawn is seen as a stage by many designers in which chemical usage is most intense. The private zone of the backyard is often very different. Intended more for the activities of the home owners, the backyard is less manicured and more personal.

The evolution of the lawn has not been without a scientific presence. The lawn industry got its start in 1901 when the U.S. Congress allotted $17,000 to ascertain the best turf grass species for lawns and pleasure grounds. In 1920 the U.S. Golf Association began working with the U.S. Department of Agriculture to devise a species of grass that would remain green year-round. Today grass-research centers are available at most agricultural universities. The industry now mixes science, aesthetics, and marketing. Interestingly, advertising is most often carried out by successful golfers to represent lawn-care companies. While composed of elements such as a garden, the lawn has clearly become a social landscape for Americans—one that provides important statements about a person's standing in society. In many communities the pursuit of the perfect lawn is reinforced by peer pressure. The physical aesthetic is relatively simple: the space contains only healthy, green grass and few weeds and is consistently cut so that it maintains a low, even height.

Of course, such a lawn is not attuned to particularities of place. Significant technology is required to insert such a garden site in areas of varied climate and rainfall. Through marketing skills and advertising, lawn-and-garden companies were able to sell their products and gradually shape the concept of the lawn to meet their desire for increased profit. Michael Pollan writes that the industrial lawn also has become a significant symbol in American life: "Since we have traditionally eschewed fences and hedges in America, the suburban vista can be marred by the negligence—or dissent—of a single property owner. This is why lawn care is regarded as such an important civic responsibility in the suburbs."

The industrial lawn has also spurred the exportation of the lawn mystique to other parts of the world. While many nations include gardens and pasture near homes, the standardized lawn is considered an American creation. Today, the image of American prosperity has aided the dissemination of the lawn aesthetic globally, particularly into wealthier homes. This is also demonstrated by the popularity of other related forms, such as golf courses in Asia and elsewhere. Regardless of the nation's garden preferences, such lawn design is directly modeled after the American form. The lawn is considered so uniquely American that Canadian scholars created a museum exhibit in 1998 titled "The American Lawn," which contained historical developments as well as design replicas. Although Americans may prefer that other nations acknowledge its natural wonders or technological developments, for many international observers the lawn has become a symbol of the United States' successful era of consumption.

While the lawn may be the closest many Americans come to a natural environment, its maintenance exacts a serious ecological toll. The lawn is not a naturally occurring ecosystem, so it requires chemical and other maintenance. For instance, massive amounts of water are required to maintain turf grass in arid or semiarid regions such as the American southwest. In many of these areas, home owners have implemented other ideas while still maintaining a public outdoor buffer. One of the most interesting gardening methods is Xeriscaping, in which one uses species native to the natural surroundings. In place of turf grass, the use of cacti and scrub or prairie grasses reduces maintenance significantly.

Clearly, the lawn of green grass is a social and cultural product of the age of conspicuous consumption. Its roots, however, fall within the realm of gardening. Ideas such as Xeriscaping reintroduce the ethic of gardening, while requiring that such a human-managed environment still function within the natural ecosystem.

Further Reading

Bormann, F. Herbert, et al., *Redesigning the American Lawn: A Search for Environmental Harmony,* New Haven, Connecticut: Yale University Press, 1993; 2nd edition, 2001

Jenkins, Virginia Scott, *The Lawn: A History of an American Obsession,* Washington, D.C.: Smithsonian Institution Press, 1994

Pollan, Michael, *Second Nature: A Gardener's Education,* New York: Dell Books, 1991

Schuyler, David, *Apostle of Taste: Andrew Jackson Downing, 1815–1852,* Baltimore, Maryland: Johns Hopkins University Press, 1996

Teyssot, Georges, editor, *The American Lawn,* New York: Princeton Architectural Press, 1999

Brian Black

Lawson, Thomas 1630–1691

English Botanist

Although the herbals of William Turner (ca. 1508–68) and John Gerard (1545–1612) included descriptions and localities for some plant species in the London area, the earliest-known printed account of organized botanical excursions in the British Isles did not appear until 1629, with the work of Thomas Johnson (ca. 1604–44). From this work developed the idea of carefully studying the geographical distribution of plants in Britain, an idea primarily advanced by John Ray (1629–1705), whose *Catalogus Plantarum Anglia* (Catalog of Plants in England) appeared in 1670. By 1695 Edmund Gibson's edition of Camden's *Britannia* published county lists of plants to a wide audience, and regional floras came of age.

One of several amateurs who became fascinated by botanical recording as its popularity grew in mid- to late- 16th-century England was the Quaker schoolmaster Thomas Lawson. The locations of English wild plants that Lawson discovered can still be found in modern regional floras, and his original notebook is preserved by the Linnean Society of London.

In contributing to the early recording of plant locations, Thomas Lawson systematically and accurately prepared records from some of the most remote English counties. He made a particular contribution to the early recording of wild plants from the northwest of England, especially the Lake District, where Lawson's field records have earned him the soubriquet the Father of Lakeland Botany. The Lake District was beloved by 19th-century romantic poets such as William Wordsworth, and today the rich flora of these uplands is conserved within the Lake District National Park. However, at the time of Lawson's botanical studies, such wild English landscapes were profoundly unpopular with English travelers and writers. Both Daniel Defoe and Celia Fiennes viewed the Lake District as "barren" with "very terrible" mountains.

Born in 1630, Thomas Lawson was baptized at Lawkland, an upland village in the northwest of England. After school in Giggleswick at the time of the Civil War between Parliament and King, he secured a place at Christ's College, Cambridge University. Scholarships for poor students were rarely adequate, and Thomas Lawson would have found himself a poor man in a rich man's world. This may account for why he left Cambridge in 1652 without completing his studies.

Lawson, though probably not ordained, offered his services as a preacher at a small chapel in the upland village of Rampside near Morecombe Bay. Here he was persuaded by the wandering preacher George Fox to become a Quaker. Nearby lay Swarthmoor Hall, where Fox befriended Margaret Fell. She, with apparent support from her husband, encouraged Fox to use Swarthmoor as the center of the Quaker movement. Lawson found himself at the very heart of this religious movement; he worked closely with Margaret Fell and Fox over the next few years and traveled widely throughout England to spread Quaker ideas.

In 1658–59 Thomas Lawson settled in the northern village of Great Strickland, where he was married in a Quaker ceremony. His marriage brought him customary tenancies that provided a steady income, sufficient to raise a small family. Although the restoration of the monarchy in 1660 promised greater religious toleration, many Quakers found themselves worse off than under the Commonwealth. Lawson continued to struggle for religious freedom away from Swarthmoor, writing pamphlets and engaging in activities that occasionally led to his arrest and imprisonment. However, after becoming more settled at Great Strickland, Lawson began a school. It was never officially sanctioned and became difficult to maintain after the 1662 Act of Uniformity. In 1664 Lawson was excommunicated for teaching without a license; his school was declared illegal and closed down in the early 1670s.

In 1674 Thomas returned to Swarthmoor Hall to make a living as a private tutor. He showed a particular interest in teaching botany, an interest that may have been encouraged by publication of John Ray's first edition of *Catalogus Angliae,* the first pocket flora of England, in 1670.

After a short while Lawson was joined at Swarthmoor Hall by Fox, who was by now married to Judge Fell's widowed wife. Fox and Lawson began work on religious publications and shared a mutual interest in botany and science. The Baconian ideal of learning from practical observation came to be particularly associated with the Quakers, who sought a system of schooling that mastered the practical sciences. Fox directly advocated schools that taught "the nature of herbs, roots and trees," and, with William Penn and others, he tried unsuccessfully to purchase a piece of land near London for the use of a garden school in which one or two of each sort of English plants were to be planted along with exotic plants.

In 1677, Thomas Lawson combined the task of taking a religious manuscript to London with a special itinerary of detours and stops that enabled him to study a range of wild plant localities. Both on his way to London and on his return, the botanical side of the journey was recorded in a notebook that already contained some of the first plant records for counties in the northwest of

England. Lawson's approach to botany was distinctly geographical. Before setting out on his journey he listed, county by county, what little was already known about the distribution of plants in England. The compilation of individual county lists had hardly begun by this date, although a provisional list for Oxfordshire was published the same year that Lawson traveled to London. He was probably the first amateur naturalist to seriously develop biological recording on a county by county basis, although John Ray and other botanists of the period had mooted the idea and should be credited with pioneering early interest in this approach.

Lawson extracted preliminary geographical lists from what little had been published and added his own discoveries as he toured. Thomas Lawson's project is put in perspective if we consider that it was not until 1695, some 20 years later, that Camden's *Britannia* appeared. This substantial geographical encyclopedia of Britain included information on a region's botany, and when it first introduced readers to the subject it included several records from Lawson's travels.

In about 1680 Thomas left Swarthmoor Hall for Great Strickland, where he helped to build a Quaker Meeting House. Over the next decade Lawson became widely known as an English botanist and the foremost authority on the flora of the Lake District. His opinion came to be respected and his plant records found their way into many published works. Lawson supplied Ray with many records and specimens of rare plants from northern England, and his herbarium came to be regarded as a reference collection on the flora of northern England.

From 1689, following the English Revolution, there was an improved atmosphere of tolerance toward Quakers in England, and Thomas Lawson was allowed to reopen his school. In his personal life the end of the decade also brought a gradual mellowing of the religious divide, for his much-loved daughter married an Anglican clergyman. By this time Lawson's interest in natural history had broadened. He collected fossils for John Ray, sending him his first parcel in 1689; when in 1690 Ray looked for enthusiasts to help collect insects, the study of which had hardly started, Lawson also participated. Thomas Lawson died in 1691 and is buried at the Friends Burial Ground, Great Strickland.

In conclusion, though Lawson was praised by his contemporary John Ray as a "diligent, industrious and skilful botanist" and earned a reputation as the *Father of Lakeland Botany,* one is drawn to a comment by his recent biographer, Jean Whittaker, that "in approaching Lawson one is always left with the impression that the man is greater than his remains." Certainly he has been the subject of few biographies, and there may yet be more to discover.

Biography

Born in Lawkland, North Yorkshire, England, 1630. Studied at Cambridge until 1652; became Quaker after meeting George Fox in mid 1650s; settled in Great Strickland, Cumbria, England, 1658/59; opened a school, 1674; moved to Swarthmoor Hall, Cumbria (Quaker center established by Fox), and made living as private tutor, with particular interest in botany; traveled to London (with many detours along the way) and recorded distribution of plants in each county visited, 1677; returned to Great Strickland, 1680, where he helped establish Quaker Meeting House and eventually opened another school; became widely know as botanist and as foremost authority on flora of Lake District. Died in Great Strickland, Cumbria, England, 1691.

Further Reading

Raistrick, Arthur, *Quakers in Science and Industry,* London: Bannisdale Press, and New York: Philosophical Library, 1950; new edition, Newton Abbot, Devon: David and Charles, 1968

Whittaker, E. Jean, *Thomas Lawson, 1630–1691: North Country Botanist, Quaker, and Schoolmaster,* York, North Yorkshire: Sessions Book Trust, 1986

DAVID SOLMAN

Lawson, William 1554–1635

English Garden Author

The Reverend William Lawson's main claim to fame lies in his presumed authorship of *The Country Housewife's Garden* (1618), the first of a new genre of books in England: women's gardening books. Whether or not Lawson was the author, he was undoubtedly the first to succeed in bringing a book of this genre into print, albeit bound with a book intended for what was generally held to be a male preserve (orchards and fruit) and given second billing. The cloak of anonymity given by Lawson to the small *Country Housewife's Garden,* and its later incorporation into a popular compendium written largely by Gervase Markham, suggests that there may be more to discover about the authorship of the first women's gardening book to have been published in England.

Bound with the first edition of *The Country Housewife's* Garden, and equally interesting, was A *New Orchard and Garden* (1618). This marks Lawson as the first author of a published book about gardening in northern England. More important (as indicated by the word *New* in its title), the book was entirely original in content. Both the title page and preface proclaim the text to be the culmination of 48 years' personal experience, placing Lawson's book firmly in the mold of the Baconian Renaissance idea of advancing human knowledge through direct observation. At a time when gardening books by English authors were almost unknown and relied heavily on foreign writings and folklore, Lawson's book stood out from the mainstream.

Lawson certainly did not lack the education or ability to draw heavily on the learned works of others; his book contains occasional quotes from Vermigli and Erasmus, and he successfully studied for ordination into the priesthood at Durham Cathedral, becoming vicar of Ormesby in Yorkshire. His approach, though not altogether different from Gervase Markham's in *The English Husbandman* (1613), probably represents true innovation: Lawson's accomplishment has been acclaimed as "the first original book on horticulture based upon personal experience and with no dependence on earlier sources" (Harvey). Moreover, *A New Orchard and Garden* became the first of a genre of popular and largely original writings about the natural world to be undertaken by English village parsons over the next 200 years. Of these, *The Natural History of Selborne* (1789) by the Reverend Gilbert White is the best-known example.

Lawson's *Country Housewife's Garden* and *A New Orchard and Garden* complemented each other, the one dealing with the traditionally female preserve of the kitchen garden and the other with the traditionally male preserve of the orchard. They became much sought after in Stuart times, selling out repeatedly and passing through numerous reprints and editions throughout the 17th century. Most of these editions were bound with other books written, selected, or adapted by Lawson or by Gervase Markham, the English poet and prolific country-life author believed by some to have been the rival poet referred to in Shakespeare's sonnets. These compilations sometimes included Simon Harward's *The Art of Propagating Plants* (1623?) and *The Husbandman's Fruitful Orchard* (1623), a rewritten and abbreviated version of *The Fruiterer's Secrets* (1604), whose original authorship is unclear, together with a number

Title page from William Lawson, *New Orchard and Garden,* revised and enlarged edition, 1623

of Markham's popular works bound with Lawson's in Markham's *A Way to Get Wealth* (1631).

Lawson's writings give much useful horticultural information, and Lawson, together with his contemporary Markham, did much to fill gaps in the knowledge about the formal design and symmetry of English gardens before changes in taste produced more naturalistic approaches. Important though they are, Lawson's books have not been without their critics. John Beale in his *Herefordshire Orchards* (1657) disagreed with a number of Lawson's assertions, and Miles Hadfield took the view that Lawson's instructions for laying out a garden were "not very helpful." Lawson himself twice corrected—and enlarged—his works, the opportunity being provided to him as earlier editions sold out.

A New Orchard and Garden professes to advise on the best way for planting, grafting, and making good any ground for an orchard and garden of formal design, particularly in the north of England and generally for the whole kingdom. Lawson's own success in furnishing "this my northerne orchard and countrey garden with needfull plants and usefull herbes" enabled him to offer practical tips and advice on the "best, surest, and readiest way to make a good orchard and garden," through, for example, choice of site, use of particular techniques of soil preparation, and approaches to layout, fence design, tree planting, and grafting. *The Country Housewife's Garden* covers some of the same topics, but the emphasis is on the kitchen garden. It offers advice on herbs of common use, such as their practical and ornamental value and when they were in season. It also describes designs for knot gardens and plots, with a view to improving the formal design and order of grounds and walks. Toward the end, it gives one subject touched on in *A New Orchard and Garden,* the husbandry of bees, particular treatment.

Lawson's books drew directly on his experience of life and gardening in Yorkshire. Local names appear in the text, such as Wilton in Cleveland, of which Lawson wrote, "I know [of] . . . a pear tree of a great age, blown close to the earth." Wilton lay close to his home, the parish of Ormesby in Cleveland on the south bank of the river Tees, a few miles from the Yorkshire coast. In the 17th century it would have been a beautiful landscape of rural charm. Lawson's personal contentment with the site of his orchard led him to proudly advise the reader, "I could . . . commend your orchard if . . . hard by it there should run a pleasant river with silver streams, you might sit in your mount, and angle a peckled trout, sleighty eel, or some other dainty fish."

In the 19th century Lawson's orchard and garden became part of the suburbs of the city of Middlesbrough. Today, the silver streams are no more, but close by lies the North Yorkshire Moors National Park, which still displays great beauty and includes the Hackness estate of Lady Margaret Hoby, the first woman diarist in England. Her diaries indicate that she had known Lawson since at least 1600 and would have shared his piety and love of gardening. Lawson's acquaintance with her is implicit in *A New Orchard and Garden.* In his discussion of beehives Lawson mentions "some (as that honourable Lady at Hackness, whose name doth much grace mine orchard) use to make seats for them (that is, bee-holes) in the stone walls of their Orchard, or Garden." It was her name, Margaret (Marguerite daisy; *Leucanthemum vulgare*), that graced Lawson's orchard about 30 miles (48 km) away, the plant, incidentally, that reportedly inspired the plant hunter John Bartram to study botany.

While the great Elizabethan and early Stuart writers were fashioning poems and plays to take an enduring place in English literature, other branches of literary activity of a more practical nature began to develop. Lawson's works were early examples of this innovation, "not only original, but of outstanding charm and simplicity of style, constituting a true masterpiece" (Harvey). His work can be seen as a direct consequence of the intellectual and cultural achievements of Renaissance and Reformation Europe: changing social characteristics and the development of the printing press gradually led to an explosion of new communication and learning.

Biography

Born in Yorkshire, England, 1554. Took religious orders at Durham Cathedral, became vicar of Ormesby, North Yorkshire; provided observations to augment second edition of poem by John Dennys, *The Secrets of Angling,* 1613; published *New Orchard and Garden* and *Country Housewife's Garden,* London, 1618; both were corrected and enlarged in 1623 and 1626. Died 1635.

Selected Publications

A New Orchard and Garden; or, The Best Way for Planting, Grafting, and to Make Any Ground Good, for a Rich Orchard, 1618

The Country Housewife's Garden, 1618

Further Reading

Archibald, William Arthur Jobson, "Lawson, William," in *Dictionary of National Biography: From the Earliest Times to 1900,* edited by Leslie Stephen and Sidney Lee, vol. 11, London, 1882; reprint, Oxford: Oxford University Press, 1973

Blomfield, Reginald Theodore, and F. Inigo Thomas, *The Formal Garden in England,* London, 1892; reprint, London: Waterstone, 1985

Desmond, Ray, *Dictionary of British and Irish Botanists and Horticulturists,* London: Taylor and Francis, 1977; revised edition, 1994

Hadfield, Miles, *A History of British Gardening,* London: Hutchinson, 1960; 3rd edition, London: John Murray, 1979

Harvey, John, "William Lawson and His Orchard—A 17th-Century Gardening Writer Identified," *Country Life* 172 (October 1982)

Henrey, Blanche, *British Botanical and Horticultural Literature,* 3 vols., Oxford: Oxford University Press, 1975; see especially vol. 1

Johnson, George William, *A History of English Gardening,* London, 1829; reprint, New York: Garland, 1982

Moody, Joanna, editor, *The Private Life of an Elizabethan Lady: The Diary of Lady Margaret Hoby, 1599–1605,* Stroud, Gloucestershire: Sutton, 1998

Taboroff, June, "Wife Unto Thy Garden: The First Gardening Books for Women," *Garden History* 11, no. 1 (1983)

DAVID SOLMAN

Laxenburg

Lower Austria, Austria

Location: approximately 7 miles (11.3 km) south of Vienna

Laxenburg, a park of about 620 acres (250 ha), is situated in a plain. Originally it was an oak wood traversed by several arms of the river Schwechat. Laxenburg park was created in several phases between 1750 and 1850. It is a significant example of early romanticism in European garden design, an ecological preserve in a predominantly agricultural environment, and a popular recreation area for the local residents as well as for the Viennese. Its dreamy atmosphere and the iconography that represents the medieval past of the Hapsburg family form a contrast with the classic imperial character of Schönbrunn.

The hunting ground of Laxenburg was Hapsburg property since the 14th century. About 1500 the emperor Maximilian I established a "Dutch pleasure garden" near a square castle of medieval origin. Until the middle of the 18th century Laxenburg was mainly used as the imperial residence in spring, when the court went there to hunt herons and pheasants.

A new era began with the imperial couple Maria Theresia and Franz Stephan I. In the 1740s Laxenburg and Schönbrunn were connected by a straight allée of about eight miles (13 km). About 1755 it was decided that a more comfortable new garden palace should be erected near the old castle, designed by Nicolo Pacassi. South of the old castle a radial system of allées was cut into the wood of the game preserve with a pavilion of green trelliswork (Grünes Lusthaus, or Temple of Diana) in the center, where the empress loved to play cards. Even further south a section of one of the arms of the river was transformed into a straight canal, the earliest part of today's Forstmeisterkanal, which now goes from one end of the park to the other. There were also ambitious plans for an extended formal pleasure garden east of the new palace, but the realization was rather modest. This so-called Waderlgarten was probably designed by artists from Lorraine—at the very same time a group of immigrants who had come with Franz Stephan from his native country were known to have been working in the gardens of Schönbrunn. At the beginning of the 19th century the Waderlgarten was fundamentally transformed into a landscape garden.

Of great importance for the next phase of the park was the visit of Emperor Joseph II to Ermenonville in 1777, where this sovereign, who admired the ideas of the Enlightenment, saw the gardens of the Marquis de Girardin with their sceneries inspired by Rousseau. In 1782 Joseph II ordered the transformation of Laxenburg into a natural *jardin anglais*. This work was planned by Isidore Ganneval (Canevale) in 1782–85 and carried out by the garden architect Lefèvre d'Archambault and the gardener Christoph Lübeck from Dessau in the 1780s. Ganneval's plan included some formal features. The geometric network of allées was retained, only in the spaces between one could find irregularly shaped meadows and clumps of trees. Some traces of this period are still left around the Temple of Concordia (erected in 1795 by G.A. Moretti) south of the Forstmeisterkanal.

The final and most important transformation and extension took place in the early years of the emperor Franz II (Francis I of Austria), who ruled from 1792 to 1835, and his vivacious wife, Maria Theresia II of Naples, who spent a great amount of energy and money on the renovation and decoration of the park. Laxenburg remained the emperor's favorite residence for all his life. He had decided to learn gardening (as all male members of the Hapsburgs were required to learn a trade) and so watched over the activities in the park with great interest and engagement. In the 1790s the young imperial couple initiated the construction of numerous follies that evoked the admiration of the contemporary public. These included a Turkish mosque designed by G. Nigelli, three structures—the Hermitage, a Chinese bridge, and the Haus der Laune (House of Caprice)—all designed by the architect J.F. Hetzendorf von Hohenberg, and a fisherman's village.

The Haus der Laune had some unusual features: it was formed of Gothic and Egyptian elements, as well as of painted sheaves of corn, barrels, etc. The cellars were under the roof, some inscriptions had to be read from right to left, and the interior contained several bizarre surprises. This house represented a topsy-turvy world and was probably meant to be a defense of *deraison* in the contemporary discussion of enlighted and romantic ideas. It was transformed into a harmless "Pavilion in the Oak Grove" in 1814. Since World War II only ruins are left, but a very exact and well-preserved model of the original Haus der Laune can be seen in the Historical Museum of Vienna.

About 1800 the park's iconography shifted from light-hearted pastoral follies to a romantic celebration of the Middle Ages and the medieval origins of the Habsburg dynasty. The construction of the Rittergau (district of chivalry) in a landscape with an artificially dammed lake and several islands is the greatest achievement of Austrian garden architecture of this time. The designer of this picturesque extension east of Ganneval's *jardin anglais* was Johann Michael Riedl, chief surveyor of the buildings and gardens of Laxenburg from 1798 to 1849. On the western lakeside Hohenberg and some other architects were commissioned to design a grotto with a model of the Hapsburg's native castle on top. From this project the Gothic bridge (finished in 1808) and the Grotto (finished in 1821) were carried out, but the Hapsburg castle was never built. The various neogothic structures, the castle Franzensburg, the Tilt-Yard, the Gothic bridge, Knight's Column, and Knight's Tomb were constructed in co-operation with the architect and sculptor Franz Jäger, the elder.

About 1815 the famous garden designer Peter Joseph Lennè from Berlin worked in Laxenburg (documented in a plan at the Graphic Collection Albertina in Vienna). He tried to modify the geometric axes with picturesque groups of trees and curved paths. In the years from 1820 to 1849 the lake was extended to the east, where a neo-Gothic pavilion was finished on Mariannen Island in 1840.

Especially in the Rittergau plants had been selected and composed to evoke various sentiments, an effect that can still be seen today, although the progress of growth has blurred the original intentions of the 19th century. Groups of plane trees on wide meadows, a circle of poplars on the western lakeside (a reference to Rousseau's tomb in Ermenonville), weeping willows near the water and the bridges, groups of pine trees on the artificial hills of the Rittergau, as well as yew and juniper in the troughs yield a pattern of iconographic planting. About 1800 a nursery for exotic trees was established in Laxenburg. The trees were mainly used for decorative planting in the park but also were sold to other garden owners.

In 1918, with the end of the Hapsburg monarchy, Laxenburg became public property. After World War II it was occupied by the Russian army. The park underwent decay and devastation for about 40 years before it became the property of the provinces Lower Austria and Vienna in 1963, and a management company was established, which initiated the restoration of the buildings and the park.

Synopsis

1755–80	Radial system of allées south of old castle; formal gardens east of new palace
1782–85	Isidore Ganneval (Canevale) designs *jardin anglais* that still retains some formal axes
1783	Emperor Joseph II opens park to public
1792–98	Construction of several pastoral follies, especially *Haus der Laune*
1798–1807	Park extended in east by Michael Riedl; layout of lakes; construction of *Rittergau*
1820–49	Completion of easternmost part of lakes

Further Reading

Brock, Annedore, *Das Haus der Laune im Laxenburger Park bei Wien,* Frankfurt and New York: Peter Lang, 1996

Hainisch, Erwin, *Der Architekt Johann Ferdinand Hetzendorf von Hohenberg,* Innsbruck, Austria: Rohrer, 1949

Hajós, Géza, *Romantische Gärten der Aufklärung,* Vienna: Böhlau, 1989

Hajós, Géza, "Der Laxenburger Park," in *Historische Gärten in Österreich,* edited by Österreichische Gesellschaft für historische Gärten, Vienna: Böhlau, 1993

Hajós, Géza, Edith Bódi, and Michaela Schober, *Der Schloßpark Laxenburg,* Laxenburg, Austria: Schloss Laxenburg Betriebsgesellschaft, 1998

Zykan, Josef, *Laxenburg,* Vienna: Herold, 1969

Beatrix Hajós

Łazienki Park

Warsaw, Poland

Location: Central Warsaw

Łazienki Park, in its present form, was established as a summer residence for King Stanislaus Augustus Poniatowski during the period 1766–95, when he created parkways and numerous buildings, including the Palace on Water, and opened the garden to the public. Earlier, however, the land was a deer park connected with the Ujazdowski castle. As such it belonged to the princes who ruled Mazovia from the 13th to the 15th century, and was part of a greater Ujazdowski ensemble. After their rule ended, a series of new owners transformed the area. The most dramatic changes were effected by King Stanislaus; during a 30-year period he turned the land into a classical park, at the same time that Warsaw became the center of the Polish Enlightenment. During the 19th century, the park was modified under the ownership of the Russian czar, becoming more casual and losing some of its features. A post–World War I renovation was later ruined by Germans during World War II. Łazienki Park was again restored during the period from 1950 to 1965, and modern features were added from 1960 to 1975. Now encompassing 76 hectares (188 acres), the park is part of the center of Warsaw.

The Ujazdowski lands became the property of the Polish kings when the duchy of Mazovia was incorporated into the kingdom of Poland in the 16th century. Warsaw became the capital in 1611 and was therefore turned into an important place of residence for the Polish nobility. Since 1674 the deer park belonged to the family of crown prince Lubomirski, who landscaped the grounds by creating a small pond and a rectangular island, with the *Hippocrene* bath pavilion on it, and an Italian garden. During the period from 1720 to 1764, King Augustus II (1670–1733) and King Augustus III (1696–1763) rented the deer park as a hunting ground. Augustus II constructed a canal (*Kanal Saski*) on the northern end of the park to partially drain the waterlogged deer park and extended the southern end. In 1744 the first stage of garden construction under Augustus III was completed.

Under Stanislaus's direction, the park underwent dramatic changes. The central theme of the park became the Palace on Water, which replaced the bath pavilion. It is situated on an artificial rectangular island in an enlarged pond that is itself placed within a deer park under the slope of a postglacial valley. The park surrounding it has three levels: the lower level is a terrace, the middle is on the slope of the postglacial valley, and the upper is on the postglacial plain. The eastern side of the original bathhouse facing the Vistula river had an Italian garden, made up of two rectangular fields cut by eight radial avenues. The beautiful, original bath pavilion called the *Hippocrene* functioned as a bath place and social gatherings venue.

The construction of the king's new garden began by draining the deer park and planting trees. In 1766–68 the baroque garden-town ensemble was designed and called the Stanislaus Axis or the Kite. Roundpoints were constructed on the eastern side of the Ujazdowski Palace. An 820-meter (897-yd.) canal was reconstructed in the deer park. A system of roundpoints connected by avenues was constructed on the western side of the 7.5-kilometer (12-mi.) access alley. Organized avenues and a square were constructed during 1766–67. During the 1770s the style of the park was baroque with Italian accents, which were remnants of the Lubomirski influence.

Two big ponds were made on the southern and northern sides of the Palace on Water. The northern pond ends in a bridge with a 1788 statue of King John III Sobieski (ruled 1674–1696) on a horse. The southern pond with fancifully sculptured banks has an island with artificial Herculean ruins as a theatrical stage. Busts of poets were placed at the edge of the amphitheater in 1790. The lower southern pond is joined to the upper southern pond by a cascade.

Stanislaus's transformation involved the presentation of architectonic and geometric structures in association with the surrounding environment, with informal plantings in separated parts. The landscaping and accessories were applied quite economically to create a perfect example of a classical garden. The king preserved classical constructions of certain parts of the garden and thus did not completely succumb to the English styles that were then in fashion. Gardeners who implemented these changes were J.Ch. Schuch (1752–1813), J.M. Tietz (1781–95), and K.L. Agricola (1773–79). The grand project was actually made in 1775–76. At that time the royal gardeners were Schneider and Schulz. A.F. Moszyński (1732–86), the chief planner of the Stanislaus Axis, was also a likely participant. Other architects were D. Merlini (1730–97), J.Ch. Kamsetzer (1753–95), and J.B. Plersch (1732–1817)

The Palace on Water, the Old Orangery, and the White House reflected the antique rule of *insulae beatae*. All residential buildings, such as the Palace on Water, White House, hermitage, cadet house, and the cistern modeled after the Roman grave of Cecilia Meteli, were constructed in 1774–78. The Palace on Water was expanded after 1782, as were the small theater, Turkish house, the Old Orangery with theater, guardhouse, farm house, Sybilla's shrine, and the Egyptian bridge. Among these, the small theater, Turkish house, and many other buildings no longer exist. The king collected sculptures in the Old Orangery that initiated the academy of art. After his dethronement in 1795 the park became neglected, animals disappeared, and the orangeries, porcelain factory, and brickyard were leased out.

In 1817 the park's inheritor sold the property to the Russian Czar Alexander I. Care of the buildings was given to J. Kubicki (1758–1833); during his tenure orangeries (1822), the pinery (1828), and the palm house (1870) were built. In 1812 a new botanical garden, the Belvedere palace together with the romantic garden, had been separated from the park. The Belvedere was reserved for the czar. In the 1830s the whole area was surrounded by a fence. During the czar's rule canals around the White House, the berceau along the Kings Promenade, and the Chinese Bridge upon the Chinese Way were destroyed, rendering the park more informal in character. After World War I the park was completely renovated, and a rose garden with a statue of the Polish composer Frederick Chopin was created. In 1936 the Belvedere garden was rejoined to the park. During World War II the park was destroyed, and about a quarter of the trees were damaged. German troops burned the Palace on Water after looting all of its valuables. The park required a complete restoration after the war.

The current composition of the park is the result of 300 years of transformation. Stylistically it can be divided into three historic parts. The oldest segment originates from the late 18th century and occupies the central region of the park, including the Palace on Water, three ponds, an amphitheater, Myśliwiecki Palace, the White House, the Old Orangery, and a hermitage. The bosquets, landscaped areas, and forest zone are part of this area. The part of the park dating from the first half of the 19th century is comprised of the beautiful Belvedere garden, king's promenade, and an exotic garden with a palm house. The newest section includes the periphery adapted as park area during the 20th century; the southern region that forms a modernistic parterre of Aurora, and the upper terrace shaped as a sunken rosarium with Chopin's statue. Currently, nearly half of the total park area is wooded. Native plants dominate in the oldest areas and exotic kinds appear in the sections created during the 19th and 20th centuries. There were 300 taxons represented in trees and shrubs in the park in 1976, and there are presently 216 taxons.

The park is now part of the town center and, therefore, is isolated within the city and devoid of its historical views. It is situated on the eastern side of the Vistula river in an area known as the Slope of Warsaw, which is treated as a natural cultural reserve, and together with the valley constitutes the basic elements of the city's ecological system. This area is troubled by a water deficit in both quality and quantity, which necessitates supplementation using contaminated water from the Vistula river. Other problems faced by the park are polluted urban air, erosion of the slope, overgrown vegetation, and the large number of people visiting the park.

The park and its architecture are an important contribution to Polish art. They represent the beginning of mature classicism in architecture and romanticism in garden art. The park also serves as a pleasure resort for the Polish people and foreign visitors, as a reminder of the nation's history. Because of its service as a living museum, the park has legal monument protection and is administered by the National Museums.

Synopsis

13th–15th C.	Ujazdów (former Jazolów) estate owned by princes of Mazovia
15th century	Ujazdów the estate of Queen Bona
1674	Ujazdów became property of Lubomirskis; pond within a rectangular, artificial island, bath pavilion (called Hippocrene), and Italian garden built in deer park
1720–64	Deer park used by kings Augustus II and Augustus III of Poland; drainage canal called Kanał Saski built, and deer park enlarged
1744	First stage of garden construction completed
1764	King Stanislaw II Augustus Poniastowski buys deer park
1765	First map of deer park by H.G. Marx
1766–67	Construction of main park ways, Łazienki became a baroque garden with some Renaissance features
1766–68	Construction of 7.5 kilometer (4.6 mi.) Stanislaus Axis (called *kite*) as baroque town-garden ensemble, and reconstruction of canal
1775–76	Elaboration of grand plan of garden
1794	Park opened to public
1795	King Stanislaw II dethroned, and park began to deteriorate
1817	Łazienki Park sold to Russian czar
1822–70	Construction of new buildings, botanical garden created, and with removal of Chinese Bridge, *berceau*, and canals, park became more informal
1918	General renovation and restoration, and park opened fully to the public
1936	Reannexation of the romantic park of Belvedere to Łazienki, and construction of a hippodrome
1939–45	Palace on water and park destroyed; Ujazdów castle burned down
1950–65	Restoration of palace on water and park
1960–75	Rosarium and parterre of Aurora built, both in modern style
1970s	Restoration of the Ujazdów castle

Further Reading

Tatarkiewicz, Władysław, *Łazienki Warszawskie*, Warsaw: Arkady, 1957; 3rd edition, 1972

Marek Siewniak

Leasowes

West Midlands, England

Location: approximately 15 miles (24 km) southwest of Birmingham

The creation of The Leasowes, southwest of Birmingham in the Midlands of England close to the town of Halesowen, by the poet William Shenstone (1714–63) was one of the seminal moments in garden history. Shenstone settled on his modest estate, which provided him with an income of £300 a year, in 1739–40. It was a hill farm, probably established in the late Middle Ages, set in a matrix of oak and beech woodlands and watered by two streams, tributaries of the river Stour. The principal valley to the north, below the farmhouse, already contained a string of fishponds. In 1788 Shenstone's friend and biographer Richard Graves described the first rather random efforts at enhancing the estate:

> On coming on board with his tenant at the Leasowes [Shenstone] cut a straight walk through his wood, terminating by a small building of rough stone; and in a sort of gravel or marl-pit, in the corner of a field, amongst some hazels, he scooped out a sort of cave, stuck a little cross of wood over the door, and called it a hermitage; and, a few years after, had built an elegant little summerhouse in the water under the fine group of beeches.

These were very much the precocious efforts of a young man, down from Oxford, and it seems from this description that The Leasowes was destined to be a typical product of the early landscape movement, with straight walks leading to "grotesque" buildings—a grotto, hermitage, and a summerhouse.

The fashionable idea of the *ferme ornée* provided Shenstone with a set of associated principles around which he could organize his estate without compromising it for the purpose of providing him with an income. Philip Southcote's famous "farm" at Woburn in Surrey was its precedent, although the immediate inspiration was the seat of Morgan Graves, the elder brother of Richard Graves, at Mickleton in Gloucestershire, who had been influenced by Southcote's work. At Woburn the farm was viewed from a circuit walk and enhanced by various "decorations"—seats, alcoves, bridges, etc. Shenstone was also familiar with Batty Langley's *New Principles of Gardening* (1728), which summarized the views of Addison and Pope and recommended establishing serpentine paths around an estate, passing through a variety of scenery including cattle enclosures, cornfields, and a farmyard. Serpentine paths and streams were to become ubiquitous elements in Shenstone's landscape, as Robert Dodsley's 1765 *Description of the Leasowes* indicates. As a working farm, however, The Leasowes ultimately failed to sustain its creator. Yet it reflected an Arcadian ideal of self-sufficiency that found sentimental support among cultivated circles in the mid-18th century. Some of Shenstone's paintings certainly convey the impression that it was a farm, and in his *Letters* (1777) Joseph Heely always refers to The Leasowes as "the farm" and describes the "milky heifer and deserving steed" enjoying the "luxuriant fields." The pasture produced hay, which was stacked in ricks, fancifully regarded by Shenstone as pyramids.

The *ferme ornée* provided the unifying framework for the estate, but its simplicity and purity could easily be compromised by too much polish and artifice. Imitating the techniques of the landscape painter, Shenstone thought it was necessary "to collect ye Beauties of Nature into a compass proper for its observation." If necessary, some of the painter's tricks could also be deployed, such as falsifying perspective and more important, introducing props to improve nature and amplify its different moods. He believed that "ground should first be considered with an eye to its peculiar character; whether it be the grand, the savage, the sprightly, the melancholy, the horrid, or the beautifull." With a "poet's feeling" scenery could thus be enhanced "by means of art."

Application of such techniques is demonstrated in one of Shenstone's earliest projects, the creation of Virgil's Grove in the valley immediately beneath the house. This eventually became the climax of the tour of the estate, but in the 1740s it was relatively isolated. Located in the deepest part of the valley within a thick wood, it provided opportunities for a display of artistry without clashing with the pastoral scenery outside. The water was manipulated to provide a spectacular display of cascades. The grove contained an obelisk to Virgil and a seat dedicated to the poet James Thomson, who had visited The Leasowes in 1746. Both memorials had inscriptions; a further inscription on a seat beneath some large tree roots epitomized how Shenstone felt about his creation. All visitors agreed this was the most delightful spot, but Shenstone had some doubts, relating to Lady Luxborough in 1749 that his planting had made it look very much like a garden. Nature, he thought, may have been compromised here by tipping the balance in favor of art.

Unlike the landscapes provided by professional improvers, The Leasowes had no blueprint, only a set of loose principles and aspirations. Throughout the 1740s and 1750s Shenstone developed other viewpoints and stations around the perimeter of the farm. As early as 1744 he wrote to his friend Richard Jago, "I have an alcove, six elegies, a seat, two epitaphs (one upon myself), three ballards, four songs, and a serpentine river to show you when you come." Poetry and gardening were, it seems, indivisible activities for Shenstone, and eventually The Leasowes had in the region of 40 wooden seats (each with its inscription), some with elaborate Gothic backs, others simply ad hoc arrangements of planks and logs. They acted as punctuation marks within the landscape, reminding visitors that there was something to see and providing them with verbal advice on how they should see it. By the late 1740s Shenstone began to view the farm as a single composition, although not until 1759 did the wandering path reach every corner.

In the early 1750s Shenstone turned his attention to the secondary valley, southwest of the house, creating a waterfall about 137 meters (150 yd.) long. At its foot was a root house dedicated to the earl of Stamford, and nearby stood an urn to a friend, William Somerville. Shenstone had a predilection for urns and erected one to Maria Dolman, his cousin who died of smallpox in 1754, and also proposed one for James Thomson. Urns, he thought, should be large and plain, to reflect solemnity, and should be placed in shade. The urns and other commemorative objects turned The Leasowes into a memorial garden and contributed greatly to its pensive atmosphere.

Alterations in the vicinity of Maria Dolman's urn, sited above the Lovers' Walk, brought Shenstone up on to the western ridge, which bounded his estate and where he had commenced landscaping in 1740. A Gothic screen was placed here in the long walk leading to the Temple of Pan. At about the same time, close to the house, where the visitors gathered, Shenstone planted a "shrubbery"; Shenstone is credited with the first use of this term. It was planted informally around a goldfish pool with flowering shrubs such as syringia, laburnum, myrtles, orange trees, laurel of Portugal, and geraniums placed in pots. Among his last works was the ruined Priory, sited on the promontory where the two streams joined. Apart from its focal position in the landscape, it provided some comfortable rooms for a tenant and some income for its creator. Finally, in 1760 Shenstone began to excavate the Priory Pool, a triangular area of water at the confluence of the streams. He died in February 1763 still waiting for it to fill.

Shenstone's great achievement was his creation of a seamless work of art. The path around the farm took the visitor from one scene to another, but these were so carefully managed that even within a few yards different views and perspectives could be enjoyed. Prospects were numerous, but too many of these were likely to cloy, so he frequently alternated them with interior views or "home scenes." The seats, alcoves, and urns in their carefully contrived settings drew the visitor's attention toward the minutiae of the landscape. At each station the inscription set the tone, usually elegiac, with fanciful references to the spirits who inhabited the spot—a veiled reference to Shenstone's own sensibilities. The recorded responses of many different visitors indicate that his judgment on the distinct character of each scene was very much in tune with the age. Even the most worldly tourist, such as the Honorable John Byng, felt there was an appropriateness in the manner in which language and the landscape were fused, creating a harmonious work of art. Thus many visitors saw The Leasowes as a literary artifact, to be read as a text. The tour provided a narrative, unfolding like an 18th-century novel, with the inscriptions providing literary digressions and the climax coming in Virgil's Grove.

In a broader context The Leasowes stood on the threshold of a major shift in the intellectual outlook of the 18th century, especially among the middle classes. They began to reject the elitist objective culture, based on classical canons, which had held sway from the 16th century, and instead embraced a more expressive sentimental culture, rooted in the subjective. Gardens akin to The Leasowes, developed with feeling, replaced overtly emblematic gardens such as Stowe. In this sense The Leasowes is the first truly picturesque garden devoted to "pleasing the imagination by scenes of grandeur, beauty or variety."

Following Shenstone's death The Leasowes passed through the hands of ten owners in ten years. It became a talisman among successful industrialists who either failed to sustain Shenstone's creative energy or struggled with his burgeoning plantations. Attrition led to decline. Some of the owners, such as Mr. Horne, launched a campaign of restoration and improvement, but this was equally unsatisfactory, and Geoffrey Lipscombe in 1799 found many of the garden buildings renewed. Horne also rebuilt the house and erected a walled kitchen garden above the long cascade, to the south of the house. In 1797 an embankment for the Dudley canal cut off the bottom of the Priory Pool and blocked the view to Halesowen.

Visitors, many of them literary figures, came in droves to The Leasowes in the late 18th century. These included Thomas Whateley, William Gilpin, John Parnell, Thomas Gray, Oliver Goldsmith, Thomas Jefferson, Samuel Johnson, Joseph Heely, John Byng, John Wesley, and innumerable minor figures. Visitors commented on the decline but were generally impressed by what they found. Some, such as Gilpin, who preferred a

Shropshire garden at Leasowes, designed by William Shenstone, ca. 1811
Copyright Mary Evans Picture Library

purer manifestation of the Picturesque, found it rather affected. Nevertheless, journals, essays, letters and literary accounts of The Leasowes proliferated, so that there was hardly a decade in the next century when some review or assessment was not being published. As John Byng put it rather sardonically on his visit in 1781, "Penmanship has the power of puffing inferior places and rendering them visitable by the curious, and admired by the ignorant." Dodsley's *Description of the Leasowes* was published in the second edition of Shenstone's collected works in 1765 and was in the hands of most visitors who thus followed the tour in the manner recommended by its creator.

The wider influence of The Leasowes is more difficult to assess. It certainly stimulated an interest in the Picturesque, but the movement developed so rapidly in the decades after Shenstone's death that his contribution went largely unacknowledged by proponents of the Picturesque such as Humphry Repton, Sir Uvedale Price, Richard Payne Knight, and John Claudius Loudon. They may have wanted to distance themselves from the apparent artificiality of The Leasowes. Thomas Jefferson visited the estate in 1786. Although he found it disappointing, his description shows he had read Dodsley, and the idea of the *ferme ornée* put down deep roots in the United States in part through his influence. In France the marquis de Girardin erected a bust to Shenstone at Ermenonville, and throughout Britain The Leasowes became the model for Picturesque gardening on a small scale, eventually to be eclipsed by Loudon's "gardenesque."

The flourishing literary record ensured that The Leasowes was never forgotten. Indeed, decay enhanced its elegiac and melancholic associations—decay was the most tangible ingredient of the Picturesque. The landscape, many felt, was in mourning for the "plaintive Shenstone." Ironically, as the alcoves and seats disappeared and nature took control, the imagination of visitors, fed on the copious literature of The Leasowes and the story of its creator, began to resonate even more strongly.

See also Ferme Ornée

Synopsis

1739–40	William Shenstone takes possession of father's estate near Halesowen
1740–43	Shenstone carries out first measures of enhancement, including straight walk, hermitage, and summerhouse on Beech Water
1743–49	Leasowes described as *ferme ornée;* Virgil's Grove developed; alcoves and seats placed at viewpoints; improvements became part of larger plan
1746	Poet James Thomson visits Leasowes
1748	Virgil's Grove painted by Thomas Smith and subsequently engraved
1749	Lord Lyttelton, William Pitt, and Sanderson Miller visit
1751	Shenstone purchases land to north of farm to complete circuit walk
1754	Urn to Maria Dolman erected at head of Lovers' Walk
1758	Work completed on southern part of estate; Priory constructed
1759	Estate mapped by William Lowe to provide plan for proposed guide
1760	Priory Pool excavated
1762–73	Ten successive owners of the estate
1763	Shenstone dies 11 February
ca. 1775–95	Estate occupied and restored by Mr. Horne
1786	Thomas Jefferson visits
1797	Canal embankment constructed
1800–1865	Estate belongs to Attwood family
1901	Halesowen Golf Club takes control of estate
1934	Leasowes passed into hands of local authorities
1991	Dudley Metropolitan Borough Council proposes to restore Leasowes
1997	Heritage Lottery fund awards £1.3 million for restoration

Further Reading

Andrews, C. Bruyn, editor, *The Torrington Diaries,* 4 vols., London: Eyre and Spottiswoode, 1934; abridged edition, as *Rides round Britain,* edited by Donald Adamson, London: Folio Society, 1996

Batey, Mavis, and David Lambert, *The English Garden Tour,* London: Murray, 1990

Dodsley, Robert, editor, *The Works in Verse and Prose of William Shenstone, Esq.,* 2 vols., London, 1764; 2nd edition, London, 1765; reprint, London: Hughs, 1968

Galigani, Giuseppe, "Shenstone's The Leasowes: A British Landscape Garden of Words," *Museologia Scientifica* 9 (1992)

Gallagher, Christopher, "The Leasowes: A History of the Landscape," *Garden History* 24 (1996)

Graves, Richard, *Recollections of Some Particulars in the Life of the Late William Shenstone, Esq., in a Series of Letters from an Intimate Friend of His, i.e. Richard Graves to William Seward, Esq.,* London, 1788

Heely, Joseph, *Letters on the Beauties of Hagley, Envil, and The Leasowes,* London, 1777; reprint, New York: Garland, 1982

Humphreys, Arthur Raleigh, *William Shenstone,* Cambridge: Cambridge University Press, 1937; New York: AMS Press, 1976

Hunt, John Dixon, *Gardens and the Picturesque,* Cambridge, Massachusetts: MIT Press, 1992

Hunt, John Dixon, and Peter Willis, *The Genius of the Place: The English Landscape Garden, 1620–1820,* London: Elek, and New York: Harper and Row, 1975

Jacques, David, *Georgian Gardens,* London: Batsford, 1983

Laird, Mark, *The Flowering of the English Landscape Garden,* Portland, Oregon: Timber Press, 1983

Lipscomb, Geoffrey, *Journey into South Wales through the Counties of Oxford, Warwick, Worcester, Herford, Salop, Stafford, Buckingham, and Herford, in the Year 1799,* London, 1802

Mallam, Duncan, editor, *The Letters of William Shenstone,* Minneapolis: Minnesota University Press, and London: Oxford University Press, 1939

Richardson, Tim, "The Leasowes, West Midlands," *Country Life* 4 (March 1999)

Riely, John, "Shenstone's Walks: The Genesis of the Leasowes," *Apollo* (September 1979)

Sambrook, James, "Parnell's Garden Tours: Hagley and the Leasowes," *Eighteenth Century Life* 8 (1983)

Whately, Thomas, *Observations on Modern Gardening,* London, 1770; reprint, New York: Garland, 1982

Williams, Marjorie, *William Shenstone: A Chapter in Eighteenth-Century Tastes,* Birmingham, West Midlands: Cornish, 1935

Williams, Marjorie, editor, *The Letters of William Shenstone,* Oxford: Blackwell, 1939

DAVID WHITEHEAD

Le Blond, Alexandre-Jean-Baptiste 1679–1719

French Architect and Garden Designer

Alexandre Jean-Baptiste Le Blond was one of the most original architects of his time. His father, Jean Le Blond, was a painter, engraver, and print publisher. He was a member of the Royal Academy of Painting and Sculpture in Paris. Le Blond studied architecture with his uncle Jean Girard, the royal architect Jules Hardouin Mansart, and André Le Nôtre, who designed the gardens of Vaux le Vicomte and Versailles. Le Blond created the plates that accompanied *Le traité sur la théorie et la pratique du jardinage* (1709; The Theory and Practice of Gardening) by A.-J. Dézallier d'Argenville, which was the definitive manual of the grand style of Le Nôtre and the first book devoted to pleasure gardens since André Mollet's *Le jardin de plaisir* (1651; The Pleasure Garden). It went through multiple editions and was widely diffused throughout Europe. Originally published anonymously, on some of the editions Le Blond was mistakenly identified as the author. Le Blond also reedited the *Cours d'architecture* (Lessons in Architecture) by Augustin-Charles D'Aviler in 1710. This edition was the most popular architecture manual of the period. He also designed several private residences such as Chaulnes-Vendôme and the Hôtel Clermont on Rue de Varenne.

Le Blond's greatest accomplishments lie in the designs of the palaces and gardens of St. Petersburg. In the three years he lived in Russia, before his early death, he designed Peterhof and Strelna, two suburban residential complexes for the czar, and the Summer Garden, the garden of the official residence of the czar in St. Petersburg. He also designed private residences and trained young Russian architects and garden designers.

Le Blond is considered the most gifted of the architects who worked under Peter the Great, an illustrious, international group that included Mikhail Zemtsov, Domenico Trezzini, Bartolommeo Francesco Rastrelli, and Andreas Schlüter, the head architect of the king of Prussia. In 1716 Le Blond met the czar, who wanted to build St. Petersburg, founded in 1703, in western European styles. Although the czar hadn't yet visited Versailles—he would the following year—he was familiar with French architecture and wished to build a Versailles-inspired palace and garden that would outshine it. Le Blond, who by then was an established authority on town planning, architecture, and landscape design, greatly impressed the czar, who engaged him as the architect general in charge of the overall planning of St. Petersburg and its environs. No building project was to proceed without his consent.

Le Blond arrived in St. Petersburg in August 1716, accompanied by a team of French painters, woodcarvers, and decorators. He immediately set up an Office of Construction, which would review all designs for approval. In 1717, at the czar's request, Le Blond prepared and published a magnificent plan for the development of St. Petersburg. From Vasilevskii Island, which was envisioned as the center of the city and the site of a grand palace, four thoroughfares were to radiate, terminating in squares with cathedrals. The czar did not adopt the plan, partly because of the cost. However, Le Blond's model of a private residence was implemented as one of three types of residences, resulting in a number of French *hôtels* along the bank of the Neva.

Le Blond's most important project was the design of the palace and gardens of Peterhof, the czar's summer seaside residence on the Gulf of Finland, about 18.5 miles (30 km) from St. Petersburg. The 300-acre (121.5 ha) park is divided into upper and lower gardens and features remarkable water gardens. Beneath the palace, which stands on an imposing natural terrace, the water flows down the marble steps of the impressive double cascade into the basin with the Samson Fountain. Peter the Great began to plan an elaborate park with a grotto and fountains in 1710. In 1716 Le Blond replaced J.F. Braunstein as the head architect for Peterhof. Only the main outline of Le Blond's master plan was realized, but his contribution was the most significant in the layout of the palace and the gardens. The park was laid out along well-defined axes, with the palace as the central pivot. A great number of trees were planted in straight lines, creating a forest pierced by broad rides with spectacular vistas, in the manner of Le Nôtre. In 1720, a year after Le Blond's death, an excellent water source was discovered in Ropsha, about 12 miles (20 km) away. A canal was built, and the water gardens became much more elaborate. Niccolo Michetti designed some of the countless fountains, water jets, cascades, and pavilions. Water flows from the basins in the upper garden to the lower garden through cascades and fountains and out to the sea. The upper garden, which extends behind the palace, was composed of formal parterres with walkways bordered by clipped trees. The lower and more complex garden radiated out in three directions from the great cascade.

Le Blond redesigned the Summer Garden according to the principles of French landscape architecture, starting in 1716. The garden, dating from 1704, was the first garden of the czar, who oversaw its construction. The Summer Garden is situated in the heart of St. Petersburg, on the bank of the Neva. Although at 27 acres (11 ha.) it is now less extensive, it is still the most important green space in the city. By the time Le Blond arrived, many fountains had been built, and Jan Roosen had laid out a garden of symmetrical parterres. Le Blond rearranged the park into a series of ornamental and geometrical patterns in the style of Versailles. Green walls, tunnels, and simple geometric shapes were formed out of clipped trees. A great variety of trees and flowers were collected from all over the country. Le Blond worked on a pavilion known as the Grotto, which Andreas Schlüter started in 1714. Its interior was decorated with mother-of-pearl and colored stones. In the 1720s an elaborate labyrinth, a variant of the one at Versailles, was designed, and classical statues were purchased in Italy and installed, eventually numbering more than 200.

The palace at Strelna, about 14 miles (22 km) west of St. Petersburg, was begun in 1710 on the same natural terrace overlooking the Gulf of Finland as Peterhof, also with upper and lower gardens and a system of canals and fountains. Of four different plans prepared by four architects between 1716 and 1718, only the plans of Le Blond and Michetti were adopted. Le Blond's plan, which was the most striking, featured three canals from the terrace flowing to the sea. With a fourth canal the park was divided into rectangles with an impressive range of designs. Only the essentials of the plan, the canals and the lime avenues, were implemented. Michetti, who succeeded Le Blond, designed the details of the park, including a grotto and a cascade.

See also Petrodvorets; Summer Garden

Biography

Born in Paris, 1679. Pupil of Le Nôtre, he designed several residences in Paris; illustrated *Le traité sur la théorie et la pratique du jardinage,* by Dézallier d'Argenville, published in 1709; member of Royal Academy of Architecture; went to St. Petersburg, Russia, as architect general to Peter the Great, 1716; designed palace and gardens of Peterhof, creating gardens in the style of Versailles; worked on Summer Garden, St. Petersburg, palace and gardens of Strelna, Russia, palace of Apraxine, Russia, as well as numerous private residences; elaborate plan for development of St. Petersburg, 1717, was not adopted. Died in St. Petersburg, Russia, 1719.

Selected Designs

1705–6	Garden, Hôtel de Vendôme, Paris, France
1708	Garden, Hôtel de Clermont, Paris, France
1716–19	Design of palace and gardens of Peterhof, St. Petersburg Oblast, Russia; redesign of Summer Garden, St. Petersburg, Russia; design of palace and gardens of Strelna, St. Petersburg Oblast, Russia; design of palace and gardens of Apraxine (does not exist today)
1717	Plan of St. Petersburg (not realized)

Selected Publications

Le traité sur la théorie et la pratique du jardinage, by Dézallier d'Argenville, 1709 (illustrations)

Further Reading

Bérélowitch, Wladimir, and Olga Medvedkova, *Histoire de St.-Pétersbourg,* Paris: Fayard, 1996

Cracraft, James, *The Petrine Revolution in Russian Architecture,* Chicago: University of Chicago Press, 1988

Hamilton, George Heard, *The Art and Architecture of Russia,* Baltimore, Maryland: Penguin, 1954; 3rd edition, New Haven, Connecticut: Yale University Press, and New York: Penguin, 1983

Shvidkovskii, Dmitrii Olegovich, and Alexander Orloff, *Saint-Pétersbourg: L'architecture des tsars,* Paris: Mengés, 1995; as *St. Petersburg: Architecture of the Tsars,* translated by John Goodman, New York: Abbeville Press, 1996

HAZEL HAHN

Ledebour Garden

Prague, Malá Strana, Czech Republic

Location: Prague 1, Malá Strana, Valdštejnské Square 3

Above Valdštejnská Street, on the Malá Strana slopes stretching upward to the foot of Prague Castle, there is a unique ensemble consisting of six palace terrace gardens, which are called the Palace Gardens, on the Southern Slope of Prague Castle. When proceeding from Valdštejn Square to Klárev, that is, from east to west, this ensemble includes the Ledebour Garden

(0.18 hectares [0.44 acres]), the Small Pálffy Garden (.07 hectares [0.17 acres]), the Large Pálffy Garden (0.2 hectares [0.5 acres]), the Kolovrat Garden (.07 hectares [9.17 acres]), the Small Fürstenberg Garden (.09 hectares [0.22 acres]), and the Large Fürstenberg Garden (1.5 hectares [3.7 acres]). Until the time when the courtyard of the Kolovrat Palace was arranged as the entrance area, the way into the Ledebour Garden was made through a carriageway and, linked with it, a little courtyard of the Ledebour Palace, land-registry number 162 in Malá Strana, this courtyard being an organic part of this number.

When vineyards of medieval origin ceased to exist on the southern slope below Prague Castle, this slope probably remained a wasteland for a long time, where grass and shrubbery caught fire during a conflagration that ravaged Malá Strana in 1541. From there the fire spread as far as Prague Castle. Subsequently, a small Renaissance terrace vineyard came into being in that part of the slope where the Ledebour Garden is now. Alongside, a smaller terrace garden owned by Jan Václav of Kolovrat was laid out in 1665.

On the low level of this smaller garden, the laying out of the baroque garden of Marie Karolína and Leopold Antonín of Trauttmansdorf began before 1710. Properly speaking, the garden should be named the Trauttmansdorf Garden, as they were the first to set it up. The beginnings of the establishment of this baroque garden are supposed to be linked with the construction of a *sala terrena*. However, it has not yet been determined unequivocally who created it, whether the Czech architect and builder Jan Blažej Santini-Aichl (1677–1723), who came from an Italian family settled in Bohemia, or an architect of Italian origin, Giovanni Battista Alliprandi (ca. 1665–1720), who worked in Bohemia from the end of the 17th century. It has recently been recognized, however, that this garden may also be the work of the Czech architect František Maxmilián Kaňka (1674–1766). The base of the flat parterre part of the garden also came into being in connection with the *sala terrena*. This base is an impressive area in the form of a spacious ceilingless hall. The *sala terrena* opens into it through an arcade with pillars. The painted decoration on the *sala terrena*, showing scenes from ancient mythology and excavations at Pompeii, was made in about 1730 by an eminent Czech baroque fresco painter, Václav Vávřinec Reiner (1689–1743). The fresco *A Battle of Romans against Turks*, painted on the massive main retaining wall supporting the slope above the parterre in front of the *sala terrena*, was also his work.

The second phase of the arrangement of the garden was between 1787 and 1797. This phase is notable for the fact that, at the time of arising classicism and romanticism, the arrangements made here were still in the spirit of the lingering late baroque style. In addition to the reconstruction of the palace, the creation of the parterre area in front of the *sala terrena* was completed during this phase; the terraces were built and the construction of the terrace part of the garden finished on a complicated terrain, whose overall difference in altitude is 25 meters (27.3 yd) (the elevation above sea level being between 205 and 230 meters). All this construction was ordered by the then owner Josef Krakovský of Kolovrat, who inherited the palace complex. Ignác Jan Palliardi (1737–1821), a member of another Italian family that had settled in Prague, was its architect and builder.

The parterre area was enriched by a monumental scenery wall with double-flight stairs and Hercules' Fountain counterbalancing the *sala terrena*. The fountain was placed on the longitudinal axis of the parterre. The left arm of the scenery wall provided for communication with the terracelike part of the garden. Up to the highest level the individual terraces were linked by double-flight stairs and stairs set in the axis. On the highest level the terraces ended with a polygonal pavilion, added to the northern boundary wall, which is also an abutment wall, whose line is made rhythmical by niches and blind arcades. As Reiner's fresco on the main retaining wall of the parterre was already destroyed at that time, its copy, made by Antonín Machek, was substituted for it at the end of Palliardi's reconstruction.

Composed in an architecturally demanding way, the garden subsequently was rearranged and repaired, but it was also affected by lack of interest, causing the critical state of the garden and its closure, lasting from 1977 to its comprehensive renovation between 1988 and 1995. Work concerning civil engineering, the utilities network, and restoration had to be done in addition to the renewal of vegetation in the garden. Period plans, from which the original appearance and composition according to individual species could be read, have not been preserved, however. There was no other way than to merely hint at original vegetation while also reacting to the new circumstances and the present use of the garden. By a cross consisting of paths, the parterre area between the *sala terrena* and the opposite scenery wall with Hercules' Fountain wall has been divided into four grass fields, whose center is decorated with a fountain. At their periphery these fields have been emphasized by doubled borders consisting of clipped common box (*Buxus sempervirens*). As Machek's copy of Reiner's fresco *A Battle of Romans against Turks*, painted on the massive retaining wall bearing the terrace part, was also destroyed, in 1940, and a 1958 modern tendentiously conceived sgrafitto *My Native Country* did not resist the onset of the static blocking of the retaining wall during the rehabilitation carried out between 1988 and 1995, a treillage consisting of three plastic arcs was used to achieve the illusory effect. Creeping woody species, namely common trumpet creeper *(Campsis radicans)* and woodbine (*Lonicera periclymenum*), were planted to the treillage. Outside the projection of the terrace part of the garden, riverbank grape (*Vitis riparia*) and wild grape (*Vitis coignetiae*) are noticeable in the adjacent section of the retaining wall with massive pillars.

On individual terraces the lateral areas with vegetation have an identical arrangement, different on each of the terraces. *Broderie* mirrors are marked off by borders consisting of clipped common box and, in the season, are made more colorful through the use of estival plants. The color effect is also emphasized by peonies (*Paeonia* 'Edulis superba', *P.* 'Festiva maxima'), creeping roses (*Rosa* 'Sympathie', *R.* 'Coral Dawn', *R.* 'Casino', *R.* 'Schwanensee') on metal structures or on wooden treillages at the retaining walls, where riverbank grape and wild grape are conspicuous again. Lavender (*Lavandula angustifolia*) and St. John's wort (*Hypericum densiflorum*) are grown on the strips between the stairs and the retaining walls. An Atlantic cedar (*Cedrus atlantica*) grows on the first terrace.

In season terra-cotta flowerpots are put on the step-like platforms on both sides of the stairs; geraniums (*Pelargonium*) are planted in these flowerpots, while flowerpots with lemon trees (*Citrus*) and hibiscus (*Hibiscus*) are transferred to the higher parts of the garden; the growing of other species has also been tried.

In the ensemble of palace gardens on the southern slope of the Prague Castle, the Ledebour Garden is one of the works conceived with great care as to its architecture. The impressiveness of this garden is enhanced by vistas of other gardens that form part of the ensemble, of the roofs of the Malá Strana palaces constituting its foot, with the dome of St. Nicholas's Church, the Petřín hill, and a part of the city panorama in general. The Ledebour Garden is part of the magic world of the ancient garden nooks, which are a result of the unique synthesis of rational as well as sensuous creativity and of an immensely stimulating complementary relationship to the environment.

Synopsis

1541 Fire engulfs Malá Strana and Prague Castle

1665 Jan Václav of Kolovrat lays out small terrace garden next to small Renaissance vineyard

ca. 1710 Baroque garden for Marie Karolína and Leopold Antonín Trauttmansdorf laid out; includes construction of *sala terrena;* ground of adjacent area leveled, with its arrangement and slope secured by massive retaining wall; designer possibly J.B. Santini-Aichl, G.B. Alliprandi, or F.M. Kaňka

ca. 1730 Václav Vavřinec Reiner paints inside of *sala terrena* and illustrated fresco on retaining wall

1787–97 Terrace part of garden set up by architect and builder Jan Ignác Palliardi for Josef Krakovský of Kolovrat

1797 Copy by A. Machek substituted for Reiner's destroyed fresco on retaining wall

1852 Palace complex, including garden, bought by Ledebour family

1852–56 Adolf of Ledebour has retaining walls and balustrades repaired under direction of Heger

1932 Balustrades on retaining walls repaired

1940 Massive retaining wall between parterre and terrrace parts of garden falls in, destroying Machek's copy of Reiner's illustrated fresco *A Battle of Romans against Turks*

1942 Main retaining wall rebuilt

1950–60 Reconstruction of garden according to design by team of employees from State Institute for the Reconstruction of Historic Towns and Properties in Prague; designs include number of new elements, particularly an oblong pond designed by architect Kříž and decorated with B. Kafka's statues for parterre, as well as brick annexes added to terrace part of garden

1977–88 Garden closed because of critical disrepair

1988–95 Extensive rehabilitation of garden according to multistage design drawn by architect Josef Lešetický and civil engineer Václav Pína with other collaborators, including architect Marie Pospíšilová, landscape gardener Božena Mackovičová, statics specialist Karel Fantyš, electrical engineer Miroslav Pečenka, and landscape gardener Jana Pyšová

Further Reading

Bašeová, Olga, *Pražské zahrady* (Prague Gardens), Prague: Panorama, 1991

Dokoupil, Zdeněk, et al., *Historické zahrady v Čechách a na Moravě* (Historic Gardens in Bohemia and Moravia), Prague: Nakl. Československých Výtvarných Umělcu, 1957

Merhout, Cyril, *Paláce a zahrady pod Pražským hradem* (Palaces and Gardens below Prague Castle), Prague: Orbis, 1954

Pacáková-Hošt'lková, Božena, et al., *Zahrady a parky v Čechách, na Moravě a ve Slezsku* (Gardens in Bohemia, Moravia, and Silesia), Prague: Libri, 1999

Wirth, Zdeněk, *Pražské zahrady* (Prague Gardens), Prague: Karel Poláček, 1943

BOŽENA PACÁKOVÁ-HOŠT'ÁLKOVÁ

Lednice-Valtice Cultural Landscape

Southern Moravia, Czech Republic

Location: Near Břeclav and the Austrian border

The cultural landscape of Lednice-Valtice is unique evidence of the gradual influence of humankind on the European landscape, from the impact of the oldest utilization to the grand artistic intentions in the 17th through the 19th centuries.

This land has been inhabited since Paleolithic times. A famous amber path went through this place in ancient times. In the period of the Roman Empire, military fortresses existed there, related to the nearby limit of Roman rule (*Limes romanum*). In the eighth century the first Slavonic state arose (the Great Moravian Empire). South Moravia later became part of the Czech state. The Liechtenstein family first came to Lednice (Eisgrub in German) in the mid-13th century. At the end of the 14th century they also acquired nearby Valtice (Feldsberg in German). Both of the demesnes remained in their hands for several centuries (Lednice for almost 700 years) and became the centers of extensive family possessions.

When Karl I of Liechtenstein was given the title of prince in the early 17th century, Valtice became his main residence and Lednice his summer seat. The two estates and the neighboring Břeclav estate were eventually united by a grandly conceived organizational and compositional plan, and they formed an impressive area that served both the recreational and prestigious purposes of the prince's family. The vast ducal residences, the châteaus at Lednice and Valtice, formed the compositional cores of the landscape.

The adaptation of the landscape was inspired by the ideal of Arcadia. Models for this arrangement could be found in the royal gardens at Stowe and the Royal Botanic Garden, Kew, in England. The landscape at Lednice-Valtice differs from them in the monumental scale of its landscape adaptations and its individual buildings and generous seeding of North American tree species. The artistic composition of the landscape includes large ponds, forest massifs, and agricultural land. Similar adaptations occurred later in Potsdam and at Muskau (Cottbus, Poland).

Both residential châteaus have a role as the focus of the landscape's composition. The château in Valtice is one of the most significant works of baroque architecture in central Europe. The original medieval castle (1192) underwent Renaissance, mannerist, and baroque reconstructions. The latter changes are connected with the names of Johann Bernard Fischer of Erlach, Domenico Martinelli, and Anton Johann Ospel. Along with the baroque church of the Assumption of the Virgin Mary, the château provides a characteristic dominant feature, important in distant views. The baroque outline of landscape composition—a system of avenues from the 17th and 18th centuries—connects with the château.

The Lednice château, which fits in well with the romantic atmosphere of the area, does not itself appear in the distant view. Instead, its exotic minaret fulfills the role of a dominant feature in the landscape. The château in Lednice was originally a Renaissance villa (ca. 1570) that was adapted gradually in baroque (1640, 1690, 1715), classical (1775, 1815), and neo-Gothic (1850) styles. The last reconstruction brought the château in Lednice to a state corresponding well with the atmosphere of the landscape. The continuous mingling of two compositional principles—baroque and Romantic—forms the basis of the appeal of the whole grounds. The connections of the architecture with the garden and landscape are substantial.

An important part of the pleasure of the landscape is the range of woody species planted there and the strategy of their distribution. Several classes of plants can be identified. An extremely varied assortment was used in the parks, with a predominance of exotic trees in places. Characteristic conifers include pencil cedars (*Juniperus virginiana*) and Weymouth pines (*Pinus strobus*), as well as domestic types—albeit montane—Norway spruces (*Picea abies*) and European larches (*Larix decidua*). Frequently used broad-leaved shrubs and trees

Valtice, Frontier Castle, Moravia, Czech Republic

include London planes (*Platanus* × *hispanica*), tulip trees (*Liriodendron tulipifera*), black locusts (*Robinia pseudoacacia*), black walnuts (*Juglans nigra*), and honey locusts (*Gleditsia triacanthos*). Also characteristic are groups of Scots pines (*Pinus sylvestris*). Copper beeches (*Fagus sylvatica* f. *purpurea*), white poplars (*Populus alba*), and grey poplars (*Populus canescens*) add color to the countryside.

The manor, where exotic trees or shrubs are scarcely to be found any longer, is also called a park. Domestic varieties, mainly oaks (most frequently the pedunculate oak [*Quercus robur*]), were planted in parklands and around some of the structures: their picturesque crowns harmonized particularly well with the elegance of the follies and temples. Pastures, preserves, and meadows were treated in a similar way: they featured copses and solitary trees, which were even planted in the fields. The borders of wooded areas, both the floodplain forests along the Dyje River and the artificially established Boří les forest, were adjusted as well. The agricultural countryside was crisscrossed with straight baroque avenues of trees as well as the so-called English avenues (*Englische Wegen*), picturesquely winding roads lined with groups of trees. All this made up a single whole where the dramatic combination of the parks changed continuously to form an epic composition of parklike pastures and preserves. The bucolic atmosphere was further enhanced by herds of sheep and horses. The Lednice-Valtice area is therefore one of the largest examples of an ornamental farm.

It is important to note that the landscaped aspect of the area matured and developed throughout the entire 19th and the first third of the 20th centuries from how it had looked when it was landscaped by Johann I Joseph (1760–1836) (architects included Bernhard Petri, Joseph Hardtmuth, Joseph Kornhäusel, Franz Engel, and J. Poppelack) to how it appeared during the time of Prince Johann II Joseph (r. 1858–1929). Johann II showed a keen interest in the art of gardening from an early age. He lived in Valtice and reputedly rode a horse to Lednice almost every day until he was well advanced in years. A student of the greatest landscape architects, such as J.H. Pückler, Peter Josef Lenné, Gustav Meyer, C. Schneider, and Gertrude Jekyll, he completed the modification of the countryside during his long term in office (71 years). At that time Lednice acquired a new appearance (by the architects A. Hampe and K. Weinbrenner), and the development of the parks of the Lednice and Valtice stately homes was completed. Both were extended to include regular gardens and collections of trees and shrubs (the landscape architects were V. Michelli, A. Czullik, and W. Lauche).

The beginning of deliberate landscaping dates to the baroque period. Aside from four ponds built at an earlier date, the first steps toward reshaping the Lednice and Valtice were the establishing of game reserves with star-shaped vistas and the planting of an avenue of trees. The avenues, which connected Valtice with important places in its surroundings, were certainly conceived and probably also planted by Prince Karl Eusebius (1611–84) in the second half of the 17th century. This is indicated by some of his ideas expounded in his *Work on Architecture*. Originally, spruce trees brought mainly from the Ruda estate in north Moravia were probably planted there. However, they did not thrive in the prevailing conditions and were gradually replaced by broad-leaved trees. In 1716–17, over 2,000 lime trees, horse chestnuts, ash trees, and poplars were planted in the Lednice avenue.

The system of avenues of trees, based on the ideas of the great Renaissance architects so admired by Prince Karl Eusebius, has survived until today. The system functions to give the landscape an order and stresses Valtice as a center. It is not a visual art composition because the avenues are not optical links and are not compositionally related to each other.

In addition to avenues of trees, the countryside features another geometrical pattern of vistas in forests and game reserves. Until at least 1692, the eastern part of the Lednice park contained the "Star" (Eisgruber Stern), which was an approximately octagonal game reserve or park, with avenues along its diagonals and probably a pavilion at its center. This pattern was first graphically recorded in the 1723 map of the Lednice estate. In 1790, during the time of Prince Alois I Joseph (1759–1805), the reconstruction of the Star began. It became a part of an extended garden of the stately home and an important focus of its composition. In 1794 a new pavilion called the Temple of the Sun, the Stars, or Diana was built at the center of the Star in place of the older structure. It was a classic monopteros "single wing" built on an approximately three-meter (3.3 yd) terrace and covered with a dome resting on eight columns.

A system of vistas also exists in the Boří les forest between Lednice and Valtice, but it is probably more recent, from the end of the 18th century. It is an organizational structure (which had not much to do with the composition of the landscape and was very freely connected with the avenue system). This structure unintentionally works as a bearer of a certain order in the landscape and participates in giving it its character, as with the avenues.

The ideas of Prince Karl Eusebius continued to influence his successors, particularly Princes Johann Adam Andreas (1657–1712), Anton Florian (1656–1721), Joseph Wenzel (1696–1772) and Alois I Joseph, until the turn of the 18th century. Prince Johann Joseph I was the first to create a landscape in a new spirit. He left the old organizational structure in place; in fact he further refined it. In 1805 he built a new stone dam for the Hlohovecký pond exactly along the axis of the Lednice avenue, which finally made it a perfectly straight line. Halfway down the avenue, he had an obelisk built (by Hardtmuth). To identify the midpoint of the Ladenská avenue, he planted an avenue of eastern white pines from there to Nový dvůr farm. Another avenue of exotic trees (honey locusts) goes from Nový dvůr farm to the Ladenská avenue toward the Rendezvous folly.

After 1805 the concept of an "English-style" park began to prevail on the Liechtenstein estate. It was introduced and implemented by Prince Johann I and his estate manager, Bernhard Petri, who had established an English-style park in Loosdorf in Lower Austria for him. In 1805–8, he rebuilt the park of Lednice. In a masterfully simple way he raised the level of the park above the level threatened by the flooding of the Dyje River: he excavated a 1.3-meter (1.4-yd.)-deep pond and used the soil to build islands and raise the rest of the parkland by 60 to 100 centimeters (23.4 to 39 in.). The work continued even after Petri left (1808) until 1811, most probably according to his plan. In the last stage of the work, a new riverbed for the Dyje was dug outside the park, and the Dyje was channeled there to prevent further damage to the garden. In those six years 300 to 700 people worked in Lednice from early spring to late autumn. They moved almost a half-million cubic meters (approx. 5.5 million cubic yd.) of soil at a cost of 2 million guilders to Prince Johann I, which did not include the cost of establishing the park itself.

Petri's activities were not limited to parks in Lednice and Valtice. The prince also created English-style parks (in German, the so-called *Englische Anlagen*) around the Mlýnský, Prostřední, and Hlohovecký fishponds. Their banks were filled in or indented to create more varied shapes, and islands were built in them. Roads were built around the ponds with trees alongside. The original pattern was clearly based on the principles of the English landscape architect Lancelot "Capability" Brown. The road around the circumference was lined with almost regular clumps, while the space around the ponds was enclosed with narrow belts in some places, which served as a background for interesting structures. In places, roads were lined with a single row of trees. It was only later that the parks were designed according to more modern concepts. Simple parkland landscaping was also used around structures scattered in the area, outside the large park around the ponds.

The task of enhancing the beauty of the countryside between Lednice and Valtice with Romantic structures was given to the architect Joseph Hardtmuth. He had already built a spa for Prince Alois I in Lednice (1794, demolished 1804), the Sun Temple (1794, demolished 1838), a complex of farm buildings (1794–97, largely demolished in 1882; the remaining parts now used as the Mansion Hotel and restaurant), the Chinese pavilion (1795, demolished 1891), the minaret (1797–1804), an obelisk halfway to Přítluky (1798), the Belvedere folly (1802), and probably some other buildings in the Lednice park, for example a Gothic house, and an artificial ruin of a portal. For Prince Johann I Joseph, Hardtmuth designed and built an aqueduct (1805) and a spa (1806, later demolished) in the Lednice park, the hunters' folly (1806) and Janohrad (Hansenburg-Johann's Castle, 1807–10) east of Lednice, and the Temple of Muses (1807–8) at the end of the Lednice orangery. He rebuilt the Nový dvůr farm (1809–10) south of Lednice, designed and started the construction of the Pohansko (1810–12) and Lány follies (1810–12) south of Břeclav, the Memorial to Father and Brothers (1810–12) at Homole (Rajstna) near Valtice, and an obelisk halfway between Lednice and Valtice (1811, damaged by lightning and collapsed in 1867).

In 1812 Joseph Kornhäusel was appointed the prince's architect and completed structures started or designed by Hardtmuth—the Memorial to Father and Brothers (colonnade) in 1812–17, and the Rendezvous, a folly built like the Arc de Triomphe (1812–13). In 1814–15 Kornhäusel adapted the Lednice residence and built its garden wing, in 1814–16 he built the fishpond folly and in 1818 the Temple of Apollo.

In early 1819 Kornhäusel was replaced by Franz Engel. Using Kornhäusel's plans, Engel completed the Temple of Apollo and the Katzeldorf folly. He extended Hardtmuth's Nový dvůr farm by adding the so-called rotunda to it, a circular pavilion with a glass wall partitioning off a cow shed originally intended for a herd of 20 rare Bern cattle. In 1824 he built the Temple of Three Graces over the southern bank of the Prostřední (middle) fishpond, opposite the fishpond manor on the western bank of the Hlohovecký fishpond, originally as a Romantic castle to counterbalance the Temple of Apollo. On 13 October 1825, however, Engel became mentally ill; he died in an asylum in 1827. The border manor was then built under the supervision of the architect J. Poppelack in 1826–27, but it is not clear whether he drew the plans himself or used Engel's undocumented plans, or whether it was Kornhäusel's work, as the scholar Paul Taussig believes. The last structure of the pleasance to be built was a chapel of St. Hubertus in the Boří les forest, following a design by George Wingelmüller (1854).

The Lednice-Valtice cultural landscape went through two stages. In the first stage a sentimental garden of the scale of the château park (192 hectares [474 acres]) was built. The assortment of smaller buildings (the obelisk, Sun Church, victory arch, Gothic house, mosque with minaret, spas, caves, aqueduct, and Chinese pavilion) was similar to the furnishing of gardens in, for example, Stowe and Kew (England), Schwetzingen and Wörlitz (Germany), Laxenburg (Austria), and Pavlovsk and Tsarskoye Selo (Russia). Unlike these other gardens, however, Lednice went through a second stage, during which it became a Romantic garden on an epic scale, with an area of approximately 71 square miles (184 square km). Medieval monuments are organically integrated into the landscape plan (the fortification from the time of the Great Moravian Empire, eighth to ninth centuries, and the ruins of the 13th-century castle in Pálava), as are Renaissance, baroque, classical, and Romantic monuments.

In terms of its quality, extent, and scale, the Lednice-Valtice cultural landscape is the most significant work of landscaping in the Czech Republic and is quite rare on a world scale.

Synopsis

1192	Lednice castle is built
1249–1946	Liechtenstein family in possession of Lednice castle
1395	Adjoining property of Valtice acquired by Liechtenstein family
1570	Lednice château constructed
1688–96	Baroque portion of horse stables designed and built by B. Fischer
1716–17	Over 2,000 lime, horse chestnut, ash, and poplar trees planted in the Lednice avenue
1790	Prince Alois Joseph orders reconstruction of Star (octagonal game reserve in the eastern part of Lednice park)
1802	Joseph Hardtmuth builds Belvedere folly, used primarily for breeding pheasants
1805	Prince Johann Joseph I builds new stone dam for Hlohovecký pond and an obelisk commemorating the 1797 peace agreement between France and Austria
1805–8	Prince Johann I rebuilds Lednice park in English style; botanist Richard van der Schott designs plans for park and provides 36,000 nonnative (mainly North American) plants
1806	Hunting lodge designed and built by Joseph Hardtmuth

Garden fountain at Lednice, Moravia, Czech Republic
Copyright C.A. Wimmer

1812 Temple of Diana, designed by Joseph Hardtmuth, built in center of Star
1820 Rotunda built on Nový dvůr, the agricultural estate
ca. 1825 Architect Karl Engel builds Temple of Three Graces
1842–43 Lednice renovated on large scale; Englishman E. Devien adds large glasshouse to house
1845 Final reconstruction of château in neo-Gothic style by George Wingelmüller
ca. 1854 Chapel of St. Hubertus, designed by George Wingelmüller in neo-Gothic style, built in Boří les Forest
1859 Formal flower gardens laid out
1996 UNESCO includes park on World's Heritage list

Further Reading

Charvátová-Sedlacková, E., and B. Storm, *Lednice: Státní zámek* (Lednice: State Castle), Prague, 1958
Dokoupil, Zdeněk, *Historické zahrady v Čechách a na Moravě* (Historic Gardens in Bohemia and Moravia), Prague: Nakl. Československých Výtvarných Umelcu, 1957
Hieke, Karel, *Moravské zámecké parky a jejich dřeviny* (Moravian Castle Parks and Their Tree Species), Prague: Staní Zemedelské Nakl., 1985
Pacáková-Hoštálková, Božena, et al., *Zahrady a parky v Čechách, na Moravě a ve Slezsku* (Gardens and Parks in Bohemia, Moravia, and Silesia), Prague: Libri, 1999
Schneider, Camillo, *Die gartenanlagen Österreich-Ungarn in Wort und Bild,* Vienna: Tempsky, 1909–14

ZDENĚK NOVÁK

Leiden, Universiteit Hortus Botanicus

Netherlands

Location: approximately 23 miles (37 km) southwest of Amsterdam

The University of Leiden ("Lijden"), the oldest in the Netherlands, was founded by William the Silent in 1575 as a reward for resisting the Spaniards during the year-long siege that ended on 3 October 1574. He first mentioned the possibility of an academy in a letter of 28 December 1574 to the state assemblies of Zeeland and Holland, which contained Leiden. The two provinces finally established their academy by charter issued on 6 January 1575, still under the authority of Philip II. The new Academia Lugduno Batava was required in the context of the foundation of the new state, both religiously and politically hostile to what it was replacing. The inauguration took place on 8 February 1575, and after two moves into former convent premises, the academy moved in 1581 to the convent premises of the White Nuns, now known as the New Academy, which still houses its administration.

In 1587 in a field behind the New Academy, the famous botanical garden, the *Hortus botanicus,* intended to be a garden of medicinal herbs, was established. Botanical gardens had already been founded at Padua and Pisa, but it was the religious coloring of Leiden that momentously made it the refuge needed by the celebrated Charles de l'Ecluse, generally known as Carolus Clusius, who was appointed its first professor of botany in 1593 and held this appointment until his death. He introduced the tulip into the Netherlands, as well as other species, including varieties of ranunculus, anemone, iris, and narcissus. He also introduced the potato into France, Germany, Austria, and the Netherlands.

Clusius is said to have asked prices for tulips so high that many were eventually stolen from the still-small botanical garden behind the university building, which subsequently was to provide the stock from which the Dutch flower industry took off. Clusius was helped extensively, more than used to be thought, by the first curator of the garden, Dirk Outgaertszoon Cluyt, a botanist and pharmacist from Delft who also wrote a book about beekeeping. The *hortus* of the new academy under Clusius and Cluyt introduced many exotics, experimented scientifically with their cultivation and hybridization, and served as the laboratory whose scientific work far exceeded in value what could have been expected of a standard Renaissance garden of medicinal plants. It is scarcely too much to claim for the Leiden *hortus* that it saw the emergence of scientific plant science from its servitude to medicine.

Leiden is most notable for the large number of newly introduced plants distributed over a long period of time to other European gardens. Everard Vorstius, Hortus Prefect in the mid-16th century, introduced plants from the East Indies and North America, including the Staghorn sumac (*Rhus typhina*) and some species of *Oenothera.* Florens Schuyl followed Vorstius as prefect and concentrated on introducing plants from South Africa, including *Pelargoniums, Mesembryanthemums,* and some species of *Gladiolus.*

Many of the prefects were famous botanists. Paul Hermann (1640–95) introduced 200 new species to the garden and after a visit to the Oxford Botanic Garden reorganized the planting on more systematic lines. Hermann Boerhaave (1668–1738), perhaps the greatest botanist at Leiden since Clusius, almost doubled the number of species grown at the garden and published *Hortus brevis historia* and *Index alter* in 1720, a two-volume history and descriptive catalog of the garden. Adriaan van Royen became prefect after Boerhaave, and soon afterward he, together with Carl Linnaeus, devised a planting plan for the garden on new systematic lines.

During the 19th and early 20th centuries, Leiden continued to introduce new plants. Philip Franz Balthazar von Siebold, surgeon-major of the army, collected extensively while in Japan and shared many of what he collected with Leiden. Notable introductions include cultivars of *Paeonia, Chrysanthemum,* and *Lilium,* as well as Japanese shrubs and trees. Willem Hendrik de Vriese significantly expanded the orchid collection while prefect to 720 species, although by 1930 it had declined to 300 species.

The Leiden Botanic Garden collaborated and finally merged with the Rijksherbarium in 1989. There have also been further organizational changes. The three major Netherlands university herbaria, Leiden, Utrecht, and Wageningen, have merged to form the Nationaal Herbarium Nederland (NHN), with its headquarters at Leiden, at the old Rijksherbarium. The NHN has a collection of 5.6 million specimens. The three botanical gardens will be maintained or enlarged, and the research fields are to be extended.

The Leiden Botanic Garden now has four main sections. The Clusius garden is laid out according to a plan in Clusius's hand dating from 1594. It contains the medicinal plants and is the garden in which the first Dutch tulip was planted. The second section, the von Siebold Memorial Garden, is Japanese in style, in memory of the botanist who brought wisteria and hortensia from Japan to the Netherlands about 1830. Some 15 of the original plants are still alive. Third are the tropical greenhouses, containing plants brought from Dutch colonies abroad, including carnivorous plants, slipper orchids, and Victoria amazonica, a giant waterlily that flowers only at night. Finally, there is the orangery. Its subtropical plants are moved inside for the winter. The interest of the Leiden Botanic Garden is now primarily historical and scientific.

Synopsis

1590	University and Town Council of Leiden found botanical garden
1593	Carolus Clusius appointed professor of botany at University of Leiden and first Hortus Prefect of the garden; Dirk Outgaertszoon Cluyt (Clutius) appointed first curator
1594	Planting of *hortus botanicus* completed, designed by Clusius
1735	Fourth expansion of site; new conservatory built; Carl Linnaeus visits and works with Adriaan van Royen, Hortus Prefect, to replant garden on new systematic lines
1816	Site quadrupled in size and redesigned in English landscape style
1898	Modern botanical laboratory built
ca. 1930s	Garden reconstructed according to Clusius's plans
1989	Garden joined with Rijksherbarium to form first research institute within faculty of Mathematics and Natural Sciences of University of Leiden
1999	Merger of three major Dutch university herbaria—Leiden, Utrecht, and Wageningen—into National Herbarium Nederland

Further Reading

Hunger, Friedrich Wilhelm Tobias, *Charles de l'Escluse (Carolus Clusius): Nederlandsch Kruidkundige, 1526–1609,* Amsterdam: Nijhoff, 1927; reprint, 1943

Juriaanse, Maria Wilhelmina, *The Founding of Leyden University,* Leiden: Brill, 1965

Morren, Edouard, *Charles de l'Escluse: Sa vie et ses œuvres, 1526–1609,* Liège, Belgium: s.n., 1875

Roze, Ernest, *Charles de l'Escluse d'Arras,* Paris, 1899; reprint, S.l.: Landré et Meesters, and Kew Books, 1976

ANTHONY H.T. LEVI

Lenné, Peter Joseph 1789–1866

German Landscape Designer

Peter Joseph Lenné was one of the most influential German garden designers in the 19th century. Born in Bonn, a son of the electoral head gardener by the same name, he apprenticed under his uncle Clemens Weyhe at Brühl Castle. As usual at that time, he then traveled, journeying to southern Germany, Austria, Italy, France, and England. His style was strongly influenced by the Paris garden designer André Thouin. In 1814–15 Lenné continued his professional training at Laxenburg near Vienna. After the Rhineland, his home country, became a Prussian province in 1815, he turned to the Prussian court and was employed as a journeyman by the royal garden director in Potsdam, Johann Gottlob Schulze. From this beginning he drew up many new designs for royal parks such as Sanssouci and Neuer Garten in an elegant style and makeup.

The first work he did on his own was the pleasure ground at Klein-Glienicke. His high ambitions led him to a more independent position in the royal garden staff in 1824, when he was appointed a member of the garden superintendence. In 1828 he was elected successor to garden director Schulze. But his influence on Prussian gardening was not restricted merely to his position as garden director. Following his suggestions, the Royal State Nursery (Landesbaumschule) was founded in 1824, and Lenné became its director. Together with the Royal State Nursery, which supplied an impressive assortment of ornamental plants to Prussia and the adjoining countries, the Royal Gardeners' Education Institute (Gärtnerlehranstalt) was founded in Potsdam, with Lenné as its director. This was the first school for gardeners worldwide, and it attracted many young people from various countries. As director of these three institutions, Lenné had enormous influence on gardening. In addition the Horticultural Promotion Society

(Verein zur Beförderung des Gartenbaues) in the Prussian states was founded in 1822. Even if here Lenné only served as a committee chairman, this society provided an important lobby for his intentions. He was supported by a staff of court gardeners and teachers who worked according to the master's principles of design, including the head gardener Hermann Sello, who created Charlottenhof Park in 1826, and the "garden conductors" Gerhard Koeber, responsible for the Berlin Tiergarten, and Gustav Meyer, who drew up most of Lenné's plans from 1843 to 1866. Many of the numerous royal gardens were redesigned by Lenné during his 50-year career in Prussia. He worked on the estates of the royal family around Potsdam and Berlin as well as on the more remote ones, for example, on the Rhine River and in Silesia. Foreign sovereigns commissioned their own estates to the Prussian garden director, including the duke of Mecklenburg in Remplin and Schwerin, the prince of Anhalt in Ballenstedt, and the king of Bavaria in Feldafing. Inquiries even came from as far as Mallorca, Spain.

Lenné also involved himself with developing public parks, first laying out the Klosterberge Garden in Magdeburg (1824). Later he redesigned the Berlin Tiergarten and created new public parks in Leipzig, Dresden, and Frankfurt.

Landscape gardening on a large scale was one of Lenné's predominant ambitions. He was well acquainted with the models of ornamental farms in England. As early as 1825 he drew up a plan for the Reichenbach Estate (Pomerania, now Poland). He aimed to create a unity of agricultural land, pastures, and orchards with refined landscaping, curved alleys, and pictorial gardens. King Friedrich Wilhelm IV supported these intentions with great impetus from 1840 onward. It was the king's vision to transform all of Potsdam's surroundings into "the most glorious and magnificent living landscape painting." Already in 1833 Lenné drew up an "Improvement Plan for the Isle of Potsdam," which contained many ideas that were executed in the 1840s. This glacial region, characterized by flat woody hills and many stretching lakes, was accentuated by Friedrich Wilhelm's Italianate buildings, including the Heilandskirche (Savior's Church) on the Havel banks, the grandiose belvedere on Pfingstberg, and the great cupola of Potsdam's main church, Saint Nicolai. Prince Wilhelm, later Emperor Wilhelm I, added a Gothic-style estate, Babelsberg Castle, where Lenné also began with the park design, later commissioned to Prince Pückler. From Peacock Island (Pfaueninsel) to Caputh, the area of ornamental landscaping around Potsdam measures approximately 11 miles (18 km).

In addition to his work with parks and gardens, Lenné became involved in 1840 with town planning. Friedrich Wilhelm IV himself produced the sketches for streets, squares, and channels in the newly developed quarters adjoining Berlin in the south (now the district of Kreuzberg), which Lenné carried out. Lenné also designed the area around today's Platz der Republik, now the location of the Reichstag and the Federal Chancellor's Office, as well as other expansion sites of the town. Lenné planted Berlin's first public squares with lawns and flower beds according to the original models he had studied in London on his earlier grand tour.

As director of the State Nursery at Potsdam, Lenné promoted the distribution of newly introduced plants throughout Germany. For example, around 1850 he distributed *Pterocarya, Cryptomeria, Thujopsis, Chamaecyparis, Deutzia, Weigela,* Japanese *Hydrangea, Forsythia, Paulownia, Cotoneaster* from Himalaya, *Rhododendron,* and *Wellingtonia* shortly after their introduction to Europe. In his aim to express art not nature, Lenné made use of his rich and decorative assortment of plants. He wrote in 1824:

> Tree and shrubs serve to insert distinctive forms into the waving picture, defining the characteristic and individual features more poignantly, thus producing the unity, which we desire for our satisfaction. The formation of individual and characteristic compositions is an essential of planting design. The more distinct the contour of this composition and the livelier the contrasting colours, the more effective will be the result.

A great number of Lenné's designs are preserved at Potsdam and listed in a voluminous catalog (Günther and Harksen). Lenné embellished hundreds of sites. As a theoretician, however, he was less effective. He left no written monograph but only two rather extensive contributions in the journal *Verhandlungen des Vereins zur Beförderung des Gartenbaues* (Transactions of the Horticultural Promotion Society) on his work in Magdeburg and Reichenbach. His plantings were highly artistic and more closely resembled John Claudius Loudon's gardenesque style than the nature-expressive style of Whately and the Picturesque school. This is mostly due to the young Lenné's French education: all of the plans he drew during this time excel with elegantly curving paths and well-colored groups of trees. Later, under the reign of Friedrich Wilhelm IV, Lenné had to retract his landscaping style to a certain degree because of the king's love for the Italianate style. Many of the smaller gardens laid out by Lenné or his assistant Meyer during this time, such as the Sicilian Garden at Sanssouci, show elaborate geometric designs. Through this coexistence of formal and informal garden design, Lenné can be connected to the period of eclecticism.

There was strong solidarity among the numerous pupils of Lenné and Meyer, who established the so-called

Lenné-Meyer School of Garden Design, which prevailed—at least in central Germany—until 1900. The modernists rejected Lenné and the landscape garden itself. In 1937 the garden designer Gerhard Hinz, a colleague of Albert Speer, published his thesis, which initiated a Lenné renaissance. Today, Lenné is considered Germany's best-known historic landscape architect.

See also Berlin, Tiergarten; Charlottenburg; Klein-Glienicke; Sanssouci

Biography
Born in Bonn, Germany, 1789. Apprenticed to his uncle Clemens Weyhe, at Brühe Castle, Bonn, 1805–8; toured Europe, visiting southern Germany, Austria, Italy, France, and England, 1809–15; worked in Laxenburg, Austria, 1814–15; employed as journeyman by Prussian royal garden director, Johann Gottlob Schulze, Potsdam, Brandenburg, Germany, 1816–24; appointed member of garden superintendent staff, Potsdam, 1824; Prussian royal garden director, 1816–66; designed or redesigned virtually every royal garden in Prussia; planted Berlin's first public squares, from 1840; created new public parks for Leipzig, Dresden, and Frankfurt, Germany; inspired Lenné-Meyer school of garden design (which prevailed in central Germany until 1900). Died in Potsdam, Brandenburg, Germany, 1866

Selected Designs

1816	Pleasure grounds, Klein-Glienicke, Potsdam, Brandenburg, Germany
1820	Reichenbach Estate, Pomerania, Poland
1824	Klosterberge Garden, Magdeburg, Saxony-Anhalt, Germany
1826–35	Charlottenhof Park, Sanssouci, Potsdam, Brandenburg, Germany
1832–43	Park, Babelsberg Castle, Potsdam, Brandenburg, Germany
1833–40	Tiergarten, Berlin, Germany
1835	Public park (Wallanlagen, now called Lennépark), Frankfurt, Brandenburg, Germany
1840–42	Estate of the Duke of Mecklenburg, Schwerin, Mecklenburg, Germany
1851	Estate of the Duke of Mecklenburg, Remplin, Mecklenburg, Germany
1855	Estate of the King of Bavaria, Feldafing, Bavaria, Germany
1857	Public park (Johannapark), Leipzig, Saxony, Germany
1859	Estate of the Prince of Anhalt, Ballenstedt, Saxony-Anhalt, Germany
1860	Sicilian Garden, Sanssouci, Potsdam, Brandenburg, Germany

Selected Work
"Über die Anlage eines Volksgartens bei der Stadt Magdeburg," *Verhandlungen des Vereins zur Beförderung des Gartenbaues* 2 (1826); English summary in *The Gardener's Magazine* 8 (1831)
"Über Trift- und Feldpflanzungen," *Verhandlungen des Vereins zur Beförderung des Gartenbaues* 2 (1826)

Further Reading
Buttlar, Florian von, editor, *Peter Joseph Lenné: Volkspark und Arkadien*, Berlin: Nicolai, 1989
Günther, Harri, and Sibylle Harksen, *Peter Joseph Lenné: Katalog der Zeichnungen*, Tübingen, Germany: Wasmuth, 1993
Hinz, Gerhard, *Peter Josef Lenné und seine bedeutendsten Schöpfungen*, Berlin: Deutscher Kunstverlag, 1937; enlarged as *Peter Joseph Lenné: Das Gesamtwerk des Gartenarchitekten und Städteplaners*, Hildesheim and New York: Olms, 1989
Verhandlungen des Vereins zur Beförderung des Gartenbaues in den Königlich Preussischen Staaten 2 (1826)

CLEMENS ALEXANDER WIMMER

Le Nôtre, André 1613–1700

French Landscape Architect

André Le Nôtre (or Le Nostre) was born into a family that occupied a central place in the art of gardening in France. His father was Jean Le Nôtre (d. 1655), chief gardener to King Louis XIII at the Tuileries in Paris after having worked as first gardener there under Claude Mollet. It is usually assumed that his grandfather was Pierre Le Nôtre (who worked between ca. 1570–1610), one of Catherine de Medici's chief gardeners in the

Tuileries. Pierre was a master gardener skilled in trellis work and arbors, and was put in charge of the restoration of the garden's parterres in 1594, after the civil war. At the end of the century, he was a senior member of the Corporation of Gardeners of Paris. The records do show the name of another contemporary named Rene Le Nôtre, who was active as a gardener in the 1570s and who could also possibly be the grandfather. In either case, André was a third generation gardener with a perfect background for his future career. Nor did his gardening connections end there. Le Nôtre had three sisters, Françoise, Elisabeth, and Marie, two of whom married gardeners. Françoise married Simon Bouchard, who had special responsibility for the care and maintenance of the orangeries at the Tuileries. Elisabeth married Pierre Desgots, who was also a gardener at the Tuileries; and her son Claude, also brought up as a gardener, was later to work with his uncle.

From an early age Le Nôtre showed both interest and ability as a draftsman and painter. He studied art with Simon Vouet (1590–1649), King Louis XIII's principal painter, and it was here that he first came into contact with Charles Le Brun (1619–90), with whom he was to collaborate so successfully at Vaux le Vicomte. A fellow student was the artist Eustache Le Sueur (1616–55). Simon Vouet had traveled extensively before settling in Paris. He reputedly went to England at the age of 14, and at 21 went to Constantinople before moving on to Rome, via Venice. He was in Italy from 1613 to 1627, during which time he traveled widely in the country. Scholar Ernest De Ganay theorizes that Vouet introduced Le Nôtre to many concepts of design from his drawings of gardens in Constantinople that were created for the Byzantine emperors by Greek gardeners. Likewise, while in Italy he apparently recorded many views of the classical Italian gardens that would have been an inspiration to his pupil.

Le Nôtre also took a keen interest in architecture. De Ganay suggests three possible tutors under whom he might have studied: Jaques Lemercier, Pierre Le Muet, and François Mansart. There is a certain logic, as well as some appeal, to the idea that he might have studied with Mansart. The logic follows from the point made by Kenneth Woodbridge that as an architect Mansart was unusually careful with the setting of his buildings. Woodbridge describes him as not only the leading and most original architect of his time, a generally accepted assessment, but also as an important figure in the history of landscape design.

Le Nôtre worked first in the Tuileries under the direction of his father, but in 1635 was appointed as first gardener to the king's younger brother, Gaston D'Orleans (1608–65) at the Luxembourg Palace. He worked here until 1642, when he found himself working under François Mansart. Mansart was the architect principally involved on work at the Chateau of Blois. It has been argued that Mansart gave Le Nôtre the opportunity to participate in other schemes on which he was working elsewhere. Later schemes for the chateaux of Petit Bourg and Maisons, both on the Seine, have been suggested as Mansart designs in which Le Nôtre had some involvement, and these would have been undertaken after he had left D'Orleans's service in 1642. Le Nôtre's father, anxious to ensure his son's future, had in the meantime petitioned the king that on his own retirement, his son should take over his position of "gardener for the two great parterres opposite the Grand Pavilion of the Tuileries." This petition was granted in 1637, and Le Nôtre took over the post in 1649. Already by 1643 he had been designated Dessinateur des Parterres de tous les Jardins du Roi. A more powerful position was presented to him in 1657 when he was appointed Controller General des batiments du Roi; these three posts combined gave him a considerable income.

Le Nôtre's first recorded design of any significance was probably one begun in 1645 for a parterre garden associated with an orangery at the royal palace of Fontainebleau. It was on the town side of the palace, which was originally an enclosed courtyard garden known as the Queen's Garden. Le Nôtre's design called for new parterres and the conversion of an older aviary into an orangery. Le Nôtre's subsequent and more significant work at Fontainbleau was undertaken nearly 20 years later with the development of the connection between the grand parterres and the canal-shaped lake that now forms an extension of the axis of the parterre gardens. Another of his many smaller designs from this period was the garden created for the Archbishop of Meaux, in which the outline of the garden is the shape of a bishop's mitre. If this was by chance—as De Ganay insists—it was one that Le Nôtre exploited with great wit: the garden has a cruciform layout and the planting and paths copy the design form usually shown on a mitre.

In 1556 Le Nôtre found a special opportunity. This was the year he embarked, with his student friend Charles Le Brun and architect Louis Le Vau, on the development of Vaux le Vicomte. Their client was Nicholas Fouquet, one of the two co-superintendents of the finance ministry. He had inherited a small property from his father in 1640. It had, according to Woodbridge, no particular advantages, except the fact that the land sloped southward from the access road and that at the bottom of the shallow valley there flowed a small river. Further land belonging to the property was on ground that continued to rise to the south, giving it a favorable topographical situation during the colder months. Fouquet has been recognized as a person of discernment and taste, and it is evident that his gardens had been started well before beginning what would be a great masterpiece. French gardens of this period are typically organized around a central axis, usually but not always centered on the house. This is the case at Vaux, and it may be that this axis was established before the new works began, since earlier writers had complimented Fouquet on his fine gardens. The trio of Le Vau, Le Brun, and Le Nôtre completed their work in a remarkably short time of just five years; the nature of their background training and their relationships makes it reasonable to assume that they did not work in an isolated or individual way but combined their skills throughout.

It will probably never be possible to attribute individual responsibilities accurately, but we know that Le Nôtre had studied architecture and that architects traditionally were involved in the layout of gardens, if not the selection of plants. This was well-established practice from Du Cerceau to François Mansart, and was followed by Le Vau himself. Nevertheless the proportions of the garden spaces are usually attributed to Le Nôtre by garden historians. In particular he is credited with the very precise management of levels achieved at Vaux and the visual effects resulting from them. The vertical alignment is such that from the terrace in front of the house, the river drops out of the view and it appears that the rectangular pool that breaks the line of the central axis is immediately in front of a grotto. It is in fact set back many meters from the river, on its other bank. This has the effect of foreshortening the garden from this position and creates a surprise when this additional unexpected lower space is revealed. Much is made by modern experts of Le Nôtre's skill in marrying the traditions of the Italian garden with terraces and the French tradition of flat gardens, both largely developed as a result of prevailing topography. Le Nôtre employed gentle slopes and subtle changes of level, the "demi-cote" as it is called in France. In the context of designs in which all was subjugated to the authority of man, the French sensibility for nuance is displayed in Le Nôtre's gardens, nowhere more so than at Vaux.

The story of the great celebrations for the completion of Fouquet's masterpiece is well known. It is perhaps the most famous example of the way in which the garden of this period was a stage for displays and entertainments, plays, masques, ballets, firework displays, and the reenactment of historic events. On 17 August 1661 Fouquet entertained the court at a great feast, and the gardens were the scene for theatrical events. A play by Molière, *Les Facheurs*, was specially commissioned for the occasion and was supported by all sorts of mechanical spectacles such as moving trees and rocks that broke open to reveal dancing nymphs; the prologue to the play was delivered by a naiad who emerged from a giant shell. This splendor led to Fouquet's downfall, however. King Louis XIV was stung by the majesty of the proceedings and, suspecting embezzlement on Fouquet's part, threw him into jail for the remainder of his life. For the designers, however, the future was to be very different; they were to be employed immediately by the man who, it can be argued, became the most powerful and influential king in European history. This commission was the palace of Versailles. Le Nôtre had already, in the year following commencement of work for Fouquet, been given the title "Controller of all the King's buildings."

Drawings by Le Nôtre are very rare, so the attribution of his work is often difficult to authenticate. Records of payments to him from the privy purse, letters from landowners and their agents, and estate accounts have established his involvement in different places. A discussion has gone on for years over Le Nôtre's travels; it had been thought that he went to Italy in his early life, though now the assumption is that such travels were only made later in life, when he was 66. His designs for Marly are thought to show the influence of what he saw in Italy, though it was after this visit that he delivered the judgement that the Italians were absolutely ignorant of the art of making gardens! The most frequently raised question among English speakers is whether he ever visited England. For many years it was suggested he had done so in connection with the design for the great parterre at Greenwich. A request for Le Nôtre's services apparently came to the French king through an intermediary from King Charles II in 1662, to which Louis XIV replied that although he needed Le Nôtre to work for him daily, he would allow him to make a tour of England. There is no clear evidence, however, that Le Nôtre did visit the country, and the silence on this subject by contemporary figures such as John Evelyn makes it seem unlikely. There is a famous drawing of the park at Greenwich apparently prepared by a French designer, with the title and notes in French, which has additional annotations authenticated as being by Le Nôtre himself. From 1658 André and Gabriel Mollet, who must have been well acquainted with Le Nôtre, are known to have worked in England. The Greenwich plan was found in the library of the Institut de France in the early 20th century, but its exact use and significance, and whether the drawing itself ever even left France, is unclear. The year 1662 was, after all, when Le Nôtre was developing the designs for the first stage of the park at Versailles, made to complement Le Vau's new rebuilding or "envelope" as it was called, encompassing Louis's father's hunting lodge. He was also developing designs for other royal palaces.

Le Nôtre's original work at Versailles centered mainly on creating the principal axis, laying out the Latona Basin, the Allée Royale (or Tapis Vert), and the great canal that continued this line. In many cases scholars are unsure just what role Le Nôtre played in the further and continuous development of Versailles. His relationship with the king was such that it is likely he would have been a confidential consultant on nearly all proposed changes. Belated work at Versailles continued long after Le Nôtre's death, and that of Louis XIV, a case in point being the Basin de Neptune beyond the Parterre du Nord at the foot of the Allée d'Eau. This element was designed by Le Nôtre in 1679 but not carried out until 1741. At the Grand Trianon (1687), he designed an original and interesting garden, now gone, called the Jardin des Sources. This occupied the space between the two wings of the building and comprised a series of minute water channels criss-crossing the garden. Small enough to step over, they separated some 20 islands of turf, on which tables and chairs could be placed.

The great parterre at Fontainbleau had been carried out by Le Nôtre in 1661, prior to starting work at Versailles. This was a reworking of an area that had been designed by Alessandro Francini around the beginning of the century. In 1663 Le Nôtre began another work, which is usually identified as his personal favorite, the remarkable composition he undertook for the Grand Conde at Chantilly. His design, while respecting the important existing elements, completely reoriented the whole site in a dramatic and exciting way. Because of these sites, and the witty work done for the Bishop of Meaux, Le Nôtre became known for his very clever handling of levels and proportion in ways that resulted in interesting and sometimes surprising visual effects.

In 1693 Le Nôtre was awarded the Order of St. Michael by the king, with whom he seems to have had a unique relationship. Now an old man, he had gained and retained Louis XIV's affection. Le Nôtre was known for his straightforward and honest ways and had a warm and spontaneous manner. It seems he lived very simply, although he was a great collector of paintings and objets d'art. He modestly attributed his considerable wealth to good financial management by his wife. Although he had been given a house by the king in the town of Versailles, he probably spent most of his last years at his own property near the Tuileries. He retained his inherited duties at the Tuileries, and in 1692 a decree was made stating that the office would pass to the grandson of Claude Mollet, André, but only after Le Nôtre's death. In the same year the controllership of the king's buildings was devolved on his nephew Claude Desgots and Jean Michel Le Bouteux.

In France and elsewhere his nephew and others continued Le Nôtre's work. Although by the beginning of the 18th century the English had begun to embrace a new style, gardens in the French manner—the manner of Le Nôtre—flourished on the Continent. An important contribution to this phenomenon was the very lucid *La théorie et la practique du jardinage* (1709) by A.J. Dézallier d'Argenville. Authoritative and widely read, it was even translated into English by John James. Desgots worked on designs for Het Loo in Holland and for Windsor Castle in England. These works and sites, including Schonbrunn and the Belvederes in Vienna, Herrenhausen in Hanover, the Nymphenburg in Munchen, and Peterhof in St. Petersburg, as well as examples from Scandinavia to Hungary, show the influence of Le Nôtre's genius. His influence is even seen in L'Enfants plan for Washington, D.C.

See also Anet; Chantilly; Fontainebleau; London Parks; Luxembourg Gardens; Sceaux; Tuileries; Vaux-le-Vicomte; Versailles

Biography

Born in Paris at father's house beside Tuileries, 12 March 1613. Studied painting with Simon Vouet; worked first with father, Jean, who was gardener in charge of parterres in royal gardens of Tuileries in Paris; appointed first gardener to Duc d'Orléans, brother of King Louis XIII, at Luxembourg Palace, Paris, 1635; married Françoise Langlois, daughter of Sieur de Hamel, 1640; designed Orangery garden at royal palace of Fontainebleau, 1645; took over father's post at Tuileries, 1649; employed with Louis Le Vau and Charles Le Brun in 1656 to create Vaux-le-Vicomte for finance minister Fouquet; appointed comptroller general of king's buildings; employed at Versailles to create setting for Le Vau's new palace for King Louis XIV, 1661–68 (involvement with Versailles continued almost until his death); worked on designs for Chantilly for Prince de Condé, 1663–86; worked on Sceaux for Colbert, 1670–77; visited Italy and had audience with the Pope, 1679; worked on Anet with Claude Desgots, his pupil, for the Duc de Vendôme, 1681–88; awarded Order of Saint-Michel by Louis XIV, 1693. Died in Paris, 15 September 1700.

Selected Designs

1635– Luxembourg, Paris, France (as gardener, it is thought he redesigned parterres for "Monsieur," Gaston, Duc d'Orléans)
1643–44 Garden for the bishop of Meaux, east of Paris
1645–47 Parterre garden for Orangery, Fontainebleau, Seine-et-Marne, France
1656–61 Vaux-le-Vicomte (estate of Nicolas Fouquet), Seine-et-Marne, France
1661–64 Grand Parterre, Fontainebleau, Seine-et-Marne, France
1661–1690 Versailles, Yvelines, France
1663–75 St. Germain-en-Laye, Yvelines, France (for the Duc d'Orléans)
1663–86 Le Canadiàre gardens (estate of the Prince de Condé), Chantilly, Oise, France

1665	St. Cloud, Hauts-de-Seine, France (for "Monsieur," Gaston, Duc d'Orléans)
1666	Tuileries (redesign for Louis XIV), Paris, France; Castries, Hérault, France
after 1666	Bishop's palace, Castres, Tarn, France
1670–77	Sceaux, Haute Seine (now known as Hauts-de-Seine), France
1671–85	Dijon, Côte-d'Or, France
1672–	Conflans, Paris, France
1674–76	Clagny, Seine-et-Oise, France
1675	Dampierre, Yvelines, Seine-et-Oise, France
1676–	Maintenon (estate of Madame de Maintenon), Eure-et-Loire, between rambouillet and Chartres
1679	Basin de Neptune, Versailles, Yvelines, France
1679–83	Marly, Seine-et-Oise, France
1679–	Meudon, great parterre (estate of the Marquis de Louvois), Hauts-de-Seine, France
ca. 1680	Choisy, Choisy le Roi, Seine et Marne
1681–88	Anet (estate of Duc de Vendôme), Eure-et-Loire, France (alternatively attributed to Claude Desgots
1686	Navarre (estate of Duc de Bouillon), France
ca. 1694	Pontchartrain, Seine-et-Oise, France

Further Reading

Adams, William Howard, *The French Garden, 1500–1800,* New York: Braziller, and London: Scolar Press, 1979

Bazin, Germain, *Paradeisos, ou, l'art du jardin,* Paris: Chêne, 1988; as *Paradeisos: The Art of the Garden,* London: Cassell, and Boston: Little Brown, 1990

De Ganay, Ernest, *Andre le Nostre, 1613–1700,* Paris: Vincent Fréal, 1962

Fox, Helen M., *Andre le Notre: Garden Architect to Kings,* New York: Crown, 1962; London: Batsford, 1963

Gollwitzer, Gerder, "The Influence of Le Nostre on the European Garden of the Eignteenth Century," in *The French Formal Garden,* edited by Elisabeth B. MacDougall and F. Hamilton Hazlehurst, Washington: Dumbarton Oaks Trustees, 1974

Hazlehurst, F. Hamilton, "Le Notre at Conflans, Garden of the Archbishop of Paris," in *The French Formal Garden,* edited by Elisabeth B. MacDougall and F. Hamilton Hazlehurst, Washington: Dumbarton Oaks Trustees, 1974

Hazlehurst, F. Hamilton, *Gardens of Illusion: The Genius of Andre Le Nostre,* Nashville, Tennesee: Vanderbilt University Press, 1980

Marie, Alfred, *Jardins français classiques des XVIIe and XVIIIe siècles,* Paris: Vincent Fréal, 1949

Strandberg, Runa, "The French Formal Garden after Le Nostre," in *The French Formal Garden,* edited by Elisabeth B. MacDougall and F. Hamilton Hazlehurst, Washington, D.C.: Dumbarton Oaks Trustees, 1974

Woodbridge, Kenneth, *Princely Gardens: The Origins and Development of the French Formal Style,* London: Thames and Hudson, and New York: Rizzoli, 1986

M.F. DOWNING

Les Cèdres

Saint-Jean-Cap-Ferrat, France

Location: between Nice and Monaco, on northwest half of peninsula of Saint-Jean-Cap-Ferrat, on Bay of Villefranche

Jutting out from the French Riviera between Nice and Monaco extends a peninsula at Saint-Jean-Cap-Ferrat that contains numerous secluded gardens and villas. Among the most exotic of these is Les Cèdres, one of the world's most important private botanical gardens, as noted for its evocative beauty as its singular botanical research. An estate of over 35 acres (14 ha), roughly quadrangular in shape, Les Cèdres rises from the southeast corner of the Bay of Villefranche along the upper western half of the peninsula.

First laid out in the middle of the 19th century by a wealthy merchant from Nice, David Désiré Pollonais, his estate came to be surrounded by the expanding estate of King Leopold II of Belgium. The monarch purchased the Pollonais estate at the beginning of the 20th century, giving the name Les Cèdres for its identifying cypresses, and expanded the residence, a white three-story villa of palatial grandeur in a classical Italianate style. This villa lies along the back portion of the grounds, looking out from a peak to the Mediterranean and the landscape of the Riviera.

In 1924 Alexandre Marnier-Lapostelle, the creator of the orange-based liqueur Grand Marnier, acquired Les Cèdres, its already extensive gardens attracting him for the possibility they offered for botanical and citric plant experiment. It was to be a complement to rare and exotic plants he was cultivating at his Villa Africaine in Nice. These estates were exceptionally situated, lying in a climate between the tropical and temperate, having rainfall of almost 76 centimeters (30 in.) a year and summer temperatures reaching into the 80 and 90 degrees Fahrenheit (26.7 and 32.2 degrees C).

Marnier-Lapostelle's son Julien nurtured Les Cèdres into a premier botanical garden and traveled the world for rare plants. Although his work was gravely interrupted during World War II, Julien Marnier-Lapostelle continued it with renewed dedication after the war. Today Les Cèdres holds 16,000 species, rivaling the Jardin des Plantes in Paris as a major center of French and worldwide botanical research, particularly for rare tropical plants.

The most noted families of plants at Les Cèdres are the Asclepiadaceae, Cactaceae, Euphorbiaceae, and Bromeliaceae. Distinguished specimens in the first family include 158 species of the small cactiform Stapeliae plants. Les Cèdres has over a thousand cacti species, many from Mexico, assuming shapes and flowering in extraordinary manners. Within two genera of cacti, Les Cèdres has almost all of the species known. There are 44 genera of Euphorbiaceae, gathered from Mexico, Ethiopia, Madagascar, and South Africa. Les Cèdres preserves species that have disappeared in these native habitats. It also has about 500 species of the Bromeliaceae, with its often waxlike flowers.

In hundreds of species orchids grow both indoors and out. Due to their epiphytic nature they frequently grow among the branches of trees, such as the Brazilian *Cattleya guttata* or the Himalayan *Dendrobium nobile*.

Plants at Les Cèdres grow both in planned gardens and in cultivated "wild" areas. The latter occupies the major part of the grounds, providing the entire area with a sense of the natural environment of the plants. Due to occasional frost and even snowfall in the region, over two dozen specialized hothouses and temporary shelters are located throughout the grounds. Approximately three dozen gardeners, technicians, grounds keepers, and scientists maintain Les Cèdres. The numerous species that bear the Marnier name testify to the originality of research done by the staff.

Throughout the estate wind roads and pathways. Formal gardens, terraces, and a lake are set near the villa. Away from this upper core are the less formal areas, which even include a stretch of plain. In one direction from the house a formal path extends to a pergola garden, reached through tropical palms and ferns. In another direction a promenade extends to the lake. On its surface lie giant *Victoria regia* from the Amazon floating with platterlike leaves so big that children can sit on them. In the Garden of Bacchus a solitary white statue of the god of wine airily lifts his arm, dwarfed by a monumental circle of *Washingtonia robusta*. Farther away rise groves of bamboo, some species several stories high. On the plain are some of the great trees of Les Cèdres, including numerous species of acacia, cedars, and eucalyptus from Asia, Australia, and the Americas. Palm trees, the emblem of the Riviera, grow in both the formal and wild areas. A palmarium holds some of the more delicate species.

The scientific uniqueness of Les Cèdres lies in the density of the rich variety and rarity of its specimens, which are cultivated and preserved with the utmost care and available to scientists worldwide as an exceptional resource for botanical and environmental research. The aesthetic satisfaction of Les Cèdres arises from its balance of contrasts in nature between the giant and jewel-like, the wild and cultivated, brilliant and subdued, and surreal and refined.

Synopsis

ca. 1850 David Désiré Pollonais acquires site of Les Cèdres

1904 King Leopold II of Belgium acquires Pollonais estate and names it Les Cèdres due to presence of several prominent cedar trees

1921 Wealthy British aristocrat Sir Edward Cassel buys Les Cèdres

1924 With death of Sir Edward Cassel, Alexandre Marnier-Lapostelle, creator of liqueur Grand Marnier, buys Les Cèdres to grow oranges and other citrus fruits that are ingredients of Grand Marnier

1946 Julien Marnier-Lapostelle, son of Alexandre, successfully clears area of hundreds of land mines planted by Germans during World War II and resumes planting at Les Cèdres; within less than two decades, more than 10,000 species and almost a dozen plant houses

1976 Management of Les Cèdres passed to Société des Produits Marnier-Lapostelle, which opens it to plant scientists for research

Further Reading

Demoly, Jean-Pierre, *Les Cèdres: An Exceptional Botanical Garden,* Paris: Picard, 1999

Hyams, Edward, and Edward MacQuitty, "Les Cèdres," in *Great Botanical Gardens of the World,* by Hyams and MacQuitty, London: Nelson, and New York: Macmillan, 1969

Racine, Michel, Ernest J.-P. Boursier-Mougenot, and Françoise Binet, *The Gardens of Provence and the French Riviera,* Cambridge, Massachusetts: MIT Press, 1987

EDWARD A. RIEDINGER

Lesser, Ludwig 1869–1957

German Landscape Architect

Ludwig Lesser was an unusually influential landscape architect in Germany from the beginning of the 20th century until he was forced to leave the country in 1939 because of the rise of National Socialism. His knowledge and professional training was comprehensive. From 1884 to 1885 he worked as an apprentice in the renowned Palmengarten (Palm Garden) in Frankfurt am Main and then in the Berlin horticultural firm and seed company of van der Smissen and Schwartz from 1885 to 1887. His interests in garden and landscape architecture, however, were broader than the experience an apprenticeship could offer. He therefore traveled widely in Europe and privately studied garden art, horticulture, city planning, and related fields by reading, attending lectures, and working in painters' studios. He furthered his knowledge in the rose nursery of Kölle and Company in Augsburg, who in those days delivered more than 1,000 different roses to customers in Germany and elsewhere in Europe; in the gardens of the Baroness Rothschild in Pregny near Geneva, Switzerland; and in the garden art and commercial gardening firm of Heinrich Henkel in Darmstadt, Germany, prior to purchasing his own horticultural business in Freiburg/Breisgau, Germany, in 1893. He continued to operate this business until 1902, when Berlin, the city of his birth, again attracted his attention.

Lesser first worked in Berlin until 1908 as a combination landscape architect-landscape contractor, which was quite common in the early days of professionalism in landscape architecture in Germany. Berlin was a boomtown at that time, and land speculation was rife. Private associations developed land for increasing numbers of people who hoped for a future in the city and its environs. In the 1880s Lesser's father, Richard, had an office for land acquisition in the suburbs of Berlin. In 1908 Lesser became garden director for two similar private associations, the Berliner Terrain-Zentrale and the Zehlendorf-West Terrain A.G. He developed open spaces such as the Ludolfinger Platz, the Zeltinger Platz, the Rosenanger, the Frohnau cemetery, and others in the garden city of Frohnau located in the northern periphery of Berlin. Although there is no source that can verify the connection, the idea for the Villenkolonie (a suburb consisting mainly of villas) of Frohnau seems to have been influenced by Frederick Law Olmsted's earlier design for the Chicago suburb of Riverside, Illinois.

In 1913 Lesser established the Deutscher Volksparkbund (German People's Park Association), which was clear evidence of his sensitivity to the needs of ordinary people in the last years of a German empire whose ruling class had become more and more reactionary. This same sensitivity is also reflected in his engagement as docent for garden art and horticulture at the Humboldt High School (Humboldt-Hochschule), a school for adults that was established in 1913 to enable working people to enhance their knowledge through evening courses. The school was closed by the Nazis in 1933. During World War I Lesser consulted as landscape architect to the Oberpräsident, the lord lieutenant of the Prussian province of East Prussia, in the reconstruction of cities such as Hohenstein, Ortelsburg, and Neidenburg, which had been destroyed by warfare. In Berlin he was head of the Berlin war gardens and served as docent for the Red Cross in hospitals and, after the war, for the German Archive for Settlement Affairs (Deutsches Archiv für Siedlungswesen) from 1919 to 1921. In 1920 Lesser briefly taught at the Agricultural University of Berlin (where, in 1929, the first chair for garden art would be established and given to Erwin Barth).

In 1919 Lesser was elected to the board of the Deutsche-Gartenbau-Gesellschaft (German Horticulture Association). He served as its president from 1923 to 1933. In 1923 he prevented the sale of the library of the German Horticulture Association, later to be incorporated into the Bücherei des deutschen Gartenbaus

(Library of German Horticulture) in Berlin, which today is one of the most valuable sources for research in horticulture and landscape architecture in Germany. As representative of the German Horticulture Association, Lesser was a member of the board of trustees of the Lehr- und Forschungsanstalt für Gartenbau (Institution for Teaching and Research in Horticulture) in Berlin-Dahlem from 1925 onward. As a permanent contributor to the Funkstunde A.G. (Radio Transmission Hour, Inc.), where he directed the department for agriculture and horticulture from 1925, he was a pioneer of radio broadcasting. His most important book, *Volksparke Heute und Morgen* (People's Parks Today and Tomorrow) appeared in 1927. In 1931 and 1932 Lesser was horticultural consultant and head of the exhibitions of the nonprofit Gemeinnützige Berliner Ausstellungs-, Messe- und Fremdenverkehrsgesellschaft (Berlin Exhibition, Fair, and Tourism Association). From 1928 to 1933 he formed a team with his son Richard, who also was trained as a landscape architect and who had worked for him since 1922. In all, Lesser designed some 700 open spaces, some 300 of them private parks and gardens, prior to 1933.

After the National Socialist takeover in January 1933 the Lessers could no longer acquire commissions from the public institutions that had until then been their main source of income. In April 1933 Ludwig Lesser was forced to step down from his office as president of the German Horticulture Association and his post as head of its orchid section because of National Socialist pressure. Humboldt People's High School dismissed him as a docent by the end of May 1933. After he had lost all public commissions, he was deprived of private commissions as well. Until 1936 he was allowed to publish the Deutscher Gartenbau-Kalender (German Horticulture Calendar), but then his books could no longer be printed. In December 1936 membership in the National Socialist Reichs Chamber for Literature (Reichsschrifttumskammer) was made a precondition for further co-operation with the publisher. Although Lesser himself, his parents, and his siblings had been baptized as Lutheran-reformists in 1884, Lesser was not admitted to the literary group because of his Jewish descent, which made him a "full Jew" in National Socialist terms. Aged 70, Lesser was forced in January 1939 to add the name "Israel'" to his first name; in November 1941 he was deprived of his German citizenship. Luckily for him, he had decided to emigrate to Sweden in the spring of 1939 with the help of his son Rudolf, who had left Germany for Sweden after the 1936 Olympic Games. In 1948 Lesser received Swedish citizenship. He never felt the need to return to Germany and died in Vallentuna, Sweden, in 1957. More than 40 years later the German Horticulture Association had not seen fit to rehabilitate its one-time president.

Biography

Born in Berlin, Germany, 1869. Apprenticed at Palmengarten (Palm Garden), Frankfurt, Germany, 1884–85, and in the horticultural firm of Van der Smissen and Schwartz, Berlin, 1885–87; traveled widely in Europe; ran a horticultural business in Freiburg, Germany, 1893–1902; practiced as a landscape architect and contractor in Berlin, designing some 700 open spaces, 1902–33; garden director for private associations, from 1908; established the Deutscher Volksparkbund (German People's Park Association), 1913; president of the German Horticulture Association, 1923–33; directed radio programs on agriculture and horticulture for Funkstunde A.G., 1925–33; forced to resign from all public and private positions by the National Socialists, 1933; emigrated to Sweden, 1939; received Swedish citizenship, 1948. Died in Vallentuna, Sweden, 1957.

Selected Designs

1906–11 Sports park, Frohnau (near Berlin), Germany
1908–10 Open spaces for garden city Frohnau, Berlin, Germany
1910 Cemetery, Frohnau (near Berlin), Germany; park cemetery, Hermsdorf (near Berlin), Germany; garden at country seat Janson, Frohnau (near Berlin), Germany
1911 Private garden Weidemann, Frohnau near Berlin, Germany
1912 Railroad Station place, Hermsdorf (near Berlin), Germany
1913 Park system for city of Jüterbog, Germany
1919 Private garden Samek, Berlin-Dahlem, Germany
1925 Open spaces, Hennigsdorfer Siedlungs, Berlin-Neubrück, Germany; color garden, Horticulture Exhibition Kroll, Berlin, Germany
1928 Open spaces for residential quarter "Weiße Stadt" (White City), also known as "Schillerpromenade," Berlin, Germany
1928 Private garden for architect Otto Rudolf Salvisberg, Berlin, Germany
1929 Private park Zoellner, Klosterheide in der Mark, Germany
1930 Cemetery-in-the-woods, Saarow near Berlin, Germany; Park around Lindner Factory, Berlin-Wittenau, Germany
1931 Deutsche Bau-Ausstellung (German Building Exhibition) open spaces and garden examples, Berlin, Germany
1932 Exhibition Sonne, Luft und Haus für alle (sun, air, and home for all exhibition),

examples for allotment gardens, Berlin, Germany

Selected Publications
"Die Platzanlagen in Frohnau," *Bauwelt* 1 (1910)
Der Kleingarten, seine zweckmäßige Anlage und Bewirtschaftung, 1915
"Siedlung ist Gartenbau!" *Gartenflora* 68 (1919)
"Volkshäuser und Volksgärten," *Das Volkshaus - Mitteilungen des deutschen Volkshausbundes* 2 (1920)
"Ein Stauden-Garten," *Gartenflora* 73 (1924)
Volksparke heute und morgen, 1927
"Der Waldfriedhof in Frohnau," *Gartenschönheit* 8 (1927)
"Der Golfplatz in Bad Saarow bei Berlin," *Gartenkunst* 43 (1930)
"Ein Wochenendlandsitz in der Mark Brandenburg," *Gartenflora* 79 (1930)
100 Ratschläge für alle Gärten (with Fritz Eggers), 1933
100 Ratschläge für die häusliche Blumenpflege, 1933
100 Ratschläge für den Gemüsegarten, 1934
Der Gräber Schmuck und Pflege, 1935
"Schönheit der Arbeit, Maschinenfabrik mitten im Grünen," *Gartenkunst* 48 (1935)
100 Ratschläge für den Obstgarten, 1936

Further Reading
De Michelis, Marco, "The Green Revolution: Leberecht Migge and Reform of the Garden in Modernist Germany," in *The History of Garden Design,* edited by Monique Mosser and Georges Teyssot, London: Thames and Hudson, 1991
Gröning, Gert, and Joachim Wolschke-Bulmahn, "Zur Entwicklung und Unterdrückung freiraumplanerischer Ansätze der Weimarer Republik," *Das Gartenamt* 34, no. 6 (1985)
Gröning, Gert, and Joachim Wolschke-Bulmahn, *Die Liebe zur Landschaft,* Teil 1, "Natur in Bewegung," in *Arbeiten zur sozialwissenschaftlich orientierten Freiraumplanung,* vol. 7, Münster: LIT Verlag, 1995
Gröning, Gert, and Joachim Wolschke-Bulmahn, *Grüne Biographien, Biographisches Handbuch zur Landschaftsarchitektur des 20. Jahrhunderts in Deutschland,* Berlin: Patzer Verlag, 1997
Lesser-Sayrac, Katrin, "Ludwig Lesser (1869–1957)," *Beiträge zur Denkmalpflege in Berlin* 4 (1995)

GERT GRÖNING

Levens Hall

Levens, Cumbria, England

Location: 5 miles (8 km) south of Kendal and approximately 60 miles (96.5 km) north-northwest of Manchester

The park and gardens of Levens Hall, Cumbria, laid out by M. Guillaume Beaumont for Colonel James Grahme between 1689 and 1710, are an outstanding example of late-17th-century garden layout. In their historical context they belong to the period when French and Dutch influence on English gardens was at its peak, roughly from 1660 to 1720. Many gardens were created in the grand manner at this time, including Hampton Court, Kensington Palace, and many others laid out as adjuncts to country houses of the period.

The French style, with its axial planning, geometric layout of straight vistas and cross vistas, parterres, avenues, and allées, was fashionable after the restoration of the monarchy in 1660. After the accession of William of Orange to the throne in 1689, Dutch ideas on gardens infiltrated, and English gardens embraced the classic Dutch style of intimate, hedged enclosures with intricate parterres and a profusion of clipped evergreens. Tastes were soon to change, and although popular at the time, topiary work was ridiculed by the cognoscenti such as the poet Alexander Pope, who criticized the cutting of figures into "mathematical shapes" and remarked that, "[i]nstead of humoring nature," gardeners were seeking to "deviate from it as much as possible," and that "the mark of the scissors was on every plant and bush." Other critics included Joseph Addison, who criticized the art of topiary in his essay in *The Spectator.*

In 1689 Beaumont (a pupil of André Le Nôtre), a highly respected gardener who worked for James II until his abdication in 1688, came to Levens Hall to suggest improvements to Grahme's newly acquired estate. Grahme, close to the king in his office of the Privy Purse,

Topiary garden, Levens Hall, Cumbria, Westmorland, England
Copyright Nick Meers/Garden Picture Library

was in touch with the latest ideas on gardens from the Continent, and the gardens were to become a suitable setting for an updated and enlarged Tudor house.

Beaumont's work at Levens was ahead of its time in that it linked the formal and informal elements of the estate into a coherent whole—an unusual innovation at this early date. He extended the gardens beyond the formal gardens into the meadow and medieval deer park, demarcating the boundary of the formal garden by building a bastion wall and ha-ha, a device never before seen in England but recommended by Antoine-Joseph Dézallier d'Argenville in his book on the laying out of gardens, *La théorie et la pratique du jardinage* published in 1709 (*The Theory and Practice of Gardening*, translated from the French by John James in 1712).

Beaumont's designs for the formal gardens included the 500-yard-long (457 m) Beech Walk, which was broken by a rondel encircled with beech, and a parterre with grass plats and flower beds edged with box and centered on clipped evergreens of yew (*Taxus baccata*) and box. In all, 90 pieces of topiary were planted. He also laid out a rose garden planted with Provence and velvet (gallica) roses, a fountain garden, and a bowling green.

Beaumont planted clumps of chestnuts, limes, and firs in the meadow to frame the distant view of the limestone sear. Later, an avenue of oaks was planted (170 trees on each side, 12 yards [11 m] apart), stretching for nearly a mile and leading to a seat beside the river Kent, placed at a point where the river makes a turn and enters a gorge. William Gilpin, an exponent of the picturesque in landscape gardening, wrote that it was "a happy combination of everything that is lovely and great in landskip." The romantic character of Beaumont's river views has been likened to the paintings of Dutch landscape painters of the period. Today the landscape, marred only by the proximity of the busy A6 road that separates park and garden, still remains. Public outcry prevented a link road to the M16 being built in the late 1960s and early 1970s.

Beaumont died in 1721 and Colonel Grahme died in 1730, but the formal gardens remained, preserved by Grahme's daughter Catherine, who became countess of Suffolk. At a time when many formal gardens were being swept away by landscape gardeners such as William Kent and Lancelot "Capability" Brown, and informal landscape gardens laid out in their place, with grass coming up to the house itself, the Levens Hall Gardens escaped destruction, it is said, because of the lack of fashion-conscious male heirs.

After Catherine's death in 1760, Levens, no longer a primary residence of the family, went through a period of neglect until the arrival of Alexander Forbes in 1792 as head gardener. There followed a period of restoration, coinciding with the revival of interest in Elizabethan and 17th-century garden styles during the early Victorian period. By the time of his death in 1862, Forbes had reinstated the topiary pieces and probably added to them the golden yews (*Taxus baccata*), the Howard device of the Crowned Lion, the Judge's wig, and the letter B (Bagot family initial). Forbes's work reflects the importance of the role of head gardener in the conservation of the garden. These pieces, together with topiaries of the great umbrellas, the chess pieces, and Queen Elizabeth and her maids of honor, as well as four peacocks, still exist today. There are now over 90 pieces in all.

The age of some of the topiaries is conjectural, but yew is remarkably resilient and withstands drastic clipping. During the late Victorian and Edwardian periods, the revival of interest in old manor houses and "old-fashioned" gardens, which carried on into the 20th century, further enhanced the reputation of Levens as the celebrated period garden that it is today.

In 1990 Hal Bagot, descendant of the original owner, took on the house and gardens and, despite the labor-intensive nature of the garden, instituted a program of restoration, putting back features of Beaumont's original design but reinterpreting them in the modern idiom. The bowling green, fountain garden with tunneled lime arbors, the herb garden, vegetable borders, nuttery, and wilderness are period features that have been reinstated, adapted to suit the needs of today.

The parterre with its topiary pieces has flower beds filled with seasonal flowers, for which 15,000 plants are grown every year, including pansies, violas, forget-me-nots, polyanthus, and tulips in the spring, and heliotrope, verbena, *Artemisia* 'Powis Castle', and argyranthemums in summer. A more modern feature is the double herbaceous borders, which lie on the main axial pathways on either side of the beech circle, and which are lined up with the avenue of trees on the far side of the ha-ha.

Synopsis

1688	James Grahme acquires Levens Hall with its run-down Tudor house and gardens
1689–92	Guillaume Beaumont lays out gardens
1693	Work proceeds in garden, on vegetable borders, ha-ha (first ha-ha constructed in England), and trees
1697	Flower garden laid out, greens (evergreens) planted, and chestnuts and limes in park planted
1700	Rose garden planted with Provence roses, damasks, and rosa mundi velvet roses; 60 Scotch firs planted in park
1701	Seven hundred trees destroyed in storm; graveling of Beaumont's Beech Walk and bowling green laid out
1702–3	Park wall rebuilt
1727	Beaumont dies
1730	Grahme dies, gardens inherited by his daughter Catherine
1730–1803	Levens owned by Mrs. Greville Howard, Viscountess Andover, who lets gardens go to seed
1792	Alexander Forbes becomes head gardener
early 1800s	Forbes reinstates topiary, adding yews and other pieces, and replants 9 miles (14.5 km) of box edging
early 1900s	Tennis court replaces part of garden
1940s–60s	Part of gardens dug up for vegetable production
1950s	Rose garden laid out as parterre
1990s	Hal Bagot starts garden restoration program, restores bowling green, lays out 17th-century garden, and plants vegetable borders, nuttery, and wilderness
1994	Fountain garden reinstated

Further Reading

Elliott, Brent, *Victorian Gardens,* London: Batsford, and Portland, Oregon: Timber Press, 1986

DIANA BASKERVYLE-GLEGG

Lighting

For many centuries, the torch lighted the way. In A.D. 200 in Caesar's Rome, early attempts at street lighting were made, and lamps were hung in front of each house on the more prominent streets. Lamps were also placed in front of the entrances of theaters and public baths so that the Romans might readily identify these public places from a distance. Until the 16th century very little changed. In 1558 the Paris municipality installed pitch-burning vases throughout the city at important street corners. Later, candle-burning lanterns replaced them. The major cities of Europe followed the Paris example. Taxes for street lighting were introduced to finance this improvement. In 1745 polished reflectors were introduced in France. In the United States, the cities of Philadelphia, Boston, and Baltimore were among the leaders in street lighting. Benjamin Franklin introduced the flat panes of glass for the oil-burning lanterns. These panes were less expensive to replace than the imported globes. Gas lighting was introduced in London in 1809, and the first city to use it in the United States was Baltimore in 1815.

Electricity made its first appearance in London and Paris in 1878 and in Cleveland in 1879. The incandescent lightbulb did not gain wide acceptance for street lighting until the introduction of gas-filled lamps in 1915. Thus began the era of modern street lighting and general outdoor lighting.

The improvement of the lightbulb and its use in house and street lighting created exciting new dimensions in outdoor living. By lighting the areas surrounding the home, the designer was able to achieve a total home environment combining maximum aesthetic appeal with efficiency and security.

Functions

Outdoor lighting offers an extension of the daylight hours for a variety of activities. Today the field of lighting design is a highly developed and specialized technology that is constantly changing with the introduction of new developments in materials, light sources, and the understanding of light energy.

Outdoor lighting is both a practical and a design consideration. Good lighting extends the use of the outdoor space, contributes to the sense of security and safety, and adds charm and drama to the nighttime landscape.

Lighting can be divided into three functional design categories: security and safety lighting, area lighting, and lighting for special effects. Security and safety lighting are practical considerations that enter and impact every design project. The purpose of this type of lighting is to create a sufficient and minimal level of light that will provide a sense of security and safety for people using the site at night.

Area lighting refers to a lighting system that is designed to extend the daylight hours by creating a high level of light spread uniformly over the area. This type of lighting is associated with athletic fields, high-use public spaces, and highway interchanges. Its design requires special attention to lighting distribution patterns, selection of the light source, and color.

Lighting for special effects is used to decorate special details of intrinsic beauty and features of special interest. It may be a specimen tree, a flower bed, a fountain, or any other salient feature. Capturing and highlighting the drama and mystery of a designed site at night is the key to designing lighting for special effects. Other than beautification and the creation of a focal point, the lighting for special effects includes identification in the form of lighted signs, outlining circulation patterns, and illuminated information. Lighting for special effects requires special attention to the viewer's line of approach, light location and direction, brightness level, and contrast. The lighting equipment and the light source should be totally concealed to create the special effects, and if the lighting equipment cannot be totally concealed, it should be as inconspicuous as possible and should harmonize with its surroundings.

Landscape lighting equipment can be classified in two ways: light source and light distribution pattern. The "light source" is the appliance that produces light, such as the lightbulb. The "distribution pattern" refers to the function of the fixture (the luminaire) that houses the light source. Two families of light sources are used for outdoor lighting applications. The incandescent lamp has a bulb with a metallic filament sealed inside through which an electric current flows; because of the filament's resistance to the passage of electricity, it glows and gives out light. It has very low luminous efficiency, and more than 75 percent of the energy input is dissipated in the form of heat. The incandescent lamps include the common lightbulb as well as sealed-beam, low-voltage, quartz, and halogen lamps. The output is a near white light that renders colors close to daylight conditions.

The electric discharge lamps involve running electric current through carbon rods, slightly separated. Some of the carbon vaporizes, and as the current flows through the carbon, vapor light is produced. The arc lamp principle is the same for today's mercury vapor, sodium vapor fluorescent, and metal halide lamps.

Design

The design of outdoor lighting requires the understanding of the light sources, the equipment selection, their effect on the objects to be illuminated, and the decisions on desired lighting effects. In many sites, it is equally as important to determine what not to light as to determine what to light. Poor lighting layout and design can create hazardous conditions. Glare is considered a major inhibitor of good visibility and causes the most visual discomfort. It is a major problem when exposed light sources can be seen directly. Luminaire location, mounting height, and lamp intensity must be carefully selected to maximize light distribution and minimize glare.

A variety of effects can be achieved by creative placement and aiming of light sources. Six lighting effects that are most frequently used in outdoor situations are up lighting, moonlighting, silhouette lighting, spotlighting, spread lighting, and path lighting.

Up lighting is the most striking of all lighting effects. Because it counters our normal experience of the daylight casting from above, up lighting can always be counted on to achieve a dramatic and often spectacular effect. To create it, light sources are ground mounted or recessed into the ground (well lights), directed upward and away from the viewer, and preferably concealed to prevent glare. If the objective is to create all-around viewing (e.g., when an object, such as a tree, can be seen from any direction), well lights with louvers should be installed as close to the root ball as possible to capture the tree trunk and foliage.

Moonlighting (down lighting) exhibits a more natural and subdued quality. Actual effects will vary, depending on mounting height of the light sources and the direction angle. The most effective way is to mount the light fixture high on a tree, which produces a soft, natural filtering of light that illuminates foliage and the lawn area while creating dramatic shadow patterns on ground surfaces and walls.

Silhouette lighting is achieved by positioning the light fixture behind and below the object and aiming the light at a vertical surface, such as a wall or fence located several feet in the back. By lighting the background, the object in the foreground appears as only an outlined mass.

Signage, statuary, specimen plants, and other interesting features can become a focal point through judicious use of high-intensity spotlighting (accent lighting). Ideal choices are shielded, tree-mounted, well-shielded, and narrow-beam light sources. By mounting lights overhead in trees and structures, glare and fixture distraction can be eliminated. When ground-mounted fixtures are used, they should be concealed with plants, rocks, and so on. The key in spotlighting design is to create sharp contrast with the surrounding elements. Therefore, in addition to spotlighting, this contrast can be created by down lighting, up lighting, or any other combination.

Spread lighting is designed to produce circular patterns of illumination for general visibility or to highlight an area. This is effective for lighting ground covers, low shrubs, flower beds, walks, and steps. Size and intensity of the spread area are determined by the height of the source fixture.

Path lights are a specific use of spread lights, being placed at a lower height. By placing low-mounted lights normally below eye level, glare is minimized to allow the pedestrian a full view of the landscape.

To call special attention to unique texture, relief lights can be created (grazing) in which the light fixture is placed several inches away from the textured wall of a facade using down lighting or up lighting. In order to fill areas between other lighting effects without exposing the actual light source, bouncing light can be used. Bouncing light is created by directing the light source against a reflective surface that distributes the light to the desired area. The effect is also called indirect lighting.

Regardless of the design effect, outdoor lighting is an important design element in extending the hours of use of outdoor spaces for security and aesthetics. Outdoor lighting designs must be flexible as spaces change with each season and time. It must take into consideration plant growth and how adjustments can be made over time. Each design must be fine-tuned at the site to be sure that the lighting appearance matches the site plan.

Further Reading

Harris, Charles Ward, and Nicholas T. Dines, editors, *Time Saver Standards for Landscape Architecture: Design and Construction Data,* New York: McGraw Hill, 1988

IES Lighting Handbook, New York: Illuminating Engineering Society of North America, 1947; 5th edition, edited by John E. Kaufman, 1972

Lam, William M.C., *Perception and Lighting as Formgivers for Architecture,* edited by Christopher Hugh Ripman, New York: McGraw Hill, 1977

Landphair, Harlow C., and Fred Klatt, Jr., *Landscape Architecture Construction,* New York: Elsevier, 1979; 3rd edition, Upper Saddle River, New Jersey: Prentice Hall, 1999

Moyer, Janet Lennox, *The Landscape Lighting Book,* New York: Wiley, 1992

ALON KVASHNY

Ligorio, Pirro ca. 1513–1583

Italian Architect and Antiquary

Pirro Ligorio was an Italian architect, painter, and antiquarian, best known for his study of Hadrian's Villa at Tivoli and for his design of the casino of Pius IV in the Vatican and the gardens at the Villa d'Este, also at Tivoli. Born in Naples, Ligorio moved to Rome in 1534 and began his work there on decorative paintings. He soon became interested in archaeology and in 1549 entered the service of Cardinal Ippolito d'Este of Ferrara as archaeologist and court painter. In the 1550s he published three maps of Rome, two of which were reconstructions of the ancient city.

In 1555 Ligorio began to work for Pope Pius IV, a fellow Neapolitan, and in 1558 was appointed architect of the Vatican palace. It was in this capacity that Ligorio designed the casino, set in the grounds of the Vatican for the pope to retire to in the afternoons. The casino was completed in 1562. Both the building and the surrounding gardens were modeled on ancient villas, especially the oval courtyard, with the entrance arches at each end, and the separate loggia, which was based on reconstructions of the naumachia, or the artificial lake, known from antique coins.

In 1565, however, Ligorio was accused of financial malfeasance, and when Pius V was elected in 1566, Ligorio moved away from papal service. In 1567 he sold to Cardinal Alessandro Farnese the manuscript of his encyclopedia of antiquities, the *Libro delle antichità di Roma,* now in the library in Naples, as well as his collection of ancient medals. Ligorio was appointed court antiquary to Alfonso II d'Este, duke of Ferrara, in 1568, which allowed him to continue his study of Hadrian's Villa and to work on the ever-growing designs for the gardens of Villa d'Este at Tivoli.

Many of the names Ligorio gave to the parts of Hadrian's Villa have now been abandoned for more neutral descriptive terms—as with the Canopus and the Piazza d'Oro. Nonetheless, the account Ligorio made of the villa became immensely important for antiquarians because it contains descriptions of remains that are now lost. He also used his account of the villa in his own work on the Villa d'Este, borrowing, for example, the idea of water ornaments, covering virtually every section with fountains and water games and promenades and grottoes. He also included statues taken from Hadrian's Villa. Some details of the Villa d'Este originated from Bramante's wall fountains at the Belvedere court at the Vatican; Ligorio, making full use of the precipitousness of the site, went even further and filled the garden with sounds and light and coolness in ways that would dazzle visitors for many centuries, however much tastes changed.

The remainder of Ligorio's work was in Ferrara. When the city was damaged in an earthquake in 1570, he took the opportunity to do more antiquarian work there. He also produced a number of designs for the Castello on the genealogy of the d'Este family, which was later completed by other artists. In 1580, as a reward for his services, Ligorio was made an honorary citizen of Ferrara.

See also Este, Villa d'

Biography

Born in Naples, Italy, ca. 1513. Moved to Rome and worked as decorative painter, 1534; entered service of Cardinal Ippolito d'Este as archeologist and court painter, 1549; employed by Pope Pius IV, 1555; employed as architect for Vatican Palace, Rome, 1558–66; accused of financial malfeasance and left employment at Vatican, 1566; employed by Alfonso II d'Este, Duke of Ferrara, 1568; designed gardens at Villa d'Este, Tivoli, Italy, 1568–70; moved to Ferrara and continued antiquarian work, 1568. Died in Ferrara, Italy, 1583.

Selected Designs

1558–62	Casino of Pius IV and gardens, Vatican Palace, Rome, Italy
1560	Gardens and villa, Villa Pia, Vatican Palace, Rome, Italy
1561–4	Palazzina Pia, Rome, Italy
1568–70	Gardens and villa, Villa d'Este, Tivoli, Lazio, Italy

Selected Publications

Delle antichità di Roma, 1553

Further Reading

Coffin, David, *The Villa in the Life of Renaissance Rome,* Princeton, New Jersey: Princeton University Press, 1979

Mandowsky, Erna, and Charles Mitchell, editors, *Pirro Ligorio's Roman Antiquities: The Drawings in MS XIII.B.7 in the National Library in Naples,* London: Warburg Institute, University of London, 1963

DAVID CAST

Linnaeus, Carl 1707–1778

Swedish Botanist

Linnaeus, as he is commonly known outside Sweden, was born Carl Linnaeus, his father Nils Ingemarsson Linnaeus having adopted the surname from a venerable lime tree (Swedish, *lind*) on ancestral property, and upon ennoblement Carl chose the linguistic medley of Carl von Linné. Although born into a clerical family and despite familial expectations for him to follow a similar career, Linnaeus was encouraged in botany by his father's enthusiasm for gardens and, more specifically, by his schoolteacher Johan Rothman at Växjö, the physician and amateur botanist Kilian Stobaeus at Lund, and at Uppsala the professors Olof Rudbeck the Younger and Olof Celsius.

Linnaeus's ideas took shape during his first period at the University of Uppsala (1728–35) through his work there as a student and demonstrator and through his scientific expeditions to Lapland (1732) and Dalarna (Dalecarlia) (1734). His reputation was made by the publication (in 14 books) of his ideas during a sojourn of three years in the Netherlands, where he was for a time director of the private garden at Hartekamp of the wealthy banker George Clifford. Linnaeus's subsequent career at Uppsala enabled him to refine and hugely expand his initial work. Like Aristotle he was primarily both an investigator with superb eyesight and an instinctive cataloger. His principal contributions to science are the invention of a workable sexual system of botanical taxonomy, the formulation of a binomial nomenclature for botany and zoology, and the establishment of a specific botanical Latin.

Although taxonomy—classification through affinities—is connatural to human thought, it was first used to any appreciable extent as a scientific tool by Aristotle, whose *Historia Animalium* in Latin translation was known to Linnaeus as a boy, and specifically for botany by Theophrastus, Aristotle's successor as head of the Peripatetic school. Nonetheless, only in the later 16th and 17th centuries were substantial attempts at an all-embracing botanical classification made, most notably by the Englishman John Ray and the Frenchman Joseph Pitton de Tournefort. But the principle on which classification was to be based nevertheless remained problematic, systematizers choosing either observed phenomena or preconceived notions or even a mixture of both. However, the role of flowers as the sexual organs of plants had been recently argued by the Frenchman Sébastien Vaillant, whose little-known research (though foreshadowed by the work of Theophrastus in the late fourth century B.C.), together with that of de Tournefort, had been introduced to Linnaeus already by Rothman at Växjö.

The first evidence of Linnaeus's practical interest in botanical sexuality is a manuscript written when he was only 22 entitled *Praeludia sponsaliorum plantarum* (Introduction to Plants' Marriages), which, although a poetic description of vegetal "love life," shows awareness of Julius Pontedera's recent opposition to Vaillant in his refutation of the former's observation on the mulberry and specifically describes the sexual functions of stamens and pistils. More serious interest is shown in a manuscript submitted to the Uppsala Society of Science in 1730 on the "marriages and sexes of plants" and in his catalog of the university's botanic garden at Uppsala (*Hortus Uplandicus,* in various manuscript versions; eventually published in 1888) put together during his first stay there. Through such work and stimulated by friendly rivalry with Petrus Artedi, who devised a new system for classifying umbellate plants and whose work of classification of fish Linnaeus had printed after the author's unfortunately early death in 1735, Linnaeus decided on a sexual basis of affinities to create a workable system of classification. He first set this forth in print in his *Fundamenta botanica* (1735; Foundations of Botany) and *Systema naturae* (also 1735; System of Nature), while his continual commentary on the 365 aphorisms of the former culminated in the *Philosophia botanica* (1751; Botanical Philosophy).

All plants were hereby divided into 24 classes, the last (*Cryptogamia*) comprising mosses, etc., which appeared flowerless. The remaining classes were distinguished by the number, form, proportionate size, and disposition of the male organs, namely, the stamens. These classes were in turn divided into orders distinguishable by female organs, namely, the styles and stigmas. Linnaeus was swiftly accused, even by quite serious scientists, of lewdness, a charge inspired by his floral definitions in overtly sexual human terms, such as his description of hermaphroditic flowers as having husband and wife in the same bedchamber. Far more important criticism came from, most notably, French botanists such as the Comte de Buffon, who argued for a more "natural system," whereas Linnaeus believed that his largely mathematical method was the only practical, albeit provisional, means of embracing in a single system the rapidly growing number of species known and that a "natural" system was incapable of construction until all plants had been discovered. Although embraced by few disciples and soon overtaken by systems based on the evolutionary theory, Linnaeus's system briefly marked the pinnacle of human attempts at classification and laid the groundwork for the identification keys important in modern botany.

Prior to the publication in 1753 of Linnaeus's *Species plantarum* (his gargantuan attempt to list all known species), the scientific community had given plants Latin names ranging in length from one word to many, whereas Linnaeus now rigorously assigned each species a single, precise, two-word Latin (or Latinized) name. Although in this he had been anticipated over a century before by the Swiss botanist Gaspard Bauhin's *Pinax theatri botanici* (1623; Register of the Botanical Theater) and indeed was conforming with the simple brevity of both common Greek practice in antiquity and that of the vernacular of most languages, his influence ensured the system's universal acceptance by the scientific community. His binomial nomenclature, which for consistency extended even to monotypic genera, is based, following Aristotle, on recognition of the importance of the genus, which is itself divided into separate species (Linnaeus was aware of varieties but generally paid them little attention). Thus his early *Genera plantarum* (1737) places a heavy emphasis on the genera, already listing 935, of which 686 were examined from living material. The name of the genus, in accord with Aristotelian scholastic logic, was to give the "essential" or "natural character," while that of the species was to indicate the "specific differences." His initial belief, however, that each species' name should be diagnostic could not withstand the discovery of further species sharing the same diagnostic characteristic. Consequently, in place of the traditional renaming of species upon new discoveries, he accepted the practical expedience of the use of "trivial" (imprecise or even nondescriptive) names that could be used for species in perpetuity. Thus even a genus could be named *Andromeda* through its resemblance to the mythical daughter of Cepheus chained to a cliff and sorrowfully hanging her head in anticipation of death, while Linnaeus is notorious for naming species of *Lepidoptera* quite arbitrarily after heroes of Homer's *Iliad*. Nevertheless, because of its obvious practical convenience, his nomenclature became increasingly authoritative, and since 1905 the first edition of *Species plantarum* has been accepted as the starting point for all botanical nomenclature, with the exception of fossil plants and certain lower cryptogams. Similarly, the tenth edition of his *Systema naturae* (1758) is the starting point for binomial zoological nomenclature, in which his definition of man as *homo sapiens* both reflected and incited development of the theory of evolution. In both areas his nomenclatural system reflects a hierarchical classification and a quest for underlying unity, both of which were Aristotelian legacies.

Despite the utilitarian simplicity of his binomial system, Linnaeus understood that an accurate identification of a plant involved a more detailed description. However, although the universally accepted language of European science was Latin, he realized its imprecision both in ancient authors such as Pliny the Elder (the most important Roman source) and in current practice, an imprecision ever aggravated by new discoveries of the microscope and by the rapidly growing number of exotic plants collected. Therefore, beginning in his earliest catalogs of the gardens at Uppsala and Hartekamp and in the descriptions of plants from his first Swedish expeditions, he strove to create what was in many ways a new linguistic tool. Thus, whereas Pliny had, for instance, used the word *calyx* to refer to no fewer than seven botanical parts, Linnaeus by strict stipulative definition made one word specify but one thing. Moreover, since Latin is a language of paltry vocabulary, Linnaeus not only coined new Latin terminology on correct philological principles but, also in common with current practice, followed Roman tradition going back at least as far as Varro and Cicero in the first century B.C. in using technical Greek vocabulary with Latin terminations. In addition, he simplified Latin grammar and by example created a model of precisely ordered description still followed in the formal and official Latin descriptions of newly found plants. It is thus largely through Linnaeus's personal efforts that scientists today possess a highly accurate and universally understood language, which would have been quite unintelligible to the Romans (and is to modern classicists).

For Linnaeus the closely related activities of naming and precisely describing species were the primary duties of a botanist, tasks wherein he fully realized his own preeminence to the extent of publicly comparing himself with Adam, to whom God had given the task of naming the animals (Genesis 2:19). Consequently, Linnaeus considered other forms of botanical investigation such as physiology to be largely of secondary importance, thus provoking other scientists to criticize him for narrow-mindedness, a criticism aggravated by Linnaeus's arrogance and interpretation of scholarly disagreement with himself as malicious and personal attack. Nonetheless, he made many such discoveries, some of which appeared in the 186 dissertations (published in various volumes of *Amoenitates Academicae* [1749–69; Academic Pleasures]) publicly defended in Latin by his students but, in accordance with the academic convention of the time, written by the professor himself. Among other things he discovered that plants "sleep," described their altered appearances in that state, demonstrated in terms of a "floral clock" the fixed diurnal rhythm of plants opening and closing their flowers, and sedulously studied the timing of longer-term floral activities such as fructification, which he related to mammalian and agricultural phases to create a natural calendar.

Linnaeus could not, however, completely overcome his clerical upbringing, which inculcated a creationism dictating a fixity of species or at least of numerous divine prototypes (genera) that controlled future speciation. Familiarity with the mule and hinny persuaded him to believe that even vegetal hybridization was matroclinal, and he seems to have been unaware of Joseph Gottlieb Kölreuter's botanical experiments published in the 1760s. Nevertheless, in 1757–58 he produced the first artificial fertile hybrid (*Trapopogon pratensis* × *T. porrifolius*) and even came to accept the inheritance of acquired characteristics, a theory systematized by his younger contemporary the French encyclopedist Jean-Baptiste Pierre Antoine de Monet de Lamarck and later made notorious by the 20th-century Russian geneticist Trofim Lysenko. Linnaeus attempted to put this belief to the practical advantage of his native country.

Since its imperialist ambitions had ended in its defeat by the Russians at Poltava in 1709 and the death of Karl XII nine years later, Sweden had become increasingly inward looking, an attitude further encouraged by the influence of German "cameralists," financial theoreticians who promoted national mercantile protectionism. Linnaeus consequently advocated the progressive naturalization of tropical plants to render expensive imports unnecessary and was supported in this transmutational botany by the state; but the harsh Swedish climate rendered null his plans for tea plantations and rice paddies around the Baltic and groves of cinnamon in Lapland.

One of the attractions in Linnaeus's move as a youth from Lund to Uppsala was the existence there of a botanic garden (i.e., a garden for scientific research rather than public display). It had been founded by Olof Rudbeck the Elder in 1655 and at its peak had contained about 1,870 different plants, although it could boast barely 300 by the 1720s. Here, Linnaeus, while still a student, was invited to give his first botanical demonstrations and began to work out in his catalogs of the garden's plants the presentation of his sexual system. Upon his appointment as professor in 1741, he persuaded the university to restore the garden and greatly expand it with an orangery, a small menagerie, and a rebuilt house for his own quarters. With the help of Dietrich Nietzel, previously the head gardener of Clifford at Hartekamp, and up to 12 assistants, he planted the garden to demonstrate, through approximately 3,000 species, the 24 classes of his sexual system, although because of the botanic garden's swampy location, he grew plants also at the nearby Hammarby estate, which he bought in 1758.

Linnaeus's collections of plants, both live for his gardens and dried for his associated herbarium (now largely in England and Sweden), were enhanced by his own early expedition to Lapland and later expeditions to Öland and Gotland (1741), Västergötland (1746), and Skåne (1749), as well as increasingly by gifts from more southerly botanic gardens and by exotic specimens gathered by his pupils, whom he called his "apostles" as they spread the word of Linnaean botany through the world. Among these apostles, some of whom succumbed to the hazards of life in remote parts on expeditions which Linnaeus had often helped to organize himself, were Daniel Carl Solander and Anders Sparrman, botanists of James Cook's first and second circumnavigations of the world respectively, Pehr Forsskal in the Ottoman Empire and the Arabian peninsula, Frederik Hasselquist in Egypt and the Middle East, Johan Petter Falck in the Caucasus and western Siberia, Carl Peter Thunberg in Japan, Pehr Löfling in Spain and South America, and Pehr Kalm in North America.

While his international scientific reputation as the great taxonomer is very high, in Sweden Linnaeus is a national hero familiar to the public principally through his writings in the vernacular (including the accounts of his later expeditions), in which he displays extraordinary powers of perception, a perpetual zest for the delights of the world's natural phenomena, and a poetic touch stimulated by his early and never-forgotten reading of the Roman poets Vergil and Ovid.

See also Leiden, Universiteit Hortus Botanicus; Uppsala Universitet Botaniska Trädgården

Biography

Born in Råshult, Kronoberg, Smaland, Sweden, 23 May (new style) 1707. Educated at universities of Lund, Malmöhus, Sweden, 1727–28, and Uppsala, Sweden, 1728–35; lectured in botany, mineralogy, and dietetics at Uppsala University, Sweden; made scientific expeditions to Lapland, 1732, Dalarna (Dalecarlia), 1734, Öland and Gotland, 1741, Västergötland, 1746, and Skane, 1749; took medical degree at Harderwijk, Gelderland, Netherlands, 1735; worked as director of private garden of George Clifford, Hartekamp, Netherlands, where he first established reputation through his publications; visited England and France, 1735–38; returned to Sweden, served as physician in Stockholm, 1738–41; cofounded Royal Swedish Academy of Sciences and became first president, 1739; appointed professor, Uppsala University, 1741; restored Uppsala University botanic garden; ennobled, 1762; published numerous scientific books and papers, which established sexual system for botanic classification, binomial nomenclature, and botanical Latin (last two still in universal use today). Willed his university chair to son Carl von Linné the Younger. Died in Uppsala, Sweden, 1778.

Selected Publications

Systema Naturae, 1735; 10th edition, 1758
Fundamenta Botanica, 1735 [incorrectly dated 1736]
Flora Lapponica, 1737
Genera Plantarum, 1737; 5th edition, 1754
Hortus Cliffortianus, 1737
Oratio de Telluris Habitabilis Incremento, 1744
Flora Suecica, 1745
Hortus Upsaliensis, 1748
Philosophia Botanica, 1751 (major revision of *Fundamenta Botanica*)
Species Plantarum, 1753
Flora Alpina, 1756
Systema Vegetabilium, 1774

Further Reading

Blunt, Wilfrid, and William T. Stearn, *The Compleat Naturalist: A Life of Linnaeus,* London: Collins, and New York: Viking Press, 1971
Broberg, Gunnar, editor, *Linnaeus: Progress and Prospects in Linnaean Research,* Stockholm: Almqvist and Wiksell, and Pittsburgh, Pennsylvania: Hunt Institute for Botanical Documentation, 1980
Broberg, Gunnar, Allan Ellenius, and Bengt Jonsell, *Linnaeus and His Garden,* Uppsala: Swedish Linnaeus Society, 1983
Duris, Pascal, *Linné et la France, 1780–1850,* Geneva: Droz, 1993
Frängsmyr, Tore, editor, *Linnaeus: The Man and His Work,* Berkeley: University of California Press, 1983;

revised edition, Canton, Massachusetts: Science History, 1994
Fries, Theodor Magnus, *Linné: Lefnadsteckning,* 2 vols., Stockholm: Fahlcrantz, 1903
Goerke, Heinz, *Carl von Linné: Artz — Naturforscher — Systematiker,* Stuttgart, Germany: Wissenschaftlichen Verlagsgesellschaft, 1966; 2nd edition, 1989; as *Linnaeus,* translated by Denver Lindley, New York: Scribner, 1973
Hagberg, Knut, *Carl Linnaeus,* Stockholm: Natur och Kultur, 1939; as *Carl Linnaeus,* translated by Alan Blair, London: Cape, 1952, and New York: Dutton, 1953
Koerner, Lisbet, *Linnaeus: Nature and Nation,* Cambridge, Massachusetts: Harvard University Press, 1999
Larson, James L., *Reason and Experience: The Representation of Natural Order in the Work of Carl von Linné,* Berkeley: University of California Press, 1971
Stafleu, Frans Antonie, *Linnaeus and the Linnaeans: The Spreading of Their Ideas in Systematic Botany, 1735–1789,* Utrecht, The Netherlands: Oosthoek, 1971

A.R. LITTLEWOOD

Liselund

Møn, Denmark

Location: northeast coast of the island of Møn (Möen), approximately 45 miles (72.5 km) south of Copenhagen

Liselund traditionally enjoys a reputation as the best-known and most beautiful Danish landscape garden. It was laid out between 1791 and 1800, following upon the earliest experiments with this new horticultural paradigm in Denmark.

In 1783, having been appointedgovernor of the islands of Möen and Falster, situated south of Zealand, Antoine Bosc de la Calmette acquired the easternmost tip of Möen. The idea was to create a fashionable country residence for occasional retreat from the family's principal seat, the nearby Marienborg estate, where farming remained at the core. The name Liselund, literally meaning "Lise's grove," after Calmette's beloved wife, Lisa, was bestowed in 1784.

A landscape garden already adorned Marienborg, and Calmette, like many of his European contemporaries, took an active interest in the horticultural and aesthetic layout of his gardens. His military background, his talents as a draftsman, and his wide-ranging artistic interests were very useful in this respect.

In 1790 Calmette and his wife set out on their first tour to gardens and other sights in Germany and Switzerland, returning home the following year with numerous ideas. A second journey (1798–99) to German and Bohemian gardens also seems to have had a significant impact on the garden project. A general plan for the Liselund grounds was drawn up by a local surveyor in 1791. Construction of Liselund's main building, usually referred to as the Old Castle, had then just begun. The architect A.J. Kirkerup and the decorative painter J.C. Lillie, who designed the interiors, were highly esteemed in the Copenhagen art world of those days.

Placed in a bowl-shaped clearing in the woods, the Old Castle (completed 1793) looks very much like a *fabrique* (ornamental building in a garden). It is modest in size, has whitewashed walls, and blends vernacular motifs, such as the thatched roof, with neoclassical motifs. The area around the Old Castle contains two dammed ponds, which beautifully mirror the building; the picture is completed by a softly undulating lawn on the southern side of the castle and a lush yet carefully sculpted forest rising behind it. The circular structure in the form of a South Sea cabin, placed on the adjacent slope, originally served as an icehouse, while the gardener lived in the so-called Swiss chalet. A privy was disguised as a woodshed and placed in the scrub.

The progression of the work at Liselund is very poorly documented. Practically all prepatory drawings or models have vanished. Yet the travel notes of Calmette and his secretary have survived, and this material indicates how specific motifs in the gardens Calmette visited in Altona and Potsdam, in Machern near Leipzig, Wörlitz and Oranienbaum near Dessau, Teplice (Teplitz) and Krasnij Dvur (Schönhof) on the southern side of the Bohemian Alps found their way to Möen. Moreover, the strong emphasis on sentimental motifs clearly reflects the German influence.

The Old Castle at Liselund, Møn (Möen), Denmark
Copyright Margrethe Floryan

Möen has an unusually varied natural scenery, and this was the primary point of departure in the garden layout. The blue-green and never resting surface of the Baltic Sea is omnipresent; chalk cliffs make up the coastline; and numerous natural gorges and chasms, springs, and water sources cut through the territory. All of these were made constituent parts of the landscape garden, and much effort was directed toward selecting and clearing specific sites for architectural or sculptural elements. Measures were also taken to dam up some of the rich waters. Oak and beech predominated in the planting scheme, followed by chestnuts. Other plants were primarily chosen to stress the meaning of a specific architectural tableau, such as the conifers placed next to the Norwegian cottage or the weeping willow at the Chinese pavilion. Both buildings were furnished with exquisite interiors designed by J.C. Lillie.

Next to these examples of the more common repertoire of late 18th-century landscape gardens, much attention was devoted to imbuing the garden with personal associations. A series of spots were designed so as to reflect the Calmettes' humanistic and connubial ideals. Yet despite speaking the language of the few initiates, these motifs were unequivocal to the learned of the period. A rotunda, reliefs, benches, bridges, water sources, and viewpoints thus commemorated the owners, their reciprocal affection and friendship, and their activities in service of the muses. The recently restored Monument à la Bonne Harmonie, a broken pyramid with a sphinx on top of it, stands out from the rest of these motifs because of a rather majestic scenography and its broader meaning. Following the rivulet behind the Old Castle, a path wends its way up to a plateau with two oblong ponds, where an artificial island is dominated by the restored monument.

An imposing ruined battery and a Gothic chapel were no less important ingredients of Liselund's diversified architectural program. Both structures were part of a setting recalling the Bohemian Alps, which Calmette knew from firsthand experience. His enjoyment of the outdoors was also reflected in the construction of a simple bathing hut. A freshwater source supplied the bathing water. In the 20th century repeated landslides demolished this part of the layout, including Liselund's modest botanical collection.

The Liselund house and garden have traditionally been associated with the aesthetics of the Louis XVI period. This judgment has of course found support in the Calmette family's French origin, their consistent use of the French language, and their immediate adherence to the French-oriented part of Danish cultural life in the Enlightenment period. As a member of the Reformed Church, Calmette's father had fled France under Louis XIV. However, the influence of Germany on the royal Danish court and on the country's political and cultural elite was very strong from the 1750s. And Calmette's turning to German, Swiss, and Bohemian garden models may be seen as characteristic of this trend.

Liselund was thus firmly anchored in the aesthetics and moral values of the Continent, and its landscape garden struck the same sentimental chord as some of the larger and better-known gardens in the German-speaking countries of the late 18th and early 19th centuries. Moreover, from early on, Liselund became a favorite subject of the young generation of Danish landscape painters. Today the Liselund property is under the auspices of the Danish ministry for cultural affairs, and it is open to the public.

Synopsis

1783	Antoine Bosc de la Calmette acquires the land
1784	Calmette names the estate Liselund (Lise's grove) after his wife
1790–93	Construction of main building, named Old Castle, designed by A.J. Kirkerup and J.C. Lillie
1791	Drawing of initial plan for the Liselund garden
1791–1800	Layout of the landscape garden
1886–87	Construction of new main building
1902–5	Liseland's botanical collection and one-fifth of the pleasure grounds disappeared into the Baltic Sea due to repeated landslides
1964–68	Old Castle and part of garden restored
1998	Restoration of Norwegian Cottage

Further Reading

Andrup, Otto, "Liselund," in *Danske slotte og herregaarde,* edited by Arthur Gerhard Hassø, vol. 5, Copenhagen: Hassings, 1944

Elling, Christian, *Den romantiske have,* Copenhagen: Gyldendalske Boghandel, 1942; 2nd edition, 1979

Scavenius, Bente, *Liselund—En romantisk have,* Copenhagen: Borgen, 1994

MARGRETHE FLORYAN

Literature, Garden in

The use of gardens and garden imagery in Western literary tradition tends to vary widely. They are employed most often as framing devices that in some way structure, contain, or illuminate the main narrative, but they can also convey thematic content of their own. When this somehow relates to the larger narrative context, they become "frame narratives," and a visually oriented subtext is created (although it is verbally defined), which often emphasizes cultural or aesthetic values. In rare instances the garden's presence establishes parameters in such a way that the narrative cannot exist or move beyond the boundaries that the garden sets up, whether they are physical, cultural, economic, or aesthetic. In poetry or drama the garden's presence tends to be more noticeable, often functioning as an important thematic or narrative element. But in general the garden plays a supporting, and often not very noticeable, role.

It is necessary to distinguish between the idea of *garden* and *landscape,* for while a garden is by definition a landscape, the reverse is not always true, although in recent times the boundaries between them have begun to blur. The most useful distinction, perhaps, is that a garden is a physical construct based on and reflecting in its form a synthesis of cultural, economic, and aesthetic values. In this sense it is a cultural as well as a literary landscape. Nevertheless, the difficulty in distinguishing between "nature" and "garden" continues to increase in the modern era, and if the contemporary eye is less discriminating in this respect, its vision is more inclusive.

As a literary and historical phenomenon the garden has appeared in virtually every branch of literature. Its earliest and perhaps most memorable presence in Western literature is the biblical Garden of Eden—Nature before the Fall—which functions on many levels: symbolical, allegorical, and as a setting or background for the seminal events depicted in the book of Genesis. It also functions metaphorically in the book of Ecclesiastes (2:10–13): "For everything there is a season, . . . a time to plant, and a time to pluck up that which is planted." In the Song of Solomon (4:12–16) a more literal description is found:

> . . . an orchard [garden] of pomegranates,
> With precious fruits, henna with spikenard plants,
> Spikenard and saffron, calamus and cinnamon,
> With all trees of frankincense; myrrh and aloes,
> With all the chief spices.

The Koran also evokes images of the rewards that true believers will reap in heavenly Islamic "paradise" gardens, wherein believing families will be reunited, while Taoism encourages a nature-oriented philosophy, earthly visions of which appear in the gardens of China and Japan. In the ancient world the garden appears in secular guise in Egyptian papyri and tomb paintings, and even in verses that would today be the equivalent of a love letter.

In the fourth century B.C. Theophrastus, a botanist and student of Aristotle, produced the *Historia Plantarum,* in which he writes about species as diverse as cotton, fig trees, pepper, cinnamon, and myrrh, familiar to him through the discoveries of Alexander the Great in Asia. In a different literary context the numerous surviving letters of the Roman aristocrat Pliny the Younger, describing his various Tuscan villas in great (even interminable) detail, have come down to us as epistolary landscapes that have been of enormous value to contemporary garden historians both as "tour guides" and revealing social commentary. Equally valuable are the writings of the Greek Pedanius Dioscorides, a biologist and pharmacologist, as well as a physician in the Roman army under Nero at the end of the first century A.D. Dioscorides's record of some 500 plants in *De materia medica* was considered by botanists and scholars as the definitive text on the subject for 1500 years.

Interest in gardens has ebbed and flowed over time, and the literature of any given historical period invariably reflects contemporary attitudes. During the Middle Ages ornamental horticulture and garden design declined sharply from the scale and level of sophistication that it had enjoyed during the Pax Romana. Despite its often modest dimensions, however, the medieval garden became a microcosmic lens through which Catholic humanity's view of the hereafter could be focused. Both secular and monastic gardens looked to the Bible, classical records, and the returning Crusaders' experiences of Islamic paradise gardens for spiritual and aesthetic inspiration. In religious communities labor in kitchen, medicinal, or cloister gardens was viewed as beneficial to both the body and the spirit and served as a daily reminder of better times in Eden. Secular gardens, meanwhile, retreated behind the walls of the keep in a turbulent and dangerous era so that they might continue to fulfill their traditional role of providing respite and pleasure, in spite of a greatly condensed—a medievalist might say distilled—cosmogony and physical setting.

While clerics were relatively silent on the subject of gardens and gardening during the medieval period, they produced some extraordinary illuminated manuscripts, richly embellished prayer books such as the renowned *Tres riche heures* of Jean, duke of Berry, and meticulously delineated herbals, often featuring beautifully rendered garden images and botanical drawings. Dioscorides's *De materia medica* was not supplanted until botanists of the 16th and later centuries rapidly expanded their repertory under the influence of new discoveries and imported species, although information from India, China, Tibet, and the East Indies had begun to make its way to Europe as early as the 1100s. The herbals produced during this period would be fully "fleshed out" by the mid-16th century with the increasingly widespread awareness and knowledge of the flora of the New World. During the 16th century accurate illustrations also began to accompany texts and botanical gardens appeared, especially in Italy in 1545 at Padua and Pisa. By the 1590s the phenomenon had spread across much of Europe. Herbals were also gradually transformed into "gardens on paper," or *herbaria,* as well as gardens in situ.

Secular writers were not under the same restraints as clerics. In *L'Morte d'Arthur,* for example, Sir Thomas Malory sent Queen Guinevere "a-Maying" into the woods—nature's garden—from whence she was abducted by Sir Mellyagraunce and rescued by Sir Lancelot. During the Renaissance Boccaccio used garden settings in his *Decameron* that made detailed descriptive references to earthly paradises, while in England Sir Philip Sidney's *Arcadia* revived the ancient ideal of the Golden Age of Greece (i.e., nature as garden). Scenes of Eden-like beauty also occurred in works as diverse as Milton's epic poetry and romances such as Guillaume de Lorri's *Le Roman de la Rose.*

For much of the 17th century, after the 16th-century wave of interest in herbals and botanical gardens had reached its peak, gardening essays and books on gardening tended to dominate, continuing a tradition that reached back to Greece and Rome and the works of Theophrastus and Dioscorides, while anticipating the modern era. It was during the 18th century that the garden came into its own as a literary phenomenon, especially in the British Isles. In few (if any) other centuries has there occurred such a convergence of the fine and applied arts, including history, philosophy, literature, painting, architecture, and especially landscape gardening, which, during this period more than any other, seems to summarize and encapsulate all that was happening in both the fine and applied arts.

A fascination with classical Greco-Roman culture was reflected during this period in names such as "Arcadia" or "Elysian Fields" bestowed by the gentry on the grander private estates. The essays of Alexander Pope and Joseph Addison that appeared in weekly newspapers such as *The Spectator* rejected French and Dutch overburdens that obscured the native English landscape and its traditions. Garden architecture often drew on classical themes to embellish the informal Picturesque landscapes rapidly displacing rigidly geometric garden designs. In his *Epistle to Richard, Lord Burlington,* Pope penned his well-known lines regarding the dominant role that nature should play in the design of 18th-century landscape gardens:

> Consult the Genius of the *Place* in all,
> That tells the waters or to rise, or fall,
> Or helps th' ambitious Hill the heav'ns to scale,
> Or scoops in circling Theatres the Vale,
> Calls in the Country, catches opening Glades,
> Joins willing Woods, and varies Shades
> from Shades,
> Now breaks, or now directs, th' intending
> Lines,
> *Paints* as you plant, and as you work,
> *Designs.*

The visions of Claude Lorraine, Salvator Rosa, and Nicholas Poussin were also everywhere evident, serving as visual texts to which landscape gardeners appear to have made frequent reference in their designs for estates such as Stourhead and Stowe in England.

More obviously literary manifestations also abound in the 18th century. Voltaire infused *Candide* (1759) with metaphorical wisdom through his sadder-but-wiser hero's response to the philosophical meanderings of Dr. Pangloss: "That is well said . . . but let us cultivate our garden." In the same year Samuel Johnson's *Rasselas* departs the gardenlike Happy Valley with rather similar results. Samuel Richardson's *Clarissa* abandons reputation and security as she stands at the garden gate poised to flee an unsuitable marriage, while in Henry Fielding's *Tom Jones,* "our hero" is exiled from his paradisiacal boyhood home, described in considerable picturesque detail by the author. Indeed, these works suggest that 18th-century literary gardens were often created solely for purposes of abandonment.

The novels of Jane Austen are of special interest with respect to the place of the garden in 18th-century literature, for they abundantly reflect the contemporary interest in landscape and landscape-related cultural values. Serving as aesthetic icons, vehicles for satire, or models of morality, the influence of garden landscapes is strongly felt, if not often expressed, in her six complete novels and two fragments. Ranging from a few words to several paragraphs, which frame as well as direct the narrative, Austen's landscapes serve as a means by which the gap between the late 18th and early 19th centuries may be bridged. *Northanger Abbey* and *Sense and Sensibility* each satirize the preferred landscape style of the period called the Picturesque, a school of aesthetics influential in architecture and garden design and closely associated with the 18th-century cult of sensibility, which emphasized the cultivation of feeling at the expense of reason. Whether employed as a Gothic parody in the former or as a vessel for the overwrought emotions of the heroine in the latter, the presence of the landscape garden is never long absent from Austen's novels. In *Pride and Prejudice* it is reinterpreted in a more restrained and elegant mode at Pemberley, Mr. Darcy's beautiful estate in Derbyshire, where Elizabeth Bennet has a memorable encounter with its owner and her future husband.

Austen's later novels return to this theme, especially *Mansfield Park,* in which the real-life Humphry Repton is mentioned several times during a dinner-table discussion involving the "improvement" of estates, specifically neighboring Sotherton Court, which serves as a metaphor for conflicting social values, a device to reveal character, and a bellwether of changing morality. *Emma* elevates its rural agrarian settings as models of respectability, firmness of character, and socioeconomic stratification expressed in landscape. This is especially evident in the strawberry-gathering party that takes place in Mr. Knightly's gardens at Donwell Abbey when the character of Mrs. Elton is revealed in all her shallowness and petty hypocrisy. *Persuasion,* Austen's last complete novel, reveals a gentle melancholy, identified as the state of mind most appropriate for proper appreciation of picturesque scenery. The tone of its opening scenes reflects the emotions, "so sweet and so sad," associated with country autumns, as opposed to "the white glare of Bath" to which the heroine later removes for purposes of plot resolution. Finally, the unfinished *Sanditon* expresses an emergent Romantic consciousness in its images of the sea, "dancing and sparkling in sunshine and freshness."

The garden appears in many literary guises during the 19th century. Romantic literature often employs it as a metaphor, and poetry of the period is rich with images of nature and its idealized interpretations. Often appearing to advantage in a ruined or beleaguered state, the garden could also serve as a medium for divine or supernatural phenomena fraught with symbolism and angst. The garden at Thornfield in Charlotte Brontë's

Jane Eyre, where Rochester first declares his love for his penniless governess, calls forth such a response: the old chestnut tree "writhed and groaned while the wind roared in the laurel walk." The next morning reveals that a lightning strike in the midst of a nocturnal thunderstorm has split the ancient tree.

During this period there also occurred a diminishing of the garden as a unifying aesthetic statement or influence; its limited vistas were perhaps too confining for the Romantic vision. The aesthetic concord that characterized the 18th century also fragmented, as art, science, and religion began to diverge. The cult of sensibility metamorphosed into unrestrained Romanticism, perhaps a response to creeping Darwinism and the runaway pace of unrestrained technological progress. Transcendentalism, the medievalism of the pre-Raphaelites, the Arts and Crafts movement, and the widespread belief in the redemptive influence of nature and natural environments on human behavior added to the confusion. Books on gardening advocating various systems appeared with increasing frequency, while the "ordered wildness" of the Picturesque landscape decayed into the stylistic confusion of the "gardenesque." Hothouse cultivation of exotic species, specimen planting of new imports, floral carpet bedding, and a general weariness with the landscapes of the unrelentingly green 18th century added to the confusion of the new style. Gardens became increasingly private spaces and lost both the accessibility and openness of Versailles and the English landscape gardens.

In literary forms this movement culminated at the beginning of the 20th century in Francis Hodgson Burnett's *The Secret Garden,* in which "Paradise" lost is gradually regained, both literally and metaphorically speaking. T.H. White's *Mistress Masham's Repose* also revolves around the secrets concealed by a decayed garden, in this case a secret and abandoned English landscape garden of the 18th century. As (supposedly) a children's book, it has much of the same charm as, and a good deal in common with, fairy tales such as *Sleeping Beauty* or *Beauty and the Beast.*

In spite of the tendency toward insularity during the 20th century, the garden became increasingly diverse and idiosyncratic in its literary expressions. They tend to be highly individualized statements isolated from each other in time, space, and cultural context. In fiction garden landscapes appear in such divergent formats as historical novels, mysteries, science fiction, fantasy, and children's books, as well as in more serious works that are now valuable to us as quasi-historical records.

The leisurely narrative of Vita Sackville-West's *The Edwardians,* a historical novel of aristocratic manners, morality, and social change, emerges in sharp focus when the young duke, Sebastian, escorts his aged grandmother on a stroll through the gardens of Chevron, the family estate. Her inbred sense of superiority extends to every aspect of existence, from the inherited privileges of the upper classes to the head gardener's artistic defects: "Diggs never had any taste beyond begonias." The garden provides both the framing structure of the narrative and a highly visible and symbolic manifestation of a soon-to-vanish way of life.

Edith Wharton's *Italian Villas and Their Gardens* provides a glimpse into that world as it existed in another country. It is something of an illustrated "guidebook"; the lavish period paintings by artist Maxfield Parrish combine with Wharton's elegant text to present a set of richly romantic landscape images the likes of which is rarely seen in contemporary literature of the genre, with its widespread use of color photography.

James Hilton's *Lost Horizon* offers a refuge from the ruins of 19th-century aristocratic lifestyle and the impending repetition of the catastrophic events that caused the downfall of much of European society as the result of World War I. In this novel, however, it is the cultural legacy of civilization itself that is at stake. In his vision of Shangri La, Hilton creates a repository for all that is best (or might eventually remain) of Western culture, preserving it for the future in an inaccessible, tightly constricted, and intensely gardened environment—a cultural oasis in the worldwide desert to come.

Gardens are often associated with mysterious doings. In Daphne Du Maurier's *Rebecca* the gardens of Manderley are not only scenes of fantasy and loveliness but also carry the dark legacy of their former mistress. Seldom has a mystery novel succeeded in its use of the garden in so many capacities, functioning as setting, symbol, and even at times in the role of a character—especially at the beginning of the narrative—whose influence works continually on the novel's nameless and all but invisible narrator/protagonist. As a trysting place with the past, it is exceptional in this context, for gardens as (romantic) trysting places are exceedingly common in literature.

J.R.R. Tolkien, author of the Lord of the Rings trilogy, a work of fantasy and medievalism, invokes numerous and powerful garden images in his epic. The Shire is essentially a gardenlike environment, and it is no accident that Sam Gamgee, one of the Ringbearers and the Shire's future mayor, is a gardener by trade (it is worth mentioning that Queen Guinevere in Parke Godwin's Arthurian novels, *Firebrand* and *Beloved Exile,* is also a ruler/gardener). Rivendell and Lothlorien, also both gardenlike environments, hold both time and the forces of the Shadow at bay. Here are additional variations of Eden, maintained by the impregnability of their magical, invisible walls, but not without great effort and sacrifice. Even "Ithilien, the garden of Gondor now desolate kept still a disheveled dryad loveliness" in its state of decline and abandonment.

Literary gardens are not always possessed of charming qualities. Sebastian Venable's corrupt garden in Tennessee Williams's *Suddenly, Last Summer* is the antithesis of all the virtues with which gardens are traditionally associated, a symbol of evil. Its carnivorous plants embody the horrific events to be revealed at the end of the play. John Berendt's novel *Midnight in the Garden of Good and Evil* evokes of the same responses, for the scenes set in this Savannah cemetery invoke the power of a "garden" whose identity is shrouded in moral ambiguity.

The 20th century also saw the expansion of the idea of the garden into a larger literary landscape context. John Steinbeck's *The Grapes of Wrath,* in which a sense of oneness with the land is lost through ignorance, neglect, and socioeconomic and natural forces beyond the control of any single individual. A similar theme was explored half a hemisphere away in Pearl H. Buck's slightly earlier work, *The Good Earth.* Both novels end on an ambiguous note, unlike Frank Herbert's *Dune,* in which the processes connected with the idea of landscape as "garden" are reversed, and an entire desert planet is destined to become a new paradise by means of a total restructuring of its ecology. Herbert's novel established an entire new literary genre known as "ecofiction," which has attracted several highly respected authors. Ursula Le Guin's *The Left Hand of Darkness,* Brian Aldiss's Helliconia trilogy, and Kim Stanley Robinson's Mars quartet are excellent examples of this new genre. The garden, like historical writing in general, seems to be equally subject to the revisionism that has become commonplace in recent decades. In the 21st century its boundaries may become even more blurred in an era of increasing ecological awareness and appreciation of nature and a corresponding redefinition of the garden idea in both landscape and literature.

Further Reading

Batey, Mavis, *Jane Austen and the English Landscape,* London: Barn Elms, and Chicago, Chicago Review Press, 1996

Clayton, Virginia Tuttle, *Gardens on Paper: Prints and Drawings, 1200–1900,* Washington, D.C.: National Gallery of Art, 1990

Daiches, David, and John Flower, *Literary Landscapes of the British Isles: A Narrative Atlas,* New York: Paddington Press, 1979, and London: Bell and Hyman, 1979

Fairbrother, Nan, *Men and Gardens,* London: Hogarth Press, and New York: Knopf, 1956

Hobhouse, Penelope, *Plants in Garden History,* London: Pavilion Books, 1992; as *Penelope Hobhouse's Gardening through the Ages,* New York: Simon and Schuster, 1992

Kazin, Alfred, *A Writer's America: Landscape in Literature,* New York: Knopf, 1988

McGuire, Diane Kostial, *American Garden Design: An Anthology of Ideas That Shaped Our Landscape,* New York: Prentice Hall, 1994

Russell, Vivan, *Edith Wharton's Italian Gardens,* Boston: Little Brown, 1997

Wharton, Edith, and Maxfield Parrish, *Italian Villas and Their Gardens,* New York: Century, 1903; London: Lane, 1904; reprint, New York: Da Capo Press, 1988

ROBERT A. BENSON

Little Sparta

Stonypath, Dunsyre, Lanarkshire, Strathclyde, Scotland

Location: 20 miles (32 km) southwest of Edinburgh on the A702

Ian Hamilton Finlay created the garden at Little Sparta in Scotland. A poet and artist, Finlay was described by a friend as being of the "rebel" party. He made his reputation originally for his writing, in particular his contribution to what is called concrete poetry. He studied briefly at the Glasgow School of Art and is internationally recognized for his sculpture.

Little Sparta is on the slopes of the Pentland Hills, south of Edinburgh; the whole garden is an expression of Finlay's art, poetry, and philosophy. It is an intensely personal statement of his stance as a revolutionary, his "determination to be in perpetual opposition to the times," as Alec Finlay describes it, and his stylistic espousal of neoclassicism. His outlook is epitomized at Little Sparta by a quotation carved in large Roman capitals: "The present order is the disorder of the future—Saint Just." It is set on a series of large flat-topped stones laid out by the lake, each word carved on a separate stone. Saint Just was a leader of the Revolution in 18th-century France, who together with Robespierre was guillotined in 1794.

Stonypath was originally a shepherd's cottage and small holding to which the Hamilton Finlays moved in 1966, later giving his creation there the name of Little Sparta. They laid out the garden in 1968, which is set out on approximately four acres (1.6 ha) of comparatively infertile land around and between the cottage and its associated buildings. It displays a markedly eclectic design approach, ranging from the formality of the front garden, including the sunken area, and the Roman garden to the natural setting of Lochan Eck, with its borrowed landscape of the Pentland Hills. Garden features include the Temple Pool within the enclosed area between the buildings, the Temple of Philemon and Bacchus, the grotto dedicated to Aeneas and Dido, Vergil's Spring, the Claude Bridge, and the pyramid dedicated to Caspar David Friedrich. Even the vegetable growing area is described as the Epicurean Garden. Literary allusions are everywhere. What unifies the garden are the ideas it presents of revolution, the challenge to established authority, and the way in which the features typical of the neoclassical 18th-century garden are given a new meaning by Hamilton Finlay's juxtaposition of them with other harsher references. The 18th century cultivated an appreciation of the sublime, as defined by Edmund Burke, those aspects of nature whose scale was overpowering, the elements too great and powerful to be controllable by humanity, and great terrors wrought by man or nature, but which could be experienced without any sense of real danger. Finlay's sublime is presented not in visual terms but as ideas. The connection to the 18th century and to neoclassicism is sustained with allusions to the French Revolution as well as Hellenic legends and the Spartan Wars of ancient Greece. A sharper thrust is achieved by the inclusion of visual references to more modern events and experiences.

The name *Little Sparta* was introduced in 1978 as a result of disagreements with the Strathclyde Regional Council, the local authority, and its policy for collecting rates—annual taxes on property—which are calculated according to the use of the property concerned. The council ruled that the exhibition building at Stonypath was a commercial premises; Finlay argued that it was a temple and defended his position vigorously—and physically—with the help of friends and supporters who came to be known as the Saint-Just Vigilantes. The new name symbolizes the parallels experienced here with the difficulties in the times of ancient Sparta of not only political life but also the harshness of the physical living conditions experienced.

Hamilton Finlay and Stonypath have been compared with the 18th-century figure of William Shenstone, the amateur poet and landscape gardener whose small estate in the midlands of England at the Leasowes featured allusions to classical ideas and times. As those of Shenstone were more pastoral and gently ironic in their character than Finlay's Little Sparta, it is more appropriate to make that comparison with Finlay's garden in its earlier stages than with the more aggressive later concepts. Finlay acknowledges Shenstone's "Unconnected Thoughts on Gardening" (1764) in his own writing of "Unconnected (or Disconnected) Sentences on Gardening" (undated and privately printed). One such sentence echoes closely the ideas of his predecessor: "Superior gardens are composed of Glooms and Solitudes and not of plants and trees."

Any belief that here is a gentle rustic idyll or Arcadian pastoral allegory is quickly dispelled by the decoration of the facade of the cottage, where Apollo is invoked at his most warlike, and as he could only be seen by present-day commentators. The motto "To Apollo—his music—his missiles—his muses," in large letters, is offset by Corinthian colonnades. The gilded head of "Apollon Terroriste" elsewhere in the garden, the Hypothetical Gateway to an Academy of Mars, the god of war, the introduction in the Grotto of Aeneas and Dido of Jove's thunder in the form of the emblem of the SS, the Battle of Midway stone inscription, and the Pacific Air War Inscribed Stone all bring the disparate ideas of classicism, poetry, revolution, conflict, and terror together across the centuries.

Another source of Finlay's images is the sea. An emphasis on the form of ships occurs frequently in his drawings and sculpture, and many visitors recognize the many evocations of the sea at Little Sparta. Beside the Loch is to be found the sinister outline of the black "Nuclear Sail." Across the Loch, taking the visitor back, in contrast, to the 18th century is the column dedicated to Finlay's hero, Saint Just.

Hamilton Finlay's personal agenda becomes clear to visitors of Little Sparta. His synthesis of ideas and images from different ages and areas is well summarized in the definition of the word *Arcadian* in his *New Arcadian Dictionary:* "Arcadian, adj. Leafy, dangerous; n. a native of Arcadia, variously a shepherd, a commando, a nymph, a satyr, a Waffen-SS man; according to Lord Byron, a blackguard."

Synopsis

1966 Hamilton Finlays move to Stonypath
1968 Garden created by Ian Hamilton Finlay
1978 Garden named Little Sparta because of dispute with local authorities

Further Reading
Abrioux, Yves, *Ian Hamilton Finlay: A Visual Primer,* Edinburgh: Reaktion Books, 1985; 2nd edition, Cambridge, Massachusetts: MIT Press, and London: Reaktion Books, 1992
Adams, William Howard, and Everett H. Scott, *Grounds for Change: Major Gardens of the Twentieth Century,* Boston: Little Brown, 1993
Asensio Cerver, Francisco, and Francisco López Parón, *Landscape Art,* Barcelona: s.n., 1995
Asensio Cerver, Francisco, and Patricia Barberá, *The World of Landscape Architects,* Barcelona: Arco Editorial Board, 1995
Finlay, Alec, editor, *Wood Notes Wild: Essays on the Poetry and Art of Ian Hamilton Finlay,* Edinburgh: Polygon Books, 1995
Finlay, Ian Hamilton, *New Arcadian Dictionary,* 1973
Macmillan, Duncan, *Scottish Art, 1460–1990,* Edinburgh: Mainstream, 1990; updated edition, as *Scottish Art, 1460–2000,* 2000
Shenstone, William, "Unconnected Thoughts on Gardening," in *The Works in Verse and Prose,* by Shenstone, vol. 2, edited by Robert Dodsley, London, 1764; 2nd edition, London, 1765; reprint, London: Hughs, 1968

M.F. DOWNING

Liu Yuan

Suzhou, Jiangsu Province, China

Location: outside the west city gate, Changmen of Suzhou

The meaning of the name *Liu Yuan* is "the lingering garden." Liu Yuan is one of the four most famous gardens in Suzhou and one of the most spacious gardens in Suzhou. In 1961 the State Council listed the garden Liu Yuan as one of the Chinese national heritages for preservation. The garden now makes up the east part of the original garden that was constructed in 1521–65 by then owner Xu Taishi (Jiongqing), a top official of the Ming dynasty. He built two gardens: Dong Yuan (East Garden) and Xi Yuan (West Garden). The West Garden later became a Buddhist temple garden called Jiezhuanglisi (Set of Monastic Regulations Temple), while the East Garden remained a private garden occupying an area of about two hectares (5 acres). In 1823, during the reign of Emperor Jiaqing of the Qing dynasty, the former East Garden was rebuilt by Liu Shu and named Han Bi Shanzhuang (Cold-Emerald Mountain-Villa).

Liu Shu was fond of strange and precious stones, so 12 monolithic stone peaks taken from Taihu Lake were erected and placed in the garden. In 1876, during the reign of Emperor Guangxu, ownership of the garden changed to Sheng Kang (Xu Ren), who oversaw rebuilding and expanded construction in what are now the eastern and western sections of the garden. More buildings were erected and the garden received its current name of Liu Yuan. Ownership of the garden has changed several times, and the garden had seen both splendor and decay. The last reconstruction was in 1953 according to the style of the late Qing dynasty.

The garden comprises four areas. The central area, the quintessential part of the garden, was originally the Han Bi Shanzhuang, which has been under intermittent care and management for the longest period of all parts of the garden. All the other sections, the eastern, northern, and western parts, were added to the original garden after 1873. The layout of the central area is based on the features of mountain and water with rockeries and pools. A large pond dominates the very center of this area, surrounded by stone hillocks, a few buildings and pavilions connected by long corridors, and bridges penetrating the garden space that is enclosed by a garden wall with scenic windows. A long and narrow corridor has been set between the residential section and the central area of the garden. Entering from the main entrance opening to the street, this corridor has played a role as a guide and simultaneously a spirit preparation for a visit to the garden.

The essence of the eastern area is architecture, as a residential section for the garden owner. The spatial composition of the buildings and the corridors is one of the highlights of Chinese classical gardens, with numerous small- and medium-size open-air spaces and courtyards. There are many magnificent and spacious halls,

The Riverside Pavilion at Liu Yuan garden
Copyright Robert M. Craig

pavilions with courtyards, and corridors focused on a hall in this area called Wu Feng Xian Guan (The Five-Peaks Celestial Hall). The hall is constructed with *nanmu* and is the largest hall in Suzhou gardens. In the front courtyard of this hall is a composition of five stone peaks. The northeastern part of the garden contains a figurative stone peak that remains from the Song dynasty named Guanyun Feng (Cloud Topping Peak).

The western area is based on large rockeries with a highest hillock of the garden, from which one could view the whole city. The northern area contains a landscape of rural villages, with a bamboo picket fence enclosing a small garden of bonsai made up of many famous species. The original buildings in this area no longer exist.

Liu Yuan is a large garden connected by numerous buildings and 700 meters (766 yd.) of corridors. It represents a pinnacle of space composition in classical gardens. The garden's ornaments, partition, windows, and pavement are also the quintessence of classical Chinese gardens.

Synopsis

1522–66	Dong Yuan (East Garden), the first construction by the owner Xu Shi-tai (Jiongqing)
1823	Han Bi Shanz Huang (Cold Emerald Mountain Villa), owned by Liu Shu (also called Liu Yuan, after the name of the owner); 12 Taihu Lake stones erected along with a reconstruction
1876	Liu Yuan (Lingering Garden) owned by Sheng Kang (Xu Ren); overall reconstruction and expansion
1953	Reconstruction
1961	National Heritage for Preservation listing

Further Reading

Chinese Encyclopedia, Architecture, Landscape Architecture and Urban Planning, Shanghai: 1988

Liu, Tun-chen, *Su-chou ku tien yüan lin,* Beijing: China Architecture and Building Press, 1979; as *Chinese Classical Gardens of Suzhou,* translated by Chen Lixian, edited by Joseph C. Wang, New York: McGraw-Hill, 1993

Suzhon Institute of Landscape Architectural Design, *Su-chou yüan lin* (Suzhou Gardens), Beijing: Chung-kuo chien chu kung yeh ch'u pan she, 1999

Yang, Hung-hsün, *Chian nan yüan lin lun; A Treatise on the Garden of Jiangnan,* Shanghai: Shang-hai jen min ch'u pan she, 1994 (with summaries in English)

ZHENG SHILING

Loddiges Family 1694–1865

The Loddiges family embraces several generations of German and Anglo-German gardeners spanning some of the most important events in the heyday of the nursery trade. The earliest known plantsman in the family worked in Hanover at the royal gardens of Herrenhausen and encouraged his son Caspar Burchart Loddiges (1694–1770) to find similar employment with noblemen in the principality. Little more is known about the first and second generations of cultivators in the Loddiges family, but the outstanding achievements of later generations are described below.

Joachim Conrad Loddiges (1738–ca. 1820)

Joachim Conrad Loddiges, the most eminent plantsman of the Loddiges family, was born at Hertzberg in 1738 and brought up in Hildesheim, near Hanover, although a number of biographers have assumed he was Dutch. Following a brief period in the Low Countries—which accounts for his fluency in Dutch—he spent several years in England as a landscape gardener to Dr. John Silvester in the village of Hackney near London. Here he introduced seeds of the Turkish rhododendron, *Rhododendron ponticum,* into Britain. In his early 30s Joachim married an English girl and sought to establish his own business to support his family. An opportunity arose when fellow German gardener and landscape designer John (Johann) Busch prepared to leave England to work for Catherine the Great at Tsarskoye Selo near St. Petersburg in Russia. Busch owned a small seed business in Hackney, established in 1756, which grew North American plants from seed collected by William Bartram. On Busch's departure in 1771, the business was gradually transferred to Joachim Conrad Loddiges, although Busch retained some involvement. Joachim successfully expanded sales, advertising exotic stock by publishing one of the earliest multilingual plant catalogs (German, English, and Latin).

After about 15 years of commercial success, Joachim dispensed with Busch's scattered garden plots and secured a single site on which to build his family house and grow and display rare garden and greenhouse plants. The Paradise Field Nursery (1787–1816), as it became known in some quarters, slowly began to attract visitors eager to see hitherto unknown herbaceous plants blossom in a garden near London: alpine clematis (*Clematis alpina*), sweet-smelling garlic (*Tulbaghia violacea*), purple broom (*Chamaecytisus purpurea*), great-flowered betony (*Stachys macrantha*), glaucous heath (*Erica glauca*), porcelain-flowered gentian (*Gentiana decumbens*), Tartarian mulberry (*Morus alba tatarica*), Caucasian rhododendron (*Rhododendron caucasicum*), Siberian squill (*Scilla siberica*), prickly comfrey (*Symphytum asperum*), Caucasian scabious (*Scabiosa caucasica*), and many more. Some of the rarities were named after Joachim Conrad Loddiges, such as the oxalis-leaved loddigesia, *Loddigesia oxalidifolia* (now in the genus *Hypocalyptus*), a member of the legume family. These and many others became illustrated in leading botanical journals of the time, especially *Botanical Magazine*.

Joachim's progress was slow but consistent. Not until 50 years after his birth into a German gardener's family did he become the proud owner of a large London nursery on its own site. His career mirrors the gradual rise in importance of commercial plant nurseries, which began to experience rapid development from the mid-18th century onward. It has been suggested by the garden historian John Harvey that the real heyday of the nursery as a major factor in social life for those with wealth and title lasted from about 1760 to 1840. This approximately coincides with the Loddiges family's involvement in the nursery trade and explains how they were able to amass a small fortune.

William (1776–1849) and George Loddiges (1786–1846)

By the early 19th century, transportation and communication links had improved, allowing plant enthusiasts to travel long distances in the pursuit of unusual specimens. The development of reliable small-bore water pipes (enabling smoke-free central heating) and improvements in glazing technology offered new opportunities for the growth and display of plants. A commercial plant nursery could now be designed to lure visitors from afar. Realizing this, Joachim's two sons, William and George, began to supplement the Hackney Field Nursery with a world-class arboretum and experimental hothouses. The horticultural journalist John Claudius Loudon referred to the new attraction as the Hackney Botanic Nursery Garden, which occupied about six hectares (14 acres) from 1816–54. The complete layout was drawn for the second edition of Loudon's *Encyclopaedia of Gardening* (1834).

Through its main entrance the visitor passed at once to a range of hothouses the sheer size of which is difficult to imagine. The centerpiece of the scheme was the Grand Palm House, which was described by Loudon as "the largest hothouse in the world": a structure 25 meters (27 yd.) long, 18 meters (19.6 yd.) wide, and 12 meters (13 yd.) high, containing the greatest collection of tropical palm trees on display in the world. Inside this glass-and-iron paraboloid was an elegant stage, 9 meters (10 yd.) high, from which to view tropical palms, ferns, and orchids. Impressed with this sight, one foreign visitor, Jacob Rinz, commented, "I cannot describe the raptures I experienced on seeing that immense palm house. All that I had before seen of the kind appeared nothing to me compared with this. I fancied myself in the Brazils; and especially at that moment when Mr Loddiges had the kindness to produce, in my presence, a shower of artificial rain."

The near-perfect tropical conditions created by George Loddiges's technological achievements earned him scientific recognition and enabled the nursery to become the first in the world to successfully cultivate many tropical plants, including cycads such as *Zamia loddigesii*, palm trees such as the blue latan palm, *Latania loddigessii*, bromeliads such as *Tillandsia anceps*, and orchids such as *Cattleya loddigesii*. By 1839 Loddiges's nursery was able to publish a catalog devoted entirely to orchids, listing more than 1,600 species and varieties propagated in their hothouses. The list included Loddiges's acropera, *Acropera loddigesii* (now *Gongora galeata*), a splendid tropical orchid named by John Lindley, professor of botany at University College London, in George's honor.

After the Palm House, the visitor entered a Dry Stove House, then a 37-meter-long (40-yd.-long) double Camellia House; these buildings formed a square in the center of which were beds of herbaceous and potted plants available for purchase. The visitor then crossed over a footbridge and onward to a series of decreasing spiral walks one-and-a-half kilometers (0.9 mi.) long, with specimen trees and nursery stock laid out alphabetically: an "A-to-Z" arboretum, starting with *Acer* on the right-hand side of the path. The stock in the front row was left to grow into natural shapes, the stock behind being for sale. "There is no garden scene about London so interesting," exclaims Loudon in the *Gardener's Magazine* (1833). On the left side of the spiral lay huge collections of roses, followed by herbaceous plants. At the end lay a special American garden. In Loudon's opinion, Loddiges's selection of hardy trees and shrubs was unsurpassed: in the *Gardener's Magazine* (1826) he writes admiringly, "There is no such collection of hardy trees and shrubs in the world," and adds, possibly with overstatement, that "in this department Messrs Loddiges have done more than all the royal and botanic gardens put together."

Trees and shrubs introduced into cultivation in Britain by the Loddiges nursery included black bamboo (*Phyllostachys nigra*), Siberian larch, weeping arborvitae, and western red cedar. Others, such as Chinese wisteria, flowered at Loddiges's nursery for the first time outside of their native country. Many were first described scientifically from specimens grown at the nursery, sometimes by members of the Loddiges family themselves, as in the case of the North American shrub *Fothergilla major*. The nursery also put new cultivars into worldwide commerce, such as fern-leaved beech and golden yew. So popular did the nursery become that botanical gardens throughout the world applied for stock. In England the nursery contributed to the Derby Arboretum (1840) and established a second A-to-Z arboretum—which for a time became the largest in the world—at Abney Park Cemetery (1838–40) north of London. Containing 2,500 different species and varieties, this garden cemetery scheme was a horticultural curiosity, being laid out strictly in alphabetical order as in the nursery, with no regard to arrangement by soil preference or country of origin.

Besides its 19th-century specialization in outdoor trees and shrubs and hothouse exotics, the nursery also took a leading role in the development of the Victorian fern craze. By 1825 the nursery grew more than one hundred exotic ferns and had a near monopoly of the fern trade. Forty years later, when the Royal Botanic Garden, Kew, near London, published its text on ferns of the world, it credited the spread of fern cultivation to Loddiges's nursery.

Ferns, tropical plants, outdoor trees and shrubs, and many other plants for which the nursery became famous were promoted through its own publication, the *Botanical Cabinet* (1817–33). Two thousand of the nursery's plants were illustrated in this publication, accompanied by a brief text explaining where the seeds had been collected or how they had arrived at the nursery. The whole Loddiges family was deeply religious, finding expression for this in the *Botanical Cabinet* and through family links with Methodist ministers.

Many of the nursery's achievements in the 19th century were due to the initiative of George Loddiges rather than that of his older brother, William. George was especially quick to understand the link between science and good plantsmanship, being elected to many of the learned societies of his day. He was an expert microscopist and one of several founding members of the Microscopical Society (now the Royal Microscopical Society). George planned and built his own centrally heated house at the nursery, linking it to a new range of stove houses. Inside the house he amassed the largest collection of hummingbirds in the world in the early 19th century. Two hummingbirds were named in his honor: *Trochilus loddigesia* and Loddiges's marvellous spatuletail, *Loddigesia miriabilis*. The ornithologist John Gould, known as "the hummingbird man," used these and many others as subjects for his bookplates and ornithological descriptions. One of George's most lasting scientific contributions was his demonstration of a means of safely transporting tender young plants across the world; a technique based on the use of glazed airtight (Wardian) cases. Use of these cases later enabled imperial powers to establish tea in India, bananas in Asia and Africa, and quinine-producing plants in Europe. They continued to be used by Kew Gardens until the 1940s.

Conrad Loddiges (1821–65)

George and William Loddiges died in the late 1840s, and thereafter the Paradise Field Nursery passed into the hands of George's 28-year-old son Conrad. He shared his family's interest in horticulture and science but had to contend with the pressures of a rapidly changing world. The heyday of the nursery as a cultural icon was passing, the value of exotic plants was falling as they became more commonplace, and rising land values and worsening air quality were forcing nurseries to close or move further from cities such as London. On expiration of the Botanic Nursery Garden's leases, Conrad closed the business entirely rather than take a more prosaic option. It last traded in 1854, although Conrad retained the family's freehold nursery house and garden and continued his learned scientific and horticultural interest in plants, especially orchids, until his death in 1865.

The Loddiges family witnessed vast changes in the nature and role of gardening and plant commerce during the 18th and early 19th centuries. Keeping abreast of these changes, and leading others, they helped create one of the most influential commercial plant nurseries in correspondence with collectors and gardens all over the world. Today botanical gardens from as far afield as Adelaide, Australia; Zurich, Switzerland; and Berlin, Germany, can trace a connection to the family.

Loddiges, Joachim Conrad 1738–ca. 1820

Biography

Born in Hertzberg, Germany, 1738, and raised in Vristbergholtzen, Hanover, Germany. Traveled to Low Countries and England, ca. 1760; specialized as seed merchant and nurseryman near London, importing seeds from William Bartram of North America, ca. 1770; published early trilingual plant catalog, 1777; introduced outdoor and greenhouse flowers from collectors and correspondents worldwide into cultivation near London, ca. 1770–87; established Paradise Field Nursery near London, 1787–1816. Died 1820s.

Loddiges, George 1784–1846, and William 1776–1849

Biography

George born in Hackney, London, 1784; William born in Hackney, 1776. Together, they establish Hackney Botanic Nursery Garden, 1816–40s, with experimental hothouses, largest palm house in world, and world-class arboretum; becomes first commercial nursery to grow tropical orchids successfully; specializes in tropical plants and outdoor trees and shrubs; botanical gardens from Adelaide to Zurich and Bonn develop connections with Loddiges's nursery; George links scientific developments and societies to nursery; becomes expert painter, microscopist, and taxidermist; amasses largest collection of hummingbirds in world; develops technique for safely transporting tender young plants across salt seas. William died in 1840s; George died in Hackney, 1846.

Loddiges, Conrad 1821–1865

Biography

Born, 1821. Closes family nursery, ca. 1854; continues private interest in plants. Died in Hackney, 1865.

Selected Designs

1816–40 Hackney Botanic Nursery Garden, near London, England

1838–40 Abney Park Cemetery, near London, England

Selected Publications

The Botanical Cabinet, 20 vols., 1817–33

Further Reading

Best, Barbara Joyce, *George William Francis: First Director of the Adelaide Botanic Garden: A Biography,* Adelaide, Victoria: Botanic Gardens of Adelaide, 1986

Cross, Anthony, "Russian Gardens, British Gardeners," *Garden History* 19, no. 1 (1991)

Desmond, Ray, *A Celebration of Flowers: Two Hundred Years of Curtis's Botanical Magazine,* Kew: Royal Botanic Gardens, 1987

Hadfield, Miles, *Gardening in Britain,* London: Hutchinson, and Newton, Massachusetts: Branford, 1960; as *A History of British Gardening,* London: Penguin, 1985

Harvey, John Hooper, *Early Nurserymen,* London: Phillimore, 1974

Harvey, John Hooper, *Mid-Georgian Nurseries of the London Region,* London: London and Middlesex Archaeological Society, 1975

Joyce, Paul, *A Guide to Abney Park Cemetery,* London: Save Abney Park Cemetery, 1984

Leighton, Ann, *American Gardens in the Eighteenth Century: "For Use or for Delight,"* Boston: Houghton Mifflin, 1976

Loudon, John Claudius, *Arboretum et Fruticetum Britannicum,* 8 vols., London, 1838; 2nd edition, as *Arbotetum et Fruticetum Britannicum; or, The Trees and Shrubs of Britain,* 8 vols., London, 1844; abridged edition, as *An Encyclopaedia of Trees and Shrubs: Being the Arboretum et Fruticetum Britannicum Abridged,* New York, 1869

Solman, David, *Loddiges of Hackney: The Largest Hothouse in the World,* edited by Jane Straker, London: Hackney Society, 1995

David Solman

Lomonosov. *See* Oranienbaum (Lomonosov)

London, George d. 1714

English Garden Designer and Nurseryman

At the end of the 17th century, the names of George London and his partner, Henry Wise, were familiar to every owner of an English country estate. The restoration of the monarchy in 1660 encouraged a massive boom in the creation and renovation of properties neglected or destroyed during the Civil War, with members of the nobility striving to emulate the French formal gardens of André Le Nôtre.

London, a young man of unknown descent, was apprenticed to John Rose, gardener to Lord Essex at Essex House in the Strand and reputedly a pupil of Le Nôtre's. Rose took London to visit France in the early 1670s and introduced him to Henry Compton, bishop of London, who employed him as a gardener at Fulham Palace. The bishop was influential in London's career as a fervent Protestant, a supporter of William of Orange, and a passionate plant collector. London left his service in 1681 to set up the Brompton Park Nursery with three other experienced gardeners; it was located on a 100-acre (40-ha) site between the present Kensington and Brompton roads. In 1687 he was joined by Wise, and the nursery continued under their partnership to supply

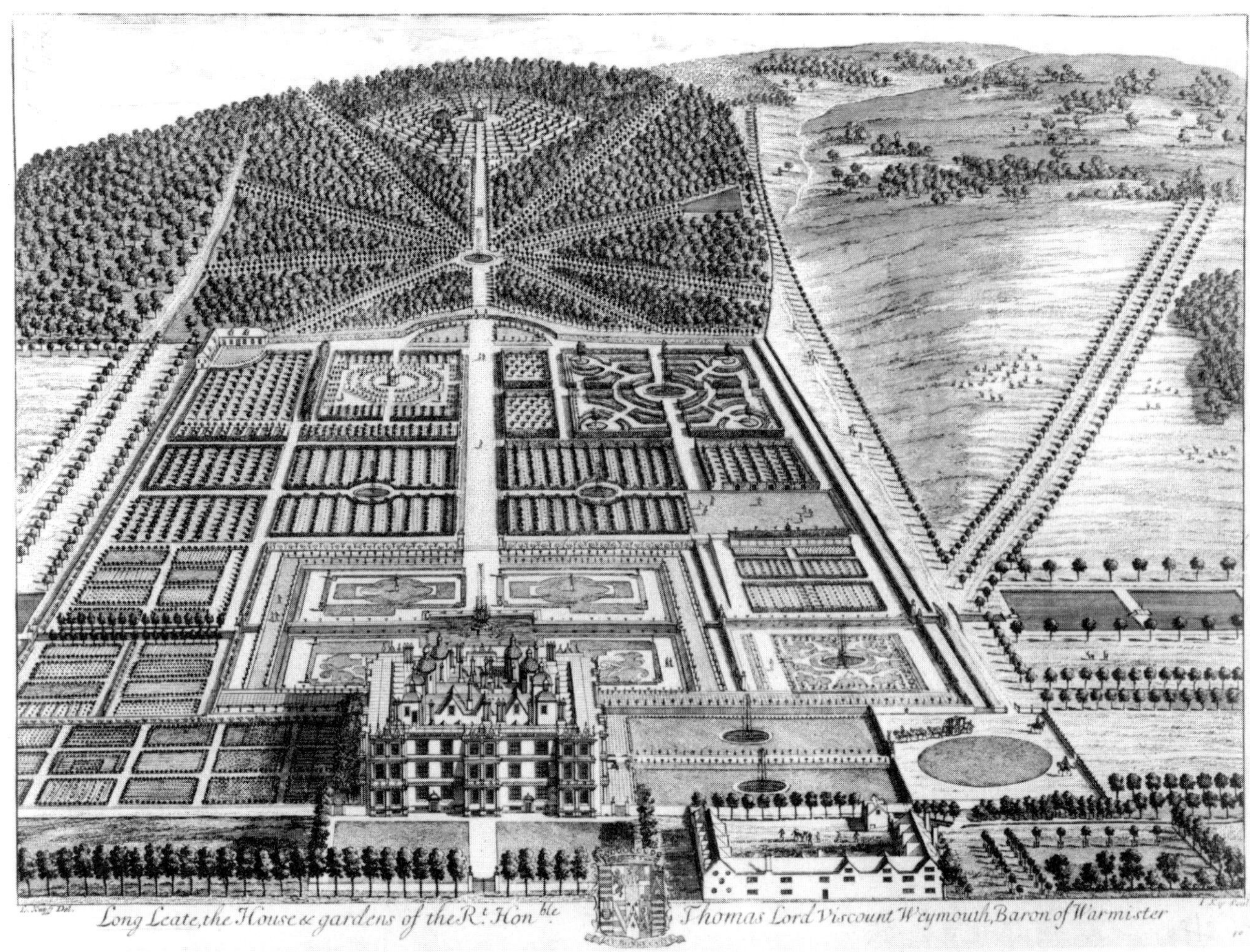

Bird's-eye view of Longleat House and gardens
Courtesy of British Library

plants for royalty and most of the country estates in England until London's death in 1714, by which time its reputation was already greatly diminished. London's early work was completed for his patron, King William, at Hampton Court, where he worked on the Wilderness and Privy Garden, and subsequently at the king's new country retreat at Kensington Palace.

With no known portrait of London, the only description of him is provided by Stephen Switzer in his *Ichnographica Rustica* (1715). Switzer recalls an immensely energetic person who rode up to 60 miles (97 km) a day visiting clients all over England. He also comments on London's expertise in the growing of fruit trees and his unusual knowledge of shrubs, trees, flowers, and exotics, adding that "he might not always come up to the highest pitch of design."

With the Brompton Park partnership involved in more than 60 gardens over 20 years, London's involvement as a designer varied from project to project; sometimes it was limited to supplying a plan or giving planting instructions to a local gardener.

As illustrated in an engraving by Knyff and Kip, an early project for Longleat House (an extensive late 17th-century formal garden in Luittshire) shows a typical London layout. Although the plan was influenced by the contemporary French formal garden, there are certain conspicuous differences, such as the repositioning of the axis to the side of the house. The parterre, its design often borrowed from contemporary pattern books, is one of the constant features of London's gardens, made either in cut turf (as at Chatsworth) or planted in box, with myrtles, hollies, and standard honeysuckles and underplanted with a range of plants and bulbs (as at Dyrham). Wildernesses, as proposed for Badminton, Castle Howard, and Chatsworth, are another feature of London's designs, together with bowling greens.

The once formal gardens of Dyrham Park, described in Switzer's *Ichnographica Rustica* and recorded in an engraving by Kip (1712), have been almost entirely lost beneath later landscaping. Traces of Wanstead Park, London's last and most ambitious project, can still be found in a public park, but the only scheme surviving almost untouched is the garden of Melbourne Hall in Derbyshire. Although intended to evoke Versailles, the garden is diminutive in size and, with its overgrown topiary hedges, is green and luxuriant as only an English garden can be.

See also Chatsworth Gardens; Gardenesque Style; Hampton Court Palace and Bushy Park

Biography
Place and date of birth unknown. Apprenticed to John Rose, gardener to Lord Essex at Essex House, 1661–77; traveled with Rose to France, where he probably met André Le Nôtre in early 1670s; introduced to Henry Compton, Bishop of London, and worked as his gardener at Fulham Palace; with Protestant bishop, became involved in political moves to bring William of Orange to English throne; junior partner in setting-up of Brompton Park Nursery, 1681; took Henry Wise as partner, 1688; appointed deputy superintendent of royal parks under William Bentinck, 1688; traveled to Holland and met Paul Hermann, cultivator of plants from the Cape; met architect William Talman in late 1680s and maintained lifelong collaboration and friendship; countrywide travel to supervise design and construction of gardens, 1690s. Died at Edgar, Hertsfordshire, England, 12 January 1714.

Selected Designs

1683–1714	Longleat House (with Brompton Park partners), Wiltshire, England
1688–95	Chatsworth House, Derbyshire, England
1689–99	Privy Garden, Hampton Court (work for William and Mary), Middlesex, England
1689	Kensington Gardens (work for William and Mary), London, England
1692	New Park, Richmond, Surrey, England
1699	Castle Howard, Yorkshire, England
1700	Dyrham Park, Gloucestershire, England
1704	Melbourne Hall, Derby, England; Marshal Tallard's garden, Nottingham, England
1706	Wanstead Park, Essex, England
1706–14	Canons Gardens, Middlesex, England (unfinished at time of London's death)

Selected Publications
The Compleat Gard'ner (with Henry Wise), a translation from the French by Jean de la Quintinie, 1699
The Retir'd Gard'ner (with Henry Wise), a translation from the French by Francois Gentil, 1706

Further Reading

Blomfield, Reginald, *The Formal Garden in England,* London, 1892; reprint, London: Waterstone, 1985; 3rd edition, London and New York: Macmillan, 1901; reprint, New York: AMS Press, 1972

Harris, John, *William Talman, Maverick Architect,* London and Boston: Allen and Unwin, 1982

Jacques, David, and Arend Jan Van der Horst, *The Gardens of William and Mary,* London: Helm, 1988

La Quintinie, Jean de, *Instruction pour les jardins fruitiers et potagers, avec un Traité des orangers, suivy de quelgues Réflexions sur l'agriculture,* 2 vols., Paris, 1690; reprint, Arles: Actes Sud, 1999; as *The Compleat Gard'ner; or, Directions for Cultivating and Right Ordering of Fruit-Gardens and Kitchen Gardens,* translated by John Evelyn, London, 1693; reprint, New York: Garland, 1982

Switzer, Stephen, *Ichnographia Rustica; or, The Nobleman, Gentleman, and Gardener's Recreation,* London, 1715; reprint, 3 vols., New York: Garland, 1982

Thacker, Christopher, *The History of Gardens*, London: Croom Helm, and Berkeley: University of California Press, 1979

SANDRA MORRIS

London Parks

London, England

London is a green capital. Today, in the metropolis of Greater London as a whole, 2,000 parks or open spaces have been laid out or altered in some way. They range in size from Epping Forest (2,500 ha [6,178 acres]) and the Lea Valley Regional Park (4,000 ha [9,884 acres]) to many that are small and highly specialized.

London's parks can be divided into three main historical types: (1) the original "public promenades," for example, the great royal parks of Central London whose landscape has evolved gradually since the 17th century; (2) the "public park proper," a later, mainly 19th-century phenomenon representing a conscious expression of metropolitan improvement and town planning; (3) the "parks of the recent period," a characteristic of which has been diversification and differentiation.

Public Promenade Park

The original purpose of parks in London was healthful exercise—synonymous with walking—which led to the creation of ornamental pleasure grounds with pleasant places to promenade. As early as the 17th century, open space close to the City of London began to be laid out or altered for this purpose. The earliest example was Moorfields, where public walks, shaded by elm trees, were laid out in 1605–7. Today only a tiny part remains, called Finsbury Circus.

Better known, and surviving more completely, are the great royal parks of Central London; an interlinked complex of open spaces comprising Hyde Park, Green Park, St. James's Park, and Kensington Gardens. In these parks a great many walks have been established over the centuries, each shaded by vast numbers of oaks, planes, limes, horse chestnuts, and (at one time) elms. The finest promenades lead all the way from St. James's Park through Hyde Park to Kensington Palace, a distance of 3.5 kilometers (2.2 mi.). Since the time of George III trees have been planted on either side of the principal walks at equal distances and lighted in the dark season to great effect.

The largest of the parks through which these great promenades pass is Hyde Park, the northeast side of which is the famous Speakers' Corner, where people are free to speak their mind. Informal access to Hyde Park has long been possible since it lay unenclosed after its acquisition by Henry VIII as a royal hunting chase, but regular public use was not intended by the Crown until the 1630s, initially for horseback riding and then for promenading. The concept of public promenading was developing elsewhere in Europe at this time: the Tiergarten in Berlin was made accessible to the public for *Lustwandeln* (pleasure-strolling) in 1649, and the Chamars, in Besançon, one of France's earliest public promenades, was planted with lime trees to improve public enjoyment in 1653. A year later in England, the diarist John Evelyn became the first to apply the term *avenue* to tree-lined walks, the public and private popularity of which was increasing.

In London public promenading in Hyde Park was interrupted during the Commonwealth interregnum of the mid-17th century, when the land was temporarily sold and access charges introduced. Access was also limited throughout the 18th century whenever Hyde Park—by then secured behind a perimeter wall—was needed for private, royal or military purposes. Free public access for promenading was more consistently expressed at St. James's Park, which was set aside for public walks after the Restoration.

In terms of landscape design these promenade parks have evolved gradually, reflecting changes in use and fashion. The design of St. James's Park as a public promenade was executed in about 1660 by the French architect and landscape designer André Le Nôtre. Le Nôtre incorporated the ideas of André Mollet about axial tree-lined walks laid out in exact proportions, as explained in his book *Le jardin de plaisir* (1651). A similar geometric approach to ornamental water features and waterside paths led to construction of the canal, which, now in a more natural style, still accommodates the park's collection of exotic ducks. Such formality of design—more art than nature—was the vogue for promenades in the late 17th century. Later, a group of writers, especially Alexander Pope, mocked Le Nôtre's stiff and formal style and the excesses of the formal park in general. The massive Serpentine River, constructed in Hyde Park at the request of George II's wife, Caroline, reflected this criticism, being laid out in a more sinuous, naturalistic style under the supervision of William Kent.

In the early 19th century the wide range of trees and shrubs becoming available in botanical gardens and nurseries offered an opportunity to make public walks more interesting and educational. Before long, London's famous Loddiges Nursery was called upon to supply rare trees and shrubs for walks in St. James's Park and Kensington Gardens. So painstakingly were these specimens labeled that the horticultural journalist and polymath John Claudius Loudon recommended they be used as a reference collection.

Later, in common with many Victorian parks, bedding plants were introduced: geraniums and roses in summer, tulips and hyacinths in spring. In other ways too the central London royal parks became increasingly similar to the new public parks, copying their cafés, monuments, and boating facilities. The simple promenade had given way to much more complex and elaborate uses.

Public Park Proper

To provide for a wide range of healthy outdoor pursuits, a public park movement emerged in London in the early 19th century, aiming to establish new, multipurpose parks in all districts. The rudiments of a plan for a multitude of new parks in the London area had been prepared long before by Evelyn, author of *Silva* (1664), the Royal Society's publication about forest trees. Following the Great Fire of London in 1666, Evelyn had advocated a ring of new parks around the city, each planted with fragrant trees and shrubs.

Evelyn's proposal lay dormant until the early 19th century, when interest in public parks was reawakened and the park ideal enlarged upon. Contributing to this development was the work of social and civic reformers, writers, and thinkers, including, among others, Loudon; the precedent set by Regent's Park, a new purpose-built public park; and a report by a select committee of the House of Commons, which recommended the establishment of public parks for poorer districts.

In 1829 Loudon fostered the debate by describing parks as "breathing zones" and publishing a remarkable scheme for green spaces at regular intervals around London. Later, he embellished this idea by suggesting that "the beau ideal" for public parks was to be found at the Loddiges' Botanic Nursery Garden in Hackney, where visitors could immerse themselves in a landscape of exotic trees and shrubs from all over the world.

Those who supported Loudon's plans for a series of new public parks in London invariably looked to the example set by the Crown at the latest royal park, Regent's Park. It was not a perfect model, however. Regent's Park was not fully open to the public until the 1840s; its original design was never fully completed; and to Loudon's way of thinking, its selection of trees and shrubs was poor. Nonetheless, the park's design (1812–26) by John Nash was of great distinction. It consisted of two concentric circles comprising an area of 149 hectares (368 acres); the inner circle contained gardens, the outer Regency terraces and imposing gateways. When completed, the park included the London Zoo, the Regent's Canal, a fine boating lake with colorful species of birds, a bandstand, fragrant flower gardens, and much more.

Interest in Regent's Park led members of Parliament to consider whether similar public parks should be built in less fashionable districts; a view supported by the parliamentary Select Committee on Public Walks in 1833. As a result Victoria Park (1845) was created in London's poverty-stricken East End. It was the first sizeable public park in London that was not strictly a royal park. Although greatly admired by many, Victoria Park was seen by some as a missed opportunity. The design, for which James Pennethorne, a protégé of John Nash, was largely responsible, did not satisfy the botanist John Lindley, who wrote a damning article in the *Gardeners' Chronicle.* Perhaps to fend off such critics, the design of Battersea Park (ca. 1853–59) was assisted by John Gibson, a protégé of Joseph Paxton. At this date Paxton's design for Britain's first truly municipal park at Birkenhead (1843–47) was seen as the exemplar of the public park. Battersea Park's eventual design centered on a grand avenue that bisected the park. At one end were a lake and islands, and, from the 1870s onward, a rock garden that quickly became the most famous rockery in a public park in the country. The park also became renowned in the 1860s for Gibson's subtropical garden.

After 1856 responsibility for planning new parks passed from Parliament to a newly elected body for the capital's local government, the Metropolitan Board of Works (later called the London County Council and thereafter the Greater London Council). It set forth a program to lay out additional open spaces, many of which were simply small churchyards or playgrounds. These smaller projects, however, did not compromise the board's main objective of creating a large park in each district of the capital. This involved the purchase or donation of a wide range of terrain: market gardens for Southwark Park (1864); ancient common land and farmland for Peckham Rye Park and Common (1894); existing fine parkland with cedars, chestnuts, and a rare tree collection, as well as a historic common, for Clissold Park (1889).

Although the topography and vegetation were different in each case, the new district public parks characteristically adopted common design elements. Unless the parks were intended to be seminatural (though these were usually acquired and maintained by the Corporation of London, which had its own program) they usually included entrance pillars, perimeter railings, gates and lodges, drinking fountains, carriage drives, flowerbeds, aviaries, bandstands, ornamental or recreational water features, and tree-lined promenades. Background planting frequently made use of smoke-tolerant trees such as the London plane, but many of the new public parks also incorporated a range of exotic trees planted in Loudon's "gardenesque" style or in separate botanical collections. The most unusual and impressive trees were sought out and described in print in the early 20th century by enthusiasts such as Kate Hall and A.D. Webster. The late Victorian birdlife of London's parks was also extensively written about, especially by the journalist and travel writer W.H. Hudson.

The highest design standard achieved among the large Victorian parks in London is generally attributed to Paxton's imaginative Crystal Palace Park (1854), which was also intended to be scientifically instructive. Islands in the park's lake represented different strata in the Earth's crust and were adorned with life-size models of prehistoric animals.

Parks of the Recent Period

In modern times, and more particularly in the last two decades of the 20th century, there has been a continuing diversification in the design and role of public parks in London. A notable development has been the emergence of the ecological park, a phenomenon that largely dates from the early 1980s. Examples include the Camley Street Natural Park near King's Cross (1985) and the Wildlife Garden Centre (1988) in East Dulwich, south

London. Elsewhere there has been a major revival of interest in the potential of the 19th-century garden cemeteries as public parks. This idea was encouraged by Loudon, who had suggested a century earlier that garden cemeteries "might become a school of architecture, sculpture, landscape gardening, arboriculture and botany." Abney Park Cemetery in north London is now being used as a park; a visitor center opened in 1990. Here the original 19th-century design incorporated an unusual A-to-Z arboretum by George Loddiges, a little of which remains today. Most popular of all is Highgate Cemetery in north London, promoted since the 1980s as a tourist attraction.

As these new types of park have emerged, less emphasis has been given to designing large multipurpose parks in the metropolis itself. Nonetheless, in south and east London two such parks, Burgess Park and Mile End Park, have been slowly taking shape. One important factor in the dearth of large new parks in London has been the development of regional parks and country parks beyond the city fringe. At the end of the century, however, as city planning began to focus increasingly on reducing commuting distances it seemed an opportune time to consider once again how best to plan for parks in London.

Synopsis

17th–18th Century: Public Promenade Park

1605–7	Moorfields, London, laid out as early example of pleasant public promenade (today only Finsbury Circus remains)
1630s	Hyde Park brought into regular public use, initially for equestrian purposes, then for promenading
mid-17th C.	Hyde Park sold and access charges imposed
1660	St. James's Park designed as public promenade park with canal, by André Le Nôtre
1700–1800	Alexander Pope mocks original, formal design of St. James's Park; in Hyde Park, Serpentine River laid out in naturalistic style supervised by William Kent
1828	St. James's Park layout changed by John Nash, canal turned into lake

19th Century: Public Park Proper

1812–26	Regent's Park designed by John Nash, as exemplar of purpose-designed park, including London Zoo and Regent's Canal
1829	J.C. Loudon publishes remarkable scheme for green spaces ("breathing zones") at equal intervals around London
1833	Parliamentary Select Committee on Public Walks recommends new public parks for less fashionable districts of London
1840s	Regent's Park fully opened to public
1845	Victoria Park opens in London's poverty-stricken East End, designed by James Pennethorne (first large park in capital not strictly a royal park)
ca. 1853–59	John Gibson, protégé of Joseph Paxton, designs Battersea Park in south London
1854	Paxton's imaginative Crystal Palace Park opens in south London
1856	Responsibility for planning new parks in London passes to Metropolitan Board of Works
1856–99	Many new district parks established in London, such as Southwark Park, Clissold Park, and Peckham Rye Park and Common
1870s	Rockwork in Battersea Park completed

20th Century: Parks of the Recent Period

1950s–90s	Two large new multipurpose parks laid out painstakingly slowly in London: Burgess Park and Mile End Park
1960s–90s	Regional and country parks laid out for London
1980s	Restoration and improvement of 19th-century garden cemeteries as public parks, including Highgate Cemetery
1980s	Opening of ecological parks such as Camley Street Natural Park near King's Cross

Further Reading

Forshaw, Alec, and Theo Bergstrom, *The Open Spaces of London,* London: Allison and Busby, 1986

Galinou, Mireille, editor, *London's Pride: The Glorious History of the Capital's Gardens,* London: Anaya, 1990

Grove, A.B., and Creswell, Roy W., *City Landscape,* London and Boston: Butterworths, 1983

Hall, Kate M., *Nature Rambles in London,* London: Hodder and Stoughton, 1908

Hudson, William Henry, *Birds in London,* London and New York, 1898; reprint, New York: AMS Press, 1968; Newton Abbot: David and Charles, 1969

Joyce, Paul, *A Guide to Abney Park Cemetery,* London: A Save Abney Park Cemetery Publication, 1984; 2nd edition, Abney Park Cemetery Trust, 1994

Kent, Douglas H., *The Historical Flora of Middlesex: An Account of the Wild Plants Found in the Watsonian Vice-County 21 from 1548 to Present Time,* London: Ray Society, 1975
Lasdun, Susan, *The English Park: Royal, Private, and Public,* London: Deutsch, 1991; New York: Vendome Press, 1992
Loudon, John Claudius, *On the Laying Out, Planting, and Management of Cemeteries: And on the Improvement of Churchyards,* London, 1843; reprint, Ilkley, Yorkshire: Scolar Press, 1981
Nussey, Helen G., *London Gardens of the Past,* London: John Lane, 1939
Sexby, J.J., *The Municipal Parks, Gardens, and Open Spaces of London: Their History and Associations,* London: Elliot Stock, 1898
Simo, Melanie Louise, *Loudon and the Landscape: From Country Seat to Metropolis, 1783–1843,* New Haven, Connecticut: Yale University Press, 1988
Solman, David, *Loddiges of Hackney, the Largest Hothouse in the World,* London: Hackney Society, 1995
Thornbury, Walter, and Edward Walford, editors, *Old and New London: A Narrative of Its History, Its People, and Its Places,* 6 vols., London, 1873–78; as *London Recollected: Its History, Lore, and Legend,* London: Alderman Press, 1985–
Webster, Angus Duncan, *London Trees: Being an Account of the Trees that Succeed in London,* London: Swarthmore Press, 1920
Wroth, Warwick William, and Arthur Edgar Wroth, *The London Pleasure Gardens of the Eighteenth Century,* London and New York, 1896; reprint, Hamden, Connecticut: Archon Books, and London: Macmillan, 1979

DAVID SOLMAN

Loudon, John Claudius 1783–1843

English Author, Architect, and Landscape Designer

Loudon, Jane Webb 1807–1858

English Gardening Writer

John Claudius Loudon lived at a time of great change in England, a period of discovery, opportunity, and social mobility. The vehicle of progress was the industrial revolution, a process that had begun during the 18th century but which had leapt forward with increased mechanization at the beginning of the 19th century. The resultant commercial and occupational opportunities created an expanded and affluent middle class, whose members could afford to move from the overcrowded cities to new villas with gardens on the countryside fringe. Loudon was not always a shrewd businessman, but he was a man of vision. He saw the inhabitants of suburban villas as a new class of garden owners who needed guidance to design and cultivate their gardens according to individual preference rather than fashionable taste. Although Loudon's prolific literary output between 1803 and 1845 encompasses horticulture, agriculture, and architecture in addition to garden matters, it was primarily for these new garden owners that he wrote many of his books and magazines.

At the beginning of the 19th century, Loudon's views on design were influenced by the theories of Sir Uvedale Price, who believed that a garden should espouse the qualities of a landscape painting. When Loudon moved from Scotland to England soon after the turn of the century, his practice as a landscape gardener provided him with the opportunity to introduce variety, intricacy, irregularity, and the rugged beauty of Price's picturesque ideal into his garden designs of this period. A notable example was Barnbarrow, near Wigton, portrayed in one of Loudon's early works, *A Treatise on Forming, Improving, and Managing Country Residences* (1806).

Rheumatic fever prevented Loudon from continuing practical landscaping at this time, and he turned his attention to farming, leasing Wood Hall Farm, near Pinner, Middlesex, for his convalescence. The opportunity to make structural changes to the house at Wood Hall Farm fueled Loudon's developing interest in architecture, which until then was mainly confined to garden structures such as summerhouses and hothouses. Furthermore, he decided to demonstrate the superiority of Scottish farming methods over the English and with his father went on to create a successful working farm there, described in *Designs for Laying Out Farms and Farm-Buildings in the Scotch Style* (1811). Loudon was asked to manage General Stratton's vast estate at Tew Lodge in Oxfordshire, where he created a grand *ferme ornée* (ornamental farm) and established one of the earliest agricultural colleges in England.

Following the Napoleonic Wars Loudon traveled extensively throughout Europe, collecting material for his most important work, the comprehensive *An Encyclopaedia of Gardening* (1822). This work provided a wealth of information for all gardeners and garden owners, presenting not only the practical, technical, and horticultural aspects of gardening but also a historical overview of British gardens. Moreover, during the period of his travels abroad, Loudon, who had always been fascinated by the effect of the constraints placed on plants grown under artificial conditions, applied his technical knowledge to glasshouse construction. He invented a form of roof construction called *ridge and furrow;* more important, he provided a solution to the problem of increasing natural light in a glasshouse by inventing a wrought-iron curved glazing bar to replace the thick wooden struts otherwise required to support the weight of the glass. The first curvilinear structure, based on Loudon's principles, was at Bretton Hall, Yorkshire, built in 1827.

By the 1820s Loudon's views on laying out gardens were further influenced by the classical gardens of Europe visited on his travels and by his reading of the theories of the Neoplatonist Quatremere de Quincy. Quatremere argues that, to be considered a work of art, a garden must be distinguishable from nature, rather than an idealized copy of it. Loudon began to promote the idea of a more formal regular garden in which "lines, surfaces and forms . . . should be different, and in some degree opposed to those of general nature" (*Encyclopaedia of Gardening*). The importance of distinguishing the work of humankind from that of nature is also reflected in Loudon's proposals for a new style of planting, which he termed the *gardenesque.* For most designed landscapes this means that trees and plants should be placed individually in a regular layout rather than as natural groups. Alternatively, Loudon proposed that artificiality could be emphasised by using among indigenous species exotic plants brought back by plant hunters. However, Loudon later refined the term *gardenesque,* his new definition in *The Suburban Gardener and Villa Companion* (1838) being more concerned with horticultural practice than the philosophy of artifice: "All the trees, shrubs and plants in the gardenesque style are planted and managed in such a way as that each may arrive at perfection and display its beauties to as great advantage as if it were cultivated for that purpose alone."

By the 1830s Loudon was also associated with a variation on the gardenesque style of gardening, one that is recognizably artificial but at the same time is based on a more naturalistic, informal design. This style, dubbed *rococo revival* (a term taken from a contemporary style of interior design) by Brent Elliott, made complementary use of symmetrical organization and irregular shapes, such as C- and S-shapes, half moons, and scrolls. Loudon's design and planting principles had the advantage of adapting with ease to the smaller villa residence and gardens planted on gardenesque principles popular in England at the time.

Although publications such as *An Encyclopaedia of Gardening* were considered essential reference books, the spread of contemporary horticultural knowledge and garden fashions was made possible through the increasing number of garden journals available. Loudon's articles in his innovative *Gardener's Magazine* (first published in 1826) had popular appeal, and flower-bed designs based on gardenesque and rococo-revival principles were published for his readers to copy.

Loudon's belief in the importance of artifice and his increasing appreciation of the garden as a functional outside space clearly signaled that he had philosophically moved on from the picturesque theories of Uvedale Price. Despite earlier criticisms of the work of the landscape designer Humphry Repton, Loudon's position was now closer to Repton's view that gardens were "not to be laid out with a view to their appearance in a picture, but to their uses, and the enjoyment of them in real life" (Repton). Loudon's delayed admiration of Repton's work came as a result of Repton's later interest in villa gardens and was demonstrated when Loudon edited the designer's collected works in 1840.

Loudon's work output was prodigious, despite poor health and constant pain caused by rheumatic fever—he could not walk easily, his left arm was almost useless, and his right arm had been amputated. In 1830, at the age of 47, he was fortunate in meeting Jane Wells Webb, a 23-year-old author of fiction and verse. After they married Jane devoted herself to making his life comfortable and assisting him in his work, becoming his amanuensis when Loudon's disabilities prevented him from writing. They made their home at Porchester Terrace in London's Bayswater, living in the three-story semidetached villa designed by Loudon in 1823 (which still exists today). There, in his beautifully planned garden, Loudon was able to cultivate his favorite plants and conduct his horticultural experiments.

With his wife's practical help and support, Loudon's volume of work increased during the 1830s. The two traveled extensively in England, describing the gardens visited in articles for *The Gardener's Magazine.* Loudon completed several more comprehensive works, including the well-received *Encyclopaedia of Cottage, Farm, and Villa Architecture and Furniture* (1833), the success of which gave rise to *Architectural Magazine* in 1834. Less financially successful was the eight-volume, lavishly illustrated *Arboretum et Fruticetum Britannicum* (1838), which describes all native and exotic trees and shrubs grown in Britain.

An Encyclopeadia of Gardening offers guidelines for the laying out of private gardens, ranging from the functional cottage garden to the pleasure grounds of a country mansion. However, Loudon reaffirmed his commitment to the middle-class villa owner in *The Suburban Gardener and Villa Companion,* remarking that "a suburban residence with a small portion of land attached, will contain all that is essential to happiness." In this well-known publication Loudon extends his earlier classifications of villa gardens. His hierarchy now ranges from first- to fourth-rate gardens, dependent on the size of the garden, the distance of the house from the entrance gate, and whether there is a park or farm attached and separate pleasure grounds, lawns, and kitchen garden. His recommendations for laying out each rate of garden are dependent on the social status of the owner and include the siting of garden features, appropriate plants, and the likely costs involved. One of Loudon's favorite gardens was at Mrs. Lawrence's villa in Drayton Green, an example of what could be achieved in a second-rate garden of two to ten acres (0.8 ha to 4 ha).

In England in the 1830s, the escape from congested city centers was paralleled by a realization that the expansion in building programs was gradually eroding public open space and the opportunity for healthy leisure pursuits. Although Loudon encouraged his readers to garden for physical and psychological benefits, he was also an advocate of public access to the well-known gardens of the day and for the provision of parks and other public open spaces. He was instrumental in changing the wall in the Bayswater Road around Kensington Gardens to iron railings to allow passersby a view in. Many early parks open to the public (at a charge) were privately owned; Loudon's designs for the Birmingham Botanic Garden (1830) and Terrace Garden in Gravesend (1836) fell into this category. His later acclaimed design for the Derby Arboretum, built for Joseph Strutt in 1840 and still in existence, provided Loudon with the opportunity to both create a public landscape and put into practice gardenesque planting on a large scale. The ground plan includes a sinuous peripheral walk and two main axes, with sidewalks leading to the main areas, all fully described in Loudon's *The Derby Arboretum* (1840).

The last few years of Loudon's life were an attempt to ward off bankruptcy and, despite constant illness, a continuation of his punishing writing schedule. He also became involved in the planning and laying out of cemeteries (*On the Laying Out, Planting, and Managing of Cemeteries: And on the Improvement of Churchyards* [1843]). Loudon also started writing *Self-Instruction for Young Gardeners* (1845), a manual aimed at the newly emerging gardening profession, whose working conditions and knowledge he was keen to improve. After several bouts of pneumonia, on 14 December 1843, while dictating to his wife, Loudon collapsed and died. He is buried in Kensal Green Cemetery near his home in Bayswater.

Although ignorant of horticulture when she met her husband, after her marriage Jane Loudon studied the subject and between 1830 and 1855 published 19 books on horticulture and botany, mostly aimed at women gardeners. Like her husband, Jane Loudon wanted to educate her readers; her books contained not only factual accounts but practical advice to women in the Victorian period, when a lady was not expected to engage in robust tasks such as digging. For example, in one of her best-known works, *Instructions in Gardening for Ladies* (1840), she comments that "digging appears at first sight . . . particularly unfitted to delicately formed hands and feet" but could be simplified by a little "attention to the principles of mechanics and the laws of motion." Jane Loudon's other well-known works include *The Lady's Companion to the Flower Garden* (1841) and the journal *The Ladies' Flower Garden,* which she founded and edited from 1839. She was also the first editor of *The Ladies' Companion,* published from 1849. After her husband's death in 1843, Jane Loudon completed his last book, *Self-Instruction for Young Gardeners,* and revised and republished his works.

John Claudius Loudon was a man of integrity and vision, often severe in his criticisms of others but concerned with improving the human condition. Jane Loudon, in her way, was equally formidable but undoubtedly more compassionate. Her description of her husband in "A Short Account of the Life and Writings of John Claudius Loudon" (1845) provides a rare insight into the personality of this driven and remarkable man: "Mr. Loudon was not a man of many words, and he was never fond of showing the knowledge he possessed; but it was astonishing how much he did know on every subject to which he turned his attention."

See also Derby Arboretum; London Parks

Loudon, John Claudius 1783–1843

Biography

Born in Cambuslang, Lanarkshire, Scotland, 1783.
Following apprenticeship to landscape gardener in

Scotland, settled in London, 1803, and elected Fellow of Linnean Society, 1806; began writing on gardening and agriculture, including several encyclopedic works, from 1806; suffered from rheumatism, after 1806, and took up farming; sold farm at Tew Lodge in Oxfordshire, 1811, and traveled throughout Europe collecting material for his *Encyclopaedia of Gardening,* published 1822; started and edited *Gardener's Magazine,* from 1826, *Magazine of Natural History,* from 1829, and short-lived *Architectural Magazine,* from 1834–1838; married Jane Webb, 1830, who revised and republished his writings after his death. Died in Bayswater, London, 1843.

Selected Designs

1806	Barnbarrow, Scotland
ca. 1808–11	*Ferme ornée,* Tew Lodge, Great Tew, Oxfordshire, England
1823	Garden, Loudon's home, Porchester Terrace, Bayswater, London, England
1831	Birmingham Botanic Garden, Birmingham, West Midlands, England
1836	Terrace Garden, Gravesend, Kent, England
1840	Derby Arboretum, Derby, Derbyshire, England

Selected Publications

Treatise on Forming, Improving, and Managing Country Residences, *1806*

Designs for Laying Out Farms and Farm-Buildings in the Scotch Style, Adapted to England, 1811

Encyclopaedia of Gardening, 1822; 4th edition, edited by Jane Webb Loudon, 1834

Gardener's Magazine, 19 vols., 1826–43

Encyclopaedia of Cottage, Farm, and Villa Architecture and Furniture, 1833; 2nd edition, 1842; 3rd edition, edited by Jane Webb Loudon, 1846

Architectural Magazine, 5 vols., 1834–38

Arboretum et Fruticetum Britannicum, 8 vols., 1838

The Suburban Gardener, and Villa Companion, 1838; 2nd edition, as *The Villa Gardener,* edited by Jane Webb Loudon, 1850

Derby Arboretum, 1840

Landscape Gardening and Landscape Architecture of the late Humphry Repton, 1840

On the Laying Out, Planting, and Managing of Cemeteries: And on the Improvement of Churchyards, 1843

Self-Instruction for Young Gardeners, Foresters, Bailiffs, Land-Stewards, and Farmers, with Jane Webb Loudon, 1845

Loudon, Jane Webb 1807–1858

Biography

Born in Birmingham, England, 1807. Began as writer of fiction and verse; married John Claudius Loudon, 1830; helped Loudon in compilation of books and periodicals, 1830–43; published 19 books on plants and gardens, mainly for female readers, 1839–48. Died in London, 13 July 1858.

Selected Publications

Ladies' Flower Garden, 1839–48

Instructions in Gardening for Ladies, 1840

Ladies' Companion to the Flower Garden, 1841

"A Short Account of the Life and Writings of John Claudius Loudon," in *Self-Instruction for Young Gardeners, Foresters, Bailiffs, Land-Stewards, and Farmers,* by John Claudius Loudon, with Jane Webb Loudon, 1845

Amateur Gardener's Calendar, 1847

Further Reading

Boniface, Priscilla, editor, *In Search of English Gardens: The Travels of John Claudius Loudon and His Wife Jane,* Wheathampstead, Hertfordshire: Lennard, 1987

Elliott, Brent, *Victorian Gardens,* London: Batsford, 1986

Gloag, John, *Mr. Loudon's England: The Life and Works of John Claudius Loudon, and His Influence on Architecture and Furniture Design,* Newcastle upon Tyne, Northumberland: Oriel Press, 1970

Howe, Bea, *Lady with Green Fingers: The Life of Jane Loudon,* London: Country Life, 1961

Price, Uvedale, *A Review of the Landscape, a Didactic Poem: Also an Essay on the Picturesque,* London, 1795; reprint, Washington, D.C.: Woodstock, 2000

Repton, Humphry, *Sketches and Hints on Landscape Gardening,* London, 1794

Taylor, Geoffrey, *Some Nineteenth-Century Gardeners,* London: Skeffington, 1951

Barbara Simms

Lutyens, Edwin 1869–1944

English Architect

Sir Edwin Lutyens is generally regarded as the foremost English architect of his time. During his long and prolific career, he demonstrated mastery of a wide variety of styles, ranging from the eclectic Arts and Crafts design of his early country houses to the monumental classical architecture of his later public buildings.

Lutyens's background was a rather unusual one for an architect. He was the 11th of 12 children born to Charles Lutyens, a soldier turned painter, and because of frequent illness as a youth, he received little formal education. Growing up in Surrey, southwest of London, during a time when the county was experiencing a boom in development, he had the opportunity to observe firsthand local builders and craftsmen at work—an experience that instilled in him a deep appreciation for traditional building forms and materials. In 1887, after dropping out of the South Kensington School of Art in London, he was taken on as an apprentice in the architectural firm of Sir Ernest George. Hardly more than a year later he received his first commission, for a cottage in Littleworth, Surrey. This and Lutyens's other early designs owed much to the picturesque vernacular style of George as well as to the work of Philip Webb and R. Norman Shaw, two other prominent Arts and Crafts domestic architects.

In 1889, about the time Lutyens was setting up his own practice, he met the noted garden designer and writer Gertrude Jekyll. A generation older than Lutyens, she became something of a mentor to him, teaching him the "simplicity of intention and directness of purpose" stressed by her friend John Ruskin; she also introduced him to numerous clients, as well as the woman he eventually married, Lady Emily Lytton. Jekyll gave Lutyens his first major commission: a new house in her maturing garden at Munstead Wood, Godalming, Surrey. After first building two other cottages on the site, Lutyens completed the main house in 1896. Constructed of local stone, the new house featured sloping roofs, high buttressed chimneys, gables, and small doorways offset by long rows of windows. Jekyll's influence is reflected in the close relationship between house and garden. The subtle use of traditional materials in the house itself and in the carefully delineated garden paths helped link the house organically to its setting.

Over the next three decades, as Lutyens's practice continued to grow, he and Jekyll collaborated on approximately one hundred gardens. Their work together represented an original approach to garden design, with Lutyens responsible for the geometric and formal planning of the structure and Jekyll lending softness and rhythm through her luxurious plantings and sympathetic handling of color. They further explored the concepts pioneered at Munstead Wood in such masterpieces as Orchards, Godalming (1898–99), Tigbourne Court, Witley, Surrey (1899), and Deanery Garden, Sonning, Berkshire (1901). The houses Lutyens built at these sites reveal increasingly his mastery of mass and volume, while the gardens were conspicuous for their combination of the formal and the picturesque. At Deanery Garden, for instance, a stone retaining wall, balustrade, and circular steps border the formal garden spaces that enclosed the house. Plantings along the wall helped to soften the stonework and to establish a transition from the formal areas to an outlying pastoral landscape of orchards and fields.

Throughout the late 1890s and early 1900s, Lutyens freely adapted varied styles of the past to the requirements of contemporary domestic architecture. His houses of this period are notable for their classical and other historical allusions, which were always contained within a range of local building traditions and materials. Beginning in 1906, however, Lutyens's classicist tendencies begin to dominate. His designs for Heathcote, near Ilkey, Yorkshire, exemplify this important turning point in his development. He had been attracted from the beginning of his career by the symmetry and geometry of classical architecture. By 1903 he was praising the style of Andrea Palladio as the "High Game"; in a letter to fellow architect Herbert Baker, Lutyens wrote that the High Game "is so big—few appreciate it now and it requires considerable training to value and realize it. The way Christopher Wren handled it was marvelous." Heathcote signified Lutyens's enthusiastic embrace of what would become the Edwardian style of architecture—a revival of the Palladian manner with a strong allegiance to the English baroque of Wren. A massive suburban villa that Lutyens finished in 1906, Heathcote resembles a Renaissance palazzo. Completely symmetrical in design, the house features a comprehensive system of coupled columns, among other classical elements. From this point on Lutyens remained committed to the Doric and Ionic orders.

Although Lutyens continued to design private residences, including several castles—such as the spectacular Castle Drogo, near Drewsteignton, Devon (1910–30)—the creation of large public buildings dominated his later career. In 1912 he received his most important commission when he was selected to advise on the planning of the imperial capital of India at New Delhi. He played a major role in determining the city layout, which was based in part on Pierre-Charles L'Enfant's plan for Washington, D.C., and Wren's plan for London after the Great Fire; he also designed the capital's main building, the Viceroy's House (1912–30; now the Presidential Palace). The layout of New Delhi incorporated a vast hexagonal grid and broad, symmetrically aligned avenues. Lutyens's idea for lavish plantings along the two-mile-long (3.2 km) processional way that leads to the hill on which the Viceroy's House is situated derived from the English garden-city pattern. The synthesis of the formal and the naturalistic that is found in the city layout also appears in the monumental Viceroy's House, which includes a huge Mogul garden. As large as the Palace of Versailles, the Viceroy's House features simplified classical forms, with occasional touches of Indian vernacular motifs, such as Mogul domes and a type of flat cornice suited to the intense sunlight. Inspired by the famed water gardens of India, Lutyens created for the Mogul garden an intricate pattern of terraces, fountains, pools, and pergolas. The end result is one of the most brilliant buildings of the 20th century. Generations of French and American architects had been trained at the École des Beaux-Arts in Paris toward the design of such a grand classical monument; it is ironic that the opportunity went to an Englishman, especially one of Lutyens's humble background.

Lutyens was knighted in 1918. By the time of his death in 1944, he had also been awarded the Order of Merit and elected president of the Royal Academy. Although many of his contemporaries considered him the greatest English architect since Wren, his reputation suffered somewhat in the years following his death, in part because of the influence of exponents of the International Style who criticized Lutyens for his adoption of classicism. The 1980s, however, saw the beginning of a revival of interest in his work, and Lutyens was the subject of major exhibitions in both New York City and London. It is for his capacity for invention along traditional lines, as well as for the sheer range of his architecture, that he will likely be remembered.

See also Hestercombe; Jekyll, Gertrude; Munstead Wood

Biography

Born in London, 29 March 1869. Studied briefly at South Kensington School of Art, London, and joined architectural firm headed by Sir Ernest George, 1887; received first commission, for cottage in Littleworth, Surrey, 1889; came under influence of landscape gardener Gertrude Jekyll, who commissioned him to build new house in garden at Munstead Wood, Godalming, Surrey, completed 1896; collaborated with Jekyll on gardens of many houses during the following three decades; from 1906, designs grew more monumental and classical in style; among notable later works are designs for government buildings in New Delhi, India, including Viceroy's House, 1912–30, and World War I memorials such as Cenotaph, London, 1919–20, and Thiepval Memorial Arch, near Arras, France, 1924. Knighted, 1918. Died in London, 1 January 1944.

Selected Designs

1889	Cottage in Littleworth, Surrey, England
1890	Crooksbury Lodge, near Farnham, Surrey, England
1896	Munstead Wood, Godalming, Surrey, England
1898–99	Orchards, near Munstead, Surrey, England
1899	Tigbourne Court, near Witley, Surrey, England
1900	Grey Walls, Gullane, East Lothian, England
1901	Deanery Gardens, Sonning, Berkshire, England
1902	Little Thakeham, near Pullborough, Sussex, England
1903	Papillon Hall, Lubenham, Leicestershire, England
1903–4	Lindisfarne Castle (restoration), Holy Island, Northumberland, England
1904	Country Life Building, Tavistock Street, Covent Garden, London, England
1905	Nashdom, Taplow, Buckinghamshire, England
1906	Heathcote, near Ilkley, Yorkshire, England
1908	Middlefield, Great Shelford, Cambridgeshire, England
1909–13	Hampstead Garden Suburb (St. Jude's Church, Free Church, manse and houses in North Square), London, England
1910–30	Castle Drogo, near Drewsteignton, Dartmoor, Devon, England
1911	Theosophical Society, Tavistock Square, London, England
1912–30	Viceroy's House and other major buildings, New Delhi, India
1919–20	Cenotaph, London, England
1920	Britannic House, Finsbury Circus, London, England
1921	Midland Bank, 126 Picadilly, London, England
1924	Thiepval Memorial Arch, near Arras, France
1928	British Embassy, Washington, D.C., United States

Selected Publications
"The Work of the Late Philip Webb," *Country Life* 37, no. 619 (1918)
"What I Think of Modern Architecture," *Country Life* 69, nos. 775–777 (1931)

Further Reading
Brown, Jane, *Gardens of a Golden Afternoon: The Story of a Partnership: Edwin Lutyens and Gertrude Jekyll,* London: Lane, and New York: Van Nostrand Reinhold, 1982; updated edition, New York and London: Penguin, 1994
Brown, Jane, *Lutyens and the Edwardians: An English Architect and His Clients,* New York: Viking, 1996; London: Penguin, 1997
Bryon, Robert, "New Delhi," *Architectural Review* 69 (1931)
Butler, Arthur Stanley George, George Stewart, and Christopher Hussey, *The Architecture of Sir Edwin Lutyens,* 3 vols., London: Country Life, and New York: Scribner, 1950
Homberger, Eric, "The Story of the Cenotaph," *Times Literary Supplement* (12 November 1976)
Hussey, Christopher, *The Life of Sir Edwin Lutyens,* London: Country Life, and New York: Scribner, 1950; special edition, 1953
Hussey, Christopher, "An Early Lutyens Castle in the Air," *Country Life* 125 (1959)
Lutyens, Mary, *Edwin Lutyens: A Memoir by His Daughter,* London: Murray, 1980; revised edition, London: Black Swan, 1991
Lutyens, Robert, *Sir Edwin Lutyens: An Appreciation in Perspective,* London: Country Life, 1942
O'Neill, Daniel, *Sir Edwin Lutyens: Country Houses,* London: Lund Humphries, 1980; New York: Whitney Library of Design, 1981
Pevsner, Nikolaus, "Building with Wit: The Architecture of Sir Edwin Lutyens," *Architectural Review* 109 (1951)
Stamp, Gavin, "The Rise and Fall and Rise of Edwin Lutyens," *Architectural Review* (November 1981)

SHERMAN J. HOLLAR

Luxembourg Gardens

Paris, France

Location: 15 rue de Vaugirard, in Saint-Germain des Prés, Paris

The Luxembourg Gardens, in the fashionable Saint-Germain district of Paris, is one of the most famous and popular public parks in France. Now almost 400 years old, its popularity with Parisians for exercise and fresh air is as great now as when the English diarist John Evelyn visited in 1644 and found the gardens freely open to "persons of quality" and full of "gallants and ladies . . . melancholy friars . . . studious scholars . . . jolly citizens, some sitting or lying on the grass, others running and jumping; some playing at bowls and ball, others dancing and singing, and all this without the least disturbance, by reason of the largeness of the place." Substitute jogging and playing tennis for "running and jumping" and not much has changed.

The story of the Luxembourg Gardens begins with the melancholy event of the assassination of Henri IV in 1610. His son, Louis XIII, became king, and his widow, Marie de Médicis, preferred not to live in the Louvre. In 1611 she bought a house from François de Luxembourg on what was then the edge of the city. The house had an old-fashioned enclosed garden, which was removed and was somewhat hemmed in by other properties; these Marie began buying up in 1613. Marie's instructions to her architect, Salomon de Brosse, were to produce a grand mansion similar to her childhood home, the Pitti Palace in Florence; instead de Brosse built a château in the French style, similar to Verneuil (designed by Jacques Androuet Du Cerceau) and Coulommiers, another chateau by de Brosse. The Palais du Luxembourg was highly symmetrical, with three ranges around a great court, closed on the street side by a low arcaded wing. Building began in 1615 and was not finished until 1631. Marie had moved in earlier and in the same year was forced by the king to leave.

The Palais du Luxembourg has the distinction of being the first palace in Paris to be set in an extensive park—the gardens. The layout of the gardens was innovative and little resembled the Boboli Gardens (the gardens of the Pitti Palace) in Florence, which Marie wished to reproduce. For the first time in France a unified, monumental, and dignified scheme was devised. The architectural quality of thc gardens and their integral relationship with the palace suggest that de Brosse may have had a key role in their design. However, the finished product was the creation of a team, which included the top designers in France at the time. The great parterre was designed by Jacques Boyceau de la Barauderie, and the waterworks were installed by Thomas Francini, who also built the terraces and balustrades and the aqueduct, which brought water from springs at Arceuil, outside Paris. The Francini family remained in control of the waterworks until 1780.

The core of the gardens survives more or less in its original form, although detail has been lost and much replanting has taken place. The new gardens were begun in 1611, with the planting of allées by the gardener Nicolas Deschamps. Their shape was dictated by the availability of land. To the south of the palace lay a Carthusian monastery. Expansion in this direction was therefore limited, and a longer cross axis, with a central allée of elms, was made to the west. A plan of 1615 by François Quesnel and Claude Vellefaux shows that only a circular bosquet in the southeast corner of the park, with radiating and circular rides, had been planted by that date. In the same year another gardener, Guillaume Boutin, was planting elms around a windmill next to the bosquet. After that, radical change took place. On the south front of the palace, a broad gravel cross walk was made, to the south of which was the main axis of the gardens, 340 meters (372 yd.) long, extending to the boundary with the monastery. Dominating it was a huge square parterre, with a large central octagonal basin and a semicircular extension at the end. Flanking the parterre were sloping banks and two tiers of terracing, from which to view the parterre, bounded by low walls and marble balustrades. Boyceau designed for this sunken space one of the first and finest *parterres de broderie*, the design for which was published in his posthumous *Traité de jardinage selon les raisons de la nature et de l'art* (1638). A swirling symmetrical pattern, divided among a number of geometric beds, was set out in dwarf box hedging. Evelyn was full of praise: "so rarely designed and accurately kept cut." The central axis was framed by tall palisades of hornbeam and on either side were bosquets of lime and elm, with walks cut through them. The gardens were ornamented with pools, fountains, and statues, some placed on pedestals on the parterre wall, some in the bosquets.

Terminating the vista at the east end of the cross walk in front of the palace was another famous feature of the gardens, the Grotte du Luxembourg, or Fontaine Médicis. This was built in 1623–30 and although called a fountain, it was not supplied with water until the 19th century. Originally built against existing buildings in the rue d'Enfer, it was a Mannerist facade divided into three niches; over the central niche was the coat of arms of Marie de Médicis. On either side of this were statues by Pierre Biard representing the rivers Rhône and Seine. The author of this building is thought probably to have been Alexandre Francini, brother of Thomas, who designed a very similar one at Wideville (1636), near Poissy.

In 1631 the king's brother, Gaston d'Orleans, took over. Work was still continuing at that time on the waterworks. By 1635 the up-and-coming architect André le Nôtre was in charge in the gardens, a position he kept until 1642. Evelyn, on his visit in 1644, found the gardens in "exquisite order." However, by the end of the century the gardens were neglected and in their unkempt state were the inspiration for paintings by Jean-Antoine Watteau. It was at this stage that the gardens began to shrink. In 1782–91 the comte de Provence, Louis XVI's brother, sold the area west of the present boundary (rue Guynemer). After the Revolution the monastery was destroyed, and this enabled the main axis to be extended southwards in 1798 with an avenue to the Observatoire (1668–72 by Claude Perrault). At the same time the palace became the home of the senate. Its buildings and gardens were restored and altered by Jean-François Chalgrin. His main contribution in the gardens was the addition of semicircular bays on each side of the parterre.

The last major changes to the gardens came in the 1860s as part of the great city planning scheme of Napolean III's prefect, Georges-Eugène Haussmann. Had a petition of 12,000 signatures not been circulated in their defense, the gardens would have been completely mutilated. As it was, some outer areas were destroyed. In 1862 the cutting of the rue de Médicis east of the palace involved the relocation of the Grotte du Luxembourg northward to its present position. Now a freestanding structure, its statues were replaced, and Pan and Diana were added in the side niches. At the back is a bas-relief, the Fontaine de Léda, installed earlier, in 1855. In the central niche a large group depicting Polyphemus discovering Acis and Galatea, by Auguste Louis-Marie Ottin, was inserted. A short canal, now rather dark and overhung by trees, was made in front, with rows of vases on pedestals on either side. Another area to go was a nursery to the west of the Observatoire avenue, which was cut off when the east-west rue Auguste Comte was made in 1866. To its north an informal *jardin anglais* was made. The Ecole Nationale Supérieure occupies the corresponding area to the east of the main axis. Very little original stonework and statuary survive from the 17th century.

Today the bosquets are adorned with statues, including the queens of France and famous 19th-century women. Evelyn found the gardens "perfectly beautiful and magnificent" in 1644. The public's continuing use and appreciation of them ensures that they remain so today.

Synopsis

1611 Marie de Médicis buys François de Luxembourg's property, Nicolas Deschamps plants allées

Israel Silvestre, *Veuë du Palais d'Orleans du costé du jardin* (Garden View of the Palace of Orleans), Luxembourg Gardens, Paris, France
Courtesy of Bibliothèque Nationale de France

1615 Work begins on palace, architect Salomon de Brosse
1615–31 Most of gardens laid out
1623–30 Building of Grotte du Luxembourg (also called Fontaine Médicis)
1629 Completion of land acquisition
1631 Marie de Médicis leaves and Gaston d'Orléans takes over gardens
1635–42 André Le Nôtre in charge of gardens for Gaston d'Orléans
1644 Visit of John Evelyn, who gives detailed description of gardens
1694 Gaston d'Orléans's grand-daughter gives property to Louis XIV
1782–91 Comte de Provence, brother of Louis XVI, sells part of garden to pay for restoration
1798 With monastery destroyed in Revolution, south axis extended with avenue to Observatoire; semi-circular bays added to parterre by Chalgrin; palace altered to become home of Senate
1862 Grotte du Luxembourg moved northward to present location and altered
1866 Southwest part of gardens, used as nursery, removed when Rue Auguste Comte cut; *Jardin anglais* made to north

Further Reading

Adams, William Howard, *The French Garden, 1500–1800,* London: Scolar Press, and New York: Braziller, 1979

Charageat, Marguerite, "La Nymphée de Wideville et la grotte du Luxembourg," *Bulletin de la Societé de l'histoire de l'art français* (1934)

Evelyn, John, *The Diary of John Evelyn*, 6 vols., edited by E.S. de Beer, Oxford: Clarendon Press, 1955

Hazlehurst, F. Hamilton, *Jacques Boyceau and the French Formal Garden,* Athens: University of Georgia Press, 1966

Hustin, Arthur, *Le Luxembourg: Son histoire domanial, archicturale, decorative et anecdotique,* 2 vols., Paris: Du Sénat, 1910–11

Hustin, Arthur, "La création du jardin du Luxembourg par Marie de Médicis," *Archives de l'Art Francais* 8 (1916)

Woodbridge, Kenneth, *Princely Gardens: The Origins and Developments of the French Formal Style,* London: Thames and Hudson, and New York: Rizzoli, 1986

ELISABETH WHITTLE

Lvov, Nikolai Alexandrovitch 1751–1803

Russian Architect and Garden Designer

Nikolai Alexandrovitch Lvov, the son of a Russian aristocrat, was born in Nikolskoye-Cherenchitsy, the family estate in the district of Tver in the northern part of central Russia. In 1767 he became an officer in the imperial guards in St. Petersburg and entered a circle of courtiers devoted to the ideas of French Enlightenment. In 1775–76 he visited France, Germany, and the Netherlands. His career as a garden designer and architect began after his return to Russia in the late 1770s.

In 1782 Lvov became one of the highest officers of the imperial post service, and in this position he created the designs for many landscapes and structures. Through his chief, Count A.A. Bezborodko, Lvov became close to Empress Catherine II and, in accordance with her idea, created an "educational garden" for her grandson, the future emperor Alexander I. This garden, called Alexandrova Datcha, was conceived as a series of pictures from a fairy-tale written by the august grandmother for her grandson. At the same time Lvov took part in designing the ideal country landscape for the Model School of Agriculture near Tsarskoye Selo, which was headed by A.A. Samborsky.

Lvov is one of the main figures in the creation of the Russian estate garden of the second half of the 18th century. His own estate, Nikolskoye-Cherenchitsy, became the model in garden art as well as in the Russian gentry's artistic philosophy of landscape. Estate houses, parks, and garden pavilions for more than 20 estates were built according to his designs. In architecture Lvov combined Palladianism with the use of motifs from French classicism of the mid-18th century. In making gardens he preferred landscape parks with pavilions in antique or rural tastes.

Lvov was also a poet, composer, and music theorist, as well as a talented engineer. He wrote the first Russian treatises on heating and ventilation; he was also the author of the first study on the history of ancient Russian architecture. Among his wide literary output the treatise on gardening, called *The Design of Count Bezborodko's Garden,* is of exceptional interest. In this work Lvov promotes a combination "of principles by Kent and Lenotre." To a great extent he based these ideas on *The Theory of Garden Art* by the Danish emissary and scholar Christian Cay Lorenz Hirshfeld; a copy of this book, annotated by Lvov, was found in the library of the Moscow Museum of Fine Arts.

Biography

Born on family estate Nikolskoye-Cherentchitsy in Tver Province, north of Moscow, 1751. Received education at home; entered military service, 1769; military tours to France and Italy, 1775–76; beginning of architectural activity, design for St. Joseph Cathedral in Mogilev, 1780s; designs for houses and gardens in estates of Tver Province, including Nikolskoye-Cherentshitsy, Mitino, Vasilyevo, Pryamukhino, and Znamenskoye-Rayok, 1780s to mid-1790s; creation of imperial garden of Alexandrova Datcha in Tsarskoye Selo, near St. Petersburg, for Grand Duke Alexander (future emperor Alexander I), 1782; design for garden of Count A.A. Bezborodko in Moscow, accompanied by Lvov's written commentaries on art of landscape gardening, 1797; creation of Prioratsky palace and park in Gatchina for Emperor Paul I, 1798–99. Died, Moscow, 1803.

Selected Designs

1780s–early 1790s	Main house, park, and pavilions of Nikolskoye-Cherenchitsy estate, district of Tver, Russia
1782–87	Alexandrova Datcha park and pavilions in Tsarskoye Selo, district of St. Petersburg, Russia
1780s	Garden pavilions in estates Mitino, Vasilyevo, and Pryamukhino, district of Tver, Russia
1788–90	Znamenskoye-Rayok estate, district of Tver, Russia; Stolnoye estate, Ukraine
1790–95	Voronovo estate near Moscow, Russia
1791	Garden house in Lyalichi estate, Ukraine
1797–99	Garden of Count Bezborodko in Moscow, Russia
1798–99	Prioratsky palace and garden cascade, Gatchina, Russia
late 1790s	Zvanka estate, district of Novgorod, Russia
1799–1800	Vvedenskoye estate near Moscow, Russia

Selected Publications

The Design of Count Bezborodko's Garden, late 1790s, manuscript held by the Library of Fine Arts Museum, Moscow

Further Reading

Budylina, M.V., O.U. Braitseva, and A.M. Kharlamova, *Arkhitektor N.A. Lvov* (The Architect N.A. Lvov), Moscow: Gos. Izd-vo Lit-ry po Stroitel'stvu, Arkhitekture i Stroit. Materialam, 1961

Grimm, G.G., "The Design of Bezborodko Garden in Moscow," *Newsletter of the Institute of Art History* 4–5 (1954)

DMITRY SHVIDKOVSKY

M

Madama, Villa

Rome, Italy

Location: west of Tiber river, approximately 1.5 miles (2.4 km) north of Vatican, on Via di Villa Madama

After Donato Bramante died in 1514, Raphael was appointed director of works at St. Peter's in Rome. The following year he was appointed prefect of inscriptions, in 1517 superintendent of antiquities, and in 1518 master of roads. At the time he was designing the Medici villa on the slopes of Monte Mario in conjunction with Antonio da Sangallo the Younger and several other assistants. The villa was commissioned by Cardinal Giuliano de' Medici, later Pope Clement VII. Construction started late in 1518 and was in progress at the time of Raphael's death on 6 April 1520. Work continued under the direction of Raphael's assistant Giulio Romano but was subsequently abandoned when it was less that half finished.

The complex was badly damaged during the Sack of Rome in 1527 and has never been finished or completely restored. The gardens were not completely constructed as planned and were neglected for hundreds of years, so little remains, although the Italian State has laid out an attractive garden on the hillside. The Medici complex is now known as the Villa Madama after Margaret of Austria, natural daughter of Emperor Charles V and first wife of Alessandro de' Medici, duke of Florence, and later of Ottavio Farnese, nephew of Pope Paul III and the future duke of Parma, through whom the villa passed to the kings of Naples and eventually to the Italian State. The government uses the estate for its original purpose of housing distinguished visitors.

The Villa Madama was the first great Roman villa of the Renaissance outside the city walls. The owner, artists, and designers were almost all from central and northern Italy, although the villa was entirely Roman in design and decoration, inspired by the classical buildings of antiquity. The villa was the largest secular undertaking of the 16th century in Italy. It was thought of as one of the Florentine landmarks in Rome much admired by contemporaries. Although the magnificent garden design was never fully executed, the Villa Madama is the earliest complete example of Roman Renaissance design to survive.

The villa was designed to provide a delightful residence at the gates of the city of Rome for important visitors to be housed and entertained, giving them an opportunity to rest after a long journey and before making the ceremonial entry into the city. As such the complex included accommodation for both people and animals, rooms for entertainment and reception, extensive gardens, and a racecourse, or exercise ground, for horses.

Raphael completely rebuilt the complex for the cardinal, entirely enveloping the villa that had previously stood on the site. Raphael and his patron envisaged a villa *all'antica* with loggias, a theater, a hippodrome, a nymphaeum, baths, fishponds, and extensive terraced gardens.

Raphael's designs were fully in the spirit of the classical revival and incorporated elements of Nero's recently discovered Domus Aurea, Vitruvius's writings, and Pliny's ideas about villas and gardens as well as existing ancient buildings such as the Temple of Fortune at Praeneste (present-day Palestrina). This idealization of the antique Roman villa was combined with the influence of the palace of Urbino, which Raphael had known since boyhood, with its *all' antica* decoration, remarkable architectural design, and hillside site.

Because the original designs of the complex are known from a recently discovered letter by Raphael, it is clear that the interpenetration of the house and garden was planned from the very beginning. Designed on a horizontal axis, the villa was intended to have a series of loggias and reception rooms and a great central courtyard that gave on to a theater "in the Greek style" set into the hillside. The elongated rectangular complex, with the theater on one side, was divided roughly into three: in the center, the upper story, courtyard, and theater; on the southeast side, the entrance court and walled gardens; and on the northwest side, the terrace garden and fishpond. From the theater, across the great courtyard, the central shorter axis leads down to the Ponte Molle over the Tiber. The great hippodrome and stables for 400 horses were planned to run parallel to the villa. The elaborate parterres planned for the hillside below the villa were intended perhaps to emulate, perhaps to surpass the terraces designed by Bramante for the Cortile del Belvedere of the Vatican.

In Raphael's description of his plans for the villa, he indicates a fountain set into the hillside and decorated with seashells and supplied with seats for use as a *diaeta* in very hot weather. The seashell decoration was carried out elsewhere in the garden, and seashell grottoes became very popular in Italian gardens later in the 16th century. Shell grottoes and houses then became very fashionable in 18th-century England. The parterres were particularly appreciated first in Italy and were much emulated. The hillside terraces were also first imitated in Italy. Raphael's ideas about including viewpoints in the design of the house and garden were influential in the history of English landscape design.

The general influence of the Villa Madama complex can be traced first in the gardens of the Doria villa in Genoa, the Villa d'Este at Tivoli, the Villa Giulia, the Villa Farnese at Caprarola, the Villa Lante at Bagnaia, and the Aldobrandini villa at Frascati. The influence of these Renaissance villas and gardens spread throughout Europe and is still important today.

Synopsis

1515 Raphael designs large complex on slopes of Monte Mario for Cardinal Giulio de' Medici
1520 Death of Raphael; project continued by assistants
1527 Sack of Rome; unfinished complex badly damaged
ca. 1537 Occupied by Margaret of Austria, from whom inherited by kings of Naple
present Owned by Italian State

Further Reading

Bafile, Mario, *Il giardino di Villa Madama,* Rome: Istituto Poligrafico dello Stato, 1942
Biermann, Hartmut, "Der Runde Hof: Betrachtungen zur Villa Madama," *Mitteilungen des Kunsthistorischen Institutes in Florenz* 30, no. 3 (1986)
Cable, Carole, *The Villa Madama: A Renaissance Villa in Rome,* Monticello, Illinois: Vance Bibliographies, 1982
Coffin, David R., *The Villa in the Life of Renaissance Rome,* Princeton, New Jersey: Princeton University Press, 1979
Dewez, Guy, *Villa Madama: Memoria sul progetto di Raffaello,* Rome: Edizioni dell'Elefante, 1990; as *Villa Madama: A Memoir Relating to Raphael's Project,* London: Lund Humphries, and New York: Princeton University Press, 1993
Frommel, Christoph Luitpold, Stefano Ray, and Manfredo Tafuri, *Raffaello architetto,* Milan: Electa, 1984
Lefevre, Renato, *Villa Madama,* Rome: Istituto Poligrafico dello Stato, 1964; 2nd edition, Rome: Editalia, 1984
Masson, Georgina, *Italian Gardens,* London: Thames and Hudson, and New York: Abrams, 1961; new edition, 1966
Moreti, Andrea, "Forma e posizione delle villa degli Horti Lucullani secondo i rilievi rinascimentali: La loro influenza sui progetti del Belvedere e del ville Madama, Barbaro e Aldobrandini," part 1, *Palladio* 6, no. 12 (1993), and part 2, *Palladio* 7, no. 13 (1994)
Shearman, J., "A Functional Interpretation of Villa Madama," *Römisches Jahrbuch für Kunstgeschichte Wien* 20 (1983)
Weiermann, Herbert, "Bemerkungen zur Villa Madama und ihren Gartenlagen," in *Festschrift Luitpold Dussler: 28 Studien zür Archäologie und Kunstgeschichte,* by J.A. Schmoll gen. Eisenwerth, Marcell Restle, and Herbert Weiermann, Munich: Deutscher Kunstverlag, 1972

JULIA KING

Madinat al-Zahra'

Córdoba, Spain

Location: on Avenida Medina Azahara (route C 431) approximately 6 miles (9.6 km) west of Córdoba

Madinat al-Zahra' was the rural palace estate built by the Umayyad caliph 'Abd al-Rahman III al-Nasir (reigned 912–61) and his son al-Hakam II (r. 961–76). Begun on 19 November 936, the mosque and most of the principal residences of the palatine complex were completed by 941. Although Córdoba was ringed by handsome villas (called *munyas*) with gardens and orchards offering their owners pleasant relief from the crowded walled city, this estate, measuring 1518 by 745 meters (1670 by 814 yd.), was so much larger than its predecessors that it was called a city (*madina*).

Extending across three stepped terraces cut into the lower slope of a range of high hills, the palatine city was a rectangular, double-walled complex with splendid halls, residences, mosques, a mint, zoo, aviary, and workshops for artisans. Most of these buildings were planned around courtyards and large gardens, with the open spaces defining the character of the city on equal terms with the built components. Much of the food consumed by the residents (which included servants and troops stationed there) was grown in the palace's kitchen gardens, and fish were raised in enormous ponds as well.

Of the formal gardens of Madinat al-Zahra', three have been studied by archaeologists. The first is a large enclosed garden (163 by 144 m [178 by 157 yd.]) that faces the reception hall known today as the Salon Rico. The Salon Rico was built in 953–7, probably replacing an older building, and the garden can be dated to the period between 941 and 957. Because the Salon Rico was cut into the sloping site, it lacked windows except on its face, which looked to the garden through an arcade of five arches on columns. Thus, the hall served as a kind of opera box, directing vision toward the verdant scene beyond it. The garden was divided into four quadrants by walkways bordered by irrigation channels. Two parallel walkways ran along the north side in front of the Salon Rico, one slightly lower than the other, connected by ramps in the corners of the garden quadrants. Opposite the Salon Rico and situated along the north-south axis of the garden, was a pavilion that, although no longer standing, probably resembled the Salon Rico on a smaller scale. This small pavilion was surrounded by rectangular tanks of water, the largest of which stood between the small pavilion and Salon Rico, reflecting each on its silvery surface.

A garden of equal size and similar plan lay some 14 meters (15 yd.) below and to the west of the Salon Rico garden. This lower garden was cross-axially planned with pavements marking the quadrants. Although this was not part of the elite zone of the Salon Rico terrace, where important ambassadorial receptions were held and feast days were marked with great ceremony, the lower garden could be viewed from above at the westernmost point of the east-west axis of the Salon Rico garden. Indeed, the garden was probably meant to be seen from that elevated perspective, since it is the only place where the lower garden's mirroring of the axial layout of the upper garden was discernable.

Above and to the north of the lower garden was a small residence that faced a small walled garden through columned porticoes. This garden was divided into halves by a thin strip of pavement and water channels that culminated in a rectangular tank of water at the western end. Unlike the Salon Rico garden, which was observed and described by contemporary historians who attended court festivities and ceremonies, this garden escaped mention in their chronicles, perhaps because it was the private dwelling of a high ranking (but unknown) member of the court.

Seventy-four years after its founding, the city of magnificent halls and handsome gardens was destroyed in a civil war over dynastic succession between the Ummayads, who were the legitimate rulers of Islamic Spain, and the sons of the powerful vizier Almanzor (al-Mansur). Because the Umayyad supporters used Madinat al-Zahra' as their headquarters, the palace was eventually sacked and burned by their opponents. Decades later the historian Ibn Hayyan would write sadly of the palace's neglected state: "With this ruin that carpet of the world was folded up and that beauty which had been an earthly paradise was disfigured."

Thereafter the derelict estate was ignored except for the occasional medieval visitor, and by the 16th century (Córdoba was conquered by the Christians in 1236) its identity was forgotten. The site was rediscovered in 1843 and excavations commenced in 1910. Although the archaeological unearthing of Madinat al-Zahra' continues today, it has been limited to the examination of buildings in the upper elite zones of the palatine city and has rarely focused on the gardens. Without archaeological excavation of the soil layers of these Islamic

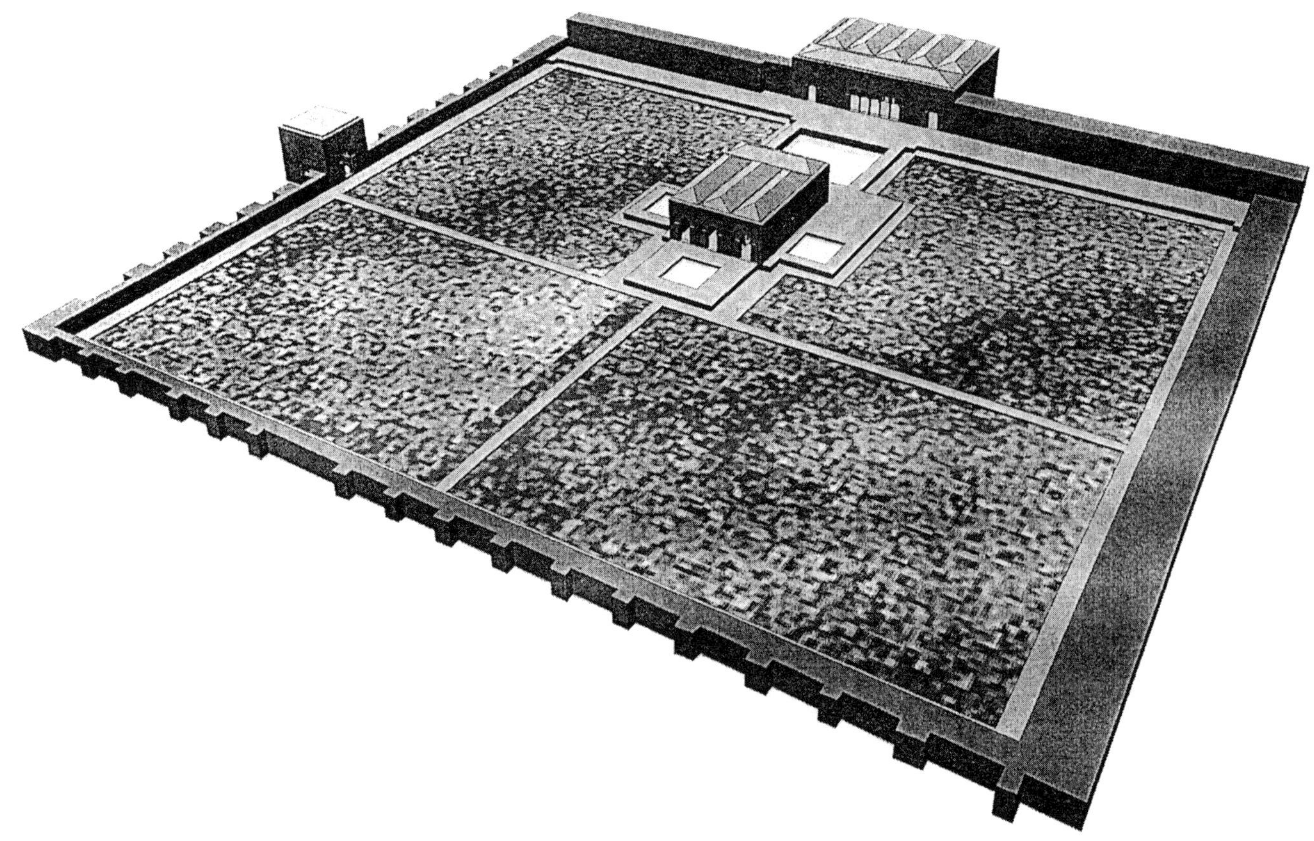

Upper garden and Salon Rico at Madinat al-Zahra', Córdoba, Spain
Courtesy of D. Fairchild Ruggles and H. Wilke

gardens, it is not known what specific plants were cultivated there, nor is the design of the plantings evident. However, comparison with later gardens in Seville and Granada, and information gleaned from the many Hispano-Arabic gardening and agricultural manuals written from the 11th to the 14th centuries, suggests the garden beds were sunken below the level of the paved walkways. They would have been planted with a seasonally changing display of flowers such as narcissus, irises, violets, and marguerites intermingled with trellised vines such as roses, shrubs such as oranges, and fruit trees, all of which were admired as much for their blooms and fragrance as for their fruit.

See also Vista Garden

Synopsis

936–41 Mosque and most of palatine complex completed by Umayyad caliph ʿAbd ar-Rahman III al-Nasir
941–57 Enclosed garden facing Salon Rico built
953–57 Salon Rico built
1010 Madinat al-Zahra' destroyed and abandoned
1843 Derelict site recognized as Madinat al-Zahra'
1910– Excavations begun

Further Reading

Hernández Giménez, Félix, *Madinat al-Zahra': Arquitectura y decoración,* Granada: Patronato de la Alhambra, 1985
Jiménez Martín, Alfonso, "Los jardines de Madinat al-Zahra'," *Cuadernos de Madinat al-Zahra'* 1 (1987)
Ruggles, D. Fairchild, "Historiography and the Rediscovery of Madinat al-Zahra'," *Islamic Studies* (Islamabad) 30 (1991)
Ruggles, D. Fairchild, "Il giardini con pianta a croce nel Mediterraneo islamico," in *Il giardino islamico: Architettura, natura, paesaggio,* edited by Attilio Petruccioli, Milan: Electa, 1994
Ruggles, D. Fairchild, *Gardens, Landscape, and Vision in the Palaces of Islamic Spain,* University Park:

Pennsylvania State University Press, 2000
Vallejo Triano, Antonio, "Madinat al-Zahra': The Triumph of the Islamic State," in *Al-Andalus: The Art of Islamic Spain,* edited by Jerrilynn Dodds, New York: Metropolitan Museum of Art, 1992

D. FAIRCHILD RUGGLES

Magazine

Unlike other forms of garden journalism, such as books and almanacs, garden magazines did not develop until the 18th century. It is believed that the first British gardening periodical was that created by Richard Bradley, *A General Treatise of Husbandry and Gardening,* started in 1721. This was followed by William Curtis's *Botanical Magazine* in 1787, which continued in publication until 1984, when it was incorporated into the publication *The Kew Magazine.* At the time it was introduced, the style of the *Botanical Magazine,* with its wide use of colored engravings, became extremely popular and much replicated.

In 1797 two magazines patterning themselves after the *Botanical Magazine* debuted. These were the *Botanist's Repository,* published by H.C. Andrews (which lasted until 1815), and *Botanical Register.* Seeing a successful formula, both publishers decided it was best to replicate the style of the *Botanical Magazine,* and these initial successes were soon followed by a series of competing periodicals such as the extremely successful *Transactions,* published by the Horticultural Society of London from 1807 to 1848. By the middle of the 19th century, as periodicals became cheaper to produce and to purchase, the competition intensified and became too great for expensive magazines that catered only to the gentry.

The result was a new breed of magazines aimed at the average person, not only "gentlemen." This new type included the *Gardener's Magazine,* founded in 1826 by John Claudius Loudon, which ran for almost 20 years. He also edited several other periodicals together with his wife, Jane; at one point they were producing five monthly publications at a time. Loudon was met with competition by the equally prolific Joseph Paxton, who published the *Horticultural Register and General Magazine* from 1831 to 1836, which featured both horticulture and natural history.

George Glenny published the first weekly horticultural paper, *The Gardeners' Gazette,* from 1837 to 1844. This was soon followed by a competing weekly created by Joseph Paxton in 1841, *The Gardeners' Chronicle.* It became one of the most respected and well-known periodicals of the time and featured distinguished gardeners and botanists. Another well-regarded and long-standing publication, *The Journal of the Royal Horticultural Society,* was founded in 1866, as was *Amateur Gardening,* started by noted garden writer Shirley Hibberd in 1884.

Perhaps the most famous of the British magazines and journals were those published by William Robinson. They are *The Garden,* founded in 1871, which is also noteworthy for featuring the writing of famed gardening expert Gertrude Jekyll, who started writing for the magazine in 1875. The other was *Gardening Illustrated,* begun in 1879.

Most of the British magazines in the 19th century were characterized by their plant illustrations, which were initially made by copper engravings, until the invention of lithography replaced copper in the 1840s. These illustrations were hand-colored, resulting in a wide range of quality between the different periodicals. It was also during the 19th century that the first specialized periodicals were produced. This began with the publication of *The Orchid Review* in 1893.

Garden magazines in other European countries also began to appear in the 18th century and to flourish in the 19th century. The first periodical published in France was the long-running *Le bon jardinier,* which debuted in 1784 and ceased publication in 1933. The initial success of *Le bon jardinier* led to the publication of several highly popular French magazines in the first half of the 19th century. These include the *Annales de la société d'horticulture de Paris,* published from 1827 to 1854; *Journal et Flore des Jardins,* published from 1832 to 1845; and *Revue horticole,* published from 1829 to 1866. In Germany the first garden magazine also appeared in the 18th century. This was the *Journal für die Gartenkunst,* first published in 1783. One of Germany's longest running periodicals was *Gartenflora,* published from 1852 to 1940. Other notable German publications included *Der teutsche Obstgartner,* first published from 1794 to 1804. It later changed its name and focus from strictly fruit to become *Allgemeines teutsches Gartenmagazin* from 1804 to 1811.

Gardening magazines in the United States were also firmly established in the 19th century. The first U.S.

magazine to feature a horticultural section was the *Massachusetts Agricultural Repository,* published from 1793 to 1832. However, the first U.S. periodical devoted solely to gardening was the *Floral Magazine and Botanical Repository,* published by the noted Philadelphia nursery family, the Landreths.

In 1845 the magazine *The Horticulturist* was founded by Andrew Jackson Downing and became the United States's leading gardening magazine. Other U.S. magazines created during this time include *The American Gardener,* by William Cobbett (begun 1854), Thomas Meehan's *Gardener's Monthly* (1859), the premier U.S. magazine of its time, and the long-running *Sunset Magazine* (1898). At one point in the 19th century, there were over 500 gardening periodicals published in the United States.

The period from 1900 to 1940 saw a dramatic increase in both the popularity of amateur gardening and gardening journalism in the United States, particularly in the growth of garden magazines. Many of the best-known magazines of the present day began during this time, such as *Better Homes and Gardens, House and Garden,* and *House Beautiful,* which featured writing from such noted garden experts as Louise Beebe Wilder, Grace Tabor, Fletcher Steele, Wilhelm Miller, and Francis King. During this same time the *Horticulture Magazine* of the American Horticultural Society was established (1922).

Although new magazines continued to be established after the war, there was a considerable lull in garden writing until the end of the 1960s. One new periodical from this period, founded in 1942, was *Organic Gardening and Farming,* published by Jerome I. Rodale; the first issue featured the writings of Charles Darwin and Sir Albert Howard.

Other magazines established during the latter part of the 20th century included the bimonthly *Plant and Soil,* a journal from The Hague, and the *Whole Earth Catalog,* founded by Howard Rheingold in 1968.

In the early 1970s gardening, particularly organic gardening, experienced a surge in popularity due to the increase in concern for the environment, the establishment of the first Earth Day in 1970, and a back-to-the-land movement. This awareness also extended to the desire to study and analyze gardening history. As a result, in 1972 the Garden History Society established its own journal, entitled *Garden History.*

Another important change in gardening journalism occurred during the 1970s. This was the renaming in 1975 of the *Journal of the Royal Horticultural Society* (first published in 1866), to *The Garden.* Some other periodicals created in the 1970s and 1980s included *Pacific Horticulture Magazine* (1976) and *Garden Design Journal,* first published by the American Society of Landscape Architects in 1982.

In the mid-1990s amateur gardening and home and garden magazines became extremely popular in the United States. By the end of the 1990s there were at least 41 magazines on the newsstands devoted to home and garden topics. In order to remain competitive, many have merged, including *Popular Gardening* and *Amateur Gardening.* At the same time there has been an increase in the number of both trade association periodicals, as well as specialized and society-sponsored periodicals. While many of them are new, some bear familiar titles that have been reintroduced, including the quarterly *Green Prints: "The Weeder's Digest" Magazine* (1991), *Home Garden* (1995), *Garden Design* (1995), *Country Living Gardener* (1996), *Kitchen Gardening Magazine* (1996), a new version of *House and Garden* (1996), and *Organic Gardening* (1996).

Further Reading

Bailey, Liberty H., editor, *Cyclopedia of American Horticulture,* 4 vols., New York: Macmillan, and Toronto, Ontario: Virtue, 1900–1902; revised edition, as *The Standard Cyclopedia of Horticulture,* 6 vols., New York: Macmillan, 1914–17

Desmond, Ray, *A Celebration of Flowers: Two Hundred Years of Curtis's Botanical Magazine,* Kew: Royal Botanic Gardens, 1987

Hobhouse, Penelope, *Plants in Garden History,* London: Pavilion Books, 1992; as *Penelope Hobhouse's Gardening through the Ages,* New York: Simon and Schuster, 1992

Isaacson, Richard T., *Gardening: A Guide to the Literature,* New York: Garland, 1985

Lyon, Thomas, editor, *This Incomperable Lande: A Book of American Nature Writing,* Boston: Houghton Mifflin, 1989

Marranca, Bonnie, editor, *American Garden Writing: Gleanings from Garden Lives Then and Now,* New York: PAJ, 1988

The New York Botanical Garden Illustrated Encyclopedia of Horticulture, 10 vols., edited by Thomas H. Everett, New York: Garland, 1980–82

Thacker, Christopher, *The History of Gardens,* Berkeley: University of California Press, and London: Croom Helm, 1979

Wheeler, David, editor, *Penguin Book of Garden Writing,* London and New York: Viking, 1996

JUDITH GERBER

Maksimir

Zagreb, Croatia

Location: eastern edge of the city of Zagreb

Maksimir is the largest and most valuable of Croatia's public gardens. Originally conceived in the 18th century and completed in the first half of the 19th century, Maksimir was the first public park, not only in Croatia, but also in all of southeastern Europe. Maksimir was named after its founder, the Zagreb bishop Maksimilian Vrhovac of Ehrenberg and Rakitovec (1752–1827). For a short while in the 19th century, the name of the park was Jurjaves, after Bishop Juraj (George) Haulik of Varaly (1788–1869), who actually realized Vrhovac's idea of a public park.

When it was created Maksimir was quite far from the city, but today it is an integral part of Zagreb's urban structure. The land set aside for the park was once covered by a forest of common oak (*Quercus robur*), alder (*Alnus* sp.), poplar (*Populus* sp.), and willow (*Salix* sp.). In the park's northern, higher part, the sessile oak (*Quercus petrae*) and hornbeam (*Carpinus betulus*) forest still survives. The park and surrounding forests covered an area of 402 hectares (993 acres). This was a very large park for what was then a fairly small city; when the park was planned and built during the first half of the 19th century, the population of Zagreb stood at about 10,000.

When Vrhovac became the bishop of Zagreb in 1787, he decided to present the residents of the city with a park for rest and recreation following the strict French style. The main promenade road leading from the entrance to a hilltop pavilion is the only remnant of the park's early baroque composition; it was later incorporated into a Romantic garden design. The first stage of development came in 1794, when the park was officially opened to the public. But Maksimir at that time was more a forest than a fully developed park.

When Juraj Haulik became the bishop of Zagreb in 1837, he turned this forest into a lovely, artistically valuable park. Haulik wished to set an example in agriculture, stimulate garden art, and improve standards of taste, as well as make the surrounding countryside more beautiful and give local residents a place to relax their bodies and minds. Work on the park proceeded from 1838 to 1847. During this time, thousands of oak trees were cut down, the ground was leveled, pits were dug out for lakes, meadows were opened, paths were laid out, and bridges were built. Numerous exotic trees, shrubs, and flowers were planted including *Abies pectinata, Acer rubrum, A. striatum, Aesculus pavia, A. lutea, A. carnea, Berberis canadensis, B. sibirica, B. cretica, Celtis australia, Cornus florida, Fraxinus americana, F. lentiscifolia, Gleditschia inermis, Laurus sassafras, Liriodendron tulipifera, Pinus canadensis, P. balsamea, Paulownia imperialis, Philadelphus coronarius, P. grandiflorus, Quercus ilicifolia, Ginkgo biloba, Syringa persica, S. chinensis, Taxus canadensis, Tilia americana, Ulmus americana, U. suberosa,* etc.

Though originally conceived in the baroque style, Maksimir became a distinctly Romantic park. Many of its architectural structures belong to the period of Romantic Classicism, coinciding with the Biedermeier style, and have elements of historicism. The park's baroque origins are now seen only in the 800-meter (875-yd.) central promenade and a star-like crossroads. The baroque star was transformed into a point from which seven views can be seen from the hilltop known as Vidikovac (*Belvedere*) or Kiosk.

At the time of its creation, Maksimir was a major garden project of the Austrian monarchy, to which Croatia then belonged. Accordingly, the garden's design was based on a park surrounding the Habsburg summer residence at Laxenburg near Vienna. Maksimir was thus planned as a park with two lakes. The most attractive and romantic lake was the lower lake, once a fish pond with row boats.

The design of Maksimir park is the work of several persons, and no single designer or architect could claim authorship. The person who contributed most to the garden plan was Haulik. It was at Laxenburg that he found his architects, gardeners, and sculptors. The leading name among this group was the landscape architect Michael Riedel, captain of the imperial manors of Schönbrunn, Hetzendorf, and Laxenburg. A second figure was Franz Schücht, imperial supervisor of architectural works, and later captain of the imperial manor of Laxenburg. The chief gardener was Franjo Serafin Körbler, while the sculptures were the work of Josip (Joseph) Kässmann and Antun Dominik Fernkorn.

Maksimir once had a large number of architectural structures, but many have disappeared. The classicist buildings date from 1839 to 1847; they included Echo Pavilion (*Latern-Tempel*), the Bishop's Summer House, the Belvedere (*Kiosk*), Umbrella (*Parapluie*), Nature Temple (*Bellevue*), People's Temple (*Volks-Tempel*), Gloriet, Moorish Pavilion, Swiss (Tyrolean) House, Quiet Hut (Peaceful Sleep) and Birch Hut (Fisher's Cottage).

There were three sculptures in the park by Kässmann (Reaping Woman, Group of Boys, and Fisher) and one sculpture by the very popular Fernkorn (a figure of St. George). In the Valley of Dahlias there was an obelisk,

Maksimir, *First Lake with Swans and Ducks,* from the graphic album "Jurjaves," Vienna, 1853
Courtesy of Hrvatske Bratske Zajednice BB

at the bottom of the Druid Grove was a toll cross made of black marble, and close to the main entrance was a figure of the Madonna.

A number of appropriately named specialty gardens were planned for the park, including a rose garden, hydrangea garden, bee garden, animal garden (deer garden), Valley of Dahlias, Swiss Valley, Nightingale Grove, and Druid Grove.

Synopsis

1787	Bishop Maksimilian Vrhovec of Zagreb has idea for establishment of baroque public park, the first in southeastern Europe
1794	First part of park officially opened to public
1838–43	Bishop Juraj Haulik finishes creation of park, designed by Michael Riedel and Franz Schücht
1839–47	Classical buildings built
1846	Upper lake completed
1847	Sculptures installed in park
1853	Graphic album *Park Jurjaves* (Jurjaves is a synonym for Maksimir) published in Vienna
1892	Pleasure ship sailed on Maksimir lakes

Further Reading

Maruševski, Olga, and Sonja Jurković, *Maksimir: The Famed Croatian Landscaped Garden,* Zagreb: Školska Knjiga, 1992

Obad Šćitaroci, Mladen, "Maksimir: A Romantic Episcopal Park in Zagreb, Croatia," *Journal of Garden History* 14, no. 2 (1994)

MLADEN OBAD ŠĆITAROCI
AND BOJANA BOJANIĆ OBAD ŠĆITAROCI

Malaysia

The history of gardens in Malaysia is comparatively recent. The botanical diversity of the forests and their economic importance, particularly for commercial hardwoods—whether pre- or post-British colonization—meant that horticulture, garden and park design, and their traditions remained relatively undeveloped until the second half of the 20th century. Since the advent of independence in 1963, however, greater emphasis has been placed upon garden and landscape creation.

The exceptions are the gardens directly associated with royal or sultanate palaces, which have a long history. There are, for example, written references to forbidden gardens and pleasure gardens of the Malaccan sultanate and the ornamental gardens of the Kelantan sultanate (Tanah Serendah Sekebun Bunga). The abundance of flowers, herbs, and fruit orchards of the Malay villages is mentioned by Munshi Abdullah in *The Travels of Abdullah* and remarked upon by other travelers in the late 1700s and early 1800s. Gardens and lawns were, during these times, associated with mosques and palaces, with banyan and frangipani trees and flowers planted in conjunction with Buddhist temples and cemeteries.

With British occupation, first as the Straits Settlements and then as the Federated States of Malaya, the concepts of town planning, ornamental gardens and parks, economic and botanic gardens, hill-station gardens, and forest reserves were introduced. Several gardens and lawns were also established by the British in direct association with their administrative offices, admiralty and gubernatorial residences, fort enclosures, and cemeteries, in places such as George Town, Ipoh, Taiping, Port Swettenham, Malacca, Singapore, Kuching, and with *padangs* associated with British administrative buildings and their recreation clubs. Singapore, originally one of the Straits Settlements, which became independent in 1965, is strongly intertwined with the garden and landscape history of Malaysia.

The various directors of the Singapore Botanic Gardens, especially during the Straits Settlements period, played an influential role in establishing an economic and botanic garden and a forestry system throughout the peninsula. Research within this institution directed the mass planting of roadside trees, hardwood forest plantations, and arboretums in various sultanates, and oversaw the introduction of rubber plantations and the establishment of botanic gardens at Penang and Malacca. The Penang "Waterfall" Gardens, established in 1884 and designed by Charles Curtis, remains today the only botanic garden in Malaysia and played a significant role in quietly enabling research at the Singapore Botanic Gardens. In the 1920s a forest research institute (Forest Research Institute of Malaysia, or FRIM) was established at Kepong, north of Kuala Lumpur, which today possesses an extensive collection of forest trees set in lawns with a series of plantations and plant-propagation areas.

With the development of rubber plantations in the early 1900s (particularly in the lowland forests on the west coast of the peninsula, occupying some 12 percent of the land mass) the British established a series of hill-station resorts and sanatoriums in conjunction with lakes and parklands in these cool temperate climates. Settlements at Cameron Highlands, Fraser's Hill near Kuala Lumpur, Bukit Larut (Maxwell's Hill) in Taiping, Penang Hill on Pulau Pinang, and Bukit Tunku (Kenny Hill) above Kuala Lumpur resulted in the establishment of small villages with architecture reminiscent of rural English villages. Often accompanying the villages and resorts were golf courses, plantations of conifers and deciduous trees, and fields of temperate vegetables and carnations. The residential area of Bukit Tunku and the 22 hectare (54 acre) Lake Gardens (1898) adjacent to the parliament buildings in Kuala Lumpur are illustrative of these developments. The Taiping Lake Gardens in Perak, opened in 1910 on the site of abandoned mining pools, and the more recent opening up of the Genting Highlands above Kuala Lumpur are extensions of this style. The latter were part of the British concept of recreation and urban greens. The adoption of this planning concept was aided by the appointment in 1921 of Charles Reade, a proponent of the "garden cities" movement and former government town planner for South Australia, as the colonial town planner. Under this policy notable landmarks, such as the Tudor-styled Selangor Club and its *padang* and the Bukit Tunku residential area, came into existence.

New settlement designs in the 1970s and 1980s continued this tradition. These include Shah Alam and Taman Tasik Shah Alam (commemorating the 25th anniversary of the sultan of Selangor's coronation), and parks such as Taman Tasik Permaisuri, inspired by the old royal garden, Laman Permaisuri in Cheras (created to honor retiring queen Raja Permaisuri Agong and influenced by the traditional Malay garden), Taman Tasik Titiwangsa in Kuala Lumpur, Taman Tasik Melati in Perlis, and Monument Park and Reservoir Park in Kuching, which are illustrative of Western planning and landscape design philosophies reinterpreted for a modern tropical environment. A second strand includes theme parks, such as David Ooi's Butterfly Farm (1986) in Penang, the Orchid Garden (1986) in the Lake Gardens founded in conjunction with the Pacific Area Travel Association, and the Hibiscus Garden (1989) in Kuala Lumpur, opened in conjunction with the meeting of the Commonwealth heads of government. A third strand consists of forest parks, such as Templer's Park

(1954), with its camping, cabin, swimming, and resort facilities near Kuala Lumpur, the nearby Serendah and Sungai Kanching Forest Reserves, the Matang Family Park in Sarawak, and the Kepong FRIM grounds.

Recent history has seen the development of the landscape architecture profession in Malaysia, aided by returning expatriates and recent Malaysian graduates trained in England and the United States. Part of the development has been due to the economic strategic planning by the Malaysian government, which is guided by five-year plans. The Second Malaysia Plan (1971–75) recognized that urbanization and industrialization were essential to growth, but the sprawl of large urban centers was restricted in the Third Malaysia Plan (1976–80) and an emphasis placed upon greening of the landscape and sustainability. In 1985 the first landscape architecture course was established at the Institut Teknologi MARA (ITM) under Puan Kamariyah Kamsah, and in the 1990s several other courses were established throughout Malaysia. In 1996 a separate federal Department of Landscape Architecture, previously within a Department of Town and Country Planning, was established.

Shifts in government policies, in line with the successive economic plans, have seen several initiatives unfold. A series of national parks, including Taman Negara on the central peninsula, Mount Kinabalu in Sabah, and Gunung Mulu and Bako in Sarawak, reflect an attempt to preserve the diminishing forests and untouched environments on the peninsula and in Borneo. Urban development projects have included an extensive urban park designed by Roberto Burle Marx in conjunction with the Petronas Towers, the Sarawak Riverfront in Kuching, the Klang River valley linear city, and the new international terminal at Sepang airport. Major landscape design programs were associated with the sporting complexes built for the 1997 Commonwealth Games, and strategic action plans have been initiated to conserve the historic places of Malacca and George Town. A number of golf courses and golf course suburbs have been developed, and there have been public-spirited attempts to increase the area of national parks and to conserve the character and landscapes of Taiping, George Town, and Penang Hill.

See also Singapore Botanic Gardens

Synopsis

1786 George Town, Penang, established by the British
1818 Singapore established by Stamford Raffles
1826 Straits Settlements, comprising Penang, Malacca, and Singapore, established
1884 "Waterfall" Botanic Gardens established in Penang
1895 Kuala Lumpur established as the British resident general's headquarters
1910 Taiping Lake Gardens opened
1921 Charles Reade appointed government town planner
1963 Malaysia granted independence
1965 Singapore gains independence from Malaysia
1985 First landscape architecture course established at Institut Teknologi MARA (ITM)
1995 Roberto Burle Marx commissioned to design an urban park in Kuala Lumpur
1996 Federal Department of Landscape Architecture established

Further Reading

Banfield, F.S., *Guide to the Botanic (Waterfall) Gardens, Penang,* Penang, Malaysia: Sinaran Bros. Sdn. Bhd., 1949

Beautiful Gardens of Malaysia: Landscaping to Better Living, Kuala Lumpur, Malaysia: Malaysian Agricultural Research and Development Institute, 1993

Bruce, Allan, "Notes on Early Mosques of the Malaysian Peninsula," *Journal of the Malaysian Branch of the Royal Asiatic Society* 69, no. 271 (1966)

Cartier, Carolyn L., "Creating Historic Open Space in Melaka," *Geographical Review* 83, no. 4 (1993)

Cockburn, P.F., "Tropical Botanic Gardens: Science of Public Amenity?" in *The Role and Goals of Tropical Botanic Gardens,* Kuala Lumpur, Malaysia: Penerbit Universiti Malaya, 1977

"Historical Notes on the Rubber Industry," *Agricultural Bulletin of the Straits and Federated Malay States* 9, no. 6 (1910)

Hosking, Sam, "Kapitan Keling Mosque Conservation Project," *View Australia* 5 (1996)

Jones, David, "The 'Waterfall' Botanic Garden on Pulau Pinang: The Foundations of the Penang Botanic Gardens, 1884–1910," *Journal of the Malaysian Branch of the Royal Asiatic Society* 70, no. 273 (1997)

Kamsah, Kamariyah, "Malaysian Landscape Architecture: Challenges for Educators," *Landscape Australia* 16, no. 3 (1994)

Khoo Kay Kim, Dato', "Taiping (Larut): The Early History of a Mining Settlement," *Journal of the Malaysian Branch of the Royal Asiatic Society* 64, no. 260 (1991)

Khoo Su Nin, *Streets of George Town, Penang,* Penang, Malaysia: Janus Print and Resources, 1993

Munshi, Mohamed Ibrahim, *The Voyages of Mohamed Ibrahim Munshi,* translated by Amin Sweeney and Nigel Phillips, Kuala Lumpur, Malaysia, and New York: Oxford University Press, 1975

Ridley, Henry Nicholas, "The History and Development of Agriculture in the Malay Peninsula,"

Agricultural Bulletin of the Straits and Federated Malay States 4, no. 8 (1905)
Teh Tiong Sa, "An Inventory of Green Space in the Federal Territory of Kuala Lumpur," *Malaysian Journal of Tropical Geography* 20 (1989)
Yueh-Kwong Leong, "Nature Reserves and Botanical Gardens in Malaysia," in *Proceedings of the International Association of Botanic Gardens, 10th General Meeting, 2–7 August 1987*, edited by K. Larsen, Brian Morley, and G. Schoser, Frankfurt: International Association of Botanic Gardens, 1989

DAVID JONES

Manning, Warren H. 1860–1938

United States Landscape Designer

Born into a well-established New England family, Warren Manning began working in his father's plant nursery as a boy. Through this experience and self-education, the young Manning acquired a thorough knowledge of plants, which led landscape architect Frederick Law Olmsted to hire him as an apprentice in 1888. Working in the Olmsted office as planting supervisor until 1896, Manning was involved in more than 100 projects, including the final installation of plants for the 1893 World's Columbian Exposition in Chicago; the planning of metropolitan park systems in Boston, Louisville, and Milwaukee; and the preparation and implementation of landscape designs for Biltmore, George W. Vanderbilt's massive North Carolina estate.

After leaving the Olmsted firm and opening his own Boston office in 1896, Manning quickly established himself as one of the nation's leading landscape designers and urban and regional planners. Among the more than 1,600 commissions that Manning worked on until his death in 1938 were projects for cities including Hopedale, Massachusetts, Harrisburg, Pennsylvania, and Birmingham, Alabama; designs for the model villages of Warren, Arizona, Gwinn, Michigan, and Goodyear Heights, Ohio; and campus plans, including proposals for the University of Minnesota and University of Virginia. In his work Manning also developed innovative methods to organize and display environmental data, which he first employed in his hometown of Billerica, Massachusetts, in 1910 and later used in preparing a national plan for the United States. An early advocate of participatory planning in the improvement of public spaces, Manning and his associates often organized "Community Days"—voluntary work sessions that brought people together to work on local landscape-related projects.

Manning expressed both his knowledge of plants and design skills in the large estate gardens he developed for several wealthy industrialists: Walden, Cyrus McCormick's mansion in Lake Forest, Illinois; Gwinn, for William Mather in suburban Cleveland; and Stan Hywet, Frank Seiberling's estate in Akron. Often termed *wild gardens* by Manning, the estate designs sought to capitalize on and emphasize local site features and qualities. The affiliation with Mather, president of the Cleveland-Cliffs Iron Company (CCI), extended from 1896 to 1930 and was especially important in the evolution of Manning's career. Mather hired Manning to prepare plans and landscape designs for CCI properties in northern Michigan, a region where the company had large iron-ore holdings. In addition to the model village of Gwinn, Manning provided designs for nurseries, office buildings, shaft houses, executives' homes, schools, and churches and also prepared master plans for local communities and a regional plan for Michigan's Upper Peninsula.

Manning served as mentor to a number of leading landscape designers, including Helen Bullard, Marjorie Sewell Cautley, Charles Gillette, Dan Kiley, Fletcher Steele, and Albert Taylor. He also wrote extensively on a wide range of landscape-related topics and was a founding member of both the American Park and Outdoor Art Association (later the American Civic Association) in 1897 and the American Society of Landscape Architects (ASLA) in 1899. While serving as president of the ASLA (1914–15), Manning promoted the creation of a National Park Service, which occurred in 1916. Following his death in 1938, *Landscape Architecture* noted Manning's "vital urge to accommodate a new world to the best uses of mankind" and his "extraordinary power of synthesis."

Biography

Born in Reading, Massachusetts, 1860. Worked in family's plant nursery for several years; apprenticed with Frederick Law Olmsted as planting design supervisor, 1888–96, collaborated on more than 100 commissions, including Biltmore estate and World's Columbian Exposition; opened Boston office, 1896; carried out more than 1,600 commissions in 40 states, including city park systems, city plans, model industrial villages, and estate gardens; prepared 927-page unpublished national plan for United States, 1919; played major role in formation of both American Park and Outdoor Art Association, 1897, and American Society of Landscape Architects, 1899; promoted creation of National Park Service while president of American Society of Landscape Architects, 1914–15. Died 1938.

Selected Designs

1894–1936	Walden estate of Cyrus McCormick, Lake Forest, Illinois, United States
1896–1932	Designs, various properties of the Cleveland-Cliffs Iron Company, northern Michigan, United States
1901–30s	City and park plans, Harrisburg, Pennsylvania, United States
1906	Model village of Warren, Arizona, United States
1906–14	Gwinn estate of William G. Mather, Cleveland, Ohio, United States
1907–25	Model village of Gwinn, Michigan, United States
1910	Environmental plan, Billerica, Massachusetts, United States
1911–16	Stan Hywet estate of Frank Seiberling, Akron, Ohio, United States
1915–19	"National Plan for the United States" (unpublished manuscript)
1917–23	Agassiz Park, Calumet, Michigan, United States
1919	City plan for Birmingham, Alabama, United States
1929	Regional plan, Upper Peninsula, Michigan, United States

Selected Publications

"Establishment of Public Parks," *American Gardening* (October 1897)

Stout Manual Training School: A Handbook for Planning and Planting Small Home Grounds, 1899

"History of Village Improvement in the United States," *Craftsman* (February 1904)

"Villages and Homes for Working Men," *Western Architect* (August 1910)

"Field of Landscape Design," *Landscape Architecture* (April 1912)

"A Step towards Solving the Industrial Housing Problem," *American City* (April 1915)

"Standardizing Scientific Name Abbreviations and Common Names of Plants," *Landscape Architecture* (October 1915)

"National Parks, Monuments, and Forests," *Landscape Architecture* (April 1916)

Warren H. Manning's City Plan of Birmingham, 1919

"National Plan Study Brief," with W. Harold Manning, *Landscape Architecture* (July 1923)

"A National Park System," *Parks and Recreation* (January 1924)

"Landscaping on an Iron Range," *Explosives Engineer* (August 1924)

"Agassiz Park of Calumet, Michigan, Built by Local Effort," *Parks and Recreation* (November-December 1927)

"Travelways of Beauty," *Landscape Architecture* (July 1930)

Further Reading

Alanen, Arnold R., and Lynn Bjorkman, "Plats, Parks, Playgrounds, and Plants: Warren H. Manning's Landscape Designs for the Mining Districts of Michigan's Upper Peninsula, 1899–1932," *IA: Journal of the Society for Industrial Archeology* 24, no. 1 (1998)

Alanen, Arnold R., and Lynn Bjorkman, "Early Twentieth-Century National Planning in the United States: The Vision of Warren H. Manning," *Annual Meeting Proceedings* (American Society of Landscape Architects) (1999)

Child, Susan, "Warren Manning, 1860–1938: The Forgotten Genius of the American Landscape," *Journal of the New England Garden History Society* 1 (Fall 1991)

Karson, Robin S., *The Muses of Gwinn: Art and Nature in a Garden Designed by Warren H. Manning, Charles A. Platt, and Ellen Biddle Shipman,* Sagaponack, New York: Sagapress, 1995

Karson, Robin S., "Manning, Warren Henry," in *Pioneers of American Landscape Design,* edited by Charles A. Birnbaum and Karson, New York: McGraw Hill, 2000

Neckar, Lance M., "Developing Landscape Architecture for the Twentieth Century: The Career of Warren H. Manning," *Landscape Journal* 8, no. 2 (1989)

ARNOLD R. ALANEN AND LYNN BJORKMAN

Market Garden

Market gardening is defined as growing fresh vegetables for the purpose of marketing the crops directly to the consumer. Therefore, the primary purpose for having a market garden is to make money. This is in contrast to the typical vegetable garden of the amateur or home gardener, whose primary purpose is to raise a supply for family or private use.

The concept of the market garden dates to the growth of vegetable and fruit gardens in early Rome. These gardens, called *hortus,* contained vegetables such as leeks, cabbage, beets, endive, and asparagus. Some evidence from Roman towns such as Pompeii indicates the existence of market gardening within the walls of the city. Some scholars speculate that this also occurred throughout Europe and in Britain. The Romans used the *hortus* not only for feeding their families but also as a market garden to earn money. Out of these market or kitchen gardens, the *villa rustica* of the wealthier Italian classes later developed. The *villa rustica* was a country house and garden that provided fruit, wine, and vegetables.

Later, market gardens in Rome continued to grow in order to meet the demand for vegetables from those who lived in cities. From these early market gardens the truck gardener trade developed. These truck gardeners formed into a guild around 1030.

During the Middle Ages in Europe, monasteries became the centers of horticulture. As such, they were the first to include vegetable gardens, specifically kitchen gardens. They took over the tradition of the *villa rusticas* of early Rome and supported their communities with fruits and vegetables.

Market gardening as we know it today began in England in the 16th century, although there were fruit, flower, and herb markets dating back to the 14th century. However, the charter for the first guild in England, the Gardeners' Company and the Fruiters' Company, was not granted until 1605. As towns such as London grew, a market for fresh fruits and vegetables developed. Soon, gardeners began selling their surplus produce from their gardens to earn extra money. Close to the roads, produce was being grown and sold directly to the public. The first market gardens from this period were always just on the outskirts of town, and as the town moved out, so would they. They provided a range of flowers, fruit, and vegetables to town and city dwellers.

Market gardens around London became plentiful during this time. The market gardens of the Westminster area were known as Neat House gardens. These Neat House gardens provided Londoners with their fresh produce for over 200 years. The varying periods of famine in the late 16th century that resulted in England's shift from a grain-dependent diet to one that included more vegetables provided an additional incentive for market gardens.

Market gardening, brought over from England, was among the first businesses in North America. In fact, the oldest family business remaining in the United States today is New Hampshire's Tuttle Market Gardens, a farm and retail market dating back to 1640. U.S. market gardens continued to grow from the 17th to the 19th century. The crops that were grown in these gardens were those that were easily cultivated by horse power. Some of the most popular crops included cabbage, tomatoes, watermelon, muskmelons, and sweet potatoes.

By the end of the 19th century, several books on market gardening had been published, including Peter Henderson's *Gardening for Profit* (1867), *Truck Farming in the South,* by A. Oemler (1883), *How to Make the Garden Pay,* by T. Greiner (1890), and *Market Gardening and Farm Notes,* by Burnet Landreth (1893).

Without the development of commercial vegetable production, modern market gardens would never have developed. However, vegetable market gardening differs from commercial production. In commercial production vegetables are marketed strictly through wholesalers, packers, and retailers to get to the consumer. In addition, commercial producers are large-scale producers who require storage facilities to market their crop year-round. Market gardeners, on the other hand, are small-scale producers. They sell all of their produce directly to the consumer during the growing season and develop their own markets.

Traditionally, the market garden was defined as a small area of up to ten acres (4 ha) that produced a range of crops such as vegetables, fruits, and some flowers. Today, the definition of a market garden still closely matches the traditional one. Basically, a market garden is a small acreage farm or garden, on high-value suburban land, whose primary marketing outlets are consumers, direct and local, meaning that the market gardener grows products such as vegetables and flowers to supply to consumers of a nearby city. Generally, they are found on farms of 2 to 20 acres (0.8 to 8 ha) having similar production, marketing, and seasonal problems. Because the area cultivated is typically small, the goal of the market gardener is to use every inch of the area throughout the growing season, meaning that many gardeners rely on companion cropping. To aid in this effort, high fertility of the soil is crucial. Therefore, gardeners use heavy fertilizing and successive crops to obtain continuous returns from the land. They also grow products that can be planted close together. Unlike the home vegetable garden, which focuses on a large variety of crops, the market garden focuses on a few crops.

With the advent of the train and then the automobile in the 19th and 20th centuries, market gardening led to the development of truck farming. Often, the term *truck farming* is used interchangeably with the practice of market gardening. However, there are differences between the two. Truck farming refers to growing one or more vegetable crops on a large scale in order to ship them to distant markets. The market garden is more of a local garden; it sells its products in the city or region where they are grown. Truck farming is usually less diverse and less intensive than market gardening. For example, the market garden requires that crops be spaced close together in order to obtain the large returns necessary to make a profit, whereas truck farmers rely on crops that require more space to grow.

When it was first developed, truck farming depended entirely on local and regional markets. As railroads and large-capacity trucks were developed, and refrigerated carriers were introduced, truck farms spread to the cheaper lands of the western and southern United States. This enabled farmers to ship seasonal crops to distant markets where their cultivation is limited by climate. Truck-gardening areas are located based on climate, soil, and shipping facilities. The major truck-farming areas in the United States are in California, Texas, Florida, along the Atlantic Coastal Plain, and in the Great Lakes area. Among the most important truck crops are tomatoes, lettuce, melons, beets, broccoli, celery, radishes, onions, cabbage, and strawberries.

The industrial revolution also helped the market garden gain in popularity. For example, the types of machines and equipment used by the modern gardener, such as tractors or planting machines, have greatly increased productivity. Another important development to the growth of both market and truck gardens was the introduction of overhead irrigation. This enabled hundreds of acres to be watered more quickly and efficiently. In addition, developments in plant nutrition, pest and disease control, and plant breeding have all helped to increase the market gardeners' yields.

Since they rely on direct marketing to consumers, most market gardeners today sell their products in a variety of ways, including roadside stands, local and regional farmers' markets, local restaurants, pick-your-own farms, and community-supported agriculture shares and subscriptions. Many market gardeners focus on growing only organic produce in order to compete with local farmers' markets and supermarkets. Still others specialize in certain crops that are not as profitable for larger growers to produce. Some market gardeners use a commission agent and sell their products strictly to local restaurants, florists, or local grocers. The most common crops for market gardeners are beets, onions, celery, radishes, parsley, lettuce, beans, broccoli, Brussels sprouts, cabbage, corn, cucumbers, gourds, pumpkins, leeks, herbs, tomatoes, squash, and sugar peas.

Further Reading

Gras, Norman Scott Brien, *A History of Agriculture in Europe and America,* London: Pitman, and New York: Crofts, 1925; 2nd edition, New York: Crofts, 1946

Henderson, Peter, *Gardening for Profit: A Guide to the Successful Cultivation of the Market and Family Garden,* New York, 1867; new and enlarged edition, 1918; reprint, Chillicothe, Illinois: American Botanist Booksellers, 1997

Staines, Ric, *Market Gardening: Growing and Selling Produce,* Golden, Colorado: Fulcrum, 1991

Thacker, Christopher, *The History of Gardens,* London: Croom Helm, and Berkeley: University of California Press, 1979

Webber, Ronald, *Market Gardening: The History of Commercial Flower, Fruit, and Vegetable Growing,* Newton Abbot, Devon: David and Charles, 1972

Wright, Richardson Little, *The Story of Gardening: From the Hanging Gardens of Babylon to the Hanging Gardens of New York,* London: Routledge, and New York: Dodd, Mead, 1934; reprint, New York: Dover, 1963

JUDITH GERBER

Marly

Marly-le-Roi, Yvelines, France

Location: approximately 10 miles (16.6 km) west of Paris city center, between Saint Germain-en-Laye and Versailles, exit 6 on the A13 autoroute

Marly is probably the greatest lost garden of Europe. It was created and constantly altered by Louis XIV (1638–1715) in the last 35 years of his life, lingered on during the 18th century, and was finally destroyed at the beginning of the 19th century. Now a ghostly layout of grassy terraces, a pond (the Abbreuvoir), and some trees are all that remains of a garden that was once hailed as one of the most spectacular and innovative in Europe.

In the late 1670s Louis XIV, at the height of his success, decided to move the court from Saint-Germain-en-Laye to Versailles, his former retreat. Versailles was vastly enlarged, and in 1682 the court moved in. The king, in need of a new retreat, chose the unpromising but secluded valley of Marly, north of Versailles. The site consisted of a narrow, marshy, steep-sided valley orientated north-south. The Duc de Saint-Simon called it "this great cesspool." Its slopes were wooded and also well watered by copious springs, which gave endless construction and maintenance problems. The royal architect, Jules Hardouin-Mansart, in collaboration with the artist Charles le Brun, produced an architectural design of great originality for the valley. The scheme was unified and deliberately hierarchical. It was dictated partly by the site and had clear Italianate influences. At the head of the valley (the south end), was the king's château, the Pavillon Royal, a square building based loosely on Palladio's Villa Rotunda, with a large central octagonal salon. In front, down the central axis of the valley, was a formal arrangement of large water basins, dominated by Le Grand Miroir, flanked on either side by four long terraces. At regular intervals along both top terraces were six small pavilions, with trompe l'oeil architectural facades designed by le Brun, featuring the signs of the zodiac. These two-bedroomed buildings were for the king's privileged guests at Marly, an honor eagerly sought ("Sire, Marly?" was the question on everyone's lips) and sparingly given. The main approach, from Versailles, was down the steep east side of the valley to the Pavillon Royal. The initial plan had a simple layout of bosquets on the flanks of the valley: on the east the Bosquet de Louveciennes or du Levant, on the west the Bosquet de Marly or du Couchant. These remained but were later increasingly elaborated and extended. Above the Bosquet du Levant the Bois de la Princesse was given an irregular layout of tortuous, serpentine walks for Louis XIV's granddaughter, the Duchesse de Bourgogne, in 1697–98. This was an interesting, almost rococo, departure from the ubiquitous rectilinearity of garden layouts of the day.

From an early stage enormous efforts were made to bring water to the garden in large quantities; it was to become the chief adornment of the gardens. Three large reservoirs were constructed above the valley in 1681, and in 1684 the Machine de Marly, a huge, elaborate, and noisy pump on the river Seine, built by Arnold de Ville, began lifting water into an aqueduct leading to the reservoirs.

In 1683 Louis XIV gave his first entertainment at Marly, while it was virtually a building site and the fountains were not yet working. After a slow start, his personal involvement was about to increase dramatically. In the same year he took over the supervision of the project, working closely with Mansart on buildings and from 1684, on the gardens with Louis de Rusé, who had worked at Saint-Germain for the king. Mansart, jealous of de Rusé's influence, finally managed to have him sacked in 1699. There is no evidence that the royal gardener, André Le Nôtre, was involved at Marly; in August 1700 the king himself gave Le Nôtre, aged 87 and close to the end of his life, a conducted tour of the gardens.

The main planting of the gardens took place between 1685 and 1695, and during this time the king developed a passion for garden design. From 1686 onward it became the main occupation of his leisure time. The style and content of the Marly gardens therefore reflected not only the general prevailing ideas but also the king's personal tastes and enthusiasms. The result was that within the overall framework there was constant change, both in style and content.

The acerbic Duc de Saint-Simon, who ironically was the savior of Marly after the king's death, said that the king "se plut à tyranniser la nature, à la dompter à force d'art et de trésors" (likes to tyrannize nature by torturing it into art forms and ornaments). Certainly, planting on the terraces and in the walks and *salles de verdure* (green rooms) in the bosquets was exceptionally formal. Mature trees—lime, elm, sycamore, maple, sweet chestnut, and horse chestnut—were brought in from local forests or Flanders. They were trained up elaborate frameworks and clipped into arcades (*portiques* and *berceaux* [arbors and tunnel arbors]), walls (*charmilles,* often of hornbeam), and even more tortured shapes, such as the parasol over the basin and statue of *Diana* (by Anselme Flamen [1695]), at the north end of the Bosquet de Marly, which required a substantial iron framework. Within the bosquets outdoor rooms, with names such as Le Grand Vestibule, Le Grand Salon, and Le Grand Ovale, were created and constantly rearranged. Basins, fountains, statues, benches, games, railings, trees, and topiary appeared, were altered, moved, and disappeared.

Topiary, in box, yew, juniper, phillyrea, myrtle, and holly, played an important part. Bulbs and other flowers filled the parterres around the Pavillon Royal. Hyacinths, tulips, irises, double anemones, daffodils, and peonies came pouring in from the nurseries at Le Roule, near Paris. The king developed an enthusiasm for exotics and ordered a plant-hunting expedition to North America. In 1700 Sieur Loitron was commissioned to make "un petit jardin de fleurs rares" (a little garden of rare flowers) in a warm spot in the nearby village in order to cultivate the new introductions, but the climate and soil of Marly proved unsuitable. The king turned his attention to carp.

Vue du Château et du Parc de Marly
Copyright Garden Picture Library

The years 1695 to 1700 were Louis XIV's period of fondness for *rocaille* (rock- and shellwork) and lavish, complicated fountains. In style the basins and fountains were similar to those of Versailles—baroque, heavily elaborate, colorful, and already outdated in an era that was moving toward the rococo and a simpler, more classical style. The Cascade Champêtre in the Bosquet du Levant, completed in 1702 and encrusted in rock-work and oyster shells, exemplified this style.

The central axis was dominated by water. On the steep slope at the south end La Rivière, a spectacular cascade of 52 steps (the number of weeks in the year, not insignificant, given the symbolism in the gardens of the diurnal cycle, months of the year and so on) designed by Father Sébastien Truchet, was built in 1697–99. This was the king's pride and joy, particularly as it outshone his brother's at St. Cloud. At its foot were two basins, the Bassin du Fer a Cheval and the Bassin de la Demi-Lune des Vents. On the other side of the Pavillon Royal was the Bassin des Quatre Gerbes (jets), below which was the largest pool, Le Grand Miroir, initially adorned with five jets, later reduced to one. An elaborate cascade led down to the pool of Les Grandes Nappes at the lower end of the garden. Beyond was the Abbreuvoir, a pool for watering horses. In 1698 the central axis was extended further north and the view opened up, by the removal of a hill and the planting of an avenue as far as a final high jet, La Grande Gerbe.

After about 1704 all *rocaille* work was removed and replaced with marble. The Cascade Champêtre was demolished and rebuilt in marble in 1706; La Rivière was remodeled with polychrome marble in 1706 and 1707. Marble statues of the *Seine* and *Marne,* by Antoine Coysevox (now in the Louvre, Paris) were put in place on either side of the head of the cascade in 1702. At about this time some pools and fountains were removed and many of the fountains were simplified in order to save water; it was found that the Machine de Marly was not powerful enough to keep up with the proliferation of fountains. In this way the routine of operating them from nine in the morning until nine at night could be continued. Among many other changes, the *salle de verdure* called Le Parnasse was completely remodeled in 1701, its former three jets being replaced by a single one 26 meters (28.5 yd.) high. The highest fountain at Marly was the Fontaine du Senat, which replaced a small reservoir in 1701. Its single jet was 29 meters high.

It was also about 1702 that the king developed a passion for carp. Gifts flooded in from the estates of fawning courtiers and elsewhere, and the four Bassins des Carpes were made either side of the Pavillon Royal especially to house them. These basins were probably the most lavishly decorated of all the many pools at Marly, and they underwent several transformations. The fish were more or less treated as pets, given names and mourned when they died, as they frequently did. The only basin in which the carp thrived was Le Grand Miroir.

The final style innovation at Marly was the introduction of polychrome ceramic tiles to line the Bassins des Carpes in 1712–14. The designs were geometric, in black, green, blue, and yellow. This was a startling and dramatic departure from the traditions of Versailles. Unfortunately, the tiles lasted a very short time, as in 1716 the basins were filled in.

At first sculpture played little part at Marly, with recycled pieces being used; the lead children from the Allee d'Eau at Versailles were sent to Marly in 1689. Eventually a great deal, in marble and bronze, both contemporary and antique, was amassed. The dominant theme was arcadian and pastoral. From 1694 Louis XIV commissioned special works, many of them by Antoine Coysevox, who was aided by his nephews Nicolas and Guillaume Coustou. The famous pair of *Chevaux de Marly* by Guillaume (now in the Louvre), which flanked the Abbreuvoir, were in fact not put in place until 1745. The final statues in the Bassins des Carpes were two pairs of "runners" from classical mythology, *Hippomenes and Atalanta* (1711) and *Apollo and Daphne* (1713). Most of the statuary, except that in lead, was saved when the gardens were destroyed, and much is now in the Louvre. The only statues now at Marly are the two Meleagris groups by Nicolas Coustou, which have been returned.

Games were another element of the garden, meant to amuse the courtiers and visitors; Louis himself preferred to walk. The most spectacular was the Ramasse or Roulette, a primitive roller coaster 260 meters (284 yd.) long, which was installed in the Bosquet du Levant in 1691. In the same year a huge swing, the Escarpolette, was put up in the Bosquet du Couchant but was replaced by a carp pool in 1702. A primitive croquet course, or Jeu du Mail, was laid out in walks in the same bosquet, and several of the *salles de verdure* had facilities for parlor games adapted for outdoors.

Soon after Louis XIV's death in 1715, the regent, Philippe d'Orléans, threatened destruction on the grounds of expense of upkeep, which was astronomical. A scurrilous poem current in Paris in 1717 echoed this view:

> A quoi nous sert en ce pays
> Ce colifichet de Marly?
> Envoyons-le au Mississippi!
>
> What use is this bauble Marly
> To us in this day and age?
> Send it to the Mississippi!

The Duc de Saint-Simon recognized Marly's historic and artistic importance and gained a reprieve. The gardens were simplified; Louis XV took the finest statuary to the Tuileries, and in 1727 La Rivière was destroyed and grassed over. The courts of Louis XV and XVI spent occasional days here, and the garden gradually took on a more romantic character as the trees grew freely. The public was given access on Sundays and public holidays. The last great commission for Marly was Guillaume Coustou's *Chevaux de Marly*. Finally, in 1781 the court abandoned Marly, and in 1792 it was appropriated by the state. The contents of the palace were sold, the gardens plundered. In 1803 Marly became the property of one Alexandre Sagniel, who set up a weaving mill, eventually went bankrupt, and then demolished all the buildings. By the time Napoléon I bought Marly in 1811, it was little more than ground to hunt over.

During the early 18th century Marly's influence spread throughout the courts of Europe. At La Favorite, in Germany, Lothar Franz Count Schönborn, archbishop and elector of Mainz, made a similar layout on the banks of the Rhine in 1700. It became known as "Little Marly" and was destroyed by French troops in 1793. Peter the Great, emperor of Russia, visited Marly in 1717 and in 1722 began Marly, Peterhof, on the Gulf of Finland. Its main cascade was a copy of the Cascade Champêtre. La Granja, Spain, laid out in 1720–46 by Louis XIV's grandson, Philip V, was clearly influenced by Marly, with a cascade very similar to La Rivière and statues by Frémin, Thierry, and Bousseau, all of whom had worked at Marly. In order to understand something of the character of Marly, it is these sites that should be visited, together with the Richelieu wing of the Louvre, in Paris, which houses much of the remaining statuary. Only faint echoes of Louis XIV's last great garden are now apparent at Marly itself.

Synopsis

1679–83 Construction of main buildings and layout of garden, designed by Jules Hardouin-Mansart and Charles Le Brun

1683 First entertainment at Marly, hosted by Louis XIV
1684 Machine de Marly comes into service pumping water from Seine
1685–95 Planting of garden
1691 *Ramasse* (elaborate roller coaster) and *escarpolette* (giant swing) installed in garden to entertain visitors
1693 Work on fountains, cascades, and pools begun
1697–98 Bois de la Princesse laid out with serpentine walks for Louis XIV's granddaughter, duchesse de Bourgogne
1697–99 La Rivière built, designed by Father Sébastien Truchet
1699– Innumerable changes to *salles de verdure*
1700 Louis XIV orders plant nursery for exotics in neighboring village
1702 Statues of Renommé and Mercure de Pégase by Antoine Coysevox installed on either side of Abbreuvoir
1702– Bassins des Carpes stocked with carp
1704– All *rocaille* (rock and shell) work removed from basins and replaced with marble
1712–14 Bassins des Carpes relined with polychrome ceramic tiles
1714 Fontaine de la Nymphe constructed, the last before Louis XIV's death (demolished 1716)
1715 Philippe d'Orléans threatens to demolish Marly to save money
1716– Basins filled in
1727 La Rivière destroyed and slope grassed over
1745 Statues of Renommé and Mercure de Pégase moved to Tuileries gardens and replaced by Chevaux Cabrés by Guillaume Coustou
1781 Marly abandoned by court
1792 Marly appropriated by State
1803 Bought by Alexandre Sagniel
1806 Sagniel demolishes all buildings
1811 Estate bought by Napoléon I

Further Reading

Adams, William Howard, *The French Garden: 1500–1800,* London: Scolar Press, and New York: Braziller, 1979

Delille, Jacques, *Les jardins, ou, L'art d'embellir les paysages: Pöeme,* Paris, 1782; as *The Gardens: A Poem,* London, 1798

Mabille, Gérard, Louis Benech, and Stéphane Castelluccio, *Vues des Jardins de Marly: Le roi jardinier,* Paris: Alain de Gourcuff, 1998, as *Views of the Gardens at Marly: Louis XIV, Master Gardener,* translated by Barbara Mellor, Paris: Gourcuff, 1998

Magne, Émile, *Le château de Marly: D'après des documents inédits,* Paris: Calmann-Lévy, 1934

Woodbridge, Kenneth, *Princely Gardens: The Origins and Development of the French Formal Style,* London: Thames and Hudson, and New York: Rizzoli, 1986

ELISABETH WHITTLE

Marot, Daniel 1661–1752

French Architect, Interior Designer, and Garden Designer

Daniel Marot was a late 17th-century designer and architect, who was especially important for translating the French style in England and Holland during the reign of William III of England. The corpus of over 300 engravings that he produced, which were widely known throughout Europe, described and defined the style of Louis XIV more completely than the work of any of his contemporaries. Marot was born in Paris, where his father Jean Marot was also a designer and producer of engravings, most importantly the so-called "Petit Marot" (1654–60) and "Grand Marot" (1670) volumes. The son began work in Paris, first in his father's studio and then under Jean Berain, an important figure in the organization of Versailles, who commissioned from him some of his first engraved works.

In 1685, the 24-year-old Marot, as a Huguenot, chose to leave France after the Edict of Nantes and settled in Holland. In 1686, he published his first set of engraved designs and received a commission from William Adrian of Nassau-Odijk, who had recently served as ambassador to France. Marot was commissioned to design the staircase, other interiors, and garden buildings at Slot Zeist in Utrecht. That same year, he worked

Parterre de broderie, designed by Daniel Marot
Courtesy of Wageningen UR Library

for the future Queen Mary at Honslaardijk, where he used elements such as oval-mirrored panels and stucco work on the ceiling that were typical of his later work; he also created a large chimney piece with steps for displaying porcelain.

It was at Zeist that Marot met the architect Jacob Roman with whom he was to collaborate closely, most importantly at the Royal Palace at Het Loo, the country residence of William III, near Appledorn (1687–1702) and on the house De Voorst (1697–1700), built for Joost van Keppel, the Earl of Albemarle. What Marot did at Het Loo was typical of the range of his work. For if he was still referred to as *maître-ornemaniste* rather than architect, he was able here, as elsewhere, to design all the interiors and also layout the gardens and garden buildings, occasionally designing an exterior facade. The work he did at Het Loo established Marot's reputation, and he was afterwards often busy within the royal circles of Holland and England.

When in 1688 William III became king of England, Marot was called in to help with many of the decorations and redecorations of the royal residences, most notably at Hampton Court, which was extended in the 1690s. Here William Talman and Christopher Wren were responsible for the design of the new buildings and the fountain court, but Marot supplied designs for chimney pieces, gilt pier suites, textile hangings, and the decoration of the king's private dining room, which was similar to what he had done at Het Loo. He was probably also responsible for the interiors of Queen Mary's apartments in the Water Gallery, which were later demolished. It is also probable that Marot worked on the gardens; while the general design was the responsibility of the royal gardeners, George London and Henry Wise, the plan of the parterre before the east front, known to us now only in the view by Jan Knip in *Britannia Illustrata* (1708), bears all the trademarks of Marot's style.

Marot is also known to have worked at this time for the duke of Montague at Petworth House, Boughton, and Montague House; some of the details of designs at Boughton exist as drawings in Marot's hand, and the colors there, mainly red, blue, and green, were those that had been employed by him at Het Loo. His designs for state beds, made during this period with the Huguenot craftsman Francis Lapierre, were also very popular. Their lively contours and headboards, carved with putti and lattice, were too florid for Holland, but they fit well with the more formal and luxurious interiors in England.

Marot seems to have left England in 1697; although he may have returned in 1706, he was based in Holland. He stayed largely in The Hague, except for the period from 1705 to 1713 when he was in Amsterdam. The pension granted to him by William III in 1698 was confirmed on William's death by the States-General. He was then free to continue working with a number of middle-class and official patrons, most notably for the Friesian Stadt-holder Johan Willem at Schloss Oranienstein (1707–9) and Slot Oranjewoud, Herrenveen (1707). After about 1715 he worked mostly as an architect; his notable projects include the Huis Schuylenburch (1715), a combination of traditional Dutch structure with Louis XIV-style ornamentation; the Huis Wassenaar-Obdam (1716–17); and the Hôtel Hugueton, now the Royal Library (1734–39).

Marot's designs for interiors were copied continually in Holland, and even the essentially baroque style of his architecture had an influence in the southern Netherlands, most notably through Jan Peter van Baurscheit (1699–1768), who worked with him at the Hôtel Hugueton. The publication of volumes of his plates, the first in 1709, another in 1713, and a later two-volume edition with some 237 plates, continued to keep his work known to many beyond the court.

Much of Marot's work is now gone, especially in England where his interior designs were soon superseded by the Palladian tradition of Lord Burlington and William Kent. The gardens, like all gardens, were changed by nature and by the taste of later designers in pursuit of a more natural style. But Marot's ways of designing are still recoverable at Het Loo, which was carefully restored from 1979 to 1984; it was this building that had kept his fame alive through published plates, most importantly those by Romeyn de Hooghe beginning in 1708, and reprints that stopped in 1776, with those of the Amsterdam publisher G.W. van Egmond.

See also Het Loo Palace

DAVID CAST

Biography

Born in Paris, 1661. Began work as engraver and designer in Paris studio of father, engraver and architect Jean Marot, and then under Jean Berain; as a Huguenot, chose to leave France after revocation of Edict of Nantes, 1685, settled in Netherlands; published first set of engravings, 1686; commissioned by William Adrian of Nassau-Odijk to design interiors and garden buildings, 1686; designed interiors and laid out gardens at Het Loo for William of Orange, 1687–1702; went with William of Orange to England when he became King William III in 1688 and designed apartments and gardens at Hampton Court, London, 1689–90s; returned to The Hague, Netherlands, 1697, and with exception of a short period in Amsterdam from 1705 to 1713, remained there designing interiors for private and official patrons. Died in The Hague, Netherlands, 1752.

Selected Designs

1685–86	Slot Zeist, Utrecht, Netherlands (with Jacob Roman)
1689–1695	Gardens and apartments, Het Loo, Apeldoorn, Gelderland, Netherlands
1688–90s	Parterre and interiors, Hampton Court, London, England
1695–1700	De Voorst, Gelderland, Netherlands

Selected Publications

Nouveaux livre d'ornaments, 1706

Further Reading

Hunt, John Dixon, editor, *The Dutch Garden in the Seventeenth Century,* Washington, D.C.: Dumbarton Oaks Research Library and Collection, 1990

Jackson-Stops, Gervase, "Daniel Marot and the 1st Duke of Montague," *Nederlands Kunsthistorisch Jaarboek* 31 (1981)

Lane, Arthur, "Daniel Marot: Designer of Delft Vases and of Gardens at Hampton Court," *Connoisseur* 123 (1949)

Ozinga, Murk D., *Daniel Marot: De schepper van den Hollandischen Lodewijk XIV-Stijl,* Amsterdam: Paris, 1939

Thurley, S., *The King's Privy Garden at Hampton Court Palace: 1689–1995,* London: Apollo, 1995

Mason, William Hayton 1724–1797

English Poet and Gardener

William Mason was the author of the didactic poem *The English Garden*, published in four books between 1772 and 1781. Although often regarded as a long and tedious poem, it celebrated the rise of the English landscape garden and its apogee in the work of Lancelot "Capability" Brown. In the poem Mason connects the gardening world of Alexander Pope and William Kent with the Picturesque perceptions of the late 18th century. Book 4, in which Mason describes Nerina's Bower, breaks new ground by providing a precocious essay on the beauties of the flower garden, which had hitherto been ignored by landscape improvers such as Brown. Mason helped re-create this romantic flower garden at Nuneham Courtenay in Oxfordshire for the second earl of Harcourt in 1777.

As an early disciple of the Picturesque, Mason recommended an Italian tour and the study of the paintings of Claude Lorraine by garden makers, so that they could bring back to England "on memory's tablet drawn" suitable scenes that could be combined with local color to produce the ideal garden. True taste, he believed, could only be expressed with a "poet's feeling and painter's eye." Just as the poet uses words and the painter pigments, so the gardener has his spade, seeds, and plants, which, when employed with a discriminating eye and the help of nature, were capable of creating a work of art. Hence, Mason attributed the origins of the English landscape style to Pope and Kent and, like Thomas Whately and William Shenstone, saw gardening as an activity that could teach moral lessons. *The English Garden* is dedicated to simplicity, by which Mason meant a lack of artifice and affectation; like his mentor Pope, he warned against ignoring the "genius of the place." In this sense Mason was a Georgic poet of the Virgilian mode, celebrating prosperous and populous landscapes, modified by the hands of taste to produce an aesthetic bonus.

Mason came into the public eye with *An Heroic Epistle to Sir William Chambers* (1773), a satirical poem in the style of Pope, written in response to Chambers's *Dissertation on Oriental Gardening* (1772). Chambers launched an attack on the vapid landscapes of Brown and wished to replace them with greater variety and intricacy, but unfortunately, his infatuation with imaginary Chinese novelties invited a defense of the solid achievements of the English landscape school, which Mason provided. The *Heroic Epistle* quickly went through 14 editions in four years and was much admired by the literati of the period, including Horace Walpole, with whom Mason had a long and significant correspondence.

Following the *Heroic Epistle* Mason was forever linked in the public mind as an apologist of Brown. He composed the epitaph on Brown's memorial in Fenstanton Church in Huntingdonshire and introduced him to the second earl Harcourt in 1778. But by the time Mason came to compose the final part of *The English Garden* between 1779 and 1781, there was much that he held precious that was at odds with the "untutor'd Brown." Brown's lack of painterly credentials was especially galling for a promoter of Picturesque susceptibilities. Brown also found Mason's minor amendments to his plans for Nuneham Courtenay irksome. Mason's fastidious concern for "hide and discover" views and his opposition to Brown's proposal to break an avenue connecting the house and church, which Mason regarded as a "long Cathedral aisle of shade" undermined Brown's professionalism. Other aspects of an earlier era of gardening were beginning to appeal to Mason, like the "gothic extravaganza" created for Queen Caroline by Kent at Richmond, which had been swept away by Brown in 1765.

Acander's landscaping activities in book 4 of *The English Garden* were mostly on a small scale and the antithesis of Brown's intrusive gestures. Acander's delight in the Gothic and the possession of a grotto (an icon for the disciples of Pope) suggest the survival of a taste for the rococo, while Nerina's Bower, with its glades of flowers, looks away from Brown toward William Gilpin's "forest scenery" or back toward Philip Southcote's *ferme orneé*. The enclosed flower garden itself, which Mason designed at Nuneham Courtenay, albeit placed in an out-of-the-way situation, represented the very antithesis of Brown's broad-brush approach to the landscape. Ironically, it embraced a degree of formality condemned in the *Heroic Epistle* and was filled with the flowers recommended by Chambers for his Chinese garden. Mason, it seems, eventually joined the opponents of Brown, and Oliver Goldsmith, one of his more vigorous adversaries, would have applauded Mason's token reprieve for all those villagers cast out of Brown's empty landscapes. They were freely allowed to enjoy Lord Harcourt's flower garden, which, as it happened, was on the site of the old village graveyard. Sir Uvedale Price was perhaps the first to notice that "Mr. Mason's poem on modern gardening is as real an attack on Brown's system as what I have written."

The Nuneham flower garden, laid out and altered at least once by Mason, took its inspiration from Rousseau's *Julie; ou, La nouvelle Héloïse* (1761; *Julie; or The New Eloise*) and was a "romantic garden before there was romanticism" (Batey, 1973). It was enclosed and without prospects, designed in the Picturesque manner as a series of vignettes, to be viewed as Gilpin recommended, from "stations" along serpentine paths. It was enhanced with a great deal of emblematic statuary while the island beds—kidney shaped and round—were planted with a studious desire for asymmetry and variety, in a cottage garden style that in time became the essence of the Picturesque. Although elements of the planning and planting had a retrospective quality—the borders were at first edged in box—Mark Laird believes that Mason established a "new mode of planting," which was eventually reflected in numerous gardens of the late 18th and 19th centuries.

Mason's espousal of the Picturesque came from his appreciation of the English landscape, especially in its more rugged form. In this he owed a great deal to two giants of the landscape movement—Thomas Gray and William Gilpin. Gray taught Mason to love Gothic architecture and mountainous countryside, and on Gray's death in 1771 Mason became his literary executor and published his *Life and Letters* (1774). Mason also corresponded for many years with Gilpin, drawing attention in the *Life* to Gray's "Tour of the Lakes," which was passed around in manuscript among an ever-widening audience. In 1782 Mason persuaded Gilpin to publish his *Observations on the River Wye,* a tour originally completed in 1772. It was dedicated to his friend. Mason also read Gilpin's *Forest Scenery* before it was published in 1791 and had in his possession the manuscript of the Western Tour of 1777 when he died in 1797.

Thus, Mason nurtured two key figures in the development of Picturesque sensibilities and was particularly upset in 1794 when Richard Payne Knight and Sir Uvedale Price—"the two Dilettanti Coxcombs"—appeared to be attacking Gilpin's version of Picturesque beauty. Walpole urged Mason to defend the reputation of Brown, but Mason found this distasteful, as he probably agreed with many of Knight's and Price's criticisms. Nevertheless, he deplored Knight's "Jacobinical" attempt at guillotining the reputation of the hapless Brown. Knight was hurt when the anonymous *Sketch from the Landscape* (1794)—written by his Herefordshire neighbor John Matthews of Belmont—accused him of borrowing Mason's ideas; he claimed in the second edition of *The Landscape* (1795) that he had never read *The English Garden*. Mason explained in private to Gilpin that he had no appetite for a public debate with Knight and Price, in part because the latter had treated him civilly in his *Essay on the Picturesque.*

Humphry Repton spoke highly of Mason and claimed that *The English Garden* was one of the key texts he read in the 1780s before embarking on a career as a landscape gardener. Although, as a practitioner rather than a theorist, he played down the affinity between painting and gardening, many of Repton's books quote passages from Mason, implying that Repton understood that his clients recognized the canonical authority of *The English Garden.* Moreover, increasingly they wanted flower gardens, and Mason was indelibly associated with this genre. Thomas Johnes told Gilpin in 1787 that he had laid out his gardens at the Hafod, near Aberystwyth, with *The English Garden* in his hand and that his daughter Marianne replicated Nerina's Bower in her elevated flower garden. As the county surveys of historic gardens in England are being published, the full extent of Mason's influence upon the florescence of the late Georgian flower garden is being revealed.

John Claudius Loudon also borrowed from Mason when he was asked to produce a flower garden at Scone Palace (1803) in Scotland, but as the flower garden was taken more and more for granted in the 19th century, the pivotal position of *The English Garden* was forgotten. But Mason's reputation in his own time was rediscovered with the publication of his correspondence with Walpole, Gray, Richard Hurd, and Gilpin, which ensured that, in any discussion of Georgian landscape aesthetics, his name was hard to ignore. As Gilpin predicted in his brief memoir on his friend (*A Short Account of Different People . . .*), Mason's poetry may have lacked "spirit and vivacity" but his letters, "animated with little strokes of satire," would long be appreciated.

See also Nuneham Courtenay

Biography

Born in Hull, East Yorkshire, England, February 1725. Educated at St. John's College, Cambridge, 1743–49; elected fellow of Pembroke College, Cambridge, 1749, using the influence of his friend poet Thomas Gray; introduced to Richard Hurd, ca. 1750; became rector of Aston, near Rotherham, South Yorkshire, 1754; appointed prebendary of York Minster, York, England, 1756, and chaplain to George III, 1757; married Mary, daughter of William Sherman of Hull; inherited small estate near Richmond, North Yorkshire, 1768; corresponded with Horace Walpole, 1763–96, and with William Gilpin, 1775–97; published poem in four volumes, *The English Garden,* 1772–81, which had a great influence on garden designers; published Thomas Gray's *Life and Letters,* 1774. Died after an injury to his shin, in Aston, 1797.

Selected Designs

1754	William Mason's garden, Aston Rectory, Aston, Yorkshire, England
1750s	Richard Hurd estate, Thurcaston, Leicestershire, England

1777 Estate of the second earl of Harcourt, Nuneham Courtenay, Oxfordshire, England
ca. 1780 Frogmore House, Windsor, Berkshire, England
ca. 1780 William Lee and Lady Elizabeth (nee Harcourt) estate, Hartwell, Buckinghamshire, England

Selected Publications

The English Garden: A Poem, 4 vols., 1772–81; collected edition, 1783
An Heroic Epistle to Sir William Chambers, 1773
The Life and Letters of Thomas Gray, 1774
Secular Odes, 1788

Further Reading

Barbier, Carl Paul, *Samuel Rogers and William Gilpin: Their Friendship and Correspondence,* London and New York: Oxford University Press, 1959
Batey, Mavis, "William Mason, English Gardener," *Garden History* 1 (1973)
Batey, Mavis, "The English Garden in Welsh," and "Two Romantic Picturesque Flower Gardens," *Garden History* 22 (1994)
Daniels, Stephen, *Humphry Repton: Landscape Gardening and the Geography of Georgian England,* New Haven, Connecticut: Yale University Press, 1999
Hunt, John Dixon, *The Figure in the Landscape: Poetry, Painting, and Gardening during the Eighteenth Century,* Baltimore, Maryland: Johns Hopkins University Press, 1976
Hunt, John Dixon, and Peter Willis, editors, *The Genius of the Place: The English Landscape Garden, 1620–1820,* London: Elek, and New York: Harper and Row, 1975
Hurd, Richard, *The Correspondence of Richard Hurd and William Mason, and Letters of Richard Hurd to Thomas Gray,* edited by Leonard Whibley, Cambridge: University Press, 1932
Hussey, Christopher, *The Picturesque: Studies in a Point of View,* London and New York: Putnam, 1927; reprint, London: Cass, 1983
Jacques, David, *Georgian Gardens: The Reign of Nature,* London: Batsford, and Portland, Oregon: Timber Press, 1983
Laird, Mark, "'Our Equally Favorite Hobby Horse': The Flower Gardens of Lady Elizabeth Lee at Hartwell and the 2nd Earl Harcourt at Nuneham Courtenay," *Garden History* 18 (1990)
Pett, Douglas Ellory, *The Parks and Gardens of Cornwall,* Penzance, Cornwall: Hodge, 1998
Price, Uvedale, *Essays on the Picturesque,* 2 vols., London, 1794–98; reprint, 3 vols., Farnborough, Hampshire: Gregg International, 1971
Simo, Melanie Louise, *Loudon and the Landscape: From Country Seat to Metropolis, 1783–1843,* New Haven, Connecticut: Yale University Press, 1988
Stroud, Dorothy, *Capability Brown,* London: Country Life, 1950; new edition, London: Faber, 1975
Stuart, David C., *Georgian Gardens,* London: Hale, 1979
Walpole, Horace, *The Correspondence of Horace Walpole, Earl of Orford, and the Rev. William Mason,* edited by J. Mitford, 2 vols., London, 1851

DAVID WHITEHEAD

Mattern, Hermann 1902–1971

German Landscape Designer

Reactions to social circumstances mark the stages of Hermann Mattern's life. Pious parents of different faiths brought him up to be liberal but aloof. At the age of ten he rejected hypocritical middle-class conventions by joining the Wandervogel, a division of the German youth movement in which boys and girls explored their native land together. The experiences of his older brother in World War I made him a pacifist.

Because of his affinity toward landscaping and the urge to be independent quickly, Mattern became a gardener. After his apprenticeship and some time traveling, he studied from 1924 to 1926 at the Institute for the Study and Research of Horticulture in Berlin-Dahlem. His major interest was in landscaping, but he also attended lectures at the Weimar Bauhaus by Walter Gropius and Oskar Schlemmer.

In Berlin in the 1920s Mattern became acquainted with Expressionism and modernism through his friendship and contacts with Hugo Häring, Arthur Korn, the Luckhardt brothers, Hans Scharoun, Bruno and Max

Taut, and Martin Wagner. He worked with the garden architects Georg Bela Pniower in Berlin and Leberecht Migge in the artist colony of Worpswede, both of whom leaned toward social reform ideals.

Karl Foerster, a world-renowned plant breeder and garden writer, brought the young and gifted Mattern to Bornim, near Potsdam, to be the director of his drafting studio in 1927. Here, Mattern was incorporated into the liberal and humanistic group that became known as the Bornim Circle of gardeners, architects, musicians, authors, artists, and scholars gathered around Karl Foerster, including Wilhelm Kempff, Hermann Hesse, Carl Zuckmayer, and Käthe Kollwitz.

With this background Mattern, Karl Foerster, and Herta Hammerbacher developed in the artificial landscape of Potsdam created by Peter Josef Lenné a new style of garden called the Bornim Style, known in England as the Foerster-Mattern School. What was the difference between the Bornim style and the established styles?

Regarding the need for prestige in the German empire and the struggle for reform in the youth movement, Germany developed a combination of Art Nouveau and classicism with geometric, strongly architectural garden spaces, as exemplified by Hermann Muthesius, Max Läuger, and Erwin Barth.

The gardens by Gertrude Jekyll in England, with their delicate compositions of color in perennials, summer flowers, and shrubs, had become even closer to nature and more extensively cultivated under the hand of William Robinson and were highly influential on the Continent. In Germany Willy Lange in particular propagated the perennials found in the wild at forest edges, in order to form gardens according to natural motifs. Thereby he strongly influenced Foerster and his cultivating goals—to develop perennials immune to changes in climate along with selected wild plants and grasses that could thrive in gardens. With Bornim's contemporary orientation and undogmatic attitude came informal, livable landscape gardens that provided easy transitions from house to garden. Mattern comprehended the innermost form of a site and built his gardens and landscapes as works of art—simple, generous, emphasizing roominess by modeling the lay of the land and by plantings outlining and concentrating the landscape. The garden vistas of the Bornim Style were influenced by the new science of ecology. Foerster's cultivation made possible condensed ecological views without the need to pay attention to plant sociology. Mattern remarked that no one could make a garden with ecology alone, and he experimented with long-lasting, easy-care groupings of perennials, grasses, bulb plants, and shrubs.

Mattern's first large work, which still exists in its basic outlines, was a 1927 Cubistic garden on a steep hillside in Heidelberg, built for the Nobel Prize winner Dr. Friedrich Bergius as a conglomerate of stone cubes, water, and overflowing plantings. This commission was followed by many domestic gardens, often for prominent clients, as well as public gardens and layouts for housing estates.

In the years following 1930, when the National Socialist activities became stronger and more encompassing, Mattern, together with many other intellectuals and artists, joined the Communist Party, seeing there the only hope for a democratic opposition. As a result, during the next years he was kept under surveillance and sometimes excluded from public contracts.

During this time there were private clients, such as Albert Speer, who in 1935 contracted for a house garden in Berlin. In the early 1940s he repeatedly offered Mattern a professorship, but Mattern declined such a position "under the current government." Another client was the Jewish factory owner Silbermann in Brandenburg, for whom Mattern, together with Scharoun, built a sheltered pool garden in 1937.

In 1936 Mattern and the architect Gerhard Graubner won first prize in the design competition for the Reichsgartenschau (Garden Exhibition of the German State) of 1939 in Stuttgart-Killesberg, also known as the "World Garden," and therefore not "nationalistic." The design was heavily opposed in National-Socialistic journals and lectures because of its liberal layout without regard to any axis or symmetry. A rich assortment of perennials, shrubs, and trees, combined with local spontaneous vegetation, led from one setting to another, interspersed with wider aspects and views. The Killesberg became the best-known of Mattern's works and became the accepted style with the wider public.

In 1936 the Reichslandschaftsanwalt (Landscaping Counsel of the State) Alwin Seifert was able to engage Mattern as an Autobahn landscaper, using the argument that he didn't need a party member for such work, just the best professional. During the war this position was altered into a "Consultant for Nutrition and the Promotion of Fruits and Vegetables" under the Organisation Todt. Mattern laid out large fruit and vegetable gardens, especially in Russia and France, carried out landscaping for housing estates in Germany, and designed a system for green spaces in Prague according to social reform principles. Such contracts kept Mattern from military service.

After the war Mattern's sensitivity and intuition, as opposed to dogmatic narrow-mindedness, made him decide early for the West. From then on Mattern worked on a broad scale. In addition to innumerable private and public gardens, he designed garden exhibitions, health resorts, student villages, cemeteries, allotments, housing-estate landscaping, and numerous houses. He was engaged both theoretically and practically in housing estates and city landscapes. Mattern wanted to create a livable landscape in which humans could live—that is, to dwell, to work, to find refreshment, and to work for the community. He promoted the intense and concentrated use of space in order to protect the environment from any further misuse. He propagated the idea of planning the structure of a landscape with a goal not only of preserving but also of developing and strengthening it.

In 1948 Mattern became a consultant for the reestablishing of the Werkakademie (Technical Academy) at Kassel in the Bauhaus model. He was one of the founders of the revitalized German Garden Society, was a founding member of the art exhibition "documenta," and in 1961 was called to the position of professor at the Technical University of Berlin. In 1965 he established the Karl Foerster Foundation for the applied study of vegetation. In 1966 he initiated the Peter Josef Lenné Prize for young garden and landscape architects, which now receives worldwide participation. He arranged the preservation of the Bücherei des Deutschen Gartenbaus (Library of German Horticulture), was a member of the Arts Academy of Berlin, and copublished the book series *Bauwelt Fundamente* (Fundamentals of the World of Architecture), started in 1964, and the journal *Pflanze und Garten* (Plant and Garden), started in 1950. With his frequent coauthor Beate zur Nedden, his second wife, he wrote numerous articles and several books about gardens and environmental problems.

Biography

Born in Hofgeismar, Germany, 1902. Passed examination for gardeners after two years of study and began gardening professionally, 1921; studied at Lehr- und Forschungsanstalt für Gartenbau (Institute for the Study and Research of Horticulture) in Berlin-Dahlem, and audited lectures at the Bauhaus in Weimar, 1924–26; served as technical gardening consultant for Magdeburg city expansion commission and in Worpswede with Leberecht Migge, 1926; directed Karl Foerster's garden design studio in Bornim, 1927–35; married Herta Hammerbacher, a fellow garden architect, 1928; married photographer Beate zur Nedden, 1935, who photographed his works and edited most of his books, articles, and lectures; founded his own design studio, and partnership of Foerster, Mattern, and Hammerbacher, 1935; served as landscape consultant for Autobahn construction and as Consultant for Nutrition and the Promotion of Fruits and Vegetables for Todt organization, 1936–45; called to Kassel to reestablish and reorganize the Werkakademie (today Gesamthochschule [Polytechnic University]) as professor of landscape architecture, 1948; served as consultant for setting up city of Bonn as provisional seat of government, 1949; director of the Institute for Landscape Architecture, Berlin University, 1961–70; established Karl Foerster Foundation for Applied Study of Vegetation, 1965; initiated Peter Josef Lenné Prize for young garden and landscape architects, 1966. Died in Greimharting, on the Chiemsee in Upper Bavaria, 1971.

Selected Designs

Approximately 5,000 designs are archived in the Design Collection of the Technical University, Berlin.

1927	Garden for Dr. Friedrich Bergius, Heidelberg, Germany
1927–39	Numerous domestic gardens, including those for Fritz Lang and Thea von Harbou, and for Hans and Marlene Poelzig in Berlin, Germany; for Fritz Schminke in Löbau, Germany; for Wilhelm Kempff in Potsdam, Germany; for Dr. Anthony van Hoboken in Vienna, Austria; for Oskar Moll in Berlin, Germany
1930	Grounds of the IG Farben administrative buildings in Frankfurt, Germany
1939	Reichsgartenschau (Garden Exhibition of the German State), Stuttgart-Killesberg; Freundschaftsinsel (Island of Friendship), Potsdam, Germany
1945–53	Refugee settlement Hinrichssegen in Upper Bavaria: settlement grounds and several buildings, including interior furnishings
1949	Garden layout at Villa Hammerschmidt, Schaumburg Palace, and Bundeshaus in Bonn, Germany
1950	German Garden Exhibition, Stuttgart-Killesberg, Germany
1955	2. Bundesgartenschau (2nd Garden Exhibition of the Federal Republic of Germany), Kassel, Germany
1956–58	Resettlement of approximately 200 agricultural establishments from crowded villages in Baden-Württemberg, Franconia, and Hessen, Germany
1958	World exhibition in Brussels, Belgium (special exhibition agriculture)
1948–69	Numerous domestic gardens for individuals in Germany, France, Sweden, and Switzerland; health resort parks including Bad Oeynhausen; castle gardens, such as Dyck on the lower Rhine; public green spaces, including those for the Philharmonic in Berlin, and the government in Detmold, Germany; green spaces for housing estates, such as Hansa Quarter and Tegel South in Berlin; memorials including Gregenstein near Kassel, Germany

Further Reading

Gröning, Gert, and Joachim Wolschke-Bulmahn, "Mattern," in *Grüne Biographien*, Berlin: Patzer, 1997

Heinrich, Vroni, "Mattern," in *Neue Deutsche Biographie*, vol. 16, Berlin: Duncker and Humblot, 1991

Heinrich, Vroni, "Hausgärten von Hermann Mattern," *Gartenpraxis* 5 (1996)

Heinrich, Vroni, "Hermann Mattern: Leben und Werk," in *Kontinuität oder Brüche? Werkstattberichte zur Landspflege in der Nachkriegszeit*, Munich: Technische Universität München, 1996

Heinrich, Vroni, *Die Idee der Stadtlandschaft bei Hermann Mattern*, in *Beiträge zur räumlichen Planung*, vol. 50, Hannover: Universität Hannover, 1999

Heinrich, Vroni, ed., *Hermann Mattern, 1902–1971: Gärten, Gartenlandschaften, Häuser* (exhib. cat), Berlin: Akademie der Künst, 1982

Reitsam, Charlotte, "Hermann Mattern," *Garten und Landschaft* 12 (1998)

VRONI HEINRICH

Mawson, Thomas Hayton 1861–1933

English Landscape Architect and Town Planner

Thomas Mawson was the first to call himself a landscape architect when he founded his practice in the Lake District in 1884. His two brothers, Isaac and Robert, ran the nursery and contracting side of the business, while Thomas handled commissions for the design of gardens on a consultancy basis. Since leaving school at the age of 12, he had spent as much time as possible reading books and visiting gardens whenever he could. He admired particularly the work of the English garden designers John Claudius Loudon and Edward Kemp.

Mawson's first commission of any size came in 1889, when Colonel Sandys asked him to design a garden for his new house, Graythwaite Hall, near Lake Windermere. Mawson placed the formal area near the house and planned an informal garden of sloping lawns, rhododendrons, and azaleas, with woodland beyond. His practice grew steadily as clients recommended him to their friends, and commissions came in for larger gardens in the northwest of England and Scotland and then from the south. In 1900 he published a book on landscape architecture titled *The Art and Craft of Garden Making*, using examples of his own work. The book eventually ran to five editions, the last being published in 1924. It brought in a number of commissions from all over the country and from abroad, and in order to reduce to some extent the time he spent traveling, Mawson moved his office to Lancaster, opening a small London office.

Mawson was a religious person—a Congregationalist—and an active fundraiser for his local church. One man he approached was Sir William Lever, later to become Lord Leverhulme, who made a donation and asked for advice on a new garden he was planning for his home at Thornton Hough near Port Sunlight. This was the beginning of a long and fruitful association and indeed friendship, which ended only in 1924 on Lord Leverhulme's death. There were three gardens designed by Mawson as his client had two additional homes—one at Rivington, near Bolton, and the other at Hampstead, London. The former was a barren west-facing hillside on which thousands of deciduous and coniferous trees were planted, as well as many species of rhododendrons. There were terraces, loggias, and pergolas, a watchtower, lawns, a Japanese garden, a lake, and waterfalls. The Hill at Hampstead was much smaller and enclosed on the heath side by a pergola, which, after the third phase of development was 800 feet (244 m) long. Before the outbreak of World War I, Mawson persuaded Lord Leverhulme to found a chair of civic design at Liverpool University. This delighted Mawson as he had felt for a long time that the United Kingdom was well behind the United States in this respect; he was equally pleased when invited to become the first visiting lecturer.

In 1908 Mawson was nominated as the British entrant for, and won, the international competition for the design of the gardens to surround the Peace Palace in The Hague. The aim in the laying out of the six-acre (2.5 ha) garden was to unite the palace with the natural beauty of the park on a monumental scale, while bringing both into a proper topographical relationship with the city. Mawson favored bringing the building well forward, with entrances recessed into the ground. In his planting scheme he sought the impression of restfulness and spaciousness.

In the first decade of the 20th century, a number of local authorities held competitions for the design of

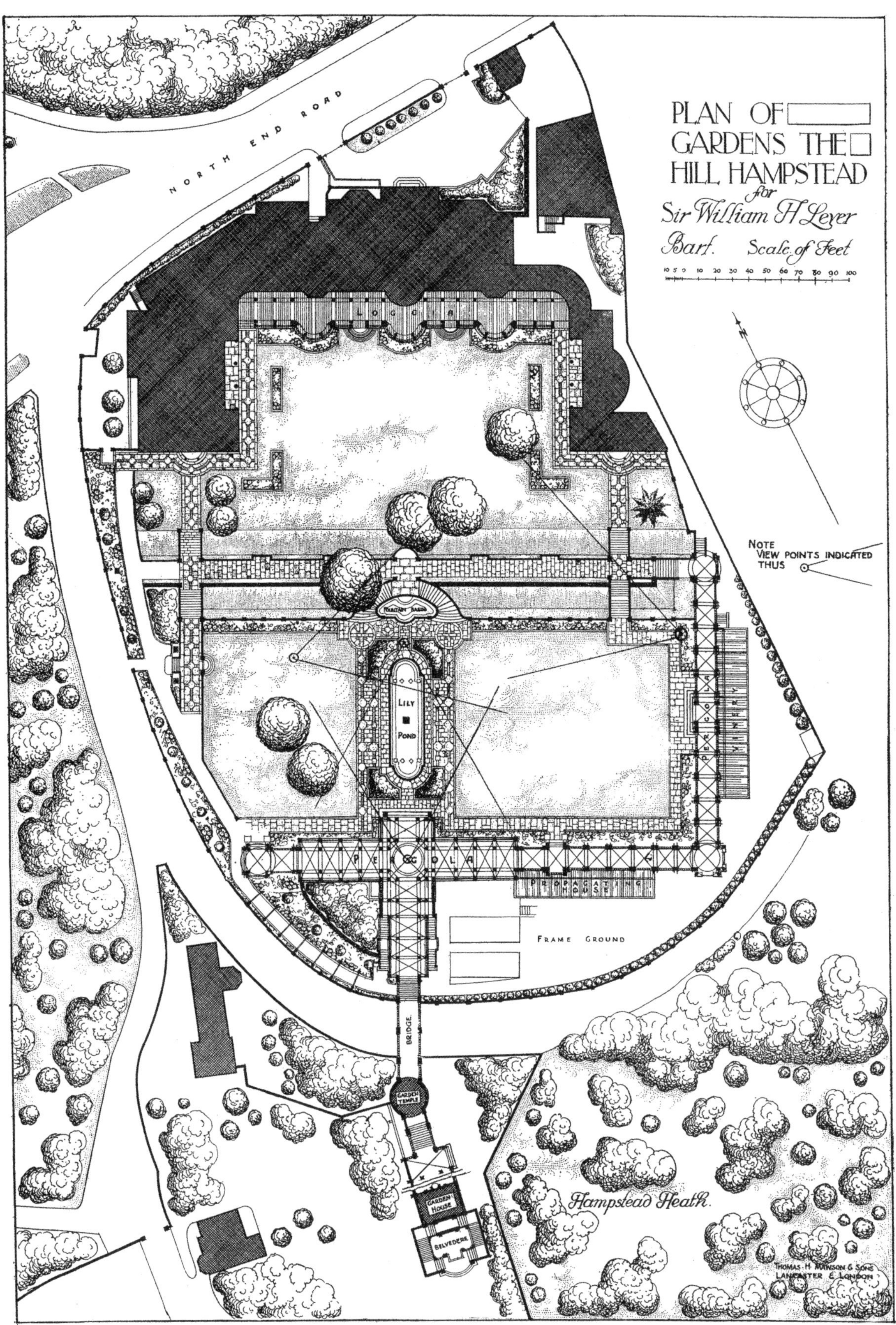

Site plan for the Hill at Hampstead garden, designed by Thomas Mawson, from Thomas Mawson, *The Art and Craft of Garden Making*, 1912

public parks, the building of which would give employment to men who were out of work at that difficult time. Mawson won one such competition, which was for a park at Newport in South Wales. Other park commissions followed, one being on an old pottery factory tip at Hanley near Stoke-on-Trent. On the sloping site he planned a pavilion in a formal garden on the higher ground, along with a bowling green and tennis courts, with lawns surrounded by oak trees and beech trees running down to a boating lake at the bottom of the site.

This type of work was spiritually rewarding for Mawson, as he felt strongly that he wanted to improve the life of those on very low incomes in urban areas; such was his sincere social conscience. His work for local authorities led him into the town planning sphere, as at times he was asked to lay out housing schemes adjacent to his parks. He therefore set about learning as much as possible by reading books on the subject and visiting as many cities in the United Kingdom and abroad as he could.

After a few years Mawson felt skilled enough to write his second book, which was entitled *Civic Art, Studies in Town Planning, Parks, Boulevards and Open Spaces,* and he published it in 1907. As a result of this book, he was invited to make lecture tours, initially in the United Kingdom, but later abroad, thus bringing him more commissions. He approached town planning, not surprisingly, from the standpoint of a consultant landscape architect, which profession he always described as the "master art." He was invited to make a tour across Canada in 1911, delivering lectures to the city fathers of most of the major cities. This tour brought in commissions for improvements to the open spaces in cities such as Regina (Saskatchewan), Vancouver (British Columbia), and Calgary (Alberta), and the design of the new resort of Banff, in Alberta. While en route to Canada for a second tour, he received a cable from the king and queen of Greece inviting him to plan improvements around the Acropolis, to the royal palace gardens, and in other areas of Athens.

The outbreak of World War I in 1914 caused many of Mawson's landscape and town planning projects to come to a halt, and most of his staff joined the forces. In order to keep himself occupied fruitfully, he initiated a project for the building of villages for partially disabled ex-servicemen. He wrote a report on the topic entitled "An Imperial Obligation" directed toward the government. However, it took several years of pressure by Mawson before this concept of government responsibility was accepted and the first village built at Lancaster.

In 1917, with the war still not over, Mawson was asked by the Greek government to replan the northern city of Salonika, which had been burnt to the ground in an accidental fire. He set up an office there helped by his two eldest sons and staffed by men drawn from the British and French armies. His philosophy was to divide the new city into three sectors, separated by public open spaces, which had the secondary but important role of firebreaks. After the war Mawson was invited to set up an office in Athens and carry out further work for the government, but he declined the offer as he felt it would be a business risk if he did so.

The practice of T.H. Mawson and Sons was never to recover fully from the effects of the war, although some clients asked for their postponed projects to be completed. There were more public parks in England, at Blackpool and Weston-Super-Mare, and town planning schemes for Northampton and Hastings and St. Leonards. In the mid-1920s Mawson was diagnosed as suffering from Parkinson's disease, becoming increasingly crippled, and handed his work over to his sons. He was, however, elected president of the Institute of Landscape Architects and the Town Planning Institute; he was also appointed a founding member of the Royal Fine Arts Commission.

Summarizing his career, one cannot but be impressed by his extremely dedicated efforts to elevate his profession. From the founding of his firm in 1884 until his health began to fail, he carried out over 125 garden designs and 50 town planning and park schemes. Mawson strove for the sincere approach to his art, dispensing with clutter and picturesque wavy lines, which had been popular with the mid-Victorians. His town planning work was very much on classical principles, with grand vistas and symmetry where appropriate. His persistence, culminating in the founding of the chair in civic design, undoubtedly advanced the establishment of further training courses in the United Kingdom. He was without question the leading landscape architect in England of the late-Victorian and Edwardian periods, but as so many of his garden schemes were labor intensive, and with high maintenance costs of the hard-landscaping, many of them have deteriorated. It is likely, however, that he will in due course take his place among the important landscape architects of the world.

Biography

Born near Lancaster, England, 1861. Worked for nurseryman outside London; decided to become landscape architect and not horticulturist; studied many books, visited numerous gardens, and set up own practice in Windermere, 1884; designed over 125 gardens and 50 public parks and town-planning schemes in the United Kingdom, Europe, and Canada; won international competition for design of gardens surrounding Peace Palace at The Hague, Holland, 1910; numerous lecture tours in Canada on Civic Design, 1910–14, from which town-planning commissions followed; carried out various town-planning and garden projects in Athens for Greek Royal Family; redesigned Salonika, 1917, after disastrous fire; designed industrial villages for disabled ex-servicemen from World War I; president of Town-Planning Institute and appointed founder member of

Royal Fine Arts Commission, 1923; elected first president of Institute of Landscape Architects, 1929; T.H. Mawson and Sons carried on by his sons, Edward P. and John W. Mawson. Died in Lancaster, England, 1933.

Selected Designs

1889 Graythwaite Hall, Sawrey, Lancashire, England
1899 Mount Stuart, Isle of Bute, Scotland
1902 Foots Cray Place, Kent, England
1904 Skibo Castle, Dornoch, Scotland
1905–12 Thornton Manor, Thornton Hough, Cheshire, England
1906 Duffryn, Cardiff, Wales; Roynton Cottage, Rivington, Lancashire, England
1906–24 The Hill, Hampstead, London, England
1908 Huidöre, Copenhagen, Denmark
1908–10 Peace Palace, The Hague, Netherlands

Public Parks

1910 Hanley, Stoke, Staffordshire, England
1911 Belle Vue, Newport, Gwent, Wales; West Park, Wolverhampton, West Midlands, England
1912 Wascana, Regina, Saskatchewan, Canada; Royal Palace, Athens, Greece
1913 British Columbia University, Vancouver, Canada
1920 Moor Park Golf Course, Hertfordshire, England
1922 Stanley Park, Blackpool, Lancashire, England
1923 Marine Gardens, Weston-Super-Mare, Somerset, England

Selected Publications

Art and Craft of Garden Making, 1900; 5th ed., 1926
Civic Art: Studies in Town Planning, Parks, Boulevards, and Open Spaces, 1911
City of Calgary, Past, Present, and Future, 1914
Bolton As It Is and As It Might Be, 1916
An Imperial Obligation: Industrial Villages for Partially Disabled Soldiers, Sailors and Flying Men, 1917
Northampton: A Scheme of Development and Reconstruction, 1925
Life and Work of an English Landscape Architect, 1927

Further Reading

Beard, Geoffrey, and Joan Wardman, *Thomas H. Mawson, 1861–1933: The Life and Work of a Northern Landscape Architect* (exhib. cat.), Lancaster: University of Lancaster, 1976
Brown, Jane, *Gardens of a Golden Afternoon: The Story of a Partnership: Edwin Lutyens and Gertrude Jekyll,* London: Allen Lane, 1982; updated edition, London and New York: Penguin, 1994
Brown, Jane, *The English Garden in Our Time: From Gertrude Jekyll to Geoffrey Jellicoe,* Woodbridge, Suffolk: Antique Collectors' Club, 1986; revised edition, as *The English Garden through the Twentieth Century,* Woodbridge, Suffolk: Garden Art, 1999
Forsyth, Alastair, *Yesterday's Gardens,* London: HMSO, 1983
Harvey, Sheila, and Stephen Rettig, editors, *Fifty Years of Landscape Design, 1934–84,* London: Landscape Press, 1985
Holme, Charles, editor, *The Gardens of England in the Northern Counties,* London and New York: The Studio, 1911
Leverhulme, William H.L., *Viscount Leverhulme,* London: Allen and Unwin, and Boston and New York: Houghton Mifflin, 1927
Mawson, David, "Thomas H. Mawson, 1861–1933," *Landscape Design* 127 (August 1979)
Ottewill, David, *The Edwardian Garden,* New Haven, Connecticut: Yale University Press, 1989
Plumptre, George, *Great Gardens, Great Designers,* London: Ward Lock, 1994
Pugsley, Steven, editor, *Devon Gardens: An Historical Survey,* Stroud, Gloucestershire: Sutton, 1994
Smith, M.D., *Leverhulme's Rivington,* Chorley, Lancashire: Nelson, 1984
Wright, Myles, *Lord Leverhulme's Unknown Venture: The Lever Chair and the Beginnings of Town and Regional Planning, 1908–48,* London: Hutchinson Benham, 1982

DAVID MAWSON

Maze

Many people use the words *maze* and *labyrinth* synonymously, while others make a distinction between them. Some use the term *maze* to refer to the 17th-century development of hedge mazes and *labyrinth* to refer to the structures described by the writers of antiquity or as a general term for any confusing arrangement of paths. Both words have come to signify a complex path of some kind and so for purposes here will be used interchangeably.

The first recorded labyrinth in history was built in the north of Egypt at the time of King Amenemhet (1841–1797 B.C.). The Greek writer Herodotus provides a fairly detailed description of this massive building complex, which was part tomb, part shrine, part initiatory complex, and part storehouse. Heredotus states that "all of the works and buildings of the Greeks put together would certainly be inferior to this labyrinth as regards labor and expense" and also describes it as "greater than the Pyramids." After this, the most famous labyrinth of antiquity was that of Knossos on Crete, built for King Minos around 1600 B.C. by the engineer Daedalus to contain the Minotaur, a monster half man and half bull. The palace ruins show evidence of the cult of the bull and of sacrificial killing with the double ax or *labrys:* this symbol of Minoan power is thought to be the origin of the word *labyrinth*. But during the same period, or perhaps earlier, people along the Baltic coasts were also building stone labyrinths for ritual purposes. Sweden still has about 280 of these labyrinths, and Finland another 140.

Labyrinths have been used as ornament or magical protection on a variety of artifacts from coins, jewelry, and baskets to church bells, stone crosses, and doorposts. On a larger scale labyrinths have been cast in bronze, made of pebble and boulders, cut into turf, laid as gravel or brick pathways, and marked with hedges, walls, wooden fences, or wire mesh. However and wherever they have existed, the basic theme of the labyrinths has been of penetrability and entrapment. They have also been used magically for the trapping of malevolent spirits. Labyrinths can be made large enough for people to walk in or small enough to be a talismanic jewel. The puzzle hedge maze may be the most familiar labyrinth large enough for people to walk in.

As Europe emerged from the Middle Ages into the Renaissance in the 15th century, knot gardens and garden labyrinths became fashionable. In 1477 in France the Roi René, duc d'Anjou, had a *daedalus* (labyrinth) at the Château de Bauge. Jacques Androuet Du Cerceau created a cypress maze at Tuileries and two hedge mazes about 1520 at the Château de Gaillon near Rouen. In the latter part of the 17th century, J. Hardouin-Mansart laid out the extravagant and famous labyrinth for Louis XIV at Versailles. Charles Perrault described it in 1677 in his book titled *Labyrinthe de Versailles*. This maze with rectilinear and curving pathways contained 39 hydraulic statues representing the Aesop fables. The labyrinth was destroyed in 1775 and replaced by the Bosquet de la Reine.

The earliest-known maze in Holland was at the royal palace of Het Loo, which later inspired the creation of the maze at Hampton Court in England. The hedge maze at Hampton Court is probably the world's most famous hedge and is certainly the oldest in England. Although it may have originated in Elizabethan times, the present maze was planted as part of the gardens laid out for William of Orange in 1690. Its unusual trapezoidal shape is due to the symmetrical layout of baroque paths in the Wilderness, the area in which the maze is located. The maze covers about a quarter of an acre (0.1 ha), and its longest side measures 68 meters (74 yd.).

In the late 17th and early 18th centuries, block mazes became popular. Block mazes were a variation of the hedge maze in which the pathway was made through an otherwise solid block of shrubs or a thicket. In addition to the maze at Versailles, other examples of block mazes in France at this time could be found at Choisy-le-Roi and Chantilly. Some of the maze designs of Batty Langley, published in his *New Principles of Gardening* (1728), derived from the French model, being block mazes with spiral and serpentine pathways, statuary, and refuges. As the *jardin anglais* garden style became popular, designers changed the formal French and Italian gardens to reflect this new fashion in garden design. For many gardens almost everything that had existed before, Renaissance, mannerist, baroque, and rococo, were wiped out. The decline in the formal garden also meant a decline for mazes.

In the late 18th and much of the 19th centuries, mazes were a component of pleasure gardens and tea gardens, although the great mazes of this period were found in the gardens of stately homes and public parks. William Nesfield designed many mazes during this time. Somerleyton Hall, near Lowestoft in Suffolk, still contains a puzzle maze laid out by him in 1846. In addition to designing the Somerleyton maze, Nesfield also prepared plans for the Royal Botanic Gardens, Kew, but his most famous maze design was that in the Royal Horticultural Society's gardens at South Kensington, which was destroyed in the 1880s by building development.

Many influential gardeners of the early 20th century shunned mazes because they could not be accommodated within their more naturalistic design themes. In his book *The English Flower Garden* (1883), William Robinson expressed the typical view regarding mazes: "The Maze is one of the notions about gardening which arose when people had very little idea of the dignity and infinite beauty of the garden flora as we now know it." Yet not everyone agreed. The most striking maze made at this time was at Hever Castle, near Edenbridge, Kent, designed by William Waldorf Astor. Four hundred years after King Henry VIII courted Anne Boleyn at Hever Castle, Astor purchased, restored, and further developed the site, which included adding a yew maze that was completed in 1905 (see Plate 23).

The period from World War I until after World War II saw little new construction of mazes and the loss of many others due to neglect and other economic priorities. A resurgence of maze building began in the 1970s. One of the largest mazes in England was designed by Greg Bright and laid out in 1978 at Longleat House, Warminster, Wiltshire. This puzzle maze had curving paths, wooden bridges, a complete lack of symmetry, and immense size (116 by 54 meters [127 by 59 yd.]). A maze craze in Japan in the 1980s resulted in the construction of over 200 three-dimensional wooden mazes. The symbolism, romanticism, magic, and entertainment that mazes provide explain why mazes continue to be a component of gardens, regardless of the fashion of the time.

Further Reading

Fisher, Adrian, and Georg Gerster, *Labyrinth: Solving the Riddle of the Maze,* New York: Harmony Books, 1990

Kern, Hermann, *Labyrinth: Erscheinungsformen und Deutungen: 5000 Jahre Gegenwart eines Urbilds,* Munich: Prestel-Verlag, 1982; 4th edition, 1999; as *Through the Labyrinth: Designs and Meanings over 5,000 Years,* Munich and New York: Prestel, 2000

Matthews, W.H., *Mazes and Labyrinths: A General Account of Their History and Developments,* London and New York: Longmans Green, 1922; reprint, New York: Dover, 1970

Pennick, Nigel, *Mazes and Labyrinths,* London: Hale, 1990

CANDICE A. SHOEMAKER

Medici Family

The Medicis were a Florentine family of international bankers, humanists, and art connoisseurs who rose to power during the Italian Renaissance. Through many generations, they played a vital role in the political, cultural, and artistic life of Florence, and despite their bourgeois origins in the late 13th century, they eventually joined the highest nobility of Europe.

The Medicis loved the idea of country life, and the retreat to the villa, *la villegiatura.* This interest was defined for them by Cosimo the Elder, patriarch of the family in the early years of the 15th century, who first attended seriously to developing and building on the various properties they had acquired beyond the city. This concern with country life, with varying degrees of interest, continued in the family for most of the subsequent generations. The number of villas and estates owned by the Medicis, the history of which is not always easy to reconstruct now, was remarkable, as was also the interest shown in decorating these properties with the works of the finest artists.

Cosimo the Elder (1389–1464) was concerned first with two sites, both in the valley of the Mugello to the northeast of Florence (the area from which the Medici originated), at Castello and at Il Trebbio, and then also at a property at Cafaggiolo. He was the first Medici to exert cultural influence by his patronage of artists and writers and his encouragement of learning, an example of which was his employment of Michelozzo Michelozzi (1396–1472), a pupil of Brunelleschi (1377–1446), as chief architect. Michelozzo transformed Il Trebbio, a castellated hunting lodge, into a villa with a walled garden in about 1451 and rebuilt the Villa Medici, Cafaggiolo (1451). The latter was transformed into a summer residence, to which were added, as we can see in a later representation, carefully planted gardens, groves, and fountains. Both buildings now perhaps seem dark and forbidding, but Michelozzo, required to keep them as castles with their medieval plans, was able to introduce into some parts classical details of the kind becoming fashionable in the architecture being built in Florence.

Cafaggiolo, where Cosimo died in 1464, was a retreat he liked very much, together with Careggi, a villa a few miles to the north of Florence, a property which had been bought in 1417 by his brother, Giovanni, and acquired by him in 1457. Michelozzo redesigned the castellated manor of Careggi with a double loggia overlooking the garden, an imitation of a Roman villa garden of clipped evergreens, pomegranates, quinces, lavender, and scented herbs and flowers. Orange and lemon trees in pots lined the paths and were grouped around the fountains, for one of which Verrocchio (1435–88) designed his "Putto with a Dolphin." Careggi became the literary and artistic center of the Medicean court. Here Cosimo invited the founding members of the Platonic Academy, under the leadership of Marsillio Ficino (1433–99), to discuss philosophy in the garden of the villa in imitation of his "divine" Plato. The treatise *De re aedificatoria* by Alberti (1404–72) was influential in the design of the garden at Careggi.

Cosimo had other properties, at Cerveto, near Empoli, acquired from the Guidi family, at Lecceto, and at Montelupo, to the west of Florence, near Lastra a Signa. He also had property in Fiesole after 1450, where, with his son Giovanni in charge, again Michelozzo worked on the reconstruction of an older castle, bought from the Bardi family, turning this into the Villa Belcanto, now the Villa Mozzi. Michelozzo also built a villa for Cosimo at Fiesole between 1458 and 1461.

This structure was a new classical building with two long terraces cut out of the hillside, overlooking the Arno valley. The first true Renaissance villa of Italy, it became one of the many residences of Lorenzo the Magnificent, and the Platonic Academy later moved here.

Cosimo's son Lorenzo the Magnificent (1449–92), who became head of the family in 1469, continued the programs of decorations and plantings at the various villas, especially at Cafaggiolo, where he laid out a garden in his youth, and his love of flowers and the countryside is evident in the poems he wrote there. In the Utens lunette, the villa has a topiary bower and circular fountain at the front, with simple square beds and small vine pergolas behind. He also acquired additional properties, such as the Villa Castello in 1477, one at Poggio a Caiano in 1479, and the Villa Spedaletto in 1486, on the slopes of the Val d'Elsa, near Pienza, which he had decorated with frescoes by Botticelli, Filippino Lippi, Perugino, and Domenico Ghirlandaio, all of which were destroyed by fire in the 1820s. Of all these buildings perhaps the villa at Poggio a Caiano, some 12 miles to the northwest of the city, was the most spectacular. Here Giuliano da Sangallo was brought in to turn an existing building into a full fledged Renaissance palace, complete with rich classical details. Later, in the 1520s, decorations were added by Pontormo and Andrea del Sarto. At Careggi, where, like his grandfather, Lorenzo died, he gave much attention to the plantings and flowers, establishing here one of the first botanical gardens in Europe. From a letter of 1480 it is clear that the gardens could be compared to those of antiquity: an olive grove sacred to Minerva, the myrtle of Venus, the oak sacred to Jupiter, and all around plants and flowers, like those perhaps to be seen in the myth of Venus described by Botticelli in his painting *Primavera* (1486).

The first Renaissance villa overlooking Rome was built by a member of the Medici family, Cardinal Giulio de Medici (1478–1534), later Pope Clement VII. The Villa Madama was begun in about 1516 on the slopes of the Monte Mario, designed partly by Raphael (1483–1520) as a series of open courts and loggias for entertaining. Intended as a reconstruction of a great classical villa of imperial Rome, with marvelous views and extensive use of sculptures, only a portion was ever completed, but its design had a far-reaching effect.

The expulsion of the Medici from Florence in 1494 ended any further serious activities in architecture and garden design by the Medicis for several years. When Cosimo I (1519–74) assumed the Dukedom of Florence in 1537, however, he began to show something of the same energy and interest as had Cosimo and Lorenzo, being first especially concerned with decorating the Palazzo Pitti that had been acquired by his wife Eleonora of Toledo in 1549 (the facade was remodeled and the great courtyard and gardens were built around and behind the palace).

Cosimo I was brought up at Castello, one of the oldest Medici villa properties. After his accession in 1537, he recalled Tribolo (1500–1550) from Bologna, to draw up plans for remodeling the gardens at Castello with a complex system of artificial waterworks. This scheme was first to embody an iconographical program devised by the scholar Benedetto Varchi (1503–65) to symbolize the Medici's defeat of their enemies and the extent of their domain. After Tribolo's death, Ammannati (1511–92) and Buontalenti (1536–1608) completed the work. The garden's major features were placed on the central axis and the whole derived its beauty from fountains, plantings, and sculptures. Vasari (1511–74) described it as "the most rich, magnificent and ornamental garden in Europe." The central fountain was crowned by the bronze figure of Hercules crushing Antaeus by Ammannati (1559–60). Beneath the terrace was a rustic grotto (ca. 1546–69) decorated with shell mosaics and stalactites and populated with realistic bronze animals whose claws, beaks, wings, ears, and noses spurted water. On the upper terrace backed by woods is Ammannati's statue-fountain of Appennino, or January (1559).

Cosimo I's son Francesco I (1541–87), who reigned from 1574, was able to initiate a full program of building with the architect, military engineer, and director of *spettacoli* Bernardo Buontalenti in something of the scale of his forbears. The wonders of the gardens of Pratolino (ca. 1569–81), acquired in 1569 by Francesco I for his second wife Bianca Cappello, were probably created by Buontalenti. The garden, intended as a showpiece of scientific ingenuity designed to outshine the Villa d'Este at Tivoli, became famous for its grottoes, *giochi d'acqua* (water jokes), and automata that made music and noises. Once the most famous of all the Medici villas, all that remains today is Giambologna's colossal statue of Appennino seated on a rock (1579–80).

Ferdinand I (1549–1609) who succeeded his brother Francesco in 1587, had a taste for opulence and enthusiasm for building. An avid collector of classical sculptures, he bought the Villa Medici in Rome to house them and in 1599 commissioned Giusto Utens (d. 1609) to paint a series of 14 lunettes depicting the Medici villas.

The Boboli Gardens, the last major creation of the Medicis, was the setting for many splendid pageants and lavish entertainments during the 17th century. In 1549 Cosimo I commissioned Tribolo to design the whole layout of the hill behind the Pitti Palace, creating an amphitheater out of the natural hollow, and beyond, a series of terraces. Later, Cosimo III (1642–1713) had a *giardino segreto* here. Buontalenti designed the upper story of the entrance facade and three interior grottoes of *La grotta grande* (1583–93). The first grotto has four statues of slaves by Michaelangelo (1475–1564), while the third contains a nude statue of Venus (1592) by Giovanni Bologna (1529–1608). It also contained *giochi*

View of the Medici Villa at Pratolino by Giusto van Utens, 1599
Copyright Alinari/Art Resource, New York

d'acqua. The *Viottolone* avenue leads along the western axis of the garden to the *Piazzale dell'Isolotto*—the Ocean Fountain (1567–76)—by Giovanni Bologna.

The Medicis entered the aristocracy of Europe through the marriage of Catherina de' Medici (1519–89) to the heir to the French throne, the future Henri II. This French alliance carried the influence of Italian garden design to France. Catherine (as she was known in France) created the Tuileries (1564–72) just outside the walls of Paris and remarkable for its size at the time (600 meters long [656 yd.]). There was a ceramic grotto by Bernard Palissy (ca. 1510–90), whose *Dessein du jardin delectable* (1563) was dedicated to Catherine. She created a garden at Montceaux-en-Brie and remodeled the gardens of Chenonceaux and Fontainebleau, using them for lavish celebrations.

Maria de' Medici (1573–1642), wife of Henry IV of England, began the palace and gardens of the Luxembourg Palace in 1612, inspired partly by the Pitti Palace and the Boboli Gardens, where she had lived in her youth. A large sunken parterre was laid out with *broderies* incorporating Marie's monogram. Saint-Germain-en-Laye was completed by Henri IV with terraced gardens and grottoes with automata, similar to those at Pratolino.

The subsequent fate of the Medici villas has varied. Il Trebbio was sold by Ferdinando II and passed through various hands until in 1862, together with Caffagiolo, it became the property of Marcantonio Borghese; it is now in private hands. The Villa Ambrogiana is still standing, but it is used now as a prison. The Villa Lapeggi, known also as the Villa Dupré, was partly demolished in the mid-17th century, and then, in 1895, it was badly damaged by an earthquake. The villa at Poggio Imperiale, which is now in the possession of the Istituto della Santissima Annunziata, was transformed into a neo-classical building in the late 18th century, as was the Villa Petraia, which passed into the possession of the House of Savoy and was much altered in the 1860s by King Victor Emmanuel II. The Villa Mozzi in Fiesole was sold by Grand Duke Cosimo III and renovated, a century later, for the Countess of Orford, sister-in-law of Horace Walpole, from which it passed through the hands of several English families. Pratolino is gone: in 1814 it was demolished, and the grounds were turned into an English garden, purchased in 1872 by Prince Paul Demidoff (many of the surviving statues were removed to the Boboli Gardens). The happiest story is perhaps that of Poggio a Caiano, which, after several changes to the original building and an English garden being designed there from 1819 to 1830 by Pasquale Poccianti, has now become the property of the state and is fully restored.

Further Reading

Acidini, Cristina, editor, *Giardini Medicei: Giardini di palazzo e di villa nella Firenze del Quattrocento,* Milan: Motta, 1996

Alberti, Leon Battista, *De pictura praestantissme, et numquamsatis laudata arte, libri tres absolutissimi,* Basel, 1540; reprint, as *De pictura praestantissima,* Portland, Oregon: Collegium Graphicum, 1972; as *On Painting,* translated by C. Grayson, and edited by M. Kemp, London: Penguin, 1991

Avery, Charles, *Florentine Renaissance Sculpture,* London: Murray, and New York: Harper and Row, 1970

Brion, Marcel, *Le siècle des Médicis,* Paris: Albin Michel, 1969; as *The Medici: A Great Florentine Family,* London: Elek Books, and New York: Crown, 1969

Cleugh, James, *The Medici: A Tale of Fifteen Generations,* New York: Doubleday, 1975; London: Hale, 1976

Cresti, Carlo, and Massimo Listri, *Civiltà delle ville Toscane,* Udine: Magnus, 1992; as *Villas of Tuscany,* New York: Vendome Press, 1993; London: Cassell, 1994

Fara, Amelio, *Buontalenti, archittetura e teatro,* Florence: nuova Italia, 1979

Hale, John Rigby, *Florence and the Medici: The Pattern of Control,* London: Thames and Hudson, 1977

Lazzaro, Claudio, *The Italian Renaissance Garden: From the Conventions of Planting, Design, and Ornament to the Grand Gardens of Sixteenth-Century Central Italy,* New Haven, Connecticut: Yale University Press, 1990

Masson, Georgina, *Italian Gardens,* London: Thames and Hudson, and New York: Abrams, 1961; new edition, 1966

Mignani, Daniela, *Le ville Medicee di Giusto Utens,* Florence: Arnaud, 1980; new edition, 1993; as *The Medicean Villas by Giusto Utens,* Florence: Arnaud, 1991; 2nd edition, 1995

Morisani, Ottavio, *Michelozzo architetto,* Turin: Einaudi, 1951

Rubin, Patricia Lee, and Alison Wright, *Renaissance Florence: The Art of the 1470s,* London: National Gallery, 1999

Shepherd, John C., and Geoffrey A. Jellicoe, *Italian Gardens of the Renaissance,* New York: Scribner, and London: Benn, 1925; reprint, New York: Princeton Architectural Press, 1993; London: Academy Editions, 1994

Tavernor, Robert, *On Alberti and the Art of Building,* New Haven, Connecticut: Yale University Press, 1998

Vasari, Giorgio, *Le vite de più eccellenti architetti, pittori, e scultori italiani,* 3 vols., Florence: Torrentino, 1550; 2nd edition, Florence: Florence: Apresso i Giunti, 1568; as *Lives of the Painters, Sculptors, and Architects,* 2 vols., translated by Gaston du C. de Vere (1912), edited by David Ekserdjian, New York: Knopf, and London: Campbell, 1996

DAVID CAST AND CHARLOTTE JOHNSON

Medieval Garden Style

It is claimed that Europe's monasteries were the pioneers of medieval garden style. The truth is, however, that the monasteries simply took over from Roman Italy the idea of *academe,* "schools in a garden," along with the their concept of *villa rustica,* that is, the community supporting itself with self-grown produce.

The medieval church with its attached cloister was the ecclesiastical version of the museum, exedra, and portico of the Roman philosopher's garden, with the court around the cloister mimicking the Roman peristyle. Byzantine basilicas had adjoining porticos, planted as gardens or *paradeisos* (paradises), serving as a courtyard where excommunicated church members mulled over their sins and waited before being received back, literally, into the church.

Although borrowed, the cloister garden was the first true garden of medieval Europe. One of the oldest recorded cloister gardens is the eighth-century garden of San Paolo Fuori, composed solely of trees and flowers pleasing to the eye, thus giving lie to the idea that all monastic gardens were mere vegetable and herb gardens. Nevertheless, thanks primarily to St. Benedict, whose sixth-century *Rule* enjoins self-sufficiency and work in the garden for all, working vegetable and herb gardens were the norm, with beauty and pleasure taking a back seat. In fact, until the sixth century, the Church considered such attributes to be "heathenish." Enjoyment was limited to the flowering tree and herb, the mainstay of the early medieval garden. However, when the Church reversed itself, growing flowers for pleasure quickly caught on. St. Benedict, borrowing rose gardening from Italy, planted a monastic rose garden, or rosary, in the sixth century. The first known reference connecting the rosary to the Virgin Mary is in a description of a seventh-century oratory rosary adjoining the hospice of St. Flacre, the Irish patron saint of gardening, dedicated to "Our Lady."

Charlemagne's *Capitulare de Villis* (ca. 800), although containing a smaller list than does Pliny the Elder, enumerates, as part of a decree regarding plants, a number of plants not mentioned in classical literature that were nevertheless growing in various parts of his empire. While listing mostly herbs, to ensure the availability of essential medicines, the list includes *Lilium* and roses (probably the red *Rosa gallica officinalis* and the white *R. alba*). Charlemagne also listed clary (*Salvia viridis*), fennel, flag iris (*Iris* × *germanica* ?), mallow (*Malva sylvestris*), rosemary, rue, sage, southernwood, sweet bay (laurel), and tansy, all flowering herbs, but omitted balm, hyssop, the lavenders, and violets, all popular plants in his day. Preserved in the Abbey of St. Gall in Switzerland is a copy of a supplement to the *Capitulare,* presented to the abbot about 816, laying out the ideal monastic garden and undoubtedly the basis for that monastery's garden. A detailed diagram of St. Gall's garden as it appeared between 820 and 830 provides us with considerable information about gardening in the ninth century, which was still monastic. Although more expansive, St. Gall's was essentially the Italian *academe* built around a central "paradise," complete with the "flowery mead garden" (which later was to come into vogue) and common wildflowers growing in the grass and four rectangular flower beds. Situated close to the hospital and monastery school was the physic garden for the infirmarian, containing 16 raised beds of medicinal herbs, including roses, lilies (*Lilium candidum*), and rosemary, the mainstay of Italian gardens, and a number of herbs used today primarily for culinary purposes. The majority of the herbs were of the flowering variety, attesting that the modern flower garden finds its roots in the herb garden. The school had its own peristyle with its own garden. Even the cemetery was a garden planted with shade and fruit trees set in straight rows, each row being of a single variety, with tombstones between, further proof that the garden's architect had used Charlemagne's *Capitulare.*

Although the medieval garden rose out of the cloister garden, the ideal medieval garden was visualized mystically, with its heritage in the Old Testament Song of Solomon: "A garden enclosed is my sister, my spouse: a spring shut up, a fountain sealed." For both medieval Christian and Muslim, the Song of Solomon was viewed as a mystical reference to the Garden of Eden. Later, as Jewish Kaballic thought began to crystallize, it too developed the same mystical meaning.

This mystical fantasy contributed such horticultural words as *husbandry* and phrases as "groom the garden" to language. The "husband" of the Song of Solomon is understood as Christ, the husband of the Church, which is the Divine Garden (the allegorical Garden of Eden). *Husbandry* is the role of the divine husband, Christ, as he *grooms* the divine bride (divine garden), the Church. This analogy further applies to humans invested with the task of the stewardship of creation, nurturing the land "as a husband his wife." The origin of the term *groom,* as in "groom the garden," is obvious.

Hildebert de Laverdin's highly popular and imaginative poem "De ornatu mundi" (1099) echoes the garden spirit at the beginning of the millennium, drawing its imagery from both the *pairi-daeza* parks of Islam and mythological descriptions of the Garden of Eden and the Trees of Knowledge and Life. Like Hildebert's poem, allegorical Islamic and Christian medieval poetry was frequently set in the medieval Edenic garden. The mystical 13th-century love poem *Roman de la Rose* (begun in 1237 by Guillaume de Lorris and finished in 1277 by Jean de Meun) shows us a highly stylized Persian garden where it is always spring and trees bear fruit and blossom simultaneously, nurtured by gentle mists and woodland breezes—a place where meadows are alive with flowers and the singing of birds, as with the voice of angels. In the outer court of the garden, the Lover, Amant, roams in search of the perfect rose. Eventually Lady Idleness opens the door to the inner court, the Holy of Holies, as it were, and upon entering, Amant realizes that this is the place where he has always belonged, a place "happy and gay and full of joy." Poet and forester Geoffrey Chaucer (ca. 1340–1400) picks up the same theme in *The Frankeleyns Tale,* describing a garden of heavenly delights planted with the oriental linden, sweet bay, olive, and a number of native plants, including the "firre" (fir). Chaucer's trees were "in assyse"—spaced in rows—as was the style in his day. Significantly, this garden, although idealized, was the model of the 14th-century medieval garden.

This mystical approach to gardening gave rise to some strange ideas. Perhaps the most bizarre artistic interpretation of the mystical garden theme is found in the 13th-century cathedral of Indres, France, where a fresco shows Eve encountering a female serpent entwined around a giant branching, slightly toxic, hallucinogenic mushroom common in Europe—the *Amanita muscaria.*

Art as well as the literature of the period prominently featured gardens and individual plants, illustrating for us the details of the medieval garden. A French miniature from about 1400 illustrated *Roman de la Rose* as a circular walled symmetric garden with animals and birds among trees interspersed with flowery paths. Other works such as the five illuminated manuscripts found in the Casanatense Library in Rome illustrate plants introduced into northern gardens by the Romans as they extended their empire. Included are sweet and sour cherries, plums, mulberries, peaches, almonds, figs, chestnuts, kale, dill, fennel, and beets, along with the all-important rose and rosemary; many of these plants, including the rose, rosemary, and citrus, perhaps even the sour cherry, found their way into Rome via Islamic traders.

For the medieval Christian, the gardens approaching the closest to the mystical paradise were Islamic. Islamic gardens were seen as mystical representations of Christ and the Holy Church (Christ's bride) bearing "fruits of the Spirit." The symmetric Islamic garden pathway became the pathway to heaven, and the Islamic rose became the symbol of the Virgin, the mystical "beloved" bride of the Song of Solomon. The medieval horticultural reference, *hortus conclusus,* thoroughly explores theologically and horticulturally this mystical theme.

The medieval Islamic garden was greatly influenced by the gardens of Dar-al-Islam (570–ca. 1000). These gardens were modeled after an even older Persian style, a style echoing Mesopotamian and older cultures. The gardens of Dar-al-Islam were rectangular, enclosed, architectural, and formal and consisted of fountains, pavilions, and many large shade trees, characteristics that describe both medieval and modern Islamic gardens.

The gardens of Dar-al-Islam were essentially turf-carpeted parterres with geometric patterns carried out by colored pebbles. These pebble designs evolved into the well-known mosaic patterns that typify the later Moorish gardens. A prominent feature of the gardens of Dar-al-Islam was artificial trees made of precious metals and gems, an idea that later was enthusiastically copied by the Khans (1162–1227). Islamic *pairi-daeza* used flowers sparingly, if at all. The few flowers used were selected for their scent rather than color and potted in urns or cut and placed in vases. An exception was the use of strategically placed rose bushes and rosaries. For Islam, the rose is the most significant of all plants. The specific Persian word for rose, *gul,* is also the generic Persian word for flower.

Next to the rose came the fruit tree in import, as the Islamic gardener recognized no other tree to be more ornamental or aromatic. This is particularly true of the citrus, introduced into Persia from China early in the second century B.C. Fruit trees were planted in orderly rectangular designs, often with each tree shaped or espaliered. Central to Persian garden design is a small body of water, either a basin or pond, always circular or oval in shape, with one lip lower so that the water could flow out. Water courses were geometrically laid out and ornamentally designed. Large gardens contained a series of tiered terraces with ponds, each with its own ornamental style, with the water coursing from pond to pond.

Although the Islamic garden style had evolved considerably by the medieval period, it never lost the Dar-al-Islamic style. This is significant because all the gardens of Dar-al-Islam were destroyed by war. Fortunately, the Moors of the northern African regions of Dar-al-Islam took it upon themselves as their religious duty to restore the *pairi-daeza*s of Dar-al-Islam. Under Moorish restoration Islamic *pairi-daezas* reached new heights, evolving into magnificent, mosaic-tiled canals surrounding parterres made of turf or stone, each with a shade tree planted at each corner. The parterres, when covered with carpet, became the social and spiritual centers of the garden.

As the Moors moved into medieval Iberia, not only did they bring with them their plants, especially the rose, they brought with them their unique garden style. The Moorish garden was a fascinating mixture of Dar-al-Islamic with Berber, Arab, Byzantine, and Jewish influences. As the Moors created their *pairi-daeza*s in Iberia, they imported Jewish, Greek, and Egyptian craftsmen to oversee the work, adding even more design elements to "paradise." The medieval Islamic historian Al-Makkari tells us that by the tenth century the countryside about Córdoba was one great garden consisting of 50,000 villas, each with their own *pairi-daeza.* Al-Makkari records that these gardens used the already-existing Roman villas as building material, perhaps incorporating a bit of Roman character as well.

Iberian Moorish gardens featured symmetrical, highly colored, paved mosaic paths embellished with Arab, Byzantine, and Egyptian geometric designs, lined with clipped box, bay, and myrtle hedges that geometrically divided the larger garden into smaller plots. Paths were set along straight lines using canal-fed fountains and pools as the focal point. Canals (also used to geometrically divide the garden), fountains, and pools were embellished with precious metal and stone ornamentation. The embellished design motif, used throughout the garden, often mimicked the artificial trees of Dar-al-Islam. Lawns were virtually nonexistent, and other than the few places left for planting trees, vines, and roses, the garden was completely tiled. What few flowers were used, like their Dar-al-Islamic counterparts, were chosen solely for scent and were either potted or placed cut in vases.

The 12th-century Arab agronomist Abu Zakariya postulated that all garden doorways should be framed with clipped evergreens and that cypress should be used to line paths and be grouped to mark intersections. An added benefit of choosing evergreens and cypress is that they served to fumigate the air, and if the garden was properly laid out, the breeze would carry the scent into the dwelling. Zakariya further suggested that canals be lined with shade trees to prevent excessive loss of water by evaporation and adamantly stated that evergreens and deciduous trees should never be grouped together. Rounding out his instruction on building the ideal *pairi-daeza* is a list of mostly aromatic trees and herbs, and vines. This design was only slightly altered by the influx of new plants and styles from Spain and Portugal's New World colonies.

The gardens of Dar-al-Islam also significantly influenced the medieval royal gardens of India, imposing the symmetrical lines and geometric designs of Islamic gardening upon the traditional Buddhist garden. Indian medieval gardens were large square plots, usually in excess of 50 acres (20 ha), subdivided into smaller square plots, with a great central pavilion (which later was to served as a tomb for the royal builder) serving as the overall focal point. The smaller plots, generally defined by blue-tiled canals, were raised platforms of turf or stone, sheltered by a tree at each corner and covered with carpets, in Dar-al-Islamic fashion. Feeding the smaller canals was a main canal, possibly bordered with herbaceous perennials, bulbs, aromatic shrubs, or roses running the entire length. Following Islamic fashion, Indian gardens generally were enclosed. Countering the Islamic influence was the preferred elaborate waterfall of the Roman style. The medieval Indian garden style reached its zenith during the reign of Jahangir and his garden-loving Persian wife. Although medieval Indian gardeners borrowed from both Islam and the Romans, they made at least one noted contribution to European garden design: The flowering tree-lined garden alley of medieval Europe draws on the Indian medieval style of using ornamental trees to line paths and public streets.

While almost nothing is known about the gardens of medieval Turkey, it was the Turks who introduced domesticated bulbous plants such as onions, garlic, and the saffron crocus into Europe via the gardens of Dar-al-Islam and later the Moors. In addition to giving Europe the domesticated bulb, the Turks also contributed to the wide variety of domesticated roses available to medieval gardens. As the Ottoman army began to spread across eastern Europe in the mid-14th century, every soldier's sack, it is claimed, contained potted bulbs and roses.

While the garden style of the Islamic Moors never made it past Iberia, an almost identical style of *paradeiso* did find its way into northern Europe (as far north as Germany) and the British Isles, imported by traveling monks and returning Crusaders, who also returned with ideas from other Islamic regions, one significant contribution being the introduction of the Oriental marble garden foot bath. Sicily became a major source of Islamic ideas, as the "baptized sultans" of the ruling Norman Hauteville family (ca. 1060–ca. 1261) claimed the Islamic *pairi-daeza*s of the deposed Muslim emirs. In Germany the chief proponent of the "Sicilian style" was Emperor Frederick II Hohenstaufen (1194–1250), who also happened to be the ruler of Sicily and southern Italy. Frederick incorporated some features of the Islamic *pairi-daeza* into his own garden in Germany, while basing his garden in Palermo, in turn, on the Europeanized Roman style then prevalent in Germany.

How did these influences play out in medieval European gardens? At least as early as the mid-11th century, gardens were admired for their beauty as well as their practicality. We read of William Rufus, who wanted to visit the convent at Romsey "to admire the roses and other flowering shrubs," an admirable desire even if his true wish was to catch a glimpse of Edith of Scotland. The horticulturist Alexander of Necham (b. 1157) writes in his *De Naturis Rerum* (The Investigation of Nature)of how as a young man he adorned his garden with flowers pleasing to the senses, recommending and listing these flowers, many which have no known value other than their beauty, as the ingredients of a pleasing garden.

Columella's 12 volume *De Re Rustica* (Of the Country) and *De Arburibus* (On Agriculture and Trees) were by this time in wide use as a gardening reference, thus we can assume that period gardens were becoming more than merely a source of food. A 12th-century description of the Cistercian Abbey at Clairvaux provides us with a detailed picture of a period monastic garden.

> Behind the abbey, but within the walls of the cloister, there is a wide level ground; here there is an orchard, with a great many fruit trees, quite like a small wood. It is close to the infirmary and very comforting to the brothers, providing a wide promenade for those who want to walk, and a pleasant resting place for those who prefer rest. Where the orchard leaves off, the garden begins, divided into several beds, or better still, cut up by little canals, which, though of standing water, do flow more or less. . . . The water fulfils the double purpose of nourishing the fish and watering the vegetables.

What is particularly noteworthy about this description is the emphasis on the garden and orchard being a place of community and rest.

About the same time that Clairvaux was being described, the Saxon theologian Hugo of St. Victor describes a *hortus,* or garden, in France as "beautiful with the adornment of trees, delightful with flowers, pleasant with green grass . . . offering the benefit of shade, agreeable with the murmur of a spring, filled with divers fruits, praised by the song of birds," a description reminiscent of the idealized Garden of Eden. Writing almost concurrently with Hugo, William of

Maimesbury raises gardening to a form of art: "There is a competition between nature and art, and what one fails in the other produces."

The monk-scholar-theologian Albertus Magnus provides us with the first real description of a medieval pleasure gardener in his *De Vegatabilibus et. Plants* (On Vegetables and Plants), written about 1260 (probably copied from a now-missing section of work completed by Bartholomew de Granville in 1240). For Magnus the pleasure gardener was simply the one who planted for his own pleasure and took delight in the beauty wrought by his labor. About 50 years later, in 1305, Pietro de' Crescenzi quotes Magnus almost verbatim in his chapter "On Pleasure Gardens" in Book 8 of his *Liber ruralium commodorum* (Library of Rural Agriculture). It was Pietro who advanced the garden style that, while greatly influencing European medieval garden style, in essence defined Renaissance garden style. *Liber ruralium commodorum* was the garden bible for well over 200 years, translated into Italian, French, and German and reprinted many times.

Magnus details the basic ingredients for a typical medieval enclosed garden of the 13th century, quite reminiscent of the monastic garden: Attached to the manor house (or monastery), the pleasure garden plays the leading role, centered between, and separating the house from, infirmary and kitchen gardens. The ideal pleasure garden, according to Magnus, has an open sunlit central lawn with a fountain and is surrounded by scented herbs and flowers and hosts raised turf benches shaded by fruit trees or vines.

Pietro's *Liber ruralium commodorum* deals with three styles of gardens: small ones (a fountain, lawn, and a few flower or herb beds), midsized ones (up to two acres [0.8 ha]), and large gardens for the nobility of 20 acres (8 ha) or more, noting that the Sicilian style was ideal for large gardens. Pietro dealt not only with garden design but also included chapters of instructions for crafting turf seats, shady arbors, walks, and waterways. Horticulturally, he touches on grafting, budding, topiary, and pleaching. Thanks to Pietro and the earlier Albertus Magnus and Bartholomew de Granville, useful and practical horticultural knowledge was now widely available. Magnus tells of using "mild heat" to force plants to flower out of season, not unusual, as long before Magnus, Roman gardeners had perfected forcing houses made from mica sheets. However, by Magnus's time these forcing houses had evolved into orangeries with wood-burning stoves for heat. During the same period we read of extensive nurseries for grafting and seedlings.

Medieval horticulturists were primarily cosmopolitan observers and compilers, drawing heavily on the classical botanists and encyclopedists, as well as what they had observed in their travels. At the same time, however, they were part of the new scientific method brewing among medieval scholars and took active part in the philosophical debate regarding the essence of nature. Bartholomew tells us the difference between tree and animal—the tree has "no soule of felynge" (no soul of feeling)—a notable departure from then current opinion. Yet Magnus wonders if the souls of the ivy and the tree upon which it is intertwined are united. Even the "scientific" Bartholomew writes at some length about how black pepper results from the scorching of white pepper. According to Bartholomew, white pepper was grown high in the Caucasus in a region inhabited by a vicious breed of snake that could only be driven off by fire when the pickers needed to harvest the peppercorn, hence black pepper. Nor was horticulturist knowledge far removed from its mythical, although now Christianized, roots. The 13th-century biographical *Life of St. Louis* speaks of ginger, rhubarb, aloes, and cinnamon as remnants of the earthly paradise, appearing as if by magic in the morning on the spread nets of the fishermen of the lower Nile.

Myth aside, according to Pietro the essential fundamentals of good garden design were "expectation and surprise." To achieve these, Pietro, drawing on the design of both Moorish and Italian gardens, suggested that a series of small gardens separated by walls or hedges be built; interconnected by walks, steps, gates, bridges, and watercourses. The medieval poem *Roman de la Rose* with the fountain of its "flowery mead" garden feeding a stream flowing beneath trellises to garden after garden is the perfect picture of Pietro's garden. In fact, Pietro even provided a design for laying out the "flowery mead garden" consisting of mixed sweet grasses and flowers. It included a seat shaded by climbing plants, a pleached evergreen, or perhaps a fruit tree or two and was to be placed so that the lady's bower opened upon it: a true lady's garden. The principal flowers were roses, violets, and marigolds.

The design and building of arbors and pergolas as elements of expectation and surprise became highly developed art forms. Legend tells of one pergola said to be covered with a single rose of such size that it gave shade to 12 knights. As the craft developed, the pergola soon gave rise to the more substantial "summer pavilions."

Another feature of the medieval garden instilling the essential element of expectation was an ancient garden feature of unknown origin—the maze. There are two general styles of garden mazes: the maze proper, with its dead ends, and the labyrinth. (The labyrinth technically is not a maze as it does not contain dead ends.) The maze proper probably originated in ancient eastern Mediterranean cultures (the oldest-known maze is Cretan), while the labyrinth's origin is most likely found in the "old religion" of the druids. In myth, both seem to have a connection with the "horned god," giving credence to the theory that the maze is a stylized sacred grove.

A tapestry woven in 16th-century Tournai depicts woodcutters clearing a forest to make an enclosed garden in which deer roam and trees are bowed over with fruit—the "hunting park." One of the earliest hunting parks was created by Frederick Barbarossa in 1161. Continental Europe's hunting parks often reflected Persian influence in that large acreage was enclosed within a wall and planted in park fashion with trees and stocked with game that could be hunted at leisure. While not properly gardens, they often contained formal gardens and essentially followed medieval garden design. The less formal English hunting parks were generally not walled (although a few were fenced) and in time gave way to the deer park of the English Renaissance. Continental hunting parks were stocked with native game and often with exotic animals such as lions and giraffes. Peacocks, with their mystical symbolism, also roamed many medieval parks and gardens.

By the 14th century pleasure gardening had made its way down to the burgess class. Late in the 14th century a Le Ménager de Paris wrote instructions for his young wife on how to run her house and garden. What makes this treatise remarkable is the amount of horticulture advice it contained, demonstrating that horticultural knowledge was not limited to a select few but available even to the working class who provided the bulk of the garden work. Le Ménager's advice is as current as the advice in modern gardening books: violets, for example, need to be kept indoors in pots during the winter and gradually hardened off in spring. Le Ménager instructs on how to graft, prune, and clip roses, when to sow hyssop, and how to import cuttings of rosemary from the Mediterranean (wrapped in waxed cloth, sewn up, and sealed with honey, then "powdered with wheaten flour").

As with Le Ménager's wife, it was women who were the medieval gardeners, planting gardens of vegetables, herbs, and flowers in well-organized parterres, along with "flowery mead" gardens as laid out by Pietro. In addition to the lady's garden, the well-heeled nobleman's estate probably also included a *pleasance* or tree garden, consisting of fruit trees with an occasional broad-leafed tree for shade. In the German *pleasance,* linden trees were an essential element.

The poet-philosopher Petrarch (1340–74) gives us much detail about the style of garden preferred by the Italian burgess class in the margins of his copy of Palladius's treatise on agriculture, jotting down his garden designs along with his successes and failures—not unlike present-day garden journals. The garden was to be the center of family life, with perhaps a small bath or vine-covered pergola. Of particular importance to Petrarch was the lawn, which was to be a miniature meadow of grass and wildflowers with a few fruit trees planted in the symmetrical Roman manner. Plants included aromatic herbs, especially hyssop and the much-favored rosemary. Smaller gardens, or perhaps a smaller garden within a larger garden, ideally were enclosed within walls or clipped hedges. From other sources we know that the medieval burgher's garden also included roses, lilies, and violets, with even the smallest garden having at least one topiary. Following the Italian custom, plants such as citrus were grown in giant pots, taken in under cover in winter.

One of the first true botanical gardens, that is, a garden grown for the sake of collecting species of plants, was begun about 1335 by Henry Daniel, a Dominican monk and doctor, living outside of London. Daniel's garden cataloged 252 different kinds of plants, and his written records are full of practical plant knowledge and behavior, as well as formulas for drugs concocted from plants. To add to the value of his writings is the fact that he frequently references all the major classical herbalists and medieval plant encyclopedists and provides an almost complete translation of Platearius's *Circa instans* (ca. 1190), a work on the medicinal properties of plants. In his writing Daniel gives attention to distinguishing between indigenous and nonindigenous plants and their habitats, encouraging the cultivation of indigenous as well as the more exotic.

By the 14th century many works were available that listed not only plants and trees but gave detailed suggestions for training and shaping plants in ways that "make a pleasing garden." Prior to the publication of the earliest technical work on English gardening, *The Feate of Gardening* by one Mayster Ion Gardener (ca. 1400), we have little idea beyond a few scattered suggestions as to how the gardens of the medieval British Isles differed from those of the Continent. All we really know for certain, is that they tended to be more modest than Continental gardens of that period. Of the 97 plants named by Mayster Gardener, at least 27 were plants foreign to the British Isles, and mostly medicinal herbs rather than ornamentals.

The mid 1400s saw the beginning of the humanist movement, which was soon to usher in the Renaissance. This movement literally began in the style of an *academe* in a garden owned by Cosimo de' Medici. It was only natural then that the humanist movement would give rise to the "humanist garden" of the late Middle Ages. The landscape architect who set the style for the humanist garden was Leono Battista Alberti, laying out their design in his *De re aedificatoria* (On Buildings), written between 1445 and 1452 as a gift for Pope Nicholas V. It was first published in 1485.

Alberti believed that the first consideration in garden design was for its inhabitants, as a garden was to be inhabited as a home. For Alberti the proper design was that of "villa": a combined house and garden, ideally set upon a hillside with a view, in the style of an Italian villa. The house and garden should interpenetrate, with loggias—half living room, half garden room—serving as the links between the two. Paths within both garden and loggia were to be defined with symmetrically planted, or potted, plants, including pomegranates (highly prized by the Italians for their decorative features). Climbing roses should be placed to grow over the trees. Paths should also be lined with clipped and aromatic squared hedges, perhaps rosemary, always popular in Italian gardens. Geometric parterres of the same plants were to be used to interrupt the path. Alberti also urged the incorporation of vine-covered pergolas made of marble columns and as many fountains as possible. And if there was enough room, include a shady grove of cypress, juniper, and myrtle, overshadowed by oaks, with ivy growing freely throughout—an idea borrowed from Pliny the Elder.

Borrowing from both Roman and Islamic tradition, the rose was the most important flower in the humanist garden. Along with roses came climbing vines. Ivy, jasmine from Sicily, convolvulus, clematis, and domesticated honeysuckle were popular vines. Ground plants included *Gladiolus byzantinus,* hyacinth, narcissus, iris, buttercup, forget-me-nots, and orchids. By the close of the Middle Ages, it was custom to take a predinner stroll through a garden "dedicated to the honorable pleasures of rejoicing the eye, refreshing the nose and renewing the spirit" (Erasmus, *Convivium Religiosum* [1522; Religious Feasts]).

Further Reading

Crisp, Frank, *Mediaeval Gardens,* 2 vols., edited by Catherine Childs Paterson, London: Lane, 1924; reprint, New York: Hacker Art Books, 1966

Hammond, P.W., *Food and Feast in Medieval England,* Dover, New Hampshire, and Stroud, Gloucestershire: Sutton, 1993

Hobhouse, Penelope, *Plants in Garden History,* London: Pavilion Books, 1992; as *Penelope Hobhouse's Gardening through the Ages,* New York: Simon and Schuster, 1992

Hyman, Edward, *A History of Gardens and Gardening,* New York: Praeger, 1971

Landsburg, Sylvia, *The Medieval Garden,* New York: Thames and Hudson, 1995

Stokstad, Marilyn Jane, and Jerry Stannard, *Gardens of the Middle Ages* (exhib. cat.), Lawrence: Spencer Museum of Art, University of Kansas, 1983

FRANK MILLS

Mesopotamia, Ancient

The land between the Tigris and Euphrates Rivers, Mesopotamia (present-day Iraq) is often called the Cradle of Civilization, for it is here that city-states grew and flourished and created a city-centered culture. Legend also places the mythic Garden of Eden in Mesopotamia, where the first human couple lived in a garden paradise. This legend finds a curious echo in the ancient village of Al-Qurna, where a tree stands with a sign, in English and Arabic, reading "The Tree of Adam." Nearby, the waters of the Tigris and the Euphrates meet, and local legend asserts that the tree marks the spot where Eden once flourished, where God himself became the divine gardener. Throughout Iraq loom ziggurat temples dating from 3,000 B.C. that recall the legend of the Tower of Babel. One such ziggurat is Aqar-Quf (now a suburb of present-day Baghdad), which once was the capital of the kingdom of the Cassites. In the south lie the ruins of Sumer, where the Sumerian culture flourished 5,000 years ago. It was the Sumerians who invented writing, and they recorded their literature, business transactions, prayers, and royal decrees on tablets of baked clay, using a curious wedge-shaped alphabet, which we now call cuneiform. Many of these tablets preserve fascinating descriptions of everyday life, including the first organized and detailed set of instructions on when to plant and when to harvest.

The civilization of Mesopotamia lasted some 3,000 years, from its earliest beginnings to the Sumerian culture and the Assyrian and the Babylonian empires. By the time Alexander the Great conquered Babylon in the fourth century B.C., the Mesopotamian civilization had been under the rule of the Persians for almost 200 years.

The archaeological record that provides us with details about ancient Mesopotamia comes from the various city centers that constituted the entire civilization. The major centers included Sumer, Ur, Parthia, Babylon, Assyria, and Sassanids.

Sumer (4000–2000 B.C.) was in the southern region of ancient Mesopotamia, and later the southern part of Babylon, now south-central Iraq. An agricultural civilization flourished here during the third and fourth millennia B.C. The Sumerians built canals, established an irrigation system, and were skilled in the use of metals (silver, gold, copper) to make pottery, jewelry, and weapons. Various kings founded dynasties at Kish, Erech, and Ur. King Sargon of Agade brought the region

Illustration of a hanging garden
Copyright North Wind Picture Archives

under the Semites (ca. 2600 B.C.), who blended their culture with the Sumerians. The final Sumerian civilization at Ur fell to Elam, and when Semitic Babylon under Hammurabi (ca. 2000 B.C.) controlled the land, the Sumerian nation vanished.

Ur (3000–250 B.C.), an ancient Babylonian city, was settled in the fourth millennium B.C. It prospered during its first dynasty (3000–2600 B.C.) and during its third dynasty became the richest city in Mesopotamia. A century later it was destroyed by the Elamites, only to be rebuilt and destroyed again by the Babylonians. After Babylon came under the control of Persia, the city was abandoned (third century B.C.).

Parthia (250 B.C.–A.D 226), an ancient country in west Asia, was originally a province in the Assyrian and Persian empires. It became part of the Macedonian Empire of Alexander the Great and the Syrian Empire. Led by Arsaces, its first king, Parthia freed itself from the rule of the Seleucids (ca. 250 B.C.) and reached the height of its power under Mithridates (first century B.C.) The empire was overthrown about A.D. 226 by Ardashir, the first Sassanid ruler of Persia.

Babylon (2000–323 B.C.) was an ancient city of Mesopotamia located on the Euphrates River about 55 miles (89 kilometers) south of present-day Baghdad. Settled since prehistoric times, it was made the capital of the Babylonian Empire by Hammurabi (r. 1792–1750 B.C.). The city was completely destroyed in 689 B.C. by the Assyrians, under Sennacherib. After restoration it flourished and became noted for its hanging gardens, one of the seven wonders of the world. In 275 B.C. the city was abandoned when the Seleucid dynasty built a new capital at Seleucia.

Assyria (1530–612 B.C.) reached its greatest extent in the seventh century B.C., during Ashurbanipal's reign. He subjected its people to merciless repression, inflicted by his army; he ruled through an efficient administrative system supervised by the central government. Assyrian rule collapsed and was followed by a brief resurgence of Babylonian rule.

Sassanids, or Sassanians, the last native dynasty of Persian kings, was founded by Ardashir in A.D. 226. There were approximately 25 Sassanid rulers, the most important after Ardashir (r. A.D. 226–40) being Shapur II (r. 309–79), Khosrau I (r. 531–79), who invaded Syria, and Khosrau II (r. 590–628), whose conquest of Egypt marked the height of the dynasty's power. The line ended when Persia fell to the Arabs in A.D. 641.

Very little rain falls in Mesopotamia, and the fertility of the land depends on the rich floodplains of the Tigris and Euphrates—the very word *Mesopotamia* is a Greek term meaning "the land in-between [two rivers]." But if the soil is regularly moistened, the arid land can yield rich harvests. Thus, the constant struggle of the Mesopotamian civilization was irrigation, and from earliest times great effort was put into creating and maintaining an effective canal system that would keep the land watered and the crops growing. Consequently, it is not surprising that the digging of a canal was deemed a holy task, a sacred duty for any ruler.

Canals are mentioned in the earliest texts of the Sumerians, and by the time of King Hammurabi (r. 1792–1750 B.C.), they are an integral part of civilized life; Hammurabi mentions them in his famous law code, stating that canals are to be kept clear of rushes and water weeds and that they must be regularly and continuously dredged. Special officials oversaw the maintenance and smooth operation of the canals.

Given this great concern with irrigation, it is only natural that the Mesopotamian civilization highly prized and aggressively built not only an efficient agricultural system but also countless private, sacred, and royal gardens and parks. The first association of gardens and Mesopotamia occurs in the myth of Eden, that place of perfect bliss, east of which was a garden tended by God himself. Within this garden lived the first human couple, Adam and Eve, the parents of all humankind. The name of this garden can be traced back to the third millennium B.C., when Sumerian records mention a place called "Edin," or Eden. In Sumerian *Eden* meant "a cultivated place" and perhaps even "a fertile plain."

Consequently, gardens became the watermark of civilization in Mesopotamia, which is the fertile plain framed by the rivers Tigris and Euphrates. Gardens represented not only the taming of nature but also the channeling of nature into the sphere of human activity. This drive to make gardens, therefore, has proceeded undiminished from the most ancient times down to the present. Mesopotamia is largely a hot dusty area, where gardens provide much-needed shade, running water, fragrant flowers, fresh fruits, and vegetables—in short, a semi-Eden set amid the harshness of a hot, unforgiving land.

In the earliest Sumerian period (ca. third century B.C.) no distinction was made between a garden and an orchard. In the *Epic of Gilgamesh* (an epic poem dating from ca. 2000 B.C.) we are told that the city of Uruk was one-third built-up habitation, one-third field, and one-third gardens. Thus, from the earliest times there has been an association of a cultivated place (gardens) set within a civilized (citified) place. It was also during this time that a new variety of wheat was found: long-eared and large-grained (similar to einkorn or emmer).

By at least the second millennium B.C., kings had royal gardens in which banquets and religious festivals were held. The large courtyards of palaces were planted with trees, flowers, and even vegetables. A typical royal garden contained palm trees, tamarisk trees, a large stone pond, beds for flowers and vegetables, walkways, and a well beside which would be built a trough and a pavilion. Such gardens can be clearly seen at Mari (in the middle Euphrates), dating from the 19th century B.C., and at Ugarit from the 15th century B.C. Records from this period also show that the royalty and the wealthy employed gardeners. Thus already we see evidence of a highly developed and skilled profession.

Gardens were not the exclusive preserve of royalty. Temples were surrounded by fruit trees and contained pools of water where vegetables and flowers thrived in tended beds. Fresh flowers and fruit were important components of temple ritual, since they were needed as offerings for the gods. Temples would often plant orchards and gardens in honor of a deity. Fruit, flowers, and vegetables from these dedicated gardens and orchards would be offered specifically to that deity. Gardens were also used as places wherein oaths were sworn before judges, especially in gardens dedicated to the sun god Shamash (the judge of the world). No doubt gardens and orchards were deemed sacred and perhaps even a manifestation of divinity. It is not known for certain how gardens within temples were laid out. But we can speculate that, since temples were often ziggurat-shaped, bushes and trees may have been planted on the various stages of the ascending temple.

By the first millennium B.C. we learn of large public parks in Assyria established by Tiglath-Pileser I (r. 1114–1076 B.C.). He was a great collector of animals and exotic plants and trees, and in the parks he let loose herds of deer, gazelles, and ibex, where the animals could roam amid imported trees such as cedar, box, oak, and various fruit trees.

Another Assyrian king renowned for his gardens was Ashurnasirpal (r. 883–859 B.C.) of Nimrud. He had mountain water diverted from the Upper Zab River into the city through a rock-cut channel so that various orchards could be watered. These were great orchards of cedar, cypress, juniper, almond, date, ebony, olive, oak, tamarisk, terebinth, ash, pomegranate, fir, pear, quince, fig, and apple tress and countless vines and flowers. Many of these trees and plants were collected from other lands where Ashurnasirpal campaigned.

Sargon II (r. 721–705 B.C.) created gardens throughout his new capital of Khorsabad, which lay northeast of Nineveh. The key feature of these gardens was the addition of small pavilions. These gardens were extensive enough to allow Sargon to hunt lions and practice falconry amid the trees.

Sennacherib (704–681 B.C.) moved the capital back to Nineveh and created more gardens to commemorate this move. To water these gardens he diverted mountain streams to the city and planted imported trees and plants, including cotton bushes, mountain vines, and olives. In one garden he also re-created the marshes of southern Babylon by flooding the area and making a swamp; he then filled it with canebrakes and wild boar. This garden soon became a home for many herons that came to nest there. Esarhaddon (680–669 B.C.) succeeded Sennacherib and created a great garden in Nineveh that emulated the environs of the Amanus mountains in Syria; he filled this garden with fruit and resinous trees.

These royal gardens were not gardens as such, but parks, where the king feasted and hunted amid the shade of many trees and the fragrance of many flowers from the farthest regions of the Babylonian Empire.

Certainly palace gardens existed, but we do not have a great deal of information on them. However, temple gardens flourished as well during this time, and archaeological records allow us to document the layout of a typical garden temple. The temple of the New Year Festival, which lies outside the city walls of Ashur, reveals a quadrangle-shaped area where fruit trees lined flower and vegetable beds. Channels of water that formed a grid across the garden watered these. As in earlier times, it was essential for temples to have immediate access to fresh fruits, vegetables, and flowers as offerings to the gods, whose idols stood in the inner sanctum of the temple.

The wealthy often possessed gardens in the countryside surrounding the city; surviving records describe such gardens as being part of estates of the wealthy. These records also note the plants that could be found in such gardens. Mention is made of various vines and fruit trees, along with vegetable plots, flowers, poplars, and the unknown *hulupu* tree. Pools, ponds, and wells irrigated these gardens, and there were gardeners whose job it was to look after such gardens and supply the owner, usually living in the city proper, with fresh fruits and vegetables on a daily basis.

Another important document that clearly states the types of plants available to the Babylonians is a cuneiform text that names the various plants found in the garden of King Merodach-Baladan II (r. 721–710 B.C.). It may be this king's garden that would become the forerunner of the famous Hanging Gardens of Babylon. The various plants are listed in differing categories, perhaps reflecting the many plots and beds in which these plants could be found. This list, however, mentions no fruit trees; there may have been a separate list for trees that is no longer extant. Or perhaps this garden was a roof garden (hence the absence of trees), which would become the forerunner of the famous Hanging Gardens.

The plants mentioned in this cuneiform text are mostly of the edible variety and include leeks, onions, garlic, and salad vegetables such as lettuce, radish cucumbers, and gherkins. There are spices and herbs such as cardamom, caraway, dill, thyme, oregano, and fennel, coriander, cumin, and fenugreek, as well as some clearly curative herbs such as rue, colocynth, sagapenum, and lucerne, which may have been imported from Turkey by Sargon II in 714 B.C. Some 67 plants have not been identified. It is also interesting to note that the names of many of these plants are Aramaic loanwords, suggesting that most of these plants were imported, thus further suggesting a fairly sophisticated trade in plants and trees.

Mesopotamian civilization reached its apex during the reign of Naboplashar (r. 625–605 B.C.). It was his son, Nebuchadnezzar (r. 604–562 B.C.), who was the builder of the legendary Hanging Gardens of Babylon, deemed by the ancients as one of the seven wonders of the known world. Legend has it that Nebuchadnezzar built the Hanging Gardens to please his wife, Amyitis, who had been brought up in Media and continually yearned for the tree-covered mountains of her land. Unfortunately, we have no Babylonian records concerning the Hanging Gardens; there are only the accounts given by Greek writers such as Berossus, Diodorus Siculus, Strabo, and Philo of Byzantium, none of whom ever saw these fabled gardens. Nebuchadnezzar ruled for some 43 years, and he was responsible for making Babylon a wondrous city in its own right. It included an array of temples (each with statues of gods in solid gold), well-laid streets, palaces, high walls, fortresses, and the famous ziggurat temple to the god Marduk (perhaps the original Tower of Babel). But nowhere is there any record of the Hanging Gardens. Even Herodotus (writing in 450 B.C.) is silent on the subject, although he gives an extensive description of the city of Babylon, down to exact measurements of the high walls.

The Greek writers that do mention these gardens give details that seem to be precise yet can also be vague. For example, Strabo the geographer reports that the garden was a series of raised terraces one on top of another and that the entire structure rested upon square pillars. He then states that these terraces were hollow and filled with earth, deep enough to easily sustain large trees. The entire structure was constructed of baked bricks. The garden was irrigated by means of an "engine" that raised water from the Euphrates up to the various high-set terraces.

Theorists believe that this "engine" was probably a chain pump, or Doria, which consists of two wheels set atop each other and linked by a chain. Below the bottom wheel would be the water source (the Euphrates, for example). Attached to the chain are a series of buckets, and as the wheel is turned, the buckets dip into the water, fill, and are pulled up to the upper wheel, where the buckets tip over and empty the water into an upper pool. The chain carries the empty buckets down below again to be filled. The pool at the top would release the water into channels, which ran the length of the garden and irrigated it. Slaves, who rotated the bottom wheel with a handle, would power the Doria.

Since stone is scare in Mesopotamia, all construction was done with brick, made of clay, mixed with chopped straw, and then hardened in the sun. These bricks easily dissolved in water, but because rain was rare the city dwellers of ancient Mesopotamia did not need to improve their bricks. The mortar used to hold these bricks together was bitumen. But given this fact, how did the gardens avoid having bricks dissolve under continuous watering?

Diodorus Siculus tells us that the platforms on which the gardens stood were made of large slabs of rock (a rare commodity in ancient Mesopotamia). These were then covered with layers of reed, asphalt, and tiles. On top, sheets of lead were placed to keep out the moisture so that the foundation would not rot. Upon this insulation was piled soil, and trees, bushes, and flowers were planted.

The result would indeed be a wonder—a green, treed artificial mountain rising some 25 yards (23 meters) above the arid plain. The rising terraces were lined with fragrant flowers, fruit trees, and tamarisk and palm trees, the tops of which could be visible from a considerable distance. The illusion created was a garden hanging or hovering in the flat plain. The term "Hanging Gardens" is a misnomer, being a mistranslation of the Greek *kremastos,* which literally means "hanging over," very much like plants or vines hanging from a balcony. This is how one should perceive the Hanging Gardens themselves—as plants and trees overhanging a terrace.

The only archaeological record that we have that could possibly be the real Hanging Gardens was discovered by the German archaeologist Robert Koldewey in 1899. While digging for the Southern Citadel of the city, he found a substructure of 14 large rooms with stone arch ceilings. Ancient records tell us that there were only two locations in the city of Babylon that had stone construction—the north wall of the Northern Citadel (previously excavated and found indeed to be partially constructed of stone) and the Hanging Gardens. Koldewey concluded that he had found the cellar of the gardens. He continued digging and soon found a room with three large holes in the floor. These, concluded Koldewey, were where the Doria stood that raised the water to the upper terraces of the gardens.

Ancient Mesopotamia lost its vigor under a series of weak kings who followed Nebuchadnezzar. Finally, in 539 B.C. Babylon fell to Cyrus the Great and was subsumed by the Persian Empire. Some 200 years later the Persians were routed by Alexander the Great, and after Alexander the area fell prey to ravaging Bedouin tribes who had little regard for cities, given their nomadic way of life. Populations moved, and the land become less inhabited. As a result the canals fell into disrepair and eventually silted up and became dry, the encroaching desert slowly and persistently taking its toll.

Ancient Mesopotamia

3000–2340 B.C.	Early dynastic period (Sumerians)
2340–2180 B.C.	Akkadian period
2125–2025 B.C.	Neo-Sumerian period

2025–1790 B.C.	Isin-Larsa period
1790–1595 B.C.	First Babylonian Empire
1595–1160 B.C.	Kassite Dynasty
1350–612 B.C.	Assyrian period
625–539 B.C.	Late Babylonian period
331 B.C.–A.D. 226	Greco-Roman period
A.D. 226–641	Sassanian (Persian) period

Gardening Chronology of Mesopotamia

8000 B.C.	Domestication of certain cereals and pulses, such as wheat (emmer and einkorn), barley, lentil, pea, bitter vetch, chickpea, and fava bean
3000 B.C.	Written manuals on the use of medicinal herbs
2500 B.C.	Cultivation of fig, grape, pomegranate, and date
1750 B.C.	Code of Hammurabi written, dealing with proper maintenance of irrigation canals and ditches, and laws are outlined which define and regulate gardens and gardening, and state when crops are planted and harvested
1000 B.C.	Tiglath-Pileser I constructs many gardens and parks
500 B.C.	Hanging Gardens of Babylon built by Nebuchadnezzar II

Further Reading

Kramer, Samuel Noah, *From the Tablets of Sumer,* Indian Hills, Colorado: Falcon's Wing Press, 1956; 3rd edition, as *History Begins at Sumer: Thirty-Nine Firsts in Man's Recorded History,* Philadelphia: University of Pennsylvania Press, 1981

Mallowan, Max Edgar Lucien, *Early Mesopotamia and Iran,* London: Thames and Hudson, and New York: McGraw Hill, 1965

Rohde, Eleanour Sinclair, *Garden-Craft in the Bible: And Other Essays,* London: Jenkins, 1927; reprint, Freeport, New York: Books for Libraries Press, 1967

Roux, Georges, *Ancient Iraq,* Cleveland, Ohio: World, and London: Allen and Unwin, 1964; 3rd edition, London and New York: Penguin, 1992

NIRMAL DASS

Mexico

Spanish invaders of Mexico were surprised to find extensive gardens, a discovery that destroyed their preconceptions of an unsophisticated people. Near what is now Mexico City the floating gardens of Xochimilco were a floral Venice. The famous floating gardens were artificial islands, known as *chinampas*. Lake Xochimilco was dominated by the *chinampas* by the early part of the 16th century. A few *chinampas* of Xochimilco remain, growing gardenias, hibiscus, and roses.

Terraces, waterworks, and aqueducts testified to precolonial local gardening expertise. The royal Aztec hunting lodge at Chapultepec, later occupied by the palace of many Mexican presidents, included grottoes and belvederes and was maintained by 300 gardeners.

The Aztecs grew flowers for flowers' sake and refused to grow produce in areas they set aside as ornamental gardens. Evidence suggests that not only the rich and famous had gardens but also the average citizens. The great 19th-century historian of Mexico, William Prescott, discussed the importance of the different flora in Mexico:

> It would obviously be out of place to enumerate in these pages all the varieties of plants, many of them of medicinal virtue, which have been introduced from Mexico into Europe. Still less can I attempt a catalogue of its flowers which, with their variegated and gaudy colors, form the greatest attraction of our greenhouses. The opposite climates embraced within the narrow latitudes of New Spain have given it probably the richest and most diversified flora to be found in any country of the globe. These different products were systematically arranged by the Aztecs, who understood their properties and collected them into nurseries more extensive than any then existing in the Old World. (quoted in Hyams)

Nonetheless, it is the Spanish colonial tradition that has most influenced Mexican gardens. Through the years they have been characterized by privacy, pottery, and patios. Vines (particularly bougainvillea in profusion), fountains, tile, ironwork, and whimsical ornaments stand out. Guava, avocado, poinsettia (called the Christmas flower in Mexico), white sapodillas, and cacti are among other favorite plants.

The Moorish-Mexican influence displays itself in the affection for courtyards, although in contrast to the strong courtyard tradition, there is also the ubiquitous central square. This public landscaping often still reflects the last part of the 19th century when, after the French military invasion in the 1860s, some Mexican gardens were remodeled to include formal parterres and loggias. Parks acquired elaborate bandstands, often with a restaurant on the ground floor and the band perched above. The rural haciendas grew into monumental estates or rural palaces whose owners could afford bucolic settings with European garden art of a high Victorian flavor. The Alameda Park in downtown Mexico City retains an atmosphere of circular gloriettas and bronze nymphs. So do the Borda Gardens in Cuernavaca, but they are older than Alameda, and its ornamental lake dates to 1783. They were much enhanced in 1865, when the Emperor Maximilian and Empress Carlota established summer residences and staged elaborate garden parties.

Perhaps in reaction to the lush past, modern Mexican architects designed minimalist gardens rivaling the Japanese in discipline. Those of architect Luis Barragn at Pedregal depend on the vast lava outcrops rather than plants. Jose de Yturbe has carried this to the point of excluding plants altogether from designs, relying on walls to frame views of distant trees. Javier Sordo Madaleno has presented designs dependent on stone surfaces and shallow pots. Minimalism has perhaps had as much or more influence on garden design in Mexico as anywhere in the world. More recently, possibly influenced by restoration of the gardens at the Chapultepec Palace (once the Royal Botanical Garden), the surrealistic creations of Edward James in Xilitla, and Robert Brady's estate at Cuernavaca, less austere gardens are again fashionable.

The Mexican garden style has also become a force in gardening in the United States. The growing number of Mexican-Americans is part of the reason for increased enthusiasm in the United States for things Mexican, which includes not only food but gardens. As Witynski and Carr (1997) have noted, "In desert gardens, on tropical patios, or inside courtyards and stairwells, the furniture, vessels, and implements of Old Mexico inspire the natural beauty of a space, inviting quiet contemplations or spirited conversation."

Continuing economic crisis has restricted large garden construction, but the country's enthusiasm for gardens is still strong. Significant creations and restorations include the properties of the Rodolfo Morales Cultural Foundation in Oaxaca, the courtyard of the Franz Meyer Museum in Mexico City, San Angel Inn in San Angel, the market turned into a fantastic conservatory known as Cosmovitral in Toluca, and the gardens at the University of the Americas in Cholula, Puebla State, with sculptures by leading Mexican artists and opulent collections of period roses, alpines, and semitropical plants. For the garden enthusiast a comparison of the lush and social Cholula gardens, with their vast variety of plants, and the severe landscaping of the sprawling state university in Mexico City gives a unique insight into the continuing dialogue in Mexican garden design. But some of the most interesting gardens of recent construction remain, in the oldest of Mexican garden traditions, intensely private and behind high walls.

Garden clubs have never been strong in Mexico, the Sociedad Mexicana de Cactologia being an exception. It has a number of chapters and an excellent quarterly journal, *Cactaceas y suculentas Mexicana,* begun in 1955. Mexico has about 850 species of cactus, about 45 percent of the cactus family found in North America. Particularly important are *Mammillaria* and *Opuntia,* both in diversity and distribution. The *Agave* family, with about 155 species, is also significant.

See also Chapultepec Park; Chinampas; Huaxtepec Park; Pre-Columbian Gardens

Further Reading

Bradley-Hole, Christopher, *The Minimalist Garden,* New York: Monacelli Press, and London: Beazley, 1999

Damaz, Paul F., *Art in Latin American Architecture,* New York: Reinhold, 1963

Haas, Antonio, and Nicolas Sapieha, *Gardens of Mexico,* New York: Rizzoli, 1993

Hyams, Edward, *A History of Gardens and Gardening,* London: Dent, and New York: Praeger, 1971

Kirby, Rosina Greene, *Mexican Landscape Architecture from the Street and from Within,* Tucson: University of Arizona Press, 1972

O'Gorman, Patricia Waberer, *Patios and Gardens of Mexico,* New York: Architectural Book, 1979

Peterson, Jeanette Favrot, *The Paradise Garden Murals of Malinalco: Utopia and Empire in Sixteenth-Century Mexico,* Austin: University of Texas Press, 1993

Rendón Garcini, Ricardo, *Haciendas de México,* Mexico: Banamex-Accivla, 1994; as *Haciendas of Mexico,* Mexico: Banamex-Accivla, 1994

Shipway, Verna Cook, and Warren Shipway, *Houses of Mexico: Origins and Traditions,* New York: Architectural Book, 1970

Witynski, Karen, and Joe P. Carr, *Mexican Country Style,* Salt Lake City, Utah: Gibbs Smith, 1997

Witynski, Karen, and Joe P. Carr, *The New Hacienda,* Salt Lake City, Utah: Gibbs Smith, 1999

PAUL RICH

Meyer, Gustav 1816–1877

German Garden Architect and Urban Designer

Gustav Meyer was most influential as Director of City Gardens in Berlin during the 1870s. As a young garden architect he was employed in the office of Peter Josef Lenné in Potsdam, Germany. Working with Lenné on the redesign of the Marlygarten, and the designs for the Nordic garden, Sicilian garden, and Fasanerie at Sans Souci, Meyer was exposed to the stylistic tendencies of Italian Renaissance gardens. These gardens were characterized by axial alignments, symmetry, and a subordination of the role of plants to primarily evergreens. In the Sicilian garden, however, potted palms, flowering myrtle, African lilies, and Jerusalem cherries were used. At Sans Souci Meyer was also introduced to the work of architect Fredrich Karl Schinkel and Schinkel's use of ancient forms such as the hippodrome. Most of Meyer's work for Lenné concerned private, estate gardens. Lenné had resigned from working on the Tiergarten, the site of the first public zoo garden, yet Meyer's interest in the notion of urban public parks went undaunted.

In 1846, with the support of Dr. Rudolf Virschow and local officials, Meyer began to design urban parks for family excursions and recreation. The Revolution of 1848 and subsequent uprising by workers made evident the social needs of working people. City officials in Berlin sought to provide workers and their families spaces for recreation and education. Meyer believed that urban parks could be developed within the city specifically for those who could not afford holiday travel. These parks would be aesthetically pleasing and would provide the setting for social interaction and the newly emerging forms of recreational activity such as formalized sports and games, outdoor gymnastics, and gardening. Fusing this social initiative with the idea of an urban park, Meyer designed Friedrichs-Hain, Treptower Park, and Humboldt Hain in Berlin. In these parks Meyer illustrated his ability to use the historical styles that characterized his early estate work in an entirely different context and for a different patronage: public parks for the proletariat in Berlin.

At Friedrichs-Hain Park, Meyer created architecturally defined spaces with Renaissance elements combined with a network of curvilinear paths heavily planted at intersections. He used many of the traditional forms and spatial patterns developed for royal gardens but adapted these forms and spaces to suit the social needs of the day. For example, the spatial division of smaller gardens found in the royal pleasure garden were translate as areas for specific recreational uses in Meyer's park. The hippodromes became sites for the newly popular gymnasium equipment, rectilinear parterres became school gardens, and open lawns became spaces for formalized games. Maintaining these traditional forms but adapting them for new uses, Meyer established recreational parks in Berlin.

Meyer's book *Lehrbuch der schönen Gartenkunst* was highly influential in the field of garden design. He encouraged designers to create functional yet beautiful gardens that could serve utilitarian and social purposes. Meyer's pragmatism overshadowed any original contributions he might have made to park and garden design. However, his ability to envision parks as an essential social tool for improving the lives of the working classes earned him great respect in the burgeoning German nation. In 1870, a year prior to the unification of the German Empire, Meyer was asked to be the first director of city gardens in Berlin.

In this post Meyer was able to bridge the concerns of urban design, recreation planning, and reform with his designs for numerous plazas, streetscapes, and recreational parks in Berlin. Meyer's ability was greatly needed in Berlin during the 1870s. The establishment there of the Reichstag and the subsequent development of urban industry that followed unification brought an unprecedented population of factory workers into the city. Meyer's design of plazas, streetscapes, and parks uniquely addressed these changed social circumstances.

Meyer's urban plaza and streetscape designs adapted the more geometric and regularized patterns indicative of the French landscape architect Jean-Charles-Adolphe Alphand's proposals in *Les Promenades de Paris*. Meyer's formal style and pragmatic use of historical imitation in these designs was a precursor to the *architekturgarten* (architectural garden) and "city beautiful" garden styles of the early 20th century. In Meyer's design for the Koppenplatz, axial paths and geometric panels gave clear spatial articulation to the plaza not only as a place for social interaction but as a decorative green space within the urban fabric. Meyer's work on the celebrated avenue Unter den Lindens from Luisenstrasse to Parisner Platz, which entailed plans for plumbing lines and replanting, also adhered to the regularized, rectilinear layout of his plaza work. However, Meyer's layout did not simply reflect a historical composition but the rational organization of the street and underlying infrastructure.

A year before his death, Meyer redesigned Treptower Park, which was the first people's park in Berlin. Treptower Park spreads out along the banks of the Spree River and provides spectacular views of Berlin. As one of the largest green, open spaces in eastern Berlin today,

Treptower Park is still enjoyed by residents and tourists. Meyer's designs for parks, plazas, and streetscapes in Berlin provided visual continuity in a time of political transition. His proclivity for replicating historical styles and forms for new uses cogent to social programs was more ameliorating than revolutionary. As part of the advent of both the city beautiful and the small park and playground movement, Meyer helped to substantiate the importance of garden design to the urban reform programs that would characterize the early 20th century landscape.

Biography

Born in Frauendorf/Oder, 1816. Employed in drawing office of Peter Josef Lenné, 1836–59; in Lenné's office, worked on design of gardens at Sans Souci, Potsdam, Germany, and private estates in Wannsee and Grünewald; worked on park projects in Berlin, 1845–77, and became director of city gardens in Berlin, 1870; promoted social utility of public open spaces for both active and passive recreation; designer of first people's park in Berlin, Treptower Park, in 1864 and 1876. Died in Berlin, 1877.

Selected Designs

1846 Marlygarten at Sans Souci (with Peter Josef Lenné), Potsdam, Germany
1846–75 Friedrichs-Hain Park, Berlin, Germany
1851–60 Fasanerie at Sans Souci (with Peter Josef Lenné), Potsdam, Germany
1857 Sicilian gardens at Sans Souci (with Peter Josef Lenné), Potsdam, Germany
1857 Nordic gardens at Sans Souci (with Peter Josef Lenné), Potsdam, Germany
1864–76 Treptower Park, Berlin, Germany
1869–73 Humboldt-Hain Park, Berlin, Germany
1875 Koppenplatz, Berlin, Germany
1876 Unter den Lindens, from Luisenstrasse to Parisner Platz, Berlin, Germany
1877 Arkona-Platz, Berlin, Germany

Selected Publications

Lehrbuch der Schönen Gartenkunst, 1860

Further Reading

Gartenflore 56 (1907)
Heinrich, Vroni, and Goerd Peschken, *Gustav Meyer Zum 100. todestag 27.5.1977,* Berlin: Institut für Landwirtschafts- und Freiraumplanung der Technischen Unversität Berlin, 1978
Hennebo, Dieter, and Alfred Hoffmann, *Geschichte der deutschen Gartenkunst,* 3 vols., Hamburg, Germany: Broschek, 1962–65
"Meyer, Gustav," in *Neue deutsche Biographie,* vol. 17, Berlin: Duncker und Humblot, 1994
Wendland, Folkwin, *Berlins Gärten und Parke,* Frankfurt, Berlin, and Vienna: Proplyäen-Verlag, 1979
Wimmer, Clemens Alexander, *Geschichte der Gartentheorie,* Darmstadt, Germany: Wissenschaftliche Buchgesellschaft, 1989

SUSAN HERRINGTON

Michaux Family

French Explorers and Plant Collectors

André and François André Michaux were as important to the United States as they were to their native France. Although they originally traveled to North America to collect plants at the command of Louis XVI of France, which had decimated its own forests and was seeking satisfactory replacements, very soon their explorations took on wider implications. Not only did they leave some of the best descriptions of late 18th- and early 19th-century North America, but they wrote the first books on trees of the continent—André's *Flora Boreali-Americana* and *Histoire des chênes de l'Amerique* and François André's *Mémoire sur la naturalisation des arbres forestiers de l'Amerique* and *The North American Sylva.* Although André died at a comparatively early age, François André continued with his work in the most sympathetic way and became even more well renowned in his own right. The two made good friends and acquaintances soon after their arrival in North America, influential men in the world of botany such as Thomas Jefferson, George Washington, and the Bartrams. Their journeys were far encompassing and stretched from northern Canada to Florida, from the East Coast to beyond the Alleghenies, and from the sources of the Mississippi and Missouri Rivers to the sea. During all these journeys they collected seeds, samples of minerals, and bird and animal skins.

André undertook the journey to northern Canada on his own, noting the changing vegetation the further north he went but always collecting, in particular, larch, birch, a new azalea, and *Sarracenia purpurea* (common pitcher plant). Father and son undertook the journey to Florida together, accompanied by Indian guides and traveling in canoes. They found some familiar plants, such as *Magnolia grandiflora, Quercus phellos, Pinus taeda,* hickories, and wax myrtles, and new ones such as *Erythrina* and *Andromeda formossissima*. There were other journeys together, to the Carolinas in particular, where *Nyassa ogeche, Zizania palustris,* a new *Kalmia,* and *Calla palustris,* all new plants, were collected.

François André undertook the journey beyond the Alleghenies and down the Ohio River after his father's death in 1802. He took particular note of the oaks—*Quercus alba, Q. rubra,* and *Q. tinctoria* (now *Q. velutina*)—used for building, as well as other trees, including *Carya cordifomis,* a nut tree, *Cerasus virginica* (probably chokecherry), and an unnamed pine used for masts. He remarked on the density of the forests, the size of the trees, and the great variety. In almost all cases the American trees were larger than those of France. He also commented how fertile the land of Virginia was. Going on to Kentucky, he noted the fine horses and was fascinated by the "Barrens" with its underground water and land he felt would be good for viniculture as it was similar to parts of France. On a later journey to Tennessee, along the banks of Roaring River, he came upon a wonderful collection of magnolias, all in one area, and made an excellent collection of seeds.

Another aspect of the Michauxs's collecting was the exchange of plants. Not only were plants taken from North America but new ones were planted in North America, such as *Lagestroemia indica* (crape myrtle), *Ginkgo biloba, Firmiana platanifolia* (Chinese parasol tree), and *Albizia julibrissin,* all of which André had brought back from Persia. On his first arrival in North America, André had quickly decided that a garden in which to cultivate some of the seeds he collected was necessary; one was laid out and a house built on land he acquired six miles from New York on the Hudson River. It was here that more collecting was organized by the Frenchman who had accompanied the Michauxs from France and who continued dispatching seeds and plants after the departure of the Michauxs and the death of André. Another garden was established at Charleston, South Carolina, and a more permanent home built. It was here the new imported trees for the continent were grown.

The Michauxs were the first to realize and appreciate that the North American forests were not inexhaustible and that they should not be destroyed in the name of progress. There had been incredible waste in the cutting down of trees when clearing land. The result was that wood was at a very high price at the time of their arrival. The Michauxs were the first to advise regeneration. Through a critical period in the history of the United States—after the revolution and the establishment of the U.S. government and administration—they had enormous influence over the establishment of a forestry department. It was through their ideas that land was acquired for forest, the department set up, and planting of seedlings started. They also pointed out that land which had been thought of as of no use could, in fact, grow trees.

Michaux, André 1746–1802

Biography

Born at Satory, Versailles, France, 1746. Son of farmer in service of Louis XV at Versailles; started farming with brother; sold share of family farm and began to study botany at Le Trianon, Versailles, 1777; traveled to England to meet botanists of the day; traveled to Persia to collect plants, 1781–85; sent by Louis XVI to North America to collect forest trees, 1785–96, where he established two nurseries for plants to be sent back to France, one in New Jersey and one in Charleston, South Carolina (where plants being introduced to North America were also raised, including *Ginkgo biloba*); joined expedition to Australia but disembarked at Mauritius, 1800; traveled to Madagascar, established a garden. Died in Madagascar, 1802.

Selected Publications

Histoire des chênes de l'Amerique, 1801
Flora Boreali-Americana, 1803

Michaux, François André 1769–1855

Biography

Born 1769. His father was botanist and plant collector André Michaux; accompanied father to America to collect forest trees and oversee the Charleston nursery, 1685–90; sent back to Paris for education, 1790; from 1796, undertook to edit, illustrate, and print father's books and then began writing himself; sent to America by minister of agriculture to investigate state of gardens established in New Jersey and Charleston by his father and to collect plants, 1801–3, and again in 1806; returned to Paris in 1808 and settled to write books; moved to Vaureal, outside Paris, and established gardens, orchards, and nursery for tree seedlings, 1821; started to plant Harcourt Arboretum, Eure, France, 1853. Died at Vaureal, France, 1855.

Selected Publications

Mémoire sur la naturalisation des arbres forestiers de l'Amerique, 1805

Michaux, François André, "Notice sur Les Îles Bermudes," *Annales du Museum d'histoire naturelle a Paris* 8 (1806)
Histoire des arbres forestiers de l'Amerique septentrionale, 1810–13; as *The North American Sylva,* translated by Augustus L. Hillhouse, 1817–19

Further Reading

Duval, Marguerite, *La planète des fleurs,* Paris: Laffout, 1977; as *The King's Garden,* Charlottesville: University Press of Virginia, 1982
Jefferson, Thomas, *Thomas Jefferson's Garden Book, 1766–1824: With Relevant Extracts from His Writings,* edited by Edwin Morris Betts, Philadelphia, Pennsylvania: American Philosophical Society, 1944
Leighton, Ann, *American Gardens in the Eighteenth Century: "For Use or for Delight,"* Boston: Houghton Mifflin, 1976
Sargent, C.S., "André Michaus," *Arnold Arboretum* (December 1888)
Savage, Henry, and Elizabeth J. Savage, *André and François André Michaux,* Charlottesville: University Press of Virginia, 1986

JILL COLLETT

Migge, Leberecht 1881–1935

German Landscape Architect

Leberecht Migge was a thought-provoking early 20th-century German landscape architect. His ideas not only stimulated fellow landscape architects but also people who were involved in the garden city, peoples' parks, and allotment garden movements. Migge first worked as a garden designer for middle-class clientele. Later in his life he turned to the garden-related needs and interests of so-called lower social groups of the urban population. Migge's social orientation became more explicit in his writings as well as in his planning and design work after World War I. In this second phase of his professional career, Migge focused on the needs and interests of the users of parks and gardens and continued to develop aesthetically pleasing design solutions. Quite frequently he collaborated with architects of the Neue Sachlichkeit (New Objectivity) such as Ernst May, Bruno Taut, and Martin Wagner.

Migge's professional career began at the end of the 19th century as a gardener's apprentice. From 1904 to 1913 he worked as garden technician and later as artistic director for the well-known landscape architecture office of Jacob Ochs in Hamburg. Most of his designs for private gardens for the middle and upper class date from this period. He also designed numerous public parks and peoples' parks (*Volksparks*), cemeteries, and other open spaces during these years. In 1913 Migge started his own landscape architecture office in Hamburg-Blankenese. In the same year his book *Die Gartenkultur des 20. Jahrhunderts* (Garden Culture for the 20th Century) appeared. Migge proved to be an enthusiastic garden writer. He compassionately discussed tasks and perspectives of landscape architecture in its various facets, many of which have shaped professional developments in German landscape architecture during the 20th century.

With the beginning of World War I, Migge's work became more and more centered on the social dimension of gardens and parks. Such publications as *Laubenkolonien und Kleingärten* (1914; Arbor Colonies and Allotment Gardens), "Jugendparks als Kriegerdank" (1916; Youth Parks in Gratitude for Soldiers), and *Jedermann Selbstversorger* (1918; Everybody a Self Starter) give evidence of this focus. During the Weimar Republic Migge systematically developed concepts of garden design for many mass housing programs in Berlin, Frankfurt, and other cities, especially for lower-income housing projects implemented by city administrations and building cooperatives as a response to the extreme housing shortage. For the city of Frankfurt Migge designed specific types of gardens for mass housing projects. Because many of the inhabitants had little experience with gardening, the plans also advised what plants to cultivate.

During the 1920s Migge engaged in the discussion of the so-called "coming garden." Opposed to other landscape architects such as Gustav Allinger, Gudmund Nyeland Brandt, and Alwin Seifert, he decisively expressed his ideas about the future of garden design in Germany. In numerous publications Migge predicted a definite social orientation in landscape architecture. In his 1927 article "The Coming Garden," Migge stated his primary goals:

> To make the way free for many gardens, for the garden of everybody—that is the genuine garden

> architecture we need. For that not so much aesthetic abilities and learned disciplinary formulae are required, but rather knowledge of people's economy and of the social and technical conditions, this is the basis upon which gardens come into existence (Migge, 1927).

Migge consequently considered a discussion of specific garden styles as superfluous: "The garden style of our time? We do not have to care about it. It will come, if it has to, without our help" (Migge, 1927).

There was a strong missionary element in Migge's ideas about garden design. For him the "coming garden" should be "a productive garden, a work garden and—it will be a glass garden" (Migge, 1927). This statement was clearly influenced by Migge's knowledge of poor living conditions in Germany in the late 1920s, especially for those in the lower social strata. He wanted to help these people by providing them with garden plots. Advanced gardening techniques could allow them to grow fruits and vegetables to improve their diet. Migge therefore recommended highly technical gardens in sharp contrast to the more romantic attitude in garden design favored by many of his colleagues (see Plate 24).

During the 1920s, a period of increasing economic problems, the idea of self-supply, enabling a large number of urbanites to produce their own fruits and vegetables, became a basic element of Migge's garden philosophy. Together with landscape architect Max Schemmel, he founded the Siedlerschule Worpswede (homesteader school) in the town of Worpswede near the city of Bremen. It was created to promote the idea of self-supply and teach people how to grow vegetables and fruits. Migge had a special interest in the cultivation of vegetables under glass and the use of human feces as manure.

Migge contributed to many garden and architectural expositions, among them the 1928 International Exhibition of Garden Design in London. He published numerous books and articles on garden design, gardening, the design of peoples' parks, city planning, and regional planning. In the context of the discussion of a draft for a Preußisches Städtebaugesetz (Prussian Town Planning Act) he published the 1925 article "Wirtschaftlicher Städtebau und wirtschaftliche Landesplanung" (Economical City Planning and Thrifty Regional Planning), in which he predicted the professional development from garden to landscape design.

In the 1920s, Migge was a member of the Bund Deutscher Gartenarchitekten (BDGA; Association of German Garden Architects). He left the association because he fundamentally disagreed with leading members of the BDGA about professional politics. During all of his career Migge did not avoid conflicts. His publications often criticized the work of colleagues in a competent and polemical way. He therefore had numerous enemies and became more and more isolated within the profession. Migge died two years after the takeover of National Socialism in 1935. In an obituary notice, Migge's estrangement from the profession of landscape architects was characterized by garden architect Camillo Schneider as being due to a personal propensity for fighting and Marxist leanings.

Biography

Born in Danzig, Germany, 1881; apprenticed as gardener; worked for Jacob Ochs' Hamburg landscape architecture firm, 1904–13, where he designed numerous private gardens, cemeteries, public parks, and other open spaces; started landscape architecture practice in Hamburg-Blankenese, 1913; began focusing on social dimensions of parks and gardens as WWI began; developed garden designs for mass housing projects in Berlin, Frankfurt, and other cities during Weimar Republic; focused on concept of self-supply in 1920s; with landscape artchitect Max Schemmel founded Siedlerschule (homesteader school) Worpswede near Berlin, 1920–21. Died in Flensburg, 1935.

Selected Designs

1909	Public garden Hamburg-Fuhlsbüttel
1912	Gardens of silk weaving mill Michels and Company, Nowawes near Potsdam (architect Hermann Muthesius)
1912–13	Collaboration for garden city Leipzig-Marienbrunn
before 1913	Gardens of military hospital Altona; gardens of Unteroffiziersschule (school for sergeants), Weilburg; Zoological garden, Hamburg
1913–14	Mariannenpark, Leipzig
1913–20	Peoples' park, Rüstringen
1916	Youth park Groß-Berlin Halbinsel Pichelswerder
1915–16	Navy cemetery, Wilhelmshaven; war cemetery Brüssel-Evere
1917	Open space plan Rüstringen
1918–19	Lindenhof housing estate Berlin-Schöneberg (architect Martin Wagner)
1920–21	Green belt Grünberg
1920s	Sonnenhof, Worpswede
1922	Green belt, city of Kiel (together with Wilhelm Hahn)
ca. 1923	Gardens for glass factory Bicheroux, Herzogenrath
1924–26	Housing estate Georgsgarten, Celle (architect Otto Haesler)
late 1920s	Housing estate Berlin-Britz

late 1920s	Hufeisensiedlung, Berlin (architects Martin Wagner, Bruno Taut)
1924	Housing estate of German Garden City Association, Berlin-Staaken (architect Erwin Gutkind)
1924–25	Housing estate Obernigk, Breslau (with Max Schemmel)
ca. 1927	Garten Bruno Taut
1927–28	Housing estate Römerstadt, Frankfurt (architect Ernst May)
1927–28	Housing estate Praunheim, Frankfurt (architect Ernst May)
1928	Housing estate Dessau-Ziebigk (architect Leopold Fischer)
1929	"Waldsiedlung" Zehlendorf-Schönow, Berlin (architects Rossius-Rhyn and Dr. Rehme)
1929–31	Open space planning for Siemensstadt, Berlin (architects Hans Scharoun et al.)
1930	Housing estate Duisburg-Neudorf (architects Kramer and Kremer)
1931–33	Reemtsma Estate, Altona near Hamburg

Selected Publications

Der Hamburger Stadtpark und die Neuzeit, 1909
"Willy Lange," *Die Gartenkunst* 11 (1909)
"Der öffentliche Park als sozialer Faktor," *Raumkunst,* no. 3 (1909)
"Max Laeuger und seine Gärten," *Die Kunst* 13 (1910)
"Mehr Ökonomie," *Die Gartenstadt* 4, no. 10 (1910)
"Wirtschaft und Kunst in der Gartenkultur," *Die Gartenkunst* 13, no. 6 (1911)
Die Gartenkultur des 20. Jahrhunderts, 1913
"Außenpark Rüstringen," *Die Gartenkunst* 16 (1914)
"Die Gartenbauausstellung Altona 1914," *Die Gartenkunst* 16, no. 2 (1914)
"Die Gartenmission der Städte," *Die Gartenkunst* 16, no. 6 (1914)
Laubenkolonien und Kleingärten, Flugschrift des Dürerbundes 167 (ca. 1914)
"Ein Wendepunkt in der Grünpolitik der Städte?" *Die Gartenkunst* 17, no. 12 (1915)
"Jugendparks als Kriegerdank," *Möllers Deutsche Gärtner-Zeitung* 31, no. 27 (1916)
"Kriegerdank-Stätten," *Möllers Deutsche Gärtner-Zeitung* 31, no. 21 (1916)
"Wie baue ich eine grüne Stadt?" *Der Städtebau* 14 (1917)
Jedermann Selbstversorge! Eine Lösung der Siedlungsfrage durch neuen Gartenbau, 1918
"Das grüne Manifest," *Eugen Diederichs Blätter zur neuen Zeit*, no. 12/13 (1919)
"Natürliche Architektur (Etappenbauweise)," *Der Siedler*, no. 2 (1921)
"Rücksicht auf die wirtschaftliche Lage bei Pflege der öffentlichen Grünanlagen," *Die Gartenkunst* 23 (1921)
"10 Leitsätze für den Kleingärtnerbeirat und entwickelnde Begründung," *Zeitschrift für Kommunalwirtschaft* 13, no. 3 (1923)
"Gartentechnik und Gartenkunst," *Die Gartenschönheit* 6, no. 4 (1925)
"Die heutige Parkpolitik der Städte," *Der Deutsche Gartenarchitekt* 2, no. 9 (1925)
"Wirtschaftlicher Städtebau durch wirtschaftliche Landesplanung," *Der Deutsche Gartenarchitekt* 2, no. 12 (1925)
Deutsche Binnenkolonisation: Sachgrundlagen des Siedlungswesens, 1926
"Hie Gartenarchitekt, hie Gartenbeamter," *Behörden-Gartenbau* 3, no. 11 (1926)
"Höfe und Gärten bei Mietshausblöcken," *Die Wohnungswirtschaft* 4, no. 20 (1927)
"Der kommende Garten," *Die Gartenschönheit* 8, no. 3 (1927)
"Der technische Gartentypus unserer Zeit," *Die Gartenschönheit* 8 (1927)
"Dezentralisations-Probleme der Großstadt, begründet mit neuer Grün- und Siedlungspolitik," *Die Baugilde*, no. 20 (1927)
"Die Großsiedlung," *Die Gartenschönheit* 9, no. 2 (1928)
"Grünpolitik der Stadt Frankfurt am Main," *Der Städtebau* 24, no. 2 (1929)
"Groß-Berliner Siedlungsgrün," *Die Wohnung* 5 (1930)
"Weltstadt-Grün: Ein Aufruf zur rentablen Parkpolitik," *Wasmuths Monatshefte für Baukunst und Städtebau* 25, no. 5 (1930)
"Siedlung und Arbeitslosigkeit," *Die Gartenstadt* 15, no. 2 (1931)
Die wachsende Siedlung nach biologischen Gesetzen, 1932
Eine Weltstadt kolonisiert, 1932
"Siedlungspolitik der Städte," *Die Gartenschönheit* 14, no. 10 (1933)
"Gartenglas und Kleinhaus," *Zentralblatt der Bauverwaltung* 54 (1934)

Further Reading

Gröning, Gert, and Joachim Wolschke-Bulmahn, *Grüne Biographien: Biographisches Handbuch zur Landschaftsarchitektur des 20. Jahrhunderts in Deutschland,* Berlin: Patzer, 1997
Hesse, Frank Peter, "Öffentlicher Garten in Fuhlsbüttel: Ein Reformbeitrag von Leberecht Migge," in *Was nützet mir ein schöner Garten: Historische Parks und Gärten in Hamburg,* edited by Hesse, Sylvia

Borgmann, and Jörg Haspel, Hamburg: VSA-Verlag, 1990
Jarlöv, Lena, *Stadsekologi och trädgårdskultur, porträtt av en kretsloppspionjär, Leberecht Migge, 1881–1935*, Stockholm: Byggforskningsrådet, 1996
Krause, Gerlinde Marianne, "Zur Entwicklung ökologischer Ansätze in der Stadtplanung: Werk und Wirkung des Gartenarchitekten Leberecht Migge (1881–1935) und seine Bedeutung für die Entwicklung der sozialistischen Stadtplanung in der DDR," Ph.D. diss., Hochschule für Architektur und Bauwesen Weimar, 1987
Leberecht Migge, 1881–1935: Gartenkultur des 20. Jahrhunderts, Worpswede, Germany: Worpsweder Verlag, 1981
Leberecht Migge: Der Sonnenhof in Worpswede als Siedlungsmodell, Worpswede, Germany: Worpsweder, Osterholz-Scharmbeck, 1982
Rohde, Michael, "Ein Volkspark des 20. Jahrhunderts in Leipzig von Migge und Molzen," *Die Gartenkunst* 8, no. 1 (1996)
Wolschke-Bulmahn, Joachim, "'The Peculiar Garden': The Advent and the Destruction of Modernism in German Garden Design," in *The Modern Garden in Europe and the United States: Proceedings of the Garden Conservancy Symposium Held at the Paine Webber Building in New York, New York, March 12, 1993,* edited by Robin Karson, Cold Spring, New York: Garden Conservancy, 1994
Wolschke-Bulmahn, Joachim, "Avantgarde und Gartenarchitektur in Deutschland," *Zolltexte* 7, no. 12 (1997)
Wolschke-Bulmahn, Joachim, and Gert Gröning, *1913–1988: 75 Jahre Bund Deutscher Landschaft-architekten BDLA*, vol. 1, *Zur Entwicklung der Interessenverbände der Gartenarchitekten in der Weimarer Republik und im Nationalsozialismus,* Bonn: Bund Deutschen Landschaftsarchitekten, 1988

JOACHIM WOLSCHKE-BULMAHN

Miller, Philip 1691–1771

English Horticulturist and Author

Philip Miller is primarily remembered as the curator and gardener of the Chelsea Physic Garden from 1722 to1770, but his influence and work spread farther than those titles would imply. In an age of exploration and discovery, new plants were needed and wanted for many purposes. He was one of the 18th century's greatest horticulturists, cultivating hundreds of new plants that were sent to him from all quarters of the globe. He discovered and described the best way to grow these plants, how to propagate them, and how to bring them to fruition. He also wrote *The Gardeners and Florists Dictionary* (1724), the first work of its kind.

Miller was probably born at Deptford near London. His father was a Scot and gardener to a gentleman at Bromley before founding his own market gardening business at Deptford. Miller's father taught him foreign languages and the sciences, particularly gardening. He was able to travel and study throughout England before visiting Flanders and Holland. He also worked in his father's business, where he decided to pursue ornamental and kitchen gardening. He established his own nursery business at St. George's Fields, Southwark (later the site of the King's Bench Prison). In 1722 at the recommendation of Sir Hans Sloane, president of the Royal Society, Miller took up the post of curator of the Chelsea Physic Garden, which Sloane had donated to the Society of Apothecaries.

From 1722 Miller lived in the garden, but by 1734 he and his family had moved to a house in nearby Swan Walk. Chelsea at this time was occupied by many nurserymen, and in 1724 Miller took up their suggestions to publish a small gardeners' dictionary. He wrote his first *Gardeners and Florists Dictionary* in two volumes. No one else had written such a book; it contained not only lists of plants, but also methods of cultivation, and discussions of the kitchen garden, fruit garden, flower garden, and "the wilderness," by which he meant a shrub and tree area. The book was immediately popular and was ordered not only by rich men with copious libraries but also by academic subscribers such as the provost of Oriel, University of Oxford, and professors of botany at Dublin and Edinburgh. It was also purchased by nurserymen and enthusiastic clergy gardeners, such as the dean of Rochester and Gilbert White. The books were republished in eight editions over the next 40 years, gradually expanding to include the Linnean system of nomenclature and new plants. The books are not illustrated because the additional cost would have made the book out of reach for most purchasers. The illustrations were published in separate volumes.

Miller became engaged in voluminous correspondence with acquaintances in England and Scotland, as well as in Europe and the United States. He was in constant communication with the professor of Leyden University and the Royal Gardeners in Paris. It was through these contacts that he met Carl Linnaeus, the Swedish botanist who reformed the nomenclature of plants and who visited him at Chelsea. Miller did not approve of Linnaeus's work to start with, but eventually adopted Linnaeus's now universal system. Miller's correspondence also included plant collectors in the United States. John Bartram, who traveled the American wilderness, dispatched hundreds of plants to Miller and other rich collectors. These consignments included forest trees and shrubs as well as herbaceous plants. Bartram's letters very often included advice on methods of growing, and he received many requests for plants from rich, influential men such as Lord Petre, who was planting a large estate and wished to experiment with new types of trees for England. A Quaker named Peter Collinson was also a close friend and correspondent. Not only did he have a fine garden, he also kept up a detailed correspondence with influential men in America and facilitated further collections of plants. The Reverend Gilbert White of Selbourne was another correspondent and visitor to Chelsea. His requests were more humble—how to grow cucumbers successfully.

Under Miller, the Chelsea Physic Garden became a center for the receipt, cultivation, and distribution of a remarkable number of plants. Illustrators were drawn to the garden as a resource, and in an age without cameras, illustration played an important role in both informing the knowledgeable and teaching students. Individuals including George D. Ehret, Jacob van Huysum, J.S. Miller, and Elizabeth Blackwell came to Chelsea, where they found Miller insistent on accuracy and the best illustration of the plants.

During his long career as curator, Miller controlled the garden's activities in fact, if not in name. The Society of Apothecaries was meant to administer the garden by committee, but their poorly kept minutes of meetings (started in 1731) do not detail more than a few everyday tasks. Miller carried on with his horticultural tasks, vast correspondence, and book writing. For 30 years he was left very much to his own devices, although in 1750 the committee expressed its satisfaction with his work and the state of the garden. In fact the group hardly ever met until 1770, when a new committee was formed and new inventories of every kind were demanded. Miller, by this time an old man, objected to these orders. He was told to move out of the garden, and despite some sort of reconciliation, he did. Another curator was hired, and Miller died the next year.

See also Chelsea Physic Garden

Biography

Born in Deptford, England, 1691. Commercial florist at St. George's Fields; served as curator and gardener for Chelsea Physic Garden, 1722–70. Died in London, England, 1771.

Publications

Gardeners and Florists Dictionary, 1724; 8th ed., 1768
The Gardeners Kalendar, 1732; 15th ed., 1769

Further Reading

Fisher, John, *The Origin of Garden Plants,* London: Constable, 1982
Fleming, Laurence, and Alan Gore, *The English Garden,* London: Joseph, 1979
Leighton, Ann, *American Gardens in the Eighteenth Century,* Boston: Houghton Mifflin, 1976

JILL COLLETT

Milotice

Milotice, Brno County, Moravia, Czech Republic

Location: 31 miles (50 km) from Brno, 68.3 miles (110 km) from Vienna, 186 miles (300 km) from Prague, 10.5 miles (17 km) from Hodonin

Outdoor entertaining among Austro-Hungarian nobility during the 18th and 19th centuries reached its peak at country estates such as Milotice, far from the dust, heat, and noise of cities but near enough to attract guests for parties and soirees. Originally a moated stone citadel built in the 14th century, Milotice lies in southeastern Moravia (Morava), an ancient Slavic province in what is now the Czech Republic. The adjacent town, also known as Milotice, has about 2,000 residents.

The remaining Gothic and Renaissance structures—moat, bridge, and corner towers—are incorporated into the renovated baroque château, which, along with its garden, has undergone various reconstructions over several centuries. Visitors today enter the estate from the east side, crossing the ancient moat on a bridge containing sculptures by Jakub Kristof Schletterer. The château and garden are currently owned and managed by the State Heritage Institute of Brno. The restored historical interiors on the first floor opened to visitors in 1974.

Following the garden's most recent renovation in the 1960s and its replanting in 1974, the maintenance staff's major task has been to preserve the formal French baroque garden in its best possible state. A staff of eight, led by administrator Evžen Bocek, maintains the garden and its greenhouse, which protects tender plants such as palms and succulents.

As is the case with other strategic outposts at this historical crossroads of Europe, Milotice has endured the effects of social and political upheaval. Its architectural style, ornamentation, and current plantings reflect the influences of foreign as well as domestic Slavic traditions. The oldest known garden was established in the 16th century outside the battlement on the west side of the château. (The Czech equivalent of *château, zámek,* means a mansion or small castle.) Bernard Ludvik Tomar of Enezesfeld, who owned Milotice from 1586 to 1597, conducted the Renaissance reconstruction, expanding the château by three wings and corner towers. Following the Thirty Years' War Gabriel Serenyi bought Milotice in 1648. In 1705 Hungarian soldiers led by Baron Ferene Rakocz in an uprising against the Habsburgs burned the château and its tower and severely damaged the garden. Since then the château has been renovated, but the original garden was never renewed.

Partial reconstruction of the devastated château began in 1717 in the spirit of the high baroque, with construction of a new garden on the east side of the building completed first. It was then that Milotice became an official summer residence of the Serenyi dynasty. The family's Milotice branch retained ownership from 1780 to 1811, when Baron Karl Antonin Serenyi's line ended. In 1888 the aristocratic family Seilern, from Porynska Falce, gained the château through marriage.

Baroque-period reconstruction in 1717 was to include the establishment of a new garden and pheasantry, minor alterations on the building's ground floor, and the addition of a grand outer staircase leading to the park-like garden. The garden's designer, well-known garden architect Anton Zinner, catered to the nobility throughout the Austro-Hungarian Empire. He designed gardens in Jaroměřice and Rokytnou, Mikulov, in Austerlitz, and the famous Belvedere Palace in Vienna owned by Eugen of Savoyen.

Inspired by the symmetry of formal French gardens, Zinner completed the Milotice garden in 1721. It soon became a favorite of Franz Khevenhueller-Metsch, the lord high steward at Marie Therese's court. Zinner's strategy was to give Milotice's east-facing landscape the appearance of a "grand garden salon." By dividing it only by an arbor and allées of linden and chestnut trees, he could take advantage of summer breezes and afternoon shade to cool the salon and its guests.

Zinner's plan called for three fountains, also meant to soothe the guests in summer. One came from Svatobořice, another seat of the Serenyi family about two miles (3.2 km) from Milotice. The other two were probably built especially for Milotice. However, none has been preserved, probably because they were made of wood. Today, the central path through the château park incorporates a pool and fountain.

In the 1740s two orangeries were erected, followed in the 1760s by a shooting pavilion constructed in the pheasantry, which is adjacent to the garden. By the end of the 18th century, visitors to Milotice were enjoying four entertainment pavilions—built at the end of the garden—including a billiards house and a skittles house. An aviary added yet another attraction to this portion of Zinner's grand garden salon.

In the 1830s Maxmillian Erras attempted a reconstruction of the baroque garden; however, his goal was to transform it into an English park. His plan was never realized, and by the end of the 19th century, Zinner's grand garden salon had deteriorated. It remained largely untended through the first half of the 20th century.

In the 1960s garden architect Dušan Riedel launched a reconstruction of Milotice's garden. However, not having Zinner's plans at his disposal, he relied on inspiration from a "baroque spirit" rather than precise documentation of the formal garden plan. He also looked to other baroque gardens for inspiration, such as André Le Nôtre's in France.

No known documentation is available that describes changes in the plantings throughout the various ownerships of Milotice. It is worth noting, however, that the existing allée is composed of linden trees, which play prominent roles in Slavic folklore, history, and tradition. The garden also contains specimens of trees, shrubs, and groundcovers that are native to North America, the Orient, western Asia, Africa, and the British Isles, as well as to central and southeastern Europe.

No known documentation is available that describes changes in the plantings throughout the various ownerships of Milotice. It is worth noting, however, that the existing allée is composed of linden trees, which play prominent roles in Slavic folklore, history, and tradition. The garden also contains specimens of trees, shrubs, and groundcovers that are native to North America, Asia, Africa, and the British Isles, as well as to central and southeastern Europe.

Synopsis

1300s	Gothic citadel on site of future château and garden constructed (portion of moat survives today)
1586–97	Bernard Ludvik Tomar of Enezesfeld completes Renaissance reconstruction of Milotice, expanding château with three wings and corner towers
16th C.	Oldest known garden at Milotice established outside battlement on west side
1618–48	Milotice emptied of inhabitants during Thirty Years' War
1648	Gabriel Serenyi purchases Milotice
1705	Hungarian forces led by Baron Ferene Rakocz nearly destroy Milotice during uprising against Habsburgs, burning château and tower, and trampling and severely damaging garden
1717–21	Serenyi family reconstructs part of devastated château; garden relocated to east side of château, along with pheasantry, garden designed by Anton Zinner
1740s	Two orangeries (helioglasshouses) erected
1760s	Serenyi family adds shooting pavilion to pheasantry
late 1700s	Serenyi family constructs four entertainment pavilions and aviary at end of garden
1780–1811	Milotice branch of Serenyi family continues ownership of estate, ending with last of Baron Karl Antonin Serenyi's line
1830s	Maxmillian Erras attempts reconstruction of baroque garden, but goal of English-style park never achieved
1888	Seilern family from Porynska Falce acquires château and garden through marriage
1900–1960s	Milotice deteriorates, remaining largely untended
1960s	Garden architect Dušan Riedel launches reconstruction of garden
1974	Garden replanted, and château's restored first floor opened to public
2001	State Heritage Institute of Brno owns and maintains château and garden

Further Reading

Jerabek, Tomas, *Milotice Chateau: Monument to the Baroque,* Brno: State Heritage Institute, 1998

Kudelka, Zdeník, editor, *Umění baroka na Moravě a ve Slezku,* Prague: Academia, 1996

Petrů, Jaroslav, *Státní zámek Milotice,* Brno: State Heritage Institute, 1971

ELIZABETH CERNOTA CLARK

Missouri Botanical Garden

St. Louis, Missouri, United States

Location: 4344 Shaw Boulevard, south of Interstate 44, 3 miles (4.8 km) west-southwest of St. Louis city center

The Missouri Botanical Garden, originally referred to as Shaw's Garden, was established in St. Louis in 1859 by businessman Henry Shaw (1800–1889). Shaw provided further funding and provisions from his personal fortune in his will, specifying the garden's goal of research, display, and education for the scientific community and the public. It has been designated a National Historic Landmark (1971) and remains a world-renowned research center, library, and public garden whose mission is "To discover and share knowledge about plants and their environment, in order to preserve and enrich life."

Shaw was born in Sheffield, England, in 1880 and settled in St. Louis at the age of 18. He imported precision tools from his native hometown and built a successful business in real estate investment. Three extended tours of England and the Continent between 1840 and 1851 enlightened Shaw and acquainted him with botanical and pleasure gardens. His visit to the estate of Chatsworth, Derbyshire, inspired him to create his own version of the site at his property on the Missouri prairie. The centerpiece of his country estate was an Italianate villa named Tower Grove (designed by George I. Barnett, 1849). Today it is surrounded by the 79-acre (32-ha) Missouri Botanical Garden and the adjacent 289-acre (101-ha) Tower Grove Park, a Victorian masterpiece based on English precedent and designed by Shaw in 1867 to complement his garden.

The original plan (drawn by Shaw in 1856) was based on a tripartite organization of flower gardens, an arboretum, and a fruticetum, reflecting Shaw's adherence to the writings of J.C. Loudon. The grounds were planted in a typically Victorian manner, mixing S-shaped beds and elaborate compartments with exotic and native specimens. Flanking the Palm House was a square parterre—the Sunken Garden—embellished with carpet bedding and giant agaves, with a sculpture of Juno marking the principle axis. An onion-domed observatory just to the south anchored concentric circles of shrubs. The Linnaean house (the oldest continuously operating display conservatory in the United States, built in 1882 and still extant) overlooked the Victoria Pool, which housed the collection of water lilies bred by head gardener James Gurney, who was trained at the Royal Botanic Society's garden at Regent's Park, London, and employed by Shaw in 1867, and Kew-trained, English horticulturalist George Pring, who came to the garden in 1906.

The design of the garden has evolved, reflecting changing fashion and taste. A 1905 plan by the Olmsted brothers was partially implemented, creating a "synoptical collection" of trees indigenous to North America. Evoking the pastoral work of the Olmsted firm, it provided a lesson in botanical classification. This wooded area was transformed in 1977 into a 14-acre (5.6-ha) Japanese "garden of pure, clear harmony and peace," *Seiwa-En*. Designed by Professor Koichi Kawana of the University of California, Los Angeles, it makes reference to Japanese philosophy, symbolizing heaven, man, and earth, in both plan and plant choice. During 1912–14 major changes were implemented to accommodate new conservatories. The previous arrangement, with numerous small beds and intricate walks, was replaced with a rolling landscape that was English in character, and planted with shrubs, flowers, and long stretches of lawn. Landscape architect John Noyes emphasized the axes from Tower Grove house into the gardens, reorienting the plan and adding cohesiveness to the whole. An Italian garden that served as context for the main conservatory also dates to this period. In 1960 the main staircase of this conservatory was incorporated into the newest building on the site, the Climatron, a 70-foot (21-m) tall geodesic dome based on futuristic prototypes by Buckminster Fuller. Constructed of aluminum and hexagonal, plexiglass panels (now replaced with reflective glass), this tropical greenhouse provides diverse variations of temperature and moisture via a climate-control system. Built during the directorship of Frits Went, it continues to represent the garden's commitment to public education through botanical displays.

The scientific aim of the garden can be traced to Shaw's close consultation in the 1850s with William Jackson Hooker, director of the Royal Botanic Garden at Kew, who was the figure responsible for transforming Kew into a world-class institution. In formulating his garden, Shaw also worked closely with Harvard University botanist Asa Gray and St. Louis physician and botanist George Engelmann. The purchase of reference books and botanical specimens, in particular a major herbarium owned by J.J. Bernhardi of Erfurt, Germany, began in 1857 when Engelmann traveled to Europe for that specific purpose. Gray emphasized the importance of education, establishing the Henry Shaw School of Botany at Washington University, St. Louis, in 1885. Gray also recommended the first director to succeed Shaw, botanist William Trelease, who was committed to research and teaching in the spirit of the garden's founder.

The herbarium was increased by contributions from Bernhardi, Engelmann, Trelease, Nicholas Riehl, and others, growing from 160,000 specimens in 1889 to over 4 million in 1998. The collection of vascular plants and bryophytes includes North American species from the Mississippi River valley and the Southwest, as well as South American flora. The personal library of Henry Shaw provided the nucleus for today's reference library. Shaw's collection consisted of writings on aesthetics and landscape gardening including Uvedale Price's *Essay on the Picturesque*, Humphry Repton's collected works *Landscape Gardening and Landscape Architecture*, and J.C. Loudon's *Arboretum et Fruticetum Britannicum*. The library, housed in the new Monsanto Center, includes in its holdings the Sturtevant Pre-Linnaean Collection, consisting of 1,100 volumes dated 1474–1753, and the 900-volume Linnaean Collection. The rare book collection includes Michaux's and Nuttall's *North American Sylva* and a first edition of Charles Darwin's *On the Origin of Species*. Illustrations in the folio collection include Banks's *Florilegium* and Mark Catesby's *The Natural History of Carolina, Florida and the Bahama Islands*.

Since the 1920s, the garden has increasingly focused on the practical application of research addressing problems of air and water pollution, cancer, and sustainable agriculture. In 1925 land on the Meramec River in Gray Summit, Missouri, was purchased to serve as an arboretum and location for housing portions of the living plant collection, particularly orchids. Today the arboretum's 2,500 acres (1,012 ha) serve as a site for ecological research, habitat restoration, and an outdoor laboratory promoting public awareness of native plants. Garden projects include the 12-volume *Flora of Panama,* initiated in 1942 as a comprehensive account of the 9,000 native species of plants of the region. The garden is home to the National Center for the Study of African Plants, which owns the country's largest collection, more than 400,000 specimens. Taxonomic research and tropical ecology remain a focus.

An interest in tropical botany dates to the garden's inception, and field research continues in the tropical environments of Peru, Panama, and Madagascar. The garden is an important center for scientists from around the world, particularly from Central and South America and Africa. Dr. Peter Raven, director since 1971, continues to successfully balance the priorities outlined by Shaw in 1859. An emphasis on research, display, and the education of professionals and the public remains the primary concern of the Missouri Botanical Garden.

Synopsis

1851–55	Henry Shaw formulates plans for a botanical garden at his country estate, Tower Grove
1856	Shaw draws up original plan of gardens
1859	Garden opened, known as Shaw's Garden
1860	Museum and library built
1867	Tower Grove Park established adjacent to Shaw's Garden, as a complement to it
1870	Palm House erected
1872	Tower Grove Park opened to public
1877	Joseph Hooker, director of Royal Botanic Gardens, Kew, visits garden and park
1882	Linnaean conservatory opened
1889	Henry Shaw dies
1896–1905	Consultation for new garden plan with Olmsted firm, Brookline, Massachusetts
1912–14	Major changes in design and plantings: new conservatory and plant houses built, reorientation of garden axis, formal parterres replaced by rolling landscape and natural garden
1925	Shaw Arboretum at Gray Summit, Missouri, established
1960	Climatron opened
1971	Garden designated National Historic Landmark
1977	Japanese Garden opened
1982	Completion of the Flora of Panama project
1984	Opening of Ridgway Center: educational facility and visitor's center that makes reference architecturally to Joseph Paxton's building for Great Exhibition, London (1851)
1998	Monsanto Center opened: example of "green architecture" in its sustainable design, recycled materials, and conservation of resources

Further Reading

Bry, Charlene, Marshall R. Crosby, and Peter H. Loewer, *A World of Plants: The Missouri Botanical Garden,* New York: Abrams, 1989

Dimmock, Thomas, "Henry Shaw, a Biographical Sketch," *Report of the Missouri Botanical Garden* 1 (1889)

Faherty, William Barnaby, *Henry Shaw: His Life and Legacies,* Columbia: University of Missouri Press, 1987

Faherty, William Barnaby, *A Gift to Glory In: The First Hundred Years of the Missouri Botanical Garden (1859–1959),* Ocean Park, Washington: Harris and Friedrich, 1989

Gray, Asa, and William Trelease, editors, *The Botanical Works of the Late George Engelmann, Collected for Henry Shaw, Esq.,* Cambridge, Massachussetts, 1887

Grove, Carol, "Aesthetics, Horticulture, and the Gardenesque: Victorian Sensibilities at Tower Grove Park," *Journal of the New England Garden History Society* 6 (Fall 1998)

"Henry Shaw's Idea of a Botanical Garden," *Missouri Botanical Garden Bulletin* 31, no. 7 (September 1943)

Kramer, Gerhardt, "Henry Shaw's Architectural Legacy to the Missouri Botanical Garden," *Gateway Heritage* 5, no. 1 (1984)

MacAdam, David H., *Tower Grove Park of the City of St. Louis,* St. Louis, Missouri, 1883

"Missouri Botanical Garden, 125th Anniversary Issue," *Gateway Heritage* 5, no. 1 (Summer 1984)

Raven, Peter, "Systematics vs. Aesthetics vs. Use," *American Association of Botanical Gardens and Arboreta Bulletin* (October 1978)

Rudolph, Emanuel D., "One Hundred Years of the Missouri Botanical Garden," *Annals of the Missouri Botanical Garden* 78, no. 1 (1991)

Stein, Bruce A., editor, *The Unseen Garden: Research at the Missouri Botanical Garden*, St. Louis, Missouri: Botanical Garden, 1987

CAROL GROVE

Modernism

Modernism in landscape architecture, unlike that in painting, sculpture, and architecture, has not been well covered in the existing literature. Architectural modernism is often narrowly defined by external characteristics prevailing during the period between 1918 and 1933, the era of the Bauhaus and the major proposals of the architect Le Corbusier. This was the era of white buildings, flat roofs, big windows, and cantilevering. While historians nowadays are slightly more relaxed about such a restrictive definition, they have generally searched for the roots of modernism—the sources of modern architecture—in the last quarter of the 18th century, following the rise of industrialization. Others take modernism as starting from the beginning of modern science and technology in the 17th century. According to Kenneth Frampton, *Modern Architecture: Critical History A* (1985), such accounts examine the relationship between "cultural, territorial and technical transformations from which modern architecture emerged."

Twentieth-century modernist landscape architects have generally rejected stylistic references to baroque gardens (because of the symbolism of a centralized power) and to the landscape school (because of the associations with the Whig supremacy). At the same time they have reacted against the English Arts-and-Crafts-style gardens—which some years earlier had been welcomed as an alternative to the baroque and landscape styles—as inappropriate (i.e., not suiting local characteristics), common, and backward looking. Stylistic references therefore were seen as an important tool to express alternative ideologies. By the end of the 19th century the rise of socialism, the growing industrialization of the Western world, with an increased population, and concern about the environment all contributed to demands for an alternative approach that addressed these issues.

One of the first responses was the search for more natural gardens at the end of the 19th century, but it was not until the first decade of the 20th century that scientific principles were applied to achieve "nature gardens." Another trend was the search for inspiration in Continental farmhouse gardens, which were thought to have developed over the centuries following functional requirements. (In Germany both nature gardens and the farmhouse garden afterward became intertwined with the national socialism of the Nazi era.) Undesigned landscapes, such as the English commons, which served as public open space, were similarly highly regarded as a source of inspiration. These followed functional requirements and were simple and informal. This functionalism reacted against allusions to grandeur or size and against "lack of clarity." It ought to be apparent, the functionalists argued, how a design arose, how it was contrived, and how it worked. These criteria were translated as "legibility" until the 1960s, when this word was vulgarized by Kevin Lynch and others.

With healthy living as a prime objective, "fitness for purpose," one of the main slogans of modernist architecture, could equally well be applied to landscape design. There was an emphasis on providing space for sun bathing, sports (such as swimming and tennis), and seating. These utilitarian and functional requirements often determined the layout. Landscape designers were to perform a subservient part in this process; their hand should not be detectable, as if the project might have been realized without their participation. In the early 20th century the German landscape architect Leberecht Migge suggested that beautiful gardens did not have to be created but that "they would grow to be beautiful." Migge was one of the main exponents of the German self-sufficiency movement in the era of the Weimar Republic (after World War I). This movement made extensive use of technology to improve recycling and simplify maintenance. Additionally, a whole range of new materials was being used in gardens, including concrete, steel, aluminium, and glass, in, for example, concrete paving, steel arbors, aluminium play equipment, and glass screens.

Examples of "less-designed" approaches might be distinguished in the Scandinavian countries, Germany, Austria, Switzerland, and the Netherlands. These generally set out to respect existing vegetation and features and to work with the natural irregularities and topography of the site. In Sweden and Finland modern landscape was dominated by architects, with excellent examples emerging from the Stockholm Parks Department, headed by Holger Blom. The Finn Alvar Aalto deserves a special position in achieving what has often been referred to as a symbiotic relationship between his buildings and the surrounding landscape. This symbiosis is also visible in the work of Swedes Gunnar Asplund and Sigurd Lewerentz, whose Stockholm Woodland Cemetery has become one of the 20th century's design icons. In Denmark the architect Jørn Utzon provided some remarkable housing schemes in Helsingør (1956) and Fredensborg (1962–63) in a country with an otherwise well-developed landscape profession. G.N. Brandt, Georg Boye, and Georg Georgsen were some of those landscape architects who provided both interesting public landscapes and private gardens. In Germany the division of those who worked with the Nazi ideology and with modern principles was a delicate one. The group of landscape architects who best represented modernism included several who had in some way been associated with the Karl Foerster nursery: Hermann Mattern, Herta Hammerbacher, Adolf Haag, Gustav Lüttge, and Otto Valentien. In the Netherlands some of the largest projects associated with the creation of new polders were carried out with the advice of J.T.P. Bijhouwer, while Mien Ruys concentrated on social housing, and Hans Warnau and Wim Boer were active in the postwar era. In this context the green planning of Amsterdam by the president of the International Congress of Modern Architecture (CIAM) Cor van Eesteren deserves a special mention, because he moved away from Beaux Arts aesthetics and developed the city on rational principles in an organic way. While landscape architecture has had little impact as a profession in southern Europe, the work of Pietro Porcinai in Italy and of the architect Dimitri Pikionis around the Acropolis in Athens is particularly worth noting.

The popular face of the "modernist" landscape, however, has largely been determined by design virtuosity: the cubist gardens in France; organically shaped gardens by Roberto Burle Marx in Brazil; the colorful architectural gardens of Luis Barragan in Mexico; the geometry of C.Th. Sørensen in Denmark; the free-form gardens by the native Californian Thomas Church, which were representative of "Western living" in the United States. These examples have captured the attention of the press, which therefore sees late-20th-century "design" trends as a natural extension of them. In fact, these purely visual approaches have rather distorted the ideology of the modern movement.

Further Reading

Bramwell, Anna, *Ecology in the 20th Century,* New Haven, Connecticut: Yale University Press, 1986

Brown, Jane, *The English Garden in Our Time,* Woodbridge, Suffolk: Antique Collectors' Club, 1986

Burckhardt, Lucius, editor, *The Werkbund: History and Ideology, 1907–1933,* Woodbury, New York: Barron's, 1980; as *The Werkbund: Studies in the History and Ideology of the Deutscher Werkbund, 1907–1933,* London: The Design Council, 1980

Enis, Ruth, "On the Pioneering Work of Landscape Architects in Israel: A Historical Review," *Landscape Journal* 11, no. 1 (1992)

Giedion, Sigfried, *Space, Time, and Architecture,* Cambridge, Massachusetts: Harvard University Press, and London: Oxford University Press, 1941; 5th edition, revised and enlarged, Cambridge, Massachusetts: Harvard University Press, 1967

Groening, Gert, and Joachim Wolschke-Bulmahn, "Changes in the Philosophy of Garden Architecture in the 20th Century and Their Impact upon Social and Spatial Environment," *Journal of Garden History* 9, no. 2 (1989)

Hauxner, Malene, *Fantasiens have,* Copenhagen: Arkitektens Forlag, 1993

Imbert, Dorothée, *The Modernist Garden in France,* New Haven, Connecticut: Yale University Press, 1993

Mader, Günter, *Gardenkunst des 20. Jahrhunderts: Garten- und Landschaftsarchitektur in Deutschland,* Stuttgart: Deutsche Verlags- Anstalt, 1999

Mosser, Monique, and Georges Teyssot, editors, *The History of Garden Design,* London: Thames and Hudson, 1991

Treib, Marc, editor, *Modern Landscape Architecture,* Cambridge, Massachusetts: MIT Press, 1993

Tunnard, Christopher, *Gardens in the Modern Landscape,* London: Architectural Press, 1938; 2nd revised edition, London: Architectural Press, and New York: Scribner, 1950

Vroom, Meto J., editor, *Buitenruimten: Ontwerpen van Nederlandse tuin- en landschaps-architecten in de periode na 1945; Outdoor Space: Environments Designed by Dutch Landscape Architects in the Period since 1945* (bilingual Dutch-English edition), Amsterdam: Thoth, 1992; 2nd edition, 1995

Warnau, Hans, "Landschapsarchitectuur en de Moderne Stroming in de Bouwkunde," in *Nederlandse landschapsarchitectuur: Tussen traditie en experiment,* edited by Gerrit Smienk, Amsterdam: Thoth, 1993

Woudstra, Jan, "Danish Landscape Design in the Modern Era (1920–1970)," *Garden History* 23, no. 2 (1995)

Woudstra, Jan, and Peter Blundell Jones, "Some Modernist Houses and Their Gardens," *Die Gardenkunst* 11, no. 1 (1999)

Wrede, Stuart, and William Howard Adams, editors, *Denatured Visions: Landscape and Culture in the Twentieth Century,* New York: Museum of Modern Art, 1991

JAN WOUDSTRA

Moen, Olav Leif 1887–1951

Norwegian Landscape Architect

Olav L. Moen was the most prominent figure in Norwegian landscape architecture during the first half of the 20th century. Most importantly, he was the first professor of landscape architecture in the Department of Garden Art, established at the Agricultural University of Norway in 1919 as the first academic program in this field in Europe. He held the position for more than 30 years, until his death in 1951.

Moen's work as a teacher during the infancy of landscape architecture is by far his most important contribution. He was involved in so many professional affairs that he is considered the father of Norwegian landscape architecture. He established the profession as one acknowledged at the agricultural university, and by society in general. He was also an active practitioner and the author of some of the most significant design projects of his time. He designed villa gardens, city parks, cemeteries, and residential areas. He won a number of prizes in competitions on urban gardens and developments in Norway as well as Germany. In addition he was a prominent critic and writer. He published articles on garden architecture and landscape gardening in newspapers, magazines, and books in Norway.

Moen was born in Trondheim in 1887 and received his training as a gardener at Hylla Gardening College in Nord-Trøndelag before he started as an apprentice at the Department of Horticulture at the Agricultural University of Norway in 1908. During 1909–16 he worked at landscape gardening and garden architecture offices in Norway, Denmark, Germany, and Switzerland. During 1916–18 he earned a degree in horticulture at the Agricultural University of Norway. In 1920 he got a grant to qualify for a professorship related to the new study program of garden architecture. He was appointed as docent in 1921. In 1939 he was promoted to professor of garden architecture.

Throughout his career Moen's designs were influenced by the neoclassical style, although in his writing he turned more functionalist after 1930. In some of his early articles he mentions Renaissance and baroque gardens as inspirations for the new garden. Later he took a different position. In *Gartnernæringen i Norge* (1935; The Gardening Professions in Norway), he wrote: "The garden has become simpler, its compartments easier, and its form extremely objective. Even the natural parts of our gardens are designed more rationally and genuinely, than was the case during the whole 19th century landscape gardens." In his articles he mainly refers to Norwegian and Scandinavian examples, but his unpublished lectures show that he was also inspired by people such as Reginald Blomfield and Thomas Mawson of England and Leberecht Migge of Germany. He argued against both the traditional gardenesque style and the new ideas about the natural garden, promoted above all by the German landscape architect Willy Lange, whom he had met during his studies at Berlin-Dahlem.

Moen's principal work is the park at the agricultural university, begun in 1924. This project contains many of Moen's most important motifs: clearly defined spaces designed for activities, connections with axes and vistas, and proportions strongly related to the architecture of the buildings. The park is reasonably well maintained and is today one of the best examples of this style in the Nordic countries. The project may have been inspired

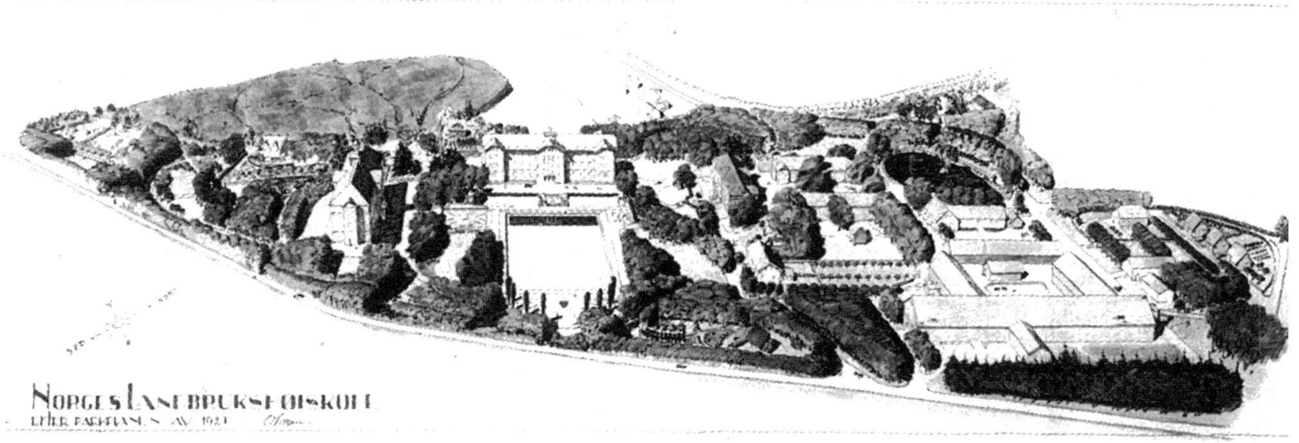

Perspective of the Norwegian Agricultural University Park by Olav L. Moen, 1930
Courtesy of Lars Olav Moen

by the Stadtpark Hamburg (1909) by Fritz Schumacher, which he visited during his studies in Berlin-Dahlem in 1920–21. This park features some of the same elements: a modern, functional *volkspark* for people to use combined with a rather strict formalist design. The focal point in the agricultural university park is a 100 by 50 meter (109 by 55 yd.) sunken green lawn surrounded by groups of trees and the main buildings of the university. Another interesting feature of the park is its seamless connections between the neoclassical style element from 1924 and the old landscape-style sections designed and built during 1860–1900.

In 1938 Moen received first prize in all three sections of a competition on farmhouse gardens (small, medium, and big farms) and in 1941 he received both first and second prize (together with O. Reisaeter) in a competition for urban development of a part of Namsos destroyed in the bombings of 1940. Other significant designs are Norsk Hydro in Notodden from 1930 and central people's parks in Drøbak (1931), Mysen (1938), Horten (1945), and Harstad (1947). In all these projects he shows variations of formal design in an informal setting.

Moen engaged in public debate on both professional and social issues. In the 1930s he was involved in the discussion about the Vigelandsparken in Oslo. The famous Norwegian sculptor Gustav Vigeland was granted a huge area at Frogner near central Oslo for displaying his art. Vigeland presented a plan for the design of the landscape without consulting any landscape architects, and the result, which was accepted by the city council without discussion, caused outrage. Moen was one of the sharpest critics and was quoted in all the main newspapers: "No other European city would even consider building anything as bad as this," he said. In his view, the plan was based on "an extensive use of avenues with no starting or ending points, cutting the whole area in pieces of useless sizes and shapes. The potentials in the existing landscape are totally neglected, and the use of vegetation give no value in bounding the area against the city outside." The critical comments only resulted in slight modifications of Vigeland's project, and its formal and functional deficiencies are obvious today. Nevertheless it is still one of the main tourist attractions in Oslo.

Biography

Born in Trondheim, Sør-Trøndelag, Norway, 14 January 1887. Raised under relatively poor conditions (mother died from tuberculosis when he was six); studied gardening at Hylla Gardening College, Nord-Trøndelag, Norway, 1905, and at Møre College, Ørsta, 1906; worked as apprentice in Department of Horticulture, Agricultural University, Ås, Norway; county gardener in Trøgstad and Askim, Norway, 1909–12; worked as landscape gardener and garden architect in Denmark, Germany, and Switzerland, 1912–16 (e.g., at Atelier für Gartenkunst and for landscape gardener Herman Burkhart, both in Zurich, Switzerland); studied horticulture at Agricultural University of Norway, Ås, 1916–18; lectured at state Gardeners College, Oslo, 1918–20; study grant from agricultural university to qualify for professorship in garden architecture at new Department of Garden Architecture, 1920; won competition in Berlin on design of colony garden area (communal garden plots), 1921; returned from six-month study tour in England, 1921; was first director of Norwegian Association of Garden Architects when it was formed in 1929; won all three sections of national competition in Norway on design of farmstead gardens, 1937; promoted to professor of garden architecture, 1939; imprisoned 1942–43 by German occupation authorities. Died in Ås, Norway, 1951.

Selected Designs

1919 Garden, Halvorsen estate, Smestad, Norway
1919 Garden, Nor estate, Kongsvinger, Norway
1920 The Finnish Legation, Oslo, Norway
1924– The Agricultural University, Ås, Norway
1926 Restoration plan, Borregaard estate, Sarpsborg, Østfold, Norway
1930 Norsk Hydro, Notodden, Telemark, Norway
1931 Bathing park (people's park), Drøbak, Akershus, Norway
1931 National Radium Hospital, Oslo, Norway
1938 People's Park, Mysen, Norway
1945 People's Park, Horten, Vestfold, Norway
1947 People's Park, Harstad, Norway

Selected Publications

"Lidt om blomsternes anvendelse i de forskjellige havestiler," *Norsk Gartnerforenings Tidsskrift* (1920)
"Har vi noget at lære av gammel norsk havekunst?" *Norsk Gartnerforenings Tidsskrift* (1922)
"Tidsmessige kirkegaarde," *Norsk Gartnerforenings Tidsskrift* (1922)
"Våre kirkegårder og deres beplantning," *Norsk Gartnerforenings Tidsskrift* (1926)
"Moderne Kirkegårdskunst," *St. Halvard* (1929)
"Hagekunst," "Offentlige grønnanlegg," "Gravplasser og kirkegårder," chapters in *Gartnernaeringen i Norge Nationaltrykkeriet Oslo,* 1935
"Aktuelle spørsmål i hagekunsten," *Norsk Hagetidend* (1938)
"Havekunstens historie i Norge," in *Nordisk illustreret Havebrugsleksikon,* 1945–48

Further Reading

Blichner, Bente, "Olav L. Moen: Landskapsarkitekt i spenningen mellom nyklassisisme og

funksjonalisme," master's thesis, Agricultural University of Norway, 1989
Jørgensen, Karsten, "Olav L. Moen og nyklassisismen i norsk landskapsarkitektur," *Byggekunst* 3 (1988)
Jørgensen, Karsten, "Equality and the Modern Way of Death," *Topos: European Landscape Magazine* 2 (1993)

KARSTEN JØRGENSEN

Mogul Gardens

The history of Indian gardens and gardening is deep rooted in its cultural and geographical conditions. India is a very fertile land with rivers running through it. There are six distinct seasons, and each season has its own species of fruits and flowers.

Gardening traditions in India started very early; there are many references to flowers and fruit groves in ancient scriptures such as old Buddhist texts and Sanskrit plays written in Vedic times (1500–500 B.C.). The sacred groves around the Buddhist shrines were among the earliest forms of gardening. But what remained over the ages and what was recorded by chroniclers were gardens built by the Muslim rulers in India, who started settling in India by A.D. 1100. Until the mid-14th century, kings and emperors rose and fell with astonishing rapidity, which left little peace and time for leisure that the craft of gardening demands. The comparatively long reign of Feroz Shah (r. 1351–88), however, proved more peaceful than that of his predecessors. During his reign one hundred gardens were built around his capital of Ferozabad (now Delhi).

The conducive geographical conditions and vast natural abundance were fully tapped and formed by the Moguls, who came to India in 1526. The Mogul dynasty, a Muslim dynasty that lasted for six generations, was a line of Muslim emperors who reigned in India for more than 200 years, from 1526 to 1858. The first of the Mogul emperors, Babur, found tremendous delight in the lush greenness of India since as a descendant of Timur and Genghis Khan, he had come from the dry and tough terrain of west Asia.

Babur's artistic traditions and religious ideals left a distinct impact on the gardening styles that followed in India under him and his descendants. Babur had come equipped with the knowledge of irrigated gardens, which were already a fashion and were well developed in Persia and Turkestan. The first garden laid out by Babur, Rambagh in Agra, was the earliest prototype of what has come to be known as the Mogul garden. Sprawling along the banks of the river Yamuna, it was Babur's attempt to re-create gardens from Farghana (his native country in west Asia) in Agra. The garden has all the important elements of a Persian garden—terraces of varying heights, water courses, and pavilions. Babur laid out and improved many of the gardens around Kabul, some of which are described at great length in his memoirs.

Babur's purpose for creating gardens lay in his artistic pursuit and also a desire to build a home away from home in India. Rulers who preceded Babur had a different impetus in the creation of gardens. The Lodhis (1451–1526), who directly preceded the Moguls, built gardens around the tombs of the dead. It seems, like the Moguls, that they also believed in the concept of the paradise garden. This concept of garden craft was inspired by the Koran. In the Koran it is written that God first planted a garden. The garden had eight parts (*chahar-bagh* concept), terraces with running streams of water, and shade-giving trees. The Lodhi Garden, which still exists in Delhi, is a vast landscape of trees and flowering vines and shrubs that encloses five tombs and one mosque. Thus, it seems that these rulers believed that they were burying the dead in paradise.

The idea of paradise as a garden is one of humankind's oldest ideals. Since the beginning of history, most probably in prehistory, societies with nothing else in common shared the concept of paradise as the ideal garden, secure and everlasting. Almost universal in human experience, this concept of paradise, in which humankind transcends its frail human condition, has persisted while many of the civilizations that adhered to it have disappeared. The image of a place of perfect and eternal peace and plenty can make a difficult temporal existence meaningful and its transitory nature acceptable. The English word *paradise* is a transliteration of the Old Persian word *pairidaeza,* referring to a walled garden, which is a simple combination of *pairi* (around) and *daeza* (wall). From the Greek *paradeisoi,* it became the Latin *paradisus* and first appeared in Middle English as *paradis* in 1175 in a biblical passage: "God ha hine brohte into paradis."

The first Mogul garden before the creation of the Taj Mahal of a tomb set in a paradise garden was that of Humayun's tomb. Humayun was Babur's son and second emperor of the Mogul dynasty. His tomb is enclosed in a paradise garden, now situated in Delhi, still beautiful even in its present state.

Lodhis were much behind their Mogul counterparts, who developed their architecture in close relation with perfectly planned and landscaped gardens. These gardens provided perfect complements for palaces, mosques, tombs, and retreats. The Mogul gardens, copied from the earlier gardens of Turkestan and Persia, are invariably square or rectangular in shape and are divided into a series of smaller square parterres. Nowhere in the world, perhaps, is spring more wonderful than in the high tableland of Persia and the mountainous countries lying east and west of it. The contrasts of climate in this area are great—summer's heat and winter's cold alternately strip the country bare of color—but the brief spring, into which is crowded the entire flowering season of the year, provides a wealth of bloom. This concentration of growth and beauty into a brief period deeply affected the imagination of the people, and all their arts reflect the national love of flowers.

The other great influence, that of religion, is explained by the restrictions of the Koran, which forbade the delineation of human beings or animals, so that the artists of the faithful were confined to floral or geometrical designs. The Shia sect of Aryan Persia never held very closely to this restriction and painted humans and animals freely; but flowers, fruits, and foliage remained the chief motifs on the tiles and carpets for which they are so famous, lending to their work a greater beauty and interest than appears in that of their stricter Sunni brethren of Baghdad, Cairo, and Damascus, for whom geometrical designs were most in favor.

The spirit of the paradise gardens of Europe hides in the flowers, the grass, the trees, but the soul of an Eastern garden is centered in the running water, which makes its other beauties possible. The Eastern paradise gardens were beautifully crafted in and around natural water bodies or artificial water tanks. The need for irrigation dictated the whole plan and arrangement of these gardens. The water would run in a stone- or brick-edged canal down the whole length of the enclosure, falling from level to level in smooth cascades, or rushing in a tumult of white foam over carved water chutes (*chaddars*). Below these waterfalls the canal would flow into a smaller tank called the *hauz*.

The creation of this cool and airy system was a necessity in this semi-arid climate. Shade-giving trees were planted around the square or rectangular outer enclosing walls in a symmetrical pattern. The area inside the enclosure was divided into a smaller square pattern, which would be planted with shade-giving fruit trees, such as mangoes, orange, blackberries, and pomegranates.

The principal pavilion was placed in the middle of the largest of the water sheets, forming a cool and airy retreat in the scorching heat. Serrated battlements and imposing gateways adorned the outer walls. Small octagonal buildings marked the angles of outer walls, usually matching the architectural style adopted in the Moguls' palaces and tombs.

Notable among Babur's descendants in the art of developing gardens was Shah Jahan, who was fifth in the line of the Mogul dynasty. Shah Jahan was an artistic ruler who carried out town planning with great style. It was Shah Jahan who gave the world one the largest architectural marvels of modern times, the Taj Mahal. All his buildings and palaces were enclosed by these paradise gardens. But he gave the garden craft its individuality by choosing Kashmir as the spot for laying three beautiful gardens, the Chashma Shahi, Shalimar, and Nishat *baghs* (gardens).

In the Shalimar *bagh* and Nishat *bagh,* Shah Jahan gave the natural mountain terrain an artistic form by creating waterways and ground terraces. Kashmir, with Dal Lake, snow-capped mountains, and its weather, created a perfect atmosphere for a paradise garden, of which Shah Jahan made full use. These large *baghs* included flower gardens confined around the principal canals and squares that bordered on them. The sides of the *baghs* had trees planted in the middle. These trees were surrounded by a raised platform of masonry or grass for the feasts and gatherings that the Moguls loved.

The park areas were specifically designed to accommodate the Mogul court and Mogul royal entourages, which would move from place to place in order to administer the vast Mogul Empire. These shady retreats were carefully planned and maintained for the visiting emperor. Where there was no garden kept in readiness for the coming emperor, a naturally beautiful site would be chosen near a water body and tents carefully pitched with great regard for form, about which the Moguls were very particular. These sites would often develop into future garden retreats.

The Moguls also considered gardening to be a pious act. Planting trees and providing shade for the travelers against the heat became a sacred gesture. The orchards provided fruit for the hungry people. Thus, the Moguls practiced garden craft not just as an artistic pursuit but also for beneficial purposes.

Each of the great Mogul emperors contributed his particular aesthetic interests and endeavors to the establishment of what has subsequently been called the Mogul style, a style that blended the Persian patterns brought by the Moguls with the indigenous genius for fine craftsmanship. The amazing achievements in the Mogul architectural tradition owe much to the great talent of Indian artisans and the wealth of material found in India, including the abundance of stone. Each emperor used local materials and indigenous forms and craftsmanship to nurture and bring out a unique and enduringly beautiful architectural tradition.

The Mogul Empire reformed government, encouraged artistry, and tried to unite its subjects. Each ruler improved the craft of gardening, some inspired by their religious beliefs, some by their artistic beliefs, and some by their economic and practical beliefs. Each ruler contributed in his own way to the development of this craft and its preservation over the ages, and each gave his creation a new design and purpose. The last Mogul emperors allowed the empire to break apart, however. As a result, the Mogul Empire came to an end and India came under British control.

See also Agra Fort; Babur; Chashma Shahi; Nishat Bagh; Red Fort; Taj Mahal

Mogul Dynasty

Babur (the founder of the Mogul empire; Reign of Babur 1526–1530)
Humayun (succeeded the throne in 1530)
Akbar (Reign of Akbar 1556–1605)
Jahangir (Reign of Jahangir 1605–1627)
Shah Jahan (Reign of Shah Jahan 1628–1658)
Aurangzeb (Reign of Aurangzeb 1658–1707; the last of the great Moguls)

Further Reading

Crowe, Sylvia, et al., *The Gardens of Mughul India*, London: Thames and Hudson, 1972
Gascoigne, Bamber, *The Great Moghuls*, New York: Harper and Row, and London: Cape, 1971
Hambly, Gavin, *Cities of Mughul India*, New York: Putnam, and London: Paul Elek, 1968
Hussain, Mahmood, Abdul Rehman, and James L. Wescoat, Jr., editors, *The Mughal Garden: Interpretation, Conservation, and Implications*, Rawalpindi, Pakistan: Ferozsons, 1996
Jairazbhoy, R.A., "Early Garden-Palaces of the Great Mughals," *Oriental Art* 4 (summer 1958)
Mathur, N., *Red Fort and Mughal Life*, New Delhi: National Museum, 1964
Moynihan, Elizabeth, *Paradise As a Garden: In Persia and Mughal India*, New York: Braziller, 1979; London: Scolar Press, 1980
Nath, R., *History of Mughal Architecture*, 3 vols., New Delhi: Abhinav, 1982–94
Prawdin, Michael, *The Builders of the Mogul Empire*, London: Allen and Unwin, 1963
Smith, Vincent Arthur, *Akbar the Great Mogul*, Oxford: Clarendon Press, 1917; 2nd edition, 1919
Villiers-Stuart, C.M., *Gardens of the Great Mughals*, London: Black, 1913; reprint, New Delhi: Cosmo, 1979
Wescoat, James L., Jr., and Joachim Wolschke-Bulmahn, editors, *Mughal Gardens: Sources, Places, Representations, and Prospects*, Washington, D.C.: Dumbarton Oaks Research Library and Collection, 1996

JANA DAS

Mollet Family

French Family of Garden Designers and Writers

While the lives of the Mollet family members remain relatively obscure, their combined work, dating from the late 16th century, had considerable impact on garden history. Some 11 members were actively engaged in creating gardens for the French, English, Dutch, and Swedish royal courts and nobility. The two most important members of the Mollet dynasty were Claude I and his son André. Both are known not only for their practical work, but also as authors of influential treatises on garden architecture. Their books, *Théâtre des plans et iardinages* (1652; Theater of Plants and Gardens) and *Le jardin de plaisir* (1651; *The Garden of Pleasure*) together with Jacques Boyceau de la Barauderie's *Traité du jardinage* (1638; Treatise on Gardening), are the dominant French garden treatises of the 17th century.

Although Claude's *Théâtre des plans et iardinages* was published posthumously in 1652, in order of genesis it is the earliest of these three books, written about 1615. It reveals him as a man of profound practical knowledge who is perfectly aware of his role as an innovator, as the mentioning of "des Secrets et des Inventions" in the subtitle of his book shows. It gives accurate, detailed information on the practice of garden architecture, the author's own work, and his role in the development of garden architecture during the reigns of Henri IV and Louis XIII.

Chapter 33 gives a short history of the development of parterre design from the late 16th century; the author describes himself as indebted to the architect and gardener Etienne Du Pérac, who after his return from Italy in 1582 taught young Claude "comme il falloit faire de beaux Iardins" (how to make beautiful gardens). He followed Du Pérac's instructions for parterre design, and so the *parterre de broderie* was born: "Ce sont les premiers Parterres & Compartimens de Broderie qui ayent esté faits en France" (These are the first *parterres* and *compartiments de broderie* in France). Claude was also the first French gardener to cultivate box for extended use in parterres. His parterre layouts for the gardens of Saint-Germain-en-Laye, Fontainebleau, and the Tuileries are shown on plates in Olivier de Serres's *Le Théâtre d'Agriculture et Mesnage des Champs* (1600; Theater of Agriculture and Land Management). Claude's own treatise is complemented by 22 plates that were engraved and signed by him and his sons André, Jacques, and Noël. They date from the same period as the text, about 1615, and show above all parterres and among them designs "de nouvelle invention de broderie" (new inventions of *broderie*).

This collaboration between father and his sons shows an important characteristic of French garden architecture in the 17th and early 18th centuries: practical knowledge and methods were transmitted within a few families of gardeners, functions and posts were handed down from one family member to another. Claude's treatise shows a strong pedagogic impetus and a benevolent regard toward his younger colleagues. Among his pupils were not only his sons, but also his collaborator Jean Le Nôtre's son André, who was to become the most illustrious creator of *jardins à la française*. Several generations later, Armand-Claude Mollet seems to have worked in Le Nôtre's entourage.

André Mollet must have had his father's manuscript at hand when in autumn 1650 he prepared his *Jardin de Plaisir*, which was published six months later. Moved by veneration for his father, he introduces Claude's portrait instead of his own in the frontispiece. André's professional knowledge is based on his father's, but his treatise sums up his own experience as a garden architect in several European countries: France, Netherlands, England, and Sweden. It talks explicitly and systematically about pleasure gardens. With a variety of motifs that surpasses Boyceau, André's plates illustrate his text, proceeding from general garden layouts to single garden elements such as types of parterres, bosquets, and labyrinths. His book, like Boyceau's, is written for gardeners who don't see themselves as craftsmen, but as artists making their contribution to the development of the arts.

The obvious social rise of garden architects in the course of the 17th century is certainly promoted by books like *Jardin de plaisir*. It is also the first European book on pleasure gardens that from the beginning could be read in several modern languages. The first edition appeared in French, German, and Swedish, and an English edition, prepared by the author before his death in 1665, followed. This is certainly due to André's international activities: while his father and Boyceau's nephew Jacques de Menours had leading roles in the royal gardens in France, in 1629–30 André was called to the royal court of England by Charles I and his wife Henrietta Maria, a sister of Louis XIII of France. When Le Nôtre's rise began in France, André Mollet agreed to serve at the Swedish court in the autumn of 1646 and arrived there in 1648. He worked for the Swedish nobility and above all for the ambitious Queen Christina, who made great efforts to form her court on the French model. Thus a renewal of garden art began in Sweden, a development which was to be continued by André's son Jean after 1653. It is important to consider that the diffusion of the *jardin à la française* in Europe started as early as with André Mollet, not only with André Le Nôtre.

See also Fontainebleau; Tuileries

Family Biographies

From late 16th century, several generations of Mollet family made important contributions to development of garden history, but little is known of their personal biographies: Jacques I (worked in royal gardens; leading gardener in Anet in service of the duc d'Aumale, from 1582); his son Claude I (born ca. 1564; appointed leading gardener of Tuileries in 1630; one of most important members of family for activity in royal gardens, and as teacher of his sons and André Le Nôtre; died not long before or in 1649); Claude I's sons Pierre (worked in Tuileries until 1671, and in Louvre garden), Claude II (born ca. 1600; gets financial support for education as gardener in 1618; one of nearest collaborators of his father, worked with him in Tuileries; worked in Versailles in 1630s; called himself *Jardinier ordinaire et dessinateur des plan(t)s, parcs et jardins des maisons royales* in 1632; died not later than 1664), André (born ca. 1600; worked in London for King Charles I and Queen Henrietta Maria, ca. 1629–30; in Netherlands for Frederik Hendrik, Prince of Orange 1633–ca. 1635; England in 1641–42; Sweden in 1648, where as leading garden architect of Queen Christina he obtained title of *Maistre des Jardins de la Sérénissime Reine de Suède*; left country in 1653, handing down responsibility for royal gardens to son Jean; whereabouts unknown in next years, but in late 1650s lived in England where he seems to have set up commerce of plants and flowers together with nephew Charles in Paris; employed by English King Charles II to keep St. James's Park, London in 1661; died 1665 in London), Jacques II (worked in gardens of Fontainebleau from 1612, where he died before 1622), and Noël (known only for collaboration on Claude I's treatise); Claude's II sons Charles (worked in royal gardens, mostly Louvre, until 1693; involved in uncle André's business, see above) and Gabriel (assisted uncle André in London in early 1660s, died before 1663); André's son Jean (trained in Tuileries garden by grandfather Claude, assisted father in Sweden, where he took over father's charge as royal gardener in 1653; worked for Swedish court and nobility until death); Charles's son Armand-Claude, architect and garden architect (born in 1660; took over father's charge in royal service in 1694, responsible for garden layout; academy member from 1699; appointed *Contrôleur général* in Versailles, 1704; ennobled in 1722; obtained title of *Architecte ordinaire de Sa Majesté* in 1735; died in 1742).

Selected Designs

Jacques I

from 1582	Anet
1608	Inventor of new parterres in Fontainebleau

Claude I

1595	Charged by Henri IV to plant new parterres in garden of Château Neuf/ Saint-Germain-en-Laye, following design by Etienne Du Pérac
mid 1590s	Jardin des Pins at Fontainebleau; new parterres in Tuileries; Montceaux-en-Brie

Claude II

1630s	Layout of parterres in Versailles
1639	alterations of these parterres
1656	designs for royal gardens, including new Louvre garden

André

1633–35	Layout of parterres in Buren and Honselaarsdijk, Netherlands; Wilton House
1641–42	Worked in Wimbledon House, England
1648–1653	Alterations in several royal gardens; parterres in king's garden and in front of queen's palace, Stockholm

Jean

1660s	garden of Rosersberg, Sweden, for Gabriel Gabrielsson Oxenstierna

Armand-Claude

1699–	Several parterre designs in Paris (for example, Hôtel de Louvois, 1699)
1718	Hôtel d'Evreux (now the Palais de l'Elysée), Paris
after 1714	Château and garden of Stains near Paris

Selected Publications

Mollet, Claude, *Théâtre des plans et iardinages: contenant des secrets et des inventions*, 1652; as *Théâtre des jardinages*, 1663, 1670, 1678

Mollet, André, *Le jardin de plaisir,* 1651; as *The Garden of Pleasure*, 1670

Further Reading

Conan, Michel, ["Postface"], in *Le jardin de plaisir* (1651), by André Mollet, Paris: Éditions du Moniteur, 1981

Guiffrey, Jules, "Traités du XVIIe siècle sur le dessin des jardins et la culture des arbres et des plants," *Archives de l'art français* 7 (1913)

Hopper, Florence, "The Dutch Classical Garden and André Mollet," *Journal of Garden History* 2, no. 1 (1982)

Karling, Sten, *Trädgårdskonstens historia i Sverige intill le Nôtrestilens genombrott,* Stockholm: Bonnier, 1931

Karling, Sten, "André Mollet and His Family," in *The French Formal Garden,* edited by Elisabeth B. MacDougall and F. Hamilton Hazlehurst, Washington, D.C.: Dumbarton Oaks Trustees, 1974

Krause, Katharina, *Die maison de plaisance: Landhäuser in der Île-de-France (1660–1730),* Munich and Berlin: Deutscher Kunstverlag, 1996

Pattacini, Laurence, "André Mollet, Royal Gardener in St. James's Park, London," *Garden History* 26, no. 1 (1998)

Stavenow, Åke, *Tidskrift för Konstvetenskap* 8 (1923/24)

IRIS LAUTERBACH

Monastic Garden

From the beginning gardens have had a significant place in the monasteries of Christianity and Buddhism. The first Christian monks in the deserts of Egypt and Palestine practiced the biblical mandate that one must eat from the labor of one's own hands, a sentiment to be echoed a few centuries later by St. Benedict in his rule: "They are true monks who live by the labor of their hands, as did the Fathers and Apostles." Buddhism teaches that the Buddha is to be found in the garden. In fact, Anathapindika, the merchant, built in the garden of Prince Jeta a monastery for the reception of the Buddha and his disciples during the Buddha's lifetime. Another garden built as a place for the Buddha to mystically reside was the fifth-century monastery of Nalanda. The Chinese pilgrim Yuang Chwang (Huien Tsang) describes the garden as "varigated with ponds with great profusion of blue lotuses, while mango groves checkered the landscape with their grateful shade."

One of the very first Christian monks, St. Antony (270–356), wrote about gardening in his journal: "These vines and the little trees did he plant; the pool did he contrive, with much labor for the watering of his garden; with his rake did he break up the earth for many years." Gardening, and the enjoyment of the garden, came to be seen for both Christian and Buddhist monks as a way to elevate the human spirit to the level of the ultimate Creator of beauty, perhaps more so for the Buddhist monk than the Christian, because the sacraments were the prime source of experiencing God for the Christian monk.

Most monastic communities have had almost from the beginning of the movement a garden area set aside for meditation. In Christian monasteries these areas were often covered, or "cloistered," arbors separated from the gardens proper by arches creating frames for viewing the beauty of the garden. By the medieval period many of the cloisters were laid out with formal gardens and ornamental fountains and pools (many remnants of primitive watering courses) becoming focal points. While these gardens were primarily utilitarian—the pools in Christian monasteries, for example, often providing fish for fast days—most were also tranquil places given to inspire meditation upon the grandeur of the Creator and, if we are to believe the writings of some, such as Hildegard of Bingen, places where mystical experiences took place. Mendel, for example, began to formulate the laws of genetics while strolling through

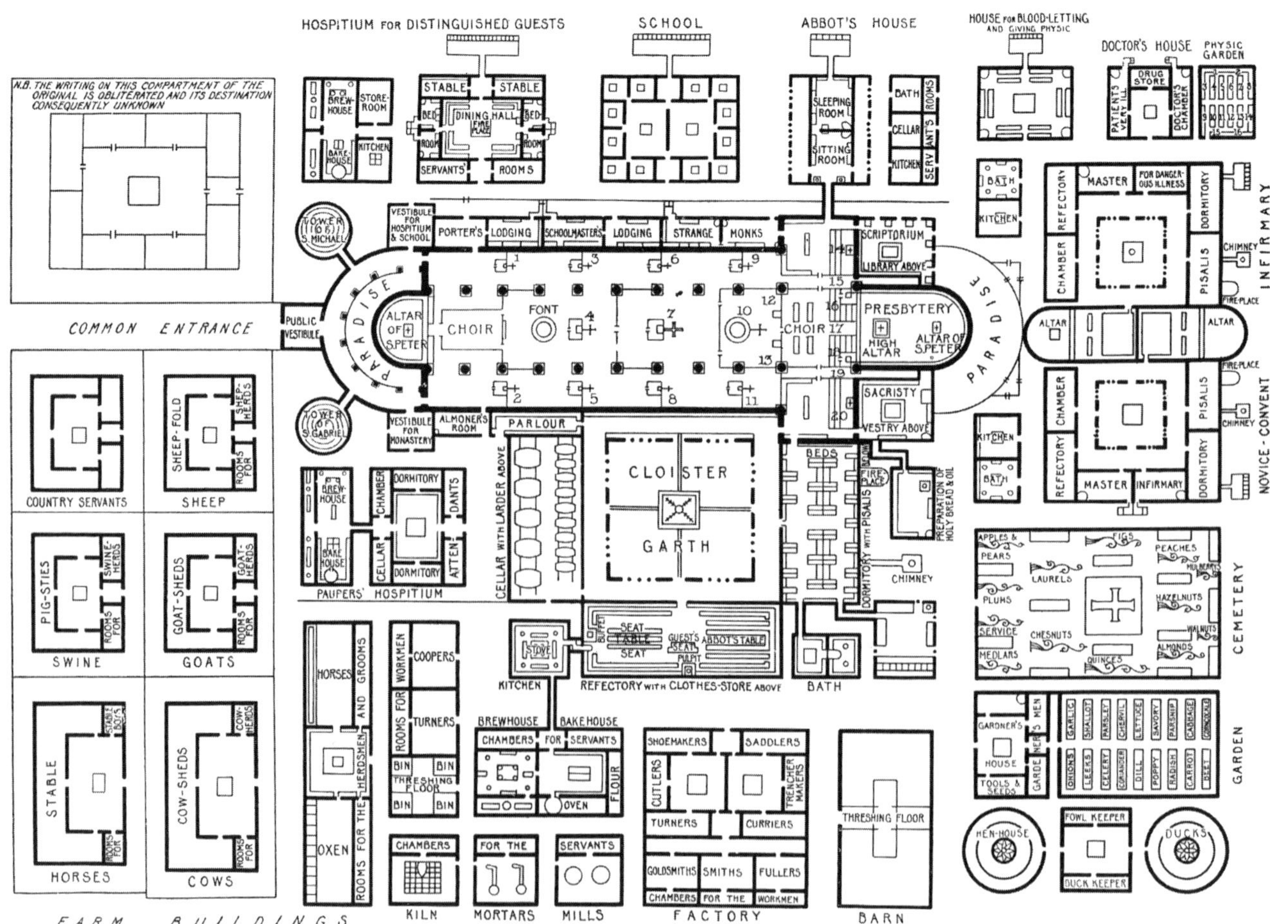

Plan of the Benedictine Monastery of St. Gall, 830, by the Rev. R. Willis

the cloister gardens and meditating upon the different flowers of the sweet-pea patch and how God allowed for so much variety.

Until recently very little seems to have been written about a Christian theology of gardening. Perhaps this has to do in part with the view of the Roman Church, which up to the sixth century held that taking pleasure from flowers was "heathenish" and the cultivation of herbs "Satanic," a view, thankfully for the advancement of Western horticulture, not shared by the Eastern and Celtic Churches or for that matter many early Roman abbots. Unlike Christianity, Islam and the Eastern religions did develop a theology of gardening, or more specifically, of re-creating paradise. The philosophies developed into the Islamic *pairi-daeza* as a re-creation of paradise, a place where Allah communed with his creation, and subsequently greatly influenced medieval Christian monastic gardens.

Although a bit later than its Christian monastic counterparts, it was during the medieval period that the Buddhist style of monastic gardening came into its own. In the 1500s Musō Kokushi, considered by some to be the father of Japanese gardening, following the principal known as *yugen,* that is, "endowing the garden with mysterious, or mystical, depth," created what is said to be the first *karesansui* garden (dry mountain water garden), what we now know as the Zen garden. Musō's *karesansui,* originally built as part of a monastic temple complex, still exists much in its original form as part of Kyōto's Saihō-ji (temple of the western paradise) gardens, providing much insight into the practical application of the garden theology of Buddhism.

When people consider gardens in Buddhist monasteries, they almost always think Zen gardens. It must, however, be remembered that not all Buddhist monasteries are Zen Buddhist monasteries, although throughout schools of Buddhism virtually the same philosophy of gardening is found. Buddhist monastic gardens are designed upon a principal of harmony: the idea that opposing forces, *yin* and *yang,* need to be in balance. Buddhist philosophy teaches that the Buddha only resides in a "balanced garden," the *Gokurakujō*, or paradise. This philosophy of harmony is similar to a Shinto philosophy known as *shi,* or binding. In Buddhism the concept of *shi* finds its fullest expression in the gardens of Zen Buddhism. Inherent in the Shinto philosophy of *shi* is the idea of "making holy." *Shime,* the binding of place (garden plot), *Shizen,* the binding of agriculture (garden plants), and *iwakora,* the binding of rock (garden appointments) must each be in balance with each other as well, as with the gardener. To preserve the harmony each school of Buddhism, like each Christian monastic order, also has its rules; some such as the *Sekiya* cover the etiquette of urinating, defecating, and spitting in the garden.

All Buddhist monastic gardens had low and high *asanas,* or seats. The low *asanas* were provided as places for monks to sit while meditating or delivering sermons to the disciples sitting at their feet. The high *asanas* served as a place to set offerings of flowers. The gardens also included *patima-guha,* image houses (shrines); *dagobas,* ritual baths for devotes who arrived from outside the monastery; and perhaps a *sanghavasa,* a cave hermitage.

Unfortunately, many of Western Buddhism's monastic gardens, while in theory still preserving the philosophy of harmony, have fallen prey to Western pragmatic thinking and have become more of a contemplative garden than a *Gokurakujō* to mystically experience the Buddha. This perhaps is also true for the modern Christian monastic garden with the emphasis on doing meditation rather than on mystical experience.

When during the sixth century the Roman Church finally came to accept the cultivation of flowers and herbs, coming full circle back to St. Antony, they began to realize that plants offered powerful symbols of various Christian virtues. The saints and the Virgin Mary particularly benefited from these virtuous associations. By the late medieval age many Roman monasteries had what came to be known as saint's gardens and Mary gardens, eventually evolving into today's familiar small shrines surrounded by flower beds and foliage. The first reference of an actual garden dedicated to Mary is found in the *Life* of the Irish patron of gardening, St. Fiacre. The saint we are told tended a small garden he built in honor of "Our Lady" at his seventh-century monastery in France, which became famous as a hospice for the poor and infirm. The first reference to a monastic Mary garden by name is found in the accounting records of a 15th-century monastic community at Norwich Priory in England. The first record of a flower actually named for Mary is found in a 1373 English recipe for a spell to ward off the plague. In this recipe the herb calendula, or pot marigold, is referred to as *seint mary gouldes* (St. Mary's Gold). It is important, the recipe claims, that *seint mary gouldes* is brewed while saying a certain prayer, or charm. Here ironically is the very thing that the Roman Church hoped to stop. Unfortunately, the Church's practice of associating flowers with Christian virtues had in time the unfortunate consequence of creating disarray among those studying horticulture, creating a lack of uniformity among the oldest names of herbs. For example, what Celts and Anglo-Saxons knew as meadowsweet became known as brides-wort or Mary's wort in honor of the Virgin Mary.

Christian monastic communities were until the 13th century mostly vegetarian, as are still those of Buddhism, with the monks tending to the raising of most of the produce. In the Christian tradition, after worship, gardening was the primary task of the monk in most

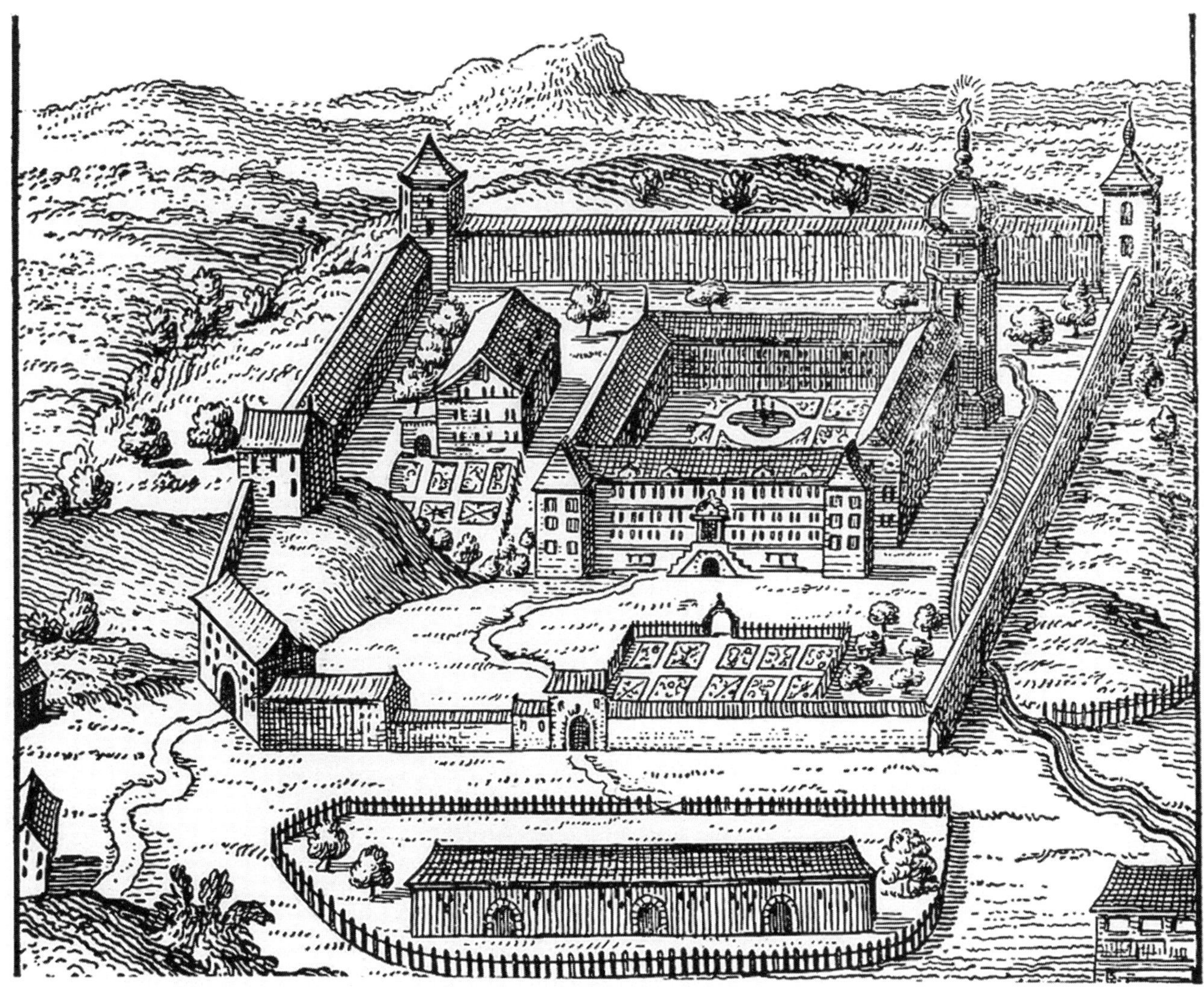

Abbey of Pfäffers as in 1723, with a Cloister Garden surrounded by the main buildings and two gardens within the outside wall

monasteries. Buddhist monasteries have always been vegetarian, although the practice of gardening varied. In some, it was the task of the monk, while in others the task fell to the laity so that the monks could devote themselves to meditation. Sites chosen for the monastic retreat were usually wild and inaccessible. Gradually the forests were cleared and the land worked into farms and gardens, but in Christian monasteries rarely were gardens purely for the sake of pleasure. On the other hand, with the emphasis primarily on meditation, Buddhist monasteries and Islamic mosques almost always had pleasure gardens. Such a contrast notes well the differing views of "pleasure" between Roman Christianity and Islam and Buddhism. By the late medieval period the monasteries associated with the Benedictine Black Monks ceased agricultural production, and to some extent the study of plants and gardens focused more on enjoyment than on produce. However, seeking to keep pleasure in its "proper place" came the reform movement of the Cistercians, who sought to reestablish the "old order" of agriculture and gardening.

We are fortunate to have detailed drawings of the layout of the gardens of the monastery of St. Gall in Switzerland, which provides us with much information about what we may surmise to be a typical ninth- or tenth-century Christian monastic garden. St. Gall's 16 garden beds contained medicinal and potherbs along with ornamentals, trees (fruit and nut), and various fruits and grapevines. The beds included onions, leeks, coriander, dill, poppy (*Papaver*), magones, radish, chard, garlic, shallot, parsley, chervil, lettuce, peppermint, parsnips, cabbage, fennel, lily, rose, climbing bean, pepperwort, costmary, Greek hay, rosemary, mint (*Menthe*), sage, rue, iris (gladiola), pennyroyal, cumin, lovage, and watercress. Records from other monastic communities suggest that to these we may add dandelion, wild carrot, primrose, sweet violet, viola, calendula, thyme, marigold, nuts, and legumes. Almost all of the gardens incorporated ornamental and fruit-bearing trees and vines. With the possible exception of the physic garden, it was the practice, at least in the pre- to late mid-medieval monasteries, not to segregate flowers, herbs, and vegetables into separate plots. At St. Gall's, as in many monasteries, it was the task of the monks, in addition to gardening, to copy ancient herbals and re-create the old healing formulas. One of the first of these, *De cultura hortorum* (*On the Cultivation of Gardens*), written by Walafrid Strabo (ca. 808–49), abbott of the Abbey of Reichenau, sings in poetic form the praises, or spiritual virtues, of gardening, a "holy occupation." In the 12th century the Abbess Hildegard of Bingen wrote two volumes on the nutritional and medicinal value of plants, which echoed the praises of gardening from Strabo to the monks of the time of St. Antony and recorded the truth which they all sought to practice: All things of creation live in a dependent relationship of harmony. There is a rhythm of season, an inner goodness of all creation, and natural laws, all of which maintain harmony and balance, a view not unlike that of Buddhism.

Further Reading

Davidson, Audrey Ekdahl, *The "Ordo Virtutum" of Hildegard of Bingen,* Kalamazoo, Michigan: Medieval Institute Publications, Western Michigan University, 1992

Hildegard, Saint, *The Letters of Hildegard of Bingen,* 2 vols., translated by Joseph L. Baird and Radd K. Ehrman, New York: Oxford University Press, 1994–98

Horn, Walter William, and Ernest Born, *The Plan of St. Gall: A Study of the Architecture and Economy of and Life in a Paradigmatic Carolingian Monastery,* 3 vols., Berkeley: University of California Press, 1979

Nitschke, Günter, *Gartenarchitektur in Japan: Rechter Winkel und natürliche Form,* Cologne, Germany: Taschen, 1991; as *Japanese Gardens: Right Angle and Natural Form,* translated by Karen Williams, Cologne, Germany: Taschen, 1993

Payne, R., and W. Blunt, *The Hortus of Walafrid Strabo,* Pittsburgh, Pennsylvania: University of Pittsburgh Press, 1966

Rubenson, Samuel, *The Letters of St. Antony: Monasticism and the Making of a Saint,* Minneapolis, Minnesota: Fortress Press, 1995

Schipperges, Heinrich, *HvB: Ein Zeichen für unsere Zeit,* Frankfurt: Knecht, 1981; as *Hildegard of Bingen: Healing and the Nature of the Cosmos,* translated by John A. Broadwin, Princeton, New Jersey: Wiener, 1997

Whiteman, Robin, and Rob Talbot, *Brother Cadfael's Herb Garden: An Illustrated Companion to Medieval Plants and Their Uses,* London: Bulfinch, 1997

Wilds, Nancy A., *Church Grounds and Gardens,* New York: Seabury Press, 1964

FRANK MILLS

Montpellier Botanic Garden

Montpellier, Hérault, France

Location: Near ancient city gate "Tour des pins" in center of Montpellier, approximately 80 miles (129 km) west of Marseille

Montpellier Botanic Garden was founded in 1593 under the direction of the physician Pierre Richer de Belleval (1564–1632). Montpellier is an old French commercial and university town located on the Mediterranean seaside. It suffered extensive damage due to several sieges in the course of religious wars in France at the end of the 16th century.

Henri IV, the young Protestant king of France, thought to stabilize the situation in part by promoting scientific activities at Montpellier University (founded in 1289). He donated a botanic garden for the medical faculty, intended as an institution for medical and pharmacological teaching. The garden foundation was also connected to promotion of agriculture as one of the king's main political objectives in the attempt to improve the nutritional situation of the rural population. The introduction of silk production in southern France was intended to diversify the rural economy. Mulberry trees originally planted as food for the caterpillars and still found throughout southern France are relicts from this time.

Due to his engagement during an epidemic disease in the area, Henri IV personally appointed Pierre Richer de

Belleval to the position of director and professor of the medical faculty. Richer de Belleval studied medicine in Montpellier and Avignon from 1584 to 1587. Until 1593 he practiced medicine as a resident physician outside Montpellier. In 1593 he started his work for the garden, which was inaugurated in 1596. Following its destruction in 1622 during yet another siege, the garden was reconstructed by Richer de Belleval himself. Some of the principal elements of the original garden have remained in their original place until today.

At the beginning the garden was rather modest in area, only 7,200 to 7,400 square meters (8,611 to 8,850 sq. yd.). (Since then, however, the garden has grown sixfold to 44,400 square meters [53,100 sq. yd.] at the present day.) It consisted of a terraced hill, called the Montagne, the labyrinth, a prototype of an aquatic garden with sectors of different humidity, and the *hortus medicus* where all simples—plants of medical interest—were cultivated.

The oldest surviving layout of the garden in conjunction with a professional description is found in a letter from the Dutch medical student Outgaert Cluyt, written in Montpellier on 30 November 1602:

> The garden lies near the city gates in a very pleasant setting. It contains several plots in alternation of cultivated nutritive with wild savage beds. A hill is orientated south and turned off from the northern winds. The sections are rough, rocky, sandy, exposed to the sun or shaded by undergrowth. There is also a labyrinth in which you can find it shady, moist with high humidity and ultimately swampy. It is 35 geometrical feet deep in which the plants grow very well. The garden is a jewel of the academy and the city. (quoted in Jarry)

An artificially terraced earthen pyramid, the Montagne provides specialized plant habitats while still permitting easy access for visitors. The Montagne is oriented from west to east and has five steps on each side and a walkway on top. The lowest level appears to have been dug down below the garden surface, and the walkways are even deeper. It was originally 15 to 20 meters (16.4 to 22 yd.) wide, 20 to 25 meters (22 to 27 yd.) long, and approximately three meters (3.2 yd.) tall. There is no evidence of a direct predecessor. Its development was closely followed by other professionals. Olivier de Serres, a famous French landscape gardener, described Richer de Belleval's Montagne in his fundamental work on horticulture and garden layout entitled *Théâtre d'agriculture* (1600; Spectrum of Agriculture).

The Montagne was based on the idea of having all climatic conditions represented in a small area, that is, a microcosm in a macrocosm. From the onset the Montagne was the section of the garden dedicated to scientific botany, in which unknown local plants were cultivated. Assignment of a plant was made less in conjunction with preconceived notions as with regard to its soil and climatic needs at its original site. In this way an ecological system of planting led to an ecological plant classification developed in Richer de Belleval's unpublished *Flora of the Languedoc*.

Independent of their medical or agricultural value, species such as mastic shrubs (*Pistacia lentiscus*), laurustinus (*Viburnum tinus*), rock laurel (mock privet) (*Phillyrea latifolia*), zistrose (*Cistus monspeliensis*), western straw-

Copper engraving of the Montpellier Botanic Garden as it looked when first created in 1596
Courtesy of Montpellier Botanic Garden

berry tree (*Arbutus unedo*), thorny oak (*Quercus coccifera*), evergreen oak (*Quercus ilex*), turpentine pistachio (*Pistacia terebinthus*), stech juniper (*Juniperus oxycederus*), rosemary (*Rosmarinus officinalis*), true lavender (*Lavandula angustifolia*), and others were cultivated. The few species mentioned give an inadequate picture of the total extent. Richer de Belleval reported in 1598 a total of 1,332 species in his garden, and it can be postulated that the Montagne contained approximately 800 species in 1600 (estimated planted surface of 200 square meters [239 sq. yd.] with four plants per square meter). The oldest plant living today is a mighty mock privet (*Phillyrea latifolia*) on the Montagne, which was planted during Richer de Belleval's lifetime.

Of all the new sections of the garden, the labyrinth, a prototype of an aquatic garden, was the most original creation. There were two passageways on a width of approximately ten meters (11 yd.) and a total depth of 10.5 meters (11.5 yd.) coiling downward around the fountain. Paths led on both sides to flower beds in which shrubs and other plants were growing in moist and shaded areas. At the end of each path was a depressed courtyard about three-and-a-half meters (3.8 yd.) long and one-and-a-half meters (1.6 yd.) wide, completely surrounded by beds full of plants. The "grotto" fashion, trendy at the time and originating in Italy, as well as the most famous contemporary "grottist," the ceramics designer Bernard Palissy, are worthy of mention. Historical sources cannot be found, but since Palissy was employed by Henri IV, a personal connection in relation with the garden in Montpellier is apparent. Richer de Belleval's *Onomatologia, seu nomenclatura stirpium* (1598; Nomenclator, Register of Plant Names) contains the first mention of the aquatic type of plants, including white water lilies (*Nymphaea alba*), water plantain (*Alisma plantago-aquatica*), and marsh marigold (*Caltha palustris*). The aquatic plant garden disappeared from the records following the destruction in 1623 and does not exist today.

Pharmaceutical plants were cultivated after 1603 south of the Montagne in the *hortus medicus* to protect them from the wind. Six parallel, elevated beds were west-east oriented and separated by paths. The plants were planted on both sides of elongated mounds for viewing. The mounds were 80 centimeters (2.6 ft.) in width, and the bordering wall 55 centimeters (1.8 ft.) high on both sides. The upper edge was fortified with shaped stones that had a number on one side and a channel on the other to feed water to any section of the mound as desired.

Newly introduced exotic sand and shore plants were to be seen behind the Montagne, including a date-palm (*Phoenix dactylifera*) and a prickly pear (*Opuntia ficus-indica*), an import from Peru. The *florilegium* with numerous flowers and exotic species decorated the main entrance. The *seminarium* existed as of 1603 and was later called the nursery. It contained foreign, exotic, and especially alpine plants. A natural history museum also formed part of the garden. All of these sections of the garden no longer exist.

Richer de Belleval's garden contains a remarkable conglomerate of different garden sections, which can be explained in part by the fact that the garden was acquired and established piece by piece over the course of decades. But even those sections designed by Richer de Belleval are marked by a mixture of various principles of garden layout. The pyramid, labyrinth, and the orchard came from the antique and medieval world. The pharmaceutical teaching garden and the natural history museum originated in the Renaissance.

The strict delimitation of individual garden sections with pinnacled walls fits best in a medieval conception of the *hortus conclusus* rather than in the Renaissance. Openness and symmetry are lacking as the important elements of the Renaissance garden. This explains the remarks of the Renaissance architect Peiresc to Charles de l'Ecluse: "If I would try to completely describe to you all of the details of a garden which is the most unordered and confusing one I have ever seen, it will be much too extensive to write it all down."

As such, the garden in Montpellier can be placed at the transition from medieval times to the Renaissance. However, the scientific-botanical concept and rededication of individual elements to new functions were unique in this form and set new standards.

Synopsis

1593 Foundation of Montpellier Botanic Garden and appointment of Pierre Richer de Belleval as director and professor of medical faculty
1596 Inauguration of garden
1598 Richer de Belleval publishes first printed register of plants, containing more than 1,200 species
1603 Inauguration of *hortus medicus*
1622 Destruction of garden during siege of Montpellier
1623 Reconstruction by Richer de Belleval, enlargement of Montagne (terraced hill)
17th C. Pierre Magnol (1638–1715) active as researcher and publisher in garden
19th C. Augustin-Pyramus de Candolle (1778–1841) garden director
1992 Declaration as French national historical monument
1993 400th anniversary of garden

Further Reading

Dulieu, Louis, *La médecine à Montpellier du XIIe au XXe siècle,* 6 vols., Paris: Hervas, 1975–77

Gilibert, Jean Emmanuel, "Figures des plantes de P. Richer de Belleval," in Claret de la Tourrette, Marc-Antoine-Louis, and François Rozier, *Démonstrations élémentaires de botanique à l'usage de l'École royal vétérinaire,* 2 vols., Lyon, 1766; 4th edition, 4 vols., 1796 (see especially vol. 1, series 2)
Guiraud, Louise, "Le premier jardin des plantes français: Création et restauration du Jardin du Roi à Montpellier par Pierre Richer de Belleval (1593–1632): Étude historique et documents," *Archives de la ville de Montpellier, inventaires et documents* 4 (1911)
Jarry, Daniel, "Le premier jardin de Richer de Belleval (1596–1622)," *Monspeliensis Hippocrates* 48 (1970)
Peiresc, Nicolas Claude Fabri de, *Lettres de Peiresc,* 7 vols., edited by Philippe Tamizey de Larroque, Paris, 1888–98; see especially vol. 7
Serres, Olivier de, *Le théâtre d'agriculture et mesnage des Champs,* 2 vols., Paris, 1804–5
Rath, Ulrich von, *Botanik und Pharmakologie in der Renaissance: Die Gründungsgeschichte des Botanischen Gartens Montpellier 1593 und seine Rezeption im nördlichen Mitteleuropa unter besonderer Berücksichtigung eines botanischen Frühdrucks der Lübecker Stadtbibliothek,* Lübeck, Germany: Bibliothek der Hansestadt Lübeck, 1998
Rath, Ulrich von, "The Function and Architecture of the Botanic Garden of the University of Montpellier (1593–1622)," *Polish Botanical Studies* 20 (1998)
Richer de Belleval, Pierre, "Onomatologia: Seu nomenclatura stirpium quae in horto regio Monspeliensi recens constructo coluntur (1598)," in *Opuscules de Pierre Richer de Belleval,* Paris, 1785
Rioux, Jean-Antoine, editor, *Le jardin des plantes de Montpellier: Quatre siècles d'histoire,* Graulhet, France: Odyssée, 1994

ULRICH VON RATH

Moscow University Botanic Garden

Moscow, Russia

Location: Old Territory (Apothecary Garden) at Prospekt Mira 26, approximately 2 miles (3.2 km) north of Kremlin; New Territory at foot of main building of Moscow State University on Vorobyovy Gory (Sparrow Hills) in southwest Moscow

The Botanic Garden of Moscow University is the oldest garden of its kind in Russia. Its origin has much in common with that of other early European botanic gardens. The old territory of the garden, still surviving on the original site, was founded by Peter the Great in 1706 as the Apothecary Garden, a source for medicinal plants in Moscow. It is quite likely that the first contributions to the newly established garden came from the ancient royal residence Izmailovo, near Moscow, famous for its vast collection of medicinal and other useful plants.

According to legend, the tsar, with his own hands, planted three conifer trees here: a fir, a silver fir, and a Siberian larch (*Larix sibirica*). The latter species was his favorite tree and still survives in the garden.

The garden originally belonged to the Moscow Hospital and subsequently to the Medical Academy. T. Gerber, invited from the University of Leipzig to become the first director of the garden, was appointed in 1735. As both a doctor of medicine and a prominent botanist, he taught botany to students at the academy and grew medicinal plants as well as botanical curiosities. He was the initiator of the botanical collections of the garden. Although very little is known about the plant species in the garden at that time, there is some evidence that, together with a relatively conventional range of local medicinal herbs, there were some contemporary rarities, such as rhubarb, which had been recently introduced from Western Europe.

There is no mention of any landscape architect in the available sources. The initial layout owed as much to the predominant formal garden style as to the practicality of the garden's major functions: teaching and plant raising. Most of the garden was covered with a network of straight paths forming square or rectangular compartments, edged by trees and shrubs, which were in turn split up into finer bedding. In the 18th century an artificial pond, also rectangular, was excavated to store rainwater for irrigation.

By the end of the 18th century, the garden had lost its original character as a physic garden and had become far more botanical, with systematically ordered collections of largely scientific value. By then, the first wooden hothouses, of which only the location is known, were built.

In 1804 the academy, which owned the site, moved to St. Petersburg, the capital of Russia since 1703. The site was abandoned and threatened with residential development. In a fortunate coincidence, however, Moscow University was in need of a new plot for a botanic garden. In 1805 the former Apothecary Garden was purchased by the university and then dramatically transformed into a proper botanic garden. Since then it has remained the property of the university.

One of the garden's most successful directors was Georg Franz Hoffmann, who had left the University of Göttingen to become professor of botany in Moscow. Soon after his arrival, the new botanic garden became an example of gardening excellence and abundance. When Hoffmann published, in Latin, the first description of the garden, *Hortus Mosquensis* (1808), he listed a total of 3,594 species (more than there are today) in the open ground and under glass. The first plan of the garden, with a detailed description, also in Latin, was engraved and attached to the edition. Although not very accurate, the plan is an invaluable depiction of how the garden might have looked in its heyday, about 200 years ago.

The garden suffered a severe setback during the French occupation of Moscow in 1812. Most of the greenhouses were destroyed, and many plants were lost together with a part of the library and herbarium. After the French retreat, from 1814 onward, the garden was gradually restored. Funds were limited, and it became necessary to sell off some of the land, reducing the area of the garden from 9 to 6.5 hectares (22 to 16 acres). The success of the restoration was due in part to the very generous donations of plants of Count Razumovsky, who at the time owned a famous botanic garden on his Gorenki estate on the outskirts of Moscow. Having miraculously survived throughout subsequent wars and revolutions, several old specimens remain in the garden's glasshouses, including some palms as much as 150 years old and one cycad (*Cycas circinalis*) that is more than 200 years old. Presumably, these are all that remain of Razumovsky's gifts.

During Catherine the Great's reign, the fashion for Picturesque gardens reached Russia, and some 50 years later influenced the garden's layout. In the early 1850s some of the paths were deliberately curved in the English style; freestanding trees and lawns appeared, and the pond was given the shape of a natural lake. The arboretum, however, is still bordered by three straight alleés, which are thought to date from the early layout. Along the alleés and throughout the garden are some spectacular trees that survive from the 18th- and 19th-century plantings. Among them is a white willow (*Salix alba*) near the pond believed to be around 300 years old—the oldest tree in central Moscow—a few lime trees (*Tilia cordata* and *T. platyphylla*); elms (*Ulmus laevis*); and others, many of which are the oldest specimens of their taxa in the city.

There are two major glasshouses in the garden. The Palm House (1891) contains the tropical plants, including specimens up to 12 meters (13.2 yd.) high. The Subtropical House (1870s), with water lily pools of later date (1905), protects various collections of tender plants that could not survive outdoors in the climate of Moscow. The Subtropical House is built on the foundations of the early 19th-century wooden glasshouses. In the garden's modest office building, the construction of which was sponsored by Moscow traders in 1882, portions of the original laboratory interiors and equipment have remained intact.

After the university expanded to Sparrow Hills in the southwestern part of the city in 1953, a new botanic garden was established there, and the original garden subsequently declined. An assessment of the historical value of the earlier site resulted in 1973 in conferment of the status of historical monument. In 1995 a long-term restoration project was begun. To avoid the confusion with the newer University Botanic Garden and the other four botanic gardens in Moscow, it was decided to revive the original name—Aptékarsky Ogoród (Apothecary Garden).

Synopsis

1706 Peter the Great founds new Apothecary Garden in northern outskirts of Moscow
1735 T. Gerber from Leipzig University appointed first director
1804 Medical Academy moves to Saint Petersburg
1805 Neglected garden sold to Moscow University
1807 G.F. Hoffmann from University of Göttingen put in charge of garden
1808 First plan and plant catalog of garden published
1812 Invasion by Napoléon and Moscow fire
1814 Restoration after war
1835 Some of garden's land sold
1850s New layout for pond and arboretum
1870s Building of Subtropical House
1882 Construction of laboratory and library building completed
1891 Palm House built
1953 New territory in Sparrow Hills (southwest of Moscow) established
1973 Status of historical monument conferred
1995 Restoration project commenced
1998 Original name revived

Further Reading

Hayden, Peter, "The Renaissance of Russia's Oldest Botanic Garden," *Garden History Society Newsletter* 51 (Winter 1997)

Hoffmann, Georg Franz, *De Hortis Botanico-Medicis: Oratio in Anniversariis Solennibus Inaugurationis Universitatis Caesareae Literarum Mosquensis:*

D. 2 Jul. a. 1807 (bilingual Latin-Russian edition), Moscow, 1807

Hoffmann, Georg Franz, *Hortus Mosquensis*, Moscow, 1808

Parshin, Artyom Y., editor, *Enumeratio plantarum Horti Botanici Universitatis Mosquensis* (The Plant Lists of the Botanic Garden of Moscow University "Apothecary Garden"), Moscow: Poltex, 2001

ARTYOM PARSHIN

Mount

The term *mount* usually refers to an artificial hill constructed within a garden with the primary objective of affording a view, either over the garden itself or beyond. In this form it seems to have been a particularly English idea and, with some earlier examples, principally developed in the 17th century. It is commonly suggested that the mount heralded the opening up of the broader landscape in both design and aesthetic terms.

For centuries the idea of the *hortus conclusus*, the enclosed garden, away from the world and inward looking, had prevailed, both for reasons of physical protection and because it was away from the realities of the world. Some early mounts may have been constructed for purely defensive purposes, with no thought of aesthetics, and it is thought that, with more settled times and as ideas changed, the visual pleasures of viewing the more extensive landscape were recognized. England in the 17th century is generally acknowledged to have lagged behind the Continent in the development of designs, and this may account for the late use of such features as the mount. In his essay "On Gardens" (1625), Francis Bacon describes his ideal for a "princelike" garden ("not well to be under thirty acres of ground"). It would contain

> in the very middle a very fair mount, with three ascents and alleys, enough for four to walk abreast; which I would have to be perfect circles without any bulwarks or embossments; and the whole mount to be thirty feet high, and some fine banqueting-house with some chimneys neatly cast, and without too much glass.

The garden mount would either be in the middle or set at the edge of the garden; indeed, elsewhere in his essay Bacon speaks of a mount being created "to look abroad into the fields." William Lawson, in his *New Orchard and Garden* (1617), proposed that there should be a mount at each corner of the garden.

A number of mounts were found in the colleges of the old universities in England, in particular the circular mount at Wadham College and the rectangular one at New College, Oxford. The arrangement of the latter, with its different directions and angles of steps and intermediate walkways, illustrates well the earlier comment of John Leland about care for easing the ascent to its top. Writing in his *Itinerary* of about 1540, he describes the park at Wressel (Wresehall) in East Yorkshire, where "in the orchardes were mounts opere topiarii writhen about with degrees like turnings of cockell-shells to cum to the top without paine."

The mount at Elvetham in Hampshire was described as having circles of privet creeping up it. This was apparently about 12 meters (13 yd.) in diameter and 6 meters (6.5 yd.) high. The Elvetham park was probably constructed in the late 16th century and had provided the setting for a great entertainment for Elizabeth I in 1591. The mount was on an island in the lake and was described as a "snayle" mount rising to four circles of "privie" (privet).

A mount at Hampton Court erected in the 1530s had a glazed arbor on its summit. Theobalds, also developed in the 16th century, and later a royal property, had a mount as well. This was a small round hill of earth with a labyrinth around and was called Venusberg. Ben Johnson spoke of the mount at Penshurst "to which the dryads do resort," and even Alexander Pope in the 18th century had one large and two small mounts at his Twickenham Villa.

All those mentioned so far are mounts of earth and were probably created, as Batty Langley was to suggest at a very late date for these features, by using soil from foundations and other excavations "raised up to make a mount." The idea of the mount was accepted early in the 16th century; and they featured in several theatrical entertainments that depended on what must have been highly elaborate and spectacular constructions. In 1528 Henry VIII entertained French ambassadors at Greenwich, and in the temporary banqueting house was built "a goodly mount, walled in with towers" and constructed with crystals and ruby-colored rocks, decorated with roses and pomegranates, and with seats for eight lords. This mount had a cave within it. At the Masque of Flowers staged at Grays Inn in 1614, the mount designed by Bacon probably in 1608–9 was a prominent element in the set. It was apparently decorated with turrets and arcading and planted with honeysuckle and eglantine.

The derivation of the mount from a defensive viewing platform within the walls seems most likely, but other possible influences cannot be discounted, and indeed there are some other forms to which the term has been attached. The application of the term *mount* to a raised walk at the side of a garden extensive enough to play bowls on may at first seem nonsensical. Such features were, however, classed as mounts and conform to the concept of a defensive viewing platform. Others have suggested that the term should include timber constructions and other buildings, arguing that these fulfilled the same function as early as in Roman times. It seems far-fetched, however, to describe the tree houses, garden pavilions, belvederes, and watchtowers that adorned Roman gardens as mounts. Nonetheless, a belvedere did afford Nero a vantage point from which to view the destruction of Rome by fire. Other influences are more plausible; for example, in Italy and France the development of mounts with a special horticultural purpose related to the growth of medicinal plants. As described by Olivier de Serres in *Le théâtre d' agriculture* (1600; The Setting of Agriculture), the botanical gardens of Padua, Pisa, and Genova all developed raised structures in which their different aspects suited different kinds of plants. They were structures in which either caves or internal storage areas would be created; these could be used for the wintering of delicate plants. Salomon de Caus describes something of the kind in his *Les raisons des forces mouvant* (1615; Understanding Fluid Forces) as does de Serres, who describes two mounts, one of which had a base of 100 meters (109 yd.), a hollow interior, and a 50-meter (55 yd.) flat top. At Montpelier the 16th-century Jardin des Plantes of Richer de Belleval comprised oblong terraces running north and south with a hollow base. In Paris the Jardin du Roi, founded in 1626 based on designs by Jean Robin, had an extensive "mount area" comprising two ridges topped by a small conical hillock.

Further Reading

Bacon, Francis, *Essays,* London: Dent, 1973
Batey, Mavis, *The Historic Gardens of Oxford and Cambridge,* London: Macmillan, 1989
Blomfield, Reginald Theodore, and F. Inigo Thomas, *The Formal Garden in England,* London, 1892; reprint, London: Waterstone, 1985
Strong, Roy, *The Renaissance Garden in England,* London: Thames and Hudson, 1979
Thacker, Christopher, *The Genius of Gardening,* London: Weidenfeld and Nicholson, 1994
Woodbridge, Kenneth, *Princely Gardens: The Origins and Development of the French Formal Style,* London: Thames and Hudson, and New York: Rizzoli, 1986

M.F. DOWNING

Mount Auburn Cemetery

Cambridge, Massachusetts, United States

Location: 580 Mount Auburn Street, Cambridge, approximately 5 miles (8 km) west-northwest of Boston city center

Mount Auburn was the first rural garden cemetery in the United States and has been a place of beauty and serenity for New England families since it was founded in 1831. It continues to offer a tranquil landscape of trees, shrubs, and flowers and provides a sanctuary for birds and other wildlife, including exquisite butterflies. And while it is best known for its landscape and for burials and monuments of historic significance, Mount Auburn continues to be a working cemetery.

The consecration and dedication of Mount Auburn Cemetery took place on 24 September 1831. Its creation is primarily attributed to the influence of Dr. Jacob Bigelow, a lecturer in botany at Harvard College and its medical school and the author of the first definitive botanical study of New England. Evidently a man of high standing in botanical circles, Bigelow earned a commendation from the Royal Horticultural Society of London and a certificate of *hommage* from the Société Linéénne of Paris.

In 1825 Bigelow invited several of his friends to join a committee for the formation of a landscaped extramural cemetery for Boston. Given Boston's sense of historical importance in founding a commonwealth independent of British rule, the committee included active members of the Bunker Hill Monument Association who shared Bigelow's interest in devising ways to strengthen its cultural and historic identity. Preserving the memory of important Bostonians by creating a landscape that would honor them offered a practical step in this direction. The group was also influenced by similar landscape developments in Europe, notably Père Lachaise Cemetery (1804) in Paris.

As with burial reform in Europe, Mount Auburn was intended to be a major departure from traditional city graveyards whose "mephitic vapours" caused health hazards, where conditions were increasingly cramped, and further expansion was becoming expensive given rising land prices. Also, the purpose and design of Mount Auburn were influenced by social welfare and utilitarian values similar to those emerging at about the same time among groups of city fathers and urban reformers in Europe.

The concept behind the Mount Auburn project was also strongly influenced by Romanticism, a cluster of attitudes that were developed by the *literati* from the late 18th century onward. The Romantics accorded an intrinsic value to wilderness and nature in opposition to the dominant imperialist view attributed to Francis Bacon (1561–1626), which saw nature as a resource to be used for its practical benefits to mankind, with the value to be ascertained through careful scientific observation.

Because of its size and landscape design, Mount Auburn was able to offer a place for quiet contemplation and mourning yet also provide the city with a park-like attraction, indeed a showcase, that would promote monuments and memorials to famous Bostonians. As a place of interest for visitors to the city and a recreational space for Bostonians, it was an important predecessor to the American public parks that developed later in the century, influencing the first such space, New York City's Central Park.

To understand the design of Mount Auburn, it is important to know that many of its founders were Unitarians. For religio-historical reasons they expressly sought a nondenominational approach to landscape and monument design, resisting conventional church architecture and symbolism such as gothic designs and the cross. Unitarians encouraged a new range of forms and motifs, sometimes from outside the tradition of European Christian symbolism. For example, the entranceway's design looked to Egyptology for inspiration. This was no doubt appropriate because of the importance that ancient Egypt accorded to the dead (as exhibited by the great pyramids), but its true significance lay in the fact that the entranceway itself symbolized the religious independence of the founders.

The closest European parallel to Mount Auburn is Abney Park Cemetery, London's first nondenominational garden cemetery (designed 1838–40). This cemetery also was founded primarily by Unitarians, had a strong horticultural emphasis, and was set in a landscape chosen for romantic associations. Abney Park's entrance ensemble also shared Mount Auburn's Egyptian design theme, a feature that was much too radical for Augustus Pugin and the ecclesiological movement in Britain.

If Mount Auburn achieved one distinction above all, in comparison with other garden cemeteries of the 19th century, it lay in the supreme quality of its natural landscape and the high horticultural standards of its supplementary planting scheme. Endowed with beautiful undulating topography, vistas, woodland, and water features, Mount Auburn had been a much sought after property well before the idea of a garden cemetery was proposed. Reflecting this natural charm, the name of Mount Auburn is generally believed to be inspired by the Oliver Goldsmith poem *The Deserted Village* (London, 1770), which reads, "Sweet Auburn! Loveliest village of the plain."

To add to its celebrated qualities, Bigelow and friends, including General Henry Dearborn, president of the Massachusetts Horticultural Society, set standards in horticulture and landscape design that established its superiority among the early garden cemeteries. They effectively adorned Mount Auburn with a botanical garden and arboretum, going well beyond what was presaged by the cemetery's opening address by Judge Joseph Story "to plant and embellish [Mount Auburn Cemetery] with shrubbery, and flowers, and trees, and walks, and other rural ornaments." Even the curving roadways, which followed natural contours, were named after native trees and shrubs.

Today Mount Auburn Cemetery occupies a site of about 70 hectares (173 acres) and is listed on the National Register of Historic Places. It continues to excite horticultural interest year round, displaying over 300 species and 700 varieties of native and exotic trees, together with over 130 species of shrub and groundcover.

Synopsis

1825 Distinguished North American botanist Jacob Bigelow forms committee to create garden cemetery near Boston

1825 Stone's Wood near Harvard (popularly known as Sweet Auburn) purchased by George Brimmer

1829 Massachusetts Horticultural Society incorporated

1830 Brimmer agrees to sell Sweet Auburn for Bigelow's and Horticultural Society's garden cemetery

1831 Massachusetts General Court passes act authorizing Horticultural Society to establish garden cemetery; Bigelow's committee agrees to purchase initial 72 acres (29 ha) of Sweet Auburn on behalf of the Horticultural Society as soon as there are 100 subscribers for lots at $60 each

Engraving of Lowell's Monument, Willow Avenue, at Mount Auburn Cemetery, by James Smillie, ca. 1847
Courtesy of Mount Auburn Cemetery, Cambridge, Massachusetts

1831 One hundred lots bought, subcommittee established (Henry Dearborn [president of the Horticultural Society], Bigelow, and Brimmer) to plan layout of cemetery

1831 Public consecration and dedication of Mount Auburn Cemetery

1831 Dearborn supervises site layout and transplanting of trees, and Bigelow names ponds, avenues, and places

1832 First interments, entrance gate constructed (rebuilt 1842), and deeds transferred to Horticultural Society

1835 Massachusetts General Court passes act to incorporate proprietors of cemetery as new corporation distinct from Horticultural Society

1830s–50s Mount Auburn influences garden cemeteries and landscape design throughout America and Europe, landscape improvements continued (Auburn Lake created)

1870s Cemetery begins to lose its prestige and appeal, as modernism replaces Romanticism and public parks assume role cemetery formerly played

1986 Friends of Mount Auburn Cemetery established to promote its cultural, historic, and natural appreciation, to secure landscape conservation, and to improve ecology

2000 Millennium interpretive approach developed for visitors

Further Reading

Bigelow, Jacob, *A History of the Cemetery of Mount Auburn*, Boston, 1860; reprint, as *A History of Mt.*

Auburn Cemetery, Cambridge, Massachusetts: Applewood Books, 1988
Goldsmith, Oliver, *The Deserted Village, and Other Poems*, London: Phoenix, 1996 Leighton, Ann, *American Gardens in the Eighteenth Century*, Boston: Houghton Mifflin, 1976
Linden-Ward, Blanche, *Silent City on a Hill: Landscapes of Memory and Boston's Mount Auburn Cemetery*, Columbus: Ohio State University Press, 1989
Sweet Auburn: The Newsletter of the Friends of Mount Auburn, 6 (1991)
Wooley, M.E., "The Development of the Love of Romantic Scenery in America," *American Historical Review* 3 (October 1897)

DAVID SOLMAN

Mount Stewart

Greyabbey, County Down, Northern Ireland

Location: 5 miles (8 km) southeast of Newtownards, about 15 miles (24 km) east of Belfast

Mount Stewart, a fine late-Georgian classical mansion, is the Irish seat of the Stewarts, marquesses of Londonderry. It is set within a small landscaped park and is situated in the northern part of the Ards Peninsula, with the Irish Sea to the east and Strangford Lough, a large, shallow inlet, to the west.

The 80-acre (32-ha) park, dating from the latter half of the 18th century, contains a seven-acre (2.6 ha) lake and, crowning a hill, a magnificent octagonal building, the Temple of the Winds, designed by the architect James ("Athenian") Stuart, who modeled it after the Tower of Andronicus Cyrrhestes (Tower of the Winds) in Athens. The temple, sometimes termed a belvedere, was a banqueting house. Built of locally quarried stone, it contains fine plasterwork and inlaid floors made of wood extracted from local bogs. Given its position, the Temple of the Winds commands views of the sea, lough, and distant mountains. In all, it is generally regarded as one of the most elegant garden buildings in Ireland.

The landscape park, on the other hand, seems never to have been exceptional. As in many other Irish demesnes, belts and clumps of trees, dense evergreen shrubberies, and some unremarkable flower beds were the main features until the early 1900s. A 7.5-acre (three ha) walled garden, one mile from the house, served to supply the household with vegetables, fruits, and cut flowers.

Mount Stewart was not the main residence of the sixth marquess and marchioness of Londonderry until after the close of World War I. Charles Stewart (1878–1949) had succeeded to the title in 1915, but with the war in progress he and his wife, Edith, lived mainly at Londonderry House in central London. Mount Stewart was used only occasionally and was a convalescent hospital during the war. Lady Londonderry was a celebrated hostess, entertaining members of the royal family, politicians, artists, and other prominent people. A group of friends who were regularly entertained at Londonderry House formed the Ark, an informal society whose members joined only by invitation and were required to adopt as a pseudonym the name of a real or imaginary beast. Edith was known as Circe the Sorceress, while, for example, Winston Churchill was Winston the Warlock.

From 1919 the Londonderrys made Mount Stewart their family home, and Lady Londonderry began to lay out the present garden. She made rough designs herself and, encouraged by the government to provide employment for ex-servicemen, engaged 20 men to begin the transformation of the estate, to make the environs of the mansion "not only more cheerful and liveable, but beautiful as well." They levelled and terraced the ground to the south and west of the house for a series of formal garden compartments. The main compartment, the Italian garden, shares a boundary with the long terrace across the south front of Mount Stewart. Lady Londonderry got the idea for her Italian garden from the gardens of the Villa Gamberaia near Florence and the Villa Farnese at Caprarola, in Italy, but she modified them in a remarkable way. She engaged a local man, Thomas Beattie, to build balustrades and make a spectacular series of sculptures in concrete. A pair of dodos flank an out-of-scale Noah's Ark—and immediately the symbolism becomes clear, for these beasts are reminders of the members of her dining circle, the Ark. There are tall monkey-pot pillars and numerous animals, real and imaginary—rabbits, a mermaid, squirrels, frogs, dogs, horses, hedgehogs, baboons, gnomes, and gryphons. Twin pairs of classical columns, surmounted by the heraldic dragons statant of the Londonderry coat-of-arms, mark the entrance to the Spanish garden, so called because the roof tiles for

Mount Stewart Palace and Gardens, County Down, Northern Ireland
Copyright Paul Miles Picture Collection

the summerhouse came from Spain. To the east, behind the Dodo Terrace, is the elegant Mairi garden, named after the Londonderrys' youngest daughter, who was the subject of the small lead statue, by Margaret Wrightson, that forms the fountain centerpiece. To the west of the house is the Sunk garden and beyond that the Shamrock garden, which contains a topiary harp, the emblem of Ireland, and in the center of the paved trefoil a bed shaped like a left hand, the "Bloody Hand of Ulster," the crest of the McDonnells of Antrim.

Although Lady Londonderry herself stated that "no architect has been employed on the design and make of the gardens," Gertrude Jekyll produced designs and planting plans for the Sunk garden in 1920. Michael Tooley has shown that Jekyll's plans, albeit modified, were followed.

Beyond the lake, to the north of the house, Lady Londonderry created Tir-n'an Oge ("Land of the Ever Young"), a private burial ground where she and her husband were later interred. The gazebos, like the stone walls elsewhere, were built by an elderly local stonemason, Joe Girvan.

All of this would perhaps be unremarkable although eccentric, but when the plants that grow exuberantly at Mount Stewart are added to the equation, this garden becomes outstanding. Lady Londonderry was a keen plantswoman; she subscribed to plant collecting expeditions including those of Frank Kingdon Ward, so there are many uncommon plants in Mount Stewart. At the start she was "incited" by two exceptional gardeners, Sir John Ross-of-Bladensburg and Sir Herbert Maxwell, to grow outdoors numerous plants, trees, and shrubs usually grown only in greenhouses. Both men had gardening experience in the milder parts of Ireland and Britain, where the influence of the relatively warm waters of the North Atlantic Drift (commonly called the Gulf Stream) ensures a frost-free, equable climate despite the latitude (54°N). As long as shelter is provided from cold easterly winds, plants from subtropical habitats can thrive, especially those from the Southern Hemisphere. Ross's garden at Rostrevor, also on the east coast of Northern Ireland, was renowned for its collection of tender plants: "Dear Lady Londonderry," he retorted during one of her visits, "never mention Kew to me again. I can grow things here that Kew has never heard of." Thus Mount Stewart boasts not only rare rhododendrons from the Himalayas but also sheltering groves of gigantic gum trees (*Eucalyptus* spp.) from Australia and flourishing cabbage palms (*Cordyline australis*) from New Zealand. The Jubilee Avenue, planted to commemorate the silver jubilee in 1935 of the reign of King George V and Queen Mary, has a red, white, and blue theme based on South American plants: red-flowered Chilean fire-bushes (*Embothrium coccineum*), white-blossomed *Eucryphia cordifolia,* and the blue potato vine, *Solanum crispum* 'Glasnevin'.

In 1955 Lady Londonderry transferred the gardens to the care of the National Trust with the financial assistance of the government of Northern Ireland. She wanted them to be "permanently preserved and maintained in the future." Under the National Trust, the gardens have not been "fossilized" but are actively and continually renewed and enriched with new plants. With the advice of such eminent horticulturists as Graham Stuart Thomas, and through the skill of the successive head gardeners and their staff, Mount Stewart remains an extraordinary place, in terms of both its design and especially its plants, fulfilling Edith Londonderry's own valediction, penned in January 1956: "I feel I can safely leave to the imagination of visitors to these gardens what they will look like when another fifty years or so have passed—The Gardens of Devonshire and Cornwall will not only be equalled, but may even be surpassed."

Synopsis

1744	Mount Pleasant purchased by Alexander Stewart and renamed Mount Stewart
1782–ca. 1786	Temple of Winds built for Hon. Robert Stewart (later Marquess of Londonderry), designed by architect James Stuart
1804–25	Mount Stewart house built by second and third marquesses
1919–27	Lady Londonderry designs, lays out, and plants present gardens
1920	Gertrude Jekyll produces designs for Sunk garden
1935	Jubilee Avenue planted
1955	Gardens transferred by Lady Londonderry to National Trust

Further Reading

De Courcy, Anne, *Circe: The Life of Edith, Marchioness of Londonderry,* London: Sinclair-Stevenson, 1992
Howley, James, *The Follies and Garden Buildings of Ireland,* New Haven, Connecticut: Yale University Press, 1993
Jupp, Belinda, compiler, *Heritage Gardens Inventory, 1992,* Belfast: University of Belfast, 1992
Lacey, Stephen, *Gardens of the National Trust,* edited by Marilyn Inglis, London: The National Trust, 1996
Lamb, Keith, and Patrick Bowe, *A History of Gardening in Ireland,* Dublin: National Botanic Gardens, 1995
Malins, Edward Greenway, and Patrick Bowe, *Irish Gardens and Demesnes from 1830,* London: Barrie and Jenkins, 1980
Malins, Edward Greenway, and the Knight of Glin, *Lost Demesnes: Irish Landscape Gardening, 1660–1845,* London: Barrie and Jenkins, 1976
Nelson, E. Charles, editor, and Mary Forrest, compiler, *Trees and Shrubs Cultivated in Ireland,* Kilkenny, Ireland: Boethius Press, 1985
Northern Gardens: Gardens and Parks of Outstanding Historic Interest in Northern Ireland, Belfast: Ulster Architectural Heritage Society, 1982
Tooley, Michael J., "Gertrude Jekyll and Mount Stewart," *Moorea* 4 (1985)
Vane-Tempest-Stewart, Edith, *Mount Stewart,* Belfast: Nicholson and Bass, 1956

E. CHARLES NELSON

Mount Vernon

Mount Vernon, Virginia, United States

Location: approximately 15 miles (24 km) south of downtown Washington, District of Columbia, and 8 miles (12.8 km) south of Alexandria, Virginia, overlooking the Potomac River

Mount Vernon, site of one of the most popular historic sites in northern Virginia, was the home of George Washington, first president of the United States (1789–97). Its garden, along with that of Thomas

View of a kitchen garden in Mount Vernon, Virginia
Copyright Lawrence D. Thornton/Archive Photos

Jefferson at Monticello, is considered one of the most successful and comprehensive historic landscape gardens in Virginia. Washington intended to create a landscape garden that would use extensive acreage as part of a large, well-considered artistic plan.

The property first came into the Washington family in 1669 when John Washington, George's great-grandfather, and Nicholas Spencer applied for a patent for land along the Potomac River between Dogue Creek and Little Hunting Creek, the name by which the plantation was first known. Augustine Washington, George's father, bought the plantation from his sister (1726), built a house on half of the property in 1735, and moved his family there. In 1743 Lawrence Washington, George's half-brother, inherited Hunting Creek and renamed the estate Mount Vernon in honor of Edward Vernon, a British admiral under whom he served. After Lawrence died (1752) and the complications of his will were settled, George Washington purchased Mount Vernon from his widowed sister-in-law in 1754.

After years in his country's military service, Washington returned to Mount Vernon in 1783 to what he considered the most "pleasantly situated" estate in the United States. Until 1789, when he became president, he replaced outbuildings, reshaped the gardens, created new lawns, and realigned several roads and lanes. Washington took his basic designs from popular landscape books of the time and from the writings and drawings of prominent gardeners and architects, many of whom visited Mount Vernon, but he was helped by his practical surveyor's eye, which allowed him to bring different landscape elements together, an impressive achievement that created a feeling of concealment and privacy in a natural way, with groves cut through with twisting paths. Compared to Mount Vernon, most other known plantation gardens were more exposed.

Washington was an agricultural innovator who carefully planted seeds gathered from all over the world in his Virginia garden and who despaired when not one of his 200 seeds imported from China germinated. He considered his experiments in the "new husbandry" as much a civic duty as a personal pleasure. He foresaw with startling clarity that the United States was destined to become the "storehouse and granary for the world" and that by gardening he was leading his country to greatness. In a letter to Sir Edwin Newebham (20 April 1797), Washington described gardening as "amongst the most rational avocations," and he asked, "What can be more pleasing than to see the work of one's hands fostered by care and attention, rising to maturity in beautiful display of those advantages and ornaments, is always regaling to the eye or the palate, when the fruit is in season?"

During his lifetime Washington increased the size of his estate from 2,126 acres (860 ha) to more than 8,000 (3,239 ha) on five independently managed farms, including the Mansion House Farm with its gardens, greenhouse, lawns, and woods. Eventually Mount Vernon included a greenhouse and a gardener's house. Washington was involved with the design and management of the grounds throughout his adult life and always looked forward to his return to his plantation for the opportunity to surround himself with the natural beauty and sense of quiet and solitude that his garden offered. When he and his wife, Martha, headed home after one of their many absences, Martha wrote ahead to say she hoped the gardener would have "every thing in his garden that would be ne[ce]ssary in the House keeping way as vegetable is the best part of our living in the country."

In agriculture Washington's great love was trees, and he observed, collected, and planted hundreds of them, often searching his nearby lands for the best specimens, surrounding his mansion with them, including hundreds of fruit trees. Mount Vernon's four-acre (1.62 ha) fruit garden was laid out with berry patches and 25 varieties of apple, plum, peach, pear, and cherry trees. In the fall field orchards produced as much as 120 gallons (126 l) of hard and sweet cider and homemade brandy a day. The gardens and orchards fed Washington's family and guests, while 300 slaves grew "garden truck" to supplement their daily ration of a quart of cornmeal and five ounces of salt herring.

The upper or north garden, originally planted with fruit and nut trees, became an elaborate and colorful pleasure garden in 1785 with the addition of flower beds, which included lilies, larkspur (*Consolida*), foxglove (*Digitalis*), crown imperial (*Frittalaria imperialis*), Persian jasmine, and guelder roses. One guest described these scented bowers as "wonderful in their appearance, exquisite in their perfume and delightful to the eye." The beds have now been restored to their original size based on archaeological excavations. Two boxwood parterres have been re-created with the French fleur-de-lis that Washington admired. The greenhouse, built in 1784, housed a large number of rare and exotic plants along with orange and lemon trees, a sago palm (*Cycas*), and two oleander (*Nerium*) shrubs.

The lower or south garden, which functioned as a sort of kitchen garden for vegetables and fruits, was first enclosed in the 1760s to protect it from deer and other animals; it was reshaped in 1786 as part of Washington's new landscape plan and contained vegetables, herbs, and fruits. It was intended as a nursery for young or transplanted trees, and there was a vineyard that doubled as a small orchard. This garden was planted in squares and rectangles and was partly terraced due to the sloping ground. Weekly reports submitted by Mount Vernon's head gardener reflect the yearly cycle of gardening, beginning in late fall with "wheeling dung into the gardens," to increase the soil's fertility, to harvesting of the crops in summer and early fall. This required as many as 74 man-days of the two to four slaves who worked in the kitchen garden.

Several fruit trees are still located in the kitchen and upper gardens, but Washington's most important orchard, located between the stables and his tomb, was restored in the late 1990s from new evidence discovered through archaeological excavations and research. About a dozen trees from Washington's original plantings still survive.

Closer to the mansion, behind the spinning house, in another small enclosed area, Washington maintained a botanical garden where he could experiment with new plant varieties, sow untested seeds, and test climate and soil changes. He grew alfalfa and oats, which he considered important to increase the productivity of his fields. Today this garden is continuously reseeded to reflect Washington's experiments and his attempts to improve the plant life of Mount Vernon.

Much of Washington's thoughts about his gardens are found in his letters and diaries. For example, he betrayed a certain melancholy that his trees would outlast him, lamenting that "I have had my day." In a diary entry for 25 March 1785, Washington wrote of planting some pine trees to help enclose the "court yard": "Planted some of the largest Pine trees on the Circular bank (the mound) which is intended to inclose the court yard. Shrubberies, &ca. and Staked most of these w[hi]ch had been planted in the two Wildernesses." In 1792 gravel walks were laid through these "wildernesses" on both sides of the lawn west of the house, and in 1798, as a sort of perpetual memorial to himself, he planted boxwoods that continue to provide striplings to Mount Vernon visitors.

After Washington died in 1799, his wife lived there until her death in 1802; after that the estate passed to various family members, who found its management increasingly difficult. The family tried unsuccessfully to persuade the U.S. Government or the Commonwealth of Virginia to maintain the land in trust for the American people.

In 1853 Ann Pamela Cunningham of South Carolina, moved by her mother's description of the rundown condition of the plantation and its grounds, decided to restore it to its original splendor. She created the Mount Vernon Ladies' Association (MVLA) of the Union to preserve the estate and began efforts to raise the $200,000 to buy Mount Vernon. In 1858 the association was able to purchase the mansion, major outbuildings, and 200 acres (80.1 ha), including the gardens. Since then the MVLA has engaged in research, preservation, and routine maintenance to keep Mount Vernon open to the public. By 1988 the gardens at Mount Vernon were restored to their 18th-century simplicity and dignity favored by Washington. In the early 1990s a tree-planting project using the seeds from American holly (*Ilex opaca*) trees taken from Mount Vernon was initiated to give individuals and communities a chance to bring a part of U.S. history into their own backyards.

Synopsis

1669 John Washington, George's great-grandfather, and Nicholas Spencer apply for a patent for land along the Potomac between Dogue Creek and Little Hunting Creek

1674 Patent for land along the Potomac granted

1726 Augustine Washington, George's father, buys plantation from his sister

1735 Augustine Washington builds a house on half of the property, called Hunting Creek

1743 Lawrence Washington, George's half-brother, inherits Hunting Creek and renames it Mount Vernon

1754 George Washington purchases Mount Vernon from his widowed sister-in-law

1760s Lower garden enclosed to protect it from animals

1783 After years in his country's military service, Washington returns to Mount Vernon as a farmer and gardener

1784 Greenhouse built

1785 Washington transforms upper garden into an elaborate pleasure garden

1786 Walls around lower or south garden are extended and reshaped as part of new landscape plan for a vegetable and fruit garden

1792 Gravel walks laid through the "wildernesses" on both sides of the lawn west of the house

1798 Boxwoods planted that continue to provide saplings to visitors to plantation

1799 Upon George Washington's death, followed by that of his wife, Martha, three years later, estate passed through long line of heirs unable to maintain the buildings and grounds

1856 Ann Cunningham of South Carolina creates the Mount Vernon Ladies' Association of the Union to preserve the estate

1858 Commonwealth of Virginia grants the association a charter of incorporation, which gives them legal authority to purchase Mount Vernon for $200,000

1860 Mansion, major outbuildings, and 200 acres become property of the association

1988 Completion of project to restore gardens to their 18th-century state

Further Reading

Dalzell, Robert F., Jr., and Lee Baldwin Dalzell, *George Washington's Mount Vernon: At Home in Revolutionary America,* New York: Oxford University Press, 1998

De Forest, Elizabeth Kellam, *The Gardens and Grounds at Mount Vernon: How George Washington Planned and Planted Them,* Mount Vernon, Virginia: Mount Vernon Ladies' Association of the Union, 1982

Dubovoy, Sina, "Mount Vernon (Virginia, U.S.A.)," in *International Dictionary of Historic Places,* 5 vols., edited by Trudy Ring, Chicago: Fitzroy Dearborn, 1994–96

Filler, Martin, "George Washington's Gardens," *House and Garden* 161, no. 5 (May 1989)

Griswold, Mac K., *Washington's Gardens at Mount Vernon: Landscape of the Inner Man,* Boston: Houghton Mifflin, 1999

Johnson, Gerald W., *Mount Vernon: The Story of a Shrine,* New York: Random House, 1953

Lopez, Jane F., "Washington Weeded Here," *Saturday Evening Post* 261, no. 5 (July 1989)

Martin, Peter, *The Pleasure Gardens of Virginia: From Jamestown to Jefferson,* Princeton, New Jersey: Princeton University Press, 1991

Nevins, Deborah, "The Gardens," *The Magazine Antiques* 135, no. 2 (February 1989)

Sale, Edith Tunis, editor, *Historic Gardens of Virginia,* Richmond, Virginia: Byrd Press, 1923

Washington, George, *The Diaries of George Washington,* 6 vols., edited by Donald Jackson and Dorothy Twohig, Charlottesville: University of Virginia Press, 1976–79

MARTIN J. MANNING

Munstead Wood

Heath Lane, Busbridge, Surrey, England

Location: 1 mile (1.6 km) southeast of Godalming off B2130, approximately 30 miles (48.4 km) southwest of London

Munstead Wood, once the home and garden of the preeminent gardener and writer Gertrude Jekyll, is considered the perfect expression of the symbiotic nature of house and garden. It became a legend during Jekyll's lifetime through the many books and articles written by Jekyll as well as through personal visits paid by writers, horticulturists, garden designers, and architects from around the world. Few houses better express their owner's characters and personalities than Munstead Wood, this due to the happy combination of a skilled architect and a determined client. And perhaps no garden better exemplifies a gardener's passionate interest in using plants to create "pictures." Like most personal gardens, those at Munstead Wood evolved over time (nearly 50 years) rather than follow a prescribed plan. In most cases, the gardens were fully developed before the house was built, and the architect's ingenious design inextricably married the house and garden.

Before she moved to Munstead Wood in the mid 1890s, Gertrude Jekyll lived at Munstead House, where her knowledge of horticulture and unique approach to planting design solidified. Not all of her gardens at Munstead House were a success—her 240-foot-long flower border was far too ambitious—however, these early lessons in her career paid off at Munstead Wood. She started gardening at Munstead House in 1878, but by 1883 she had run out of room. As it turned out, she was able to acquire 15 acres (6 ha) in the immediate neighborhood. The land was mostly heath, or what she described as the "poorest possible soil." Nonetheless, she used what natural advantages she found there as inspiration, developing the former Scots pine plantation into woodland gardens and the poor arable field into her working gardens, reserving the central chestnut copse for the site of her house, which was not built until 1896.

The woodland gardens were inspired to some extent by William Robinson's pivotal book *The Wild Garden* (1870), which promoted the use of native plants in naturalistic groupings. Jekyll followed Robinson's suggestions, underplanting areas with masses of rhododendrons and giving each woodland path a specific interest, whether ferns and bracken or lilies or dog's tooth violets, to complement the selected groupings of birches, chestnuts, or oaks. Groups of silver birch, for instance, mingled with large plantings of salmon and pink rhododendrons, such as 'Bianchii', which gave way to white-flowered types in the denser woodland. She planted a so-called river of daffodils along the ancient pack-horse tracts that ran through the woodlands and established a garden devoted to native heaths. Where the lawn met the woods, she planted clumps of lilies, ferns, asters, and other shrubbery-edge plantings.

As she explains in *Colour in the Flower Garden* (1908), Jekyll established a number of ornamental gardens at Munstead Wood that were devoted to flowers of one season. These included a spring garden, a naturalistic primrose garden (filled with her famous "Munstead bunch" primrose), a June-blooming cottage garden, September-blooming aster borders, and an October-blooming Michaelmas daisy border. Perhaps her most widely acclaimed creation was the main hardy flower border. Some 200 feet (61 m) long and 14 feet (4.3 m) deep, it was backed by an 11-foot (3.3 m) high stone wall that separated it from the spring garden. The border had a complex and intricate color scheme based on harmonious color relationships. Perhaps inspired by one of J.M.W. Turner's paintings, the large central portion had fiery reds fading to orange and deep yellow. The colors continued to fade to paler yellow and pink, culminating at both ends with blues and lilacs in a ground of gray foliage.

On the south side of the house, a long terrace facing the woodlands was planted with borders of China roses (*Rosa* × *odorata* 'Pallida'), rosemary, hydrangeas, and vines, with a broad flight of steps leading to the lawn. On the north side, a paved court was decorated with pots of hostas, ferns, and lilies, with a fragrant *Clematis montana* on the wall and a square tank, the only formal water feature in the garden, linked up with established shrub borders.

Approximately two acres (.8 ha) were given over to working gardens, including a kitchen garden, nursery, and a large orchard. Numerous cottage-style borders were filled with China asters, hollyhocks, delphiniums, roses, irises, and lupines, and a variety of plants with gray foliage. The large nursery supplied plants for Jekyll's garden design commissions, while the kitchen garden kept the house supplied with fruits and vegetables.

In Edwin Lutyens, Gertrude Jekyll found an architect who shared her vernacular sensibilities for home building and could create a house worthy of her gardens. Her love of simple materials and excellence in craftsmanship extended to the planning and building of all aspects of Munstead Wood, not only the house. Before settling on a design for the house, which Lutyens eventually built in 1896, he built two other cottages on the site: the

Munstead Wood, Surrey, England
Courtesy of Gertrude Jekyll Collection, Environmental Design Archives, University of California, Berkeley

gardener's cottage and the Hut, where Gertrude Jekyll lived for two years while the main house was being built. All three buildings were steeped in the regional Surrey vocabulary, using half-timbering, deeply hipped roofs, and plastered walls. Gertrude Jekyll's esteem for the Arts and Crafts movement, seen in her study of numerous crafts, extended to the interior layout and furnishing of her house as well as to the building craftsmanship.

Although Lutyens had little to do with the design of the gardens at Munstead Wood, the close compatibility of Lutyens's and Jekyll's ideas led to a fruitful design partnership that resulted in some of the most renowned gardens of the early 20th century, including Orchards, Deanery Garden, Hestercombe, and Folly Farm. These gardens were based, in part, on concepts that had been conceived at Munstead Wood.

Even though the character of Munstead Wood was lost after Jekyll's death in 1932, her many books, articles, and extensive photographic records serve to keep its significance alive today. Munstead Wood went out of family hands in 1948, and is occasionally open to the public. In recent years parts of the garden have been replanted, using the vast store of information available about the site. A field survey carried out under the aegis of the Royal Commission on Historical Monuments of England was initiated in 1991 after storm damage destroyed many historic trees on the property. Research findings uncovered much technical information that was invaluable to the recent restoration.

Synopsis

1883	15-acre (6-ha) tract of land acquired by Gertrude Jekyll, who begins development of woodland gardens
1887	*Chamaecyparis lawsoniana* hedge installed to partially enclose large, triangular kitchen garden
1889	Edwin Lutyens, future architect of Munstead Wood, meets Gertrude Jekyll
early 1890s	Garden walls built; spring garden, ornamental flower borders, kitchen gardens, and garden paths laid out
1892–93	Lutyens prepares site plan and initial sketches for Hut, gardener's cottage, and main house
1894	Construction of the Hut (where Gertrude Jekyll lives until main house is built) and gardener's cottage
1895	Construction of thunderhouse in kitchen garden
1896	Construction of main house
1897	Gertrude Jekyll moves into new house
1909	Stables and loft buildings renovated by Lutyens
1932	Death of Gertrude Jekyll at Munstead Wood
1948	Sale of house, auction of household contents; property subsequently split into five divisions
1991	Survey of property by Royal Commission on Historical Monuments of England
1993	Partial restoration of gardens based on vintage photographs, descriptions, and survey findings

Further Reading

Jekyll, Gertrude, *Home and Garden: Notes and Thoughts, Practical and Critical, of a Worker in Both,* London: Longmans Green, 1900; reprint, Woodbridge, Suffolk: Antique Collectors' Club, 1982

Jekyll, Gertrude, *Colour in the Flower Garden,* London: Country Life, 1908; reprint, edited by Graham Stuart Thomas, Portland, Oregon: Sagapress/Timber Press, 1995

Jekyll, Gertrude, and Lawrence Weaver, "A Garden in West Surrey," in *Gardens for Small Country Houses,* London: Country Life, and New York: Scribner, 1912; revised as *Arts and Crafts Gardens: Gardens for Small Country Houses,* Woodbridge, Suffolk: Garden Art Press, 1997

King, Stephen, "Restoring Miss Jekyll," *Garden Design* 16, no. 4 (June–July 1997)

"Munstead Wood, Godalming, the Residence of Miss Jekyll," in *Gardens, Old and New: The Country House and Its Garden Environment,* vol. 2, edited by John Leyland, London: Country Life, and New York: Scribner, 1903

"Munstead Wood, Surrey, Client Report," London: Royal Commission on the Historical Monuments of England, 1994

Tankard, Judith B., "The Garden before Munstead Wood," *Hortus* 20 (1991)

Tankard, Judith B., "Miss Jekyll's True Colours (Autochrome Photographs of Munstead Wood)," *Country Life* (15 May 1997)

Tankard, Judith B., and Martin A. Wood, *Gertrude Jekyll at Munstead Wood,* Stroud, Gloucestershire: Sutton, and Sagaponack, New York: Sagapress, 1996

Tankard, Judith B., and Michael R. Van Valkenburgh, *Gertrude Jekyll: A Vision of Garden and Wood,* New York: Sagapress, and London: Murray, 1989

Tipping, H. Avray, "Munstead Wood," in *English Gardens,* London: Country Life, and New York: Scribner, 1925

Weaver, Lawrence, *Houses and Gardens by E.L. Lutyens,* London: Country Life, 1913; New York: Scribner, 1914; reprint, Woodbridge, Suffolk: Antique Collectors' Club, 1985

Wood, Martin A., "Gertrude Jekyll's Munstead Wood," in *Gertrude Jekyll: Essays on the Life of a Working Amateur,* edited by Michael Tooley and Primrose Arnander, Witton-le-Wear, Durham: Michaelmas Books, 1995

JUDITH B. TANKARD

Muso Soseki. *See* Kokushi (Muso Soseki)

Music in the Garden

In 1776 the English music historian John Hawkins reported from London that "music seemed to be essential" in the "gardens of the inn of court, the park." He called special attention to the earl of Ranelagh, who "had erected a spacious building of timber, of a circular form, and within it an organ, and an orchestra capable of holding a numerous band of performers" in his garden. That music was not only "essential" here, and that special edifices for music making and dancing were erected in gardens, is an aspect of horticulture that can be traced back to antiquity. The Hellenistic-Roman ornamental garden (*xystus*), for example, had open bowers (*stibadium*) in which in the first century B.C., according to Pliny the Younger, freemen and slaves made music and danced. Since then, the garden, in the west as well as in China, India, and the Near East, has not only been a styled space that can be visually experienced but also a *hortus musicus,* a specific area acoustically and physically animated by rhythms and sounds.

In the Middle Ages conviviality of all sorts was enjoyed during the summer in the orchards, palisade gardens, rose gardens, and labyrinths. Courtly poetry and miniature paintings document the custom of singing and playing instruments on the grassy bank, as well as round and pair dances in the open meadow, in tents, or in open bowers. A statute of the town of Wismar, Mecklenburg, from 1343 states that town minstrels were to play for the citizens in the public rose garden (*Roseto*) in the afternoon on Sundays and holidays. By the end of the 14th century, the city of Feldkirch in Vorarlberg, Austria, had a public dance hall "im Bomgarten" (in the orchard). The local women are recorded as dancing in the orchard of the Silesian monastery Heinrichau on feast days.

During the 16th century the number of pleasure gardens (*viridantiae*), also called dance gardens, grew in Italy, France, and Germany. Dancers would circle around fountains or individual trees. Grottoes were also built in these gardens for their echo effects, and sculptures were installed of figures with musical instruments as attributes (e.g., Orpheus and Apollo). The Renaissance garden, in which theater could also be performed, was, as an open-air banqueting hall, filled with life. Since that time horticulture has been the art in which the other arts have harmoniously come together to form the *gardino harmonico.* After the Reformation this spirited activity was officially forbidden in some parts of Europe, for example, in 1587 in the Swiss canton of Bern.

In Islamic palaces from the early to the modern period, music, like poetry, was a popular courtly entertainment, and concerts were often staged in garden pavilions, in which the pleasing sounds of fountains and singing birds compounded the pleasure of hearing the lute, pipes, tambourine, and the human voice.

In the 17th and early 18th centuries the full range of courtly pomp manifested itself in the presentation of music in the garden. Gallant *concerts champêtres* (music in the landscape) were organized, and figure dances such as the minuet were performed in serpentine lines that garden designers could also make visible in the layout of paths and plantings. Gardeners sang special "gardeners' tunes" (*giardiniero*) while working. Even waterworks were planned as musical metaphors, for example, in Vienna, "where one teaches water to dance,/And hinders it from flowing through marble basins" (Aloys Blumauer, 1784). An excellent example of the use of musical metaphors is the park of the pleasure palace Hellbrunn, near Salzburg. It contains a hedge theater (1612–19), sculptures whose themes were taken from early Italian opera, an Orpheus grotto, a bird-song grotto (*Vogelsang grotte*), *The Sound of Music* pavilion, and a *hydraulos* (hydraulic organ), hence all facets of a baroque autocratic play world. Moreover, the image of the garden was transformed in poetry and music as an absolute metaphor. Numerous collections of vocal works and dances appeared with titles such as *Musikalischer Lustgarten* (1691; Musical Pleasure Garden), *Hortus Musicus* (1687; Garden of Music), *Pratum spirituale* (1620; Spiritual Meadow), and *Venus-Gärtlein* (1656; The Garden of Venus). Music houses were constructed for performances, for example, in 1683 in Sadler Garden at Islington. Europe's first freestanding concert hall was built in the Bagno of Steinfurt, Westphalia, in 1770.

After 1750, besides the sounds of natural horns and glass harmonicas, Aeolian harps hung from trees and in grottoes marked the tonal aura, above all, of the English gardens. Around 1800 singing folk or other popular songs in the garden to the accompaniment of a harp or guitar became a favored pastime. Wind ensembles, too, the *Hautboistencorps* or *Harmoniemusiken* (oboe bands), found especially in gardens and parks the desired resonance as a part of "pleasure gardening." Through the vogue for chinoiserie, the ambience was enriched with bell chimes. The use of hunting horns was intended to bring the beauty of the landscape closer to the soul by means of their naturelike sound. Staged shepherds' idylls and singspiel (for example, Johann Wolfgang von Goethe's 1782 forest and aquatic drama *Die Fischerin* (The Fisherwoman) in the park of Tiefurt Castle near Weimar) were performed by preference in the open air in Weimar, Wörlitz, and other places. In the gardens of inns that had dance halls or were equipped with "bandstands," garden or coffee concerts and *concerts d'été* (summer concerts) were increasingly offered for paying audiences. While diverse listeners assembled in the pleasure gardens of the large cities, players of light music served a distinguished audience in the parks and avenues of the spas, in so-called spa concerts; only the exclusive court society was admitted to the concert hall built in 1782 by Czarina Catherine II in the park of Tsarskoye Selo.

In the 19th and 20th centuries musical entertainments continued to be offered to the general public. In London's Surrey Gardens these were even expanded around 1840 to veritable "Concerts Monstres" with up to 1,000 participants. The domestic ideology, on the other hand, encouraged the retreat of the middle classes into the private sphere with tranquil music on the garden bench, for example, with Antonin Dvorák's "Prípoved lásky" (op. 27, no. 3; "Love Song in the Garden"). (See Plate 25.)

Further Reading

Albert, Heinrich, *Musicalische Kürbs-Hütte,* edited by Joseph M. Müller-Blattau, Kassel, Germany: Bärenreiter, 1932

Brown, Andrew M.C., *The Aeolian Harp in European Literature, 1591–1892,* Cambridge: Bois de Boulogne, 1970

Busch-Salmen, Gabriele, Walter Salmen, and Christoph Michel, *Der Weimarer Musenhof,* Stuttgart, Germany: Metzler, 1998

Coeyman, Barbara, "Social Dance in the 1668 *Feste de Versailles:* Architecture and Performance Context," *Early Music* 26, no. 2 (1998)

Defant, Christine, "Johann Adam Reinckens 'Hortus Musicus': Versuch einer Deutung als Metapher für die hochbarocke Musikauffassung in Deutschland," *Die Musikforschung* 42 (1989)

Fehrle-Burger, Lili, *Die Welt der Oper in den Schlossgärten von Heidelberg und Schwetzingen,* Karlsruhe, Germany: Braun, 1977

Hennebo, Dieter, *Gärten des Mittelalters,* Munich: Artemis Verlag, 1987

Jeans, Susi, "Water Organs," in *Music, Libraries, and Instruments,* London and New York: Hinrichsen, 1961

Meyer, Rudolf, *Hecken- und Gartentheater in Deutschland im XVII. und XVIII. Jahrhundert,* Emsdetten, Germany: Lechte, 1934

Morrow, Mary Sue, *Concert Life in Haydn's Vienna,* Stuyvesant, New York: Pendragon, 1989

Paradisus Musicus: Muziek en samenleving in Rubens' tijd (exhib. cat.), Antwerp: Stadt Antwerpen, 1977

Salmen, Walter, *Haus- und Kammermusik,* Leipzig: Deutscher Verlag für Musik, 1969

Salmen, Walter, *Das Konzert,* Munich: Beck, 1988

Salmen, Walter, "Reichardts Garten in Halle-Giebichenstein," *Die Gartenkunst* 6 (1994)

Salmen, Walter, "Chinoiserie in der Musik- und Tanzgeschichte bis 1800," in *Festschrift Christoph-Hellmut Mahling zum 65. Geburtstag,* edited by Axel Beer, Kristina Pfarr, and Wolfgang Ruf, Tutzing, Germany: Schneider, 1997

Sands, Mollie, "Music of the 18th-Century Pleasure Gardens," *The Monthly Musical Record* 64 (1939)

Shenstone, William, "Unconnected Thoughts on Gardening," in *The Works in Verse and Prose,* by Shenstone, vol. 2, edited by Robert Dodsley, London, 1764; 2nd edition, London, 1765; reprint, London: Hughs, 1968

Southgate, T., "Music at the Public Gardens of the 18th Century," *Proceedings of the Royal Music Association* 38 (1911/12)

WALTER SALMEN

N

National Botanic Gardens Glasnevin. *See* Glasnevin, National Botanic Gardens

National Trust Gardens

Now one of the great private institutions of England and Wales, the National Trust was founded in 1895 as a result of the concerns about the way the English countryside was changing. Three individuals determined to form an association of private citizens who would act for the entire nation to acquire and manage land and buildings worthy of preservation. All three had a strongly developed sense of philanthropy. They were Octavia Hill, a Christian socialist and champion of the London poor, Sir Robert Hunter, a lawyer, chief solicitor to the Post Office, who was active in the preservation of historic rights of way, commons, and countryside access, and H.D. Rawnsley, canon of Carlisle Cathedral, whose chief concern had been protection of the Lake District. Hill's contribution had been particularly practical, purchasing run-down London tenements, improving them, providing gardens, and letting them at fair rents. All three were already fighting the profit-led expansion of towns and industry and the enclosure of public land. Hill and Hunter had worked together in the Commons Preservation Society beginning in the 1860s.

The 19th century had been one of an explosion of population, vast increases in the size of cities, uncontrolled development, and encroachment on the countryside. The three founders of the National Trust were representative of many who wished to see the countryside protected and some of its historic treasures saved for the future. At the time a number of organizations already existed that were devoted to individual causes, and some questioned whether this new organization would survive, let alone achieve its objectives. However, even while Hunter was writing the statutes of the Trust, its first property had already been pledged. In 1894 Mrs. Talbot, a landowner in West Wales, had a small area of coastal land near the town of Barmouth for which she had a great fondness. Her motivation in making the gift was, she said, to put it into the custody of some society "that will never vulgarise it or prevent wild nature from having its own way." Dinas Oleu, or the Fortress of Light, a five-acre (2 ha) tract of cliff top, is still recorded in the National Trust handbook. Since that first gift the Trust has amassed a huge estate comprising 673,740 acres (272,700 ha) of countryside, as well as over 200 houses and gardens and 49 industrial monuments. It has been described as the largest private landowner anywhere in the world. Included in the landownership is 600 miles (372 km) of important coastline. For many of its supporters the most appreciated part of the Trust's estate is the collection of historic houses and gardens; the great extent of its countryside ownership is less generally recognized. While the total preservation of areas such as Dinas Oleu is an accepted policy, the same is not always the case with domestic properties.

The houses acquired at the beginning were of historic interest rather than being the reminders of gracious living more commonly associated in the present day with the National Trust. The first, in 1896, was a dilapidated 14th-century half-timbered clergy house at Alfriston in Sussex, bought for the sum of ten pounds. The second, bought four years later, was another early building, at Long Crendon in Buckinghamshire, a courthouse that had been in use from the 15th to the 19th century. The purchase of Barras Head in Cornwall from the earl of Wharncliffe was made in the same year as the clergy house. This raised questions about the long-term protection of properties; the Trust was after all young and its future not assured.

An Act of Parliament drafted for the National Trust in 1907 by Hunter addressed this issue and placed the Trust in a unique position by allowing it to declare its properties "inalienable"; that is, they cannot be mortgaged or sold, and no one can take them from the Trust. This provided the protection sought by many of the donors. The Act enabled the Trust to undertake certain operations and activities but placed on it a prohibition on fencing or charging admission to common land. Another important milestone came almost 30 years later with the development of what came to be known as the Country House Scheme. In the 1930s many landowners were faced with increasing difficulties in managing estates as well as with crippling death duties. The marquess of Lothian inherited his estates in 1930. In 1934 he proposed that the Trust work out a scheme with the government so that, rather than forcing estates to be split up and destroyed as a consequence of death duties, estates could be taken over, together with some endowment. Houses could already be left to the nation in lieu of death duties, but the endowment necessary to support the estate could not.

By Lord Lothian's scheme properties could be gifted to the Trust with sufficient funds for their upkeep, public access ensured, and the owner or the family could continue to live there as tenants. The Trust had in principle always believed that their properties should not just be museums but lived-in properties. Lothian left Blickling Hall in Norfolk to the Trust in 1940, together with 4,600 acres (1,862 ha). At about the same time the important 13,000-acre (32,120-ha) estate of the Trevelyan family of Wallington Hall in Northumberland was left to the Trust with similar tenancy arrangements. These two legacies formed the basis of the Trust's future operations and were followed by many others, which have served the nation well as far as the preservation of its heritage is concerned. These arrangements were made possible as a result of an Act of Parliament of 1937 drafted by the National Trust with the agreement of the inland Revenue and the Treasury.

In its first ten years the National Trust attracted 500 members; by 1997 the membership had grown to over 250,000, and during 1996, the year after the centenary, more than 11.5 million visits were paid to the 263 properties for which entry charges are made. This is some measure of the service to the nation the Trust performs.

Further Reading

Greeves, Lydia, and Michael Trinick, *The National Trust Guide: A Complete Introduction to the Buildings, Gardens, Coast, and Country Owned by the National Trust,* revised edition, London: National Trust, 1990

The National Trust Handbook for Members and Visitors (annual; 1987–)

Newby, Howard, editor, *The National Trust: The Next Hundred Years,* London: National Trust, 1995

Thomas, Graham Stuart, *Gardens of the National Trust,* London: The National Trust, 1979

Waterson, Merlin, *The National Trust: The First Hundred Years,* London: BBC Books, 1994

Weideger, Paula, *Gilding the Acorn: Behind the Façade of the National Trust,* New York: Simon and Schuster, 1994

Williams-Ellis, Clough, *On Trust for the Nation,* London: Elek, 1947

M.F. DOWNING

Natural Garden (Wild Garden)

The creation of naturalistic or ecologically inspired gardens is one of the major facets of contemporary gardening. The burgeoning of interest in natural gardening has been very much a 20th-century phenomenon, although a celebration of the natural landscape and wild plants in cultivated gardens has had prominence to a greater or lesser extent in previous centuries. One of the fascinating aspects of the current trend is the wide range of approaches that is encompassed under the general heading of wild or natural gardens.

One of the turning points that led to the current approach to natural gardening was a change in scale and focus in garden fashion during the later stages of the 18th-century English landscape movement. Although the English landscape school, typified by Lancelot "Capability" Brown, is associated with "naturalistic" gardens, these were large-scale set-piece arrangements using the building blocks of landform, woodlands, and water, and they were very much designed to be looked at rather than intimately experienced. The natural content itself was sanitized: smooth, rounded, and nonthreatening, with none of the dynamism and unpredictability of real nature. As a reaction to this, the proponents of the Picturesque style celebrated the roughness and excitement of nature and in many ways focused attention on the small-scale detail and intimate associations of natural elements and plants. It is this view of nature that has generally captivated those involved in natural gardening ever since, on both sides of the Atlantic.

The great exponent of a more relaxed approach to garden planting in the late 19th and early 20th centuries was William Robinson, who through his books *The Wild Garden* (1870) and *The English Flower Garden* (1883), as well as many other publications, vigorously promoted the cultivation of hardy plants in natural situations, such as meadows, woodland copses, and wetlands, where they could spread and colonize. His inspiration for doing so was to emulate the dramatic and beautiful effects he had observed in vegetation in the wild. Robinson's philosophy was to thoroughly understand the environmental conditions of a site or part of a garden and to choose plants suited to those conditions that would flourish there with minimal maintenance, and which would create beautiful natural associations. This approach still captures the essence of the natural garden.

A number of contemporary strands in natural, wild, or ecological gardens can be identified. It is important to distinguish between the *naturalistic* garden, where the appearance of nature is given, and the purely *native* garden, in which an attempt is made to reproduce plant communities from the wild. The native plant garden is perhaps the purest form of natural gardening. The use of only native plants, in both naturalistic and more contrived settings, is passionately put forward by its followers. An early and influential advocate was the U.S. landscape designer Jens Jensen, who aimed to reflect the character of the American Midwest landscape and vegetation in the gardens and parks within which he worked in the early 20th century. The native plant movement is still particularly strong in the United States and in Australia. In both these instances a primary motivation is to exploit local, regional, and national diversity in plant material and design inspiration as a counter to the predominant standard European style. A further important consideration is the preservation or conservation in a garden setting of plants or habitats that are threatened in the wild.

The native-plant-only enthusiasts are, nonetheless, a minority. Most natural gardeners reason that, because the garden itself is an artificial environment, the inclusion of nonnative species does not hinder the achievement of a naturalistic appearance and can in fact enhance visual and wildlife value. For those who advocate wildlife gardening, a natural garden includes the totality of life, not just the plants. Plants are chosen for their potential food and shelter value to birds, mammals, and invertebrates, and this may involve a cosmopolitan mix of native and exotic plant species.

The Robinsonian tradition continues in the so-called new-wave perennial gardening that has been strongly influenced by developments in Germany and the Netherlands. This movement is a major force in contemporary gardening. Plant selection is based on both ecological requirements and aesthetic considerations, often resulting in very beautiful and visually striking garden pictures. The design approach to the use of plants builds on the painterly associations of color, form, and texture of the Gertrude Jekyll school, but it also gives equal weight to the forms, rhythms, and textures of nature.

The natural garden is associated with a naturelike appearance, but many natural gardeners are equally concerned with natural processes and environmental sustainability. A natural garden may therefore contain high levels of recycling of organic matter and water and aim to reduce or eliminate the use of inorganic fertilizers, herbicides, and pesticides.

Further Reading

Druse, Kenneth, *The Natural Habitat Garden,* New York: Clarkson Potter, 1994

Hansen, Richard, and Friedrich Stahl, *Die Stauden und ihre Lebensbereiche in Gärten und Grünanlagen,* Stuttgart, Germany: Ulmer, 1981; as *Perennials and Their Garden Habitats,* translated by Richard Ward, Cambridge and New York: Cambridge University Press, and Portland, Oregon: Timber Press, 1993

Jensen, Jens, *Siftings,* Chicago: Seymour, 1939; reprint, Baltimore, Maryland: Johns Hopkins University Press, 1990

Robinson, William, *The Wild Garden,* London, 1870; 7th edition, 1929; reprint of 5th edition (1895), Portland, Oregon: Sagapress/Timber Press, 1994

NIGEL DUNNETT

Neoclassicism

The term *classical* is related to the so-called classic period of ancient Greek culture, but it also means creations influenced by the spirit of antiquity or tradition in any century. Since the rediscovery of the architectural rules of Vitruvius in the Renaissance, architecture was based on Vitruvius through the baroque period. The castles of Versailles and Blenheim are, in some sense, classically intended, even though they originated from baroque style.

Strictly speaking neoclassical covers the style of architecture that replaced the baroque style about 1750 and prevailed to about 1850. Neoclassical architecture is characterized by straight, restful forms and reduced ornaments derived from the ancients only. The developments leading to the Renaissance, which freed the arts from the Gothic style, and led to Palladianism, were repeated in a similar way with the rise of neoclassicism and neo-Palladianism.

The rise of neoclassicism in the 18th century is closely connected to the rise of the landscape garden. Many neo-Palladian buildings, such as the famous examples at Stourhead, Claremont, Prior Park, and Wörlitz, are situated in landscape parks very modern in their times. Therefore, it can be supposed that landscape gardens are neoclassical, too, despite their informal (i.e., not straight-lined) appearance. This may be well argued in some cases, if classical thoughts are readable in an iconographic program expressed in statuary, follies, or inscriptions. Classic temples, rotundas, ruins, urns, and Palladian bridges are frequent elements of landscape gardens. Very little was known about the true appearance of original ancient gardens, and this gave a vast scope for interpretation. Indeed, in designing their parks the first promoters of the English landscape garden had kept in mind classical landscapes from Italy, as depicted in paintings in their collections. The first appearances of the English landscape garden, at least, represented for example by William Kent, were dominated by classical themes. Some authors term this garden type as the *classical landscape garden.*

To correlate one particular category of gardens with the term *neoclassical* is not without problems, however. The geometric garden style must also be regarded under the heading of classicism. The period of André Le Nôtre's geometrical garden has been described as classic garden style because it was the great age of domination of the French style in Europe. This garden style, however, must not be misinterpreted as neoclassical, and it would better termed *baroque garden style.*

The German art historian Iris Lauterbach (1990) has drawn attention to a particular classic garden style in France at the end of the Ancien Régime. Here parallel phenomena between architecture and gardens can be usefully compared. English landscape gardens were imitated in France after 1764, but at the same time geometric style was preserved and partly developed as well. The classical movement in France between 1750 and 1775 is characterized by *la modeste simplicité,* regarded as more natural than the forgoing, rococo style. Louis XV and his architects Jean-François Blondel and Jacques-Anges Gabriel were responsible for adherence to what was called French national style.

From 1771 onward the advantages and disadvantages of geometric gardens were intensively discussed in France. Not all authors advocated the landscape garden, and the poet Jaques Delille wrote in his famous poem *Les Jardins* (1781) "Je ne décide point entre Kent et Le Nôtre" (I can't decide between Kent and Le Nôtre). Even until 1789, several mostly unexecuted designs made use of the geometric style for urban gardens, palace gardens, and public gardens, sometimes mixed with irregular parts. Some designers related directly to older patterns contriving parterre and labyrinth features as used in the Renaissance. Italian terraces, stairs, and hippodromes had a great influence on the French architects of the revolution on their grand tours, and their designs tried to imitate ancient garden traces. Such gardens may be justifiably called neoclassical.

Similar neoclassical gardens sometimes were found in other countries. A synoptic overview of neoclassical gardens has never been published, so some samples are given here.

The Pensil Garden at Queluz, created by the French architect Jean-Baptiste Robillon for Dom Pedro of Portugal in 1758–60 may be called an extraordinary example of classical garden layout preserved in a perfect manner today. Prince Henry of Prussia created a classical island parterre at Rheinsberg near Berlin in 1762. The grass parterre is ornamented with statues and two great flower baskets. In Sweden, the architect Fredrik Magnus Piper (1746–1824), having visited Italy and England, drew plans of very imposing geometrical gardens from 1780 onward.

In Spain, the architect Juan de Villanueva designed in 1771–72 the charming gardens of Casita del Infante and Casita del Principe near El Escorial for the sons of King Charles III. Both terraced gardens, being completely symmetrically arranged, are in perfect unity with the buildings. In Padova, the Prato della Valle was designed in 1775. It is a large urban square, dominated by an elliptic channel bordered with statues of Paduan celebrities, that enclosed an island crossed by star-ways and originally ornamented by four *tempiettos.* The public park of Villa Giulia, Palermo, was also designed in the 1770s; its star-shaped outlines and hedged quarters are closely related to Renaissance models. Czar Paul I created in the 1780s and 90s several classical gardens within his landscape parks at Pavlovsk and Gatchina near St. Petersburg. The architects were Charles Cameron and Vincenzo Brenna. The geometrical Private Garden at Pavlovsk was copied by the Russian princess Maria Pavlovna in Belvedere at Weimar after 1806.

An example for Colonial neoclassicism can be found in what is now the Huguenots Museum at Franschoek near Cape Town, built by Louis Michel Thiebault in 1791. Two pavilions behind the main building are connected by a colonnade, surmounted by imposing mountains.

During and after the French Revolution, classical garden design continued. It diminished as neo-Gothic and other eclectic styles emerged during the 19th century, but it survived in the Italianate style in the midcentury.

In 1805 the Italian architect Antonio Basoli laid out a grand design for Napoléon's park at Zola Predosa near Bologna. It was perfectly geometrical, but it was never completed. The castle garden in Stuttgart was designed by the architect Nikolaus Friedrich von Thouret with a central axis and several tree-lined rondels in 1806. In front of the castle he planned a cascade with an elliptical basin. The spaces outside the geometrical pattern were laid out in the landscape style.

The neoclassical Capitol in Washington has long served as a model for public buildings. Similar public buildings were designed in the same style of simple grandeur in other countries, such as the Lustgarten at the Old Museum by Schinkel in Berlin (1834) or the Königsplatz by Klenze in Munich.

About 1900 some architects, such as U.S. landscape architect Charles Platt and German architect Peter Behrens, newly invented classicism. Platt preferred to copy Italian gardens; Behrens designed gardens adapted to classical villas. The great plan for Chicago by Daniel M. Burnham and Edward H. Bennett from 1909 shows a similar monumental, axial design of the park system. This style was vastly expanded by the totalitarian regimes of Hitler, Stalin, Franco and others. Public buildings have always demanded a monumental, classic garden design for their surroundings. On the northern side of the royal palace in Madrid, for example, a neoclassical terrace garden was created in 1934–49.

Further Reading

Lauterbach, Iris, *Der französische Garten am Ende des Ancien Régime,* Worms, Germany: Werner, 1987

Mosser, Monique, and Georges Teyssot, editors, *L'architettura dei giardini d'Occidente,* Milan: Electa, 1990; as *The Architecture of Western Gardens,* Cambridge, Massachusetts: MIT Press, 1991; as *The History of Garden Design,* London: Thames and Hudson, 1991

CLEMENS ALEXANDER WIMMER

Nesfield, William Andrews 1794–1881

English Painter and Landscape Gardener

Before turning to landscape gardening, Willaim Nesfield began his professional life as a soldier and then as a watercolor painter, experiences that were important influences on his later career. Nesfield's training at the Royal Military Academy, Woolwich from 1809 to 1812 included lessons in architecture and perspective taught by Thomas Paul Sandby, son of the famous watercolorist Paul Sandby; and his talent for painting showed itself while he served in the army in Spain and Canada. On leaving the military he decided to pursue a career as a painter specializing in landscapes, and between 1823 and 1852 he exhibited regularly at the Old Watercolour Society. He was ultimately forced to resign from the society due to pressure from his landscape practice.

During the 1820s and 1830s Nesfield traveled throughout the British Isles painting and sketching. His contemporaries included David Cox (1753–1859), John Varley (1778–1842), Clarkson Stanfield (1793–1867), and James Duffied Harding (1797–1863). He turned to landscape gardening in the 1830s, initially working alongside his brother-in-law, the architect Anthony Salvin (1799–1881).

Nesfield's earliest commission appears to have come in the mid-1830s at Methley Hall, West Yorkshire, and a few years later his design for the garden at his London home in Fortis Green, Muswell Hill was featured in John Claudius Loudon's *The Gardener's Magazine* in February 1840. Nesfield's reputation was such that Loudon declared that his "opinion is now sought for by gentlemen of taste in every part of the country." Both of these gardens display Nesfield's predilection for formal parterres and flower beds, which were to become his hallmark.

Nesfield is principally remembered for these elaborate, geometrical parterre designs comprising scrolls, volutes, crosses, scallops, and other shapes that were delineated with colored gravels, low box hedges, grass, small shrubs, architectural features, and a variety of summer and winter plantings. These kinds of elements are seen in his work at Stoke Edith, Herefordshire; Crewe Hall, Cheshire; Eaton Hall, Cheshire; and Oxenhoath, Kent. However, his practice was considerably varied, and in addition to creating pleasure gardens, rosaria, and arboreta, he was called upon to install fountains and create waterways, as at Castle Howard, North Yorkshire; Witley Court, Worcestershire; and Holkham Hall, Norfolk. He designed entranceways and approaches to houses, as at Arley Hall, Cheshire; and screened railways from properties, as at Crewe Hall, Staffordshire; Greenwich Park; and Barham Court, Kent. In other commissions, Nesfield supervised new tree plantations and thinned existing woodlands, recommended suitable flowers, shrubs, and trees, as well as numerous other related operations, such as moving individual shrubs and statues and designing architectural and sculptural features.

Nesfield became the premier landscape gardener of early Victorian England and was the first practitioner to avail himself of the advantages of modern railway transportation. It was his custom to travel the country tirelessly, carrying with him two essential volumes: a copy of Bradshaw's railway timetables and an anthology of parterre designs, which he would show to prospective clients. Copied from 17th century French Baroque parterres, these designs were self-consciously historical. Nesfield was thus a man who mixed comfortably with the old and the modern.

Among his unpublished writings and correspondence, he frequently mentioned adhering to the teachings of the "Old Masters" of gardening. By these he meant such French Baroque landscape architects as André Le Nôtre (1613–1700), André Mollet (died ca. 1665), and Jacques Boyceau (died ca. 1633), whose designs he had copied into his anthology. English influences from the same period included Sir Thomas Hanmer (1677–1746), John Evelyn (1620–1706), the designs of George London (1650–1714) and Henry Wise (1653–1738), and the bird's-eye views of Leonard Knyff (1650–1721) and Jan Kip (1653–1722). Nesfield was outspoken in his contempt for the garden designs of William Kent (1684–1748) and Lancelot "Capability" Brown (1715–1783), but among the more recent landscape gardeners and writers of which he approved were William Gilpin (1762–1843), Humphry Repton (1752–1818), Loudon (1783–1843), and, most importantly, Uvedale Price (1747–1829), whose writings on the Picturesque underpinned Nesfield's own views on the subject.

Years of practice as a landscape painter also influenced Nesfield's principles of garden design. In a letter of 2 February 1846 to Sir William Hooker at the Royal Botanic Gardens, Kew, he declared landscape gardening to be "the Art of painting with Nature's materials." His usual practice when beginning a project was to make a report on the existing property, noting its defects and giving a series of general recommendations which could embrace gardens, woodlands, the wider landscape, and even the architecture of the house in question. These reports would subsequently be supplemented with illustrated designs and proposals of a more specific nature. In the absence of fuller documentation, it is not always clear to what extent, if any, some or all of these recommendations were implemented, especially at properties which no longer exist.

Contemporary opinion was initially full of approval for Nesfield's designs. His parterre at Worsley Hall, Lancashire was described as "in the most perfect unison with the mansion" in an 1846 issue of *The Gardener's Chronicle*; his proposals for Buckingham Palace were also praised in the same journal. In 1860 Nesfield's designs for the Royal Horticultural Society's garden in Kensington were admired and he was referred to as "the first landscape gardener of the day" in *The Florist*, and illustrations of a number of his parterres appeared in E. Adveno Brooke's *The Gardens of England* (1857). There were dissenting voices, however, especially among gardeners who were opposed to his complicated flower schemes. In 1852 his flower beds at Eaton Hall, Cheshire were dismissed as "useless" and "ridiculous" in *The Cottage Gardener.* Nesfield's popularity declined as fashion turned away from elaborate parterre designs and polychrome effects toward more horticultural arrangements, a move led by William Robinson (1838–1935). Hugely expensive to maintain, many of his parterres also began to be simplified or erased by the end of the 19th century, and very few survive today.

In later years Nesfield was assisted by his two sons: William Eden Nesfield (1835–1888), who was better known as an architect and partner of Richard Norman Shaw (1831–1912), and Markham Nesfield, who attracted attention with his work on the Italian Gardens in Regent's Park, London, before his untimely death in 1874.

See also Duncombe Park

Biography

Born near Chester-le-Street, Durham, England, 19 February 1794. Trained at Royal Military Academy, Woolwich, including lessons on architecture and perspective taught by Thomas Paul Sandby (son of Paul Sandby), 1809–12; gazetted as 2nd Lieutenant in 95th Rifle Regiment, 1812; witnessed action in Wellington's Peninsular campaign in 1813 and subsequently in Canada during War of 1812; on leaving army pursued career as watercolor painter, touring the Continent,

England, Wales, and Scotland; following his marriage in 1833, began 40-year career as professional landscape gardener, during which he was consulted at more than 200 sites in British Isles; majority of clients owners of country houses, but worked at a number of public parks and gardens, including Royal Botanical Gardens, Kew, and Regent's Park, London; assisted by sons, William Eden and Markham, who became well-known in their own right (William as an architect and Markham for his work on the Italian Gardens in Regent's Park). Died in Regent's Park, London, 1881.

Selected Designs

mid 1830s	Methley Hall, West Yorkshire, England
late 1830s	Nesfield's London home, Fortis Green, Muswell Hill, north London, England
1840–60	Crewe Hall, Staffordshire, England
1842–47	Arley Hall, Cheshire, England
1843–46	Keele Hall, Staffordshire, England
ca. 1844	Alton Towers, Staffordshire, England
1844–48	Royal Botanical Gardens, Kew, London, England
1846–47	Stoke Rochford, Lincolnshire, England; Worsley Hall, Lancashire, England; Oxenhoath, Kent, England
1848–51	Buckingham Palace (unexecuted), London, England
1849–58	Holkham Hall, Norfolk, England
1849–64	Castle Howard, North Yorkshire, England
1850–60	Eaton Hall, Cheshire, England
1853–60	Stoke Edith, Herefordshire, England
1855–58	Broughton Hall, West Yorkshire, England
1859–65	Witley Court, Worcestershire, England
1860–61	Royal Horticultural Society Garden, Kensington, London, England
1863–70	The Avenue Gardens, Regent's Park, London, England

Further Reading

Brown, M., and G. Stansfield, *The Fountains of Witley Court,* York and Great Witley, Worcestershire: Village/Peter Huxtable Designs, 1992

Elliott, Brent, "Master of the Geometric Art," *Journal of the Royal Horticultural Society* 106 (1981)

Elliott, Brent, *Victorian Gardens,* London: Batsford, and Portland, Oregon: Timber Press, 1986

Evans, S., "Master Designer," *The Antique Collector* 63 (October 1992)

Evans, S., "Talented Twice Over," *Country Life* 187 (April 1993)

Evans, S., *Nesfield's Monster Work: The Gardens of Witley Court,* Great Witley, Worcestershire: Peter Huxtable Designs, 1994

Evans, S., "Genius of Pattern," *Country Life* 188 (May 1994)

Laurie, I.C., "Nesfield in Cheshire," *Garden History* 15 (1987)

Nelson, E.C., "A Nesfield Plan for Lyrath, County Kilkenny," *Garden History* 13 (1985)

Ridgway, Christopher, "Dream in Progress," *Country Life* 183 (July 1989)

Ridgway, Christopher, "William Andrews Nesfield: Between Uvedale Price and Isambard Kingdom Brunel," *Journal of Garden History* 13 (1993)

Ridgway, Christopher, editor, *William Andrews Nesfield, Victorian Landscape Architect,* York: Institute of Advanced Architectural Studies, University of York, 1996

Tooley, M.J., *William Andrews Nesfield, 1794–1881: Exhibition Guide,* Witton-le-Wear: Michaelmas Books, 1994

Tooley, M.J., editor, *William Andrews Nesfield: Essays to Mark the Bicentenary of His Birth,* Witton-le-Wear: Michaelmas Books, 1994

CHRISTOPHER RIDGWAY

Netherlands

In no other European country has the character of the land so influenced the way of life of its inhabitants, including their garden and botanical activities. The Netherlands covers approximately 41,000 square kilometers (15,830 sq. mi.); its landscape was first formed by the sea, rivers, ice caps, and melting water and subsequently by the formation of peat. About 60 percent of the surface area is formed by the rivers Maas (Meuse), Rijn (Rhine), and Schelde (Scheldt), and about 24 percent, mostly in the west and the north, is below sea level.

Little is known of the Dutch medieval garden, although paintings, miniatures, and household accounts give evidence of their existence. Particularly notable were the gardens of the counts of Holland at Het Binnenhof, The Hague, laid out between 1350 and 1460, and the gardens of the dukes of Gelder at Rosendael. Binnenhof was created as a series of outdoor rooms closely integrated with the castle and contained "flowery medes" embellished with turf seats, arbors, trellised roses, lavender, and carnations, as well as an ornate pavilion whose roof was adorned with gilded statues of the counts of Holland.

The designs of Hans Vredeman de Vries, a 16th-century Frisian artist and engineer, reveal the elaboration, within a medieval framework, of Flemish mannerist intricacy and artifice. De Vries is the author of the first independent series of garden designs published in early modern Europe, *Hortorum viridariumque formae* (ca. 1583; Forms of Gardens and Orchards). Through his work abroad and the dissemination of his engraved garden designs, de Vries's mannerist gardens extended well beyond the Dutch borders.

The establishment of the Leiden Botanic Garden in 1587 and the appointment of Carolus Clusius, Europe's first scientific horticulturist and taxonomist, as its director helped propel the Netherlands into a leading role in horticulture. Leiden's most notable function for a long time was the distribution of a large number of newly introduced plants to other European gardens. Geranium (*Pelargonium)* and evening primrose (*Oenothera*) are well-known examples, but the most significant introductions were the many bulb species such as narcissi, crocus, hyacinth, Siberian iris, and particularly the tulip, which led to tulipomania in 1634–37.

The fight for liberation from Spain, which began in 1568, led to an independent Dutch Republic in 1581. The strength of the young republic was the enormous wealth generated by the merchants. The Dutch East India Company was founded in 1602, and the Dutch West India Company in 1621. By the mid-17th century the Netherlands had become the world's leading commercial power. The country's prosperity led to a flowering of the arts of painting, architecture, and gardening.

In the 17th and 18th centuries the Dutch garden played a significant role in northern European culture, as well as in the Dutch colonies in Brazil, South America, and Indonesia. Having begun to cast off its Renaissance features at the end of the 16th century, the Dutch garden developed generally as a series of rectangular compartments, independent of each other but aligned, surrounded by hedges and pergolas. De Vries's engravings illustrate one of the features that influenced the northern European gardens of the 17th century, the *parterre de piéces coupées* (cutwork). Inspired by the Dutch passion for flowers, this type of parterre consisted of an intricate pattern of various elements, each of which, differently designed and separated from the others by narrow passageways, created a bed for the cultivation of rare plants and exotic flowers.

Small country estates became popular among the regents and merchants of the Netherlands and also became fashionable at the court of Orange. The specific demands of the landscape—the surplus of water, the sandy dune land, and the strong winds—made numerous measures necessary for creating a garden. In particular, avenues designed as windbreaks formed an integral part of virtually all gardens designed in the 17th century and gave the garden a sense of enclosure, an inward-looking orientation. Land for the country estates was often purchased over a period of time since the land distribution system was of small parceled plots of land, thus limiting any grand architectural organization. This situation, combined with the ditches and moats needed for drainage meant that orchards, vegetable gardens, and decorative parterres often were created as individual garden spaces, without any architectural interrelation.

The earliest known design of an actual Dutch garden is Prince Maurits's Buitenhof in The Hague (ca. 1620). The Buitenhof manifests the Albertian ideal of abstract design with its purely geometric structure and arrangement of the integrated parts. The shape was a double square totally enclosed with a crenellated brick wall and a canal. Each square contained a circular arbor and corner arbor pavilions, with another pavilion at the point where the two circles touched. Inside the circles were *parterres de broderie* (embroidery parterres), perhaps the earliest in the Netherlands, centered on fountains.

Classicism also influenced the shape of gardens in a fundamental manner. The house and gardens of Elswout (ca. 1657) near Haarlem and the princely gardens of Frederik Hendrik are early examples. Elswout, a country house built on a virgin site, displayed a striking and harmonious design of house and garden, inspired by classical and Italian examples. Visitors from abroad toured on tow barges the numerous waterways on which these *villa suburbanae* appeared almost uninterruptedly.

When Frederik Hendrik laid out new gardens for the mansion at Honselaarsdijk (ca. 1621), he employed the highly mathematical Dutch approach and the Italian theories of proportion. Canals defined three rectangles one within the other. The innermost was the house with its forecourt, set within the gardens and orchards, the heart of which were two bosquets laid out in double circles and corner pavilions, similar to Buitenhof. Honselaarskijk served as a model of the Dutch classical canal garden throughout the 17th century and influenced garden layouts in many parts of northern Europe. The general layout and the proportions of the garden evidently inspired André Mollet, who designed two parterres at Honselaarskijk about 1633. Engravings of these designs appear in Mollet's *Le Jardin de Plaisir* (1651; *The Garden of Pleasure*), which also includes a design that provides Mollet's conception of Honselaarsdijk's complete layout (unrealized). Hendrik followed the mathematical approach in designing the gardens at Rijswijk, but the details were French, as seen in the use of parterres, statues, fountains, and trelliswork.

Jacob van Campen was the principal architect to further develop the Italianate classical influence on the new garden style and to promote it, attempting much the same as Inigo Jones at the English court. Van Campen's most influential patrons of Hendrik's court were Constantijn Huygens and Johan Maruits, count of Nassau-Siegen. Van Campen assisted with town houses in The Hague for both Huygens and Maurits beginning about 1633 and designed Huygens's country estate, Hofwijck. Hofwijck had a rigid rectangular framework, intersected and surrounded by canals, with a sylvan Edenic garden whose layout, with one of the earliest essays in the informal planting of trees, derived from the proportions of the Vitruvian human figure. Other Italianate gardens included Elswout, Nijenrode, and Huis ten Bosch, which was laid out by Pieter Post for Hendrik in 1647, recalling the Villa d'Este at Tivoli.

During the second half of the 17th century, Stadholder William III of Orange and his wife Mary, daughter of James II of England, began to develop the gardens of their royal residences in a style that was to become known as the Franco-Dutch garden. The royal gardens of Het Loo in Gelderland embodied most perfectly the French-inspired designs, primarily André Le Nôtre's model. Such royal gardens, and Het Loo in particular, rapidly became famous, influencing the construction of gardens throughout the Protestant north of Europe. Their style took root particularly in Great Britain after 1689, when William and Mary moved there with their entire court on becoming king and queen of England.

Renamed "William and Mary" in England, this style amounted to a transition between the Renaissance tradition and the French baroque model. Canals acted as boundaries to geometrical structures reminiscent of the Italian tradition, while the parterres now had the flowing lines characteristic of the French and were planted with hundreds of bulbs imported to the Netherlands from remote countries. If architecture was predominant in the Italian Baroque garden and the emphasis on the plant element was special to the French garden, the Franco-Dutch garden gave particular importance to a balanced though contrasting relationship between geometrical design and natural form, between structures and flowers. Notable gardens are Zeist, Het Loo, and de Voorst, all presumably laid out by Jacob Roman, architect to William III.

Originally designed by court architect Jacob Roman and extended and embellished by the French architect Daniel Marot, Het Loo (realized between 1686 and 1695) may be regarded as the ultimate expression of William and Mary's gardening tastes. Dutch in layout and French in ornamentation, the garden clearly bore the mark of its two designers. The geometrical layout followed the criterion of the central axis and a symmetrical structure, with a rich array of fountains, canals, and cascades. All the gardens had *parterres de broderie,* Italo-Franco fountains and sculpture, and geometrical forms of topiary, as well as such Renaissance vestiges as *berceaux* (tunnel arbors), mazes, and trellis arbors. The Franco-Dutch garden, particularly Het Loo, was widely imitated above all in England but also in Germany and Russia.

The early 18th century witnessed the innovative development of the Dutch Régence garden (ca. 1720), which in plan reflected a change in attitude toward the relationship between art and nature and in conception foreshadowed the Picturesque garden. The Dutch Régence gardens were laid out near Haarlem by members of the Amsterdam bourgeoisie. These gardens were closer in conception to the rococo and Picturesque gardens, as they embodied elements of intimacy, contrast and movement, grace and charm, pictorial asymmetry and *utile dulci* (a combination of the useful and the beautiful). The house was secondary to the garden, whose main structure of woods engulfed the house and nearly eclipsed parterres. Ideal and self-contained landscapes were created within the enclosed confines of the garden, excluding any direct connection with the surrounding countryside, a characteristic that continued throughout the 18th and 19th centuries. Grass parterres, *bassins, boulingrins,* allées, *vertugadins,* and still ponds were employed for ornamentation.

The gardens of Waterland, Noord-Holland, embody the ideals of the Dutch Régence garden, of which they were an early example (ca. 1720). The gardens were conceived as a labyrinth. The main feature was a large pond from which five avenues radiated through woods terminating in such pictorial elements as an intimate verdant room with a triumphal arch, a Turkish tent, and moving pictures of boats on a lake nearby, provided by a camera obscura in a tunnel. The presence of these last two features in a garden was unprecedented, one evoking distant lands and the other representing science in the service of nature.

A synthesis of the Dutch Régence garden and intricate and artificial rococo gardens designed by Daniel Marot, such as Meer-en-Berg and Huis ten Bosch, reflected the early Dutch landscape garden after 1750. The schematic plans were in the spirit of Stephen Switzer. Along irregular lakes of ponds, rectilinear avenues linked circular or symmetrical curving paths, such as at Woestduin (1766) by A. Snoeck and Beechestijn (1772) by J.G. Michael, the Netherlands's first landscape architect. By the end of the 18th century the French Picturesque garden was a predominant influence.

The most influential landscape architect of the 19th century in the Netherlands was J.D. Zocher the Younger (1791–1870). His romantic landscape parks based on Brownian-Reptonian principles reflected a synthesis of French, German, and English landscape parks. Zocher's plans demonstrate a mastery of integrating natural scenery with structure, skillfully adapted to the site and its surroundings. Examples of his work include Haarlemmerhout (1827), Twickel (ca. 1830), and Rosendael (1836). Zocher also designed the first public park, Vondelpark in Amsterdam, completed in 1877.

In the first half of the century, their interpretation of the English landscape style to the Netherlands landscape became one of the dominant styles of the time. For example, the English landscape style was applied to the public walks on the dikes of towns such as Haarlem, Breda, and Utrecht. The cottage garden was another principal style during the first half of the 20th century, influencing designers such as J.P. Fokker, J.F. Tersteeg, John Bergmans, and Mien Ruys. Ruys began her career designing borders for the garden architecture department of her father's nursery. After broadening her experience and education, she became a key figure in the development of the modern garden in the Netherlands. Jan Thijs Pieter Bijhouwer and Willem Christiaan Johannes Boer were also instrumental in the evolving modern landscape and garden style.

Bijhouwer applied his considerable knowledge of the landscape in developing methods of ecological analysis and design, which have become standard practice. He was a pioneer in the profession of landscape architecture, particularly its relationship with architecture and town planning. Boer designed communal gardens, public open spaces, parks, and urban areas. His views on the development of the design of gardens, parks, and urban landscape design in relation to architecture and town planning were also influential in the modern movement.

The ecological approach to design also significantly influenced the development of gardens and landscapes in the 20th century. The *heem* park and garden is now a feature of many cities. The most notable is the J.P. Thijsse woodland park in Amstelveen near Amsterdam by Broerse and Landwehr, constructed in 1940. The ecological approach began in the 1920s with Jaques P. Thijsse, who was concerned with the rapid expansion of towns and industries that was occurring without apparent appreciation of the natural landscape. The ecological movement has since spread to the park system, as well as to roads and housing estates.

See also Amsterdamse Bos; Het Loo Palace; Keukenhof; Leiden, Universiteit Hortus Botanicus; Thijsse Park; Zeist

Further Reading

Blerck, Henk van, and Jörg Dettmar, *Landscape: 9 + 1 Young Dutch Landscape Architects* (exhib. cat.), Rotterdam: NAi, 1999

Boer W.C.J., "Changing Ideas in Urban Landscape Architecture in the Netherlands," in *Learning from Rotterdam: Investigating the Process of Urban Park Design,* by M.J. Vroom and J.H.A. Meeus, London: Mansell, and New York: Nichols, 1990

Groen, Jan van der, *Den Nederlandtsen hovenier,* Amsterdam, 1668

Hunt, John Dixon, editor, *The Dutch Garden in the Seventeenth Century,* Washington, D.C.: Dumbarton Oaks Research Library and Collection, 1990

Hunt, John Dixon, and Erik de Jong, editors, *The Anglo-Dutch Garden in the Age of William and Mary; De Gouden eeuw van de Hollandse tuinkunst* (exhib. cat.; bilingual English-Dutch edition), London: Taylor and Francis, 1988

Jacques, David, and Arend Jan van der Horst, *The Gardens of William and Mary,* London: Helm, 1988

Jong, E. de, *Nature and Art: Dutch Garden and Landscape Architecture, 1650–1740,* Philadelphia: Universitiy of Pennsylvania Press, 2001

Kuyper, W., *Dutch Classicist Architecture: A Survey of Dutch Architecture, Gardens, and Anglo-Dutch Architectural Relations from 1625 to 1700,* Delft, The Netherlands: Delft University Press, 1980

Oldenburger-Ebbers, Carla S., "Garden Design in the Netherlands in the Seventeenth Century," in *The History of Garden Design,* edited by Monique Mosser and Georges Teyssot, London: Thames and Hudson, 1991

Oosten, Henrik van, *Die niederländische Garten,* Wolffenbüttel, Germany, 1706; as *The Dutch Gardener: or, The Compleat Florist,* London, 1703; 2nd edition, 1711

Ruff, Allan R., *Holland and the Ecological Landscape,* Manchester: Department of Town and Country Planning, the University of Manchester, 1979

CANDICE A. SHOEMAKER

Neugebäude

Vienna, Austria

Location: approximately 5 miles (8 km) southeast of Vienna, near Simmering

Maximilian II's gardens near Vienna were given the simple designation *Neugebäude*—new building—because Maximilian died before its completion and without giving a proper name to the complex. Thus, the name was adopted after his death. Only scattered sources and a few depictions that lack detail (e.g., Matthäus Merian, *Topographia Provinciarum Austriacarum* [1649],

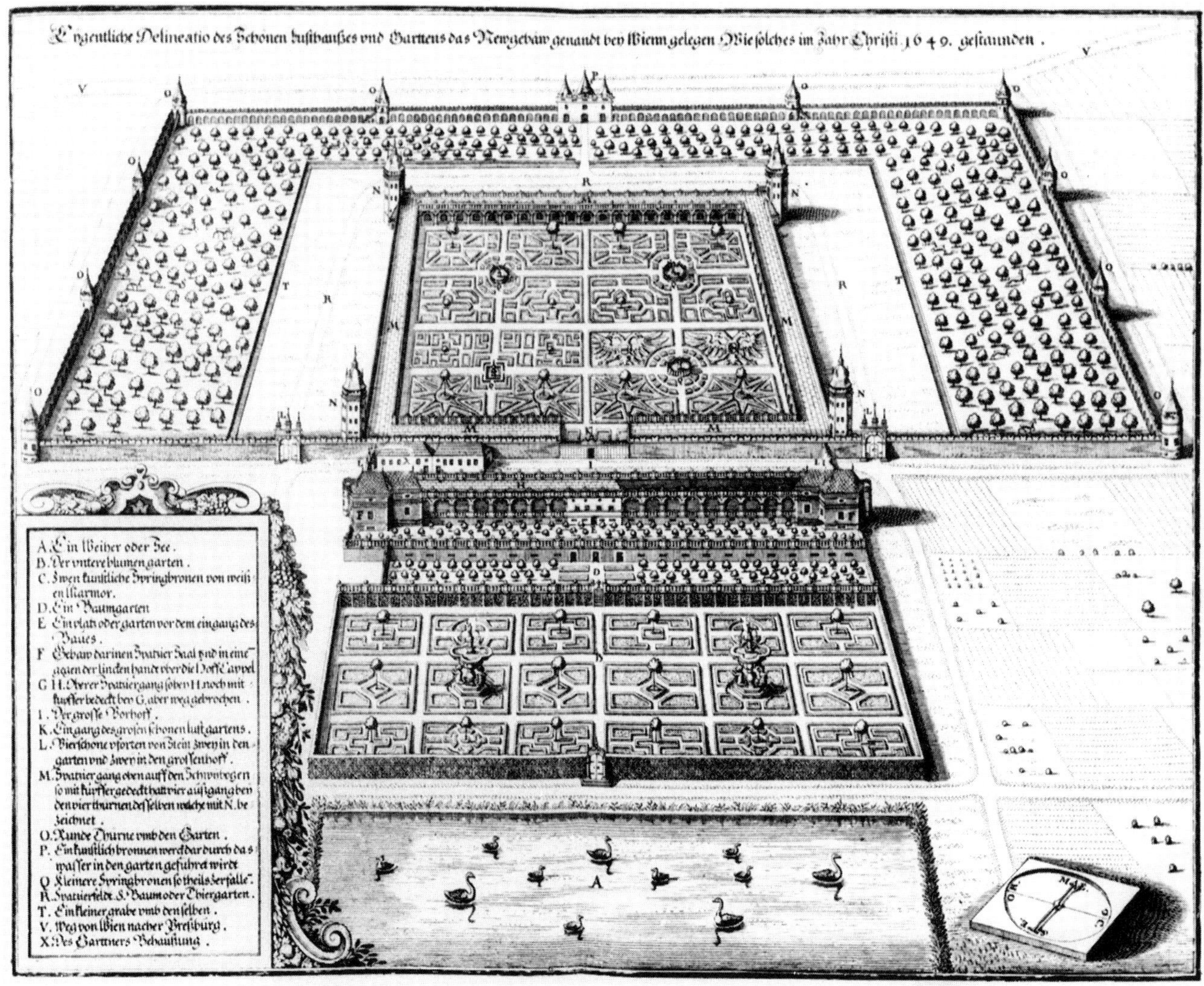

The Neugebäude in Matthäus Merian, *Typographia Provinciarum Austriacorum,* 1649
Courtesy of Österreichische National Bibliothek

Johann Adam Delsenbach, *Anfang Einiger Vorstellungen* [ca. 1715]) provide us with an impression of this important garden complex.

As did his parents, Maximilian had an affinity for pleasure gardens and an interest in botany. The Belvedere garden in Prague, realized on his father's, Ferdinand I's, command, certainly was a model for Maximilian's new garden near Vienna. He also may have remembered Moorish gardens in Spain, where he had grown up. This European context formed the artistic horizon for the gardens of the Neugebäude. Since 1564 Maximilian was in correspondence with his ambassadors in Venice and Rome in order to receive antique sculptures and plans of gardens and garden buildings. A letter from Hans Jakob Fugger to Jacopo Strada (November 1568) mentions the latter's invention of a *palazzo di piacere* or *palazzo di natura* near Vienna, which is the Neugebäude. Strada was the central figure for the transmission of Italian architectural models to the imperial court, although it is not possible to name a specific Italian model for this new garden complex.

Another possible model for the structure of the complex has been much discussed. Written sources, and the fact that the later Turkish invasion in 1683 spared the Neugebäude, nourished the legend that the site chosen by Maximilian was the place where in 1529 the besieger of Vienna, Sultan Süleyman, had set up his tents. This symbolic triumph over the permanent Turkish menace is perhaps expressed in the structure of the complex surrounded by defensive walls and towers.

The complex opens to the Danube plain on the north and is located on several levels of the steep hillside. The building is situated on the edge; the upper garden is divided into an outer field and an inner pleasure garden, and the part below the building shows terraces, a flower garden, and a fishpond. Some of the parterres—

parterres de pièces coupées—show the imperial double eagle and other heraldic motifs; no other details that might allow a more complex iconographic interpretation are known. After Maximilian's death the foreign plants and trees brought here were no longer cared for, and the conduits for the complicated system of watercourses, fountains, and the emperor's bath fell in decay.

Strada, who had also designed the gallery of antiques in the electoral residence of Munich, the so-called Antiquarium, conceived the main building of the Neugebäude as a gallery for the imperial collection of antique and modern sculptures. The Neugebäude and its gardens were not meant to serve as a permanent residence but as a *villa suburbana* conceived for imperial self-representation through works of art and festivities.

Synopsis

1566–68	Emperor Maximilian II has pheasantry (*Fasangarten*) laid out at estate of Ebersdorf
1568	Maximilian decides to have garden and building laid out south of pheasantry on steep bank of Danube river; planting work in all parts of new garden begun
since 1569	Fruit trees and grafts brought from the royal gardens in Prague
1573	Gardens with enclosure buildings finished; main building begun
1576	Maximilian II dies, and building never finished
1577	His successor, Rudolf II, continues architectural work, but stops interior decoration
1775	Columns, friezes, and reliefs removed for use in construction of *fabriques* in garden of Schönbrunn
since 1922	Construction of crematory in upper garden field
since 1970s	Discussion among curators of monuments and architectural historians about preservation, reconstruction, and new use of building and surrounding complex

Further Reading

Feuchtmüller, Rupert, *Das Neugebäude,* Vienna and Hamburg: Zsolnay, 1976

Fürstenhöfe der Renaissance: Giulio Romano und die klassische Tradition (exhib. cat.), Vienna: Kunsthistorisches Museum, 1989

Hajós, Geza, "The Laying-Out of the Garden at the Neugebäude: Opportunities and Dangers of a Reconstruction," *Journal of Garden History* 7, no. 2 (1987)

Lietzmann, Hilda, *Das Neugebäude in Wien: Sultan Süleymans Zelt, Kaiser Maximilians II. Lustschloß: Ein Beitrag zur Kunst- und Kulturgeschichte der zweiten Hälfte des sechzehnten Jahrhunderts,* Munich: Deutscher Kunstverlag 1987

Lietzmann, Hilda, "Das Neugebäude und Böhmen," in *Prag um 1600: Kunst und Kultur am Hofe Kaiser Rudolfs II.* (exhib. cat.), vol. 3, Freren, Germany: Luca Verlag, 1988

Zimmermann, Reinhard, "Ästhetische und ideelle Aspekte der Gartenanlagen des Neugebäudes bei Wien," *Arx* 9, no. 2 (1987)

Zimmermann, Reinhard, "Iconography in German and Austrian Renaissance Gardens," in *Garden History: Issues, Approaches, Methods,* Washington, D.C.: Dumbarton Oaks Research Library and Collection, 1989

IRIS LAUTERBACH

New York, Central Park. *See* Central Park

New Zealand

The first humans to reach New Zealand were the ancestors of the Maori people, probably not more than 800 years ago. They found three main islands (spread from 35(S to 47(S longitude) with large areas under temperate lowland forest characterized by long-lived podocarps, abundant epiphytes, vines, and numerous ferns—from tiny, filmy species to tall tree ferns. Other regions had been blanketed with recent volcanic deposits and supported shrubs and bracken fern. In drier eastern areas were tussock grasslands where natural fires had prevented regeneration. The Maori successfully introduced tropical root crops such as the sweet potato to the warmer North Island and northern coasts of the South Island, combining long-fallow swiddening with intensive practices such as mound and basin cultivation, ditching for water control, gravel mulching, and composting. Although there is little to indicate that they grew any purely ornamental plants, a strong aesthetic element is evident in the layout and high standard of care of their vegetable gardens, as described by the first European visitors in the late 18th century.

After a period of exploitation of timber, seals, and whales, missionaries settled among the Maori from 1815, rapidly introducing European fruits, vegetables, and flowers from the earlier Australian settlements. Once New Zealand was annexed by Britain in 1840, organized immigration brought a cross section of British society to the colony, including professional gardeners and nurserymen. Like the botanical explorers who preceded them, they valued the distinctive character of the endemic flora, especially the ferns, the subtropical-looking palms and flaxes, and the coastal shrubs tolerant of salt spray and wind. Many native plants (e.g., *Hebe* and *Pittosporum* spp.) were introduced to Europe during the 19th century, and the trade expanded further in the 20th century when transportation problems were overcome. Other immigrants, however, preferred the garden flora of their homelands. Once shelter belts were established—predominantly North American conifers, Lombardy poplars, and Australian eucalyptus—homesteaders sought oak, elm, beech, and other European trees for their pleasure gardens. The style of both rural and suburban gardens in the second half of the 19th century was strongly influenced by the Victorian gardenesque, characterized by lawns dotted with specimen trees and annual flower beds, with fringing shrubberies. Every major garden fashion in Britain was quickly adopted in New Zealand, from ferneries, rockeries, and roseries to carpet bedding.

The leaders of the new settlements followed town plans that provided garden space for each dwelling, plus recreation areas and green belts to enhance public health. They were able to implement ideals unattainable in old European cities. Most towns developed public gardens within one or two decades of establishment. Amenity societies dedicated to tree planting, beautification of public land, and the preservation of picturesque scenery sprang up beginning in the late 1880s. The common quarter-acre suburban section enabled families to grow fruit and vegetables and keep poultry at the rear and to devote the front to ornamental gardening. Unfortunately, the model they followed had been devised for more expansive properties, and many villas were soon dwarfed by giant conifers planted as specimen trees.

In the larger rural gardens, enlightened owners (sometimes working with garden designers such as Alfred Buxton) were better able to fulfill the potential of the New Zealand landscapes and climates. Although they continued to be influenced by British movements such as the Surrey style—exemplified by Gertrude Jekyll's woodland gardening—and Arts and Crafts water features and pergolas, they diversified the planting material to include many Southern Hemisphere species, successfully integrating exotic and native plants. By the 1920s several large rural gardens (such as Douglas Cook's Eastwoodhill near Gisborne) had effectively become arboretums, while others were as elegantly and expensively laid out as a Surrey country estate.

The adoption of dominion status in 1907 coincided with growing local interest in native flora, including the challenging alpine species. The pioneer plant ecologist Leonard Cockayne established the Otari Native Plant Museum in Wellington in 1927, which demonstrated the horticultural potential of plants that had been formerly regarded as useless impediments to agricultural expansion and ruthlessly burned. But few gardeners were prepared to exclude exotic plants completely, preferring to interplant tree ferns, fuchsias, and other small native trees with magnolias, camellias, and rhododendrons, plants that enjoyed similar acidic soil types and climatic conditions. In Taranaki and other well-watered regions, amateurs such as Bernard Hollard and Felix and Les Jury turned from farming to plant breeding, developing cultivars of magnolias, rhododendrons, and other connoisseurs' plants, which are now internationally renowned (e.g., *Magnolia* 'Iolanthe' and *Rhododendron* 'Kaponga').

Rhododendrons were also a specialty of the Dunedin Botanic Gardens (from 1914) and of the outstanding Pukeiti Garden created since 1950 in cutover native rainforests on the flanks of Mount Taranaki. Essentially, these extensive gardens use woodland-style meandering paths, glades, and layered planting of exotic and native species to achieve an "enhanced" naturalistic effect. The introduction of the vireya rhododendrons from islands in Southeast Asia and New Guinea saw similar woodland gardens develop in Auckland, but with a more tropical look. The Eden Gardens, situated in an old quarry, are a prime example.

Following World War II, U.S. influences in house design toward open-plan living also saw a more conscious integration of house and garden. Along with patios, barbecues, and decks came the raised planters and swimming pools of the Californian or "Sunset" style. This style proved better suited to small suburban sections than the woodland garden and now has subtropical and Mediterranean variants. An informal coastal style of gardening has also evolved in New Zealand, combining succulents, massed daisies, and geraniums with sun-loving bulbs and perennials from South Africa and Australia.

New Zealand has not developed any single distinctive garden style and given its climatic range, will never do so. But it has certainly contributed much to international horticulture, in the form of native plants introduced to Europe and North America and within New Zealand itself and the integration of natives with a wider range of exotic species than can be grown in countries with continental climates. New Zealand gardeners have used these to create gardens that are colorful, largely informal, and of year-round interest. Recent surveys have shown that gardening is the preferred leisure activity of New Zealanders, one that is increasingly subject to fashion trends. Nonetheless, there are a handful of designers, including the Auckland artist Ted Smyth, who have created gardens that unite the house, its immediate surroundings, and the distant landscape of sea and islands with a classic simplicity that transcends fashion.

Further Reading

Barber, Laurie, "A History of Horticulture in the Waikato," *Annual Journal of the Royal New Zealand Institute of Horticulture* 15 (1988)

Bradbury, Matthew, editor, *A History of the Garden in New Zealand,* Auckland and New York: Viking Press, 1995

Challenger, S., "Commercial Availability of Conifers in New Zealand, 1851–1873," *Annual Journal of the Royal New Zealand Institute of Horticulture* 14 (1986–87)

Challenger, S., "Amenity Horticulture in Canterbury, 1850–1880," *Annual Journal of the Royal New Zealand Institute of Horticulture* 16 (1989)

Cook, Walter, "Wellington's Town Belt—A People's Park and a Heritage for Everyone," *Horticulture in New Zealand* 2, no. 2 (1991)

Dann, Christine, *Cottage Gardening in New Zealand,* Wellington, New Zealand: Allen and Unwin New Zealand, 1990

Gabites, Isobel, and Rob Lucas, *The Native Garden: Design Themes from Wild New Zealand,* Auckland, New Zealand: Godwit, 1998

Goldsmith, Susette, and Verne Barrell, *The Gardenmakers of Taranaki,* New Plymouth, New Zealand: Ratanui Press, 1997

Greenfield, Pat, *Pukeiti: New Zealand's Finest Rhododendron Garden,* Auckland, New Zealand: Bateman, 1997

Leach, Helen May Keedwell, *1,000 Years of Gardening in New Zealand,* Wellington, New Zealand: Reed, 1984

Leach, Helen May Keedwell, "Native Plants and National Identity in New Zealand Gardening: An Historical Review," *Horticulture in New Zealand* 5, no. 1 (1994)

Leach, Helen May Keedwell, "Analysing Change in the New Zealand Home Garden—By Style or Element?" *New Zealand Garden Journal* 1, no. 2 (1996)

McGeorge, Pamela, "An Artist as Landscaper," *New Zealand Gardener* 54, no. 5 (1998)

Nelson, E.C., "An Archaic Duet—New Zealand's Contribution to Ireland's Garden Heritage," *Annual Journal of the Royal New Zealand Institute of Horticulture* 16 (1989)

Shepherd, Winsome, "Thomas Mason (1818–1903): The Finest Garden in the Southern Hemisphere: 'The Gums,' Taita, Wellington," *Horticulture in New Zealand* 2, no. 2 (1991)

Strongman, Thelma, *The Gardens of Canterbury,* Wellington, New Zealand: Reed, 1984

Tipples, Rupert, *Colonial Landscape Gardener Alfred Buxton of Christchurch, New Zealand, 1872–1950,* Canterbury, New Zealand: Department of Horticulture and Landscape, Lincoln College, 1989

Tipples, Rupert, "Christchurch—The First Garden City?" *Horticulture in New Zealand* 3, no. 1 (1992)

HELEN LEACH

Nieborów

Mazovia, Poland

Location: 9 miles (14.5 km) southeast of Łowicz, and approximately 40 miles (64 km) west-southwest of Warsaw

The Nieborów palace and garden complex is one of the major and best-preserved baroque residencies in Poland. Axially designed, it is a classic example of the *entre cour et jardin* palace. In front of the palace is a village and a vast courtyard framed with outbuildings and an orangery. The back of the palace is occupied by a geometrical garden with an axis reaching beyond its border into the fields surrounding the residence and the forest on the horizon.

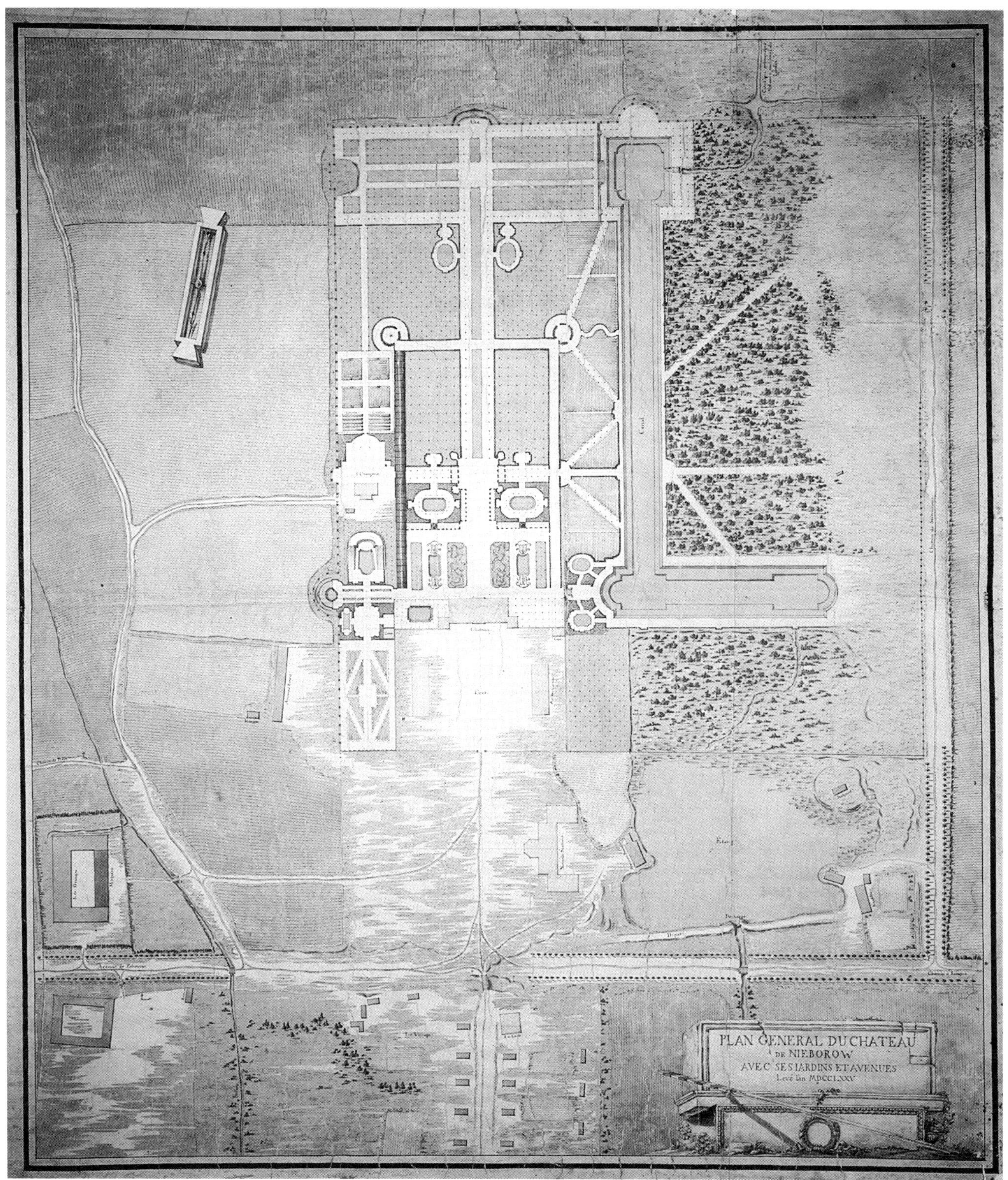

Plan of the palace and garden of Nieborów, designed by Szymon Bogumił Zug, ca. 1775
Copyright Muzeum Narodowe w Warszawie

The garden exemplifies French style, with some elements revealing Dutch influence. It was laid out by an architect of Dutch origin, Tylman van Gameren, near the end of the 17th century for Primate Stefan Radziejowski and was originally rectangular (186 by 120 yd. [170 by 110 m]); it consisted of a parterre and hornbeam and linden bosquets lined on three sides by linden alleys with a circular arbor at their crossing point. Along the main axis runs an *allée verte,* which is intersected by a narrower alley forming a transverse axis. Later the garden was closed from the west by a canal whose perpendicular branch, together with an additional narrow, slanted canal, formed the letter "Ł"—a reference to the Łochockis, who then owned the residence. In the second half of the 18th century the garden grew twice as big; it was enlarged toward the south, east, and west by sections planted with fruit trees and linden. The length of the alley along the main axis was doubled, and a double line of linden trees was planted along the canal.

The second major stage in the evolution of the Nieborów garden goes back to its first owners, the Radziwiłł princes, who possessed Nieborów until the property was taken over by the state in 1945. To transform the garden, they employed Szymon Bogumił Zug, an eminent architect during the Polish Enlightenment and the creator of many English-style gardens. It was then that the enclosure of the garden using a ditch—a ha-ha—was created, which is now one of the best examples of a ha-ha in Poland. Zug transformed the forest beyond the canal into a grove for strolling. This grove has a stream and small lakes, and it is inhabited by animals such as roe deer. About this time a magnificent collection of orange trees was bought from the famous Dresden collection of exotic plants owned by the Moszyńskis (in the first half of the 19th century the trees were given to the Łazienki Palace in Warsaw, which was at the time a residence of Czar Alexander I). In the 19th and 20th centuries the garden was adorned with ancient, medieval, and neoclassical sculptures.

When Nieborów became part of the National Museum in Warsaw in 1945, Professor Gerard Ciołek, an expert on the history of Polish gardens and an architect and conservator, attempted a reconstruction of the plantings and water system in the garden based on Zug's design. Located close to the Bolimów Forest nature reserve, the garden is inhabited by many birds, as well as hares, hedgehogs, and martens.

Synopsis

1695	Rebuilding of 16th-century mansion into palace for Primate Stefan Radziejowski, and planting begun of rectangular garden; both works carried out by architect Tylman van Gameren
after 1763	"Ł"-shaped canal built
1774	Planting of plane trees (preserved until today) adjacent to palace; Nieborów becomes property of Radziwiłłs
1774–75	Arrangement of enlarged geometric garden by architect Szymon Bogumił Zug; construction of Old Orangery
1796	New Orangery in Nieborów built, designed by Zug
1945	Palace in Nieborów, together with garden and park in Arkadia nearby, became part of National Museum in Warsaw
1947–51	Garden restored according to plan by Gerard Ciołek, including partial reconstruction of New Orangery pulled down in mid-19th century

Further Reading

Bowe, Patrick, *Gardens in Central Europe,* New York: Train/Scala Books, 1991

Ciołek, Gerard, *Ogrody polskie,* Warsaw: Arkady, 1954; 2nd edition, 1978 (summary in English)

Czartoryska, Princess Izabela, *Myślirózne o sposobie zakładania ogrodów* (Thoughts on the Manner of Planting Gardens), Warsaw, 1804

Jabłoński, Krzysztof, and Włodzimierz Piwkowski, *Nieborów, Arkadia,* Warsaw: Wydawn Sport i Turystyka, 1988

Knox, Brian, "The Arrival of the English Landscape Garden in Poland and Bohemia," in *The Picturesque Garden and Its Influences outside the British Isles,* edited by Nikolaus Pevsner, Washington, D.C.: Dumbarton Oaks, 1974

Lorentz, Stanisław, and Andrzej Rottermund, *Neoclassicism in Poland,* translated by Jerzy Bałdyga, Warsaw: Arkady, 1986

Piwkowski, Wlodzimierz, *Nieborów,* Warsaw: Arkady, 1978

Radziwiłł, Princess Helena, *Le guide d'Arcadie,* Berlin, 1800

MALGORZATA SZAFRAŃSKA

Nikitsky Botanical Garden

Yalta, Crimea, Southern Ukraine

Location: approximately 3.6 miles (6 km) from Yalta

Overlooking the sea at a distance of approximately 3.6 miles (6 km) from Yalta, in Crimea, the Nikitsky Botanical Garden contains species representing flora from all subtropical areas of the earth. Its creation in the early 19th century was associated with the concurrent extensive development of the southern lands. Both viticulture and horticulture were becoming the staple branches of farming in the southern Crimea: the beneficial climate favored the development of decorative gardening. The establishment of a standard state botanical garden could guide the development of southern horticulture and supply it with planting stock.

On 10 June 1811 a decree was signed in St. Petersburg concerning the establishment in Crimea of the Imperial Botanical Garden. Christian Steven, a young scientist, became its first director. Land plots for the garden were to be allotted near the village of Nikita, founded several centuries before by Greek settlers. Yalta was then a small village linked to Alushta by just a riders' path.

The first plantings were made in September 1812, the date that actually marked the birth of the Nikitsky Botanical Garden. Three years later the garden published its successes in the first catalog of the plants available from its nurseries. In 12 years of work Steven established contacts with 40 institutions and private persons who sent seeds and saplings from various parts of Europe. In total he gathered 450 species of decorative plants into the collection. In 1817 the garden established Russia's first collection of fruit trees. From its first years the garden cultivated roses for essential oil, tobacco, dye plants, and plants used for making textile fabrics and in medicine.

In 1826 Nikolai Gartwiss became director of Nikitsky, and decorative horticulture and fruit growing made a steady progress under his management. A grape collection was planted. Over 20 years the collection of tree species more than doubled. Contacts with many trade companies of Europe and the United States strengthened.

After the October Revolution (1917) and termination of the Civil War, the garden began to develop as a scientific research institution. Departments and laboratories were organized, and a staff of scientific workers was created. The strengthening of links with agricultural practice has become a prominent feature of the garden's work. Toward the 1950s the long-term testing of new varieties of fruit, essential oil-bearing, medical, and ornamental plants grown in the pre- and postwar years was completed, and the garden recommended varieties for industrial cultivation.

In 2000 the Nikitsky Botanical Garden became a National Scientific Center. With its branches (production and experimental departments) it occupies an area over 2,000 hectares (4,942 acres). The garden's scientists study world plant resources in order to use them in the national economy, carry on introduction and selection of fruit-bearing, nut-bearing, essential oil-bearing, medical, dye, and ornamental plants, and work out methods of their mass reproduction and protection from pests and diseases. Researchers' attention has become ever more attracted by the most urgent problems of protecting nature, the beautiful landscapes of the Crimea being a resort area of nationwide importance. The garden's plant collections are rich and varied. The total number of species, hybrids, and varieties possessed by the garden exceeds 28,000.

The garden descends to the seashore in picturesque terraces; its four parks make a magnificent living museum in the open air.

The Upper Park was created from 1880 to 1937. There are 850 species and forms of trees and shrubs, including a 500-year-old English yew (a wild coniferous specimen of the Crimean flora that has survived from the past centuries), an allée of pyramidal cypresses planted in 1886, and the best varieties of Soviet- and foreign-bred roses.

The Lower Park is the oldest section of the garden, where the first plantings were made in Christian Steven's tenure. Surviving from those times are magnificent specimens of pines, oaks, olive trees, and other species whose numerous descendants now adorn the gardens and parks of the South Coast of the Crimea.

The Seaside Park was created for the 100th anniversary of the garden, and it has the warmest microclimate and contains the most tender subtropical plants, including seven species of palms, coniferous exotics, fragrant olives, and Mediterranean shrubs.

In 1973 on Cape Martian, east of the Seaside Park, a state wildlife preserve was created. It is a research model for nature protection in the Crimea. It spreads over 120 hectares (297 acres) of land and the same area offshore in the Black Sea. More than 500 plant species that make up one-fifth of the mountainous Crimea's flora grow on Cape Martian. The wildlife preserve is the habitat for 146 species of birds, 17 mammal species, 11 species of amphibians and reptiles, almost 200 species of sea animals, and numerous invertebrates. All are under safe protection.

The park on Cape Montedor also includes coniferous exotics, as well as evergreen sequoias.

The product of several generations of labor, the Nikitsky Botanical Garden maintains a rich and varied living collection. The renown of the garden is international; it is visited by a half-million tourists annually.

Synopsis

1811 Decree signed creating Nikitsky Botanical Garden
1812 First plantings
1817 Fruit trees planted
1912 Pavilion with colonnade built, creation of Seaside Park
1973 Creation of wildlife preserve "Cape Martian"
2000 Nikitsky becomes national scientific center

Further Reading

Chernova, N.M., *Putevoditel po Nikitskomu botanicheskomu sadu imeni Molotova* (A Guide to the Nikitsky Botanical Garden Named for Molotov), Yalta, Ukraine: Krymgosizdat, 1938

Golubeva, Irina Vladimirovna, and Aleksandr Mikhaiovich Kormilitsyn, *Nikits'kyi botanichnyi sad: Fotoal'bom; Nikitsky botanichesy sad; Nikitsky Botanical Garden* (trilingual Ukrainian-Russian-English edition), Kiev, Ukraine: "Mystetstvo," 1979

Golubeva, Irina Vladimirovna, and S.I. Kuznetsov, *Nikitsky botanichesky sad: Putevoditel'* (Nikitsky Botanical Garden: A Guide), 2nd edition, Simferopol', Ukraine: "Tavriya," 1985; 4th edition, 1985 (4th edition with summaries in English, French, and German)

Howard, Richard A., Burdette L. Wagenknecht, and Peter S. Green, *International Directory of Botanical Gardens,* Utrecht: International Bureau for Plant Taxonomy and Nomenclature, 1963; 5th edition, by Christine A. Heywood, Vernon H. Heywood, and Peter Wyse, Koenigstein, Germany: Koeltz Scientific Books, 1990

Hyams, Edward, and William MacQuitty, *Great Botanical Gardens of the World,* New York: Macmillan, and London: Nelson, 1969

Lapin, P.I., *Botanical Gardens of the USSR,* Moscow: Kolos, 1984

Rikhter, A.A., et al., *Kratkie itogi rabot Nikitskogo botanicheskogo sada im. Molotova, 1812–1938 gg.* (A Short Summary of the Work of the Nikitsky Botanical Garden Named for Molotov), Yalta, Ukraine: Gos. Nikitsky Botanichesky Sad im. Molotova, 1938

VALERY EZHOV

Nishat Bagh

Srinagar, Jammu and Kashmir, India

Location: Jammu and Kashmir province, on road along southeast shore of Dal Lake, approximately 400 miles (643.5 km) north-northwest of Delhi

The Nishat Bagh (Garden of Gladness) was a pleasure estate built about 1620 by Asaf Khan (d. 1641), the older brother of Empress Nur Jahan and trusted advisor to Shah Jahan when the latter ascended the throne in 1628. Because it was not imperial and lacked ceremonial importance, the garden had no need of the throne rooms and reception halls of the Shalamar Bagh. However, its spectacular setting and large size more than compensated for the absence of fine buildings, and Shah Jahan mentioned it as one of his favorite gardens. It was situated on the east shore of Dal Lake and reached by a boat passing under the bridge of the causeway that cut across the lake at that point. From the lake's edge the landscape rises steeply to the foot of a vertiginous and often snow-capped peak. Thus, in the pause of a moment the visitor's gaze encompasses the dramatic contrast of the placid lake against the mountains' grandeur with the garden mediating visually between the two.

The Nishat Bagh formed a long rectangle, 220 meters wide by more than 350 meters long (240 by 383 yd.). It was organized in 12 stepped terraces—likened by one witness to "the layers of heaven" and certainly associated with the signs of the zodiac—and water coursed from one level to the next via a central channel (3 m [3.3 yd.] wide) with a row of water jets running down the middle. Nestled close to the mountain, the steep slope of the landscape sent the water rushing through the channel and splashing noisily into pools and down water chutes (*chadars*), imitating a natural mountain

Nishat Bagh with a view of Lake Dal
Copyright D. Fairchild Ruggles

stream with cascades. In places, stone slabs bridge the water channel, inviting the visitor to sit and enjoy the water's sound and spray. The splendid abundance of water in these gardens in the Mogul period (much scarcer today) was one of their most pleasing aspects and must have been a welcome contrast to the more parsimonious water displays of gardens in Delhi, Agra, and Fatehpur Sikri. In addition to its aesthetic role, the water served a practical purpose as well, irrigating the flowers and orchards flanking the central stream.

The estate was divided into two parts. The lower levels were for the use of Asaf Khan and his male visitors. The lowest of these bordered the lake and was lined with plane trees with a pavilion between them from which visitors could be greeted, but this garden level is now marred by the modern lake road that traverses it. Although the pavilion that stands there today is two stories, the original was probably one story so as not to impede the view. The *zenana* (harem) gardens at the topmost level were for the private use of the women of the family. This terrace was separated from the others by an elevated retaining wall, 6 meters (6.6 yd.) high, ornamented with blind arches and designed with octagonal stone pavilions at either end, each three stories high. From here the women had excellent views of the activities of men in the lower terraces, the lake, and beyond to Akbar's hilltop fort on the opposite bank.

Synopsis

ca. 1620 Nishat Bagh (Garden of Gladness) built by Asaf Khan

Further Reading

Brookes, John, *Gardens of Paradise: The History and Design of the Great Islamic Gardens,* New York: New Amsterdam, and London: Wiedenfeld and Nicolson, 1987

Crowe, Sylvia, et al., *The Gardens of Mughal India,* London: Thames and Hudson, 1972
Jellicoe, Susan, "The Development of the Mughal Garden," in *The Islamic Garden,* edited by Elisabeth B. MacDougall and Richard Ettinghausen, Washington, D.C.: Dumbarton Oaks, 1976
Moynihan, Elizabeth B., *Paradise as a Garden in Persia and Mughal India,* New York: Braziller, 1979
Thackston, W.M., "Mughal Gardens in Persian Poetry," in *Mughal Gardens: Sources, Places, Representations, and Prospects,* edited by James L. Wescoat, Jr., and Joachim Wolschke-Bulmahn, Washington, D.C.: Dumbarton Oaks Research Library and Collection, 1996
Villiers-Stuart, Constance M., *Gardens of the Great Mughals,* London: Black, 1913

D. FAIRCHILD RUGGLES

Niven, James 1776–1827

Scottish Horticulturist and Plant Collector

Scotland was the home of many of the best plant collectors and gardeners of the 18th and 19th centuries, and James Niven was one of the most significant. He visited the Cape of Good Hope, where he made substantial collections of herbarium specimens, seeds, and bulbs. Many new species were described using his specimens or plants raised from his seeds.

Niven was the third child and second son of John Niven, a weaver, and his wife, Anne, of Penicuik, a village situated south of Edinburgh. Undoubtedly he received the standard education provided for Scottish children at that period and in March 1795 was apprenticed to Robert Menzies, head gardener at the Botanic Garden, Leith Walk, Edinburgh. His apprenticeship ended a year later, and Niven then moved to England to the duke of Northumberland's garden, Syon House, on the northern bank of the river Thames opposite the Royal Botanic Gardens, Kew. At Syon House he worked under Thomas Hoy and became known to the wealthy garden owner and plant enthusiast George Hibbert.

Hibbert engaged Niven to travel to the Cape Colony. The exact dates of Niven's two visits to the Cape of Good Hope are not known, but he was certainly collecting near Cape Town by August 1799 and may have arrived there as early as mid-1798. He stayed in the region until 1803, when Britain returned control of the Cape Colony to the Dutch.

Back in England, Niven was engaged for a second time to travel to southern Africa by a consortium of wealthy gardeners that included the Empress Josephine and James Lee, a nurseryman of Hammersmith, London. Niven reached Cape Town again early in 1805 and spent six more years at the Cape of Good Hope. During his tours in southern Africa, Niven traveled as far north as Kamiesberg in Namaqualand and as far east as the Gamtoos River about 40 kilometers (25 mi.) from Humansdorp.

After his second tour, Niven settled in Penicuik and abandoned botanical and horticultural pursuits. He married and fathered five children before his death on 9 January 1827.

Niven's contribution to horticulture and botany was as a collector of the Cape of Good Hope's remarkable flora. He must have gathered thousands of herbarium specimens, but the plants he introduced to European gardens, either as seeds or bulbs, were in general not hardy and, being often difficult to cultivate, were grown mainly by connoisseurs. Niven's introductions included many species of *Erica* (Cape heaths)—he is credited with about 30 new species—which were then very fashionable greenhouse plants, and several species of *Protea* and its relatives. Few of his introductions have become common garden plants in temperate regions.

Several of the sumptuously illustrated botanical works published in the early 19th century contain portraits of plants raised in English and French gardens from Niven's collections. Niven himself is commemorated in the Cape genus *Nivenia*, a shrubby member of the Iris family.

Biography

Born in Penicuik, Scotland, 28 September 1776. Apprentice gardener at Botanic Garden, Leith Walk, Edinburgh, March 1795–February 1796; gardener at Syon House, Surrey, England, ca. 1796–98; traveled to Cape of Good Hope to collect plants, ca. 1798–ca. 1803 and ca. 1805–12; settled in Penicuik, 1812. Died in Penicuik, 9 January 1827.

Further Reading

Gunn, Mary, and L.E. Codd, *Botanical Exploration of Southern Africa,* Cape Town: Balkema, 1981

Nelson, E.C., and J.P. Rourke, "James Niven (1776–1827), a Scottish Botanical Collector at the Cape of Good Hope: His *Hortus Siccus* at the National Botanic Gardens, Glasnevin, Dublin, and the Royal Botanic Gardens, Kew," *Kew Bulletin* 48 (1993)

E. CHARLES NELSON

Noguchi, Isamu 1904–1988

United States Artist and Garden Designer

Isamu Noguchi was one of the 20th century's most visionary artists, whose legacy is 60 years of innovative work in sculpture, garden design, set design, furniture design, and designs for public open space. Noguchi was a pioneer in collaborating with other disciplines. He believed that art could play a larger role than the purely aesthetic object and sought a socially conscious role for his art and environments.

Noguchi's mother was an American writer and teacher, his father a renowned Japanese poet, and for much of his

Sunken Garden for Chase Manhattan Bank Plaza in New York City, New York, ca. 1961–64
Courtesy of Isamu Noguchi Foundation

life Noguchi divided his time between the two countries. This life within two cultures forged both his sense of personal identity and his artistic sensibility. He developed his ideas for public space from his studio in New York and his understanding of the contemplative object and landscape from his stone-carving studio in Japan.

Constantin Brancusi, Buckminster Fuller, and Martha Graham were key to Noguchi's development as an artist. Brancusi, an acclaimed sculptor, instilled in him a sensitivity to tools and materials, as well as an approach to both abstract art and the design of utilitarian objects. Fuller, a philosopher/scientist, inspired Noguchi's interest in synthesizing aesthetics and technology with a utopian vision, while Graham's innovative choreography revealed new relationships between the body and space.

In the 1930s Noguchi traveled to Japan and was particularly inspired by the unified sculptural landscape of Japanese gardens. He began to use these ideas in seminal projects such as *Play Mountain* and in set designs for Martha Graham—projects that expanded upon traditional notions of sculpture. *Play Mountain* was an innovative playground proposal that created an integrated landscape of terraces, slopes, and pools.

Noguchi realized his first major work in the landscape at the gardens for the United Nations Educational, Scientific, and Cultural Organization (UNESCO) in Paris (1956–58), using the elements of a traditional Japanese garden in nontraditional ways. Concrete blocks are juxtaposed with found rocks. The biomorphic curves in the garden draw upon surrealism, and simple geometric seating is inspired both by his work with Brancusi and the tea ceremony.

Noguchi's environmental designs of the 1960s demonstrate a powerful integration of sculpture and landscape. Two of his projects, the Beinecke Library at Yale University, New Haven, Connecticut (1960–64), and the Chase Manhattan Bank Plaza in New York (1961–64), are sunken gardens. One cannot enter these gardens physically; like the Zen gravel gardens, they are for contemplation only. At Chase Manhattan the circular garden is a meditation on stone and water. A shallow pool with sprays interact with river-worn rocks and geometric pavers. At Yale Noguchi created his most abstract garden. Made entirely of white marble and containing only a pyramid, cube, and circle, the project investigates Eastern art and Western geometry. Noguchi used the stroll garden—another archetype of Japanese garden design, and one that is designed for movement—in the Billy Rose Sculpture Garden at the Israel Museum in Jerusalem (1960–65) and a later garden, *California Scenario* (1980–82), a plaza in Costa Mesa, California.

The Isamu Noguchi Garden Museum in New York was opened to the public in 1985 and continues to present Noguchi's sculpture and gardens as he wanted them to be seen. The artistic dialogues that were crucial to him are visible in this setting: East and West, nature and culture, object and environment.

Biography

Born in Los Angeles, California, 1904. Began career as sculptor in New York, 1924, by creating figurative sculpture and busts; worked with sculptor Constantin Brancusi in Paris, 1927; inspired by trip to Japan in 1931, began to propose theoretical sculptural landscapes of monuments and playgrounds; began 30-year collaboration with dancer and choreographer Martha Graham, 1935; inspired by surrealism in 1940s, exemplified by stone sculptures exploring biomorphic interlocking forms, a vocabulary he adapted to create functional objects; travel to ancient symbolic sites around the world, 1949–51, inspiring artistic investigations into primordial nature of stone and ritualistic nature of public space; received first commission for public open-space designs, for gardens of UNESCO in Paris 1956–58; creation of both sculpture and environments continued in the 1960s (Whitney Museum retrospective exhibition, gardens at Chase Manhattan Bank and Yale University); art and design showcased in important exhibitions and in public commissions, 1970s and 1980s; designed Dodge Fountain and Hart Plaza, Detroit, Michigan, United States, 1972–79; Isamu Noguchi Garden Museum officially opened in New York, 1985; represented United States at Venice Biennale, 1986. Died in New York City, 1988.

Selected Designs

1933 *Play Mountain* and *Monument to the Plow* (both unrealized)
1938 Fountain, Ford Motor Company Building, New York World's Fair, New York, United States (destroyed)
1941 *Contoured Playground* (unrealized)
1945 Jefferson Memorial Park (with Edward Durrell Stone), St. Louis, Missouri, United States (unrealized)
1951 Hiroshima Bridges, Hiroshima, Japan; garden for Lever House (with Gordon Bunshaft of Skidmore, Owings, and Merrill), New York City, New York, United States
1956–57 Gardens, Connecticut General Life Insurance Company (now CIGNA Corporation), Bloomfield, Connecticut, United States
1956–58 Gardens, UNESCO headquarters, Paris, France
1960–61 Sculptures, First National City Bank Building Plaza, Fort Worth, Texas, United States

1960–64 Sunken Garden, Beinecke Rare Book and Manuscript Library, Yale University, New Haven, Connecticut, United States
1960–65 The Billy Rose Sculpture Garden, Israel Museum, Jerusalem, Israel
1961–64 Sunken Garden, Chase Manhattan Bank Plaza, New York City, New York, United States
1964 Gardens, IBM Headquarters, Armonk, New York, United States
1968 *Red Cube* sculpture, 140 Broadway, New York City, New York, United States
1970 Fountains, Expo 70, Osaka, Japan
1972–79 Horace E. Dodge Fountain and Phillip A. Hart Plaza, Detroit, Michigan, United States
1975 *Landscapes of Time* sculptures, Jackson Federal Building, Seattle, Washington, United States
1975–76 Playscapes playground, Piedmont Park, Atlanta, Georgia, United States
1977–78 Interior, *Tengoku* (Heaven), Sogetsu Flower Arranging School, Tokyo, Japan
1978–86 Lillie and Roy Cullen Sculpture Garden, Museum of Fine Arts, Houston, United States
1980–82 *California Scenario,* South Coast Plaza, Costa Mesa, California, United States
from 1980 Bayfront Park, Miami, Florida, United States
1981–83 Isamu Noguchi Garden Museum, Long Island City, New York, United States
1984 Water garden, Domon Ken Museum, Sakata, Japan
1988– Public park, Sapporo, Japan

Selected Publications
A Sculptor's World, 1968
The Isamu Noguchi Garden Museum, 1987

Further Reading
Altshuler, Bruce, *Isamu Noguchi,* New York: Abbeville Press, 1994
Apostolos-Cappadona, Diane, and Altshuler, Bruce, editors, *Isamu Noguchi: Essays and Conversations,* New York: Abrams, 1994
Ashton, Dore, *Noguchi East and West,* New York: Knopf, 1992
Friedman, Martin L., *Noguchi's Imaginary Landscapes,* Minneapolis, Minnesota: Walker Art Center, 1978
Grove, Nancy, *Isamu Noguchi: A Study of the Sculpture,* New York: Garland, 1985
Hunter, Sam, *Isamu Noguchi,* New York: Abbeville Press, 1978

REBECCA KRINKE

Norway

Little is known about Norwegian gardens in the Middle Ages. The small, enclosed garden containing plants for food and other practical use, which can still be seen in the Norwegian countryside, may be the last remains of the Viking horticultural tradition. It is often rectangular or square and is detached from the farmhouse. Very little documentation remains of other medieval gardens, such as monastery gardens that existed from the 11th century.

It is not until the 16th and 17th centuries that we find well-documented examples of Renaissance gardens in Norway. Some are even to a certain degree preserved; others have been restored. These gardens were mainly inspired by the Flemish gardens of the time. Typically they were created by immigrant Flemish gardeners themselves, such as Master Adrian in the Bishop's Garden in Bergen, which was constructed at the end of the 16th century. The most outstanding example of this type still surviving is the old garden at the barony of Rosendal in Hardanger, laid out in the 1660s (see Plate 26). The surrounding landscape forms a dramatic and interesting contrast to the flat parterre, and although we have no direct evidence, the position of dominating mountains in the vicinity probably influenced the orientation of house and garden.

One example of the few and modest gardens in the baroque style that still exists is Rød Herregård near Halden, Østfold, overlooking the bay. It contains a park or pleasure grounds with walks close to the sea and up to a hill that provides views over the sea and back toward the house. On the terraces closest to the house are flower beds and ornamental areas; farther down are the orchard and kitchen gardens. Hazel (*Corylus*) alleys border the garden on each side. A pleached lime tree tunnel forming the end of the formal garden remains intact from the garden, which was laid out in the 1770s.

With the development of the English landscape style, Norway followed fashion to a much higher degree than before. In the late 18th century, several gardens in this style developed in Norway. Bogstad Gård, beside the lake of

Bogstadvannet near Oslo and laid out in the 1780s, is an original example of this style. Here we find the prescribed green lawns with clumps of trees, all in a beautiful landscape setting. The garden has been maintained quite well.

The need for more scientific approaches in the field of agriculture led to the establishment of the Agricultural College at Ås in 1859, which later became the Agricultural University of Norway. The university, together with the park and arboretum, established in 1860, became an important center for Norwegian arboriculture, horticulture, and eventually also landscape architecture. This development was mirrored by a shift in the art of landscape gardening. In the first half of the 19th century, landscape gardening became more a purely horticultural affair. In 1815–18 the Tøyen Botanical Garden at the University of Oslo was established, the first in the country. A smaller botanical garden was established in 1899 at the University of Bergen; this is now the university garden and has been recently replaced by the Milde Arboretum. These gardens have no doubt raised the general level of awareness concerning horticulture, but they have not played a major role in the aesthetic aspects of garden design. At the turn of the 20th century, a new trend became visible. Some of the horticulturists trained at the Norges Landbrukshøgskole (Agricultural University of Norway) became the pioneers of the landscape profession in the country.

The central figure in Norwegian landscape architecture in this initial period was Olav L. Moen (1887–1951). He received a degree in horticulture from the Agricultural University of Norway in 1918 and was appointed as the first lecturer and later professor of the Department of Garden Art, which was established in 1919, the first of its kind in Europe. Moen's contribution as a teacher over a 30-year period in the pioneer age of the profession, together with his great effort as a designer and writer, makes him worthy of the title "Father of Norwegian Landscape Architecture."

Karen Reistad (1900–1993) was another outstanding garden designer of the 20th century. Both in her projects and her published lectures and articles, she represented a poetic functionalism in landscape architecture. Many of her private gardens have a strikingly silent obviousness and simplicity. Her most important works are the many war cemeteries she designed. The largest one, dating from 1954, is situated in Tjøtta, Nordland, where more than 8,000 Russian soldiers killed during World War II are buried. The project displays peaceful isolation and at the same time, contact with the sky and far mountains through a transparent curtain of low birches.

Since the 1950s Norwegian landscape planning has made noteworthy achievements within several sectors, such as hydropower development, highway improvement, conservation of historic landscapes, and urban design. The profession has grown considerably and is today well acknowledged in the society. A large proportion of planning institutions from the municipal level to the national level have landscape architects in key positions on staff, and in the private sector a large number of landscape design companies have been established in the last two to three decades. In 1960 Egil Gabrielsen and Morten Grindaker designed the Hydro Park in Oslo, which set a new trend in public garden design in Norway. It is geometrically shaped and contains stone walls sculpted by the artist Odd Tandberg. Gabrielsen was later professor of landscape architecture at the Agricultural University of Norway, while Grindaker has continued as a consultant up to the present day. Another landscape designer is Bjarne Aasen, who was responsible for the University Park in Trondheim as well as the new university in Tromsø. He is a partner in the group called 13.3. that has designed the landscape of Aker Brygge, a waterfront commercial area in Oslo beginning in 1988. Chief designer Terje Vedal sculpted the floor in the central plaza with hills and steps, and the area has become extremely popular. A group called CUBUS, with landscape designer Arne Saelen, has made noteworthy achievements, for example in the Vetrelidsalmenningen (Vetrelid Common, 1993), a boulevard in Bergen. Many companies combine landscape architecture with architecture, planning, and interior design, such as the company Snøhetta in Oslo, which designed the new Alexandria Library completed in 2000.

Even though there are many excellent landscape designers in Norway, it is hard to detect specific influences that Norwegian landscape design has had on other countries. Norway is part of the Nordic tradition, which can be characterized by a certain relation to nature, and by bringing so-called unspoiled nature into designed areas such as cemeteries or urban housing areas. This can be seen as a Nordic contribution to international landscape design.

Further Reading

Bruun, Magne, "Historic Gardens in Norway," in *Monuments and Sites: Norway, a Cultural Heritage,* edited by Luce Hinsch et al., Oslo: Universitetsforlaget, 1987

Bruun, Magne, "Landscape Planning in Norway,"*Byggekunst* 72, no. 4 (1990)

Jørgensen, Karsten, "Nature and Garden Art in Norway," *Journal of Garden History* 17 (1997)

Treib, Marc, "Landscape on the Edge," *Byggekunst* 72, no. 4 (1990)

KARSTEN JØRGENSEN

Nuneham Courtenay

Nuneham Courtenay, Oxfordshire, England

Location: approximately 5 miles (8 km) southeast of Oxford

The house and gardens of Nuneham Courtenay near Oxford owe their formative creation to the first earl of Harcourt (1714–77) and his son Lord Nuneham (1736–1809), from 1777 the second earl of Harcourt. In 1760 the first earl shifted the family seat from the low-lying ancestral home at Stanton Harcourt to high ground overlooking the river Thames where Stiff Leadbetter had designed a new house. In 1764 James Stuart helped the earl replace the medieval church with a classical temple. The temple would serve both as a place of worship and as a feature of the evolving Picturesque pleasure ground. The initial phase was completed in the 1770s under Lord Nuneham with help from the poet William Mason. Thereafter, the second earl of Harcourt consulted Lancelot "Capability" Brown on improvements while remodeling parts of the house; in the 19th century William Sawrey Gilpin oversaw additional plantings.

Garden historians have long considered Nuneham Courtenay important for several reasons. First, the village of Nuneham, which was removed and rebuilt by the first earl after 1760, has been associated with Oliver Goldsmith's poem *The Deserted Village* (1770). The poem describes the effect on the peasantry of village removal to make way for a Brownian landscape park. Second, the celebrated flower garden, which Lord Nuneham and Mason first laid out in 1771–72, has been associated with Jean-Jacques Rousseau's *Julie; ou, La Nouvelle Héloïse* (1761; *Julie; or, The New Eloise*). During the philosopher's exile in England in 1766, the radically inclined Nuneham gave him lodging on the family estate. After the first earl's death in 1777, the second earl of Harcourt added a bust of Rousseau to his circuit walk to accompany the inscription, "Si l'Auteur de la nature est grand dans les grandes choses il est très grand dans les petites" (If nature's author is great in the great things, he is even greater in the small ones). Third, and above all, Mason's garden is often regarded as the starting point of the "romantic" flower garden, signifying a renewed interest in herbaceous plants after the presumed disappearance of flowers in the early landscape garden.

The influence of Nuneham is unquestionable. Its novel look was disseminated through engravings from Paul Sandby's watercolors of 1777, which circulated widely after 1778. The publication of Nathaniel Swinden's *The Beauties of Flora Display'd* (1778), with its diagrams of conical flower beds, apparently codified the Nuneham prototype. William Watts's view of Wrotham, Hertfordshire, shows the dispersal of this circular form in the following decade—a dispersal further corroborated by the appearance of flower beds in renewed layouts of the 1780s and 1790s, from Syon House, Middlesex, to Hartwell House, Buckinghamshire. Furthermore, Richard Woods's design of 1780 for an "Elysium Garden" for Sir John Griffin at Audley End seems modeled on the second earl of Harcourt's "Elysée." As late as 1803 Humphry Repton could still praise the composition of Mason's flower garden for its blend of art and nature: "seats, temples, statues, vases, or other ornaments" harmonized with a "profusion of flowers and curious plants." And William Combe's account of a visit in 1792 concluded that Nuneham's "flower-garden transcends all rivalry, and is itself alone."

It is clear, nonetheless, that Mason's garden was not a complete novelty, despite its enormous influence and preeminent status. The overall structure and disposition of beds in a self-contained Picturesque enclosure had already been anticipated in Thomas Wright's design of 1760 for the duchess of Beaufort at Netheravon, Wiltshire. And the method of displaying flowers as "nosegays" in grass had been pioneered as early as the 1730s by Richard Bateman at Grove House, Berkshire—a method further developed by Philip Southcote, Joseph Spence, and Richard Woods in the following years. Indeed, Nuneham's arrangement of circles, ellipses, and kidney-shaped beds can be traced back through the mediation of Wright to Robert Furber's "Borders of Cut Work" in *A Catalogue of English and Foreign Trees* (1727).

The pictorial evidence of Picturesque flower gardens before Nuneham goes hand in hand with horticultural evidence from the nursery trade. According to John Harvey, in the mid-18th century "the growing of herbaceous plants put on a spurt." This was especially true from 1750, perhaps due to a lull in the influx of North American shrubs and trees after the 1730s and 1740s. John Webb's catalogs of 1753 and 1760 indicate that, in a period of just seven years, his supply of flower seeds jumped from around 211 types to well over 588. Surviving nursery bills itemizing flowers delivered between 1750 and 1770 to sites such as Redlynch, Somerset, confirm a resurgent interest in flower gardening.

Difficulties in tracing the lineage of Mason's flower garden at Nuneham have resulted from the disappearance of the original plans drawn up in 1771–72. A letter from Mason to Lord Nuneham, dated 26 September 1772, refers to "your plan of the Flower garden and another traced from it in which I have drawn a gravel walk round it and altered the form of the beds and also

Watercolor of the flower garden and Temple of Flora at Nuneham Courtenay by Paul Sandby, ca. 1777
Courtesy of Paul Mellon Centre

(with a horrible green wash) notified what ought to be grass." It appears from this correspondence that the gardener, Walter Clarke, had a hand in the initial scheme, which Mason dismissed as a "blistering plaister," and that late in 1772 the poet was still shaping the second version with its circuit path around a lawn studded with flower beds.

The schematic depiction of Mason's flower garden on Capability Brown's large improvement plan of 1779 (which roughly corresponds to the Sandby watercolors of 1777) is the earliest plan still extant. It indicates that the layout of 1772 consisted of a rather tidy arrangement of beds that only gradually evolved into the more relaxed disposition described and sketched by Repton in 1798. It remains uncertain whether the shift was due to the dramatic impact in the 1780s or 1790s of Gilpin's ideas of "forest lawn" or to dynamic horticultural processes in tandem with changing aesthetics. Certainly the colored plan of Nuneham in 1785 (after alterations in 1783–84) indicates a gradual spreading and coalescence of the original beds that continued into the 1790s.

While the three almost-identical plans of the garden that are assumed to date from the second phase of alterations in 1794 indicate a surprising adherence to the spatial organization of the first scheme, they confirm such organic changes. These occurred along the circuit walk at the Temple of Flora as well as in the shapes and contents of beds and shrubberies. Thus, Lord Harcourt worked with the effects of growth over time. The fact that of the three versions of the plan, one made its way into the duke of Manchester's papers lends credibility to the notion that Nuneham was the garden everybody wished to emulate. Thus in 1799, when the second earl of Harcourt's sister, Lady Elizabeth Lee, came to remodel her flower garden at Hartwell, Buckinghamshire, she followed the Nuneham prototype. Yet in placing the flower beds beneath the windows of her house, Lady Elizabeth departed from her brother's sequestered enclosure, pointing the way to the return of the grand floral parterres in the early 19th century.

Synopsis

1760	First Earl Harcourt moves family seat to Nuneham Courtenay and removes and rebuilds village of Nuneham
1764	Classical temple built on site of medieval church by James Stuart
1766	Jean-Jacques Rousseau resides at Nuneham Courtenay during exile from France
1770s	Design of pleasure grounds by first earl's son Lord Nuneham, with help from poet William Mason
1771–72	Flower garden laid out
1777	Paul Sandby's watercolors disseminate Nuneham's novel look
after 1777	Second Earl Harcourt consults Lancelot "Capability" Brown regarding design of garden
1778	Nathaniel Swinden's *Beauties of Flora Display'd* published, with diagrams of Nuneham flower beds
1779	Capability Brown completes improvement plan
19th C.	William Sawrey Gilpin oversees additional plantings

Further Reading

Batey, Mavis, "Romantic Vision in a Flower-Garden," *Country Life* (12 September 1968)

Batey, Mavis, *Nuneham Courtenay, Oxfordshire,* Oxford: University of Oxford Press, 1979

Batey, Mavis, *Regency Gardens,* Princes Risborough, Buckinghamshire: Shire Publications, 1995

Batey, Mavis, "Two Romantic Picturesque Flower Gardens," *Garden History* 22, no. 2 (1995)

Bending, Stephen, "William Mason's 'An Essay on the Arrangement of Flowers in Pleasure-Grounds,'" *Journal of Garden History* 9, no. 4 (1989)

Combe, William, *An History of the Principal Rivers of Great Britain,* 2 vols., London, 1794–96

Harris, John, "Some Imperfect Ideas on the Genesis of the Loudonesque Flower Garden," in *John Claudius Loudon and the Early Nineteenth Century in Great Britain,* edited by Elisabeth B. MacDougall, Washington, D.C.: Dumbarton Oaks, 1980

Harris, John, "Garden of the Mason School," *Country Life* (3 October 1985)

Harris, John, "A Pioneer in Gardening: Dickie Bateman Re-assessed," *Apollo* (October 1993)

Laird, Mark, "'Our Equally Favorite Hobby Horse': The Flower Gardens of Lady Elizabeth Lee at Hartwell and the 2nd Earl Harcourt at Nuneham Courtenay," *Garden History* 18, no. 2 (1990)

Laird, Mark, *The Flowering of the Landscape Garden: English Pleasure Grounds, 1720–1800,* Philadelphia: University of Pennsylvania Press, 1999

Mason, William, *The English Garden,* London, 1772–81; see especially vol. 4

Soye-Mitchell, Brigitte de, "Nuneham Courteny: Jardin secret d'un poète," in *Jardin et paysages: Le style anglais,* edited by André Parreaux and Michèle Plaisant, Villeneuve-d'Ascq, France: Publications de l'Université de Lille III, 1977

Swinden, Nathaniel, *The Beauties of Flora Display'd,* London, 1778

MARK LAIRD

Nurserymen

Nurseries first appeared in the Netherlands. A fruit-tree trade is recorded as early as 1466 at Boskoop, and other market gardens before 1500 are recorded at Gouda and Leiden. In 1611, 20 market gardens were located at Boskoop.

In England, market gardeners, who dealt not only with fruits and vegetables but also with ornamental exotic plants, existed in the mid-17th century. The oldest recorded English catalogs were printed by John Tradescant (1634 and 1656) and George Rickets (1667). Tradescant, Jr., offered the first North American plants. Robert Standard had for sale in 1684 limes (*Citrus aurantifolia*), firs (*Abies* spp.), arborvitae (*Thuja* spp.), horse chestnuts (*Aesculus* spp.), persian lilacs (*Syringa* × *persica*), firethorn (*Pyracantha* spp.), planes (*Platanus* spp.), oranges (*Citrus sinesnsis*), myrtles (*Myrtus* spp.), and pomegranates (*Punica granatum*). By 1700 printed plant trade catalogs were not unusual in London.

Nurseries also began to appear in England: famous nurseries were London and Wise (founded in 1681), Gray (shortly before 1700), Robert Furber (shortly after 1700), James Gordon (after 1742), Lee and Kennedy (around 1745), and Busch/Loddiges (around 1754). Standish and Noble and Waterer and Veitch became the most famous. George London and Henry Wise also translated the French-written works of La Quintinie, Liger, and Gentil into English.

In 1730 a London society of gardeners, which included Furber, Gray, and Miller, printed supposedly the most splendid *Catalogus plantarum* of all time. Containing 21 colored plates by Jacob van Huysum, the most famous flower painter of this time, with English plant descriptions, it was an artful and scientific work, but it did not give prices. Then in about 1737 Christopher Gray printed a *Catalogue of American Trees and Shrubs*. He had, according to Mark Catesby, "a greater variety of American forest trees and shrubs than in any other place in England," including *Magnolia grandiflora*.

The American Quaker farmer John Bartram (1699–1777) of Philadelphia collected unknown plants from unsettled parts of the country, and the London merchant Peter Collinson (1694–1768) received seeds from him from 1733. The English scientist-gardener Philipp Miller and the London nurseries Gordon, Gray and Furber made the newly introduced plants well-known and distributed them throughout Europe. In 1764 a German plant-lover wrote that Collinson's seed boxes reached England each January or February and contained more than 100 tree and shrub species with Bartram's printed catalog "always on the ground of the box."

Prices were often added to the early printed catalogs by hand. Hand-written prices were found first in a catalog from 1754, containing approximately 170 trees and shrubs and 32 garden roses. The highest-valued plants were citrus, Cedar of Lebanon (*Cedrus libani*), and tulip trees (*Liriodendron tulipifera*). Increasing demand led to increasing supply and production, and prices fell rapidly. Plant sizes were not indicated in the early catalogs.

During the early 18th century, mainly forest trees, hollies, Laurustinus (*Viburnum tinus*), and clipped yews were demanded. The number of tree and shrub species offered increased from 40 in 1730 to 100 in 1760. About 1760 there existed approximately 100 nurseries in England.

The introduction of several American plants to Europe between 1753 and 1795 is attributed to James Lee and Lewis Kennedy at Hammersmith (Lee translated Linnaeus's *Philosophia Botanica* [1751] into English). Loudon called the firm "unquestionably the first nursery in Britain, or, the world." It existed until about 1900.

The German Johann Busch founded the Hackney Nursery, which introduced *Rhododendron ponticum, Fothergilla alnifolia,* and others species. John Bartram sent seeds to Busch via Peter Collinson. Busch traded plants mostly in tubs and pots, avoiding demolition of the roots on transport. His international trade potential, however, was dependent upon commissioned American seed boxes. So long as park owners possessed vast grounds and a great garden staff, seeds were more important trade goods than plants. Landowners created nurseries for their own requirements: if a complete plant was necessary, they bought one specimen only and propagated it themselves. The early commercial nurseries, therefore, offered a vast assortment rather than many specimens of one sort. Orders for American seeds to Busch from Germany are recorded from 1760 on. Busch's pupil Johann Andreas Gräfer, also a German, introduced *Aucuba japonica* and *Malus baccata.*

When Busch went to Russia in 1771, another German, Conrad Loddiges (1738–1826), became owner of the Hackney Nursery. He received American plants from André Michaux and William Bartram and Siberian ones from Busch. Loddiges laid out a famous arboretum and became a specialist in andromedas, azaleas, rhododendrons, and kalmias, which were very high-priced. He claimed to have introduced 151 new plants into Britain and aimed at cultivating all plant species of the world. In 1817 he founded the *Botanical Cabinet*, a journal with hand-colored engravings illustrating 2,000 plants. Publication of the journal continued until 1833.

By the time Loddiges's sons ran the nursery, the Hackney collection surpassed the plant stocks at the Royal Botanic Gardens, Kew, and the firm had the best reputation in all of Europe. In spite of this success, the firm was liquidated in 1852.

Throughout Europe the demand for exotic trees and shrubs increased about 1775. The great nurserys of Lee and Kennedy, Malcolm, Russel, and Loddiges employed their own plant collectors in North and South America during the explosion of the plant trade between 1790 and 1837. Some nurserymen had reputations as botanists, too, such as Thomas Fairchild (1667–1729).

Specialist nurseries became more prevalent in the 19th century, such as Waterer in Knap Hill, Surrey, which was famous for its rhododendron propagation. William Jackman founded a nursery in 1810 that released *Clematis jackmanii* in 1859 and became a specialist in this genus.

John Standish and Charles Noble, in business together since 1846, introduced *Jasminum nudiflorum* and *Cryptomeria japonica* into the trade. Joseph Dalton Hooker gave them his rhododendrons collected in the Himalayas, and Standish hybrizided them with other species from 1838. *Mahonia japonica* was introduced into the trade by Noble in 1858. Fortune contributed new plants from China and Japan to the firm of Standish and Noble.

Harvey recorded 100 nursery catalogs from 1675–1800, 90 from 1800–1836, and 110 from 1837–50. The nursery of James Veitch (1792–1863), Exeter, became the greatest English one after the liquidation of Loddiges's nursery. This firm employed the plant hunters Thomas and William Lobb. Lindley wrote in 1851 that nowhere in the world were more new and precious plants in Europe, excluding Kew, than at Veitch's nursery. James Veitch, Jr. (1815–69), moved the firm to Chelsea. His son John Gould Veitch (1839–70) collected plants from China and Japan in 1860. His brother Sir Harry James (1840–1924) brought the firm to the peak of its fame. Henry Wilson collected for James in China (Veitch, 1906), but the firm closed down in 1914.

John Banister wrote the first American plant catalog for export in 1679, published by John Ray in England. The seed catalogs of John Bartram were hand-written. Bernard M'Mahon (1775?–1816), Philadelphia, published a printed seed catalog in 1806. M'Mahon became important by negotiating for plant materials from the Pacific coast, such as the *Mahonia,* named in his honor. His *Gardener's Calendar,* first edited in 1806, was a very successful handbook for over 50 years.

Chinese nurseries at Canton functioned similarly, as trade places for Chinese plants before the great European plant hunting expeditions into the Chinese continent began.

The 19th century catalogs mostly contain prices, partly because the sale conditions had changed. Several species were sold by the dozen, or in lots of 60 or 100 pieces, and fast-growing trees were separated by height. James Booth offered forest trees in six classes up to 12 feet high in 1807: stem diameter and replanting times were frequently stated. Outstanding specimens were sold on request. Seeds from trees were never sold as extensively as in the 18th century. Several ornamental plants were sold as standard-trees, such as red hawthorns, laburnums, roses, and globose locusts. Most nurseries also offered assortments of roses, evergreens, azaleas, or ornamental shrubs, assembled by the firm itself, for a reduced price.

Dutch nurseries of the 18th century with an international clientele were Johann Rosencrantz; Kebs, Groenewoud and Morbeeck of Haarlem; and Haazen of Leiden. There is a printed catalog by Haazen from about 1760 containing four magnolias, 11 oaks, and 133 citrus cultivars. The German Ernst Heinrich Krelage founded at Haarlem the leading Dutch firm of the 19th century in 1811, which specialized in bulbs. It closed in 1921.

Belgium became a horticultural hub of Europe in the 19th century. Ambroise Verschaffelt (1825–86) and Louis van Houtte (1810–76) owned the most famous nurseries at Gent. From 1845 onward Van Houtte published the highly esteemed plant journal *Flore de Serres et des Jardins.* His establishment was a mecca for gardeners and garden lovers of the world. His rhododendron and *Erica* assortments were famous. In 1842, he was one of the first to offer *Paulownia.*

In France, early nurseries were founded by E. Simon at Plantières near Metz in 1753, by Abbé Nolin for the king at Roule in 1772, and by André Leroy at Angers in 1780. The firm Vilmorin-Andrieux, founded by Andrieux in 1745, is still famous today, and it has published the garden calendar *Le bon jardinier* since 1755.

The nursery of Baumann at Bollwiller, Elsace, was founded in 1740 with fruit trees and became the most celebrated French nursery in the first half of the 19th century. The Baumann brothers offered conifers in pots in 1825, for ease of transport and planting. The hybrid chestnut *Aesculus hippocastanum* 'Baumannii' only confirms the fame of this vanished nursery today.

Victor Lemoine (1823–1911) founded a specialized nursery in 1850 made famous by its hybrids from the genuses *Chaenomeles, Clematis, Deutzia, Hydrangea, Philadelphus, Spiraea, Syringa* and *Weigela.* Its greatest successes were double-flowered lilacs, such as 'Madame Lemoine' and 'Monique Lemoine'.

In Germany, several princes promoted the cultivation of fruit plants in their countries from the time of elector August of Saxonia in the 16th century. The first commercial nursery is thought to be Boeckmann's in Hamburg. A second firm owned by the family Klefeker appeared in Hamburg about 1700. It seems that both had close connections to Dutch and English nurseries. Most German plant lovers of the 18th century ordered plants directly from these companies. Frederick the Great received for Sanssouci plane treess, tulip trees, and acacias from Philipp Miller, Chelsea, in 1746. The first guides to how a nursery can be started were published in Germany in 1770 by Otto von Münchhausen and Samuel Daniel Ludwig Henne. The exchange and trade of trees and shrubs grown in Germany was at this time mainly a profession of the princes, noble landed gentry, and their gardeners, which caused some trouble for the latter with their patrons.

Commercial nurseries in Germany increased in number since the 1770s, such as Buek's in Hamburg, Börner's in Dresden, Reichert's in Weimar, and Corthum's at Zerbst. Two German institutes traded with American seed boxes, such as the Leipzig "Intelligenz-Comptoir" and Friedrich Ludwig August von Burgsdorff's Wood Seeds Institute near Berlin. Burgsdorff's had commissioners also in Vienna, Paris, Stockholm, Warsaw, and St. Petersburg.

The most famous German nurseries of the 19th century were founded by the James Scot Booth near Hamburg, Count Hoffmannsegg and Seidel in Dresden, the merchant Johann Gottlieb Nathusius near Magdeburg, garden director Peter Josef Lenné at Potsdam, and Heinrich and Philipp Siesmayer near Frankfurt. The greatest German nursery was built up by Franz Späth in Berlin after 1860, which still exists today.

Robert Prince, at Flushing, Long Island, is said to be the first American nurseryman, handling fruit trees since 1735. His firm, later extended to ornamental plants, was kept by his descendants through the fourth generation (until 1865). Bartram's nursery was also managed by his sons into the 19th century. The gardens of Prince and Bartram are preserved today. The well-known author on roses, Samuel Parsons (1819–1906), was owner of another important nursery on Long Island. Thomas Meehan (1826–1901) opened a nursery near Philadelphia and became a professor and famous writer. Among his publications was the periodical *Meehans' Monthly,* published from 1859 on.

Further Reading

Harvey, John, *Early Gardening Catalogues: With Complete Reprints of Lists and Accounts of the 16th–19th Centuries,* London: Phillimore, 1972

Harvey, John, *Early Nurserymen: with Reprints of Documents and Lists,* London: Phillimore, 1974

Harvey, John, "The Stocks Held by Early Nurseries," *Agricultural History Review* 22 (1974)

Heriz-Smith, Shirley, "The Veitch Nurseries of Killerton and Exeter," *Garden History* 16 (1988)

Heriz-Smith, Shirley, "James Veitch and Sons of Exeter and Chelsea," *Garden History* 17 (1989)

Jarvis, P.J., "North American Plants and Horticultural Innovation in England, 1550–1700," *Geographical Review* 63 (1973)

Le Rougetel, Hazel, "Philip Miller/John Bartram: Botanical Exchange," *Garden History* 14 (1986)

Le Rougetel, Hazel, *The Chelsea Gardener: Philip Miller 1691–1771,* Portland, Oregon: Sagapress/Timber Press, and London: Natural History Museum, 1990

Solman, David, *Loddiges of Hackney,* London: Hackney Society, 1995

Spongberg, Stephen A., *A Reunion of Trees: The Discovery of Exotic Plants and Their Introduction into North American and European Landscapes,* Cambridge, Massachusetts: Harvard University Press, 1990

Veitch, James Herbert, *Hortus Veitchii: A History of the Rise and Progress of the Nurseries of Messrs. James Veitch and Sons, together with an Account of the Botanical Collectors and Hybridists Employed by Them and a List of the Most Remarkable of Their Introductions,* London: Veitch, 1906

Vrugtman, Ina, "Nursery and Seed Trade Catalogues," *Heritage Seed Program* 4, no. 3 (1991)

Willson, Eleanor Joan, *James Lee and the Vineyard Nursery, Hammersmith,* London: Hammersmith Local History Group, 1961

Willson, Eleanor Joan, *West London Nursery Gardens: The Nursery Gardens of Chelsea, Fulham, Hammersmith, Kensington, and a Part of Westminster, Founded before 1900,* London: Fulham and Hammersmith Historical Society, 1982

Willson, Eleanor Joan, *Nurserymen to the World: The Nursery Gardens of Woking and North-West Surrey and Plants Introduced by Them,* London: s.n., 1989

CLEMENS ALEXANDER WIMMER

Nymphenburg, Palace of

Munich, Germany

Location: Approximately 1.2 miles (2 km) west of Munich city center

The Palace of Nymphenburg was the gem of Bavarian royalty. A creation of the Wittlesbach family, it evolved from a simple gift of endearment to a complex garden whose sole purpose was to delight its guests. The garden was influenced by both the baroque style and the landscape style, creating a unique merger of tastes from two different eras. Nymphenburg enchanted the royal court with a stately palace, distinctive garden pavilions, impressive water features, grandiose parterres, and extensive parklands.

The palace gardens are divided into two distinct areas: the entrance drive and garden. Nymphenburg's grand entrance is designed to impress. It includes a more-than 1,600-meter-long (1,749 yd.) tree-lined canal that extends from the nearby city into the heart of the palace complex, terminating in a large fountain and reflecting pools. Along the canal a stately drive leads to the semicircular palace buildings, which embrace these water elements. The main palace serves as the dominant feature in the center of this space and anchors the end of the canal. Additional buildings connected by open-air galleries symmetrically flank the main structure. These galleries allow the first views into the gardens beyond the palace.

The garden side of the palace is composed of the great parterre embodying the baroque style. Although modified throughout the years, it still maintains its formal

The Principal Parterre at Nymphenburg, Munich, Germany, from Matthias Diesel, *Erlustierende Augenweide,* 1717–22

appearance. Large lawn spaces are edged with gravel walks, flower beds, and statuary of gods and goddesses lining either side of the parterre.

The entrance canal separates around the palace and great parterre and then converges again into one canal leading away from the palace into the distance. The great marble cascade, located approximately 91 meters (99.5 yd.) beyond the great parterre, acts as a terminus to the canal. Located on either side of this part of the canal is the Parkburgen (forested park), created in the landscape style. This area was formerly a baroque woodland penetrated by formal allées and gardens. Today it consists of large informal open spaces, two lakes, and the original garden pavilions built before the transformation.

Nymphenburg began as a gift from Elector Ferdinand Maria to his wife, Henriette Adelaide, out of gratitude for bearing the heir to the Bavarian throne (1663). A garden pavilion at the Italian palace Venaria Reale inspired the naming of this country estate. This pavilion featured frescoes of mythological figures (nymphs), hence the name, "Nymphenburg." Henriette subsequently commissioned Italian architect Agostino Barelli to create her summer palace. Barelli designed a simple five-story structure with a grand exterior staircase. As buildings were added to the main structure over the next century, they were sited so as to create a symmetrical arc, with the original palace as the axial focus. The semicircular space created enclosure and provided definition to the entrance drive, or Rondell.

The reign of Max Emanuel (1680–1726), the son whose celebrated birth initiated the creation of Nymphenburg, greatly influenced the appearance and function of the palace. Elector Max Emanuel was a spirited leader who loved sport and adventure. In honor of his mother, he continued to expand both building and garden at Nymphenburg, transforming the grounds to fulfill his recreational desires. During his reign he solidified a grandiose garden scheme, adding pavilions and weaving intricate water features throughout the Nymphenburg grounds. In 1701 he commissioned Frenchman Charles Carbonet to implement a vast baroque garden influenced by both French and Dutch styles. Construction ceased in 1704 when Max Emanuel left Germany to partake in the War of the Spanish Succession.

Upon returning to Nymphenburg in 1715, Max Emanuel commissioned court architect Joseph Effner and court garden superintendent Dominique Girard to prepare a site plan of the palace gardens. This plan continued the baroque tradition begun by Carbonet. The existing great parterre was now flanked on each side by smaller formal garden rooms. These rooms contained popular French garden features at the time, including a maze, outdoor theater, bowling green, and open spaces for sport. Beyond the great parterre the immense Parkburgen was developed. A grand canal, continuing along the axis of the great parterre, split the Parkburgen into two halves. Each half contained a network of radial allées penetrating woodlands.

Halfway down and perpendicular to the axis of the great canal were two special garden features designed by Effner: the Badenburg (1718–21) and Pagodenburg (1716–19) pavilions. On a cross axis to the canal, the Pagodenburg was constructed to the north and the Badenburg to the south. The Pagodenburg, named after Chinese god figures, provided a place of rest after partaking in sport. The Badenburg, celebrating the element of water, served as a bathing pavilion.

Prior to his death, Max Emanuel began construction on his third garden pavilion, a secluded hermitage known as the Magdalenenklause (1725–28). Another Effner design, the Magdalenenklause was concealed in the woodlands northwest of the great parterre and functioned as a chapel.

The successor to Max Emanuel, Elector Karl Albrecht (r. 1726–45), expanded the Rondell by constructing grandiose reflecting pools in its center. In the late 1720s a canal was dug from these reflecting pools on an axis away from the palace, creating the impressive entrance that exists today. Albrecht also constructed Nymphenburg's fourth garden pavilion, the Amalienburg (1734–39), as a gift for his wife to satisfy her love of hunting. It is one of the finest examples of rococo style in the world, designed by court architect François Cuvilliés, Sr.

In 1804 Elector Maxmilian Joseph commissioned German court garden superintendent Ludwig von Sckell to update the garden by incorporating current design trends. For almost 20 years Sckell transformed large portions of the formal gardens into an informal landscape park but left the baroque parterre, believing its relationship to the formal palace too important. The Dutch-influenced canals also remained, maintaining the overall arrangement of the gardens. However, beyond the parterre all was transformed into the popular landscape style.

Although all the garden pavilions remained, the landscape surrounding them greatly changed. Formal gardens were replaced with informal lakes and large open lawns. Tree groves perceived as accidental were in actuality carefully planned to restrict and broaden views to garden landmarks.

The Palace of Nymphenburg is a wonderful example of one garden comprising two stylistic trends: the baroque style typifying the early 18th century and the landscape style epitomizing the early 19th century, an illustration of contrary styles that embodied extravagant pleasure and prominence. A royal palace that began as a simple act of endearment to one still delights many today.

Synopsis

1663	Elector Ferdinand Maria gives wife Henriette Adelaide land for country estate outside Munich
1664	Construction of Nymphenburg Palace begins under direction of Italian architect Agostino Barelli
1671	First garden design in Italian style
1674	Architect Enrico Zuccalli replaces Barelli to finish building
1702	Elector Max Emanuel commissions architect Antonio Viscardi to expand palace construction; Charles Carbonet designs baroque garden with Dutch-influenced canals
1716–19	Construction of Pagodenburg garden pavilion by architect Joseph Effner
1718–21	Construction of Badenburg garden pavilion by architect Joseph Effner
1725–28	Construction of the Magdalenenklause or Hermitage by architect Joseph Effner
1728	Construction of Rondell (entrance court)
1730	Construction of canals and tree-lined avenues leading into city
1733	Construction of garden walls
1734–39	Construction of Amalienburg hunting pavilion by court architect François Cuvilliés, Sr.
1762	Pump house to supply large parterre fountain and palace with water constructed between Amalienburg and Badenburg pavilions
1769	Marble added to cascade located at west end of garden canal
1803	Joseph Bader rebuilds Green Pump House
1804–1823	Friedrich Ludwig von Sckell transforms most of Baroque garden into one influenced by landscape style
1807	Joseph Bader constructs pump works for fountains on palaces

	entrance side within existing Orangery Buildings pump house; construction of hot-houses north of great parterre; reconstruction of small parterre near palace from designs by Friedrich von Sckell
1820 and 1860	Construction of two additional hot-houses from Sckell's plans
1835	Waterworks for entrance fountains installed in pump house of northern-side building
1865	Construction of Monopteris as garden monument
1952–58	Restoration of Badenburg and Magdalenenklause
1956–58	Restoration of Amalienburg
1970–71	Restoration of main building facade's original colors

Further Reading

Berrall, Julia S., *The Garden: An Illustrated History,* New York: Viking Press, 1966

Dohna, Ursula, *Private Gardens of Germany,* London: Weidenfeld and Nicholson, and New York: Harmony Books, 1986

Hyams, Edward, *A History of Gardens and Gardening,* London: Dent, and New York: Praeger, 1971

Klingensmith, Samuel John, *The Utility of Splendor: Ceremony, Social Life, and Architecture at the Court of Bavaria, 1600–1800,* Chicago: The University of Chicago Press, 1993

Laird, Mark, *The Formal Garden: Traditions of Art and Nature,* New York: Thames and Hudson, 1992

Mosser, Monique, and Georges Teyssot, editors, *L'architettura dei giardini d'Occidente,* Milan: Electa, 1990; as *The Architecture of Western Gardens,* Cambridge, Massachusetts: MIT Press, 1991; as *The History of Garden Design,* London: Thames and Hudson, 1991

Ogrin, Dušan, *The World Heritage of Gardens,* London: Thames and Hudson, 1993

Quest-Ritson, Charles, *The Garden Lover's Guide to Germany,* New York: Princeton Architectural Press, 1998

Schlapper, Fee, *Schloss Nymphenburg,* Munich: Nymphenburger Verlagshandluing, 1972

Schmid, Elmar D., *Nymphenburg,* Munich: Suddeutscher Verlag, 1979

Thacker, Christopher, *The History of Gardens,* London: Croom Helm, and Berkeley: University of California Press, 1979

LISA NUNAMAKER ORGLER

O

Olmsted Family

United States Family of Landscape Architects

For about a hundred years beginning in the 1880s, American landscape architecture was dominated by one family and its firm. It was the combined achievement of three members of this family: Frederick Law Olmsted (1822–1903), his stepson and nephew John Charles Olmsted (1852–1920), and his son Frederick Law Olmsted, Jr. (1870–1957). During that time the firm took on about 6,000 commissions, of which half were implemented.

Frederick Law Olmsted's commitment to landscape architecture really started in 1857 when he became superintendent of Central Park, New York, and then, together with the English-born architect Calvert Vaux, became the park's codesigner and director of construction from 1858 to 1861. From the end of the Civil War up to his retirement in 1895, Olmsted committed his life to his ultimate goal: to civilize the urban frontier with the help of nature and shaped by the landscape architect. To Olmsted the foremost problem of American development in the decades after 1865 was rapid urbanization, which produced a population "little socially rooted" and "isolated . . . from humanizing influences and with . . . constant practice of heart-hardening and taste smothering habits" (quoted in Beveridge and Rocheleau). In this he perceived a threat to an individual's character as well as to democracy at large. Following the ideal of the 18th-century English gentleman, he hoped for the day when all Americans would have achieved gentility—refinement, aesthetic values, a sense of propriety—in short, good taste.

With his strong sense of duty and dedication, Olmsted set a high standard for the landscape architect, a profession established by him—and a term he originated together with Vaux. The landscape architect was to be a teacher of taste and its role in society, was to raise the general cultural level of society, and was to counteract the negative concomitants of industrialization and urbanization. The place to do so most effectively was the city park, a pastoral place in the midst of, and yet set apart from, teeming city life. It would be a place of democratic interaction insofar as people from all classes would mingle in it and in this way would reduce the potential for class conflict—a place where the lower classes would be educated in gentility and where all city dwellers would experience the restorative powers of nature. Here people could "inhale" the spirit of "communitiveness," a sense of shared community and concern for the common good he highly valued. To Olmsted, then, the park was much more than a piece of nature within the artificiality of the city. He considered it an institution of culture and recreation with far-reaching repercussions on both the private and public life of Americans.

Having been to visit several European countries, Olmsted was much impressed by the tradition of English landscape gardening, especially by the art of Lancelot "Capability" Brown. Olmsted was also well versed in the ideas of John Ruskin, Thomas Carlyle, Ralph Waldo Emerson, and James Russell Lowell and was a committed member of the City Beautiful movement. With Andrew Jackson Downing (1815–52), who has been called the first important American landscape gardener, Olmsted shared an appreciation of family, home, and gentility as a counterpoise to change and the crowded and unhealthful conditions of the urban environment.

A look at Olmsted's wide-ranging activities and works shows that he well deserves the attributes of leading American landscape architect of the post-Civil War years and father of American landscape architecture. He created parks, perhaps the best known being Central Park, New York, and Prospect Park in Brooklyn, both together with Vaux; park systems, the first in Buffalo, New York, later Boston's "Emerald Necklace"; residential communities, such as Riverside, Illinois; academic campuses; the grounds of thc 1893 World's Fair in

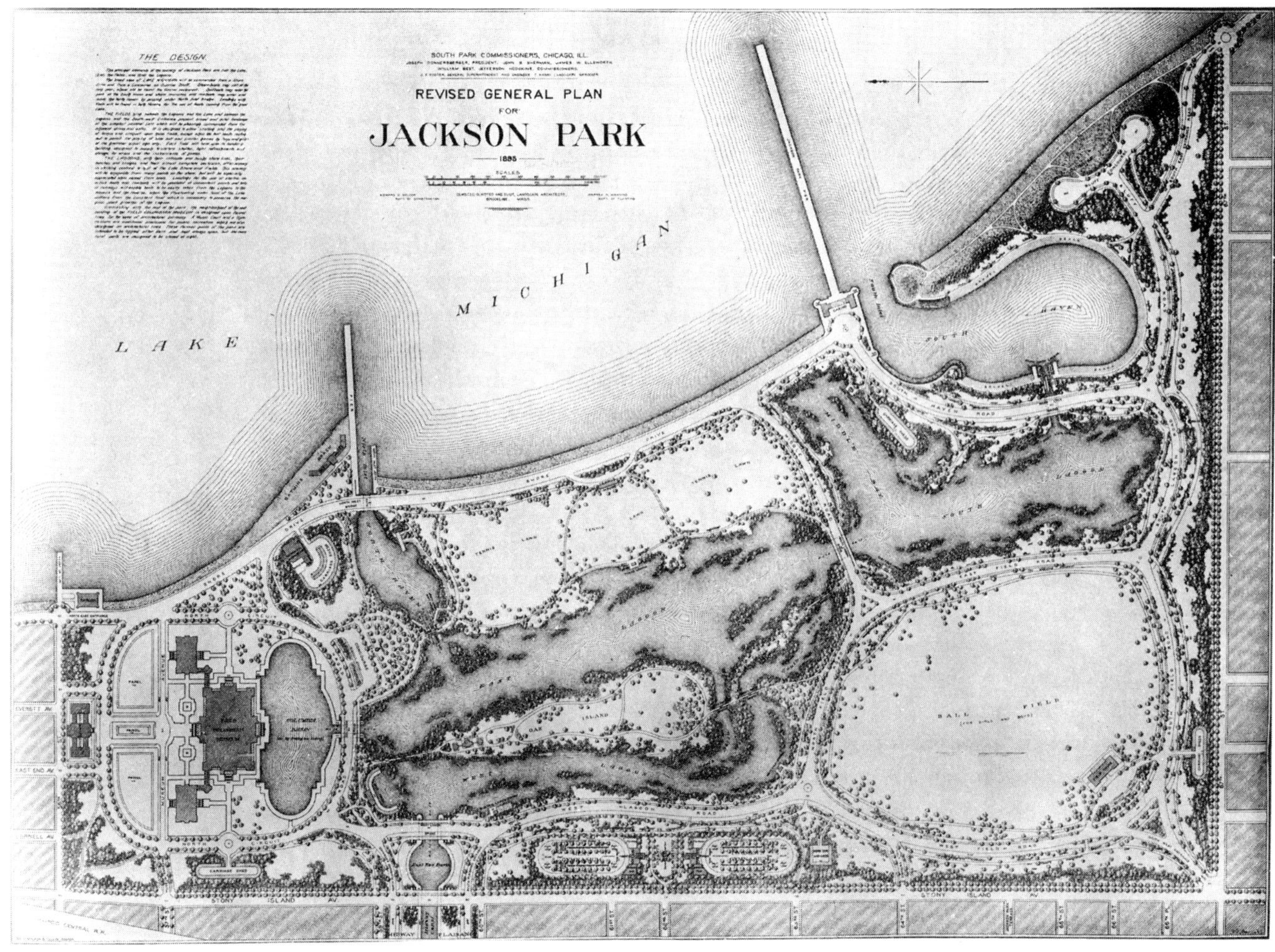

Revised general plan of Jackson Park, Chicago, Illinois, ca. 1895
Courtesy of National Park Service, Frederick Law Olmsted National Historic Site

Chicago; and the grounds of some 200 private estates. He was a leader in the campaign to establish the Niagara Reservation and as head of the first commission was involved in the struggle to keep the Yosemite Valley free from the encroachment of commercial and industrial uses and in this way preserve an area of great natural beauty for public enjoyment. On the estate of George Vanderbilt near Asheville, North Carolina, he began to construct the largest arboretum in the world—although it was never completed.

When Frederick Law Olmsted married his brother's widow in 1859, he adopted their children, John Charles being one of them. John Charles entered his stepfather's firm in 1875, to become, together with Frederick Law Olmsted, Jr., senior partner of Olmsted Brothers in 1898. John Charles Olmsted added his skills in art, architecture, engineering, and photography and his management expertise to the practice, which in those years turned to an efficient business that was able to expand its commissions from about 600 to 3,500. Just like his half-brother, John Charles continued the elder Olmsted's principles yet adapted them to the economic and social conditions of an expanding industrial nation. With an accelerated march of brick and mortar, he thus shifted the emphasis from the pastoral to the architectural and recreational. Believing that haphazard building should be controlled to prevent beautiful vistas and areas of scenic beauty from being destroyed, he worked on parks and park systems created by his stepfather and designed parks and exposition grounds himself in order to provide recreational zones he held indispensable for the modern city dweller. Perhaps his most lasting contribution is his influence on the pattern of cities, since he stressed parks and generous spaces as essential elements to make urban life agreeable.

Frederick Law Olmsted, Jr., an able organizer and systematizer, as well as a designer with a strong sense of duty and social usefulness, concentrated much of his

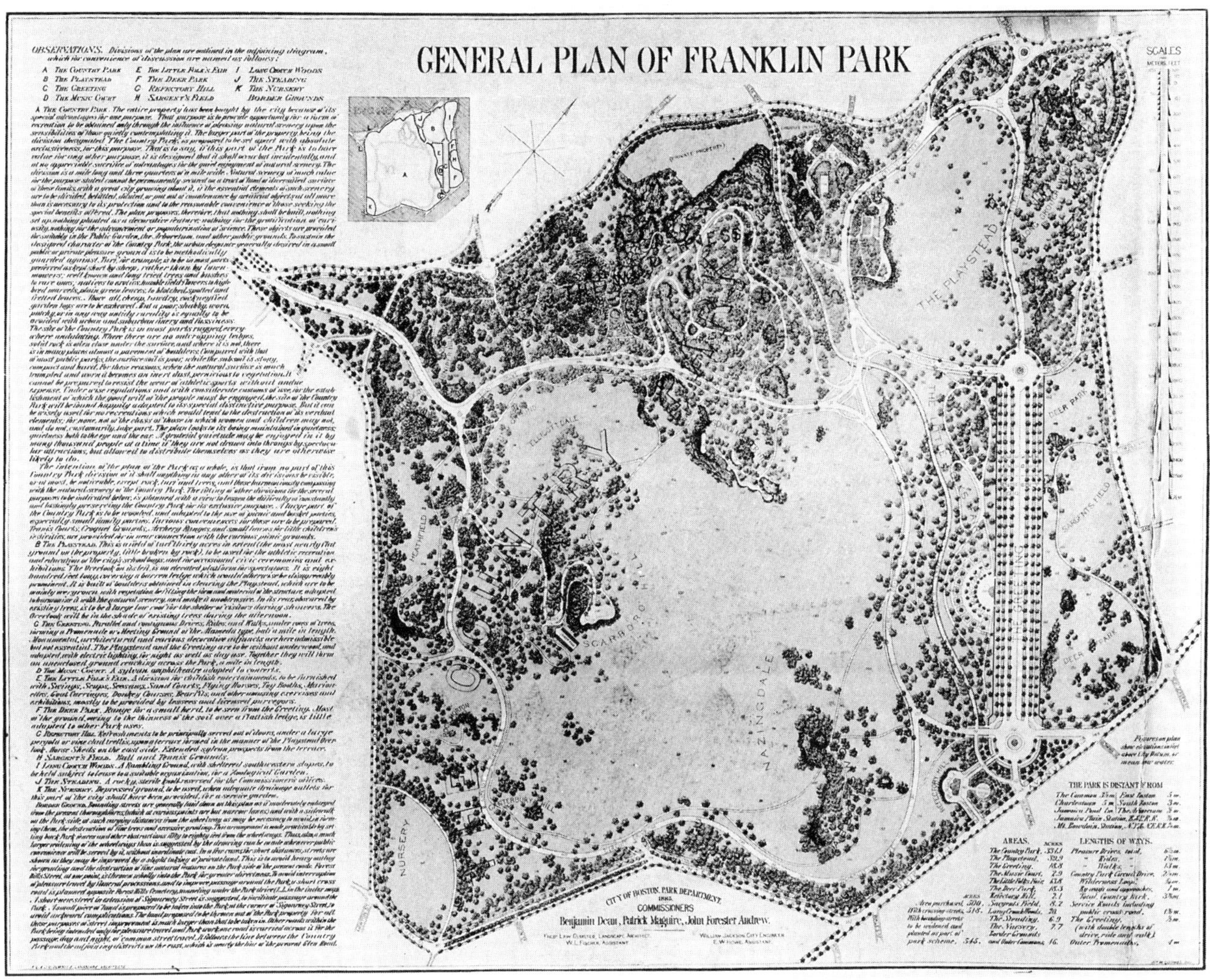

General plan of Franklin Park, Boston, Massachusetts, ca. 1881
Courtesy of National Park Service, Frederick Law Olmsted National Historic Site

time on the institutional and planning aspect of the profession. He played a decisive role in promoting the institutionalization of landscape architecture when he laid down the theoretical foundations of the new profession. He did so in his prolific writings and services on various boards and commissions, for instance, as a founding member and later president of the American Society of Landscape Architects. After having been appointed instructor in landscape architecture at Harvard University in 1900, he devised the first formal training program for the profession in the United States. As a member of the McMillan Commission, he worked on the plan that was to shape the nation's capital in the 20th century, not as something fixed forever but rather something capable of adapting to changing conditions. While he himself devised a blueprint for a system of parks for the whole region, the commission's report as a whole profoundly affected reformers and improvement societies all over the country, for it fostered the belief that the "City Beautiful" was simply a question of adequate planning. In addition to planning and landscape design, Frederick Law Olmsted, Jr., shared with his father an interest in the conservation movements. He even played an active role at one of the same places that drew the attention of his father, Yosemite, where the younger Olmsted was on the board of advisers. All three Olmsteds devoted their working lives to make nature—molded by landscape architecture—an integral part of the urban environment.

See also Arnold Arboretum; Biltmore House; Central Park; Stanford University

Olmsted, Frederick Law 1822–1903

Biography

Born in Hartford, Connecticut, 1822. After 1837 worked with civil engineers and farmers, was a clerk in New York City for seven months, traveled to China for one year, and spent one semester at Yale University, New Haven, Connecticut; practiced scientific agriculture on his farm, Staten Island, New York, 1849–57; completed a six-month tour of the British Isles in 1850, and again in 1856, together with visits to France, Germany, and Italy, and in once again to Britain and France, 1859; traveled twice through the U.S. South in the early 1850s; partner in the publishing firm Dix and Edwards and managing editor of *Putnam's Monthly Magazine,* 1855–57; appointed superintendent of Central Park, New York, and submitted design plan for park with Calvert Vaux, 1857; chief architect and director of construction, 1858–61; between 1858 and his retirement in 1895, he and his partners designed 20 major urban parks, over 100 other public recreation grounds, 50 residential communities, the grounds of some 200 private estates, and planned 55 academic campuses and residential institutions. His stepson and partner, John Charles Olmsted, and his son, Frederick Law Olmsted, Jr., carried on his design tradition. Died in Brookline, Massachusetts, 1903.

Selected Designs

1858–63	Central Park (with partner Calvert Vaux), New York City, New York, United States
1865–73	Prospect Park, Brooklyn, New York, United States
1868–70	Residential community in Riverside, Illinois, United States
1874–91	Capitol grounds, Washington, District of Columbia, United States
1876–93	Boston public parks, Boston, Massachusetts, United States
1886–91	Stanford University, Palo Alto, California, United States
1887	Niagara Reservation, Niagara Falls, New York, United States
1888–93	Site plan for and grounds of the World's Columbian Exposition, Chicago, Illinois, United States
1888–95	Biltmore estate of George W. Vanderbilt, Asheville, North Carolina, United States

Selected Publications

Walks and Talks of an American Farmer in England, 2 vols., 1852
A Journey through Texas; or, A Saddle-Trip on the Southwestern Frontier, 1857
A Journey in the Back Country, 1860
The Cotton Kingdom: A Traveller's Observations on Cotton and Slavery in the American Slave States, 2 vols., 1861
Yosemite and the Mariposa Grove: A Preliminary Report, 1865
Public Parks and the Enlargement of Towns, 1870
A Consideration of the Justifying Value of a Public Park, 1881
The Spoils of the Park, with a Few Leaves for the Deep-Laden Note-Books of "A Wholly Unpractical Man," 1882

Olmsted, John Charles 1852–1920

Biography

Born in Geneva, Switzerland, 1852. Joined the 40th Parallel survey teams in Nevada and Utah, 1869–71; received a Ph.D. from Sheffield Scientific School, Yale University, New Haven, Connecticut, 1875; entered the firm of his stepfather, Frederick Law Olmsted, 1875; full partner in the firm, 1884; senior partner, from 1895 (together with Frederick Law Olmsted, Jr., from 1898), when the practice grew from ca. 600 to total of 3,500 commissions; founding member and first president of the American Society of Landscape Architects, 1899; like Frederick Law, Jr., he continued the elder Olmsted's principles in extending his designs (in Boston, Massachusetts; Hartford, Connecticut; Atlanta, Georgia; Rochester, New York; and Brooklyn, New York), and in his own comprehensive park systems and residential communities (e.g., Dayton, Ohio; Seattle, Washington; Spokane, Washington; Essex County, New Jersey; Portland, Oregon; and Portland, Maine), as well as parks (e.g., Charleston, South Carolina; New Orleans, Louisiana; and Chicago, Illinois); also designed exposition grounds in Seattle, Washington, and Winnipeg, Manitoba. Died in Brookline, Massachusetts, 1920.

Selected Designs

1896–1922	Mount Holyoke College (with Frederick Law Olmsted, Jr.), South Hadley, Massachusetts, United States
1900–	Orange Park, Essex County, New Jersey, United States
1901–10	University of Chicago (with Frederick Law Olmsted, Jr.), Chicago, Illinois, United States
1903–19	Johns Hopkins University (with Frederick Law Olmsted, Jr.), Baltimore, Maryland, United States
1904	South Parks (today McGuane Park), Chicago, Illinois, United States
1915	Grounds, San Diego exposition, San Diego, California, United States

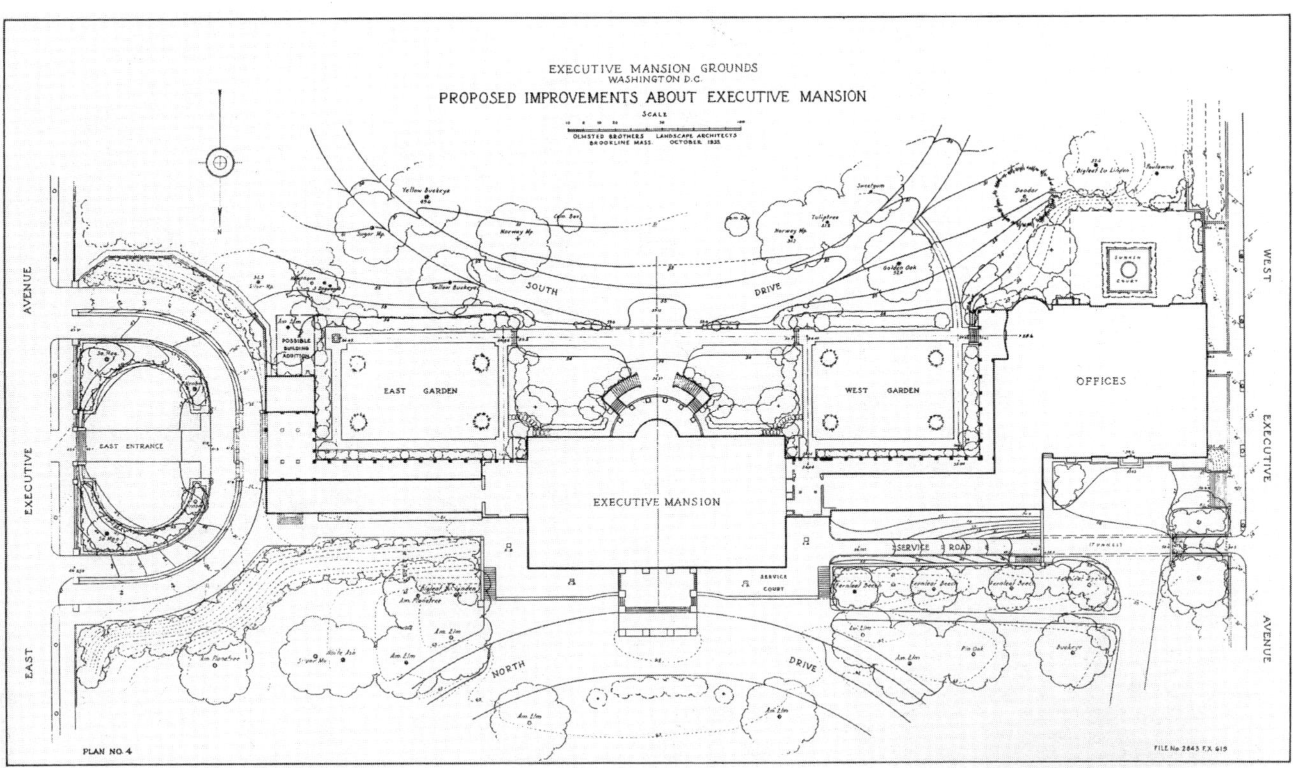

Proposed improvements for grounds surrounding the Executive Mansion (White House grounds), Washington, D.C., ca. 1935, Olmsted Brothers Landscape Architects
Courtesy of National Park Service, Frederick Law Olmsted National Historic Site

Selected Publications

The Projected Park and Parkways on the South Side of Buffalo: Two Reports by the Landscape Architects, 1888

Report of Olmsted Brothers on a Proposed Parkway System for Essex County, N.J., 1915

Olmsted, Frederick Law, Jr. 1870–1957

Biography

Born on Staten Island, New York, 1870. Accompanied his father to job sites and on European study trips from his early years, continued to travel widely throughout his career; received an A.B. from Harvard University, Cambridge, Massachusetts, 1894; became a partner in the Olmsted firm, 1898 (which was renamed Olmsted Brothers in same year); worked as landscape architect on the Biltmore estate, Asheville, North Carolina, 1888–95; designed residential communities and urban parks and park systems, 1905–15 (e.g., planning reports for Detroit, Michigan; Boulder, Colorado; Pittsburgh, Pennsylvania; New Haven, Connecticut; and Rochester, New York); active as an organizer and public servant; founding member of the American Society of Landscape Architects, 1899, and president, 1908–9 and 1919–23; instructor in landscape architecture at Harvard University, 1900–1917, where he created the first university course in landscape architecture in the United States; appointed to the Park Improvement Commission for the District of Columbia (the McMillan Commission), 1901; head of the National Conference on City Planning, from 1910; organizer of the American City Planning Institute in 1917; member of the National Capital Park Planning Commission, 1926–32; advisor to the National Park Service on managing Yosemite National Park, 1928–40 and 1951–56; equal partner with John Charles Olmsted in firm renamed Olmsted Brothers, 1898–1902; senior partner in the largest office of landscape architecture in the world, 1920–49; retired in 1949. Died in Malibu, California, 1957.

Selected Designs

1898–1920 Boston Metropolitan Park System, Boston, Massachusetts, United States

1901 McMillan report for the future development of Washington, District of Columbia, United States

1902–	Roland Park, Baltimore, Maryland, United States
1910–13	Forest Hills Gardens, New York, United States
1913	Suburban development, Newport, Rhode Island, United States
1927	Residential community of Palos Verdes Estates, near Los Angeles, California, United States

Selected Publications

The Smoke Nuisance, 1908; 2nd edition, 1911
The Improvement of Boulder, Colorado, 1910
Pittsburgh Main Thoroughfares and the Down Town District; Improvements Necessary to Meet the City's Present and Future Needs, 1911
Report of State Park Survey of California, 1929

Further Reading

Beveridge, Charles E., and Paul Rocheleau, *Frederick Law Olmsted: Designing the American Landscape,* New York: Rizzoli, 1995; revised edition, New York: Universe, 1998
Hall, Lee, *Olmsted's America: An "Unpractical" Man and His Vision of Civilization,* Boston: Little Brown, 1995
Kalfus, Melvin, *Frederick Law Olmsted: The Passion of a Public Artist,* New York: New York University Press, 1990
Klaus, Susan L., "Efficiency, Economy, Beauty: The City Planning Reports of Frederick Law Olmsted, Jr., 1905–1915," *Journal of the American Planning Association* 57 (1991)
Roper, Laura Wood, *FLO: A Biography of Frederick Law Olmsted,* Baltimore, Maryland: Johns Hopkins University Press, 1973
Rybczynski, Witold, *A Clearing in the Distance: Frederick Law Olmsted and America in the Nineteenth Century,* New York: Scribner, 1999
Whiting, Edward Clark, and William Lyman Phillips, "Frederick Law Olmsted, 1870–1957: An Appreciation of the Man and His Works," *Landscape Architecture* 48 (April 1958)

ANGELA SCHWARZ

Ontario, Royal Botanical Gardens

Hamilton, Ontario, Canada

Location: Highway 2, 1 mile (1.6 km) east of intersection of Highways 403 and 6, between cities of Hamilton and Burlington, approximately 30 miles (48.4 km) southwest of Toronto

Conceived as a gateway garden to one of Canada's most diverse cities, Royal Botanical Gardens has grown into a public amenity and a center for botanical research. It is the largest botanical garden in Canada, including approximately 300 acres (120 ha) of cultivated garden areas and over 2,500 acres (1,010 ha) of nature sanctuaries and wetlands.

The genesis of this institution was in the vision and work of Thomas Baker McQuesten, a lawyer and member of Provincial Parliament for the city of Hamilton, Ontario. In the early 1920s Canada had only two formal botanical institutions: the Central Experimental Farm in Ottawa and University of British Columbia's Botanical Garden in Vancouver. Spurred by a desire for civic beautification and development, McQuesten, then chairman for public works for the city of Hamilton, and C.V. Langs, chair of the City of Hamilton Board of Park Management, undertook the development of what would emerge as the Royal Botanical Gardens. Focusing on the northwest entrance to the city, the parks board began acquiring lands as public park space. The first properties purchased by the city included 258 acres (104.5 ha) of wooded land and 119.5 acres (48.5 ha) of wetland called Westdale Park. By securing this area the board set the tone for subsequent development of the gardens as public garden space and protected natural areas.

Key to the development of the park concept was the large Great Lakes coastal wetland area called Cootes Paradise. Named after a British army officer stationed in the area at the time of the American Revolution, Cootes Paradise is a complex system of wetlands and ravines that extends inland from Hamilton Harbour, itself a bay of Lake Ontario. As early as 1887 civic and provincial governments were concerned about the protection of the marsh as a wildlife and bird sanctuary and took steps to protect it from filling and development. As a result the majority of the marsh has remained intact, although it has suffered significant degradation as a result of pollution and the effects of carp, an introduced species of fish. In the early part of the 20th century, squatters lived in a shanty town along the shore of the marsh, drawn there by a lack of city interference and abundance of natural resources.

In December 1929 the parks board gave approval to a suggestion that the name of Westdale Park be changed to Royal Botanical Gardens. The onset of the Great Depression severely limited the available resources, and funding from the federal government as a make-work program allowed construction of one feature, the Rock Garden, to begin in November 1929. Carl Borgstrom, who was strongly influenced by Fredrick Law Olmsted, won the 1928 gateway design competition.

At about the same time, construction began on the campus of McMaster University, which had been founded in Toronto and subsequently moved to Hamilton. The McMaster campus was established directly adjacent to Westdale Park. Thus, the city gardens were envisioned as both the entranceway to the city and to the university. As the Rock Garden was being built, part of Westdale Park adjacent to the university was developed as a Sunken Garden, including steps with balustrades and a concrete pool area. The site of the Sunken Garden and 130 acres (52 ha) of Royal Botanical Gardens property was sold to McMaster University in 1963. The Sunken Garden was eventually demolished in order to build a new teaching hospital complex on the site.

As construction of the Rock Garden progressed, King George V of England granted a Royal Charter for use of the name "Royal Botanical Gardens," initially applied to the original 400-acre (161-ha) site. Several other parcels of land were added to the growing park system in subsequent years. Later in 1930 a 122-acre (49-ha) property called Hendrie Valley Farm was given to the city by George M. Hendrie. The farm consisted of sloping woodlands and a broad valley to the north and east of Cootes Paradise. The original Westdale Park site, the Rock Gardens, and Hendrie Valley Farm (now called Hendrie Park) were combined together in 1932 as Royal Botanical Gardens.

The combination of cultivated public spaces and natural lands changed the original concept of Royal Botanical Gardens from that of a contained, cultivated showpiece to an outward-looking institution that included conservation and interpretation of natural habitats as part of its objectives. Royal Botanical Gardens was subsequently separated from the City of Hamilton Board of Parks Management and was made an agency of the Province of Ontario on 1 April 1941.

Land acquisition remained an important focus for Royal Botanical Gardens throughout the 1940s. By the end of the decade, almost 2,000 acres (800 ha) had been acquired. A significant addition of 400 acres (160 ha) on the north shore of Cootes Paradise brought most of the wetlands under its management. Much of the garden design work commenced following the land acquisitions of the 1940s, under the continuing supervision of Borgstrom.

A formal association between faculty of McMaster University and the management of Royal Botanical Gardens developed in the 1940s. The first director of Royal Botanical Gardens, Dr. Norman W. Radforth, was given joint appointments as director of the gardens, full professor, and head of the botany department at McMaster University in 1946. Radforth served as director until 1953, when he retired from the gardens to devote his full attention to the university's biology department.

For a time during the 1940s Royal Botanical Gardens planned a residential training institute in park management and horticulture under Radforth's direction. Known as the Royal Botanical Gardens Institute of Parks and Recreation, it was to be housed in a small hotel purchased for that purpose. Unfortunately this program was canceled, but it had a lasting effect through the hiring of Leslie Laking, who became Royal Botanic Gardens' longest serving director.

By 1950 the various properties within Royal Botanical Gardens totaled 1,800 acres (720 ha). That same year the problematic effects of introduced carp on the wetland ecosystem of Cootes Paradise were first noted. A large fish native to Europe and Asia, carp enter shallow waters to spawn each spring. The turbidity caused by tens of thousands of adult carp spawning in Cootes Paradise has been one of the most important factors causing the most visible change in the marsh: the dying back of emergent vegetation to a small remnant of its original coverage.

Royal Botanical Gardens established a carp control program in May and June of 1950 that resulted in the removal of three tons of carp from the marsh. This project proved to be ineffective but was only the first effort directed at remediation of the damage caused by carp. In the 1990s a major rehabilitation program entitled Project Paradise was created by Royal Botanical Gardens, including both direct habitat restoration projects and fund-raising to sustain the habitat rehabilitation work. This program, centered on the Cootes Paradise Fishway, is keeping most carp out of the marsh, allowing the vegetation to recover.

Concerns over the quality of the environment of Cootes Paradise have a long history. As early as the mid-1940s, unexplained deaths of turtles and fish in the marsh were causing concern. In October 1946 the City of Hamilton Health Department was found to have been spraying DDT on the marsh in an effort to control mosquitoes. Research began into the characteristics of the marsh and the effects of human impacts and pollution, research that continues to the present day.

Upon Radforth's retirement from Royal Botanical Gardens in 1953, Dr. Leslie Laking was appointed as the second director. During the 1950s relatively little new property was added, and efforts focused instead on the development of formal garden areas and facilities. Creation of a rose garden began in April 1951. That same year construction began on the Spring Garden (see Plate 27), consisting largely of peonies and irises. The opportunity to develop some of the lands adjacent to the Cootes Paradise marsh as an arboretum was also realized, with construction beginning in 1953.

Under the direction of John Lamoureux, an extensive trail system was developed throughout the nature sanctuary areas. Beginning in the 1950s the trail system was constructed largely around existing pathways, and in some cases, historical carriage-ways and old roads. The trails provide access to the nature sanctuaries and venues for guided walks and courses.

Development of both the horticultural garden areas and facilities for visitors has continued more or less continuously since the 1960s. In 1964 a Rose Garden, designed by J. Austin Floyd, was built in Hendrie Park. A fountain court area was constructed in 1965. The last major parcel of property to come to Royal Botanical Gardens was more than 600 acres (243 ha) of the Cootes Paradise marsh, turned over by the Hamilton Harbour Commission in December 1977. This acquisition gave Royal Botanical Gardens ownership of nearly all of Cootes Paradise, permitting extensive and integrated management of the marsh.

Throughout the 1980s development focused on formal garden areas and improved visitor services. The construction of a new conservatory housing the Mediterranean Garden was begun in 1984 and completed in 1986.

The history and significance of Royal Botanical Gardens was formally acknowledged by the government of Canada in May 1998, with its designation as a Site of National Historical and Architectural Significance.

Royal Botanical Gardens has developed extensive educational programs, beginning in 1947 with the opening of the Children's Garden. In the early 1960s the educational programs included interpretation of maple bush operations. In 1977 it introduced a horticultural therapy program to Ontario. Six courses taught therapists to apply horticultural activities as components of health care. Outdoor education and nature interpretation were given a boost in 1968 with the opening of the Nature Interpretive Centre.

In addition to the cultivated gardens and nature sanctuaries, six important functions are contributing to the garden's growth: a popular gardening information service, a rich educational program, home demonstration gardens, special events such as garden festivals and flower shows, the large reference and lending library, and an annual plant sale.

Five major cultivated garden areas now comprise the formal sections of Royal Botanical Gardens. The Arboretum occupies a site on the north shore of Cootes Paradise, with a Nature Interpretive Centre and horticultural plant propagation facilities. The Arboretum also houses the lilac collection, representing the living specimens of the world type registry of French hybrid lilacs of the genus *Syringa,* which Royal Botanical Gardens maintains. The Laking Garden is devoted to perennials, with major collections of irises and peonies. The Rock Garden is now a historic site, and Hendrie Park has been developed to include several important theme gardens, including the Rose Garden, the World of Botany garden, the Thyme Garden, the Woodland Garden, and the Medicinal Plants Garden. Adjacent to Hendrie Park, Royal Botanical Gardens Centre includes the Mediterranean Garden conservatory and the Children's Discovery Garden.

The nature sanctuaries exhibit substantial biological diversity, with nearly 1,000 species of spontaneously occurring plants, 25 species of mammals, and 248 recorded bird species (of which 38 are aquatic birds). Nearly 60 species of fish are present in the Cootes Paradise marsh and adjacent waters. The rehabilitation of Cootes Paradise continues as one of Royal Botanical Gardens' most important projects. These wetlands are one of the few remaining major spawning areas for native fish on the lower Great Lakes.

Synopsis

1887 Cootes Paradise wetland under government protection

1920s Hamilton city purchases Westdale Park

1928 Creation of gateway parks along major road connecting city to provincial capital

1929 Sod turning and first rock laid at Rock Garden, adjacent to Burlington High Level Bridge, as part of city of Hamilton beautification program; parks board approves change of name from Westdale Park to Royal Botanical Gardens

1930 Royal Charter granted by King George V for name, Royal Botanical Gardens, for original 400-acre (162-ha) site; Hendrie Valley Farm property added 122 acres (49 ha)

1932 Westdale park site, Rock Garden, and Hendrie Valley Farm combined into Royal Botanical Gardens

1942 Rock Garden opened to public

1947 Opening of Children's Garden

1963 Sunken Garden sold to McMaster University and later demolished

1968 Nature Interpretive Centre opened on north shore of Cootes Paradise
1986 Mediterranean Garden (conservatory adjacent to RBG Centre) opened to public
1996 Children's Discovery Garden opened adjacent to RBG Centre
1997 Cootes Paradise Fishway in full operation

Further Reading

Best, John, *Thomas Baker McQuesten: Public Works, Politics, and Imagination,* Hamilton, Ontario: Corinth Press, 1991

Track, Norman, *Canada's Royal Garden: Portraits and Reflections,* Toronto, Ontario: Viking Books, 1994

DAVID ALLEN GALBRAITH

Oranienbaum (Lomonosov)

Lomonosov, St. Petersburg Oblast, Russia

Location: approximately 20 miles (32 km) west of St. Petersburg

Russians still often refer to Oranienbaum, considered too Germanic a name, by its revolutionary title Lomonosov, the family name of the founder of the nearby 18th-century colored-glass manufacturer Mikhail Vassilievich. After Peterhof (Petrodvorets), Tsarskoye Selo (Pushkin), and perhaps Pavlovsk, it is the grandest of the remaining 18th-century summer palaces. It is also the only one that did not lie within Nazi-occupied territory during World War II or undergo the consequent systematic destruction suffered by the others. It escaped with constant bombardment and much hardship, but comparatively little physical damage. On the south coast of the Gulf of Finland, about 25 miles (40 km) west of St. Petersburg and 7 miles (12 km) west of Peterhof, it is the most westerly of the summer palaces. Its contents are much less magnificent than those of Peterhof and Tsarskoye Selo, but its parks are more peaceful and less crowded. It was once joined to the gulf by a canal.

Oranienbaum is an ensemble of parks, museums, and several palaces, none of which is visible from any of the others. It is said to lack Peterhof's beauty, Pushkin's elegant splendor, and Pavlovsk's severe nobility but to surpass the others in refined charm. In 1713, shortly after Peter the Great had begun to build Peterhof, his close companion Alexander Danilovich Menshikov began to build Oranienbaum on land given to him by the czar in 1707.

The architects D. Fontana in 1710 and G. Shedel (from 1710 to 1727) built the Grand Palace on the estate, a huge structure, concave to the north, with graceful elongated wings curling northward and flanked by domed pavilions at each end. The upper and lower gardens were laid out while the Great Palace was under construction. Fountains and sculptures were scattered throughout the lower garden, at the front of the house, to the north and nearer the sea. It was a paradigm of parks laid out in Russia in the French style during the first half of the 18th century, although the parterres between the palace and the road contain beds that are rhomboid and circular rather than rectilinear.

Oranienbaum served briefly as a hospital but was finally given to the future czar Peter III, husband of the future Catherine the Great, and it became his summer residence beginning in 1743, during which time B.F. Rastrelli reconstructed the Grand Palace. Construction at Oranienbaum continued for several decades. Peter III had the Peterstadt fortress ensemble built on the banks of the Karost River. Before Peter III's marriage and accession Antonio Rinaldi built for him the small Peter III Palace, with a tower crowned by a spire, in the southeast corner of the lower park, between the lower lake to the north and the upper lake to the south. The ceremonial archway remains, but the original moat, barracks, and fortifications have now disappeared. West and south of the Great Palace lies the upper park, laid out in rectilinear paths within which a network of paths on a diagonal axis is now lost to the undergrowth. The upper park is formal in design and contains canals, bridges, ponds, and mixed woodland of firs, oaks, limes, and birch, but very few curves. It was Catherine the Great's favorite part of the estate; after her husband's death she commissioned Rinaldi to build here what are generally considered to be Oranienbaum's two best buildings, the Sliding (or "Skating") Hill and the Chinese Palace.

On the north side of the upper park lies the Stone Hall, where Catherine dressed for costume balls and was known to emerge in a chariot, dressed as Minerva. Farther to the west, in its northwest corner, is

Gardens at Oranienbaum
Copyright Paul Miles Picture Collection

the three-story pleasure pavilion known as the Sliding Hill, which contains a model of the original west side of the park, with a one-third-mile (0.5 km) roller coaster flanked on both sides by elevated drives on which guests raced their horses, using sledges in winter and wheeled carts in summer.

South of the park is the baroque "Chinese Palace," which Catherine called her private *dacha,* although she is known to have spent only 48 days here during her 34-year reign. Official literature describes Rinaldi's work as rococo, mixed with "bright, festival baroque" and "severe and strictly logical classicism." Except for the admittedly sometimes considerable elements of interior chinoiserie, certainly little about Oranienbaum is oriental in anything other than name and little exists here of the exquisite delicacy of the finest Bavarian rococo. World War II left the buildings in urgent need of maintenance and sometimes restoration, now duly completed, but the parks were relatively unharmed.

Synopsis

1707 Czar Peter the Great gives land for Oranienbaum to Prince Alexander Danilovich Menshikov
1713 Menshikov starts to build Oranienbaum
1727 Menshikov exiled on death of Catherine I
1743 Oranienbaum became summer residence of future czar Peter III, who begins reconstruction work
1762 Accession and death of Peter III; Catherine the Great commissions Antonio Rinaldi to build Sliding Hill Pavilion and Chinese Palace
1946 Reopening of Upper Park after World War II
1959 Full reopening of Oranienbaum

Further Reading

Alexander, John T., *Catherine the Great: Life and Legend,* New York: Oxford University Press, 1989

Hansmann, Wilfried, *Gartenkunst der Renaissance und des Barock,* Cologne, Germany: DuMont, 1983
Michael, Prince of Greece, *Imperial Palaces of Russia,* translated by Catherine O'Keeffe, London: Tauris Parke, 1992
Mosser, Monique, and Georges Teyssot, editors, *L'architettura dei giardini d'Occidente,* Milan: Electa, 1990; as *The Architecture of Western Gardens,* Cambridge, Massachusetts: MIT Press, 1991; as *The History of Garden Design,* London: Thames and Hudson, 1991
Murrell, Kathleen Berton, *St. Petersburg: History, Art, and Architecture,* S.l.: Troika, 1993; London: Flint River, 1995
Vasilevskaia, Nina, and Elena Vasilevskaia, *St. Petersburg: A Guide to the Architecture,* translated by Yelena Kazey, Saint Petersburg: Bibliopolis, 1994

ANTHONY H.T. LEVI

Ornament, Garden

The use of garden ornaments is recorded as early as the ancient Egyptians. Wall paintings and architectural reliefs discovered in tombs show not only the layout of the gardens but the use of vine trellises, pools, gates, paths, obelisks, garden pavilions, and large earthenware pots for plants and statues.

After conquering Egypt and Mesopotamia in the seventh century, the ancient Persians had considerable influence on ornamental garden design. Their traditions provided the foundation for Islamic garden design. Information about Islamic gardens comes from paintings, patterns woven into Persian carpets, and sculptural reliefs. The Islamic religion forbids graven images; therefore, Islamic gardens contained no statues. Water became an important feature in Islamic gardens due to its scarcity; small, narrow pools were used both to store water and to provide an environment with a cooling effect. Fountains used water sparingly, with single jets spouting small streams of water. Islamic gardens were also known for their use of tile and masonry on paths, patios, and on structures. Other garden ornaments included terra-cotta pots, benches, and window seats.

The ancient Greeks' significant contribution to landscape design was their ability to take full advantage of a site when placing temples and shrines. Little evidence exists as to the design of the areas around the temples and shrines since there are no remaining artifacts. However, Greek literature suggests that these areas contained gardens and used decorative statuary, vases, and urns.

Ancient Romans built extravagant gardens in the hills around Rome. The Roman garden integrated the exterior with the interior of the villa. Frequent garden ornaments in these gardens included pools, fountains, and fine sculptures made of bronze or marble, as well as mosaic tile paving, grottoes, furniture, trellises, and arbors. Most of the gardens and garden ornaments of ancient Rome were destroyed after the fall of the Roman Empire and almost completely disappeared from the landscape.

The garden styles of China and Japan were greatly influenced by religion, art, and nature. Chinese gardens were designed to produce an allusion, making use of the surrounding nature. Poetry and paintings greatly influenced Chinese garden design. Elements of Chinese gardens included structures, plants, hills, rocks, water, and animal life. These components were sparingly enhanced with garden ornaments. Ceramic pots containing plants were carefully placed, sometimes as a contrast against the roughness of a rock. A bench or fence with shelves was also sometimes used to display the potted plants. Gardens might have some statuary, but rocks were carefully chosen and placed in the garden to symbolize mountains, various plants, animals, and birds. Bridges were used to link spaces and were artfully designed with shapes and decorations that contributed to the garden aesthetics. Bridges often had a zigzag shape to slow the visitor's walk so the scenery could be enjoyed. Fences were used to separate spaces or to block views; openings in fences were often filled with intricate grilles. Gates connected spaces and were usually an open design so the visitor could see into the next space. Calligraphy, carved on stone, rock, or wood, was used throughout the garden to identify buildings or a scene or even express the writer's philosophy.

Japanese gardens were designed to reflect nature on a smaller scale. Symbolism was attached to every element in the garden. Such gardens included rock, stone, water, plants, and structures. Ornaments were primarily found in tea gardens. Stone lanterns light the path to the teahouse, and wash basins, usually outside the teahouse, offer an opportunity to cleanse the body and spirit. Stepping stones, carefully chosen for their shape and size, lead the visitor to the teahouse. A *shishi odoshi* (deer scarer) is a bamboo pipe that fills with water and then tips to dump the water into a basin. The tipping motion makes a clatter to frighten wildlife.

The Italian Renaissance, with its renewed interest in learning and the fine arts, inspired garden designers and created a greater interest in the ornamental features of the garden. Key elements of Italian gardens included flowing water, terraces, statuary, and knot gardens. The Italian Renaissance gardens are best known for their fountains. Italian gardens were built on hillsides to capture the cool breezes, which also allowed garden designers to build fabulous cascades and fountains using gravity to build sufficient water pressure. At times water was also contained in still pools with fine statuary as ornamentation.

Italian Renaissance gardens were modest and based on a human scale, unlike the scale used by the French as demonstrated in the gardens at Versailles, created in the 17th century for Louis XIV. France's topography differs greatly from Italy's and was not suitable for building great fountains. Nonetheless, that did not stop Louis XIV from building grand gardens with extensive water features. Immense and diverse fountains, pools, and canals, along with parterres, urns, vases, statuary, topiary, an orangery, paths, and vistas, surround his great palace. Garden ornaments at Versailles reflect the skills of designers and artists to create gardens and art that was appropriate not only in materials but to the scale of the place.

Until the 18th century English gardens were greatly influenced by the Italians, French, and Dutch, the latter being expert nurserymen. In the 18th century a new type of garden appeared in England. Working on a larger scale than William Kent, garden designer Lancelot "Capability" Brown removed the geometry of the previous garden styles and replaced them with a picturesque style influenced by 17th-century landscape paintings. Streams were dammed to form lakes, and trees were planted in clumps, an influence of William Kent. However, it is to the Italians and French that the garden designer Gertrude Jekyll looked to for examples of garden ornaments by the late 19th century.

The overall appearance and function of garden ornaments have changed little through history. The greatest changes have been in materials—to adapt to various climates and styles—and in scale, to adapt to the region's topography and influence of current leadership or religion. Particular types of garden ornaments have helped define the gardens of each period in history.

Statuary, first introduced by the Greeks, has always been an important element in the garden. Statues were generally of political leaders, religious figures, or elements of nature. Early statues were made of marble, which was not suited to the harsher climates of England, for example, where the more durable materials of stone or lead were used.

Gardens in the 18th century often used urns as terminal points in vistas, sitting in niches or placed atop balustrades or posts. Originally designed as a footed vessel with a lid and meant to hold the ashes of the dead, urns in time became more ornate and were used as vases to display plants. Little distinction is made between urns and vases since both have the same function.

Pergolas and trellises provide support for vines and other types of climbing plants. Usually made of wood, they may also be made of metal or a combination of stone, masonry, and wood. Their function has not changed; even today their primary use is as support for climbing plants.

Garden seats provide not only a place to rest but also a place from which to enjoy the garden. Historically, designers have generally felt that garden seats should not be conspicuous but in keeping with the surroundings of the garden. Location, materials, size, and style are all important considerations for placing a seat in the garden.

One of the more popular garden ornaments that has survived the test of time is the sundial. Even with the invention of watches and clocks, the desire to have a sundial in the garden has never lessened. Some are mounted on walls and others on pedestals.

Today garden ornaments come in all styles, forms, and materials. As garden history has demonstrated, however, the most successful garden ornaments are chosen for their suitability to the site, with scale, materials, and style as guidelines.

Further Reading

Bibb, Elizabeth, *In the Japanese Garden,* Washington, D.C.: Starwood, and London: Cassell, 1991

Dongchu, Hu, *The Way of the Virtuous: The Influence of Art and Philosophy on Chinese Garden Design,* Beijing: New World Press, 1991

Douglas, William Lake, et al., *Garden Design: History, Principles, Elements, Practice,* Scarborough, Ontario: Prentice-Hall Canada, 1983; New York: Simon and Schuster, and London: Macdonald, 1984

Israel, Barbara, *Antique Garden Ornament: Two Centuries of American Taste,* New York: Abrams, 1999

Jellicoe, Geoffrey, and Susan Jellicoe, *The Landscape of Man: Shaping the Environment from Prehistory to the Present Day,* New York: Viking Press, and London: Thames and Hudson, 1975; 3rd edition, expanded and updated, New York: Thames and Hudson, 1995

Jekyll, Gertrude, *Garden Ornament,* London: Country Life, and New York: Scribner, 1918; reprint, Woodbridge, Suffolk: Antique Collectors' Club, 1982

Llewellyn, Roddy, *Roddy Llewellyn's Elegance and Eccentricity,* edited by Robert Holt, London: Lock,

1989; as *Ornamental English Gardens*, New York: Rizzoli, 1990
Morris, Alistair, *Antiques from the Garden*, Woodbridge, Suffolk: Garden Art Press, 1996; 2nd edition, 1999
Newton, Norman T., *Design on the Land: The Development of Landscape Architecture*, Cambridge, Massachusetts: Harvard University Press, 1971
Plumptre, George, *Garden Ornament: Five Hundred Years of History and Practice*, London: Thames and Hudson, and New York: Doubleday, 1989
Smith, Linda Joan, *Smith and Hawken Garden Ornament*, New York: Workman, 1998
Yang, Hung-hsün; *The Classical Gardens of China: History and Design Techniques*, translated by Wang Hui Min, New York: Van Nostrand Reinhold, 1982

MARILYN MAGNUSON

Ornamental Plant

Throughout the history of humankind, plants have been used primarily for food and medicine, but many medicinal herbs were also beautiful, and fruit trees bore lovely blossoms as well as fruit. Humankind's ornamental use of plants can be traced through 7,000 years of archaeological evidence, architectural fragments, artifacts, historical records, literature, and art. Not surprisingly, the greatest evidence of plants' decorative value comes from times of peace and prosperity when concerns could rise above mere survival.

Archaeologists studying ancient gardens employ a variety of techniques to determine time periods, hardscape features, and relationships to adjoining buildings. They can determine the age of a garden and its relationship to nearby structures if the garden features exist in the same level of soil as the buildings. These features might include gravel or stone pathways. Darker-colored soil would indicate the position and size of planting beds enriched for cultivation. The size of planting holes indicate the size of the plants themselves. In more modern restoration efforts subtle depressions or other variations in the surface of the overall landscape may indicate patterns of pathways or planting beds. Although pollen analysis has not proved particularly useful, plant varieties can be ascertained through documentary evidence such as drawings, painting, plans, or decorative motifs.

In Mesopotamia, the "cradle of civilization" dating back 7,000 years, archaeologists have found evidence of formal irrigated temple gardens. Trees were central features, and fruit was considered a sacred offering to the gods. Clearly recognizable Madonna lilies (*Lilium candidum*) appear in various architectural fragments, along with other unidentifiable stylized flowers.

As early as 2000 B.C. ornamental plants were being used in Egypt as religious offerings. Plant motifs decorate architectural fragments and burial relics. Papyrus (*Cyperus papyrus*) represents resurrection, the palm (*Phoenix dactylifera*), fertility; the sacred blue lotus (*Nymphaea caerulea*) appeared most often, decorating temples, walls, domestic objects, wreaths, and jewelry. Other floral images include daisies, lilies, roses, iris, blue annual cornflowers (*Centaura depressa*), red field poppy (*Papaver choeas*), and opium poppy (*Papaver somniferum*).

In the Grecian isles archaeologists have found evidence of ornamental plants in terra-cotta pots outside the Minoan palace (ca. 2100–1600 B.C.), most likely palm trees, scented myrtle, pomegranates, roses, Madonna lilies, and irises. By 400 B.C. the Isle of Rhodes was legendary for its roses, grown with crocus, dianthus, hyacinth, iris, lily, narcissus, and scented violets. The Greek philosophers of Plato's era (fourth century B.C.) walked among plane, poplar, olives, bay laurel, cypress, oak, pine, and fir trees transplanted from the forests. Many of today's most common ornamentals bear the names of Greek gods, such as iris, goddess of the rainbow, and peony, named for Paeon, a mythic Greek physician.

The 11th-century B.C. Assyrian king Tiglath-Pigeser I collected plants as he conquered neighboring kingdoms to the west and south, including cedars, box, rare fruit trees, jasmine, rose, lilies, irises, tulips, hollyhocks, mallows, anemones, buttercups, daisies, chamomiles, helichrysums, crocuses, and poppies.

East of Mesopotamia from 900 to 400 B.C., the Persians developed walled gardens whose name evolved into the English word *paradise*. Planted always with trees for shade and fruit, and employing gravity-fed irrigation, these gardens also featured beds of cultivated wildflowers that have since been adopted as ornamental staples, including yellow roses (*Rosa hemispherica*), narcissus, lily, tulip, stocks, dianthus, jasmine, violets, violas, hollyhocks, marigolds, and lilacs.

Islam spread rapidly through the Middle East following Mohammed's death in A.D. 632. Ornamental gardening reached new heights under Muslim rule, reflecting the belief that man's earthly gardens should provide a foretaste of heaven. A list of plants from Abu Raihan Muhammed al-Biruni (A.D. 1050) includes roses, white and yellow jasmine, lavender, anemone coronaria, cholchicums, mallow, narcissus, opium poppy, violets, Madonna lily, and oleanders.

Gardens were a major architectural feature of classical Rome and its empire. Flowers were grown for commerce; ivy and grape garlands topped columns; and periwinkle, myrtle, and bay wreaths crowned statues. Roman gods governed plant fertility and share their names with many of the favorite flowers of modern times. Marcus Terentius Varro's *De Re Rustico* (40 B.C.; Three Books on Farming) and Lucius Junius Maderatus Culumella's *De de Rustica,* book 10 (A.D. 60; On Agriculture) refer to snowdrops, marigolds, narcissus, lilies, corn flag, violets, and roses. Pliny the Elder in the first century A.D. described topiary in his *Natural History.*

Post-Roman European gardens grew within castle and monastery walls, with a heavy emphasis on food crops and medicinal herbs. No formal records exist of European gardens between the fall of the Roman Empire and beginnings of the Renaissance in 1400. However, the Romans had introduced *Rosa gallica,* Madonna lily, violets, periwinkle, and the Christmas rose (*Helleborus niger*). Monk Wilifred Strabo's *Hortulus* (A.D. 100) mentions ornamentals grown as altar decorations—white roses, for instance, signifying the Virgin Mary's purity, and red roses, martyrs' blood.

Until the mid-16th century European ornamentals were largely collected from the wild, including viola, campion, sweet rocket, leopard's bane, stock, snowdrop, hollyhocks, violets, columbine, primrose, foxglove, and English daisies (*Bellis perennis*). In medieval monasteries ornamental gardens dedicated to the Virgin Mary featured white flowers (symbolic of her purity) and blossoms bearing her name: our lady's bedstraw—thyme, sweet woodruff, and groundsel—said to have filled the manger, our lady's garters (ribbon grass), our lady's slipper (orchid), our lady's tresses (prunella), our lady's bunch of keys (cowslip), our lady's thimble (harebell), our lady's tears (lily of the valley), our lady's gloves (foxglove), costmary (lungwort), marigold (actually calendula), lady's mantle, and rosemary, named for the Virgin's blue cloak.

The Renaissance spurred a great interest in gardening as an art form. As European monarchs established diplomatic ties to Constantinople (1554), the horticultural treasures of the Islamic world flooded into northern gardens. Most notable were the tulip, fritallaria, and all manner of exotic bulbs, as well as irises, carnation, and lilac. Twenty times as many new plants arrived in Europe in the proceeding 100 years as had been absorbed in the past 2,000.

The influx of exotic plants, together with the Renaissance hunger for horticultural beauty, gave rise to the science of botany and plant classification, fueling the curiosity of succeeding generations of plant discoverers who not only scoured Europe's wild areas in search of new flora but also struck out into China, Japan, and North and South America. North American trees, shrubs, and wildflowers (rhododendron, mountain laurel, true marigolds, sunflowers, canna, and nasturtiums) were eagerly adopted into English and European horticulture along with the tree peony, chrysanthemum, hydrangea, clematis, and other Chinese and Japanese treasures. From the Southern Hemisphere came tropical ornamentals (zinnias, cannas, petunias) propagated in manor greenhouses for annual bedding. Hybridizers zealously set out to perfect the display qualities of the newly discovered and old-time favorite plants. The newest and rarest ornamentals were sought first by wealthy plant collectors, arboretums, and commercial nurserymen before eventually making their way into mainstream gardens.

Due to technological advances in agricultural food production and unprecedented prosperity, ornamental gardening is no longer reserved for the wealthy and powerful. But even as commercial nurseries avidly compete to introduce the latest hybrids, and plant collectors race to remote mountainsides for rare specimens, classic heirlooms handed down through history form the backbone of many modern borders.

Today there is a great interest in rediscovering historic landscapes and the heirloom flowers originally featured in their planting beds. The greatest challenges to recreating these gardens lie in discovering the original planting schemes and finding current sources of plant materials that have long fallen from popular use. Such determinations can be especially confusing since many older gardens reflected the horticultural fashions of more than one historical period.

Aiding in such discoveries, a number of government, academic, for-profit, and nonprofit organizations around the world are conducting research and restoration efforts. As a result some of the world's most unusual and beautiful gardens are being restored. Within these living history museums visitors may for the first time see and experience in context many historic ornamentals. Those interested in determining the original planting schemes of a particular historic property can benefit from the intensive research being done on original documents or peruse these ancient "herbals" themselves. Local historical societies can often provide photographs or descriptions of properties, historic events, or social occasions that include reference to specific planting schemes. A number of old and current books and periodicals provide information about heirloom varieties popular in specific time periods and geographic regions. In response to the growing interest in garden restoration and heirloom plants, a growing number of specialty nurseries and seed-saver exchanges now offer extensive listings of rare old seeds and plants and will take requests for others not listed.

Further Reading

Berrall, Julia S., *The Garden,* New York: Viking, and London: Thames and Hudson, 1966

Camp, Wendell Holmes, *The World in Your Garden,* Washington, D.C.: National Geographic Society, 1937

Clarkson, Rosetta E., *Green Enchantment: The Magic Spell of Gardens,* New York: Macmillan, 1940

Coats, Peter, *Flowers in History,* New York: Viking Press, and London: Weidenfeld and Nicolson, 1970

Fairbrother, Nan, *Men and Gardens,* New York: Knopf, and London: Hogarth Press, 1956

Hobhouse, Penelope, *Plants in Garden History,* London: Pavilion Books, 1992; as *Penelope Hobhouse's Gardening through the Ages,* New York: Simon and Schuster, 1992

Hyams, Edward, *A History of Gardens and Gardening,* New York: Praeger, and London: Dent, 1971

Martin, Laura C., *Garden Flower Folklore,* Chester, Connecticut: Globe Pequot Press, 1987

Tice, Patricia M., *Gardening in America, 1830–1910* (exhib. cat), Rochester, New York: Strong Museum, 1984

TRESA JONES

Orsini, Villa

Bomarzo, Lazio, Italy

Location: approximately 10 miles (16.6 km) northeast of Viterbo and 40 miles (66.6 km) north of Rome

In 1542 Pier Francesco ("Vicino") Orsini, a military captain, poet, and member of one of Rome's oldest noble families, inherited a fiefdom comprising the small hill town of Bomarzo near the city of Viterbo. During his youth he participated with papal forces in a military campaign in Germany (1546); in a second campaign he was captured at the siege of Hesdin (1553) and released only in 1555. Between these military campaigns he began (ca. 1552) to decorate a wooded hillock some 350 meters (383 yd.) west of Bomarzo with sculpture and garden architecture, including several fountains. Described as a Sacro Bosco or Sacred Wood in one of the numerous inscriptions composed by Orsini in the wood, the irregularly shaped area was about 265 meters (290 yd.) long and 120 meters (131 yd.) at its widest. The Sacred Wood covered a hillock whose eastern boundary was a small brook set in a deep valley. In 1561 Orsini dammed up the southern end of the brook to form a large artificial lake about 100 meters (109 yd.) long, which was lost when the dam broke from neglect.

The original entrance to the wood was at the northeast end, where once stood two pillars capped by sphinxes. The inscription on one pillar read, "You who enter here, take heed," and the other likened the monuments in the area to the ancient Seven Wonders of the World. Unfortunately, the present owner has moved the sphinxes to the center of the brook, where a wooden bridge affords a modern entrance to the area. Just beyond the original entrance a visitor would encounter the Leaning House (Casa Pendente), a two-story square tower built in a leaning position so that a spectator in the upper chamber looks out on a world askew. The house bears an inscription dedicating it to Cardinal Cristoforo Madruzzo, a friend of Orsini, who bought the nearby hill town of Soriano in 1561, which presumably establishes a date *postquam* for the building.

Beyond the house are a small open theater and a *nymphaeum.* A small obelisk nearby is inscribed with the date 1552. This is the earliest extant date in the woods, suggesting that this pastoral section was the first part undertaken by Orsini. A path beyond, along the edge of the brook, is lined with several pieces of sculpture and fountains, all carved out of the rocky outcrops of the hillock, as is the lower story of the Leaning House. Most of the sculpture is over-life-size. There is a fountain of a boat, a fountain with the winged Pegasus jumping off Mount Parnassus in Greece to create in its hoof prints the Fountain of the Muses, and a figure of a gigantic tortoise on whose back rides a figure of Fame blowing twin trumpets. There is a colossal group of the hero *Orlando,* insane with frustrated love, tearing apart a youthful woodcutter, as related in Ariosto's epic poem *Orlando Furioso.* The sculptor of the group was probably the youthful Simone Moschino, who was active at Bomarzo in the mid-1570s.

On the north side of the hill above the theatrical exedra is a series of terraces with more colossal sculpture.

Leaning house and amphitheater, Villa Orsini, Bomarzo, Lazio, Italy
Copyright John Bethell/Garden Picture Library

On the terrace behind the upper story of the Leaning House are rows of large urns, a river god or *Oceanus,* a group of a winged dragon attacked by a lion and a lioness, and a freestanding, life-size elephant bearing a small castle on its back and carrying a dead Roman soldier in its trunk. Cut into the hill behind the elephant is a grotto whose facade is a gigantic *Hell's Mask*. The mouth is the entrance, and the tongue within served as a table, for the grotto was a summer dining room. The remains of an inscription around the mouth is a paraphrase of a line from Dante's *Inferno,* reading in translation, "Leave aside all care you who enter here."

The terrace above the grotto is outlined by large acorns in the form of an ancient hippodrome, an area often included in ancient Roman gardens. The acorns were probably a reference to the golden age of antiquity. A drawing by the artist Giovanni Guerra (1604) seems to depict two flower beds or parterres in the center of the hippodrome. If so, this is the only evidence of floriculture in the wood.

The stairs from this terrace to the summit of the hill are guarded at their base by a statue of *Cerberus,* the three-headed dog, guardian of the ancient underworld. On the summit is a small, domed classical temple, derived from that of an ancient Etruscan temple; Bomarzo is in ancient Etruria, and the wood contains several references to Etruscan culture. The historian Francesco Sansovino, a friend of Orsini, described the view from the loggia in the Orsini palace in the town of Bomarzo down upon the temple dedicated to Orsini's wife, Giulia Farnese, who died early in the 1560s. Orsini revived the ancient Roman tradition of a wooded funerary precinct at the edge of town.

There has never been a completely satisfactory explanation of the iconography of the entire layout, and because it includes so many personal references, there may never be one. In fact, many of the garden features seem to be autobiographical. For example, in a series of letters Orsini describes his passion for his young mistress, Laura, who abandoned him in 1574 for a young lover. The group of *Orlando,* insane from his unrequited love of Angelica, tearing apart the young woodcutter, is undoubtedly a reference to Orsini's state of mind. The blanket on the back of the elephant is decorated with the Orsini insignia of roses, probably as a reference to his military campaigns and imprisonment at Hesdin. The slow-moving tortoise bearing Fame reflects the slowness of fame Orsini earned from his long involvement in the northern wars, and the myth of Pegasus with the Fountain of the Muses refers to Orsini's role as a poet and friend of several contemporary poets and writers.

In his preface to Jacopo Sannazaro's poem *Arcadia,* Sansovino mentions that Arcadia reminds him of Bomarzo and that the sacred wood in Arcadia has features similar to those of Bomarzo, including a figure of Pan and a "cave," a figure of Oceanus, and a tomb of a beloved. But Bomarzo is certainly not a re-creation of Arcadia. There is at Bomarzo a general overall theme of entering a fearsome, awesome wood with fierce, threatening beasts and unnatural architecture. A general ascent past these features to the more pastoral hippodrome area planted with flowers, then past *Cerberus,* the guardian of Hades, leads to the summit and the quiet serenity of the *tempietto* (small temple). A Dantean overlay visible in the *Hell's Mask* with its inscription and in *Cerberus* accents this theme.

Orsini continued to work in his wood almost until his death in January 1585. From his letters one learns that in 1574–75 he was experimenting with coloring some of the statues, and slight traces of paint on some of the figures have been discovered. During the last decade of Orsini's life, his sole preoccupation was to show his wood to friends and visitors.

Synopsis

1542 Vicino Orsini inherits fief of Bomarzo
1552 Orsini decorates wooded hillock with sculpture and garden architecture, and probably completes theater area
1561 Artificial lake created by Orsini
1564 Major part of Sacro Bosco completed
1574 Some statues painted
1585 Death of Orsini

Further Reading

Bredekamp, Horst, and Wolfram Janzer, *Vicino Orsini und der Heilige Wald von Bomarzo: Ein Fürst als Künstler und Anarchist,* 2 vols., Worms, Germany: Werner, 1985; 2nd edition, 1991

Bruschi, Arnaldo, "Nuovi date documentari sulle opere Orsiane di Bomarzo," *Quaderni dell'Istituto di storia dell'architettura* 10 (1963)

Bruschi, Arnaldo, "II problema storico di Bomarzo," *Palladio* 13 (1963)

Coffin, David R., *Gardens and Gardening in Papal Rome,* Princeton, New Jersey: Princeton University Press, 1991

Darnell, Margaretta, and Mark S. Weil, "Il Sacro Bosco di Bomarzo: Its 16th-Century Literary and Antiquarian Context," *Journal of Garden History* 4 (1984)

Lazzaro, Claudia, *The Italian Renaissance Garden: From the Conventions of Planting, Design, and Ornament to the Grand Gardens of 16th-Century Central Italy,* New Haven, Connecticut: Yale University Press, 1990

Settis, Salvatore, "Contributi a Bomarzo," *Bollettino d'Arte* 6, no. 51 (1966)
Zander, Giuseppe, "Gli elementi documentari sul Sacro Bosco," *Quaderni dell' Istituto di storia dell'architettura* 7–9 (1955)

DAVID COFFIN

Orto Botanico dell'Università di Padova. *See* Padova, Orto Botanico dell'Università di

Orto Botanico dell'Università di Palermo. *See* Palermo, Orto Botanico dell'Università de

Orto Botanico dell'Università di Pisa. *See* Pisa, Orto Botanico dell'Università di

Otari-Wilton's Bush Native Botanic Garden and Forest Reserve

Wellington, New Zealand

Location: suburb of Wilton, 3 miles (4.8 km) from Wellington city center

Otari is the only botanic garden in New Zealand dedicated solely to native species. With two hectares (5 acres) in cultivation, it is the foremost native plant collection in the country, containing 874 of the 2,500 indigenous higher plant taxa of New Zealand. There is a special emphasis on growing species threatened with extinction, and one-quarter of the country's currently listed threatened plants are represented in Otari. Along with cultivated gardens Otari contains 75 hectares (185 acres) of mature and regenerating lowland forest, which forms a valuable part of Wellington's Outer Town Belt.

In 1902 concern among local residents about the demise of native forest elsewhere around Wellington focused attention on this valley, which was mostly undeveloped native reserve land granted to Maori during the colonization process. A petition to the government for protection of the forest was endorsed by the newly established Scenery Preservation Commission. Leonard Cockayne, internationally acclaimed for pioneering the field of plant ecology during the early 1900s, was an advisor to the commission and was instrumental in gaining Scenic Reserve status for the forest remnant (a new Scenery Preservation Act of 1903 made this possible), and he later became a member of the board managing the Otari Scenic Reserve.

Although the reserve was purchased by a government department, the city council had a financial interest and finally purchased it outright in 1918, giving citizens a much greater say in its future. During the 1920s, after several substantial additions to the reserve, including a mature forest stand protected by one of the early European farmers Job Wilton, interest grew among citizens for having an indigenous plant collection within easy reach of the city.

The director of Parks and Reserves nominated Otari as the site for this collection. With the appointment of Leonard Cockayne as director of the "Open-Air Plant Museum," as it was known in 1926, the concept flourished. Within five years his Alpine Garden contained 300 species, and specialist beds were being developed. In subsequent years beds have been formed for *Dracophyllum, Olearia, Hebe, Linum,* grasses and sedges, *Pomaderris, Sophora* (kowhai), *Clematis, Pseudopanax,* and *Coprosma;* beds that illustrate unique characteristics of New Zealand's flora such as divaricating juvenile forms; and geographic collections such as the North Auckland and Marlborough borders.

Cockayne set clear guidelines that still direct the management of the garden today: to collect all the New Zealand species possible to be cultivated in the garden (arranged as far as practical in families), focusing especially on cultivating hybrids for scientific interest; to reproduce examples of vegetation associations of primitive New Zealand; to restore the existing forest as far as possible to its original structure and composition; and to illustrate to visitors the horticultural uses of indigenous plants for their gardens.

Under Cockayne's guidance Stan Reid made an ecological study of the forest in 1934, which was repeated 50 years later, providing invaluable insight into the revegetation dynamics of Wellington. One of the more whimsical legacies of Cockayne's direction is the naming of paths through the reserve. They record the names of botanists who have advanced the knowledge of the flora and vegetation of New Zealand.

Cockayne was director of the Otari Open-Air Plant Museum for eight years until his death in 1932 and is buried in the botanic garden. A large rock is his simple memorial, symbolically surrounded with a garden representing the flora of the Wellington region.

Synopsis

1839 New Zealand Company colonizes Wellington, purchasing land from Maori tribes and surveying 100-acre lots (40 ha), one tenth of which are allocated back to dispossessed Maori

1847 Further native reserves allocated as compensation for lost cultivations, including Otari Block in Kaiwharawhara Survey District

1860 Job Wilton buys and develops 100-acre (40 ha) Lot 1, but preserves stand of mature forest

1902 Maori owners of undeveloped portion of Otari Block desire to sell, and concerned citizens successfully lobby government to buy and reserve land

1906 Otari Scenic Reserve created

1918 Wellington City Council purchases Scenic Reserve as reserve "in Trust for Recreation purposes and for the preservation of Native Flora"

1925 Owner of Job Wilton's bush block dies, and city acquires 6.8 hectares (2.75 acres) to add to Otari Reserve; Otari Open-Air Native Plant Museum opened in part of Otari Reserve

1934 Stan Reid completes ecological study of Otari forest

1937 Native Plant Preservation Society takes on role of propagation and planting

1947–62 Walter Brockie curator and adds 264 species to collection

1962–92 Raymond Mole curator, awarded Loder Cup for contribution to horticulture

1970s Vigorous public campaigning prevents major road from bisecting Otari, and subsequently Outer Town Belt policy is adopted

1980 Visitor center built, recognizing new educational objectives in Otari's management

1991 One curator appointed for all four Wellington Botanic Gardens

1992 Major possum-control program undertaken, and significant recovery of forest health evident within two years

1999 New treetop bridge; redevelopment of visitor center and car parks; new alpine garden with tarn completed

Further Reading

Gabites, Isobel, *Wellington's Living Cloak: A Guide to the Natural Plant Communities,* Wellington, New Zealand: Victoria University Press and Wellington Botanical Society, 1993

Reid, S., "Bracken Fern and Scrub Communities in Otari Reserve, Re-observed after Fifty Years," *Wellington Botanical Society Bulletin* 45

ISOBEL GABITES

Oxford Botanic Garden

Oxford, England, and Nuneham Courtenay, Oxfordshire, England

Location: two sites: opposite Magdalen College across the High Street on Rose Lane in Oxford, and at Nuneham Courtenay, approximately 5 miles (8 km) south-southeast of Oxford

The University of Oxford Botanic Garden now has two sites, the original 4.5-acre (1.8-ha) site opposite Magdalen College bordering the Cherwell River and the 80-acre (32.4-ha) Harcourt Arboretum at Nuneham Courtenay nine miles (5.6 km) south of Oxford, which opened in 1968. The site at Magdalen College contains the most compact yet diverse collection of plants in the world, with 8,000 species from over 90 percent of the higher-plant families, newly renovated rock and bog gardens, and seven display glasshouses providing environments ranging from tropical aquatic through rain forest to arid desert. It is the oldest botanic garden in Great Britain, third oldest in the world (after Padua and Leiden), and was founded in 1621 as a physic garden growing plants for medicinal research, the fruit of a gift of £5,000 (today above £3.5 million) by Henry Danvers, later first earl of Danby, for "the glorification of the works of God and for the furtherance of learning."

The chosen site belonged—and still belongs—to Magdalen College, of which the garden is a tenant. Part of the site had been a Jewish burial ground before the expulsion of the Jews in 1293, and the ground had to be raised to avoid the frequent flooding that occurred in the rest of Christ Church meadow. The university scavenger provided "4,000 loads of mucke and dunge" for the purpose (Allen and Walker). The walls and arches (which did not need restoration until recently) were completed in 1633, by which time the money was gone and the garden subsequently was used as a timber store.

The first garden superintendent, Jacob Bobart, was appointed in 1642 but his salary of £40 a year fell seven years in arrears, and he had to earn his living by selling fruits from the garden. The three varieties of medlar available today were growing in the garden by 1648. The first professor of botany was Robert Morison, physician to Charles II, who had a particular interest in the naming and grouping of plants.

When Morison died in 1683, both he and Bobart were replaced by Bobart's son, Jacob Bobart the younger, who began to catalog, collect, and exchange seeds with other gardeners, inaugurating the seed trade in Europe. After Bobart retired in 1719, the garden fell into decay and was refounded by William Sherard, who gave it £500 and endowed a chair of botany. Its incumbent was to be appointed by the Royal College of Physicians, thus ensuring that the position went to a scientist rather than a clergyman.

The first Sherardian professor was Jacob Dillenius, who was greatly interested in the new classification of species but is best remembered for the careless introduction of the Oxford ragwort from Mount Etna that spread up along the Cherwell River and later along the line of the new railway to London. Dillenius died in 1747 and was succeeded by Humphrey Sibthorp, during whose tenure the first glasshouses were built in 1766. They were heated by carts of red-hot coals wheeled through them by junior members of staff. The garden was kept going by its staff, which included John Foreman, superintendent for 57 years from 1756 to 1813, and James Benwell, who worked in the garden until he retired at the age of 78 in 1813.

Sibthorp was succeeded by his industrious son, John, professor from 1787 to 1796. He collected widely in the Aegean, taking with him the botanical artist Ferdinand Bauer who produced the drawings and paintings for the ten-volume *Flora Graeca* published between 1806 and 1840. Foreman's successor, William Baxter, *Praefectus* from 1813 to 1847, had to combine his superintendent duties with lecturing as another professor neglected the garden.

Then came Charles Daubeny, who was professor of chemistry and professor of surgery as well as professor of botany. He succeeded in swiftly raising a large sum of money and, with William Baxter, Jr., who had succeeded his father, replanned the garden, removing the six miles (3.7 km) of long, narrow beds and regrouping the plants, already rearranged according to place of origin rather than medicinal function. Daubeny left the British plants grouped according to Linnaeus's system, made the shape of the beds irregular, built new glasshouses, and changed the name of the garden to "botanic." His combined specialisms led him to experiment with plant nutrition and fertilizers.

Daubeny's successor was interested more in the anatomy and histology of plants, and the reorganization of science in the university nearly led to a move for the garden. When it was decided to leave it on its present site, the glasshouses were rebuilt in 1893. During the late 19th century, close cooperation developed with the Royal Botanic Gardens, Kew, where many of the finest Oxford specimens ended up and whose own system of oblong beds Oxford adopted.

Isaac Balfour, professor from 1884 to 1888, initiated a program to label every plant with name and country of origin and left the garden much as it is today. The rock garden, which needed calcareous stone for the alpine plants, was constructed in 1925. After World War II, Christ Church offered the garden extra space at a very low rent, and the herbaceous borders were laid out. The glasshouses were again rebuilt. The year 1950 saw the construction of the pond and 1951 the planting up of the bog garden. The garden now became a university department in its own right, although the keeper is still the professor of botany.

The garden today reflects the interests of its most recent keepers, responsible to a board of curators. One keeper, a geneticist, had beds laid out to show the development of the modern rose, and another put together a collection of over 400 species showing variegation. A recent superintendent had a special interest in carnivorous plants, now reflected in the collection of the Succulent House. In 1963 the Harcourt Arboretum was annexed to the garden.

Over the years the garden and the arboretum have had to raise money, respond to public demand, satisfy the needs of the university science departments, undertake national scientific functions, cope with changes of personnel and university organization, and survive the vagaries of weather-inflicted damage. A storm on 25 January 1990 caused massive destruction and led to replanting programs in both the garden and the arboretum. As a happy augury, the *Agave ferox*, planted in 1894 and said to flower only after it has lived for a full century, duly flowered in the spring of 1995.

Synopsis

1293	Jewish burial ground closed after expulsion of Jews, land later acquired by Magdalen College
1621	Henry Danvers donates £5,000 for physic garden
1633	Walls and arches completed
1642	Jacob Bobart appointed first superintendent
1648	First inventory of garden drawn up
1683	Death of first professor of botany, Robert Morison, physician to King Charles II
1683–1719	Jacob Bobart the Younger acts as both superintendent and professor
1720s	Garden in decline until William Sherard donates £500 and endows Sherardian Chair of Botany
1747	Death of Jacob Dillenius, first Sherardian Professor of Botany
1766	First glasshouses built
1850	Major reorganization of garden by Charles Daubeny, who changes name to Oxford Botanic Garden
1851	New glasshouses built
1873	Project to move garden defeated
1884–88	Isaac Balfour labels plants
1925	Rock garden constructed
1945	Major expansion undertaken with space offered by Christ Church college; herbaceous borders laid out
1950	Construction of pond
1951	Garden becomes university department in its own right, with post of keeper still filled by Sherardian Professor of Botany
1963	Harcourt Arboretum at Nuneham Courtenay annexed to garden
1995	Flowering of *Agave ferox* in Succulent House (planted in 1894)

Further Reading

Allen, Louise, and Timothy Walker, *The University of Oxford Botanic Garden*, Oxford: Oxford Botanic Garden, 1995

Guide to the Oxford Botanic Gardens, Oxford: Clarendon Press, 1971

ANTHONY H.T. LEVI